Modern
Advanced
Accounting

Ninth Edition

E. John Larsen
University of Southern California

Boston Burr Ridge, IL Dubuque, IA Madison, WI New York San Francisco St. Louis
Bangkok Bogotá Caracas Kuala Lumpur Lisbon London Madrid Mexico City
Milan Montreal New Delhi Santiago Seoul Singapore Sydney Taipei Toronto

McGraw-Hill Higher Education &

*A Division of The **McGraw-Hill** Companies*

MODERN ADVANCED ACCOUNTING

Published by McGraw-Hill/Irwin, a business unit of The McGraw-Hill Companies, Inc., 1221 Avenue of the Americas, New York, NY, 10020. Copyright © 2003, 2000, 1997, 1994, 1991, 1988, 1983, 1979, 1975 by The McGraw-Hill Companies, Inc. All rights reserved. No part of this publication may be reproduced or distributed in any form or by any means, or stored in a database or retrieval system, without the prior written consent of The McGraw-Hill Companies, Inc., including, but not limited to, in any network or other electronic storage or transmission, or broadcast for distance learning.

Some ancillaries, including electronic and print components, may not be available to customers outside the United States.

This book is printed on acid-free paper.

domestic   2 3 4 5 6 7 8 9 0 CCW/CCW 0 9 8 7 6 5 4 3
international   1 2 3 4 5 6 7 8 9 0 CCW/CCW 0 9 8 7 6 5 4 3 2

ISBN 0-07-250290-8

Publisher: *Brent Gordon*
Executive editor: *Stewart Mattson*
Editorial coordinator: *Heather Sabo*
Marketing manager: *Richard Kolasa*
Project manager: *Natalie J. Ruffatto*
Production supervisor: *Gina Hangos*
Freelance design coordinator: *Laurie J. Entringer*
Senior producer, Media technology: *Ed Przyzycki*
Supplement producer: *Matthew Perry*
Cover design: *John Resh*
Typeface: *10/12 Times Roman*
Compositor: *Techbooks*
Printer: *Courier Westford*

Library of Congress Cataloging-in-Publication Data

Larsen, E. John.
    Modern advanced accounting / E. John Larsen.--9th ed.
      p. cm.
    Includes index.
    ISBN 0-07-250290-8 (alk. paper)--ISBN 0-07-119846-6 (international : alk. paper)
    1. Accounting.   I. Title.
HF5635 .L3267 2008
657'.046—dc21

2002019863

INTERNATIONAL EDITION ISBN 0-07-119846-6
Copyright © 2003. Exclusive rights by The McGraw-Hill Companies, Inc.
for manufacture and export. This book cannot be re-exported from the country to which it is sold by McGraw-Hill.
The International Edition is not available in North America.

www.mhhe.com

Preface

June 2001 was a milestone month in the annals of financial and governmental accounting. June 30 was the end of a highly controversial accounting method: the pooling-of-interests method of accounting for certain business combinations. Also, the first phase-in of the significantly revised financial reporting model for state and local governmental units was established for fiscal years beginning after June 15. Both of these events are described and illustrated in this ninth edition of *Modern Advanced Accounting.*

The ninth edition of *Modern Advanced Accounting* may be used as the primary textbook in a conventional one-semester or two-quarter advanced accounting course, or as a secondary source in a course that emphasizes technical pronouncements on accounting standards as the primary reference materials. The emphasis throughout the book is on financial accounting concepts and on the application of these concepts to problems arising in both business and nonbusiness organizations. Specialized accounting entities such as partnerships and affiliated companies and topics such as international accounting standards and business segments are dealt with in terms of current-day accounting issues.

The ninth edition also continues the emphasis on case studies involving analytical and conceptual thinking on both accounting and ethical issues, some of which require students to research suggested references on the Internet. The ninth edition has cases that require the students to stretch their thinking beyond the basic accounting issues. For example, Case 1–2 requires the student to evaluate the usefulness of ethics rules of the AICPA, FEI, and IMA in relation to quotations from the *Meditations* of Marcus Aurelius Antoninus; Case 1–12 involves identifying "cookie-jar reserves" in a case of fraudulent financial reporting; and Case 12–3 requires students to analyze a publicly owned enterprise's compliance with selected disclosure requirements of *FASB Statement No. 133,* "Accounting for Derivative Instruments and Hedging Activities."

As in previous editions, the ninth edition of *Modern Advanced Accounting* includes the ethics codes of the AICPA, FEI, and IMA; summaries of numerous SEC Accounting and Auditing Enforcement Releases; illustrations of financial accounting and reporting from public companies' financial reports; and a glossary of key terms.

NEW FEATURES OF THE NINTH EDITION

The ninth edition of *Modern Advanced Accounting* has the following new features:

- Relegation of the discussion of pooling-of-interests accounting to an appendix in Chapter 5, to provide a historical context.

- Elimination of the eighth edition chapter devoted to consolidated financial statements for a pooling-type business combination, and consequent reduction of total chapters to 19.

- Discussion and, as appropriate, illustration of the following Financial Accounting Standards Board and Governmental Accounting Standards Board *Statements:*

FASB Statement No. 141,   "Business Combinations" in Chapter 5

FASB Statement No. 142,   "Goodwill and Other Intangible Assets" in Chapter 5

FASB Statement No. 144,   "Accounting for the Impairment or Disposal of Long-Lived Assets" in Chapter 13

GASB Statement No. 33,   "Accounting and Reporting for Nonexchange Transactions," in Chapter 19

GASB Statement No. 34,   "Basic Financial Statements—and Management's Discussion and Analysis—for State and Local Governments" in Chapters 17–19

GASB Statement No. 35,   "Basic Financial Statements—and Management's Discussion and Analysis—for Public Colleges and Universities" in Chapter 19

GASB Statement No. 37,   "Basic Financial Statements—and Management's Discussion and Analysis—for State and Local Governments: Omnibus" in Chapter 19

GASB Statement No. 38,   "General Financial Statement Note Disclosures" in Chapter 19

- Discussion of the *Proposed FASB Statement,* "Accounting for Financial Instruments with Characteristics of Liabilities, Equity, or Both" in Chapter 6

- Introduction of International Accounting Standards Board in Chapter 11.

- Substantial excerpt from the FASB's *The IASC-U.S. Comparison Project: A Report on the Similarities and Differences Between IASC Standards and U.S. GAAP* in Chapter 11.

- A table in Chapter 11 summarizing the complex derivative instruments accounting standards set forth in *FASB Statement No. 133,* "Accounting for Derivative Instruments and Hedging Activities."

- Illustrative financial statements of the McGraw-Hill Companies, Inc., in Chapter 13 and of The Kenneth T. and Eileen L. Norris Foundation in Chapter 16.

ORGANIZATION OF SUBJECT MATTER

I believe that the organization of 18 of the 19 chapters into five areas of concentration is useful to both instructors and students. This arrangement should facilitate the planning and presentation of the subject matter and, I anticipate, make it easier for students to learn and retain the concepts and procedures presented. A brief description of the five parts follows.

Part One: Accounting for Partnerships and Branches (Chapters 2 through 4)

Following ethical issues in Chapter 1, the first section deals with the accounting principles and procedures for partnerships, joint ventures, and branch operations. Partnerships (limited liability, general, and limited) and joint ventures are covered in Chapters 2 and 3, which take the student from the basic concepts of partnership accounting often presented in an introductory accounting course to the more complex problems of income sharing, realignment of partners' equities, and liquidation. Chapter 4, which deals with home office–branch relationships and combined financial statements, provides a logical stepping-stone to the six chapters dealing with business combinations and consolidated financial statements.

Part Two: Business Combinations and Consolidated Financial Statements (Chapters 5 through 10)

The sequencing of topics in Chapters 5 through 10 is designed to take the student from the less complex date-of-business combination accounting and financial statement display issues to the more rigorous features of post-combination accounting and display matters. Where appropriate, provisions of the FASB's proposed *Statement,* "Consolidated Financial Statements: Purpose and Policy," are discussed in Chapters 6 through 10.

Part Three: International Accounting; Reporting of Segments, for Interim Periods, and to the SEC (Chapters 11 through 13)

The many complex matters involved in international accounting are discussed in Chapters 11 and 12, which emphasize the increasing importance and impact of the International Accounting Standards Board and the International Organization of Securities Commissions. The three topics covered in Chapter 13 are indirectly related to the subject matter of Chapters 11 and 12 and thus are included here.

Part Four: Accounting for Fiduciaries (Chapters 14 and 15)

The fourth section of the book includes chapters entitled "Bankruptcy: Liquidation and Reorganization" and "Estates and Trusts." Although some instructors may not cover these two traditional topics in their courses, I believe that it is imperative to include them for those who wish to do so. Many accountants in today's practice environment must assist clients with problems of bankruptcy, liquidation, reorganization, and the accounting for estates and trusts.

Part Five: Accounting for Nonbusiness Organizations (Chapters 16 through 19)

In Chapters 17 through 19, students progress from accounting and financial statement display issues for a governmental entity's general fund through its other governmental-type funds to its proprietary and fiduciary funds and its comprehensive annual financial report. No specific type of nonprofit organization is emphasized in Chapter 16; instead, an overview of accounting and reporting issues for various such organizations are dealt with; and in Chapter 19 students are referred to a *Journal of Accountancy* that illustrates a city's financial statements.

Pedagogical Element

This icon is used to help faculty identify ethical issues integrated throughout this textbook. Because Chapter 1 is entirely about ethics, this icon is not used in that chapter.

REVIEW QUESTIONS, EXERCISES, CASES, AND PROBLEMS

The learning and assignment material provided at the end of each chapter is divided into four groups: review questions, exercises, cases, and problems. Most end-of-chapter material has been tested in class by the author.

The review questions may be used by students as a self-testing and review device to measure their comprehension of key points in each chapter.

An exercise typically covers a specific point or topic and does not require extensive computations. Instructors may use the exercises to supplement problem assignments, for class discussion, and for examinations.

The cases require analytical reasoning but generally involve little or no quantitative data. Students are required to analyze business situations, to apply accounting standards, and to propose or evaluate a course of action. However, they are not required to prepare lengthy working papers or otherwise to manipulate accounting data on an extensive scale. The cases have proved to be an effective means of encouraging students to take positions in the argument of controversial accounting and ethical issues.

Several problems demonstrate the concepts presented in the theoretical discussion included in the chapter. Probably no more than a third of the problems would be used in a single course; consequently, ample opportunity exists to vary homework assignments from term to term.

SUPPLEMENTS WITH THE NINTH EDITION

As was the case with previous editions, the ninth edition of *Modern Advanced Accounting* is accompanied by a comprehensive package of supplementary items for both students and instructors.

For Students

1. The **Study Guide/Working Papers** (0072502932) supplement is available for students to purchase. The Study Guide, prepared by the author, is designed to help students measure their progress by providing immediate feedback. It contains an outline of the important points for each chapter, plus a variety of objective questions, short exercises, and a case. Answers to the questions, exercises, and case are at the end of each Study Guide chapter to help students evaluate their understanding of the subject matter.

   Accounting Working Papers for the problems are included in the same supplement as the Study Guide. On these working papers the organization names, problem numbers, numerous headings, and some preliminary data (such as trial balances) have been entered to save students time and to facilitate review by the instructor.

2. *Check Figures* are provided for many exercises and problems. In this edition of *Modern Advanced Accounting* the check figures are included with the exercises and problems. The purpose of the figures is to aid students in verifying intermediate amounts in problem solutions and in discovering errors.

For Instructors

1. An **Instructor's Resource Guide** (0072502924), prepared by the author of the text, is a teaching aid designed to assist instructors in preparing assignments and in covering the material in class. The author's goals in providing this supplement are to

make the task of instructors easier and to enable them to use their time more efficiently, so that the students' learning process can be enhanced.

A Solutions Manual also makes up part of the Instructor's Resource Guide. The Solutions Manual contains answers to all review questions, exercises, cases, and problems in the text. In addition, at the beginning of each chapter, there are short descriptions, time estimates, and difficulty ratings for each of the problems, to help instructors choose problems that best fit the needs of their individual courses in terms of scope, level, and emphasis.

2. A **Test Bank** (0072502940), prepared by the author of the text, with text material arranged chapter by chapter, is available at no charge. It contains true-or-false and multiple-choice questions, short problems, and a case for each chapter. Instructors should find the booklet a useful source of material for assembling examinations, because they may emphasize those topics or chapters covered in their course outline. Complete answers are provided for all questions, problems, and cases.

3. A **Computerized Test Bank** (0072502959), the computerized version of the Test Bank, is delivered in the Brownstone Diploma shell. It can be used to create different versions of the same test, change the answer order, edit and add questions, and conduct online testing.

4. *Solutions Transparencies* (0072502916) are available for many of the problems in the text. The transparencies are considered by many instructors to be an effective means of showing desired organization and format of solutions.

5. A book specific website, new to this edition, includes updates to the text, PowerPoint® slides, the Instructor's Resource Guide, and links to relevant sites. The website can be found at www.mhhe.com/Larsen9e.

A POINT OF PERSONAL PRIVILEGE

The demise of the pooling-of-interests method of accounting for business combinations is especially gratifying to the author. In 1970, during a California Society of Certified Public Accountants committee discussion of the *Exposure Draft* of what was ultimately *APB Opinion No. 16,* "Business Combinations, he was the only committee member to vote to *prohibit* pooling accounting. Vindication at last!"

Acknowledgments

I am deeply grateful to the following key players in the development of the ninth edition of *Modern Advanced Accounting:*

- My dear wife Kathleen, whose enthusiasm for the ninth edition—the seventh that she has assisted me in producing—led to her finding time in her busy career for support in proofreading and making suggestions on content of chapters.

- The primary Irwin/McGraw-Hill editors with whom I dealt: Sponsoring Editor Stewart Mattson, who provided many innovative suggestions for the edition; and Editorial Coordinator Heather Sabo, who skillfully dealt with original manuscript, communication with copyright waiver grantors, and overall logistical problems, always with patience and warmth.

- The McGraw-Hill/Irwin book team—Marketing Manager Rich Kolasa, Marketing Specialist Melissa Larmon, Project Manager Natalie Ruffatto, Designer Laurie Entringer, Production Supervisor Gina Hangos, and Supplement Coordinator Matthew Perry—for their encouragement, patience, and overall professionalism.

- The Financial Accounting Standards Board and the Governmental Accounting Standards Board, for permission to quote from *Statements, Discussion Memoranda, Interpretations,* and *Exposure Drafts.* Portions of various FASB documents, copyright by Financial Accounting Standards Board, 401 Merritt 7, P.O. Box 5116, Norwalk, Connecticut 06856-5116, U.S.A., are reprinted with permission. Complete copies of these documents are available from the FASB. Portions of various GASB documents, copyright by Governmental Accounting Standards Board, 401 Merritt 7, P.O. Box 5116, Norwalk, Connecticut 06856-5116, U.S.A., are reprinted with permission. Complete copies of these documents are available from the GASB.

- The McGraw-Hill Companies for permission to reproduce in Chapter 13 excerpts from the 2000 annual report of The McGraw-Hill Companies and the company's quarterly news release for June 30, 2001.

- Ronald R. Barnes, Executive Director/Trustee of The Kenneth T. and Eileen L. Norris Foundation, for permission to reproduce the Foundation's financial statements in Chapter 16.

Reviewers of the eighth edition for their helpful comments and suggestions:

Frank Marino
Assumption College

Dave Nichols
University of Mississippi

John F. Reardon
LaSalle University

Phillip Korb
University of Baltimore

William Parrott
University of South Florida

Dale A. Brenning
DeVry Institute of Technology

James Yang
Montclair State University

Barbara R. Stewart
Towson University

David J. Medved
Davenport University

William D. Stout
University of Louisville

Robert Zwicker
Pace University

John Biondo
SUNY College at Old Westbury

Alan Mayer-Sommer
Georgetown University

Arlette C. Wilson
Auburn University

William Cooper
North Carolina A&T University

As indicated by the foregoing acknowledgments, although only my name appears on the spine of this textbook, countless others have played major roles in its development and production. However, any shortcomings are solely my responsibility: "The buck stops here"!

E. John Larsen

Brief Contents

Contents

PART THREE
INTERNATIONAL ACCOUNTING: REPORTING OF SEGMENTS, FOR INTERIM PERIODS, AND TO THE SEC 490

Chapter 11
International Accounting Standards; Accounting for Foreign Currency Transactions 490

Chapter 12
Translation of Foreign Currency Financial Statements 517

Chapter 19
Governmental Entities: Proprietary Funds, Fiduciary Funds, and Comprehensive Annual Financial Report 793

Chapter One

Ethical Issues in Advanced Accounting

Scope of Chapter

Why begin the study of advanced accounting with a discussion of ethical issues? Because in recent years much attention has been devoted to the ethical conduct of accountants, both in industry and in public practice. Critics have alleged that ethical standards of accountants have deteriorated and that the interests of users of financial statements and financial reports have been subordinated to the desires of preparers of such reports to present the most favorable picture of the financial status of a reporting entity. Terms such as the following have been incorporated in the vocabulary of accountants:

Cute accounting to describe stretching the *form* of accounting standards to the limit, regardless of the *substance* of the underlying business transactions or events

Cooking the books to indicate fraudulent financial reporting

Many topics of advanced accounting have been the subject of both cute accounting and cooking the books by accounting executives of business enterprises. Because the chief financial officer, the controller, the chief accounting officer, and the accounting staffs of business enterprises have the primary responsibility for preparing financial statements and financial reports and disseminating them to users, this chapter deals with the ethical standards appropriate for those preparers. In this and subsequent chapters, Securities and Exchange Commission (SEC) enforcement actions dealing with fraudulent financial reporting are described for the topics covered in those chapters.

WHAT IS FRAUDULENT FINANCIAL REPORTING?

The following covers misstatements in financial statements that are caused by fraudulent financial reporting, and the reasons for and methods of committing fraud:

Misstatements arising from fraudulent financial reporting are intentional misstatements or omissions of amounts or disclosures in financial statements to deceive financial statement users. Fraudulent financial reporting may involve acts such as the following:

- Manipulation, falsification, or alteration of accounting records or supporting documents from which financial statements are prepared

- Misrepresentation in, or intentional omission from, the financial statements of events, transactions, or other significant information
- Intentional misapplication of accounting principles relating to amounts, classification, manner of presentation, or disclosure

Fraud frequently involves the following: (*a*) a pressure or an incentive to commit fraud and (*b*) a perceived opportunity to do so. . . . For example, fraudulent financial reporting may be committed because management is under pressure to achieve an unrealistic earnings target.

Fraud may be concealed through falsified documentation, including forgery. For example, management that engages in fraudulent financial reporting might attempt to conceal misstatements by creating fictitious invoices.

Fraud also may be concealed through collusion among management, employees, or third parties. For example, through collusion, false evidence that control activities have been performed effectively may be presented.[1]

AN EXAMPLE OF FRAUDULENT FINANCIAL REPORTING

The SEC's *Accounting and Auditing Enforcement Release No. 923,* "Securities and Exchange Commission v. Joseph C. Allegra, David Hersh, J. Ledd Ledbetter and H. Flynn Clyburn . . ." (AAER 923), issued June 11, 1997, provides an example of fraudulent financial reporting carried out by the president and chief executive officer; the chief financial officer, treasurer, and secretary; the chief operating officer and senior executive vice president; and another executive vice president of a national provider of alternate site health care services. According to the SEC, the four officers overstated the company's net income for the quarters ended December 31, 1992, and March 31, 1993, by taking the following "cooking the books" actions:

1. Recognizing January 1993 revenues in December 1992 and April 1993 revenues in March 1993 and artificially accelerating product delivery schedules at the end of both quarters.

2. Deferring writeoffs of uncollectible accounts past the end of the appropriate quarter.

Also, according to the SEC, the chief financial officer (a CPA) overstated quarterly income by:

1. Recognizing in the quarter ended March 31, 1993, a gain from the sale of an asset during the quarter ended June 30, 1993.

2. Recognizing as assets certain expenses incurred during the quarters ended December 31, 1992, and March 31, 1993.

3. Making fictitious journal entries in connection with business combinations accomplished in March 1993, the effect of which was to understate doubtful accounts expense.

In a "consent decree" in which the four officers neither admitted nor denied the SEC's allegations, they agreed to numerous monetary and other penalties.

---

[1] *AICPA Professional Standards.* vol. 1, "U.S. Auditing Standards," sec. 316.

ETHICAL STANDARDS FOR PREPARERS OF FINANCIAL STATEMENTS AND FINANCIAL REPORTS

Until recently, most efforts to develop ethical standards for accountants have focused on CPAs in the practice of public accounting—primarily auditing. For example, although the first code of ethics of the American Institute of Certified Public Accountants (AICPA) was adopted in 1917, prior to 1988 few of its provisions applied to AICPA members in industry. The Institute of Management Accountants (IMA), an organization devoted primarily to the interest of accountants in industry, first issued its *Standards of Ethical Conduct for Management Accountants* in 1983. The Financial Executives Institute (FEI), an organization of financial vice presidents, controllers, and treasurers of business enterprises, first issued its *Code of Ethics* in 1985.

Presumably, the lack of formal ethical standards for management accountants and financial executives prior to 1983 stemmed from the view that the first line of defense against improper financial reporting was provided by independent CPAs who audited financial statements of business enterprises, and that preparers of those statements had only a secondary role in assuring quality financial reporting. This view was prevalent even though the AICPA had long included statements such as the following in its pronouncements on auditing:

> The financial statements are management's responsibility. The auditor's responsibility is to express an opinion on the financial statements. Management is responsible for adopting sound accounting policies and for establishing and maintaining an internal control structure that will, among other things, record, process, summarize, and report financial data that is consistent with management's assertions embodied in the financial statements. The internal control structure should include an accounting system to identify, assemble, analyze, classify, record, and report an entity's transactions and to maintain accountability for the related assets and liabilities. The entity's transactions and the related assets and liabilities are within the direct knowledge and control of management. The auditor's knowledge of these matters is limited to that acquired through the audit. Thus, the fair presentation of financial position, results of operations, and cash flows in conformity with generally accepted accounting principles is an implicit and integral part of management's responsibility. The independent auditor may make suggestions about the form or content of the financial statements or draft them, in whole or in part, based on information from management's accounting system. However, the auditor's responsibility for the financial statements he has audited is confined to the expression of his opinion on them.[2]

Significant Events in the Establishment of Ethical Standards for Management Accountants and Financial Executives

The Seaview Symposium of 1970

An early effort to establish ethical standards for preparers of financial statements occurred at a 1970 symposium of members of the AICPA, the FEI, the Financial Analysts Federation, and the Robert Morris Associates (an organization of credit grantors), which took place at Seaview Country Club, Absecon, New Jersey. Papers and discussions at this symposium criticized the lack of a code of ethics for members of the FEI, given that the other three participating organizations had such codes.[3]

---

[2] *AICPA Professional Standards*, vol. 1, "U.S. Auditing Standards," sec. 110.02 (prior to amendment).
[3] John C. Burton, ed., *Corporate Financial Reporting: Ethical and Other Problems* (New York: AICPA, 1972), pp. 7, 51–52, 109, 420–421.

The Equity Funding Fraud of 1973

In 1973, a major fraud, of about nine years' duration, was discovered at Equity Funding Corporation of America (Equity), a seller of mutual fund shares that were pledged by the investors to secure loans to finance life insurance premiums. During the nine-year period, at least $143 million of fictitious pretax income was generated—a period in which Equity reported a total net income of $76 million, instead of the real pretax losses totaling more than $67 million.[4] The fraud was carried out by at least 10 executives of Equity, including the chief executive officer (CEO), chief financial officer (CFO), controller, and treasurer; several of the executives were CPAs with public accounting experience. The fraudulent conduct of these CPAs, all of whom presumably had at one time been subject to the AICPA's *Code of Professional Ethics* during their public accounting careers, furnished clear evidence of the need for ethics codes for management accountants and other financial executives.

Action by the IMA

In 1983, the IMA issued *Standards of Ethical Conduct for Practitioners of Management Accounting and Financial Management,* the third in a series of *Statements on Management Accounting.* The IMA standards, which are presented in Appendix 1 at the end of this chapter (pages 8 through 10), cover the management accountant's obligations as to competence, confidentiality, integrity, and objectivity, and they provide guidance for resolutions of ethical conflict. Noteworthy in the preamble to the standards (pages 8–9) is the management accountant's obligation not to condone violations of the standards by others in the organization.

Action by the FEI

The *Code of Ethics* promulgated by the FEI in 1985 is in Appendix 2 (page 11). Although briefer than the IMA standards, the FEI's code covers essentially the same areas of professional conduct as do the IMA standards.

Treadway Commission Recommendations

The National Commission on Fraudulent Financial Reporting (Treadway Commission), which had been sponsored by the AICPA, the IMA, the FEI, the American Accounting Association (composed primarily of accounting educators), and the Institute of Internal Auditors, issued its report in 1987. Defining *fraudulent financial reporting* as "intentional or reckless conduct, whether act or omission, that results in materially misleading financial statements,"[5] the Treadway Commission made 49 recommendations for curbing such reporting. The recommendations dealt with the public company; the independent public accountant; the SEC, financial institution regulators, and state boards of accountancy; and education. Stating that "the responsibility for reliable financial reporting resides first and foremost at the corporate level,"[6] the Treadway Commission included the following among its recommendations for the public company:

> <u>Recommendations:</u> *Public companies should maintain accounting functions that are designed to meet their financial reporting obligations.*
>
> A public company's accounting function is an important control in preventing and detecting fraudulent financing reporting. The accounting function must be designed to allow the company and its officers to fulfill their statutory financial disclosure obligations.

---

[4] *Report of the Trustee of Equity Funding Corporation of America,* October 31, 1974, p. 12.
[5] *Report of the National Commission on Fraudulent Financial Reporting* (New York: 1987), p. 2.
[6] Ibid., p. 6.

As a member of top management, the chief accounting officer helps set the tone of the organization's ethical conduct and thus is part of the control environment. Moreover, the chief accounting officer is directly responsible for the financial statements, and can and should take authoritative action to correct them if necessary. He generally has the primary responsibility for designing, implementing, and monitoring the company's financial reporting system and internal accounting controls. The controller may serve as the chief accounting officer, or the chief financial officer also may perform the functions of a chief accounting officer.

The chief accounting officer's actions especially influence employees who perform the accounting function. By establishing high standards for the company's financial disclosures, the chief accounting officer guides others in the company toward legitimate financial reporting.

Moreover, the chief accounting officer is in a unique position. In numerous cases, other members of top management, such as the chief executive officer, pressure the chief accounting officer into fraudulently manipulating the financial statements. An effective chief accounting officer is familiar with the company's financial position and operations and thus frequently is able to identify unusual situations caused by fraudulent financial reporting perpetrated at the divisional level.

The chief accounting officer has an obligation to the organization he serves, to the public, and to himself to maintain the highest standards of ethical conduct. He therefore must be prepared to take action necessary to prevent fraudulent financial reporting. His efforts may entail bringing matters to the attention of the CEO, the CFO, the chief internal auditor, the audit committee, or the entire board of directors.

The Financial Executives Institute (FEI) and the [Institute of Management Accountants (IMA)] play active roles in enhancing the financial reporting process by sponsoring research, technical professional guidance, and continuing professional education and by participating in the shaping of standards. Both organizations also have promulgated codes of conduct that strongly encourage reliable financial reporting. Public companies should encourage their accounting employees to support these organizations and adhere to their codes of conduct.[7]

Revision of AICPA Ethics Rules

In 1988, the members of the AICPA approved a revised **Code of Professional Conduct** to replace the **Code of Professional Ethics** that previously had been in effect. This action was triggered by the 1986 **Report of the Special Committee on Standards of Professional Conduct for Certified Public Accountants** (Anderson Committee), which recommended restructuring the AICPA's ethics code to improve its relevance and effectiveness.[8] A key element of the Anderson Committee recommendations was extension of applicability of the Rules of Professional Conduct of the revised **Code of Professional Conduct** to AICPA members who are not practicing in a CPA firm.[9] Thus, Rules 102, 201, 202, 203, 302, and 501 of the **Code of Professional Conduct** in Appendix 3 (pages 11 through 23) apply to **all** AICPA members, including those in private industry, governmental entities, nonprofit organizations, and academia.

Analysis of Ethical Standards for Management Accountants and Financial Executives

A review of the contents of the IMA, FEI, and AICPA ethics pronouncements in Appendixes 1, 2, and 3 reveals several similarities. All three require members of the re-

---

[7] Ibid., pp. 36–37.
[8] *Report of the Special Committee on Standards of Professional Conduct for Certified Public Accountants* (New York: AICPA, 1986), p. 1.
[9] Ibid., p. 23.

spective organizations to be competent, act with integrity and objectivity, maintain confidentiality of sensitive information, and avoid discreditable acts. The IMA and AICPA codes specifically prohibit conflicts of interest, but the FEI code only indirectly addresses such conflicts in its confidentiality provision. Only the IMA and FEI codes specifically require communication of complete information to users of their members' reports; AICPA members indirectly are comparably obligated by Rule 202.

Rule 203 of the AICPA code requires compliance with generally accepted accounting principles. One might prefer that both the IMA and the FEI codes had comparable explicit provisions, given management accountants' and financial executives' primary responsibility for financial statements and financial reports.

Other differences among the three ethics codes include the following:

1. The IMA standards in essence require members to *report* violations of the standards by members of their organizations to responsible officials of the organizations. The FEI and AICPA codes have no such requirements.

2. The FEI code requires members to conduct their *personal,* as well as their *business,* affairs with honesty and integrity. The IMA and AICPA standards do not address personal affairs.

The issues of **conflicts of interest** and **discreditable acts** are discussed further in the following sections.

Conflicts of Interest

Conflicts of interest result when individuals reap inappropriate *personal* benefits from their acts in an *official* capacity. For example, a chief accounting officer might cook the books to overstate pretax income of the employer corporation in order to obtain a larger performance bonus. Alternatively, the controller of a publicly owned corporation might engage in **insider trading**[10] to maximize gains or minimize losses on purchases or sales of the employer corporation securities. For example, in **Accounting and Auditing Enforcement Release (AAER) 344** (December 10, 1991), the SEC reported the permanent disbarment from practice of the controller, a CPA, of a publicly owned company, who had allegedly engaged in insider trading and thus avoided losses of more than $73,000 on sales of the employer company's common stock. According to the SEC, the controller had acted with senior management of the company to overstate the company's earnings by more than $38,000,000 over a two-and-one-half-year period. The controller was ordered to disgorge the $73,000 and pay a penalty of the same amount.

Discreditable Acts

None of the three ethics codes presented in appendixes to this chapter defines **discreditable acts.** Probably the term cannot be adequately defined or circumscribed; what is a discreditable act to one observer might not be so construed by another. For example, and returning to the FEI's requirement of integrity in its members' *personal* affairs, might an FEI member observing another member's substance abuse construe the act as discreditable to the abusive member, the member's employer, the FEI, or other members of the FEI? Such questions are difficult to answer in a society in which some condone personal actions that are condemned by others.

---

[10] Section 21A of the Securities Exchange Act of 1934 defines *insider trading* as "purchasing or selling a security while in possession of material, nonpublic information . . . or . . . communicating such information in connection with a securities transaction."

Concluding Observations

In considering episodes of cooking the books, described in subsequent chapters, the reader should keep in mind that, although the Treadway Commission stated, "The incidence of fraudulent financial reporting cannot be quantified with any degree of precision,"[11] it also gave the following data:

1. The number of SEC proceedings against reporting companies from 1981 to 1986 was less than 1% of the number of financial reports filed with the SEC during that period.

2. The Chairman of the Federal Deposit Insurance Corporation contended that management fraud (presumably including cooking the books) contributed to one-third of bank failures.

3. Ten percent of total bankruptcies in a study authorized by the Treadway Commission involved fraudulent financial reporting.

4. Former SEC Chairman John Shad estimated that all fraudulent securities activities amount to a fraction of 1% of the $50 billion of corporate and government securities traded daily.[12]

Thus, cooking the books episodes, though serious and despicable, apparently do not indicate a wholesale breakdown of ethical conduct by management accountants and financial executives of business enterprises.

An important question to consider is: Can the codes of conduct for management accountants and financial executives recently established or revised by the IMA, the FEI, and AICPA help those key players in corporate financial reporting to resist pressures, often from top management but sometimes from within themselves, to falsify financial statements and financial reports? Or is it too much to expect such individuals, whose livelihoods and careers depend a great deal on what is in those statements and reports, to be completely impartial in their preparation? Ralph E. Walters, CPA, former Director of Professional Conduct for The California Society of Certified Public Accountants, has considered this thorny question:

> An obligation to be *impartial* seems to me to place a new and possibly unrealistic burden on the management accountant. Traditionally, most employees have felt an obligation, within the bounds of honesty and integrity, to put the best face upon their employer's affairs. For example, there is still some latitude in selection and judgment in the application of GAAP [generally accepted accounting principles]. Some managers consistently opt for the most aggressive principle or application. The aggregate effect is to bias the financial statements. They may be in accordance with GAAP, but the quality of earnings is suspect. They are not impartial. This condition is not uncommon in practice (it is a principal reason we need independent auditors). An accountant associated with this condition is literally violating the AICPA Code. The [IMA] Code is less clear.
>
> Is this interpretation realistic? Do management accountants generally understand this? I doubt it. In fairness to their members and to the public, the AICPA and the [IMA] need to put their heads together and agree how much objectivity management accountants can be expected to live with, including some examples in real-life situations. The positions should be consistent and must be made clear to all management accountants.[13]

---

[11] *Report of the National Committee on Fraudulent Financial Reporting*, p. 25.
[12] Ibid., pp. 25–26.
[13] Ralph E. Walters, "Ethics and Excellence," *Management Accounting*, January 1990, p. 12.

The questions raised in the foregoing paragraph are difficult to answer. However, the SEC has emphasized the importance of objectivity as follows, in rejecting the "good soldier" rationalization of unethical conduct by a corporate controller (a CPA):

> The Commission cannot condone [the controller's] conduct. [The controller] has or had available to him more than sufficient information to be aware that the financial statements he prepared and the periodic reports he signed were materially inaccurate. Under the circumstances, and as a senior level financial officer and the highest level CPA within [the corporation] involved in the financial reporting process, [the controller] owed a duty to [the corporation] and its shareholders not to assist in, or even acquiesce in, [the corporation's] issuance of such financial statements. Although [the controller] may have made the appropriate recommendations to his corporate supervisors, when those recommendations were rejected, [the controller] acted as the "good soldier," implementing their directions which he knew or should have known were improper.[14]

In like vein, the SEC commented as follows on the behavior of a corporate controller who, despite his knowledge of cooking the books activities directed by the company's former CEO and former CFO, took no remedial actions:

> As controller, [the CPA] had a duty to satisfy himself that [the company's] financial statements were properly stated under GAAP. [The controller] knew or recklessly disregarded facts indicating that, as a result of the fraudulent entries, [the company's] reported financial statements during fiscal year 1990 . . . were materially false and misleading. Although [the company's] former CEO and CFO devised and directed the improper practices resulting in [the company's] false recording and reporting, in the Commission's view, this does not justify [the controller's] failure to take sufficient steps to satisfy himself that the transactions were properly recorded . . . This failure was inconsistent with his duties as . . . controller.[15]

At the beginning of their professional careers, students of advanced accounting might well reflect on their sense of ethical values and decide on a course of action if they find themselves in a position such as the foregoing ones.

Institute of Management Accountants Standards of Ethical Conduct for Practitioners of Management Accounting and Financial Management*

Practitioners of management accounting and financial management have an obligation to the public, their profession, the organization they serve, and themselves to maintain the highest standards of ethical conduct. In recognition of this obligation, the Institute of Management Accountants has promulgated the following standards of ethical con-

---

[14] *AAER 93*, ". . . In the Matter of Michael R. Maury," March 26, 1986.
[15] *AAER 538*, ". . . In the Matter of Michael V. Barnes," March 11, 1994.
* From Institute of Management Accountants, *Statements on Management Accounting: Standards of Ethical Conduct for Management Accountants,* Statement No. 1C (10 Paragon Drive, Montvale, NJ 07645, April 1997). Reprinted with permission.

duct for practitioners of management accounting and financial management. Adherence to these standards, both domestically and internationally, is integral to achieving the Objectives of Management Accounting. Practitioners of management accounting and financial management shall not commit acts contrary to these standards nor shall they condone the commission of such acts by others within their organization.

COMPETENCE

Practitioners of management accounting and financial management have a responsibility to:

- Maintain an appropriate level of professional competence by ongoing development of their knowledge and skills.
- Perform their professional duties in accordance with relevant laws, regulations, and technical standards.
- Prepare complete and clear reports and recommendations after appropriate analysis of relevant and reliable information.

CONFIDENTIALITY

Practitioners of management accounting and financial management have a responsibility to:

- Refrain from disclosing confidential information acquired in the course of their work except when authorized, unless legally obligated to do so.
- Inform subordinates as appropriate regarding the confidentiality of information acquired in the course of their work and monitor their activities to assure the maintenance of that confidentiality.
- Refrain from using or appearing to use confidential information acquired in the course of their work for unethical or illegal advantage either personally or through third parties.

INTEGRITY

Practitioners of management accounting and financial management have a responsibility to:

- Avoid actual or apparent conflicts of interest and advise all appropriate parties of any potential conflict.
- Refrain from engaging in any activity that would prejudice their ability to carry out their duties ethically.
- Refuse any gift, favor, or hospitality that would influence or would appear to influence their actions.
- Refrain from either actively or passively subverting the attainment of the organization's legitimate and ethical objectives.
- Recognize and communicate professional limitations or other constraints that would preclude responsible judgment or successful performance of an activity.

- Communicate unfavorable as well as favorable information and professional judgments or opinions.

- Refrain from engaging in or supporting any activity that would discredit the profession.

OBJECTIVITY

Practitioners of management accounting and financial management have a responsibility to:

- Communicate information fairly and objectively.

- Disclose fully all relevant information that could reasonably be expected to influence an intended user's understanding of the reports, comments, and recommendations presented.

RESOLUTION OF ETHICAL CONFLICT

In applying the standards of ethical conduct, practitioners of management accounting and financial management may encounter problems in identifying unethical behavior or in resolving an ethical conflict. When faced with significant ethical issues, practitioners of management accounting and financial management should follow the established policies of the organization bearing on the resolution of such conflict. If these policies do not resolve the ethical conflict, such practitioner should consider the following courses of action:

- Discuss such problems with the immediate superior except when it appears that the superior is involved, in which case the problem should be presented initially to the next higher managerial level. If a satisfactory resolution cannot be achieved when the problem is initially presented, submit the issues to the next higher managerial level.

  If the immediate superior is the chief executive officer, or equivalent, the acceptable reviewing authority may be a group such as the audit committee, executive committee, board of directors, board of trustees, or owners. Contact with levels above the immediate superior should be initiated only with the superior's knowledge, assuming the superior is not involved. Except where legally prescribed, communication of such problems to authorities or individuals not employed or engaged by the organization is not considered appropriate.

- Clarify relevant ethical issues by confidential discussion with an objective advisor (e.g., IMA Ethics Counseling Service) to obtain a better understanding of possible courses of action.

- Consult your own attorney as to legal obligations and rights concerning the ethical conflict.

- If the ethical conflict still exists after exhausting all levels of internal review, there may be no other recourse on significant matters than to resign from the organization and to submit an informative memorandum to an appropriate representative of the organization. After resignation, depending on the nature of the ethical conflict, it may also be appropriate to notify other parties.

Appendix 2

FEI Code of Ethics*

As a member of Financial Executives Institute, I will:

- Conduct my business and personal affairs at all times with honesty and integrity.

- Provide complete, appropriate and relevant information in an objective manner when reporting to management, stockholders, employees, government agencies, other institutions and the public.

- Comply with rules and regulations of federal, state, provincial, and local governments, and other appropriate private and public regulatory agencies.

- Discharge duties and responsibilities to my employer to the best of my ability, including complete communication on all matters within my jurisdiction.

- Maintain the confidentiality of information acquired in the course of my work except when authorized or otherwise legally obligated to disclose. Confidential information acquired in the course of my work will not be used for my personal advantage.

- Maintain an appropriate level of professional competence through continuing development of my knowledge and skills.

- Refrain from committing acts discreditable to myself, my employer, FEI or fellow members of the Institute.

Appendix 3

AICPA Code of Professional Conduct†
COMPOSITION, APPLICABILITY, AND COMPLIANCE

The Code of Professional Conduct of the American Institute of Certified Public Accountants consists of two sections—(1) the Principles and (2) the Rules. The Principles provide the framework for the Rules, which govern the performance of professional services by members. The Council of the American Institute of Certified Public Accountants is authorized to designate bodies to promulgate technical standards under the Rules, and the bylaws require adherence to those Rules and standards.

---

* From Financial Executives Institute, *Code of Ethics* (10 Madison Avenue, Morristown, NJ 07962-1938). Reprinted with permission.
† From American Institute of Certified Public Accountants, *Code of Professional Conduct.* Copyright © 2000 by American Institute of Certified Public Accountants, Inc. (New York). Reprinted with permission. (Not included are the Statements on Standards for Tax Services incorporated in the Code in 2000.)

The Code of Professional Conduct was adopted by membership to provide guidance and rules to all members—those in public practice, in industry, in government, and in education—in the performance of their professional responsibilities.

Compliance with the Code of Professional Conduct, as with all standards in an open society, depends primarily on members' understanding and voluntary actions, secondarily on reinforcement by peers and public opinion, and ultimately on disciplinary proceedings, when necessary, against members who fail to comply with the Rules.

OTHER GUIDANCE

Interpretations of Rules of Conduct consist of interpretations which have been adopted, after exposure to state societies, state boards, practice units and other interested parties, by the professional ethics division's executive committee to provide guidelines as to the scope and application of the Rules but are not intended to limit such scope or application. A member who departs from such guidelines shall have the burden of justifying such departure in any disciplinary hearing. *Interpretations* which existed before the adoption of the Code of Professional Conduct on January 12, 1988, will remain in effect until further action is deemed necessary by the appropriate senior technical committee.

Ethics Rulings consist of formal rulings made by the professional ethics division's executive committee after exposure to state societies, state boards, practice units and other interested parties. These rulings summarize the application of Rules of Conduct and Interpretations to a particular set of factual circumstances. Members who depart from such rulings in similar circumstances will be requested to justify such departures. *Ethics Rulings* which existed before the adoption of the Code of Professional Conduct on January 12, 1988, will remain in effect until further action is deemed necessary by the appropriate senior technical committee.

Publication of an Interpretation or Ethics ruling in *The Journal of Accountancy* constitutes notice to members. Hence, the effective date of the pronouncement is the last day of the month in which the pronouncement is published in *The Journal of Accountancy.* The professional ethics division will take into consideration the time that would have been reasonable for the member to comply with the pronouncement.

A member should also consult, if applicable, the ethical standards of his state CPA society, state board of accountancy, the Securities and Exchange Commission, and any other governmental agency which may regulate his client's business or use his report to evaluate the client's compliance with applicable laws and related regulations.

SECTION I: PRINCIPLES

PREAMBLE

Membership in the American Institute of Certified Public Accountants is voluntary. By accepting membership, a certified public accountant assumes an obligation of self-discipline above and beyond the requirements of laws and regulations.

These Principles of the Code of Professional Conduct of the American Institute of Certified Public Accountants express the profession's recognition of its responsibilities to the public, to clients, and to colleagues. They guide members in the performance of their professional responsibilities and express the basic tenets of ethical and professional conduct. The Principles call for an unswerving commitment to honorable behavior, even at the sacrifice of personal advantage.

ARTICLE I: RESPONSIBILITIES

In carrying out their responsibilities as professionals, members should exercise sensitive professional and moral judgments in all their activities.

As professionals, certified public accountants perform an essential role in society. Consistent with that role, members of the American Institute of Certified Public Accountants have responsibilities to all those who use their professional services. Members also have a continuing responsibility to cooperate with each other to improve the art of accounting, maintain the public's confidence, and carry out the profession's special responsibilities for self-governance. The collective efforts of all members are required to maintain and enhance the traditions of the profession.

ARTICLE II: THE PUBLIC INTEREST

Members should accept the obligation to act in a way that will serve the public interest, honor the public trust, and demonstrate commitment to professionalism.

A distinguishing mark of a profession is acceptance of its responsibility to the public. The accounting profession's public consists of clients, credit grantors, governments, employers, investors, the business and financial community, and others who rely on the objectivity and integrity of certified public accountants to maintain the orderly functioning of commerce. This reliance imposes a public interest responsibility on certified public accountants. The public interest is defined as the collective well-being of the community of people and institutions the profession serves.

In discharging their professional responsibilities, members may encounter conflicting pressures from among each of those groups. In resolving those conflicts, members should act with integrity, guided by the precept that when members fulfill their responsibility to the public, clients' and employers' interests are best served.

Those who rely on certified public accountants expect them to discharge their responsibilities with integrity, objectivity, due professional care, and a genuine interest in serving the public. They are expected to provide quality services, enter into fee arrangements, and offer a range of services—all in a manner that demonstrates a level of professionalism consistent with these Principles of the Code of Professional Conduct.

All who accept membership in the American Institute of Certified Public Accountants commit themselves to honor the public trust. In return for the faith that the public reposes in them, members should seek continually to demonstrate their dedication to professional excellence.

ARTICLE III: INTEGRITY

To maintain and broaden public confidence, members should perform all professional responsibilities with the highest sense of integrity.

Integrity is an element of character fundamental to professional recognition. It is the quality from which the public trust derives and the benchmark against which a member must ultimately test all decisions.

Integrity requires a member to be, among other things, honest and candid within the constraints of client confidentiality. Service and the public trust should not be subordinated to personal gain and advantage. Integrity can accommodate the inadvertent error and the honest difference of opinion; it cannot accommodate deceit or subordination of principle.

Integrity is measured in terms of what is right and just. In the absence of specific rules, standards, or guidance, or in the face of conflicting opinions, a member should test decisions and deeds by asking: "Am I doing what a person of integrity would do? Have I retained my integrity?" Integrity requires a member to observe both the form and the spirit of technical and ethical standards; circumvention of those standards constitutes subordination of judgment.

Integrity also requires a member to observe the principles of objectivity and independence and of due care.

ARTICLE IV: OBJECTIVITY AND INDEPENDENCE

A member should maintain objectivity and be free of conflicts of interest in discharging professional responsibilities. A member in public practice should be independent in fact and appearance when providing auditing and other attestation services.

Objectivity is a state of mind, a quality that lends value to a member's services. It is a distinguishing feature of the profession. The principle of objectivity imposes the obligation to be impartial, intellectually honest, and free of conflicts of interest. Independence precludes relationships that may appear to impair a member's objectivity in rendering attestation services.

Members often serve multiple interests in many different capacities and must demonstrate their objectivity in varying circumstances. Members in public practice render attest, tax, and management advisory services. Other members prepare financial statements in the employment of others, perform internal auditing services, and serve in financial and management capacities in industry, education, and government. They also educate and train those who aspire to admission into the profession. Regardless of service or capacity, members should protect the integrity of their work, maintain objectivity, and avoid any subordination of their judgment.

For a member in public practice, the maintenance of objectivity and independence requires a continuing assessment of client relationships and public responsibility. Such a member who provides auditing and other attestation services should be independent in fact and appearance. In providing all other services, a member should maintain objectivity and avoid conflicts of interest.

Although members not in public practice cannot maintain the appearance of independence, they nevertheless have the responsibility to maintain objectivity in rendering professional services. Members employed by others to prepare financial statements or to perform auditing, tax, or consulting services are charged with the same responsibility for objectivity as members in public practice and must be scrupulous in their application of generally accepted accounting principles and candid in all their dealings with members in public practice.

ARTICLE V: DUE CARE

A member should observe the profession's technical and ethical standards, strive continually to improve competence and the quality of services, and discharge professional responsibility to the best of the member's ability.

The quest for excellence is the essence of due care. Due care requires a member to discharge professional responsibilities with competence and diligence. It imposes the obligation to perform professional services to the best of a member's ability with concern for the best interest of those for whom the services are performed and consistent with the profession's responsibility to the public.

Competence is derived from a synthesis of education and experience. It begins with a mastery of the common body of knowledge required for designation as a certified public accountant. The maintenance of competence requires a commitment to learning and professional improvement that must continue throughout a member's professional life. It is a member's individual responsibility. In all engagements and in all responsibilities, each member should undertake to achieve a level of competence that will assure that the quality of the member's services meets the high level of professionalism required by these Principles.

Competence represents the attainment and maintenance of a level of understanding and knowledge that enables a member to render services with facility and acumen. It also establishes the limitations of a member's capabilities by dictating that consultation or referral may be required when a professional engagement exceeds the personal competence of a member or a member's firm. Each member is responsible for assessing his or her own competence—of evaluating whether education, experience, and judgment are adequate for the responsibility to be assumed.

Members should be diligent in discharging responsibilities to clients, employers, and the public. Diligence imposes the responsibility to render services promptly and carefully, to be thorough, and to observe applicable technical and ethical standards.

Due care requires a member to plan and supervise adequately any professional activity for which he or she is responsible.

ARTICLE VI: SCOPE AND NATURE OF SERVICES

A member in public practice should observe the Principles of the Code of Professional Conduct in determining the scope and nature of services to be provided.

The public interest aspect of certified public accountants' services requires that such services be consistent with acceptable professional behavior for certified public accountants. Integrity requires that service and the public trust not be subordinated to personal gain and advantage. Objectivity and independence requires that members be free from conflicts of interest in discharging professional responsibilities. Due care requires that services be provided with competence and diligence.

Each of these Principles should be considered by members in determining whether or not to provide specific services in individual circumstances. In some instances, they may represent an overall constraint on the nonaudit services that might be offered to a specific client. No hard-and-fast rules can be developed to help members reach these judgments, but they must be satisfied that they are meeting the spirit of the Principles in this regard.

In order to accomplish this, members should

- Practice in firms that have in place internal quality-control procedures to ensure that services are competently delivered and adequately supervised.

- Determine, in their individual judgments, whether the scope and nature of other services provided to an audit client would create a conflict of interest in the performance of the audit function for that client.

- Assess, in their individual judgments, whether an activity is consistent with their role as professionals.

SECTION II: RULES

APPLICABILITY

The bylaws of the American Institute of Certified Public Accountants require that members adhere to the Rules of the Code of Professional Conduct. Members must be prepared to justify departures from these Rules.

INTERPRETATION ADDRESSING THE APPLICABILITY OF THE AICPA CODE OF PROFESSIONAL CONDUCT

For purposes of the applicability section of the Code, a "member" is a member or international associate of the American Institute of CPAs.

1. The Rules of Conduct that follow apply to all professional services performed except (a) where the wording of the rule indicates otherwise and (b) that a member who is practicing outside the United States will not be subject to discipline for departing from any of the rules stated herein as long as the member's conduct is in accord with the rules of the organized accounting profession in the country in which he or she is practicing. However, where a member's name is associated with financial statements under circumstances that would entitle the reader to assume that United States practices were followed, the member must comply with the requirements of Rules 202 and 203.

2. A member shall not knowingly permit a person, whom the member has the authority or capacity to control, to carry out on his or her behalf, either with or without compensation, acts which, if carried out by the member, would place the member in violation of the rules. Further, a member may be held responsible for the acts of all persons associated with him or her in the practice of public accounting whom the member has the authority or capacity to control.

3. A member (as defined in interpretation 101-9 [ET section 101.11]) may be considered to have his or her independence impaired, with respect to a client, as the result of the actions or relationships of certain persons or entities, as described in rule 101 [ET section 101.01] and its interpretations and rulings, whom the member does not have the authority or capacity to control. Therefore, nothing in this section should lead one to conclude that the member's independence is not impaired solely because of his or her inability to control the actions or relationships of such persons or entities.

DEFINITIONS

Client. A client is any person or entity, other than the member's employer, that engages a member or a member's firm to perform professional services or a person or entity with respect to which professional services are performed. For purposes of this paragraph, the term "employer" does not include—

a. Entities engaged in the practice of public accounting; or
b. Federal, state, and local governments or component units thereof provided the member performing professional services with respect to those entities—
    i. Is directly elected by voters of the government or component unit thereof with respect to which professional services are performed; or
    ii. Is an individual who is (1) appointed by a legislative body and (2) subject to removal by a legislative body; or
    iii. Is appointed by someone other than the legislative body, so long as the appointment is confirmed by the legislative body and removal is subject to oversight or approval by the legislative body.

Council. The Council of the American Institute of Certified Public Accountants.

Enterprise. For purposes of the Code, the term *enterprise* is synonymous with the term *client.*

Financial statements. A presentation of financial data, including accompanying notes, if any, intended to communicate an entity's economic resources and/or obligations at a point in time or the changes therein for a period of time, in accordance with generally accepted accounting principles or a comprehensive basis of accounting other than generally accepted accounting principles.

Incidental financial data to support recommendations to a client or in documents for which the reporting is governed by Statements on Standards for Attestation Engagements and tax returns and supporting schedules do not, for this purpose, constitute financial statements. The statement, affidavit, or signature of preparers required on tax returns neither constitutes an opinion on financial statements nor requires a disclaimer of such opinion.

Firm. A form of organization permitted by state law or regulation whose characteristics conform to resolutions of Council that is engaged in the practice of public accounting, including the individual owners thereof.

Institute. The American Institute of Certified Public Accountants.

Interpretations of rules of conduct. Pronouncements issued by the division of professional ethics to provide guidelines concerning the scope and application of the rules of conduct.

Member. A member, associate member, or international associate of the American Institute of Certified Public Accountants.

Practice of public accounting. The practice of public accounting consists of the performance for a client, by a member or a member's firm, while holding out as CPA(s), of the professional services of accounting, tax, personal financial planning, litigation support services, and those professional services for which standards are promulgated by bodies designated by Council, such as Statements of Financial Accounting Standards, Statements on Auditing Standards, Statements on Standards for Accounting and Review Services, Statements on Standards for Consulting Services, Statements of Governmental Accounting Standards, and Statements on Standards for Attestation Engagements.

However, a member or a member's firm, while holding out as CPA(s), is not considered to be in the practice of public accounting if the member or the member's firm does not perform, for any client, any of the professional services described in the preceding paragraph.

Professional Services. Professional services include all services performed by a member while holding out as a CPA.

Holding Out. In general, any action initiated by a member that informs others of his or her status as a CPA or AICPA-accredited specialist constitutes holding out as a CPA. This would include, for example, any oral or written representation to another regarding CPA status, use of the CPA designation on business cards or letterhead, the display of a certificate evidencing a member's CPA designation, or listing as a CPA in local telephone directories.

RULES

RULE 101 INDEPENDENCE

A member in public practice shall be independent in the performance of professional services as required by standards promulgated by bodies designated by Council.

RULE 102 INTEGRITY AND OBJECTIVITY

In the performance of any professional service, a member shall maintain objectivity and integrity, shall be free of conflicts of interest, and shall not knowingly misrepresent facts or subordinate his or her judgment to others.

RULE 201 GENERAL STANDARDS

A member shall comply with the following standards and any interpretations thereof by bodies designated by Council.

A. *Professional Competence.* Undertake only those professional services that the member or the member's firm can reasonably expect to be completed with professional competence.

B. *Due Professional Care.* Exercise due professional care in the performance of professional services.

C. *Planning and Supervision.* Adequately plan and supervise the performance of professional services.

D. *Sufficient Relevant Data.* Obtain sufficient relevant data to afford a reasonable basis for conclusions or recommendations in relation to any professional services performed.

RULE 202 COMPLIANCE WITH STANDARDS

A member who performs auditing, review, compilation, management consulting, tax, or other professional services shall comply with standards promulgated by bodies designated by Council.

RULE 203 ACCOUNTING PRINCIPLES

A member shall not (1) express an opinion or state affirmatively that the financial statements or other financial data of any entity are presented in conformity with generally accepted accounting principles or (2) state that he or she is not aware of any material modifications that should be made to such statements or data in order for them to be in conformity with generally accepted accounting principles, if such statements or data contain any departure from an accounting principle promulgated by bodies designated by Council to establish such principles that has a material effect on the statements or data taken as a whole. If, however, the statements or data contain such a departure and the member can demonstrate that due to unusual circumstances the financial statements or data would otherwise have been misleading, the member can comply with the rule by describing the departure, its approximate effects, if practicable, and the reasons why compliance with the principle would result in a misleading statement.

RULE 301 CONFIDENTIAL CLIENT INFORMATION

A member in public practice shall not disclose any confidential client information without the specific consent of the client.

This rule shall not be construed (1) to relieve a member of his or her professional obligations under rules 202 and 203, (2) to affect in any way the member's obligation to comply with a validly issued and enforceable subpoena or summons, or to prohibit a member's compliance with applicable laws and government regulations, (3) to prohibit review of a member's professional practice under AICPA or state CPA society or Board of Accountancy authorization, or (4) to preclude a member from initiating a complaint with, or responding to any inquiry made by, the ethics division or trial board of the Institute or a duly constituted investigative or disciplinary body of a state CPA society or Board of Accountancy.

Members of any of the bodies identified in (4) above and members involved with professional practice reviews identified in (3) above shall not use to their own advantage or disclose any member's confidential client information that comes to their attention in carrying out those activities. This prohibition shall not restrict members' exchange of information in connection with the investigative or disciplinary proceedings described in (4) above or the professional practice reviews described in (3) above.

RULE 302 CONTINGENT FEES*

A member in public practice shall not

1. Perform for a contingent fee any professional services for, or receive such a fee from, a client for whom the member or the member's firm performs
   a. an audit or review of a financial statement; or
   b. a compilation of a financial statement when the member expects, or reasonably might expect, that a third party will use the financial statement and the member's compilation report does not disclose a lack of independence; or
   c. an examination of prospective financial information;
   or
2. Prepare an original or amended tax return or claim for a tax refund for a contingent fee for any client.

The prohibition in (1) above applies during the period in which the member or the member's firm is engaged to perform any of the services listed above and the period covered by any historical financial statements involved in any such listed services.

Except as stated in the next sentence, a contingent fee is a fee established for the performance of any service pursuant to an arrangement in which no fee will be charged unless a specified finding or result is attained, or in which the amount of the fee is otherwise dependent upon the finding or result of such service. Solely for purposes of this rule, fees are not regarded as being contingent if fixed by courts or other public authorities, or, in tax matters, if determined based on the results of judicial proceedings or the findings of governmental agencies.

A member's fees may vary depending, for example, on the complexity of services rendered.

RULE 401 [RESERVED]

RULE 501 ACTS DISCREDITABLE

A member shall not commit an act discreditable to the profession.

RULE 502 ADVERTISING AND OTHER FORMS OF SOLICITATION

A member in public practice shall not seek to obtain clients by advertising or other forms of solicitation in a manner that is false, misleading, or deceptive. Solicitation by the use of coercion, over-reaching, or harassing conduct is prohibited.

---

* Laws or board of accountancy rules of some states prohibit the receipt of contingent fees by CPAs. (Author's note)

RULE 503 COMMISSIONS AND REFERRAL FEES*

A. **Prohibited Commissions**

A member in public practice shall not for a commission recommend or refer to a client any product or service, or for a commission recommend or refer any product or service to be supplied by a client, or receive a commission, when the member or the member's firm also performs for that client

a. an audit or review of a financial statement; or

b. a compilation of a financial statement when the member expects, or reasonably might expect, that a third party will use the financial statement and the member's compilation report does not disclose a lack of independence; or

c. an examination of prospective financial information.

This prohibition applies during the period in which the member is engaged to perform any of the services listed above and the period covered by any historical financial statements involved in such listed services.

B. **Disclosure of Permitted Commissions**

A member in public practice who is not prohibited by this rule from performing services for or receiving a commission and who is paid or expects to be paid a commission shall disclose that fact to any person or entity to whom the member recommends or refers a product or service to which the commission relates.

C. **Referral Fees**

Any member who accepts a referral fee for recommending or referring any service of a CPA to any person or entity or who pays a referral fee to obtain a client shall disclose such acceptance or payment to the client.

RULE 504 *[There is currently no rule 504.]*

RULE 505 FORM OF ORGANIZATION AND NAME

A member may practice public accounting only in the form of organization permitted by law or regulation whose characteristics conform to resolutions of Council.

A member shall not practice public accounting under a firm name that is misleading. Names of one or more past owners may be included in the firm name of a successor organization.

A firm may not designate itself as "Members of the American Institute of Certified Public Accountants" unless all of its owners are members of the Institute.

APPENDIX A: COUNCIL RESOLUTION DESIGNATING BODIES TO PROMULGATE TECHNICAL STANDARDS

FINANCIAL ACCOUNTING STANDARDS BOARD

WHEREAS: In 1959 the Council designated the Accounting Principles Board to establish accounting principles, and

WHEREAS: The Council is advised that the Financial Accounting Standards Board (FASB) has become operational, it is

---

* Laws or board of accountancy rules of some states prohibit the payment or receipt of commissions by CPAs. (Author's note)

RESOLVED: That as of the date hereof the FASB, in respect of statements of financial accounting standards finally adopted by such board in accordance with its rules of procedure and the bylaws of the Financial Accounting Foundation, be, and hereby is, designated by this Council as the body to establish accounting principles pursuant to rule 203 and standards on disclosure of financial information for such entities outside financial statements in published financial reports containing financial statements under rule 202 of the Rules of the Code of Professional Conduct of the American Institute of Certified Public Accountants provided, however, any accounting research bulletins, or opinions of the accounting principles board issued or approved for exposure by the accounting principles board prior to April 1, 1973, and finally adopted by such board on or before June 30, 1973, shall constitute statements of accounting principles promulgated by a body designated by Council as contemplated in rule 203 of the Rules of the Code of Professional Conduct unless and until such time as they are expressly superseded by action of the FASB.

GOVERNMENTAL ACCOUNTING STANDARDS BOARD

WHEREAS: The Governmental Accounting Standards Board (GASB) has been established by the board of trustees of the Financial Accounting Foundation (FAF) to issue standards of financial accounting and reporting with respect to activities and transactions of state and local governmental entities, and

WHEREAS: The American Institute of Certified Public Accountants is a signatory to the agreement creating the GASB as an arm of the FAF and has supported the GASB professionally and financially, it is

RESOLVED: That as of the date hereof, the GASB, with respect to statements of governmental accounting standards adopted and issued in July 1984 and subsequently in accordance with its rules of procedure and the bylaws of the FASB, be, and hereby is, designated by the Council of the American Institute of Certified Public Accountants as the body to establish financial accounting principles for state and local governmental entities pursuant to rule 203, and standards on disclosure of financial information for such entities outside financial statements in published financial reports containing financial statements under rule 202.

AICPA COMMITTEES AND BOARDS

WHEREAS: The membership of the Institute has adopted rules 201 and 202 of the Rules of the Code of Professional Conduct, which authorizes the Council to designate bodies to promulgate technical standards with which members must comply, and therefore it is

ACCOUNTING AND REVIEW SERVICES COMMITTEE

RESOLVED: That the AICPA accounting and review services committee is hereby designated to promulgate standards under rules 201 and 202 with respect to unaudited financial statements or other unaudited financial information of an entity that is not required to file financial statements with a regulatory agency in connection with the sale or trading of its securities in a public market.

AUDITING STANDARDS BOARD

RESOLVED: That the AICPA auditing standards board is hereby designated as the body authorized under rules 201 and 202 to promulgate auditing and attest standards and procedures.

RESOLVED: That the auditing standards board shall establish under statements on auditing standards the responsibilities of members with respect to standards for disclosure of financial information outside financial statements in published financial reports containing financial statements.

MANAGEMENT CONSULTING SERVICES EXECUTIVE COMMITTEE

RESOLVED: That the AICPA management consulting services executive committee is hereby designated to promulgate standards under rules 201 and 202 with respect to the offering of management consulting services, provided, however, that such standards do not deal with the broad question of what, if any, services should be proscribed.

AND FURTHER RESOLVED: That any Institute committee or board now or in the future authorized by the Council to issue enforceable standards under rules 201 and 202 must observe an exposure process seeking comment from other affected committees and boards, as well as the general membership.

ATTESTATION STANDARDS

RESOLVED: That the AICPA accounting and review services committee, auditing standards board, and management consulting services executive committee are hereby designated as bodies authorized under rules 201 and 202 to promulgate attestation standards in their respective areas of responsibility.

APPENDIX B: COUNCIL RESOLUTION CONCERNING RULE 505—FORM OF ORGANIZATION AND NAME

A. RESOLVED: That with respect to a member engaged in the practice of public accounting in firm or organization which performs (1) any audit or other engagement performed in accordance with the Statements on Auditing Standards, (2) any review of a financial statement performed in accordance with the Statements on Standards for Accounting and Review Services, or (3) any examination of prospective financial information performed in accordance with the Statements on Standards for Attestation Engagements, or which holds itself out as a firm of certified public accountants or uses the term "certified public accountant(s)" or the designation "CPA" in connection with its name, the characteristics of such a firm or organization under rule 505 are as set forth below.

  1. A majority of the ownership of the firm in terms of financial interests and voting rights must belong to CPAs. The non-CPA owner would have to be actively engaged as a firm member in providing services to the firm's clients as his or her principal occupation. Ownership by investors or commercial enterprises not actively engaged as firm members in providing services to the firm's clients as their principal occupation is against the public interest and continues to be prohibited.
  2. There must be a CPA who has ultimate responsibility for all the services provided by the firm and by each business unit[1] performing the services described in A, above. Compilation services and other engagements governed by Statements on Auditing Standards or Statements on Standards for Accounting and Re-

---

[1] "Business unit" is meant to indicate geographic (such as offices) and functional arrangements (such as tax and management consulting services).

view Services and non-CPA owners could not assume ultimate responsibility for any such services or engagements.

3. Non-CPAs becoming owners after adoption of Council's resolution would have to possess a baccalaureate degree and, beginning in the year 2010, have obtained 150 semester hours of education at an accredited college or university.

4. Non-CPA owners would be permitted to use the title "principal," "owner," "officer," "member" or "shareholder," or any other title permitted by state law, but not hold themselves out to be CPAs.

5. Non-CPA owners would have to abide by the AICPA Code of Professional Conduct. AICPA members may be held responsible under the Code for acts of co-owners.

6. Non-CPA owners would have to complete the same work-related CPE requirements as set forth under AICPA bylaw section 2.3 for AICPA members.

7. Owners shall at all times own their equity in their own right and shall be the beneficial owners of the equity capital ascribed to them. Provision would have to be made for the ownership to be transferred, within a reasonable period of time, to the firm or to other qualified owners if the owner ceases to be actively engaged in the firm.

8. Non-CPA owners would not be eligible for membership in the AICPA.

B. RESOLVED: The characteristics of all other firms or organizations are deemed to be whatever is legally permissible under applicable law or regulation except as otherwise provided in paragraph C below.

C. RESOLVED: That with respect to a member engaged in the practice of public accounting in a firm or organization which is not within the description of a firm or organization set forth in paragraph A above, but who performs compilations of financial statements performed in accordance with the Statements on Standards for Accounting and Review Services, the characteristics of such a firm or organization under Rule 505 are as set forth below.

1. There must be a CPA who has ultimate responsibility for any financial statement compilation services provided by the firm and by each business unit performing such compilation services and non-CPA owners could not assume ultimate responsibility for any such services.

2. Any compilation report must be signed individually by a CPA, and may not be signed in the name of the firm or organization.

Review Questions

1. What are **cute accounting** and **cooking the books**?

2. Why is the Equity Funding Corporation of America fraud significant for management accountants and financial executives?

3. Identify the four components of ethical conduct for management accountants, set forth in **Standards of Ethical Conduct for Practitioners of Management Accounting and Financial Management** of the Institute of Management Accountants.

4. How did the National Commission on Fraudulent Financial Reporting (Treadway Commission) define **fraudulent financial reporting**?

5. What Rules of Professional Conduct of the American Institute of Certified Public Accountants apply to all members of the AICPA, including management accountants?

6. Do the ethics codes of the Institute of Management Accountants and the Financial Executives Institute require their members to comply with generally accepted accounting principles? Explain.

7. What is *insider trading* of corporate securities?

8. Does the Securities and Exchange Commission accept a "good soldier" rationalization for fraudulent financial reporting? Explain.

9. What are the obligations of management accountants regarding *conflicts of interest*?

10. Does the *Code of Ethics* of the Financial Executives Institute require FEI members to maintain the confidentiality of information acquired in the course of their work in all circumstances? Explain.

11. Does the *Code of Professional Conduct* of the American Institute of Certified Public Accountants require AICPA members in industry to maintain the appearance of independence? Explain.

12. Differentiate between the *Interpretations of Rules of Conduct* and the *Ethics Rulings* components of the AICPA's *Code of Professional Conduct*.

Exercises

Select the best answer for each of the following multiple-choice questions:

(Exercise 1.1)

1. The bylaws of the AICPA require members to adhere to the Code of Professional Conduct section entitled:
   a. Principles
   b. Rules
   c. Interpretations
   d. Ethics Rulings

2. A rule of the AICPA Code of Professional Conduct that does not apply to AICPA members in private industry is:
   a. Rule 101   Independence.
   b. Rule 102   Integrity and Objectivity.
   c. Rule 201   General Standards.
   d. Rule 203   Accounting Principles.
   e. None of the foregoing.

3. Conduct of a member's personal affairs is addressed in the ethics code or codes of the:
   a. American Institute of Certified Public Accountants only.
   b. Financial Executives Institute only.
   c. Institute of Management Accountants only.
   d. Three organizations cited above.

4. According to the National Commission on Fraudulent Financial Reporting (Treadway Commission), the responsibility for reliable financial reporting lies first and foremost:
   a. At the corporate level.
   b. With the SEC.
   c. With independent auditors.
   d. With state boards of accountancy.

5. Does *fraudulent financial reporting* include:

	Cooking the Books?	Cute Accounting?
a.	No	Yes
b.	No	No
c.	Yes	Yes
d.	Yes	No

6. According to the AICPA, are financial statements of a business enterprise that have been drafted by the enterprise's independent auditors the representations of the enterprise's:

	Management?	Independent Auditors?
a.	Yes	Yes
b.	Yes	No
c.	No	Yes
d.	No	No

7. ***Standards of Ethical Conduct for Practitioners of Management Accounting and Financial Management*** of the Institute of Management Accountants deal with all of the following except:

   a. Competence.
   b. Confidentiality.
   c. Independence.
   d. Integrity.
   e. Objectivity.

8. The ***Report of the National Commission on Fraudulent Financial Reporting*** did not include recommendations for:

   a. Financial institution regulators.
   b. Legal counsel of business enterprises.
   c. Educators.
   d. State boards of accountancy.

9. Are conflicts of interest addressed *directly* in the ethics codes of the:

	IMA?	FEI?	AICPA?
a.	Yes	Yes	Yes
b.	Yes	No	Yes
c.	No	Yes	Yes
d.	No	No	Yes

10. Compliance with generally accepted accounting principles is required by the ethics code of the:

    a. AICPA only.
    b. AICPA and FEI.
    c. AICPA and IMA.
    d. AICPA, FEI, and IMA.

11. According to ***Standards of Ethical Conduct for Practitioners of Management Accounting and Financial Management*** of the Institute of Management Accountants, management accountants faced with significant ethical issues should first:

    a. Discuss the issue with the immediate superior, except when it appears the superior is involved.
    b. Clarify relevant concepts by confidential discussion with an objective adviser.
    c. Discuss the issue with the audit committee of the board of directors.
    d. Follow the established policies of the business enterprise bearing on the resolution of such issues.

12. The section of the American Institute of Certified Public Accountants Code of Professional Conduct that governs the performance of professional services by AICPA members is the:

    a. Principles
    b. Rules
    c. Bylaws
    d. Technical standards

Cases

(Case 1.1) Suppose you were to participate in a debate of the following resolution:

Resolved, that the following sentence from the Preamble to Section I: Principles of the AICPA Code of Professional Conduct is overly idealistic in today's society:

The Principles call for an unswerving commitment to honorable behavior, even at the sacrifice of personal advantage.

Instructions
Would you support the affirmative or the negative side of the debate? Explain.

(Case 1.2) In his *Meditations,* the Roman emperor Marcus Aurelius Antoninus wrote as follows (Books III and VII):

A man must stand erect, not be kept erect by others. . . .

Be thou erect or be made erect.

Instructions
Evaluate the usefulness of the ethics rules of the AICPA, FEI, and IMA in relation to the foregoing quotations.

(Case 1.3) Chief executive officers (CEOs) of business enterprises often pressure enterprise chief financial officers (CFOs) or controllers to cook the books.

Instructions
Evaluate the ethics rules of the IMA, FEI, and AICPA as guidelines for resisting the pressures described above.

(Case 1.4) General Instruction D(2)(a) of Form 10-K, Annual Report, requires the report, filed with the SEC, to be signed by the registrant company's principal financial officer and controller or principal accounting officer. Similarly, General Instruction G of Form 10-Q, Quarterly Report, requires the report, filed with the SEC, to be signed by the principal financial or chief accounting officer of the registrant company.

Instructions
How should the chief financial officer (CFO) and the controller of an SEC registrant enterprise view the obligation to sign the registrant's Form 10-K and Form 10-Q reports to the SEC? Explain.

(Case 1.5) According to Ralph E. Walters (page 7 of the text): "An obligation to be *impartial* seems to me to place a new and possibly unrealistic burden on the management accountant."

Instructions
Do you agree with Walters? Explain.

(Case 1.6) In a classroom discussion of ethics for financial executives, student Marcia opined that the Financial Executives Institute erred in requiring its members to conduct their *personal affairs* as well as their *business affairs* at all times with honesty and integrity. According to Marcia, such a requirement is an unwarranted invasion of FEI members' privacy. Student Ross disagreed, stating that FEI members' conduct in business affairs is significantly affected by their conduct in personal affairs, and therefore conduct in both areas appropriately is subjected to the same high standards by the FEI.

Instructions
Do you agree with student Marcia or student Ross? Explain.

(Case 1.7)   Vernon Cass, chief financial officer of Tingley Corporation, a publicly owned enterprise, asked his subordinate, John Conroy, CPA and controller of Tingley, if any accounting changes might be made before the forthcoming close of the fiscal year to enhance Tingley's earnings for the year. Conroy suggested that he might extend economic lives of plant assets, reduce the percentage used to estimate doubtful accounts expense based on net credit sales, and defer, rather than expense, certain advertising costs that consistently had been recognized as expenses in prior years. Cass instructed Conroy to formalize a proposal incorporating those suggestions, for consideration by the audit committee of Tingley's board of directors.

Instructions
Evaluate the actions of Vernon Cass and John Conroy. (Suggestion: Consider the provisions of *APB Opinion No. 20,* "Accounting Changes," and *Statement on Auditing Standards No. 57,* "Auditing Accounting Estimates," in your discussion.)

(Case 1.8)   The following excerpt is from *Standards of Ethical Conduct for Practitioners of Management Accounting and Financial Management* of the Institute of Management Accountants:

> If [an] ethical conflict still exists after exhausting all levels of internal review, there may be no other recourse on significant matters than to resign from the organization and to submit an informative memorandum to an appropriate representative of the organization.

Instructions
What is your opinion of the foregoing excerpt? Explain.

(Case 1.9)   Certified public accountants (CPAs) typically are subject to codes of ethics or conduct enacted by state boards of accountancy that license the accountants.

Instructions
Given that CPAs are subject to oversight by state boards of accountancy, what is the incentive—if any—for CPAs in management accounting to be members of the AICPA, the FEI, or the IMA? Explain.

(Case 1.10)   You are the chief financial officer of Playthings, Inc., a newly organized, publicly owned manufacturer of toys and games. Roy Weber, the chairman of the audit committee of the company's board of directors, asks you to consider at what point, under generally accepted accounting principles, the company can recognize revenue for "bill and hold" sales of toys to retailers. He stresses that it is imperative for the company to comply with federal and state securities laws.

Instructions
Prepare a memorandum to answer the audit committee chairman after you have researched the following:

> *Statement of Financial Accounting Concepts No. 6,* "Elements of Financial Statements," pars. 78, 79.

> *Statement of Financial Accounting Concepts No. 5,* "Recognition and Measurement in Financial Statements of Business Enterprises," pars. 83, 84.

> *Uniform Commercial Code,* secs. 401, 501.

> *SEC Accounting Series Release No. 292,* ". . . In the Matter of Arthur Andersen & Co."

> *SEC Accounting and Auditing Enforcement Release No. 108,* ". . . In the Matter of Stewart Parness."

> *SEC Accounting and Auditing Enforcement Release No. 817,* ". . . In the Matter of Cypress Bioscience Inc. . . ."

(Case 1.11) The following excerpts from notes to financial statements of two publicly owned enterprises are from the Fifty-Fourth Edition of *Accounting Trends & Techniques,* pages 79 and 80 (Copyright © 2000, American Institute of Certified Public Accountants, Inc.):

BANTA CORPORATION (DEC)

NOTES TO CONSOLIDATED FINANCIAL STATEMENTS

Note 1 (In Part): Summary of Accounting Policies

Inventories At January 1, 2000, the Corporation's inventories are stated at the lower of cost or market using the first-in, first-out (FIFO) method. Effective January 3, 1999, certain operations (comprising approximately one third of the Corporation's inventories) changed from the last-in, first-out basis to FIFO. The change in accounting principles was made to provide a better matching of revenue and expenses. This accounting change was not material to the financial statements, and accordingly, no retroactive restatement of prior years' financial statements was made. Inventories include material, labor and manufacturing overhead.

WILLAMETTE INDUSTRIES, INC. (DEC)

NOTES TO CONSOLIDATED FINANCIAL STATEMENTS
(Dollar amounts, except per share amounts, in thousands)

Note 4: Property, Plant and Equipment

Effective January 1, 1999, the company changed its accounting estimates relating to depreciation. The estimated service lives for most machinery and equipment were extended five years. The change was based upon a study performed by the company's engineering department, comparisons to typical industry practices and the effect of the company's extensive capital investments which have resulted in a mix of assets with longer productive lives due to technological advances. As a result of the change, 1999 net income was increased $51,900, or $.046 per diluted share.

Instructions

In your opinion, do either, both, or neither of the foregoing notes represent *cute accounting,* as defined on page 1 of the text? Explain, by reference to paragraphs 15, 16, and 17 of *Accounting Principles Board Opinion No. 20,* "Accounting Changes."

(Case 1.12) In a September 1998 speech, former Securities and Exchange Commission Chairman Arthur Levitt used the term *cookie-jar reserves* to describe a "cooking the books" technique used by some publicly owned companies to manage earnings. The technique involved establishing fictitious liabilities for bogus expenses or realized and earned revenues in a highly profitable quarter or fiscal year, and reversing the liabilities in subsequent low earnings periods.

Instructions

a. Obtain and study *SEC AAER 1140,* "In the Matter of W. R. Grace & Co., Respondent" (June 30, 1999) and describe the "cookie-jar reserves" technique used by Grace.

b. Review the *Staff Accounting Bulletins* issued by the SEC subsequent to June 30, 1999, and briefly describe the provisions of a *Bulletin* dealing with the Grace matter and the SEC staff's resultant requirements.

Chapter **Two**

Partnerships: Organization and Operation

Scope of Chapter

The Uniform Partnership Act, which has been adopted by most of the states, defines a *partnership* (often referred to as a *firm*) as *"an association of two or more persons to carry on, as co-owners, a business for profit."* In this definition, the term *persons* includes individuals and other partnerships, and in some states, corporations. Partnerships generally are associated with the practice of law, medicine, public accounting, and other professions, and also with small business enterprises. In some states licensed professional persons such as CPAs are forbidden to incorporate because the creation of a corporate entity might weaken the confidential relationship between the professional person and the client. However, a number of states have approved legislation designed to permit *professional corporations,* which have various requirements as to professional licensing of stockholders, transfers of stock ownership, and malpractice insurance coverage.

The traditional form of partnership under the Uniform Partnership Act has been the *general partnership,* in which *all* partners have unlimited personal liability for unpaid debts of the partnership. However, laws of several states now permit the formation of *limited liability partnerships (LLPs),* which have features of both general partnerships and professional corporations. Individual partners of LLPs are personally responsible for their own actions and for the actions of partnership employees under their supervision; however, they are not responsible for the actions of other partners. The LLP as a whole, like a general partnership, is responsible for the actions of all partners and employees. Since many of the issues of organization, income-sharing plans, and changes in ownership of now-prevalent LLPs are similar to those of general partnerships, LLPs are discussed in this section. The organization of limited liability partnerships and income-sharing plans and changes in ownership of such partnerships are discussed and illustrated first, followed by an explanation of the characteristics of, accounting for, and financial statements of *limited partnerships* (which differ significantly from LLPs). The chapter ends with a description of SEC enforcement actions involving unethical violations of accounting standards for partnerships.

ITION OF A LIMITED LIABILITY PARTNERSHIP

Characteristics of an LLP

The basic characteristics of an LLP are:

Ease of Formation   In contrast with a corporation, a limited liability partnership may be created by an oral or a written contract between two or more persons, or may be *implied by their conduct.* This advantage of convenience and minimum cost of the formation of a partnership in some cases may be offset by certain difficulties inherent in such an informal organizational structure. LLPs that are accounting or law firms generally must register with the state licensing authority.

Limited Life   An LLP may be ended by the death, retirement, bankruptcy, or incapacity of a partner. The admission of a new partner to the partnership legally *dissolves* the former partnership and establishes a new one.

Mutual Agency   Each partner has the authority to act for the limited liability partnership and to enter into contracts on its behalf. However, acts beyond the normal scope of business operations, such as the obtaining of a bank loan by a partner, generally do not bind the partnership unless specific authority has been given to the partner to enter into such transactions.

Co-Ownership of Partnership Assets and Earnings   When individuals invest assets in an LLP, they retain no claim to those specific assets but acquire an *ownership equity in net assets* of the partnership. Every member of an LLP also has an interest in partnership earnings; in fact, participation in earnings and losses is one of the tests of the existence of a partnership.

Deciding between an LLP and a Corporation

One of the most important considerations in choosing between a limited liability partnership and the corporate form of business organization is the income tax status of the enterprise and of its owners. An LLP pays no income tax but is required to file an annual *information return* showing its revenue and expenses, the amount of its net income, and the division of the net income among the partners. The partners report their respective shares of the *ordinary net income* from the partnership and such items as dividends and charitable contributions in their individual income tax returns, regardless of whether they received more or less than this amount of cash from the partnership during the year.

A corporation is a separate legal entity subject to a corporate income tax. The net income, when and if distributed to stockholders as dividends, also is taxable income to stockholders. Certain corporations with few stockholders may elect to be taxed as partnerships, provided their net income or loss is assumed by their stockholders. These corporations file information returns as do partnerships, and their stockholders report their respective shares of the year's net income or loss on individual tax returns. Thus, a limited liability partnership may incorporate as a *Subchapter S Corporation* to retain the advantages of limited liability but at the same time elect to be taxed as a partnership. Income tax rates and regulations are subject to frequent change, and new interpretations of tax laws often arise. The tax status of the owners also is likely to change from year to year. For these reasons, management of a business enterprise should review the tax implications of the limited

liability partnership and corporate forms of organization so that the enter
adapt most successfully to the income tax environment.

The burden of taxation is not the only factor influencing a choice between
ited liability partnership and the corporate form of organization. Perhaps the fa   ...t
most often tips the scales in favor of incorporation is the opportunity for obtaining
larger amounts of capital when ownership may be divided into shares of capital stock,
readily transferable, and offering the advantages inherent in the separation of ownership and management. Another reason for choosing the corporate form of organization
is the limited liability of *all* stockholders for unpaid debts of the corporation.

Is the LLP a Separate Entity?

In accounting literature, the legal status of partnerships often has received more emphasis than the fact that they are business enterprises. It has been common practice to
distinguish a partnership from a corporation by saying that a partnership is an "association of persons" and a corporation is a separate entity. Such a distinction stresses
the ***legal form*** rather than the ***economic substance*** of the business organization. In
terms of managerial policy and business objectives, limited liability partnerships are as
much business and accounting entities as are corporations. Limited liability partnerships typically are guided by long-range plans not likely to be affected by the admission or withdrawal of a single partner. In these firms the accounting policies should reflect the fact that the partnership is an accounting entity apart from its owners.

Treating the LLP as an economic and accounting entity often will aid in developing financial statements that provide the most meaningful presentation of financial position and results of operations. Among the accounting policies to be stressed is continuity in asset valuation, despite changes in the income-sharing ratio and changes in
ownership. Another appropriate policy may be recognizing as operating expenses the
salaries for personal services rendered by partners who also hold managerial positions.
In theoretical discussions, considerable support is found for treating every business enterprise as an accounting entity, apart from its owners, regardless of the form of organization. A managing partner under this view is both an employee and an owner, and
the salary for the personal services rendered by a partner is an operating expense of
the partnership.

The inclusion of partners' salaries among operating expenses has been opposed by
some accountants on grounds that partners' salaries may be set at unrealistic levels and
that a partnership is an association of individuals who are owners and not employees
of the partnership, despite their managerial or other functions.

A limited liability partnership has the characteristics of a separate entity in that it
may hold title to property, may enter into contracts, and in some states may sue or be
sued as an entity. In practice, most accountants treat limited liability partnerships as
separate entities with continuity of accounting policies and asset valuations not inter-
rupted by changes in ownership.

The Partnership Contract

Although a partnership may exist on the basis of an oral agreement or may be implied
by the actions of its members, good business practice requires that the partnership contract be in writing. The most important points covered in a contract for a limited liability partnership are the following:

1. The date of formation and the planned duration of the partnership, the names of the
   partners, and the name and business activities of the partnership.

2. The assets to be invested by each partner, the procedure for valuing noncash investments, and the penalties for a partner's failure to invest and maintain the agreed amount of capital.

3. The authority of each partner and the rights and duties of each.

4. The accounting period to be used, the nature of accounting records, financial statements, and audits by independent public accountants.

5. The plan for sharing net income or loss, including the frequency of income measurement and the distribution of the income or loss among the partners.

6. The drawings allowed to partners and the penalties, if any, for excessive withdrawals.

7. Insurance on the lives of partners, with the partnership or surviving partners named as beneficiaries.

8. Provision for arbitration of disputes and liquidation of the partnership at the end of the term specified in the contract or at the death or retirement of a partner. Especially important in avoiding disputes is agreement on procedures such as binding arbitration for the valuation of the partnership assets and the method of settlement with the estate of a deceased partner.

One advantage of preparing a partnership contract with the aid of attorneys and accountants is that the process of reaching agreement on specific issues will develop a better understanding among the partners on many issues that might be highly controversial if not settled at the outset. However, it is seldom possible to cover in a partnership contract every issue that may later arise. Revision of the partnership contract generally requires the approval of all partners.

Disputes arising among partners that cannot be resolved by reference to the partnership contract may be settled by binding arbitration or in the courts. A partner who is not satisfied with the handling of disputes always has the right to withdraw from the partnership.

Ledger Accounts for Partners

Accounting for an LLP differs from accounting for a single proprietorship or a corporation with respect to the sharing of net income and losses and the maintenance of the partners' ledger accounts. Although it might be possible to maintain partnership accounting records with only one ledger account for each partner, the usual practice is to maintain three types of accounts. These partnership accounts consist of (1) *capital* accounts, (2) *drawing* or *personal* accounts, and (3) accounts for *loans* to and from partners.

The original investment by each partner is recorded by debiting the assets invested, crediting any liabilities assumed by the partnership, and crediting the partner's capital account with the current fair value of the *net assets* (assets minus liabilities) invested. Subsequent to the original investment, the partner's equity is *increased* by additional investments and by a share of net income; the partner's equity is *decreased* by withdrawal of cash or other assets and by a share of net losses.

Another possible source of increase or decrease in partners' ownership equity results from changes in ownership, as described in subsequent sections of this chapter.

The original investment of assets by partners is recorded by credits to the capital accounts; *drawings* (withdrawals of cash or other assets) by partners in anticipation of net income or drawings that are considered salary allowances are recorded by debits to the drawing accounts. However, a large withdrawal that is considered a permanent reduction in the ownership equity of a partner is debited directly to the partner's capital account.

At the end of each accounting period, the net income or net loss in the partnership's Income Summary ledger account is transferred to the partners' capital accounts in accordance with the partnership contract. The debit balances in the drawing accounts at the end of the period also are closed to the partners' capital accounts. Because the accounting procedures for partners' ownership equity accounts are not subject to state regulations as in the case of capital stock and other stockholders' equity accounts of a corporation, deviations from the procedures described here are possible.

Loans to and from Partners

Occasionally, a partner may receive cash from the limited liability partnership with the intention of repaying this amount. Such a transaction may be debited to the Loans Receivable from Partners ledger account rather than to the partner's drawing account.

Conversely, a partner may make a cash payment to the partnership that is considered a loan rather than an increase in the partner's capital account balance. This transaction is recorded by a credit to Loans Payable to Partners and generally is accompanied by the issuance of a promissory note. Loans receivable from partners are displayed as assets in the partnership balance sheet and loans payable to partners are displayed as liabilities. The classification of these items as current or long-term generally depends on the maturity date, although these **related party transactions** may result in noncurrent classification of the partners' loans, regardless of maturity dates.

If a substantial unsecured loan has been made by a limited liability partnership to a partner and repayment appears doubtful, it is appropriate to offset the receivable against the partner's capital account balance. If this is not done, partnership total assets and total partners' equity may be misleading. In any event, the disclosure principle requires separate listing of any receivables from partners.

Valuation of Investments by Partners

The investment by a partner in the firm often includes assets other than cash. It is imperative that the partners agree on the current fair value of nonmonetary assets at the time of their investment and that the assets be recognized in the accounting records at such values. Any gains or losses resulting from the disposal of such assets during the operation of the partnership, or at the time of liquidation, generally are divided according to the plan for sharing net income or losses. Therefore, equitable treatment of the individual partners requires a starting point of current fair values recorded for all noncash assets invested in the firm. Thus, partnership gains or losses from disposal of noncash assets invested by the partners will be measured by the difference between the disposal price and the current fair value of the assets when invested by partners, adjusted for any depreciation or amortization to the date of disposal.

INCOME-SHARING PLANS FOR LIMITED LIABILITY PARTNERSHIPS

Partners' Equity in Assets versus Share in Earnings

The equity of a partner in the net assets of the limited liability partnership should be distinguished from a partner's share in earnings. Thus, to say that David Jones is a one-third partner is not a clear statement. Jones may have a one-third equity in the net assets of the partnership but have a larger or smaller share in the net income or losses of the firm. Such a statement might also be interpreted to mean that Jones was entitled to one-third of the net income or losses, although his capital account represented much more or much less than one-third of the total partners' capital. To state the matter concisely, partners may agree on any type of *income-sharing plan (profit and loss ratio),* regardless of the amount of their respective capital account balances. The Uniform Partnership Act provides that if partners fail to specify a plan for sharing net income or losses, *it is assumed that they intended to share equally.* Because income sharing is of such great importance, it is rare to find a situation in which the partnership contract is silent on this point.

Division of Net Income or Loss

The many possible plans for sharing net income or loss among partners of a limited liability partnership are summarized in the following categories:

1. Equally, or in some other ratio.

2. In the ratio of partners' capital account balances on a particular date, or in the ratio of average capital account balances during the year.

3. Allowing interest on partners' capital account balances and dividing the remaining net income or loss in a specified ratio.

4. Allowing salaries to partners and dividing the resultant net income or loss in a specified ratio.

5. Bonus to managing partner based on income.

6. Allowing salaries to partners, allowing interest on capital account balances, and dividing the remaining net income or loss in a specified ratio.

These alternative income-sharing plans emphasize that the value of personal services rendered by individual partners may vary widely, as may the amounts of capital invested by each partner. The amount and quality of managerial services rendered and the amount of capital invested often are important factors in the success or failure of a limited liability partnership. Therefore, provisions may be made for salaries to partners and interest on their respective capital account balances as a preliminary step in the division of income or loss. Any remaining income or loss then may be divided in a specified ratio.

Another factor affecting the success of a limited liability partnership may be that one of the partners has large personal financial resources, thus giving the partnership a strong credit rating. Similarly, a partner who is well known in a profession or an industry may make an important contribution to the success of the partnership without participating actively in the operations of the partnership. These two factors may be incorporated in the income-sharing plan by careful selection of the ratio in which any remaining net income or loss is divided.

The following examples show how each of the methods of dividing net income or loss may be applied. This series of illustrations is based on data for Alb & Bay LLP, which had a net income of $300,000 for the year ended December 31, 2002, the first year of operations. The partnership contract provides that each partner may withdraw $5,000 cash on the last day of each month; both partners did so during 2002. The drawings are recorded by debits to the partners' drawing accounts and are not a factor in the division of net income or loss; all other withdrawals, investments, and net income or loss are entered directly in the partners' capital accounts.

Partner Alb invested $400,000 on January 1, 2002, and an additional $100,000 on April 1. Partner Bay invested $800,000 on January 1 and withdrew $50,000 on July 1. These transactions and events are summarized in the following Capital, Drawing, and Income Summary ledger accounts:

Ledger Accounts for Alb and Bay

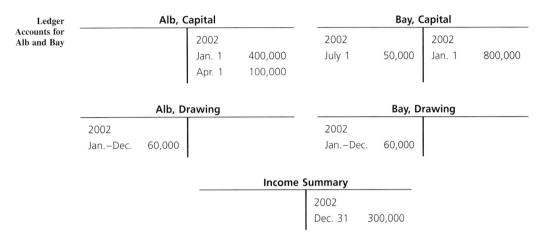

Division of Earnings Equally or in Some Other Ratio

Many limited liability partnership contracts provide that net income or loss is to be divided equally. Also, if the partners have made no specific agreement for income sharing, the Uniform Partnership Act provides that an intent of equal division is assumed. The net income of $300,000 for Alb & Bay LLP is transferred by a closing entry on December 31, 2002, from the Income Summary ledger account to the partners' capital accounts by the following journal entry:

Journal Entry to Close Income Summary Ledger Account

Income Summary	300,000	
Alb, Capital		150,000
Bay, Capital		150,000
To record division of net income for 2002.		

The drawing accounts are closed to the partners' capital accounts on December 31, 2002, as follows:

Journal Entry to Close Drawing Accounts

Alb, Capital	60,000	
Bay, Capital	60,000	
Alb, Drawing		60,000
Bay, Drawing		60,000
To close drawing accounts.		

After the drawing accounts are closed, the balances of the partners' capital accounts show the ownership equity of each partner on December 31, 2002.

If Alb & Bay LLP had a net loss of, say, $200,000 during the year ended December 31, 2002, the Income Summary ledger account would have a debit balance of $200,000. This loss would be transferred to the partners' capital accounts by a debit to each capital account for $100,000 and a credit to the Income Summary account for $200,000.

If Alb and Bay share earnings in the ratio of 60% to Alb and 40% to Bay and net income was $300,000, the net income would be divided $180,000 to Alb and $120,000 to Bay. The agreement that Alb should receive 60% of the net income (perhaps because of greater experience and personal contacts) would cause Partner Alb to absorb a larger share of the net loss if the partnership operated unprofitably. Some partnership contracts provide that a net income is to be divided in a specified ratio, such as 60% to Alb and 40% to Bay, but that a net loss is divided equally or in some other ratio. Another variation intended to compensate for unequal contributions by the partners provides that an agreed ratio (60% and 40% in this example) shall be applicable to a specified amount of income but that any additional income shall be shared in some other ratio.

Division of Earnings in Ratio of Partners' Capital Account Balances

Division of partnership earnings in proportion to the capital invested by each partner is most likely to be found in limited liability partnerships in which substantial investment is the principal ingredient for success. To avoid controversy, it is essential that the partnership contract specify whether the income-sharing ratio is based on (1) the original capital investments, (2) the capital account balances at the beginning of each year, (3) the balances at the end of each year (before the distribution of net income or loss), or (4) the average balances during each year.

Continuing the illustration for Alb & Bay LLP, assume that the partnership contract provides for division of net income in the ratio of *original capital investments.* The net income of $300,000 for 2002 is divided as follows:

Division of Net Income in Ratio of Original Capital Investments

$$\text{Alb: } \$300,000 \times \$400,000/\$1,200,000 = \$100,000$$
$$\text{Bay: } \$300,000 \times \$800,000/\$1,200,000 = \$200,000$$

The journal entry to close the Income Summary ledger account would be similar to the journal entry illustrated on page 36.

Assuming that the net income is divided in the ratio of capital account balances at the **end of the year** (before drawings and the distribution of net income), the net income of $300,000 for 2002 is divided as follows:

Division of Net Income in Ratio of End-of-Year Capital Account Balances

$$\text{Alb: } \$300,000 \times \$500,000/\$1,250,000 = \$120,000$$
$$\text{Bay: } \$300,000 \times \$750,000/\$1,250,000 = \$180,000$$

Division of net income on the basis of (1) original capital investments, (2) yearly beginning capital account balances, or (3) yearly ending capital account balances may prove inequitable if there are material changes in capital accounts during the year. Use of average balances as a basis for sharing net income is preferable because it reflects the capital actually available for use by the partnership during the year.

If the partnership contract provides for sharing net income in the ratio of average capital account balances during the year, it also should state the amount of drawings each partner may make without affecting the capital account. In the example for Alb & Bay LLP, the partners are entitled to withdraw $5,000 cash monthly. Any additional withdrawals or investments are entered directly in the partners' capital accounts and therefore influence the computation of the average capital ratio. The partnership contract also should state whether capital account balances are to be computed to the nearest month or to the nearest day.

The computations of average capital account balances to the nearest month and the division of net income for Alb & Bay LLP for 2002 are as follows:

ALB & BAY LLP
Computation of Average Capital Account Balances
For Year Ended December 31, 2002

Partner	Date	Increase (Decrease) in Capital	Capital Account Balance	Fraction of Year Unchanged	Aver Capit Account Balances
Alb	Jan. 1	400,000	400,000	$\frac{1}{4}$	100,000
	Apr. 1	100,000	500,000	$\frac{3}{4}$	375,000
					475,000
Bay	Jan. 1	800,000	800,000	$\frac{1}{2}$	400,000
	July 1	(50,000)	750,000	$\frac{1}{2}$	375,000
					775,000
	Total average capital account balances for Alb and Bay				1,250,000

Division of net income:
To Alb: $300,000 × $475,000/$1,250,000   114,000
To Bay: $300,000 × $775,000/$1,250,000   186,000
   Total net income   300,000

Interest on Partners' Capital Account Balances with Remaining Net Income or Loss Divided in Specified Ratio

In the preceding section, the plan for dividing the entire net income in the ratio of partners' capital account balances was based on the assumption that invested capital was the dominant factor in the success of the partnership. However, in most cases the amount of invested capital is only one factor that contributes to the success of the partnership. Consequently, many partnerships choose to divide only a portion of net income in the capital ratio and to divide the remainder equally or in some other specified ratio.

To allow interest on partners' capital account balances at 15%, for example, is the same as dividing a part of net income in the ratio of partners' capital balances. If the partners agree to allow interest on capital as a first step in the division of net income, they should specify the interest rate to be used and also state whether interest is to be computed on capital account balances on specific dates or on average capital balances during the year.

Again refer to Alb & Bay LLP with a net income of $300,000 for 2002 and capital account balances as shown on page 35. Assume that the partnership contract allows interest on partners' average capital account balances at 15%, with any remaining net income or loss to be divided equally. The net income of $300,000 for 2002 is divided as follows:

Division of Net Income with Interest Allowed on Average Capital Account Balances

	Alb	Bay	Combined
Interest on average capital account balances:			
Alb: $475,000 × 0.15	$ 71,250		$ 71,250
Bay: $775,000 × 0.15		$116,250	116,250
Subtotal			$187,500
Remainder ($300,000 − $187,500)			
divided equally	56,250	56,250	112,500
Totals	$127,500	$172,500	$300,000

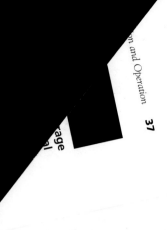

The journal entry to close the Income Summary ledger account on December 31, ...2, is similar to the journal entry illustrated on page 35.

...s a separate case, assume that Alb & Bay LLP had a net loss of $10,000 for the ...ended December 31, 2002. If the partnership contract provides for allowing in... ...on capital accounts, this provision ***must be enforced regardless of whether op-*** ***...ns are profitable or unprofitable.*** The only justification for omitting the ...nce of interest on partners' capital accounts during a loss year would be in the ...' a partnership contract containing a specific provision requiring such omission. Note in the following analysis that the $10,000 debit balance of the Income Summary ledger account resulting from the net loss is increased by the allowance of interest to $197,500, which is divided equally:

Division of Net Loss

	Alb	Bay	Combined
Interest on average capital account balances:			
Alb: $475,000 × 0.15	$ 71,250		$ 71,250
Bay: $775,000 × 0.15		$116,250	116,250
Subtotal			$187,500
Resulting deficiency ($10,000 + $187,500)			
divided equally	(98,750)	(98,750)	197,500
Totals	$(27,500)	$ 17,500	$ (10,000)

The journal entry to close the Income Summary ledger account on December 31, 2002, is shown below:

Closing the Income Summary Ledger Account with a Debit Balance

Alb, Capital	27,500	
Income Summary		10,000
Bay, Capital		17,500
To record division of net loss for 2002.		

At first thought, the idea that a net loss of $10,000 should cause one partner's capital to increase and the other partner's capital to decrease may appear unreasonable, but there is sound logic to support this result. Partner Bay invested substantially more capital than did Partner Alb; this capital was used to carry on operations, and the partnership's incurring of a net loss in the first year is no reason to disregard Bay's larger capital investment.

A significant contrast between two of the income-sharing plans discussed here (the capital-ratio plan and the interest-on-capital-accounts plan) is apparent if one considers the case of a partnership operating at a loss. Under the capital-ratio plan, the partner who invested more capital is required to bear a larger share of the net loss. This result may be considered unreasonable because the investment of capital presumably is not the cause of a net loss. Under the interest plan of sharing earnings, the partner who invested more capital receives credit for this factor and is charged with a lesser share of the net loss, or may even end up with a net credit.

Using interest allowances on partners' capital accounts as a technique for sharing partnership earnings equitably has no effect on the measurement of the net income or loss of the partnership. Interest on partners' capital accounts ***is not an expense of the partnership,*** but interest on loans from partners is recognized as expense and a factor in the measurement of net income or loss of the partnership. Similarly, interest earned on loans to partners is recognized as partnership revenue. This treatment is consistent with the point made on page 33 that loans to and from partners are assets and liabilities, respectively, of the limited liability partnership.

Another item of expense arising from dealings between a partnership and one of its partners is commonly encountered when the partnership leases property from a lessor who is also a partner. Rent expense is recognized by the partnership in such situations. The lessor, although a partner, also is a lessor to the partnership.

Salary Allowance with Resultant Net Income or Loss Divided in Specified Ratio

Salaries and drawings are not the same thing. Because the term *salaries* suggests weekly or monthly cash payments for personal services that are recognized as operating expenses by the limited liability partnership, accountants should be specific in defining the terminology used in accounting for a partnership. This text uses the term **drawings** in only one sense: a withdrawal of cash or other assets that reduces the partner's equity but has no part in the division of net income. In the discussion of partnership accounting, the word **salaries** means an operating expense included in measuring net income or loss. When the term **salaries** is used with this meaning, the division of net income is the same, regardless of whether the salaries have been paid.

A partnership contract that authorizes partners to make regular withdrawals of specific amounts should state whether such withdrawals are intended to be a factor in the division of net income or loss. For example, assume that the contract states that Partner Alb may make drawings of $3,000 monthly and Partner Bay $8,000. If the intent is not clearly stated to include or exclude these drawings as an element in the division of net income or loss, controversy is probable, because one interpretation will favor Partner Alb and the opposing interpretation will favor Partner Bay.

Assuming that Partner Alb has more experience and ability than Partner Bay and also devotes more time to the partnership, it seems reasonable that the partners will want to recognize the more valuable contribution of personal services by Alb in choosing a plan for division of net income or loss. One approach to this objective would be to adopt an unequal ratio: for example, 70% of net income or loss to Alb and 30% to Bay. However, the use of such a ratio usually is not a satisfactory solution, for the same reasons mentioned in criticizing the capital ratio as a profit-sharing plan. A ratio based only on personal services may not reflect the fact that other factors are important in determining the success of the partnership. A second point is that if the partnership incurs a loss, the partner rendering more personal services will absorb a larger portion of the loss.

A solution to the problem of recognizing unequal personal services by partners is to provide in the partnership contract for different salaries to partners, with the resultant net income or loss divided equally or in some other ratio. Applying this reasoning to the continuing illustration for Alb & Bay LLP, assume that the partnership contract provides for an annual salary of $100,000 to Alb and $60,000 to Bay, with resultant net income or loss to be divided equally. The salaries are paid monthly during the year. The net income of $140,000 for 2002 is divided as follows:

	Alb	Bay	Combined
Salaries	$100,000	$ 60,000	$160,000
Net income ($300,000 − $160,000)			
divided equally	70,000	70,000	140,000
Totals	$170,000	$130,000	$300,000

Division of $140,000 Net Income after Salaries Expense

The following journal entries are required for the foregoing:

1. Monthly journal entries debiting Partners' Salaries Expense, $13,333 ($160,000 ÷ 12 = $13,333) and crediting Alb, Capital, $8,333 ($100,000 ÷ 12 = $8,333) and Bay, Capital, $5,000 ($60,000 ÷ 12 = $5,000).

2. Monthly journal entries debiting Alb, Drawing, $8,333 and Bay, Drawing, $5,000 and crediting Cash, $13,333.

3. End-of-year journal entry debiting Income Summary, $140,000, and crediting Alb, Capital, $70,000 and Bay, Capital, $70,000.

Bonus to Managing Partner Based on Income

A partnership contract may provide for a bonus to the managing partner equal to a specified percentage of income. The contract should state whether the basis of the bonus is net income without deduction of the bonus as an operating expense or income after the bonus. For example, assume that the Alb & Bay LLP partnership contract provides for a bonus to Partner Alb of 25% of net income and that the remaining income is divided equally. The net income is $300,000. After the bonus of $75,000 ($300,000 × 0.25 = $75,000) to Alb, the remaining $225,000 of income is divided $112,500 to Alb and $112,500 to Bay. Thus, Alb's share of income is $187,500 ($75,000 + $112,500 = $187,500), and Bay's share is $112,500; the bonus *is not* recognized as an operating expense of the limited liability partnership.

If the partnership contract provided for a bonus of 25% of income *after the bonus* to Partner Alb, the bonus is computed as follows:

$$\text{Bonus} + \text{income after bonus} = \$300,000$$

Bonus Based on Income after Bonus

$$\text{Let } X = \text{income after bonus}$$
$$0.25X = \text{bonus}$$
$$\text{Then } 1.25X = \$300,000 \text{ income before bonus}$$
$$X = \$300,000 \div 1.25$$
$$X = \$240,000$$
$$0.25X = \underline{\underline{\$60,000}} \text{ bonus to Partner Alb}[1]$$

Thus, the prebonus income of $300,000 in this case is divided $180,000 to Alb and $120,000 to Bay, and the $60,000 bonus *is* recognized as an operating expense of the partnership.

The concept of a bonus is not applicable to a net loss. When a limited liability partnership operates at a loss, the bonus provision is disregarded. The partnership contract also may specify that extraordinary items or other unusual gains and losses are to be excluded from the basis for the computation of the bonus.

Salaries to Partners with Interest on Capital Accounts

Many limited liability partnerships divide income or loss by allowing salaries to partners and also interest on their capital account balances. Any resultant net income or loss is divided equally or in some other ratio. Such plans have the merit of recognizing that the value of personal services rendered by different partners may vary,

---

[1] An alternative computation consists of converting the bonus percentage to a fraction. The bonus then may be computed by adding the numerator to the denominator and applying the resulting fraction to the income before the bonus. In the preceding example, 25% is converted to $\frac{1}{4}$; and adding the numerator to the denominator, the $\frac{1}{4}$ becomes $\frac{1}{5}$(4 + 1 = 5). One-fifth of $300,000 equals $60,000, the bonus to Partner Alb.

and that differences in amounts invested also warrant recognition in an equitable plan for sharing net income or loss.

To illustrate, assume that the partnership contract for Alb & Bay LLP provides for the following:

1. Annual salaries of $100,000 to Alb and $60,000 to Bay, recognized as operating expense of the partnership, with salaries to be paid monthly.

2. Interest on average capital account balances, as computed on page 37.

3. Remaining net income or loss divided equally.

Assuming income of $300,000 for 2002 before annual salaries expense, the $140,000 net income [$300,000 − ($100,000 + $60,000) = $140,000] is divided as follows:

	Alb	Bay	Combined
Interest on average capital account balances:			
Alb: $475,000 × 0.15	$71,250		$ 71,250
Bay: $775,000 × 0.15		$116,250	116,250
Subtotal			$187,500
Resulting deficiency ($187,500 − $140,000)			
divided equally	(23,750)	(23,750)	(47,500)
Totals	$47,500	$ 92,500	$140,000

Division of Net Income after Salaries Expense

The journal entries to recognize partners' salaries expense, partners' withdrawals of the salaries, and closing of the Income Summary ledger account are similar to those described on page 40.

Financial Statements for an LLP

Income Statement

Explanations of the division of net income among partners may be included in the partnership's income statement or in a note to the financial statements. This information is referred to as the ***division of net income section*** of the income statement. The following illustration for Alb & Bay LLP shows, in a condensed income statement for the year ended December 31, 2002, the division of net income as shown above and the disclosure of partners' salaries expense, a ***related party*** item:

ALB & BAY LLP Income Statement For Year Ended December 31, 2002		
Net sales		$3,000,000
Cost of goods sold		1,800,000
Gross margin on sales		$1,200,000
Partners' salaries expense	$160,000	
Other operating expenses	900,000	1,060,000
Net income		$ 140,000
Division of net income:		
Partner Alb	$ 47,500	
Partner Bay	92,500	
Total	$140,000	

Note that because a partnership is not subject to income taxes, there is no income taxes expense in the foregoing income statement. A note to the partnership's financial statements may disclose this fact and explain that the partners are taxed for their shares of partnership income, including their salaries.

Statement of Partners' Capital

Partners and other users of limited liability partnership financial statements generally want a complete explanation of the changes in the partners' capital accounts each year. To meet this need, a *statement of partners' capital* is prepared. The following illustrative statement of partners' capital for Alb & Bay LLP is based on the capital accounts presented on page 35 and includes the division of net income illustrated in the foregoing income statement.

ALB & BAY LLP Statement of Partners' Capital For Year Ended December 31, 2002			
	Partner Alb	**Partner Bay**	**Combined**
Partners' original investments, beginning of year	$400,000	$800,000	$1,200,000
Additional investment (withdrawal) of capital	100,000	(50,000)	50,000
Balances before salaries, net income, and drawings	$500,000	$750,000	$1,250,000
Add: Salaries	100,000	60,000	160,000
Net income	47,500	92,500	140,000
Subtotals	$647,500	$902,500	$1,550,000
Less: Drawings	100,000	60,000	160,000
Partners' capital, end of year	$547,500	$842,500	$1,390,000

Partners' capital at end of year is reported as owners' equity in the December 31, 2002, balance sheet of the partnership as illustrated below.

Balance Sheet

A condensed balance sheet for Alb & Bay LLP on December 31, 2002, is presented below.

ALB & BAY LLP Balance Sheet December 31, 2002				
Assets		**Liabilities and Partners' Capital**		
Cash	$ 50,000	Trade accounts payable		$ 240,000
Trade accounts		Long-term debt		370,000
receivable	40,000	Total liabilities		$ 610,000
Inventories	360,000	Partners' capital:		
Plant assets (net)	1,550,000	Partner Alb	$547,500	
		Partner Bay	842,500	1,390,000
		Total liabilities and partners'		
Total assets	$2,000,000	capital		$2,000,000

Statement of Cash Flows

A statement of cash flows is prepared for a partnership as it is for a corporation. This financial statement, the preparation of which is explained and illustrated in intermediate accounting textbooks, displays the net cash provided by operating activities, net cash used in investing activities, and net cash provided or used in financing activities of the partnership. A statement of cash flows for Alb & Bay LLP under the indirect method, which includes the net income from the income statement on page 41 and the investments and combined drawings from the statement of partners' capital on page 42, is as follows:

ALB & BAY LLP
Statement of Cash Flows (indirect method)
For Year Ended December 31, 2002

Cash flows from operating activities:		
Net income		$ 140,000
Adjustments to reconcile net income to net cash provided by operating activities:		
Partners' salaries expense	$ 160,000	
Depreciation expense	20,000	
Increase in trade accounts receivable	(40,000)	
Increase in inventories	(360,000)	
Increase in trade accounts payable	240,000	20,000
Net cash provided by operating activities		$ 160,000
Cash flows from investing activities:		
Acquisition of plant assets		$(1,200,000)
Cash flows from financing activities:		
Partners' investments	$1,300,000	
Partners' withdrawal	(50,000)	
Partners' drawings	(160,000)	
Net cash provided by financing activities		1,090,000
Net increase in cash (cash at end of year)		$ 50,000
Exhibit I *Noncash investing and financing activity: Capital lease obligation incurred for plant assets*		$ 370,000

Correction of Partnership Net Income of Prior Period

Any business enterprise, whether it be a single proprietorship, a partnership, or a corporation, will from time to time discover errors made in the measurement of net income in prior accounting periods. Examples include errors in the estimation of depreciation, errors in inventory valuation, and omission of accruals of revenue and expenses. When such errors are discovered, the question arises as to whether the corrections should be treated as part of the measurement of net income for the current accounting period or as *prior period adjustments* and entered directly to partners' capital accounts.

The correction of prior years' net income is particularly important when the partnership's income-sharing plan has been changed. For example, assume that in 2002 the net income for Alb & Bay LLP was $300,000 and that the partners shared the net income equally, but in 2003 they changed the income-sharing ratio to 60% for Alb and 40% for Bay. During 2003 it was determined that the inventories at the end of 2002 were overstated by $100,000 because of computational errors. The $100,000 reduction in the net income for 2002 should be divided $50,000 to each partner, in accordance with the income-sharing ratio in effect for 2002, the *year in which the error occurred.*

Somewhat related to the correction of errors of prior periods is the treatment of non-operating gains and losses. When the income-sharing ratio of a partnership is changed, the partners should consider the differences that exist between the carrying amounts of assets and their current fair values. For example, assume that Alb & Bay LLP owns land acquired for $20,000 that had appreciated in current fair value to $50,000 on the date when the income-sharing ratio is changed from 50% for each partner to 60% for Alb and 40% for Bay. If the land were sold for $50,000 just prior to the change in the income-sharing ratio, the $30,000 gain would be divided $15,000 to Alb and $15,000 to Bay; if the land were sold immediately after establishment of the 60 : 40 income-sharing ratio, the gain would be divided $18,000 to Alb and only $12,000 to Bay.

A solution sometimes suggested for such partnership problems is to revalue the partnership's assets to current fair value when the income-sharing ratio is changed or when a new partner is admitted or a partner retires. In some cases the revaluation of assets may be justified, but in general the continuity of historical cost valuations in a partnership is desirable for the same reasons that support the use of that valuation principle in accounting for corporations. A secondary objection to revaluation of assets is that, with a few exceptions such as marketable securities, satisfactory evidence of current fair value is seldom available. The best solution to the problem of a change in the ratio of income sharing usually is achieved by making appropriate adjustments to the partners' capital accounts rather than by a restatement of carrying amounts of assets.

CHANGES IN OWNERSHIP OF LIMITED LIABILITY PARTNERSHIPS

Accounting for Changes in Partners

Most changes in the ownership of a limited liability partnership are accomplished without interruption of its operations. For example, when a large LLP promotes one of its employees to partner, there is usually no significant change in the finances or operating routines of the partnership. However, from a legal viewpoint a partnership is *dissolved* by the retirement or death of a partner or by the admission of a new partner.

Dissolution of a partnership also may result from the bankruptcy of the firm or of any partner, the expiration of a time period stated in the partnership contract, or the mutual agreement of the partners to end their association.[2] Thus, the term *dissolution* may be used to describe events ranging from a minor change of ownership interest not affecting operations of the partnership to a decision by the partners to terminate the partnership.

Accountants are concerned with the *economic substance* of an event rather than with its *legal form.* Therefore, they must evaluate all the circumstances of the individual case to determine how a change in partners should be recorded. The following sections of this chapter describe and illustrate the principal kinds of changes in the ownership of a partnership.

---

[2] The *dissolution* of a partnership is defined by the Uniform Partnership Act as "the change in the relation of the partners caused by any partner ceasing to be associated in the carrying on as distinguished from the winding up of the business."

Accounting and Managerial Issues

Although a partnership is ended in a legal sense when a partner withdraws or a new partner is admitted, the partnership often continues operations with little outward evidence of change. In current accounting practice, a partner's interest often is considered a share in the partnership that may be transferred, much as shares of a corporation's capital stock are transferred among stockholders, without disturbing the continuity of the partnership. For example, if a partner of a CPA firm retires or a new partner is admitted to the firm, the contract for the change in ownership should be planned carefully to avoid disturbing client relationships. In a large CPA firm with hundreds of partners, the decision to promote an employee to the rank of partner generally is made by a committee of partners rather than by action of all partners.

Changes in the ownership of a partnership raise a number of accounting and managerial issues on which an accountant may serve as consultant. Among these issues are the setting of terms for admission of a new partner, the possible revaluation of existing partnership assets, the development of a new plan for the division of net income or loss, and the determination of the amount to be paid to a retiring partner.

Admission of a New Partner

When a new partner is admitted to a firm of two or three partners, it is particularly appropriate to consider the fairness and adequacy of past accounting policies and the need for correction of errors in prior years' accounting data. The terms of admission of a new partner often are influenced by the level and trend of past earnings, because they may be indicative of future earnings. Sometimes accounting policies such as the use of the completed-contract method of accounting for construction-type contracts or the installment method of accounting for installment sales may cause the accounting records to convey a misleading impression of earnings in the years preceding the admission of a new partner. Accordingly, adjustments of the partnership accounting records may be necessary to restate the carrying amounts of assets and liabilities to current fair values before a new partner is admitted.

As an alternative to revaluation of the existing partnership assets, it may be preferable to evaluate any differences between the carrying amounts and current fair values of assets and adjust the terms for admission of the new partner. In this way, the amount invested by the incoming partner may be set at a level that reflects the current fair value of the net assets of the partnership, even though the carrying amounts of existing partnership assets remain unchanged in the accounting records.

The admission of a new partner to a partnership may be effected either by an ***acquisition*** of all or part of the interest of one or more of the existing partners or by an ***investment*** of assets by the new partner with a resultant increase in the net assets of the partnership.

Acquisition of an Interest by Payment to One or More Partners

If a new partner acquires an interest from one or more of the existing partners, the event is recorded by establishing a capital account for the new partner and decreasing the capital account balances of the selling partners by the same amount. No assets are received by the partnership; the transfer of ownership is a private transaction between two or more partners.

As an illustration of this situation, assume that Lane and Mull, partners of Lane & Mull LLP, share net income or losses equally and that each has a capital account balance of $60,000. Nash (with the consent of Mull) acquires one-half of Lane's interest in the partnership by a cash payment to Lane. The journal entry to record this change in ownership follows:

Nash Acquires One-Half of Lane's Interest in Partnership	Lane, Capital ($60,000 × ½)	30,000
	Nash, Capital	30,000
	To record transfer of one-half of Lane's capital to Nash.	

The cash paid by Nash for half of Lane's interest may have been the carrying amount of $30,000, or it may have been more or less than the carrying amount. Possibly no cash price was established; Lane may have made a gift to Nash of the equity in the partnership. Regardless of the terms of the transaction between Lane and Nash, the journal entry illustrated above is all that is required in the partnership's accounting records; no change has occurred in the partnership assets, liabilities, or *total* partners' capital.

To explore further some of the implications involved in the acquisition of an interest by a new partner, assume that Nash paid $40,000 to Lane for one-half of Lane's $60,000 equity in the partnership. Some accountants have suggested that the willingness of the new partner to pay $10,000 [$40,000 − ($60,000 × ½) = $10,000] in excess of the carrying amount for a one-fourth interest in the total capital of the partnership indicates that the total capital is worth $40,000 ($10,000 ÷ 0.25 = $40,000) more than is shown in the accounting records. They reason that the carrying amounts of partnership assets should be written up by $40,000, or goodwill of $40,000 should be recognized with offsetting credits of $20,000 each to the capital accounts of the existing partners, Lane and Mull. However, most accountants take the position that the payment by Nash to Lane is a personal transaction between them and that the partnership, which has neither received nor distributed any assets, should prepare no journal entry other than an entry recording the transfer of one-half of Lane's capital to Nash.

What are the arguments for these two opposing views? Those who advocate a write-up of assets stress the **legal concept** of dissolution of the former partnership and formation of a new partnership. This change in identity of owners, it is argued, justifies a departure from the going-concern principle and the revaluation of partnership assets to current fair values to achieve an accurate measurement of the capital invested by each member of the new partnership.

The opposing argument, that the acquisition of an interest by a new partner requires only a transfer from the capital account of the selling partner to the capital account of the new partner, is based on several points. First, the partnership did not participate in negotiating the price paid by Nash to Lane. Many factors other than the valuation of partnership assets may have been involved in the negotiations between the two individuals. Perhaps Nash paid more than the carrying amount because Nash was allowed generous credit terms or received more than a one-fourth share in partnership net income. Perhaps the new partner was anxious to join the firm because of the personal abilities of Lane and Mull or because of the anticipated growth of the partnership. Further, goodwill, defined as the excess of the cost of an acquired company over the sum of its identifiable net assets,[3] attaches only to a business *as a whole*.[4] For these and other reasons, one may conclude that the cash paid for a partnership interest by a new

---

[3] *FASB Statement No. 142*, "Goodwill and Other Intangible Assets," par. F1.
[4] *Ibid.*

partner to an existing partner does not provide sufficient evidence to support changes in the carrying amounts of the partnership's assets.

Investment in Partnership by New Partner

A new partner may gain admission by investing assets in the limited liability partnership, thus increasing its total assets and partners' capital. For example, assume that Wolk and Yary, partners of Wolk & Yary LLP, share net income or loss equally and that each has a capital account balance of $60,000. Assume also that the carrying amounts of the partnership assets are approximately equal to current fair values and that Zell owns land that might be used for expansion of partnership operations. Wolk and Yary agree to admit Zell to the partnership by investment of the land; net income and losses of the new firm are to be shared equally. The land had cost Zell $50,000, but has a current fair value of $80,000. The admission of Zell is recorded by the partnership as follows:

New Partner Invests Land	Land	80,000
	Zell, Capital	80,000
	To record admission of Zell to partnership.	

Zell has a capital account balance of $80,000 and thus owns a 40% [$80,000 ÷ ($60,000 + $60,000 + $80,000) = 0.40] interest in the net assets of the firm. The fact that the three partners share net income and losses equally does not require that their capital account balances be equal.

Bonus or Goodwill Allowed to Existing Partners

In a profitable, well-established firm, the existing partners may insist that a portion of the investment by a new partner be allocated to them as a bonus or that goodwill be recognized and credited to the existing partners. The new partner may agree to such terms because of the benefits to be gained by becoming a member of a firm with high earning power.

Bonus to Existing Partners

Assume that in Cain & Duke LLP, the two partners share net income and losses equally and have capital account balances of $45,000 each. The carrying amounts of the partnership net assets approximate current fair values. The partners agree to admit Eck to a one-third interest in capital and a one-third share in net income or losses for a cash investment of $60,000. The net assets of the new firm amount to $150,000 ($45,000 + $45,000 + $60,000 = $150,000). The following journal entry gives Eck a one-third interest in capital and credits the $10,000 **bonus** ($60,000 − $50,000 = $10,000) equally to Cain and Duke in accordance with their prior contract to share net income and losses equally:

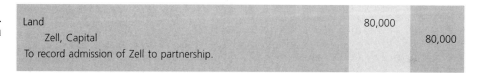

Recording Bonus to Existing Partners	Cash	60,000
	Cain, Capital ($10,000 × ½)	5,000
	Duke, Capital ($10,000 × ½)	5,000
	Eck, Capital ($150,000 × ⅓)	50,000
	To record investment by Eck for a one-third interest in capital, with bonus of $10,000 divided equally between Cain and Duke.	

Goodwill to Existing Partners

In the foregoing illustration, Eck invested $60,000 but received a capital account balance of only $50,000, representing a one-third interest in the net assets of the firm. Eck might prefer that the full amount invested, $60,000, be credited to Eck's capital account. This might be done while still allotting Eck a one-third interest if **goodwill** is recognized by the partnership, with the offsetting credit divided equally between the two existing partners. If Eck is to be given a one-third interest represented by a capital account balance of $60,000, the indicated total capital of the partnership is $180,000 ($60,000 × 3 = $180,000), and the total capital of Cain and Duke must equal $120,000 ($180,000 × ⅔ = $120,000). Because their present combined capital account balances amount to $90,000, a write-up of $30,000 in the net assets of the partnership is recorded as follows:

Recording Implied Goodwill	Cash	60,000	
	Goodwill ($120,000 − $90,000)	30,000	
	Cain, Capital ($30,000 × ½)		15,000
	Duke, Capital ($30,000 × ½)		15,000
	Eck, Capital		60,000
	To record investment by Eck for a one-third interest in capital, with credit offsetting goodwill of $30,000 divided equally between Cain and Duke.		

Evaluation of Bonus and Goodwill Methods

When a new partner invests an amount larger than the carrying amount of the interest acquired, the transaction should be recorded by allowing a bonus to the existing partners. The bonus method adheres to the valuation principle and treats the partnership as a going concern.

The alternative method of recording the goodwill implied by the amount invested by the new partner *is not considered acceptable by the author.* Use of the goodwill method signifies the substitution of estimated current fair value of an asset rather than valuation on a cost basis. The goodwill of $30,000 recognized in the foregoing example was not paid for by the partnership. ***Its existence is implied*** by the amount invested by the new partner for a one-third interest in the firm. The amount invested by the new partner may have been influenced by many factors, some of which may be personal rather than economic in nature.

Apart from the questionable theoretical basis for such recognition of goodwill, there are other practical difficulties. The presence of goodwill created in this manner is likely to evoke criticism of the partnership's financial statements, and such criticism may cause the partnership to write off the goodwill.[5] Also, if the partnership were liquidated, the goodwill would have to be written off as a loss.

Fairness of Asset Valuation

In the foregoing examples of bonus or goodwill allowed to the existing partners, it was assumed that the carrying amounts of assets of the partnership approximated current

---

[5] As indicated on page 46, only acquired goodwill should be recognized, and, as explained in Chapter 5, it currently must be written off, in whole or in part, when it is determined to be *impaired.*

fair values. However, if land and buildings, for example, have been owned by the partnership for many years, their carrying amounts and current fair values may be significantly different.

To illustrate this problem, assume that the net assets of Cain & Duke LLP, carried at $90,000, were estimated to have a current fair value of $120,000 at the time of admission of Eck as a partner. The previous example required Eck to receive a one-third interest in partnership net assets for an investment of $60,000. Why not write up the partnership's *identifiable* assets from $90,000 to $120,000, with a corresponding increase in the capital account balances of the existing partners? Neither a bonus nor the recognition of goodwill then would be necessary to record the admission of Eck with a one-third interest in net assets for an investment of $60,000 because this investment is equal to one-third of the total partnership capital of $180,000 ($120,000 + $60,000 = $180,000).

Such restatement of asset values would not be acceptable practice in a corporation when the market price of its capital stock had risen. If one assumes the existence of certain conditions in a partnership, adherence to cost as the basis for asset valuation is as appropriate a policy as for a corporation. These specific conditions are that the income-sharing ratio should be the same as the share of equity of each partner and that the income-sharing ratio should continue unchanged. When these conditions do not exist, a restatement of net assets from carrying amount to current fair value may be the best way of achieving equity among the partners.

Bonus or Goodwill Allowed to New Partner

A new partner may be admitted to a limited liability partnership because it needs cash or because the new partner has valuable skills and business contacts. To ensure the admission of the new partner, the present firm may offer the new partner a larger equity in net assets than the amount invested by the new partner.

Bonus to New Partner

Assume that the two partners of Farr & Gold LLP, who share net income and losses equally and have capital account balances of $35,000 each, offer Hart a one-third interest in net assets and a one-third share of net income or losses for an investment of $20,000 cash. Their offer is based on a need for more cash and on the conviction that Hart's personal skills and business contacts will be valuable to the partnership. The investment of $20,000 by Hart, when added to the existing capital of $70,000, gives total capital of $90,000 ($20,000 + $70,000 = $90,000), of which Hart is entitled to one-third, or $30,000 ($90,000 × ⅓ = $30,000). The excess of Hart's capital account balance over the amount invested represents a $10,000 *bonus* ($30,000 − $20,000 = $10,000) allowed to Hart by Farr and Gold. Because those partners share net income or losses equally, the $10,000 bonus is debited to their capital accounts in equal amounts, as shown by the following journal entry to record the admission of Hart to the partnership:

Recording Bonus to New Partner

Cash	20,000	
Farr, Capital ($10,000 × ½)	5,000	
Gold, Capital ($10,000 × ½)	5,000	
Hart, Capital		30,000
To record admission of Hart, with bonus of $10,000 from Farr and Gold.		

In outlining this method of accounting for the admission of Hart, it is assumed that the net assets of the partnership were valued properly. If the admission of the new partner to a one-third interest for an investment of $20,000 was based on recognition that the net assets of the existing partnership were worth only $40,000, consideration should be given to writing down net assets by $30,000 ($70,000 − $40,000 = $30,000). Such write-downs would be appropriate if, for example, trade accounts receivable included doubtful accounts or if inventories were obsolete.

Goodwill to New Partner

Assume that the new partner Hart is the owner of a successful single proprietorship that Hart invests in the partnership rather than making an investment in cash. Using the same data as in the preceding example, assume that Farr and Gold, with capital account balances of $35,000 each, give Hart a one-third interest in net assets and net income or losses. The *identifiable* tangible and intangible net assets of the proprietorship owned by Hart are worth $20,000, but, because of its superior earnings record, a current fair value for the *total* net assets is agreed to be $35,000. The admission of Hart to the partnership is recorded as shown below:

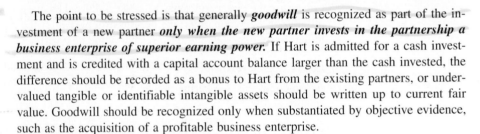

New Partner Invests Single Proprietorship with Goodwill	Identifiable Tangible and Intangible Net Assets	20,000	
	Goodwill ($35,000 − $20,000)	15,000	
	Hart, Capital		35,000
	To record admission of Hart; goodwill is attributable to superior earnings of single proprietorship invested by Hart.		

The point to be stressed is that generally **goodwill** is recognized as part of the investment of a new partner *only when the new partner invests in the partnership a business enterprise of superior earning power.* If Hart is admitted for a cash investment and is credited with a capital account balance larger than the cash invested, the difference should be recorded as a bonus to Hart from the existing partners, or undervalued tangible or identifiable intangible assets should be written up to current fair value. Goodwill should be recognized only when substantiated by objective evidence, such as the acquisition of a profitable business enterprise.

Retirement of a Partner

A partner retiring from a limited liability partnership usually receives cash or other assets from the partnership. It is also possible that a retiring partner might arrange for the sale of his or her partnership interest to one or more of the continuing partners or to an outsider. Because the accounting principles applicable to the latter situation already have been considered, the discussion of the retirement of a partner is limited to the situation in which the retiring partner receives assets of the partnership.

An assumption underlying this discussion is that the retiring partner has a right to withdraw under the terms of the partnership contract. A partner always has the *power* to withdraw, as distinguished from the *right* to withdraw. A partner who withdraws in violation of the terms of the partnership contract, and without the consent of the other partners, may be liable for damages to the other partners.

Computation of the Settlement Price

What is a fair measurement of the equity of a retiring partner? A first indication is the retiring partner's capital account balance, but this amount may need to be adjusted before it represents an equitable settlement price. Adjustments may include the correction of errors in accounting data or the recognition of differences between carrying amounts of partnership net assets and their current fair values. Before making any adjustments, the accountant should refer to the partnership contract, which may contain provisions for computing the amount to be paid to a retiring partner. For example, these provisions might require an appraisal of assets, an audit by independent public accountants, or a valuation of the partnership as a going concern according to a prescribed formula. If the partnership has not maintained accurate accounting records or has not been audited, it is possible that the partners' capital account balances are misstated because of incorrect depreciation expense, failure to provide for doubtful accounts expense, and other accounting deficiencies.

If the partnership contract does not contain provisions for the computation of the retiring partner's equity, the accountant may obtain written authorization from the partners to use a specific method to determine an equitable settlement price.

In most cases, the equity of the retiring partner is computed on the basis of current fair values of partnership net assets. The gain or loss indicated by the difference between the carrying amounts of assets and their current fair values is divided in the income-sharing ratio. After the equity of the retiring partner has been computed in terms of current fair values for assets, the partners may agree to settle by payment of this amount, or they may agree on a different amount. The computation of an estimated current fair value for the retiring partner's equity is a necessary step in reaching a settlement. An independent decision is made whether to recognize the current fair values and the related changes in partners' capital in the partnership's accounting records.

Bonus to Retiring Partner

The partnership contract may provide for the computation of **internally generated** goodwill at the time of a partner's retirement and may specify the methods for computing the goodwill. Generally, the amount of the computed goodwill is allocated to the partners in the income-sharing ratio. For example, assume that partner Lund is to retire from Jorb, Kent & Lund LLP. Each partner has a capital account balance of $60,000, and net income and losses are shared equally. The partnership contract provides that a retiring partner is to receive the balance of the retiring partner's capital account plus a share of any internally generated goodwill. At the time of Lund's retirement, goodwill in the amount of $30,000 is computed to the mutual satisfaction of the partners. *In the opinion of the author, this goodwill should not be recognized in the accounting records of the partnership* by a $30,000 debit to Goodwill and a $10,000 credit to each partner's capital account.

Serious objections exist to recording goodwill as determined in this fashion. Because only $10,000 of the goodwill is included in the payment for Lund's equity, the remaining $20,000 of goodwill *has not been paid for* by the partnership. Its display in the balance sheet of the partnership is not supported by either the valuation principle or reliable evidence. The fact that the partners "voted" for $30,000 of goodwill does not meet the need for reliable evidence of asset values. As an alternative, it would be possible to recognize only $10,000 of goodwill and credit Lund's capital account for the same amount, because this amount was paid for by the partnership as a condition of Lund's retirement. This method is perhaps more justifiable, but reliable evidence that goodwill exists still is lacking. (As indicted on page 46, *FASB Statement No. 142,* "Accounting for Goodwill . . . ," provides that goodwill attaches only to a business *as a whole* and is recognized only when a business is *acquired.*) The most satisfactory method of accounting for the retirement of partner Lund is to record the amount paid to Lund for goodwill as a $10,000 *bonus.* Because the settlement with Lund is for the balance of Lund's capital account of $60,000, plus estimated goodwill of $10,000, the following journal entry to record Lund's retirement is recommended:

Bonus Paid to Retiring Partner

Lund, Capital	60,000	
Jorb, Capital ($10,000 × ½)	5,000	
Kent, Capital ($10,000 × ½)	5,000	
Cash		70,000
To record payment to retiring partner Lund, including a bonus of $10,000.		

The bonus method illustrated here is appropriate whenever the settlement with the retiring partner exceeds the carrying amount of that partner's capital. The agreement for settlement may or may not use the term ***goodwill;*** the essence of the matter is the determination of the amount to be paid to the retiring partner.

Bonus to Continuing Partners

A partner anxious to escape from an unsatisfactory business situation may accept less than his or her partnership equity on retirement. In other cases, willingness by a retiring partner to accept a settlement below carrying amount may reflect personal problems. Another possible explanation is that the retiring partner considers the net assets of the partnership to be overvalued or anticipates less partnership net income in future years.

In brief, there are many factors that may induce a partner to accept less than the carrying amount of his or her capital account balance on withdrawal from the partnership. Because a settlement below carrying amount seldom is supported by objective evidence of overvaluation of assets, the preferred accounting treatment is to leave net asset valuations undisturbed unless a large amount of impaired goodwill is carried in the accounting records as a result of the prior admission of a partner as described on page 50. The difference between the retiring partner's capital account balance and the amount paid in settlement should be allocated as a ***bonus*** to the continuing partners.

For example, assume that the three partners of Merz, Noll & Park LLP share net income or losses equally, and that each has a capital account balance of $60,000. Noll retires from the partnership and receives $50,000. The journal entry to record Noll's retirement follows:

Bonus to Continuing Partners

Noll, Capital	60,000	
Cash		50,000
Merz, Capital ($10,000 × ½)		5,000
Park, Capital ($10,000 × ½)		5,000
To record retirement of Partner Noll for an amount less than carrying amount of Noll's equity, with a bonus to continuing partners.		

The final settlement with a retiring partner often is deferred for some time after the partner's withdrawal to permit the accumulation of cash, the measurement of net income to date of withdrawal, the obtaining of bank loans, or other acts needed to complete the transaction.

Death of a Partner

Limited liability partnership contracts often provide that partners shall acquire life insurance policies on each others' lives so that cash will be available for settlement with the estate of a deceased partner. A ***buy-sell agreement*** may be formed by the partners, whereby the partners commit their estates to sell their equities in the partnership and the surviving partners to acquire such equities. Another form of such an agreement gives the surviving partners an ***option to buy,*** or ***right of first refusal,*** rather than imposing on the partnership an obligation to acquire the deceased partner's equity.

LIMITED PARTNERSHIPS

The legal provisions governing ***limited partnerships*** (not to be confused with limited liability partnerships) are provided by the Uniform Limited Partnership Act. Among the features of a limited partnership are the following:

1. There must be at least one general partner, who has unlimited liability for unpaid debts of the partnership.

2. Limited partners have no obligation for unpaid liabilities of the limited partnership; only general partners have such liability.

3. Limited partners have no participation in the management of the limited partnership.

4. Limited partners may invest only cash or other assets in a limited partnership; they may not provide services as their investment.

5. The surname of a limited partner may not appear in the name of the partnership.

6. The formation of a limited partnership is evidenced by a ***certificate*** filed with the county recorder of the principal place of business of the limited partnership. The certificate includes many of the items present in the typical partnership contract of a limited liability partnership (see pages 31–32); in addition, it must include the name and residence of each general partner and limited partner; the amount of cash and other assets invested by each limited partner; provision for return of a limited partner's investment; any priority of one or more limited partners over other limited partners; and any right of limited partners to vote for election or removal of general partners, termination of the partnership, amendment of the certificate, or disposal of all partnership assets.

Membership in a limited partnership is offered to prospective limited partners in ***units*** subject to the Securities Act of 1933. Thus, unless provisions of that Act exempt a limited partnership, it must file a registration statement for the offered units with the Securities and Exchange Commission (SEC) and undertake to file periodic reports with the SEC. The SEC has provided guidance for such registration and reporting in ***Industry Guide 5: Preparation of Registration Statements Relating to Interests in Real Estate Limited Partnerships.***

Large limited partnerships that engage in ventures such as oil and gas exploration and real estate development and issue units registered with the SEC are termed ***master limited partnerships.***

Accounting for Limited Partnerships

The accounting for business transactions and events of limited partnerships parallels the accounting for limited liability partnerships, except that limited partners do not have periodic drawings debited to a Drawing ledger account. With respect to additions and retirements of limited partners, who may be numerous, the limited partnership should maintain a subsidiary limited partners' ledger, similar to the stockholders' ledger of a corporation, with capital accounts for each limited partner showing investment units, increases for net income and decreases for net losses, and decreases for retirements.

Financial Statements for Limited Partnerships

In *Staff Accounting Bulletin 40,* the SEC provided standards for financial statements of limited partnerships filed with the SEC, as follows.[6]

> The equity section of a [limited] partnership balance sheet should distinguish between amounts ascribed to each ownership class. The equity attributed to the general partners should be stated separately from the equity of the limited partners, and changes in the number of equity units . . . outstanding should be shown for each ownership class. A statement of changes in partnership equity for each ownership class should be furnished for each period for which an income statement is included.
>
> The income statements of [limited] partnerships should be presented in a manner which clearly shows the aggregate amount of net income (loss) allocated to the general partners and the aggregate amount allocated to the limited partners. The statement of income should also state the results of operations on a per unit basis.

Although the foregoing standards are mandatory only for limited partnerships subject to the SEC's jurisdiction, they are appropriate for other limited partnerships.

To illustrate financial statements for a limited partnership, assume that Wesley Randall formed Randall Company, a limited partnership that was exempt from the registration requirements of the Securities Act of 1933. On January 2, 2002, Wesley Randall, the general partner, acquired 30 units at $1,000 a unit, and 30 limited partners acquired a total of 570 units at $1,000 a unit. The limited partnership certificate for Randall Company provided that limited partners might withdraw their net equity (investment plus net income less net loss) only on December 31 of each year. Wesley Randall was authorized to withdraw $500 a month at his discretion, but he had no drawings during 2002. Randall Company had a net income of $90,000 for 2002, and on December 31, 2002, two limited partners withdrew their entire equity interest of 40 units.

The following condensed financial statements (excluding a statement of cash flows) incorporate the foregoing assumptions and comply with the provisions of *Staff Accounting Bulletin 40:*

RANDALL COMPANY (a limited partnership) Income Statement For Year Ended December 31, 2002		
Revenue		$400,000
Costs and expenses		310,000
Net income		$ 90,000
Division of net income ($150* per unit based on 600 weighted-average units outstanding):		
To general partner (30 units)	$ 4,500	
To limited partners (570 units)	85,500	
Total	$90,000	

*$90,000 ÷ 600 units outstanding throughout 2002 = $150.

[6] *Staff Accounting Bulletin 40,* Topic F, Securities and Exchange Commission (Washington, DC: 1981).

RANDALL COMPANY (a limited partnership) Statement of Partners' Capital For Year Ended December 31, 2002						
	General Partner		**Limited Partners**		**Combined**	
	Units	**Amount**	**Units**	**Amount**	**Units**	**Amount**
Initial investments, beginning of year	30	$30,000	570	$570,000	600	$600,000
Add: Net income		4,500		85,500		90,000
Subtotals	30	$34,500	570	$655,500	600	$690,000
Less: Redemption of units			40	46,000	40	46,000
Partners' capital, end of year	30	$34,500	530	$609,500	560	$644,000

RANDALL COMPANY (a limited partnership) Balance Sheet December 31, 2002			
Assets		**Liabilities and Partners' Capital**	
Current assets	$ 240,000	Current liabilities	$ 100,000
Other assets	760,000	Long-term debt	256,000
		Total liabilities	$ 356,000
		Partners' capital ($1,150* per unit based on 560 units outstanding):	
		General partner $ 34,500	
		Limited partners 609,500	644,000
		Total liabilities and	
Total assets	$1,000,000	partners' capital	$1,000,000

*$644,000 ÷ 560 = $1,150.

SEC ENFORCEMENT ACTIONS DEALING WITH WRONGFUL APPLICATION OF ACCOUNTING STANDARDS FOR PARTNERSHIPS

In 1982, the Securities and Exchange Commission (SEC) initiated a series of *Accounting and Auditing Enforcement Releases* (AAERs) to report its enforcement actions involving accountants. Following are summaries of two AAERs dealing with violations of accounting standards for partnerships.

AAER 202

AAER 202, "Securities and Exchange Commission v. William A. MacKay and Muncie A. Russell" (September 29, 1988), deals with a general partnership formed by the former chief executive officer (CEO) and chief financial officer (CFO) (a CPA) of American Biomaterials Corporation, a manufacturer of medical and dental products. The SEC alleged that the partnership, Kirkwood Associates, ostensibly an executive search firm, had received more than $410,000 from American Biomaterials for nonexistent services. The partnership had no offices or employees, and its telephone number and address were those of a telephone answering and mail collection service. Although its

CEO and CFO directly benefited from the $410,000 payments, American Biomaterials did not disclose this ***related-party transaction*** in its report to the SEC. The CEO and the CFO, without admitting or denying the SEC's allegations, consented to the federal court's permanently enjoining them from violating the federal securities laws.

AAER 214

In ***AAER 214,*** "Securities and Exchange Commission v. Avanti Associates First Mortgage Fund 84 Limited Partnership et al." (January 11, 1989), the SEC reported on a federal court's entry of a permanent injunction against the general partner (a CPA) of a limited partnership that in turn was the general partner of a second limited partnership that made and acquired short-term first mortgage loans on real property. According to the SEC, the financial statements of the second limited partnership, filed with the SEC in ***Form 10-K,*** included a note that falsely reported the amount and nature of a related-party transaction. Correct reporting of the related-party transaction would have disclosed that the CPA had improperly profited from a kickback scheme involving payments made by borrowers from the limited partnership to a distant relative of the CPA. In a related enforcement action, reported in ***AAER 220,*** ". . . In the Matter of Richard P. Franke . . ." (March 24, 1989), the SEC permanently prohibited appearing or practicing before it by the CPA who had ostensibly audited the limited partnership's financial statements that were included in ***Form 10-K.***

Review Questions

1. In the formation of a limited liability partnership, partners often invest nonmonetary assets such as land, buildings, and machinery, as well as cash. Should nonmonetary assets be recognized by the partnership at current fair value, at cost to the partners, or at some other amount? Explain.

2. Some large CPA firms have thousands of staff members, and hundreds of partners, and operate on a national or an international basis. Would the professional corporation form of organization be more appropriate than the limited liability partnership form for such large organizations? Explain.

3. Explain the limited liability partnership balance sheet display of loans to and from partners and the accounting for interest on such loans.

4. Explain how partners' salaries should be displayed in the income statement of a limited liability partnership, if at all.

5. List at least five items that should be included in a limited liability partnership contract.

6. List at least five methods by which net income or losses of a limited liability partnership may be divided among partners.

7. Ainsley & Burton LLP admitted Paul Craig to a one-third interest in the firm for his investment of $50,000. Does this mean that Craig would be entitled to one-third of the partnership's net income or losses?

8. Duncan and Eastwick are negotiating a partnership contract, with Duncan to invest $60,000 and Eastwick $20,000 in the limited liability partnership. Duncan suggests that interest at 8% be allowed on average capital account balances and that any remaining net income or losses be divided in the ratio of average capital account balances. Eastwick prefers that the entire net income or losses be divided in the ratio of average capital account balances. Comment on these proposals.

9. The partnership contract of Peel & Quay LLP is brief on the sharing of net income and losses. It states: "Net income is to be divided 80% to Peel and 20% to Quay, and each partner is entitled to draw $2,000 a month." What difficulties do you fore-

see in implementing this contract? Illustrate possible difficulties under the assumption that the partnership had a net income of $100,000 in the first year of operations.

10. Muir and Miller operated Muir & Miller LLP for several years, sharing net income and losses equally. On January 1, 2002, they agreed to revise the income-sharing ratio to 70% for Muir and 30% for Miller, because of Miller's desire for semiretirement. On March 1, 2002, the partnership received $10,000 in settlement of a disputed amount receivable on a contract completed in 2001. Because the outcome of the dispute had been uncertain, no trade account receivable had been recognized. Explain the accounting treatment you would recommend for the $10,000 cash receipt.

11. Should the carrying amounts of a limited liability partnership's assets be restated to current fair values when a partner retires or a new partner is admitted to the firm? Explain.

12. A new partner admitted to a limited liability partnership often is required to invest an amount of cash larger than the carrying amount of the interest in net assets the new partner acquires. In what way might such a transaction be recorded? What is the principal argument for each method?

13. Two partners invested $2,000 each to form a limited liability partnership for the construction of a shopping center. The partnership obtained a bank loan of $800,000 to finance construction, but no payment on this loan was due for two years. Each partner withdrew $50,000 cash from the partnership from the proceeds of the loan. How should the investment of $4,000 and the withdrawal of $100,000 be displayed in the financial statements of the partnership?

14. A CPA firm was asked to express an auditors' opinion on the financial statements of a limited partnership in which a corporation was the general partner. Should the financial statements of the limited partnership and the auditors' report thereon include the financial statements of the general partner?

15. How do the financial statements of a limited partnership differ from those of a limited liability partnership?

16. Differentiate between a *limited liability partnership* (LLP) and a *limited partnership.*

Exercises

(Exercise 2.1)   Select the best answer for each of the following multiple-choice questions:

1. The partnership contract of Lowell & Martin LLP provided for salaries of $45,000 to Lowell and $35,000 to Martin, with any remaining income or loss divided equally. During 2002, pre-salaries income of Lowell & Martin LLP was $100,000, and both Lowell and Martin withdrew cash from the partnership equal to 80% of their salary allowances. During 2002, Lowell's equity in the partnership:

   a. Increased more than Martin's equity.
   b. Decreased more than Martin's equity.
   c. Increased the same amount as Martin's equity.
   d. Decreased the same amount as Martin's equity.

2. When Andrew Davis retired from Davis, Evans & Fell LLP, he received cash in excess of his capital account balance. Under the bonus method, the excess cash received by Davis:

    a. Reduced the capital account balances of Evans and Fell.

    b. Had no effect on the capital account balances of Evans and Fell.

    c. Was recognized as goodwill of the partnership.

    d. Was recognized as an operating expense of the partnership.

3. A large cash withdrawal by Partner Davis from Carr, Davis, Exley & Fay LLP, which is viewed by all partners as a permanent reduction of Davis's ownership equity in the partnership, is recorded with a debit to:

    a. Loan Receivable from Davis.

    b. Davis, Drawing.

    c. Davis, Capital.

    d. Retained Earnings.

4. The partnership contract for Gore & Haines LLP provided that Gore is to receive an annual salary of $60,000, Haines is to receive an annual salary of $40,000, and the net income or loss (after partners' salaries expense) is to be divided equally between the two partners. Net income of Gore & Haines LLP for the fiscal year ended December 31, 2002, was $90,000. The closing entry for net income on December 31, 2002, is a debit to Income Summary for $90,000 and credits to Gore, Capital and Haines, Capital, respectively, of:

    a. $54,000 and $36,000.

    b. $55,000 and $35,000.

    c. $45,000 and $45,000.

    d. Some other amounts.

5. Which of the following is an expense of a limited liability partnership?

    a. Interest on partners' capital account balances.

    b. Interest on loans from partners to the partnership.

    c. Both *a* and *b*.

    d. Neither *a* nor *b*.

6. The CPA partners of Tan, Ullman & Valdez LLP shared net income and losses 25%, 35%, and 40%, respectively. On January 31, 2002, by mutual consent of the partners, Julio Valdez withdrew from the partnership, receiving $162,000 for his $150,000 capital account balance. The preferable journal entry (explanation omitted) for the partnership on January 31, 2002, is:

a. Valdez, Capital	150,000	
Tan, Capital ($12,000 × 25/60)	5,000	
Ullman, Capital ($12,000 × 35/60)	7,000	
Cash		162,000
b. Valdez, Capital	162,000	
Goodwill	12,000	
Valdez, Capital ($162,000 − $150,000)		12,000
Cash		162,000
c. Goodwill ($12,000 ÷ 0.40)	30,000	
Valdez, Capital	162,000	
Tan, Capital ($30,000 × 0.25)		7,500
Ullman, Capital ($30,000 × 0.35)		10,500
Valdez, Capital ($30,000 × 0.40)		12,000
Cash		162,000

d. Valdez, Capital ($12,000 × 0.40)	4,800	
Valdez, Capital ($150,000 − $4,800)	145,200	
Tan, Capital ($12,000 × 0.25)	3,000	
Ullman, Capital ($12,000 × 0.35)	4,200	
Loss on Withdrawal of Partner	4,800	
Cash		162,000

7. The two partners of Adonis & Brutus LLP share net income and losses in the ratio of 7 : 3, respectively. On February 1, 2002, their capital account balances were as follows:

   Adonis $70,000
   Brutus   60,000

   Adonis and Brutus agreed to admit Cato as a partner with a one-third interest in the partnership capital and net income or losses for an investment of $50,000. The new partnership will begin with total capital of $180,000. Immediately after Cato's admission to the partnership, the capital account balances of Adonis, Brutus, and Cato, respectively, are:

   a. $60,000, $60,000, $60,000.
   b. $63,000, $57,000, $60,000.
   c. $63,333, $56,667, $60,000.
   d. $70,000, $60,000, $50,000.
   e. Some other amounts.

8. According to this text, the recognition of goodwill in the accounting records of a limited liability partnership may be appropriate for:

   a. The admission of a new partner for a cash investment.
   b. The retirement of an existing partner.
   c. Either of the foregoing situations.
   d. Neither of the foregoing situations.

9. The partnership contract for Clark & Davis LLP provides that "net income or losses are to be distributed in the ratio of partners' capital account balances." The appropriate interpretation of this provision is that net income or losses should be distributed in:

   a. The ratio of beginning capital account balances.
   b. The ratio of average capital account balances.
   c. The ratio of ending account balances (before distribution of net income or loss).
   d. One of the foregoing methods to be specified by partners Clark and Davis.

10. Salaries to partners of a limited liability partnership typically should be accounted for as:

    a. A device for sharing net income.
    b. An operating expense of the partnership.
    c. Drawings by the partners from the partnership.
    d. Reductions of the partners' capital account balances.

11. The income-sharing provision of the contract that established Early & Farber LLP provided that Early was to receive a bonus of 20% of income after deduction of the bonus, with the remaining income distributed 40% to Early and 60% to

Farber. If income before the bonus of Early & Farber LLP was $240,000 for the fiscal year ended August 31, 2002, the capital accounts of Early and Farber should be credited, respectively, in the amounts of:

a. $120,000 and $120,000.
b. $124,800 and $115,200.
c. $96,000 and $144,000.
d. $163,200 and $76,800.
e. Some other amounts.

12. Which of the following typical expenses of a corporation is not relevant for a limited liability partnership?

a. Salaries expense.
b. Interest expense.
c. Income taxes expense.
d. Pension expense.
e. None of the above.

13. Are the results of operations on a *per unit* basis displayed in the income statement of a:

	Limited Liability Partnership?	Limited Partnership?
a.	Yes	Yes
b.	Yes	No
c.	No	Yes
d.	No	No

(Exercise 2.2) On January 2, 2002, Carle and Dody established Carle & Dody LLP, with Carle investing $80,000 and Dody investing $70,000 on that date. The income-sharing provisions of the partnership contract were as follows:

CHECK FIGURE

Credit Dody, capital, a total of $9,975.

1. Salaries of $30,000 *per annum* to each partner.
2. Interest at 6% *per annum* on beginning capital account balances of each partner.
3. Remaining income or loss divided equally.

Pre-salary income of Carle & Dody LLP for the *month* of January 2002 was $20,000. Neither partner had a drawing for that month.

   Prepare journal entries for Carle & Dody LLP on January 31, 2002, to provide for partners' salaries and close the Income Summary ledger account. Show supporting computations in the explanations for the entries.

(Exercise 2.3) Activity in the capital accounts of the partners of Webb & Yu LLP for the fiscal year ended December 31, 2002, follows:

CHECK FIGURE

b. Net income to Yu, $28,000.

	Webb, Capital	Yu, Capital
Balances, Jan. 1	$40,000	$80,000
Investment, July 1	20,000	
Withdrawal, Oct. 1		40,000

Net income of Webb & Yu LLP for the year ended December 31, 2002, amounted to $48,000.

   Prepare a working paper to compute the division of the $48,000 net income of Webb & Yu LLP under each of the following assumptions:

a. The partnership contract is silent as to sharing of net income and losses.

b. Net income and losses are divided on the basis of average capital account balances (not including the net income or loss for the current year).

c. Net income and losses are divided on the basis of beginning capital account balances.

d. Net income and losses are divided on the basis of ending capital account balances (not including the net income or loss for the current year).

(Exercise 2.4)

The partnership contract of Ray, Stan & Todd LLP provided that Ray was to receive a bonus equal to 20% of income and that the remaining income or loss was to be divided 40% each to Ray and Stan and 20% to Todd. Income of Ray, Stan & Todd LLP for 2002 (before the bonus) amounted to $127,200.

Explain two alternative ways in which the bonus provision might be interpreted, and prepare a working paper to compute the division of the $127,200 income of Ray, Stan & Todd LLP for 2002 under each interpretation.

✻ (Exercise 2.5)

The partnership contract of Jones, King & Lane LLP provided for the division of net income or losses in the following manner:

CHECK FIGURE

Net income to Jones, $27,000.

1. Bonus of 20% of income before the bonus to Jones.
2. Interest at 15% on average capital account balances to each partner.
3. Residual income or loss equally to each partner.

Net income of Jones, King & Lane LLP for 2002 was $90,000, and the average capital account balances for that year were Jones, $100,000; King, $200,000; and Lane, $300,000.

Prepare a working paper to compute each partner's share of the 2002 net income of Jones, King & Lane LLP.

(Exercise 2.6)

The partnership contract of Ann, Bud & Cal LLP provides for the remuneration of partners as follows:

CHECK FIGURE

Debit bonus expense, $10,000.

1. Salaries of $40,000 to Ann, $35,000 to Bud, and $30,000 to Cal, to be recognized annually as operating expense of the partnership in the measurement of net income.
2. Bonus of 10% of income after salaries and the bonus to Ann.
3. Remaining net income or loss 30% to Ann, 20% to Bud, and 50% to Cal.

Income of Ann, Bud & Cal LLP before partners' salaries and Ann's bonus was $215,000 for the fiscal year ended December 31, 2002.

Prepare journal entries for Ann, Bud & Cal LLP on December 31, 2002, to (1) accrue partners' salaries and Ann's bonus and (2) close the Income Summary ledger account (credit balance of $100,000) and divide the net income among the partners. Show supporting computations in the explanation for the second journal entry.

(Exercise 2.7)

The partnership contract for Bates & Carter LLP provided for salaries to partners and the division of net income or losses as follows:

CHECK FIGURE

Net income to Bates, $42,400.

1. Salaries of $40,000 a year to Bates and $60,000 a year to Carter.
2. Interest at 12% a year on beginning capital account balances.
3. Remaining net income or loss 70% to Bates and 30% to Carter.

For the fiscal year ended December 31, 2002, Bates & Carter LLP had presalaries income of $200,000. Capital account balances on January 1, 2002, were $400,000 for Bates and $500,000 for Carter; Bates invested an additional $100,000 in the partnership on September 30, 2002. In accordance with the partnership contract, both partners drew their salary allowances in cash from the partnership during the year.

Prepare journal entries for Bates & Carter LLP on December 31, 2002, to (1) accrue partners' salaries and (2) close the Income Summary (credit balance of $100,000) and drawing accounts. Show supporting computations in the journal entry closing the Income Summary account.

(Exercise 2.8) Emma Neal and Sally Drew are partners of Neal & Drew LLP sharing net income or losses equally; each has a capital account balance of $200,000. Sally Drew (with the consent of Neal) sold one-fifth of her interest to her daughter Paula for $50,000, with payment to be made to Sally Drew in five annual installments of $10,000, plus interest at 15% on the unpaid balance.

Prepare a journal entry for Neal, Drew & Drew LLP to record the change in ownership, and explain why you would or would not recommend a change in the valuation of net assets in the accounting records of Neal, Drew & Drew LLP.

(Exercise 2.9) On January 31, 2002, Nancy Ross and John Clemon were admitted to Logan, Marsh & Noble LLP (CPA firm), which had net assets of $120,000 prior to the admission and an income-sharing ratio of Logan, 25%; Marsh, 35%; and Noble, 40%. Ross paid $20,000 to Carl Logan for one-half of his 20% share of partnership net assets on January 31, 2002, and Clemon invested $20,000 in the partnership for a 10% interest in the net assets of Logan, Marsh, Noble, Ross & Clemon LLP. No goodwill was to be recognized as a result of the admission of Ross and Clemon to the partnership.

CHECK FIGURE

Credit Clemon, capital, $14,000.

Prepare separate journal entries on January 31, 2002, to record the admission of Ross and Clemon to Logan, Marsh, Noble, Ross & Clemon LLP.

(Exercise 2.10) Partners Arne and Bolt of Arne & Bolt LLP have capital account balances of $30,000 and $20,000, respectively, and they share net income and losses in a 3:1 ratio.

Prepare journal entries to record the admission of Cope to Arne, Bolt & Cope LLP under each of the following conditions:

CHECK FIGURE

b. Credit Arne, capital, $19,500.

a. Cope invests $30,000 for a one-fourth interest in net assets; the total partnership capital after Cope's admission is to be $80,000.

b. Cope invests $30,000, of which $10,000 is a bonus to Arne and Bolt. In conjunction with the admission of Cope, the carrying amount of the inventories is increased by $16,000. Cope's capital account is credited for $20,000.

(Exercise 2.11) Lamb and Meek, partners of Lamb & Meek Limited Liability Partnership who share net income and losses 60% and 40%, respectively, had capital account balances of $70,000 and $60,000, respectively, on June 30, 2002. On that date Lamb and Meek agreed to admit Niles to Lamb, Meek & Niles Limited Liability Partnership with a one-third interest in total partnership capital of $180,000 and a one-third share of net income or losses, for a cash investment of $50,000.

Prepare a working paper to compute the balances of the Lamb, Capital, Meek, Capital and Niles, Capital ledger accounts on June 30, 2002, following the admission of Niles to Lamb, Meek & Niles Limited Liability Partnership.

(Exercise 2.12) Floyd Austin and Samuel Bradford are partners of Austin & Bradford LLP who share net income and losses equally and have equal capital account balances. The net assets of the partnership have a carrying amount of $80,000. Jason Crade is admitted to Austin, Bradford & Crade LLP with a one-third interest in net income or losses and net assets. To acquire this interest, Crade invests $34,000 cash in the partnership.

CHECK FIGURE

b. Credit Crade, capital, $34,000.

Prepare journal entries to record the admission of Crade in the accounting records of Austin, Bradford & Crade LLP under the:

a. Bonus method.

b. Revaluation of net assets method, assuming partnership inventories are overstated.

(Exercise 2.13)

On August 31, 2002, Logan and Major, partners of Logan & Major Limited Liability Partnership who had capital account balances of $80,000 and $120,000, respectively, on that date and who shared net income and losses in a 2:3 ratio, agreed to admit Nelson to Logan, Major & Nelson Limited Liability Partnership with a 20% interest in net assets and net income in exchange for a $60,000 cash investment. Logan and Major were to retain their prior income-sharing arrangement with respect to the 80% remainder of net income (100% − 20% = 80%). On September 30, 2002, after the closing of the partnership's revenue and expense ledger accounts, the Income Summary ledger account had a credit balance of $50,000.

Prepare journal entries for Logan, Major & Nelson Limited Liability Partnership to record the admission of Nelson on August 31, 2002, and to close the Income Summary ledger account on September 30, 2002.

(Exercise 2.14)

On January 31, 2002, partners of Lon, Mac & Nan LLP had the following loan and capital account balances (after closing entries for January):

Loan receivable from Lon	$ 20,000 dr
Loan payable to Nan	60,000 cr
Lon, Capital	30,000 dr
Mac, Capital	120,000 cr
Nan, Capital	70,000 cr

The partnership's income-sharing ratio was Lon, 50%; Mac, 20%; and Nan, 30%.

On January 31, 2002, Ole was admitted to the partnership for a 20% interest in *total capital* of the partnership in exchange for an investment of $40,000 cash. Prior to Ole's admission, the existing partners agreed to increase the carrying amount of the partnership's inventories to current fair value, a $60,000 increase.

Prepare journal entries on January 31, 2002, for Lon, Mac, Nan & Ole LLP to record the $60,000 increase in the partnership's inventories and the admission of Ole for a $40,000 cash investment.

(Exercise 2.15)

On May 31, 2001, Ike Loy was admitted to Jay & Kaye LLP by investing Loy Company, a highly profitable proprietorship having identifiable tangible and intangible net assets of $600,000, at carrying amount and current fair value. Prior to Loy's admission, capital account balances and income-sharing percentages of Jay and Kaye were as follows:

	Capital Account Balances	Income-Sharing Percentages
Jay	$400,000	60%
Kaye	500,000	40%

The partnership contract for the new Jay, Kaye & Loy LLP included the following provisions:

1. Loy was to receive a capital account balance of $660,000 on his admission to the partnership on May 31, 2001.

2. Income for the fiscal year ending May 31, 2002, and subsequent years was to be allocated as follows:

   a. Bonus of 10% of income *after the bonus* to Loy.

   b. Resultant net income or loss 30% to Jay, 20% to Kaye, and 50% to Loy.

Income *before the bonus* for the year ended May 31, 2002, was $132,000.

Prepare journal entries for Jay, Kaye & Loy LLP on May 31, 2001, and May 31, 2002 (the latter to accrue Loy's bonus and to close the Income Summary ledger account having a credit balance of $120,000).

(Exercise 2.16) The inexperienced accountant for Fox, Gee & Hay LLP prepared the following journal entries during the fiscal year ended August 31, 2002:

CHECK FIGURE

Credit Hay, capital, a net amount of $12,000.

2001			
Sept. 1	Cash	50,000	
	Goodwill	150,000	
	Fox, Capital ($150,000 × 0.25)		37,500
	Gee, Capital ($150,000 × 0.75)		112,500
	Hay, Capital		50,000

To record admission of Hay for a 20% interest in net assets, with goodwill credited to Fox and Gee in their former income-sharing ratio. Goodwill is computed as follows:

Implied total capital, based on Hay's investment ($50,000 × 5)	$250,000	
Less: Net assets prior to Hay's admission	100,000	
Goodwill	$150,000	

2002			
Aug. 31	Income Summary	30,000	
	Fox, Capital ($30,000 × 0.20)		6,000
	Gee, Capital ($30,000 × 0.60)		18,000
	Hay, Capital ($30,000 × 0.20)		6,000

To divide net income for the year in the residual income-sharing ratio of Fox, 20%; Gee, 60%; Hay, 20%. Provision in partnership contract requiring $40,000 annual salary allowance to Hay is disregarded because income before salary is only $30,000.

Prepare journal entries for Fox, Gee & Hay LLP on August 31, 2002, to correct the accounting records, which have not been closed for the year ended August 31, 2002. Assume that Hay's admission to the partnership should have been recorded by the bonus method. Do not reverse the foregoing journal entries.

(Exercise 2.17) On June 30, 2002, the balance sheet of King, Lowe & More LLP and the partners' respective income-sharing percentages were as shown on the next page.

KING, LOWE & MORE LLP
Balance Sheet
June 30, 2002

Assets

Curent assets	$185,000
Plant assets (net)	200,000
Total assets	$385,000

Liabilities and Partners' Capital

Trade accounts payable	$ 85,000
Loan payable to King	15,000
King, capital (20%)	70,000
Lowe, capital (20%)	65,000
More, capital (60%)	150,000
Total liabilities and partners' capital	$385,000

King decided to retire from the partnership on June 30, 2002, and by mutual agreement of the partners the plant assets were adjusted to their total current fair value of $260,000. The partnership paid $92,000 cash for King's equity in the partnership, exclusive of the loan, which was repaid in full. No goodwill was to be recognized in this transaction.

Prepare journal entries for King, Lowe & More LLP on June 30, 2002, to record the adjustment of plant assets to current fair value and King's retirement.

(Exercise 2.18) The partners' capital (income-sharing ratio in parentheses) of Nunn, Owen, Park & Quan LLP on May 31, 2002, was as follows:

Nunn (20%)	$ 60,000
Owen (20%)	80,000
Park (20%)	70,000
Quan (40%)	40,000
Total partners' capital	$250,000

On May 31, 2002, with the consent of Nunn, Owen, and Quan:

1. Sam Park retired from the partnership and was paid $50,000 cash in full settlement of his interest in the partnership.
2. Lois Reed was admitted to the partnership with a $20,000 cash investment for a 10% interest in the net assets of Nunn, Owen, Quan & Reed LLP.

No goodwill was to be recognized for the foregoing events.

Prepare journal entries on May 31, 2002, to record the foregoing events.

(Exercise 2.19) The accountant for Tan, Ulm & Vey LLP prepared the following journal entry on January 31, 2002:

2002			
Jan. 31	Goodwill ($12,000 ÷ 0.40)	30,000	
	Vey, Capital ($150,000 + $12,000)	162,000	
	Tan, Capital ($30,000 × 0.25)		7,500
	Ulm, Capital ($30,000 × 0.35)		10,500
	Vey, Capital ($30,000 × 0.40)		12,000
	Cash		162,000
	To record withdrawal of Ross Vey, with a cash payment of $162,000, compared with his prewithdrawal capital account balance, and recognition of implicit goodwill, allocated in partners' income-sharing ratio of 25% : 35% : 40%.		

Prepare a journal entry for Tan, Ulm & Vey LLP on January 31, 2002, to **correct,** not **reverse,** the foregoing entry. Show supporting computations in the explanation for the entry.

(Exercise 2.20)   Macco Company (a limited partnership) was established on January 2, 2002, with the issuance of 10 units at $10,000 a unit to Malcolm Cole, the general partner, and 40 units in the aggregate to five limited partners at $10,000 a unit. The certificate for Macco provided that Cole was authorized to withdraw a maximum of $24,000 a year on December 31 of each year for which net income was at least $100,000 and that limited partners might withdraw their equity for cash or promissory notes on December 31 of each year only. For 2002 Macco Company had a net income of $300,000, and on December 31, 2002, Cole withdrew $24,000 cash and a limited partner redeemed 10 units, receiving a two-year promissory note bearing interest at 10%.

Prepare a statement of partners' capital for Macco Company (a limited partnership) for the fiscal year ended December 31, 2002.

Cases

(Case 2.1)   The author of *Modern Advanced Accounting* takes the position (page 31) that salaries awarded to partners of a limited liability partnership should be recognized as operating expenses of the partnership. Some other accountants maintain that partners' salaries should be accounted for as a step in the division of net income or losses of a limited liability partnership.

Instructions
Which method of accounting for partners' salaries do you support? Explain.

(Case 2.2)   During your audit of the financial statements of Arnold, Bright & Carle LLP for the fiscal year ended January 31, 2002, you review the following general journal entry:

2001			
Feb. 1	Cash	120,000	
	Goodwill	60,000	
	Arnold, Capital ($60,000 × 0.60)		36,000
	Bright, Capital ($60,000 × 0.40)		24,000
	Carle, Capital		120,000

To record admission of Carla Carle to Arnold & Bright LLP
for a one-third interest in total capital, with implicit goodwill
allocated to Arnold and Bright in their income-sharing ratio.
Goodwill is computed as follows:

Implied total capital of partnership based		
on Carle's investment ($120,000 × 3)	$360,000	
Less: Total capital of Arnold and Bright	(180,000)	
Cash invested by Carle	(120,000)	
Goodwill	$ 60,000	

Instructions

Is recognition of goodwill in the foregoing journal entry in accordance with generally accepted accounting principles? Explain.

(Case 2.3) In a classroom discussion of accounting standards for limited liability partnerships, student Ronald suggested that interest on partners' capital account balances, allocated in accordance with the partnership contract, should be recognized as an operating expense by the partnership.

Instructions

What is your opinion of student Ronald's suggestion? Explain.

(Case 2.4) The partners of Arch, Bell & Cole LLP had the following capital account balances and income-sharing ratio on May 31, 2002 (there were no loans receivable from or payable to partners):

Partner	Capital Account Balance	Income-Sharing Ratio
Arch	$120,000	35%
Bell	210,000	25
Cole	90,000	40
Totals	$420,000	100%

The partners are considering admission of Sidney Dale to the new Arch, Bell, Cole & Dale LLP for a 25% interest in partnership capital and a 20% share of net income. They request your advice on the preferability of Dale's investing cash in the partnership compared with their selling Dale one-fourth of each of their partnership interests.

Instructions

Present the partners of Arch, Bell & Cole LLP with the advantages and disadvantages of the two possible methods of the admission of Dale. Disregard income tax considerations.

(Case 2.5)   During your audit of Nue & Olde LLP for its first year of operations, you discover the following end-of-year adjusting entry in the partnership's general journal:

2002			
Dec. 31	Partners' Income Taxes Expense	40,000	
	Partners' Income Taxes Payable		40,000
	To provide for income taxes payable on Nue's and Olde's individual income tax returns based on their shares of partnership income for 2002.		

Instructions

Is the recognition of income taxes expense in the foregoing journal entry in accordance with generally accepted accounting principles? Explain, including in your explanation the accepted definitions of *expense* and *income taxes expense.*

(Case 2.6)   Dee, Ern & Fay LLP, whose partners share net income and losses equally, had an operating income of $30,000 for the first year of operations. However, near the end of that year, the partners learned of two unfavorable developments: (*a*) the bankruptcy of Sasha Company, maker of a two-year promissory note for $20,000 payable to Partner Dee that had been indorsed in blank to the partnership by Dee at face amount as Dee's original investment, and (*b*) the appearance on the market of new competing patented devices that rendered worthless a patent with a carrying amount of $10,000 that had been invested in the partnership by Ern as part of Ern's original investment.

Dee, Ern & Fay LLP had retained the promissory note made by Sasha Company with the expectation of discounting it when cash was needed. Quarterly interest payments had been received regularly prior to the bankruptcy of Sasha, but present prospects were for no further collections of interest or principal.

Fay argues that the $30,000 operating income should be divided $10,000 to each partner, with the $20,000 loss on the uncollectible note debited to Dee's capital account and the $10,000 loss on the worthless patent debited to Ern's capital account.

Instructions

Do you agree with Fay? Explain.

(Case 2.7)   A series of substantial net losses from operations has resulted in the following balance sheet drafted by the controller of Nobis, Ortho & Parr LLP:

NOBIS, ORTHO & PARR LLP
Balance Sheet
July 31, 2002

Assets

Current assets		$420,000
Plant assets (net)		550,000
Total assets		$970,000

Liabilities and Partners' Capital

Current liabilities		$380,000
Long-term debt		420,000
Total liabilities		$800,000
Art Nobis, capital	$130,000	
June Ortho, capital	(120,000)	
Carl Parr, capital	160,000	
Total partners' capital		170,000
Total liabilities and partners' capital		$970,000

Concerned about the partnership's high debt-to-equity ratio of 470.6% ($800,000 ÷ $170,000 = 470.6%), the partners consult with Jack Julian, CPA, controller of the partnership, who is a member of the AICPA, FEI, and IMA (see Chapter 1), regarding the propriety of converting partner Ortho's capital deficit to an account receivable. Ortho shows Julian a personal financial statement showing net assets of more than $400,000; Ortho points out that the bulk of her assets are in long-term investments that are difficult to liquidate to obtain cash for investment in the partnership. Partner Ortho is willing to pledge high-grade securities in her personal portfolio of investments to secure the $120,000 amount.

Instructions
May Jack Julian ethically comply with the request of the partners of Nobis, Ortho & Parr LLP? Explain.

(Case 2.8) Jean Rogers, CPA, is a member of the AICPA, the IMA, and the FEI (see Chapter 1); she is employed as the controller of Barnes, Egan & Harder LLP. On June 30, 2002, the end of the partnership's fiscal year, partner Charles Harder informed Rogers that the proceeds of a $100,000 personal loan to him by Local Bank on a one-year, 8% promissory note had been deposited in the partnership's checking account at Local Bank. Showing Rogers a memo signed by all three partners that approved the partnership's repayment of Harder's personal loan, including interest, Harder instructed Rogers to account for the loan proceeds as a credit to his partnership capital account and to recognize the partnership's subsequent payments of principal and interest on the loan with debits to Charles Harder, Drawing and Interest Expense, respectively.

Instructions
May Jean Rogers ethically comply with Charles Harder's request? Explain.

(Case 2.9) Carl Dobbs and David Ellis formed Dobbs & Ellis LLP on January 2, 2002. Dobbs invested cash of $50,000, and Ellis invested cash of $20,000 and marketable equity securities (classified as available for sale) with a current fair value of $80,000. A portion of the securities was sold at carrying amount in January 2002 to provide cash for operations of the partnership.

The partnership contract stated that net income and losses were to be divided in the capital ratio and authorized each partner to withdraw $1,000 monthly. Dobbs withdrew $1,000 on the last day of each month during 2002, but Ellis made no withdrawals during 2002 until July 1, when he withdraw all the securities that had not been sold by the partnership. The securities that Ellis withdrew had a current fair value of $41,000 when invested in the partnership on January 2, 2002, and a current fair value of $62,000 on July 1, 2002, when withdrawn. Ellis instructed the accountant for Dobbs & Ellis LLP to record the transaction by reducing Ellis's capital account balance by $41,000, which was done. Income from operations of Dobbs & Ellis LLP for 2002 amounted to $24,000.

Instructions

Determine the appropriate division of net income of Dobbs & Ellis LLP for 2002. If the income-sharing provision of the partnership contract is unsatisfactory, state the assumptions you would make for an appropriate interpretation of the partners' intentions. Describe the journal entry, if any, that you believe should be made for Dobbs & Ellis LLP. (Disregard income taxes.)

(Case 2.10)   George Lewis and Anna Marlin are partners of Lewis & Marlin LLP, who share net income and losses equally. They offer to admit Betty Naylor to Lewis, Marlin & Naylor LLP for a one-third interest in net assets and in net income or losses for an investment of $50,000 cash. The total capital of Lewis & Marlin LLP prior to Naylor's admission was $110,000. Naylor makes a counteroffer of $40,000, explaining that her investigation of Lewis & Marlin LLP indicates that many trade accounts receivable are past due and that a significant amount of the inventories is obsolete. Lewis and Marlin deny both of these allegations. They contend that inventories are valued in accordance with generally accepted accounting principles and that the accounts receivable are fully collectible. However, after prolonged negotiations, the admission price of $40,000 proposed by Naylor is agreed upon.

Instructions

Explain two ways in which the admission of Naylor might be recorded by Lewis, Marlin & Naylor LLP, and indicate which method is preferable.

(Case 2.11)   Lowyma Company LLP, a partnership of Ed Loeser, Peter Wylie, and Herman Martin, has operated successfully for many years, but Martin now plans to retire. In discussions of the settlement to be made with Martin, the point was made that inventories had been valued at last-in, first-out cost for many years. Martin suggested that because the partnership had begun managing inventories by the just-in-time system, the first-in, first-out cost of the inventories should be determined and the excess of this amount over the carrying amount of the inventories should be recognized as a gain to the partnership to be shared equally by the three partners. Loeser objected to this suggestion on grounds that any method of inventory valuation would give reasonably accurate results provided it were followed consistently and that a departure from the long-established last-in, first-out method of inventory valuation used by the partnership would produce an erroneous earnings record for the life of the partnership to date.

Instructions

Evaluate the objections of Ed Loeser by reference to *APB Opinion No. 20,* "Accounting Changes."

Problems

(Problem 2.1) Among the business transactions and events of Oscar, Paul & Quinn LLP, whose partners shared net income and losses equally, for the month of January 2002, were the following:

Jan. 2 With the consent of Paul and Quinn, Oscar made a $10,000 cash advance to the partnership on a 12% demand promissory note.

6 With the consent of Oscar and Paul, Quinn withdrew from the partnership merchandise with a cost of $4,000 and a fair value of $5,200, in lieu of a regular cash drawing. The partnership uses the perpetual inventory system.

13 The partners agreed that a patent with a carrying amount of $6,000, which had been invested by Paul when the partnership was organized, was worthless and should be written off.

27 Paul paid a $2,000 trade account payable of the partnership.

Instructions

Prepare journal entries for the foregoing transactions and events of Oscar, Paul & Quinn LLP and the January 31, 2002, adjusting entry for the note payable to Oscar.

(Problem 2.2) The condensed balance sheet of Gee & Hawe LLP on December 31, 2001, follows:

CHECK FIGURE

a. Credit Ivan, capital, $120,000; *b*. Net income to Hawe, $12,000.

GEE & HAWE LLP Balance Sheet December 31, 2001			
Assets		**Liabilities and Partners' Capital**	
Current assets	$100,000	Liabilities	$300,000
Plant assets (net)	500,000	Louis Gee, capital	200,000
		Ray Hawe, capital	100,000
Total	$600,000	Total	$600,000

Gee and Hawe shared net income or losses 40% and 60%, respectively. On January 2, 2002, Lisa Ivan was admitted to Gee, Hawe & Ivan LLP by the investment of the net assets of her highly profitable proprietorship. The partners agreed to the following current fair values of the identifiable net assets of Ivan's proprietorship:

Current assets	$ 70,000
Plant assets	230,000
Total assets	$300,000
Less: Liabilities	200,000
Net assets	$100,000

Ivan's capital account was credited for $120,000. The partners agreed further that the current fair values of the net assets of Gee & Hawe LLP were equal to their carrying amounts and that the accounting records of the old partnership should be used for the new partnership. The following partner-remuneration plan was adopted for the new partnership:

1. Salaries of $10,000 to Gee, $15,000 to Hawe, and $20,000 to Ivan, to be recognized as expenses of the partnership.
2. A bonus of 10% of income after deduction of partners' salaries and the bonus to Ivan.

3. Remaining income or loss as follows: 30% to Gee, 40% to Hawe, and 30% to Ivan.

For the fiscal year ended December 31, 2002, Gee, Hawe & Ivan LLP had income of $78,000 before partners' salaries and the bonus to Ivan.

Instructions

Prepare journal entries for Gee, Hawe & Ivan LLP to record the following (include supporting computations in the explanations for the entries):

a. The admission of Ivan to the partnership on January 2, 2002.

b. The partners' salaries, bonus, and division of net income for the year ended December 31, 2002.

(Problem 2.3) Ross & Saye LLP was organized and began operations on March 1, 2001. On that date, Roberta Ross invested $150,000, and Samuel Saye invested land and building with current fair values of $80,000 and $100,000, respectively. Saye also invested $60,000 in the partnership on November 1, 2001, because of its shortage of cash. The partnership contract includes the following remuneration plan:

	Ross	Saye
Annual salary (recognized as operating expense)	$18,000	$24,000
Annual interest on average capital account balances	10%	10%
Remainder	60%	40%

The annual salary was to be withdrawn by each partner in 12 monthly installments.

During the fiscal year ended February 28, 2002, Ross & Saye LLP had net sales of $500,000, cost of goods sold of $280,000, and total operating expenses of $100,000 (including partners' salaries expense but excluding interest on partners' average capital account balances). Each partner made monthly cash drawings in accordance with the partnership contract.

Instructions

a. Prepare a condensed income statement of Ross & Saye LLP for the year ended February 28, 2002. Show the details of the division of net income in a supporting exhibit.

b. Prepare a statement of partners' capital for Ross & Saye LLP for the year ended February 28, 2002.

(Problem 2.4) Partners Lucas and May formed Lucas & May LLP on January 2, 2002. Their capital accounts showed the following changes during:

	Lucas, Capital	May, Capital
Original investments, Jan. 2, 2002	$120,000	$180,000
Investments: May 1	15,000	
July 1		15,000
Withdrawals: Nov. 1	(30,000)	(75,000)
Capital account balances, Dec. 31, 2002	$105,000	$120,000

The income of Lucas & May LLP for 2002, before partners' salaries expense, was $69,600. The income included an extraordinary gain of $12,000.

Instructions

Prepare a working paper to compute each partner's share of net income of Lucas & May LLP for 2002 to the nearest dollar, assuring the following alternative income-sharing plans:

a. The partnership contract is silent as to division of net income or loss.

b. Income before extraordinary items is shared equally after allowance of 10% interest on average capital account balances (computed to the nearest month) and after salaries of $20,000 to Lucas and $30,000 to May recognized as operating expenses by the partnership. Extraordinary items are shared in the ratio of original investments.

c. Income before extraordinary items is shared on the basis of average capital account balances, and extraordinary items are shared on the basis of original investments.

d. Income before extraordinary items is shared equally between Lucas and May after a 20% bonus to May based on income before extraordinary items after the bonus. Extraordinary items are shared on the basis of original investments.

(Problem 2.5) Alex, Baron & Crane LLP was formed on January 2, 2002. The original cash investments were as follows:

CHECK FIGURE

a. Net income to Alex, $11,760; *b.* Crane, capital, $202,540.

Alex	$ 96,000
Baron	144,000
Crane	216,000

According to the partnership contract, the partners were to be remunerated as follows:

1. Salaries of $14,400 for Alex, $12,000 for Baron, and $13,600 for Crane, to be recognized as operating expenses by the partnership.
2. Interest at 12% on the average capital account balances during the year.
3. Remainder divided 40% to Alex, 30% to Baron, and 30% to Crane.

Income before partners' salaries for the fiscal year ended December 31, 2002, was $92,080. Alex invested an additional $24,000 in the partnership on July 1; Crane withdrew $36,000 from the partnership on October 1; and, as authorized by the partnership contract, Alex, Baron, and Crane each withdrew $1,250 monthly against their shares of net income for the year.

Instructions

a. Prepare a working paper to divide the $92,080 income before partners' salaries of the Alex, Baron & Crane LLP for the year ended December 31, 2002, among the partners. Show supporting computations.

b. Prepare a statement of partners' capital for the Alex, Baron & Crane LLP for the year ended December 31, 2002.

Problem (2.6) Partner Eng plans to withdraw from Chu, Dow & Eng LLP on July 10, 2002. Partnership assets are to be used to acquire Eng's partnership interest. The balance sheet for the partnership on that date follows:

CHECK FIGURE

a. Debit Chu, capital, $2,400; *c.* Debit Chu, capital, $15,000.

CHU, DOW & ENG LLP
Balance Sheet
July 10, 2002

Assets		Liabilities and Partners' Capital	
Cash	$ 74,000	Liabilities	$ 45,000
Trade accounts receivable (net)	36,000	Chu, capital	120,000
Plant assets (net)	135,000	Dow, capital	60,000
Goodwill (net)	30,000	Eng, capital	50,000
Total	$275,000	Total	$275,000

Chu, Dow, and Eng share net income and losses in the ratio of 3 : 2 : 1, respectively.

Instructions

Prepare journal entries to record Eng's withdrawal from the Chu, Dow & Eng LLP on July 10, 2002, under each of the following independent assumptions:

a. Eng is paid $54,000, and the excess paid over Eng's capital account balance is recorded as a bonus to Eng from Chu and Dow.

b. Eng is paid $45,000, and the difference is recorded as a bonus to Chu and Dow from Eng.

c. Eng is paid $45,000, and goodwill currently in the accounting records of the partnership, which arose from Chu's original investment of a highly profitable proprietorship, is reduced by the total amount of impairment implicit in the transaction.

d. Eng accepts cash of $40,500 and plant assets (equipment) with a current fair value of $9,000. The equipment had cost $30,000 and was 60% depreciated, with no residual value. (Record any gain or loss on the disposal of the equipment in the partners' capital accounts.)

(Problem 2.7) Yee & Zane LLP has maintained its accounting records on the accrual basis of accounting, except for the method of handling uncollectible account losses. Doubtful accounts expense has been recognized only when specific trade accounts receivable were determined to be uncollectible.

The partners of Yee & Zane LLP are anticipating the admission of Arne to the firm on December 31, 2002, and they retain you to review the partnership accounting records before this action is taken. You suggest that the firm change retroactively to the allowance method of accounting for doubtful accounts receivable so that the planning for admission of Arne may be based on the accrual basis of accounting. The following information is available:

Year Trade Accounts Receivable Originated	Trade Accounts Receivable Written Off			Additional Estimated Uncollectible Accounts
	2000	2001	2002	
1999	$1,200	$ 200		
2000	1,500	1,300	$ 600	$ 450
2001		1,800	1,400	1,250
2002			2,200	4,800
Totals	$2,700	$3,300	$4,200	$6,500

The partners shared net income and losses equally until 2001. In 2002 the income-sharing plan was changed as follows: salaries of $8,000 and $6,000 to Yee and Zane, respectively, to be expensed by the partnership; the resultant net income or loss to be divided 60% to Yee and 40% to Zane. Income of Yee & Zane LLP for 2002 was $52,000 before partners' salaries expense.

Instructions

a. Prepare a journal entry for Yee & Zane LLP on December 31, 2002, giving effect to the change in accounting method for doubtful accounts expense. Support the entry with an exhibit showing changes in doubtful accounts expense for the year ended December 31, 2002.

b. Assume that after you prepared the journal entry in *a* above, Yee's capital account balance was $48,000, Zane's capital account balance was $22,000, and Arne invested $30,000 for a 20% interest in net assets of Yee, Zane & Arne LLP and a 25% share in net income or losses. Prepare a journal entry for Yee, Zane & Arne LLP to record the admission of Arne on December 31, 2002, by the bonus method.

(Problem 2.8) Following are financial statements and additional information for Alef, Beal & Clarke LLP:

ALEF, BEAL & CLARKE LLP
Income Statement
For Year Ended December 31, 2002

Revenue and gain:		
Fees		$480,000
Gain on disposal of equipment		600
Total revenue and gain		$480,600
Expenses:		
Depreciation	$ 3,220	
Other	427,670	
Total expenses		430,890
Net income		$ 49,710
Division of net income:		
Partner Alef	$ 22,280	
Partner Beal	5,150	
Partner Clarke	22,280	
Total	$ 49,710	

ALEF, BEAL & CLARKE LLP
Statement of Partners' Capital
For Year Ended December 31, 2002

	Alef	*Beal*	*Clarke*	*Combined*
Partners' capital, beginning of year	$ 9,805	$10,680	$12,089	$32,574
Add: Net income	22,280	5,150	22,280	49,710
Goodwill recognized on partner Beal's retirement	1,000	1,000	1,000	3,000
Subtotals	$33,085	$16,830	$35,369	$85,284
Less: Drawings	(16,735)	(4,830)	(15,700)	(37,265)
Retirement of partner Beal		(12,000)		(12,000)
Partners' capital, end of year	$16,350	$ -0-	$19,669	$36,019

ALEF, BEAL & CLARKE LLP
Comparative Balance Sheets
December 31, 2002, and 2001

	Dec. 31, 2002	Dec. 31, 2001	Increase (Decrease)
Assets			
Current assets:			
Cash	$ 8,589	$ 3,295	$ 5,294
Trade accounts receivable	12,841	8,960	3,881
Allowance for doubtful accounts	(930)	(1,136)	(206)*
Supplies	983	412	571
Total current assets	$21,483	$11,531	$ 9,952
Investments:			
Cash surrender value of life insurance policies	$ 4,060	$ 5,695	$ (1,635)
Plant assets:			
Land	$ 4,200	$ 4,200	$ 0
Buildings and equipment	40,800	30,090	10,710
Accumulated depreciation of buildings and equipment	(12,800)	(13,480)	(680)†
Net plant assets	$32,200	$20,810	$11,390
Goodwill	$ 3,000		$ 3,000
Total assets	$60,743	$38,036	$22,707
Liabilities and Partners' Capital			
Current liabilities:			
Note payable to bank	$ 3,330		$ 3,330
Trade accounts payable	1,681	$ 2,984	(1,303)
Accrued liabilities	1,913	2,478	(565)
Current portion of long-term debt	5,600		5,600
Total current liabilities	$12,524	$ 5,462	$ 7,062
Long-term debt:			
Equipment contract payable, due $300 monthly plus interest at 6%	$ 4,200		$ 4,200
Note payable to retired partner, due $2,000 each July 1 plus interest at 5%	8,000		8,000
Total long-term debt	$12,200		$12,200
Total liabilities	$24,724	$ 5,462	$19,262
Partners' capital:			
Partner Alef	$16,350	$ 9,805	$ 6,545
Partner Beal		10,680	(10,680)
Partner Clarke	19,669	12,089	7,580
Total partners' capital	$36,019	$32,574	$ 3,445
Total liabilities and partners' capital	$60,743	$38,036	$22,707

* A *decrease* in the allowance and an *increase* in total current assets.
† A *decrease* in accumulated depreciation and an *increase* in net plant assets.

Additional Information

1. Alef, Beal, and Clarke shared net income and losses equally. On July 1, 2002, after the $15,450 net income of the partnership for the six months ended June 30, 2002, had been divided among the partners, Andrew Beal retired from the partnership, re-

ceiving $2,000 cash and a 5%, five-year promissory note for $10,000 in full settlement of his interest. The partners agreed to recognize goodwill of $3,000 prior to Beal's retirement and to retain Beal's name in the partnership name. Alef and Clarke agreed to share net income and losses equally following Beal's retirement.

2. Following Beal's withdrawal, the insurance policy on his life was canceled, and the partnership received the cash surrender value of $3,420.

3. The partnership had acquired equipment costing $15,210 on August 31, 2002, for $6,210 cash and an equipment contract payable $300 a month at the end of each month beginning September 30, 2002, plus interest at 6%. The partnership made required payments when due.

4. On September 30, 2002, the partnership had disposed of equipment that had cost $4,500 for $1,200, recognizing a gain of $600.

5. The partnership had borrowed $3,330 from the bank on a six-month, 8% promissory note due April 15, 2003.

Instructions

Prepare a statement of cash flows under the indirect method for Alef, Beal & Clarke LLP for the year ended December 31, 2002. A working paper is not required.

(Problem 2.9)   Southwestern Enterprises (a limited partnership) was formed on January 2, 2002, with the issuance of 1,200 units, $1,000 each, as follows:

CHECK FIGURE:

Net income to limited partners, $360,000.

Laurence Douglas, general partner, 400 units	$ 400,000
10 limited partners, 800 units total	800,000
Total (1,200 units)	$1,200,000

The trial balance of Southwestern Enterprises on December 31, 2002, the end of its first year of operations, is as follows:

SOUTHWESTERN ENTERPRISES (a limited partnership)
Trial Balance
December 31, 2002

	Debit	Credit
Cash	$ 20,000	
Trade accounts receivable	90,000	
Allowance for doubtful accounts		$ 10,000
Inventories	100,000	
Plant assets	1,500,000	
Accumulated depreciation of plant assets		100,000
Note payable to bank		20,000
Trade accounts payable		50,000
Accrued liabilities		30,000
Laurence Douglas, capital		400,000
Laurence Douglas, drawings	0	
Limited partners, capital		800,000
Limited partners, redemptions	260,000	
Net sales		1,400,000
Cost of goods sold	700,000	
Operating expenses	140,000	
Totals	$2,810,000	$2,810,000

Additional Information

1. The Limited Partners, Capital and Limited Partners, Redemptions ledger accounts are controlling accounts supported by subsidiary ledgers.

2. The certificate for Southwestern Enterprises provides that general partner Laurence Douglas may withdraw cash each December 31 to the extent of his unit participation in the net income of the limited partnership. Douglas had no drawings for 2002. The certificate also provides that limited partners may withdraw their net equity only on June 30 or December 31 of each year. Two limited partners, each owning 100 units in Southwestern Enterprises, withdrew cash for their equity during 2002, as shown by the following Limited Partners, Redemptions ledger account:

Limited Partners, Redemptions

Date	Explanation	Debit	Credit	Balance
2002				
June 30	100 units @ $1,100	110,000		110,000 dr
Dec. 31	100 units @ $1,500	150,000		260,000 dr

3. Net income of Southwestern Enterprises for the year ended December 31, 2002, was subdivided as follows:

Six months ended June 30, 2002	$120,000
Six months ended Dec. 31, 2002	440,000
Net income, year ended Dec. 31, 2002	$560,000

4. The 10%, six-month bank loan had been received on December 31, 2002.

5. There were no disposals of plant assets during 2002.

Instructions

Prepare an income statement, a statement of partners' capital, a balance sheet, and a statement of cash flows (indirect method) for Southwestern Enterprises (a limited partnership) for the year ended December 31, 2002. Show net income per weighted-average unit separately for the general partner and the limited partners in the income statement, and show partners' capital per unit in the balance sheet. A working paper is not required for the statement of cash flows.

(Problem 2.10)   The partners of Noble & Roland LLP have asked you to *review* the balance sheet on page 79. (*AICPA Professional Standards*, vol. 2, "Compilation and Review of Financial Statements," sec. AR100.04 defines *review* as follows:

Review of financial statements. Performing inquiry and analytical procedures that provide the accountant with a reasonable basis for expressing limited assurance that there are no material modifications that should be made to the statements in order for them to be in conformity with generally accepted accounting principles or, if applicable, with another comprehensive basis of accounting.

Also, sec. AR100.35 states: "Each page of the financial statements reviewed by the accountant should include a reference such as 'See Accountant's Review Report.' ")

NOBLE & ROLAND LLP
Balance Sheet
June 30, 2002

Assets

Current assets:

Cash and cash equivalents	$ 3,000
Short-term investments in marketable equity securities, at cost	10,000
10% note receivable, due on demand	20,000
Trade accounts receivable	40,000
Short-term prepayments	1,000
Total current assets	$ 74,000
Equipment, net of accumulated depreciation $4,000	50,000
Total assets	$124,000

Liabilities and Partners' Capital

Current liabilities:

Trade accounts payable		$ 15,000
Accrued liabilities		2,000
Total current liabilities		$ 17,000
Long-term debt:		
8% note payable, due June 30, 2006		5,000
Total liabilities		$ 22,000
Partners' capital:		
Partner Anne Noble	$62,000	
Partner Janice Roland	40,000	
Total partners' capital		102,000
Total liabilities and partners' capital		$124,000

Your review of the foregoing balance sheet disclosed the following:

1. The partners had requested your review because the bank considering their application for a 30-day, 12%, unsecured loan of $5,000 had requested a review because of concern about the partnership's high current ratio of $4.35 to $1 ($74,000 ÷ $17,000 = $4.35 to $1).

2. The short-term investments, properly classified as *available for sale,* had a current fair value of $6,000. Because of the substantial unrealized loss on the investments, the partnership had no present plans to dispose of them in the near future.

3. The note receivable had been executed by partner Janice Roland two years ago; because interest had been paid to June 30, 2002, the partnership had no present plans to demand payment of the principal.

4. Trade accounts receivable totaling $5,000 are estimated to be doubtful of collection.

5. Payee of the note payable was partner Anne Noble.

6. Interest rates on the note receivable and note payable, and depreciation of the equipment, appeared appropriate.

Instructions

a. Prepare journal entries to correct the accounting records of Noble & Roland LLP as of June 30, 2002. Allocate all entries affecting income statement accounts to the partners' capital accounts in their income-sharing ratio: Noble, 60%; Roland, 40%.

b. Prepare a corrected balance sheet for Noble & Roland LLP as of June 30, 2002.

In preparing the solution, refer to the following sources:

Accounting Research Bulletin No. 43, "Restatement and Revision of Accounting Research Bulletins," chs. 1A5 and 3A4.

APB Opinion No. 12, "Omnibus Opinion—1967," pars. 2 and 3.

Statement of Financial Accounting Standards No. 57, "Related Party Disclosures," par. 2.

Statement of Financial Accounting Standards No. 115, "Accounting for Certain Investments in Debt and Equity Securities," pars. 12b, 13, and 17.

Statement of Financial Accounting Standards No. 130, "Reporting Comprehensive Income," pars. 26 and 33a.

Chapter **Three**

Partnership Liquidation and Incorporation; Joint Ventures

Scope of Chapter

This chapter deals with the liquidation of limited liability partnerships (LLPs) and limited partnerships. It also covers accounting issues related to incorporation of a limited liability partnership. The final section of the chapter discusses and illustrates accounting for both corporate and unincorporated joint ventures—business enterprises with features similar to those of general partnerships.

LIQUIDATION OF A PARTNERSHIP

The Meaning of Liquidation

The *liquidation* of a limited liability partnership means winding up its activities, usually by selling assets, paying liabilities, and distributing any remaining cash to the partners. In some cases, the partnership net assets may be sold as a unit; in other cases, the assets may be sold in installments, and most or all of the cash received must be used to pay partnership creditors. This process of liquidation may be completed quickly, or it may require several months.

When the decision is made to liquidate a limited liability partnership, the accounting records of the partnership should be adjusted and closed, and the net income or loss for the final period of operations entered in the capital accounts of the partners.

The liquidation process usually begins with the *realization* (conversion to cash) of noncash assets. Absent provisions of the partnership contract to the contrary, the losses or gains from realization of assets are divided among the partners in the income-sharing ratio and entered in their capital accounts. The amounts shown as their respective equities at this point are the basis for settlement. However, before any payment to partners, all outside creditors of the limited liability partnership must be paid in full. If the cash obtained from the realization of assets is insufficient to pay liabilities in full, an unpaid creditor may act to enforce collection from the personal assets of any solvent partner whose actions caused the partnership's insolvency, regardless of whether that partner has a credit or a debit capital account balance. As pointed out in Chapter 2, a partnership is treated as an entity for many purposes such as changes in partners, but it may not use the shield of a separate entity to protect culpable partners personally against the claims of unpaid partnership creditors.

Division of Losses and Gains during Liquidation

The underlying theme in accounting for the liquidation of a limited liability partnership may be stated as follows: ***Divide the loss or gain from the realization of noncash assets before distributing cash.*** As assets are realized, any loss or gain is allocated to the partners' capital accounts in the income-sharing ratio. The income-sharing ratio used during the operation of the partnership is applicable also to the losses and gains during liquidation, unless the partners have a different agreement.

When the net loss or gain from liquidation is divided among the partners and outside creditors have been paid, the final ***credit*** balances of the partners' capital and loan ledger accounts will be equal to the cash available for distribution to them. ***Payments are then made in the amounts of the partners' respective equities in the partnership.***

Distribution of Cash or Other Assets to Partners

The Uniform Partnership Act lists the order for distribution of cash by a liquidating partnership as (1) payment of creditors in full, (2) payment of loans from partners, and (3) payment of partners' capital account credit balances. The indicated priority of partners' loans over partners' capital appears to be a legal fiction. This rule is nullified for practical purposes by an established legal doctrine called the ***right of offset.*** If a partner's capital account has a debit balance (or even a potential debit balance depending on possible future realization losses), any credit balance in that partner's loan account must be offset against the deficit (or potential deficit) in the capital account. ***However, if a partner with a loan account receives any cash, the payment is recorded by a debit to the loan account to the extent of the balance of that account.***

Because of the right of offset, the total amount of cash received by a partner during liquidation always will be the same as if loans to the partnership had been recorded in the partner's capital account. Furthermore, the existence of a partner's loan account will not advance the time of payment to any partner during the liquidation. Consequently, in the preparation of a ***statement of realization and liquidation*** (see page 83), the number of columns may be reduced by combining the amount of a partner's loan with the amount shown in the partner's capital account. Thus, the statement of realization and liquidation will include only one column for each partner; the first amount in the column will be the total equity (including any loans) of the partner at the beginning of liquidation.

Combining the capital and loan ledger account balances of a partner in the statement of realization and liquidation does not imply combining these accounts in the partnership ledger. Separate ledger accounts for capital and for loans should be maintained to provide a clear record of the terms under which assets were invested by the partners.

A partner may choose to receive certain noncash assets, such as computers or office furniture, ***in kind*** rather than to convert such property to cash. Regardless of whether noncash assets are distributed to partners, it is imperative to follow the rule that no distribution of assets may be made to partners until after all outside partnership creditors have been paid.

The following section of this chapter illustrates a series of liquidations in which the realization of noncash assets is completed before any payments are made to partners. Another section illustrates liquidation in installments; that is, payments to partners after a portion of the noncash assets has been realized and all liabilities to outsiders have been paid, but with the final loss or gain from realization of the remaining assets not known. The installment payments to partners are computed by a method that provides a safeguard against overpayment.

PAYMENTS TO PARTNERS OF AN LLP AFTER ALL NONCASH ASSETS REALIZED

Equity of Each Partner Is Sufficient to Absorb Loss from Realization

Assume that Abra and Barg, who share net income and losses equally, decide to liquidate Abra & Barg LLP. A balance sheet on June 30, 2002, just prior to liquidation, follows:

Balance Sheet of Limited Liability Partnership Prior to Liquidation

ABRA & BARG LLP			
Balance Sheet			
June 30, 2002			
Assets		**Liabilities and Partners' Capital**	
Cash	$10,000	Liabilities	$20,000
Other assets	75,000	Loan payable to Barg	20,000
		Abra, capital	40,000
		Barg, capital	5,000
Total	$85,000	Total	$85,000

As a first step in the liquidation, the noncash assets with a carrying amount of $75,000 realized cash of $35,000, with a resultant loss of $40,000 absorbed equally by Abra and Barg. Because Barg's capital account balance is only $5,000, the partnership's accountant exercises the right of offset by transferring $15,000 from Barg's loan ledger account to Barg's capital account. The statement of realization and liquidation below, covering the period July 1 through 15, 2002, shows the division of the realization loss between the partners, the payment of outside creditors, the offset of Barg's capital deficit against Barg's loan, and the distribution of the remaining cash to the partners. (The income-sharing ratio appears next to each partner's name.)

ABRA & BARG LLP						
Statement of Realization and Liquidation						
July 1 through 15, 2002						
	Assets				**Partners' Capital**	
				Barg,	**Abra**	**Barg**
	Cash	**Other**	**Liabilities**	**loan**	**(50%)**	**(50%)**
Balances before liquidation	$10,000	$75,000	$20,000	$20,000	$40,000	$ 5,000
Realization of other assets at a loss of $40,000	35,000	(75,000)			(20,000)	(20,000)
Balances	$45,000		$20,000	$20,000	$20,000	$(15,000)
Payment to creditors	(20,000)		(20,000)			
Balances	$25,000			$20,000	$20,000	$(15,000)
Offset Barg's capital deficit against Barg's loan				(15,000)		15,000
Balances	$25,000			$ 5,000	$20,000	$ -0-
Payments to partners	(25,000)			(5,000)	(20,000)	-0-

In the foregoing statement of realization and liquidation, Barg's loan account balance of $20,000 and capital account balance of $5,000 might have been combined to obtain an equity of $25,000 for Barg. As stated earlier, such a procedure would be appropriate because the legal priority of a partner's loan account has no significance in determining either the total amount of cash paid to a partner or the timing of cash payments to partners during liquidation.

In the foregoing illustration, Partner Abra received cash of $20,000 and Partner Barg received $5,000. Neither partner received cash until after partnership creditors had been paid in full. Because the only partnership asset is $25,000 cash at this point, it is reasonable to assume that checks to Abra and Barg for $20,000 and $5,000, respectively, were prepared and delivered to the partners at the same time. It is thus apparent that a partner's loan account has no special significance in the liquidation process. Therefore, succeeding illustrations do not show a partner's loan ledger account in a separate column of the statement of realization and liquidation. Whenever a partner's loan account is involved, its balance may be combined with the partner's capital account balance in the statement of realization and liquidation.

Equity of One Partner Is Not Sufficient to Absorb that Partner's Share of Loss from Realization

In this case, the loss on realization of assets, when distributed in the income-sharing ratio, results in a debit balance in the capital account of one of the partners. It may be assumed that the partner with a debit balance has no loan account or that the total of the partner's capital account and loan account combined is less than the partner's share of the loss on realization. To fulfill an agreement to share a specified percentage of partnership losses, the partner must pay to the partnership sufficient cash to eliminate any capital deficit. If the partner is unable to do so, the deficit must be absorbed by the other partners as an additional loss to be shared in the same proportion as they have previously shared net income or losses among themselves. To illustrate, assume the balance sheet below for Diel, Ebbs & Frey LLP just prior to liquidation:

Balance Sheet for Limited Liability Partnership to Be Liquidated

DIEL, EBBS & FREY LLP			
Balance Sheet			
May 20, 2002			
Assets		**Liabilities and Partners' Capital**	
Cash	$ 20,000	Liabilities	$ 30,000
Other assets	80,000	Diel, capital	40,000
		Ebbs, capital	21,000
		Frey, capital	9,000
Total	$100,000	Total	$100,000

The income-sharing ratio is Diel, 20%; Ebbs, 40%; and Frey, 40%. The other assets with a carrying amount of $80,000 realized $50,000 cash, resulting in a loss of $30,000. Partner Frey is charged with 40% of this loss, or $12,000 ($30,000 × 0.40 = $12,000), which creates a deficit of $3,000 in Frey's capital account. In the statement of realization and liquidation on page 85, it is assumed that Frey pays the $3,000 to the partnership.

| DIEL, EBBS & FREY LLP
Statement of Realization and Liquidation
May 21 through 31, 2002 | | | | | | |
| | Assets | | | Partners' Capital | | |
	Cash	Other	Liabilities	Diel, (20%)	Ebbs (40%)	Frey (40%)
Balances before liquidation Realization of other assets at a loss of $30,000	$20,000 50,000	$80,000 (80,000)	$30,000	$40,000 (6,000)	$21,000 (12,000)	$ 9,000 (12,000)
Balances Payment to creditors	$70,000 (30,000)		$30,000 (30,000)	$34,000	$ 9,000	$(3,000)
Balances Cash received from Frey	$40,000 3,000			$34,000	$ 9,000	$(3,000) 3,000
Balances Payments to partners	$43,000 (43,000)			$34,000 (34,000)	$ 9,000 (9,000)	$ -0- -0-

**Illustration of Completed
Liquidation of Limited
Liability Partnership**

Next, change one condition of the foregoing illustration by assuming that partner Frey was not able to pay the $3,000 capital deficit to the partnership. If the cash available after payment of creditors is to be distributed to Diel and Ebbs without a delay to determine the collectibility of the $3,000 claim against Frey, the statement of realization and liquidation would appear as illustrated below:

**Illustration of Incomplete
Liquidation of Limited
Liability Partnership**

| DIEL, EBBS & FREY LLP
Statement of Realization and Liquidation
May 21 through 31, 2002 | | | | | | |
| | Assets | | | Partners' Capital | | |
	Cash	Other	Liabilities	Diel, (20%)	Ebbs (40%)	Frey (40%)
Balances before liquidation Realization of other assets at a loss of $30,000	$20,000 50,000	$80,000 (80,000)	$30,000	$40,000 (6,000)	$21,000 (12,000)	$ 9,000 (12,000)
Balances Payment to creditors	$70,000 (30,000)		$30,000 (30,000)	$34,000	$ 9,000	$(3,000)
Balances Payments to partners	$40,000 (40,000)			$34,000 (33,000)	$ 9,000 (7,000)	$(3,000)
Balances				$ 1,000	$ 2,000	$(3,000)

The cash payments of $33,000 to Diel and $7,000 to Ebbs leave both with a sufficient capital account credit balance to absorb their share of the additional loss if Frey is unable to pay $3,000 to the partnership. The income-sharing ratio is 20% for Diel and 40% for Ebbs; consequently, the possible additional loss of $3,000 would be charged to them in the proportion of $2/6$, or $1,000, to Diel and $4/6$, or $2,000, to Ebbs. The payment of the $40,000 cash available to partners is divided between them in a manner that reduces Diel's capital account balance to $1,000 and Ebbs's balance to $2,000.

If the $3,000 is later collected from Frey, this amount will be divided $1,000 to Diel and $2,000 to Ebbs. The foregoing statement of realization and liquidation then may be completed as follows:

Completion of Liquidation; Capital Deficit Paid by Partner Frey

| | Assets | | | Partners' Capital | | |
	Cash	Liabilities	Diel (20%)	Ebbs (40%)	Frey (40%)
Balances (from page 85)			$1,000	$2,000	$(3,000)
Cash received from Frey	$3,000				3,000
Payments to partners	(3,000)		(1,000)	(2,000)	

However, if the $3,000 receivable from Frey is uncollectible, the statement of realization and liquidation would be completed with the write-off of Frey's capital deficit shown as an additional loss absorbed by Diel and Ebbs as follows:

Completion of Liquidation; Partner Frey Unable to Pay Capital Deficit

| | Assets | | | Partners' Capital | | |
	Cash	Liabilities	Diel (20%)	Ebbs (40%)	Frey (40%)
Balances (from page 85)			$1,000	$2,000	$(3,000)
Additional loss from Frey's uncollectible capital deficit			(1,000)	(2,000)	3,000

Equities of Two Partners Are Not Sufficient to Absorb Their Shares of Loss from Realization

It already has been noted that inability of a partner to pay the partnership for a capital deficit causes an additional loss to the other partners. A partner may have sufficient capital, or combination of capital and loan accounts, to absorb any direct share of loss on the realization of noncash assets, but not sufficient equity to absorb additional actual or potential losses caused by inability of the partnership to collect the deficit in another partner's capital account. In brief, one capital deficit, if not collectible, may cause a second capital deficit that may or may not be collectible.

Assume that Judd, Kamb, Long, and Marx, partners of Judd, Kamb, Long & Marx LLP, share net income and losses 10%, 20%, 30%, and 40%, respectively. Their capital account balances for the period August 1 through 15, 2002, are as shown in the statement of realization and liquidation on page 87, supported by the table that follows.

Table 3.1 on page 87, which supports the statement of realization and liquidation on that page, shows that the $20,000 of available cash may be distributed $16,000 to Judd and $4,000 to Kamb. If the $24,000 deficit in Marx's capital account proves uncollectible, the additional loss to be divided among the other three partners will cause Long's capital account to change from a $6,000 credit balance to a $6,000 debit balance (deficit). Therefore, Long is not eligible to receive a cash payment. If this deficit in Long's capital account proves uncollectible, the balances remaining in the capital accounts of Judd and Kamb, after the cash payments to them totaling $20,000, will be equal to the amounts ($2,000 and $4,000, respectively) needed to absorb the additional loss shifted from Long's capital account.

	Assets			Partners' Capital			
JUDD, KAMB, LONG & MARX LLP **Statement of Realization and Liquidation** **August 1 through 15, 2002**							
	Cash	**Other**	**Liabilities**	**Judd** **(10%)**	**Kamb** **(20%)**	**Long** **(30%)**	**x** **(40%)**
Balances before liquidation	$ 20,000	$200,000	$120,000	$30,000	$32,000	$30,000	$ 8,000
Realization of other assets at a loss of $80,000	120,000	(200,000)		(8,000)	(16,000)	(24,000)	(32,000)
Balances	$140,000		$120,000	$22,000	$16,000	$ 6,000	$(24,000)
Payment to creditors	(120,000)		(120,000)				
Balances	$ 20,000			$22,000	$16,000	$ 6,000	$(24,000)
Payments to partners **(Table 3)**	(20,000)			(16,000)	(4,000)		
Balances				$ 6,000	$12,000	$ 6,000	$(24,000)

TABLE 3.1

	Partners' Capital			
JUDD, KAMB, LONG & MARX LLP **Computation of Cash Payments to Partners** **August 15, 2002**				
	Judd (10%)	**Kamb (20%)**	**Long (30%)**	**Marx (40%)**
Capital account balances before distribution of cash to partners	$22,000	$16,000	$ 6,000	$(24,000)
Additional loss to Judd, Kamb, and Long if Marx's deficit is uncollectible (ratio of 10:20:30)	(4,000)	(8,000)	(12,000)	24,000
Balances	$18,000	$ 8,000	$ (6,000)	
Additional loss to Judd and Kamb if Long's deficit is uncollectible (ratio of 10:20)	(2,000)	(4,000)	6,000	
Amounts that may be paid to partners	$16,000	$ 4,000		

Partnership Is Insolvent but Partners Are Solvent

If a limited liability partnership is *insolvent,* it is unable to pay all outside creditors, and at least one and perhaps all of the partners will have debit balances in their capital accounts. In any event, the total of the capital account debit balances will exceed the total of the credit balances. If the partner or partners with a capital deficit pay the required amount to the partnership, it will have cash to pay its liabilities in full. However, the partnership creditors may demand payment from *any solvent* partner whose actions caused the partnership's insolvency, regardless of whether the partner's capital account has a debit balance or a credit balance. In terms of relationships with creditors, the limited liability partnership is not a separate entity. A partner who makes payments to partnership creditors receives a credit to his or her capital account. As an illustration of an insolvent partnership whose partners are solvent (have personal assets in excess of liabilities), assume that Nehr, Ordo & Page LLP, whose partners share net income and losses equally, had the following balance sheet just prior to liquidation on May 10, 2002:

NEHR, ORDO & PAGE LLP
Balance Sheet
May 10, 2002

Assets		Liabilities and Partners' Capital	
Cash	$ 15,000	Liabilities	$ 65,000
Other assets	85,000	Nehr, capital	18,000
		Ordo, capital	10,000
		Page, capital	7,000
Total	$100,000	Total	$100,000

On May 12, 2002, the other assets with a carrying amount of $85,000 realize $40,000 cash, which causes a loss of $45,000 to be divided equally among the partners. The total cash of $55,000 is paid to the partnership creditors, which leaves unpaid liabilities of $10,000. Partner Nehr's capital account has a credit balance of $3,000 after absorbing one-third of the loss. Partners Ordo and Page owe the partnership $5,000 and $8,000, respectively. Assuming that on May 30, 2002, Ordo and Page pay in the amounts of their deficiencies, the partnership will use $10,000 of the $13,000 available cash to pay the remaining liabilities and will distribute $3,000 to Nehr. These events are summarized in the statement of realization and liquidation below.

NEHR, ORDO & PAGE LLP
Statement of Realization and Liquidation
May 12 through 30, 2002

	Assets			Partners' Capital		
	Cash	Other	Liabilities	Nehr (⅓)	Ordo (⅓)	Page (⅓)
Balances before liquidation	$15,000	$85,000	$65,000	$18,000	$10,000	$ 7,000
Realization of other assets at a loss of $45,000	40,000	(85,000)		(15,000)	(15,000)	(15,000)
Balances	$55,000		$65,000	$ 3,000	$ (5,000)	$ (8,000)
Partial payment to creditors	(55,000)		(55,000)			
Balances	$ -0-		$10,000	$ 3,000	$(5,000)	$ (8,000)
Cash invested by Ordo and Page	13,000				5,000	8,000
Balances	$13,000		$10,000	$ 3,000		
Final payment to creditors	(10,000)		(10,000)			
Balances	$ 3,000			$ 3,000		
Payment to Nehr	(3,000)			(3,000)		

It should be noted that if a limited liability partnership is insolvent because of an adverse award of damages in a lawsuit, and the partner or partners responsible for the damages are solvent, they alone of the partners must pay the amount of damages that the insolvent LLP is unable to pay. However, if such partners also are insolvent, both they and the LLP may have to file for liquidation under Chapter 7 of the U.S. Bankruptcy Code, which is discussed in Chapter 14 of this textbook. The partners of the LLP not responsible for the award of damages, unless they too were insolvent, apparently would not have to undertake bankruptcy proceedings.

General Partnership Is Insolvent and Partners Are Insolvent

In the foregoing illustration of an insolvent *limited liability* partnership, the partners were solvent and therefore able to pay their capital deficits to the partnership. Now consider an insolvent *general* partnership in which one or more of the partners are insolvent. This situation raises a question as to the relative rights of two groups of creditors: (1) creditors of the partnership and (2) creditors of the partners. The relative rights of these two groups of creditors are governed by the provisions of the Uniform Partnership Act relating to the *marshaling of assets.* These rules provide that assets of the general partnership (including partners' capital deficits) are first available to creditors of the partnership and that assets of the partners are first available to their creditors. After the liabilities of the partnership have been paid in full, the creditors of an individual partner have a claim against the assets (if any) of the partnership to the extent of that partner's equity in the partnership.

After the creditors of a partner have been paid in full from the assets of the partner, any remaining assets of the partner are available to partnership creditors, regardless of whether the partner's capital account has a credit balance or a debit balance. *Such claims by creditors of the partnership are permitted only when these creditors are unable to obtain payment from the partnership.*

To illustrate the relative rights of creditors of an insolvent general partnership and personal creditors of an insolvent partner, assume that the Rich, Sand & Toll Partnership, a general partnership whose partners share net income and losses equally, has the partnership balance sheet below just prior to liquidation on November 30, 2002:

Balance Sheet of General
Partnership Prior
to Liquidation

RICH, SAND & TOLL PARTNERSHIP
Balance Sheet
November 30, 2002

Assets		Liabilities and Partners' Capital	
Cash	$ 10,000	Liabilities	$ 60,000
Other assets	100,000	Rich, capital	5,000
		Sand, capital	15,000
		Toll, capital	30,000
Total	$110,000	Total	$110,000

Assume also that on November 30, 2002, the partners have the following assets and liabilities other than their equities in the partnership:

Partners' Personal Assets
and Liabilities

Partner	Personal Assets	Personal Liabilities
Rich	$100,000	$25,000
Sand	50,000	50,000
Toll	5,000	60,000

The realization of other assets of the partnership results in a loss of $60,000, as shown in the following statement of realization and liquidation for the period December 1 through 12, 2002:

RICH, SAND & TOLL PARTNERSHIP Statement of Realization and Liquidation December 1 through 12, 2002						
	Assets			**Partners' Capital**		
	Cash	**Other**	**Liabilities**	**Rich ($\frac{1}{3}$)**	**Sand ($\frac{1}{3}$)**	**Toll ($\frac{1}{3}$)**
Balances before liquidation	$10,000	$100,000	$60,000	$ 5,000	$15,000	$30,000
Realization of other assets at a loss of $60,000	40,000	(100,000)		(20,000)	(20,000)	(20,000)
Balances	$50,000		$60,000	$(15,000)	$ (5,000)	$10,000
Partial payment to creditors	(50,000)		(50,000)			
Balances			$10,000	$(15,000)	$ (5,000)	$10,000

Liquidation of General Partnership Not Completed

The creditors of the partnership have received all the cash of the general partnership and still have unpaid claims of $10,000. They cannot collect from Sand or Toll because the assets of these two partners are just sufficient or are insufficient to pay their liabilities. However, the partnership creditors may collect the $10,000 in full from Rich, who is solvent. By chance, Rich has a capital deficit of $15,000, but this is of no concern to creditors of the partnership, who may collect in full from any partner who has sufficient assets, regardless of whether that partner's capital account has a debit balance or a credit balance. The statement of realization and liquidation is now continued below to show Rich's payment of the final $10,000 owed to partnership creditors. Because the assumptions about Rich's finances showed that Rich had $100,000 of assets and only $25,000 of liabilities, Rich is able to invest in the partnership the additional $5,000 needed to offset Rich's capital deficit. This $5,000 cash is paid to partner Toll, the only partner with a capital account credit balance.

Continuation of Statement of Realization and Liquidation for General Partnership

	Cash	**Liabilities**	**Partners' Capital**		
			Rich ($\frac{1}{3}$)	**Sand ($\frac{1}{3}$)**	**Toll ($\frac{1}{3}$)**
Balances (from above)		$ 10,000	$(15,000)	$(5,000)	$10,000
Payment by Rich to partnership creditors		(10,000)	10,000		
Balances			$ (5,000)	$(5,000)	$10,000
Cash invested by Rich	$5,000		5,000		
Balances	$5,000			$(5,000)	$10,000
Payment to Toll (or Toll's creditors)	(5,000)				(5,000)
Balances				$(5,000)	$ 5,000

The continued statement of realization and liquidation now shows that Sand owes $5,000 to the partnership; however, Sand's assets of $50,000 are exactly equal to Sand's liabilities of $50,000. Under the Uniform Partnership Act, all the assets of Sand will go to Sand's creditors; therefore, the $5,000 deficit in Sand's capital account represents an additional loss to be shared equally by Rich and Toll. To conclude the liquidation, Rich, who is solvent, pays $2,500 to the partnership, and the $2,500 will be paid to Toll or to

Toll's creditors, because Toll is insolvent. These payments are shown below to complete the statement of realization and liquidation for the Rich, Sand & Toll Partnership:

Completion of Liquidation of General Partnership

	Cash	Partners' Capital		
		Rich ($\frac{1}{3}$)	Sand ($\frac{1}{3}$)	Toll ($\frac{1}{3}$)
Balances (from page 90)			$(5,000)	$ 5,000
Write-off of Sand's capital deficit as uncollectible		$(2,500)	5,000	(2,500)
Balances		$(2,500)		$(2,500)
Cash invested by Rich	$ 2,500	2,500		
Balances	$ 2,500			$ 2,500
Payment to Toll (or Toll's creditors)	(2,500)			(2,500)

The final results of the liquidation show that the partnership creditors received payment in full because of the financial status of partner Rich. Because Rich was solvent, the creditors of Rich also were paid in full. The creditors of Sand were paid in full, thereby exhausting Sand's assets; however, because Sand failed to pay the $5,000 capital deficit to the partnership, an additional loss of $5,000 was absorbed by Rich and Toll. The creditors of Toll received all of Toll's separate assets of $5,000 and also $7,500 from the partnership, representing Toll's equity in the firm. However, Toll's creditors were able to collect only $12,500 ($5,000 + $7,500 = $12,500) on their total claims of $60,000.

INSTALLMENT PAYMENTS TO PARTNERS

In the foregoing illustrations of partnership liquidation, all the partnership noncash assets were realized and the total loss from liquidation was divided among the partners before any cash payments were made to them. However, the liquidation of some partnerships may extend over several months. In such extended liquidations, the partners usually will want to receive cash as it becomes available rather than wait until all noncash assets have been realized. Installment payments to partners are appropriate if necessary safeguards are used to ensure that all partnership creditors are paid in full and that no partners are paid more than the amount to which they would be entitled after all losses on realization of assets are known.

Liquidation in installments is a process of realizing some assets, paying creditors, paying the remaining available cash to partners, realizing additional assets, and making additional cash payments to partners. The liquidation continues until all noncash assets have been realized and all cash has been distributed to partnership creditors and partners.

The circumstances of installment liquidations of partnerships vary; consequently, the approach of this text is to emphasize the general principles guiding liquidation in installments rather than to provide illustrations of all possible liquidation situations. Among the variables that cause partnership liquidations to differ are the sufficiency of each partner's capital to absorb that partner's share of the possible losses remaining after each installment payment of cash, the shifting of losses from one partner to another because of inability to collect a capital deficit, the offsetting of loan account balances against capital deficits, and the possible need for setting aside cash to pay future liquidation costs or unrecorded partnership liabilities.

General Principles Guiding Installment Payments

The critical element in installment liquidations is that the liquidator authorizes cash payments to partners before all losses that may be incurred in the liquidation are known. If payments are made to partners and later losses cause deficits in the partners' capital accounts, the liquidator will have to request the return of the payments. If the payments cannot be recovered, the liquidator may be liable to the other partners for the loss caused them by the inappropriate distribution of cash. Because of this danger, the only safe policy for determining installment cash payments to partners is the following *worst-case scenario:*

1. Assume a total loss on all remaining noncash assets, and provide for all possible losses, including potential liquidation costs and unrecorded liabilities.

2. Assume that any partner with a potential capital deficit will be unable to pay anything to the partnership; thus, distribute each installment of cash as if no more cash will be forthcoming, either from realization of assets or from collection of capital deficits from partners.

Under these assumptions, the liquidator will authorize a cash payment to a partner only if that partner has a capital account credit balance (or in capital and loan accounts combined) in excess of the amount required to absorb a portion of the maximum possible loss that may be incurred on liquidation. A partner's "share of the maximum possible loss" would include any loss that may result from the inability of partners to pay any potential capital deficits to the partnership.

When installment payments are made according to these rules, the effect will be to bring the equities of the partners to the income-sharing ratio as quickly as possible. *When installment payments have proceeded to the point that the partners' capital and loan account balances (equities) correspond with the income-sharing ratio, all subsequent payments may be made in that ratio,* because each partner's equity will be sufficient to absorb an appropriate share of the maximum possible remaining loss.

Determining Appropriate Installment Payments to Partners

The amounts of cash that may be distributed safely to the partners each month (or at any other point in time) may be determined by computing the impact on partners' equities (capital and loan account balances) of the maximum possible loss on noncash assets remaining to be realized and the resultant potential impact on partners' capital. To illustrate, assume that the partners of Urne, Vint & Wahl LLP, who share net income and losses in a 4 : 3 : 2 ratio, decide to liquidate the partnership and to distribute cash in installments. The balance sheet for Urne, Vint & Wahl LLP just prior to the beginning of liquidation on July 5, 2002, is as follows:

Balance Sheet of Limited Liability Partnership Prior to Liquidation in Installments

URNE, VINT & WAHL LLP Balance Sheet July 5, 2002			
Assets		**Liabilities and Partners' Capital**	
Cash	$ 8,000	Liabilities	$ 61,000
Other assets	192,000	Urne, capital	40,000
		Vint, capital	45,000
		Wahl, capital	54,000
Total	$200,000	Total	$200,000

To simplify the illustration, assume that noncash assets were realized as follows:

Realization of Other Assets by Liquidating Partnership

URNE, VINT & WAHL LLP Realization of Other Assets July 6 through September 30, 2002			
Date, 2002	Carrying Amount of Assets Realized	Loss on Realization	Cash Received by Partnership
July 31	$ 62,000	$13,500	$ 48,500
August 31	66,000	36,000	30,000
September 30	64,000	31,500	32,500
Totals	$192,000	$81,000	$111,000

Thus, on July 31, 2002, $56,500 ($8,000 + $48,500 = $56,500) of cash is available for distribution. The first claim to the cash is that of partnership creditors; because their claims total $61,000, the entire $56,500 available on July 31 is paid to creditors, leaving an unpaid balance of $4,500 ($61,000 − $56,500 = $4,500), and the partners receive nothing on that date.

On August 31, 2002, $30,000 cash is available for distribution; the first $4,500 is paid to creditors, leaving $25,500 ($30,000 − $4,500 = $25,500) available for distribution to partners. Under the worst-case scenario described on page 92, the appropriate distribution of the $25,500 to partners is determined as follows:

Determination of Cash Distributions to Partners, Aug. 31, 2002

	Urne	Vint	Wahl
Capital account balances, July 5, 2002	$ 40,000	$45,000	$54,000
Allocation of loss on July 31, 2002, realization of noncash assets ($13,500)	(6,000)	(4,500)	(3,000)
Allocation of loss on Aug. 31, 2002, realization of noncash assets ($36,000)	(16,000)	(12,000)	(8,000)
Capital account balances, Aug. 31, 2002	$ 18,000	$28,500	$43,000
Allocation of maximum potential loss on remaining noncash assets ($64,000)	(28,445)	(21,333)	(14,222)
Potential capital account balances	$(10,445)	$ 7,167	$28,778
Allocation of potential loss from uncollectibility of Urne's potential capital deficit in ratio of 3 : 2	10,445	(6,267)	(4,178)
Appropriate cash payments to partners, Aug. 31, 2002	$ 0	$ 900	$24,600

A technique similar to that above would be used to determine the appropriate payment to partners of the $32,500 cash available on September 30, 2002.

Preparation of a Cash Distribution Program

Although the method for determining cash payments to partners illustrated in the foregoing section is sound, it is somewhat cumbersome. Furthermore, it does not show at the ***beginning*** of the liquidation how cash might be divided among the partners as it becomes available. For these reasons, it is more efficient to prepare in advance a complete *cash distribution program* to show how cash may be divided during liquidation. If such a program is prepared, any amounts of cash received from the realization of partnership assets may be paid immediately to partnership creditors and the partners as specified in the program.

Using the data for Urne, Vint & Wahl LLP illustrated on page 93, the following cash distribution program may be prepared; the working paper supporting the cash distribution program and an explanation of the preparation of the working paper are below and on pages 95 and 96:

		Creditors	Urne	Vint	Wahl
URNE, VINT & WAHL LLP					
Cash Distribution Program					
July 5, 2002					
First	$ 61,000	100%			
Next	24,000				100%
Next	25,000			60%	40%
All over	$110,000		$\frac{4}{9}$	$\frac{3}{9}$	$\frac{2}{9}$

Procedures for developing the following working paper:[1]

1. The "capital account balances before liquidation" represent the *equities* of the partners in the partnership, that is, the balance of a partner's capital account, plus or minus the balance (if any) of a loan made by a partner to the partnership or a loan made by the partnership to a partner.

2. The capital account balance before liquidation for each partner is divided by each partner's income-sharing ratio to determine the amount of capital per unit of income (loss) sharing for each partner. This procedure is critical because it (1) identifies the partner with the largest capital per unit of income (loss) sharing who, therefore, will be the first to receive cash, (2) facilitates the ranking of partners in the order in which they are entitled to receive cash, and (3) provides the basis for computing the amount of cash each partner receives at various stages of liquidation. Because Wahl's capital per unit of income (loss) sharing is largest ($27,000), Wahl is the first partner to receive cash (after all partnership creditors have been paid), followed by Vint and finally by Urne.

3. Wahl receives enough cash to reduce Wahl's capital of $27,000 per unit of income (loss) sharing to $15,000, equal to the balance for Vint, the second-ranking partner. To accomplish this, Wahl's capital per unit of income (loss) sharing must be reduced by $12,000, and because Wahl has two units of income (loss) sharing, Wahl receives $24,000 ($12,000 × 2 = $24,000) before Vint receives any cash.

---

[1] The procedure for preparing a cash distribution program illustrated herein may be used regardless of the number of partners involved or the complexity of the income-sharing ratio. For example, assume that partners share net income and losses as follows: Abt 41.2%, Bry 32.3%, Cam 26.5%. The income-sharing ratio may be stated as 412 for Abt, 323 for Bry and 265 for Cam to apply the techniques illustrated in this section.

	URNE, VINT & WAHL LLP		
	Working Paper for Cash Distributions to Partners during Liquidation		
	July 5, 2002		
	Urne	**Vint**	**Wahl**
Capital account balances before liquidation	$40,000	$45,000	$54,000
Income-sharing ratio	4	3	2
Divide capital account balances before liquidation by income-sharing ratio to obtain **capital per unit of income (loss) sharing** for each partner	$10,000	$15,000	$27,000
Required reduction in capital per unit of income (loss) sharing for Partner Wahl to reduce Wahl's balance to equal the next largest balance (for Partner Vint). This is the amount of the first cash distribution to a partner **per unit of the partner's income (loss) sharing.** Because Wahl has 2 units of income (loss) sharing, Wahl receives the first $24,000 ($12,000 × 2 = $24,000)	———	———	(12,000)
Capital per unit of income (loss) sharing after payment of $24,000 to Wahl	$10,000	$15,000	$15,000
Required reduction in capital per unit of income (loss) sharing for Partners Vint and Wahl to reduce their balances to equal Partner Urne's balance, which is the smallest capital per unit of income (loss) sharing. The required reduction is multiplied by each partner's income-sharing ratio to compute the amount of cash to be paid. Thus, Vint receives $15,000 ($5,000 × 3 = $15,000), and Wahl receives $10,000 ($5,000 × 2 = $10,000)	———	(5,000)	(5,000)
Capital per unit of income (loss) sharing after payment of $15,000 to Vint and $34,000 to Wahl. **Remaining cash may be distributed in the income-sharing ratio**	$10,000	$10,000	$10,000

4. At this point, the capital per unit of income (loss) sharing for both Vint and Wahl is $15,000, indicating that they are entitled to receive cash until their capital per unit of income (loss) sharing is reduced by $5,000 to the $10,000 balance for Urne, the lowest-ranking partner. Because Vint has three units and Wahl has two units of income (loss) sharing, Vint receives $15,000 ($5,000 × 3 = $15,000) and Wahl receives an additional $10,000 ($5,000 × 2 = $10,000) before Urne receives any cash. After Wahl receives $24,000, Vint and Wahl would share any amount of cash available to a maximum amount of $25,000 in a 3 : 2 ratio.

5. After Vint has received $15,000 and Wahl has received $34,000 ($24,000 + $10,000 = $34,000), the capital per unit of income (loss) sharing is $10,000 for each partner, and any additional cash is paid to the partners in the income-sharing ratio (4 : 3 : 2), because their capital account balances have been reduced to the income-sharing ratio. This is illustrated on the next page.

Reduction of Capital
Account Balances to
Income Sharing Ratio

	Urne ($^4/_9$)	Vint ($^3/_9$)	Wahl ($^2/_9$)
Capital account balances before liquidation	$40,000	$ 45,000	$54,000
First payment of cash to Wahl			(24,000)
Second payment of cash to Vint and Wahl in 3 : 2 ratio	_____	(15,000)	(10,000)
Capital account balances (in income-sharing ratio of 4 : 3 : 2) after payment of total of $49,000 to Vint and Wahl	$40,000	$ 30,000	$20,000

Only when installment payments reach the point at which partners' capital account balances correspond with the income-sharing ratio may subsequent cash payments be made in that ratio.

A cash distribution program such as the one on page 94 also may be used to ascertain an equitable distribution of noncash assets to partners. The current fair value of noncash assets such as marketable securities, inventories, or equipment distributed to partners is treated as equivalent to cash payments. If a distribution of noncash assets departs from the cash distribution program by giving one of the partners a larger distribution than that partner is entitled to receive, subsequent distributions should be adjusted to allow the remaining partners to "make up" the distribution prematurely made to one of the partners. In such cases, a ***revised cash distribution program must be prepared,*** because the original relationship among the partners' capital account balances has been disrupted.

Any losses or gains on the realization of assets during liquidation are allocated to the partners in the income-sharing ratio, unless the partnership contract specifies another allocation procedure. Thus, the degree to which the capital account balances do not correspond with the income-sharing ratio is not altered by such losses or gains. Consequently, losses or gains from the realization of assets in the course of partnership liquidation do not affect the cash distribution program prepared prior to the start of liquidation.

To illustrate how the cash distribution program on page 94 may be used, assume that the realization of other assets by Urne, Vint & Wahl LLP from July 6 through September 30, 2002, is as shown on page 93. The cash available each month is paid to creditors and partners according to the cash distribution program on page 94. The distributions of cash are summarized below:

URNE, VINT & WAHL LLP					
Distributions of Cash to Creditors and Partners					
July 6 through September 30, 2002					
			Partners' Capital		
Date	Cash	Liabilities	Urne ($^4/_9$)	Vint ($^3/_9$)	Wahl ($^2/_9$)
July 31 (includes $8,000 on hand on July 5)	$ 56,500	$56,500			
August 31	30,000	4,500			$24,000⎱
				$ 900	600⎰
September 30	32,500			14,100	9,400⎱
			$4,000	3,000	2,000⎰
Totals	$119,000	$61,000	$4,000	$18,000	$36,000

The entire cash balance of $56,500 available on July 31 is paid to creditors, leaving $4,500 in unpaid liabilities. When $30,000 becomes available on August 31, $4,500 is paid to creditors, leaving $25,500 to be paid to the partners according to the cash distribution program on page 94. The program requires Wahl to receive 100% of the first $24,000 available for distribution to partners, and for Vint and Wahl to share the next $25,000 in a 3 : 2 ratio. On August 31 only $1,500 ($30,000 − $4,500 − $24,000 = $1,500) is available for payment to Vint and Wahl; thus, they receive $900 and $600, respectively. Of the $32,500 available on September 30, the first $23,500 is paid to Vint and Wahl in a 3 : 2 ratio, or $14,100 and $9,400, respectively, in order to complete the distribution of $25,000 to Vint and Wahl before Urne participates; this leaves $9,000 ($32,500 − $23,500 = $9,000) to be distributed to Urne, Vint, and Wahl in the 4 : 3 : 2 income-sharing ratio.

A complete statement of realization and liquidation for Urne, Vint & Wahl LLP follows.

	Assets			Partners' Capital		
URNE, VINT & WAHL LLP **Statement of Realization and Liquidation** **July 6 through September 30, 2002**						
	Cash	**Other**	**Liabilities**	**Urne (⁴/₉)**	**Vint (³/₉)**	**Wahl (²/₉)**
Balances before liquidation	$ 8,000	$192,000	$ 61,000	$ 40,000	$ 45,000	$ 54,000
July 31 installment:						
Realization of other assets at a loss of $13,500	48,500	(62,000)		(6,000)	(4,500)	(3,000)
Balances	56,500	$130,000	$ 61,000	$ 34,000	$ 40,500	$ 51,000
Payment to creditors	$(56,500)		(56,500)			
Balances	$ -0-	$130,000	$ 4,500	$ 34,000	$ 40,500	$ 51,000
Aug. 31 installment:						
Realization of other assets at a loss of $36,000	30,000	(66,000)		(16,000)	(12,000)	(8,000)
Balances	$ 30,000	$ 64,000	$ 4,500	$ 18,000	$ 28,500	$ 43,000
Payment to creditors	(4,500)		(4,500)			
Balances	$ 25,500	$ 64,000		$ 18,000	$ 28,500	$ 43,000
Payments to partners	(25,500)				(900)	(24,600)
Balances	$ -0-	$ 64,000		$ 18,000	$ 27,600	$ 18,400
Sept. 30 installment:						
Realization of other assets at a loss of $31,500	32,500	(64,000)		(14,000)	(10,500)	(7,000)
Balances	$ 32,500			$ 4,000	$ 17,100	$ 11,400
Payments to partners	(32,500)			(4,000)	(17,100)	(11,400)

The journal entries to record the realization of assets and to complete the liquidation of Urne, Vint & Wahl LLP are as follows:

Journal Entries to Record Liquidation of Limited Liability Partnership in Installments

2002			
July 31	Cash	48,500	
	Urne, Capital	6,000	
	Vint, Capital	4,500	
	Wahl, Capital	3,000	
	Other Assets		62,000
	To record realization of assets and division of $13,500 loss among partners in 4 : 3 : 2 ratio.		
July 31	Liabilities	56,500	
	Cash		56,500
	To record payment to creditors.		
Aug. 31	Cash	30,000	
	Urne, Capital	16,000	
	Vint, Capital	12,000	
	Wahl, Capital	8,000	
	Other Assets		66,000
	To record realization of assets and division of $36,000 loss among partners in 4 :3 : 2 ratio.		
31	Liabilities	4,500	
	Vint, Capital	900	
	Wahl, Capital	24,600	
	Cash		30,000
	To record payment to creditors and first installment to partners.		
Sept. 30	Cash	32,500	
	Urne, Capital	14,000	
	Vint, Capital	10,500	
	Wahl, Capital	7,000	
	Other Assets		64,000
	To record realization of remaining assets and division of $31,500 loss among partners in 4 :3 : 2 ratio.		
30	Urne, Capital	4,000	
	Vint, Capital	17,100	
	Wahl, Capital	11,400	
	Cash		32,500
	To record final installment to partners to complete the liquidation of the partnership.		

Withholding of Cash for Liabilities and Liquidation Costs

As previously emphasized, partnership creditors are entitled to payment in full before anything is paid to partners. However, in some cases the liquidator may find it more convenient to set aside sufficient cash required to pay certain recorded liabilities, and to distribute the remaining cash to the partners. The withholding of cash for payment of recorded liabilities is appropriate when for any reason it is not practicable or advisable (as when the amount of the claim is in dispute) to pay the liabilities before cash is distributed to partners. An amount of cash set aside, and equal to ***recorded unpaid*** liabilities, is not a factor in computing possible future liquidation losses; the possible future loss is measured by the amount of noncash assets, any ***unrecorded*** liabilities, and any liquidation costs that may be incurred.

Any costs incurred during the liquidation of a partnership are deducted from partners' capital account balances to compute the cash available for distribution to partners. Costs of liquidation thereby are treated as part of the total loss from liquidation. However, in some cases, the liquidator may wish to withhold cash in anticipation of future liquidation costs. The amount of cash set aside for future liquidation costs or for payment of unrecorded liabilities should be combined with the amount of noncash assets in the computation of the maximum possible loss that may be incurred to complete the liquidation of the partnership.

Liquidation of Limited Partnerships

Most of the discussion of the liquidation of limited liability partnerships and general partnerships, in preceding sections of this chapter, applies to the liquidation of limited partnerships. However, the Uniform Limited Partnership Act provides that after outside creditors of a limited partnership have been paid, the equities of the limited partners must be paid before the general partner or partners may receive any cash. Further, the limited partners may agree that one or more of them may have priority over the others regarding payments in liquidation of the limited partnership.

INCORPORATION OF A LIMITED LIABILITY PARTNERSHIP

Partners may evaluate the possible advantages to be gained by incorporating a partnership. Among such advantages are limited liability of stockholders, ease of attracting additional capital, and possible income tax advantages.

To ensure that each partner receives an equitable portion of the capital stock issued by the new corporation, the assets of the partnership must be adjusted to current fair value before being transferred to the corporation. Any identifiable intangible asset or goodwill developed by the partnership is included among the assets transferred to the corporation.

To illustrate the incorporation of a partnership, assume that Blair and Benson, partners of Blair & Benson LLP, who share net income and loss in a 4 : 1 ratio, organize B & B Corporation to take over the net assets of the partnership. The balance sheet of the partnership on June 30, 2002, the date of incorporation, is as follows:

Balance Sheet of Limited Liability Partnership Prior to Incorporation (continued)

BLAIR & BENSON LLP Balance Sheet June 30, 2002		
Assets		
Cash		$12,000
Trade accounts receivable	$28,100	
Less: Allowance for doubtful accounts	600	27,500
Inventories, first-in, first-out cost		25,500
Equipment, at cost	$60,000	
Less: Accumulated depreciation of equipment	26,000	34,000
Total assets		$99,000

(continued)

BLAIR & BENSON LLP		
Balance Sheet (concluded)		
June 30, 2002		
Liabilities and Partners' Capital		
Liabilities:		
Trade accounts payable		$35,000
Partners' capital:		
Blair, capital	$47,990	
Benson, capital	16,010	64,000
Total liabilities and partners' capital		$99,000

After an appraisal of the equipment and an audit of the partnership's financial statements, the partners agree that the following adjustments are required to restate the net assets of the partnership to current fair value:

1. Increase the allowance for doubtful accounts to $1,000.

2. Increase the inventories to current replacement cost of $30,000.

3. Increase the equipment to its reproduction cost new, $70,000, less accumulated depreciation on this basis, $30,500; that is, to current fair value, $39,500.

4. Recognize accrued liabilities of $1,100.

5. Recognize goodwill of $10,000.

B & B Corporation is authorized to issue 10,000 shares of $10 par common stock. It issues 5,500 shares of common stock valued at $15 a share to the partnership in exchange for the net assets of the partnership. The 5,500 shares received by the partnership are divided between the partners on the basis of the adjusted balances of their capital accounts. (Partners may withdraw small amounts of cash to round their capital account balances to even amounts, thus avoiding the issuance of fractional shares of common stock.) This procedure completes the dissolution and liquidation of the partnership.

Although the accounting records of the partnership may be modified to serve as the records of the new corporation, it is customary to use a new set of accounting records for the corporation. If this alternative is followed, the procedures required are:

In Accounting Records of Partnership:

1. Prepare journal entries for revaluation of assets, including recognition of goodwill.

2. Record any cash withdrawals necessary to adjust partners' capital account balances to round amounts. (In some instances, the contract may require transfer to the corporation of all assets except cash.)

3. Record the transfer of assets and liabilities to the corporation, the receipt of the corporation's common stock by the partnership, and the distribution of the common stock to the partners in settlement of the balances of their capital accounts.

The journal entries to adjust and eliminate the accounting records of the Blair & Benson LLP on June 30, 2002, are as follows:

Journal Entries for Blair & Benson LLP

Inventories ($30,000 − $25,500)	4,500	
Equipment ($70,000 − $60,000)	10,000	
Goodwill	10,000	
Allowance for Doubtful Accounts ($1,000 − $600)		400
Accumulated Depreciation of Equipment		
($30,500 − $26,000)		4,500
Accrued Liabilities Payable		1,100
Blair, Capital ($18,500 × 0.80)		14,800
Benson, Capital ($18,500 × 0.20)		3,700
To adjust assets and liabilities to agreed amounts and to divide net gain of $18,500 between partners in 4:1 ratio		
Receivable from B & B Corporation ($64,000 + $18,500)	82,500	
Trade Accounts Payable	35,000	
Accrued Liabilities Payable	1,100	
Allowance for Doubtful Accounts	1,000	
Accumulated Depreciation of Equipment	30,500	
Cash		12,000
Trade Accounts Receivable		28,100
Inventories		30,000
Equipment		70,000
Goodwill		10,000
To record transfer of assets and liabilities to B & B Corporation.		
Common Stock of B & B Corporation (5,500 × $15)	82,500	
Receivable from B & B Corporation		82,500
To record receipt of 5,500 shares of $10 par common stock valued at $15 a share in payment for net assets transferred to B & B Corporation.		
Blair, Capital ($47,990 + $14,800; 4,186 × $15)	62,790	
Benson, Capital ($16,010 + $3,700; 1,314 × $15)	19,710	
Common Stock of B & B Corporation		82,500
To record distribution of common stock of B & B Corporation to partners: 4,186 shares to Blair and 1,314 shares to Benson.		

In Accounting Records of Corporation:

1. Record the acquisition of assets and liabilities (including obligation to pay for the net assets) from the partnership at current fair values.

2. Record the issuance of common stock at current fair value in payment of the obligation to the partnership.

The journal entries in the accounting records of B & B Corporation on June 30, 2002, are illustrated on the next page:

Journal Entries for B & B Corporation

Cash	12,000	
Trade Accounts Receivable	28,100	
Inventories	30,000	
Equipment	39,500	
Goodwill	10,000	
Allowance for Doubtful Accounts		1,000
Trade Accounts Payable		35,000
Accrued Liabilities Payable		1,100
Payable to Blair & Benson LLP		82,500
To record acquisition of assets and liabilities from Blair & Benson LLP.		
Payable to Blair & Benson LLP	82,500	
Common Stock, $10 par (5,500 × $10)		55,000
Paid-In Capital in Excess of Par		27,500
To record issuance of 5,500 shares of common stock valued at $15 a share in payment for net assets of Blair & Benson LLP.		

Note that the allowance for doubtful accounts is recognized in the accounting records of B & B Corporation because the specific accounts receivable that may not be collected are not known. In contrast, the depreciation recognized by the Blair & Benson Partnership is disregarded by B & B Corporation because the "cost" of the equipment to the new corporation is $39,500.

The balance sheet for B & B Corporation on June 30, 2002, is as follows:

B & B CORPORATION
Balance Sheet
June 30, 2002

Assets

Cash		$ 12,000
Trade accounts receivable	$28,100	
Less: Allowance for doubtful accounts	1,000	27,100
Inventories, at current replacement cost		30,000
Equipment, at current fair value		39,500
Goodwill		10,000
Total assets		$118,600

Liabilities and Stockholders' Equity

Liabilities:		
Trade accounts payable		$ 35,000
Accrued liabilities payable		1,100
Total liabilities		$ 36,100
Stockholders' equity:		
Common stock, $10 par, authorized 10,000 shares, issued and outstanding 5,500 shares	$55,000	
Additional paid-in capital	27,500	82,500
Total liabilities and stockholders' equity		$118,600

JOINT VENTURES

A *joint venture* differs from a partnership in that it is limited to carrying out a single project, such as production of a motion picture or construction of a building. Historically, joint ventures were used to finance the sale or exchange of a cargo of merchandise in a foreign country. In an era when marine transportation and foreign trade involved many hazards, individuals *(venturers)* would band together to undertake a venture of this type. The capital required usually was larger than one person could provide, and the risks were too high to be borne alone. Because of the risks involved and the relatively short duration of the project, no net income was recognized until the venture was completed. At the end of the voyage, the net income or net loss was divided among the venturers, and their association was ended.

In its traditional form, the accounting for a joint venture did not follow the accrual basis of accounting. The assumption of continuity was not appropriate; instead of the determination of net income at regular intervals, the measurement and reporting of net income or loss awaited the completion of the venture.

Present-Day Joint Ventures

In today's business community, joint ventures are less common but still are employed for many projects such as (1) the acquisition, development, and sale of real property; (2) exploration for oil and gas; and (3) construction of bridges, buildings, and dams.

The term *corporate joint venture* also is used by many large American corporations to describe overseas operations by a corporation whose ownership is divided between an American company and a foreign company. Many examples of jointly owned companies also are found in some domestic industries. A corporate joint venture and the accounting for such a venture currently are described in *APB Opinion No. 18,* "The Equity Method of Accounting for Investments in Common Stock," as follows:

> "Corporate joint venture" refers to a corporation owned and operated by a small group of businesses (the "joint venturers") as a separate and specific business or project for the mutual benefit of the members of the group. A government may also be a member of the group. The purpose of a corporate joint venture frequently is to share risks and rewards in developing a new market, product or technology; to combine complementary technological knowledge; or to pool resources in developing production or other facilities. A corporate joint venture also usually provides an arrangement under which each joint venturer may participate, directly or indirectly, in the overall management of the joint venture. Joint venturers thus have an interest or relationship other than as passive investors. An entity which is a subsidiary of one of the "joint venturers" is not a corporate joint venture. The ownership of a corporate joint venture seldom changes, and its stock is usually not traded publicly. A minority public ownership, however, does not preclude a corporation from being a corporate joint venture.

*****

> The [Accounting Principles] Board concludes that the equity method best enables investors in corporate joint ventures to reflect the underlying nature of their investment in those ventures. ***Therefore, investors should account for investments in common stock of corporate joint ventures by the equity method,*** in consolidated financial statements. [Emphasis added.]

*****

When investments in common stock of corporate joint ventures or other investments accounted for under the equity method are, in the aggregate, material in relation to the financial position or results of operations of an investor, it may be necessary for summarized information as to assets, liabilities, and results of operations of the investees to be presented in the notes or in separate statements, either individually or in groups, as appropriate.[2]

A recent variation of the corporate joint venture is the *limited liability company* (LLC) joint venture, which is the corporate version of the *limited liability partnership* discussed in Chapter 2 and this chapter. An example of the formation of two LLC joint ventures is found in the following note to the financial statements of Stone Container Corporation, a publicly owned enterprise:

Notes to Financial Statements

3. (In Part): Joint Ventures, Acquisitions and Investments

On May 30, 1996, the Company entered into a joint venture with Four M Corporation ("Four M") to form Florida Coast Paper Company, L.L.C. ("Florida Coast") to purchase a paperboard mill located in Port St. Joe, Florida, from St. Joe Paper Company for $185 million plus applicable working capital. As part of the transaction, Florida Coast sold, through a private placement, debt of approximately $165 million. Pursuant to an exchange offer, such privately-placed debt was exchanged for registered notes identical to the privately-placed notes. The Company accounts for its investment in Florida Coast under the equity method. Concurrent with the formation of the joint venture, the Company and Four M entered into output purchase agreements with Florida Coast which require each of the joint venture partners to purchase 50 percent of the production of Florida Coast. The output purchase agreements also require the Company and Four M to equally share in the funding of certain cash flow deficits of Florida Coast.

On July 12, 1996, the Company and Gaylord Container Corporation entered into a joint venture whereby the retail bag packaging businesses of these two companies were contributed to form S&G Packaging Company, L.L.C. ("S&G"). The Company accounts for its interest in S&G under the equity method. S&G produces paper grocery bags and sacks, handle sacks and variety bags, with estimated annual sales in excess of $300 million and serves supermarkets, quick service restaurants, paper distributors and non-food mass merchandisers throughout North America and the Caribbean.[3]

Accounting for a Corporate or LLC Joint Venture

The complexity of modern business, the emphasis on good organization and strong internal control, the importance of income taxes, the extent of government regulation, and the need for preparation and retention of adequate accounting records are strong arguments for establishing a separate set of accounting records for every corporate joint venture of large size and long duration. In the stockholders' equity accounts of the joint venture, each venturer's account is credited for the amount of cash or noncash assets invested. The fiscal year of the joint venture may or may not coincide with the fiscal years of the venturers, but the use of the accrual basis of accounting and periodic financial statements for the venture permit regular reporting of the share of net income or loss allocable to each venturer.

---

[2] *APB Opinion No. 18*, "The Equity Method of Accounting for Investments in Common Stock," AICPA (New York: 1971), pars. 3d, 16, 20d, as amended by *FASB Statement No. 94*, "Consolidation of All Majority-Owned Subsidiaries."

[3] AICPA, *Accounting Trends & Techniques*, 51st ed. (Jersey City, NJ: 1997), p. 58.

The accounting records of such a corporate joint ventu
accounts for assets, liabilities, stockholders' equity, revenu
accounting process should conform to generally accepted
the recording of transactions to the preparation of financial

Accounting for an Unincorporated Joint Ver

As indicated on page 103, **APB Opinion No. 18** required ven
method of accounting for investments in corporate joint venture
address accounting for investments in **unincorporated** joint vι   ⌐wever, the
AICPA subsequently interpreted **APB Opinion No. 18** as follows:

> [B]ecause the investor-venturer [in an unincorporated joint venture] owns an undivided in-
> terest in each asset and is proportionately liable for its share of each liability, the provisions
> of [**APB Opinion No. 18** related to the equity method of accounting] may not apply in
> some industries. For example, where it is the established industry practice (such as in some
> oil and gas venture accounting), the investor-venturer may account in its financial state-
> ments for its *pro rata* share of the assets, liabilities, revenues, and expenses of the venture.[4]

In view of the foregoing, it appears that either of two alternative methods of accounting may be adopted by investors in unincorporated joint ventures; thus, some investors
have the option of using either the **equity method of accounting** or a **proportionate
share method of accounting** for the investments. The two methods may be illustrated
by assuming that Arthur Company and Beatrice Company each invested $400,000 for
a 50% interest in an unincorporated joint venture on January 2, 2002. Condensed financial statements (other than a statement of cash flows) for the joint venture, Arbe
Company, for 2002 were as follows:

ARBE COMPANY (a joint venture) Income Statement For Year Ended December 31, 2002		
Revenue		$2,000,000
Less: Cost and expenses		1,500,000
Net income		$ 500,000
Division of net income:		
Arthur Company	$250,000	
Beatrice Company	250,000	
Total	$500,000	

ARBE COMPANY (a joint venture) Statement of Venturers' Capital For Year Ended December 31, 2002			
	Arthur Company	Beatrice Company	Combined
Investments, Jan. 2	$400,000	$400,000	$ 800,000
Add: Net income	250,000	250,000	500,000
Venturers' capital, end of year	$650,000	$650,000	$1,300,000

---

[4] *The Equity Method of Accounting for Investments in Common Stock: Accounting Interpretation of
APB Opinion No. 18,* No. 2, "Investments in Partnerships and Ventures," AICPA (New York: 1971).

ARBE COMPANY (a joint venture) **Balance Sheet** **December 31, 2002**		
Assets		
Current assets		$1,600,000
Other assets		2,400,000
Total assets		$4,000,000
Liabilities and Venturers' Capital		
Current liabilities		$ 800,000
Long-term debt		1,900,000
Venturers' capital:		
Arthur Company	$650,000	
Beatrice Company	650,000	1,300,000
Total liabilities and venturers' capital		$4,000,000

Under the ***equity method of accounting,*** both Arthur Company and Beatrice Company prepare the following journal entries for the investment in Arbe Company:

Venturer's Journal Entries for Unincorporated Joint Venture Under *Equity Method of Accounting*

2002			
Jan. 2	Investment in Arbe Company (Joint Venture)	400,000	
	Cash		400,000
	To record investment in joint venture.		
Dec. 31	Investment in Arbe Company (Joint Venture)	250,000	
	Investment Income		250,000
	To record share of Arbe Company net income ($500,000 × 0.50 = $250,000).		

Under the ***proportionate share method of accounting,*** in addition to the two foregoing journal entries, both Arthur Company and Beatrice Company prepare the following journal entry for their respective shares of the assets, liabilities, revenue, and expenses of Arbe Company:

Venturer's Additional Journal Entry for Unincorporated Joint Venture Under *Proportionate Share Method of Accounting*

2002			
Dec. 31	Current Assets ($1,600,000 × 0.50)	800,000	
	Other Assets ($2,400,000 × 0.50)	1,200,000	
	Costs and Expenses ($1,500,000 × 0.50)	750,000	
	Investment Income	250,000	
	Current Liabilities ($800,000 × 0.50)		400,000
	Long-Term Debt ($1,900,000 × 0.50)		950,000
	Revenue ($2,000,000 × 0.50)		1,000,000
	Investment in Arbe Company (Joint Venture)		650,000
	To record proportionate share of joint venture's assets, liabilities, revenue, and expenses.		

Use of the equity method of accounting for unincorporated joint ventures is consistent with the accounting for corporate joint ventures specified by *APB Opinion No. 18.* However, information on material assets and liabilities of a joint venture may be relegated to a note to financial statements (see footnote 2, par. 20d on page 104), thus resulting in *off–balance sheet financing.* The proportionate share method of accounting for unincorporated joint ventures avoids the problem of off–balance sheet financing but has the questionable practice of including *portions* of assets such as plant assets in each venturer's balance sheet.

Given the Financial Accounting Standards Board's statement that "Information about an enterprise gains greatly in usefulness if it can be compared with similar information about other enterprises,"[5] it is undesirable to have two significantly different generally accepted accounting methods for investments in unincorporated joint ventures. Accordingly, the FASB has undertaken a study of the accounting for investments in joint ventures, as well as the accounting for all investments for which the equity method of accounting presently is used.

In *International Accounting Standard 31 (IAS 31),* "Financial Reporting of Interests in Joint Ventures," the International Accounting Standards Board, which is discussed in Chapter 11, permits *either* the *proportionate consolidation method* (analogous to the *proportionate share method* described on page 105) *or* the equity method for a venturer's investment in a *jointly controlled entity,* which might be a corporation or a partnership. As pointed out on page 105, U.S. generally accepted accounting principles *require* the equity method of accounting for investments in corporate joint ventures but *permit* either the equity method or the proportionate share method of accounting for investments in unincorporated joint ventures.

SEC ENFORCEMENT ACTIONS DEALING WITH WRONGFUL APPLICATION OF ACCOUNTING STANDARDS FOR JOINT VENTURES

AAER 40, "Securities and Exchange Commission v. Chronar Corp." (October 3, 1984), reported a permanent injunction against a corporation engaged in research and development of solar photovoltaic technology and the design, development, and marketing of manufacturing processes and equipment for photovoltaic panels. The SEC alleged that the corporation had prematurely recognized revenue (under the proportionate share method of accounting) from a joint venture of which it was a 51% owner. The "revenue" was from the corporation itself, in transactions fraught with uncertainties. The result of the inappropriate recognition of revenue and related expenses of the joint venture by the corporation was a 48% understatement of the corporation's nine-month net loss reported to the SEC in its quarterly report on *Form 10-Q.* In a related enforcement action, reported in *AAER 78,* ". . . In the Matter of Seidman & Seidman . . ." (October 10, 1985), the CPA firm that had reviewed the corporation's nine-month financial statements was censured by the SEC and undertook to improve its professional standards.

The SEC reported in *AAER 102,* ". . . In the Matter of Ray M. VanLandingham and Wallace A. Patzke, Jr." (June 20, 1986), the issuance of an order requiring the chief accounting officer and the controller (both CPAs) of a corporate marketer of petroleum

---

[5] *Statement of Financial Accounting Concepts No. 2,* "Qualitative Characteristics of Accounting Information," FASB (Stamford, CT: 1980), par. 111.

products to comply with provisions of the **Securities Exchange Act of 1934** and related rules. The SEC found that the two executives were responsible for the corporation's failure to write down by at least $100 million its investment (carried at $311 million) in a joint venture that operated an oil refinery. The write-down was necessitated by the corporation's unsuccessful efforts to sell its investment in the joint venture at a price significantly below the carrying amount of the investment.

Review Questions

1. Alo and Bel, partners of Alo & Bel LLP, have capital accounts of $60,000 and $80,000, respectively. In addition, Alo has made an interest-bearing loan of $20,000 to the partnership. If Alo and Bel now decide to liquidate the partnership, what priority or advantge, if any, does Alo have in the liquidation with respect to the loan ledger account?

2. Explain the procedure to be followed in a limited liability partnership liquidation when a debit balance arises in the capital account of one of the partners.

3. In the liquidation of Cor, Don & Ell LLP, the realization of noncash assets resulted in a loss that produced the following balances in the partners' capital accounts: Cor, $25,000 credit; Don, $12,500 credit; and Ell, $5,000 debit. The partners shared net income and losses in a 5 : 3 : 2 ratio. All liabilities have been paid, and $32,500 of cash is available for distribution to partners. However, it is not possible to determine at present whether Ell will be able to pay in the $5,000 capital deficit. May the cash on hand be distributed without a delay to determine the collectibility of the amount due from Ell? Explain.

4. After realization of all noncash assets and distributing all available cash to creditors, the insolvent Fin, Guy & Han Partnership (a general partnership) still had trade accounts payable of $12,000. The capital account of Fin had a credit balance of $16,000 and that of Guy had a credit balance of $2,000. Creditors of the partnership demanded payment from Fin, who replied that the three partners shared net income equally and had begun operations with equal capital investments. Fin therefore offered to pay the creditors one-third of their claims and no more. What is your opinion of the position taken by Fin? What is the balance of Han's capital account? What journal entry, if any, should be made in the partnership accounting records for a payment by Fin to the partnership creditors?

5. In Ile, Job & Key, LLP, Ile is the managing partner. The partnership contract provides that Ile is to receive an annual salary of $12,000, payable in 12 equal monthly installments, and the resultant net income or loss is to be divided equally. On June 30, 2002, the partnership suspended operations and began liquidation. Because of a shortage of cash, Ile had not drawn any salary for the last two months of operations. How should Ile's claim for $2,000 of "unpaid wages" be accounted for in the liquidation of the partnership?

6. Lud and Moy, partners of the liquidating Lud & Moy LLP, share net income and losses equally. State reasons for allocation of losses incurred in the realization of assets equally or in the ratio of capital account balances.

7. Explain the basic principle to be observed in the distribution of cash in installments to partners when the liquidation of a limited liability partnership extends over several months.

8. During the installment liquidation of a limited liability partnership, it is appropriate to estimate the loss from realization of noncash assets. What journal entries, if

any, should be made to recognize in the partners' capital accounts their respective shares of the loss that may be incurred during the liquidation?

9. Nom, Orr & Pan LLP is to be liquidated over several months, with installment distributions of cash to the partners. Will the total amount of cash received by each partner under these circumstances be more, less, or the same amount as if the liquidator had retained all cash until all noncash assets had been realized and then had made a single cash payment to each of the partners?

10. Under what circumstances, if any, is it appropriate for a limited liability partnership undergoing installment liquidation to distribute cash to partners in the income-sharing ratio?

— 11. Rab, San, and Tay, partners of Rab, San & Tay LLP who share net income or losses equally, had capital account balances of $30,000, $25,000, and $21,000, respectively, when the partnership began liquidation. Among the assets was a promissory note receivable from San in the amount of $7,000. All partnership liabilities had been paid. The first assets realized during the liquidation were marketable debt securities (classified as held to maturity) with a carrying amount of $15,000, for which cash of $18,000 was received. How should this $18,000 be divided among the partners?

12. When Urb, Van & Woo LLP began liquidation, the capital account credit balances were Urb, $38,000; Van, $35,000; and Woo, $32,000. When the liquidation was complete, Urb had received less cash than either of the other two partners. What factors might explain why the partner with the largest capital account balance might receive the smallest amount of cash in liquidation?

13. Yang and Zee, partners of Yang & Zee LLP, decided to incorporate the partnership as Yang-Zee Corporation. The entire capital stock of Yang-Zee Corporation was divided equally between Yang and Zee because they had equal capital account balances in the partnership. An appraisal report obtained on the date of incorporation indicated that the land and buildings had increased in value by 50% while owned by the partnership. Should the carrying amounts of those assets be increased to appraisal value or valued at cost less accumulated depreciation to the partnership when recognized in Yang-Zee Corporation's accounting records? Explain.

14. Explain how a *joint venture* differs from a partnership.

15. What are *corporate joint ventures*? What accounting standards for such ventures were established in *APB Opinion No. 18,* "The Equity Method of Accounting for Investments in Common Stock"?

16. Compare the *equity method of accounting* with the *proportionate share method of accounting* for an investment in an unincorporated joint venture.

Exercises

(Exercise 3.1)   Select the best answer for each of the following multiple-choice questions:

1. If Jebb, a partner with a loan receivable from a liquidating limited liability partnership, receives less cash than the amount of the loan during the liquidation, the payment is recorded with a debit to the partnership's ledger account entitled:

   a. Loan Receivable from Jebb.
   b. Jebb, Capital.
   c. Jebb, Drawing.
   d. Loan Payable to Jebb.

2. Is the balance of the Loan Payable to Partner Jones ledger account combined with the balance of the Partner Jones, Capital account of a liquidating limited liability partnership in:

	The Partnership's General Ledger?	The Partnership's Statement of Realization and Liquidation?
a.	Yes	Yes
b.	Yes	No
c.	No	Yes
d.	No	No

3. In the liquidation of a limited liability partnership, a loan payable to a partner:
   a. Must be offset against that partner's capital account balance before liquidation commences.
   b. Will not advance the time of payment to that partner during the liquidation.
   c. Has the same priority as amounts payable to outside creditors of the partnership.
   d. Must be closed to that partner's drawing account.

4. In the liquidation of a limited liability partnership, cash received by a partner having a loan receivable from the partnership is debited to the partner's:
   a. Loan account.
   b. Capital account.
   c. Drawing account.
   d. Retained earnings account.

5. Prior to the beginning of liquidation, the liabilities and partners' capital of Mann, Nunn & Ogg LLP, whose partners shared net income and losses equally, consisted of Liabilities, $60,000; Loan Payable to Ogg, $21,000; Mann, Capital, $30,000; Nunn, Capital, $60,000; and Ogg, Capital, $39,000. If, after realization of all noncash assets and payment of all outsider liabilities, $60,000 cash was available for distribution to partners on January 31, 2002, partner Ogg should receive:
   a. $60,000
   b. $39,000
   c. $30,000
   d. $21,000
   e. Some other amount

6. The ***marshaling of assets*** provisions of the Uniform Partnership Act provide that unpaid creditors of an insolvent general partnership have first claim to assets of:
   a. The partnership.
   b. A solvent partner.
   c. An insolvent partner.
   d. Either the partnership or a solvent partner, as elected by the creditor.

7. May unpaid creditors of an insolvent liquidating general partnership obtain payment from a personally solvent partner whose partnership capital account has a:

	Debit Balance?	Credit Balance?
a.	Yes	Yes
b.	Yes	No
c.	No	Yes
d.	No	No

8. The ledger accounts of the liquidating Gill, Hall & James LLP included Loan Receivable from Gill, $10,000 dr; Loan Payable to Hall, $20,000 cr; Gill, Capital,

$30,000 dr; Hall, Capital, $60,000 cr; James, Capital, $50,000 cr. The partners share net income and losses 20%, 40%, and 40%, respectively. In the preparation of a cash distribution to partners during liquidation working paper, beginning capital per unit of income-sharing amounts are:

	Gill	Hall	James
a.	($40,000)	$80,000	$50,000
b.	($20,000)	$20,000	$12,500
c.	($15,000)	$15,000	$12,500
d.	-0-	$80,000	$50,000

9. In the liquidation of a limited liability partnership in installments, the partner who receives the first payment of cash after all liabilities have been paid is the partner having the largest:

   a. Capital account balance.
   b. Capital per unit of income sharing.
   c. Income-sharing percentage.
   d. Loan account balance.

10. In the preparation of a cash distribution program for the liquidating Marlo, Noble & Owen LLP, the balance of the Loan Receivable from Partner Marlo ledger account in the accounting records of the partnership is:

    a. Added to the Partner Marlo, Drawing, account balance.
    b. Deducted from the Partner Marlo, Capital, account balance.
    c. Included with the total of the noncash assets accounts.
    d. Disregarded.

11. In the installment liquidation of a limited liability partnership, the income-sharing ratio is used for cash payments to partners:

    a. At no time.
    b. Throughout the course of the liquidation.
    c. Once the partners' capital account balances have been reduced to the income-sharing ratio.
    d. Only for asset realizations that result in gains.

12. May a balance sheet prepared for a corporation on the date it was created from the incorporation of a limited liability partnership display in stockholders' equity:

	Common Stock?	Additional Paid-in Capital?	Retained Earnings?
a.	Yes	Yes	Yes
b.	Yes	Yes	No
c.	Yes	No	No
d.	Yes	No	Yes

13. The proportionate share method of accounting is appropriate for:

    a. Corporate joint ventures only.
    b. Unincorporated joint ventures only.
    c. Both corporate joint ventures and unincorporated joint ventures.
    d. Neither corporate joint ventures nor unincorporated joint ventures.

(Exercise 3.2)

CHECK FIGURE

Debit Ron, capital, $11,500.

After the realization of all noncash assets and the payment of all liabilities, the balance sheet of the liquidating Pon, Quan & Ron LLP on January 31, 2002, showed Cash, $15,000; Pon, Capital, ($9,000); Quan, Capital, $8,000; and Ron, Capital, $16,000, with ( ) indicating a capital deficit. The partners share net income and losses equally.

Prepare a journal entry for Pon, Quan & Ron LLP on January 31, 2002, to show the payment of $15,000 cash in a safe manner to the partners. Show computations in the explanation for the journal entry.

(Exercise 3.3) Archer and Bender, partners of Archer & Bender LLP, who share net income and losses in a 60 : 40 ratio, respectively, decided to liquidate the partnership. A portion of the noncash assets had been realized, but assets with a carrying amount of $42,000 were yet to be realized. All liabilities had been paid, and cash of $20,000 was available for distribution to partners. The partners' capital account credit balances were $40,000 for Archer and $22,000 for Bender.

CHECK FIGURE

Cash to Archer, $14,800.

Prepare a working paper to compute the amount of cash (totaling $20,000) to be distributed to each partner.

(Exercise 3.4) Carlo and Dodge started Carlo & Dodge LLP some years ago and managed to operate profitably for several years. Recently, however, they lost a lawsuit requiring payment of large damages because of Carlo's negligence and incurred unexpected losses on trade accounts receivable and inventories. As a result, they decided to liquidate the partnership. After all noncash assets were realized, only $18,000 was available to pay liabilities, which amounted to $33,000. The partners' capital account balances before the start of liquidation and their income-sharing percentages are shown below:

CHECK FIGURE

b. Credit Dodge, capital, $9,675.

	Capital Account Balances	Income-Sharing Percentages
Carlo	$23,000	55%
Dodge	13,500	45%

a. Prepare a working paper to compute the total loss incurred on the liquidation of the Carlo & Dodge LLP.

 b. Prepare a journal entry to record Carlo's payment of $15,000 to partnership creditors and to close the partners' capital accounts. Carlo was barely solvent after paying the partnership creditors, but Dodge had net assets, exclusive of partnership interest, in excess of $100,000.

(Exercise 3.5) The balance sheet of Rich, Stowe & Thorpe LLP on the date it commenced liquidation was as follows, with the partners' income-sharing ratio in parentheses:

CHECK FIGURE

Cash to Rich, $8,000.

RICH, STOWE & THORPE LLP
Balance Sheet
September 24, 2002

Assets		Liabilities and Partners' Capital	
Cash	$ 20,000	Liabilities	$240,000
Other assets	480,000	Rich, capital (40%)	80,000
		Stowe, capital (40%)	120,000
		Thorpe, capital (20%)	60,000
		Total liabilities and	
Total assets	$500,000	partners' capital	$500,000

On September 24, 2002, other assets with a carrying amount of $360,000 realized $300,000 cash, and $320,000 ($20,000 + $300,000 = $320,000) cash was paid in a safe manner.

Prepare journal entries for Rich, Stowe & Thorpe LLP on September 24, 2002.

(Exercise 3.6) On June 3, 2002, the partners of Ace, Bay & Cap LLP agreed (1) to liquidate the partnership, (2) to share gains and losses on the realization of noncash assets in the ratio 1:3:4, and (3) to disburse the $80,000 available cash on June 3 in a safe manner. In addition to cash, the June 3 balance sheet of the partnership had other assets, $100,000; liabilities, $50,000; Ace, capital, $60,000; Bay, capital, $40,000; and Cap, capital, $30,000. The partnership had no loans receivable from or payable to the partners.

Prepare a journal entry for Ace, Bay & Cap LLP on June 3, 2002, to record the disbursement of $80,000 cash. Show computations in the explanation for the entry.

(Exercise 3.7) After realization of a portion of the noncash assets of Ed, Flo & Gus LLP, which was being liquidated, the capital account balances were Ed, $33,000; Flo, $40,000; and Gus, $42,000. Cash of $42,000 and other assets with a carrying amount of $78,000 were on hand. Creditors' claims total $5,000. The partners share net income and losses in a 5:3:2 ratio.

CHECK FIGURE

Cash to Flo, $13,000.

Prepare a working paper to compute the cash payments (totaling $37,000) that may be made to the partners.

(Exercise 3.8) When Hale and Ian, partners of Hale & Ian LLP who shared net income and losses in a 4:6 ratio, were incapacitated in an accident, a liquidator was appointed to wind up the partnership. The partnership's balance sheet showed cash, $35,000; other assets, $110,000; liabilities, $20,000; Hale, capital, $71,000; and Ian, capital, $54,000. Because of the specialized nature of the noncash assets, the liquidator anticipated that considerable time would be required to dispose of them. The costs of liquidating the partnership (advertising, rent, travel, etc.) were estimated at $10,000.

CHECK FIGURE

Cash to Hale, $5,000.

Prepare a working paper to compute the amount of cash (totaling $5,000) that may be distributed to each partner.

(Exercise 3.9) The following balance sheet was available for Jones, Kell & Lamb LLP on March 31, 2002 (each partner's income-sharing percentage is shown in parentheses):

CHECK FIGURE

b. Cash to Lamb, $17,000.

JONES, KELL & LAMB LLP
Balance Sheet
March 31, 2002

Assets		Liabilities and Partners' Capital	
Cash	$ 25,000	Liabilities	$ 52,000
Other assets	180,000	Jones, capital (40%)	40,000
		Kell, capital (40%)	65,000
		Lamb, capital (20%)	48,000
Total	$205,000	Total	$205,000

a. The partnership was being liquidated by the realization of other assets in installments. The first realization of noncash assets having a carrying amount of $90,000 realized $50,000, and all cash available after settlement with creditors was distributed to partners. Prepare a working paper to compute the amount of cash each partner should receive in the first installment.

b. If the facts are as in *a* above, except that $3,000 cash is withheld for anticipated liquidation costs, compute the amount of cash that each partner should receive.

c. As a separate case, assume that each partner appropriately received some cash in the distribution after the second realization of noncash assets. The cash to be distributed amounted to $14,000 from the third realization of noncash assets, and other assets with a $6,000 carrying amount remained. Prepare a working paper to show how the $14,000 is distributed to the partners.

(Exercise 3.10) On November 10, 2002, May, Nona, and Olive, partners of May, Nona & Olive LLP, had capital account balances of $20,000, $25,000, and $9,000, respectively, and shared net income and losses in a 4 : 2 : 1 ratio.

a. Prepare a cash distribution program for liquidation of the May, Nona & Olive Partnership in installments, assuming liabilities totaled $20,000 on November 10, 2002.

b. How much cash was paid to all partners if May received $4,000 on liquidation?

c. If May received $13,000 cash pursuant to liquidation, how much did Olive receive?

d. If Nona received only $11,000 as a result of the liquidation, what was the loss to the partnership on the realization of assets? (No partner invested any additional assets in the partnership.)

(Exercise 3.11) Following is the balance sheet of Paul & Quinn LLP on June 1, 2002:

PAUL & QUINN LLP
Balance Sheet
June 1, 2002

Assets		Liabilities and Partners' Capital	
Cash	$ 5,000	Liabilities	$20,000
Other assets	55,000	Paul, capital	22,500
		Quinn, capital	17,500
Total	$60,000	Total	$60,000

The partners share net income and net losses as follows: Paul, 60%; Quinn, 40%. In June, other assets with a carrying amount of $22,000 realized $18,000, creditors were paid in full, and $2,000 was paid to the partners in a manner to reduce their capital account balances closer to the income-sharing ratio. In July, other assets with a carrying amount of $10,000 realized $12,000, liquidation costs of $500 were paid, and cash of $12,500 was distributed to the partners. In August, the remaining other assets realized $22,500, and final settlement was made between the partners.

Prepare a working paper to compute the amount of cash each partner should receive in June, July, and August, 2002.

(Exercise 3.12) On September 26, 2002, prior to commencement of liquidation of Orville, Paula & Quincy LLP, the partnership had total liabilities of $80,000 and partners' capital account credit balances of $120,000 for Orville, $160,000 for Paula, and $80,000 for Quincy. There were no loans to or from partners in the partnership's accounting records. The partners shared net income and losses as follows: Orville, 30%; Paula, 50%; Quincy, 20%.

Prepare a cash distribution program for Orville, Paula & Quincy LLP on September 26, 2002.

(Exercise 3.13) On January 21, 2002, the date the partners of Ang, Bel & Cap LLP decided to liquidate the partnership, its balance sheet showed cash, $33,000; other assets, $67,000; trade accounts payable, $20,000; loan payable to Ang, $12,000; Ang, capital, $28,000; Bel, capital, $18,000; and Cap, capital, $22,000. The partnership's income-sharing ratio was Ang, 50%; Bel, 30%; Cap, 20%. The accountant for the partnership prepared the following cash distribution program (to facilitate installment payments to partners) on January 21, 2002: First $20,000, 100% to creditors; next $6,000, 100% to Cap; next $14,000, ⅝ to Ang and ⅖ to Cap; all over $40,000, in income-sharing ratio. Based on the foregoing, the partners decided to pay the entire cash of $33,000 on January 21, 2002, in a safe manner consistent with the Uniform Partnership Act.

Prepare a journal entry to record the Ang, Bel & Cap LLP payment of $33,000 cash on January 21, 2002.

(Exercise 3.14) The net equities and income-sharing ratio for the partners of Ruiz, Salvo, Thomas & Urwig LLP before liquidation was authorized on May 5, 2002, were as follows:

	Ruiz	Salvo	Thomas	Urwig
Net equity in partnership	$36,000	$32,400	$8,000	$(100)
Income-sharing ratio	3	4	2	1

Assets were expected to realize cash significantly in excess of carrying amounts.

Prepare a program showing how cash should be distributed to the partners as it becomes available in the course of liquidation if liabilities of the partnership totaled $15,000 on May 5, 2002.

(Exercise 3.15) On September 30, 2002, the partners of Allen, Brown & Cox LLP, who shared net income and losses in the ratio of 5 : 3 : 2, respectively, decided to liquidate the partnership. The partnership trial balance on that date was as follows:

ALLEN, BROWN & COX LLP
Trial Balance
September 30, 2002

	Debit	Credit
Cash	$ 18,000	
Loan receivable from Allen	30,000	
Trade accounts receivable (net)	66,000	
Inventories	52,000	
Machinery and equipment (net)	189,000	
Trade accounts payable		$ 53,000
Loan payable to Brown		20,000
Allen, capital		118,000
Brown, capital		90,000
Cox, capital		74,000
Totals	$355,000	$355,000

The partners planned a lengthy time period for realization of noncash assets in order to minimize liquidation losses. All available cash, less an amount retained to provide for future liquidation costs, was to be distributed to the partners at the end of each month.

Prepare a cash distribution program for Allen, Brown & Cox LLP on September 30, 2002, showing how cash should be distributed to creditors and to partners as it becomes available during liquidation. Round amounts to the nearest dollar.

(Exercise 3.16) The balance sheet of Davis, Evans & Fagin LLP on September 29, 2002, included cash, $20,000; other assets, $262,000; liabilities, $50,000; and total partners' capital, $232,000. On that date, the three partners decided to dissolve and liquidate the partnership. The cash distribution program prepared by the partnership's accountant follows:

DAVIS, EVANS & FAGIN LLP
Cash Distribution Program
September 29, 2002

	Total	Creditors	Davis	Evans	Fagin
First	$ 50,000	100%			
Next	34,000			100%	
Next	48,000			33⅓%	66⅔%
All over	$132,000		40%	20%	40%

On September 30, 2002, noncash assets with a carrying amount of $140,000 were sold for $100,000 cash.

Prepare journal entries for Davis, Evans & Fagin LLP on September 30 to record the realization of $140,000 of noncash assets and the payment of all available cash on that date in accordance with the cash distribution program.

(Exercise 3.17) The balance sheet of Venner & Wigstaff LLP, immediately before the partnership was incorporated as Venwig Corporation, follows:

VENNER & WIGSTAFF LLP
Balance Sheet
September 30, 2002

Assets		Liabilities and Partners' Capital	
Cash	$ 10,500	Trade accounts payable	$ 16,400
Trade accounts receivable	15,900	Venner, capital	60,000
Inventories	42,000	Wigstaff, capital	52,000
Equipment (net of $18,000			
accumulated depreciation)	60,000		
Total	$128,400	Total	$128,400

The following adjustments to the balance sheet of the partnership were recommended by a CPA before accounting records for Venwig Corporation were to be established:

1. An allowance for doubtful accounts was to be established in the amount of $1,200.
2. Short-term prepayments of $800 were to be recognized.
3. The current fair value of inventories, $48,000, and the current fair value of equipment, $72,000, were to be recognized.
4. Accrued liabilities of $750 were to be recognized.

Prepare a balance sheet for Venwig Corporation on October 1, 2002, assuming that 10,000 shares of $5 par common stock were issued to the partners in exchange for their equities in the partnership. Fifty thousand shares of common stock were authorized to be issued.

(Exercise 3.18) On January 2, 2002, Yale Corporation and Zola Corporation each invested $500,000 in an unincorporated joint venture, Y-Z Company, the income or losses of which were to be shared equally. On December 31, 2002, financial statements of Y-Z Company showed total revenue, $800,000; total costs and expenses, $600,000; total current assets, $600,000; net plant assets, $1,500,000; total current liabilities, $300,000; total long-term debt, $600,000; and total venturers' capital, $1,200,000. Neither venturer had drawings during 2002.

a. Prepare journal entries for Yale Corporation for the year ended December 31, 2002, to record its investment in Y-Z Company under the equity method of accounting.

b. Prepare an additional journal entry for Yale Corporation on December 31, 2002, to complete the journal entries (together with those in *a*) required for the investment in Y-Z Company under the proportionate share method of accounting.

Cases

(Case 3.1) Professor Lewis posed the following question to students of advanced accounting: "Does the limited liability partnership form of business enterprise damage the mutual agency characteristic of a general partnership?"

Instructions
How would you answer Professor Lewis's question? Explain.

(Case 3.2) The partners of the liquidating Nance, Olson & Peale LLP have requested Nancy Lane, CPA, to assist in the liquidation. Lane discovered considerable disarray in the partnership's accounting records for liabilities, especially for trade accounts payable. Despite the condition of the accounting records, the partners have urged Lane to prepare a cash distribution program to show how cash received from the realization of noncash assets might be distributed to creditors and to partners as it became available.

Instructions
Is Nancy Lane able to prepare a cash distribution program, given the condition of the Nance, Olson & Peale LLP accounting records? Explain.

(Case 3.3) The Berg, Hancock & Loomis Partnership (a general partnership) was insolvent and in the process of liquidation under the Uniform Partnership Act. After the noncash assets were realized and the resultant loss was distributed equally among the partners in accordance with the partnership contract, their financial positions were as follows:

	Equity in Partnership	Financial Position Other Than Equity in Partnership	
		Assets	Liabilities
Jack Berg	$30,000	$110,000	$45,000
Diane Hancock	(21,000)	20,000	40,000
David Loomis	(55,000)	55,000	45,000

Several partnership creditors remained unpaid, but the partnership had no cash.

Instructions
Explain the prospects for collection by:

a. The creditors of the partnership.

b. The creditors of each partner.

c. Jack Berg from the other partners. Compute the total loss that Berg will incur on the liquidation of the partnership.

(Case 3.4) Lois Allen and Barbara Brett established a limited liability partnership and shared net income and losses equally. Although the partners began business with equal capital accounts, Allen made more frequent authorized cash withdrawals than Brett, with the result that her capital account balance became the smaller of the two. The partners decided to liquidate the partnership on June 30, 2002; on that date the accounting records were closed and financial statements were prepared. The balance sheet included capital of $40,000 for Allen and $60,000 for Brett, as well as a $10,000 loan payable to Brett.

The liquidation of the partnership was managed by Allen, because Brett was hospitalized by illness on July 1, 2002, the day after partnership operations were suspended. The procedures followed by Allen were as follows: (1) realize all the noncash assets at the best amounts obtainable; (2) pay the outside creditors in full; (3) pay Brett's loan; and (4) divide all remaining cash between Brett and herself in the 40 : 60 ratio represented by their capital account balances.

When Brett was released from the hospital on July 5, 2002, Allen informed her that through good luck and hard work, she had been able to realize the noncash assets and complete the liquidation during the five days of Brett's hospitalization. Thereupon, Allen delivered two partnership checks to Brett. One check was for $10,000 in payment of the loan; the other was in settlement of Brett's capital account balance.

Instructions

a. Do you approve of the procedures followed by Allen in the liquidation? Explain.

b. Assume that the liquidation procedures followed resulted in the payment of $24,000 to Brett in addition to the payment of her loan in full. What was the partnership's gain or loss on the realization of assets? If you believe that other methods should have been followed in the liquidation, explain how much more or less Brett would have received under the procedure you recommend.

(Case 3.5)   The Wells, Conner & Zola Partnership, a general partnership CPA firm, has been forced to liquidate because of the bankruptcy of partner Lewis Zola, which caused the dissolution of the firm. On the date of Zola's bankruptcy filing, the partnership's balance sheet was as shown below, with the partners' income-sharing percentages in parentheses.

WELLS, CONNER & ZOLA PARTNERSHIP			
Balance Sheet			
October 31, 2002			
Assets		**Liabilities and Partners' Capital**	
Cash	$ 60,000	Trade accounts payable	$140,000
Trade accounts receivable	120,000	Interest payable to Wells	10,000
Office equipment (net)	240,000	10% note payable to Wells	100,000
Library (net)	90,000	Wells, capital (50%)	280,000
Goodwill (net)	40,000	Conner, capital (30%)	80,000
		Zola, capital (20%)	(60,000)
		Total liabilities and	
Total assets	$550,000	partners' capital	$550,000

In a meeting with the three partners, you, as the partners' accountant, are asked to supervise the liquidation of the partnership. In response to partner John Wells's assertion that, according to his attorney, the partnership had to pay the note and interest payable to Wells after all trade accounts payable had been paid, you explain your understanding of the right of offset, which gives the Wells loan no priority over partners' capital. You point out that the amounts to be realized for the partnership's office equipment and library are uncertain and that in an enforced liquidation losses may be incurred on the realization of those assets. You also indicate that the impaired partnership goodwill has no realizable value and should be written off to the partners' capital accounts at once.

Your statements cause consternation to partners John Wells and Kathleen Conner. Wells points out that he has been absorbing the majority of the partnership's recent operating losses, and that his loan to the partnership was necessitated by a cash shortage. Conner objects to sharing any part of the writeoff of impaired goodwill, reminding Wells, Zola, and you that the goodwill was recognized in the admission of Zola to the former Wells & Conner partnership for his investment of his highly profitable CPA firm proprietorship. Noting that Zola's personal bankruptcy was most likely an outgrowth of his deteriorating relationship with Wells, partnership clients, and her, Conner strongly urges that Zola's capital account be charged for the entire $40,000 carrying amount of the impaired goodwill.

After further acrimonious discussion, the three partners request you to "go back to the drawing board" and return with a recommendation on how best to resolve the issues raised by Wells and Conner. In response to your inquiry, both Wells and Conner emphasize that they intend to continue the practice of public accounting in some form; Zola states that he has no future career plans until the resolution of his bankruptcy filing.

Instructions

Prepare a memo for your recommendations for the three partners in response to the issues they have raised. Include in your recommendations your views on the desirability of the partners' retaining an independent attorney to resolve the issues raised.

(Case 3.6) Anne Sanchez, chief accounting officer of the Kane & Grant Partnership (a general partnership), is a member of the IMA, the FEI, and the AICPA (see Chapter 1). Partners Jane Kane and Lloyd Grant inform Sanchez of their plans to incorporate the highly profitable partnership, with a view of a public offering to outside investors in the future. Indicating their desire for the best possible balance sheet for the new corporation, they ask Sanchez to reconsider her insistence that the partnership account for its 50% investment in KG/WM Company, an unincorporated joint venture, by the proportionate share method. Partner Kane shows Sanchez the following comparative balance sheet data for the partnership under two methods of accounting for the investment in KG/WM Company:

KANE & GRANT PARTNERSHIP
Condensed Balance Sheets
April 30, 2002

	Proportionate Share Method	Equity Method
Assets		
Investment in KG/WM Company	$ 0	$ 600,000
Other assets	3,800,000	2,400,000
Total assets	$3,800,000	$3,000,000
Liabilities and Partners' Capital		
Total liabilities	$2,000,000	$1,200,000
Partners' capital	1,800,000	1,800,000
Total liabilities and partners' capital	$3,800,000	$3,000,000

Kane points out that under the proportionate share method of accounting for the investment in KG/WM Company, the Kane & Grant Partnership's debt-to-equity ratio is 111% ($2,000,000 ÷ $1,800,000 = 111%), while under the equity method of accounting for the investment the partnership's debt-to-equity ratio is only 67% ($1,200,000 ÷ $1,800,000 = 67%).

Instructions

May Anne Sanchez ethically comply with the request of Jane Kane and Lloyd Grant? Explain.

(Case 3.7)   The Financial Accounting Standards Board is studying the accounting for investments in both corporate joint ventures and unincorporated joint ventures.

Instructions

Do you favor requiring a *single* accounting method for investments in both corporate and unincorporated joint ventures? If so, what should the accounting method be? If not, should one accounting method be mandatory for investments in corporate joint ventures, and another method mandatory for investments in unincorporated joint ventures? Or should alternative accounting methods be available for investments in both types of joint ventures? Explain.

Problems

(Problem 3.1)   During liquidation, the Doris, Elsie & Frances Partnership (a general partnership) became insolvent. On January 17, 2002, after all noncash assets had been realized and all available cash had been distributed to creditors, the balance sheet of the partnership was as follows:

DORIS, ELSIE & FRANCES PARTNERSHIP Balance Sheet January 17, 2002	
Liabilities and Partners' Capital	
Trade accounts payable	$ 60,000
Doris, capital	120,000
Elsie, capital	(160,000)
Frances, capital	(20,000)
Total liabilities and partners' capital	$ -0-

The partners shared net income and losses (including gains and losses in liquidation) in the ratio 20%, 50%, and 30%, respectively. On January 17, 2002, when the financial positions of the partners were as shown below, Elsie and Frances invested in the partnership all cash available under the marshaling of assets provisions of the Uniform Partnership Act:

Partner	Assets*	Liabilities*
Doris	$ 60,000	$ 80,000
Elsie	280,000	200,000
Frances	250,000	240,000

* Excludes equity in partnership

Instructions

Prepare journal entries for the Doris, Elsie & Frances Partnership on January 17, 2002, to record the receipt of cash from Elsie and Frances, the appropriate distribution of the cash, and the completion of the partnership liquidation.

(Problem 3.2)   Following is the balance sheet of Olmo, Perez & Quinto LLP on January 31, 2002, the date the partners authorized liquidation of the partnership. There were no unrecorded liabilities.

OLMO, PEREZ & QUINTO LLP
Balance Sheet
January 31, 2002

Assets		Liabilities and Partners' Capital	
Cash	$ 10,000	Trade accounts payable	$ 90,000
Loan receivable from Perez	50,000	Loan payable to Olmo	60,000
Other assets (net)	240,000	Olmo, capital	140,000
		Perez, capital	(70,000)
		Quinto, capital	80,000
		Total liabilities and	
Total assets	$300,000	partners' capital	$300,000

Additional Information for 2002:

1. The partners' income (loss)-sharing ratio was Olmo, 40%; Perez, 40%; and Quinto, 20%.
2. On February 1, noncash assets with a carrying amount of $180,000 realized $140,000, and all available cash was paid to creditors and to partners.
3. On February 4, noncash assets with a carrying amount of $60,000 realized $50,000, and that amount was paid to partners.
4. On February 5, Perez, who was almost insolvent, paid $30,000 on the loan from the partnership. Olmo and Quinto agreed that the partnership would receive no further cash from Perez, and they instructed the accountant to close the partnership's accounting records.

Instructions
Prepare journal entries for Olmo, Perez & Quinto LLP on February 1, 4, and 5, 2002. Disregard costs of the liquidation. Round all amounts to the nearest dollar. (Preparation of a cash distribution program as a supporting exhibit is recommended.)

(Problem 3.3) The loan and capital account balances of Hal, Ian, Jay & Kay LLP were as follows on September 25, 2002, the date that the partnership began liquidation:

	Debit	Credit
Loan receivable from Jay	$10,000	
Loan payable to Hal		$20,000
Hal, capital		50,000
Ian, capital		25,000
Jay, capital		70,000
Kay, capital		50,000

Partnership liabilities totaled $80,000 on September 25, 2002. The partners shared net income and losses and realization gains and losses as follows: Hal, 20%; Ian, 25%; Jay, 30%; and Kay, 25%.

Instructions
Prepare a cash distribution program for Hal, Ian, Jay & Kay LLP on September 25, 2002.

(Problem 3.4) Carson and Worden decided to dissolve and liquidate Carson & Worden LLP on September 23, 2002. On that date, the balance sheet of the partnership was as follows:

CHECK FIGURE

b. Oct. 1, debit Carson, capital, $4,800.

CARSON & WORDEN LLP
Balance Sheet
September 23, 2002

Assets		Liabilities and Partners' Capital	
Cash	$ 5,000	Trade accounts payable	$ 15,000
Other assets	100,000	Loan payable to Worden	10,000
		Carson, capital	60,000
		Worden, capital	20,000
Total	$105,000	Total	$105,000

On September 23, 2002, noncash assets with a carrying amount of $70,000 realized $60,000, and $64,000 was paid to creditors and partners, $1,000 being retained to cover possible liquidation costs. On October 1, 2002, the remaining noncash assets realized $18,000 (net of liquidation costs), and all available cash was distributed to partners. Carson and Worden share net income and losses 40% and 60%, respectively.

Instructions

a. Prepare a cash distribution program for Carson & Worden LLP on September 23, 2002, to determine the appropriate distribution of cash to partners as it becomes available.

b. Prepare journal entries for Carson & Worden LLP on September 23 and October 1, 2002, to record the realization of assets and distributions of cash to creditors and partners.

(Problem 3.5) The statement of realization and liquidation for Luke, Mayo & Nomura LLP was as follows:

LUKE, MAYO & NOMURA LLP
Statement of Realization and Liquidation
April 30 through June 1, 2002

	Assets		Trade Accounts Payable	Partner's Capital		
	Cash	*Other*		*Luke*	*Mayo*	*Nomura*
Balances before liquidation (April 30, 2002)	$ 20,000	$200,000	$120,000	$ 10,000	$ 30,000	$60,000
Realization of other assets at a loss of $120,000 (May 9, 2002)	80,000	(200,000)		(40,000)	(40,000)	(40,000)
Balances	$100,000		$120,000	$(30,000)	$(10,000)	$20,000
Payment to creditors (May 12, 2002)	(100,000)		(100,000)			
Balances			$ 20,000	$(30,000)	$(10,000)	$20,000
Payment by Luke to partnership creditors (May 18, 2002)			(20,000)	20,000		
Balances				$(10,000)	$(10,000)	$20,000
Cash invested by Luke and Mayo (May 25, 2002)	$ 20,000			10,000	10,000	
Balances	$ 20,000					$20,000
Payment to Nomura (June 1, 2002)	(20,000)					(20,000)

Instructions
Prepare journal entries (omit explanations) for the liquidation of Luke, Mayo & Nomura LLP on May 9, 12, 18, and 25 and June 1, 2002. Use a single Other Assets ledger account.

(Problem 3.6) On December 31, 2002, the accounting records of Luna, Nava & Ruby LLP included the following ledger account balances:

	(Dr) Cr
Luna, drawing	$(24,000)
Ruby, drawing	(9,000)
Loan payable to Nava	30,000
Luna, capital	123,000
Nava, capital	100,500
Ruby, capital	108,000

Total assets of the partnership amounted to $478,500, including $52,500 cash, and partnership liabilities totaled $150,000. The partnership was liquidated on December 31, 2002, and Ruby received $83,250 cash pursuant to the liquidation. Luna, Nava, and Ruby shared net income and losses in a 5:3:2 ratio, respectively.

Instructions
a. Prepare a working paper to compute the total loss from the liquidation of Luna, Nava & Ruby LLP on December 31, 2002.

b. Prepare a statement of realization and liquidation for Luna, Nava & Ruby LLP on December 31, 2002.

c. Prepare journal entries for Luna, Nava & Ruby LLP on December 31, 2002, to record the liquidation.

(Problem 3.7) The following balance sheet was prepared for Haye & Lee LLP immediately prior to liquidation:

HAYE & LEE LLP			
Balance Sheet (unaudited)			
March 31, 2002			
Assets		**Liabilities and Partners' Capital**	
Cash	$ 10,000	Liabilities	$ 27,000
Investments in marketable		Haye, capital	72,000
equity securities (available		Lee, capital	31,000
for sale)	44,000	Accumulated other	
Other assets	100,000	comprehensive income	24,000
Total	$154,000	Total	$154,000

Haye and Lee shared operating income or losses in a 2:1 ratio and gains and losses on investments in a 3:1 ratio. The transactions and events to complete the liquidation were as follows:

Apr. 1 Haye withdrew the marketable equity securities at the agreed current fair value of $44,000.

3 Other assets and the trade name, Haley's, were sold to Wong Products for $200,000 face amount of 12% bonds with a current fair value of $180,000. The gain on this transaction was an investment gain. The bonds were classified as available for sale.

Apr. 7 Wong Products 12% bonds with a face amount of $40,000 were sold for $35,600 cash. The loss on this transaction was an investment loss.

8 Liabilities were paid.

10 Haye withdrew $100,000 face amount and Lee withdrew $60,000 face amount of Wong Products 12% bonds at carrying amounts.

15 Available cash was paid to Haye and to Lee.

Instructions

Prepare journal entries for Haye & Lee LLP to record the foregoing transactions and events. Disregard interest on the bonds of Wong Products.

(Problem 3.8) Following is the balance sheet for Adams, Barna & Coleman LLP on June 4, 2002, immediately prior to its liquidation:

CHECK FIGURES

Final cash payments:
Adams, $100; Barna,
$16,100.

ADAMS, BARNA & COLEMAN LLP			
Balance Sheet			
June 4, 2002			
Assets		**Liabilities and Partners' Capital**	
Cash	$ 6,000	Liabilities	$ 20,000
Other assets	94,000	Loan payable to Barna	4,000
		Adams, capital	27,000
		Barna, capital	39,000
		Coleman, capital	10,000
Total	$100,000	Total	$100,000

The partners shared net income and losses as follows: Adams, 40%; Barna, 40%; and Coleman, 20%. On June 4, 2002, the other assets realized $30,700, and $20,500 had to be paid to liquidate the liabilities because of an unrecorded trade account payable of $500. Adams and Barna were solvent, but Coleman's personal liabilities exceeded personal assets by $5,000.

Instructions

a. Prepare a statement of realization and liquidation for Adams, Barna & Coleman LLP on June 4, 2002. Combine Barna's loan and capital account balances.

b. Prepare journal entries for Adams, Barna & Coleman LLP to record the liquidation on June 4, 2002.

c. How much cash would other assets have to realize on liquidation in order for Coleman to receive enough cash from the partnership to pay personal creditors in full? Assume that $20,500 is required to liquidate the partnership liabilities.

(Problem 3.9) The accountant for Smith, Jones & Webb LLP prepared the following balance sheet immediately prior to liquidation of the partnership:

CHECK FIGURE

Final cash payments:
$28,000 to each partner.

SMITH, JONES & WEBB LLP			
Balance Sheet			
April 30, 2002			
Assets		**Liabilities and Partners' Capital**	
Cash	$ 20,000	Liabilities	$ 80,000
Other assets	280,000	Smith, capital	60,000
		Jones, capital	70,000
		Webb, capital	90,000
Total	$300,000	Total	$300,000

During May 2002, noncash assets with a carrying amount of $105,000 realized $75,000, and all liabilities were paid. During June, noncash assets with a carrying amount of $61,000 realized $25,000, and in July the remaining noncash assets with a carrying amount of $114,000 realized $84,000. The cash available at the end of each month was distributed promptly. The partners shared net income and losses equally.

Instructions
Prepare a statement of realization and liquidation for Smith, Jones & Webb LLP covering the entire period of liquidation (May through July 2002) and a supporting working paper showing the computation of installment payments to partners as cash becomes available.

(Problem 3.10) Denson, Eastin, and Feller, partners of Denson, Eastin & Feller LLP, shared net income and losses in a 5 : 3 : 2 ratio, respectively. On December 31, 2002, at the end of an unprofitable year, they decided to liquidate the partnership. The partners' capital account credit balances on that date were as follows: Denson, $22,000; Eastin, $24,900; Feller, $15,000. The liabilities in the balance sheet amounted to $30,000, including a loan of $10,000 payable to Denson. The cash balance was $6,000.

The partners planned to realize the noncash assets over a long period and to distribute cash when it became available. All three partners were solvent.

CHECK FIGURE

b. Total amount realized, $61,900.

Instructions
Prepare a cash distribution program for Denson, Eastin & Feller LLP on December 31, 2002, and answer each of the following questions; prepare a working paper to show how you reached your conclusions. (Each question is independent of the others.)

a. If Eastin received $2,000 from the first distribution of cash to partners, how much did Denson and Feller each receive at that time?

b. If Denson received total cash of $20,000 as a result of the liquidation, what was the total amount realized by the partnership on the noncash assets?

c. If Feller received $6,200 on the first distribution of cash to partners, how much did Denson receive at that time?

(Problem 3.11) After several years of successful operation of Lord & Lee LLP, partners Lord and Lee decided to incorporate the partnership and issue common stock to public investors.

On January 2, 2003, Lord-Lee Corporation was organized with authorization to issue 150,000 shares of $10 par common stock, and it issued 20,000 shares for cash to public investors at $16 a share. Lord and Lee agreed to accept shares of common stock at $16 a share in amounts equal to their respective partnership capital account balances, after the adjustments indicated on page 126 and after making cash withdrawals sufficient to avoid the need for issuing less than a multiple of 100 shares to either of the two partners. In payment for such shares, the partnership's net assets were transferred to the corporation and common stock certificates were issued. Accounting records were established for the corporation.

The post-closing trial balance of Lord & Lee LLP on December 31, 2002, follows:

CHECK FIGURES

a. Jan. 2, debit Lord, capital, $72,000; *c.* Total assets, $527,550.

LORD & LEE LLP
Post-Closing Trial Balance
December 31, 2002

	Debit	Credit
Cash	$ 37,000	
Trade accounts receivable	30,000	
Inventories	56,000	
Land	28,000	
Buildings	50,000	
Accumulated depreciation of buildings		$ 17,000
Trade accounts payable		10,000
Lord, capital		63,000
Lee, capital		111,000
Totals	$201,000	$201,000

The partnership contract provided that Lord was to receive 40% of net income or losses and Lee was to receive 60%. The partners approved the following adjustments to the accounting records of the partnership on December 31, 2002:

1. Recognize short-term prepayments of $1,500 and accrued liabilities of $750.
2. Provide an allowance for doubtful accounts of $12,000.
3. Increase the carrying amount of land to current fair value of $45,000.
4. Increase the carrying amount of inventories to replacement cost of $75,000.

Instructions

a. Prepare a journal entry for Lord & Lee LLP on December 31, 2002, to record the foregoing adjustments and on January 2, 2003, to record the liquidation of the partnership.

b. Prepare journal entries on January 2, 2003, to record Lord-Lee Corporation's issuances of common stock to public investors, Lord, and Lee.

c. Prepare a balance sheet for Lord-Lee Corporation on January 2, 2003, after the foregoing transactions and events had been recorded.

Chapter **Four**

Accounting for Branches; Combined Financial Statements

Scope of Chapter

The accounting and reporting for *segments* of a business enterprise—primarily *branches* and *divisions*—are dealt within this chapter. Although branches of an enterprise are not separate legal entities, they are separate economic and accounting entities whose special features necessitate accounting procedures tailored for those features, such as *reciprocal* ledger accounts.

BRANCHES AND DIVISIONS

As a business enterprise grows, it may establish one or more branches to market its products over a large territory. The term *branch* is used to describe a business unit located at some distance from the *home office.* This unit carries merchandise obtained from the home office, makes sales, approves customers' credit, and makes collections from its customers.

A branch may obtain merchandise solely from the home office, or a portion may be purchased from outside suppliers. The cash receipts of the branch often are deposited in a bank account belonging to the home office; the branch expenses then are paid from an *imprest cash fund* or a bank account provided by the home office. As the imprest cash fund is depleted, the branch submits a list of cash payments supported by *vouchers* and receives a check or an electronic or wire transfer from the home office to replenish the fund.

The use of an imprest cash fund gives the home office considerable control over the cash transactions of the branch. However, it is common practice for a large branch to maintain its own bank accounts. The extent of autonomy and responsibility of a branch varies, even among different branches of the same business enterprise.

A segment of a business enterprise also may be operated as a *division,* which generally has more autonomy than a branch. The accounting procedures for a division not organized as a separate corporation *(subsidiary company)* are similar to those used for branches. When a business segment is operated as a separate corporation, consolidated financial statements generally are required. Consolidated financial statements are described in Chapters 6 through 10; accounting and reporting problems for business segments are included in Chapter 13.

START-UP COSTS OF OPENING NEW BRANCHES

The establishment of a branch often requires the incurring of considerable costs before significant revenue may be generated. Operating losses in the first few months are likely. In the past, some business enterprises would capitalize and amortize such ***start-up costs*** on the grounds that such costs are necessary to successful operation at a new location. However, most enterprises recognized start-up costs in connection with the opening of a branch as expenses of the accounting period in which the costs are incurred. The decision should be based on the principle that net income is measured by matching expired costs with realized revenue. Costs that benefit future accounting periods are deferred and allocated to those periods. Seldom is there complete certainty that a new branch will achieve a profitable level of operations in later years. In recognition of this fact, in 1998 the AICPA Accounting Standards Executive Committee issued ***Statement of Position 98-5*** (SOP 98-5), "Reporting on the Costs of Start-Up Activities," which required expensing of all start-up costs, including those associated with ***organizing*** a new entity such as a branch or division.[1]

ACCOUNTING SYSTEM FOR A BRANCH

The accounting system of one business enterprise with branches may provide for a complete set of accounting records at each branch; policies of another such enterprise may keep all accounting records in the home office. For example, branches of drug and grocery chain stores submit daily reports and business documents to the home office, which enters all transactions by branches in computerized accounting records kept in a central location. The home office may not even conduct operations of its own; it may serve only as an accounting and control center for the branches.

A branch may maintain a complete set of accounting records consisting of journals, ledgers, and a chart of accounts similar to those of an independent business enterprise. Financial statements are prepared by the branch accountant and forwarded to the home office. The number and types of ledger accounts, the internal control structure, the form and content of the financial statements, and the accounting policies generally are prescribed by the home office.

This section focuses on a branch operation that maintains a complete set of accounting records. Transactions recorded by a branch should include all controllable expenses and revenue for which the branch manager is responsible. If the branch manager has responsibility over all branch assets, liabilities, revenue, and expenses, the branch accounting records should reflect this responsibility. Expenses such as depreciation often are not subject to control by a branch manager; therefore, both the branch plant assets and the related depreciation ledger accounts generally are maintained by the home office.

---

[1] It is interesting to note that 23 years before the issuance of SOP 98-5, FASB member Walter Schuetze dissented to the issuance of ***Statement of Financial Accounting Standards No. 7,*** "Accounting and Reporting by Development Stage Enterprises," because it did not address the issue of accounting for start-up costs.

Reciprocal Ledger Accounts

The accounting records maintained by a branch include a Home Office ledger account that is credited for all merchandise, cash, or other assets provided by the home office; it is debited for all cash, merchandise, or other assets sent by the branch to the home office or to other branches. The Home Office account is a quasi-ownership equity account that shows the net investment by the home office in the branch. At the end of an accounting period when the branch closes its accounting records, the Income Summary account is closed to the Home Office account. A net income increases the credit balance of the Home Office account; a net loss decreases this balance.

In the home office accounting records, a *reciprocal ledger account* with a title such as Investment in Branch is maintained. This noncurrent asset account is debited for cash, merchandise, and services provided to the branch by the home office, and for net income reported by the branch. It is credited for cash or other assets received from the branch, and for net losses reported by the branch. Thus, the Investment in Branch account reflects the *equity method of accounting.* A separate investment account generally is maintained by the home office for each branch. If there is only one branch, the account title is likely to be Investment in Branch; if there are numerous branches, each account title includes a name or number to identify each branch.

Expenses Incurred by Home Office and Allocated to Branches

Some business enterprises follow a policy of notifying each branch of expenses incurred by the home office on the branch's behalf. As stated on page 128, plant assets located at a branch generally are carried in the home office accounting records. If a plant asset is acquired by the home office for the branch, the journal entry for the acquisition is a debit to an appropriate asset account such as Equipment: Branch and a credit to Cash or an appropriate liability account. If the branch acquires a plant asset, it debits the Home Office ledger account and credits Cash or an appropriate liability account. The home office debits an asset account such as Equipment: Branch and credits its Investment in Branch.

The home office also usually acquires insurance, pays property and other taxes, and arranges for advertising that benefits all branches. Clearly, such expenses as depreciation, property taxes, insurance, and advertising must be considered in determining the profitability of a branch. A policy decision must be made as to whether these expense data are to be retained at the home office or are to be reported to the branches so that the income statement prepared for each branch will give a complete picture of its operations. An expense incurred by the home office and allocated to a branch is recorded by the home office by a debit to Investment in Branch and a credit to an appropriate expense ledger account; the branch debits an expense account and credits Home Office.

If the home office does not make sales, but functions only as an accounting and control center, most or all of its expenses may be allocated to the branches. To facilitate comparison of the operating results of the various branches, the home office may charge each branch interest on the capital invested in that branch. Such interest expense recognized by the branches would be offset by interest revenue recognized by the home office and would not be displayed in the *combined* income statement of the business enterprise as a whole.

Alternative Methods of Billing Merchandise Shipments to Branches

Three alternative methods are available to the home office for billing merchandise shipped to its branches. The shipments may be billed (1) at home office cost, (2) at a percentage above home office cost, or (3) at the branch's retail selling price. The shipment of merchandise to a branch does not constitute a *sale,* because ownership of the merchandise does not change.

Billing *at home office cost* is the simplest procedure and is widely used. It avoids the complication of unrealized gross profit in inventories and permits the financial statements of branches to give a meaningful picture of operations. However, billing merchandise to branches at home office cost attributes all gross profits of the enterprise to the branches, even though some of the merchandise may be manufactured by the home office. Under these circumstances, home office cost may not be the most realistic basis for billing shipments to branches.

Billing shipments to a branch *at a percentage above home office cost* (such as 110% of cost) may be intended to allocate a reasonable gross profit to the home office. When merchandise is billed to a branch at a price above home office cost, *the net income reported by the branch is understated and the ending inventories are overstated for the enterprise as a whole.* Adjustments must be made by the home office to eliminate the excess of billed prices over cost *(intracompany profits)* in the preparation of combined financial statements for the home office and the branch.

Billing shipments to a branch *at branch retail selling prices* may be based on a desire to strengthen internal control over inventories. The Inventories ledger account of the branch shows the merchandise received and sold at retail selling prices. Consequently, the account will show the ending inventories that should be on hand at retail prices. The home office record of shipments to a branch, when considered along with sales reported by the branch, provides a perpetual inventory stated at selling prices. If the physical inventories taken periodically at the branch do not agree with the amounts thus computed, an error or theft may be indicated and should be investigated promptly.

Separate Financial Statements for Branch and for Home Office

A separate income statement and balance sheet should be prepared for a branch so that management of the enterprise may review the operating results and financial position of the branch. The branch's income statement has no unusual features if merchandise is billed to the branch at home office cost. However, if merchandise is billed to the branch at branch retail selling prices, the branch's income statement will show a net loss approximating the amount of operating expenses. The only unusual aspect of the balance sheet for a branch is the use of the Home Office ledger account in lieu of the ownership equity accounts for a separate business enterprise. The separate financial statements prepared for a branch may be revised at the home office to include expenses incurred by the home office allocable to the branch and to show the results of branch operations after elimination of any intracompany profits on merchandise shipments.

Separate financial statements also may be prepared for the home office so that management will be able to appraise the results of its operations and its financial position. However, it is important to emphasize that separate financial statements of the home office and of the branch are prepared *for internal use only;* they do not meet the needs of investors or other external users of financial statements.

Combined Financial Statements for Home Office and Branch

A balance sheet for distribution to creditors, stockholders, and government agencies must show the financial position of a business enterprise having branches as a *single entity.* A convenient starting point in the preparation of a combined balance sheet consists of the adjusted trial balances of the home office and of the branch. A working paper for the combination of these trial balances is illustrated on page 134.

The assets and liabilities of the branch are substituted for the Investment in Branch ledger account included in the home office trial balance. Similar accounts are combined to produce a single total amount for cash, trade accounts receivable, and other assets and liabilities of the enterprise as a whole.

In the preparation of a combined balance sheet, reciprocal ledger accounts are eliminated because they have no significance when the branch and home office report as a single entity. The balance of the Home Office account is offset against the balance of the Investment in Branch account; also, any receivables and payables between the home office and the branch (or between two branches) are eliminated.

The operating results of the enterprise (the home office and all branches) are shown by an income statement in which the revenue and expenses of the branches are combined with corresponding revenue and expenses for the home office. Any intracompany profits or losses are eliminated.

Illustrative Journal Entries for Operations of a Branch

Assume that Smaldino Company bills merchandise to Mason Branch *at home office cost* and that Mason Branch maintains complete accounting records and prepares financial statements. *Both the home office and the branch use the perpetual inventory system.* Equipment used at the branch is carried in the home office accounting records. Certain expenses, such as advertising and insurance, incurred by the home office on behalf of the branch, are billed to the branch. Transactions and events during the first year (2002) of operations of Mason Branch are summarized below (start-up costs are disregarded):

1. Cash of $1,000 was forwarded by the home office to Mason Branch.

2. Merchandise with a home office cost of $60,000 was shipped by the home office to Mason Branch.

3. Equipment was acquired by Mason Branch for $500, to be carried in the home office accounting records. (Other plant assets for Mason Branch generally are acquired by the home office.)

4. Credit sales by Mason Branch amounted to $80,000; the branch's cost of the merchandise sold was $45,000.

5. Collections of trade accounts receivable by Mason Branch amounted to $62,000.

6. Payments for operating expenses by Mason Branch totaled $20,000.

7. Cash of $37,500 was remitted by Mason Branch to the home office.

8. Operating expenses incurred by the home office and charged to Mason Branch totaled $3,000.

FINAL EXAM

These transactions and events are recorded by the home office and by Mason Branch as follows (explanations for the journal entries are omitted):

Typical Home Office and Branch Transactions and Events (Perpetual Inventory System)	Home Office Accounting Records Journal Entries			Mason Branch Accounting Records Journal Entries		
	1. Investment in Mason Branch	1,000		Cash	1,000	
	Cash		1,000	Home Office		1,000
	2. Investment in Mason Branch	60,000		Inventories	60,000	
	Inventories		60,000	Home Office		60,000
	3. Equipment: Mason Branch	500		Home Office	500	
	Investment in Mason Branch		500	Cash		500
	4. None			Trade Accounts Receivable	80,000	
				Cost of Goods Sold	45,000	
				Sales		80,000
				Inventories		45,000
	5. None			Cash	62,000	
				Trade Accounts Receivable		62,000
	6. None			Operating Expenses	20,000	
				Cash		20,000
	7. Cash	37,500				
	Investment in Mason Branch		37,500	Home Office	37,500	
				Cash		37,500
	8. Investment in Mason Branch	3,000		Operating Expenses	3,000	
	Operating Expenses		3,000	Home Office		3,000

If a branch obtains merchandise from outsiders as well as from the home office, the merchandise acquired from the home office may be recorded in a separate Inventories from Home Office ledger account.

In the home office accounting records, the Investment in Mason Branch ledger account has a debit balance of $26,000 [before the accounting records are closed and the branch net income of $12,000 ($80,000 − $45,000 − $20,000 − $3,000 = $12,000) is transferred to the Investment in Mason Branch ledger account], as illustrated on the next page.

Reciprocal Ledger Account in Accounting Records of Home Office Prior to Equity-Method Adjusting Entry

Investment in Mason Branch

Date	Explanation	Debit	Credit	Balance
2002	Cash sent to branch	1,000		1,000 dr
	Merchandise billed to branch at home office cost	60,000		61,000 dr
	Equipment acquired by branch, carried in home office accounting records		500	60,500 dr
	Cash received from branch		37,500	23,000 dr
	Operating expenses billed to branch	3,000		26,000 dr

In the accounting records of Mason Branch, the Home Office ledger account has a credit balance of $26,000 (before the accounting records are closed and the net income of $12,000 is transferred to the Home Office account), as shown below:

Reciprocal Ledger Account in Accounting Records of Mason Branch Prior to Closing Entry

Home Office

Date	Explanation	Debit	Credit	Balance
2002	Cash received from home office		1,000	1,000 cr
	Merchandise received from home office		60,000	61,000 cr
	Equipment acquired	500		60,500 cr
	Cash sent to home office	37,500		23,000 cr
	Operating expenses billed by home office		3,000	26,000 cr

Working Paper for Combined Financial Statements

A working paper for combined financial statements has three purposes: (1) to combine ledger account balances for like revenue, expenses, assets, and liabilities, (2) to eliminate any intracompany profits or losses, and (3) to eliminate the reciprocal accounts.

Assume that the perpetual inventories of $15,000 ($60,000 − $45,000 = $15,000) at the end of 2002 for Mason Branch had been verified by a physical count. The working paper illustrated on page 134 for Smaldino Company is based on the transactions and events illustrated on pages 131 and 132 and additional assumed data for the home office trial balance. All the routine year-end adjusting entries (except the home office entries on page 136) are assumed to have been made, and the working paper is begun with the adjusted trial balances of the home office and Mason Branch. Income taxes are disregarded in this illustration.

Note that the $26,000 debit balance of the Investment in Mason Branch ledger account and the $26,000 credit balance of the Home Office account are the balances *be-fore the respective accounting records are closed,* that is, before the $12,000 net income of Mason Branch is entered in these two reciprocal accounts. In the Eliminations column, elimination (*a*) offsets the balance of the Investment in Mason Branch account against the balance of the Home Office account. *This elimination appears in the working paper only;* it is not entered in the accounting records of either the home office or Mason Branch because its only purpose is to facilitate the preparation of combined financial statements.

Combined Financial Statements Illustrated

The following working paper provides the information for the combined financial statements (excluding a statement of cash flows) of Smaldino Company on page 135.

WORK PAPER

SMALDINO COMPANY
Working Paper for Combined Financial Statements of Home Office and Mason Branch
For Year Ended December 31, 2002
(Perpetual Inventory System: Billings at Cost)

	Adjusted Trial Balances		Eliminations	Combined
	Home Office	Mason Branch		
	Dr (Cr)	Dr (Cr)	Dr (Cr)	Dr (Cr)
Income Statement				
Sales	(400,000)	(80,000)		(480,000)
Cost of goods sold	235,000	45,000		280,000
Operating expenses	90,000	23,000		113,000
Net income (to statement of retained earnings below)	75,000	12,000		87,000
Totals	-0-	-0-		-0-
Statement of Retained Earnings				
Retained earnings, beginning of year	(70,000)			(70,000)
Net (income) (from income statement above)	(75,000)	(12,000)		(87,000)
Dividends declared	40,000			40,000
Retained earnings, end of year (to balance sheet below)				117,000
Totals				-0-
Balance Sheet				
Cash	25,000	5,000		30,000
Trade accounts receivable (net)	39,000	18,000		57,000
Inventories	45,000	15,000		60,000
Investment in Mason Branch	26,000		(a) (26,000)	
Equipment	150,000			150,000
Accumulated depreciation of equipment	(10,000)			(10,000)
Trade accounts payable	(20,000)			(20,000)
Home office		(26,000)	(a) 26,000	
Common stock, $10 par	(150,000)			(150,000)
Retained earnings (from statement of retained earnings above)				(117,000)
Totals	-0-	-0-	-0-	-0-

(a) To eliminate reciprocal ledger account balances.

SMALDINO COMPANY Income Statement For Year Ended December 31, 2002	
Sales	$480,000
Cost of goods sold	280,000
Gross margin on sales	$200,000
Operating expenses	113,000
Net income	$ 87,000
Basic earnings per share of common stock	$ 5.80

SMALDINO COMPANY Statement of Retained Earnings For Year Ended December 31, 2002	
Retained earnings, beginning of year	$ 70,000
Add: Net income	87,000
Subtotal	$157,000
Less: Dividends ($2.67 per share)	40,000
Retained earnings, end of year	$117,000

SMALDINO COMPANY Balance Sheet December 31, 2002		
Assets		
Cash		$ 30,000
Trade accounts receivable (net)		57,000
Inventories		60,000
Equipment	$150,000	
Less: Accumulated depreciation	10,000	140,000
Total assets		$287,000
Liabilities and Stockholders' Equity		
Liabilities		
Trade accounts payable		$ 20,000
Stockholders' equity		
Common stock, $10 par, 15,000 shares authorized,		
issued, and outstanding	$150,000	
Retained earnings	117,000	267,000
Total liabilities and stockholders' equity		$287,000

Home Office Adjusting and Closing Entries and Branch Closing Entries

The home office's equity-method adjusting and closing entries for branch operating results and the branch's closing entries on December 31, 2002, are as follows (explanations for the entries are omitted):

Home Office Accounting Records Adjusting and Closing Entries			Mason Branch Accounting Records Closing Entries		
None			Sales	80,000	
			Cost of Goods Sold		45,000
			Operating Expenses		23,000
			Income Summary		12,000
Investment in Mason Branch	12,000		Income Summary	12,000	
Income: Mason Branch		12,000	Home Office		12,000
Income: Mason Branch	12,000		None		
Income Summary		12,000			

Billing of Merchandise to Branches at Prices above Home Office Cost

As stated on page 130, the home offices of some business enterprises bill merchandise shipped to branches at home office cost plus a markup percentage (or alternatively at branch retail selling prices). Because both these methods involve similar modifications of accounting procedures, a single example illustrates the key points involved, using the illustration for Smaldino Company on pages 131 and 132 with one changed assumption: the home office bills merchandise shipped to Mason Branch at a markup of 50% above home office cost, or $33\frac{1}{3}$% of billed price.[2]

Under this assumption, the journal entries for the first year's events and transactions by the home office and Mason Branch are the same as those presented on page 132 except for the journal entries for shipments of merchandise from the home office to Mason Branch. These shipments ($60,000 cost + 50% markup on cost = $90,000) are recorded under the perpetual inventory system as follows:

Home Office Accounting Records Journal Entries			Mason Branch Accounting Records Journal Entries		
2. Investment in Mason Branch	90,000		Inventories	90,000	
Inventories		60,000	Home Office		90,000
Allowance for Overvaluation of Inventories: Mason Branch		30,000			

In the accounting records of the home office, the Investment in Mason Branch ledger account on page 137 now has a debit balance of $56,000 before the accounting records are closed and the branch net income or loss is entered in the Investment in Mason

---

[2] Billed price = cost + 0.50 cost; therefore, markup on billed price is 0.50/(1 + 0.50), or $33\frac{1}{3}$%.

Branch account. This account is $30,000 larger than the $26,000 balance in the prior illustration (page 133). The increase represents the 50% markup over cost ($60,000) of the merchandise shipped to Mason Branch.

Reciprocal Ledger Account in Accounting Records of Home Office, Prior to Equity-Method Adjusting Entry

Investment in Mason Branch

Date	Explanation	Debit	Credit	Balance
2002	Cash sent to branch	1,000		1,000 dr
	Merchandise billed to branch at markup			
	of 50% over home office cost, or 33⅓%			
	of billed price	90,000		91,000 dr
	Equipment acquired by branch, carried			
	in home office accounting records		500	90,500 dr
	Cash received from branch		37,500	53,000 dr
	Operating expenses billed to branch	3,000		56,000 dr

In the accounting records of Mason Branch, the Home Office ledger account now has a credit balance of $56,000, before the accounting records are closed and the branch net income or loss is entered in the Home Office account, as illustrated below:

Reciprocal Ledger Account in Accounting Records of Mason Branch Prior to Closing Entry

Home Office

Date	Explanation	Debit	Credit	Balance
2002	Cash received from home office		1,000	1,000 cr
	Merchandise received from home office		90,000	91,000 cr
	Equipment acquired	500		90,500 cr
	Cash sent to home office	37,000		53,000 cr
	Operating expenses billed by home office		3,000	56,000 cr

Mason Branch recorded the merchandise received from the home office at billed prices of $90,000; the home office recorded the shipment by credits of $60,000 to Inventories and $30,000 to Allowance for Overvaluation of Inventories: Mason Branch. Use of the allowance account enables the home office to maintain a record of the cost of merchandise shipped to Mason Branch as well as the amount of the unrealized gross profit on the shipments.

At the end of the accounting period, Mason Branch reports its inventories (at billed prices) at $22,500. The cost of these inventories is $15,000 ($22,500 ÷ 1.50 = $15,000). In the home office accounting records, the required balance of the Allowance for Overvaluation of Inventories: Mason Branch ledger account is $7,500 ($22,500 − $15,000 = $7,500); thus, this account balance must be reduced from its present amount of $30,000 to $7,500. The reason for this reduction is that *the 50% markup of billed prices over cost has become realized gross profit to the home office with respect to the merchandise sold by the branch.* Consequently, at the end of the year the home office reduces its allowance for overvaluation of the branch inventories to the $7,500 excess valuation contained in the ending inventories. The debit adjustment of $22,500 in the allowance account is offset by a credit to the Realized Gross Profit: Mason Branch Sales account, because it represents additional gross profit of the home office resulting from sales by the branch.

These matters are illustrated in the home office end-of-period adjusting and closing entries on page 140.

Working Paper When Billings to Branches Are at Prices above Cost

When a home office bills merchandise shipments to branches at prices above home office cost, preparation of the working paper for combined financial statements is facilitated by an analysis of the flow of merchandise to a branch, such as the following for Mason Branch of Smaldino Company:

SMALDINO COMPANY Flow of Merchandise for Mason Branch During 2002			
	Billed Price	**Home Office Cost**	**Markup (50% of Cost; 33⅓ % of Billed Price)**
Beginning inventories			
Add: Shipments from home office	$90,000	$60,000	$30,000
Available for sale	$90,000	$60,000	$30,000
Less: Ending inventories	22,500	15,000	7,500
Cost of goods sold	$67,500	$45,000	$22,500

The Markup column in the foregoing analysis provides the information needed for the Eliminations column in the working paper for combined financial statements below and on page 139.

SMALDINO COMPANY Working Paper for Combined Financial Statements of Home Office and Mason Branch For Year Ended December 31, 2002 (Perpetual Inventory System: Billings above Cost)				
	Adjusted Trial Balances		**Eliminations**	**Combined**
	Home Office	**Mason Branch**		
	Dr (Cr)	*Dr (Cr)*	*Dr (Cr)*	*Dr (Cr)*
Income Statement				
Sales	(400,000)	(80,000)		(480,000)
Cost of goods sold	235,000	67,500	(a) (22,500)	280,000
Operating expenses	90,000	23,000		113,000
Net income (loss) (to statement of retained earnings below)	75,000	(10,500)	(b) 22,500	87,000
Totals	-0-	-0-		-0-
Statement of Retained Earnings				
Retained earnings, beginning of year	(70,000)			(70,000)
Net (income) loss (from income statement above)	(75,000)	10,500	(b) (22,500)	(87,000)
Dividends declared	40,000			40,000
Retained earnings, end of year (to balance sheet below)				117,000
Totals				-0-

(continued)

SMALDINO COMPANY
Working Paper for Combined Financial Statements of Home Office and Mason Branch (concluded)
For Year Ended December 31, 2002
(Perpetual Inventory System: Billings above Cost)

| | Adjusted Trial Balances | | Eliminations | Combined |
| | Home Office | Mason Branch | | |
	Dr (Cr)	*Dr (Cr)*	*Dr (Cr)*	*Dr (Cr)*
Balance Sheet				
Cash	25,000	5,000		30,000
Trade accounts receivable (net)	39,000	18,000		57,000
Inventories	45,000	22,500	(a) (7,500)	60,000
Investment in Mason Branch	56,000		(c) (56,000)	
Allowance for overvaluation of inventories:				
Mason Branch	(30,000)		(a) 30,000	
Equipment	150,000			150,000
Accumulated depreciation of equipment	(10,000)			(10,000)
Trade accounts payable	(20,000)			(20,000)
Home office		(56,000)	(c) 56,000	
Common stock, $10 par	(150,000)			(150,000)
Retained earnings (from statement of				
retained earnings above)				(117,000)
Totals	-0-	-0-	-0-	-0-

(a) To reduce ending inventories and cost of goods sold of branch to cost, and to eliminate unadjusted balance of Allowance of Overvaluation of Inventories: Mason Branch ledger account.
(b) To increase income of home office by portion of merchandise markup that was realized by branch sales.
(c) To eliminate reciprocal ledger account balances.

The foregoing working paper differs from the working paper on page 134 by the inclusion of an elimination to restate the ending inventories of the branch to cost. Also, the income reported by the home office is adjusted by the $22,500 of merchandise markup that was realized as a result of sales by the branch. As stated on page 133, the amounts in the Eliminations column appear only in the working paper. The amounts represent a mechanical step to aid in the preparation of combined financial statements and are not entered in the accounting records of either the home office or the branch.

Combined Financial Statements

Because the amounts in the Combined column of the working paper on page 138 and above are the same as in the working paper prepared when the merchandise shipments to the branch were billed at home office cost, the combined financial statements are identical to those illustrated on page 135.

Home Office Adjusting and Closing Entries and Branch Closing Entries

The December 31, 2002, adjusting and closing entries of the home office are illustrated on page 140.

**End-of-Period Home Office
Adjusting and Closing Entries**

**Home Office Accounting Records
Adjusting and Closing Entries**

Income: Mason Branch	10,500	
Investment in Mason Branch		10,500
To record net loss reported by branch.		
Allowance for Overvaluation of Inventories: Mason Branch	22,500	
Realized Gross Profit: Mason Branch Sales		22,500
To reduce allowance to amount by which ending inventories of branch exceed cost.		
Realized Gross Profit: Mason Branch Sales	22,500	
Income: Mason Branch		10,500
Income Summary		12,000
To close branch net loss and realized gross profit to Income Summary ledger account. (Income tax effects are disregarded.)		

After the foregoing journal entries have been posted, the ledger accounts in the home office general ledger used to record branch operations are as follows:

**End-of-Period Balances
in Accounting Records
of Home Office**

Investment in Mason Branch

Date	Explanation	Debit	Credit	Balance
2002	Cash sent to branch	1,000		1,000 dr
	Merchandise billed to branch at markup of 50% above home office cost, or 33⅓% of billed price	90,000		91,000 dr
	Equipment acquired by branch, carried in home office accounting records		500	90,500 dr
	Cash received from branch		37,500	53,000 dr
	Operating expenses billed to branch	3,000		56,000 dr
	Net loss for 2002 reported by branch		10,500	45,500 dr

Allowance for Overvaluation of Inventories: Mason Branch

Date	Explanation	Debit	Credit	Balance
2002	Markup on merchandise shipped to branch during 2002 (50% of cost)		30,000	30,000 cr
	Realization of 50% markup on merchandise sold by branch during 2002	22,500		7,500 cr

End-of-Period Balances in Accounting Records of Home Office (concluded)

Realized Gross Profit: Mason Branch Sales

Date	Explanation	Debit	Credit	Balance
2002	Realization of 50% markup on merchandise sold by branch during 2002		22,500	22,500 cr
	Closing entry	22,500		-0-

Income: Mason Branch

Date	Explanation	Debit	Credit	Balance
2002	Net loss for 2002 reported by branch	10,500		10,500 dr
	Closing entry		10,500	-0-

In the **separate** balance sheet for the home office, the $7,500 credit balance of the Allowance of Overvaluation of Inventories: Mason Branch ledger account is deducted from the $45,500 debit balance of the Investment in Mason Branch account, thus reducing the carrying amount of the investment account to a cost basis with respect to shipments of merchandise to the branch. In the **separate** income statement for the home office, the $22,500 realized gross profit on Mason Branch sales may be displayed following gross margin on sales, $165,000 ($400,000 sales − $235,000 cost of goods sold = $165,000).

The closing entries for the branch at the end of 2002 are as follows:

Closing Entries for Mason Branch (Perpetual Inventory System)

Mason Branch Accounting Records
Closing Entries

Sales	80,000	
Income Summary	10,500	
Cost of Goods Sold		67,500
Operating Expenses		23,000
To close revenue and expense ledger accounts.		
Home Office	10,500	
Income Summary		10,500
To close the net loss in the Income Summary account to the Home Office account.		

After these closing entries have been posted by the branch, the following Home Office ledger account in the accounting records of Mason Branch has a credit balance of $45,500, the same as the debit balance of the Investment in Mason Branch account in the accounting records of the home office:

Compare this Ledger Account with Investment in Mason Branch Account

Home Office

Date	Explanation	Debit	Credit	Balance
2002	Cash received from home office		1,000	1,000 cr
	Merchandise received from home office		90,000	91,000 cr
	Equipment acquired	500		90,500 cr
	Cash sent to home office	37,500		53,000 cr
	Operating expenses billed by home office		3,000	56,000 cr
	Net loss for 2002	10,500		45,500 cr

Treatment of Beginning Inventories Priced above Cost

The working paper on pages 138–139 shows how the ending inventories and the related allowance for overvaluation of inventories were handled. However, because 2002 was the first year of operations for Mason Branch, no beginning inventories were involved.

Perpetual Inventory System

Under the perpetual inventory system, no special problems arise when the beginning inventories of the branch include an element of unrealized gross profit. The working paper eliminations would be similar to those illustrated on pages 138–139.

Periodic Inventory System

The illustration of a second year of operations (2003) of Smaldino Company demonstrates the handling of beginning inventories carried by Mason Branch at an amount above home office cost. However, assume that both the home office and Mason Branch adopted the periodic inventory system in 2003. When the periodic inventory system is used, the home office credits Shipments to Branch (an offset account to Purchases) for the home office cost of merchandise shipped and Allowance for Overvaluation of Inventories for the markup over home office cost. The branch debits Shipments from Home Office (analogous to a Purchases account) for the billed price of merchandise received.

The beginning inventories for 2003 were carried by Mason Branch at $22,500, or 150% of the cost of $15,000 ($15,000 × 1.50 = $22,500). Assume that during 2003 the home office shipped merchandise to Mason Branch that cost $80,000 and was billed at $120,000, and that Mason Branch sold for $150,000 merchandise that was billed at $112,500. The journal entries (explanations omitted) to record the shipments and sales under the periodic inventory system are illustrated below:

	Home Office Accounting Records Journal Entries		Mason Branch Accounting Records Journal Entries	
Journal Entries for Shipments to Branch at a Price above Home Office Cost (Periodic Inventory System)				
	Investment in Mason Branch	120,000	Shipments from Home Office	120,000
	Shipments to Mason Branch	80,000	Home Office	120,000
	Allowance for Overvaluation of Inventories: Mason Branch	40,000		
	None		Cash (or Trade Accounts Receivable)	150,000
			Sales	150,000

The branch inventories at the end of 2003 amounted to $30,000 at billed prices, representing cost of $20,000 plus a 50% markup on cost ($20,000 × 1.50 = $30,000). The flow of merchandise for Mason Branch during 2003 is summarized on page 143.

SMALDINO COMPANY Flow of Merchandise for Mason Branch During 2003			
	Billed Price	Home Office Cost	Markup (50% of Cost; 33⅓% of Billed Price)
Beginning inventories (from page 138)	$ 22,500	$ 15,000	$ 7,500
Add: Shipments from home office	120,000	80,000	40,000
Available for sale	$142,500	$ 95,000	$ 47,500
Less: Ending inventories	(30,000)	(20,000)	(10,000)
Cost of goods sold	$112,500	$ 75,000	$ 37,500

The activities of the branch for 2003 and end-of-period adjusting and closing entries are reflected in the four home office ledger accounts below and on page 144.

End-of-Period Balances in Accounting Records of Home Office

Investment in Mason Branch

Date	Explanation	Debit	Credit	Balance
2003	Balance, Dec. 31, 2002 (from page 140)			45,500 dr
	Merchandise billed to branch at markup of 50% above home office cost, or 33⅓% of billed price	120,000		165,500 dr
	Cash received from branch		113,000	52,500 dr
	Operating expenses billed to branch	4,500		57,000 dr
	Net income for 2003 reported by branch	10,000		67,000 dr

Allowance for Overvaluation of Inventories: Mason Branch

Date	Explanation	Debit	Credit	Balance
2003	Balance, Dec. 31, 2002 (from page 140)			7,500 cr
	Markup on merchandise shipped to branch during 2003 (50% of cost)		40,000	47,500 cr
	Realization of 50% markup on merchandise sold by branch during 2003	37,500		10,000 cr

Realized Gross Profit: Mason Branch Sales

Date	Explanation	Debit	Credit	Balance
2003	Realization of 50% markup on merchandise sold by branch during 2003		37,500	37,500 cr
	Closing entry	37,500		-0-

Income: Mason Branch

Date	Explanation	Debit	Credit	Balance
2003	Net income for 2003 reported by branch		10,000	10,000 cr
	Closing entry	10,000		-0-

In the accounting records of the home office at the end of 2003, the balance required in the Allowance for Overvaluation of Inventories: Mason Branch ledger account is $10,000, that is, the billed price of $30,000 less cost of $20,000 for merchandise in the branch's ending inventories. Therefore, the allowance account balance is reduced from $47,500 to $10,000. This reduction of $37,500 represents the 50% markup on merchandise above cost that was realized by Mason Branch during 2003 and is credited to the Realized Gross Profit: Mason Branch Sales account.

The Home Office account in the branch general ledger shows the following activity and closing entry for 2003:

Home Office

Date	Explanation	Debit	Credit	Balance
2003	Balance, Dec. 31, 2002 (from page 141)			45,500 cr
	Merchandise received from home office		120,000	165,500 cr
	Cash sent to home office	113,000		52,500 cr
	Operating expenses billed by home office		4,500	57,000 cr
	Net income for 2003		10,000	67,000 cr

The working paper for combined financial statements under the periodic inventory system, which reflects pre-adjusting and pre-closing balances for the reciprocal ledger accounts and the Allowance for Overvaluation of Inventories: Mason Branch account, is on page 145.

Reconciliation of Reciprocal Ledger Accounts

At the end of an accounting period, the balance of the Investment in Branch ledger account in the accounting records of the home office may not agree with the balance of the Home Office account in the accounting records of the branch because certain transactions may have been recorded by one office but not by the other. The situation is comparable to that of reconciling the ledger account for Cash in Bank with the balance in the monthly bank statement. The lack of agreement between the reciprocal ledger account balances causes no difficulty during an accounting period, but at the end of each period the reciprocal account balances must be brought into agreement before combined financial statements are prepared.

As an illustration of the procedure for reconciling reciprocal ledger account balances at year-end, assume that the home office and branch accounting records of Mercer Company on December 31, 2002 contain the data on page 146.

SMALDINO COMPANY
Working Paper for Combined Financial Statements of Home Office and Mason Branch
For Year Ended December 31, 2003
(Periodic Inventory System: Billings above Cost)

	Adjusted Trial Balances		Eliminations	Combined
	Home Office	Mason Branch		
	Dr (Cr)	Dr (Cr)	Dr (Cr)	Dr (Cr)
Income Statement				
Sales	(500,000)	(150,000)		(650,000)
Inventories, Dec. 31, 2002	45,000	22,500	(b) (7,500)	60,000
Purchases	400,000			400,000
Shipments to Mason Branch	(80,000)		(a) 80,000	
Shipments from home office		120,000	(a) (120,000)	
Inventories, Dec. 31, 2003	(70,000)	(30,000)	(c) 10,000	(90,000)
Operating expenses	120,000	27,500		147,500
Net income (to statement of retained earnings below)	85,000	10,000	(d) 37,500	132,500
Totals	-0-	-0-		-0-
Statement of Retained Earnings				
Retained earnings, beginning of year (from page 138)	(117,000)			(117,000)
Net (income) (from income statement above)	(85,000)	(10,000)	(d) (37,500)	(132,500)
Dividends declared	60,000			60,000
Retained earnings, end of year (to balance sheet below)				189,500
Total				-0-
Balance Sheet				
Cash	30,000	9,000		39,000
Trade accounts receivable (net)	64,000	28,000		92,000
Inventories, Dec. 31, 2003	70,000	30,000	(c) (10,000)	90,000
Allowance for overvaluation of inventories: Mason Branch	(47,500)		{(a) 40,000} {(b) 7,500}	
Investment in Mason Branch	57,000		(e) (57,000)	
Equipment	158,000			158,000
Accumulated depreciation of equipment	(15,000)			(15,000)
Trade accounts payable	(24,500)			(24,500)
Home office		(57,000)	(e) 57,000	
Common stock, $10 par	(150,000)			(150,000)
Retained earnings (from statement of retained earnings above)				(189,500)
Totals	-0-	-0-	-0-	-0-

(a) To eliminate reciprocal ledger accounts for merchandise shipments.
(b) To reduce beginning inventories of branch to cost.
(c) To reduce ending inventories of branch to cost.
(d) To increase income of home office by portion of merchandise markup that was realized by branch sales.
(e) To eliminate reciprocal ledger account balances.

Reciprocal Ledger Accounts Before Adjustments

Investment in Arvin Branch (in accounting records of Home Office)

Date	Explanation	Debit	Credit	Balance
2002				
Nov. 30	Balance			62,500 dr
Dec. 10	Cash received from branch		20,000	42,500 dr
27	Collection of branch trade accounts receivable		1,000	41,500 dr
29	Merchandise shipped to branch	8,000		49,500 dr

Home Office (in accounting records of Arvin Branch)

Date	Explanation	Debit	Credit	Balance
2002				
Nov. 30	Balance			62,500 cr
Dec. 7	Cash sent to home office	20,000		42,500 cr
28	Acquired equipment	3,000		39,500 cr
30	Collection of home office trade accounts receivable		2,000	41,500 cr

Comparison of the two reciprocal ledger accounts discloses four reconciling items, described as follows:

1. **A debit of $8,000 in the Investment in Arvin Branch ledger account without a related credit in the Home Office account.**

   On December 29, 2002, the home office shipped merchandise costing $8,000 to the branch. The home office debits its reciprocal ledger account with the branch on the date merchandise is shipped, but the branch credits its reciprocal account with the home office when the merchandise is received a few days later. The required journal entry on December 31, 2002, in the ***branch accounting records,*** assuming use of the perpetual inventory system, appears below:

Branch Journal Entry for Merchandise in Transit from Home Office

Inventories in Transit	8,000	
Home Office		8,000
To record shipment of merchandise in transit from home office.		

   In taking a physical inventory on December 31, 2002, the branch must add to the inventories on hand the $8,000 of merchandise in transit. When the merchandise is received in 2003, the branch debits Inventories and credits Inventories in Transit.

2. **A credit of $1,000 in the Investment in Arvin Branch ledger account without a related debit in the Home Office account.**

   On December 27, 2002, trade accounts receivable of the branch were collected by the home office. The collection was recorded by the home office by a debit to Cash and a credit to Investment in Arvin Branch. No journal entry was made by Arvin Branch; therefore, the following journal entry is required ***in the accounting records of Arvin Branch*** on December 31, 2002:

Branch Journal Entry for Trade Accounting Receivable Collected by Home Office

Home Office	1,000	
Trade Accounts Receivable		1,000
To record collection of accounts receivable by home office.		

3. **A debit of $3,000 in the Home Office ledger account without a related credit in the Investment in Arvin Branch account.**

On December 28, 2002, the branch acquired equipment for $3,000. Because the equipment used by the branch is carried in the accounting records of the home office, the journal entry made by the branch was a debit to Home Office and a credit to Cash. No journal entry was made by the home office; therefore, the following journal entry is required on December 31, 2002, *in the accounting records of the home office:*

Home Office Journal Entry for Equipment Acquired by Branch

Equipment: Arvin Branch	3,000	
Investment in Arvin Branch		3,000
To record equipment acquired by branch.		

4. **A credit of $2,000 in the Home Office ledger account without a related debit in the Investment in Arvin Branch account.**

On December 30, 2002, trade accounts receivable of the home office were collected by Arvin Branch. The collection was recorded by Arvin Branch by a debit to Cash and a credit to Home Office. No journal entry was made by the home office; therefore, the following journal entry is required *in the accounting records of the home office* on December 31, 2002:

Home Office Journal Entry for Trade Accounts Receivable Collected by Branch

Investment in Arvin Branch	2,000	
Trade Accounts Receivable		2,000
To record collection of accounts receivable by Arvin Branch.		

The effect of the foregoing end-of-period journal entries is to update the reciprocal ledger accounts, as shown by the following reconciliation:

MERCER COMPANY—HOME OFFICE AND ARVIN BRANCH		
Reconciliation of Reciprocal Ledger Accounts		
December 31, 2002		
	Investment in Arvin Branch Account (in home office accounting records)	Home Office Account (in branch accounting records)
Balances before adjustments	$49,500 dr	$41,500 cr
Add: (1) Merchandise shipped to branch by home office		8,000
(4) Home office trade accounts receivable collected by branch	2,000	
Less: (2) Branch trade accounts receivable collected by home office		(1,000)
(3) Equipment acquired by branch	(3,000)	
Adjusted balances	$48,500 dr	$48,500 cr

Transactions between Branches

Efficient operations may on occasion require that merchandise or other assets be transferred from one branch to another. Generally, a branch does not carry a reciprocal ledger account with another branch but records the transfer in the Home Office ledger account. For example, if Alba Branch ships merchandise to Boro Branch, Alba Branch debits Home Office and credits Inventories (assuming that the perpetual inventory system is used). On receipt of the merchandise, Boro Branch debits Inventories and credits Home Office. The home office records the transfer between branches by a debit to Investment in Boro Branch and a credit to Investment in Alba Branch.

The transfer of merchandise from one branch to another does not justify increasing the carrying amount of inventories by the freight costs incurred because of the indirect routing. The amount of freight costs properly included in inventories at a branch is limited to the cost of shipping the merchandise *directly* from the home office to its present location. Excess freight costs are recognized as expenses of the home office.

To illustrate the accounting for excess freight costs on interbranch transfers of merchandise, assume the following data. The home office shipped merchandise costing $6,000 to Dana Branch and paid freight costs of $400. Subsequently, the home office instructed Dana Branch to transfer this merchandise to Evan Branch. Freight costs of $300 were paid by Dana Branch to carry out this order. If the merchandise had been shipped directly from the home office to Evan Branch, the freight costs would have been $500. The journal entries required in the three sets of accounting records (assuming that the perpetual inventory system is used) are as follows:

In Accounting Records of *Home Office:*

Investment in Dana Branch	6,400	
Inventories		6,000
Cash		400
To record shipment of merchandise and payment of freight costs.		
Investment in Evan Branch	6,500	
Excess Freight Expense—Interbranch Transfers	200	
Investment in Dana Branch		6,700
To record transfer of merchandise from Dana Branch to Evan Branch under instruction of home office. Interbranch freight of $300 paid by Dana Branch caused total freight costs on this merchandise to exceed direct shipment costs by $200 ($400 + $300 − $500 = $200).		

In Accounting Records of *Dana Branch:*

Freight In (or Inventories)	400	
Inventories	6,000	
Home Office		6,400
To record receipt of merchandise from home office with freight costs paid in advance by home office.		

Home Office	6,700	
Inventories		6,000
Freight In (or Inventories)		400
Cash		300

To record transfer of merchandise to Evan Branch under instruction of home office and payment of freight costs of $300.

In Accounting Records of *Evan Branch*:

Inventories	6,000	
Freight In (or Inventories)	500	
Home Office		6,500

To record receipt of merchandise from Dana Branch transferred under instruction of home office and normal freight costs billed by home office.

Recognizing excess freight costs on merchandise transferred from one branch to another as expenses of the home office is an example of the accounting principle that expenses and losses should be given prompt recognition. The excess freight costs from such shipments generally result from inefficient planning of original shipments and should not be included in inventories.

In recognizing excess freight costs of interbranch transfers as expenses attributable to the home office, the assumption was that the home office makes the decisions directing all shipments. If branch managers are given authority to order transfers of merchandise between branches, the excess freight costs are recognized as expenses attributable to the branches whose managers authorized the transfers.

SEC ENFORCEMENT ACTION DEALING WITH WRONGFUL APPLICATION OF ACCOUNTING STANDARDS FOR DIVISIONS

The SEC's *AAER 35*, "Securities and Exchange Commission v. Stauffer Chemical Company" (August 13, 1984), describes a federal court's entry of a permanent injunction against a corporation engaged in the manufacture and sale of chemicals and chemical-related products. The SEC found that the corporation had overstated its earnings by means of three major misstatements, one of which was the failure to eliminate $1.1 million of intracompany profits in inventories shipped from one of the corporation's divisions to another division. The court also ordered the corporation to file timely with the SEC a *Form 8-K,* "Current Report," describing its restatement of its previously reported revenue and earnings for the effects of the three major misstatements.

Review Questions	1. Some branches maintain complete accounting records and prepare financial statements much the same as an autonomous business enterprise. Other branches perform only limited accounting functions, with most accounting activity concentrated in the home office. Assuming that a branch has a complete set of accounting records, what criterion or principle would you suggest be used in deciding whether various

types of expenses applicable to the branch should be recognized by the home office or by the branch?

2. Explain the use of *reciprocal ledger accounts* in home office and branch accounting systems in conjunction with the periodic inventory system.

3. The president of Sandra Company informs you that a branch is being opened and requests your advice: "I have been told that we may bill merchandise shipped to the branch at cost, at branch retail selling prices, or anywhere in between. Do certified public accountants really have that much latitude in the application of generally accepted accounting principles?"

4. Jesse Corporation operates 10 branches in addition to its home office and bills merchandise shipped by the home office to the branches at 10% above home office cost. All plant assets are carried in the home office accounting records. The home office also conducts an advertising program that benefits all branches. Each branch maintains its own accounting records and prepares separate financial statements. In the home office, the accounting department prepares financial statements for the home office and combined financial statements for the enterprise as a whole.

   Explain the purpose of the financial statements prepared by the branches, the home office financial statements, and the combined financial statements.

5. The accounting policies of Armenia Company provide that equipment used by its branches is to be carried in the accounting records of the home office. Acquisitions of new equipment may be made either by the home office or by the branches with the approval of the home office. Slauson Branch, with the approval of the home office, acquired equipment at a cost of $17,000. Describe the journal entries for the Slauson Branch and the home office to record the acquisition of the equipment.

6. Explain the use of and journal entries for a home office's Allowance for Overvaluation of Inventories: Branch ledger account.

7. The reciprocal ledger account balances of Meadow Company's branch and home office are not in agreement at year-end. What factors might have caused this?

8. Ralph Company operates a number of branches but centralizes its accounting records in the home office and maintains control of branch operations. The home office found that Ford Branch had an ample supply of a certain item of merchandise but that Gates Branch was almost out of the item. Therefore, the home office instructed Ford Branch to ship merchandise with a cost of $5,000 to Gates Branch. What journal entry should Ford Branch make, and what principle should guide the treatment of freight costs? (Assume that Ford Branch uses the perpetual inventory system.)

Exercises

(Exercise 4.1)   Select the best answer for each of the following multiple-choice questions:

1. May the Investment in Branch ledger account of a home office be accounted for by the:

	Cost Method of Accounting?	Equity Method of Accounting?
a.	Yes	Yes
b.	Yes	No
c.	No	Yes
d.	No	No

2. Which of the following generally is not a method of billing merchandise shipments by a home office to a branch?

   a. Billing at cost.
   b. Billing at a percentage below cost.
   c. Billing at a percentage above cost.
   d. Billing at retail selling prices.

3. A branch journal entry debiting Home Office and crediting Cash may be prepared for:

   a. The branch's transmittal of cash to the home office only.
   b. The branch's acquisition for cash of plant assets to be carried in the home office accounting records only.
   c. Either *a* or *b*.
   d. Neither *a* nor *b*.

4. A home office's Allowance for Overvaluation of Inventories: Branch ledger account, which has a credit balance, is:

   a. An asset valuation account.
   b. A liability account.
   c. An equity account.
   d. A revenue account.

5. Does a branch use a Shipments from Home Office ledger account under the:

	Perpetual Inventory System?	Periodic Inventory System?
a.	Yes	Yes
b.	Yes	No
c.	No	Yes
d.	No	No

6. A journal entry debiting Cash in Transit and crediting Investment in Branch is required for:

   a. The home office to record the mailing of a check to the branch early in the accounting period.
   b. The branch to record the mailing of a check to the home office early in the accounting period.
   c. The home office to record the mailing of a check by the branch on the last day of the accounting period.
   d. The branch to record the mailing of a check to the home office on the last day of the accounting period.

7. For a home office that uses the periodic inventory system of accounting for shipments of merchandise to the branch, the credit balance of the Shipments to Branch ledger account is displayed in the home office's separate:

   a. Income statement as an offset to Purchases.
   b. Balance sheet as an offset to Investment in Branch.
   c. Balance sheet as an offset to Inventories.
   d. Income statement as revenue.

8. If the home office maintains accounts in its general ledger for a branch's plant assets, the branch debits its acquisition of office equipment to:

   a. Home Office.
   b. Office Equipment.
   c. Payable to Home Office.
   d. Office Equipment Carried by Home Office.

9. In a working paper for combined financial statements of the home office and the branch of a business enterprise, an elimination that debits Shipments to Branch and credits Shipments from Home Office is required under:
    a. The periodic inventory system only.
    b. The perpetual inventory system only.
    c. Both the periodic inventory system and the perpetual inventory system.
    d. Neither the periodic inventory system nor the perpetual inventory system.

10. The appropriate journal entry (explanation omitted) for the home office to recognize the branch's expenditure of $1,000 for equipment to be carried in the home office accounting records is:

a. Equipment	1,000	
Investment in Branch		1,000
b. Home Office	1,000	
Equipment		1,000
c. Investment in Branch	1,000	
Cash		1,000
d. Equipment: Branch	1,000	
Investment in Branch		1,000

11. On January 31, 2002, East Branch of Lyle Company, which uses the perpetual inventory system, prepared the following journal entry:

Inventories in Transit	10,000	
Home Office		10,000
To record shipment of merchandise in transit from home office.		

When the merchandise is received on February 4, 2002, East Branch should:
    a. Prepare no journal entry.
    b. Debit Inventories and credit Home Office, $10,000.
    c. Debit Home Office and credit Inventories in Transit, $10,000.
    d. Debit Inventories and credit Inventories in Transit, $10,000.

12. If a home office bills merchandise shipments to the branch at a markup of 20% on cost, the markup on billed price is:
    a. $16\frac{2}{3}\%$.
    b. 20%.
    c. 25%
    d. Some other percentage.

13. The appropriate journal entry (explanation omitted) in the accounting records of the home office to record a $10,000 cash remittance in transit from the branch at the end of an accounting period is:

a. Cash	10,000	
Cash in Transit		10,000
b. Cash in Transit	10,000	
Investment in Branch		10,000
c. Cash	10,000	
Home Office		10,000
d. Cash in Transit	10,000	
Cash		10,000

(Exercise 4.2) On September 1, 2002, Pasadena Company established a branch in San Marino. Following are the first three transactions between the home office and San Marino branch of Pasadena Company:

Sept. 1 Home office sent $10,000 to the branch for an imprest bank account.
2 Home office shipped merchandise costing $60,000 to the branch, billed at a markup of 20% on billed price.

3 Branch acquired office equipment for $3,000, to be carried in the home office accounting records.

Both the home office and the San Marino branch of Pasadena Company use the perpetual inventory system.
Prepare journal entries (omit explanations) for the foregoing transactions:

a. In the accounting records of the home office.
b. In the accounting records of the San Marino branch.

(Exercise 4.3) On September 1, 2002, Western Company established the Eastern Branch. Separate accounting records were set up for the branch. Both the home office and the Eastern Branch use the periodic inventory system. Among the intracompany transactions were the following:

Sept. 1 Home office mailed a check for $50,000 to the branch. The check was received by the branch on September 3.
4 Home office shipped merchandise costing $95,000 to the branch at a billed price of $125,000. The branch received the merchandise on September 8.
11 The branch acquired a truck for $34,200. The home office maintains the plant assets of the branch in its accounting records.

Prepare journal entries (omit explanations) for the foregoing intracompany transactions in the accounting records of (*a*) the home office and (*b*) the Eastern Branch.

(Exercise 4.4) Among the journal entries of the home office of Watt Corporation for the month of January, 2002, were the following:

2002			
Jan. 2	Investment in Wilshire Branch	100,000	
	Inventories		80,000
	Allowance for Overvaluation of Inventories: Wilshire Branch		20,000
	To record merchandise shipped to branch.		
18	Equipment: Wilshire Branch	5,000	
	Investment in Wilshire Branch		5,000
	To record acquisition of equipment by branch for cash.		
31	Investment in Wilshire Branch	8,000	
	Operating Expenses		8,000
	To record allocation of operating expenses to branch.		

Prepare related journal entries for the Wilshire Branch of Watt Corporation; the branch uses the perpetual inventory system.

(Exercise 4.5)   Among the journal entries for business transactions and events of the Hoover Street Branch of Usc Company during January, 2002, were the following:

Jan. 12	Inventories	60,000	
	Home Office		60,000
	To record the receipt of merchandise shipped Jan. 10 from the home office and billed at a markup of 20% on billed price.		
25	Cash	25,000	
	Home Office		25,000
	To record collection of trade accounts receivable of home office.		
31	Operating Expenses	18,000	
	Home Office		18,000
	To record operating expenses allocated by home office.		

Prepare appropriate journal entries for the home office of Usc Company.

(Exercise 4.6)   Among the journal entries of the home office of Turbo Company for the month ended August 31, 2002, were the following:

2002			
Aug. 6	Investment in Lido Branch	10,000	
	Cash		10,000
	To record payment of account payable of branch.		
14	Cash	6,000	
	Investment in Lido Branch		6,000
	To record collection of trade account receivable of branch.		
22	Equipment: Lido Branch	20,000	
	Investment in Lido Branch		20,000
	To record branch acquisition of equipment for cash, to be carried in home office accounting records.		

Prepare appropriate journal entries (omit explanations) for Lido Branch of Turbo Company.

(Exercise 4.7)   Prepare journal entries in the accounting records of both the home office and the Exeter Branch of Wardell Company to record each of the following transactions or events (omit explanations):

a. Home office transferred cash of $5,000 and merchandise (at home office cost) of $10,000 to the branch. Both the home office and the branch use the perpetual inventory system.

b. Home office allocated operating expenses of $1,500 to the branch.

c. Exeter Branch informed the home office that it had collected $416 on a note payable to the home office. Principal amount of the note was $400.

d. Exeter Branch made sales of $12,500, terms 2/10, n/30, and incurred operating expenses of $2,500. The cost of goods sold was $8,000, and the operating expenses were paid in cash.

e. Exeter Branch had a net income of $500. (Debit Income Summary in the accounting records of the branch.)

(Exercise 4.8) Leland Company has a policy of accounting for all plant assets of its branches in the accounting records of the home office. Contrary to this policy, the accountant for Davis Branch prepared the following journal entries for the equipment acquired by Davis Branch at the direction of the home office:

2002			
Aug. 1	Equipment	20,000	
	Cash		20,000
	To record acquisition of equipment with an economic life of 10 years and a residual value of $2,000.		
Dec.31	Depreciation Expense	750	
	Accumulated Depreciation of Equipment		750
	To recognize depreciation of equipment by the straight-line method ($18,000 × $^5\!/_{120}$ = $750).		

Prepare appropriate journal entries for Davis Branch and the home office on December 31, 2002, the end of the fiscal year, assuming that the home office had prepared no journal entries for the equipment acquired by the Davis Branch on August 1, 2002. Neither set of accounting records has been closed.

(Exercise 4.9) The home office of Figueroa Company ships merchandise to the Nine-Zero Branch at a billed price that includes a markup on home office cost of 25%. The Inventories ledger account of the branch, under the perpetual inventory system, showed a December 31, 2002, debit balance, $120,000; a debit for a shipment received January 16, 2003, $500,000; total credits for goods sold during January, 2003, $520,000; and a January 31, 2003, debit balance, $100,000 (all amounts are home office billed prices).

Prepare a working paper for the home office of Figueroa Company to analyze the flow of merchandise to Nine-Zero Branch during January, 2003.

CHECK FIGURE

Markup in cost of goods sold, $104,000.

(Exercise 4.10) The flow of merchandise from the home office of Southern Cal Company to its 32 Branch during the month of April, 2002, may be analyzed as follows:

CHECK FIGURE

Apr. 30 balance, $20,000 credit.

SOUTHERN CAL COMPANY
Flow of Merchandise for 32 Branch
For Month Ended April 30, 2002

	Billed Price	Cost	Markup
Beginning inventories	$180,000	$150,000	$ 30,000
Add: Shipment from home office (Apr. 16)	540,000	450,000	90,000
Available for sale	$720,000	$600,000	$120,000
Less: Ending inventories	120,000	100,000	20,000
Cost of goods sold	$600,000	$500,000	$100,000

From the foregoing information, reconstruct a three-column ledger account Allowance for Overvaluation of Inventories: 32 Branch for the home office of Southern Cal Company, beginning with the March 31, 2002, balance, $30,000 credit.

(Exercise 4.11) On May 31, 2002, Portland Street Branch (the only branch) of Trapp Company reported a net income of $80,000 for May, 2002, and a $240,000 ending inventory at billed price of merchandise received from the home office at a 25% markup on billed price. Prior to adjustment, the May 31, 2002, balance of the home office's Allowance for Overvaluation of Inventories: Portland Street Branch was $200,000 credit.

Prepare journal entries (omit explanations) on May 31, 2002, for the home office of Trapp Company to reflect the foregoing facts.

(Exercise 4.12)   Tillman Textile Company has a single branch in Toledo. On March 1, 2002, the home office accounting records included an Allowance for Overvaluation of Inventories: Toledo Branch ledger account with a credit balance of $32,000. During March, merchandise costing $36,000 was shipped to the Toledo Branch and billed at a price representing a 40% markup on the billed price. On March 31, 2002, the branch prepared an income statement indicating a net loss of $11,500 for March and ending inventories at billed prices of $25,000.

CHECK FIGURE

b. Debit allowance for overvaluation of inventories, $46,000.

INVB 60400

INV 36,000

14,400

a. Prepare a working paper to compute the home office cost of the branch inventories on March 1, 2002, assuming a uniform markup on all shipments to the branch.

b. Prepare a journal entry to adjust the Allowance for Overvaluation of Inventories: Toledo Branch ledger account on March 31, 2002, in the accounting records of the home office.

(Exercise 4.13)   The home office of Glendale Company, which uses the perpetual inventory system, bills shipments of merchandise to the Montrose Branch at a markup of 25% on the billed price. On August 31, 2002, the credit balance of the home office's Allowance for Overvaluation of Inventories: Montrose Branch ledger account was $60,000. On September 17, 2002, the home office shipped merchandise to the branch at a billed price of $400,000. The branch reported an ending inventory, at billed price, of $160,000 on September 30, 2002.

CHECK FIGURE

Sept. 30, credit realized gross profit, $120,000.

Prepare journal entries involving the Allowance for Overvaluation of Inventories: Montrose Branch ledger account of the home office of Glendale Company on September 17 and 30, 2002. Show supporting computations in the explanations for the entries.

(Exercise 4.14)   On January 31, 2002, the unadjusted credit balance of the Allowance for Overvaluation of Inventories: Vermont Avenue Branch of the home office of Searl Company was $80,000. The branch reported a net income of $60,000 for January, 2002, and an ending inventory on January 31, 2002, of $81,000, at billed prices that included a markup of 50% on home office cost.

Prepare journal entries (omit explanations) for the home office of Searl Company on January 31, 2002, for the foregoing facts.

(Exercise 4.15)   The home office of Gomez Company bills its only branch at a markup of 25% above home office cost for all merchandise shipped to that Perez Branch. Both the home office and the branch use the periodic inventory system. During 2002, the home office shipped merchandise to the branch at a billed price of $30,000. Perez Branch inventories for 2002 were as follows:

CHECK FIGURE

Credit realized gross profit, $5,100.

	Jan. 1	Dec. 31
Purchased from home office (at billed price)	15,000	19,500
Purchased from outsiders	6,800	8,670

Prepare journal entries (including adjusting entry) for the home office of Gomez Company for 2002 to reflect the foregoing information.

(Exercise 4.16)   Samore, Inc., bills its only branch for merchandise shipments at a markup of 30% above home office cost. The branch sells the merchandise at a markup of 10% above billed price. Shortly after the close of business on January 28, 2002, some of the branch merchandise was destroyed by fire. The following additional information is available:

Inventories, Jan. 1 (at billed prices from home office)	$15,600
Inventories, Jan. 28, of merchandise not destroyed (at selling prices)	7,150
Shipments from home office from Jan. 1 to Jan. 28 (at billed prices)	71,500
Sales from Jan. 1 to Jan. 28	51,840
Sales returns from Jan. 1 to Jan. 28 (merchandise actually returned)	3,220
Sales allowances from Jan. 1 to Jan. 28 (price adjustments)	300

a. Prepare a working paper to compute the estimated cost (to the home office) of the merchandise destroyed by fire at the branch of Samore, Inc., on January 28, 2002.

b. Prepare a journal entry for the branch to recognize the uninsured fire loss on January 28, 2002. Both the home office and the branch use the perpetual inventory system.

(Exercise 4.17)   On May 31, 2002, the unadjusted balances of the Investment in Troy Branch ledger account of the home office of Argos Company and the Home Office account of the Troy Branch of Argos Company were $380,000 debit and $140,000 credit, respectively.

Additional Information

1. On May 31, 2002, the home office had shipped merchandise to the branch at a billed price of $280,000; the branch did not receive the shipment until June 3, 2002. Both the home office and the branch use the perpetual inventory system.

2. On May 31, 2002, the branch had sent a $10,000 "dividend" to the home office, which did not receive the check until June 2, 2002.

3. On May 31, 2002, the home office had prepared the following journal entry, without notifying the branch:

Cash	50,000	
Investment in Troy Branch		50,000
To record collection of a trade account receivable of branch.		

Prepare journal entries (omit explanations) on May 31, 2002, for *(a)* the home office and *(b)* the Troy Branch of Argos Company to reconcile the reciprocal ledger accounts.

Cases

(Case 4.1)   The management of Longo Company, which has a June 30 fiscal year and sells merchandise at its home office and six branches, is considering closing Santee Branch because of its declining sales volume and excessive operating expenses. Longo's contract with Lewis Hanson, manager of Santee Branch, provides that Hanson is to receive a termination bonus of 15% of the branch's net income in its final period of operations, but no bonus in the event of a net loss in the final period. The contract is silent as to the measurement of the branch's net income or loss.

For the period July 1 through October 31, 2002, the date Santee Branch ceased operations, its income statement prepared in the customary fashion by the branch accountant reported a net loss of $10,000. Hanson pointed out to Longo management that the loss was net of $30,000 advertising expenses that had been apportioned to the branch by Longo's home office in September, 2002, prior to Longo management's decision to close the branch on October 31. Hanson alleged that it was inappropriate for the branch to absorb advertising costs for a period in which it would no longer be making sales presumably initiated in part by the advertising. The controller of Longo responded that under the same line of reasoning, the branch's October 31, 2002, inventories, which included a $60,000 markup over home office cost, should be reduced by that amount, with a corresponding increase in the branch's net loss, because the home office would never realize the markup through future sales by Santee Branch.

Instructions

Do you agree with the Santee Branch manager, with the controller of Longo Company, with both, or with neither? Explain.

(Case 4.2) Fortunato Company, which had operated successfully in a single location for many years, opened a branch operation in another city. The products sold by Fortunato in its home office required federal and state regulatory agency approval; the home office had secured such approval long ago. However, new approval of those agencies was required before Fortunato was authorized to produce and sell the same products at the new branch.

After the branch had been established and had begun testing its manufacturing equipment and considering development of possible new products other than those manufactured by the home office, management of Fortunato met to discuss accounting for operating costs of the new branch prior to its authorization to manufacture and sell products. Controller Robert Engle pointed out that when the home office had been established, it was a *development stage enterprise* prior to obtaining approval for production and sale of its products, with specialized financial statements display requirements provided by *FASB Statement No. 7,* "Accounting and Reporting by Development Stage Enterprises." Engle added that Fortunato, as currently an operating enterprise, was not authorized to use such specialized requirements for the new branch. The vice president for legal affairs, Nancy Kubota, stated that the current regulatory agency environment was much stricter than it had been when Fortunato's home office obtained authorization for its production and sales, and that a several-month waiting period might be anticipated before approval of the branch's operations. Pending such approval, the branch could not legally even manufacture products for stockpiling in inventories.

Chief executive officer Michael Kantor expressed dismay at the prospect described by Kubota, stating that a long period of "marking time" at the branch, with no revenue available to cover operating costs, would generate substantial losses for Fortunato as a whole unless the costs could be deferred as start-up costs. Financial vice president Mary Sage asked Engle if there were any published financial accounting standards for start-up costs. Engle replied in the affirmative, pointing out that in 1998 the AICPA's Accounting Standards Executive Committee had issued *Statement of Position 98-5,* "Reporting on the Costs of Start-Up Activities," which mandated expensing of start-up costs. Sage then asked Engle if the "marking time" costs incurred by the branch prior to regulatory agency approval might be accounted for as deferred charges or intangible assets. Engle stated that he would answer that question after consulting accepted accounting definitions of *assets, intangible assets, contingent assets, expenses,* and *losses.*

Instructions

How should Robert Engle answer Mary Sage's question? Explain, after researching the foregoing definitions.

(Case 4.3) Kevin Carter, CPA, a member of the IMA, the FEI, and the AICPA (see Chapter 1), is the newly hired controller of Oilers, Inc., a closely held manufacturer of replacement parts for oil well drilling equipment. Oilers distributes its products through its home office and 14 branches located near oil fields in several southwestern states. Shortly after being employed, Carter learned that the reciprocal ledger accounts at Oilers' home office and 14 branches were out of balance by substantial amounts and that no member of the home office accounting department could remember when—if ever—the reciprocal ledger accounts had been in balance. In response to Carter's astonished inquiries, the home office chief accountant stated that:

1. Oilers, Inc., had never been audited by independent CPAs, and it had no internal audit staff.
2. Management of Oilers, in reviewing financial statements of the 14 branches, concentrated on branch income statements and was unconcerned about the out-of-balance status of the branches' Home Office ledger accounts.
3. To facilitate elimination of the reciprocal ledger account balances in the working paper for combined financial statements of the home office and 14 branches of Oilers, the chief accountant debited Miscellaneous Expense or credited Miscellaneous Revenue for the aggregate amount of the unlocated differences. These "plug" amounts were reported in the federal and state income tax returns filed by Oilers.

Instructions
What is your advice to Kevin Carter? Should he permit the practice described above to continue? If not, should he request management of Oilers to contract for an independent audit? Alternatively, should he authorize the accountant at each of the 14 branches to adjust the branch's Home Office ledger account balance to agree with the home office's reciprocal Investment in Branch account balance, with the unlocated difference debited to Miscellaneous Expense or credited to Miscellaneous Revenue, as appropriate? Should some other course of action be taken? Explain.

(Case 4.4) The management of Windsor Company, which has several branches as well as a home office, is planning to sell the net assets of Southwark Branch to an unrelated business enterprise. As controller of Windsor, you are asked by the board of directors if you can prepare separate financial statements for Southwark Branch for the prospective purchaser. Among the directors' questions are the following:

1. What specific financial statements are appropriate, and what are their titles?
2. Would there be an equity section in a balance sheet for the branch?
3. How should unrealized intracompany markup above home office cost in the branch's ending inventories be treated in the branch's separate financial statements?

Before attempting to answer the directors' questions, you consult the following sources:

AICPA Professional Standards, vol. 2, "Accounting & Review Services," etc.: AR100.04, ET 92.04.

Statement of Financial Accounting Concepts No. 1, "Objectives of Financial Reporting by Business Enterprises," par. 6.

Statement of Financial Accounting Concepts No. 6, "Elements of Financial Statements," par. 24.

Statement of Financial Accounting Standards No. 57, "Related Party Disclosures," par. 2.

Instructions
After consulting the foregoing sources, prepare a memorandum to the board of directors of Windsor Company in answer to their questions.

(Case 4.5) Langley, Inc., operates a number of branches as well as a home office. Each branch stocks a complete line of merchandise obtained almost entirely from the home office. The branches also handle their billing, approve customer credit, and make cash collections. Each branch has its own bank account, and each maintains accounting records. However, all plant assets at the branches are carried in the accounting records of the home office and are depreciated in those records by the straight-line method at 10% a year, with no residual value.

On July 1, 2002, the manager of Lola Branch acquired office equipment. The equipment had a cash price of $2,400 but was acquired on the installment plan with no down payment and 24 monthly payments of $110 beginning August 1, 2002. No journal entry was made for this transaction by the branch until August 1, when the first monthly payment was recorded by a debit to Miscellaneous Expense. The same journal entry was made in each of the four remaining months of 2002.

On December 2, 2002, the branch manager became aware that equipment could be acquired by the branches only with prior approval by the home office. Regardless of whether the home office or the branches acquired plant assets, such assets were to be carried in the accounting records of the home office, but any gain or loss on the disposal of equipment was to be recognized in the accounting records of the branches. To avoid criticism, the manager of the Lola Branch immediately disposed of the office equipment acquired July 1 by sale for $1,500 cash to an independent store. The manager then paid the balance due on the installment contract using a personal check and the $1,500 check received from sale of the equipment. In consideration of the advance payment of the remaining installments on December 3, 2002, the equipment dealer agreed to a $150 reduction in the $240 interest portion of the contract. No journal entry was prepared for the sale of the equipment or the settlement of the liability.

Assume that you are a CPA engaged to audit the financial statements of Langley, Inc. During your visit to Lola Branch you analyze the Miscellaneous Expense ledger account and investigate the five monthly debits of $110. This investigation discloses the acquisition and subsequent disposal of the office equipment. After some hesitation, the branch manager gives you a full explanation of the events.

Instructions
a. Describe (do not prepare) the journal entries that should have been made by Lola Branch for the foregoing transactions and events.
b. Describe (do not prepare) the journal entries that should have been made by the home office of Langley, Inc., for the foregoing transactions and events.
c. Prepare a single journal entry for Lola Branch on December 31, 2002, to correct its accounting records.
d. Prepare a single journal entry for the home office of Langley, Inc., on December 31, 2002, to correct its accounting records.

Problems

(Problem 4.1) Hartman, Inc., established Reno Branch on January 2, 2002. During 2002, Hartman's home office shipped merchandise to Reno Branch that cost $300,000. Billings were made at prices marked up 20% above home office cost. Freight costs of $15,000 were paid by the home office. Sales by the branch were $450,000, and branch operating expenses were $96,000, all for cash. On December 31, 2002, the branch took a physical inventory that showed merchandise on hand of $72,000 at billed prices. Both the home office and the branch use the periodic inventory system.

Instructions
Prepare journal entries for Reno Branch and the home office of Hartman, Inc., to record the foregoing transactions and events, ending inventories, and adjusting and closing entries on December 31, 2002. (Allocate a proportional amount of freight costs to the ending inventories of the branch.)

(Problem 4.2) Included in the accounting records of the home office and Wade Branch, respectively, of Lobo Company were the following ledger accounts for the month of January 2002:

Investment in Wade Branch (in Home Office accounting records)

Date	Explanation	Debit	Credit	Balance
2002				
Jan. 1	Balance			39,200 dr
9	Shipment of merchandise	4,000		43,200 dr
21	Receipt of cash		1,600	41,600 dr
27	Collection of branch trade accounts receivable		1,100	40,500 dr
31	Shipment of merchandise	6,000		46,500 dr
31	Payment of branch trade accounts payable		2,000	48,500 dr

Home Office (in Wade Branch accounting records)

Date	Explanation	Debit	Credit	Balance
2002				
Jan. 1	Balance			39,200 cr
10	Receipt of merchandise		4,000	43,200 cr
19	Remittance of cash	1,600		41,600 cr
28	Acquisition of furniture	1,200		40,400 cr
30	Return of merchandise	2,200		38,200 cr
31	Remittance of cash	2,500		35,700 cr

Instructions
a. Prepare a working paper to reconcile the reciprocal ledger accounts of Lobo Company's home office and Wade Branch to the corrected balances on January 31, 2002.
b. Prepare journal entries on January 31, 2002, for the (1) home office and (2) Wade Branch of Lobo Company to bring the accounting records up to date. Both the home office and the branch use the perpetual inventory system.

(Problem 4.3) The home office of Styler Corporation operates a branch to which it bills merchandise at prices marked up 20% above home office cost. The branch obtains merchandise only from the home office and sells it at prices averaging markups 10% above the prices billed by the home office. Both the home office and the branch maintain perpetual inventory records and both close their accounting records on December 31.

On March 10, 2002, a fire at the branch destroyed a part of the inventories. Immediately after the fire, a physical inventory of merchandise on hand and not damaged amounted to $16,500 at branch retail selling prices. On January 1, 2002, the inventories of the branch at billed prices had been $18,000. Shipments from the home office during the period January 1 to March 10, 2002, were billed to the branch in the amount of $57,600. The accounting records of the branch show that net sales during this period were $44,880.

Instructions

Prepare journal entries on March 10, 2002, to record the uninsured loss from fire in the accounting records of (a) the branch and (b) the home office of Styler Company. Show supporting computations for all amounts. Assume that the loss was reported at billed prices by the branch to the home office and that it was recorded in the intracompany reciprocal ledger accounts.

(Problem 4.4)

On December 31, 2002, the Investment in Ryble Branch ledger account in the accounting records of the home office of Yugo Company shows a debit balance of $55,500. You ascertain the following facts in analyzing this account:

1. On December 31, 2002, merchandise billed at $5,800 was in transit from the home office to the branch. The periodic inventory system is used by both the home office and the branch.

2. The branch had collected a home office trade accounts receivable of $560 on December 30, 2002; the home office was not notified.

3. On December 29, 2002, the home office had mailed a check for $2,000 to the branch, but the accountant for the home office had recorded the check as a debit to the Charitable Contributions ledger account; the branch had not received the check as of December 31, 2002.

4. Branch net income for December, 2002 was recorded erroneously by the home office at $840 instead of $480 on December 31, 2002. The credit was recorded by the home office in the Income: Ryble Branch ledger account.

5. On December 28, 2002, the branch had returned supplies costing $220 to the home office; the home office had not recorded the receipt of the supplies. The home office records acquisitions of supplies in the Inventory of Supplies ledger account.

Instructions

a. Assuming that all other transactions and events have been recorded properly, prepare a working paper to compute the unadjusted balance of the Home Office ledger account in the accounting records of Yugo Company's Ryble Branch on December 31, 2002.

b. Prepare journal entries for the home office of Yugo Company on December 31, 2002, to bring its accounting records up to date. Closing entries have not been made.

c. Prepare journal entries for Ryble Branch of Yugo Company on December 31, 2002, to bring its accounting records up to date.

d. Prepare a reconciliation on December 31, 2002, of the Investment in Ryble branch ledger account in the accounting records of the home office and the Home Office account in the accounting records of Ryble Branch of Yugo Company. Use a single column for each account and start with the unadjusted balances.

(Problem 4.5)

Trudie Company's home office bills shipments of merchandise to its Savoy Branch at 140% of home office cost. During the first year after the branch was opened, the following were among the transactions and events completed:

1. The home office shipped merchandise with a home office cost of $110,000 to Savoy Branch.

2. Savoy Branch sold for $80,000 cash merchandise that was billed by the home office at $70,000, and incurred operating expenses of $16,500 (all paid in cash).

3. The physical inventories taken by Savoy Branch at the end of the first year were $82,460 at billed prices from the home office.

Instructions

a. Assuming that the perpetual inventory system is used both by the home office and by Savoy Branch, prepare for the first year:

(1) All journal entries, including closing entries, in the accounting records of Savoy Branch of Trudie Company.

(2) All journal entries, including the adjustment of the Inventories Overvaluation account, in the accounting records of the home office of Trudie Company.

b. Assuming that the periodic inventory system is used both by the home office and by Savoy Branch, prepare for the first year:

(1) All journal entries, including closing entries, in the accounting records of Savoy Branch of Trudie Company.

(2) All journal entries, including the adjustment of the Inventories Overvaluation account, in the accounting records of the home office of Trudie Company.

(Problem 4.6) You are making an audit for the year ended December 31, 2002, of the financial statements of Kosti-Marian Company, which carries on merchandising operations at both a home office and a branch. The unadjusted trial balances of the home office and the branch are shown below:

CHECK FIGURE

c. Combined net income, $63,120.

KOSTI-MARIAN COMPANY Unadjusted Trial Balances December 31, 2002	Home Office Dr (Cr)	Branch Dr (Cr)
Cash	$ 22,000	$ 10,175
Inventories, Jan. 1, 2002	23,000	11,550
Investment in branch	60,000	
Allowance for overvaluation of branch inventories, Jan. 1, 2002	(1,000)	
Other assets (net)	197,000	48,450
Current liabilities	(35,000)	(8,500)
Common stock, $2.50 par	(200,000)	
Retained earnings, Jan. 1, 2002	(34,000)	
Dividends declared	15,000	
Home office		(51,000)
Sales	(169,000)	(144,700)
Purchases	190,000	
Shipments to branch	(110,000)	
Shipments from home office		104,500
Freight-in from home office		5,225
Operating expenses	42,000	24,300
Totals	$ -0-	$ -0-

The audit for the year ended December 31, 2002, disclosed the following:

1. The branch deposits all cash receipts in a local bank for the account of the home office. The audit working papers for the cash cutoff include the following:

Amount	Date Deposited by Branch	Date Recorded by Home Office
$1,050	Dec. 27, 2002	Dec. 31, 2002
1,100	Dec. 30, 2002	Not recorded
600	Dec. 31, 2002	Not recorded
300	Jan. 2, 2003	Not recorded

2. The branch pays operating expenses incurred locally from an imprest cash account that is maintained with a balance of $2,000. Checks are drawn once a week on the imprest cash account, and the home office is notified of the amount needed to replenish the account. On December 31, 2002, a $1,800 reimbursement check was in transit from the home office to the branch.

3. The branch received all its merchandise from the home office. The home office bills the merchandise shipments at a markup of 10% above home office cost. On December 31, 2002, a shipment with a billed price of $5,500 was in transit to the branch. Freight costs of common carriers typically are 5% of billed price. Freight costs are considered to be inventoriable costs. Both the home office and the branch use the periodic inventory system.

4. Beginning inventories in the trial balance are shown at the respective costs to the home office and to the branch. The physical inventories on December 31, 2002, were as follows:

Home office, at cost	$30,000
Branch, at billed price (excluding shipment in transit and freight)	9,900

Instructions

a. Prepare journal entries to adjust the accounting records of the home office of Kosti-Marian Company on December 31, 2002.

b. Prepare journal entries to adjust the accounting records of Kosti-Marian Company's branch on December 31, 2002.

c. Prepare a working paper for combined financial statements of Kosti-Marian Company (use the format on page 145). Compute the amounts in the adjusted trial balances for the home office and the branch by incorporating the journal entries in *(a)* and *(b)* with the amounts in the unadjusted trial balances.

(Problem 4.7) On January 4, 2002, Solis Company opened its first branch, with instructions to Steven Carr, the branch manager, to perform the functions of granting credit, billing customers, accounting for receivables, and making cash collections. The branch paid its operating expenses by checks drawn on its bank account. The branch obtained merchandise solely from the home office; billings from these shipments *were at cost to the home office.* The adjusted trial balances for the home office and the branch on December 31, 2002, were as follows:

SOLIS COMPANY
Adjusted Trial Balances
December 31, 2002

	Home Office Dr (Cr)	Branch Dr (Cr)
Cash	$ 46,000	$ 14,600
Notes receivable	7,000	
Trade accounts receivable (net)	80,400	37,300
Inventories	95,800	24,200
Investment in branch	82,700	
Furniture and equipment (net)	48,100	
Trade accounts payable	(41,000)	
Common stock, $2 par	(200,000)	
Retained earnings, Dec. 31, 2001	(25,000)	
Dividends declared	30,000	
Home office		(82,700)
Sales	(394,000)	(101,100)
Cost of goods sold	200,500	85,800
Operating expenses	69,500	21,900
Totals	$ -0-	$ -0-

The physical inventories on December 31, 2002, were in agreement with the perpetual inventory records of the home office and the branch.

Instructions
a. Prepare a four-column working paper for combined financial statements of the home office and branch of Solis Company for the year ended December 31, 2002.
b. Prepare closing entries on December 31, 2002, in the accounting records of the branch of Solis Company.
c. Prepare adjusting and closing entries pertaining to branch operations on December 31, 2002, in the accounting records of the home office of Solis Company.

(Problem 4.8) The unadjusted general ledger trial balances on December 31, 2002, for Calco Corporation's home office and its only branch are shown below and on page 166:

CALCO CORPORATION
Unadjusted Trial Balances
December 31, 2002

	Home Office Dr (Cr)	Branch Dr (Cr)
Cash	$ 28,000	$ 23,000
Trade accounts receivable (net)	35,000	12,000
Inventories, Jan. 1, 2001 (at cost to home office)	70,000	15,000
Investment in branch	30,000	
Equipment (net)	90,000	
Trade accounts payable	(46,000)	(13,500)
Accrued liabilities	(14,000)	(2,500)
Home office		(19,000)
Common stock, $10 par	(50,000)	

(continued)

	CALCO CORPORATION Unadjusted Trial Balances (concluded) December 31, 2002	
	Home Office Dr (Cr)	Branch Dr (Cr)
Retained earnings, Jan. 1, 2002	(48,000)	
Dividends declared	10,000	
Sales	(450,000)	(100,000)
Purchases	290,000	24,000
Shipments from home office		45,000
Operating expenses	55,000	16,000
Totals	$ -0-	$ -0-

Your audit disclosed the following:

1. On December 10, 2002, the branch manager acquired equipment for $500, but failed to notify the home office. The branch accountant, knowing that branch equipment is carried in the home office ledger, recorded the proper journal entry in the branch accounting records. It is Calco's policy not to recognize depreciation on equipment acquired in the last half of a year.

2. On December 27, 2002, Mojo, Inc., a customer of the branch, erroneously paid its account of $2,000 to the home office. The accountant made the correct journal entry in the home office accounting records but did not notify the branch.

3. On December 30, 2002, the branch remitted to the home office cash of $5,000, which had not been received by the home office as of December 31, 2002.

4. On December 31, 2002, the branch erroneously recorded the December allocated expenses from the home office as $500 instead of $5,000.

5. On December 31, 2002, the home office shipped merchandise billed at $3,000 to the branch; the shipment had not been received by the branch as of December 31, 2002.

6. The inventories on December 31, 2002, excluding the shipment in transit, were: home office—$60,000 (at cost); branch—$20,000 (consisting of $18,000 from home office at billed prices and $2,000 from suppliers). Both the home office and the branch use the periodic inventory system.

7. The home office erroneously billed shipments to the branch at a markup of 20% above home office cost, although the billing should have been at cost. The Sales ledger account was credited for the invoices' price by the home office.

Instructions

a. Prepare journal entries for the home office of Calco Corporation on December 31, 2002, to bring the accounting records up to date and to correct any errors. Record ending inventories by an offsetting credit to the Income Summary ledger account. Do not prepare other closing entries.

b. Prepare journal entries for the branch of Calco Corporation on December 31, 2002, to bring the accounting records up to date and to correct any errors. Record ending inventories at cost to the home office by an offsetting credit to the Income Summary ledger account. Do not prepare other closing entries.

c. Prepare a working paper to summarize the operations of Calco Corporation for the year ended December 31, 2002. Disregard income taxes and use the following column headings:

Revenue and Expenses	Home Office	Branch	Combined

(Problem 4.9) The following reciprocal ledger accounts were included in the accounting records of the home office and the Lee Branch of Kreshek Company on April 30, 2002. You have been retained by Kreshek to assist it with some accounting work preliminary to the preparation of financial statements for the quarter ended April 30, 2002.

Investment in Lee Branch

Date	Explanation	Debit	Credit	Balance
2002				
Feb. 1	Balance			124,630 dr
6	Shipment of merchandise, 160 units @ $49	7,840		132,470 dr
17	Note receivable collected by branch	2,500		134,970 dr
Mar. 31	Cash deposited by branch		2,000	132,970 dr
Apr. 2	Merchandise returned by branch		450	132,520 dr
26	Loss on disposal of branch equipment	780		133,300 dr
28	Operating expenses charged to branch	1,200		134,500 dr
29	Corrected loss on disposal of branch equipment from $780 to $250		530	133,970 dr

Home Office

Date	Explanation	Debit	Credit	Balance
2002				
Feb. 1	Balance			124,630 cr
8	Merchandise from home office, 160 units @$49		7,480	132,110 cr
14	Received shipment directly from supplier, invoice to be paid by home office		2,750	134,860 cr
15	Note receivable collected for home office		2,500	137,360 cr
Mar. 30	Deposited cash in account of home office	2,000		135,360 cr
31	Returned merchandise to home office	450		134,910 cr
Apr. 29	Paid repair bill for home office	375		134,535 cr
30	Excess merchandise returned to home office (billed at cost)	5,205		129,330 cr
30	Preliminary net income for quarter (before any required corrections)		13,710	143,040 cr

Additional Information

1. Branch equipment is carried in the accounting records of the home office; the home office notifies the branch periodically as to the amount of depreciation applicable to equipment used by the branch. Gains or losses on disposal of branch equipment are reported to the branch and included in the income statement of the branch.

2. Because of the error in recording the shipment from the home office on February 8, 2002, the sale of the 160 units has been debited improperly by the branch to cost of goods sold at $46.75 a unit.

3. On April 30, 2002, the branch collected trade accounts receivable of $350 belonging to the home office, but the branch employee who recorded the collection mistakenly treated the trade accounts receivable as belonging to the branch.

4. The branch recorded the preliminary net income of $13,710 by a debit to Income Summary and a credit to Home Office, although the revenue and expense ledger accounts had not been closed.

Instructions

a. Reconcile the reciprocal ledger accounts of the home office and Lee Branch of Kreshek Company to the correct balances on April 30, 2002. Use a four-column working paper (debit and credit columns for the Investment in Lee Branch account in the home office accounting records and debit and credit columns for the Home Office account in the branch accounting records). Start with the unadjusted balances on April 30, 2002, and work to corrected balances, including explanations of all adjusting or correcting items.

b. Prepare journal entries for Lee Branch of Kreshek Company on April 30, 2002, to bring its accounting records up to date, assuming that corrections still may be made to revenue and expense ledger accounts. The branch uses the perpetual inventory system. Do not prepare closing entries.

c. Prepare journal entries for the home office of Kreshek Company on April 30, 2002, to bring its accounting records up to date. The home office uses the perpetual inventory system and has not prepared closing entries. Do not prepare closing entries.

(Problem 4.10) Arnie's, a single proprietorship owned by Arnold Nance, sells merchandise at both its home office and a branch. The home office bills merchandise shipped to the branch at 125% of home office cost, and is the only supplier for the branch. Shipments of merchandise to the branch have been recorded improperly by the home office by credits to Sales for the billed price. Both the home office and the branch use the perpetual inventory system.

Arnie's has engaged you to audit its financial statements for the year ended December 31, 2002. This is the first time the proprietorship has retained an independent accountant. You were provided with the following unadjusted trial balances:

ARNIE'S
Unadjusted Trial Balances
December 31, 2002

	Home Office Dr (Cr)	Vida Branch Dr (Cr)
Cash	$ 31,000	$ 13,000
Trade accounts receivable (net)	20,000	22,000
Inventories	40,000	8,000
Investment in branch	45,000	
Equipment (net)	150,000	
Trade accounts payable	$ (23,000)	
Accrued liabilities		$ (2,000)
Note payable, due 2005	(51,000)	
Arnold Nance, capital, Jan. 1, 2002	(192,000)	
Arnold Nance, drawing	50,000	
Home office		(10,000)
Sales	(390,000)	(160,000)
Cost of goods sold	250,000	93,000
Operating expenses	70,000	36,000
Totals	$ -0-	$ -0-

Additional Information

1. On January 1, 2002, inventories of the home office amounted to $25,000 and inventories of the branch amounted to $6,000. During 2002, the branch was billed for $105,000 for shipments from the home office.

2. On December 28, 2002, the home office billed the branch for $12,000, representing the branch's share of operating expenses paid by the home office. This billing had not been recorded by the branch.

3. All cash collections made by the branch were deposited in a local bank to the bank account of the home office. Deposits of this nature included the following:

Amount	Date Deposited by Vida Branch	Date Recorded by Home Office
$5,000	Dec. 28, 2002	Dec. 31, 2002
3,000	Dec. 30, 2002	Not recorded
7,000	Dec. 31, 2002	Not recorded
2,000	Jan. 2, 2003	Not recorded

4. Operating expenses incurred by the branch were paid from an imprest bank account that was reimbursed periodically by the home office. On December 30, 2002, the home office had mailed a reimbursement check in the amount of $3,000, which had not been received by the branch as of December 31, 2002.

5. A shipment of merchandise from the home office to the branch was in transit on December 31, 2002.

Instructions

a. Prepare journal entries to adjust the accounting records of Arnie's home office on December 31, 2002. Establish an allowance for overvaluation of branch inventories.

b. Prepare journal entries to adjust the accounting records of Vida Branch on December 31, 2002.

c. Prepare a working paper for combined financial statements of Arnie's on December 31, 2002 (use the format on pages 138–139). Compute the amounts for the adjusted trial balances for the home office and the branch by incorporating the journal entries in (*a*) and (*b*) with the amounts in the unadjusted trial balances.

d. After the working paper in (*c*) is completed, prepare all required adjusting and closing entries on December 31, 2002, in the accounting records of Arnie's home office.

Chapter Five

Business Combinations

The Financial Accounting Standards Board has provided the following working definition of **business combination**:

> [A] *business combination* occurs when an entity acquires net assets that constitute a business or acquires equity interests of one or more other entitites and obtains control over that entity or entities.[1]

Footnotes to this definition amplify the terms **entity, business,** and **control** as follows:[2]

> *Entity*: A business enterprise, a new entity formed to complete a business combination, or a mutual enterprise—an entity, not investor-owned, that provides dividends, lower costs, or other economic benefits directly to its owners, members, or participants.
>
> *Business*: An asset group that constitutes a business as characterized by the Emerging Issues Task Force (EITF) in **EITF Issue No. 98-3,** "Determining Whether a Nonmonetary Transaction Involves Receipt of Productive Assets or of a Business."
>
> *Control*: Ownership by one company, directly or indirectly, of the outstanding voting shares of another company.

In common parlance, business combinations are often referred to as **mergers and acquisitions.**

The Financial Accounting Standards Board has suggested the following definitions for terms commonly used in discussions of business combinations.[3]

Combined enterprise The accounting entity that results from a business combination.

Constituent companies The business enterprises that enter into a business combination.

Combinor A constituent company entering into a purchase-type business combination whose owners as a group end up with control of the ownership interests in the combined enterprise.

Combinee A constituent company other than the combinor in a business combination.

Business combinations may be divided into two classes—friendly takeovers and hostile takeovers. In a **friendly takeover,** the boards of directors of the constituent companies generally work out the terms of the business combination amicably and submit

---

[1] *FASB Statement No. 141,* "Business Combintations" (Norwalk: FASB, 2001), par. 9.
[2] Ibid., pars. 9 and F1.
[3] *FASB Discussion Memorandum,* "An Analysis of Issues Related to Accounting for Business Combinations and Purchased Intangibles" (Stamford: FASB, 1976), p. 3.

the proposal to stockholders of all constituent companies for approval. A target combinee in a *hostile takeover* typically resists the proposed business combination by resorting to one or more defensive tactics with the following colorful designations:

Pac-man defense A threat to undertake a hostile takeover of the prospective combinor.

White knight A search for a candidate to be the combinor in a friendly takeover.

Scorched earth The disposal, by sale or by a spin-off to stockholders, of one or more profitable business segments.

Shark repellent An acquisition of substantial amounts of outstanding common stock for the treasury or for retirement, or the incurring of substantial long-term debt in exchange for outstanding common stock.

Poison pill An amendment of the articles of incorporation or bylaws to make it more difficult to obtain stockholder approval for a takeover.

Greenmail An acquisition of common stock presently owned by the prospective combinor at a price substantially in excess of the prospective combinor's cost, with the stock thus acquired placed in the treasury or retired.

Scope of Chapter

The first section of this chapter presents reasons for the popularity of business combinations and techniques for arranging them. Then, *purchase accounting*—the only acceptable method—for business combinations is explained and illustrated. An appendix contains a discussion of the now-prohibited *pooling-of-interests* method of accounting for business combinations.

BUSINESS COMBINATIONS: WHY AND HOW?

Why do business enterprises enter into a business combination? Although a number of reasons have been cited, probably the overriding one for *combinors* in recent years has been *growth.* Business enterprises have major operating objectives other than growth, but that goal increasingly has motivated combinor managements to undertake business combinations. Advocates of this *external* method of achieving growth point out that it is much more rapid than growth through *internal* means. There is no question that expansion and diversification of product lines, or enlarging the market share for current products, is achieved readily through a business combination with another enterprise. However, the disappointing experiences of many combinors engaging in business combinations suggest that much may be said in favor of more gradual and reasoned growth through internal means, using available management and financial resources.

Other reasons often advanced in support of business combinations are obtaining new management strength or better use of existing management and achieving manufacturing or other operating economies. In addition, a business combination may be undertaken for the income tax advantages available to one or more parties to the combination.

Critics have alleged that the foregoing reasons attributed to the "urge to merge" (business combinations) do not apply to hostile takeovers. These critics complain that the "sharks" who engage in hostile takeovers, and the investment bankers and attorneys who counsel them, are motivated by the prospect of substantial gains resulting from the sale of business segments of a combinee following the business combination.

Antitrust Considerations

One obstacle faced by large corporations that undertake business combinations is the possibility of antitrust litigation. The U.S. government on occasion has opposed concentration of economic power in large business enterprises. Consequently, business combinations frequently have been challenged by the Federal Trade Commission or the Antitrust Division of the Department of Justice, under the provisions of Section 7 of the Clayton Act, which reads in part as follows:

> No corporation engaged in commerce shall acquire, directly or indirectly, the whole or any part of the stock or other share capital and no corporation subject to the jurisdiction of the Federal Trade Commission shall acquire the whole or any part of the assets of another corporation engaged also in commerce, where in any line of commerce in any section of the country the effect of such acquisition may be substantially to lessen competition or to tend to create a monopoly.

The breadth of the preceding legislation has led to federal antitrust action against all types of business combinations: *horizontal* (combinations involving enterprises in the same industry), *vertical* (combinations between an enterprise and its customers or suppliers), and *conglomerate* (combinations between enterprises in unrelated industries or markets).

Methods for Arranging Business Combinations

The four common methods for carrying out a business combination are statutory merger, statutory consolidation, acquisition of common stock, and acquisition of assets.

Statutory Merger

As its name implies, a statutory merger is executed under provisions of applicable state laws. In a statutory merger, the boards of directors of the constituent companies approve a plan for the exchange of voting common stock (and perhaps some preferred stock, cash, or long-term debt) of one of the corporations (the *survivor*) for all the outstanding voting common stock of the other corporations. Stockholders of all constituent companies must approve the terms of the merger; some states require approval by a two-thirds majority of stockholders. The survivor corporation issues its common stock or other consideration to the stockholders of the other corporations in exchange for all their holdings, thus acquiring ownership of those corporations. The other corporations *then are dissolved and liquidated and thus cease to exist as separate legal entities,* and their activities often are continued as *divisions* of the survivor, which now owns the *net assets* (assets minus liabilities), rather than the outstanding common stock, of the liquidated corporations.

To summarize, the procedures in a statutory merger are:

1. The boards of directors of the constituent companies work out the terms of the merger.

2. Stockholders of the constituent companies approve the terms of the merger, in accordance with applicable corporate bylaws and state laws.

3. The survivor issues its common stock or other consideration to the stockholders of the other constituent companies in exchange for all their outstanding voting common stock of those companies.

4. The survivor dissolves and liquidates the other constituent companies, receiving in exchange for its common stock investments the net assets of those companies.

Statutory Consolidation

A statutory consolidation also is consummated in accordance with applicable state laws. However, in a consolidation a ***new corporation is formed to issue its common stock*** for the outstanding common stock of two or more existing corporations, ***which then go out of existence.*** The new corporation thus acquires the net assets of the defunct corporations, whose activities may be continued as divisions of the new corporation.

To summarize, the procedures in a statutory consolidation are:

1. The boards of directors of the constituent companies work out the terms of the consolidation.

2. Stockholders of the constituent companies approve the terms of the consolidation, in accordance with applicable corporate bylaws and state laws.

3. A new corporation is formed to issue its common stock to the stockholders of the constituent companies in exchange for all their outstanding voting common stock of those companies.

4. The new corporation dissolves and liquidates the constituent companies, receiving in exchange for its common stock investments the net assets of those companies.

Acquisition of Common Stock

One corporation (the ***investor***) may issue preferred or common stock, cash, debt, or a combination thereof to acquire from present stockholders a controlling interest in the voting common stock of another corporation (the ***investee***). This stock acquisition program may be accomplished through direct acquisition in the stock market, through negotiations with the principal stockholders of a closely held corporation, or through a tender offer to stockholders of a publicly owned corporation. A ***tender offer*** is a publicly announced intention to acquire, for a stated amount of consideration, a maximum number of shares of the combinee's common stock "tendered" by holders thereof to an agent, such as an investment banker or a commercial bank. The price per share stated in the tender offer usually is well above the prevailing market price of the combinee's common stock. If a controlling interest in the combinee's voting common stock is acquired, that corporation becomes ***affiliated*** with the combinor ***parent company*** as a ***subsidiary,*** but ***is not dissolved and liquidated and remains a separate legal entity.*** Business combinations arranged through common stock acquisitions require authorization by the combinor's board of directors and may require ratification by the combinee's stockholders. Most hostile takeovers are accomplished by this means.

Business combinations that result in a parent company–subsidiary relationship are discussed in Chapter 6.

Acquisition of Assets

A business enterprise may acquire from another enterprise all or most of the gross assets or net assets of the other enterprise for cash, debt, preferred or common stock, or a combination thereof. The transaction generally must be approved by the boards of directors and stockholders or other owners of the constituent companies. The selling enterprise ***may continue its existence as a separate entity or it may be dissolved and liquidated;*** it does not become an ***affiliate*** of the combinor.

Establishing the Price for a Business Combination

An important early step in planning a business combination is deciding on an appropriate price to pay. The amount of cash or debt securities, or the number of shares of preferred or common stock, to be issued in a business combination generally is determined by variations of the following methods:

1. Capitalization of expected average annual earnings of the combinee at a desired rate of return.

2. Determination of current fair value of the combinee's net assets (including goodwill).

The price for a business combination consummated for cash or debt generally is expressed in terms of the total dollar amount of the consideration issued. When common stock is issued by the combinor in a business combination, the price is expressed as a ratio of the number of shares of the combinor's common stock to be exchanged for each share of the combinee's common stock.

Illustration of Exchange Ratio

The negotiating officers of Palmer Corporation have agreed with the stockholders of Simpson Company to acquire all 20,000 outstanding shares of Simpson common stock for a total price of $1,800,000. Palmer's common stock presently is trading in the market at $65 a share. Stockholders of Simpson agree to accept 30,000 shares of Palmer's common stock at a value of $60 a share in exchange for their stock holdings in Simpson. The exchange ratio is expressed as 1.5 shares of Palmer's common stock for each share of Simpson's common stock, in accordance with the following computation:

Computation of Exchange Ratio in Business Combination

Number of shares of Palmer Corporation common stock to be issued	30,000
Number of shares of Simpson Company common stock to be exchanged	20,000
Exchange ratio: 30,000 ÷ 20,000	1.5 : 1

PURCHASE METHOD OF ACCOUNTING FOR BUSINESS COMBINATIONS

In *FASB Statement No. 141,* "Business Combinations," the FASB mandated *purchase accounting* for all business combinations entered into after June 30, 2001.[4] The key components of purchase accounting were identified as follows by the FASB:[5]

Initial recognition: Assets are commonly acquired in exchange transactions that trigger the initial recognition of the assets acquired and any liabilities assumed.

Initial measurement: Like other exchange transactions generally, acquisitions are measured on the basis of the fair values exchanged.

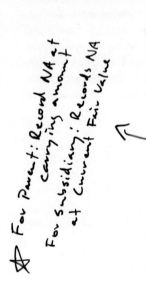

Allocating cost: Acquiring assets in groups requires not only ascertaining the cost of the asset (or net asset) group but also allocating that cost to the individual assets (or individual assets and liabilities) that make up the group.

Accounting after acquisition: The nature of an asset and not the manner of its acquisitions determines an acquiring entity's subsequent accounting for the asset.

The foregoing provide the foundation for applying the purchase method of accounting for business combinations.

[4] *FASB Statement No. 141,* par. 13.
[5] Ibid., pars. 4, 5, 7, 8.

Determination of the Combinor

Because the carrying amounts of the net assets of the combinor are not affected by a business combination, the combinor must be accurately identified. The FASB stated that in a business combination effected solely by the distribution of cash or other assets or by incurring liabilities, the combinor is the distributing or incurring constituent company.[6] For combinations effected by the issuance of equity securities, consideration of all the facts and circumstances is required to identify the combinor. However, a common theme is that the combinor is the constituent company whose stockholders as a group retain or receive the largest portion of the voting rights of the combined enterprise and thereby can elect a majority of the governing board of directors or other group of the combined enterprise.[7]

Computation of Cost of a Combinee

The cost of a combinee in a business combination accounted for by the purchase method is the total of (1) the amount of consideration paid by the combinor, (2) the combinor's **direct** "out-of-pocket" costs of the combination, and (3) any **contingent consideration** that is determinable on the date of the business combination.

Amount of Consideration

This is the total amount of cash paid, the current fair value of other assets distributed, the present value of debt securities issued, and the current fair (or market) value of equity securities issued by the combinor.

Direct Out-of-Pocket Costs

Included in this category are some legal fees, some accounting fees, and finder's fees. A **finder's fee** is paid to the investment banking firm or other organization or individuals that investigated the combinee, assisted in determining the price of the business combination, and otherwise rendered services to bring about the combination.

Costs of registering with the SEC and issuing **debt securities** in a business combination are debited to Bond Issue Costs; they are not part of the cost of the combinee. Costs of registering with the SEC and issuing **equity securities** are not direct costs of the business combination but are offset against the proceeds from the issuance of the securities. **Indirect** out-of-pocket costs of the combination, such as salaries of officers of constituent companies involved in negotiation and completion of the combination, are recognized as expenses incurred by the constituent companies.

Contingent Consideration

Contingent consideration is additional cash, other assets, or securities that may be issuable in the future, contingent on future events such as a specified level of earnings or a designated market price for a security that had been issued to complete the business combination. Contingent consideration that is **determinable** on the consummation date of a combination is recorded as part of the cost of the combination; contingent consideration **not determinable** on the date of the combination is recorded when the contingency is resolved and the additional consideration is paid or issued (or becomes payable or issuable).

---

[6] Ibid., par. 16.
[7] Ibid., par. 17.

Illustration of Contingent Consideration

The contract for Norton Company's acquisition of the net assets of Robinson Company provided that Norton would pay $800,000 cash for Robinson's net assets (including goodwill), which would be included in the Robb Division of Norton Company. The following contingent consideration also was included in the contract:

1. Norton was to pay Robinson $100 a unit for all sales by Robb Division of a slow-moving product that had been written down to scrap value by Robinson prior to the business combination. No portion of the $800,000 price for Robinson's net assets involved the slow-moving product.

2. Norton was to pay Robinson 25% of any pretax financial income in excess of $500,000 (excluding income from sale of the slow-moving product) of Robb Division for each of the four years subsequent to the business combination.

On January 2, 2002, the date of completion of the business combination, Robinson Company had firm, noncancelable sales orders for 500 units of the slow-moving product. The sales orders and all units of the slow-moving product were transferred to Norton by Robinson.

Norton's cost of the net assets acquired from Robinson includes $50,000 (500 × $100 = $50,000) for the ***determinable*** contingent consideration attributable to the backlog of sales orders for the slow-moving product. However, because any pretax accounting income of Robb Division for the next four years cannot be determined on January 2, 2002, no provision for the 25% contingent consideration is included in Norton's cost on January 2, 2002. The subsequent accounting for such contingent consideration is described on pages 184–185.

Allocation of Cost of a Combinee

The FASB required that the cost of a combinee in a business combination be allocated to assets (other than goodwill) acquired and liabilities assumed based on their estimated fair values on the date of the combination. Any excess of total costs over the amounts thus allocated is assigned to goodwill.[8] Methods for determining fair values included present values for receivables and most liabilities; net realizable value less a reasonable profit for work in process and finished goods inventories; and appraised values for land, natural resources, and nonmarketable securities.[9] In addition, the following combinee intangible assets were to be recognized individually and valued at fair value:[10]

> Assets arising from contractual or legal rights, such as patents, copyrights, and franchises.
> Other assets that are separable from the combinee entity and can be sold, licensed, exchanged, and the like, such as customer lists and unpatented technology

Other matters involved in the allocation of the cost of a combinee in a business combination are:

1. A part of the cost of a combinee is allocable to identifiable tangible and intangible assets that resulted from research and development activities of the combinee or are to be used in research and development activities of the combined enterprise. Subsequently, such assets are to be expensed, as required by ***FASB Statement No. 2,*** "Accounting for Research and Development Costs," unless they may be used for other than research and development activities in the future.[11]

---

[8] Ibid., pars. 35, 43.

[9] Ibid. par. 37.

[10] Ibid., pars. 39, A14.

[11] *FASB Interpretation No. 4,* "Applicability of *FASB Statement No. 2* to Business Combinations Accounted for by the Purchase Method" (Stamford: FASB, 1975), pars. 4–5.

2. In a business combination, leases of the combinee-lessee are classified by the combined enterprise as they were by the combinee unless the provisions of a lease are modified to the extent it must be considered a new lease.[12] Thus, unmodified capital leases of the combinee are treated as capital leases by the combined enterprise, and the leased property and related liability are recognized in accordance with the guidelines of ***FASB Statement No. 141.***

3. A combinee in a business combination may have ***preacquisition contingencies,*** which are contingent assets (other than potential income tax benefits of a loss carryforward), contingent liabilities, or contingent impairments of assets, that existed prior to completion of the business combination. If so, an ***allocation period,*** generally not longer than one year from the date the combination is completed, may be used to determine the current fair value of a preacquisition contingency. A portion of the cost of a purchased combinee is allocated to a preacquisition contingency whose fair value is determined during the allocation period. Otherwise, an estimated amount is assigned to a preacquisition contingency if it appears probable that an asset existed, a liability had been incurred, or an asset had been impaired at the completion of the combination. Any adjustment of the carrying amount of a preacquisition contingency subsequent to the end of the allocation period is included in the measurement of net income for the accounting period of the adjustment.[13]

Goodwill

Goodwill frequently is recognized in business combinations because the total cost of the combinee exceeds the current fair value of identifiable net assets of the combinee. The amount of goodwill recognized on the date the business combination is consummated may be adjusted subsequently when contingent consideration becomes issuable, as illustrated on page 184.[14]

"Negative Goodwill"

In some purchase-type business combinations (known as ***bargain purchases***), the current fair values assigned to the identifiable net assets acquired exceed the total cost of the combinee. A bargain purchase is most likely to occur for a combinee with a history of losses or when common stock prices are extremely low. The excess of the current fair values over total cost is applied pro rata to reduce (but not below zero) the amounts initially assigned to all the acquired assets except financial assets other than investments accounted for by the equity method; assets to be disposed of by sale; deferred tax assets; prepaid assets relating to pension or other postretirement benefits; and any other current assets. If any excess of current fair values over cost of the combinee's net assets remains after the foregoing reduction, it is recognized as an extraordinary gain by the combinor.[15]

Illustration of Purchase Accounting for Statutory Merger, with Goodwill

On December 31, 2002, Mason Company (the combinee) was merged into Saxon Corporation (the combinor or survivor). Both companies used the same accounting principles for assets, liabilities, revenue, and expenses and both had a December 31 fiscal year. Saxon issued 150,000 shares of its $10 par common stock (current fair value

---

[12] *FASB Interpretation No. 21,* "Accounting for Leases in a Business Combination" (Stamford: FASB, 1978), pars. 12–15.
[13] *FASB Statement No. 141,* par. 40.
[14] Ibid., par. 28.
[15] Ibid., pars. 44, 45.

$25 a share) to Mason's stockholders for all 100,000 issued and outstanding shares of Mason's no-par, $10 stated value common stock. In addition, Saxon paid the following out-of-pocket costs associated with the business combination:

Combinor's Out-of-Pocket Costs of Business Combination

Accounting fees:	
For investigation of Mason Company as prospective combinee	$ 5,000 Y
For SEC registration statement for Saxon common stock	60,000 N
Legal fees:	
For the business combination	10,000 Y
For SEC registration statement for Saxon common stock	50,000 N
Finder's fee	51,250 Y
Printer's charges for printing securities and SEC registration statement	23,000 N
SEC registration statement fee	750 N
Total out-of-pocket costs of business combination	$200,000

WOULD INCUR $

There was no contingent consideration in the merger contract.

Immediately prior to the merger, Mason Company's condensed balance sheet was as follows:

Combinee's Balance Sheet Prior to Merger Business Combination

MASON COMPANY (combinee)
Balance Sheet (prior to business combination)
December 31, 2002

Assets

Current assets	$1,000,000
Plant assets (net)	3,000,000
Other assets	600,000
Total assets	$4,600,000

Liabilities and Stockholders' Equity

Current liabilities	$ 500,000
Long-term debt	1,000,000
Common stock, no-par, $10 stated value	1,000,000
Additional paid-in capital	700,000
Retained earnings	1,400,000
Total liabilities and stockholders' equity	$4,600,000

Using the guidelines in *FASB Statement No. 141,* "Business Combinations" (see page 174), the board of directors of Saxon Corporation determined the current fair values of Mason Company's identifiable assets and liabilities (identifiable net assets) as follows:

Current Fair Values of Combinee's Identifiable Net Assets

Current assets	$1,150,000
Plant assets	3,400,000
Other assets	600,000
Current liabilities	(500,000)
Long-term debt (present value)	(950,000)
Identifiable net assets of combinee	$3,700,000

The condensed journal entries that follow are required for Saxon Corporation (the combinor) to record the merger with Mason Company on December 31, 2002, as a business combination. Saxon uses an investment ledger account to accumulate the total cost of Mason Company prior to assigning the cost to identifiable net assets and goodwill.

Combinor's Journal Entries for Business Combination (Statutory Merger)

SAXON CORPORATION (combinor)
Journal Entries
December 31, 2002

Investment in Mason Company Common Stock (150,000 × $25)	3,750,000	
Common Stock (150,000 × $10)		1,500,000
Paid-in Capital in Excess of Par		2,250,000
To record merger with Mason Company.		
Investment in Mason Company Common Stock ($5,000 + $10,000 + $51,250)	66,250	
Paid-in Capital in Excess of Par ($60,000 + $50,000 + $23,000 + 750)	133,750	
Cash		200,000
To record payment of out-of-pocket costs incurred in merger with Mason Company. Accounting, legal, and finder's fees in connection with the merger are recognized as an investment cost; other out-of-pocket costs are recorded as a reduction in the proceeds received from issuance of common stock.		
Current Assets	1,150,000	
Plant Assets	3,400,000	
Other Assets	600,000	
Discount on Long-Term Debt	50,000	
Goodwill	116,250	
Current Liabilities		500,000
Long-Term Debt		1,000,000
Investment in Mason Company Common Stock ($3,750,000 + $66,250)		3,816,250
To allocate total cost of liquidated Mason Company to identifiable assets and liabilities, with the remainder to goodwill. (Income tax effects are disregarded.) Amount of goodwill is computed as follows:		

Total cost of Mason Company ($3,750,000 + $66,250)		$3,816,250
Less: Carrying amount of Mason's identifiable net assets ($4,600,000 − $1,500,000)		$3,100,000
Excess (deficiency) of current fair values of identifiable net assets over carrying amounts:		
Current assets	150,000	
Plant assets	400,000	
Long-term debt	50,000	3,700,000
Amount of goodwill		$ 116,250

Note that no adjustments are made in the foregoing journal entries to reflect the current fair values of Saxon's identifiable net assets or goodwill, *because Saxon is the combinor in the business combination.*

Accounting for the income tax effects of business combinations is considered in Chapter 9.

Mason Company (the combinee) prepares the condensed journal entry below to record the dissolution and liquidation of the company on December 31, 2002.

Recording the Liquidation of Combinee

MASON COMPANY (combinee)
Journal Entry
December 31, 2002

Current Liabilities	500,000	
Long-Term Debt	1,000,000	
Common Stock, $10 stated value	1,000,000	
Paid-in Capital in Excess of Stated Value	700,000	
Retained Earnings	1,400,000	
Current Assets		1,000,000
Plant Assets (net)		3,000,000
Other Assets		600,000
To record liquidation of company in conjunction with merger with Saxon Corporation.		

Illustration of Purchase Accounting for Acquisition of Net Assets, with Bargain-Purchase Excess

On December 31, 2002, Davis Corporation acquired the net assets of Fairmont Corporation directly from Fairmont for $400,000 cash, in a business combination. Davis paid legal fees of $40,000 in connection with the combination.

The condensed balance sheet of Fairmont prior to the business combination, with related current fair value data, is presented below:

Balance sheet of Combinee Prior to Business Combination

FAIRMONT CORPORATION (combinee)
Balance Sheet (prior to business combination)
December 31, 2002

	Carrying Amounts	Current Fair Values
Assets		
Current assets	$ 190,000	$ 200,000
Investment in marketable debt securities (held to maturity)	50,000	60,000
Plant assets (net)	870,000	900,000
Intangible assets (net)	90,000	100,000
Total assets	$1,200,000	$1,260,000
Liabilities and Stockholders' Equity		
Current liabilities	$ 240,000	$ 240,000
Long-term debt	500,000	520,000
Total liabilities	$ 740,000	$ 760,000
Common stock, $1 par	$ 600,000	
Deficit	(140,000)	
Total stockholders' equity	$ 460,000	
Total liabilities and stockholders' equity	$1,200,000	

Thus, Davis acquired identifiable net assets with a current fair value of $500,000 ($1,260,000 − $760,000 = $500,000) for a total cost of $440,000 ($400,000 + $40,000 = $440,000). The $60,000 excess of current fair value of the net assets over their cost to Davis ($500,000 − $440,000 = $60,000) is prorated to the plant assets and intangible assets in the ratio of their respective current fair values, as follows:

Allocation of Excess of Current Fair Value Over Cost of Identifiable Net Assets of Combinee in Business Combination

To plant assets: $60,000 × $\dfrac{\$900,000}{\$900,000 + \$100,000}$	$54,000
To intangible assets: $60,000 × $\dfrac{\$100,000}{\$900,000 + \$100,000}$	6,000
Total excess of current fair value of identifiable net assets over combinor's cost	$60,000

No part of the $60,000 bargain-purchase excess is allocated to current assets or to the investment in marketable securities.

The journal entries below record Davis Corporation's acquisition of the net assets of Fairmont Corporation and payment of $40,000 legal fees:

Combinor's Journal Entries for Business Combination (Acquisition of Net Assets)

DAVIS CORPORATION (combinor)
Journal Entries
December 31, 2002

Investment in Net Assets of Fairmont Corporation	400,000	
Cash		400,000
To record acquisition of net assets of Fairmont Corporation.		
Investment in Net Assets of Fairmont Corporation	40,000	
Cash		40,000
To record payment of legal fees incurred in acquisition of net assets of Fairmont Corporation.		
Current Assets	200,000	
Investments in Marketable Debt Securities	60,000	
Plant Assets ($900,000 − $54,000)	846,000	
Intangible Assets ($100,000 − $6,000)	94,000	
Current Liabilities		240,000
Long-Term Debt		500,000
Premium on Long-Term Debt ($520,000 − $500,000)		20,000
Investment in Net Assets of Fairmont Corporation ($400,000 + $40,000)		440,000
To allocate total cost of net assets acquired to identifiable net assets, with excess of current fair value of the net assets over their cost prorated to noncurrent assets other than investment in marketable debt securities. (Income tax effects are disregarded.)		

Other Topics in Accounting for Business Combinations

Statutory Consolidation

Because a new corporation issues common stock to effect a statutory consolidation, one óf the constituent companies in a statutory consolidation must be identified as the combinor, under the criteria described on page 175. Once the combinor has been identified, the new corporation recognizes net assets acquired from the combinor at their *carrying amount* in the combinor's accounting records; however, net assets acquired from the combinee are recognized by the new corporation at their *current fair value*.

To illustrate, assume the following balance sheets of the constituent companies involved in a statutory consolidation on December 31, 2002:

LAMSON CORPORATION AND DONALD COMPANY Separate Balance Sheets (prior to business combination) December 31, 2002		
	Lamson Corporation	**Donald Company**
Assets		
Current assets	$ 600,000	$ 400,000
Plant assets (net)	1,800,000	1,200,000
Other assets	400,000	300,000
Total assets	$2,800,000	$1,900,000
Liabilities and Stockholders' Equity		
Current liabilities	$ 400,000	$ 300,000
Long-term debt	500,000	200,000
Common stock, $10 par	430,000	620,000
Additional paid-in capital	300,000	400,000
Retained earnings	1,170,000	380,000
Total liabilities and stockholders' equity	$2,800,000	$1,900,000

The current fair values of both companies' liabilities were equal to carrying amounts. Current fair values of identifiable assets were as follows for Lamson and Donald, respectively: current assets, $800,000 and $500,000; plant assets, $2,000,000 and $1,400,000; other assets, $500,000 and $400,000.

On December 31, 2002, in a statutory consolidation approved by shareholders of both constituent companies, a new corporation, LamDon Corporation, issued 74,000 shares of no-par, no-stated-value common stock with an agreed value of $60 a share, based on the following valuations assigned by the negotiating directors to the two constituent companies' identifiable net assets and goodwill:

PLUG

Computation of Number of Shares of Common Stock Issued in Statutory Consolidation	**Lamson Corporation**	**Donald Company**
Current fair value of identifiable net assets:		
Lamson: $800,000 + $2,000,000 + $500,000 − $400,000 − $500,000	$2,400,000	
Donald: $500,000 + $1,400,000 + $400,000 − $300,000 − $200,000		$1,800,000
Goodwill	180,000	60,000
Net assets' current fair value	$2,580,000	$1,860,000
Number of shares of LamDon common stock to be issued to constituent companies' stockholders, at $60 a share agreed value	43,000	31,000

44

Because the former stockholders of Lamson Corporation receive the larger interest in the common stock of LamDon Corporation ($^{43}/_{74}$, or 58%), Lamson is the combinor in the business combination. Assuming that LamDon paid $200,000 out-of-pocket costs of the statutory consolidation after it was consummated on December 31, 2002, Lam-Don's journal entries would be as follows:

Journal Entries for
New Corporation for
Business Combination
(Statutory Consolidation)

LAMDON CORPORATION
Journal Entries
December 31, 2002

Investment in Lamson Corporation and Donald Company		
Common Stock (74,000 × $60)	4,440,000	
Common Stock, no par		4,400,000
To record consolidation of Lamson Corporation and Donald Company as a purchase.		
Investment in Lamson Corporation and Donald Company		
Common Stock	110,000	
Common Stock, no par	90,000	
Cash		200,000
To record payment of costs incurred in consolidation of Lamson Corporation and Donald Company. Accounting, legal, and finder's fees in connection with the consolidation are recorded as investment cost; other out-of-pocket costs are recorded as a reduction in the proceeds received from the issuance of common stock.		
Current Assets ($600,000 + $500,000)	1,100,000	
Plant Assets ($1,800,000 + $1,400,000)	3,200,000	
Other Assets ($400,000 + $400,000)	800,000	
Goodwill	850,000	
Current Liabilities ($400,000 + $300,000)		700,000
Long-Term Debt ($500,000 + $200,000)		700,000
Investment in Lamson Corporation and Donald Company		
Common Stock ($4,440,000 + $110,000)		4,550,000
To allocate total cost of investment to identifiable assets and liabilities, at carrying amount for combinor Lamson Corporation's net assets and at current fair value for combinee Donald Company's net assets. (Income tax effects are disregarded.)		

Amount of goodwill is computed as follows:

Total cost of investment	
($4,440,000 + $110,000)	$4,550,000
Less: Carrying amount of Lamson's identifiable	
net assets	(1,900,000)
Current fair value of Donald's identifiable	
net assets	(1,800,000)
Amount of goodwill	$ 850,000

Note in the foregoing journal entry that because of the combinor's net assets' being recognized at carrying amount and because of the $110,000 direct out-of-pocket costs of the business combination, the amount of goodwill is $850,000, rather than $240,000 ($180,000 + $60,000 = $240,000), the amount assigned by the negotiating directors to goodwill in the determination of the number of shares of common stock to be issued in the combination (see page 182).

Subsequent Issuance of Contingent Consideration

As indicated on page 175, contingent consideration that is **determinable** on the date of a purchase-type business combination is included in the measurement of cost of the combinee. Any other contingent consideration is recorded when the contingency is resolved and the additional consideration becomes issuable or is issued.

Returning to the Norton Company illustration on page 176, assume that by December 31, 2003, the end of the first year following Norton's acquisition of the net assets of Robinson Company, another 300 units of the slow-moving product had been sold, and Norton's Robb Division had pre-tax financial income of $580,000 (exclusive of income from the slow-moving product). On December 31, 2003, Norton prepares the following journal entry to record the resolution of contingent consideration:

Journal Entry for Contingent Consideration Involving Subsequent Sales and Earnings

Goodwill	50,000	
Payable to Robinson Company		50,000
To record payable contingent consideration applicable to January 2, 2002, business combination as follows:		
Sales of slow-moving product (300 × $100)	$30,000	
Pretax income of Robb Division [($580,000 − $500,000) × 0.25]	20,000	
Total payable	$50,000	

Some purchase-type business combinations involve contingent consideration based on subsequent market prices of debt or equity securities issued to effect the combination. Unless the subsequent market price equals at least a minimum amount on a subsequent date or dates, additional securities, cash, or other assets must be issued by the combinor to compensate for the deficiency.

For example, assume the following journal entry for the statutory merger of Soltero Corporation and Mero Company on January 2, 2002:

Journal Entry for Business Combination (Statutory Merger)

Investment in Mero Company Common Stock (120,000 × $12)	1,440,000	
Common Stock, $5 stated value (120,000 × $5)		600,000
Paid-in Capital in Excess of Stated Value		840,000
To record merger with Mero Company as a purchase.		

Assume that terms of the Soltero–Mero business combination required Soltero to issue additional shares of its common stock to the former stockholders of Mero if the market price of Soltero's common stock was less than $12 a share on December 31, 2002. If the market price of Soltero's common stock was $10 on that date, Soltero prepares the following journal entry on that date:

<table>
<tr><td rowspan="11" style="vertical-align:top">**Journal Entry for Contingent Consideration Involving Subsequent Market Price of Common Stock**</td></tr>
</table>

Journal Entry for Contingent Consideration Involving Subsequent Market Price of Common Stock

Paid-in Capital in Excess of Stated Value (24,000 × $5)	120,000	
Common Stock to Be Issued for Contingent Consideration		120,000
To record additional shares of common stock to be issued under terms of Jan. 2, 2002, merger with Mero company, as follows:		
Required value of common stock issued in merger		
(120,000 × $12)	$1,440,000	
Less: Market value of common stock, Dec. 31, 2002		
(120,000 × $10)	1,200,000	
Market value of additional common stock to be issued	$ 240,000	
Number of additional shares of common stock to be		
issued ($240,000 ÷ $10)	24,000	

The foregoing journal entry is in accord with the following provisions of *FASB Statement No. 141,* "Business Combinations":

> The issuance of additional securities or distribution of other consideration upon resolution of a contingency based on security prices shall not affect the cost of the [combinee], regardless of whether the amount specified is a security price to be maintained or a higher security price to be achieved. When the contingency is resolved and additional consideration is distributable, the [combinor] shall record the current fair value of the additional consideration issued or issuable. However, the amount previously recorded for securities issued at the date of [the business combination] shall be simultaneously reduced to the lower current value of those securities. Reducing the value of debt securities previously issued to their later fair value results in recording a discount on debt securities. The discount should be amortized from the date the additional securities are issued.[16]

IAS 22, *"Accounting for Business Combinations"*

The International Accounting Standards Board requires purchase-type accounting for all business combinations except those deemed a **uniting of interests,** defined as a combination in which the stockholders of the constituent companies combine into one entity the whole of the net assets and operations of those companies to achieve a continuing mutual sharing of the risks and benefits of the combined enterprise. For a uniting-of-interests–type combination, pooling-of-interests accounting (see pages 190–191) **must** be used. Further, goodwill in a purchase-type business combination must be amortized over a period not exceeding 20 years.

Accounting for Acquired Intangible Assets Subsequent to a Business Combination

In *FASB Statement No. 142,* "Goodwill and Other Intangible Assets," the Financial Accounting Standards Board provided that intangible assets with finite useful lives were to be amortized over those estimated useful lives. In contrast, goodwill and other intangible assets with indefinite useful lives were **not** to be amortized but were to be tested for impairment at least annually.[17] The FASB also provided detailed procedures for impairment tests.[18] Those procedures typically are described and illustrated in intermediate accounting textbooks.

---

[16] *FASB Statement No. 141,* par. 30.
[17] *FASB Statement No. 142,* "Goodwill and Other Intangible Assets," pars. 11, 16, 18.
[18] Ibid. pars. 17, 19–25.

Financial Statements Following a Business Combination

The balance sheet for a combined enterprise issued as of the date of a business combination accomplished through a statutory merger, statutory consolidation, or acquisition of assets includes all the assets and liabilities of the constituent companies. (The *consolidated* balance sheet issued immediately following a combination that results in a parent-subsidiary relationship is described in Chapter 6.) In a balance sheet following a business combination, assets and liabilities of the combinor are at *carrying amount,* assets acquired from the combinee are at *current fair value* (adjusted for any bargain-purchase excess as illustrated on page 181), and *retained earnings is that of the combinor only.* The income statement of the combined enterprise for the accounting period in which a business combination occurred includes the operating results of the combinee *after the date of the combination only.*

Disclosure of Business Combinations in a Note to Financial Statements

Because of the complex nature of business combinations and their effects on the financial position and operating results of the combined enterprise, extensive disclosure is required for the periods in which they occur.

Following are the extensive disclosure requirements for business combinations established by the FASB:[19]

The notes to the financial statements of a combined entity shall disclose the following information in the period in which a material business combination is completed:

1. The name and a brief description of the acquired entity and the percentage of voting equity interests acquired

2. The primary reasons for the acquisition, including a description of the factors that contributed to a purchase price that results in recognition of goodwill

3. The period for which the results of operations of the acquired entity are included in the income statement of the combined entity

4. The cost of the acquired entity and, if applicable, the number of shares of equity interests (such as common shares, preferred shares, or partnership interests) issued or issuable, the value assigned to those interests, and the basis for determining that value

5. A condensed balance sheet disclosing the amount assigned to each major asset and liability caption of the acquired entity at the acquisition date

6. Contingent payments, options, or commitments specified in the acquisition agreement and the accounting treatment that will be followed should any such contingency occur

7. The amount of purchased research and development assets acquired and written off in the period . . . and the line item in the income statement in which the amounts written off are aggregated

8. For any purchase price allocation that has not been finalized, that fact and the reasons therefor. In subsequent periods, the nature and amount of any material adjustments made to the initial allocation of the purchase price shall be disclosed.

The notes to the financial statements also shall disclose the following information in the period in which a material business combination is completed if the amounts as-

---

[19] Ibid., pars. 51–55.

signed to goodwill or to other intangible assets acquired are significant in relation to the total cost of the acquired entity:

1. For intangible assets subject to amortization:
   a. The total amount assigned and the amount assigned to any major intangible asset class
   b. The amount of any significant residual value, in total and by major intangible asset class
   c. The weighted-average amortization period, in total and by major intangible asset class
2. For intangible assets *not* subject to amortization, the total amount assigned and the amount assigned to any major intangible asset class
3. For goodwill:
   a. The total amount of goodwill and the amount that is expected to be deductible for tax purposes
   b. The amount of goodwill by reportable segment (if the combined entity is required to disclose segment information in accordance with *FASB Statement No. 131.* "Disclosures about Segments of an Enterprise and Related Information," unless not practicable.

The notes to the financial statements shall disclose the following information if a series of individually immaterial business combinations completed during the period are material in the aggregate:

1. The number of entities acquired and a brief description of those entities

2. The aggregate cost of the acquired entities, the number of equity interests (such as common shares, preferred shares, or partnership interests) issued or issuable, and the value assigned to those interests

3. The aggregate amount of any contingent payments, options, or commitments and the accounting treatment that will be followed should any such contingency occur (if potentially significant in relation to the aggregate cost of the acquired entities)

4. Information regarding intangible assets and goodwill if the aggregate amount assigned to those assets acquired is significant in relation to the aggregate cost of the acquired entities.

If the combined entity is a **public business enterprise,** the notes to the financial statements shall include the following supplemental information on a pro forma basis for the period in which a material business combination occurs (or for the period in which a series of individually immaterial business combinations occur that are material in the aggregate):

1. Results of operations for the current period as though the business combination or combinations had been completed at the beginning of the period, unless the acquisition was at or near the beginning of the period

2. Results of operations for the comparable prior period as though the business combination or combinations had been completed at the beginning of that period if comparative financial statements are presented.

At a minimum, the supplemental pro forma information shall display revenue, income before extraordinary items and the cumulative effect of accounting changes, net income, and earnings per share. In determining the pro forma amounts, income taxes, interest expense, preferred share dividends, and depreciation and amortization of assets shall be adjusted to the accounting base recognized for each in recording the combination. Pro forma information related to results of operations of periods prior to the combination shall be limited to the results of operations for the immediately preceding period. Disclosure also shall be made of the nature and amount of any material, nonrecurring items reported in the pro forma results of operations.

APPRAISAL OF ACCOUNTING STANDARDS FOR BUSINESS COMBINATIONS

The accounting standards for business combinations described and illustrated in the preceding pages of this chapter may be criticized on grounds that they are not consistent with the conceptual framework for financial accounting and reporting.

The principal criticisms of purchase accounting center on the recognition of goodwill. Many accountants take exception to the *residual* basis for valuing goodwill established in *FASB Statement No. 141.* These critics contend that part of the amounts thus assigned to goodwill probably apply to other *identifiable* intangible assets. Accordingly, goodwill in a business combination should be valued *directly* by use of methods described in intermediate accounting textbooks. Any remaining cost not directly allocated to all identifiable tangible and intangible assets and to goodwill would be apportioned to those assets based on the amounts assigned in the first valuation process or recognized as a loss.

Other accountants question whether current fair values of the *combinor's* net assets—especially goodwill—should be disregarded in accounting for a purchase-type business combination. They maintain it is inconsistent to reflect current fair values for net assets of the *combinee only,* in view of the significance of many combinations involving large constituent companies.

SEC ENFORCEMENT ACTIONS DEALING WITH WRONGFUL APPLICATION OF ACCOUNTING STANDARDS FOR BUSINESS COMBINATIONS

AAER 38

AAER 38, "Securities and Exchange Commission v. Corda Diversified Technologies Inc., et al." (September 10, 1984), reports a federal court's entry of an injunction against a corporate manufacturer and marketer of residential, commercial, and industrial hardware and its CEO, CFO, and independent auditors. The SEC stated that the corporation, which formerly had been a publicly owned "shell" with no operations, had wrongly been identified as the combinor in a business combination with a privately owned company. Because the former stockholders of the privately owned corporation controlled 75% of the outstanding common stock of the "shell" following the business combination, the privately owned company was the combinor. Nonetheless, it was improperly accounted for as the combinee, and its assets were carried at current fair values in the consolidated financial statements. The result was that consolidated total assets, reported as $15,119,727, were overstated by at least $9 million. In a related enforcement action, reported in *AAER 39,* ". . . In the Matter of Smith & Stephens Accountancy Corporation and James J. Smith" (September 10, 1984), the SEC permanently prohibited the independent auditors of the manufacturing corporation from appearing or practicing before the SEC, with the proviso that, under specified conditions, the auditors could apply for reinstatement after two years.

AAER 275

In *AAER 275,* ". . . In the Matter of Charles C. Lehman, Jr." (September 28, 1990), the SEC reported the permanent disbarment of a CPA from appearing or practicing before it, with the proviso that the CPA might, if he complied with specified conditions, apply for reinstatement in 18 months. According to the SEC, the CPA, on behalf of the firm of which he was managing partner, improperly expressed an unqualified audit opinion on the financial statements of a combined enterprise following a merger in which the *survivor* was improperly identified as the *combinor.* The *merging company* actually was the combinor because following the business combination its former sole stockholder owned 82.8% of the outstanding common stock of the survivor. The consequence of the misidentification of the combinor was the overstatement of a principal asset of the combined enterprise by 12,045% ($1,342,600 compared with $11,055).

AAER 598

A significant part of *AAER 598,* ". . . In the Matter of Meris Laboratories, Inc., Stephen B. Kass, and John J. DiPitro" (September 26, 1994), deals with an independent clinical laboratory's improper accounting for direct out-of-pocket costs of business combinations. According to the SEC, included in such costs, which were capitalized as part of the total costs of the combinations, were payroll costs of employees who were to be terminated following the combinations; writeoffs of combinee accounts receivable; erroneously paid sales commissions; various recurring internal costs of operations; and payments under consulting contracts. The aggregate overstatement of income resulting from the improper accounting was 80%. The SEC ordered the clinical laboratory, its CEO, and its CFO (a CPA) to cease and desist from violating the federal securities laws.

AAERs 601, 606, and 607

The SEC undertook enforcement actions against the engagement partner and audit manager of a CPA firm and the controller of the firm's audit client as reported in the following releases:

- *AAER 601,* ". . . In the Matter of Martin Halpern, CPA" (September 27, 1994).

- *AAER 606,* ". . . In the Matter of Louis Fox, CPA" (September 28, 1994).

- *AAER 607,* ". . . In the Matter of Jeffrey R. Pearlman, CPA" (September 28, 1994).

The SEC found that the engagement partner and manager of the CPA firm had failed to comply with generally accepted auditing standards in the audit of financial statements prepared by the controller following a business combination in which the combinor was improperly identified as the combinee. The result was a nearly $18,000,000 overstatement of the combinor's patents in the financial statements of the combined enterprise. The audit manager was permanently barred from practicing before the SEC, and the engagement partner and company controller were similarly barred, but for a period of three years.

Appendix

Now-Prohibited Pooling-of-Interests Accounting for Business Combinations

The original premise of the pooling-of-interests method was that certain business combinations *involving the exchange of common stock* between an *issuer* and the *stockholders of a combinee* were more in the nature of a *combining of existing stockholder interests* than an *acquisition of assets* or *raising of capital.* Combining of existing stockholder interests was evidenced by combinations involving common stock exchanges between corporations *of approximately equal size.* The stockholders and managements of these corporations continued their relative interests and activities in the combined enterprise as they previously did in the constituent companies. Because neither of the like-size constituent companies could be considered the *combinor* under the criteria set forth on page 175, the pooling-of-interests method of accounting provided for carrying forward to the accounting records of the combined enterprise the combined assets, liabilities, and retained earnings of the constituent companies at their *carrying amounts* in the accounting records of the constituent companies. The current fair value of the common stock issued to effect the business combination and the current fair value of the combinee's net assets were *disregarded* in pooling-of-interests accounting. Further, because there *allegedly* was no identifiable combinor in a pooling-type business combination, the term *issuer* identified the corporation that issued its common stock to accomplish the combination.

ILLUSTRATION OF POOLING-OF-INTERESTS ACCOUNTING FOR STATUTORY MERGER

The Saxon Corporation–Mason Company merger business combination described on pages 177 to 178 would have been accounted for as a pooling of interests by the following journal entries in Saxon Corporation's (the survivor's) accounting records:

Survivor's Journal Entries for Pooling-Type Business Combination (Statutory Merger)

SAXON CORPORATION (survivor)
Journal Entries
December 31, 2002

Current Assets	1,000,000	
Plant Assets (net)	3,000,000	
Other Assets	600,000	
Current Liabilities		500,000
Long-Term Debt		1,000,000
Common Stock, $10 par		1,500,000
Paid-in Capital in Excess of Par		200,000
Retained Earnings		1,400,000
To record merger with Mason Company as a pooling of interests.		
Expenses of Business Combination	200,000	
Cash		200,000
To record payment of out-of-pocket costs incurred in merger with Mason Company.		

Because a pooling-type business combination is a combining of existing stockholder interests rather than an acquisition of assets, an Investment in Mason Company Common Stock ledger account, as employed in the purchase accounting illustration on page 179, was not used in the foregoing journal entries. Instead, in the first journal entry, Mason's assets, liabilities, and retained earnings are assigned their carrying amounts in Mason's premerger balance sheet (see page 178). Because the common stock issued by Saxon Corporation must be recorded at *par* (150,000 shares × $10 = $1,500,000), the $200,000 credit to paid-in capital in excess of par is a ***balancing amount*** for the journal entry. It may be verified as shown below:

<table>
<tr><td rowspan="3" style="text-align:left">**Computation of Survivor's Credit to Paid-in Capital in Excess of Par**</td><td>Total paid-in capital of Mason Company prior to merger
  ($1,000,000 + $700,000)</td><td style="text-align:right">$1,700,000</td></tr>
<tr><td>Less: Par value of Saxon Corporation common stock issued
  in merger</td><td style="text-align:right">1,500,000</td></tr>
<tr><td>Amount credited to Saxon Corporation's Paid-in Capital in
  Excess of Par ledger account</td><td style="text-align:right">$ 200,000</td></tr>
</table>

If the par value of common stock issued by Saxon Corporation had ***exceeded*** the total paid-in capital of Mason Company, Saxon's Paid-in Capital in Excess of Par ledger account would have been ***debited*** in the illustrated journal entry. If the balance of Saxon's Paid-in Capital in Excess of Par account was insufficient to absorb the debit, Saxon's Retained Earnings account would have been reduced.

In the second journal entry above ***all*** out-of-pocket costs of the business combination were ***recognized as expenses*** because a pooling-type business combination is neither an acquisition of assets nor a raising of capital. The expenses of business combination are not deductible for income tax purposes; thus Saxon Corporation does not adjust its income taxes expense and liability ledger accounts.

Mason Company's journal entry to record the dissolution and liquidation of the company would be identical to the journal entry illustrated on page 180.

POPULARITY OF POOLING ACCOUNTING

The pooling method of accounting for business combinations was sanctioned initially by the AICPA in ***Accounting Research Bulletin No. 40,*** "Business Combinations." However, ***ARB No. 40*** provided few criteria for identifying the business combinations that qualified for pooling accounting and was therefore unsatisfactory as a guide for this accounting method. Subsequently, ***ARB No. 48,*** "Business Combinations," superseded the previous pronouncement with an expanded discussion of the pooling method. ***ARB No. 48*** continued to permit pooling accounting for most business combinations involving an exchange of common stock. However, ***ARB No. 48*** also failed to provide definitive guidelines for identifying the business combinations that qualified for pooling accounting. As a result, a substantial number of business combinations arranged during the 1950s and 1960s were accounted for as poolings, despite the fact that the "combining of existing stockholder interests" aspect was absent.

Why had pooling accounting become so popular? Some of the reasons are apparent from the following comparison of the combined Saxon Corporation journal entries illustrated on pages 175 and 190 for the merger with Mason Company:

Comparison of Combinor's/Issuer's Journal Entries—Purchase and Pooling

	Purchase Accounting		Pooling Accounting	
Current Assets	1,150,000		1,000,000	
Plant Assets	3,400,000		3,000,000	
Other Assets	600,000		600,000	
Discount on Long-Term Debt	50,000			
Goodwill	116,250			
Expenses of Business Combination			200,000	
Current Liabilities		500,000		500,000
Long-Term Debt		1,000,000		1,000,000
Common Stock, $10 par		1,500,000		1,500,000
Paid-in Capital in Excess of Par		2,116,250		200,000
Retained Earnings				1,400,000
Cash		200,000		200,000
To record merger with Mason Company.				

Differences in Net Assets

The first difference to consider in comparing the foregoing journal entries is that the net assets recorded under the purchase method ($3,616,250) exceed the pooling-method net assets ($2,900,000) by $716,250. The composition of the $716,250 is summarized below:

Composition of Difference in Net Assets—Purchase Versus Pooling

Excess of purchase asset values over pooling asset values:	
Current assets ($1,150,000 − $1,000,000)	$150,000
Plant assets ($3,400,000 − $3,000,000)	400,000
Goodwill	116,250
Excess of pooling liability values over purchase liability values:	
Long-term debt [$1,000,000 − ($1,000,000 − $50,000)]	50,000
Excess of purchase net assets values over pooling net assets values	$716,250

Assuming that the $400,000 difference in plant assets was attributable to *depreciable* assets, total expenses of Saxon Corporation for years subsequent to December 31, 2002, would have been $716,250 larger under purchase accounting than under pooling accounting. Assume, for example, that the $150,000 difference in current assets was attributable to inventories that would be allocated to cost of goods sold on the first-in, first-out basis; the average economic life of the depreciable plant assets was 10 years; the goodwill would be required to be amortized over a 40-year period; and the long-term debt had a remaining five-year term to maturity.[20] Saxon Corporation's *pre-tax income* for the year ending December 31, 2003 (the year following the merger), would have been nearly $203,000 less under purchase accounting than under pooling accounting, attributable to the following larger postmerger expenses under purchase accounting:

[20] For simplicity, the discount on long-term debt is amortized by the straight-line method. Theoretically, and in actual practice, the *interest* method described in intermediate accounting textbooks is used when the difference between the two methods is material in amount.

Difference in Pre-Tax Income—Purchase Versus Pooling

Cost of goods sold	$150,000
Depreciation expense ($400,000 × $\frac{1}{10}$)	40,000
Amortization expense ($116,250 × $\frac{1}{40}$)	2,906
Interest expense ($50,000 × $\frac{1}{5}$)	10,000
Excess of 2003 pre-tax income under pooling accounting rather than under purchase accounting	$202,906

It is true that pre-tax income for the year ended December 31, 2002 (the year of the merger), is reduced $200,000 in pooling accounting, because the pooling method included the immediate ***expensing*** of the out-of-pocket costs of the business combination. However, this situation tended to be obscured by the fact that the income statements of Saxon Corporation and Mason Company would have been combined in pooling accounting for the ***entire*** year ended December 31, 2002.

In summary, the favorable effect of pooling accounting on post-combination earnings has been the main reason for the popularity of this accounting method for business combinations.

Difference in Total Paid-in Capital

The increase in Saxon Corporation's total paid-in capital is $1,916,250 less ($3,616,250 − $1,700,000 = $1,916,250) under pooling accounting than under purchase accounting. Of this difference, $1,200,000 ($1,400,000 − $200,000 = $1,200,000) is attributable to a net increase in Saxon Corporation's retained earnings under the pooling accounting method. If state laws make this $1,200,000 available as a basis for dividend declarations by Saxon, another advantage of the pooling method of accounting is readily apparent.

Impact of Different Price-Earnings Ratios

Even more dramatic than the preceding advantages inherent in the pooling-of-interests method of accounting is the potential impact on the market price of Saxon Corporation's common stock if the price-earnings ratios for Saxon's and Mason's common stock differed significantly prior to the merger. Suppose, for example, that Saxon Corporation and Mason Company had the following financial information prior to the business combination:

Selected Financial Information Prior to Business Combination

	Saxon Corporation	Mason Company
Year ended Dec. 31, 2002:		
Net income	$ 500,000*	$375,000
Basic earnings per share of common stock	$0.50	$3.75
On Dec. 31, 2002:		
Number of shares of common stock outstanding	1,000,000[†]	100,000[†]
Market price per share	$25	$30
Price-earnings ratio	50	8

* Net of $200,000 expenses of business combination.
[†] Outstanding during entire year.

After consummation of the business combination as a pooling, Saxon Corporation's income statement for the year ended December 31, 2002, would have reported the combined enterprise's net income as $875,000 ($500,000 + $375,000 = $875,000)—the total of the separate net incomes of the constituent companies. "Pooled" basic earnings per share for Saxon thus is increased to approximately $0.76. This increased amount of basic earnings per share is computed by dividing combined earnings of $875,000 by 1,150,000 (1,000,000 + 150,000 = 1,150,000), the *effective* number of shares of Saxon's common stock considered to have been outstanding during the year ended December 31, 2002. If the price-earnings ratio for Saxon's common stock continued unchanged, the stock's market price would increase after the merger to $38 a share ($0.76 × 50 = $38), a 52% increase ($13 ÷ $25 = 0.52). Saxon Corporation probably would attain the reputation of an "exciting growth company," and Saxon's directors likely would seek out other prospects for pooling-type business combinations.

Less significant advantages attributed to the pooling method of accounting for business combinations result from the fact that the carrying amounts of assets and liabilities of the combinee are not restated. Pooling accounting thus parallels income tax accounting if the business combination qualifies as a "tax-free corporate reorganization." Further, the recognition of goodwill and its subsequent amortization were not required in the pooling method.

PAST ABUSES OF POOLING ACCOUNTING AND AICPA REMEDIAL ACTIONS

The attractive features of pooling accounting described in the preceding section, together with the absence of firm guidelines for poolings in *ARB No. 48,* led to a number of serious abuses of the method in the past. These abuses led the AICPA to issue, in 1970, *APB Opinion No. 16,* which limited application of the pooling-of-interests method of accounting to business combinations that met 12 specified criteria. These criteria, *all of which were to be satisfied for pooling to be permitted,* were divided into three groups as follows:

1. *Attributes of the combining companies.* The two conditions in this group were designed to assure that the pooling-type business combination was truly a combining of two or more enterprises whose common stockholder interests were *previously independent* of each other.

2. *Manner of combining ownership interests.* The seven conditions in this group supported the requirement for pooling accounting that an exchange of stock to combine existing voting common stock interests actually took place, in substance as well as in form.

3. *Absence of planned transactions.* The three planned transactions prohibited by this group of conditions were those that would be inconsistent with the combining of entire existing interests of common stockholders.

A business combination that met the Accounting Principles Board's 12 conditions had to be accounted for as a pooling, regardless of the legal form of the combination (statutory merger, statutory consolidation, acquisition of common stock, or acquisition of assets). Inexplicably, an acquisition of assets was construed as an "exchange of voting common stock interests" if all the other specified conditions for a pooling were met!

In the nearly 31 years between the 1970 issuance of *APB Opinion No.16,* "Business Combinations," and its 2001 supersession by *FASB Statement No. 141,* "Business Combinations," which prohibited application of the pooling-of-interests method of accounting for business combinations initiated after June 30, 2001, an increasing crescendo of criticism of the method arose, sparked primarily by academic accountants, who applied nicknames such as "dirty pooling," "pooling around," and "pfooling" to the method. Thus, in retrospect, it is interesting to note the prescient dissents to the issuance of ***APB Opinion No. 16*** by 6 of the 18 members of the Accounting Principles Board, as follows:

> *The Opinion entitled "Business Combinations" was adopted by the assenting votes of twelve members of the Board. Messrs. Broeker, Burger, Davidson, Horngren, Seidman, and Weston dissented.*

Messrs. Broeker, Burger, and Weston dissent to issuance of this Opinion because they believe that it is not a sound or logical solution of the problem of accounting for business combinations. They believe that, except for combinations of companies whose relative size is such as to indicate a significant sharing of ownership risks and benefits, business combinations represent the acquisition or purchase of one company by another and that accounting should reflect that fact. While they agree that the criteria specified in this Opinion for the pooling of interests method represent, in most cases, an improvement over present criteria in practice, this action does not, in their opinion, represent a substantive response by the Accounting Principles Board to the overall problem.

Messrs. Davidson, Horngren, and Seidman dissent to the Opinion because it seeks to patch up some of the abuses of pooling. The real abuse is pooling itself. On that, the only answer is to eliminate pooling. Paragraphs 35 to 41 set forth some of the defects of pooling. The fundamental one is that pooling ignores the asset values on which the parties have traded, and substitutes a wholly irrelevant figure—the amount on the seller's books. Such nonaccounting for bargained acquisition values permits the reporting of profits upon subsequent disposition of such assets when there really may be less profit or perhaps a loss. Had the assets been acquired from the seller for cash, the buyer's cost would be the amount of the cash. Acquisition for stock should make no difference. The accounting essence is the amount of consideration, not its nature. Payment in cash or stock can be a matter of form, not substance. Suppose the seller wants cash. The buyer can first sell stock and turn over the proceeds to the seller, or the seller can take stock and promptly sell the stock for cash.

The following deal with some arguments made in the Opinion for pooling: (1) Pooling is described in paragraph 28 as a fusion resulting from "pooling equity interests." But it is the sort of fusion where a significant exchange transaction takes place. The seller parts with control over its assets and operations. In return the buyer issues stock representing an interest in its assets and operations. That interest has value and is a measure of the cost of the acquisition to the buyer. (2) Paragraph 29 declares that pooling is really a transaction among the stockholders. That just is not the fact. The buyer is always a company. (3) Paragraph 25 decries purchase accounting because it results in a write-up of only seller's assets. There is no write-up. There is only a recording of cost to the buyer. That cost is measured by the value of the assets acquired from the seller. (4) Pooling is said to avoid the difficulty of valuing assets or stock (paragraph 22). Difficulty of valuation should not be permitted to defeat fair presentation. Besides, the parties do determine values in their bargaining for the amount of stock to be issued.

Some say that to eliminate pooling will impede mergers. Mergers were prevalent before pooling, and will continue after. Accounting does not exist to aid or discourage mergers, but to account for them fairly. Elimination of pooling will remove the confusion that comes from the coexistence of pooling and purchase accounting. Above all, the elimination of pooling would remove an aberration in historical-cost accounting that permits an acquisition to be accounted for on the basis of the seller's cost rather than the buyer's cost of the assets obtained in a bargained exchange.

SEC Enforcement Action Dealing with Wrongful Application of Pooling-of-Interests Accounting Standards

In ***AAER 1272,*** "In the Matter of Cendant Corporation" (June 14, 2000), the SEC issued a cease and desist order against an enterprise that had used a "cookie jar reserve" technique to overstate the expenses of numerous pooling-of-interests business combinations, with offsets to fictitious liabilities. Subsequent to the business combinations, the enterprise would reduce the fictitious liabilities by transferring amounts to revenues or offsetting current period expenses against them. Such "cooking the books" machinations resulted, according to the SEC, in overstatements of the enterprise's income totaling $79 million over a period of three fiscal years.

Review Questions

1. Define **business combination.**
2. Differentiate between a **statutory merger** and a **statutory consolidation.**
3. Identify two methods that may be used, individually or jointly, to determine an appropriate price to pay for a combinee in a business combination.
4. How is the **combinor** in a business combination determined?
5. State how each of the following out-of-pocket costs of a merger business combination is accounted for by the combinor:
   a. Printing costs for proxy statement mailed to combinor's stockholders in advance of special meeting to ratify terms of the merger.
   b. Legal fees for negotiating the merger.
   c. CPA firm's fees for auditing financial statements in SEC registration statement covering shares of common stock issued in the merger.
   d. Printing costs for common stock certificates issued in the merger.
   e. Legal fees for SEC registration statement covering shares of common stock issued in the merger.
   f. CPA firm's fees for advice on income tax aspects of the merger.
6. Goodwill often is recognized in business combinations. Explain the meaning of **goodwill** and **negative goodwill.**
7. Define **contingent consideration** in a business combination.
8. How is the total cost of a combinee allocated in a business combination?
9. Define the term **preacquisition contingencies.**
10. What combinee intangible assets other than goodwill are to be given accounting recognition in a business combination?

Exercises

(Exercise 5.1) Select the best answer for each of the following multiple-choice questions:

1. Is one or more of the constituent companies always liquidated in a business combination carried out by means of:

	A Statutory Merger?	A Statutory Consolidation?	An Acquisition of Common Stock?
a.	Yes	Yes	Yes
b.	Yes	No	Yes
c.	Yes	Yes	No
d.	No	Yes	Yes

2. The cost of a combinee in a business combination includes all the following except:
   a. Legal fees and finder's fee.
   b. Cost of registering and issuing debt securities issued to effect the combination.

    c. Amount of consideration.

    d. Contingent consideration that is determinable.

3. A target company's defense against an unfriendly takeover that involves the disposal of one or more profitable business segments of the target is termed:

    a. Pac-man defense *b.* Scorched earth *c.* Shark repellent *d.* Poison pill

4. Are the combinees **always** liquidated in business combinations accomplished by a(n):

	Statutory Merger?	Statutory Consolidation?	Acquisition of Common Stock?	Acquisition of Assets?
a.	Yes	Yes	Yes	No
b.	Yes	Yes	No	Yes
c.	Yes	Yes	No	No
d.	Yes	No	No	Yes

5. In a "bargain purchase" business combination, the excess of the current fair value of the combinee's identifiable net assets over the cost to the combinor is:

    a. Credited to the combinor's Negative Goodwill ledger account.

    b. Offset against the balance of the combinor's Investment in Combinee Company ledger account.

    c. Credited to the combinor's Additional Paid-in Capital ledger account.

    d. Accounted for in some other manner.

6. The term **survivor** is associated with a business combination accomplished through:

    a. A statutory merger.

    b. A statutory consolidation.

    c. An acquisition of common stock.

    d. An acquisition of assets.

7. Does the date-of-combination cost of the combinee in a business combination include:

	Determinable Contingent Consideration?	Nondeterminable Contingent Consideration?
a.	Yes	Yes
b.	Yes	No
c.	No	Yes
d.	No	No

8. In the balance sheet of a combined enterprise on the date of a business combination, **unallocated** negative goodwill is displayed:

    a. In stockholders' equity.

    b. In a note to financial statements.

    c. As an offset to total assets.

    d. As a deferred credit.

    e. In some other manner.

(Exercise 5.2)

CHECK FIGURE

Debit goodwill, $90,000.

The balance sheet of Mel Company on January 31, 2002, showed current assets, $100,000; other assets, $800,000; current liabilities, $80,000; long-term debt, $240,000; common stock (10,000 shares, $10 par), $100,000; and retained earnings, $480,000. On that date, Mel merged with Sal Corporation in a business combination in which Sal issued 35,000 shares of its $1 par (current fair value $20 a share) common stock to stockholders of Mel in exchange for all their outstanding common stock. The current fair values of Mel's liabilities were equal to their carrying amounts; the current fair values of Mel's current assets and other assets (none intangible) were $120,000 and $850,000, respectively, on January 31, 2002. Also on that date, Sal paid direct out-of-pocket costs of the business combination, $40,000, and costs of registering and issuing its common stock, $70,000.

Prepare journal entries (omit explanations) for Sal Corporation to record its merger with Mel Company on January 31, 2002. (Disregard income taxes.)

(Exercise 5.3) The condensed balance sheet of Geo Company on March 31, 2002, is shown below:

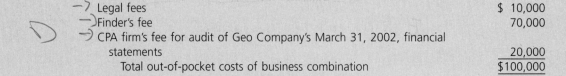

GEO COMPANY Balance Sheet (prior to business combination) March 31, 2002	
Assets	
Cash	$ 20,000
Other current assets	140,000
Plant assets (net)	740,000
Total assets	$900,000
Liabilities and Stockholders' Equity	
Current liabilities	$ 80,000
Long-term debt	200,000
Common stock, $2 par	180,000
Additional paid-in capital	120,000
Retained earnings	320,000
Total liabilities and stockholders' equity	$900,000

CHECK FIGURE

Amount of goodwill, $10,000.

On March 31, 2002, Master Corporation paid $700,000 cash for all the net assets of Geo (except cash) in a business combination. The carrying amounts of Geo's other current assets and current liabilities were the same as their current fair values. However, current fair values of Geo's plant assets and long-term debt were $920,000 and $190,000, respectively. Also on March 31, Master paid the following out-of-pocket costs for the business combination with Geo:

Legal fees	$ 10,000
Finder's fee	70,000
CPA firm's fee for audit of Geo Company's March 31, 2002, financial	
statements	20,000
Total out-of-pocket costs of business combination	$100,000

Prepare a working paper to compute the amount of goodwill or bargain-purchase excess in the business combination of Master Corporation and Geo Company on March 31, 2002. (Disregard income taxes.)

(Exercise 5.4) The balance sheet of Combinee Company on January 31, 2002, was as follows:

COMBINEE COMPANY
Balance Sheet (prior to business combination)
January 31, 2002

Assets		Liabilities and Stockholders' Equity	
Current assets	$ 300,000	Current liabilities	$ 200,000
Plant assets	600,000	Long-term debt	300,000
Other assets	100,000	Common stock, no	
		par or stated value	100,000
		Retained earnings	400,000
		Total liabilities and	
Total assets	$1,000,000	stockholders' equity	$1,000,000

On January 31, 2002, Combinor Company issued $700,000 face amount of 6%, 20-year bonds due January 31, 2022, with a present value of $625,257 at a 7% yield, to Combinee Company for its net assets. On January 31, 2002, the current fair values of Combinee's liabilities equaled their carrying amounts; however, current fair values of Combinee's assets were as follows:

Current assets	$320,000
Plant assets	680,000
Other assets (none intangible)	120,000

Also on January 31, 2002, Combinor paid out-of-pocket costs of the combination as follows:

Accounting, legal, and finder's fees incurred for combination	$ 80,000
Costs of registering 6% bonds with SEC	110,000
Total out-of-pocket costs	$190,000

Prepare journal entries (omit explanations) dated January 31, 2002, for Combinor Company to record its acquisition of the net assets of Combinee Company. (Disregard income taxes.)

(Exercise 5.5) On March 31, 2002, Combinor Company issued 100,000 shares of its $1 par common stock (current fair value $5 a share) for the net assets of Combinee Company. Also on that date, Combinor paid the following out-of-pocket costs in connection with the combination:

Finder's, accounting, and legal fees relating to business combination	$ 70,000
Costs associated with SEC registration statement	50,000
Total out-of-pocket costs of business combination	$120,000

The balance sheet of Combinee on March 31, 2002, with related current fair values, was as follows:

COMBINEE COMPANY
Balance Sheet (prior to business combination)
March 31, 2002

	Carrying Amounts	Current Fair Values
Assets		
Current assets	$200,000	$260,000
Plant assets (net)	400,000	480,000
Other assets (none intangible)	140,000	150,000
Total assets	$740,000	
Liabilities and Stockholders' Equity		
Current liabilities	$ 80,000	$ 80,000
Long-term debt	260,000	260,000
Common stock, no par or stated value	150,000	
Retained earnings	250,000	
Total liabilities and stockholders' equity	$740,000	

Prepare journal entries (omit explanations) for Combinor Company on March 31, 2002, to record the business combination with Combinee Company. (Disregard income taxes.)

(Exercise 5.6) On May 31, 2002, Byers Corporation acquired for $560,000 cash all the net assets except cash of Sellers Company, and paid $60,000 cash to a law firm for legal services in connection with the business combination. The balance sheet of Sellers on May 31, 2002, was as follows:

SELLERS COMPANY
Balance Sheet (prior to business combination)
May 31, 2002

Assets		Liabilities and Stockholders' Equity	
Cash	$ 40,000	Liabilities	$ 620,000
Other current assets (net)	280,000	Common stock, $1 par	250,000
Plant assets (net)	760,000	Retained earnings	330,000
Intangible assets (net)	120,000	Total liabilities and	
Total assets	$1,200,000	stockholders' equity	$1,200,000

The present value of Sellers's liabilities on May 31, 2002, was $620,000. The current fair values of its noncash assets were as follows on May 31, 2002:

Other current assets	$300,000
Plant assets	780,000
Intangible assets (all recognizable under generally accepted accounting principles for business combinations)	130,000

Prepare journal entries (omit explanations) for Byers Corporation on May 31, 2002, to record the acquisition of the net assets of Sellers Company except cash. (Disregard income taxes.)

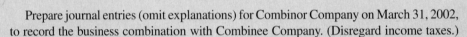

(Exercise 5.7) On September 26, 2002, Acquirer Corporation paid $160,000 cash to Disposer Company for all its net assets except cash, and $10,000 for direct out-of-pocket costs of the business combination. There was no contingent consideration. Current fair values of Disposer's identifiable net assets on September 26, 2002, were as follows:

	Current Fair Values
Cash	$ 10,000
Other current assets	120,000
Plant assets	150,000
Intangible assets (all recognizable in accordance with generally accepted accounting principles for business combinations)	50,000
Current liabilities	90,000
Long-term debt (face amount $60,000)	50,000

   Prepare journal entries (omit explanations) for Acquirer Corporation on September 26, 2002, to record the business combination. (Disregard income taxes.)

(Exercise 5.8)   On December 31, 2002, Combinor Company issued 100,000 shares of its $1 par common stock (current fair value $5 a share) in exchange for all the outstanding common stock of Combinee Company in a statutory merger. Also on that date, Combinor paid the following out-of-pocket costs in connection with the combination:

Accounting, finder's, and legal fees relating to business combination	$ 70,000
Costs associated with SEC registration statement	50,000
Total out-of-pocket costs of business combination	$120,000

The balance sheet of Combinee on December 31, 2002, was as follows:

COMBINEE COMPANY **Balance Sheet (prior to business combination)** **December 31, 2002**	
Assets	
Current assets	$200,000
Plant assets (net)	400,000
Other assets (none intangible)	140,000
Total assets	$740,000
Liabilities and Stockholders' Equity	
Current liabilities	$ 80,000
Long-term debt	260,000
Common stock, no par or stated value	150,000
Retained earnings	250,000
Total liabilities and stockholders' equity	$740,000

   The current fair values of Combinee's identifiable net assets were equal to their carrying amounts on December 31, 2002.
   Prepare journal entries (omit explanations) for Combinor Company on December 31, 2002, to record the business combination with Combinee Company. (Disregard income taxes.)

(Exercise 5.9)   The balance sheet of Combinee Company on September 24, 2002, was as follows:

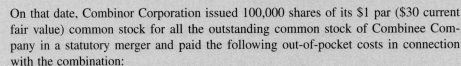

COMBINEE COMPANY			
Balance Sheet (prior to business combination)			
September 24, 2002			
Current assets	$ 200,000	Current liabilities	$ 100,000
Plant assets	700,000	Long-term debt	300,000
Other assets		Common stock, no par or	
(none intangible)	100,000	stated value	200,000
		Retained earnings	400,000
		Total liabilities and	
Total assets	$1,000,000	stockholders' equity	$1,000,000

On that date, Combinor Corporation issued 100,000 shares of its $1 par ($30 current fair value) common stock for all the outstanding common stock of Combinee Company in a statutory merger and paid the following out-of-pocket costs in connection with the combination:

Direct out-of-pocket costs of the combination	$130,000
Costs associated with SEC registration statement	50,000
Total out-of-pocket costs	$180,000

The current fair values of Combinee's identifiable net assets were equal to their carrying amounts; however, $400,000 of Combinor's cost was allocable to identifiable tangible and intangible assets of Combinee that resulted from Combinee's research and development activities. Those assets had no further use in research and development projects.

Prepare journal entries (omit explanations) on September 24, 2002, for (*a*) Combinor Corporation and (*b*) Combinee Company to record the statutory merger. (Disregard income taxes.)

(Exercise 5.10) The balance sheet of Nestor Company on February 28, 2002, with related current fair values of assets and liabilities, was as follows:

NESTOR COMPANY		
Balance Sheet (prior to business combination)		
February 28, 2002		
	Carrying Amounts	*Current Fair Values*
Assets		
Current assets	$ 500,000	$ 520,000
Plant assets (net)	1,000,000	1,050,000
Other assets (none intangible)	300,000	310,000
Total assets	$1,800,000	
Liabilities and Stockholders' Equity		
Current liabilities	$ 300,000	$ 300,000
Long-term debt	400,000	480,000
Common stock, $1 par	500,000	
Additional paid-in capital	200,000	
Retained earnings	400,000	
Total liabilities and stockholders' equity	$1,800,000	

On February 28, 2002, Bragg Corporation issued 600,000 shares of its $1 par common stock (current fair value $2 a share) to Lucy Rowe, sole stockholder of Nestor Company, for all 500,000 shares of Nestor common stock owned by her, in a merger business combination. Because the merger was negotiated privately and Rowe signed a "letter agreement" not to dispose of the Bragg common stock she received, the Bragg stock was not subject to SEC registration requirements. Thus, only $8,000 in legal fees was incurred to effect the merger; these fees were paid in cash by Bragg on February 28, 2002.

Prepare journal entries for Bragg Corporation on February 28, 2002, to record the business combination with Nestor Company. (Disregard income taxes.)

(Exercise 5.11) The condensed balance sheet of Maxim Company on December 31, 2002, prior to the business combination with Sorrel Corporation, was as follows:

CHECK FIGURE

Debit paid-in capital,
$40,060

MAXIM COMPANY **Balance Sheet (prior to business combination)** **December 31, 2002**	
Assets	
Current assets	$ 400,000
Plant assets (net)	1,200,000
Other assets (none intangible)	200,000
Total assets	$1,800,000
Liabilities and Stockholders' Equity	
Current liabilities	$ 300,000
Common stock, $1 par	400,000
Additional paid-in capital	200,000
Retained earnings	900,000
Total liabilities and stockholders' equity	$1,800,000

On December 31, 2002, Sorrel issued 800,000 shares of its $1 par common stock (current fair value $3 a share) for all the outstanding common stock of Maxim in a statutory merger. Also on December 31, 2002, Sorrel paid the following out-of-pocket costs of the business combination with Maxim:

Finder's and legal fees relating to business combination	$30,000
Costs associated with SEC registration statement	40,000
Total out-of-pocket costs of business combination	$70,000

On December 31, 2002, the current fair values of Maxim's other assets and current liabilities equaled their carrying amounts; current fair values of Maxim's current assets and plant assets were $500,000 and $1,500,000, respectively.

Prepare journal entries (omit explanations) for Sorrel Corporation on December 31, 2002, to record the business combination with Maxim Company. (Disregard income taxes.)

(Exercise 5.12) On August 31, 2002, Combinor Corporation entered into a statutory merger business combination with Combinee Company, by issuing 100,000 shares of $1 par common stock having a current fair value of $20 a share for all 50,000 outstanding shares of Combinee's no-par, no-stated-value common stock. Also, Combinor paid the following out-of-pocket costs of the combination on August 31, 2002:

Finder's and legal fees relating to business combination	$100,000
Costs associated with SEC registration statement	150,000
Total out-of-pocket costs of business combination	$250,000

On August 31, 2002, Combinee's balance sheet included the following:

	Carrying Amounts	Current Fair Values
Current assets	$ 500,000	$ 600,000
Plant assets (net)	2,600,000	2,800,000
Current liabilities	400,000	400,000
Long-term debt	1,000,000	1,000,000
Common stock	800,000	
Retained earnings	900,000	

Prepare journal entries (omit explanations) for Combinor Corporation on August 31, 2002, to record the statutory merger with Combinee Company. (Disregard income taxes.)

(Exercise 5.13) On November 1, 2002, Sullivan Corporation issued 50,000 shares of its $10 par common stock in exchange for all the common stock of Mears Company in a statutory merger. Out-of-pocket costs of the business combination may be disregarded. Sullivan tentatively recorded the shares of common stock issued at par and debited the Investment in Mears Company Common Stock ledger account for $500,000. Mears Company was liquidated and became Mears Division of Sullivan Corporation. The net income of Sullivan Corporation and Mears Company or Mears Division during 2002 was as follows:

	Jan. 1 through Oct. 31	Nov. 1 through Dec. 31
Sullivan Corporation	$420,000	$80,000*
Mears Company	350,000	
Mears Division of Sullivan Corporation		50,000

* Excludes any portion of Mears Division net income.

Condensed balance sheet information and other data for 2002 follow:

	Sullivan Corporation		Mears Company Oct. 31	Mears Division of Sullivan Corporation Dec. 31
	Oct. 31	Dec. 31		
Assets	$3,500,000	$4,080,000	$4,000,000	$4,150,000
Liabilities	500,000	500,000	1,000,000	1,100,000
Common stock, $10 par	2,000,000	2,500,000	2,000,000	
Retained earnings	1,000,000	1,080,000*	1,000,000	
Market price per share of common stock	100	130	20	

* Excludes any portion of Mears Division net income.

Neither Sullivan nor Mears Company declared or paid dividends during 2002. In recent months, Sullivan's common stock had been trading at about 40 times earnings; prior to November 1, 2002, Mears Company common stock had been trading at 10 times earnings.

Answer the following questions, ***assuming that the difference between current fair values and carrying amounts of Mears Company's identifiable net assets applies to land.*** Show supporting computations and disregard income taxes.

a. What is Sullivan's net income for the year ended December 31, 2002?

b. What is Sullivan's basic earnings per share for the year ended December 31, 2002?

c. What is the amount of Sullivan's retained earnings on December 31, 2002?

(Exercise 5.14) On December 31, 2002, Tucker Corporation acquired all the net assets of Loring Company for 100,000 shares of Tucker's $2 par common stock having a current fair value of $16 a share. Terms of the business combination required Tucker to issue additional shares of common stock to Loring on December 31, 2003, if the market price of the common stock was less than $16 a share on that date. Sufficient shares would be issued to make the aggregate market value of the total shares issued to Loring equal to $1,600,000 on December 31, 2003. The market price of Tucker's common stock on that date was $10 a share.

CHECK FIGURE

Number of additional
shares to be issued, 60,000.

Prepare a journal entry for Tucker Corporation on December 31, 2003, to record the additional shares of common stock issuable to Loring Company on that date.

Cases

(Case 5.1) You have been engaged to audit the financial statements of Solamente Corporation for the fiscal year ended May 31, 2003. You discover that on June 1, 2002, Mika Company had been merged into Solamente in a business combination. You also find that both Solamente and Mika (prior to its liquidation) incurred legal fees, accounting fees, and printing costs for the business combination; both companies debited those costs to an intangible asset ledger account entitled "Cost of Business Combination." In its journal entry to record the business combination with Mika, Solamente increased its Cost of Business Combination account by an amount equal to the balance of Mika's comparable ledger account.

Instructions

Evaluate Solamente's accounting for the out-of-pocket costs of the business combination with Mika.

(Case 5.2) You are the controller of Software Company, a distributor of computer software, which is planning to acquire a portion of the net assets of a product line of Midge Company, a competitor enterprise. The projected acquisition cost is expected to exceed substantially the current fair value of the identifiable net assets to be acquired, which the competitor has agreed to sell because of its substantial net losses of recent years. The board of directors of Software asks if the excess acquisition cost may appropriately be recognized as goodwill.

Instructions

Prepare a memorandum to the board of directors in answer to the question, after consulting the following:

Statement of Financial Accounting Concepts No. 6, "Elements of Financial Statements," par. 25.

FASB Statement No. 141, "Business Combinations," pars. 9, 43, F1 (Goodwill).

FASB Statement No. 142, "Goodwill and Other Intangible Assets," par. B67.

(Case 5.3) On February 15, 2002, officers of Shane Corporation agreed with George Merlo, sole stockholder of Merlo Company and Merlo Industries, Inc., to acquire all his common stock ownership in the two companies as follows:

1. 10,000 shares of Shane's $1 par common stock (current fair value $30 a share) would be issued to George Merlo on February 28, 2002, for his 1,000 shares of $10 par common stock of Merlo Company. In addition, 20,000 shares of Shane common stock would be issued to George Merlo on February 28, 2007, if aggregate net income of Merlo Company for the five-year period then ended exceeded $300,000.

2. $250,000 cash would be paid to George Merlo on February 28, 2002, for his 10,000 shares of $1 par common stock of Merlo Industries, Inc. In addition $250,000 in cash would be paid to George Merlo on February 28, 2007, if aggregate net income of Merlo Industries, Inc., for the five-year period then ended exceeded $300,000.

Both Merlo Company and Merlo Industries, Inc., were to be merged into Shane on February 28, 2002, and were to continue operations after that date as divisions of Shane. George Merlo also agreed not to compete with Shane for the period March 1, 2002, through February 28, 2007. Because the merger was negotiated privately and George Merlo signed a "letter agreement" not to dispose of the Shane common stock he received, the business combination was not subject to the jurisdiction of the SEC. Out-of-pocket costs of the business combination may be disregarded.

Selected financial statement data of the three constituent companies as of February 28, 2002 (prior to the merger), were as follows:

	Shane Corporation	Merlo Company	Merlo Industries, Inc.
Total assets	$25,000,000	$ 500,000	$ 600,000
Stockholders' equity	10,000,000	200,000	300,000
Net sales	50,000,000	1,500,000	2,500,000
Basic earnings per share	5	30	3

The controller of Shane prepared the following condensed journal entries to record the merger on February 28, 2002:

Assets other than goodwill	600,000	
Goodwill	10,000	
Liabilities		300,000
Common Stock		10,000
Common Stock to Be Issued		20,000
Paid-in Capital in Excess of Par		280,000

To record merger with Merlo Company, with identifiable assets and liabilities recorded at current fair values and goodwill recognized.

Assets	650,000	
Goodwill	150,000	
Liabilities		300,000
Payable to George Merlo		250,000
Cash		250,000

To record merger with Merlo Industries, Inc., with assets and liabilities of Merlo Industries, Inc., recorded at current fair values and goodwill recognized.

Instructions

Do you concur with the controller's journal entries? Explain.

(Case 5.4) Robert Frank, sole stockholder of Frank Electronics, Inc., a non-publicly owned corporation, has brought you the following balance sheets:

FRANK ELECTRONICS, INC. Balance Sheet March 31, 2002			
Assets		**Liabilities and Stockholder's Equity**	
Current assets	$150,000	Current liabilities	$ 70,000
Plant assets (net)	300,000	Long-term debt	130,000
Intangible assets (net)*	50,000	Common stock, no par or stated value, 10,000 shares authorized, issued, and outstanding	100,000
		Retained earnings	200,000
		Total liabilities and	
Total assets	$500,000	stockholder's equity	$500,000

* All recognizable under generally accepted accounting principles for business combinations.

LESTER ENTERPRISES, INC. Balance Sheet March 31, 2002			
Assets		**Liabilities and Stockholder's Equity**	
Cash	$ 50,000	Liabilities	$ 0
Common stock subscriptions receivable	5,000	Common stock, no par or stated value, 50,000 shares authorized:	
Investments in marketable equity securities (available for sale)	45,000	Issued and outstanding, 10,000 shares	80,000
		Subscribed, 5,000 shares	5,000
		Retained earnings	11,000
		Accumulated other comprehensive income	4,000
		Total liabilities and stockholder's	
Total assets	$100,000	equity	$100,000

Robert Frank states that he wants your advice on the proper accounting for a proposed business combination (statutory merger), in which Lester Enterprises would issue 12,000 shares of common stock to Robert Frank in exchange for his 10,000 shares of Frank Electronics common stock. The Lester Enterprises shares would be assigned a fair value of $40 per share; if Lester Enterprises were deemed the combinor, the $180,000 excess [(12,000 × $40) − ($100,000 + $200,000) = $180,000] would be allocated to Frank Electronics assets as follows:

Current assets	$ 40,000
Plant assets	90,000
Intangible assets	20,000
Goodwill	30,000
Total	$180,000

In response to your inquiries, Robert Frank explained that Lester Enterprises, now solely owned by George Lester, was registered with the Securities and Exchange Commission because it had been a publicly owned corporation before George Lester had "bought out" the other five shareholders. Later, George Lester sold all operating assets of Lester Enterprises to an unrelated publicly owned corporation in exchange for equity securities of that corporation (Lester Enterprises' marketable equity securities investment). Robert Frank also stated that George Lester had subscribed to 5,000 shares of Lester Enterprises common stock on March 31, 2002, and that the subscription price of $5,000 was payable on June 30, 2002.

Instructions
Would Lester Enterprises, Inc., be the combinor in the merger with Frank Electronics, Inc.? Explain.

(Case 5.5) Paragraph B121 of *FASB Statement No. 141,* "Business Combinations," reads in part as follows:

> Based on its analysis, the [Financial Accounting Standards] Board concluded that core goodwill meets the assets definition in [*Statement of Financial Accounting Concepts No. 6,* "Elements of Financial Statements"] . . .

Instructions:
After reading paragraphs B101 through B120 of *Statement No. 141,* do you agree with the FASB's conclusion? Explain.

Problems

(Problem 5.1) On January 31, 2002, La Salle Corporation acquired for $540,000 cash all the net assets except cash of De Soto Company and paid $60,000 cash to a law firm for legal services in connection with the business combination. The balance sheet of De Soto Company on January 31, 2002, prior to the business combination, was as follows:

CHECK FIGURE
Debit plant assets, $846,400.

DE SOTO COMPANY				
Balance Sheet (prior to business combination)				
January 31, 2002				
Assets			**Liabilities and Stockholders' Equity**	
Cash	$ 40,000		Liabilities	$ 620,000
Other current assets (net)	280,000		Common stock, no par or	
Plant assets (net)	760,000		stated value	250,000
Intangible assets (net)	120,000		Retained earnings	330,000
			Total liabilities and	
Total assets	$1,200,000		stockholders' equity	$1,200,000

The current fair value of De Soto's liabilities on January 31, 2002, was $620,000. The current fair values of its noncash assets were as follows on January 31, 2002:

Other current assets	$300,000
Plant assets	874,000
Intangible assets (All recognizable under generally accepted accounting principles for business combinations.)	76,000

Instructions

Prepare journal entries for La Salle Corporation on January 31, 2002, to record the acquisition of the net assets of De Soto Company except cash. Show computations in the explanations for the journal entries where appropriate. (Disregard income taxes.)

(Problem 5.2) The balance sheet of Cooper Company on August 31, 2002, with related current fair value data, was as follows:

CHECK FIGURE

Debit goodwill, $88,120.

COOPER COMPANY Balance Sheet (prior to business combination) August 31, 2002	Carrying Amounts	Current Fair Values
Assets		
Current assets	$180,000	$ 220,000
Plant assets (net)	640,000	700,000
Intangible assets (net) (All recognizable under generally accepted accounting principles for business combinations.)	80,000	90,000
Total assets	$900,000	$1,010,000
Liabilities and Stockholders' Equity		
Current liabilities	$ 80,000	$ 80,000
Long-term debt	200,000	190,000
Total liabilities	$280,000	$ 270,000
Common stock, no par or stated value	$400,000	
Retained earnings	220,000	
Total stockholders' equity	$620,000	
Total liabilities and stockholders' equity	$900,000	

On August 31, 2002, Lionel Corporation issued $1 million face amount of 10-year, 10% bonds (interest payable each February 28 and August 31), to yield 14%, for all the net assets of Cooper. Bond issue costs paid by Lionel on August 31, 2002, totaled $60,000, and the accounting and legal fees to effect the business combination, paid on August 31, 2002, were $40,000.

Instructions

Prepare journal entries on August 31, 2002, to record Lionel Corporation's acquisition of the net assets of Cooper Company. Show the computation of goodwill in the explanation of the relevant journal entry. (Disregard income taxes.)

(Problem 5.3) The journal entries for the business combination of Wabash Corporation and Indiana Company on December 31, 2002, were as follows:

WABASH CORPORATION
Journal Entries
December 31, 2002

Investment in Indiana Company Common Stock	10,000,000	
12% Bonds Payable		10,000,000
To record merger with Indiana Company as a purchase.		
Investment in Indiana Company Common Stock	150,000	
Bond Issue Costs	50,000	
Cash		200,000
To record payment of costs incurred in merger with Indiana Company.		
Current Assets ($3,140,000 + $560,000)	3,700,000	
Plant Assets ($9,070,000 + $330,000)	9,400,000	
Goodwill	400,000	
Current Liabilities		3,350,000
Investment in Indiana Company Common Stock		10,150,000

To allocate total cost of Indiana Company investment to identifiable assets and liabilities, with the remainder to goodwill. (Income tax effects are disregarded.) Amount of goodwill is computed as follows:

Total cost of investment		
($10,000,000 + $150,000)	$10,150,000	
Less: Carrying amount of		
identifiable net assets		
[($3,140,000 +		
$9,070,000) −		
$3,350,000]	$8,860,000	
Excess of current fair		
values of identifiable		
net assets over		
carrying amounts		
($560,000 +		
$330,000)	890,000	9,750,000
Amount of goodwill		$ 400,000

CHECK FIGURE

Debit plant assets $9,800,000.

Additional Information

1. The stockholders' equity section of Indiana Company's balance sheet on December 31, 2002 (prior to the merger), included the following:

Common stock, $1 par	$5,000,000
Retained earnings	3,860,000
Total stockholders' equity	$8,860,000

2. There was no contingent consideration in connection with the business combination.

Instructions

Prepare journal entries (omit explanations) for Wabash Corporation for the business combination on December 31, 2002, under the assumptions that, instead of issuing bonds, Wabash had issued 1 million shares of its no-par, no-stated-value common stock with a current fair value of $10 a share to effect the combination, that the bond issue costs were costs of issuing common stock, that the current fair value of the plant assets was $9,900,000, and that all other facts remained the same.

(Problem 5.4) The balance sheet of Combinee Company on October 31, 2002, was as follows:

CHECK FIGURE

Debit goodwill, $340,000.

COMBINEE COMPANY	
Balance Sheet (prior to business combination)	
October 31, 2002	
Assets	
Cash	$ 60,000
Other current assets	420,000
Plant assets (net)	920,000
Total assets	$1,400,000
Liabilities and Stockholders' Equity	
Current liabilities	$ 180,000
Long-term debt	250,000
Common stock, $5 par	200,000
Additional paid-in capital	320,000
Retained earnings	450,000
Total liabilities and stockholders' equity	$1,400,000

Combinor Corporation's board of directors established the following current fair values for Combinee's identifiable net assets other than cash:

Other current assets	$ 500,000
Plant assets (net)	1,000,000
Current liabilities	180,000
Long-term debt	240,000

Accordingly, on October 31, 2002, Combinor issued 100,000 shares of its $10 par (current fair value $13) common stock for all the net assets of Combinee in a business combination. Also on October 31, 2002, Combinor paid the following out-of-pocket costs in connection with the combination:

Finder's fee, accounting fees, and legal fees to effect combination	$180,000
Costs associated with SEC registration statement	120,000
Total out-of-pocket costs of business combination	$300,000

Instructions

Prepare journal entries for Combinor Corporation on October 31, 2002, to record the business combination with Combinee Company. (Disregard income taxes.)

(Problem 5.5) Condensed balance sheet data of Conner Company and Capsol Company on July 31, 2002, were as follows:

	Conner Company	*Capsol Company*
Total assets	$700,000	$670,000
Total liabilities	$300,000	$300,000
Common stock, $25 par	200,000	250,000
Additional paid-in capital	80,000	130,000
Retained earnings (deficit)	120,000	(10,000)
Total liabilities and stockholders' equity	$700,000	$670,000

CHECK FIGURE

Debit goodwill, $180,000.

On July 31, 2002, Conner and Capsol entered into a statutory consolidation. The new company, Consol Corporation, issued 45,000 shares of $10 par common stock for all the outstanding common stock of Conner and 30,000 shares for all the outstanding common stock of Capsol. Out-of-pocket costs of the business combination may be disregarded.

Instructions

Prepare journal entries for Consol Corporation on July 31, 2002, to record the business combination. Assume that Capsol is the combinor; that current fair values of identifiable assets are $800,000 for Conner and $700,000 for Capsol; that each company's liabilities are fairly stated at $300,000; and that the current fair value of Consol's common stock is $14 a share. (Disregard income taxes.)

(Problem 5.6) The condensed balance sheets of Silva Corporation, the combinor, prior to and subsequent to its March 1, 2002, merger with Marvel Company, are as follows:

CHECK FIGURE

Credit additional paid-in capital, net, $550,000.

SILVA CORPORATION		
Balance Sheets (prior to and subsequent to business combination)		
March 1, 2002		
	Prior to Business Combination	*Subsequent to Business Combination*
Assets		
Current assets	$ 500,000	$ 850,000
Plant assets (net)	1,000,000	1,800,000
Total assets	$1,500,000	$2,650,000
Liabilities and Stockholders' Equity		
Current liabilities	$ 350,000	$ 600,000
Long-term debt	100,000	150,000
Common stock, $1 par	400,000	700,000
Additional paid-in capital	310,000	860,000
Retained earnings	340,000	340,000
Total liabilities and stockholders' equity	$1,500,000	$2,650,000

50,000

Prior to the business combination, Marvel had, at both carrying amount and current fair value, total assets of $1,200,000 and total liabilities of $300,000. Out-of-pocket costs of the business combination, $50,000, were paid by Silva on March 1, 2002; consideration for the combination was common stock having a current fair value of $870,000.

Instructions

Reconstruct the journal entries (omit explanations) that Silva Corporation prepared on March 1, 2002, to record the business combination with Marvel Company. (Disregard income taxes.)

(Problem 5.7) On October 31, 2002, Solomon Corporation issued 20,000 shares of its $1 par (current fair value $20) common stock for all the outstanding common stock of Midland Company in a statutory merger. Out-of-pocket costs of the business combination paid by Solomon on October 31, 2002, were as follows:

CHECK FIGURE

Debit goodwill,
$50,870.

Direct costs of the business combination	$20,870
Costs of registering and issuing common stock	31,130
Total out-of-pocket costs of business combination	$52,000

Midland's balance sheet on October 31, 2002, follows:

MIDLAND COMPANY
Balance Sheet (prior to business combination)
October 31, 2002

Assets

Inventories	$140,000
Other current assets	80,000
Plant assets (net)	380,000
Total assets	$600,000

Liabilities and Stockholders' Equity

Payable to Solomon Corporation	$ 75,000
Other liabilities	225,000
Common stock, $3 par	30,000
Additional paid-in capital	120,000
Retained earnings	150,000
Total liabilities and stockholders' equity	$600,000

Additional Information

1. The current fair values of Midland's other current assets and all its liabilities equaled the carrying amounts on October 31, 2002.

2. Current fair values of Midland's inventories and plant assets were $170,000 and $420,000, respectively, on October 31, 2002.

3. Solomon's October 31, 2002, balance sheet included an asset entitled Receivable from Midland Company in the amount of $75,000.

Instructions

Prepare Solomon Corporation's journal entries on October 31, 2002, to record the business combination with Midland Company. (Disregard income taxes.)

(Problem 5.8) The balance sheet on March 31, 2002, and the related current fair value data for Edgar Company were as follows:

EDGAR COMPANY
Balance Sheet (prior to business combination)
March 31, 2002

	Carrying Amounts	Current Fair Values
Assets		
Current assets	$ 500,000	$ 575,000
Plant assets (net)	1,000,000	1,200,000
Patent (net)	100,000	50,000
Total assets	$1,600,000	
Liabilities and Stockholders' Equity		
Current liabilities	$ 300,000	$ 300,000
Long-term debt	400,000	450,000
Common stock, $10 par	100,000	
Retained earnings	800,000	
Total liabilities and stockholders' equity	$1,600,000	

On April 1, 2002, Value Corporation issued 50,000 shares of its no-par, no-stated-value common stock (current fair value $14 a share) and $225,000 cash for the net assets of Edgar Company, in a business combination. Of the $125,000 out-of-pocket costs paid by Value on April 1, 2002, $50,000 were accounting, legal, and finder's fees related to the business combination, and $75,000 were costs related to the issuance of common stock.

Instructions

Prepare journal entries for Value Corporation on April 1, 2002, to record the business combination with Edgar Company. (Disregard income taxes.)

(Problem 5.9) Molo Company merged into Stave Corporation in a business combination completed April 30, 2002. Out-of-pocket costs paid by Stave on April 30, 2002, in connection with the combination were as follows:

Finder's, accounting, and legal fees relating to the business combination	$15,000
Costs associated with SEC registration statement for securities issued to complete the business combination	10,000
Total out-of-pocket costs of business combination	$25,000

The individual balance sheets of the constituent companies immediately prior to the merger were as follows:

STAVE CORPORATION AND MOLO COMPANY
Balance Sheets (prior to business combination)
April 30, 2002

	Stave Corporation	Molo Company
Assets		
Current assets	$ 4,350,000	$ 3,000,000
Plant assets (net)	18,500,000	11,300,000
Patents (net)	450,000	200,000
Deferred charges	150,000	
Total assets	$23,450,000	$14,500,000

(continued)

STAVE CORPORATION AND MOLO COMPANY
Balance Sheets (prior to business combination) (concluded)
April 30, 2002

	Stave Corporation	Molo Company
Liabilities and Stockholders' Equity		
Liabilities	$ 2,650,000	$ 2,100,000
Common stock, $10 par	12,000,000	
Common stock, $5 par		3,750,000
Additional paid-in capital	4,200,000	3,200,000
Retained earnings	5,850,000	5,450,000
Less: Treasury stock, at cost, 100,000 shares	(1,250,000)	
Total liabilities and stockholders' equity	$23,450,000	$14,500,000

Additional Information

1. The current fair values of the identifiable assets and liabilities of Stave Corporation and of Molo Company were as follows on April 30, 2002:

STAVE CORPORATION AND MOLO COMPANY
Current Fair Values of Identifiable Net Assets
April 30, 2002

	Stave Corporation	Molo Company
Current assets	$ 4,950,000	$ 3,400,000
Plant assets (net)	22,000,000	14,000,000
Patents	570,000	360,000
Deferred charges	150,000	
Liabilities	(2,650,000)	(2,100,000)
Identifiable net assets	$25,020,000	$15,660,000

2. There were no intercompany transactions prior to the business combination.
3. Before the business combination, Stave had 3,000,000 shares of common stock authorized, 1,200,000 shares issued, and 1,100,000 shares outstanding. Molo had 750,000 shares of common stock authorized, issued, and outstanding.
4. Molo Company was dissolved and liquidated on completion of the merger.

Instructions

Prepare journal entries for Stave Corporation on April 30, 2002, to record the business combination with Molo Company under the following assumptions: Stave paid $3,100,000 cash and issued 10% bonds at face amount of $16,900,000 for all the outstanding common stock of Molo. The current fair value of the bonds was equal to their face amount. (Disregard bond issue costs and income taxes.)

(Problem 5.10) Coolidge Corporation agreed to pay $850,000 cash and issue 50,000 shares of its $10 par ($20 current fair value a share) common stock on September 30, 2002, to Hoover Company for all the net assets of Hoover except cash. In addition, Coolidge agreed that if the market value of its common stock was not $20 a share or more on September 30, 2003, a sufficient number of additional shares of common stock would be issued to Hoover to make the aggregate market value of its Coolidge common shareholdings equal to $1 million on that date.

The balance sheet of Hoover on September 30, 2002, with related current fair values of assets and liabilities, is as follows:

CHECK FIGURE

a. Debit patent, $95,000.

HOOVER COMPANY
Balance Sheet (prior to business combination)
September 30, 2002

	Carrying Amounts	Current Fair Values
Assets		
Cash	$ 100,000	$ 100,000
Trade accounts receivable (net)	300,000	300,000
Inventories	520,000	680,000
Short-term prepayments	20,000	20,000
10% investment in Truman Company common stock (long-term, available for sale)	180,000	180,000
Land	500,000	650,000
Other plant assets (net)	1,000,000	1,250,000
Patent (net)	80,000	100,000
Total assets	$2,700,000	
Liabilities and Stockholders' Equity		
Current liabilities	$ 700,000	$ 700,000
Long-term debt	500,000	480,000
Common stock, $5 par	600,000	
Additional paid-in capital	400,000	
Retained earnings	500,000	
Total liabilities and stockholders' equity	$2,700,000	

Out-of-pocket costs of the business combination paid by Coolidge on September 30, 2002, were as follows:

Audit fees—SEC registration statement	$ 30,000
Finder's fee	35,000
Legal fees—business combination	15,000
Legal fees—SEC registration statement	20,000
Printing costs—securities and SEC registration statement	25,000
SEC registration fee	350
Total out-of-pocket costs of business combination	$125,350

Instructions
a. Prepare the September 30, 2002, journal entries for Coolidge Corporation to reflect the foregoing transactions and events. (Disregard income taxes.)

b. Assume that on September 30, 2003, the market value of Coolidge Corporation's common stock was $16 a share. Prepare a journal entry to record the issuance of additional shares of Coolidge common stock to Hoover Company on that date and the payment of cash in lieu of fractional shares, if any.

(Problem 5.11) The board of directors of Solo Corporation is considering a merger with Mono Company. The most recent financial statements and other financial data for the two companies, both of which use the same accounting principles and practices, are shown below:

SOLO CORPORATION AND MONO COMPANY
Balance Sheets (prior to business combination)
October 31, 2002

	Solo Corporation	Mono Company
Assets		
Current assets	$ 500,000	$ 200,000
Plant assets (net)	1,000,000	1,500,000
Other assets	300,000	100,000
Total assets	$1,800,000	$1,800,000
Liabilities and Stockholders' Equity		
Current liabilities	$ 400,000	$ 100,000
Long-term debt	500,000	1,300,000
Common stock, $10 par	600,000	100,000
Additional paid-in capital	100,000	100,000
Retained earnings	200,000	200,000
Total liabilities and stockholders' equity	$1,800,000	$1,800,000

SOLO CORPORATION AND MONO COMPANY
Statements of Income and Retained Earnings (prior to business combination)
For Year Ended October 31, 2002

	Solo Corporation	Mono Company
Net sales	$5,000,000	$1,000,000
Costs and expenses:		
Cost of goods sold	$3,500,000	$ 600,000
Operating expenses	1,000,000	200,000
Interest expense	200,000	50,000
Income taxes expense	120,000	60,000
Total costs and expenses	$4,820,000	$ 910,000
Net income	$ 180,000	$ 90,000
Retained earnings, beginning of year	20,000	110,000
Retained earnings, end of year	$ 200,000	$ 200,000
Basic earnings per share	$3.00	$9.00
Price-earnings ratio	10	5

Solo's directors estimated that the out-of-pocket costs of the merger would be as follows:

Finder's fee and legal fees for the merger	$ 5,000
Costs associated with SEC registration statement	7,000
Total out-of-pocket costs of merger	$12,000

The fair values of Mono's liabilities on October 31, 2002, were equal to their carrying amounts. Current fair values of Mono's assets on that date were as follows:

Current assets (difference from balance sheet amount of $200,000 attributable to inventories carried at first-in, first-out cost that were sold during the year ended October 31, 2003)	$ 230,000
Plant assets (difference from balance sheet amount of $1,500,000 attributable to land—$60,000 and to depreciable assets with a five-year remaining economic life—$40,000)	1,600,000
Other assets (difference from balance sheet amount of $100,000 attributable to leasehold with a remaining term of four years)	120,000

Solo's board of directors is considering the following plan for effecting the merger, as follows: Issue 15,000 shares of common stock with a current fair value of $20 a share, $100,000 cash, and a 15%, three-year note for $200,000 for all the outstanding common stock of Mono. The present value of the note would be equal to its face amount.

Under the plan, Mono would be liquidated but would continue operations as a division of Solo.

Instructions

To assist Solo Corporation's board of directors in their evaluation of the plan, prepare a working paper to compute or prepare the following for the plan as though the merger had been effected on October 31, 2002 (disregard income taxes):

a. Net income and basic earnings per share (rounded to the nearest cent) of Solo for the year ended October 31, 2002.

b. Net income and basic earnings per share (rounded to the nearest cent) of Solo for the year ending October 31, 2003, assuming the same sales and cost patterns for the year ended October 31, 2002. Goodwill, if any, is not expected to become impaired.

c. Pro forma balance sheet of Solo following the business combination on October 31, 2002.

Chapter **Six**

Consolidated Financial Statements: On Date of Business Combination

Scope of Chapter

Topics dealt with in Chapter 6 include the nature of consolidated financial statements; the concept of *control* versus *ownership* as the basis for such financial statements; the preparation of consolidated financial statements involving both wholly owned and partially owned subsidiaries; the nature of minority (noncontrolling) interest and its valuation; and "push-down" accounting for separate financial statements of subsidiaries.

PARENT COMPANY–SUBSIDIARY RELATIONSHIPS

Chapter 5 includes the terms *investor* and *investee* in the discussion of business combinations involving a combinor's acquisition of common stock of a combinee corporation. If the investor acquires a controlling interest in the investee, a *parent–subsidiary relationship* is established. The investee becomes a *subsidiary* of the acquiring *parent company* (investor) but remains a separate legal entity.

Strict adherence to the legal aspects of such a business combination would require the issuance of separate financial statements for the parent company and the subsidiary on the date of the combination, and also for all subsequent accounting periods of the affiliation. However, such strict adherence to legal form disregards the substance of most parent–subsidiary relationships: A parent company and its subsidiary are a *single economic entity.* In recognition of this fact, *consolidated financial statements* are issued to report the financial position and operating results of a parent company and its subsidiaries as though they comprised a *single accounting entity.*

Nature of Consolidated Financial Statements

Consolidated financial statements are similar to the combined financial statements described in Chapter 4 for a home office and its branches. Assets, liabilities, revenue, and expenses of the parent company and its subsidiaries are totaled; intercompany transactions and balances are eliminated; and the final consolidated amounts are reported in the consolidated balance sheet, income statement, statement of stockholders' equity, and statement of cash flows.

However, the separate legal entity status of the parent and subsidiary corporations necessitates eliminations that generally are more complex than the combination eliminations described and illustrated in Chapter 4 for a home office and its branches. Before illustrating consolidation eliminations, it is appropriate to examine some basic principles of consolidation.

Should All Subsidiaries Be Consolidated?

In the past, a wide range of consolidation practices existed among major corporations in the United States. For example, the forty-second edition of *Accounting Trends & Techniques* (published in 1988), the AICPA's annual survey of accounting practices in the published financial statements of 600 companies, reported the following:[1]

1. A total of 456 companies consolidated all significant subsidiaries, but 136 companies excluded some significant subsidiaries from the consolidated financial statements. (The remaining eight companies surveyed did not issue consolidated financial statements.)

2. The principal types of subsidiaries excluded from consolidation were foreign subsidiaries, finance-related subsidiaries, and real estate subsidiaries. "Finance-related subsidiaries" included finance companies, insurance companies, banks, and leasing companies.

Such wide variations in consolidation policy were undesirable and difficult to justify from a theoretical point of view. The purpose of consolidated financial statements is to present for a single accounting entity the combined resources, obligations, and operating results of a family of related corporations; consequently, there is no reason for excluding from consolidation any subsidiary that is *controlled.* The argument that finance-related subsidiaries should not be consolidated with parent manufacturing or retailing enterprises because of their unique features is difficult to justify, considering the wide variety of production, marketing, and service enterprises that are consolidated in a *conglomerate* or highly diversified family of corporations.

In *FASB Statement No. 94,* "Consolidation of All Majority-Owned Subsidiaries," issued in 1987, the Financial Accounting Standards Board required the consolidation of nearly all subsidiaries, effective for financial statements for fiscal years ending after December 15, 1988. Only subsidiaries not actually controlled (as described in the following section) were exempted from consolidation.

The Meaning of Controlling Interest

Traditionally, an investor's direct or indirect ownership of *more than 50%* of an investee's outstanding common stock has been required to evidence the controlling interest underlying a parent–subsidiary relationship. However, even though such a common stock ownership exists, other circumstances may negate the parent company's *actual* control of the subsidiary. For example, a subsidiary that is in liquidation or reorganization in court-supervised bankruptcy proceedings is not controlled by its parent company. Also, a foreign subsidiary in a country having severe production, monetary, or income tax restrictions may be subject to the authority of the foreign country rather than of the parent company. Further, if *minority* shareholders of a subsidiary have the right effectively to *participate* in the financial and operating activities of the

---

[1] *Accounting Trends & Techniques,* 42nd ed. (New York: AICPA, 1988), p. 45.

subsidiary in the ordinary course of business, the subsidiary's financial statements should not be consolidated with those of the parent company.[2]

It is important to recognize that a parent company's control of a subsidiary might be achieved *indirectly.* For example, if Plymouth Corporation owns 85% of the outstanding common stock of Selwyn Company and 45% of Talbot Company's common stock, and Selwyn also owns 45% of Talbot's common stock, both Selwyn and Talbot are controlled by Plymouth, because it effectively controls 90% of Talbot. This effective control consists of 45% owned directly and 45% indirectly. Additional examples of indirect control are in Chapter 10.

Criticism of Traditional Concept of Control

Many accountants have criticized the traditional definition of *control* described in the preceding section, which emphasizes *legal form.* These accountants maintain that an investor owning less than 50% of an investee's voting common stock *in substance* may control the affiliate, especially if the remaining common stock is scattered among a large number of stockholders who do not attend stockholder meetings or give proxies. Effective control of an investee also is possible if the individuals comprising management of the investor corporation own a substantial number of shares of common stock of the investee or successfully solicit proxies from the investee's other stockholders.

Furthering the foregoing views, in *Financial Reporting Release No. 25,* the Securities and Exchange Commission (SEC) required companies subject to its jurisdiction to emphasize *economic substance* over *legal form* in adopting a consolidation policy.[3] Subsequently, the Financial Accounting Standards Board issued a *Discussion Memorandum,* "An Analysis of Issues Related to Consolidation Policy and Procedures," which dealt at length with the question of *ownership* (legal form) versus *control* (economic substance) as a basis for consolidation.[4]

FASB's Proposed Redefinition of Control

Following the issuance of the Discussion Memorandum described in the preceding section, the FASB issued a *Proposed Statement* that would have defined *control* of an entity as power over its assets—power to use or direct the use of the individual assets of another entity in essentially the same ways as the controlling entity can use its own assets.[5] In the face of strenuous objections by financial statement preparers to the foregoing definition, in 1999 the FASB issued a revised *Proposed Statement* that would define *control* as a parent company's nonshared decision-making ability that enables it to guide the ongoing activities of its subsidiary and to use that power to increase the benefits that it derives and limit the losses that it suffers from the activities of that subsidiary.[6] The *Proposed Statement* further stated that:

> . . . in the absence of evidence that demonstrates otherwise, the existence of control of a corporation shall be presumed if an entity (including its subsidiaries):

---

[2] *Emerging Issues Task Force (of FASB) Issue 96-16,* "Minority Shareholder Veto Rights."
[3] *Codification of Financial Reporting Policies,* Securities and Exchange Commission (Washington, 1986), Sec. 105.
[4] *FASB Discussion Memorandum,* ". . . Consolidation Policy and Procedures" (Norwalk: FASB, 1991), pars. 35–48.
[5] *Proposed Statement of Financial Accounting Standards,* "Consolidated Financial Statements: Policies and Procedures" (Norwalk: FASB, 1995), par. 10.
[6] *Proposed Statement of Financial Accounting Standards,* "Consolidated Financial Statements: Purpose and Policy" (Norwalk: FASB, 1999), par. 10.

(a) Has a majority voting interest in the election of a corporation's governing body or a right to appoint a majority of the members of its governing body

(b) Has a large minority voting interest [for example, exceeding 56% of the votes typically cast] in the election of a corporation's governing body and no other party or organized group of parties has a significant voting interest

(c) Has a unilateral ability to (1) obtain a majority voting interest in the election of a corporation's governing body or (2) obtain a right to appoint a majority of the corporation's governing body through the present ownership of convertible securities or other rights that are currently exercisable at the option of the holder and the expected benefit from converting those securities or exercising that right exceeds its expected cost.[7]

By the latter proposal, the FASB planned to repeal the long-standing requirement of majority ownership of an investee's outstanding common stock as a prerequisite for consolidation. *Objectively determined* legal form was to be replaced by *subjectively determined* economic substance as the basis for consolidated financial statements.

After nearly two years of extensive consideration of this proposal, the FASB reported that, "after careful consideration, the Board determined that, at this time, there is not sufficient Board member support to proceed with . . . a final Statement on consolidation policy . . ."[8] Accordingly, ownership of more than 50% of an investee's outstanding common stock remains the basis for consolidation of financial statements in most circumstances.

CONSOLIDATION OF WHOLLY OWNED SUBSIDIARY ON DATE OF BUSINESS COMBINATION

There is no question of *control* of a wholly owned subsidiary. Thus, to illustrate consolidated financial statements for a parent company and a wholly owned purchased subsidiary, assume that on December 31, 2002, Palm Corporation issued 10,000 shares of its $10 par common stock (current fair value $45 a share) to stockholders of Starr Company for all the outstanding $5 par common stock of Starr. There was no contingent consideration. Out-of-pocket costs of the business combination paid by Palm on December 31, 2002, consisted of the following:

Combinor's Out-of-Pocket Costs of Business Combination

Finder's and legal fees relating to business combination *Direct*	$50,000
Costs associated with SEC registration statement for Palm common stock	35,000
Total out-of-pockets costs of business combination *indirect*	$85,000

Assume also that Starr Company was to continue its corporate existence as a wholly owned subsidiary of Palm Corporation. Both constituent companies had a December 31 fiscal year and used the same accounting principles and procedures; thus, no adjusting entries were required for either company prior to the combination. The income tax rate for each company was 40%.

Financial statements of Palm Corporation and Starr Company for the year ended December 31, 2002, prior to consummation of the business combination, follow:

[7] Ibid., par. 18.
[8] *Status Report*, FASB, April 13, 2001.

PALM CORPORATION AND STARR COMPANY		
Separate Financial Statements (prior to business combination)		
For Year Ended December 31, 2002		
	Palm Corporation	Starr Company
Income Statements	*Carrying Amount used*	*CFV used*
Revenue:		
Net sales	$ 990,000	$600,000
Interest revenue	10,000	
Total revenue	$1,000,000	$600,000
Costs and expenses:		
Cost of goods sold	$ 635,000	$410,000
Operating expenses	158,333	73,333
Interest expense	50,000	30,000
Income taxes expense	62,667	34,667
Total costs and expenses	$ 906,000	$548,000
Net income	$ 94,000	$ 52,000
Statements of Retained Earnings		
Retained earnings, beginning of year	$ 65,000	$100,000
Add: Net income	94,000	52,000
Subtotals	$ 159,000	$152,000
Less: Dividends	25,000	20,000
Retained earnings, end of year	$ 134,000	$132,000
Balance Sheets		
Assets		
Cash	$100,000	$ 40,000
Inventories	150,000	110,000
Other current assets	110,000	70,000
Receivable from Starr Company	25,000	
Plant assets (net)	450,000	300,000
Patent (net)		20,000
Total assets	$835,000	$540,000
Liabilities and Stockholders' Equity		
Payables to Palm Corporation		$ 25,000
Income taxes payable	$ 26,000	10,000
Other liabilities	325,000	115,000
Common stock, $10 par	300,000	
Common stock, $5 par		200,000
Additional paid-in capital	50,000	58,000
Retained earnings	134,000	132,000
Total liabilities and stockholders' equity	$835,000	$540,000

The December 31, 2002, current fair values of Starr Company's identifiable assets and liabilities were the same as their carrying amounts, except for the three assets listed on page 224.

Current Fair Values of Selected Assets of Combinee

	Current Fair Values, Dec. 31, 2002
Inventories	$135,000
Plant assets (net)	365,000
Patent (net)	25,000

Because Starr was to continue as a separate corporation and generally accepted accounting principles do not sanction write-ups of assets of a going concern, Starr did not prepare journal entries for the business combination. Palm Corporation recorded the combination as a purchase on December 31, 2002, with the following journal entries:

Combinor's Journal Entries for Business Combination (acquisition of 100% of subsidiary's outstanding common stock)

PALM CORPORATION (COMBINOR)
Journal Entries
December 31, 2002

Investment in Starr Company Common Stock (10,000 × $45)	450,000	
Common Stock (10,000 × $10)		100,000
Paid-in Capital in Excess of Par		350,000

To record issuance of 10,000 shares of common stock for all the outstanding common stock of Starr Company in a business combination.

Investment in Starr Company Common Stock	50,000	
Paid-in Capital in Excess of Par	35,000	
Cash		85,000

To record payment of out-of-pocket costs of business combination with Starr Company. Finder's and legal fees relating to the combination are recorded as additional costs of the investment; costs associated with the SEC registration statement are recorded as an offset to the previously recorded proceeds from the issuance of common stock.

The first journal entry is similar to the entry illustrated in Chapter 5 (page 179) for a statutory merger. An Investment in Common Stock ledger account is debited with the current fair value of the combinor's common stock issued to effect the business combination, and the paid-in capital accounts are credited in the usual manner for any common stock issuance. In the second journal entry, the **direct** out-of-pocket costs of the business combination are debited to the Investment in Common Stock ledger account, and the costs that are associated with the SEC registration statement, being costs of issuing the common stock, are applied to reduce the proceeds of the common stock issuance.

Unlike the journal entries for a merger illustrated in Chapter 5, the foregoing journal entries do not include any debits or credits to record individual assets and liabilities of Starr Company in the accounting records of Palm Corporation. The reason is that Starr was not **liquidated** as in a merger; it remains a separate legal entity.

After the foregoing journal entries have been posted, the affected ledger accounts of Palm Corporation (the combinor) are as follows:

Ledger Accounts of Combinor Affected by Business Combination

Cash

Date	Explanation	Debit	Credit	Balance
2002 Dec. 31	Balance forward			100,000 dr
31	Out-of-pocket costs of business combination		85,000	15,000 dr

Investment in Starr Company Common Stock

Date	Explanation	Debit	Credit	Balance
2002 Dec. 31	Issuance of common stock in business combination	450,000		450,000 dr
31	Direct out-of-pocket costs of business combination	50,000		500,000 dr

Common Stock, $10 Par

Date	Explanation	Debit	Credit	Balance
2002 Dec. 31	Balance forward			300,000 cr
31	Issuance of common stock in business combination		100,000	400,000 cr

Paid-in Capital in Excess of Par

Date	Explanation	Debit	Credit	Balance
2002. Dec. 31	Balance forward			50,000 cr
31	Issuance of common stock in business combination		350,000	400,000 cr
31	Costs of issuing common stock in business combination	35,000		365,000 cr

Explanation for differences between page 223 to consolidated 235 on page 229

Preparation of Consolidated Balance Sheet without a Working Paper

Accounting for the business combination of Palm Corporation and Starr Company requires a *fresh start* for the consolidated entity. This reflects the theory that a business combination that involves a parent company-subsidiary relationship is an *acquisition of the combinee's net assets* (assets less liabilities) by the combinor. The operating results of Palm and Starr prior to the date of their business combination are those of two separate *economic*—as well as *legal*—entities. Accordingly, a consolidated balance sheet is the only *consolidated* financial statement issued by Palm on December 31, 2002, the date of the business combination of Palm and Starr.

The preparation of a consolidated balance sheet for a parent company and its wholly owned subsidiary may be accomplished without the use of a supporting working paper. The parent company's investment account and the subsidiary's stockholder's equity accounts do not appear in the consolidated balance sheet because they are essentially *reciprocal* (intercompany) accounts. The parent company (combinor) assets and liabilities (other than intercompany ones) are reflected at *carrying amounts,* and the subsidiary (combinee) assets and liabilities (other than intercompany ones) are reflected at *current fair values,* in the consolidated balance sheet. Goodwill is recognized to the extent the cost of the parent's investment in 100% of the subsidiary's outstanding common stock exceeds the current fair value of the subsidiary's *identifiable* net assets, both tangible and intangible.

Applying the foregoing principles to the Palm Corporation and Starr Company parent–subsidiary relationship, the following consolidated balance sheet is produced:

PALM CORPORATION AND SUBSIDIARY
Consolidated Balance Sheet
December 31, 2002

Assets

Current assets:		
Cash ($15,000 + $40,000)		$ 55,000
Inventories ($150,000 + $135,000)		285,000
Other ($110,000 + $70,000)		180,000
Total current assets		$ 520,000
Plant assets (net) ($450,000 + $365,000)		815,000
Intangible assets:		
Patent (net) ($0 + $25,000)	$ 25,000	
Goodwill	15,000	40,000
Total assets		$1,375,000

Liabilities and Stockholders' Equity

Liabilities:		
Income taxes payable ($26,000 + $10,000)		$ 36,000
Other ($325,000 + $115,000)		440,000
Total liabilities		$ 476,000
Stockholders' equity:		
Common stock, $10 par	$400,000	
Additional paid-in capital	365,000	
Retained earnings	134,000	899,000
Total liabilities and stockholders' equity		$1,375,000

The following are significant aspects of the consolidated balance sheet:

1. The first amounts in the computations of consolidated assets and liabilities (except goodwill) are the parent company's carrying amounts; the second amounts are the subsidiary's current fair values.

2. Intercompany accounts (parent's investment, subsidiary's stockholders' equity, and intercompany receivable/payable) are excluded from the consolidated balance sheet.

3. *Goodwill* in the consolidated balance sheet is the cost of the parent company's investment ($500,000) less the current fair value of the subsidiary's identifiable net assets ($485,000), or $15,000. The $485,000 current fair value of the subsidiary's identifiable net assets is computed as follows: $40,000 + $135,000 + $70,000 + $365,000 + $25,000 − $25,000 − $10,000 − $115,000 = $485,000.

Working Paper for Consolidated Balance Sheet

The preparation of a consolidated balance sheet on the date of a business combination usually requires the use of a **working paper for consolidated balance sheet,** even for a parent company and a wholly owned subsidiary. The format of the working paper, with the individual balance sheet amounts included for both Palm Corporation and Starr Company, is shown below.

Developing the Elimination

As indicated on page 225, Palm Corporation's Investment in Starr Company Common Stock ledger account in the working paper for consolidated balance sheet is similar to a home office's Investment in Branch account, as described in Chapter 4. However, Starr Company is a **separate corporation,** not a **branch;** therefore, Starr has the three conventional stockholders' equity accounts rather than the single Home Office reciprocal account used by a branch. Accordingly, the elimination for the **intercompany** accounts of Palm and Starr must **decrease to zero** the Investment in Starr Company Common Stock account of Palm and the three stockholder's equity accounts of Starr. Decreases in assets are effected by **credits,** and decreases in stockholders' equity accounts are effected by **debits;** therefore, the elimination for Palm Corporation and subsidiary on December 31, 2002 (the date of the business combination), is begun as shown at the top of page 228 (a journal entry format is used to facilitate review of the elimination):

Format of Working Paper for Consolidated Balance Sheet for Wholly Owned Subsidiary on Date of Business combination

PALM CORPORATION AND SUBSIDIARY Working Paper for Consolidated Balance Sheet December 31, 2002				
	Palm Corporation	Starr Company	Eliminations Increase (Decrease)	Consolidated
Assets				
Cash	15,000	40,000		
Inventories	150,000	110,000	135,000 -110,000 = 25,000	
Other current assets	110,000	70,000		
Intercompany receivable (payable)	25,000	(25,000)		
Investment in Starr Company common stock	500,000			
Plant assets (net)	450,000	300,000	365,000 -300,000 = 65,000	
Patent (net)		20,000	25,000 -20,000 = 5000	
Goodwill			500K - 485K = 15K next page	
Total assets	1,250,000	515,000		
Liabilities and Stockholders' Equity				
Income taxes payable	26,000	10,000		
Other liabilities	325,000	115,000		
Common stock, $10 par	400,000			
Common stock, $5 par		200,000		
Additional paid-in capital	365,000	58,000		
Retained earnings	134,000	132,000		
Total liabilities and stockholders' equity	1,250,000	515,000		

Elimination of Intercompany Accounts

Common Stock—Starr	200,000	
Additional Paid-in Capital—Starr	58,000	
Retained Earnings—Starr	132,000	
	(390,000)	
Investment in Starr Company Common Stock—Palm		500,000

The footing of $390,000 of the debit items of the foregoing partial elimination represents the *carrying amount* of the net assets of Starr Company and is $110,000 less than the credit item of $500,000, which represents the cost of Palm Corporation's investment in Starr. As indicated on page 224, part of the $110,000 difference is attributable to the excess of current fair values over carrying amounts of certain *identifiable* tangible and intangible assets of Starr. This excess is summarized as follows (the current fair values of all other assets and liabilities are equal to their carrying amounts):

Differences between Current Fair Values and Carrying Amounts of Combinee's Identifiable Assets

	Current Fair Values	Carrying Amounts	Excess of Current Fair Values over Carrying Amounts
Inventories	$135,000	$110,000	$25,000
Plant assets (net)	365,000	300,000	65,000
Patent (net)	25,000	20,000	5,000
Totals	$525,000	$430,000	$95,000

Generally accepted accounting principles do not presently permit the write-up of a going concern's assets to their current fair values. Thus, to conform to the requirements of purchase accounting for business combinations, the foregoing excess of current fair values over carrying amounts must be incorporated in the consolidated balance sheet of Palm Corporation and subsidiary by means of the elimination. *Increases* in assets are recorded by *debits;* thus, the elimination for Palm Corporation and subsidiary begun above is *continued* as follows (in journal entry format):

Use of Elimination to Reflect Current Fair Values of Combinee's Identifiable Assets

Common Stock—Starr	200,000	
Additional Paid-in Capital—Starr	58,000	
Retained Earnings—Starr	132,000	
Inventories—Starr ($135,000 − $110,000)	25,000	
Plant Assets (net)—Starr ($365,000 − $300,000)	65,000	
Patent (net)—Starr ($25,000 − $20,000)	5,000	
	(485,000)	
Investment in Starr Company Common Stock—Palm		500,000

The revised footing of $485,000 of the debit items of the foregoing partial elimination is equal to the *current fair value* of the *identifiable* tangible and intangible net assets of Starr Company. Thus, the $15,000 difference ($500,000 − $485,000 = $15,000) between the cost of Palm Corporation's investment in Starr and the current fair value of Starr's identifiable net assets represents *goodwill of Starr,* in accordance with purchase accounting theory for business combinations, described in Chapter 5 (pages 176 to 177). Consequently, the December 31, 2002, elimination for Palm Corporation and subsidiary is completed with a $15,000 **debit** to Goodwill—Starr.

Completed Elimination and Working Paper for Consolidated Balance Sheet

The completed elimination for Palm Corporation and subsidiary (in journal entry format) and the related working paper for consolidated balance sheet are as follows:

Completed Working Paper Elimination for Wholly Owned Purchased Subsidiary on Date of Business Combination

PALM CORPORATION AND SUBSIDIARY
Working Paper Elimination
December 31, 2002

(a) Common Stock—Starr	200,000
Additional Paid-in Capital—Starr	58,000
Retained Earnings—Starr	132,000
Inventories—Starr ($135,000 − $110,000)	25,000
Plant Assets (net)—Starr ($365,000 − $300,000)	65,000
Patent (net)—Starr ($25,000 − $20,000)	5,000
Goodwill—Starr ($500,000 − $485,000)	15,000
Investment in Starr Company Common Stock—Palm	500,000

To eliminate intercompany investment and equity accounts of subsidiary on date of business combination; and to allocate excess of cost over carrying amount of identifiable assets acquired, with remainder to goodwill. (Income tax effects are disregarded.)

Working Paper for Consolidated Balance Sheet for Wholly Owned Subsidiary on Date of Business Combination

PALM CORPORATION AND SUBSIDIARY
Working Paper for Consolidated Balance Sheet
December 31, 2002

	Palm Corporation	Starr Company	Eliminations Increase (Decrease)	Consolidated
Assets				
Cash	15,000	40,000		55,000
Inventories	150,000	110,000	(a) 25,000	285,000
Other current assets	110,000	70,000		180,000
Intercompany receivable (payable)	25,000	(25,000)		
Investment in Starr Company common stock	500,000		(a) (500,000)	
Plant assets (net)	450,000	300,000	(a) 65,000	815,000
Patent (net)		20,000	(a) 5,000	25,000
Goodwill			(a) 15,000	15,000
Total assets	1,250,000	515,000	(390,000)	1,375,000
Liabilities and Stockholders' Equity				
Income taxes payable	26,000	10,000		36,000
Other liabilities	325,000	115,000		440,000
Common stock, $10 par	400,000			400,000
Common stock, $5 par		200,000	(a) (200,000)	
Additional paid-in capital	365,000	58,000	(a) (58,000)	365,000
Retained earnings	134,000	132,000	(a) (132,000)	134,000
Total liabilities and stockholders' equity	1,250,000	515,000	(390,000)	1,375,000

The following features of the working paper for consolidated balance sheet on the date of the business combination should be emphasized:

1. The elimination is not entered in either the parent company's or the subsidiary's accounting records; it is only a part of the working paper for preparation of the consolidated balance sheet.

2. The elimination is used to reflect differences between current fair values and carrying amounts of the subsidiary's identifiable net assets because the subsidiary did not write up its assets to current fair values on the date of the business combination.

3. The Eliminations column in the working paper for consolidated balance sheet reflects *increases* and *decreases,* rather than *debits* and *credits.* Debits and credits are not appropriate in a working paper dealing with *financial statements* rather than *trial balances.*

4. *Intercompany receivables* and *payables* are placed on the same line of the working paper for consolidated balance sheet and are combined to produce a consolidated amount of zero.

5. The respective corporations are identified in the working paper elimination. The reason for precise identification is explained in Chapter 8 dealing with the eliminations of intercompany profits (or gains).

6. The consolidated paid-in capital amounts are those of the parent company only. Subsidiaries' paid-in capital amounts *always* are eliminated in the process of consolidation.

7. Consolidated retained earnings on the date of a business combination includes only the retained earnings of the parent company. This treatment is consistent with the theory that purchase accounting reflects a fresh start in an acquisition of net assets (assets less liabilities), not a combining of existing stockholder interests.

8. The amounts in the Consolidated column of the working paper for consolidated balance sheet reflect the financial position of a *single economic entity* comprising *two legal entities,* with all *intercompany* balances of the two entities eliminated.

Consolidated Balance Sheet

The amounts in the Consolidated column of the working paper for consolidated balance sheet are presented in the customary fashion in the *consolidated balance sheet* of Palm Corporation and subsidiary that follows. In the interest of brevity, notes to financial

PALM CORPORATION AND SUBSIDIARY Consolidated Balance Sheet December 31, 2002		
Assets		
Current assets:		
Cash		$ 55,000
Inventories		285,000
Other		180,000
Total current assets		$ 520,000
Plant assets (net)		815,000
Intangible assets:		
Patent (net)	$ 25,000	
Goodwill	15,000	40,000
Total assets		$1,375,000

(continued)

PALM CORPORATION AND SUBSIDIARY Consolidated Balance Sheet (concluded) December 31, 2002		
Liabilities and Stockholders' Equity		
Liabilities:		
Income taxes payable		$ 36,000
Other		440,000
Total liabilities		$ 476,000
Stockholders' equity:		
Common stock, $10 par	$400,000	
Additional paid-in capital	365,000	
Retained earnings	134,000	899,000
Total liabilities and stockholders' equity		$1,375,000

statements and other required disclosures are omitted. The consolidated amounts are the same as those in the consolidated balance sheet on page 226.

In addition to the foregoing **consolidated** balance sheet on December 31, 2002, Palm Corporation's published financial statements for the year ended December 31, 2002, include the **unconsolidated** income statement and statement of retained earnings illustrated on page 223 and an unconsolidated statement of cash flows.

CONSOLIDATION OF PARTIALLY OWNED SUBSIDIARY ON DATE OF BUSINESS COMBINATION

The consolidation of a parent company and its **partially owned** subsidiary differs from the consolidation of a wholly owned subsidiary in one major respect—the recognition of minority interest. **Minority interest,** or **noncontrolling interest,** is a term applied to the claims of stockholders other than the parent company (the **controlling interest**) to the net income or losses and net assets of the subsidiary. The minority interest in the subsidiary's net income or losses is displayed in the consolidated income statement, and the minority interest in the subsidiary's net assets is displayed in the consolidated balance sheet.

To illustrate the consolidation techniques for a business combination involving a partially owned subsidiary, assume the following facts. On December 31, 2002, Post Corporation issued 57,000 shares of its $1 par common stock (current fair value $20 a share) to stockholders of Sage Company in exchange for 38,000 of the 40,000 outstanding shares of Sage's $10 par common stock in a business combination. Thus, Post acquired a 95% interest (38,000 ÷ 40,000 = 0.95) in Sage, which became Post's subsidiary. There was no contingent consideration. Out-of-pocket costs of the combination, paid in cash by Post on December 31, 2002, were as follows:

Combinor's Out-of-Pocket **Costs of Business Combination**	Finder's and legal fees relating to business combination *Direct*	$ 52,250
	Costs associated with SEC registration statement *Indirect*	72,750
	Total out-of-pocket costs of business combination	$125,000

Financial statements of Post Corporation and Sage Company for their fiscal year ended December 31, 2002, prior to the business combination, are on page 232. There were no intercompany transactions prior to the combination.

POST CORPORATION AND SAGE COMPANY
Separate Financial Statements (prior to business combination)
For Year Ended December 31, 2002

	Post Corporation	Sage Company
Income Statements		
Net sales	$5,500,000	$1,000,000
Costs and expenses:		
Costs of goods sold	$3,850,000	$ 650,000
Operating expenses	925,000	170,000
Interest expense	75,000	40,000
Income taxes expense	260,000	56,000
Total costs and expenses	$5,110,000	$ 916,000
Net income	$ 390,000	$ 84,000
Statements of Retained Earnings		
Retained earnings, beginning of year	$ 810,000	$ 290,000
Add: Net income	390,000	84,000
Subtotals	$1,200,000	$ 374,000
Less: Dividends	150,000	40,000
Retained earnings, end of year	$1,050,000	$ 334,000
Balance Sheets		
Assets		
Cash	$ 200,000	$ 100,000
Inventories	800,000	500,000
Other current assets	550,000	215,000
Plant assets (net)	3,500,000	1,100,000
Goodwill (net)	100,000	
Total assets	$5,150,000	$1,915,000
Liabilities and Stockholders' Equity		
Income taxes payable	$ 100,000	$ 16,000
Other liabilities	2,450,000	930,000
Common stock, $1 par	1,000,000	
Common stock, $10 par		400,000
Additional paid-in capital	550,000	235,000
Retained earnings	1,050,000	334,000
Total liabilities and stockholders' equity	$5,150,000	$1,915,000

The December 31, 2002, current fair values of Sage Company's identifiable assets and liabilities were the same as their carrying amounts, except for the following assets:

Current Fair Values of Selected Assets of Combinee

	Current Fair Values, Dec. 31, 2002
Inventories	$ 526,000
Plant assets (net)	1,290,000
Leasehold	30,000

Sage Company did not prepare journal entries related to the business combination because Sage is continuing as a separate corporation, and generally accepted accounting principles do not permit the write-up of assets of a going concern to current fair values. Post recorded the combination with Sage by means of the following journal entries:

Test

Combinor's Journal Entries for Business Combination (acquisition of 95% of subsidiary's outstanding common stock)

POST CORPORATION (Combinor)
Journal Entries
December 31, 2002

Investment in Sage Company Common Stock		
(57,000 × $20) *CFV*	1,140,000	
Common Stock (57,000 × $1) *Par*		57,000
Paid-in Capital in Excess of Par		1,083,000
To record issuance of 57,000 shares of common stock for 38,000 of the 40,000 outstanding shares of Sage Company common stock in a business combination.		
Investment in Sage Company Common Stock	52,250	
Paid-in Capital in Excess of Par	72,750	
Cash		125,000
To record payment of out-of-pocket costs of business combination with Sage Company. Finder's and legal fees relating to the combination are recorded as additional costs of the investment; costs associated with the SEC registration statement are recorded as an offset to the previously recorded proceeds from the issuance of common stock.		

Same as 100% ownership in these JE

Explained on bottom of 231

After the foregoing journal entries have been posted, the affected ledger accounts of Post Corporation are as follows:

Ledger Accounts of Combinor Affected by Business Combination

Cash

Date	Explanation	Debit	Credit	Balance
2002				
Dec. 31	Balance forward			200,000 dr
31	Out-of-pocket costs of business combination		125,000	75,000 dr

Investment in Sage Company Common Stock

Date	Explanation	Debit	Credit	Balance
2002				
Dec. 31	Issuance of common stock in business combination	1,140,000		1,140,000 dr
31	Direct out-of-pocket costs of business combination	52,250		1,192,250 dr

Common Stock, $1 Par

Date	Explanation	Debit	Credit	Balance
2002 Dec. 31	Balance forward			1,000,000 cr
31	Issuance of common stock in business combination		57,000	1,057,000 cr

Paid-In Capital in Excess of Par

Date	Explanation	Debit	Credit	Balance
2002 Dec. 31	Balance forward			550,000 cr
31	Issuance of common stock in business combination		1,083,000	1,633,000 cr
31	Costs of issuing common stock in business combination	72,750		1,560,250 cr

Working Paper for Consolidated Balance Sheet

Because of the complexities caused by the minority interest in the net assets of a partially owned subsidiary and the measurement of goodwill acquired in the business combination, it is advisable to use a working paper for preparation of a consolidated balance sheet for a parent company and its partially owned subsidiary on the date of the business combination. The format of the working paper is identical to that illustrated on page 227.

Developing the Elimination

The preparation of the elimination for a parent company and a partially owned subsidiary parallels that for a wholly owned subsidiary described earlier in this chapter. First, the *intercompany* accounts are reduced to zero, as shown below (in journal entry format):

<table>
<tr><td rowspan="5">Elimination of Intercompany Accounts of Parent Company and Subsidiary on Date of Business Combination</td><td>Common Stock—Sage</td><td>400,000</td><td></td></tr>
<tr><td>Additional Paid-in Capital—Sage</td><td>235,000</td><td></td></tr>
<tr><td>Retained Earnings—Sage</td><td>334,000</td><td></td></tr>
<tr><td></td><td>969,000</td><td></td></tr>
<tr><td>Investment in Sage Company Common Stock—Post</td><td></td><td>1,192,250</td></tr>
</table>

The footing of $969,000 of the debit items of the partial elimination above represents the *carrying amount* of the net assets of Sage Company and is $223,250 less than the credit item of $1,192,250. Part of this $223,250 difference is the excess of the total of the cost of Post Corporation's investment in Sage Company and the *minority interest* in Sage Company's net assets over the carrying amounts of Sage's identifiable net assets. This excess may be computed as follows, from the data provided on page 232 (the current fair values of all other assets and liabilities of Sage are equal to their carrying amounts):

Differences Between Current Fair Values and Carrying Amounts of Combinee's Identifiable Assets

	Current Fair Values	Carrying Amounts	Excess of Current Fair Values over Carrying Amounts
Inventories	$ 526,000	$ 500,000	$ 26,000
Plant assets (net)	1,290,000	1,100,000	190,000
Leasehold	30,000		30,000
Totals	$1,846,000	$1,600,000	$246,000

Under current generally accepted accounting principles, the foregoing differences are not entered in Sage Company's accounting records. Thus, to conform with the requirements of purchase accounting, the differences must be reflected in the consolidated balance sheet of Post Corporation and subsidiary by means of the elimination, which is continued below:

Test

Use of Elimination to Reflect Current Fair Values of Identifiable Assets of Subsidiary on Date of Business Combination

Common Stock—Sage	400,000	
Additional Paid-in Capital—Sage	235,000	
Retained Earnings—Sage	334,000	
Inventories—Sage ($526,000 − $500,000)	26,000	
Plant Assets (net)—Sage ($1,290,000 − $1,100,000)	190,000	
Leasehold—Sage	30,000	
	⟨1,215,000⟩	
Investment in Sage Company Common Stock—Post		1,192,250

The revised footing of $1,215,000 of the debit items of the above partial elimination represents the **current fair value** of Sage Company's **identifiable** tangible and intangible net assets on December 31, 2002.

Two items now must be recorded to complete the elimination for Post Corporation and subsidiary. First, the **minority interest** in the identifiable net assets (at current fair values) of Sage Company is recorded by a **credit.** The minority interest is computed as follows:

Test

Computation of Minority Interest in Combinee's Identifiable Net Assets

Current fair value of Sage Company's identifiable net assets	$1,215,000
Minority interest ownership in Sage Company's identifiable net assets (100% minus Post Corporation's 95% interest)	0.05
Minority interest in Sage Company's **identifiable** net assets ($1,215,000 × 0.05)	$ 60,750

Second, the goodwill **acquired by Post Corporation** in the business combination with Sage Company is recorded by a **debit.** The goodwill is computed below:

Test

Computation of Goodwill Acquired by Combinor

Cost of Post Corporation's 95% interest in Sage Company	$1,192,250
Less: Current fair value of Sage Company's identifiable net assets acquired by Post ($1,215,000 × 0.95)	1,154,250
Goodwill **acquired by Post Corporation**	$ 38,000

The working paper elimination for Post Corporation and subsidiary may now be completed as follows:

**Completed Working Paper
Elimination for Partially
Owned Subsidiary on Date of
Business Combination**

POST CORPORATION AND SUBSIDIARY Working Paper Elimination December 31, 2002		
(a) Common Stock—Sage	400,000	
Additional Paid-in Capital—Sage	235,000	
Retained Earnings—Sage	334,000	
Inventories—Sage ($526,000 − $500,000)	26,000	
Plant Assets (net)—Sage ($1,290,000 − $1,100,000)	190,000	
Leasehold—Sage	30,000	
Goodwill—Post ($1,192,250 − $1,154,250)	38,000	
Investment in Sage Company Common Stock—Post		1,192,250
Minority Interest in Net Assets of Subsidiary		60,750
To eliminate intercompany investment and equity accounts of subsidiary on date of business combination; to allocate excess of cost over carrying amount of identifiable assets acquired, with remainder to goodwill; and to establish minority interest in identifiable net assets of subsidiary on date of business combination ($1,215,000 × 0.05 = $60,750). (Income tax effects are disregarded.)		

Working Paper for Consolidated Balance Sheet

The working paper for the consolidated balance sheet on December 31, 2002, for Post Corporation and subsidiary is on page 237.

Nature of Minority Interest

The appropriate classification and presentation of minority interest in consolidated financial statements has been a perplexing problem for accountants, especially because it is recognized *only in the consolidation process* and does not result from a business transaction or event of either the parent company or the subsidiary. Two concepts for consolidated financial statements have been developed to account for minority interest— the *parent company concept* and the *economic unit concept.* The FASB has described these two concepts as follows:

The parent company concept emphasizes the interests of the parent's shareholders. As a result, the consolidated financial statements reflect those stockholders' interests in the parent itself, plus their undivided interests in the net assets of the parent's subsidiaries. The consolidated balance sheet is essentially a modification of the parent's balance sheet with the assets and liabilities of all subsidiaries substituted for the parent's investment in subsidiaries.

. . . [T]he stockholders' equity of the parent company is also the stockholders' equity of the consolidated entity. Similarly, the consolidated income statement is essentially a modification of the parent's income statement with the revenues, expenses, gains, and losses of subsidiaries substituted for the parent's income from investment in the subsidiaries.

The economic unit concept emphasizes control of the whole by a single management. As a result, under this concept (sometimes called the entity theory in the accounting literature), consolidated financial statements are intended to provide infor-

POST CORPORATION AND SUBSIDIARY
Working Paper for Consolidated Balance Sheet
December 31, 2002

	Post Corporation	Sage Company	Eliminations Increase (Decrease)		Consolidated
Assets					
Cash	75,000	100,000			175,000
Inventories	800,000	500,000	(a)	26,000	1,326,000
Other current assets	550,000	215,000			765,000
Investment in Sage Company common stock	1,192,250		(a)	(1,192,250)	
Plant assets (net)	3,500,000	1,100,000	(a)	190,000	4,790,000
Leasehold			(a)	30,000	30,000
Goodwill	100,000		(a)	38,000	138,000
Total assets	6,217,250	1,915,000		(908,250)	7,224,000
Liabilities and Stockholders' Equity					
Income taxes payable	100,000	16,000			116,000
Other liabilities	2,450,000	930,000			3,380,000
Common stock, $1 par	1,057,000				1,057,000
Common stock, $10 par		400,000	(a)	(400,000)	
Additional paid-in capital	1,560,250	235,000	(a)	(235,000)	1,560,250
Minority interest in net assets of subsidiary			(a)	60,750	60,750
Retained earnings	1,050,000	334,000	(a)	(334,000)	1,050,000
Total liabilities and stockholders' equity	6,217,250	1,915,000		(908,250)	7,224,000

Working Paper for Consolidated Balance Sheet for Partially Owned Subsidiary on Date of Business Combination

mation about a group of legal entities—a parent company and its subsidiaries—operating as a single unit. The assets, liabilities, revenues, expenses, gains, and losses of the various component entities are the assets, liabilities, revenues, expenses, gains, and losses of the consolidated entity. Unless all subsidiaries are wholly owned, the business enterprise's proprietary interest (its residual owners' equity—assets less liabilities) is divided into the controlling interest (stockholders or other owners of the parent company) and one or more noncontrolling interests in subsidiaries. Both the controlling and the noncontrolling interests are part of the proprietary group of the consolidated entity, even though the noncontrolling stockholders' ownership interests relate only to the affiliates whose shares they own.[9]

In accordance with the foregoing quotation, the ***parent company concept*** of consolidated financial statements apparently treats the minority interest in net assets of a subsidiary as a ***liability***. This liability is increased each accounting period subsequent to the date of a business combination by an ***expense*** representing the minority's share of the subsidiary's net income (or decreased by the minority's share of the subsidiary's net loss). Dividends declared by the subsidiary to minority stockholders decrease the liability to them. Consolidated net income is ***net*** of the minority's share of the subsidiary's net income.

In the ***economic unit concept,*** the minority interest in the subsidiary's net assets is displayed in the stockholders' equity section of the consolidated balance sheet. The

[9] *FASB Discussion Memorandum,* ". . . Consolidation Policy and Procedures" (Norwalk: FASB, 1991), pars. 63–64.

consolidated income statement displays the minority interest in the subsidiary's net income as a ***subdivision of total consolidated net income,*** similar to the distribution of net income of a partnership (see page 41).

Absent specific accounting standards dealing with minority interest in subsidiaries, in prior years publicly owned companies used the parent company concept exclusively. Nonetheless, in 1995 the FASB expressed a preference for the economic unit concept, despite its emphasis on the legal form of the minority interest in a subsidiary.[10] This action was consistent with an earlier FASB rejection of the idea that the minority interest in net assets is a ***liability:***

> Minority interests in net assets of consolidated subsidiaries do not represent present obligations of the enterprise to pay cash or distribute other assets to minority stockholders. Rather, those stockholders have ownership or residual interests in components of a consolidated enterprise.[11]

Having abandoned its attempts to issue a pronouncement on consolidation policy and procedure (see page 222), the FASB in 2000 included the following in a ***Proposed Statement of Financial Accounting Standards,*** "Accounting for Financial Instruments with Characteristics of Liabilities, Equity, or Both":

> An equity instrument that is issued by a less-than-wholly-owned subsidiary included in the reporting entity to an entity outside the consolidated group and thus representing the noncontrolling equity interest in that subsidiary shall be reported in the consolidated financial statements as a separate component of equity.[12]

In view of the FASB's actions described in the foregoing section, the economic unit concept of displaying minority interest is stressed throughout this book.

Consolidated Balance Sheet for Partially Owned Subsidiary

The consolidated balance sheet of Post Corporation and its partially owned subsidiary, Sage Company, is on page 239. The consolidated amounts are taken from the working paper for consolidated balance sheet on page 237.

The display of minority interest in net assets of subsidiary in the equity section of the consolidated balance sheet of Post Corporation and subsidiary is consistent with the economic unit concept of consolidated financial statements. It should be noted that ***there is no ledger account for minority interest in net assets of subsidiary, in either the parent company's or the subsidiary's accounting records.***

Alternative Methods for Valuing Minority Interest and Goodwill

The computation of minority interest in net assets of subsidiary and goodwill on page 235 is based on two premises. First, the ***identifiable net assets*** of a partially owned purchased subsidiary should be valued on a single basis—***current fair value,*** in accordance with purchase accounting theory for business combinations. Second, only the subsidiary goodwill ***acquired by the parent company*** should be recognized, in accordance with the cost method for valuing assets.

---

[10] "Consolidated Financial Statements: Policy and Procedure," pars. 22–24.
[11] *Statement of Financial Accounting Concepts No. 6,* "Elements of Financial Statements" (Norwalk: FASB, 1985), par. 254.
[12] *Proposed Statement of Financial Accounting Standards,* "Accounting for Financial Instruments with Characteristics of Liabilities, Equity, or Both" (Norwalk: FASB, 2000), par. 36.

POST CORPORATION AND SUBSIDIARY
Consolidated Balance Sheet
December 31, 2002

Assets

Current assets:		
Cash		$ 175,000
Inventories		1,326,000
Other		765,000
Total current assets		$2,266,000
Plant assets (net)		$4,790,000
Intangible assets:		
Leasehold	$ 30,000	
Goodwill	138,000	168,000
Total assets		$7,224,000

Liabilities and Stockholders' Equity

Liabilities:		
Income taxes payable		$ 116,000
Other		3,380,000
Total liabilities		$3,496,000
Stockholders' equity:		
Common stock, $1 par	$1,057,000	
Additional paid-in capital	1,560,250	
Minority interest in net assets of subsidiary	60,750	
Retained earnings	1,050,000	3,728,000
Total liabilities and stockholders' equity		$7,224,000

Two alternatives to the procedure described on page 238 have been suggested. The first alternative would assign current fair values to a partially owned purchased subsidiary's identifiable net assets **only to the extent of the parent company's ownership interest therein.** Under this alternative, $233,700 ($246,000 × 0.95 = $233,700) of the total difference between current fair values and carrying amounts of Sage Company's identifiable net assets summarized on page 232 would be reflected in the aggregate debits to inventories, plant assets, and leasehold in the working paper elimination for Post Corporation and subsidiary on December 31, 2002. The minority interest in net assets of subsidiary would be based on the **carrying amounts** of Sage Company's identifiable net assets, rather than on their **current fair values,** and would be computed as follows: $969,000 × 0.05 = $48,450. Goodwill would be $38,000, as computed on page 235. Supporters of this alternative argue that current fair values of a combinee's identifiable net assets should be reflected in consolidated financial statements only to the extent (percentage) that they have been **acquired by the combinor.** The balance of the combinee's net assets, and the related minority interest in the net assets, should be reflected in consolidated financial statements at the carrying amounts in the subsidiary's accounting records. Thus, identifiable net assets of the subsidiary would be valued on a **hybrid** basis, rather than at full current fair values as required by purchase accounting theory.

The other alternative for valuing minority interest in net assets of subsidiary and goodwill is to obtain a current fair value for **100%** of a partially owned purchased subsidiary's **total** net assets, either through independent measurement of the minority interest or by **inference** from the cost of the parent company's investment in the subsidiary. Independent measurement of the minority interest might be accomplished by reference to quoted market prices of publicly traded common stock owned by minority stockholders of the subsidiary. The computation of minority interest and goodwill of Sage Company by inference from the cost of Post Corporation's investment in Sage is as follows:

<table>
<tr><td rowspan="6">**Computation of Minority Interest and Goodwill of Partially Owned Subsidiary Based on Implied Total Current Fair Value of Subsidiary**</td><td>Total cost of Post Corporation's investment in Sage Company</td><td>$1,192,250</td></tr>
<tr><td>Post's percentage ownership of Sage</td><td>0.95</td></tr>
<tr><td>Implied current fair value of 100% of Sage's total net assets
($1,192,250 ÷ 0.95)</td><td>$1,255,000</td></tr>
<tr><td>Minority interest ($1,255,000 × 0.05)</td><td>$ 62,750</td></tr>
<tr><td>Goodwill ($1,255,000 − $1,215,000, the current fair value of
Sage's *identifiable* net assets)</td><td>$ 40,000</td></tr>
</table>

Supporters of this approach contend that a ***single valuation method*** should be used for all net assets of a purchased subsidiary—including goodwill—regardless of the existence of a minority interest in the subsidiary. They further maintain that the goodwill should be attributed to the ***subsidiary,*** rather than to the ***parent company,*** as is done for a wholly owned purchased subsidiary, in accordance with the theory of purchase accounting for business combinations.

A summary of the three methods for valuing minority interest and goodwill of a partially owned purchased subsidiary (derived from the December 31, 2002, business combination of Post Corporation and Sage Company) follows:

<table>
<tr><td rowspan="2">**Comparison of Three Methods for Valuing Minority Interest and Goodwill of Partially Owned Subsidiary**</td><td rowspan="2"></td><td rowspan="2">**Total Identifiable Net Assets**</td><td>**Minority Interest in Net Assets of**</td><td rowspan="2"></td></tr>
<tr><td>**Subsidiary**</td><td>**Goodwill**</td></tr>
<tr><td></td><td>1. Identifiable net assets recorded at current fair value; minority interest in net assets of subsidiary based on identifiable net assets</td><td>$1,215,000</td><td>$60,750</td><td>$38,000</td></tr>
<tr><td></td><td>2. Identifiable net assets recorded at current fair value only to extent of parent company's interest; balance of net assets and minority interest in net assets of subsidiary reflected at carrying amounts</td><td>1,202,700*</td><td>48,450</td><td>38,000</td></tr>
<tr><td></td><td>3. Current fair value, through independent measurement or inference, assigned to total net assets of subsidiary, including goodwill</td><td>1,215,000</td><td>62,750</td><td>40,000</td></tr>
</table>

* $969,000 + ($246,000 × 0.95) = $1,202,700.

In 1995, the Financial Accounting Standards Board tentatively expressed a preference for the method of valuing minority interest and goodwill set forth in method 1 above.[13] Accordingly, that method is illustrated in subsequent pages of this book.

Bargain-Purchase Excess in Consolidated Balance Sheet

A business combination that results in a parent company–subsidiary relationship may involve an excess of current fair values of the subsidiary's identifiable net assets over the

[13] "Consolidated Financial Statements: Policy and Procedures," par. 27.

cost of the parent company's investment in the subsidiary's common stock. If so, the accounting standards described in Chapter 5 (page 177) are applied. The excess of current fair values over cost (bargain-purchase excess) is applied pro rata to reduce the amounts initially assigned to noncurrent assets other than financial assets (excluding investments accounted for by the equity method), assets to be disposed of by sale, deferred tax assets, and prepaid assets relating to pensions and other postretirement benefit plans.

Illustration of Bargain-Purchase Excess: Wholly Owned Subsidiary

On December 31, 2002, Plowman Corporation acquired all the outstanding common stock of Silbert Company for $850,000 cash, including direct out-of-pocket costs of the business combination. Stockholders' equity of Silbert totaled $800,000, consisting of common stock, $100,000; additional paid-in capital, $300,000; and retained earnings, $400,000. The current fair values of Silbert's identifiable net assets were the same as their carrying amounts, except for the following:

Current Fair Values of Selected Assets of Combinee

	Current Fair Values	Carrying Amounts	Differences
Inventories	$ 339,000	$320,000	$19,000
Long-term investments in marketable debt securities (held to maturity)	61,000	50,000	11,000
Plant assets (net)	1,026,000	984,000	42,000
Intangible assets (net)	54,000	36,000	18,000

Thus, the current fair values of Silbert's identifiable net assets exceeded the amount paid by Plowman by $40,000 [($800,000 + $19,000 + $11,000 + $42,000 + $18,000) − $850,000 = $40,000]. This $40,000 bargain-purchase excess is offset against amounts originally assigned to Silbert's plant assets and intangible assets in proportion to their current fair values ($1,026,000:$54,000 = 95:5). The December 31, 2002, working paper elimination for Plowman Corporation and subsidiary is as follows:

Working Paper Elimination for Wholly Owned Subsidiary with Bargain-Purchase Excess on Date of Business Combination

PLOWMAN CORPORATION AND SUBSIDIARY
Working Paper Elimination
December 31, 2002

(a) Common Stock—Silbert	100,000	
Additional Paid-in Capital—Silbert	300,000	
Retained Earnings—Silbert	400,000	
Inventories—Silbert ($339,000 − $320,000)	19,000	
Long-Term Investments in Marketable Debt Securities—Silbert ($61,000 − $50,000)	11,000	
Plant Assets (net)—Silbert [($1,026,000 − $984,000) − ($40,000 × 0.95)]	4,000	
Intangible Assets (net)—Silbert [($54,000 − $36,000) − ($40,000 × 0.05)]	16,000	
Investment in Silbert Company Common Stock—Plowman		850,000

To eliminate intercompany investment and equity accounts of subsidiary on date of business combination; and to allocate $40,000 excess of current fair values of subsidiary's identifiable net assets over cost to subsidiary's plant assets and intangible assets in ratio of $1,026,000:$54,000, or 95%:5%. (Income tax effects are disregarded.)

Illustration of Bargain-Purchase Excess: Partially Owned Subsidiary

The Plowman Corporation–Silbert Company business combination described in the foregoing section is now changed by assuming that Plowman acquired **98%,** rather than **100%,** of Silbert's common stock for $833,000 ($850,000 × 0.98 = $833,000) on December 31, 2002, with all other facts remaining unchanged. The excess of current fair values of Silbert's identifiable net assets over Plowman's cost is $39,200 [($890,000 × 0.98) − $833,000 = $39,200]. Under these circumstances, the working paper elimination for Plowman Corporation and subsidiary on December 31, 2002, is as follows:

Working Paper Elimination for Partially Owned Subsidiary with Bargain-Purchase Excess on Date of Business Combination

PLOWMAN CORPORATION AND SUBSIDIARY
Working Paper Elimination
December 31, 2002

(a) Common Stock—Silbert	100,000	
Additional Paid-in Capital—Silbert	300,000	
Retained Earnings—Silbert	400,000	
Inventories—Silbert ($339,000 − $320,000)	19,000	
Long-Term Investments in Marketable Debt Securities—Silbert ($61,000 − $50,000)	11,000	
Plant Assets (net)—Silbert [($42,000 − ($39,200 × 0.95)]	4,760	
Intangible Assets (net)—Silbert [$18,000 − ($39,200 × 0.05)]	16,040	
Investment in Silbert Company Common Stock—Plowman		833,000
Minority Interest in Net Assets of Subsidiary ($890,000 × 0.02)		17,800

To eliminate intercompany investment and equity accounts of subsidiary on date of business combination; to allocate parent company's share of excess ($39,200) of current fair values of subsidiary's identifiable net assets over cost to subsidiary's plant assets and intangible assets in ratio of 95%:5%; and to establish minority interest in net assets of subsidiary on date of business combination. (Income tax effects are disregarded.)

Disclosure of Consolidation Policy

Currently, the "Summary of Significant Accounting Policies" note to financial statements required by **APB Opinion No. 22,** "Disclosure of Accounting Policies," and by Rule 3A-03 of the SEC's **Regulation S-X,** which is discussed in Chapter 13, generally includes a description of consolidation policy reflected in consolidated financial statements. The following excerpt from an annual report of The McGraw-Hill Companies, Inc., a publicly owned corporation, is typical:

> *Principles of consolidation.* The consolidated financial statements include the accounts of all subsidiaries and the company's share of earnings or losses of joint ventures and affiliated companies under the equity method of accounting. All significant intercompany accounts and transactions have been eliminated.

International Accounting Standard 27

Among the provisions of *IAS 27,* **"Consolidated Financial Statements and Accounting for Investments in Subsidiaries,"** are the following:

1. Consolidation policy is based on **control** rather than solely on ownership. **Control** is described as follows:

Control (for the purpose of this Standard) is the power to govern the financial and op-erating policies of an enterprise so as to obtain benefits from its activities.

*****

Control is presumed to exist when the parent owns, directly or indirectly through subsidiaries, more than one half of the voting power of an enterprise unless, in exceptional circumstances, it can be clearly demonstrated that such ownership does not constitute control. Control also exists even when the parent owns one half or less of the voting power of an enterprise when there is:

(a) power over more than one half of the voting rights by virtue of an agreement with other investors;

(b) power to govern the financial and operating policies of the enterprise under a statute or an agreement;

(c) power to appoint or remove the majority of the members of the board of directors or equivalent governing body; or

(d) power to cast the majority of votes at meetings of the board of directors or equivalent governing body.

2. Intercompany transactions, profits or gains, and losses are eliminated in full, re-gardless of an existing minority interest.

3. The minority interest in net income of subsidiary is displayed separately in the con-solidated income statement. The minority interest in net assets of subsidiary is dis-played separately from liabilities and stockholders' equity in the consolidated bal-ance sheet. Thus, the IASC rejected both the parent company concept and the economic unit concept (see pages 236 to 237).

4. In the unconsolidated financial statements of a parent company, investments in sub-sidiaries that are included in the consolidated statements may be accounted for by either the equity method, as required by the SEC, or the cost method.

Advantages and Shortcomings of Consolidated Financial Statements

Consolidated financial statements are useful principally to stockholders and prospec-tive investors of the parent company. These users of consolidated financial statements are provided with comprehensive financial information for the economic unit repre-sented by the parent company and its subsidiaries, without regard for legal separate-ness of the individual companies.

Creditors of each consolidated company and minority stockholders of subsidiaries have only limited use for consolidated financial statements, because such statements do not show the financial position or operating results of the individual companies comprising the consolidated group. In addition, creditors of the constituent companies cannot ascer-tain the asset coverages for their respective claims. But perhaps the most telling criticism of consolidated financial statements has come from financial analysts. These critics have pointed out that consolidated financial statements of diversified companies (conglomer-ates) are impossible to classify into a single industry. Thus, say the financial analysts, con-solidated financial statements of a conglomerate cannot be used for comparative purposes. The problem of financial reporting by diversified companies is considered in Chapter 13.

"Push-Down Accounting" for a Purchased Subsidiary

A thorny question for accountants has been the appropriate basis of accounting for assets and liabilities of a subsidiary that, because of a substantial minority interest, loan agreements, legal requirements, or other commitments, issues separate financial statements to outsiders following the business combination. Some accountants have maintained that because generally accepted accounting principles do not permit the write-up of assets by a going concern, the subsidiary should report assets, liabilities, revenue, and expenses in its separate financial statements at amounts based on carrying amounts prior to the business combination. Other accountants have recommended that the values assigned to the subsidiary's net assets in the consolidated financial statements be "pushed down" to the subsidiary for incorporation in its separate financial statements. These accountants believe that the business combination is an event that warrants recognition of current fair values of the subsidiary's net assets in its separate statements.

In *Staff Accounting Bulletin No. 54,* the Securities and Exchange Commission staff sanctioned *push-down accounting* for separate financial statements of subsidiaries that are substantially wholly owned by a parent company subject to the SEC's jurisdiction.[14] (The securities laws administered by the SEC, and the SEC's own rules, sometimes require a parent company to include separate financial statements of a subsidiary in its reports to the SEC.) This action by the SEC staff was followed several years later by the FASB's issuance of a *Discussion Memorandum,* ". . . New Basis Accounting," which solicited views on when, if ever, a business enterprise should adjust the carrying amounts of its net assets, including goodwill, to current fair values, including push-down accounting situations.[15]

In the absence of definitive guidelines from the FASB, companies that have applied push-down accounting apparently have used accounting techniques analogous to quasi-reorganizations (which are discussed in intermediate accounting textbooks) or to reorganizations under the U.S. Bankruptcy Code (discussed in Chapter 14). That is, the restatement of identifiable assets and liabilities of the subsidiary and the recognition of goodwill are accompanied by a write-off of the subsidiary's retained earnings; the balancing amount is an increase in additional paid-in capital of the subsidiary.[16]

To illustrate push-down accounting, I return to the Post Corporation–Sage Company business combination, specifically to the working paper for consolidated balance sheet on page 237. To apply the push-down accounting techniques described in the previous paragraph, the following *working paper adjustment* to the Sage Company balance sheet amounts would be required:

Working Paper Adjustment for Push-Down Accounting for Subsidiary's Separate Balance Sheet

Inventories	26,000	
Plant Assets (net)	190,000	
Leasehold	30,000	
Goodwill	38,000	
Retained Earnings	334,000	
Additional Paid-in Capital		618,000
To adjust carrying amounts of identifiable net assets, to recognize goodwill, and to write off retained earnings in connection with push-down accounting for separate financial statements.		

---

[14] *Staff Accounting Bulletin No. 54,* Securities and Exchange Commission (Washington: 1983).

[15] *FASB Discussion Memorandum,* ". . . New Basis Accounting (Norwalk: FASB, 1991), pars. 1–11.

[16] Hortense Goodman and Leonard Lorensen, *Illustrations of "Push Down" Accounting* (New York: AICPA, 1985).

Sage Company's separate balance sheet reflecting push-down accounting is the following:

SAGE COMPANY		
Balance Sheet (push-down accounting)		
December 31, 2002		
Assets		
Current assets:		
Cash		$ 100,000
Inventories ($500,000 + $26,000)		526,000
Other		215,000
Total current assets		$ 841,000
Plant assets (net) ($1,100,000 + $190,000)		1,290,000
Leasehold		30,000
Goodwill		38,000
Total assets		$2,199,000
Liabilities and Stockholders' Equity		
Liabilities:		
Income taxes payable		$ 16,000
Other		930,000
Total liabilities		$ 946,000
Stockholders' equity:		
Common stock, $10 par	$400,000	
Additional paid-in capital ($235,000 + $618,000)	853,000	1,253,000
Total liabilities and stockholders' equity		$2,199,000

A note to financial statements would describe Sage Company's business combination with Post Corporation and its adjustments to reflect push-down accounting in its balance sheet.

Note that the $38,000 goodwill in Sage Company's separate balance sheet is attributed to Post Corporation in the working paper elimination on page 236. As explained in Chapter 7, the attribution to Post Corporation is required to avoid applying any amortization of the goodwill to minority stockholders' interest in net income of Sage.

SEC ENFORCEMENT ACTIONS DEALING WITH WRONGFUL APPLICATION OF ACCOUNTING STANDARDS FOR CONSOLIDATED FINANCIAL STATEMENTS

AAER 34

"Securities and Exchange Commission v. Digilog, Inc. and Ronald Moyer," reported in *AAER 34* (July 5, 1984), deals with the issue of whether Corporation A, though *in form* not a conventional subsidiary, *in substance* was controlled by Corporation B and thus should have been a party to consolidated financial statements with Corporation B, which developed, manufactured, and sold electronic equipment. In reporting a federal court's entry of a permanent injunction against Corporation B and its CEO, the SEC opined that, although Corporation A's initial issuance of 50 shares of common stock was to the CEO of Corporation B (for $50,000), Corporation B nonetheless ***substantively controlled*** Corporation A for the following reasons:

1. Corporation B provided initial working capital of $450,000 to Corporation A in exchange for promissory notes convertible within five years to 90% of the authorized common stock of Corporation A.

2. Corporation B sublet office space and provided accounting, financial, and administrative services to Corporation A.

3. Corporation B sold equipment, software, furniture, and other items to Corporation A for cash and a $92,000 interest-bearing promissory note.

4. Corporation B ultimately made loans and extended credit to, and guaranteed bank loans of, Corporation A that totaled $4.9 million.

5. All promissory notes issued by Corporation A to Corporation B were secured by the former's accounts receivable, inventories, and equipment.

Despite Corporation B's management's having been informed by its independent auditors that its financial statements need not be consolidated with those of Corporation A, the SEC ruled to the contrary, maintaining that ***substance*** prevailed over ***form*** (Corporation B's CEO, rather than Corporation B itself, owned all 50 shares of Corporation A's outstanding common stock). In a related enforcement action, reported in ***AAER 45***, " . . . In the Matter of Coopers & Lybrand and M. Bruce Cohen, C.P.A." (November 27, 1984), the SEC set forth its acceptance of the undisclosed terms of a "Consent and Settlement" with the CPA firm and its engagement partner that had audited Corporation B's unconsolidated financial statements.

Review Questions

1. Discuss the similarities and dissimilarities between consolidated financial statements for a parent company and its subsidiaries and combined financial statements for the home office and branches of a single legal entity.

2. The use of consolidated financial statements for reporting to stockholders is common. Under some conditions, certain subsidiaries may be excluded from consolidation. List the conditions under which subsidiaries sometimes are excluded from consolidated financial statements.

3. The controller of Pastor Corporation, which has just become the parent of Sexton Company in a business combination, inquires if a consolidated income statement is required for the year ended on the date of the combination. What is your reply? Explain.

4. In a business combination resulting in a parent–subsidiary relationship, the identifiable net assets of the subsidiary must be reflected in the consolidated balance sheet at their current fair values on the date of the business combination. Does this require the subsidiary to enter the current fair values of the identifiable net assets in its accounting records? Explain.

5. Are eliminations for the preparation of consolidated financial statements entered in the accounting records of the parent company or of the subsidiary? Explain.

6. Differentiate between a ***working paper for consolidated balance sheet*** and a ***consolidated balance sheet.***

7. Describe three methods that have been proposed for valuing minority interest and goodwill in the consolidated balance sheet of a parent company and its partially owned subsidiary.

8. Compare the ***parent company concept*** and the ***economic unit concept*** of consolidated financial statements as they relate to the display of minority interest in net assets of subsidiary in a consolidated balance sheet.

9. The principal limitation of consolidated financial statements is their lack of separate information about the assets, liabilities, revenue, and expenses of the individual companies included in the consolidation. List the problems that users of consolidated financial statements encounter as a result of this limitation.

10. What is ***push-down accounting***?

Exercises

(Exercise 6.1) Select the best answer for each of the following multiple-choice questions:

1. A parent company's correctly prepared journal entry to record the out-of-pocket costs of the acquisition of the subsidiary's outstanding common stock in a business combination was as follows (explanation omitted):

Investment in Sullivan Company Common Stock	36,800	
Cash		36,800

The implication of the foregoing journal entry is that the consideration issued by the parent company for the outstanding common stock of the subsidiary was:

   a. Cash.
   b. Bonds.
   c. Common stock.
   d. Cash, bonds, or common stock.

2. The traditional definition of ***control*** for a parent company–subsidiary relationship (parent's ownership of more than 50% of the subsidiary's outstanding common stock) emphasizes:

   a. Legal form.
   b. Economic substance.
   c. Both legal form and economic substance.
   d. Neither legal form nor economic substance.

3. An investor company that owns more than 50% of the outstanding voting common stock of an investee may not ***control*** the investee if:

   a. The investee is in reorganization in bankruptcy proceedings.
   b. There is a large passive minority interest in the investee.
   c. A part of the investor company's ownership is ***indirect.***
   d. The investee is a finance-related enterprise.

4. ***FASB Statement No. 94,*** "Consolidation of All Majority Owned Subsidiaries," exempts from consolidation:

   a. No subsidiaries of the parent company.
   b. Foreign subsidiaries of the parent company.
   c. Finance-related subsidiaries of the parent company.
   d. Subsidiaries not controlled by the parent company.

5. If, on the date of the business combination, C = consideration given to the former stockholders of wholly owned subsidiary Stacey Company by Passey Corporation; DOP = direct out-of-pocket costs of the combination; CA = carrying amount, and CFV = current fair value of Stacey's identifiable net assets; and GW = goodwill:

   a. C + DOP = CA + GW
   b. C − DOP = CFV − GW
   c. C + DOP = CFV + GW
   d. C = CA + GW − DOP

6. In a completed working paper elimination (in journal entry format) for a parent company and its wholly owned subsidiary on the date of the business combination, the total of the debits generally equals the:

   a. Parent company's total cost of its investment in the subsidiary.
   b. Carrying amount of the subsidiary's identifiable net assets.
   c. Current fair value of the subsidiary's identifiable net assets.
   d. Total paid-in capital of the subsidiary.

7. In a working paper elimination (in journal entry format) for the consolidated balance sheet of a parent company and its wholly owned subsidiary on the date of a business combination, the subtotal of the debits to the subsidiary's stockholders' equity accounts equals the:

   a. Current fair value of the subsidiary's ***identifiable*** net assets.
   b. Current fair value of the subsidiary's ***total*** net assets, including goodwill.
   c. Balance of the parent company's investment ledger account.
   d. Carrying amount of the subsidiary's ***identifiable*** net assets.

8. In the working paper for consolidated balance sheet prepared on the date of the business combination of a parent company and its wholly owned subsidiary, whose liabilities had current fair values equal to their carrying amounts, the total of the Eliminations column is equal to:

   a. The current fair value of the subsidiary's ***identifiable*** net assets.
   b. The total stockholder's equity of the subsidiary.
   c. The current fair value of the subsidiary's ***total*** net assets, including goodwill.
   d. An amount that is not determinable.

9. On the date of the business combination of Pobre Corporation and its wholly owned subsidiary, Sabe Company, Pobre paid (1) $100,000 to the former stockholders of Sabe for their stockholders' equity of $65,000 and (2) $15,000 for direct out-of-pocket costs of the combination. Goodwill recognized in the business combination was $10,000. The current fair value of Sabe's identifiable net assets was:

   a. $65,000   *b.* $75,000   *c.* $105,000   *d.* $115,000   *e.* $125,000

10. Differences between current fair values and carrying amounts of the identifiable net assets of a subsidiary on the date of a business combination are recognized in a:

    a. Working paper elimination.
    b. Subsidiary journal entry.
    c. Parent company journal entry.
    d. Note to the consolidated financial statements.

11. In a business combination resulting in a parent company–wholly owned subsidiary relationship, goodwill developed in the working paper elimination is attributed:

    a. In its entirety to the subsidiary.
    b. In its entirety to the parent company.

    c. To both the parent company and the subsidiary, in the ratio of current fair values of identifiable net assets.

    d. In its entirety to the consolidated entity.

12. In a consolidated balance sheet of a parent company and its partially owned subsidiary, minority interest in net assets of subsidiary is displayed as a:

    a. Liability under the economic unit concept but a part of consolidated stockholders' equity under the parent company concept.

    b. Part of consolidated stockholders' equity under the economic unit concept but a liability under the parent company concept.

    c. Liability under both the economic unit concept and the parent company concept.

    d. Part of consolidated stockholders' equity under both the economic unit concept and the parent company concept.

13. On the date of the business combination of a parent company and its partially owned subsidiary, under the computation method used in this book, the amount assigned to minority interest in net assets of subsidiary is based on the:

    a. Cost of the parent company's investment in the subsidiary's common stock.

    b. Carrying amount of the subsidiary's *identifiable* net assets.

    c. Current fair value of the subsidiary's *identifiable* net assets.

    d. Current fair value of the subsidiary's *total* net assets, including goodwill.

14. The debits in the working paper elimination (in journal entry format) for the consolidated balance sheet of Parent Corporation and 90%-owned Subsidiary Company totaled $2,080,000, including a debit of $80,000 to Goodwill—Parent. The credit elements of the elimination are:

	Investment in Subsidiary Company Common Stock—Parent	Minority Interest in Net Assets of Subsidiary
a.	$2,000,000	$ 80,000
b.	$1,880,000	$200,000
c.	$1,872,000	$208,000
d.	Some other amounts.	

15. The cost of Paul Corporation's 80% investment in Seth Company's outstanding voting common stock was $1,200,000, and the current fair value of Seth's identifiable net assets, which had a carrying amount of $1,000,000, was $1,250,000. Under the computation method used in this book, Goodwill—Paul and Minority Interest in Net Assets of Subsidiary are, respectively:

    a. $200,000 and $250,000.

    b. $200,000 and $200,000.

    c. $250,000 and $300,000.

    d. Some other amounts.

16. Has push-down accounting for a subsidiary's separate financial statements been sanctioned by the:

	FASB?	SEC?
a.	Yes	Yes
b.	Yes	No
c.	No	Yes
d.	No	No

(Exercise 6.2) On March 31, 2002, Pyre Corporation acquired for $8,200,000 cash all the outstanding common stock of Stark Company when Stark's balance sheet showed net assets of

$6,400,000. Out-of-pocket costs of the business combination may be disregarded. Stark's identifiable net assets had current fair values different from carrying amounts as follows:

	Carrying Amounts	Current Fair Values
Plant assets (net)	$10,000,000	$11,500,000
Other assets	1,000,000	700,000
Long-term debt	6,000,000	5,600,000

Prepare a working paper to compute the amount of goodwill to be displayed in the consolidated balance sheet of Pyre Corporation and subsidiary on March 31, 2002.

(Exercise 6.3) Single Company's balance sheet on December 31, 2002, was as follows:

SINGLE COMPANY
Balance Sheet (prior to business combination)
December 31, 2002

Assets

Cash	$ 100,000
Trade accounts receivable (net)	200,000
Inventories	510,000
Plant assets (net)	900,000
Total assets	$1,710,000

Liabilities and Stockholders' Equity

Current liabilities	$ 310,000
Long-term debt	500,000
Common stock, $1 par	100,000
Additional paid-in capital	200,000
Retained earnings	600,000
Total liabilities and stockholders' equity	$1,710,000

On December 31, 2002, Phyll Corporation acquired all the outstanding common stock of Single for $1,560,000 cash, including direct out-of-pocket costs. On that date, the current fair value of Single's inventories was $450,000 and the current fair value of Single's plant assets was $1,000,000. The current fair values of all other assets and liabilities of Single were equal to their carrying amounts.

a. Prepare a working paper to compute the amount of goodwill to be displayed in the December 31, 2002, consolidated balance sheet of Phyll Corporation and subsidiary.

b. Prepare a working paper to compute the amount of consolidated retained earnings to be displayed in the December 31, 2002, consolidated balance sheet of Phyll Corporation and subsidiary, assuming that Phyll's unconsolidated balance sheet on that date included retained earnings of $2,500,000.

(Exercise 6.4) Following are the December 31, 2002, balance sheets of two companies prior to their business combination:

PELERIN CORPORATION AND SOUTH COMPANY
Separate Balance Sheets (prior to business combination)
December 31, 2002
(000 omitted)

	Pelerin Corporation	South Company
Assets		
Cash	$ 3,000	$ 100
Inventories (at first-in, first-out cost, which approximates current fair value)	2,000	200
Plant assets (net)	5,000	700*
Total assets	$10,000	$1,000
Liabilities and Stockholders' Equity		
Current liabilities	$ 600	$ 100
Common stock, $1 par	1,000	100
Additional paid-in capital	3,000	200
Retained earnings	5,400	600
Total liabilities and stockholders' equity	$10,000	$1,000

* Current fair value, Dec. 31, 2002, $1,500,000.

a. On December 31, 2002, Pelerin Corporation acquired all the outstanding common stock of South Company for $2,000,000 cash. Prepare a working paper to compute the amount of goodwill to be displayed in the consolidated balance sheet of Pelerin Corporation and subsidiary on December 31, 2002.

b. On December 31, 2002, Pelerin Corporation acquired all the outstanding common stock of South Company for $1,600,000 cash. Prepare a working paper to compute the amount of plant assets to be displayed in the consolidated balance sheet of Pelerin Corporation and subsidiary on December 31, 2002.

(Exercise 6.5) The separate balance sheets of Painter Corporation and Sawyer Company following their business combination, in which Painter acquired all of Sawyer's outstanding common stock, were as follows:

PAINTER CORPORATION AND SAWYER COMPANY
Separate Balance Sheets (following business combination)
May 31, 2002

	Painter Corporation	Sawyer Company
Assets		
Inventories	$ 60,000	$ 30,000
Other current assets	140,000	110,000
Investment in Sawyer Company common stock	250,000	
Plant assets (net)	220,000	160,000
Goodwill (net)	10,000	
Total assets	$680,000	$300,000

(continued)

	PAINTER CORPORATION AND SAWYER COMPANY	
	Separate Balance Sheets (following business combination) (concluded)	
	May 31, 2002	

	Painter Corporation	Sawyer Company
Liabilities and Stockholders' Equity		
Current liabilities	$100,000	$ 70,000
Bonds payable	104,000	30,000
Common stock, $1 par	200,000	80,000
Additional paid-in capital	116,000	70,000
Retained earnings	160,000	50,000
Total liabilities and stockholders' equity	$680,000	$300,000

On May 31, 2002, the current fair values of Sawyer's inventories and plant assets (net) were $40,000 and $180,000, respectively; the current fair values of its other assets and its liabilities were equal to their carrying amounts.

Prepare a consolidated balance sheet for Painter Corporation and subsidiary on May 31, 2002, without using a working paper. (Disregard income taxes.)

(Exercise 6.6)   On May 31, 2002, Pristine Corporation acquired for $950,000 cash, including direct out-of-pocket costs of the business combination, all the outstanding common stock of Superb Company. There was no contingent consideration involved in the combination. Superb was to be a subsidiary of Pristine.

CHECK FIGURE

Debit goodwill—Superb, $50,000.

Additional Information for May 31, 2002

1. Superb's stockholders' equity prior to the combination was as follows:

Common stock, $1 par	$100,000
Additional paid-in capital	200,000
Retained earnings	450,000
Total stockholders' equity	$750,000

2. Superb's liabilities had current fair values equal to their carrying amounts. Current fair values of Superb's inventories, land, and building (net) exceeded carrying amounts by $60,000, $40,000, and $50,000, respectively.

Prepare a working paper elimination, in journal entry format (omit explanation) for the consolidated balance sheet of Pristine Corporation and subsidiary on May 31, 2002. (Disregard income taxes.)

(Exercise 6.7)   The condensed separate and consolidated balance sheets of Perth Corporation and its subsidiary, Sykes Company, on the date of their business combination, were as follows:

	Perth Corporation	Sykes Company	Consolidated
PERTH CORPORATION AND SUBSIDIARY *Separate and Consolidated Balance Sheets (following business combination)* June 30, 2002			
Assets			
Cash	$ 100,000	$ 40,000	$ 140,000
Inventories	500,000	90,000	610,000
Other current assets	250,000	60,000	310,000
Investment in Sykes Company common stock	440,000		
Plant assets (net)	1,000,000	360,000	1,440,000
Goodwill (net)	100,000		120,000
Total assets	$2,390,000	$550,000	$2,620,000
Liabilities and Stockholders' Equity			
Income taxes payable	$ 40,000	$ 35,000	$ 75,000
Other liabilities	580,600	195,000	775,600
Common stock	1,020,000	200,000	1,020,000
Additional paid-in capital	429,400	210,000	429,400
Retained earnings (deficit)	320,000	(90,000)	320,000
Total liabilities and stockholders' equity	$2,390,000	$550,000	$2,620,000

Reconstruct the working paper elimination for Perth Corporation and subsidiary on June 30, 2002 (in journal entry format), indicated by the above data. (Disregard income taxes.)

(Exercise 6.8) On November 1, 2002, Prox Corporation issued 10,000 shares of its $10 par ($30 current fair value) common stock for 85 of the 100 outstanding shares of Senna Company's $100 par common stock, in a business combination. Out-of-pocket costs of the business combination were as follows:

Legal and finder's fees associated with the business combination	$36,800
Costs incurred for SEC registration statement for Prox common stock	20,000
Total out-of-pocket costs of business combination	$56,800

On November 1, 2002, the current fair values of Senna's identifiable net assets were equal to their carrying amounts. On that date, Senna's stockholders' equity consisted of the following:

Common stock, $100 par	$ 10,000
Additional paid-in capital	140,000
Retained earnings	70,000
Total stockholders' equity	$220,000

Prepare journal entries for Prox Corporation on November 1, 2002, to record the business combination with Senna Company. (Disregard income taxes.)

(Exercise 6.9) On February 28, 2002, Ploy Corporation acquired 88% of the outstanding common stock of Skye Company for $50,000 cash and 5,000 shares of Ploy's $10 par common stock with a current fair value of $20 a share. Out-of-pocket costs of the business combination paid by Ploy on February 28, 2002, were as follows:

Finder's and legal fees relating to business combination	$15,000
Costs associated with SEC registration statement	10,000
Total out-of-pocket costs of business combination	$25,000

On February 28, 2002, Skye's stockholders' equity consisted of common stock, $1 par, $10,000; additional paid-in capital, $30,000; and retained earnings, $60,000. Carrying amounts of the three following identifiable assets or liabilities of Skye were **less than current fair values** on February 28, 2002, by the amounts indicated:

Inventories	$20,000
Plant assets (net)	80,000
Bonds payable, due February 28, 2008	30,000

a. Prepare journal entries for Ploy Corporation on February 28, 2002, to record the business combination with Skye Company. (Disregard income taxes.)

b. Prepare a working paper to compute the following amounts for the consolidated balance sheet of Ploy Corporation and subsidiary on February 28, 2002:
 (1) Goodwill (neither Ploy nor Skye had goodwill in its separate balance sheet).
 (2) Minority interest in net assets of subsidiary.

(Exercise 6.10)

Pullin Corporation acquired 70% of the outstanding common stock of Style Company on July 31, 2002. The unconsolidated balance sheet of Pullin immediately after the business combination and the consolidated balance sheet of Pullin Corporation and subsidiary were as follows:

PULLIN CORPORATION
Unconsolidated and Consolidated Balance Sheets
July 31, 2002

	Unconsolidated	Consolidated
Assets		
Current assets	$106,000	$146,000
Investment in Style Company common stock	100,000	
Plant assets (net)	270,000	370,000
Goodwill		11,100
Total assets	$476,000	$527,100
Liabilities and Stockholders' Equity		
Current liabilities	$ 15,000	$ 28,000
Minority interest in net assets of subsidiary		38,100
Common stock, no par or stated value	350,000	350,000
Retained earnings	111,000	111,000
Total liabilities and stockholders' equity	$476,000	$527,100

Of the excess payment for the investment in Style Company common stock, $10,000 was ascribed to undervaluation of Style's plant assets and the remainder was ascribed to goodwill. Current assets of Style included a $2,000 receivable from Pullin that arose before the business combination.

a. Prepare a working paper to compute the total current assets in Style Company's separate balance sheet on July 31, 2002.

b. Prepare a working paper to compute the total stockholders' equity in Style Company's separate balance sheet on July 31, 2002.

c. Prepare a working paper to show how the goodwill of $11,100 included in the July 31, 2002, consolidated balance sheet of Pullin Corporation and subsidiary was computed.

(Exercise 6.11)

Polter Corporation acquired 80% of the outstanding common stock of Santo Company on October 31, 2002, for $800,000, including direct out-of-pocket costs of the business combination. The working paper elimination (in journal entry format) on that date was as follows (explanation omitted):

POLTER CORPORATION AND SUBSIDIARY Working Paper Elimination October 31, 2002		
Common Stock—Santo	50,000	
Additional Paid-in Capital—Santo	60,000	
Retained Earnings—Santo	490,000	
Inventories—Santo	50,000	
Plant Assets (net)—Santo	100,000	
Goodwill—Polter [$800,000 − ($750,000 × 0.80)]	200,000	
Investment in Santo Company Common Stock—Polter		800,000
Minority Interest in Net Assets of Subsidiary ($750,000 × 0.20)		150,000

Assuming that a value is to be imputed for 100% of Santo Company's net assets (including goodwill) from Polter Corporation's $800,000 cost, prepare a working paper to compute the debit to Goodwill and the credit to Minority Interest in Net Assets of Subsidiary in the foregoing working paper elimination.

(Exercise 6.12)

Combinor Corporation and Combinee Company had been operating separately for five years. Each company had a minimal amount of liabilities and a simple capital structure consisting solely of common stock. Combinor, in exchange for its unissued common stock, acquired 80% of the outstanding common stock of Combinee. Combinee's identifiable net assets had a current fair value of $800,000 and a carrying amount of $600,000. The current fair value of the Combinor common stock issued in the business combination was $700,000. Out-of-pocket costs of the combination may be disregarded.

Prepare a working paper to compute the minority interest in net assets of subsidiary and the goodwill that would be displayed in the consolidated balance sheet of Combinor Corporation and subsidiary, under three alternative methods of computation as illustrated on page 240.

(Exercise 6.13)

On May 31, 2002, Pismo Corporation acquired for $760,000 cash, including direct out-of-pocket costs of the business combination, 80% of the outstanding common stock of Sobol Company. There was no contingent consideration involved in the combination. Sobol was to be a subsidiary of Pismo.

Additional Information for May 31, 2002:

1. Sobol Company's stockholders' equity prior to the combination was as follows:

Common stock, no par or stated value	$300,000
Retained earnings	400,000
Total stockholders' equity	$700,000

2. Differences between current fair values and carrying amounts of Sobol's identifiable assets were as follows (the current fair values of Sobol's other assets and its liabilities equaled their carrying amounts):

	Current Fair Values	Carrying Amounts	Differences
Inventories	$ 120,000	$ 80,000	$ 40,000
Land	300,000	250,000	50,000
Building (net)	800,000	740,000	60,000
Totals	$1,220,000	$1,070,000	$150,000

Prepare a working paper elimination, in journal entry format (omit explanation) for the consolidated balance sheet of Pismo Corporation and subsidiary on May 31, 2002. (Disregard income taxes.)

(Exercise 6.14) The working paper elimination (in journal entry format) on August 31, 2002, for the consolidated balance sheet of Payton Corporation and subsidiary is shown below. On that date, Payton acquired most of the outstanding common stock of Sutton Company for cash.

CHECK FIGURE
c. Goodwill, $6,000.

PAYTON CORPORATION AND SUBSIDIARY
Working Paper Elimination
August 31, 2002

Common Stock—Sutton	60,000	
Additional Paid-in Capital—Sutton	35,250	
Retained Earnings—Sutton	50,100	
Inventories—Sutton	3,900	
Plant Assets (net)—Sutton	28,500	
Patent—Sutton	4,500	
Goodwill—Payton	5,280	
Investment in Sutton Company Common Stock—Payton		165,660
Minority Interest in Net Assets of Subsidiary		21,870

To eliminate intercompany investment and equity accounts of subsidiary on date of business combination; to allocate excess of cost over current fair values of identifiable net assets acquired to goodwill; and to establish minority interest in net assets of subsidiary on date of business combination. (Income tax effects are disregarded.)

Answer the following questions (show supporting computations):

a. What percentage of the outstanding common stock of the subsidiary was acquired by the parent company?

b. What was the aggregate current fair value of the subsidiary's identifiable net assets on August 31, 2002?

c. What amount would be assigned to goodwill under the method that infers a total current fair value for the subsidiary's total net assets, based on the parent company's investment?

d. What amount would be assigned to minority interest in net assets of subsidiary under the method described in *c*?

Cases

(Case 6.1) In the absence of definitive guidelines from the FASB, companies that have applied push-down accounting in the separate financial statements of substantially wholly owned subsidiaries have used accounting techniques analogous to quasi-reorganizations or to reorganizations under the U.S. Bankruptcy Code. That is, the restatement of the subsidiary's identifiable assets and liabilities to current fair values and the recognition of goodwill are accompanied by a writeoff of the subsidiary's retained earnings; the balancing amount is an increase in additional paid-in capital of the subsidiary.

Instructions
What is your opinion of the foregoing accounting practice? Explain.

(Case 6.2) In paragraph 44 of *Statement of Financial Accounting Standards No. 141,* "Business Combinations," the Financial Accounting Standards Board directed that if the sum of the fair values of assets acquired and liabilities assumed in a business combination exceeds the cost of the acquired enterprise, such excess should be allocated as a pro rata reduction of amounts that otherwise would have been assigned to noncurrent assets other than specified exceptions.

Instructions
What support, if any, do you find for the action of the FASB? Explain.

(Case 6.3) On January 2, 2002, the board of directors of Photo Corporation assigned to a voting trust 15,000 shares of the 60,000 shares of Soto Company common stock owned by Photo. The trustee of the voting trust presently has custody of 40,000 of Soto's 105,000 shares of issued common stock, of which 5,000 shares are in Soto's treasury. The term of the voting trust is three years.

Instructions
Are consolidated financial statements appropriate for Photo Corporation and Soto Company for the three years ending December 31, 2004? Explain.

(Case 6.4) On July 31, 2002, Paley Corporation transferred all right, title, and interest in several of its current research and development projects to Carla Saye, sole stockholder of Saye Company, in exchange for 55 of the 100 shares of Saye Company common stock owned by Carla Saye. On the same date, Martin Morgan, who is not related to Paley Corporation, Saye Company, or Carla Saye, acquired for $45,000 cash the remaining 45 shares of Saye Company common stock owned by Carla Saye. Carla Saye notified the directors of Paley Corporation of the sale of common stock to Morgan.

Because Paley had recognized as expense the costs related to the research and development when the costs were incurred, Paley's controller prepared the following journal entry to record the business combination with Saye Company:

Investment in Saye Company Common Stock (55 × $1,000)	55,000	
Gain on Disposal of Intangible Assets		55,000
To record transfer of research and development projects to Carla		
Saye in exchange for 55 shares of Saye Company common stock.		
Valuation of the investment is based on an unrelated cash issuance of		
Saye Company common stock on this date.		

Instructions

a. Do you concur with the foregoing journal entry? Explain.

b. Should the $55,000 gain be displayed in a consolidated income statement of Paley Corporation and subsidiary for the year ended July 31, 2002? Explain.

(Case 6.5) On May 31, 2002, Patrick Corporation acquired at 100, $500,000 face amount of Stear Company's 10-year, 12%, convertible bonds due May 31, 2007. The bonds were convertible to 50,000 shares of Stear's voting common stock ($1 par), of which 40,000 shares were issued and outstanding on May 31, 2002. The controller of Patrick, who also is one of three Patrick officers who serve on the five-member board of directors of Stear, proposes to issue consolidated financial statements for Patrick Corporation and Stear Company on May 31, 2002.

Instructions

Do you agree with the Patrick controller's proposal? Explain.

(Case 6.6) In January 2002, Pinch Corporation, a chain of discount stores, began a program of business combinations with its principal suppliers. On May 31, 2002, the close of its fiscal year, Pinch paid $8,500,000 cash and issued 100,000 shares of its common stock (current fair value $20 a share) for all 10,000 outstanding shares of common stock of Silver Company. Silver was a furniture manufacturer whose products were sold in Pinch's stores. Total stockholders' equity of Silver on May 31, 2002, was $9,000,000. Out-of-pocket costs attributable to the business combination itself (as opposed to the SEC registration statement for the 100,000 shares of Pinch's common stock) paid by Pinch on May 31, 2002, totaled $100,000.

In the consolidated balance sheet of Pinch Corporation and subsidiary on May 31, 2002, the $1,600,000 [$8,500,000 + (100,000 × $20) + $100,000 − $9,000,000] difference between the parent company's cost and the carrying amounts of the subsidiary's identifiable net assets was allocated in accordance with purchase accounting as follows:

Inventories	$ 250,000
Plant assets	850,000
Patents	300,000
Goodwill	200,000
Total excess of cost over carrying amounts of subsidiary's net assets	$1,600,000

Under terms of the indenture for a $1,000,000 bond liability of Silver, Pinch was obligated to maintain Silver as a separate corporation and to issue a separate balance sheet for Silver each May 31. Pinch's controller contends that Silver's balance sheet on May 31, 2002, should value net assets at $10,600,000—their cost to Pinch. Silver's controller disputes this valuation, claiming that generally accepted accounting principles require issuance of a historical cost balance sheet for Silver on May 31, 2002.

Instructions

a. Present arguments supporting the Pinch controller's position.

b. Present arguments supporting the Silver controller's position.

c. Which position do you prefer? Explain.

(Case 6.7)

The board of directors of Purdido Corporation have just directed Purdido's officers to abandon further efforts to complete an acquisition of all the outstanding common stock of Sontee Company in a business combination that would have resulted in a parent company–subsidiary relationship between Purdido and Sontee. After learning of the board's decision, Purdido's chief financial officer instructed the controller, a CPA who is a member of the AICPA, the FEI, and the IMA (see Chapter 1), to analyze the out-of-pocket costs of the abandoned proposed combination. After some analysis of Purdido's accounting records, the controller provided the following summary to the CFO:

PURDIDO CORPORATION **Out-of-Pocket Costs of Abandoned Business Combination** **April 17, 2002**	
Legal fees relating to proposed business combination	$120,000
Finder's fee relating to proposed business combination	0*
Costs associated with proposed SEC registration statement for Purdido	
common stock to have been issued in the business combination	180,000
Total out-of-pocket costs of abandoned business combination	$300,000

* Finder's fee was contingent on successful completion of the business combination.

Noting that recognition of the entire $300,000 as expense on April 17, 2002, would have a depressing effect on earnings of Purdido for the quarter ending June 30, 2002, the CFO instructed the controller to expense only $120,000 and to debit the $180,000 amount to the Paid-in Capital in Excess of Par ledger account. In response to the controller's request for justification of such a debit, the CFO confided that Purdido's board was presently engaged in exploring other business combination opportunities, and that the costs incurred on the proposed SEC registration statement thus had future benefits to Purdido.

Instructions

May the controller of Purdido Corporation ethically comply with the CFO's instructions? Explain.

(Case 6.8)

Assume you are a CPA and a member of the AICPA, the FEI, and the IMA (see Chapter 1). You are CFO of a publicly owned corporation whose CEO is planning to become the sole stockholder of a newly established corporation in a situation with characteristics similar to those described in Securities and Exchange Commission *AAER 34,* "Securities and Exchange Commission v. Digilog, Inc. and Ronald Moyer" (described on pages 245 to 246). When you inform the CEO of the SEC's findings in *AAER 34,* the CEO informs you that the corporation's independent auditors have provided a copy of a reply by the AICPA's Technical Information Service to a question involving a situation similar to that in *AAER 34* and that the Technical Information Service answer was that consolidated financial statements were *not* required. The CEO gives you Section 1400.07, "Reporting on Company Where Option to Acquire Control Exists," of the *AICPA Technical Practice Aids* and orders you not to insist on consolidation of "his" corporation's financial statements.

Instructions

What are your ethical obligations in this matter? Explain.

(Case 6.9) In a classroom discussion of the appropriate balance sheet display of the minority interest in net assets of a consolidated subsidiary, student Michael expressed a dislike for both the economic unit concept favored by the FASB and the alternative parent company concept. According to Michael, the minority interest in net assets of a subsidiary is neither a part of consolidated stockholders' equity, as suggested by the economic unit concept, nor a liability, as indicated by the parent company concept. Michael favored displaying minority interest in the "mezzanine" section of the consolidated balance sheet, between liabilities and stockholders' equity. Michael suggested a precedent for such display in the Securities and Exchange Commission's comparable mandated display for redeemable preferred stock, per Section 211 of the SEC's *Codification of Financial Reporting Policies.* Student Roger disagreed with student Michael, pointing out that the FASB's *Statement of Financial Accounting Concepts No. 6,* "Elements of Financial Statements," does not identify an element entitled *mezzanine.*

Instructions

Do you support the view of student Michael or of student Roger? Explain.

Problems

(Problem 6.1) On September 30, 2002, Parr Corporation paid $1,000,000 to shareholders of Sane Company for 90,000 of Sane's 100,000 outstanding shares of no-par, no-stated-value common stock; additionally, Parr paid direct out-of-pocket costs of the combination totaling $80,000 on that date. Carrying amounts and current fair values of Sane's identifiable net assets on September 30, 2002, were analyzed as follows:

<table>
<tr><td>CHECK FIGURE</td><td>Common stock, no par</td><td>$400,000</td></tr>
<tr><td rowspan="2">b. Debit goodwill—Parr, $189,000.</td><td>Retained earnings</td><td>500,000</td></tr>
<tr><td>Total carrying amount of identifiable net assets</td><td>$900,000</td></tr>
<tr><td></td><td>Add: Differences between current fair value and carrying amount:</td><td></td></tr>
<tr><td></td><td>Inventories (first-in, first-out cost)</td><td>30,000</td></tr>
<tr><td></td><td>Plant assets (net)</td><td>60,000</td></tr>
<tr><td></td><td>Total current fair value of identifiable net assets</td><td>$990,000</td></tr>
</table>

Instructions

a. Prepare journal entries for Parr Corporation on September 30, 2002, to record the business combination with Sane Company. (Disregard income taxes.)

b. Prepare a working paper elimination for Parr Corporation and subsidiary (in journal entry format) on September 30, 2002. (Disregard income taxes.)

(Problem 6.2) On September 30, 2002, Philly Corporation issued 100,000 shares of its no-par, no-stated-value common stock (current fair value $12 a share) for 18,800 shares of the outstanding $20 par common stock of Stype Company. The $150,000 out-of-pocket costs of the business combination paid by Philly on September 30, 2002, were allocable as follows: 60% to finder's, legal, and accounting fees directly related to the business combination; 40% to the SEC registration statement for Philly's common stock issued in the business combination. There was no contingent consideration.

Immediately prior to the business combination, separate balance sheets of the constituent companies were as follows:

CHECK FIGURE

b. Debit goodwill—Philly, $115,000.

PHILLY CORPORATION AND STYPE COMPANY **Separate Balance Sheets (prior to business combination)** **September 30, 2002**		
	Philly *Corporation*	*Stype* *Company*
Assets		
Cash	$ 200,000	$ 100,000
Trade accounts receivable (net)	400,000	200,000
Inventories (net)	600,000	300,000
Plant assets (net)	1,300,000	1,000,000
Total assets	$2,500,000	$1,600,000
Liabilities and Stockholders' Equity		
Current liabilities	$ 800,000	$ 400,000
Long-term debt		100,000
Common stock, no par or stated value	1,200,000	
Common stock, $20 par		400,000
Retained earnings	500,000	700,000
Total liabilities and stockholders' equity	$2,500,000	$1,600,000

Current fair values of Stype's identifiable net assets differed from their carrying amounts as follows:

	Current Fair Values, *Sept. 30, 2002*
Inventories	$ 340,000
Plant assets (net)	1,100,000
Long-term debt	90,000

Instructions

a. Prepare journal entries for Philly Corporation on September 30, 2002, to record the business combination with Stype Company. (Disregard income taxes.)

b. Prepare a working paper for consolidated balance sheet and related working paper elimination (in journal entry format) for Philly Corporation and subsidiary on September 30, 2002. Amounts in the working papers should reflect the journal entries in *a*. (Disregard income taxes.)

(Problem 6.3)   Separate balance sheets of Pellman Corporation and Shire Company on May 31, 2002, together with current fair values of Shire's identifiable net assets, are as follows:

PELLMAN CORPORATION AND SHIRE COMPANY
Separate Balance Sheets (prior to business combination)
May 31, 2002

	Pellman Corporation	Shire Company Carrying Amounts	Shire Company Current Fair Values
Assets			
Cash	$ 550,000	$ 10,000	$ 10,000
Trade accounts receivable (net)	700,000	60,000	60,000
Inventories	1,400,000	120,000	140,000
Plant assets (net)	2,850,000	610,000	690,000
Total assets	$5,500,000	$800,000	
Liabilities and Stockholders' Equity			
Current liabilities	$ 500,000	$ 80,000	$ 80,000
Long-term debt	1,000,000	400,000	440,000
Common stock, $10 par	1,500,000	100,000	
Additional paid-in capital	1,200,000	40,000	
Retained earnings	1,300,000	180,000	
Total liabilities and stockholders' equity	$5,500,000	$800,000	

On May 31, 2002, Pellman acquired all 10,000 shares of Shire's outstanding common stock by paying $300,000 cash to Shire's stockholders and $50,000 cash for finder's and legal fees relating to the business combination. There was no contingent consideration, and Shire became a subsidiary of Pellman.

Instructions

a. Prepare journal entries for Pellman Corporation to record the business combination with Shire Company on May 31, 2002. (Disregard income taxes.)

b. Prepare a working paper for consolidated balance sheet of Pellman Corporation and subsidiary on May 31, 2002, and the related working paper elimination (in journal entry format). Amounts in the working papers should reflect the journal entries in *a.* (Disregard income taxes.)

(Problem 6.4) On April 30, 2002, Powell Corporation issued 30,000 shares of its no-par, no-stated-value common stock having a current fair value of $20 a share for 8,000 shares of Seaver Company's $10 par common stock. There was no contingent consideration; out-of-pocket costs of the business combination, paid by Seaver on behalf of Powell on April 30, 2002, were as follows:

Finder's and legal fees relating to business combination	$40,000
Costs associated with SEC registration statement	30,000
Total out-of-pocket costs of business combination	$70,000

Separate balance sheets of the constituent companies on April 30, 2002, prior to the business combination, were as follows:

POWELL CORPORATION AND SEAVER COMPANY
Separate Balance Sheets (prior to business combination)
April 30, 2002

	Powell Corporation	Seaver Company
Assets		
Cash	$ 50,000	$ 150,000
Trade accounts receivable (net)	230,000	200,000
Inventories	400,000	350,000
Plant assets (net)	1,300,000	560,000
Total assets	$1,980,000	$1,260,000
Liabilities and Stockholders' Equity		
Current liabilities	$ 310,000	$ 250,000
Long-term debt	800,000	600,000
Common stock, no par or stated value	500,000	
Common stock, $10 par		100,000
Additional paid-in capital		360,000
Retained earnings (deficit)	370,000	(50,000)
Total liabilities and stockholders' equity	$1,980,000	$1,260,000

Current fair values of Seaver's identifiable net assets were the same as their carrying amounts, except for the following:

	Current Fair Values, Apr. 30, 2002
Inventories	$440,000
Plant assets (net)	780,000
Long-term debt	620,000

Instructions

a. Prepare a journal entry for Seaver Company on April 30, 2002, to record its payment of out-of-pocket costs of the business combination on behalf of Powell Corporation.

b. Prepare journal entries for Powell Corporation to record the business combination with Seaver Company on April 30, 2002. (Disregard income taxes.)

c. Prepare a working paper for consolidated balance sheet of Powell Corporation and subsidiary on April 30, 2002, and the related working paper elimination (in journal entry format). Amounts in the working papers should reflect the journal entries in *a* and *b*. (Disregard income taxes.)

(Problem 6.5) On July 31, 2002, Pyr Corporation issued 20,000 shares of its $2 par common stock (current fair value $10 a share) for all 5,000 shares of outstanding $5 par common stock of Soper Company, which was to remain a separate corporation. Out-of-pocket costs of the business combination, paid by Pyr on July 31, 2002, are shown below:

Finder's and legal fees related to business combination	$20,000
Costs associated with SEC registration statement for Pyr common stock	10,000
Total out-of-pocket costs of business combination	$30,000

The constituent companies' separate balance sheets on July 31, 2002, prior to the business combination, follow:

	PYR CORPORATION AND SOPER COMPANY Separate Balance Sheets (prior to business combination) July 31, 2002	
	Pyr Corporation	*Soper Company*
Assets		
Current assets	$ 800,000	$150,000
Plant assets (net)	2,400,000	300,000
Goodwill (net)		20,000
Total assets	$3,200,000	$470,000
Liabilities and Stockholders' Equity		
Current liabilities	$ 400,000	$120,000
Long-term debt	1,000,000	200,000
Common stock, $2 par	800,000	
Common stock, $5 par		25,000
Additional paid-in capital	400,000	50,000
Retained earnings	600,000	75,000
Total liabilities and stockholders' equity	$3,200,000	$470,000

Soper's goodwill, which had resulted from its July 31, 1998, acquisition of the net assets of Solo Company, was not impaired.

Soper's assets and liabilities having July 31, 2002, current fair values different from their carrying amounts were as follows:

	Carrying Amounts	*Current Fair Values*
Inventories	$ 60,000	$ 65,000
Plant assets (net)	300,000	340,000
Long-term debt	200,000	190,000

There were no intercompany transactions prior to the business combination, and there was no contingent consideration in connection with the combination.

Instructions

a. Prepare Pyr Corporation's journal entries on July 31, 2002, to record the business combination with Soper Company as a purchase. (Disregard income taxes.)

b. Prepare a working paper elimination (in journal entry format) and the related working paper for consolidated balance sheet of Pyr Corporation and subsidiary on July 31, 2002. Amounts in the working papers should reflect the journal entries in *a*. (Disregard income taxes.)

(Problem 6.6) The unconsolidated and consolidated balance sheets of Pali Corporation and subsidiary on August 31, 2002, the date of Pali's business combination with Soda Company, are as follows:

PALI CORPORATION Unconsolidated and Consolidated Balance Sheets August 31, 2002		
	Unconsolidated	*Consolidated*
Assets		
Cash	$ 120,000	$ 160,000
Trade accounts receivable (net)	380,000	540,000
Inventories	470,000	730,000
Investment in Soda Company common stock	380,000	
Plant assets (net)	850,000	1,470,000
Goodwill		8,000
Total assets	$2,200,000	$2,908,000
Liabilities and Stockholders' Equity		
Current liabilities	$ 430,000	$ 690,000
Long-term debt	550,000	730,000
Premium on long-term debt		20,000
Minority interest in net assets of subsidiary		248,000
Common stock, $1 par	500,000	500,000
Additional paid-in capital	440,000	440,000
Retained earnings	280,000	280,000
Total liabilities and stockholders' equity	$2,200,000	$2,908,000

On August 31, 2002, Pali had paid cash of $3 a share for 60% of the outstanding shares of Soda's $1 par common stock and $20,000 cash for legal fees in connection with the business combination. There was no contingent consideration. The equity (book value) of Soda's common stock on August 31, 2002, was $2.80 a share, and the amount of Soda's retained earnings was twice as large as the amount of its additional paid-in capital. The excess of current fair value of Soda's plant assets over their carrying amount on August 31, 2002, was $1\frac{2}{3}$ times as large as the comparable excess for Soda's inventories on that date. The current fair values of Soda's cash, trade accounts receivable (net), and current liabilities were equal to their carrying amounts on August 31, 2002.

Instructions
Reconstruct the working paper elimination (in journal entry format) for the working paper for consolidated balance sheet of Pali Corporation and subsidiary on August 31, 2002. (Disregard income taxes.)

(Problem 6.7) On October 31, 2002, Pagel Corporation acquired 83% of the outstanding common stock of Sayre Company in exchange for 50,000 shares of Pagel's no-par, $2 stated value ($10 current fair value a share) common stock. There was no contingent consideration. Out-of-pocket costs of the business combination paid by Pagel on October 31, 2002, were as follows:

Legal and finder's fees related to business combination	$34,750
Costs associated with SEC registration statement for Pagel's common stock	55,250
Total out-of-pocket costs of business combination	$90,000

There were no intercompany transactions between the constituent companies prior to the business combination. Sayre was to be a subsidiary of Pagel. The separate balance sheets of the constituent companies prior to the business combination follow:

PAGEL CORPORATION AND SAYRE COMPANY
Separate Balance Sheets (prior to business combination)
October 31, 2002

	Pagel Corporation	Sayre Company
Assets		
Cash	$ 250,000	$ 150,000
Inventories	860,000	600,000
Other current assets	500,000	260,000
Plant assets (net)	3,400,000	1,500,000
Patents (net)		80,000
Total assets	$5,010,000	$2,590,000
Liabilities and Stockholders' Equity		
Income taxes payable	$ 40,000	$ 60,000
Other current liabilities	390,000	854,000
Long-term debt	950,000	1,240,000
Common stock, no-par, $2 stated value	1,500,000	
Common stock, $10 par		100,000
Additional paid-in capital	1,500,000	
Retained earnings	630,000	336,000
Total liabilities and stockholders' equity	$5,010,000	$2,590,000

Current fair values of Sayre's identifiable net assets were the same as their carrying amounts on October 31, 2002, except for the following:

	Current Fair Values
Inventories	$ 620,000
Plant assets (net)	1,550,000
Patents (net)	95,000
Long-term debt	1,225,000

Instructions

a. Prepare Pagel Corporation's journal entries on October 31, 2002, to record the business combination with Sayre Company. (Disregard income taxes.)

b. Prepare working paper eliminations (in journal entry format) on October 31, 2002, and the related working paper for the consolidated balance sheet of Pagel Corporation and subsidiary. Amounts in the working papers should reflect the journal entries in *a.* (Disregard income taxes.)

(Problem 6.8) On January 31, 2002, Porcino Corporation issued $50,000 cash, 6,000 shares of $2 par common stock (current fair value $15 a share), and a 5-year, 14%, $50,000 promissory note payable for all 10,000 shares of Secor Company's outstanding common stock, which were owned by Lawrence Secor. The only out-of-pocket costs paid by Porcino to complete the business combination were legal fees of $10,000, because Porcino's common stock issued in the combination was not subject to the registration requirements of the SEC. There was no contingent consideration, and 14% was the fair rate of interest for the promissory note issued by Porcino in connection with the business combination.

Separate balance sheets of Porcino and Secor on January 31, 2002, prior to the business combination, were as follows:

PORCINO CORPORATION AND SECOR COMPANY
Separate Balance Sheets (prior to business combination)
January 31, 2002

	Porcino Corporation	Secor Company
Assets		
Inventories	$ 380,000	$ 60,000
Other current assets	640,000	130,000
Plant assets (net)	1,520,000	470,000
Intangible assets (net)	160,000	40,000
Total assets	$2,700,000	$700,000
Liabilities and Stockholders' Equity		
Current liabilities	$ 420,000	$200,000
Long-term debt	650,000	300,000
Common stock, $2 par	800,000	
Common stock, $15 par		150,000
Additional paid-in capital	220,000	160,000
Retained earnings (deficit)	610,000	(110,000)
Total liabilities and stockholders' equity	$2,700,000	$700,000

Current fair values of Secor's identifiable net assets that differed from their carrying amounts on January 31, 2002, were as follows:

	Current Fair Values
Inventories	$ 70,000
Plant assets (net)	540,000
Intangible assets (net)	60,000
Long-term debt	350,000

Instructions

a. Prepare journal entries for Porcino Corporation on January 31, 2002, to record its business combination with Secor Company. (Disregard income taxes.)

b. Prepare a working paper for consolidated balance sheet of Porcino Corporation and subsidiary on January 31, 2002, and the related working paper elimination (in journal entry format). Amounts in the working papers should reflect the journal entries in *a*. (Disregard income taxes.)

(Problem 6.9) On June 30, 2002, Pandit Corporation issued a $300,000 note payable, due $60,000 a year with interest at the fair rate of 15% beginning June 30, 2003, for 8,500 of the 10,000 outstanding shares of $10 par common stock of Singh Company. Legal fees of $20,000 incurred by Pandit in connection with the business combination were paid on June 30, 2002.

Separate balance sheets of the constituent companies, immediately following the business combination, are shown on page 268.

PANDIT CORPORATION AND SINGH COMPANY
Separate Balance Sheets (following business combination)
Junè 30, 2002

	Pandit Corporation	Singh Company
Assets		
Cash	$ 80,000	$ 60,000
Trade accounts receivable (net)	170,000	90,000
Inventories	370,000	120,000
Investment in Singh Company common stock	320,000	
Plant assets (net)	570,000	240,000
Goodwill (net)	50,000	
Total assets	$1,560,000	$510,000
Liabilities and Stockholders' Equity		
Trade accounts payable	$ 220,000	$120,000
Income taxes payable	100,000	40,000
15% note payable, due $60,000 annually	300,000	
Common stock, $10 par	250,000	100,000
Additional paid-in capital	400,000	130,000
Retained earnings	290,000	120,000
Total liabilities and stockholders' equity	$1,560,000	$510,000

Additional Information

1. An independent audit of Singh Company's financial statement for the year ended June 30, 2002, disclosed that Singh's July 1, 2001, inventories had been overstated $60,000 due to double counting; and that Singh had omitted from its inventories on June 30, 2002, merchandise shipped FOB shipping point by a vendor on June 30, 2002, at an invoiced amount of $35,000. Corrections of Singh's inventories errors are not reflected in Singh's balance sheet.

2. Both Pandit and Singh had an income tax rate of 40%.

3. Current fair values of Singh's net assets *reported* in Singh's balance sheet on June 30, 2002, differed from carrying amounts as follows:

	Current Fair Values
Inventories	$150,000
Plant assets (net)	280,000

Instructions

a. Prepare a journal entry or entries (including income tax effects) to correct the inventories' misstatements in Singh Company's financial statements for the year ended June 30, 2002. Singh's accounting records have not been closed for the year ended June 30, 2002.

b. Prepare a working paper elimination (in journal entry format) and a working paper for the consolidated balance sheet of Pandit Corporation and subsidiary on June 30, 2002. Amounts in the working papers for Singh Company should reflect the adjusting journal entry or entries prepared in *a*. (Disregard income taxes.)

(Problem 6.10) On page 269 are the separate balance sheets of Pliny Corporation and Sylla Company on December 31, 2002, prior to their business combination.

PLINY CORPORATION AND SYLLA COMPANY
Separate Balance Sheets (prior to business combination)
December 31, 2002

	Pliny Corporation	Sylla Company
Assets		
Inventories	$ 800,000	$ 300,000
Other current assets	1,200,000	500,000
Long-term investments in marketable debt securities (held to maturity)		200,000
Plant assets (net)	2,500,000	900,000
Intangible assets (net)	100,000	200,000
Total assets	$4,600,000	$2,100,000
Liabilities and Stockholders' Equity		
Current liabilities	$1,400,000	$ 300,000
10% note payable, due June 30, 2012	2,000,000	
12% bonds payable, due Dec. 31, 2007		500,000
Common stock, $1 par	600,000	200,000
Additional paid-in capital	200,000	400,000
Retained earnings	400,000	700,000
Total liabilities and stockholders' equity	$4,600,000	$2,100,000

On December 31, 2002, Pliny paid $100,000 cash and issued $1,500,000 face amount of 14%, 10-year bonds for all the outstanding common stock of Sylla, which became a subsidiary of Pliny. On the date of the business combination, 16% was the fair rate of interest for the bonds of both Pliny and Sylla, both of which paid interest on June 30 and December 31. There was no contingent consideration involved in the business combination, but Pliny paid the following out-of-pocket costs on December 31, 2002:

Finder's and legal fees relating to business combination	$50,000
Costs associated with SEC registration statement for Pliny's bonds	40,000
Total out-of-pocket costs of business combination	$90,000

In addition to the 12% bonds payable, Sylla had identifiable net assets with current fair values that differed from carrying amounts on December 31, 2002, as follows:

	Current Fair Values
Inventories	$330,000
Long-term investments in marketable debt securities	230,000
Plant assets (net)	940,000
Intangible assets (net)	220,000

Instructions

a. Prepare journal entries for Pliny Corporation to record the business combination with Sylla Company on December 31, 2002. Use a calculator or present value tables to compute the present value, rounded to the nearest dollar, of the 14% bonds issued by Pliny. (Disregard income taxes.)

b. Prepare a working paper for consolidated balance sheet for Pliny Corporation and subsidiary on December 31, 2002, and the related working paper elimination (in journal entry format). Use a calculator or present value tables to compute the present value, rounded to the nearest dollar, of the 12% bonds payable of Sylla. Amounts in the working papers should reflect the journal entries in *a*. (Disregard income taxes.)

(Problem 6.11)

CHECK FIGURES:
a. Debit Investment account, $70,000;
b. Credit minority interest in net assets, $62,000.

You have been engaged to audit the financial statements of Parthenia Corporation and subsidiary for the year ended June 30, 2002. The working paper for consolidated balance sheet of Parthenia and subsidiary on June 30, 2002, prepared by Parthenia's inexperienced accountant, is at the bottom of this page.

In the course of your audit, you reviewed the following June 30, 2002, journal entries in the accounting records of Parthenia Corporation:

Investment in Storey Company Common Stock	220,000	
Goodwill	60,000	
Cash		280,000

To record acquisition of 4,000 shares of Storey Company's outstanding common stock in a business combination, and to record acquired goodwill as follows:

Cash paid for Storey common stock	$280,000
Less: Stockholders' equity of Storey, June 30, 2002	220,000
Goodwill acquired	$ 60,000

Expenses of Business Combination	10,000	
Cash		10,000

To record payment of legal fees in connection with business combination with Storey Company.

PARTHENIA CORPORATION AND SUBSIDIARY
Working Paper for Consolidated Balance Sheet
June 30, 2002

	Parthenia Corporation	Storey Company	Eliminations Increase (Decrease)	Consolidated
Assets				
Cash	60,000	50,000		110,000
Trade accounts receivable (net)	120,000	90,000		210,000
Inventories	250,000	160,000		410,000
Investment in Storey Company common stock	220,000		(a) (220,000)	
Plant assets (net)	590,000	500,000		1,090,000
Goodwill (net)	60,000			60,000
Total assets	1,300,000	800,000	(220,000)	1,880,000
Liabilities and Stockholders' Equity				
Current liabilities	200,000	280,000		480,000
Long-term debt	500,000	300,000		800,000
Common stock, $5 par	100,000			100,000
Common stock, $10 par		50,000	(a) (50,000)	
Additional paid-in capital	200,000	70,000	(a) (70,000)	200,000
Retained earnings	300,000	100,000	(a) (100,000)	300,000
Total liabilities and stockholders' equity	1,300,000	800,000	(220,000)	1,880,000

Your inquiries of directors and officers of Parthenia and your review of supporting documents disclosed the following current fair values for Storey's identifiable net assets that differ from carrying amounts on June 30, 2002:

	Current Fair Values
Inventories	$180,000
Plant assets (net)	530,000
Long-term debt	260,000

Instructions

a. Prepare a journal entry to correct Parthenia Corporation's accounting for its June 30, 2002, business combination with Storey Company. Parthenia's accounting records have not been closed. (Disregard income taxes.)

b. Prepare a corrected working paper for consolidated balance sheet of Parthenia Corporation and subsidiary on June 30, 2002, and related working paper elimination (in journal entry format). Amounts in the working papers should reflect the journal entries in *a.* (Disregard income taxes.)

Chapter **Seven**

Consolidated Financial Statements: Subsequent to Date of Business Combination

Scope of Chapter

Subsequent to the date of a business combination, the parent company must account for the operating results of the subsidiary: the net income or net loss and dividends declared and paid by the subsidiary. In addition, a number of intercompany transactions and events that frequently occur in a parent company–subsidiary relationship must be recorded.

In this chapter the accounting for operating results of both wholly owned and partially owned subsidiaries is described and illustrated. Accounting for intercompany transactions not involving a profit (gain) or a loss, as well as those involving a profit or a loss, are dealt with in Chapter 8.

ACCOUNTING FOR OPERATING RESULTS OF WHOLLY OWNED SUBSIDIARIES

In accounting for the operating results of consolidated subsidiaries, a parent company may choose the *equity method* or the *cost method* of accounting.

Equity Method

In the equity method of accounting, the parent company recognizes its share of the subsidiary's net income or net loss, adjusted for depreciation and amortization of differences between current fair values and carrying amounts of a subsidiary's identifiable net assets on the date of the business combination, as well as its share of dividends declared by the subsidiary. Thus, the equity method of accounting for a subsidiary's operating results is similar to home office accounting for a branch's operations, as described in Chapter 4.

Proponents of the equity method of accounting maintain that the method is consistent with the accrual basis of accounting because it recognizes increases or decreases in the carrying amount of the parent company's investment in the subsidiary when they are *realized* by the subsidiary as net income or net loss, not when they are *paid* by the subsidiary as dividends. Thus, proponents claim, the equity method stresses the *economic substance* of the parent company–subsidiary relationship because the two companies constitute a single economic entity for financial accounting. Proponents of the equity method also claim that dividends declared by a subsidiary do not constitute revenue to the parent company, as maintained by advocates of the cost method; instead, dividends are a liquidation of a portion of the parent company's investment in the subsidiary.

Cost Method

In the cost method of accounting, the parent company accounts for the operations of a subsidiary only to the extent that dividends are declared by the subsidiary. Dividends declared by the subsidiary from net income subsequent to the business combination are recognized as revenue by the parent company; dividends declared by the subsidiary in excess of postcombination net income constitute a reduction of the carrying amount of the parent company's investment in the subsidiary. Net income or net loss of the subsidiary is *not recognized* by the parent company when the cost method of accounting is used.

Supporters of the cost method contend that the method appropriately recognizes the *legal form* of the parent company–subsidiary relationship. Parent company and subsidiary are separate legal entities; accounting for a subsidiary's operations should recognize the separateness, according to proponents of the cost method. Thus, a parent company realizes revenue from an investment in a subsidiary when the subsidiary declares a dividend, not when the subsidiary reports net income. The cost method of accounting is illustrated in the appendix at the end of this chapter (pages 303 to 309).

Choosing between Equity Method and Cost Method

Consolidated financial statement amounts are the same, regardless of whether a parent company uses the equity method or the cost method to account for a subsidiary's operations. However, the working paper eliminations used in the two methods are different, as illustrated in subsequent sections of this chapter.

Illustration of Equity Method for Wholly Owned Subsidiary for First Year after Business Combination

Assume that Palm Corporation had appropriately accounted for the December 31, 2002, business combination with its wholly owned subsidiary, Starr Company (see pages 222 to 224 for a description of the business combination), and that Starr had a net income of $60,000 (income statement is on page 280) for the year ended December 31, 2003. Assume further that on December 20, 2003, Starr's board of directors declared a cash dividend of $0.60 a share on the 40,000 outstanding shares of common stock owned by Palm. The dividend was payable January 8, 2004, to stockholders of record December 29, 2003.

Starr's December 20, 2003, journal entry to record the dividend declaration is as follows:

Wholly Owned Subsidiary's Journal Entry for Declaration of Dividend

2003			
Dec. 20	Dividends Declared (40,000 × $0.60)	24,000	
	Intercompany Dividends Payable		24,000
	To record declaration of dividend payable Jan. 8, 2004, to stockholders of record Dec. 29, 2003.		

Starr's credit to the Intercompany Dividends Payable ledger account indicates that the liability for dividends payable to the parent company *must be eliminated* in the preparation of consolidated financial statements for the year ended December 31, 2003.

Under the equity method of accounting, Palm Corporation prepares the following journal entries to record the dividend and net income of Starr for the year ended December 31, 2003:

Parent Company's Equity-Method Journal Entries to Record Operating Results of Wholly Owned Subsidiary

2003			
Dec. 20	Intercompany Dividends Receivable	24,000	
	Investment in Starr Company Stock		24,000
	To record dividend declared by Starr Company, payable Jan. 8, 2004, to stockholders of record Dec. 29, 2003.		
31	Investment in Starr Company Common Stock	60,000	
	Intercompany Investment Income		60,000
	To record 100% of Starr Company's net income for the year ended Dec. 31, 2003. (Income tax effects are disregarded.)		

The parent's first journal entry records the dividend declared by the subsidiary in the Intercompany Dividends Receivable account and is the counterpart of the subsidiary's journal entry to record the declaration of the dividend. The credit to the Investment in Starr Company Common Stock account in the first journal entry reflects an underlying premise of the equity method of accounting: dividends declared by a subsidiary represent a return of a portion of the parent company's investment in the subsidiary.

The parent's second journal entry records the parent's 100% share of the subsidiary's net income for 2003. The subsidiary's net income *accrues* to the parent company under the equity method of accounting, similar to the accrual of interest on a note receivable or an investment in bonds.

The income tax effects of Palm Corporation's accrual of its share of Starr Company's net income are disregarded at this time. Income tax allocation problems associated with all aspects of parent company and subsidiary accounting are considered in Chapter 9.

Adjustment of Subsidiary's Net Income

In addition to the two foregoing journal entries, Palm must prepare a third equity-method journal entry on December 31, 2003, to adjust Starr's net income for depreciation and amortization attributable to the differences between the current fair values and carrying amounts of Starr's identifiable net assets on December 31, 2002, the date of the Palm–Starr business combination. Because such differences were not recorded by the subsidiary, the subsidiary's 2003 net income *is overstated* from the point of view of the consolidated entity.

Assume that the December 31, 2002 (date of business combination), differences between the current fair values and carrying amounts of Starr Company's net assets were as follows (see Chapter 6, pages 224 and 228):

p223

Differences Between Current Fair Values and Carrying Amounts of Wholly Owned Subsidiary's Assets on Date of Business Combination

Inventories (first-in, first-out cost)		$ 25,000
Plant assets (net):		
Land	$15,000	
Building (economic life 15 years)	30,000	
Machinery (economic life 10 years)	20,000	65,000
Patent (economic life 5 years)		5,000
Goodwill (not impaired as of December 31, 2003)		15,000
Total		$110,000

Pal*m* Corporation prepares the following additional equity-method journal entry to reflect the effects of depreciation and amortization of the differences between the current fair values and carrying amounts of Starr Company's net assets on Starr's net income for the year ended December 31, 2003:

Test

Parent Company's Equity-Method Journal Entry to Record Operating Results of Wholly Owned Subsidiary Attributable to Depreciation and Amortization of Subsidiary's Net Assets

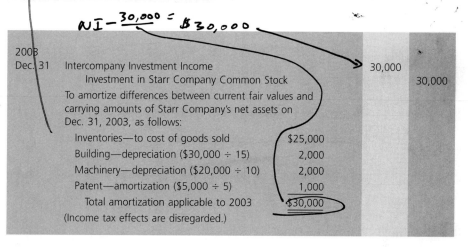

2003			
Dec. 31	Intercompany Investment Income	30,000	
	Investment in Starr Company Common Stock		30,000
	To amortize differences between current fair values and carrying amounts of Starr Company's net assets on Dec. 31, 2003, as follows:		
	Inventories—to cost of goods sold	$25,000	
	Building—depreciation ($30,000 ÷ 15)	2,000	
	Machinery—depreciation ($20,000 ÷ 10)	2,000	
	Patent—amortization ($5,000 ÷ 5)	1,000	
	Total amortization applicable to 2003	$30,000	
	(Income tax effects are disregarded.)		

After the three foregoing journal entries are posted, Palm Corporation's Investment in Starr Company Common Stock and Intercompany Investment Income ledger accounts are as follows:

Ledger Accounts of Parent Company Using Equity Method of Accounting for Wholly Owned Subsidiary

Investment in Starr Company Common Stock

Date	Explanation	Debit	Credit	Balance
2002				
Dec. 31	Issuance of common stock in business combination	450,000		450,000 dr
31	Direct out-of-pocket costs of business combination	50,000		500,000 dr
2003				
Dec. 20	Dividend declared by Starr		24,000	476,000 dr
31	Net income of Starr	60,000		536,000 dr
31	Amortization of differences between current fair values and carrying amounts of Starr's net assets		30,000	506,000 dr

Intercompany Investment Income

Date	Explanation	Debit	Credit	Balance
2003				
Dec. 31	Net income of Starr		60,000	60,000 cr
31	Amortization of differences between current fair values and carrying amounts of Starr's net assets	30,000		30,000 cr

Developing the Elimination

Palm Corporation's use of the equity method of accounting for its investment in Starr Company results in a balance in the Investment account that is a mixture of two components: (1) the carrying amount of Starr's identifiable net assets and (2) the excess on the date of business combination of the current fair values of the subsidiary's net assets (including goodwill) over their carrying amounts, net of depreciation and amortization ("current fair value excess"). These components are analyzed below:

PALM CORPORATION
Analysis of Investment in Starr Company Common Stock Ledger Account
For Year Ended December 31, 2003

	Carrying Amount	Current Fair Value Excess	Total
Beginning balances (date of business combination)	$390,000	$110,000	$500,000
Net income of Starr	60,000		60,000
Amortization of differences between current fair values and carrying amounts of Starr's identifiable net assets		(30,000)	(30,000)
Dividend declared by Starr	(24,000)		(24,000)
Ending balances	$426,000	$ 80,000	$506,000

Intercompany investment income, $30,000

The $426,000 ending balance of the Carrying Amount column agrees with the total stockholder's equity of Starr Company on December 31, 2003 (see balance sheet section of working paper for consolidated financial statements on page 280), as follows:

Common stock, $5 par	$200,000
Additional paid-in capital	58,000
Retained earnings	168,000
Total stockholder's equity	$426,000

Wholly Owned Subsidiary's Stockholder's Equity, Dec. 31, 2003

The $80,000 ending balance of the Current Fair Value Excess column agrees with the December 31, 2003, total of the unamortized balances for each of the respective assets of Starr Company, as shown on page 277.

Unamortized Differences Between Current Fair Values and Carrying Amounts of Wholly Owned Subsidiary's Assets One Year Subsequent to Business Combination

	Balances, Dec. 31, 2002 (p. 275)	Amortization for Year 2003 (p. 275)	Balances, Dec. 31, 2003
Inventories	$ 25,000	$(25,000)	
Plant assets (net):			
Land	$ 15,000		$15,000
Building	30,000 *15 yrs*	$ (2,000)	28,000
Machinery	20,000 *10 yrs*	(2,000)	18,000
Total plant assets	$ 65,000	$ (4,000)	$61,000
Patent	$ 5,000 *5 yrs*	$ (1,000)	$ 4,000
Goodwill	15,000		15,000
Totals	$110,000	$(30,000)	$80,000

It is evident from the analysis of Palm Corporation's Investment ledger account that the working paper elimination subsequent to the date of a business combination must include accounts that appear in the constituent companies' income statements and statements of retained earnings, as well as in their balance sheets, because *all three basic financial statements must be consolidated for accounting periods subsequent to the date of a business combination.* (A consolidated statement of cash flows is prepared from the three basic *consolidated* financial statements and other information, as explained in Chapter 9.) The items that must be included in the elimination are (1) the subsidiary's *beginning-of-year* stockholder's equity and its dividends, and the parent's investment; (2) the parent's intercompany investment income; (3) unamortized current fair value excesses of the subsidiary; and (4) certain operating expenses of the subsidiary. Assuming that Star Company allocates machinery depreciation and patent amortization entirely to cost of goods sold, and building depreciation 50% each to cost of goods sold and operating expenses, the working paper elimination (in journal entry format) for Palm Corporation and subsidiary on December 31, 2003, is as follows, with the component items numbered in accordance with the foregoing breakdown:

Working Paper Elimination for Wholly Owned Subsidiary for First Year Subsequent to Date of Business Combination

PALM CORPORATION AND SUBSIDIARY
Working Paper Elimination
December 31, 2003

(a)	Common Stock—Starr	200,000 (1)	
	Additional Paid-in Capital—Starr	58,000 (1)	
	Retained Earnings—Starr	132,000 (1) *Beg. year balance* ★	
	Intercompany Investment Income—Palm	30,000 (2)	
	Plant Assets (net)—Starr ($65,000 − $4,000)	61,000 (3)	
	Patent (net)—Starr ($5,000 − $1,000)	4,000 (3)	
	Goodwill—Starr	15,000 (3)	
	Cost of Goods Sold—Starr	29,000 (4)	
	Operating Expenses—Starr	1,000 (4)	
	Investment in Starr Company Common Stock—Palm		506,000 (1)
	Dividends Declared—Starr		24,000 (1)

To carry out the following:

(a) Eliminate intercompany investment and equity accounts of subsidiary **at beginning of year,** and subsidiary dividend.

(b) Provide for Year 2003 depreciation and amortization on differences between current fair values and carrying amounts of Starr's net assets as follows:

(continued)

PALM CORPORATION AND SUBSIDIARY
Working Paper Elimination (concluded)
December 31, 2003

	Cost of Goods Sold	Operating Expenses
Inventories sold	$25,000	
Building depreciation	1,000	$1,000
Machinery depreciation	2,000	
Patent amortization	1,000	
Totals	$29,000	$1,000

(c) Allocate unamortized differences between combination
date current fair values and carrying amounts of
Starr's net assets to appropriate assets.
(Income tax effects are disregarded.)

Comments on components of the foregoing working paper elimination, numbered to correspond with the four categories on page 277, follow:

(1) As indicated in Chapter 6 (page 225), the three components of the subsidiary's stockholder's equity are reciprocal to the parent company's Investment ledger account. However, because a consolidated statement of retained earnings is prepared for each year following a business combination, the subsidiary's ***beginning-of-year*** retained earnings amount is eliminated, together with the subsidiary's dividends, which are an offset to the subsidiary's retained earnings. (As illustrated in the analysis on page 276, the balance of the parent company's Investment ledger account is ***net*** of the dividends received from the subsidiary.) The elimination of the subsidiary's beginning-of-year retained earnings makes beginning-of-year consolidated retained earnings on page 280 identical to the end-of-previous-year consolidated retained earnings (see page 229 in Chapter 6).

(2) As illustrated in the analysis on page 276, the amount of the parent company's intercompany investment income is an element of the balance of the parent's Investment ledger account. In effect, the elimination of the intercompany investment income, coupled with items described in (4) below, comprises a reclassification of the intercompany investment income to the adjusted components of the subsidiary's net income in the consolidated income statement.

(3) The debits to the subsidiary's plant assets, patent, and goodwill bring into the consolidated balance sheet the unamortized differences between current fair values and carrying amounts of the subsidiary's assets on the date of the business combination (see the analysis on page 277).

(4) The increases in the subsidiary's cost of goods sold and operating expenses, totaling $30,000 ($29,000 + $1,000 = $30,000), in effect reclassify the comparable decrease in the parent company's Investment ledger account under the equity method of accounting (see the analysis on page 276) to the appropriate categories for the consolidated income statement.

Working Paper for Consolidated Financial Statements

The working paper for consolidated financial statements for Palm Corporation and subsidiary for the year ended December 31, 2003, is on page 280. The intercompany receivable and payable is the $24,000 dividend payable by Starr to Palm on December 31, 2003. (The advances by Palm to Starr that were outstanding on December 31, 2002, were repaid by Starr January 2, 2003.)

The following aspects of the working paper for consolidated financial statements of Palm Corporation and subsidiary should be emphasized:

1. The intercompany receivable and payable, placed in adjacent columns on the same line, are offset without a formal elimination.

2. The elimination cancels all intercompany transactions and balances not dealt with by the offset described in 1 above.

3. The elimination cancels the subsidiary's retained earnings balance *at the beginning of the year* (the date of the business combination), so that each of the three basic financial statements may be consolidated in turn. (*All* financial statements of a parent company and a purchased subsidiary are consolidated for accounting periods subsequent to the business combination.)

4. The first-in, first-out method is used by Starr Company to account for inventories; thus, the $25,000 difference attributable to Starr's beginning inventories is allocated to cost of goods sold for the year ended December 31, 2003.

5. Income tax effects of the elimination's increase in Starr Company's expenses are not included in the elimination. Accounting for income tax effects in consolidated financial statements is considered in Chapter 9.

6. One of the effects of the elimination is to reduce the differences between the current fair values and the carrying amounts of the subsidiary's net assets, excepting land and goodwill, on the business combination date. The effect of the reduction is as follows:

Total difference on date of business combination (Dec. 31, 2002)	$110,000
Less: Reduction in elimination (a) ($29,000 + $1,000)	30,000
Unamortized difference, Dec. 31, 2003 ($61,000 + $4,000 + $15,000)	$ 80,000

The joint effect of Palm Corporation's use of the equity method of accounting and the annual elimination will be to extinguish $50,000 of the $80,000 difference above through Palm's Investment in Starr Company Common Stock ledger account. *The $15,000 balance applicable to Starr's land will not be extinguished; the $15,000 balance applicable to Starr's goodwill will be reduced only if the goodwill in subsequently impaired.*

7. The parent company's use of the equity method of accounting results in the equalities described below:

> **Parent company net income = consolidated net income**
> **Parent company retained earnings = consolidated retained earnings**

The equalities exist when the equity method of accounting is used *if there are no intercompany profits accounted for in the determination of consolidated net assets.* Intercompany profits (gains) are discussed in Chapter 8.

Equity Method: Wholly Owned Subsidiary Subsequent to Date of Business Combination

	Palm Corporation	Starr Company	Elimination Increase (Decrease)	Consolidated
PALM CORPORATION AND SUBSIDIARY **Working Paper for Consolidated Financial Statements** **For Year Ended December 31, 2003**				
Income Statement				
Revenue:				
Net sales	1,100,000	680,000		1,780,000
Intercompany investment income	30,000		(a) (30,000)	
Total revenue	1,130,000	680,000	(30,000)	1,780,000
Costs and expenses:				
Cost of goods sold	700,000	450,000	(a) 29,000	1,179,000
Operating expenses	217,667	130,000	(a) 1,000	348,667
Interest expense	49,000			49,000
Income taxes expense	53,333	40,000		93,333
Total costs and expenses	1,020,000	620,000	30,000*	1,670,000
Net income GO BACK EQM	110,000	60,000	(60,000)	110,000
Statement of Retained Earnings				
Retained earnings, beginning of year	134,000	132,000	(a) (132,000)	134,000
Net income	110,000	60,000	(60,000)	110,000
Subtotal	244,000	192,000	(192,000)	244,000
Dividends declared	30,000	24,000	(a) (24,000)†	30,000
Retained earnings, end of year	214,000	168,000	(168,000)	214,000
Balance Sheet **Assets**				
Cash	15,900	72,100		88,000
Intercompany receivable (payable) SUB	24,000	(24,000)		
Inventories	136,000	115,000		251,000
Other current assets	88,000	131,000		219,000
Investment in Starr Company common stock	506,000		(a) (506,000)	
Plant assets (net)	440,000	340,000	(a) 61,000	841,000
Patent (net)		16,000	(a) 4,000	20,000
Goodwill			(a) 15,000	15,000
Total assets	1,209,900	650,100	(426,000)	1,434,000
Liabilities and Stockholders' Equity				
Income taxes payable	40,000	20,000		60,000
Other liabilities	190,900	204,100		395,000
Common stock, $10 par	400,000			400,000
Common stock, $5 par		200,000	(a) (200,000)	
Additional paid-in capital	365,000	58,000	(a) (58,000)	365,000
Retained earnings	214,000	168,000	(168,000)	214,000
Total liabilities and stockholders' equity	1,209,900	650,100	(426,000)	1,434,000

* An **increase** in total costs and expenses and a **decrease** in net income.
† A **decrease** in dividends and an **increase** in retained earnings.

8. Despite the equalities indicated above, ***consolidated financial statements*** are superior to ***parent company financial statements*** for the presentation of financial position and operating results of parent and subsidiary companies. The effect of the consolidation process for Palm Corporation and subsidiary is to ***reclassify Palm's $30,000 share of its subsidiary's adjusted net income to the revenue and expense components of that net income.*** Similarly, Palm's $506,000 investment in the subsidiary ***is replaced by the assets and liabilities comprising the subsidiary's net assets.***

9. Purchase accounting theory requires the exclusion from consolidated retained earnings of a subsidiary's retained earnings on the date of a business combination. Palm Corporation's use of the equity method of accounting meets this requirement. Palm's ending retained earnings amount in the working paper, which is equal to consolidated retained earnings, includes only Palm's $30,000 share of the subsidiary's adjusted net income for the year ended December 31, 2003, the first year of the parent-subsidiary relationship.

Consolidated Financial Statements

The consolidated income statement, statement of retained earnings, and balance sheet of Palm Corporation and subsidiary for the year ended December 31, 2003, are as follows. The amounts in the consolidated financial statements are taken from the Consolidated column in the working paper on page 280.

PALM CORPORATION AND SUBSIDIARY		
Consolidated Income Statement		
For Year Ended December 31, 2003		
Net sales		$1,780,000
Costs and expenses:		
Cost of goods sold	$1,179,000	
Operating expenses	348,667	
Interest expense	49,000	
Income taxes expense	93,333	
Total costs and expenses		1,670,000
Net income		$ 110,000
Basic earnings per share of common stock		
(40,000 shares outstanding)		$2.75

PALM CORPORATION AND SUBSIDIARY	
Consolidated Statement of Retained Earnings	
For Year Ended December 31, 2003	
Retained earnings, beginning of year	$134,000
Add: Net income	110,000
Subtotal	$244,000
Less: Dividends ($0.75 a share)	30,000
Retained earnings, end of year	$214,000

PALM CORPORATION AND SUBSIDIARY
Consolidated Balance Sheet
December 31, 2003

Assets

Current assets:

Cash		$ 88,000
Inventories		251,000
Other		219,000
Total current assets		$ 558,000
Plant assets (net)		841,000
Intangible assets:		
Patent (net)	$ 20,000	
Goodwill	15,000	35,000
Total assets		$1,434,000

Liabilities and Stockholders' Equity

Liabilities:		
Income taxes payable		$ 60,000
Other		395,000
Total liabilities		$ 455,000
Stockholders' equity:		
Common stock, $10 par	$400,000	
Additional paid-in capital	365,000	
Retained earnings	214,000	979,000
Total liabilities and stockholders' equity		$1,434,000

Closing Entries

After consolidated financial statements have been completed, both the parent company and its subsidiaries prepare and post closing entries, to complete the accounting cycle for the year. The subsidiary's closing entries are prepared in the usual fashion. However, the parent company's use of the equity method of accounting necessitates specialized closing entries.

The equity method of accounting disregards legal form in favor of the economic substance of the relationship between a parent company and its subsidiaries. However, state corporation laws generally require separate accounting for retained earnings available for dividends to stockholders. Accordingly, Palm Corporation prepares the closing entries illustrated below and on page 283 on December 31, 2003, after the consolidated financial statements have been completed:

Parent Company's Dec. 31, 2003, Closing Entries under the Equity Method of Accounting for Subsidiary

Net Sales	1,100,000	
Intercompany Investment Income	30,000	
Income Summary		1,130,000
To close revenue accounts.		
Income Summary	1,020,000	
Cost of Goods Sold		700,000
Operating Expenses		217,667
Interest Expense		49,000
Income Taxes Expense		53,333
To close expense accounts.		

Income Summary	110,000	
Retained Earnings of Subsidiary ($30,000 − $24,000)		6,000
Retained Earnings ($110,000 − $6,000)		104,000
To close Income Summary account; to transfer net income legally available for dividends to retained earnings; and to segregate 100% share of adjusted net income of subsidiary not distributed as dividends by the subsidiary.		
Retained Earnings	30,000	
Dividends Declared		30,000
To close Dividends Declared account.		

After the foregoing closing entries have been posted, Palm Corporation's Retained Earnings and Retained Earnings of Subsidiary ledger accounts are as shown below:

Parent Company's Ledger Accounts for Retained Earnings

Retained Earnings

Date	Explanation	Debit	Credit	Balance
2002				
Dec. 31	Balance			134,000 cr
2003				
Dec. 31	Close net income available for dividends		104,000	238,000 cr
31	Close Dividends Declared account	30,000		208,000 cr

Retained Earnings of Subsidiary

Date	Explanation	Debit	Credit	Balance
2003				
Dec. 31	Close net income not available for dividends		6,000	6,000 cr

The third closing entry excludes from Palm Corporation's retained earnings the amount of Palm's net income not available for dividends to Palm's stockholders—$6,000. This amount is computed as follows:

Adjusted net income of Starr Company recorded by Palm Corporation in Intercompany Investment Income ledger account	$30,000
Less: Dividends declared by Starr to Palm	24,000
Amount of Starr's adjusted net income not distributed as a dividend to Palm	$ 6,000

Palm's Retained Earnings of Subsidiary ledger account thus contains the amount of Starr's adjusted net income (less net losses) *since the date of the business combination* that has not been distributed by Starr to Palm as dividends. This amount is termed the ***undistributed earnings of the subsidiary*** and is equal to the net increase in the balance of Palm's Investment in Starr Company Common Stock ledger account (page 275) since December 31, 2002, the date of the business combination ($506,00 − $500,000 = $6,000). In addition, the total of the ending balances of Palm's Retained Earnings and Retained Earnings of Subsidiary ledger accounts is equal to consolidated retained earnings, as shown on page 284:

Total of Parent Company's Two Retained Earnings Account Balances Equals Consolidated Retained Earnings

Balances, Dec. 31, 2003:

Retained earnings	$208,000
Retained earnings of subsidiary	6,000
Total (equal to consolidated retained earnings, Dec. 31, 2003—see page 282)	$214,000

Illustration of Equity Method for Wholly Owned Subsidiary for Second Year after Business Combination

In this section, the Palm Corporation–Starr Company example is continued to illustrate application of the equity method of accounting for a wholly owned subsidiary for the second year following a business combination. On December 17, 2004, Starr Company declared a dividend of $40,000, payable January 6, 2005, to Palm Corporation, the stockholder of record December 28, 2004. For the year ended December 31, 2004, Starr had a net income of $90,000, and its goodwill was not impaired.

After the posting of appropriate journal entries for 2004 under the equity method of accounting, selected ledger accounts for Palm Corporation are as follows:

Ledger Accounts of Parent Company under the Equity Method of Accounting for Wholly Owned Subsidiary

Investment in Starr Company Common Stock

Date	Explanation	Debit	Credit	Balance
2002				
Dec. 31	Issuance of common stock in business combination	450,000		450,000 dr
31	Direct out-of-pocket costs of business combination	50,000		500,000 dr
2003				
Dec. 20	Dividend declared by Starr		24,000	476,000 dr
31	Net income of Starr	60,000		536,000 dr
31	Amortization of differences between current fair values and carrying amounts of Starr's net assets		30,000	506,000 dr
2004				
Dec. 17	Dividend declared by Starr		40,000	466,000 dr
31	Net income of Starr	90,000		556,000 dr
31	Amortization of differences between current fair values and carrying amounts of Starr's net assets		5,000*	551,000 dr

Intercompany Investment Income

Date	Explanation	Debit	Credit	Balance
2003				
Dec. 31	Net income of Starr		60,000	60,000 cr
31	Amortization of differences between current fair values and carrying amounts of Starr's net assets	30,000		30,000 cr
31	Closing entry	30,000		-0-

(continued)

Same Concept Y2

Intercompany Investment Income (concluded)

Date	Explanation	Debit	Credit	Balance
2004				
Dec. 31	Net income of Starr		90,000	90,000 cr
31	Amortization of differences between current fair values and carrying amounts of Starr's net assets	5,000*		85,000 cr

* Building depreciation ($30,000 ÷ 15) $2,000
    Machinery depreciation ($20,000 ÷ 10)   2,000
    Patent amortization ($5,000 ÷ 5)   1,000
        Total amortization applicable to 2004 $5,000

Developing the Elimination

The working paper elimination for December 31, 2004, is developed in much the same way as the elimination for December 31, 2003, as illustrated below (in journal entry format):

Working Paper Elimination for Wholly Owned Subsidiary for Second Year Subsequent to Date of Business Combination

PALM CORPORATION AND SUBSIDIARY
Working Paper Elimination
December 31, 2004

(a) Common Stock—Starr	200,000	
Additional Paid-in Capital—Starr	58,000	
Retained Earnings—Starr ($168,000 − $6,000)	162,000	
Retained Earnings of Subsidiary—Palm	6,000	
Intercompany Investment Income—Palm	85,000	
Plant Assets (net)—Starr ($61,000 − $4,000)	57,000	
Patent (net)—Starr ($4,000 − $1,000)	3,000	
Goodwill—Starr	15,000	
Cost of Goods Sold—Starr	4,000	
Operating Expenses—Starr	1,000	
Investment in Starr Company Common Stock—Palm		551,000
Dividends Declared—Starr		40,000

To carry out the following:

(a) Eliminate intercompany investment and equity accounts of subsidiary **at beginning of year,** and subsidiary dividend.

(b) Provide for Year 2004 depreciation and amortization on differences between current fair values and carrying amounts of Starr's net assets as follows:

	Cost of Goods Sold	Operating Expenses
Building depreciation	$1,000	$1,000
Machinery depreciation	2,000	
Patent amortization	1,000	
Totals	$4,000	$1,000

(c) Allocate unamortized differences between combination date current fair values and carrying amounts of Starr's net assets to appropriate assets.

(Income tax effects are disregarded.)

The principal new feature of the foregoing elimination is the treatment of the beginning-of-year Retained Earnings ledger account balance of the subsidiary, Starr Company. Because consolidated retained earnings of Palm Corporation and subsidiary on December 31, 2003, included the amount of $6,000, representing the undistributed earnings of the subsidiary for the year ended December 31, 2003, only $162,000 ($168,000 − $6,000 = $162,000) is eliminated from the subsidiary's retained earnings balance on January 1, 2004. In addition, the $6,000 balance (before the closing entry for 2004) of the parent company's Retained Earnings of Subsidiary ledger account is eliminated, to avoid "double counting" of the undistributed earnings of the subsidiary as of January 1, 2004, in the consolidated financial statements of Palm Corporation and subsidiary for the year ended December 31, 2004.

Working Paper for Consolidated Financial Statements

The features of the December 31, 2004, elimination for Palm Corporation and subsidiary described in the foregoing section are illustrated in the following *partial* working paper for consolidated financial statements. The net income and dividends for Palm Corporation are assumed for illustrative purposes.

Equity Method: Wholly Owned Subsidiary Subsequent to Date of Business Combination

PALM CORPORATION AND SUBSIDIARY Partial Working Paper for Consolidated Financial Statements For Year Ended December 31, 2004				
	Palm Corporation	Starr Company	Eliminations Increase (Decrease)	Consolidated
Statement of Retained Earnings				
Retained earnings, beginning of year	208,000	168,000	(a) (162,000)	214,000
Net income	245,000	90,000	(90,000)*	245,000
Subtotal	453,000	258,000	(252,000)	459,000
Dividends declared	60,000	40,000	(a) (40,000)†	60,000
Retained earnings, end of year	393,000	218,000	(212,000)	399,000
Balance Sheet				
Common stock, $10 par	400,000			400,000
Common stock, $5 par		200,000	(a) (200,000)	
Additional paid-in capital	365,000	58,000	(a) (58,000)	365,000
Retained earnings	393,000	218,000	(212,000)	399,000
Retained earnings of subsidiary	6,000		(a) (6,000)	
Total stockholders' equity	1,164,000	476,000	(476,000)	1,164,000
Total liabilities and stockholders' equity	x,xxx,xxx	xxx,xxx	(476,000)	x,xxx,xxx

* Decrease in intercompany investment income ($85,000), plus total increase in costs and expenses ($4,000 + $1,000), equals $90,000.
† A **decrease** in dividends and an **increase** in retained earnings.

The elimination of only $162,000 of the balance of the subsidiary's beginning-of-year retained earnings results in consolidated retained earnings of $214,000 at the beginning of the year (January 1, 2004). This amount is equal to consolidated retained earnings on December 31, 2003 (see page 286). In addition, the total of the parent company's two retained earnings amounts in the working paper for consolidated financial statements ($393,000 + $6,000 = $399,000) is identical to the amount of consolidated retained earnings on December 31, 2004.

Closing Entries

The amount of the undistributed earnings of Starr Company for 2004 is $45,000, computed as follows:

Adjusted net income of Starr Company recorded by Palm Corporation in Intercompany Investment Income ledger account (page 285)	$85,000
Less: Dividends declared by Starr to Palm	40,000
Amount of Starr's adjusted net income not distributed as a dividend to Palm	$45,000

In the December 31, 2004, closing entries for Palm Corporation, $45,000 of Palm's $245,000 net income for 2004 is closed to the Retained Earnings of Subsidiary ledger account. The remaining $200,000 ($245,000 − $45,000 = $200,000) is closed to the Retained Earnings account, because it is available for dividends to the stockholders of Palm. Following the posting of the closing entries, the two ledger accounts are as follows:

Parent Company's Ledger Accounts for Retained Earnings

Retained Earnings

Date	Explanation	Debit	Credit	Balance
2002				
Dec. 31	Balance			134,000 cr
2003				
Dec. 31	Close net income available for dividends		104,000	238,000 cr
31	Close Dividends Declared account	30,000		208,000 cr
2004				
Dec. 31	Close net income available for dividends		200,000	408,000 cr
31	Close Dividends Declared account	60,000		348,000 cr

Retained Earnings of Subsidiary

Date	Explanation	Debit	Credit	Balance
2003				
Dec. 31	Close net income not available for dividends		6,000	6,000 cr
2004				
Dec. 31	Close net income not available for dividends		45,000	51,000 cr

Again, the balance of Palm's Retained Earnings of Subsidiary ledger account, $51,000, is equal to the net increase in the balance of Palm's Investment in Starr Company Common Stock account (page 284) since the date of the business combination ($551,000 − $500,000 = $51,000). Further, the total of the ending balances of the foregoing retained earnings accounts, $399,000 ($348,000 + $51,000 = $399,000) is equal to consolidated retained earnings of $399,000 on December 31, 2004 (see page 286).

Accounting for Operating Results of Partially Owned Subsidiaries

Accounting for the operating results of a partially owned subsidiary requires the computation of the minority interest in net income or net losses of the subsidiary. Thus, under the economic unit concept of consolidated financial statements, the consolidated

income statement of a parent company and its partially owned subsidiary includes an allocation of total consolidated income (loss) to the parent company and the minority interest. In the consolidated balance sheet, the minority interest in net assets of subsidiary is displayed in stockholders' equity.

Illustration of Equity Method for Partially Owned Subsidiary for First Year after Business Combination

The Post Corporation–Sage Company consolidated entity described in Chapter 6 (pages 231 to 232) is used in this section to illustrate the equity method of accounting for the operating results of a partially owned subsidiary. Post owns 95% of the outstanding common stock of Sage, and minority stockholders own the remaining 5%.

Assume that Sage Company on November 24, 2003, declared a $1 a share dividend, payable December 16, 2003, to stockholders of record December 1, 2003, and that Sage had a net income of $90,000 for the year ended December 31, 2003. Sage prepares the following journal entries for the declaration and payment of the dividend:

Partially Owned Subsidiary's Journal Entries for Declaration and Payment of Dividend

2003			
Nov. 24	Dividends Declared (40,000 × $1)	40,000	
	Dividends Payable ($40,000 × 0.05)		2,000
	Intercompany Dividends Payable ($40,000 × 0.95)		38,000
	To record declaration of dividend payable Dec. 16, 2003, to stockholders of record Dec. 1, 2003.		
Dec. 16	Dividends Payable	2,000	
	Intercompany Dividends Payable	38,000	
	Cash		40,000
	To record payment of dividend declared Nov. 24, 2003, to stockholders of record Dec. 1, 2003.		

Post's journal entries for 2003, under the equity method of accounting, include the following:

Parent Company's Equity-Method Journal Entries to Record Operating Results of Partially Owned Subsidiary

2003			
Nov. 24	Intercompany Dividends Receivable	38,000	
	Investment in Sage Company Common Stock		38,000
	To record dividend declared by Sage Company, payable Dec. 16, 2003, to stockholders of record Dec. 1, 2003.		
Dec. 16	Cash	38,000	
	Intercompany Dividends Receivable		38,000
	To record receipt of dividend from Sage Company.		
31	Investment in Sage Company Common Stock ($90,000 × 0.95)	85,500	
	Intercompany Investment Income		85,500
	To record 95% of net income of Sage Company for the year ended Dec. 31, 2003. (Income tax effects are disregarded.)		

As pointed out on page 235, a business combination involves a restatement of net asset values of the subsidiary. Sage Company's net income of $90,000 does not reflect cost expirations attributable to Sage's restated net asset values, *because the restatements were not entered in Sage's accounting records.* Consequently, the depreciation and amortization of the $246,000 difference between the current fair values of Sage's *identifiable* net assets on December 31, 2002, the date of the business combination, and the carrying amounts of those net assets must be accounted for by Post Corporation. Assume, as in Chapter 6 (page 235), that the difference was allocable to Sage's identifiable assets as follows:

Differences between Current Fair Values and Carrying Amounts of Partially Owned Subsidiary's Identifiable Net Assets on Date of Business Combination		
Inventories (first-in, first-out cost)		$ 26,000
Plant assets (net):		
Land	$60,000	
Building (economic life 20 years)	80,000	
Machinery (economic life 5 years)	50,000	190,000
Leasehold (economic life 6 years)		30,000
Total		$246,000

In addition, Post had acquired in the business combination goodwill attributable to Sage in the amount of $38,000, computed as follows:

Computation of Goodwill Acquired by Combinor		
Cost of Post Corporation's 95% interest in Sage Company		$1,192,250
Less: 95% of $1,215,000 aggregate current fair values of Sage's		
identifiable net assets		1,154,250
Goodwill acquired by Post		$ 38,000

Post Corporation prepares the following journal entry on December 31, 2003, under the equity method of accounting to reflect the effects of the differences between current fair values and carrying amounts of the partially owned subsidiary's identifiable net assets:

Parent Company's Equity-Method Journal Entry to Record Amortization of Partially Owned Subsidiary's Identifiable Net Assets		
Intercompany Investment Income	42,750	
Investment in Sage Company Common Stock		42,750

To amortize differences between current fair values and carrying amounts of Sage Company's identifiable net assets on December 31, 2003, as follows:

Inventories—to cost of goods sold	$26,000
Building—depreciation ($80,000 ÷ 20)	4,000
Machinery—depreciation ($50,000 ÷ 5)	10,000
Leasehold—amortization ($30,000 ÷ 6)	5,000
Total difference applicable to 2003	$45,000
Amortization for 2003 ($45,000 × 0.95)	$42,750

(Income tax effects are disregarded.)

Assuming the goodwill acquired by Post in the business combination was not impaired as of December 31, 2003, Post prepares no journal entry to reduce the carrying amount of the goodwill.

After the foregoing journal entry is posted, Post Corporation's Investment in Sage Company Common Stock and Intercompany Investment Income ledger accounts are as follows:

Ledger Accounts of Parent
Company under Equity
Method of Accounting for

Investment in Sage Company Common Stock

Date	Explanation	Debit	Credit	Balance
2002				
Dec. 31	Issuance of common stock in business combination	1,140,000		1,140,000 dr
31	Direct out-of-pocket costs of business combination	52,250		1,192,250 dr
2003				
Nov. 24	Dividend declared by Sage		38,000	1,154,250 dr
Dec. 31	Net income of Sage	85,500		1,239,750 dr
31	Amortization of differences between current fair values and carrying amounts of Sage's identifiable net assets		42,750	1,197,000 dr

Intercompany Investment Income

Date	Explanation	Debit	Credit	Balance
2003				
Dec. 31	Net income of Sage		85,500	85,500 cr
31	Amortization of differences between current fair values and carrying amounts of Sage's identifiable net assets	42,750		42,750 cr

The $42,750 balance of Post Corporation's Intercompany Investment Income account represents 95% of the $45,000 adjusted net income ($90,000 − $45,000 = $45,000) of Sage Company for the year ended December 31, 2003.

Developing the Elimination

Post Corporation's use of the equity method of accounting for its investment in Sage Company results in a balance in the Investment ledger account that is a mixture of three components: (1) the carrying amount of Sage's identifiable net assets; (2) the "current

POST CORPORATION
Analysis of Investment in Sage Company Common Stock Ledger Account
For Year Ended December 31, 2003

	Carrying Amount	Current Fair Value Excess	Goodwill	Total	
Beginning balances	$920,550	$233,700	$38,000	$1,192,250	
Net income of Sage ($90,000 × 0.95)	85,500			85,500	} Intercompany investment income, $42,750
Amortization of differences between current fair values and carrying amounts of Sage's identifiable net assets ($45,000 × 0.95)		(42,750)		(42,750)	
Dividend declared by Sage ($40,000 × 0.95)	(38,000)			(38,000)	
Ending balances	$968,050	$190,950	$38,000	$1,197,000	

fair value excess," which is attributable to Sage's ***identifiable*** net assets; and (3) the goodwill acquired by Post in the business combination with Sage. These components are analyzed on page 290.

The minority interest in Sage's net assets (which is not recorded in a ledger account) may be analyzed similarly, except that ***there is no goodwill attributable to the minority interest:***

POST CORPORATION Analysis of Minority Interest in Net Assets of Sage Company For Year Ended December 31, 2003				
	Carrying Amount	Current Fair Value Excess	Total	
Beginning balances	$48,450	$12,300	$60,750	
Net income of Sage ($90,000 × 0.05)	4,500		4,500	Minority interest in net income of subsidiary, $2,250
Amortization of differences between current fair values and carrying amounts of Sage's identifiable net assets ($45,000 × 0.05)		(2,250)	(2,250)	
Dividend declared by Sage ($40,000 × 0.05)	(2,000)		(2,000)	
Ending balances	$50,950	$10,050	$61,000	

The $1,019,000 ($968,050 + $50,950 = $1,019,000) total of the ending balances of the Carrying Amount columns of the two foregoing analyses agrees with the total stockholders' equity of Sage Company on December 31, 2003 (see balance sheet section of working paper for consolidated financial statements on page 295), as follows:

Partially Owned Subsidiary's Stockholders' Equity, Dec. 31, 2003

Common stock, $10 par	$ 400,000
Additional paid-in capital	235,000
Retained earnings	384,000
Total stockholders' equity	$1,019,000

The $201,000 ($190,950 + $10,050 = $201,000) total of the ending balances of the Current Fair Value Excess columns of the two analyses agrees with the December 31, 2003, total of the unamortized balances for each of the respective identifiable assets of Sage Company, as follows:

Unamortized Differences Between Current Fair Values and Carrying Amounts of Partially Owned Subsidiary's Identifiable Assets One Year Subsequent to Business Combination

	Balances, Dec. 31, 2002 (p. 289)	Amortization for Year 2003 (p. 289)	Balances, Dec. 31, 2003
Inventories	$ 26,000	$(26,000)	
Plant assets (net):			
Land	$ 60,000		$ 60,000
Building	80,000	$ (4,000)	76,000
Machinery	50,000	(10,000)	40,000
Total plant assets	$190,000	$(14,000)	$176,000
Leasehold	$ 30,000	$ (5,000)	$ 25,000
Totals	$246,000	$(45,000)	$201,000

Assuming that Sage Company allocates machinery depreciation and leasehold amortization entirely to cost of goods sold, and building depreciation 50% each to cost of goods sold and operating expenses, the working paper eliminations (in journal entry format) for Post Corporation and subsidiary on December 31, 2003, are as shown below and on page 293. The reference numbers in parentheses relate to the discussion in the following paragraph.

Comments on components of the first working paper elimination follow:

1. As indicated in Chapter 6 (page 225), the three components of the subsidiary's stockholders' equity are reciprocal to the parent company's Investment account. However, because a consolidated statement of retained earnings is to be prepared for the first year following the business combination, the subsidiary's ***beginning-of-year*** retained earnings amount is eliminated, together with the subsidiary's dividends, which are an offset to the subsidiary's retained earnings. Further, the beginning-of-year minority interest, $60,750 (see page 235 of Chapter 6), is reduced by the minority interest's share of the subsidiary's dividends, $2,000, as a counterpart of the parent company's reduction of its Investment account balance by $38,000, its share of the subsidiary's dividends (see the analysis of the Investment account on page 290).

2. As illustrated in the analysis on page 290, the amount of the parent company's intercompany investment income is an element of the balance of the parent's Investment ledger account. In effect, the elimination of the intercompany investment income, coupled with items described in (4) below and on page 293, comprises a reclassification of the intercompany investment income to the adjusted components of the subsidiary's net income in the consolidated income statement.

3. The debits to the subsidiary's plant assets and leasehold bring into the consolidated balance sheet the unamortized differences between current fair values and carrying amounts of the subsidiary's identifiable assets on the date of the business combination (see the analysis on page 291). Further, the debit to the parent company's goodwill brings the amount of that asset into the consolidated balance sheet.

Working Paper Eliminations for Partially Owned Subsidiary for First Year Subsequent to Date of Business Combination

POST CORPORATION AND SUBSIDIARY Working Paper Eliminations December 31, 2003		
(a) Common Stock—Sage	400,000 (1)	
Additional Paid-in Capital—Sage	235,000 (1)	
Retained Earnings—Sage	334,000 (1)	
Intercompany Investment Income—Post	42,750 (2)	
Plant Assets (net)—Sage ($190,000 − $14,000)	176,000 (3)	
Leasehold (net)—Sage ($30,000 − $5,000)	25,000 (3)	
Goodwill—Post	38,000 (3)	
Cost of Goods Sold—Sage	43,000 (4)	
Operating Expenses—Sage	2,000 (4)	
Investment in Sage Company Common Stock—Post		1,197,000 (1)
Dividends Declared—Sage		40,000 (1)
Minority Interest in Net Assets of Subsidiary ($60,750 − $2,000) [See (d).]		58,750 (1)

(continued)

POST CORPORATION AND SUBSIDIARY
Working Paper Eliminations (concluded)
December 31, 2003

To carry out the following:

(a) Eliminate intercompany investment and equity accounts of subsidiary **at beginning of year,** and subsidiary dividends.

(b) Provide for Year 2003 depreciation and amortization on differences between current fair values and carrying amounts of Sage's identifiable net assets as follows:

	Cost of Goods Sold	Operating Expenses
Inventories sold	$26,000	
Building depreciation	2,000	$2,000
Machinery depreciation	10,000	
Leasehold amortization	5,000	
Totals	$43,000	$2,000

(c) Allocate unamortized differences between combination date current fair values and carrying amounts to appropriate assets.

(d) Establish minority interest in net assets of subsidiary at beginning of year ($60,750), less minority interest share of dividends declared by subsidiary during year ($40,000 × 0.05 = $2,000).

(Income tax effects are disregarded.)

(b) Minority Interest in Net Income of Subsidiary	2,250	
Minority Interest in Net Assets of Subsidiary		2,250

To establish minority interest in subsidiary's adjusted net income for Year 2003 as follows:

Net income of subsidiary	$90,000
Net reduction of elimination (a) ($43,000 + $2,000)	(45,000)
Adjusted net income of subsidiary	$45,000
Minority interest share ($45,000 × 0.05)	$ 2,250

4. The increases in the subsidiary's cost of goods sold and operating expenses, totaling $45,000 ($43,000 + $2,000 = $45,000), in effect reclassify the comparable decreases totaling $45,000 ($42,750 + $2,250 = $45,000) in the parent company's Investment account and the minority interest in net assets of the subsidiary, respectively (see the analyses on pages 290 and 291) to the appropriate categories for the consolidated income statement.

Working Paper for Consolidated Financial Statements

The working paper for consolidated financial statements for Post Corporation and subsidiary for the year ended December 31, 2003, is shown on page 295.

The following aspects of the working paper for consolidated financial statements of Post Corporation and subsidiary should be emphasized:

1. Income tax effects of the increase in Sage Company's costs and expenses are not included in elimination (a). Income tax effects in consolidated financial statements are considered in Chapter 9.

2. Elimination (a) cancels Sage's retained earnings balance *at the beginning of the year.* This step is essential for the preparation of all three basic consolidating financial statements.

3. The parent company's use of the equity method of accounting results in the following equalities:

> **Parent company net income = consolidated net income**
> **Parent company retained earnings = consolidated retained earnings**

These equalities exist in the equity method of accounting if there are no intercompany profits (gains) or losses eliminated for the determination of consolidated net assets. Intercompany profits are discussed in Chapter 8.

4. One of the effects of elimination (a) is to reduce the differences between the current fair values of the subsidiary's identifiable net assets on the business combination date and their carrying amounts on that date. The effect of the reduction is as follows:

Aggregate difference on date of business combination (Dec. 31, 2002)	$246,000
Less: Reduction in elimination (a) ($43,000 + $2,000)	45,000
Unamortized difference, Dec. 31, 2003 ($176,000 + $25,000)	$201,000

The joint effect of Post's use of the equity method of accounting and the annual eliminations will be to extinguish $141,000 of the remaining $201,000 difference through Post's Investment in Sage Company Common Stock ledger account. *The $60,000 applicable to Sage's land will not be extinguished.*

5. The minority interest in net assets of subsidiary on December 31, 2003, may be verified as follows:

Sage Company's total stockholders' equity, Dec. 31, 2003	$1,019,000
Add: Unamortized difference computed in **4,** above	201,000
Sage's adjusted stockholders' equity, Dec. 31, 2003	$1,220,000
Minority interest in net assets of subsidiary ($1,220,000 × 0.05)	$ 61,000

6. The minority interest in net income of subsidiary is recognized in elimination (b) in the amount of $2,250 (5% of the adjusted net income of Sage Company) as an increase in minority interest in net assets of subsidiary and in the minority interest in total consolidated income, with the remaining consolidated income being the parent's share thereof.

Equity Method: Partially Owned Subsidiary Subsequent to Date of Business Combination

	POST CORPORATION AND SUBSIDIARY Working Paper for Consolidated Financial Statements For Year Ended December 31, 2003			
	Post Corporation	**Sage Company**	**Eliminations Increase (Decrease)**	**Consolidated**
Income Statement				
Revenue:				
Net sales	5,611,000	1,089,000		6,700,000
Intercompany investment income	42,750		(a) (42,750)	
Total revenue	5,653,750	1,089,000	(42,750)	6,700,000
Costs and expenses:				
Costs of goods sold	3,925,000	700,000	(a) 43,000	4,668,000
Operating expenses	556,000	129,000	(a) 2,000	687,000
Interest and income taxes expense	710,000	170,000		880,000
Minority interest in net income of subsidiary			(b) 2,250	2,250
Total costs and expenses and minority interest	5,191,000	999,000	47,250[†]	6,237,250
Net income	462,750	90,000	(90,000)	462,750
Statement of Retained Earnings				
Retained earnings, beginning of year	1,050,000	334,000	(a) (334,000)	1,050,000
Net income	462,750	90,000	(90,000)	462,750
Subtotal	1,512,750	424,000	(424,000)	1,512,750
Dividends declared	158,550	40,000	(a) (40,000)[‡]	158,550
Retained earnings, end of year	1,354,200	384,000	(384,000)	1,354,200
Balance Sheet Assets				
Inventories	861,000	439,000		1,300,000
Other current assets	639,000	371,000		1,010,000
Investment in Sage Company common stock	1,197,000		(a) (1,197,000)	
Plant assets (net)	3,600,000	1,150,000	(a) 176,000	4,926,000
Leasehold (net)			(a) 25,000	25,000
Goodwill	95,000		(a) 38,000	133,000
Total assets	6,392,000	1,960,000	(958,000)	7,394,000
Liabilities and Stockholders' Equity				
Liabilities	2,420,550	941,000		3,361,550
Common stock, $1 par	1,057,000			1,057,000
Common stock, $10 par		400,000	(a) (400,000)	
Additional paid-in capital	1,560,250	235,000	(a) (235,000)	1,560,250
Minority interest in net assets of subsidiary			(a) 58,750⎱ (b) 2,250⎰	61,000
Retained earnings	1,354,200	384,000	(384,000)	1,354,200
Total liabilities and stockholders' equity	6,392,000	1,960,000	(958,000)	7,394,000

[†] An **increase** in total costs and expenses, and a **decrease** in net income.
[‡] A **decrease** in dividends and an **increase** in retained earnings.

Consolidated Financial Statements

The consolidated income statement, statement of retained earnings, and balance sheet of Post Corporation and subsidiary for the year ended December 31, 2003, are shown below and on page 297. The amounts in the consolidated financial statements are taken from the Consolidated column in the working paper on page 295.

POST CORPORATION AND SUBSIDIARY
Consolidated Income Statement
For Year Ended December 31, 2003

Net sales		$6,700,000
Costs and expenses:		
Cost of goods sold	$4,668,000	
Operating expenses	687,000	
Interest and income taxes expense	880,000	
Total costs and expenses		6,235,000
Total consolidated income		$ 465,000
Less: Minority interest in net income of subsidiary		2,250
Net income		$ 462,750
Basic earnings per share of common stock (1,057,000 shares outstanding)		$ 0.44

POST CORPORATION AND SUBSIDIARY
Consolidated Statement of Retained Earnings
For Year Ended December 31, 2003

Retained earnings, beginning of year	$1,050,000
Add: Net income	462,750
Subtotal	$1,512,750
Less: Dividends ($0.15 a share)	158,550
Retained earnings, end of year	$1,354,200

POST CORPORATION AND SUBSIDIARY
Consolidated Balance Sheet
December 31, 2003

Assets

Current assets:		
Inventories		$1,300,000
Other		1,010,000
Total current assets		$2,310,000
Plant assets (net)		4,926,000
Intangible assets:		
Leasehold (net)	$ 25,000	
Goodwill	133,000	158,000
Total assets		$7,394,000

(continued)

POST CORPORATION AND SUBSIDIARY Consolidated Balance Sheet (concluded) December 31, 2003		
Liabilities and Stockholders' Equity		
Liabilities		
Total liabilities		$3,361,550
Stockholders' equity:		
Common stock, $1 par	$1,057,000	
Additional paid-in capital	1,560,250	
Minority interest in net assets of subsidiary	61,000	
Retained earnings	1,354,200	4,032,450
Total liabilities and stockholders' equity		$7,394,000

Closing Entries

As indicated on page 202, legal considerations necessitate the following closing entries for Post Corporation on December 31, 2003:

Parent Company's Dec. 31, 2003, Closing Entries under the Equity Method of Accounting for Subsidiary

Net Sales	5,611,000	
Intercompany Investment Income	42,750	
Income Summary		5,653,750
To close revenue accounts.		
Income Summary	5,191,000	
Cost of Goods Sold		3,925,000
Operating Expenses		556,000
Interest and Income Taxes Expense		710,000
To close expense accounts.		
Income Summary	462,750	
Retained Earnings of Subsidiary ($42,750 − $38,000)		4,750
Retained Earnings ($462,750 − $4,750)		458,000
To close Income Summary account; to transfer net income legally available for dividends to retained earnings; and to segregate 95% share of adjusted net income of subsidiary not distributed as dividends.		
Retained Earnings	158,550	
Dividends Declared		158,550
To close Dividends Declared account.		

After the foregoing closing entries have been posted, Post's Retained Earnings and Retained Earnings of Subsidiary ledger accounts are as follows:

**Parent Company's Ledger
Accounts for Retained
Earnings**

Retained Earnings

Date	Explanation	Debit	Credit	Balance
2002				
Dec. 31	Balance			1,050,000 cr
2003				
Dec. 31	Close net income available for dividends		458,000	1,508,000 cr
31	Close Dividends Declared account	158,550		1,349,450 cr

Retained Earnings of Subsidiary

Date	Explanation	Debit	Credit	Balance
2003				
Dec. 31	Close net income not available for dividends		4,750	4,750 cr

The $4,750 balance of Post's Retained Earnings of Subsidiary ledger account represents Post's share of the undistributed earnings of Sage Company for the year ended December 31, 2003. The undistributed earnings of the subsidiary may be reconciled to the increase in Post's investment ledger account balance (see page 290) as follows:

Balance, Dec. 31, 2003	$1,197,000
Balance, Dec. 31, 2002	1,192,250
Difference—equal to undistributed earnings of subsidiary for 2003	$ 4,750

In addition, the total of the ending balances of Post's Retained Earnings and Retained Earnings of Subsidiary ledger accounts is equal to consolidated retained earnings, as shown below:

**Total of Parent Company's
Two Retained Earnings
Account Balances Equals
Consolidated Retained
Earnings**

Balances, Dec. 31, 2003:	
Retained earnings	$1,349,450
Retained earnings of subsidiary	4,750
Total (equal to consolidated retained earnings, Dec. 31, 2003—see page 297)	$1,354,200

Illustration of Equity Method for Partially Owned Subsidiary for Second Year after Business Combination

In this section, the Post Corporation–Sage Company example is continued to demonstrate application of the equity method of accounting for a partially owned purchased subsidiary for the second year following the business combination. On November 22, 2004, Sage Company declared a dividend of $50,000, payable December 17, 2004, to stockholders of record December 1, 2004. For the year ended December 31, 2004, Sage had a net income of $105,000. Post's share of the dividend was $47,500 ($50,000 × 0.95 = $47,500), and Post's share of Sage's net income was $99,750 ($105,000 × 0.95 = $99,750). The goodwill acquired by Post in the business combination was not impaired.

After the posting of appropriate journal entries for 2004 under the equity method of accounting, selected ledger accounts for Post Corporation are as follows:

Investment in Sage Company Common Stock

Date	Explanation	Debit	Credit	Balance
2002				
Dec. 31	Issuance of common stock in business combination	1,140,000		1,140,000 dr
31	Direct out-of-pocket costs of business combination	52,250		1,192,250 dr
2003				
Nov. 24	Dividend declared by Sage		38,000	1,154,250 dr
Dec. 31	Net income of Sage	85,500		1,239,750 dr
31	Amortization of differences between current fair values and carrying amounts of Sage's identifiable net assets		42,750	1,197,000 dr
2004				
Nov. 22	Dividend declared by Sage		47,500	1,149,500 dr
Dec. 31	Net income of Sage	99,750		1,249,250 dr
31	Amortization of differences between current fair values and carrying amounts of Sage's identifiable net assets		18,050*	1,231,200 dr

Intercompany Investment Income

Date	Explanation	Debit	Credit	Balance
2003				
Dec. 31	Net income of Sage		85,500	85,500 cr
31	Amortization of differences between current fair values and carrying amounts of Sage's identifiable net assets	42,750		42,750 cr
31	Closing entry	42,750		-0-
2004				
Dec. 31	Net income of Sage		99,750	99,750 cr
31	Amortization of differences between current fair values and carrying amounts of Sage's identifiable net assets	18,050*		81,700 cr

* Building depreciation ($80,000 ÷ 20)	$ 4,000	
Machinery depreciation ($50,000 ÷ 5)	10,000	
Leasehold amortization ($30,000 ÷ 6)	5,000	
Total amortization applicable to 2004	$19,000	
Post Corporation's share ($19,000 × 0.95)	$18,050	

Developing the Eliminations

The working paper eliminations for December 31, 2004, are developed in much the same way as for the eliminations for December 31, 2003, as illustrated on page 300 (in journal entry format):

POST CORPORATION AND SUBSIDIARY
Working Paper Eliminations
December 31, 2004

(a) Common Stock—Sage	400,000	
Additional Paid-in Capital—Sage	235,000	
Retained Earnings—Sage ($384,000 − $4,750)	379,250	
Retained Earnings of Subsidiary—Post	4,750	
Intercompany Investment Income—Post	81,700	
Plant Assets (net)—Sage ($176,000 − $14,000)	162,000	
Leasehold (net)—Sage ($25,000 − $5,000)	20,000	
Goodwill—Post	38,000	
Cost of Goods Sold—Sage	17,000	
Operating Expenses—Sage	2,000	
Investment in Sage Company Common Stock—Post		1,231,200
Dividends Declared—Sage		50,000
Minority Interest in Net Assets of Subsidiary		
($61,000 − $2,500)		58,500

To carry out the following:

(a) Eliminate intercompany investment and equity accounts of
subsidiary **at beginning of year,** and subsidiary dividend.

(b) Provide for Year 2004 depreciation and amortization on
differences between current fair values and carrying amounts
of Sage's identifiable net assets as follows:

	Cost of Goods Sold	Operating Expenses
Building depreciation	$ 2,000	$2,000
Machinery depreciation	10,000	
Leasehold amortization	5,000	
Totals	$17,000	$2,000

(c) Allocate unamortized differences between combination date
current fair values and carrying amounts to appropriate assets.

(d) Establish minority interest in net assets of subsidiary at beginning
of year ($61,000), less minority interest share of dividends
declared by subsidiary during year ($50,000 × 0.05 = $2,500).

(Income tax effects are disregarded.)

(b) Minority Interest in Net Income of Subsidiary	4,300	
Minority Interest in Net Assets of Subsidiary		4,300

To establish minority interest in subsidiary's adjusted net income for
Year 2004 as follows:

Net income of subsidiary	$105,000	
Net reduction in elimination (a)		
($17,000 + $2,000)	(19,000)	
Adjusted net income of subsidiary	$ 86,000	
Minority interest share ($86,000 × 0.05)	$ 4,300	

Because consolidated retained earnings of Post Corporation and subsidiary on December 31, 2003, included the amount of $4,750, representing the parent company's share of the undistributed earnings of the subsidiary for the year ended December 31, 2003, only $379,250 ($384,000 − $4,750 = $379,250) is eliminated from the subsidiary's retained earnings on January 1, 2004. In addition, the $4,750 balance (before the closing entry for 2004) of the parent company's Retained Earnings of Subsidiary ledger account is eliminated, to avoid "double counting" of the undistributed earnings of the subsidiary as of January 1, 2004, in the consolidated financial statements of Post Corporation and subsidiary for the year ended December 31, 2004.

Working Paper for Consolidated Financial Statements

The aspects of the December 31, 2004, eliminations for Post Corporation and subsidiary described in the foregoing paragraph are illustrated in the following *partial* working paper for consolidated financial statements. The amounts presented for Post Corporation are assumed.

Equity Method: Partially Owned Subsidiary Subsequent to Date of Business Combination

POST CORPORATION AND SUBSIDIARY Partial Working Paper for Consolidated Financial Statements For Year Ended December 31, 2004				
	Post Corporation	Sage Company	Eliminations Increase (Decrease)	Consolidated
Statement of Retained Earnings				
Retained earnings, beginning of year	1,349,450	384,000	(a) (379,250)	1,354,200
Net income	353,550	105,000	(105,000)*	353,550
Subtotal	1,703,000	489,000	(484,250)	1,707,750
Dividends declared	158,550	50,000	(a) (50,000)†	158,550
Retained earnings, end of year	1,544,450	439,000	(434,250)	1,549,200
Balance Sheet				
Total liabilities	x,xxx,xxx	xxx,xxx	xxx,xxx	xxx,xxx
Common stock, $1 par	1,057,000			1,057,000
Common stock, $10 par		400,000	(a) (400,000)	
Additional paid-in capital	1,560,250	235,000	(a) (235,000)	1,560,250
Minority interest in net assets of subsidiary			(a) 58,500} (b) 4,300}	62,800
Retained earnings	1,544,450	439,000	(434,250)	1,549,200
Retained earnings of subsidiary	4,750		(a) (4,750)	
Total stockholders' equity	4,166,450	1,074,000	(1,011,200)	4,229,250
Total liabilities and stockholders' equity	x,xxx,xxx	x,xxx,xxx	(1,011,200)	x,xxx,xxx

* Decrease in intercompany investment income ($81,700), plus total increase in costs and expenses ($17,000 + $2,000 + $4,300), equals $105,000.
† A **decrease** in dividends and an **increase** in retained earnings.

The December 31, 2004, balance of the minority interest in net assets of subsidiary may be verified as follows:

Proof of Minority Interest in Net Assets of Subsidiary

Sage Company's total stockholders' equity, Dec. 31, 2004	$1,074,000
Add: Unamortized difference between combination date current fair values and carrying amounts of Sage's identifiable net assets ($162,000 + $20,000)	182,000
Sage's adjusted stockholders' equity, Dec. 31, 2004	$1,256,000
Minority interest in net assets of subsidiary ($1,256,000 × 0.05)	$ 62,800

Closing Entries

Post Corporation's share of the undistributed earnings of Sage Company for 2004 is $34,200, computed as follows:

Parent Company's Share of Undistributed Earnings of Subsidiary

Adjusted net income of Sage Company recorded by Post Corporation in Intercompany Investment Income ledger account (page 299)	$81,700
Less: Post's share of dividends declared by Sage ($50,000 × 0.95)	47,500
Post's share of amount of Sage's adjusted net income not distributed as dividends	$34,200

In the December 31, 2004, closing entries for Post Corporation, $34,200 of Post's net income for 2004 is closed to the Retained Earnings of Subsidiary ledger account. The remaining $319,350 ($353,550 − $34,200 = $319,350) is closed to the Retained Earnings account, because it is available for dividends to the stockholders of Post. Following the posting of the closing entries, the two ledger accounts are as follows:

Parent Company's Ledger Accounts for Retained Earnings

Retained Earnings

Date	Explanation	Debit	Credit	Balance
2002				
Dec. 31	Balance			1,050,000 cr
2003				
Dec. 31	Close net income available for dividends		458,000	1,508,000 cr
31	Close Dividends Declared account	158,550		1,349,450 cr
2004				
Dec. 31	Close net income available for dividends		319,350	1,668,800 cr
31	Close Dividends Declared account	158,550		1,510,250 cr

Retained Earnings of Subsidiary

Date	Explanation	Debit	Credit	Balance
Dec. 31	Close net income not available for dividends		4,750	4,750 cr
Dec. 31	Close net income not available for dividends		34,200	38,950 cr

The $38,950 balance of Post's Retained Earnings of Subsidiary ledger account represents Post's share of the undistributed earnings of Sage Company since December 31, 2002, the date of the business combination. The undistributed earnings of the subsidiary may be reconciled to the increase in Post's Investment ledger account balance (see page 299) as follows:

Balance, Dec. 31, 2004	$1,231,200
Balance, Dec. 31, 2003	1,197,000
Difference—equal to undistributed earnings of subsidiary for 2004	$ 34,200

In addition, the total of the December 31, 2004, ending balances of Post's Retained Earnings and Retained Earnings of Subsidiary ledger accounts is equal to consolidated earnings, as shown below:

Total of Parent Company's Two Retained Earnings Account Balances Equals Consolidated Retained Earnings

Balances, Dec. 31, 2004:	
Retained earnings	$1,510,250
Retained earnings of subsidiary	38,950
Total (equal to consolidated earnings, Dec. 31, 2004—see page 301)	$1,549,200

Concluding Comments on Equity Method of Accounting

In today's financial accounting environment, the equity method of accounting for a subsidiary's operations is preferable to the cost method for the following reasons:

1. The equity method, which is consistent with the accrual basis of accounting, emphasizes *economic substance* of the parent company–subsidiary relationship, while the cost method emphasizes *legal form.* Financial accounting stresses substance over form.

2. The equity method permits the use of *parent company journal entries* to reflect many items that must be included in *working paper eliminations* in the cost method. Formal journal entries in the accounting records provide a better record than do working paper eliminations.

3. The equity method facilitates issuance of separate financial statements for the parent company, if required by Securities and Exchange Commission regulations or other considerations.

4. Except when intercompany profits (gains) or losses (discussed in Chapter 8) exist in assets or liabilities to be consolidated, the parent company's net income and combined retained earnings account balances are identical in the equity method to the related consolidated amounts. Thus, the equity method provides a useful self-checking technique.

For these reasons, the equity method of accounting for a subsidiary's operations is emphasized in the following chapters.

Appendix

Cost Method for Partially Owned Subsidiary

To illustrate the cost method of accounting for the operating results of a subsidiary, the Post Corporation–Sage Company business combination, which involves a partially owned subsidiary, is used. Post acquired 95% of Sage's outstanding common stock at a total cost (including out-of-pocket costs) of $1,192,250 on December 31, 2002. Sage's operations for the first two years following the business combination included the following:

Year Ended Dec. 31,	Net Income	Dividends Declared
2003	$ 90,000	$40,000
2004	105,000	50,000

ILLUSTRATION OF COST METHOD FOR PARTIALLY OWNED SUBSIDIARY FOR FIRST YEAR AFTER BUSINESS COMBINATION

If Post Corporation used the cost method, rather than the equity method, of accounting for Sage Company's operating results for the year ended December 31, 2003, Post would not prepare journal entries to record Sage's net income for the year. Post would record Sage's dividend declaration as follows on November 24, 2003:

Parent Company's Cost-Method Journal Entry to Record Dividend Declared by Partially Owned Subsidiary

Intercompany Dividends Receivable	38,000	
Intercompany Dividends Revenue		38,000
To record dividend declared by Sage Company, payable Dec. 16, 2003, to stockholders of record Dec. 1, 2003. (Income tax effects are disregarded.)		

Post's journal entry for receipt of the dividend from Sage would be the same under the cost method as under the equity method of accounting illustrated on page 208.

Working Paper for Consolidated Financial Statements

The working paper for consolidated financial statements and the related working paper eliminations (in journal entry format) for Post Corporation and subsidiary for the year ended December 31, 2003, follow:

Cost Method: Partially Owned Subsidiary Subsequent to Date of Business Combination

POST CORPORATION AND SUBSIDIARY Working Paper for Consolidated Financial Statements For Year Ended December 31, 2003				
	Post Corporation	Sage Company	Eliminations Increase (Decrease)	Consolidated
Income Statement				
Revenue:				
Net sales	5,611,000	1,089,000		6,700,000
Intercompany dividends revenue	38,000		(c) (38,000)	
Total revenue	5,649,000	1,089,000	(38,000)	6,700,000
Cost and expenses:				
Cost of goods sold	3,925,000	700,000	(b) 43,000	4,668,000
Operating expenses	556,000	129,000	(b) 2,000	687,000
Interest and income taxes expense	710,000	170,000		880,000
Minority interest in net income of subsidiary			(d) 2,250	2,250
Total costs and expenses and minority interest	5,191,000	999,000	47,250*	6,237,250
Net income	458,000	90,000	(85,250)	462,750

(continued)

POST CORPORATION AND SUBSIDIARY **Working Paper for Consolidated Financial Statements (concluded)** **For Year Ended December 31, 2003**					
	Post Corporation	**Sage Company**	**Eliminations Increase (Decrease)**		**Consolidated**
Statement of Retained Earnings					
Retained earnings, beginning of year	1,050,000	334,000	(a)	(334,000)	1,050,000
Net income	458,000	90,000		(85,250)	462,750
Subtotal	1,508,000	424,000		(419,250)	1,512,750
Dividends declared	158,550	40,000	(c)	(40,000)†	158,550
Retained earnings, end of year	1,349,450	384,000		(379,250)	1,354,200
Balance Sheet **Assets**					
Inventories	861,000	439,000	{(a) {(b)	26,000 (26,000)	1,300,000
Other current assets	639,000	371,000			1,010,000
Investment in Sage Company common stock	1,192,250		(a)	(1,192,250)	
Plant assets (net)	3,600,000	1,150,000	{(a) {(b)	190,000 (14,000)	4,926,000
Leasehold (net)			{(a) {(b)	30,000 (5,000)	25,000
Goodwill	95,000		(a)	38,000	133,000
Total assets	6,387,250	1,960,000		(953,250)	7,394,000
Liabilities and Stockholders' Equity					
Liabilities	2,420,550	941,000			3,361,550
Common stock, $1 par	1,057,000				1,057,000
Common stock, $10 par		400,000	(a)	(400,000)	
Additional paid-in capital	1,560,250	235,000	(a)	(235,000)	1,560,250
Minority interest in net assets of subsidiary			{(a) {(c) {(d)	60,750 (2,000) 2,250	61,000
Retained earnings	1,349,450	384,000		(379,250)	1,354,200
Total liabilities and stockholders' equity	6,387,250	1,960,000		(953,250)	7,394,000

* An **increase** in total costs and expenses and a **decrease** in net income.
† A **decrease** in dividends and an **increase** in retained earnings.

<table>
<tr><td rowspan="2">Working Paper Eliminations (Cost Method) for Partially Owned Subsidiary for First Year Subsequent to Date of Business Combination</td><td colspan="2">POST CORPORATION AND SUBSIDIARY
Working Paper Eliminations
December 31, 2003</td></tr>
<tr><td>

(a) Common Stock—Sage
   Additional Paid-in Capital—Sage
   Retained Earnings—Sage
   Inventories—Sage
   Plant Assets (net)—Sage
   Leasehold (net)—Sage
   Goodwill—Post
      Investment in Sage Company Common Stock—Post
      Minority Interest in Net Assets of Subsidiary

</td><td>

400,000
235,000
334,000
26,000
190,000
30,000
38,000
      1,192,250
      60,750

</td></tr>
</table>

(continued)

POST CORPORATION AND SUBSIDIARY
Working Paper Eliminations (concluded)
December 31, 2003

To eliminate intercompany investment and equity accounts of subsidiary **on date of business combination** (Dec. 31, 2002); to allocate excess of cost over carrying amounts of identifiable assets acquired, with remainder to goodwill; and to establish minority interest in net assets of subsidiary on date of business combination ($1,215,000 × 0.05 = $60,750).

(b) Cost of Goods Sold—Sage	43,000	
Operating Expenses—Sage	2,000	
Inventories—Sage		26,000
Plant Assets (net)—Sage		14,000
Leasehold (net)—Sage		5,000

To provide for Year 2003 depreciation and amortization on differences between business combination date current fair values and carrying amounts of Sage's identifiable assets as follows:

	Cost of Goods Sold	Operating Expenses
Inventories sold	$26,000	
Building depreciation	2,000	$2,000
Machinery depreciation	10,000	
Leasehold amortization	5,000	
Totals	$43,000	$2,000

(Income tax effects are disregarded.)

(c) Intercompany Dividends Revenue—Post	38,000	
Minority Interest in Net Assets of Subsidiary	2,000	
Dividends Declared—Sage		40,000

To eliminate intercompany dividends and minority interest share thereof ($40,000 × 0.05 = $2,000).

(d) Minority Interest in Net Income of Subsidiary	2,250	
Minority Interest in Net Assets of Subsidiary		2,250

To establish minority interest in subsidiary's adjusted net income for Year 2003 as follows:

Net income of subsidiary	$90,000
Net reduction in elimination (b)	(45,000)
Adjusted net income of subsidiary	$45,000
Minority interest share ($45,000 × 0.05)	$ 2,250

The points that follow relative to the cost-method working papers for Post Corporation and subsidiary should be noted.

1. The consolidated amounts in the cost-method working paper for consolidated financial statements are identical to the consolidated amounts in the equity-method

working paper (page 295). This outcome results from the use of different eliminations in the two methods.

2. Three cost-method eliminations, (a), (b), and (c), are required to accomplish what a single equity-method elimination, (a) on pages 292 and 293, does. The reason is that the parent company's accounting records are used in the equity method to reflect the parent's share of the subsidiary's adjusted net income or net loss.

3. Elimination (a) deals with the intercompany investment and subsidiary equity accounts *on the date of the business combination.* This elimination is identical to the one on page 296 of Chapter 6. This accounting technique is necessary because the parent's Investment in Sage Company Common Stock account is maintained at the *cost of the original investment* in the cost method.

4. The parent company's cost-method net income and retained earnings are not the same as the consolidated amounts. Thus, the consolidated amounts on December 31, 2003, may be proved as follows, to assure their accuracy:

Proof of Consolidated Net Income and Consolidated Retained Earnings under Cost Method	

Consolidated Net Income:

Net income of Post Corporation	$458,000
Add: Post's share of Sage Company's adjusted net income not distributed as dividends [($45,000 − $40,000) × 0.95]	4,750
Consolidated net income	$462,750

Consolidated Retained Earnings:

Retained earnings of Post Corporation	$1,349,450
Add: Post's share of adjusted net increase in Sage Company's retained earnings [($50,000 − $45,000) × 0.95]	4,750
Consolidated retained earnings	$1,354,200

Closing Entries

There are no unusual features of closing entries for a parent company that uses the cost method of accounting for a subsidiary's operating results. The Intercompany Dividends Revenue ledger account is closed with other revenue accounts to the Income Summary account. Because the parent company does not record the undistributed earnings of subsidiaries under the cost method, a Retained Earnings of Subsidiary ledger account is unnecessary in the cost method.

ILLUSTRATION OF COST METHOD FOR PARTIALLY OWNED SUBSIDIARY FOR SECOND YEAR AFTER BUSINESS COMBINATION

The only journal entry prepared by Post Corporation for the Year 2004 operating results of Sage Company under the cost method of accounting is to accrue $47,500 of intercompany dividends revenue ($50,000 × 0.95 = $47,500) on November 22, 2004. The working paper eliminations (in journal entry format) on December 31, 2004, are as follows:

POST CORPORATION AND SUBSIDIARY		
Working Paper Eliminations		
December 31, 2004		

(a) Common Stock—Sage	400,000	
Additional Paid-in Capital—Sage	235,000	
Retained Earnings—Sage	334,000	
Inventories—Sage	26,000	
Plant Assets (net)—Sage	190,000	
Leasehold (net)—Sage	30,000	
Goodwill—Post	38,000	
Investment in Sage Company Common Stock—Post		1,192,250
Minority Interest in Net Assets of Subsidiary		60,750

To eliminate intercompany investment and equity accounts of
subsidiary **on date of business combination** (Dec. 31, 2002);
to allocate excess of cost over carrying amounts of identifiable
assets acquired, with remainder to goodwill; and to establish
minority interest in net assets of subsidiary on date of business
combination.

(b) Retained Earnings—Sage	45,000	
Cost of Goods Sold—Sage	17,000	
Operating Expenses—Sage	2,000	
Inventories—Sage		26,000
Plant Assets (net)—Sage		28,000
Leasehold—Sage		10,000

To provide for Years 2003 and 2004 depreciation and amortization
on differences between business combination date current fair
values and carrying amounts of Sage's identifiable assets;
Year 2003 amounts are debited to Sage's retained earnings;
Year 2004 amounts are debited to Sage's operating expenses.

(c) Retained Earnings—Sage ($61,000 − $60,750)	250	
Minority Interest in Net Assets of Subsidiary		250

To provide for net increase in minority interest from date of
business combination to **beginning of year.**

(d) Intercompany Dividends Revenue—Post	47,500	
Minority Interest in Net Assets of Subsidiary	2,500	
Dividends Declared—Sage		50,000

To eliminate intercompany dividends and minority interest share
of dividends ($50,000 × 0.05 = $2,500).

(e) Minority Interest in Net Income of Subsidiary	4,300	
Minority Interest in Net Assets of Subsidiary		4,300

To establish minority interest in subsidiary's adjusted net income
for Year 2004 as follows:

Net income of subsidiary	$105,000
Net reduction in elimination (b)	(19,000)
Adjusted net income of subsidiary	$ 86,000
Minority interest share ($86,000 × 0.05)	$ 4,300

Because the parent company does not record depreciation and amortization applicable to the differences between the current fair values and carrying amounts of the subsidiary's identifiable net assets, elimination (b) must provide for total depreciation and amortization for **both** years since the business combination. In addition, elimination (c) must account for the net increase in the minority interest in net assets of the subsidiary from the business combination date to the beginning of the current year.

Working Paper for Consolidated Financial Statements

The following **partial** working paper for consolidated financial statements illustrates the retained earnings changes for Post Corporation and subsidiary during Year 2004. The consolidated amounts are identical to those under the equity method of accounting (see page 301):

Cost Method: Partially Owned Subsidiary Subsequent to Date of Business Combination

				POST CORPORATION AND SUBSIDIARY Partial Working Paper for Consolidated Financial Statements For Year Ended December 31, 2004	
	Post Corporation	**Sage Company**	**Eliminations Increase (Decrease)**	**Consolidated**
Statement of Retained Earnings				
Retained earnings, beginning of year	1,349,450	384,000	(a) (334,000) (b) (45,000) (c) (250)	1,354,200
Net income	319,350	105,000	(70,800)*	353,550
Subtotal	1,668,800	489,000	(450,050)	1,707,750
Dividends declared	158,550	50,000	(d) (50,000)†	158,550
Retained earnings, end of year	1,510,250	439,000	(400,050)	1,549,200

* Decrease in intercompany dividends revenue ($47,500), plus total increase in costs and expenses ($17,000 + $2,000 + $4,300), equals $70,800.
† A **decrease** in dividends and an **increase** in retained earnings.

Review Questions

1. "Consolidated financial statement amounts are the same, regardless of whether a parent company uses the equity method or the cost method to account for a subsidiary's operations." Why is this statement true?

2. When there are no intercompany profits (gains) or losses in consolidated assets or liabilities, the equity method of accounting produces parent company net income that equals consolidated net income. The equity method also results in parent company retained earnings of the same amount as consolidated retained earnings. Why, then, are consolidated financial statements considered superior to separate financial statements of the parent company when the parent company uses the equity method? Explain.

3. Describe the special features of closing entries for a parent company that accounts for its subsidiary's operating results by the equity method.

4. Strake Company, a 90%-owned subsidiary of Peale Corporation, had a net income of $50,000 for the first year following the business combination. However, the working paper elimination for the minority interest in the subsidiary's net income was in the amount of $3,500 rather than $5,000. Is this difference justifiable? Explain.

5. Discuss some of the advantages that result from the use of the equity method, rather than the cost method, of accounting for a subsidiary's operating results.

6. Both Parnell Corporation and Plankton Company have wholly owned subsidiaries. Parnell has an Intercompany Dividends Revenue ledger account, and an Intercompany Investment Income account is included in the Plankton ledger. Do both companies use the same method of accounting for their subsidiaries' operating results? Explain.

7. Plumstead Corporation's 92%-owned subsidiary declared a dividend of $3 a share on its 50,000 outstanding shares of common stock. How does Plumstead record this dividend under:

  a. The equity method of accounting?
  b. The cost method of accounting?

8. Is a Retained Earnings of Subsidiary ledger account *required* for a parent company that uses the equity method of accounting for the subsidiary's operations? Explain.

Exercises

(Exercise 7.1) Select the best answer for each of the following multiple-choice questions:

1. Concepts underlying the equity method and the cost method of accounting for the operating results of a subsidiary may be summarized as follows:

	Equity Method	*Cost Method*
a.	Legal form	Economic substance
b.	Legal form	Legal form
c.	Economic substance	Economic substance
d.	Economic substance	Legal form

2. Under the equity method of accounting for the operating results of a subsidiary, dividends declared by the subsidiary to the parent company are accounted for by the parent company as:

  a. Dividend revenue on the declaration date.
  b. A reduction of the investment in subsidiary on the payment date.
  c. Dividend revenue on the payment date.
  d. A reduction of the investment in subsidiary on the declaration date.

3. In a closing entry at the end of an accounting period, a parent company that uses the equity method of accounting for the operations of a subsidiary credits the Retained Earnings of Subsidiary account in the amount of the:

  a. Balance of the subsidiary's Retained Earnings account.
  b. Dividends declared by the subsidiary to the parent.
  c. Parent's share of the subsidiary's net income.
  d. Parent's share of the undistributed earnings of the subsidiary.

4. Under the equity method of accounting, dividends declared by the subsidiary to the parent company are credited to the parent's:

  a. Intercompany Dividends Receivable account.
  b. Investment in Subsidiary Common Stock account.
  c. Retained Earnings of Subsidiary account.
  d. Retained Earnings account.

5. After completion of the parent company's equity-method journal entries for its profitable wholly owned subsidiary's operating results, the balance of the parent's Intercompany Investment Income ledger is equal to the:

    a. Subsidiary's net income.

    b. Subsidiary's net Income, less amortization of current fair value differences of the subsidiary's identifiable net assets.

    c. Subsidiary's net income, less amortization of current fair value differences of the subsidiary's net assets, including goodwill.

    d. Increase in the after-closing balance of the subsidiary's Retained Earnings ledger account.

6. The end-of-period closing entries for a parent company that uses the equity method of accounting for the operating results of a wholly owned subsidiary include a credit to the Retained Earnings of Subsidiary ledger account in the amount of the:

    a. Ending retained earnings of the subsidiary.

    b. Net income of the subsidiary for the period.

    c. Undistributed earnings of the subsidiary for the period.

    d. Dividends declared by the subsidiary during the period.

7. The accuracy of the minority interest in net assets of a partially owned subsidiary subsequent to the date of the business combination may be verified by applying the minority interest percentage to the:

    a. Total stockholders' equity of the subsidiary.

    b. Balance of the parent company's Investment in Subsidiary Common Stock account.

    c. Total stockholders' equity of the subsidiary plus unamortized current fair value differences.

    d. Amount in *c* plus unimpaired goodwill.

8. On any date, the balance of a parent company's Retained Earnings of Subsidiary account attributable to a wholly owned subsidiary is equal to the:

    a. Balance of the subsidiary's Retained Earnings account.

    b. Net increase in the parent's Investment in Subsidiary Common Stock account since the date of the business combination.

    c. Total net income of the subsidiary since the date of the business combination.

    d. Total dividends declared by the subsidiary since the date of the business combination.

9. During a fiscal year, the balance of a parent company's Investment in Subsidiary Common Stock ledger account for a wholly owned subsidiary, for which the parent company uses the equity method of accounting, increases by the amount of the subsidiary's:

    a. Adjusted net income.

    b. Dividends.

    c. Adjusted net income plus dividends.

    d. Undistributed earnings.

10. If a parent company uses the equity method of accounting, in the working paper eliminations for the second and succeeding years following a business combination between the parent company and its wholly owned subsidiary, the amount eliminated for the subsidiary's retained earnings is the balance of the subsidiary's Retained Earnings Ledger account:

    a. At the **beginning** of the year.

    b. On the date of the business combination.

    c. At the **end** of the year.

    d. At the **beginning** of the year, *less* the balance of the parent's Retained Earnings of Subsidiary account.

11. The 80%-owned subsidiary of a parent company reported a net income of $80,000 for the year ended May 31, 2003. The parent company's appropriate journal entry under the equity method of accounting is (explanation omitted):

    a. Investment in Subsidiary Company Common Stock   80,000
       Investment Income   80,000
    b. Intercompany Investment Income   80,000
       Investment in Subsidiary Company Common Stock   80,000
    c. Investment in Subsidiary Company Common Stock   64,000
       Intercompany Investment Income   64,000
    d. Intercompany Investment Income   64,000
       Investment in Subsidiary Company Common Stock   64,000

12. The post-closing balances of the Retained Earnings ledger accounts of Panich Corporation and its 80%-owned subsidiary, Swenson Company, on February 28, 2003, were as follows (there were no intercompany profits or losses):

Panich Corporation:	
Retained earnings	$1,600,000
Retained earnings of subsidiary	80,000
Swenson Company:	
Retained earnings	460,000

    Consolidated retained earnings of Panich Corporation and subsidiary on February 28, 2003, is:

    a. $1,600,000.
    b. $1,680,000.
    c. $1,968,000.
    d. $2,060,000.
    e. Some other amount.

13. An Intercompany Dividends Receivable ledger account is used in:

    a. The cost method of accounting only.
    b. The equity method of accounting only.
    c. Both the cost method and the equity method of accounting.
    d. Neither the cost method nor the equity method of accounting.

14. Under the equity method of accounting, a parent company uses the Retained Earnings of Subsidiary ledger account for a subsidiary:

    a. For closing entries only.
    b. For dividends declared by the subsidiary only.
    c. For both dividends declared by the subsidiary and closing entries.
    d. For neither dividends declared by the subsidiary nor closing entries.

15. On May 31, 2002, the date of the business combination of Passey Corporation and its 80%-owned subsidiary, Sandy Company, for which Passey uses the equity method of accounting, the balance of Sandy's Retained Earnings account was $100,000, and on May 31, 2003, the after-closing balance was $120,000. **Prior to** Passey's May 31, 2003, closing entries, the balance of its Retained Earnings of Subsidiary ledger account was:

    a. Zero.
    b. $80,000.
    c. $100,000.
    d. An undeterminable amount.

16. At the end of an accounting period, a parent company that uses the equity method of accounting for its partially owned subsidiary closes its:

   a. Dividends Declared ledger account.
   b. Intercompany Dividends Receivable ledger account.
   c. Dividends Payable ledger account.
   d. Intercompany Dividends Payable ledger account.

(Exercise 7.2) The September 30, 2002, date-of-combination current fair value differences of the net assets of Spence Company, wholly owned subsidiary of Pence Corporation, were as shown below. In addition, goodwill of $45,000 was recognized in the Pence–Spence business combination.

	Current Fair Value	Carrying Amount	Difference
Inventories (first-in, first-out cost)	$120,000	$100,000	$ 20,000
Plant assets (depreciable over 10-year life)	680,000	560,000	120,000
Identifiable intangible assets (amortizable over 5-year life)	160,000	120,000	40,000

During the fiscal year ended September 30, 2003, the following occurred:

Sept. 1	Spence declared a dividend of $80,000 to Pence.
18	Spence paid the $80,000 dividend to Pence.
30	Spence reported a net income of $980,000 for the year to Pence.
30	The goodwill was determined to be unimpaired.

Prepare journal entries (omit explanations) for Pence Corporation to record the operating results of Spence Company for fiscal year 2003 under the equity method of accounting. (Disregard income taxes.)

(Exercise 7.3) Following are all details of three ledger accounts of a parent company that uses the equity method of accounting for its subsidiary's operating results:

Intercompany Dividends Receivable

2003		2003	
Aug. 16	36,000	Aug. 27	36,000

Investment in Subsidiary Common Stock

2002		2003	
Sept. 1	630,000	Aug. 16	36,000
2003		Aug. 31	5,000
Aug. 31	72,000		

Intercompany Investment Income

2003		2003	
Aug. 31	5,000	Aug. 31	72,000

Draft the most logical explanation for each of the transactions or events recorded in the foregoing ledger accounts.

(Exercise 7.4) The working paper elimination for a parent company and its wholly owned subsidiary on the date of their business combination was as shown below:

PRISTINE CORPORATION AND SUBSIDIARY Working Paper Elimination May 31, 2002		
Common Stock—Superb	100,000	
Additional Paid-in Capital—Superb	200,000	
Retained Earnings—Superb	450,000	
Inventories (first-in, first-out cost)—Superb	60,000	
Land—Superb	40,000	
Building—Superb	50,000	
Goodwill—Superb	50,000	
Investments in Superb Company Common Stock—Pristine		950,000

To eliminate intercompany investment and equity accounts of subsidiary on date of business combination; and to allocate excess of cost over carrying amount of identifiable net assets acquired, with remainder to goodwill. (Income tax effects are disregarded.)

Additional Information

1. For the fiscal year ended May 31, 2003, Superb had a net income of $80,000 and declared and paid a dividend of $30,000 (debited to the Dividends Declared ledger account) to Pristine.
2. Superb uses first-in, first-out cost for inventories and straight-line depreciation and amortization for plant and intangible assets.
3. On May 31, 2002, Superb's building had a remaining economic life of 10 years, and the consolidated goodwill was unimpaired as of May 31, 2003.
4. Superb includes depreciation expense in cost of goods sold.

Prepare a working paper elimination, in journal entry format (omit explanation) for Pristine Corporation and subsidiary on May 31, 2003. (Disregard income taxes.)

(Exercise 7.5) The working paper elimination (in journal entry format) for Polar Corporation and its wholly owned subsidiary, Solar Company, on July 31, 2002, the date of the business combination, was as follows:

POLAR CORPORATION AND SUBSIDIARY Working Paper Elimination July 31, 2002		
(a) Common Stock, no-par—Solar	50,000	
Retained Earnings—Solar	250,000	
Inventories (first-in, first-out cost)—Solar	30,000	
Plant Assets (depreciable, net)—Solar	120,000	
Goodwill—Solar	20,000	
Investment in Solar Company Common Stock—Polar		470,000

To eliminate intercompany investment and equity accounts of subsidiary on date of business combination; and to allocate excess of cost over carrying amount of identifiable assets acquired, with remainder to goodwill. (Income tax effects are disregarded.)

Additional Information

1. For the fiscal year ended July 31, 2003, Solar declared dividends (debiting the Dividends Declared ledger account) of $20,000 and had a net income of $50,000, for which Polar applied the equity method of accounting.

2. Solar uses a 10-year economic life for depreciable plant assets, with depreciation expense included in cost of goods sold.

3. The consolidated goodwill was unimpaired as of July 31, 2003.

Prepare a working paper elimination (in journal entry format) for Polar Corporation and subsidiary on July 31, 2003. Omit the explanation for the elimination. (Disregard income taxes.)

(Exercise 7.6) The date-of-business combination working paper eliminates (in journal entry format, explanation omitted) for the consolidated balance sheet of Paro Corporation and its wholly owned subsidiary, Savo Company, was as follows:

PARO CORPORATION AND SUBSIDIARY Working Paper Elimination February 28, 2002		
Common Stock—Savo	50,000	
Retained Earnings—Savo	80,000	
Inventories—Savo (first-in, first-out cost)	10,000	
Plant Assets (net)—Savo (10-year economic life)	60,000	
Goodwill—Savo	10,000	
Investment in Savo Company Common Stock—Paro		210,000

On February 3, 2003, Savo declared a dividend of $20,000 to its stockholder; on February 27, 2003, Savo paid the dividend; and on February 28, 2003, Savo reported a net income of $60,000 for the fiscal year then ended. Savo includes all depreciation and amortization in cost of goods sold. The consolidated goodwill was unimpaired as of February 28, 2003.

Prepare a working paper elimination (in journal entry format; omit explanation) for consolidated financial statements of Paro Corporation and subsidiary on February 28, 2003. (Disregard income taxes.)

(Exercise 7.7) The working paper elimination (in journal entry format) for Parry Corporation and subsidiary on October 31, 2002, the date of the business combination, was as follows:

PARRY CORPORATION AND SUBSIDIARY Working Paper Elimination October 31, 2002		
(a) Common Stock—Samuel	100,000	
Additional Paid-in Capital—Samuel	150,000	
Retained Earnings—Samuel	200,000	
Plant Assets (net)—Samuel (depreciable)	250,000	
Goodwill—Samuel	60,000	
Investment in Samuel Company Common Stock—Parry		760,000

To eliminate intercompany investment and equity accounts of subsidiary on date of business combination; and to allocate excess of cost over carrying amount of identifiable assets acquired, with remainder to goodwill.

For the fiscal year ended October 31, 2003, Samuel had a net income of $50,000, and on October 31, 2003, Samuel declared dividends of $20,000, payable November 16, 2003. Samuel depreciates plant assets by the straight-line method at a 10% rate with no residual value and includes plant assets depreciation in cost of goods sold. The consolidated goodwill was unimpaired as of October 31, 2003.

a. Prepare Parry Corporation's October 31, 2003, journal entries to record the operating results and dividend of Samuel Company under the equity method of accounting. (Disregard income taxes and omit explanations.)

b. Prepare the October 31, 2003, working paper elimination (in journal entry format) for Parry Corporation and subsidiary. (Disregard income taxes and omit explanation.)

(Exercise 7.8) The working paper elimination (explanation omitted) on the date of the Pulp Corporation–Stump Company business combination was as follows:

CHECK FIGURE

b. Debit goodwill—
Stump, $40,000.

PULP CORPORATION AND SUBSIDIARY Working Paper Elimination January 31, 2002		
Common Stock, no par or stated value—Stump	100,000	
Retained Earnings—Stump	180,000	
Inventories (first-in, first-out cost)—Stump	20,000	
Plant Assets—Stump (depreciable, 5-year life)—Stump	100,000	
Goodwill—Stump	40,000	
Investment in Stump Company Common Stock—Pulp		440,000

For the fiscal year ended January 31, 2003, Stump had a net income of $240,000, and on that date it declared and paid a dividend of $120,000. Stump includes plant asset depreciation expenses in cost of goods sold. The consolidated goodwill was unimpaired.

a. Prepare journal entries (omit explanations) for Pulp Corporation on January 31, 2003, to record the operations of Stump Company under the equity method of accounting. (Disregard income taxes.)

b. Prepare a working paper elimination, in journal entry format (omit explanation), for Pulp Corporation and subsidiary on January 31, 2003. (Disregard income taxes.)

(Exercise 7.9) Palmer Corporation had the following ledger account on December 31, 2004:

CHECK FIGURE

Balance, Dec. 31, 2004,
$61,000 credit.

Investment in Sim Company Common Stock

Date	Explanation	Debit	Credit	Balance
2002				
Dec. 31	Issuance of common stock in business combination	840,000		840,000 dr
31	Direct out-of-pocket costs of business combination	40,000		880,000 dr
2003				
Oct. 14	Dividend declared by Sim		20,000	860,000 dr
Dec. 31	Net income of Sim	60,000		920,000 dr

31	Amortization of differences
	  between current fair values and
	  carrying amounts of Sim's net
	  assets
			14,500	905,500 dr

				(continued)

Investment in Sim Company Common Stock (concluded)

Date	Explanation	Debit	Credit	Balance
2004				
Oct. 18	Dividend declared by Sim		50,000	855,500 dr
Dec. 31	Net income of Sim	90,000		945,500 dr
31	Amortization of differences between current fair values and carrying amounts of Sim's net assets		4,500	941,000 dr

Prepare a three-column Retained Earnings of Subsidiary ledger account for Palmer Corporation, and post appropriate closing entries for December 31, 2003, and December 31, 2004, to the account.

(Exercise 7.10) On March 31, 2002, Pitt Corporation acquired for cash 90% of the outstanding common stock of Scow Company. The $100,000 excess of Pitt's investment over 90% of the current fair value (and carrying amount) of Scow's identifiable net assets was allocable to goodwill, which was considered totally impaired as of March 31, 2003, because for the fiscal year ended that date, Scow had a net loss of $130,000 and declared no dividends.

Disregarding income taxes, prepare a working paper to compute the balance of Pitt Corporation's Intercompany Investment Income ledger account under the equity method of accounting on March 31, 2003.

(Exercise 7.11) On January 2, 2002, Ply Corporation acquired 75% of the outstanding common stock of Spade Company for $345,000 cash, including out-of-pocket costs. The investment was accounted for by the equity method. On January 2, 2002, Spade's identifiable net assets (carrying amount and current fair value) were $300,000. Ply determined that the excess of the cost of its investment over the current fair value of Spade's identifiable net assets was attributable to goodwill. Spade's net income for the fiscal year ended December 31, 2002, was $160,000. During Year 2002, Ply received $60,000 cash dividends from Spade. There were no other transactions between the two enterprises, and consolidated goodwill was unimpaired as of December 31, 2002.

CHECK FIGURE

Balance, Dec. 31, 2002, $405,000.

Prepare a working paper to compute the balance of Ply Corporation's Investment in Spade Company Common Stock ledger account (after adjustment) on December 31, 2002, disregarding income taxes.

(Exercise 7.12) On January 2, 2003, Plain Corporation acquired 80% of Sano Company's outstanding common stock for an amount of cash equal to 80% of the carrying amount (and current fair value) of Sano's identifiable net assets on that date. The balances of Plain's and Sano's Retained Earnings ledger accounts on January 2, 2003, were $500,000 and $100,000, respectively. During 2003, Plain had a net income of $200,000 under the equity method of accounting and declared dividends of $50,000, and Sano had a net income of $40,000 and declared dividends of $20,000. There were no other intercompany transactions between Plain and Sano.

CHECK FIGURE

Consolidated retained earnings, $650,000.

Prepare a working paper to compute the consolidated retained earnings of Plain Corporation and subsidiary on December 31, 2003. (Disregard income taxes.)

(Exercise 7.13) Pinson Corporation owned a 90% interest in a subsidiary, Solomon Company, which was accounted for by the equity method. During Year 2003, Pinson had income, exclusive of intercompany investment income, of $145,000, and Solomon had a net income of $120,000. Solomon declared and paid a $40,000 dividend during Year 2003.

There were no differences between the current fair values and carrying amounts of Solomon's identifiable net assets on the date of the business combination, and there was no goodwill in the business combination.

Prepare a working paper to compute the consolidated net income of Pinson Corporation and subsidiary for Year 2003. (Disregard income taxes.)

(Exercise 7.14) The working paper elimination (explanation omitted) on the date of the Pallid Corporation–Sallow Company business combination was as follows:

PALLID CORPORATION AND SUBSIDIARY **Working Paper Elimination** **January 31, 2002**		
Common Stock, no par or stated value—Sallow	50,000	
Retained Earnings—Sallow	90,000	
Inventories (first-in, first-out cost)—Sallow	10,000	
Plant Assets—Sallow (depreciable, 10-year life)	50,000	
Goodwill—Pallid	20,000	
Investment in Sallow Company Common Stock—Pallid		190,000
Minority Interest in Net Assets of Subsidiary ($200,000 × 0.15)		30,000

For the fiscal year ended January 31, 2003, Sallow had a net income of $120,000, and on that date it declared dividends totaling $60,000, to be paid February 28, 2003.

a. Prepare journal entries (omit explanations) for Pallid Corporation on January 31, 2003, to record the operations of Sallow Company under the equity method of accounting. (Disregard income taxes.) Consolidated goodwill was unimpaired as of January 31, 2003.

b. Prepare working paper eliminations, in journal entry format (omit explanations), for Pallid Corporation and subsidiary on January 31, 2003. Sallow includes depreciation in cost of goods sold. (Disregard income taxes.)

(Exercise 7.15) The retained earnings ledger accounts of Putter Corporation and its 80%-owned subsidiary, Simmer Company, were as follows for the two years following their business combination on May 31, 2002. There were no intercompany profits (gains) or losses in transactions between the two enterprises during the two years ended May 31, 2004.

Putter Corporation:

Retained Earnings

Date	Explanation	Debit	Credit	Balance
2002				
May 31	Balance			640,000 cr
2003				
May 31	Close net income available for dividends ($140,000 − $28,000)		112,000	752,000 cr
31	Close Dividends Declared account	60,000		692,000 cr
2004				
May 31	Close net income available for dividends ($180,000 − $52,000)		128,000	820,000 cr
31	Close Dividends Declared account	90,000		730,000 cr

Retained Earnings of Subsidiary

Date	Explanation	Debit	Credit	Balance
2003				
May 31	Close net income not available for dividends [($80,000 − $15,000 − $30,000) × 0.80]		28,000	28,000 cr
2004				
May 31	Close net income not available for dividends [($120,000 − $5,000 − $50,000) × 0.80]		52,000	80,000 cr

Simmer Company:

Retained Earnings

Date	Explanation	Debit	Credit	Balance
2002				
May 31	Balance			100,000 cr
2003				
May 31	Close net income		80,000	180,000 cr
31	Close Dividends Declared account	30,000		150,000 cr
2004				
May 31	Close net income		120,000	270,000 cr
31	Close Dividends Declared account	50,000		220,000 cr

Prepare the statement of retained earnings section of the working paper for consolidated financial statements of Putter Corporation and subsidiary for the year ended May 31, 2004.

(Exercise 7.16) Selected ledger account balances for Parton Corporation on May 31, 2003, were as follows:

Investment in (80% owned) Starter Company common stock ($60,000 net increase from May 31, 2002)	$620,000 dr
Intercompany investment income	95,000 cr
Dividends declared	50,000 dr
Sales (no offset accounts)	840,000 dr
Cost of goods sold	378,000 dr
Operating expenses and income taxes expense	212,000 dr

Prepare closing entries (omit explanations) for Parton Corporation on May 31, 2003.

(Exercise 7.17) The balance of Putnam Corporation's Investment in Salisbury Company Common Stock ledger account on September 30, 2003, was $265,000. The 20% minority interest in net assets of subsidiary in the consolidated balance sheet of Putnam Corporation and subsidiary on September 30, 2003, was $60,000. For the year ended September 30, 2004, Salisbury had a net income of $50,000 and declared and paid dividends of $18,750. Amortization for the year ended September 30, 2004, was as follows:

Differences between current fair values and carrying amounts of Salisbury's identifiable net assets on date of business combination	$4,500

Prepare a working paper to compute the following:

a. Balance of Putnam Corporation's Investment in Salisbury Company Common Stock ledger account on September 30, 2004.

b. Balance of Putnam Corporation's Intercompany Investment Income ledger account on September 30, 2004, before closing entry.

c. Amount of closing entry credit to Putnam's Retained Earnings of Subsidiary ledger account on September 30, 2004.

d. Minority interest in net income of subsidiary in consolidated income statement of Putnam Corporation and subsidiary for year ended September 30, 2004.

e. Minority interest in net assets of subsidiary in consolidated balance sheet of Putnam Corporation and subsidiary on September 30, 2004.

Cases

(Case 7.1) You have recently become the controller of Precision Corporation, a manufacturing enterprise that has begun a program of expansion through business combinations. On February 1, 2002, two weeks prior to your controllership appointment, Precision had completed the acquisition of 85% of the outstanding common stock of Sloan Company for $255,000 cash, including out-of-pocket costs. You are engaged in a discussion with Precision's chief accountant concerning the appropriate accounting method for Precision's interest in Sloan Company's operating results. The chief accountant strongly supports the cost method of accounting, offering the following arguments:

1. The cost method recognizes that Precision and Sloan are separate legal entities.

2. The existence of a 15% minority interest in Sloan requires emphasis on the legal separateness of the two companies.

3. A parent company recognizes revenue under the cost method only when the subsidiary declares dividends. Such dividend revenue is consistent with the revenue realization principle of financial accounting. The Intercompany Investment Income account recorded in the equity method of accounting does not fit the definition of realized revenue.

4. Use of the equity method of accounting might result in Precision's declaring dividends to its shareholders out of "paper" retained earnings that belong to Sloan.

5. The cost method is consistent with other aspects of historical-cost accounting, because working paper eliminations, rather than journal entries in ledger accounts, are used to recognize amortization of differences between current fair values and carrying amounts of Sloan's identifiable net assets.

Instructions
Prepare a rebuttal to each of the chief accountant's arguments.

(Case 7.2) John Raymond, chief financial officer of publicly owned Punjab Corporation, is concerned about the negative impact on Punjab's quarterly earnings resulting from its December 31, 2002, business combination with wholly owned Selvidge Company, its only subsidiary. With the end of the first quarter of Year 2003 approaching and the required filing of *Form 10-Q,* "Quarterly Report," with the Securities and Exchange Commission, Raymond has considered the required depreciation and amortization of the current fair value excesses resulting from the business combination, as follows:

Depreciable plant assets (5-year remaining composite economic life to Selvidge)	$200,000
Patent (3-year remaining economic life, 8-year remaining legal life to Selvidge)	96,000
Goodwill	160,000

Reviewing controller Nancy Wade's forecasts of pre-tax income of Punjab and Selvidge in their separate income statements for the three months ending March 31, 2003, Raymond made the following estimates:

Forecasted pre-tax income for 3 months ended Mar. 31, 2003:			
Punjab Corporation		$ 80,000	
Selvidge Company		40,000	
Total		$120,000	
Per share (100,000 weighted-average shares expected to be outstanding)			$1.20
Less: Depreciation and amortization of date-of-business combination current fair value excess:			
Plant assets ($200,000 $\times$ $\frac{1}{5}$ $\times$ $\frac{1}{4}$)	$10,000		
Patent ($96,000 $\times$ $\frac{1}{3}$ $\times$ $\frac{1}{4}$)	8,000		
		18,000	
Adjusted forecasted pre-tax income		$102,000	
Per share			$1.02

Pointing out to Wade that the 15% decrease in forecasted pre-tax earnings per share ($0.18 $\div$ $1.20 = 15\%$) would be difficult to explain to Punjab's board of directors, Raymond asked her to increase the remaining composite economic life of Selvidge's depreciable plant assets to 10 years from 5 years and to use the remaining legal life, rather than the remaining economic life, of the patent as its basis of amortization. In reply, Wade informed Raymond that before acquiescing to his request, she would have to research the following literature of accounting and auditing:

> **FASB Statement No. 142,** "Goodwill and Other Intangible Assets," paragraph 11
>
> **APB Opinion No. 20,** "Accounting Changes," paragraphs 10, 31, and 33
>
> **AICPA Professional Standards,** vol. 1, "U.S. Auditing Standards," Sections AU342.05 and AU420.14

Instructions
After researching the foregoing references, state your opinion as to how Nancy Wade should respond to John Raymond's request.

(Case 7.3) In a classroom discussion of accounting standards for consolidated financial statements, student Rachel questioned the propriety of displaying dividends payable to minority stockholders of a partially owned subsidiary as a liability in the consolidated balance sheet. She pointed out that, under the economic unit concept of consolidated financial statements, the minority interest in net assets of subsidiary is displayed with stockholders' equity in the consolidated balance sheet, and that dividends payable to minority stockholders clearly are a part of the interest of those stockholders in the net assets of the subsidiary. In response, student Carl contended that dividends payable to minority stockholders unquestionably meet the definition of **liabilities** in paragraph 35 of *Statement of Financial Accounting Concepts No. 6,* "Elements of Financial Statements."

Instructions

Do you support the view of student Rachel or of student Carl? Explain.

Problems

(Problem 7.1)

The working paper elimination for Prem Corporation and its subsidiary, Supp Company, on December 31, 2002, the date of the business combination, follows (in journal entry format):

CHECK FIGURES

a. Balance of Investment account, Dec. 31, 2003, $190,000 dr; *b.* Debit goodwill—Supp, $12,000.

PREM CORPORATION AND SUBSIDIARY
Working Paper Elimination
December 31, 2002

(a) Common Stock—Supp	10,000	
Additional Paid-in Capital—Supp	40,000	
Retained Earnings—Supp	50,000	
Inventories—Supp (first-in, first-out cost)	20,000	
Plant Assets—Supp (economic life 10 years)	60,000	
Goodwill—Supp	12,000	
Investment in Supp Company Common Stock—Prem		192,000

To eliminate intercompany investment and equity accounts of subsidiary on date of business combination; and to allocate excess of cost over carrying amount of identifiable assets acquired, with remainder to goodwill. (Income tax effects are disregarded.)

On December 8, 2003, Supp declared, and on December 18, 2003, paid, a dividend to Prem of $6,000, and it had a net income of $30,000 for 2003. Prem used the equity method of accounting for Supp's operating results. Consonsolidated goodwill was unimpaired as of December 31, 2003.

Instructions

a. Set up a three-column ledger account for Prem Corporation's Investment in Supp Company Common Stock ledger account, bring forward the December 31, 2002, debit balance of $192,000, and post the required entries to the account for Year 2003. (Disregard income taxes.)

b. Prepare a working paper elimination (in journal entry format) for Prem Corporation and subsidiary on December 31, 2003, disregarding income taxes. Supp Company includes straight-line depreciation expense in cost of goods sold and amortization expense in operating expenses.

(Problem 7.2)

On September 5, 2003, Soy Company, the 80%-owned subsidiary of Pro Corporation, declared a cash dividend of $1 a share on its 100,000 outstanding shares of $1 par common stock. The dividend was paid on September 26, 2003. For the fiscal year ended September 30, 2003, the first year of the Pro–Soy affiliation, Soy had a net income of $300,000. In addition to goodwill of $80,000, the September 30, 2002 (date of the business combination) working paper elimination (in journal entry format) for Pro Corporation and subsidiary included the following debits:

CHECK FIGURE

Sept. 30, debit intercompany investment income, $57,600.

Inventories (first-in, first-out cost)—Soy	$60,000
Plant assets (net) (all depreciable over a 10-year economic life, straight-line method)—Soy	80,000
Discount on long-term debt (5-year remaining term)—Soy	20,000

Instructions

Prepare journal entries for Pro Corporation on September 5, 26, and 30, 2003, to record its equity method of accounting for the operating results of Soy Company. Use the straight-line method of amortization for discount on long-term debt, and disregard income taxes. Consolidated goodwill was unimpaired as of September 30, 2003.

(Problem 7.3) The working paper elimination (in journal entry format) for Promo Corporation and subsidiary on March 31, 2002, the date of the business combination, was as follows:

CHECK FIGURE

b. Balance of Investment account, Mar. 31, 2003, $502,000; *c.* Debit goodwill—Sanz, $40,000.

PROMO CORPORATION AND SUBSIDIARY
Working Paper Elimination
March 31, 2003

(a) Common Stock, $1 par—Sanz	50,000	
Additional Paid-in Capital—Sanz	100,000	
Retained Earnings—Sanz	150,000	
Inventories—Sanz (first-in, first-out cost)	20,000	
Land—Sanz	50,000	
Other Plant Assets—Sanz (economic life 10 years)	80,000	
Goodwill—Sanz	40,000	
Investment in Sanz Company Common Stock—Promo		490,000

To eliminate intercompany investment and equity accounts of subsidiary on date of business combination; and to allocate excess of cost over carrying amounts of identifiable assets acquired, with remainder to goodwill. (Income tax effects are disregarded.)

For the fiscal year ended March 31, 2003, Sanz had a net income of $60,000. Sanz declared a cash dividend of $0.40 a share on March 1, 2003, and paid the dividend on March 15, 2003. (Sanz had not declared or paid dividends during the year ended March 31, 2002.) Sanz uses the straight-line method for depreciation expense and amortization expense, both of which are included in operating expenses. Consolidated goodwill was not impaired as of March 31, 2003.

Instructions

a. Prepare journal entries for Promo Corporation to record the operating results of Sanz Company for the year ended March 31, 2003, under the equity method of accounting. (Disregard income taxes.)

b. Prepare three-column ledger accounts for Promo Corporation's Investment in Sanz Company Common Stock and Intercompany Investment Income ledger accounts, and post the journal entries in *a*.

c. Prepare a working paper elimination for Promo Corporation and subsidiary on March 31, 2003 (in journal entry format). (Disregard income taxes.)

(Problem 7.4) Penn Corporation's October 31, 2003, journal entries to record the operations of its 80%-owned subsidiary, Soper Company, during the first year following the business combination, were as follows:

Intercompany Dividends Receivable	16,000	
Investment in Soper Company Common Stock		16,000

To record $1 a share dividend declared by Soper Company, payable Nov. 7, 2003, to stockholders of record Oct. 31, 2003.

Investment in Soper Company Common Stock	40,000	
Intercompany Investment Income		40,000

To record 80% of Soper Company's net income for the year ended Oct. 31, 2003. (Income tax effects are disregarded.)

Intercompany Investment Income	22,400	
Investment in Soper Company Common Stock		22,400

To amortize differences between current fair values and carrying amounts of Soper Company's identifiable net assets on Oct. 31, 2003:

Inventories—to cost of goods sold	$20,000
Plant assets—depreciation ($80,000 ÷ 10)	8,000
Total difference	$28,000
Amortization ($28,000 × 0.80)	$22,400

(Income tax effects are disregarded.)

Additional Information

1. Penn had acquired 16,000 shares of Soper's $1 par common stock on October 31, 2002, at a total cost, including out-of-pocket costs, of $240,000. The minority interest in net assets of subsidiary on that date was $50,000.

2. On October 31, 2003, the balances of Soper's Common Stock, Paid-in Capital in Excess of Par, and Retained Earnings ledger accounts were in the ratio of 1 : 3 : 5, respectively.

3. Soper allocates depreciation expense 75% to cost of goods sold and 25% to operating expenses.

4. Consolidated goodwill of $40,000 was unimpaired as of October 31, 2003.

Instructions

Prepare working paper eliminations (in journal entry format) for Penn Corporation and subsidiary on October 31, 2003. (Suggestion: Use T accounts to determine balances of ledger accounts of the parent company and subsidiary.) (Disregard income taxes.)

(Problem 7.5) On January 2, 2003, Pewter Corporation made the following investments:

1. Acquired for cash 80% of the 1,000 shares of outstanding common stock of Stewart Company at $70 a share. The stockholders' equity of Stewart on January 2, 2003, consisted of the following:

Common stock, no par or stated value	$50,000
Retained earnings	20,000
Total stockholders' equity	$70,000

2. Acquired for cash 70% of the 3,000 shares of outstanding common stock of Skate Company at $40 a share. The stockholders' equity of Skate on January 2, 2003, consisted of the following:

Common stock, $20 par	$ 60,000
Additional paid-in capital	20,000
Retained earnings	40,000
Total stockholders' equity	$120,000

Out-of-pocket costs of the two business combinations may be disregarded. An analysis of the retained earnings of each company for Year 2003 follows:

	Pewter Corporation	Stewart Company	Skate Company
Balances, beginning of year	$240,000	$ 20,000	$ 40,000
Net income (loss)	104,600*	36,000	(12,000)
Cash dividends declared and paid, Dec. 31, 2003	(40,000)	(16,000)	(9,000)
Balances, end of year	$304,600*	$ 40,000	$ 19,000

* Before giving effect to journal entries in *a*(2), below.

Instructions

a. Prepare journal entries for Pewter Corporation to record the following for Year 2003:

(1) Investments in subsidiaries' common stock

(2) Parent company's share of subsidiaries' net income or net loss (disregarding income taxes), under the equity method of accounting

(3) Parent company's share of subsidiaries' dividends declared, under the equity method of accounting (Do not prepare journal entries for receipt of cash.)

b. Prepare a working paper to compute the minority interest in each subsidiary's net assets on December 31, 2003.

c. Prepare a working paper to compute the amount to be reported as consolidated retained earnings of Pewter Corporation and subsidiaries on December 31, 2003.

(Problem 7.6) Analyses of the Investment in State Company Common Stock ledger account of Parks Corporation (State's parent company), the minority interest in net assets of State, and the differences between current fair values and carrying amounts of State's identifiable net assets on May 31, 2002, the date of the Parks–State business combination, were as follows for the fiscal year ended May 31, 2003:

PARKS CORPORATION
Analysis of Investment in State Company Common Stock Ledger Account
For Year Ended May 31, 2003

	Carrying Amount	Current Fair Value Excess	Goodwill	Total	
Beginning balances	$400,000	$80,000	$50,000	$530,000	
Net income of State Company	80,000			80,000	⎫ Intercompany
Amortization of differences between current fair values and carrying amounts of State's identifiable net assets		(7,200)		(7,200)	⎬ investment income,
Dividends declared by State	(30,000)			(30,000)	⎪ $72,800
Ending balances	$450,000	$72,800	$50,000	$572,800	⎭

PARKS CORPORATION **Analysis of Minority Interest in Net Assets of State Company** **For Year Ended May 31, 2003**	Carrying Amount	Current Fair Value Excess	Total	
Beginning balances	$100,000	$20,000	$120,000)	Minority
Net income of State Company	20,000		20,000	interest
Amortization of differences between current fair values and carrying amounts of State's identifiable net assets		(1,800)	(1,800)	in net income of subsidiary,
Dividend declared by State	(7,500)		(7,500)	$18,200
Ending balances	$112,500	$18,200	$130,700	

Minority interest in net income of subsidiary, $18,200

PARKS CORPORATION **Analysis of Differences between Current Fair Values and Carrying Amounts of** **State Company's Identifiable Net Assets** **For Year Ended May 31, 2003**	Balances, May 31, 2002	Amortization for Year 2003	Balances, May 31, 2003
Plant assets (net):			
Land	$ 39,000		$39,000
Buildings	36,000	$4,000	32,000
Machinery	25,000	5,000	20,000
Total plant assets	$100,000	$9,000	$91,000

State had 10,000 shares of $1 par common stock outstanding on May 31, 2003, that had been issued for $5 a share when State was organized. There has been no change in State's paid-in capital since State's organization. State includes straight-line depreciation expense of plant assets in cost of goods sold. Dividends were declared by State on May 31, 2003. Consolidated goodwill was unimpaired as of May 31, 2003.

Instructions

a. Reconstruct Parks Corporation's journal entries for the year ended May 31, 2003, to record the operating results of State Company under the equity method of accounting. (Disregard income taxes.)

b. Prepare working paper eliminations for Parks Corporation and subsidiary (in journal entry format) on May 31, 2003. (Disregard income taxes.)

(Problem 7.7) Paseo Corporation acquired 82% of Steppe Company's outstanding common stock for $328,000 cash on March 31, 2002. Out-of-pocket costs of the business combination may be disregarded. Steppe's stockholders' equity on March 31, 2002, was as follows:

Common stock, $2 par	$ 50,000
Additional paid-in capital	75,000
Retained earnings	135,000
Total stockholders' equity	$260,000

Additional Information

1. All of Steppe's identifiable net assets were fairly valued at their March 31, 2002, carrying amounts except for the following:

	Carrying Amounts	Current Fair Values
Land	$100,000	$120,000
Building (net) (10-year economic life)	200,000	250,000
Patent (net) (8-year economic life)	60,000	80,000

2. Goodwill resulting from the business combination was unimpaired as of March 31, 2003. Steppe used the straight-line method for depreciation and amortization. Steppe included depreciation expense in cost of goods sold and amortization expense in operating expenses.

3. During the fiscal year ended March 31, 2003, Steppe had a net income of $1.20 a share and declared and paid no dividends. There were no intercompany transactions between Paseo and Steppe.

Instructions

a. Prepare Paseo Corporation's journal entries to record Steppe Company's operating results for the year ended March 31, 2003, under the equity method of accounting. (Disregard income taxes.)

b. Prepare working paper eliminations (in journal entry format) for Paseo Corporation and subsidiary on March 31, 2003. (Disregard income taxes.)

(Problem 7.8) Pavich Corporation acquired 75% of the outstanding common stock of Sisler Company on October 1, 2002, for $547,500, including direct out-of-pocket costs. Sisler's stockholders' equity on October 1, 2002, was as follows:

Common stock, $5 par	$250,000
Additional paid-in capital	100,000
Retained earnings	200,000
Total stockholders' equity	$550,000

Additional Information

1. Current fair values of Sisler's identifiable net assets exceed their carrying amounts on October 1, 2002, as follows:

	Excess of Current Fair Values over Carrying Amounts
Inventories (first-in, first-out cost)	$30,000
Plant assets (net) (economic life 10 years)	50,000
Patent (net) (economic life 5 years)	20,000

2. Both Pavich and Sisler included depreciation expense in cost of goods sold and amortization expense in operating expenses. Both companies used the straight-line method for depreciation. Consolidated goodwill was unimpaired as of September 30, 2003 and 2004.

3. For the two fiscal years ended September 30, 2004, Sisler had net income and declared and paid dividends as follows:

Year Ended Sept. 30,	Net Income	Dividends
2003	$ 80,000	$10,000
2004	120,000	75,000

Instructions

a. Prepare journal entries for Pavich Corporation on September 30, 2003, and September 30, 2004, to record under the equity method of accounting the operating results of Sisler Company for the two years ended on those dates. Do not prepare entries for the declaration of Sisler's dividends; assume the dividends were received by Pavich on September 30 of each year. (Disregard income taxes.)

b. Prepare working paper eliminations (in journal entry format) for Pavich Corporation and subsidiary on September 30, 2003, and September 30, 2004. (Disregard income taxes.)

c. Prepare a three-column ledger account for Pavich Corporation's Retained Earnings of Subsidiary ledger account, showing the closing entries posted to that account on September 30, 2003, and September 30, 2004.

(Problem 7.9)　The working paper elimination for Plumm Corporation and its wholly owned subsidiary, Stamm Company, on the date of the business combination was as follows (in journal entry format):

PLUMM CORPORATION AND SUBSIDIARY
Working Paper Elimination
November 30, 2002

Common Stock—Stamm	80,000	
Additional Paid-in Capital—Stamm	200,000	
Retained Earnings—Stamm	220,000	
Inventories—Stamm	20,000	
Goodwill—Stamm	40,000	
Investment in Stamm Company Common Stock—Plumm		560,000

To eliminate intercompany investment and equity accounts of subsidiary on date of business combination; and to allocate excess of cost over carrying amounts of identifiable assets acquired, with remainder to goodwill. (Income tax effects are disregarded.)

Separate financial statements of Plumm and Stamm for the fiscal year ended November 30, 2003, were as follows:

PLUMM CORPORATION AND STAMM COMPANY
Separate Financial Statements (for first year following business combination)
For Year Ended November 30, 2003

	Plumm Corporation	Stamm Company
Income Statements		
Revenue:		
Net sales	$ 800,000	$415,000
Intercompany investment income	69,000	
Total revenue	$ 869,000	$415,000

(continued)

	Plumm Corporation	Stamm Company
PLUMM CORPORATION AND STAMM COMPANY		
Separate Financial Statements (for first year following business combination) (concluded)		
For Year Ended November 30, 2003		
Income Statements		
Costs and expenses:		
Cost of goods sold	$ 500,000	$110,000
Operating expenses	233,333	155,000
Income taxes expense	26,667	60,000
Total costs and expenses	$ 760,000	$325,000
Net income	$ 109,000	$ 90,000
Statements of Retained Earnings		
Retained earnings, beginning of year	$ 640,000	$220,000
Net income	109,000	90,000
Subtotals	$ 749,000	$310,000
Dividends	60,000	30,000
Retained earnings, end of year	$ 689,000	$280,000
Balance Sheets		
Assets		
Investment in Stamm Company common stock	$ 599,000	
Other	1,840,000	$960,000
Total assets	$2,439,000	$960,000
Liabilities and Stockholders' Equity		
Liabilities	$ 650,000	$400,000
Common stock, $1 par	500,000	80,000
Additional paid-in capital	600,000	200,000
Retained earnings	689,000	280,000
Total liabilities and stockholders' equity	$2,439,000	$960,000

Consolidated goodwill was unimpaired as of November 30, 2003.

Instructions

a. Reconstruct the journal entries for Plumm Corporation on November 30, 2003, under the equity method of accounting, to record the operating results of Stamm Company for the fiscal year ended November 30, 2003, including Stamm's dividend declared and paid on that date. (Do not prepare a journal entry for the declaration of the dividend.) (Disregard income taxes.)

b. Prepare a working paper for consolidated financial statements of Plumm Corporation and subsidiary for the year ended November 30, 2003, and the related working paper elimination (in journal entry format). (Disregard income taxes.)

(Problem 7.10) Ping Corporation acquired 80% of the outstanding common stock of Stang Company on December 31, 1999, for $120,000. On that date, Stang had one class of common stock outstanding with a carrying amount of $100,000 and retained earnings of $30,000. Ping had a $50,000 deficit in retained earnings.

CHECK FIGURE

b. Credit Investment account, $143,200.

Additional Information

1. Ping acquired the Stang common stock from Stang's major stockholder primarily to acquire control of signboard leases owned by Stang. The leases were to expire

on December 31, 2004, and Ping's executives estimated that the leases, which were not renewable, were worth at least $20,000 more than their carrying amount when the Stang common stock was acquired. Stang includes signboard leases amortization in other expenses.

2. The separate financial statements for both companies for the year ended December 31, 2003, were as follows:

PING CORPORATION AND SUBSIDIARY
Separate Financial Statements (prior to business combination)
For Year Ended December 31, 2003

	Ping Corporation	Stang Company
Income Statements		
Net sales	$420,000	$300,000
Costs and expenses:		
Cost of goods sold	$315,000	$240,000
Other expenses	65,000	35,000
Total costs and expenses	$380,000	$275,000
Net income	$ 40,000	$ 25,000
Statements of Retained Earnings		
Retained earnings, beginning of year	$ 15,000	$ 59,000
Net income	40,000	25,000
Subtotals	$ 55,000	$ 84,000
Dividends		9,000
Retained earnings, end of year	$ 55,000	$ 75,000
Balance Sheets		
Assets		
Current assets	$172,000	$199,100
Investment in Stang Company common stock	120,000	
Land	25,000	10,500
Building and equipment	200,000	40,000
Accumulated depreciation	(102,000)	(7,000)
Signboard leases (net)		8,400
Total assets	$415,000	$251,000
Liabilities and Stockholders' Equity		
Dividends payable		$ 9,000
Other current liabilities	$ 60,000	67,000
Common stock, no par or stated value	300,000	100,000
Retained earnings	55,000	75,000
Total liabilities and stockholders' equity	$415,000	$251,000

---

3. Stang declared a 9% cash dividend on December 20, 2003, payable January 16, 2004, to stockholders of record December 31, 2003. Ping carried its investment at cost and had not recorded Stang's dividend on December 31, 2003. Ping neither declared nor paid dividends during Year 2003.

Instructions

a. Prepare adjusting entries for Ping Corporation on December 31, 2003, to convert its accounting for Stang Company's operating results to the equity method of accounting. (Disregard income taxes.)

b. Prepare a working paper for consolidated financial statements of Ping Corporation and subsidiary on December 31, 2003, and the related working paper eliminations (in journal entry format). Amounts for Ping Corporation should reflect the adjusting entries prepared in *a*. (Disregard income taxes.)

(Problem 7.11) On June 30, 2003, Petal Corporation acquired for cash of $19 a share, including out-of-pocket costs, all the outstanding common stock of Sepal Company. Both companies continued to operate as separate entities. Petal adopted the equity method of accounting for Sepal's operating results.

Additional Information

1. On June 30, 2003, Sepal's balance sheet was as follows:

SEPAL COMPANY	
Balance Sheet (prior to business combination)	
June 30, 2003	
Assets	
Cash	$ 700,000
Trade accounts receivable (net)	600,000
Inventories	1,400,000
Plant assets (net)	3,300,000
Other assets	500,000
Total assets	$6,500,000
Liabilities and Stockholders' Equity	
Trade accounts payable and other current liabilities	$ 700,000
Long-term debt	2,600,000
Other liabilities	200,000
Common stock, $1 par	1,000,000
Additional paid-in capital	400,000
Retained earnings	1,600,000
Total liabilities and stockholders' equity	$6,500,000

2. On June 30, 2003, Sepal's assets and liabilities having current fair values that were different from carrying amounts were as follows:

	Current Fair Values
Plant assets (net)	$16,400,000
Other assets	200,000
Long-term debt	2,200,000

The differences between current fair values and carrying amounts resulted in a debit or credit to depreciation or amortization for the consolidated financial statements for the six-month period ended December 31, 2003, as follows:

Plant assets (net)	$500,000 debit
Other assets	10,000 credit
Long-term debt	5,000 debit
Total	$495,000 debit

3. The amount paid by Petal in excess of the current fair value of the identifiable net assets of Sepal was attributable to goodwill.

4. The Year 2003 net income (or net loss) for each company was as follows:

	Petal Corporation	Sepal Company
Jan. 1 to June 30, 2003	$ 250,000	$ (750,000)
July 1 to Dec. 31, 2003	1,070,000	1,250,000

The $1,070,000 net income of Petal included Petal's equity in the adjusted net income of Sepal for the six months ended December 31, 2003.

5. On December 31, 2003, the end of the fiscal year, the separate balance sheets for both companies were as follows:

PETAL CORPORATION AND SUBSIDIARY
Separate Balance Sheets (six months subsequent to business combination)
December 31, 2003

	Petal Corporation	Sepal Company
Assets		
Cash	$ 3,500,000	$ 625,000
Trade accounts receivable (net)	1,400,000	1,500,000
Inventories	1,000,000	2,500,000
Investment in Sepal Company common stock	19,755,000	
Plant assets (net)	2,000,000	3,100,000
Other assets	100,000	475,000
Total assets	$27,755,000	$8,200,000
Liabilities and Stockholders' Equity		
Trade accounts payable and other current liabilities	$ 1,500,000	$1,100,000
Long-term debt	4,000,000	2,600,000
Other liabilities	750,000	250,000
Common stock, $1 par	10,000,000	1,000,000
Additional paid-in capital	5,000,000	400,000
Retained earnings	6,505,000	2,850,000
Total liabilities and stockholders' equity	$27,755,000	$8,200,000

6. Consolidated goodwill was unimpaired as of December 31, 2003.

Instructions

Prepare a consolidated balance sheet for Petal Corporation and its wholly owned subsidiary, Sepal Company, on December 31, 2003. Do not use a working paper, but show supporting computations. (Disregard income taxes.)

Chapter Eight

Consolidated Financial Statements: Intercompany Transactions

Scope of Chapter

This chapter describes and illustrates the accounting and working paper eliminations for *related party transactions* between a parent company and its subsidiaries. One class of transactions does not include intercompany profits (gains) or losses; the other class does. The accounting techniques for such transactions are designed to ensure that consolidated financial statements include only those balances and transactions resulting from the *consolidated group's dealings with outsiders.* To this end, *separate ledger accounts should be established for all intercompany assets, liabilities, revenue, and expenses.* These separate accounts clearly identify the intercompany items that must be eliminated in the preparation of consolidated financial statements.

ACCOUNTING FOR INTERCOMPANY TRANSACTIONS NOT INVOLVING PROFIT (GAIN) OR LOSS

Intercompany transactions that do not include an intercompany profit or loss are loans on promissory notes or open account, leases of property under operating leases, and rendering of services.

Loans on Notes or Open Accounts

Parent companies generally have more extensive financial resources or bank lines of credit than do their subsidiaries. Also, it may be more economical in terms of favorable interest rates for the parent company to carry out all the affiliated group's borrowings from financial institutions. Under these circumstances, the parent company may make loans to its subsidiaries for their working capital or other needs. Generally, the rate of interest on such loans exceeds the parent company's borrowing rate.

To illustrate, assume that during the year ended December 31, 2004, Palm Corporation made the following cash loans to its wholly owned subsidiary, Starr Company, on promissory notes:

Loans by Parent Company to Wholly Owned Subsidiary

Date of Note	Term of Note, Months	Interest Rates, %	Amount
Feb. 1, 2004	6	10	$10,000
Apr. 1, 2004	6	10	15,000
Sept. 1, 2004	6	10	21,000
Nov. 1, 2004	6	10	24,000

To differentiate properly between intercompany loans and loans with outsiders, Palm Corporation and Starr Company would use the following ledger accounts to record the foregoing transactions (assuming all promissory notes were paid when due):

Ledger Accounts of Parent Company and Subsidiary for Intercompany Loan Transactions

PALM CORPORATION LEDGER
Intercompany Notes Receivable

2004		2004	
Feb. 1	10,000	Aug. 1	10,000
Apr. 1	15,000	Oct. 1	15,000
Sept. 1	21,000		
Nov. 1	24,000		

STARR COMPANY LEDGER
Intercompany Notes Payable

2004		2004	
Aug. 1	10,000	Feb. 1	10,000
Oct. 1	15,000	Apr. 1	15,000
		Sept. 1	21,000
		Nov. 1	24,000

Intercompany Interest Receivable

2004	
Dec. 31	1,100

Intercompany Interest Payable

	2004	
	Dec. 31	1,100

Intercompany Interest Revenue

	2004	
	Aug. 1	500
	Oct. 1	750
	Dec. 31	1,100

Intercompany Interest Expense

2004		
Aug. 1	500	
Oct. 1	750	
Dec. 31	1,100	

In the working paper for consolidated financial statements for Palm Corporation and subsidiary for the year ended December 31, 2004, the foregoing ledger accounts appear as shown below:

PALM CORPORATION AND SUBSIDIARY
Partial Working Paper for Consolidated Financial Statements
For Year Ended December 31, 2004

	Palm Corporation	Starr Company	Eliminations Increase (Decrease)	Consolidated
Income Statement				
Intercompany revenue (expenses)	2,350	(2,350)		
Balance Sheet				
Intercompany receivables (payables)	46,100*	(46,100)		

* $45,000 + $1,100 = $46,100.

It is apparent from the foregoing illustration that careful identification of intercompany ledger account balances in the accounting records of the affiliated companies is essential for correct elimination of the intercompany items in the working paper for consolidated financial statements.

Discounting of Intercompany Notes

If an intercompany note receivable is discounted at a bank by the payee, the note in effect is payable to an **outsider**—the discounting bank. Consequently, discounted intercompany notes are **not eliminated** in a working paper for consolidated financial statements.

Suppose, for example, that on December 1, 2004, Palm Corporation had discounted at a 12% discount rate the $24,000 note receivable from Starr Company. Palm would prepare the following journal entry:

Parent Company's Journal Entry for Discounting of Note Receivable from Subsidiary			
Cash ($25,200 − $1,260)		23,940	
Interest Expense ($1,260 discount − $1,000*)		260	
Intercompany Notes Receivable			24,000
Intercompany Interest Revenue ($24,000 × 0.10 × $\frac{1}{12}$)			200

To record discounting of 10%, six-month note receivable from Starr Company dated Nov. 1, 2004, at a discount rate of 12%. Cash proceeds are computed as follows:

Maturity value of note		
[$24,000 + ($24,000 × 0.10 × $\frac{6}{12}$)]	$25,200	
Less: Discount ($25,200 × 0.12 × $\frac{5}{12}$)	1,260	
Proceeds	$23,940	

* Interest on note that accrues to discounting bank during discount period.

The foregoing journal entry recognizes intercompany interest revenue for the one month the note was held by Palm. This approach is required because Starr recognizes in its accounting records one month of intercompany interest expense on the note.

To assure proper accountability for the $24,000 note, Palm should notify Starr of the discounting. Starr would then prepare the following journal entry on December 1, 2004:

Subsidiary Journal Entry for Parent Company's Discounting of Note Payable by Subsidiary to Parent Company			
Intercompany Notes Payable		24,000	
Intercompany Interest Expense		200	
Notes Payable			24,000
Interest Payable			200

To transfer 10%, six-month note payable to Palm Corporation dated Nov. 1, 2004, from intercompany notes to outsider notes. Action is necessary because Palm Corporation discounted the note on this date.

In the foregoing journal entry, Starr credited Interest Payable rather than Intercompany Interest Payable for the $200 accrued interest on the note. This approach is required because the discounting bank, not Palm, is now the payee for the total maturity value of the note.

Under the note discounting assumption, the ledger accounts related to intercompany notes would appear in the December 31, 2004, working paper for consolidated financial statements as follows:

PALM CORPORATION AND SUBSIDIARY
Partial Working Paper for Consolidated Financial Statements
For Year Ended December 31, 2004

	Palm Corporation	Starr Company	Eliminations Increase (Decrease)	Consolidated
Income Statement				
Intercompany revenue (expenses)	2,150*	(2,150)*		
Balance Sheet				
Intercompany receivables (payables)	21,700†	(21,700)†		

* $200 less than in illustration on page 334 because $24,000 discounted note earned interest for one month rather than two months.
† $21,000 note dated Sept. 1, 2004, plus $700 accrued interest.

Leases of Property under Operating Leases

If a parent company leases property to a subsidiary, or vice versa, it is essential that both affiliates use the same accounting principles for the lease. If the lease is an *operating lease,* the lessor affiliate recognizes the rental payments as intercompany rent revenue, and the lessee affiliate recognizes the payments as intercompany rent expense. (For a *sales-type/capital lease,*[1] the lessor affiliate recognizes a sale of the property, and the lessee affiliate accounts for the lease as an acquisition of the property. Accounting for a capital lease often involves intercompany profits or losses, which are discussed in a subsequent section of this chapter.)

To illustrate consolidation techniques for an intercompany *operating lease,* assume that Palm Corporation leased space for a sales office to Starr Company under a 10-year lease dated February 1, 2004. The lease required monthly rentals of $2,500 payable in advance the first day of each month beginning February 1, 2004.

In the income statement section of the working paper for consolidated financial statements for the year ended December 31, 2004, Palm's $27,500 ($2,500 × 11 = $27,500) intercompany rent revenue would be offset against Starr's intercompany rent expense in a manner similar to the offset of intercompany interest revenue and expense illustrated above. There would be no intercompany assets or liabilities to be offset in an operating lease for which rent is paid in advance at the beginning of each month.

Rendering of Services

One affiliate may render services to another, with resultant intercompany fee revenue and expenses. A common example is the *management fee* charged to subsidiaries by a parent company that is a holding company with no significant operations.

Management fees often are billed monthly by the parent company, computed as a percentage of the subsidiary's net sales, number of employees, total assets, or some other measure. No new consolidation problems are introduced by intercompany fee revenue and expenses. However, care must be taken to make certain that both the parent company and the subsidiary record the fee billings in the same accounting period.

Income Taxes Applicable to Intercompany Transactions

The intercompany revenue and expense transactions illustrated in this section do not include an element of intercompany profit (gain) or loss for the consolidated entity.

[1] The accounting for operating leases and capital leases is explained in intermediate accounting textbooks.

This is true because the revenue of one affiliate exactly offsets the expense of the other affiliate in the income statement section of the working paper for consolidated financial statements. Consequently, there are no income tax effects associated with the elimination of the intercompany revenue and expenses, whether the parent company and its subsidiaries file separate income tax returns or a consolidated income tax return.

Summary: Intercompany Transactions Not Involving Profit or Loss

The preceding sections have emphasized the necessity of clearly identifying intercompany ledger account balances in the accounting records of both the parent company and the subsidiary. This careful identification facilitates the elimination of intercompany items in the preparation of consolidated financial statements. Sometimes, the separate financial statements of a parent company and a subsidiary include differing amounts for intercompany items that should offset. Before preparation of the working paper for consolidated financial statements, journal entries should be prepared to correct intercompany balances or to bring such balances up to date.

ACCOUNTING FOR INTERCOMPANY TRANSACTIONS INVOLVING PROFIT (GAIN) OR LOSS

Many business transactions between a parent company and its subsidiaries involve a profit (gain) or loss. Among these transactions are intercompany sales of merchandise, intercompany sales of plant assets, intercompany leases of property under capital/sales-type leases, and intercompany sales of intangible assets. Until intercompany profits or losses in such transactions are *realized* through the sale of the asset to an *outsider* or otherwise, the *unrealized* profits or losses must be eliminated in the preparation of consolidated financial statements.

In addition, a parent or subsidiary company's acquisition of its affiliate's bonds *in the open market* may result in a *realized gain or loss to the consolidated entity.* Such a realized gain or loss is not recognized in the separate income statement of either the parent company or the subsidiary, but it must be recognized in the consolidated income statement.

The remainder of this chapter discusses and illustrates the working paper eliminations for intercompany transactions of the types described above. The focus is on intercompany transactions involving *profits (gains),* although such transactions also may involve losses.

Importance of Eliminating or Including Intercompany Profits (Gains) and Losses

The importance of eliminating *unrealized* intercompany profits (gains) and losses and recognizing *realized* gains or losses in the preparation of consolidated income statements cannot be overemphasized. Failure to eliminate *unrealized* profits and losses would result in consolidated income statements that report not only results of transactions with those outside the consolidated entity but also the results of *related party* activities within the affiliated group. Similarly, nonrecognition of *realized* gains and losses would misstate consolidated net income. The parent company's management would have free rein to manipulate consolidated net income ("manage earnings") if unrealized intercompany profits and losses were not eliminated in the preparation of consolidated income statements.

RCOMPANY SALES OF MERCHANDISE

Intercompany sales of merchandise are a natural outgrowth of **vertical** business combinations, which involve a combinor and one or more of its customers or suppliers as combinees. **Downstream** intercompany sales of merchandise are those from a parent company to its subsidiaries. **Upstream** intercompany sales are those from subsidiaries to the parent company. **Lateral** intercompany sales are between two subsidiaries of the same parent company.

The **intercompany sales** of merchandise between a parent company and its subsidiary are similar to the **intracompany shipments** of merchandise by a home office to a branch, described in Chapter 4.

Intercompany Sales of Merchandise at Cost

Intercompany sales of merchandise may be made at a price equal to the selling company's cost. If so, the working paper elimination is the same, whether all the goods were sold by the purchasing affiliate or whether some of the goods remained in the purchaser's inventories on the date of the consolidated financial statements. For example, assume that Palm Corporation (the parent company) during the year ended December 31, 2004, sold merchandise costing $150,000 to Starr Company (the subsidiary) at a selling price equal to the cost of the merchandise. Assume further that Starr's December 31, 2004, inventories included $25,000 of merchandise obtained from Palm and that Starr still owed Palm $15,000 for merchandise purchases on December 31, 2004. (Starr also had purchased merchandise from other suppliers during Year 2004.)

The two companies would prepare the following aggregate journal entries for the foregoing transactions, assuming that both companies used the perpetual inventory system:

Journal Entries for Parent Company's Downstream Sales of Merchandise to Subsidiary at Cost and Subsidiary's Sales of Merchandise to Outsiders

Palm Corporation Journal Entries			Starr Company Journal Entries		
Intercompany Accounts Receivable	150,000		Inventories	150,000	
Intercompany Sales		150,000	Intercompany Accounts Payable		150,000
To record sales to Starr Company.			To record purchases from Palm Corporation.		
Intercompany Cost of Goods Sold	150,000				
Inventories		150,000			
To record cost of goods sold to Starr Company.					
Cash	135,000		Intercompany Accounts Payable	135,000	
Intercompany Accounts Receivable		135,000	Cash		135,000
To record payments received from Starr Company.			To record payments made to Palm Corporation.		
			Trade Accounts Receivable	160,000	
			Sales		160,000
			To record sales.		
			Cost of Goods Sold	125,000	
			Inventories		125,000
			To record cost of goods sold.		

The working paper for consolidated financial statements for Palm Corporation and subsidiary for the year ended December 31, 2004, would include the following data with regard to intercompany sales of merchandise only:

Partial Working Paper for Consolidated Financial Statements—Intercompany Sales of Merchandise at Cost

PALM CORPORATION AND SUBSIDIARY Partial Working Paper for Consolidated Financial Statements For Year Ended December 31, 2004					
		Palm Corporation	**Starr Company**	**Eliminations Increase (Decrease)**	**Consolidated**
Income Statement Intercompany revenue (expenses)		*			
Balance Sheet Intercompany receivable (payable)		15,000	(15,000)		

* Palm Corporation's $150,000 intercompany sales and intercompany cost of goods sold are offset in Palm's separate income statement in the working paper.

Note that Starr Company's cost of goods sold for Year 2004 and inventories on December 31, 2004, are not affected by working paper eliminations. From a consolidated entity viewpoint, both Starr's cost of goods sold and Starr's inventories are stated at *cost;* no element of intercompany profit or loss is involved.

Unrealized Intercompany Profit in Ending Inventories

More typical than the intercompany sales of merchandise at cost described in the preceding section are intercompany sales involving a gross profit. The gross profit margin may be equal to, more than, or less than the margin on sales to outsiders. The selling affiliate's intercompany gross profit is *realized* through the purchasing affiliate's sales of the acquired merchandise to outsiders. Consequently, any merchandise purchased from an affiliated company that remains unsold on the date of a consolidated balance sheet results in the *overstatement* (from a *consolidated* point of view) of the purchaser's ending inventories. The overstatement is equal to the amount of the selling affiliate's *unrealized* intercompany gross profit included in the ending inventories. This overstatement is canceled through an appropriate working paper elimination in the preparation of consolidated financial statements.

Suppose, for example, that Sage Company (the 95%-owned subsidiary) during the year ended December 31, 2004, began selling merchandise to Post Corporation (the parent company) at a gross profit margin of 20%. Sales by Sage to Post for the year totaled $120,000, of which $40,000 remained unsold by Post on December 31, 2004. On that date, Post owed $30,000 to Sage for merchandise. Both companies used the perpetual inventory system.

The transactions described in the foregoing paragraph are recorded in summary form by the two companies as follows:

Journal Entries for Partially Owned Subsidiary's Upstream Sales of Merchandise to Parent Company at a Gross Profit and Parent's Sales of the Merchandise to Outsiders

Post Corporation Journal Entries			Sage Company Journal Entries		
Inventories	120,000		Intercompany Accounts Receivable	120,000	
Intercompany Accounts					
Payable		120,000	Intercompany Sales		120,000
To record purchases from Sage Company.			To record sales to Post Corporation.		
			Intercompany Cost of Goods Sold	96,000	
			Inventories		96,000
			To record cost of goods sold to Post Corporation.		
Intercompany Accounts Payable	90,000		Cash	90,000	
Cash		90,000	Intercompany Accounts Receivable		90,000
To record payments made to Sage Company.			To record payments received from Post Corporation.		
Trade Accounts Receivable	100,000				
Sales		100,000			
To record sales.					
Cost of Goods Sold	80,000				
Inventories		80,000			
To record cost of goods sold.					

The intercompany gross profit in Sage's sales to Post during the year ended December 31, 2004, is analyzed as follows:

Analysis of Gross Profit Margin in Partially Owned Subsidiary's Upstream Sales of Merchandise to Parent Company for First Year	Selling Price	Cost	Gross Profit (25% of Cost; 20% of Selling Price)
Beginning inventories			
Add: Sales	$120,000	$96,000	$24,000
Subtotals	$120,000	$96,000	$24,000
Less: Ending inventories	40,000	32,000	8,000
Cost of goods sold	$ 80,000	$64,000	$16,000

The foregoing analysis shows that the intercompany gross profit on sales by Sage to Post totaled $24,000, and that $16,000 of this intercompany profit was realized through Post's sales of the acquired merchandise to outside customers. The remaining $8,000 of intercompany profit remains **unrealized** in Post's inventories on December 31, 2004.

The following working paper elimination (in journal entry format) is required for Sage's intercompany sales of merchandise to Post for the year ended December 31, 2004:

Working Paper Elimination for First Year of Intercompany Sales of Merchandise at a Gross Profit Margin

POST CORPORATION AND SUBSIDIARY
Partial Working Paper Eliminations
December 31, 2004

(b) Intercompany Sales—Sage	120,000	
Intercompany Cost of Goods Sold—Sage		96,000
Cost of Goods Sold—Post		16,000
Inventories—Post		8,000
To eliminate intercompany sales, cost of goods sold, and unrealized intercompany profit in inventories. (Income tax effects are disregarded.)		

Handwritten margin notes:
Trans
120,000
−96000
24000
8000
————
16000
COGS overstated
8000

The effects of the foregoing elimination are as follows: First, it eliminates Sage's intercompany sales to Post and the related intercompany cost of goods sold; this avoids the overstatement of the **consolidated** amounts for sales and cost of goods sold, which should represent merchandise transactions with customers outside the consolidated entity. Second, the elimination removes the intercompany gross profit from Post's cost of goods sold, thus restating it to the cost of the **consolidated entity.** Finally, the elimination reduces the consolidated inventories to **actual cost** for the consolidated entity.

Entering the preceding elimination in the working paper for consolidated financial statements results in the consolidated amounts shown below (amounts for total sales to outsiders and cost of goods sold are assumed):

Partial Working Paper for Consolidated Financial Statements—First Year of Intercompany Sales of Merchandise at a Gross Profit

POST CORPORATION AND SUBSIDIARY
Partial Working Paper for Consolidated Financial Statements
For Year Ended December 31, 2004

	Post Corporation	Sage Company	Eliminations Increase (Decrease)	Consolidated
Income Statement				
Revenue:				
Sales	5,800,000	1,200,000		7,000,000
Intercompany sales		120,000	(b) (120,000)	
Costs and expenses:				
Cost of goods sold	4,100,000	760,000	(b) (16,000)	4,844,000
Intercompany cost of				
goods sold		96,000	(b) (96,000)	
Balance Sheet				
Assets				
Intercompany receivable				
(payable)	(30,000)	30,000		
Inventories	900,000	475,000	(b) (8,000)	1,367,000

Note that the $120,000 elimination of intercompany sales, less the $112,000 total ($16,000 + $96,000 = $112,000) of the two cost of goods sold eliminations, equals $8,000—the amount of the intercompany profit eliminated from inventories. This $8,000 unrealized intercompany profit is attributable to Sage Company—the **seller** of the merchandise—and **must be taken into account in the computation of the minor-**

Handwritten margin notes (right side): IF YOU DIDN'T DO THIS INTERCO WILL BE OVERSTATED COGS OVERSTATED / 24000 ARTIFICIAL WRITE UP / OVERSTATE CNP understate NI

ity interest in Sage's net income for the year ended December 31, 2004. The $8,000 also enters into the computation of Sage's portion of consolidated retained earnings on December 31, 2004. These procedures are illustrated in the following sections.

If the intercompany sales of merchandise are made by a *parent company* or by a *wholly owned subsidiary,* there is no effect on any minority interest in net income or loss, *because the selling affiliate does not have minority stockholders.* Thus, it is important to identify, by company name, the financial statement items that are affected by working paper eliminations for intercompany sales of merchandise, so that the minority interest in net income or loss of a partially owned subsidiary that makes upstream or lateral sales of merchandise at a gross profit may be computed correctly.

Intercompany Profit in Beginning and Ending Inventories

The working paper elimination for intercompany sales of merchandise is complicated by intercompany profits in the *beginning* inventories of the purchaser. It is generally assumed that, on a first-in, first-out basis, the intercompany profit in the purchaser's *beginning* inventories is realized through sales of the merchandise to outsiders during the ensuing accounting period. Only the intercompany profit in *ending* inventories remains unrealized at the end of the period.

Continuing the illustration from the preceding section, assume that Sage Company's intercompany sales of merchandise to Post Corporation during the year ended December 31, 2005, are:

Analysis of Gross Profit Margin in Partially Owned Subsidiary's Upstream Sales of Merchandise to Parent Company for Second Year

	Selling Price	Cost	Gross Profit (25% of Cost; 20% of Selling Price)
Beginning inventories	$ 40,000	$ 32,000	$ 8,000
Add: Sales	150,000	120,000	30,000
Subtotals	$190,000	$152,000	$38,000
Less: Ending inventories	60,000	48,000	12,000
Cost of goods sold	$130,000	$104,000	$26,000

Sage's intercompany sales and intercompany cost of goods sold for the year ended December 31, 2004, had been closed with other income statement amounts to Sage's Retained Earnings ledger account. Consequently, from a *consolidated* point of view, Sage's December 31, 2004, retained earnings was overstated by $7,600 (95% of the $8,000 unrealized intercompany profit in Post's inventories on December 31, 2004). The remaining $400 of unrealized profit on December 31, 2004, is attributable to the minority interest in net assets of Sage Company, the *seller* of the merchandise. The following working paper elimination (in journal entry format) on December 31, 2005, reflects these facts:

Working Paper Elimination for Second Year of Intercompany Sales of Merchandise at a Gross Profit Margin

POST CORPORATION AND SUBSIDIARY		
Partial Working Paper Eliminations		
December 31, 2005		
(b) Retained Earnings—Sage ($8,000 $\times$ 0.95)*	7,600	
Minority Interest in Net Assets of Subsidiary ($8,000 $\times$ 0.05)	400	
Intercompany Sales—Sage	150,000	
Intercompany Cost of Goods Sold—Sage		120,000
Cost of Goods Sold—Post		26,000
Inventories—Post		12,000
To eliminate intercompany sales, cost of goods sold, and unrealized intercompany profits in inventories. (Income tax effects are disregarded.)		

* As indicated in Chapter 7 (page 278), this elimination is posted to the **beginning-of-year** retained earnings in the statement of retained earnings section of the working paper for consolidated financial statements.

Intercompany Profit in Inventories and Amount of Minority Interest

Accountants have given considerable thought to intercompany profits in purchases and sales transactions of partially owned subsidiaries. There is general agreement that all the unrealized intercompany profit in a partially owned subsidiary's ending inventories should be eliminated for consolidated financial statements. *This holds true whether the sales to the subsidiary are downstream from the parent company or are made by a wholly owned subsidiary of the same parent.*

There has been no such agreement on the treatment of intercompany profit in the parent company's or a subsidiary's inventories from upstream or lateral sales by a partially owned subsidiary. Two alternative approaches have been suggested.

1. The first approach is elimination of intercompany profit *only to the extent of the parent company's ownership interest* in the selling subsidiary's common stock. This approach is based on the *parent company concept* of consolidated financial statements (see Chapter 6, pages 236 and 237), in which the minority interest is considered to be a *liability* of the consolidated entity. If the minority stockholders are considered *outside creditors,* intercompany profit in the parent company's ending inventories has been *realized* to the extent of the minority stockholders' interest in the selling subsidiary.

2. The second approach is elimination of *all the intercompany profit.* The *economic unit concept* of consolidated financial statements (see Chapter 6, pages 237 and 238), in which the minority interest is considered to be a *part of consolidated stockholders' equity,* underlies this approach. If minority stockholders are *part owners* of consolidated assets, their share of intercompany profits in inventories has not been realized.

The FASB expressed a preference for the second approach, in the following passage:

> The effects on equity of eliminating intercompany profits and losses on assets that remain within the group shall be allocated between the controlling interest and the non-controlling interest on the basis of their proportionate interests in the selling affiliate.[2]

[2] *Proposed Statement of Financial Accounting Standards,* "Consolidated Financial Statements: Policy and Procedures" (Norwalk: FASB, 1995), par. 19.

Consequently, intercompany profits or losses in inventories resulting from **upstream or lateral sales of merchandise by a partially owned subsidiary** must be considered in the computation of the minority interest in net income of the subsidiary, and in the computation of the portion of retained earnings of the subsidiary to be included in consolidated retained earnings. The subsidiary's net income must be **increased** by the **realized** intercompany profit in the purchasing affiliate's **beginning** inventories and **decreased** by the **unrealized** intercompany profit in the purchasing affiliate's **ending** inventories. Failure to do so would attribute the entire intercompany profit effects to the **consolidated** net income. (See page 365 for an illustration of the computation of minority interest in net income of a partially owned subsidiary that makes intercompany sales of merchandise.)

Should Net Profit or Gross Profit Be Eliminated?

Some accountants have discussed the propriety of eliminating intercompany **net profit,** rather than **gross profit,** in inventories of the consolidated entity. There is little theoretical support for such a proposal. First, elimination of intercompany net profit would in effect capitalize operating (selling and administrative) expenses in consolidated inventories. Selling expenses are always period costs, and only in unusual circumstances are some administrative expenses capitalized in inventories as product costs. Second, the measurement of net profit for particular merchandise requires many assumptions as to allocations of common costs.

INTERCOMPANY SALES OF PLANT ASSETS

Intercompany sales of plant assets differ from intercompany sales of merchandise in two respects. First, intercompany sales of plant assets between affiliated companies are rare transactions. In contrast, intercompany sales of merchandise occur frequently, once a program of such sales has been established. Second, the relatively long economic lives of plant assets require the passage of many accounting periods before intercompany gains or losses on sales of these assets are realized in transactions with outsiders. Conversely, intercompany profits in consolidated inventories at the end of one accounting period usually are realized through sale of the merchandise to outsiders during the ensuing period. These differences are illustrated in the working paper elimination for intercompany gains or losses on sales of plant assets described in the following sections.

Intercompany Gain on Sale of Land

Journal Entries for Parent Company's Downstream Sale of Land to Partially Owned Subsidiary

Suppose that, during the year ended December 31, 2004, Post Corporation (the parent company) sold to Sage Company (the partially owned subsidiary) for $175,000 a parcel of land that had cost Post $125,000. Sage acquired the land for a new building site. The two companies would record the transaction as follows (disregarding income tax effects to Post Corporation):

Post Corporation Journal Entry			Sage Company Journal Entry		
Cash	175,000		Land	175,000	
Land		125,000	Cash		175,000
Intercompany			To record acquisition of land		
Gain on Sale of Land		50,000	from Post Corporation.		
To record sale of land to Sage					
Company.					

In consolidated financial statements for the year ended December 31, 2004, the land must be valued at its historical cost to the consolidated entity. Also, the $50,000 intercompany gain must be eliminated, because it has not been ***realized*** in a transaction with an outsider. Accordingly, the following working paper elimination (in journal entry format) is required on December 31, 2004:

Working Paper Elimination for Year of Intercompany Sale of Land at a Gain

POST CORPORATION AND SUBSIDIARY
Partial Working Paper Eliminations
December 31, 2004

(c) Intercompany Gain on Sale of Land—Post	50,000	
Land—Sage		50,000
To eliminate unrealized intercompany gain on sale of land. (Income tax effects are disregarded.)		

The working paper elimination is entered as follows in the working paper for consolidated financial statements for the year ended December 31, 2004:

Partial Working Paper for Consolidated Financial Statements—Year of Intercompany Sale of Land at a Gain

POST CORPORATION AND SUBSIDIARY
Partial Working Paper for Consolidated Financial Statements
For Year Ended December 31, 2004

	Post Corporation	Sage Company	Elimination Increase (Decrease)	Consolidated
Income Statement Intercompany gain on sale of land	50,000		(c) (50,000)	
Balance Sheet Land (for building site)		175,000	(c) (50,000)	125,000

Because land is not a depreciable plant asset, in subsequent years no journal entries affecting the land would be made by Sage unless the land were resold to an outsider (or back to Post). Nevertheless, in ensuing years, as long as Sage owns the land, its $175,000 cost to Sage is overstated $50,000 for consolidated financial statement purposes. Because the gain of $50,000 on the sale of land was closed with other income statement amounts to Post's Retained Earnings ledger account on December 31, 2004, the following working paper elimination (in journal entry format) is required for Year 2005 and subsequent years:

Working Paper Elimination for Years Subsequent to Intercompany Sale of Land at a Gain

POST CORPORATION AND SUBSIDIARY
Partial Working Paper Eliminations
December 31, 2005

(c) Retained Earnings—Post	50,000	
Land—Sage		50,000
To eliminate unrealized intercompany gain in land. (Income tax effects are disregarded.)		

The foregoing working paper elimination has no effect on the minority interest in the net income or net assets of the subsidiary, because *the unrealized gain was attributable entirely to the parent company, the seller.*

Suppose that, instead of constructing a building on the land, Sage sold the land to an outsider for $200,000 during the year ended December 31, 2006. Sage would prepare the following journal entry to record the sale:

Subsidiary's Journal Entry for Sale of Land to an Outsider

Cash	200,000	
Land		175,000
Gain on Sale of Land		25,000
To record sale of land to an outsider.		

The consolidated income statement for the year ended December 31, 2006, must show that, for *consolidated* purposes, a *$75,000 gain was realized* on Sage's sale of the land. This $75,000 gain consists of the $25,000 gain recognized by Sage and the $50,000 intercompany gain on Post's sale of the land to Sage two years earlier. The following working paper elimination (in journal entry format) is required on December 31, 2006:

Working Paper Elimination to Recognize Realization of Intercompany Gain on Sale of Land

POST CORPORATION AND SUBSIDIARY
Partial Working Paper Eliminations
December 31, 2006

(c) Retained Earnings—Post	50,000	
Gain on Sale of Land—Post		50,000
To recognize $50,000 gain on Post Corporation's sale of land to Sage Company resulting from sale of land by Sage to an outsider. (Income tax effects are disregarded.)		

No further eliminations with respect to the land would be required after 2006.

Intercompany Gain on Sale of Depreciable Plant Asset

Periodic depreciation expense causes a significant difference in the working paper eliminations for an unrealized intercompany gain on the sale of a depreciable plant asset, compared with the eliminations described in the preceding section. Because the unrealized intercompany gain must be eliminated from the valuation of the depreciable asset in a consolidated balance sheet, the appropriate gain element also must be eliminated from the related depreciation expense in a consolidated income statement. This concept is illustrated in the following pages.

Intercompany Gain on Date of Sale of Depreciable Plant Asset

The date-of-sale working paper elimination for the intercompany sale of a depreciable plant asset is identical to the comparable elimination for land. On the date of sale, no depreciation expense has been recognized by the affiliate that acquired the plant asset.

To illustrate, assume that on December 31, 2004, Sage Company (the partially owned subsidiary) sold machinery to Post Corporation (the parent company). Details of the sale and depreciation policy of the machinery are as follows:

Details of Machinery Sold Upstream to Parent Company by Partially Owned Subsidiary		
Selling price of machinery to Post Corporation		$60,000
Cost of machinery to Sage Company when acquired Jan. 2, 2002		50,000
Estimated residual value:		
To Sage Company, Jan. 2, 2002		$ 4,000
To Post Corporation, Dec. 31, 2004		4,000
Economic life:		
To Sage Company, Jan. 2, 2002		10 years
To Post Corporation, Dec. 31, 2004		5 years
Annual depreciation expense (straight-line method):		
To Sage Company ($46,000 × 0.10)		$ 4,600
To Post Corporation ($56,000 × 0.20)		11,200

The two companies would account for the sale on December 31, 2004, as follows:

Journal Entries for Partially Owned Subsidiary's Upstream Sale of Machinery to Parent Company

Post Corporation Journal Entry			Sage Company Journal Entry		
Machinery	60,000		Cash	60,000	
Cash		60,000	Accumulated		
To record acquisition			Depreciation		
of machinery from			($4,600 × 3)	13,800	
Sage Company.			Machinery		50,000
			Intercompany		
			Gain on Sale		
			of Machinery		23,800
			To record sale of		
			machinery to Post		
			Corporation.		

The following working paper elimination (in journal entry format) is required for consolidated financial statements on December 31, 2004, the date of intercompany sale of the machinery:

Working Paper Elimination on Date of Intercompany Sale of Machinery at a Gain

POST CORPORATION AND SUBSIDIARY		
Partial Working Paper Eliminations		
December 31, 2004		
(d) Intercompany Gain on Sale of Machinery—Sage	23,800	
Machinery—Post		23,800
To eliminate unrealized intercompany gain on sale of machinery.		
(Income tax effects are disregarded.)		

The elimination results in the machinery's being valued in the consolidated balance sheet at its carrying amount to Sage Company—the seller—as follows:

Effect of Elimination of Unrealized Intercompany Profit on Upstream Sale of Machinery

Cost of machinery to Post Corporation (acquirer parent company)	$60,000
Less: Amount of elimination—intercompany gain	23,800
Difference—equal to carrying amount [cost ($50,000), less accumulated depreciation ($13,800)] of machinery to Sage Company (seller subsidiary)	$36,200

Elimination of the $23,800 intercompany gain on the sale of machinery *is taken into account in the computation of the minority interest in the net income of the par-*

*tially owned subsidiary—the seller—*for Year 2004. The $23,800 elimination also enters into the computation of *Sage's retained earnings,* for consolidation purposes, on December 31, 2004. These matters are also illustrated on pages 364 to 365.

Intercompany Gain Subsequent to Date of Sale of Depreciable Plant Asset

An appropriate intercompany gain element must be eliminated from depreciation expense for a plant asset acquired by one affiliate from another at a gain. The following working paper elimination (in journal entry format) for Post Corporation and subsidiary on December 31, 2005 (one year after the intercompany sale of machinery), illustrates this point:

Working Paper Elimination for First Year Subsequent to Intercompany Sale of Machinery at a Gain

POST CORPORATION AND SUBSIDIARY
Partial Working Paper Eliminations
December 31, 2005

(d) Retained Earnings—Sage ($23,800 × 0.95)	22,610	
Minority Interest in Net Assets of Subsidiary ($23,800 × 0.05)	1,190	
Accumulated Depreciation—Post	4,760	
Machinery—Post		23,800
Depreciation Expense—Post		4,760

To eliminate unrealized intercompany gain in machinery and in related depreciation. (Income tax effects are disregarded.) Gain element in straight-line depreciation computed as $23,800 × 0.20 = $4,760, based on five-year economic life.

Because Sage Company's intercompany gain on sale of the machinery was closed to Sage's Retained Earnings ledger account on December 31, 2004, the working paper elimination on December 31, 2005, corrects the overstatement of Sage's *beginning-of-year* retained earnings from the viewpoint of the consolidated entity. In addition, the minority interest's share of the overstatement in the beginning retained earnings of Sage is recorded.

The intercompany gain eliminated from Post Corporation's depreciation expense may be verified as follows:

Verification of Intercompany Gain Element in Depreciation Expense of Parent Company

Post's annual straight-line depreciation expense [($60,000 − $4,000) × 0.20]	$11,200
Less: Straight-line depreciation expense for a five-year economic life, based on Sage's carrying amount on date of sale [($36,200 − $4,000) × 0.20]	6,440
Difference—equal to intercompany gain element in Post's annual depreciation expense	$ 4,760

Intercompany Gain in Depreciation and Minority Interest

From the point of view of the consolidated entity, the intercompany gain element of the acquiring affiliate's annual depreciation expense represents a *realization* of a portion of the total intercompany gain by the selling affiliate. Depreciation, in this view, is in effect an *indirect sale* of a portion of the machinery to the customers of Post Corporation—the acquirer of the machinery. The selling prices of Post's products produced by the machinery are established at amounts adequate to cover all costs of producing the products, including depreciation expense.

Thus, the $4,760 credit to Post's depreciation expense in the December 31, 2005, working paper elimination illustrated above in effect *increases* Sage's net income for consolidated purposes. *This increase must be considered in the computation of the minority interest in the subsidiary's net income* for the year ended December 31, 2005, *and of the amount of the subsidiary's retained earnings included in consolidated retained earnings on that date,* as illustrated on page 371.

Intercompany Gain in Later Years

Working paper eliminations for later years in the economic life of the machinery sold at an intercompany gain must reflect the fact that the intercompany gain element in the *acquiring affiliate's* annual depreciation expense in effect represents a *realization* of a portion of the total intercompany gain by the *selling affiliate.* For example, the working paper elimination (in journal entry format) for Post Corporation and subsidiary on December 31, 2006 (two years following the intercompany sale of the machinery), is as follows:

<table>
<tr><td style="background:black;color:white;text-align:center">

POST CORPORATION AND SUBSIDIARY
Partial Working Paper Eliminations
December 31, 2006
</td><td></td><td></td></tr>
<tr><td>(d) Retained Earnings—Sage [($23,800 − $4,760) × 0.95]</td><td>18,088</td><td></td></tr>
<tr><td>Minority Interest in Net Assets of Subsidiary
[($23,800 − $4,760) × 0.05]</td><td>952</td><td></td></tr>
<tr><td>Accumulated Depreciation—Post ($4,760 × 2)</td><td>9,520</td><td></td></tr>
<tr><td>Machinery—Post</td><td></td><td>23,800</td></tr>
<tr><td>Depreciation Expense—Post</td><td></td><td>4,760</td></tr>
<tr><td>To eliminate unrealized intercompany gain in machinery and related depreciation. (Income tax effects are disregarded.)</td><td></td><td></td></tr>
</table>

(Margin note:) **Working Paper Elimination for Second Year Subsequent to Intercompany Sale of Machinery at a Gain**

The credit amounts of the foregoing elimination for Year 2006 are the same as those for Year 2005. The credit amounts will remain unchanged for all working paper eliminations during the remaining economic life of the machinery, because of the parent company's use of the straight-line method of depreciation. The $19,040 total ($18,088 + $952 = $19,040) of the debits to Sage's retained earnings and to the minority interest in net assets of subsidiary represents the *unrealized* portion of the total intercompany gain *at the beginning of Year 2006.* Each succeeding year, the unrealized portion of the total intercompany gain *decreases,* as indicated by the following summary of the working paper elimination *debits* for those years:

(Margin note:) **Debit Elements of Working Paper Eliminations for Third, Fourth, and Fifth Years Subsequent to Intercompany Sale of Machinery at a Gain**

POST CORPORATION AND SUBSIDIARY **Partial Working Paper Eliminations—Debits Only** **December 31, 2007 through 2009**			
		Year Ended Dec. 31,	
	2007	**2008**	**2009**
Debits			
(d) Retained earnings—Sage	$13,566	$ 9,044	$ 4,522
Minority interest in net assets of subsidiary	714	476	238
Accumulated depreciation—Post	14,280	19,040	23,800

At the end of Year 2009, the entire $23,800 of intercompany gain has been realized through Post Corporation's annual depreciation expense. Thereafter, the working paper elimination below (in journal entry format) is required for the machinery until it is sold or scrapped:

POST CORPORATION AND SUBSIDIARY		
Partial Working Paper Eliminations		
December 31, 2010		
Accumulated Depreciation—Post	23,800	
Machinery—Post		23,800
To eliminate intercompany gain in machinery and related accumulated depreciation. (Income tax effects are disregarded.)		

INTERCOMPANY LEASE OF PROPERTY UNDER CAPITAL/SALES-TYPE LEASE

Land and buildings, machinery and equipment, and other property may be transferred from one affiliate to another under a lease that is a *sales-type lease* to the lessor and a *capital lease* to the lessee.[3] If so, a number of intercompany ledger accounts must be established by both the lessor and the lessee to account for the lease.

To illustrate, assume that on January 2, 2004, Palm Corporation (the parent company) leased equipment carried in its inventory to Starr Company (the wholly owned subsidiary) under a sales-type lease requiring Starr to pay Palm $10,000 on each January 2, 2004 through 2007, with a bargain purchase option of $1,000 payable on January 2, 2008. Palm's implicit interest rate, which was known to Starr and was less than Starr's incremental borrowing rate, was 8%. The economic life of the equipment to Starr was six years, with no residual value. The cost of the leased equipment, which had been carried in Palm's Inventories ledger account, was $30,000, and there were no initial direct costs under the lease.

The present value of the minimum lease payments, which constitutes Palm's *net investment in the lease,* is computed as follows (using a calculator or present value tables):

Present value of $10,000 each year for four years at	
8% ($10,000 × 3.577097)	$35,771
Present value of $1,000 in four years at 8% ($1,000 × 0.735030)	735
Palm Corporation's net investment in the lease	$36,506

The journal entries of Palm Corporation and Starr Company for Year 2004, the first year of the lease, are on page 351, and selected ledger accounts for both companies relative to the lease are shown on pages 352 through 354.

---

[3] Accounting for leases is discussed and illustrated in intermediate accounting textbooks.

PALM CORPORATION
Journal Entries

2004			
Jan. 2	Intercompany Lease Receivables	41,000	
	[($10,000 × 4) + $1,000]		
	Intercompany Cost of Goods Sold	30,000	
	Intercompany Sales		36,506
	Unearned Intercompany Interest Revenue		4,494
	($41,000 − $36,506)		
	Inventories		30,000
	To record sales-type lease with Starr Company at inception and cost of leased equipment.		
2	Cash	10,000	
	Intercompany Lease Receivables		10,000
	To record receipt of first payment on intercompany lease.		
Dec. 31	Unearned Intercompany Interest Revenue	2,120	
	[($31,000 − $4,494) × 0.08]		
	Intercompany Interest Revenue		2,120
	To recognize interest earned for first year of intercompany sales-type lease.		

Subsidiary's (Lessee's) Journal
Entries for First Year of
Intercompany Capital Lease

STARR COMPANY
Journal Entries

2004			
Jan. 2	Leased Equipment—Capital Lease	36,506	
	Intercompany Liability under Capital Lease (net)		36,506
	To record intercompany capital lease at inception.		
2	Intercompany Liability under Capital Lease (net)	10,000	
	Cash		10,000
	To record lease payment for first year of intercompany lease.		
Dec. 31	Intercompany Interest Expense	2,120	
	[($36,506 − $10,000) × 0.08]		
	Intercompany Interest Payable		2,120
	To record accrued interest on intercompany lease obligation on Dec. 31, 2004.		
31	Depreciation Expense ($36,506 ÷ 6)	6,084	
	Leased Equipment—Capital Lease		6,084
	To record depreciation expense (straight-line method) for first year of intercompany lease. (Six-year economic life of leased equipment is used because lease contains a bargain purchase option.)		

PALM CORPORATION
Ledger Accounts

Intercompany Lease Receivables

Date	Explanation	Debit	Credit	Balance
2004				
Jan. 2	Inception of lease	41,000		41,000 dr
2	Receipt of first payment		10,000	31,000 dr
2005				
Jan. 2	Receipt of second payment		10,000	21,000 dr
2006				
Jan. 2	Receipt of third payment		10,000	11,000 dr
2007				
Jan. 2	Receipt of fourth payment		10,000	1,000 dr
2008				
Jan. 2	Receipt of purchase option		1,000	-0-

Unearned Intercompany Interest Revenue

Date	Explanation	Debit	Credit	Balance
2004				
Jan. 2	Inception of lease ($41,000 − $36,506)		4,494	4,494 cr
Dec. 31	Interest for year [($31,000 − $4,494) × 0.08]	2,120		2,374 cr
2005				
Dec. 31	Interest for year [($21,000 − $2,374) × 0.08]	1,490		884 cr
2006				
Dec. 31	Interest for year [($11,000 − $884) × 0.08]	809		75 cr
2007				
Dec. 31	Interest for year [($1,000 − $75) × 0.08]	75*		-0-

* Adjusted $1 for rounding.

Intercompany Interest Revenue

Date	Explanation	Debit	Credit	Balance
2004				
Dec. 31	Interest for Year 2004		2,120	2,120 cr
31	Closing entry	2,120		-0-
2005				
Dec. 31	Interest for Year 2005		1,490	1,490 cr
31	Closing entry	1,490		-0-
2006				
Dec. 31	Interest for Year 2006		809	809 cr
31	Closing entry	809		-0-
2007				
Dec. 31	Interest for Year 2007		75*	75 cr
31	Closing entry	75		-0-

* Adjusted $1 for rounding.

STARR COMPANY
Ledger Accounts

Leased Equipment—Capital Lease

Date	Explanation	Debit	Credit	Balance
2004				
Jan. 2	Capital lease at inception	36,506		36,506 dr
Dec. 31	Depreciation for Year 2004		6,084	30,422 dr
2005				
Dec. 31	Depreciation for Year 2005		6,084	24,338 dr
2006				
Dec. 31	Depreciation for Year 2006		6,084	18,254 dr
2007				
Dec. 31	Depreciation for Year 2007		6,084	12,170 dr
2008				
Dec. 31	Depreciation for Year 2008		6,085*	6,085 dr
2009				
Dec. 31	Depreciation for Year 2009		6,085*	-0-

* Adjusted $1 for rounding.

Intercompany Liability under Capital Lease

Date	Explanation	Debit	Credit	Balance
2004				
Jan. 2	Capital lease at inception		36,506	36,506 cr
2	First lease payment	10,000		26,506 cr
2005				
Jan. 2	($10,000 − $2,120 interest)	7,880		18,626 cr
2006				
Jan. 2	($10,000 − $1,490 interest)	8,510		10,116 cr
2007				
Jan. 2	($10,000 − $809 interest)	9,191		925 cr
2008				
Jan. 2	($1,000 − $75 interest)	925		-0-

Intercompany Interest Expense

Date	Explanation	Debit	Credit	Balance
2004				
Dec. 31	($26,506 × 0.08)	2,120		2,120 dr
31	Closing entry		2,120	-0-
2005				
Dec. 31	($18,626 × 0.08)	1,490		1,490 dr
31	Closing entry		1,490	-0-
2006				
Dec. 31	($10,116 × 0.08)	809		809 dr
31	Closing entry		809	-0-
2007				
Dec. 31	($925 × 0.08)	75*		75 dr
31	Closing entry		75	-0-

* Adjusted $1 for rounding.

Depreciation Expense

Date	Explanation	Debit	Credit	Balance
2004				
Dec. 31	($36,506 ÷ 6)	6,084		6,084 dr
31	Closing entry		6,084	-0-
2005				
Dec. 31	($36,506 ÷ 6)	6,084		6,084 dr
31	Closing entry		6,084	-0-
2006				
Dec. 31	($36,506 ÷ 6)	6,084		6,084 dr
31	Closing entry		6,084	-0-
2007				
Dec. 31	($36,506 ÷ 6)	6,084		6,084 dr
31	Closing entry		6,084	-0-
2008				
Dec. 31	($36,506 ÷ 6)	6,085*		6,085 dr
31	Closing entry		6,085	-0-
2009				
Dec. 31	($36,506 ÷ 6)	6,085*		6,085 dr
31	Closing entry		6,085	-0-

* Adjusted $1 for rounding.

Working paper eliminations (in journal entry format) for Palm Corporation and subsidiary for the first two years of the intercompany lease are as follows (intercompany interest revenue and intercompany interest expense self-eliminate on the same line of the income statement section of the working paper for consolidated fianncial statements):

Working Paper Elimination for First Year of Intercompany Sales-Type/Capital Lease

PALM CORPORATION AND SUBSIDIARY
Partial Working Paper Eliminations
December 31, 2004

(b) Intercompany Liability under Capital Lease—Starr	26,506	
Intercompany Interest Payable—Starr	2,120	
Unearned Intercompany Interest Revenue—Palm	2,374	
Intercompany Sales—Palm	36,506	
Intercompany Cost of Goods Sold—Palm		30,000
Intercompany Lease Receivables—Palm		31,000
Leased Equipment—Capital Lease—Starr ($36,506 − $30,000 − $1,084)		5,422
Depreciation Expense—Starr [($36,506 − $30,000) ÷ 6]		1,084

To eliminate intercompany accounts associated with intercompany lease and to defer unrealized portion of intercompany gross profit on sales-type lease. (Income tax effects are disregarded.)

PALM CORPORATION AND SUBSIDIARY
Partial Working Paper Eliminations
December 31, 2005

(b) Intercompany Liability under Capital Lease—Starr	18,626	
Intercompany Interest Payable—Starr	1,490	
Unearned Intercompany Interest Revenue—Palm	884	
Retained Earnings—Palm [($36,506 − $30,000) − $1,084]	5,422	
Intercompany Lease Receivables—Palm		21,000
Leased Equipment—Capital Lease—Starr ($5,422 − $1,084)		4,338
Depreciation Expense—Starr		1,084
To eliminate intercompany accounts associated with intercompany lease and to defer unrealized portion of intercompany gross profit on sales-type lease. (Income tax effects are disregarded.)		

The foregoing eliminations have features comparable with both eliminations for intercompany sales of merchandise (page 343) and eliminations for intercompany sales of plant assets (page 349). For example, the elimination of December 31, 2004, removes the parent company's intercompany sales ($36,506) and cost of goods sold ($30,000), because the leased equipment had been carried in the parent's Inventories ledger account and the sales-type lease (from the parent's viewpoint) occurred during Year 2004. The subsidiary's (lessee's) depreciation expense of $1,084 for Year 2004 represents the realization of a portion of the parent's gross profit margin on the intercompany sale. In the Year 2005 elimination, the original $6,506 ($36.506 − $30.000 = $6,506) unrealized gross profit element in the subsidiary's leased equipment has been reduced by the $1,084 reduction of the subsidiary's Year 2004 depreciation expense.

INTERCOMPANY SALES OF INTANGIBLE ASSETS

The working paper eliminations for intercompany gains on sales of intangible assets are similar to those for intercompany gains in depreciable plant assets, except that no accumulated amortization ledger account may be involved. The unrealized intercompany gain of the selling affiliate is realized through periodic amortization expense recognized by the acquiring affiliate.

To illustrate, assume that on January 2, 2005, Palm Corporation sold to Starr Company, its wholly owned subsidiary, for $40,000 a patent carried in Palm's accounting records at $32,000. The patent had a remaining economic life of four years on January 2, 2005, and was amortized by the straight-line method. The appropriate working paper elimination (in journal entry format) on December 31, 2005, follows:

PALM CORPORATION AND SUBSIDIARY
Partial Working Paper Eliminations
December 31, 2005

(c) Intercompany Gain on Sale of Patent—Palm ($40,000 − $32,000)	8,000	
Amortization Expense—Starr ($8,000 ÷ 4)		2,000
Patent—Starr ($8,000 − $2,000)		6,000
To eliminate unrealized intercompany gain in patent and related amortization. (Income tax effects are disregarded.)		

The working paper elimination (in journal entry format) for December 31, 2006, is as follows:

PALM CORPORATION AND SUBSIDIARY **Partial Working Paper Eliminations** **December 31, 2006**		
(c) Retained Earnings—Palm ($8,000 − $2,000)	6,000	
Amortization Expense—Starr ($8,000 ÷ 4)		2,000
Patent—Starr ($6,000 − $2,000)		4,000
To eliminate unrealized intercompany gain in patent and related amortization. (Income tax effects are disregarded.)		

ACQUISITION OF AFFILIATE'S BONDS

The intercompany profits (gains) or losses on intercompany sales of merchandise, plant assets, and intangible assets and on leases of property under capital/sales-type leases are, on the date of sale, *unrealized* gains or losses resulting from business transactions between two affiliated corporations. Intercompany gains and losses may be *realized by the consolidated entity* when one affiliate acquires, *in the open market,* outstanding bonds of another affiliate. The gain or loss on such a transaction is *imputed,* because the transaction is not consummated between the two affiliates. No realized or unrealized intercompany gain or loss would result from the *direct* acquisition of one affiliate's bonds by another affiliate, because the cost of the investment to the acquirer would be *exactly offset* by the proceeds of the debt to the issuer.

Illustration of Acquisition of Affiliate's Bonds

Assume that on January 2, 2004, Sage Company (the partially owned subsidiary) issued to the public $500,000 face amount of 10% bonds due January 1, 2009. The bonds were issued at a price to yield a 12% return to investors. Interest was payable annually on January 1. Bond issue costs are disregarded in this example.

The net proceeds of the bond issue to Sage were $463,952, computed as follows:[4]

Present value of $500,000 in five years at 12%, with interest paid annually ($500,000 × 0.567427)	$283,713
Add: Present value of $50,000 each year for five years at 12% ($50,000 × 3.604776)	180,239
Proceeds of bond issue	$463,952

During the year ended December 31, 2004, Sage prepared the following journal entries for the bonds, including the amortization of bond discount by the *interest method:*

---

[4] Intermediate accounting textbooks generally contain a discussion of computations of bond issuance proceeds using calculators or present value tables. (*Annual* interest payments are assumed to simplify the illustration; bonds typically pay interest *semiannually.*)

Partially Owned Subsidiary's Journal Entries for Issuance of Bonds Payable and Accrual of Interest	**2004**		
	Jan. 2 Cash	463,952	
	Discount on Bonds Payable	36,048	
	Bonds Payable		500,000
	To record issuance of 10% bonds due Jan. 1, 2009, at a discount to yield 12%.		
	Dec. 31 Interest Expense ($463,952 × 0.12)	55,674	
	Interest Payable ($500,000 × 0.10)		50,000
	Discount on Bonds Payable		5,674
	To record accrual of annual interest on 10% bonds.		

On December 31, 2004, the balance of Sage's Discount on Bonds Payable ledger account was $30,374 ($36,048 − $5,674 = $30,374).

Assume that on December 31, 2004, Post Corporation (the parent company) had cash available for investment. With a market yield rate of 15% on that date, Sage Company's 10% bonds might be acquired at a substantial discount. Consequently, Post acquired in the open market on December 31, 2004, $300,000 face amount (or 60% of the total issue of $500,000) of the bonds for $257,175 plus $30,000 accrued interest for one year ($300,000 × 0.10 = $30,000). The $257,175 acquisition cost is computed as follows:

Computation of Parent Company's Acquisition Cost for Bonds of Partially Owned Subsidiary	Present value of $300,000 in four years at 15%, with interest paid annually ($300,000 × 0.571753) $171,526
	Add: Present value of $30,000 each year for four years at 15% ($30,000 × 2.854978) 85,649
	Cost to Post Corporation of $300,000 face amount of bonds $257,175

Post prepared the following journal entry on December 31, 2004, to record the acquisition of Sage's bonds:

Parent Company's Journal Entry to Record Open-Market Acquisition of Bonds of Partially Owned Subsidiary	Investment in Sage Company Bonds	257,175	
	Intercompany Interest Receivable	30,000	
	Cash		287,175
	To record acquisition of $300,000 face amount of Sage Company's 10% bonds due Jan. 1, 2009, and accrued interest for one year.		

Upon receiving notification of the parent company's acquisition of the bonds, Sage Company prepared the following journal entry on December 31, 2004, to record the **intercompany** status of a portion of its bonds payable:

Partially Owned Subsidiary's Journal Entry to Record Parent Company's Open-Market Acquisition of Subsidiary's Outstanding Bonds

Bonds Payable	300,000	
Discount on Intercompany Bonds Payable ($30,374 × 0.60)	18,224	
Interest Payable ($50,000 × 0.60)	30,000	
Intercompany Bonds Payable		300,000
Discount on Bonds Payable		18,224
Intercompany Interest Payable		30,000
To transfer to intercompany accounts all amounts attributable to bonds acquired by parent company in open market.		

From the standpoint of the consolidated entity, Post Corporation's acquisition of Sage Company's bonds is equivalent to the **extinguishment** of the bonds at a **realized** gain of $24,601, computed as follows:

Computation of Realized Gain on Parent Company's Open-Market Acquisition of Subsidiary's Outstanding Bonds

Carrying amount of Sage Company's bonds acquired by Post	
Corporation on Dec. 31, 2004 ($300,000 − $18,224)	$281,776
Less: Cost of Post Corporation's investment	257,175
Realized gain on extinguishment of bonds	$ 24,601

The $24,601 realized gain **is not recorded** in the accounting records of either the parent company or the subsidiary. Instead, it is recognized in the working paper elimination (in journal entry format) on December 31, 2004, shown below.

Working Paper Elimination to Recognize Gain on Intercompany Extinguishment of Bonds Payable

POST CORPORATION AND SUBSIDIARY
Partial Working Paper Eliminations
December 31, 2004

(e) Intercompany Bonds Payable—Sage	300,000	
Discount on Intercompany Bonds Payable—Sage		18,224
Investment in Sage Company Bonds—Post		257,175
Gain on Extinguishment of Bonds—Sage		24,601
To eliminate subsidiary's bonds acquired by parent and to recognize gain on the extinguishment of the bonds. (Income tax effects are disregarded.)		

Disposition of Gain on Extinguishment of Bonds

The foregoing working paper elimination attributes the gain on Post Corporation's acquisition of its subsidiary's bonds to Sage Company—the subsidiary. This treatment of the gain follows from the assumption that the parent company's open-market acquisition of the subsidiary's bonds was, in substance, the extinguishment of the bonds by the subsidiary. The parent company acted as **agent** for the subsidiary in the open-market transaction; thus, the gain is attributed to the subsidiary. Under this approach, the accounting for the gain on the acquisition of the subsidiary's bonds is the same as if the **subsidiary itself** had acquired and retired the bonds.

The entire realized gain of $24,601 is displayed in the consolidated income statement of Post Corporation and subsidiary for the year ended December 31, 2004.[5] If the gain is **material,** it is displayed as an **extraordinary item,** net of applicable income taxes.[6]

---

[5] *APB Opinion No. 26,* "Early Extinguishment of Debt" (New York: AICPA, 1973), par. 20.
[6] *FASB Statement No. 64,* "Extinguishments of Debt . . ." (Stamford: FASB, 1982), pars. 1–4.

Minority Interest in Gain on Extinguishment of Bonds

As discussed in the preceding section, the gain on Post Corporation's acquisition of its subsidiary's bonds is attributed to the partially owned subsidiary. It follows that ***the gain should be considered in the computation of the minority interest in the subsidiary's net income*** for the year ended December 31, 2004. Also, the gain is included in the computation of the amount of the subsidiary's retained earnings to be included in consolidated retained earnings on December 31, 2004. These procedures are illustrated on page 365.

Accounting for Gain in Subsequent Years

In the four years following Post Corporation's acquisition of Sage Company's bonds, the gain *realized but unrecorded* on the date of acquisition is in effect *recorded* by the consolidated entity through the differences in the two affiliates' amortization and accumulation of bond discount. (It is essential that the affiliate that acquired the bonds at a discount undertake an accumulation program consistent with that of the affiliate that issued the bonds; thus, Post Corporation should adopt the interest method of amortization used by Sage.) To illustrate this concept, the accounting for the bond interest by the two companies for the year ended December 31, 2005, is below, and the ledger accounts of both companies relative to the intercompany bonds are illustrated on pages 360 and 361 for the four years the bonds remain outstanding.

Affiliated Companies' Journal Entries for Bonds for Year after Intercompany Acquisition of the Bonds

	Post Corporation Journal Entries			Sage Company Journal Entries		
2005						
Jan. 2	Cash	30,000		Intercompany Interest Payable	30,000	
	Intercompany Interest			Interest Payable	20,000	
	Receivable		30,000	Cash		50,000
	To record receipt of			To record payment of accrued		
	accrued interest on			interest on 10% bonds.		
	Sage Company's					
	10% bonds.					
				Intercompany Interest Expense	33,813	
				Interest Expense	22,542	
Dec. 31	Intercompany Interest			Intercompany Interest		
	Receivable	30,000		Payable		30,000
	Investment in Sage			Interest Payable		20,000
	Company Bonds	8,576		Discount on Intercom-		
	Intercompany			pany Bonds Payable		3,813
	Interest Revenue		38,576	Discount on Bonds		
	To accrue annual interest			Payable		2,542
	on Sage Company's			To accrue annual interest on 10%		
	10% bonds			bonds. Interest is computed as		
	($257,175 ×			follows:		
	0.15 = $38,576).			Intercompany ($300,000 −		
				$18,224) × 0.12 = $33,813		
				Other ($200,000 −		
				$12,150) × 0.12 = $22,542		

POST CORPORATION
Ledger Accounts

Investment in Sage Company Bonds

Date	Explanation	Debit	Credit	Balance
2004				
Dec. 31	Acquisition of $300,000 face amount of bonds	257,175		257,175 dr
2005				
Dec. 31	Accumulation of discount ($38,576 − $30,000)	8,576		265,751 dr
2006				
Dec. 31	Accumulation of discount ($39,863 − $30,000)	9,863		275,614 dr
2007				
Dec. 31	Accumulation of discount ($41,342 − $30,000)	11,342		286,956 dr
2008				
Dec. 31	Accumulation of discount ($43,044 − $30,000)	13,044		300,000 dr

Intercompany Interest Revenue

Date	Explanation	Debit	Credit	Balance
2005				
Dec. 31	($257,175 × 0.15)		38,576	38,576 cr
31	Closing entry	38,576		-0-
2006				
Dec. 31	($265,751 × 0.15)		39,863	39,863 cr
31	Closing entry	39,863		-0-
2007				
Dec. 31	($275,614 × 0.15)		41,342	41,342 cr
31	Closing entry	41,342		-0-
2008				
Dec. 31	($286,956 × 0.15)		43,044*	43,044 cr
31	Closing entry	43,044		-0-

* Adjusted $1 for rounding.

SAGE COMPANY
Ledger Accounts

Intercompany Bonds Payable

Date	Explanation	Debit	Credit	Balance
2004				
Dec. 31	Bonds acquired by parent company		300,000	300,000 cr

(continued)

SAGE COMPANY
Ledger Accounts (concluded)

Discount on Intercompany Bonds Payable

Date	Explanation	Debit	Credit	Balance
2004 Dec. 31	Bonds acquired by parent company	18,224		18,224 dr
2005 Dec. 31	Amortization ($33,813 − $30,000)		3,813	14,411 dr
2006 Dec. 31	Amortization ($34,271 − $30,000)		4,271	10,140 dr
2007 Dec. 31	Amortization ($34,783 − $30,000)		4,783	5,357 dr
2008 Dec. 31	Amortization ($35,357 − $30,000)		5,357	-0-

Intercompany Interest Expense

Date	Explanation	Debit	Credit	Balance
2005 Dec. 31 31	[($300,000 − $18,224) × 0.12] Closing entry	33,813	 33,813	33,813 dr -0-
2006 Dec. 31 31	[($300,000 − $14,411) × 0.12] Closing entry	34,271	 34,271	34,271 dr -0-
2007 Dec. 31 31	[($300,000 − $10,140) × 0.12] Closing entry	34,783	 34,783	34,783 dr -0-
2008 Dec. 31 31	[($300,000 − $5,357) × 0.12] Closing entry	35,357	 35,357	35,537 dr -0-

A comparison of the yearly journal entries to Post Corporation's Intercompany Interest Revenue ledger account and Sage Company's Intercompany Interest Expense account demonstrates that the difference between the annual entries in the two accounts represents the ***recording,*** in the separate companies' accounting records, of the $24,601 gain ***realized but unrecorded*** when the parent company acquired the subsidiary's bonds in the open market. A summary of the differences between the two intercompany interest amounts is as follows:

Total of Differences Between Parent's Intercompany Interest Revenue and Subsidiary's Intercompany Interest Expense Is Equal to Realized Gain on Parent's Acquisition of Subsidiary's Bonds

Year Ended Dec. 31,	Post Corporation's Intercompany Interest Revenue	Sage Company's Intercompany Interest Expense	Difference—Representing Recording of Realized Gain
2005	$ 38,576	$ 33,813	$ 4,763
2006	39,863	34,271	5,592
2007	41,342	34,783	6,559
2008	43,044	35,357	7,687
Totals	$162,825	$138,224	$24,601

Working Paper Elimination on December 31, 2005

The working paper elimination (in journal entry format) for the bonds and interest on December 31, 2005, is as follows:

POST CORPORATION AND SUBSIDIARY Partial Working Paper Eliminations December 31, 2005		
(e) Intercompany Interest Revenue—Post	38,576	
Intercompany Bonds Payable—Sage	300,000	
Discount on Intercompany Bonds Payable—Sage		14,411
Investment in Sage Company Bonds—Post		265,751
Intercompany Interest Expense—Sage		33,813
Retained Earnings—Sage ($24,601 × 0.95)		23,371
Minority Interest in Net Assets of Subsidiary ($24,601 × 0.05)		1,230
To eliminate subsidiary's bonds owned by parent company, and related interest revenue and expense; and to increase subsidiary's **beginning** retained earnings by amount of unamortized realized gain on the extinguishment of the bonds. (Income tax effects are disregarded.)		

The foregoing working paper elimination effectively reduces consolidated net income (before minority interest) by $4,763 ($38,576 − $33,813 = $4,763). As shown on page 361, the $4,763 is the difference between the eliminated intercompany interest revenue of the parent company and the eliminated intercompany interest expense of the subsidiary. Failure to eliminate intercompany interest in this manner would result in a $4,763 overstatement of pre-minority interest consolidated net income for Year 2005, because the *entire* $24,601 realized gain on the parent company's acquisition of the subsidiary's bonds was recognized in the consolidated income statement for Year 2004—the year the bonds were acquired—as evidenced by the $24,601 credited to Retained Earnings—Sage and to Minority Interest in Net Assets of Subsidiary in the elimination.

The $4,763 reduction of consolidated net income (before minority interest) is attributable to the subsidiary, because the original realized gain to which the $4,763 relates was allocated to the subsidiary. Consequently, *the $4,763 must be considered in the computation of minority interest in net income of the subsidiary* for the year ended December 31, 2005. The $4,763 also enters into the computation of the amount of the subsidiary's retained earnings included in consolidated retained earnings. These amounts associated with Sage Company's bonds are reflected in the working paper for consolidated financial statements for the year ended December 31, 2005, as illustrated on pages 368 and 369.

Working Paper Elimination on December 31, 2006

The working paper elimination (in journal entry format) on December 31, 2006, is as follows:

POST CORPORATION AND SUBSIDIARY **Partial Working Paper Eliminations** **December 31, 2006**		
(e) Intercompany Interest Revenue—Post	39,863	
Intercompany Bonds Payable—Sage	300,000	
Discount on Intercompany Bonds Payable—Sage		10,140
Investment in Sage Company Bonds—Post		275,614
Intercompany Interest Expense—Sage		34,271
Retained Earnings—Sage [($24,601 − $4,763) × 0.95]		18,846
Minority Interest in Net Assets of Subsidiary [($24,601 − $4,763) × 0.05]		992
To eliminate subsidiary's bonds owned by parent company, and related interest revenue and expense; and to increase subsidiary's **beginning** retained earnings by amount of unamortized realized gain on the extinguishment of the bonds. (Income tax effects are disregarded.)		

Comparable working paper eliminations are appropriate for Years 2007 and 2008. After Sage Company paid the bonds in full on maturity (January 2, 2009), no further working paper eliminations for the bonds would be required.

Reissuance of Intercompany Bonds

The orderly amortization of a realized gain on the acquisition of an affiliate's bonds is disrupted if the acquiring affiliate sells the bonds to outsiders before they mature. A *transaction* gain or loss on such a sale is not *realized* by the consolidated entity. Logic requires that a working paper elimination be prepared to treat the transaction gain or loss as premium or discount on the reissued bonds, as appropriate. These complex issues are rarely encountered; thus, they are not illustrated here.

ILLUSTRATION OF EFFECT OF INTERCOMPANY PROFITS (GAINS) ON MINORITY INTEREST

To illustrate the effect of intercompany profits (gains) on the computation of minority interest in the net income of a partially owned subsidiary, return to the example of Post Corporation and its 95%-owned purchased subsidiary, Sage Company. The following working paper eliminations for Post Corporation and subsidiary (in journal entry format) are taken from page 300 of Chapter 7, and from pages 341, 345, 347, and 358 of this chapter. These eliminations are followed by a *revised* elimination (which differs from the one on page 300 of Chapter 7) for minority interest in net income of subsidiary.

POST CORPORATION AND SUBSIDIARY
Working Paper Eliminations
December 31, 2004

(a) Common Stock—Sage	400,000	
Additional Paid-in Capital—Sage	235,000	
Retained Earnings—Sage ($384,000 − $4,750)	379,250	
Retained Earnings of Subsidiary—Post	4,750	
Intercompany Investment Income—Post	81,700	
Plant Assets (net)—Sage ($176,000 − $14,000)	162,000	
Leasehold—Sage ($25,000 − $5,000)	20,000	
Goodwill—Post	38,000	
Cost of Goods Sold—Sage	17,000	
Operating Expenses—Sage	2,000	
Investment in Sage Company Common Stock—Post		1,231,200
Dividends Declared—Sage		50,000
Minority Interest in Net Assets of Subsidiary ($61,000 − $2,500)		58,500

To carry out the following:

(1) Eliminate intercompany investment and equity accounts of subsidiary **at beginning of year,** and subsidiary dividends.

(2) Provide for Year 2004 depreciation and amortization on differences between current fair values and carrying amounts of Sage's identifiable net assets as follows:

	Cost of Goods Sold	Operating Expenses
Building depreciation	$ 2,000	$2,000
Machinery depreciation	10,000	
Leasehold amortization	5,000	$2,000
Totals	$17,000	$2,000

(3) Allocate unamortized differences between combination date current fair values and carrying amounts to appropriate assets.

(4) Establish minority interest in net assets of subsidiary at beginning of year ($61,000), less minority interest in dividends declared by subsidiary during year ($50,000 × 0.05 = $2,500).

(Income tax effects are disregarded.)

(b) Intercompany Sales—Sage	120,000	
Intercompany Cost of Goods Sold—Sage		96,000
Cost of Goods Sold—Post		16,000
Inventories—Post		8,000

To eliminate intercompany sales, cost of goods sold, and unrealized profit in inventories. (Income tax effects are disregarded.)

(c) Intercompany Gain on Sale of Land—Post	50,000	
Land—Sage		50,000

To eliminate unrealized intercompany gain on sale of land. (Income tax effects are disregarded.)

(continued)

POST CORPORATION AND SUBSIDIARY Working Paper Eliminations (concluded) December 31, 2004		
(d) Intercompany Gain on Sale of Machinery—Sage	23,800	
Machinery—Post		23,800
To eliminate unrealized intercompany gain on sale of machinery. (Income tax effects are disregarded.)		
(e) Intercompany Bonds Payable—Sage	300,000	
Discount on Intercompany Bonds Payable—Sage		18,224
Investment in Sage Company Bonds—Post		257,175
Gain on Extinguishment of Bonds—Sage		24,601

To eliminate subsidiary's bonds acquired by parent, and to
    recognize gain on the extinguishment of the bonds. (Income
    tax effects are disregarded.)		

(f) Minority Interest in Net Income of Subsidiary	3,940	
Minority Interest in Net Assets of Subsidiary		3,940
To establish minority interest in subsidiary's adjusted net income for Year 2004 as follows:		

Net income of subsidiary	$105,000
Adjustments for working paper eliminations:	
(a) ($17,000 + $2,000)	(19,000)
(b)	(8,000)
(d)	(23,800)
(e)	24,601
Adjusted net income of subsidiary	$ 78,801
Minority interest share ($78,801 × 0.05)	$ 3,940

In elimination *(f)* above, the effects of the other eliminations on the subsidiary's net income are applied to compute the adjusted net income of the subsidiary, for consolidation purposes. The minority interest percentage then is applied to compute the minority interest in net income of the subsidiary. The rationale for these procedures follows:

- **Elimination (a)** increases costs and expenses of the subsidiary, thus decreasing the subsidiary's net income, a total of $19,000.
- **Elimination (b)** reduces the subsidiary's gross profit margin on sales by $24,000 ($120,000 − $96,000 = $24,000); however, $16,000 of the gross profit margin was realized by the parent company in its sales to outsiders. The net effect on the subsidiary's net income is a decrease of $8,000 ($24,000 − $16,000 = $8,000).
- **Elimination (c)** removes a gain of the parent company; it does not affect the subsidiary's net income.
- **Elimination (d)** removes a gain of the subsidiary and reduces the subsidiary's net income by $23,800.
- **Elimination (e)** attributes a gain on extinguishment of bonds to the subsidiary, thus increasing the subsidiary's net income by $24,601.

Working Paper for Consolidated Financial Statements

A partial working paper for consolidated financial statements for Post Corporation and subsidiary for the year ended December 31, 2004, is on page 366. The amounts for Post Corporation and Sage Company are the same as in the illustration on page 301 of Chapter 7.

Equity Method: Partially Owned Subsidiary Subsequent to Date of Business Combination

	POST CORPORATION AND SUBSIDIARY			
	Partial Working Paper for Consolidated Financial Statements			
	° For Year Ended December 31, 2004			
	Post Corporation	Sage Company	Eliminations Increase (Decrease)	Consolidated
Statement of Retained Earnings				
Retained earnings, beginning of year	1,349,450	384,000	(a) (379,250)	1,354,200
Net income	353,550	105,000	(161,839)*	296,711
Subtotals	1,703,000	489,000	(541,089)	1,650,911
Dividends declared	158,550	50,000	(a) (50,000)†	158,550
Retained earnings, end of year	1,544,450	439,000	(491,089)	1,492,361
Balance Sheet				
Liabilities and Stockholders' Equity				
Total liabilities	x,xxx,xxx	xxx,xxx	xxx,xxx	x,xxx,xxx
Common stock, $1 par	1,057,000			1,057,000
Common stock, $10 par		400,000	(a) (400,000)	
Additional paid-in capital	1,560,250	235,000	(a) (235,000)	1,560,250
Minority interest in net assets			{(a) 58,500)	62,440
of subsidiary			{(f) 3,940)	
Retained earnings	1,544,450	439,000	(491,089)	1,492,361
Retained earnings of subsidiary	4,750		(a) (4,750)	
Total stockholders' equity	4,166,450	1,074,000	(1,067,499)	4,172,051
Total liabilities and stockholders' equity	x,xxx,xxx	x,xxx,xxx	(1,067,499)	x,xxx,xxx

*Net decrease in revenue (and gains): $81,700 + $120,000 + $50,000 + $23,800 − $24,601	$250,890
Less: Net decrease in costs and expenses: $96,000 + $16,000 − $19,000 − $3,940	89,060
Decrease in combined net incomes to compute consolidated net income	$161,839

† A **decrease** in dividends and an **increase** in retained earnings.

The foregoing working paper demonstrates that, when intercompany profits exist, consolidated net income is not the same as the parent company's net income under the equity method of accounting for the subsidiary's operations; nor is consolidated retained earnings the same as the total of the parent company's two retained earnings amounts. ($1,544,450 + $4,750 = $1,549,200; consolidated retained earnings is $1,492,361.) In the comprehensive illustration that follows, I demonstrate how consolidated net income and consolidated retained earnings may be verified when intercompany profits (gains) are involved in the consolidation process.

COMPREHENSIVE ILLUSTRATION OF WORKING PAPER FOR CONSOLIDATED FINANCIAL STATEMENTS

Chapters 6 through 8 explain and illustrate a number of aspects of working papers for consolidated financial statements. The comprehensive illustration that follows incorporates most of these aspects. The illustration is for Post Corporation and its partially owned subsidiary, Sage Company, for the year ended December 31, 2005.

The ledger accounts for Post Corporation's Investment in Sage Company Common Stock, Retained Earnings, and Retained Earnings of Subsidiary, and for Sage Company's Retained Earnings, are as follows. Closing entries for Year 2005 are not yet recorded in the retained earnings accounts. Review of these accounts should aid in understanding the illustrative working paper for consolidated financial statements on pages 368 and 369 and the related working paper eliminations (in journal entry format) on pages 370 and 371. Consolidated goodwill was unimpaired throughout the three-year period.

POST CORPORATION LEDGER ACCOUNTS

Investment in Sage Company Common Stock

Date	Explanation	Debit	Credit	Balance
2002				
Dec. 31	Total cost of business combination	1,192,250		1,192,250 dr
2003				
Nov. 24	Dividend declared by Sage		38,000	1,154,250 dr
Dec. 31	Net income of Sage	85,500		1,239,750 dr
31	Amortization of differences		42,750	1,197,000 dr
2004				
Nov. 22	Dividend declared by Sage		47,500	1,149,500 dr
Dec. 31	Net income of Sage	99,750		1,249,250 dr
31	Amortization of differences		18,050	1,231,200 dr
2005				
Nov. 25	Dividend declared by Sage		57,000	1,174,200 dr
Dec. 31	Net income of Sage	109,250		1,283,450 dr
31	Amortization of differences		18,050	

Retained Earnings

Date	Explanation	Debit	Credit	Balance
2002				
Dec. 31	Balance			1,050,000 cr
2003				
Dec. 31	Close net income available for dividends		458,000	1,508,000 cr
31	Close Dividends Declared account	158,550		1,349,450 cr
2004				
Dec. 31	Close net income available for dividends		319,350	1,668,800 cr
31	Close Dividends Declared account	158,550		1,510,250 cr

Retained Earnings of Subsidiary

Date	Explanation	Debit	Credit	Balance
2003				
Dec. 31	Close net income not available for dividends		4,750	4,750 cr
2004				
Dec. 31	Close net income not available for dividends		34,200	38,950 cr

SAGE COMPANY LEDGER ACCOUNT

Retained Earnings

Date	Explanation	Debit	Credit	Balance
2002				
Dec. 31	Balance		334,000	334,000 cr
2003				
Dec. 31	Close net income		90,000	424,000 cr
31	Close Dividends Declared account	40,000		384,000 cr
2004				
Dec. 31	Close net income		105,000	489,000 cr
31	Close Dividends Declared account	50,000		439,000 cr

Equity Method: Partially Owned Subsidiary Subsequent to Business Combination

POST CORPORATION AND SUBSIDIARY
Working Paper for Consolidated Financial Statements
For Year Ended December 31, 2005

	Post Corporation	Sage Company	Eliminations Increase (Decrease)		Consolidated
Income Statement					
Revenue:					
Net sales	5,900,000	1,400,000			7,300,000
Intercompany sales		150,000	(b)	(150,000)	
Intercompany interest revenue	38,576		(e)	(38,576)	
Intercompany investment income	91,200		(a)	(91,200)	
Intercompany revenue (expenses)	14,000	(14,000)			
Total revenue	6,043,776	1,536,000)		(279,776)	7,300,000
Costs and expenses:			(a)	17,000	
			(b)	(26,000)	
Cost of goods sold	4,300,000	950,000	(d)	(4,760)	5,236,240
Intercompany cost of goods sold		120,000	(b)	(120,000)	
Operating expenses	985,108	217,978	(a)	2,000)	1,205,036
Intercompany interest expense		33,813	(e)	(33,813)	
Interest expense	51,518	22,542			74,060
Income taxes expense	246,000	76,667			322,667
Minority interest in net income of subsidiary			(f)	4,600	4,600
Total costs and expenses and minority interest	5,582,626	1,421,000		(160,973)*	6,842,653
Net income	461,150	115,000		(118,803)	457,347

* A **decrease** in total costs and expenses and an **increase** in net income.

(continued)

POST CORPORATION AND SUBSIDIARY
Working Paper for Consolidated Financial Statements (concluded)
For Year Ended December 31, 2005

	Post Corporation	Sage Company	Eliminations Increase (Decrease)		Consolidated
Statement of Retained Earnings					
Retained earnings, beginning of year	1,510,250	439,000	(a)	(400,050)	1,492,361
			(b)	(7,600)	
			(c)	(50,000)	
			(d)	(22,610)	
			(e)	23,371	
Net income	461,150	115,000		(118,803)	457,347
Subtotal	1,971,400	554,000		(575,692)	1,949,708
Dividends declared	158,550	60,000	(a)	(60,000)*	158,550
Retained earnings, end of year	1,812,850	494,000		(515,692)	1,791,158
Balance Sheet					
Assets					
Intercompany receivables (payables)	(3,500)	3,500			
Inventories	950,000	500,000	(b)	(12,000)	1,438,000
Other current assets	760,000	428,992			1,188,992
Investment in Sage Company stock	1,265,400		(a)	(1,265,400)	
Investment in Sage Company bonds	265,751		(e)	(265,751)	
Plant assets (net)	3,700,000	1,300,000	(a)	148,000	5,128,960
			(d)	(19,040)	
Land (for building site)		175,000	(c)	(50,000)	125,000
Leasehold (net)			(a)	15,000	15,000
Goodwill	85,000		(a)	38,000	123,000
Total assets	7,022,651	2,407,492		(1,411,191)	8,018,952
Liabilities and Stockholders' Equity					
Bonds payable		200,000			200,000
Intercompany bonds payable		300,000	(e)	(300,000)	
Discount on bonds payable		(9,608)			(9,608)
Discount on intercompany bonds payable		(14,411)	(e)	(14,411)†	
Other liabilities	2,553,601	802,511			3,356,112
Common stock, $1 par	1,057,000				1,057,000
Common stock, $10 par		400,000	(a)	(400,000)	
Additional paid-in capital	1,560,250	235,000	(a)	(235,000)	1,560,250
Minority interest in net assets of subsidiary			(a)	59,800	64,040
			(b)	(400)	
			(d)	(1,190)	
			(e)	1,230	
			(f)	4,600	
Retained earnings	1,812,850	494,000		(515,692)	1,791,158
Retained earnings of subsidiary	38,950		(a)	(38,950)	
Total liabilities and stockholders' equity	7,022,651	2,407,492		(1,411,191)	8,018,952

* A **decrease** in dividends and an **increase** in retained earnings.

† A **decrease** in discount on intercompany bonds payable and an **increase** in total liabilities and stockholders' equity.

POST CORPORATION AND SUBSIDIARY		
Working Paper Eliminations		
December 31, 2005		

(a) Common Stock—Sage	400,000	
Additional Paid-in Capital—Sage	235,000	
Retained Earnings—Sage ($439,000 − $38,950)	400,050	
Retained Earnings of Subsidiary—Post	38,950	
Intercompany Investment Income—Post	91,200	
Plant Assets (net)—Sage ($162,000 − $14,000)	148,000	
Leasehold (net)—Sage ($20,000 − $5,000)	15,000	
Goodwill—Post	38,000	
Cost of Goods Sold—Sage	17,000	
Operating Expenses—Sage	2,000	
Investment in Sage Company Common Stock—Post		1,265,400
Dividends Declared—Sage		60,000
Minority Interest in Net Assets of Subsidiary		59,800

To carry out the following:

(1) Eliminate intercompany investment and equity accounts of subsidiary at **beginning** of year, and subsidiary dividend.

(2) Provide for Year 2005 depreciation and amortization on differences between current fair values and carrying amount of Sage's identifiable net assets as follows:

	Cost of Goods Sold	Operating Expenses
Building depreciation	$ 2,000	$2,000
Machinery depreciation	10,000	
Leasehold amortization	5,000	
Totals	$17,000	$2,000

(3) Allocate unamortized differences between combination date current fair values and carrying amounts to appropriate assets.

(4) Establish minority interest in net assets of subsidiary at beginning of year, excluding intercompany profits effects ($62,800), less minority interest in dividends declared by subsidiary during year ($60,000 × 0.05 = $3,000).

(Income tax effects are disregarded.)

(b) Retained Earnings—Sage	7,600	
Minority Interest in Net Assets of Subsidiary	400	
Intercompany Sales—Sage	150,000	
Intercompany Cost of Goods Sold—Sage		120,000
Cost of Goods Sold—Post		26,000
Inventories—Post		12,000

To eliminate intercompany sales, cost of goods sold, and unrealized profits in inventories. (Income tax effects are disregarded.)

(c) Retained Earnings—Post	50,000	
Land—Sage		50,000

To eliminate unrealized intercompany gain in land. (Income tax effects are disregarded.)

(continued)

POST CORPORATION AND SUBSIDIARY
Working Paper Eliminations (concluded)
December 31, 2005

(d) Retained Earnings—Sage	22,610	
Minority Interest in Net Assets of Subsidiary	1,190	
Accumulated Depreciation—Post	4,760	
Machinery—Post		23,800
Depreciation Expense—Post		4,760
To eliminate unrealized intercompany gain in machinery and in related depreciation. (Income tax effects are disregarded.)		
(e) Intercompany Interest Revenue—Post	38,576	
Intercompany Bonds Payable—Sage	300,000	
Discount on Intercompany Bonds Payable—Sage		14,411
Investment in Sage Company Bonds—Post		265,751
Intercompany Interest Expense—Sage		33,813
Retained Earnings—Sage		23,371
Minority Interest in Net Assets of Subsidiary		1,230
To eliminate subsidiary's bonds owned by parent company, and related interest revenue and expense; and to increase subsidiary's beginning retained earnings by amount of unamortized realized gain on the extinguishment of the bonds. (Income tax effects are disregarded.)		
(f) Minority Interest in Net Income of Subsidiary	4,600	
Minority Interest in Net Assets of Subsidiary		4,600
To establish minority interest in subsidiary's adjusted net income for Year 2005, as follows:		

Net income of subsidiary		$115,000
Adjustments for working paper eliminations:		
(a) ($17,000 + $2,000)	(19,000)	
(b) ($150,000 − $120,000 − $26,000)	(4,000)	
(d)	4,760	
(e) ($38,576 − $33,813)	(4,763)	
Adjusted net income of subsidiary		$ 91,997
Minority interest share ($91,997 × 0.05)		$ 4,600

Following are 12 important features of the working paper for consolidated financial statements and related working paper eliminations for Post Corporation and subsidiary for the year ended December 31, 2005:

1. Intercompany investment income of Post Corporation for Year 2005 is computed as follows:

Computation of Intercompany Investment Income

$115,000 (Sage Company's net income for Year 2002) × 0.95	$109,250
Less: $19,000 [(Year 2005 amortization of differences between current fair values and carrying amounts of Sage Company's identifiable net assets on date of business combination) × 0.95]	18,050
Intercompany investment income of Post Corporation for Year 2005	$ 91,200

2. Post Corporation's intercompany revenue of $14,000 is a management fee from Sage Company, computed as 1% of Sage's $1,400,000 net sales for Year 2005 ($1,400,000 × 0.01 = $14,000).

3. The income tax effects of Post Corporation's use of the equity method of accounting for its subsidiary's operations are not reflected in Post's income taxes expense for Year 2005. Income tax effects associated with the equity method of accounting are considered in Chapter 9.

4. Consolidated retained earnings of Post Corporation and subsidiary at the beginning of Year 2005 ($1,492,361) is identical to consolidated retained earnings at the end of Year 2004 (see page 366).

5. The net intercompany payable of Post Corporation on December 31, 2005, is computed as follows:

Computation of Net Intercompany Payable of Parent Company

Accounts payable to Sage Company for merchandise purchases		$47,500
Less: Interest receivable from Sage Company (page 359)	$30,000	
Management fee receivable from Sage Company	14,000	44,000
Net intercompany payable		$ 3,500

6. Elimination *(a)* continues the amortization of differences between current fair values and carrying amounts of the subsidiary's net assets on the date of the business combination of Post Corporation and Sage Company (see Chapter 7, page 299).

7. The $62,800 minority interest at the beginning of the year, ***excluding intercompany profits (gains) effects,*** as set forth in the explanation for elimination *(a)*(4), is computed as follows:

Computation of Minority Interest at Beginning of Year

Stockholders' equity of Sage Company, Dec. 31, 2004:		
Common stock, $10 par		$ 400,000
Additional paid-in capital		235,000
Retained earnings		439,000
Total stockholders' equity		$1,074,000
Add: Unamortized differences between current fair values and carrying amounts of Sage's identifiable net assets, Dec. 31, 2004 (see page 364):		
Plant assets	$162,000	
Leasehold	20,000	182,000
Total adjusted net assets of Sage, Dec. 31, 2004		$1,256,000
Minority interest therein ($1,256,000 × 0.05)		$ 62,800

8. Eliminations *(b)*, *(c)*, *(d)*, and *(e)* are identical to the eliminations illustrated in this chapter on pages 343, 346, 348, and 362, respectively. For posting to the working paper for consolidated financial statements, elimination *(d)* was condensed. The credit to Depreciation Expense in elimination *(d)* is posted to Cost of Goods Sold in the income statement section of the working paper.

9. The effects of eliminations *(a)* through *(e)* on the computation of the minority interest in net income of the subsidiary, in elimination *(f)*, are analyzed as follows:

- ***Elimination (a)*** increases costs and expenses of the subsidiary, thus decreasing the subsidiary's net income, a total of $19,000.

- *Elimination (b)* reduces the subsidiary's gross profit margin on sales by $30,000 ($150,000 − $120,000 = $30,000); however, $26,000 of gross profit margin was realized by the parent company in its sales to outsiders. The net effect on the subsidiary's net income is a decrease of $4,000 ($30,000 − $26,000 = $4,000).

- *Elimination (c)* does not affect the net income of the subsidiary.

- *Elimination (d)* includes a $4,760 credit to the parent company's depreciation expense, which in effect is a realization of a portion of the intercompany profit on the subsidiary's sale of machinery to the parent company (see page 349). Thus, the subsidiary's net income is increased by $4,760.

- *Elimination (e)* decreases intercompany interest revenue by $38,576 and decreases intercompany interest expense by $33,813. The difference, $4,763 ($38,576 − $33,813 = $4,763), is a reduction of the subsidiary's net income, to avoid double counting of the realized but unrecorded gain on the extinguishment of the subsidiary's bonds in the prior year (see page 362).

10. Because of the elimination of intercompany profits (gains), consolidated net income for the year ended December 31, 2005, does not equal the parent company's equity-method net income. Consolidated net income may be verified as shown below:

Verification of Consolidated Net Income

Net income of Post Corporation		$461,150
Less: Post's share of adjustments to subsidiary's net		
income for intercompany profits (gains):		
Elimination (b) ($150,000 − $120,000 − $26,000)	$(4,000)	
Elimination (d)	4,760	
Elimination (e) ($38,576 − $33,813)	(4,763)	
Total	$(4,003)	
Post's share [$(4,003) × 0.95]		(3,803)
Consolidated net income		$457,347

11. Similarly, consolidated retained earnings on December 31, 2005, does not equal the total of the two parent company retained earnings amounts in the working paper for consolidated financial statements. Consolidated retained earnings may be verified as follows:

Verification of Consolidated Retained Earnings

Total of Post Corporation's two retained earnings amounts		
($1,812,850 + $38,950)		$1,851,800
Adjustments:		
Post's share of adjustments to subsidiary's net income		(3,803)
(see above)		
Intercompany gain in Post's retained earnings—		
elimination (c)		(50,000)
Post's share of adjustments to subsidiary's beginning		
retained earnings for intercompany profits (gains):		
Elimination (b)	$ (7,600)	
Elimination (d)	(22,610)	
Elimination (e)	23,371	(6,839)
Consolidated retained earnings		$1,791,158

12. The consolidated amounts in the working paper for consolidated financial statements represent the financial position and operating results of Post Corporation and subsidiary resulting from the consolidated entity's transactions with **outsiders.** All intercompany transactions, profits (gains), and balances have been eliminated in the computation of the consolidated amounts.

SEC ENFORCEMENT ACTION DEALING WITH WRONGFUL ACCOUNTING FOR AN INTERCOMPANY ACCOUNT

AAER 992

"In the Matter of Robert Gossett and Ronald Langos, Respondents," reported in **AAER 992** (December 1, 1997), described the SEC's discovery of a number of egregious misstatements of the quarterly and fiscal year consolidated financial statements of a company and its subsidiaries that provided corrosion control engineering, monitoring services, systems, and equipment to the infrastructure, environmental, and energy markets. Among these misstatements, perpetrated primarily by the parent company's president and chief operating officer and its vice president of finance, chief financial officer, and treasurer, was an improper debit balance in the parent's Intercompany Account. Instead of being eliminated in consolidation, the Intercompany Account's debit balance included $601,000 of subcontract expenses and $700,000 attributable to the parent company's failure to record certain intercompany transfers of inventory.

Review Questions

1. How should a parent company and subsidiary account for related party transactions and balances to assure their correct elimination in the preparation of consolidated financial statements? Explain.

2. Identify five common related party transactions between a parent company and its subsidiary.

3. Primak Corporation rents a sales office to its wholly owned subsidiary under an operating lease requiring rent of $2,000 a month, payable the first day of the month. What are the income tax effects of the elimination of Primak's $24,000 rent revenue and the subsidiary's $24,000 rent expense in the preparation of a consolidated income statement? Explain.

4. Is an intercompany note receivable that has been discounted by a bank eliminated in the preparation of a consolidated balance sheet? Explain.

5. How are consolidated financial statements affected if unrealized intercompany profits (gains) resulting from transactions between a parent company and its subsidiaries are not eliminated? Explain.

6. What consolidated financial statement categories are affected by intercompany sales of merchandise at a profit? Explain.

7. How is the unrealized intercompany profit in a subsidiary's **beginning** inventories resulting from the parent company's sales of merchandise to the subsidiary accounted for in a working paper elimination (in journal entry format)? Explain.

8. How is the minority interest in net income of a partially owned subsidiary affected by working paper eliminations for intercompany profits? Explain.

9. Some accountants have advocated the elimination of intercompany profit in the parent company's ending inventories only to the extent of the parent's ownership

interest in the partially owned selling subsidiary. What is an argument in opposition to this treatment of intercompany profit in the parent company's ending inventories?

10. How do intercompany sales of plant assets and intangible assets differ from inter-company sales of merchandise?

11. Is an intercompany gain on the sale of land ever *realized?* Explain.

12. Sayles Company, a 90%-owned subsidiary of Partin Corporation, sold to Partin for $10,000 a machine with a carrying amount of $8,000, no residual value, and an economic life of four years. Explain how the intercompany gain element of Partin Corporation's annual depreciation expense for the machine is accounted for in the working paper for consolidated financial statements.

13. In what ways do working paper eliminations (in journal entry format) for inter-company leases of property under capital/sales-type leases resemble eliminations for intercompany sales of plant assets and intangible assets? Explain.

14. "No intercompany gain or loss should be recognized when a parent company acquires in the open market outstanding bonds of its subsidiary, because the trans-action is not an *intercompany* transaction." Do you agree with this statement? Explain.

15. What accounting problems result from the reissuance by a subsidiary of parent com-pany bonds that had been acquired in the open market by the subsidiary? Explain.

16. Intercompany profits (gains) or losses in inventories, plant assets, intangible as-sets, or bonds result in consolidated net income that differs from the parent com-pany's equity-method net income. Why is this true? Explain.

Exercises

(Exercise 8.1)   Select the best answer for each of the following multiple-choice questions:

1. On October 31, 2002, Sol Company, the wholly owned subsidiary of Pan Corpo-ration, borrowed $50,000 from Pan on a 90-day, 8% promissory note. On November 30, 2002, Pan discounted the note at Western National Bank at a 10% discount rate. In the journal entry to record the discounting of the note, the amount of the debit to the Cash account is:

   a. $50,000.
   b. $50,150.
   c. $50,333.
   d. $51,000.
   e. Some other amount.

2. On February 28, 2002, Pylon Corporation discounted at Bank of Los Angeles at a 15% discount rate a $120,000, 60-day, 12% note receivable dated February 19, 2002, made by Sullivan Company, a wholly owned subsidiary of Pylon. In its jour-nal entry to record the discounting of the note, Pylon:

   a. Debits Cash, $119,799 ($122,400 − $2,601).
   b. Credits Discount on Intercompany Notes Receivable, $2,601 ($122,400 × 0.15 × $51/_{360}$).
   c. Credits Intercompany Interest Revenue, $2,400 ($120,000 × 0.12 × $60/_{360}$).
   d. Credits Notes Receivable, $120,000.
   e. Prepares none of the foregoing debits or credits.

3. Intercompany loans, operating leases of property, and rendering of services do not include an element of intercompany profit (gain) or loss for the consolidated entity because:

   a. The affiliated companies do not profit at each other's expense.
   b. The revenue of one affiliate exactly offsets the expense of the other affiliate.
   c. The transactions are not with outsiders.
   d. The intercompany amounts are eliminated in the working paper for consolidated financial statements.

4. A subsidiary's journal entry to record the parent company's discounting of a note receivable from the subsidiary at a bank includes:

Debit	Credit
a. Notes Payable	Interest Payable
b. Intercompany Notes Payable	Interest Payable
c. Intercompany Notes Payable	Intercompany Interest Payable
d. Notes Payable	Intercompany Interest Payable

5. A working paper elimination (in journal entry format) for intercompany sales of merchandise generally includes a credit to:

   a. Intercompany Cost of Goods Sold only.
   b. Cost of Goods Sold only.
   c. Both Intercompany Cost of Goods Sold and Cost of Goods Sold.
   d. Neither Intercompany Cost of Goods Sold nor Cost of Goods Sold.

6. Does a parent company's open-market acquisition of its subsidiary's bonds at a cost less than their carrying amount result, from a consolidated viewpoint on the date of acquisition, in:

	A Realized Gain?	An Unrealized Gain?
a.	Yes	Yes
b.	Yes	No
c.	No	Yes
d.	No	No

7. This sentence appears in **ARB No. 51,** "Consolidated Financial Statements": "The amount of intercompany profit or loss to be eliminated . . . is not affected by the existence of a minority interest." The foregoing statement is consistent with the:

   a. Parent company concept.
   b. Economic unit concept.
   c. Equity method of accounting.
   d. Purchase method of accounting.

8. In a working paper elimination (in journal entry format) dated March 31, 2003, for the elimination of intercompany sales, cost of goods sold, and intercompany profit in inventories resulting from a parent company's sales of merchandise to its partially owned subsidiary, the intercompany profit in the April 1, 2002 (beginning-of-year) inventories of the subsidiary is:

   a. Debited to Inventories—Subsidiary.
   b. Credited to Inventories—Subsidiary.
   c. Debited to Retained Earnings—Parent.
   d. Debited to Retained Earnings—Subsidiary and Minority Interest in Net Assets of Subsidiary.

9. During the year ended March 31, 2003, Puritan Corporation sold merchandise costing $120,000 to its 75%-owned subsidiary, Separatist Company, at a gross profit rate of 40%. In the relevant working paper elimination (in journal entry format) on March 31, 2003, Intercompany Sales—Puritan is debited for:

    a. $156,000.
    b. $168,000.
    c. $180,000.
    d. $200,000.
    e. Some other amount.

10. A debit to Minority Interest in Net Assets of Subsidiary is *inappropriate* in a working paper elimination (in journal entry format) for intercompany sales of merchandise by a:

    a. Parent company to a partially owned subsidiary.
    b. Partially owned subsidiary to another partially owned subsidiary.
    c. Partially owned subsidiary to a wholly owned subsidiary.
    d. Partially owned subsidiary to the parent company.

11. On August 31, 2002, Polanski Corporation acquired for $84,115 (a 14% yield), $100,000 face amount of 10%, 20-year bonds due August 31, 2008, of Skowalksi Company, its wholly owned subsidiary. The bonds had been issued by Skowalksi to yield 12%. In a working paper elimination (in journal entry format) for the fiscal year ended February 28, 2003, Polanski debits the Intercompany Interest Revenue ledger account for:

    a. $5,000.   b. $5,888.   c. $6,000.   d. $8,412.   e. Some other amount.

12. A working paper elimination (in journal entry format) debiting Retained Earnings—Parent and crediting Land—Subsidiary is prepared in the accounting period or periods:

    a. Of the sale of the land only.
    b. Following the period of the sale of the land only.
    c. Both of the sale of the land and following the period of the sale of the land.
    d. Neither of the sale of the land nor following the period of the sale of the land.

13. If a machine is sold by a wholly owned subsidiary to the parent company at a gain at the end of the affiliates' fiscal year, the appropriate working paper elimination (in journal entry format) will not include a(n):

    a. Debit to Retained Earnings—Subsidiary.
    b. Debit to Intercompany Gain on Sale of Machinery—Subsidiary.
    c. Credit to Machinery—Parent.
    d. Explanation.

14. If there is a $60,000 intercompany gain on the sale of machinery by a parent company to its subsidiary, and the subsidiary establishes a five-year economic life, straight-line depreciation, and no residual value for the machinery, the amount of the debit to Retained Earnings—Parent in the working paper elimination at the end of the third year of the machinery's economic life is:

    a. $24,000.
    b. $36,000.
    c. $48,000.
    d. $60,000.
    e. An indeterminable amount.

(Exercise 8.2)

On March 13, 2002, Parker Corporation loaned $100,000 to its subsidiary, Sark Company, on a 90-day, 8% promissory note. On April 12, 2002, Parker discounted the Sark note at First National Bank at a 10% discount rate.

Prepare a working paper to compute the debit to the Cash ledger account in Parker Corporation's April 12, 2002, journal entry to record the discounting of the Sark Company note. Round to the nearest dollar.

(Exercise 8.3)

On March 1, 2002, Payton Corporation loaned $10,000 to its subsidiary, Slagle Company, on a 90-day, 7% promissory note. On March 31, 2002, Payton discounted the Slagle note at a bank at a 9% discount rate.

Prepare Payton Corporation's journal entry on March 31, 2002, to record the discounting of the Slagle Company note. Round all amounts to the nearest dollar.

(Exercise 8.4)

On March 31, 2002, Scully Company, the wholly owned subsidiary of Planke Corporation, prepared the following journal entry at the instruction of Planke:

Intercompany Notes Payable	18,000	
Intercompany Interest Expense	135	
Notes Payable		18,000
Interest Payable		135

To transfer 9%, 60-day note payable to Planke Corporation dated March 1, 2002, from intercompany notes to outsider notes. Action is necessary because Planke discounted the note at 10% on this date.

Prepare a journal entry for Planke Corporation on March 31, 2002, to record the discounting of the Scully Company note with the bank. Use a 360-day year.

(Exercise 8.5)

Palos Verdes Corporation had the following events and transactions with its 90%-owned subsidiary, South Gate Company, during the fiscal year ended May 31, 2003:

2002
June 1 Palos Verdes loaned South Gate $120,000 on a 90-day, 12% promissory note.
July   1 Palos Verdes discounted the South Gate note at a bank at a 15% discount rate.

2003
May   1 South Gate declared a dividend totaling $80,000.
May 10 South Gate paid the dividend declared May 1, 2000.
May 31 South Gate reported a net income of $200,000 for the year ended May 31, 2003.

Prepare journal entries for Palos Verdes Corporation (omit explanations) for the foregoing transactions and events. Use the equity method of accounting where appropriate. (Disregard income taxes.)

(Exercise 8.6)

Peggy Corporation supplies all the merchandise sold by its wholly owned subsidiary, Sally Company. Both Peggy and Sally use the perpetual inventory system. Peggy bills merchandise to Sally at a price 25% in excess of Peggy's cost. For the fiscal year ended November 30, 2003, Peggy's sales to Sally were $120,000 at billed prices. At billed prices, Sally's December 1, 2002, inventories were $18,000, and its November 30, 2003, inventories were $24,000.

Prepare for Peggy Corporation and subsidiary an analysis of intercompany sales, cost of goods sold, and gross profit in inventories for the year ended November 30, 2003. Your analysis should show selling price, cost, and gross profit for each of the three intercompany items.

(Exercise 8.7) The intercompany sales of merchandise by Patter Corporation to its wholly owned subsidiary, Smatter Company, for the fiscal year ended February 28, 2003, may be analyzed as follows:

CHECK FIGURE

Credit cost of goods sold—Smatter, $187,500.

	Selling Price	Cost	Gross Profit
Beginning inventories	$100,000	$ 75,000	$ 25,000
Add: Sales	800,000	600,000	200,000
Subtotals	$900,000	$675,000	$225,000
Less: Ending inventories	150,000	112,500	37,500
Cost of goods sold	$750,000	$562,500	$187,500

Prepare a working paper elimination for Patter Corporation and subsidiary on February 28, 2003. Omit explanation and disregard income taxes.

(Exercise 8.8) Pele Corporation acquired 70% of the outstanding common stock of Shad Company on August 1, 2002. During the fiscal year ended July 31, 2003, Pele sold merchandise to Shad in the amount of $120,000; the merchandise was priced at 20% above Pele's cost. Shad had 30% of this merchandise in inventories on July 31, 2003.

CHECK FIGURE

Credit intercompany cost of goods sold—Pele, $100,000.

Prepare a working paper elimination (in journal entry format) for Pele Corporation and subsidiary on July 31, 2003. (Disregard income taxes.)

(Exercise 8.9) During the fiscal year ended December 31, 2003, Spring Company, a 75%-owned subsidiary of Polydom Corporation, sold merchandise costing $600,000 to Solano Company, a 90%-owned subsidiary of Polydom, at a markup of 25% on selling price. Included in Solano's December 31, 2003, inventories were goods acquired from Spring at a billed price of $200,000, representing a $40,000 increase over the comparable inventories on December 31, 2002.

CHECK FIGURE

Debit minority interest, $10,000.

Prepare a working paper elimination (in journal entry format) for Polydom Corporation and subsidiaries on December 31, 2003. (Disregard income taxes.)

(Exercise 8.10) Polar Corporation entered into business combinations with Solar Company, an 80%-owned subsidiary, and Stellar Company, a 70%-owned subsidiary, on September 30, 2002. During the fiscal year ended September 30, 2003, intercompany sales of merchandise by the two subsidiaries were as follows:

CHECK FIGURE

Credit cost of goods sold—Solar, $45,000.

	Solar Sales to Stellar	Stellar Sales to Solar
Cost of merchandise sold	$120,000	$180,000
Markup on selling price	20%	25%
Selling price of merchandise (cost to purchaser) in Sept. 30, 2003, inventories of purchaser	$ 40,000	$ 60,000

Prepare working paper eliminations (in journal entry format; omit explanations) for Polar Corporation and subsidiaries on September 30, 2003. (Disregard income taxes.)

(Exercise 8.11) Among the working paper eliminations (in journal entry format) of Parke Corporation and subsidiary on December 31, 2003, was the following (explanation omitted):

Retained Earnings—Selma ($18,750 × 0.90)	16,875	
Minority Interest in Net Assets of Subsidiary ($18,750 × 0.10)	1,875	
Accumulated Depreciation—Parke	12,500	
Machinery—Parke		25,000
Depreciation Expense (straight-line)—Parke ($25,000 ÷ 4)		6,250

Answer the following questions:

a. What is the probable explanation of the foregoing elimination?

b. How many years have elapsed since the underlying intercompany transaction? Explain.

c. How does the credit to Depreciation Expense—Parke enter into the measurement of consolidated net income for Parke Corporation and subsidiary for the year ended December 31, 2003? Explain.

(Exercise 8.12)

On October 1, 2003, the beginning of a fiscal year, Patria Corporation acquired equipment for $14,500 from its 90%-owned subsidiary, Selena Company. The equipment was carried at $9,000 in Selena's accounting records and had an economic life of 10 years on October 1, 2003. Patria uses the sum-of-the-years' digits depreciation method.

Prepare a working paper elimination (in journal entry format) for Patria Corporation and subsidiary on September 30, 2005. (Disregard income taxes.)

(Exercise 8.13)

On January 2, 2003, Steve Company, an 80%-owned subsidiary of Paulo Corporation, sold to its parent company for $20,000 a machine with a carrying amount of $16,000, a five-year economic life, and no residual value. Both Paulo and Steve use the straight-line method of depreciation for all machinery.

Compute the missing amounts in the working paper eliminations (in journal entry format) for Paulo Corporation and subsidiary that follow. Use the identifying numbers for the missing amounts in your solution.

	December 31, 2005		December 31, 2007	
Minority Interest in Net Assets of Subsidiary	(1)		(4)	
Retained Earnings—Steve	(2)		(5)	
Accumulated Depreciation—Paulo	(3)		(6)	
Machinery—Paulo		4,000		4,000
Depreciation Expense—Paulo		800		800
To eliminate unrealized intercompany gain in machinery and in related depreciation. (Income tax effects are disregarded.)				

(Exercise 8.14)

The working paper elimination (in journal entry format) on December 31, 2003, the date that Pelion Corporation entered into a sales-type lease with its subsidiary, Styron Company, was as shown below:

Intercompany Liability under Capital Lease—Styron	15,849	
Unearned Intercompany Interest Revenue—Pelion	4,151	
Intercompany Sales—Pelion	20,849	
Intercompany Cost of Goods Sold—Pelion		17,000
Intercompany Lease Receivables—Pelion		20,000
Leased Equipment—Capital Lease—Styron		
($20,849 − $17,000)		3,849
To eliminate intercompany accounts associated with intercompany lease and to defer unrealized portion of intercompany gross profit on sales-type lease. (Income tax effects are disregarded.)		

Pelion's (the lessor's) implicit interest rate, known to Styron (the lessee) and less than Stryon's incremental borrowing rate, was 10%, and the leased equipment had a 10-year economic life with no residual value. Five lease payments of $5,000 each, beginning on December 31, 2003, were required under the lease. Styron uses the straight-line method of depreciation.

Prepare a working paper elimination (in journal entry format) for Pelion Corporation and subsidiary on December 31, 2004. (Disregard income taxes.)

(Exercise 8.15) On March 1, 2003, the beginning of a fiscal year, Smart Company, the wholly owned subsidiary of Pawley Corporation, sold to Pawley for $80,000 a patent with a carrying amount of $60,000 and a four-year remaining economic life. Pawley credits amortization directly to intangible asset ledger accounts and includes amortization with operating expenses.

Prepare a working paper elimination for Pawley Corporation and subsidiary on February 29, 2004. (Omit explanation and disregard income taxes.)

(Exercise 8.16) Solaw Company, the wholly owned subsidiary of Polka Corporation, issued 10%, five-year bonds on May 1, 2003, at their face amount of $100,000. Interest is payable annually each May 1, beginning Year 2004. On April 30, 2004, the end of a fiscal year, Polka acquired in the open market 40% of Solaw's outstanding bonds at a 12% yield, plus accrued interest for one year.

Prepare a working paper to compute the amount of cash paid by Polka Corporation for Solaw Company's bonds on April 30, 2004, and the gain on the extinguishment of the bonds. Round all computations to the nearest dollar. (Disregard income taxes.)

(Exercise 8.17) On November 1, 2003, the beginning of a fiscal year, Sinn Company, the 90%-owned subsidiary of Parr Corporation, issued to the public $100,000 face amount of five-year, 9% bonds, interest payable each November 1, beginning Year 2004, for $103,993—an 8% yield. Bond issue costs may be disregarded. On October 31, 2004, Parr acquired in the open market $60,000 face amount of Sinn's 9% bonds for $58,098—a 10% yield. The realized gain on the transaction displayed in the October 31, 2004, consolidated income statement of Parr Corporation and subsidiary was $3,889. Sinn and Parr use the interest method of amortization of bond premium and accumulation of bond discount.

Prepare a working paper to compute the missing amounts in the working paper elimination (in journal entry format) below. Round all amounts to the nearest dollar. (Disregard income taxes.)

PARR CORPORATION AND SUBSIDIARY Partial Working Paper Eliminations October 31, 2005		
Intercompany Interest Revenue—Parr	(1)	
Intercompany Bonds Payable—Sinn	60,000	
Premium on Intercompany Bonds Payable—Sinn	(2)	
Investment in Sinn Company Bonds—Parr		(3)
Intercompany Interest Expense—Sinn		(4)
Retained Earnings—Sinn		(5)
Minority Interest in Net Assets of Subsidiary		389
To eliminate subsidiary's bonds owned by parent company, and related interest revenue and expense; and to increase subsidiary's beginning retained earnings by amount of unamortized realized gain on the extinguishment of the bonds. (Income tax effects are disregarded.)		

(Exercise 8.18) Palimino Corporation acquired a 70% interest in Sokal Company in 2002. For the fiscal years ended December 31, 2003 and 2004, Sokal had a net income of $80,000 and $90,000, respectively. During Year 2003, Sokal sold merchandise to Palimino for $10,000 at a gross profit of $2,000. The merchandise was resold during Year 2004 by Palimino to outsiders for $15,000.

Compute the minority interest in Sokal Company's net income for the years ended December 31, 2003 and 2004. (Disregard income taxes.)

Cases

(Case 8.1) Powell Corporation has begun selling idle machinery from a discontinued product line to a wholly owned subsidiary, Seeley Company, which needs the machinery in its operations. Powell had transferred the machinery from the Machinery ledger account to an Idle Machinery account, had written down the machinery to current fair value based on quotations from used machinery dealers, and had terminated depreciation of the idle machinery when the product line was discontinued.

During the fiscal year ended December 31, 2003, Powell's sales of idle machinery to Seeley totaled $50,000 and were accounted for by Powell and Seeley in the following aggregate journal entries:

POWELL CORPORATION Journal Entries		
Cash	50,000	
Sales of Idle Machinery		50,000
To record sales of idle machinery to Seeley Company.		
Cost of Idle Machinery Sold	40,000	
Idle Machinery		40,000

SEELEY COMPANY Journal Entries		
Machinery	50,000	
Cash		50,000
To record acquisition of used machinery from Powell Corporation.		
Depreciation Expense	5,000	
Accumulated Depreciation of Machinery		5,000
To provide, in accordance with regular policy, depreciation for one-half year in year of acquisition of machinery, based on economic life of five		

On December 31, 2003, the accountant for Powell Corporation prepared the following working paper elimination (in journal entry format):

Retained Earnings—Powell	10,000	
Machinery—Seeley		10,000
To eliminate unrealized intercompany gain in machinery.		

Instructions

Evaluate the foregoing journal entries and working paper elimination.

(Case 8.2) Sawhill Company, one of two wholly owned subsidiaries of Peasley Corporation, is in liquidation under Chapter 7 of the U.S. Bankruptcy Code. On October 31, 2003, the close of a fiscal year, Sawhill sold trade accounts receivable with a carrying amount of $50,000 to Shelton Company, the other wholly owned subsidiary of Peasley Corporation, for a gain of $10,000. Shelton debited the $10,000 to a deferred charge ledger account, which was to be amortized to expense in proportion to the amounts collected on the trade accounts receivable Shelton had acquired from Sawhill. The $10,000 gain was displayed in the consolidated income statement of Peasley Corporation and Shelton Company for the year ended October 31, 2003; Sawhill Company was not included in the consolidated financial statements on that date because it was in liquidation. Peasley used the equity method of accounting for its investments in both Shelton and Sawhill.

Instructions

Evaluate the accounting described above.

(Case 8.3) You are the newly hired controller of Winston Corporation, whose founder and sole owner, Harold Winston, engaged you to "straighten out the books" in anticipation of the company's "going public" in about three years. In reviewing the accounting records of Winston Corporation and its wholly owned subsidiary, Cranston Company, you find that both companies have used the periodic inventory system, but neither company had kept adequate records of Winston's sales of its only product to Cranston, which sold that product and other products obtained from unrelated suppliers to Cranston customers. You learned from Harold Winston that no uniform markup had been applied to products sold to Cranston; the markups varied from 15% to 25% of Winston's production costs. You also learn that the two companies had filed separate income tax returns, prepared by a local CPA firm, in past years. Your initial investigation indicates that, on the advice of the engagement partner of the local CPA firm, both Winston and Cranston had taken accurate physical inventories in past years.

Instructions

Is it possible for you to prepare fairly presented consolidated financial statements for Winston Corporation and subsidiary as of the end of the first fiscal year of your controllership? Explain.

(Case 8.4) As independent auditor of a new client, Aqua Water Corporation, you are reviewing the working paper for consolidated financial statements prepared by Arthur Brady, Aqua Water's accountant. Aqua Water distributes water to homeowners in a suburb of a large city. Aqua Water purchases the water from its subsidiary, Aqua Well Company. Aqua Water organized Aqua Well five years ago and acquired all its common stock for cash on that date.

During the course of your audit, you have learned the following:

1. Both Aqua Water and Aqua Well are public utilities subject to the jurisdiction of the state's Public Utilities Commission.

2. Aqua Well charges Aqua Water for the transmission of water from wells to consumers. The transmission charge, at the customary utility rate, was approved by the state's Public Utilities Commission.

3. Aqua Well charges Aqua Water separately for the volume of water delivered to Aqua Water's customers.

4. Your audit working papers show the following audited amounts for the two companies' separate financial statements:

	Aqua Water Corporation	Aqua Well Company
Total revenue	$3,500,000	$ 300,000
Net income	300,000	50,000
Total assets	5,700,000	1,000,000
Stockholders' equity	2,500,000	600,000

The working paper for consolidated financial statements prepared by Aqua Water Corporation's accountant appears in order, except that Aqua Well's Transmission Revenue amount of $60,000 is not offset against Aqua Water's Transmission Expense amount of $60,000. The accountant explained that, because the transmission charge by Aqua Well is at the customary utility rate approved by the state's Public Utilities Commission, the charge should not be treated as intercompany revenue and expense. Furthermore, Brady points out, the working paper for consolidated financial statements does offset Aqua Well's Water Sales amount of $200,000 against Aqua Water's Purchases amount of $200,000.

Instructions
Do you concur with the accountant's (Brady's) position? Explain.

(Case 8.5) You are a sole practitioner CPA specializing in forensic (investigative) accounting. The audit committee of Padgett Corporation, a nonpublic enterprise with ten shareholders, has requested you to investigate possible misstatements in the following condensed consolidated financial statements of Padgett and its wholly owned subsidiary, Seacoast Company:

PADGETT CORPORATION AND SUBSIDIARY
Consolidated Income Statement
For Year Ended December 31, 2003

Revenue and gains:		
Net sales		$2,000,000
Gain on sale of land		200,000
Total revenue and gains		$2,200,000
Costs and expenses:		
Cost of goods sold	$1,400,000	
Selling, general and administrative expenses	300,000	
Income taxes expense	170,000	
Total costs and expenses		1,870,000
Net income		$ 330,000
Basic earnings per share		$5.50

PADGETT CORPORATION AND SUBSIDIARY
Consolidated Balance Sheet
December 31, 2003

Assets

Current assets	$ 3,000,000
Property, plant, and equipment (net)	7,000,000
Total assets	$10,000,000

Liabilities and Stockholders' Equity

Current liabilities		$ 2,000,000
Long-term debt		5,000,000
Total liabilities		$ 7,000,000
Stockholders' equity:		
Common stock, no par or stated value; 60,000 shares authorized, issued and outstanding (no change during year)	$1,200,000	
Retained earnings (no dividends during year)	1,800,000	
Total stockholders' equity		3,000,000
Total liabilities and stockholders' equity		$10,000,000

Your investigation disclosed the following:

1. The majority stockholder, chairman of the board, and president of Padgett had authorized the sale of part of Padgett's land, having a carrying amount of $800,000, to Seacoast in 2003 for a $1,000,000, five-year, noninterest-bearing, unsecured promissory note. A fair rate of interest on the note is 8%. The $200,000 intercompany gain ($1,000,000 − $800,000 = $200,000) had not been eliminated in the preparation of the consolidated income statement of Padgett and Seacoast.

2. On December 31, 2003, Padgett had sold to Seacoast finished goods with a cost of $500,000, at Padgett's usual markup of 30% on cost. Neither the intercompany sales nor the intercompany cost of goods sold had been eliminated in the preparation of the consolidated income statement of Padgett and Seacoast. None of the finished goods had been sold by Seacoast to outsiders on December 31, 2003.

Instructions
Write a letter to the audit committee of Padgett Corporation's board of directors, describing your findings and their impact on the assets, liabilities, stockholders' equity, revenue and gains, expenses, and basic earnings per share of Padgett Corporation and subsidiary. Do not prepare revised financial statements.

Problems

(Problem 8.1)

CHECK FIGURE

a. Intercompany interest revenue, $208.

On October 21, 2003, Prentiss Corporation loaned to its 92%-owned subsidiary, Scopes Company, $100,000 on a 90-day, $7\frac{1}{2}$% promissory note. On October 31, 2003, Prentiss discounted the Scopes note at City Bank, at a discount rate of 9% a year.

Instructions
Prepare journal entries for the foregoing business transactions and events:

a. In the accounting records of Prentiss Corporation.

b. In the accounting records of Scopes Company.

Round all amounts to the nearest dollar.

(Problem 8.2) Pillsbury Corporation has begun making working capital loans to its wholly owned subsidiary, Sarpy Company, on $7\frac{1}{2}\%$ promissory notes. The following 120-day loans were made prior to June 30, 2003, the close of the fiscal year:

May 1, 2003	$15,000
May 31, 2003	20,000

CHECK FIGURE

a. June 6, credit intercompany interest revenue, $113.

On June 6, 2003, Pillsbury discounted the May 1 note at a bank, at a 9% discount rate. The bank used a 360-day year and based the discount on the maturity value of the note.

Instructions

Prepare journal entries to record the note transactions and related June 30, 2003, adjustments:

a. In the accounting records of Pillsbury Corporation.

b. In the accounting records of Sarpy Company.

Round all amounts to the nearest dollar.

(Problem 8.3) Pittsburgh Corporation completed a business combination with Syracuse Company on April 30, 2002. Immediately thereafter, Pittsburgh began making cash advances to Syracuse at a 10% annual interest rate. In addition, Syracuse agreed to pay a monthly management fee to Pittsburgh of 2% of monthly net sales. Payment was to be made no later than the tenth day of the month following Syracuse's accrual of the fee.

CHECK FIGURE

c. Intercompany revenue (expenses), $6,911.

During your audit of the financial statements of Pittsburgh Corporation and Syracuse Company as of July 31, 2002, the end of the fiscal year, you discovered that each company has set up only one ledger account—entitled Intercompany Account—to record all intercompany transactions. Details of the two accounts on July 31, 2002, are as follows:

PITTSBURGH CORPORATION LEDGER				
Intercompany Account—Syracuse Company				
Date	*Explanation*	*Debit*	*Credit*	*Balance*
2002				
May 2	Cash advance paid	4,500		4,500 dr
May 27	Cash advance paid	9,000		13,500 dr
June 11	Management fee received		2,000	11,500 dr
June 12	Repayment of May 2 advance and interest		4,550	6,950 dr
June 21	Cash advance paid	10,000		16,950 dr
July 11	Management fee received		2,200	14,750 dr
July 27	Repayment of May 27 advance and interest		9,150	5,600 dr
July 31	Cash advance paid	5,000		10,600 dr

SYRACUSE COMPANY LEDGER				
Intercompany Account—Pittsburgh Corporation				
Date	*Explanation*	*Debit*	*Credit*	*Balance*
2002				
May 3	Cash advance received		4,500	4,500 cr
May 28	Cash advance received		9,000	13,500 cr
June 10	Management fee paid			
	($100,000 × 0.02)	2,000		11,500 cr
June 11	Repayment of May 2 advance			
	and interest	4,550		6,950 cr
June 22	Cash advance received		10,000	16,950 cr
July 10	Management fee paid			
	($110,000 × 0.02)	2,200		14,750 cr
July 26	Repayment of May 27 advance			
	and interest	9,150		5,600 cr

Your audit working papers show audited net sales of $330,000 for Syracuse Company for the three months ended July 31, 2002. You agreed to the companies' use of a 360-day year for computing interest.

Instructions

a. Prepare correcting entries for Pittsburgh Corporation on July 31, 2002. Establish appropriate separate intercompany accounts in the journal entries.

b. Prepare correcting entries for Syracuse Company on July 31, 2002. Establish appropriate separate intercompany accounts in the journal entries.

c. Prepare a partial working paper for consolidated financial statements to include the intercompany accounts established in *a* and *b*.

(Problem 8.4)

CHECK FIGURE

Credit gain on
extinguishment, $1,736.

Parley Corporation owns 90% of the outstanding common stock of Silton Company. Both Parley and Silton have a February 28 (or 29) fiscal year-end. On March 1, 2003, Silton sold to Parley for $100,000 a warehouse carried in Silton's Leasehold Improvements ledger account on that date at a net amount of $80,000. Parley was amortizing the warehouse on the straight-line basis over the remaining term of the operating lease, which was to expire February 28, 2013.

On March 1, 2004, Parley acquired in the open market for $48,264 cash (a 10% yield) one-half of Silton's $100,000 face amount 8% bonds due February 28, 2006. The bonds had been issued at their face amount on March 1, 2001, with interest payable annually on February 28, beginning in 2002. Both Silton and Parley use the interest method of amortization and accumulation of bond discount.

Instructions

Prepare working paper eliminations (in journal entry format) on February 28, 2005, for Parley Corporation and subsidiary. (Disregard income taxes.)

(Problem 8.5)

CHECK FIGURE

Debit minority interest in
net assets, $1,875.

Peke Corporation sells merchandise to its 75%-owned subsidiary, Stoke Company, at a markup of 25% on cost. Stoke sells merchandise to Peke at a markup of 25% on selling price. Merchandise transactions between the two companies for the fiscal year ended June 30, 2004, were as follows, at selling prices:

	Peke Sales to Stoke	Stoke Sales to Peke
July 1, 2003, inventories of purchaser	$ 48,000	$ 30,000
Sales during year	600,000	800,000
Subtotals	$648,000	$830,000
Less: June 30, 2004, inventories of purchaser	60,000	40,000
Cost of goods sold during year	$588,000	$790,000

Instructions

Prepare working paper eliminations (in journal entry format) on June 30, 2004, for Peke Corporation and subsidiary. (Disregard income taxes.)

(Problem 8.6) For the fiscal year ended April 30, 2003, Scala Company, the 90%-owned subsidiary of Padua Corporation, had a net income of $120,000. During the year ended April 30, 2003, the following intercompany transactions and events occurred:

1. Padua sold merchandise to Scala for $180,000, at a markup of 20% on Padua's cost. Merchandise acquired from Padua in Scala's inventories totaled $54,000 on May 1, 2002, and $84,000 on April 30, 2003, at billed prices.

2. On May 1, 2002, Scala sold to Padua for $80,000 a machine with a carrying amount to Scala of $56,000. Padua established a remaining economic life of eight years, no residual value, and the straight-line method of depreciation for the machine.

3. On April 30, 2003, Padua acquired in the open market $200,000 face amount of Scala's 10%, ten-year bonds for $158,658, a yield rate of 14%. Scala had issued $400,000 face amount of the bonds on October 31, 2002, for $354,120, a yield rate of 12%. The bonds paid interest each April 30 and October 31; Padua acquired its bond investment after the interest for April 30, 2003, had been paid to the previous bondholders. Both Scala and Padua use the interest method of amortization or accumulation of bond discount.

Instructions

Prepare working paper eliminations (in journal entry format) for Padua Corporation and subsidiary on April 30, 2003, including the minority interest in net income of subsidiary. Disregard the elimination for the intercompany investment in the subsidiary's common stock; also disregard income taxes.

(Problem 8.7) On July 1, 2002, the beginning of a fiscal year, Pacific Corporation and its wholly owned subsidiary, Sommer Company, entered into the following intercompany transactions and events:

1. Pacific sold to Sommer for $16,000 a machine with a carrying amount of $12,000 ($30,000 cost less $18,000 accumulated depreciation). Sommer estimated a remaining economic life of eight years and no residual value for the machine. Sommer uses the straight-line method of depreciation for all plant assets.

2. Pacific acquired in the open market for $361,571 (a 12% yield) four-fifths of Sommer's outstanding 8% bonds due June 30, 2005 (after June 30, 2002, interest had been paid on the bonds). Sommer's accounting records on July 1, 2002, included the following ledger account balances:

8% bonds payable, due June 30, 2005	$500,000 cr
Discount on 8% bonds payable	24,870 dr

The 8% bonds (interest payable each June 30) had been issued by Sommer July 1, 2000, to yield 10%. Bond issue costs may be disregarded. Interest expense recognized by Sommer through Year 2002 was as follows:

Year ended June 30, 2001	$46,209
Year ended June 30, 2002	46,830

Both Sommer and Pacific use the interest method of amortization or accumulation of bond discount.

Instructions

a. Prepare journal entries for Pacific Corporation to record the two transactions or events with Sommer Company on July 1, 2002, and intercompany interest revenue for the year ended June 30, 2003. (Disregard income taxes.)

b. Prepare working paper eliminations (in journal entry format) for Pacific Corporation and subsidiary on June 30, 2003. (Disregard income taxes.)

(Problem 8.8)

CHECK FIGURE

b. Aug. 31, 2004, credit gain on extinguishment, $31,227.

On August 31, 2003, the end of a fiscal year, Silver Company, a wholly owned subsidiary of Pollard Corporation, issued to the public, at a yield rate of 11%, $800,000 face amount of 10%, ten-year bonds with interest payable each February 28 and August 31. Bond issue costs may be disregarded. On August 31, 2004, after Silver's interest payment, Pollard acquired in the open market $600,000 face amount of Silver's 10% bonds for $533,034, at a yield rate of 12%. On that date, Silver's Discount on Bonds Payable account had a debit balance of $44,985. Both companies use the interest method of amortization or accumulation of bond discount, and both companies close their accounting records only at the end of the fiscal year.

Instructions

a. Set up three-column ledger accounts for Pollard Corporation's Investment in Silver Company Bonds and Intercompany Interest Revenue and for Silver Company's Intercompany Bonds Payable, Discount on Intercompany Bonds Payable, and Intercompany Interest Expense. Record in the ledger accounts all transactions involving Silver's 10% bonds from August 31, 2004, through August 31, 2005. Round all amounts to the nearest dollar. Disregard income taxes, and do not prepare closing entries.

b. Prepare working paper eliminations (in journal entry format) for Pollard Corporation and subsidiary on August 31, 2004, and August 31, 2005. (Disregard income taxes.)

(Problem 8.9)

CHECK FIGURES

b. Credit leased equipment: Dec. 31, 2003, $28,242; Dec. 31, 2004, $23,535.

On December 31, 2003, Procus Corporation entered into a three-year sales-type lease with its 90%-owned subsidiary, Stoffer Company, for equipment having an economic life of six years, no residual value, and a cost in Procus's Inventories ledger account of $32,000. The lease required Stoffer to pay Procus $20,000 on December 31, 2003, 2004, and 2005, and $5,000 (a bargain purchase option) on December 31, 2006. Procus's implicit interest rate (known to Stoffer and less than Stoffer's incremental borrowing rate) was 7%, and Stoffer uses the straight-line method of depreciation. The present value of the minimum lease payments was $60,242.

Instructions

a. Set up three-column ledger accounts for Procus Corporation's Intercompany Lease Receivables, Unearned Intercompany Interest Revenue, and Intercompany Interest Revenue ledger accounts and for Stoffer Company's Leased Equipment—Capital Lease, Intercompany Liability under Capital Lease, and Intercompany Interest Expense accounts; record in the accounts all transactions and events related to the leased property for the six years ended December 31, 2009. (Round all amounts to the nearest dollar; disregard income taxes.)

b. Prepare working paper eliminations (in journal entry format) for Procus Corporation and subsidiary on December 31, 2003, and December 31, 2004. (Disregard income taxes.)

(Problem 8.10)

Patrick Corporation issued 100,000 shares of its $10 par common stock (current fair value $2,205,000) to acquire all the outstanding $10 par common stock of Shannon Company on December 31, 2002, the end of a fiscal year, in a business combination. In addition, Patrick acquired for $220,424, at a 12% yield rate, $250,000 face amount of Shannon's 9%, ten-year bonds due June 30, 2008, with interest payable each June 30 and December 31. (The current fair values of Shannon's net assets equaled their carrying amounts.) After completion of the business combination and journal entries to transfer merchandise transactions between Patrick and Shannon prior to the business combination to appropriate intercompany ledger accounts, the separate financial statements of the two companies were as follows:

CHECK FIGURE

Consolidated retained earnings, $4,799,576.

PATRICK CORPORATION AND SHANNON COMPANY
Separate Financial Statements (following business combination)
For Year Ended December 31, 2002

	Patrick Corporation	Shannon Company
Income Statements		
Revenue:		
Net sales	$15,000,000	$10,000,000
Intercompany sales (prior to business combination)		600,000
Total revenue	$15,000,000	$10,600,000
Costs and expenses:		
Cost of goods sold	$ 6,000,000	$ 6,000,000
Intercompany cost of goods sold (prior to business combination)		480,000
Operating expenses	5,350,000	2,137,000
Interest expense	150,000	108,000
Income taxes expense	1,400,000	750,000
Total costs and expenses	$12,900,000	$ 9,475,000
Net income	$ 2,100,000	$ 1,125,000
Statements of Retained Earnings		
Retained earnings, beginning of year	$ 3,530,000	$ 275,000
Add: Net income	2,100,000	1,125,000
Subtotals	$ 5,630,000	$ 1,400,000
Less: Dividends declared	800,000	270,000
Retained earnings, end of year	$ 4,830,000	$ 1,130,000

(continued)

PATRICK CORPORATION AND SHANNON COMPANY
Separate Financial Statements (following business combination) (concluded)
For Year Ended December 31, 2002

	Patrick Corporation	Shannon Company
Balance Sheets		
Assets		
Cash	$ 750,000	$ 300,000
Trade accounts receivable (net)	1,950,000	450,000
Intercompany accounts receivable (prior to business combination)		300,000
Inventories	2,100,000	950,000
Investment in Shannon Company common stock	2,205,000	
Investment in Shannon Company bonds	220,424	
Plant assets (net)	4,660,000	2,000,000
Other assets	564,576	350,000
Total assets	$12,450,000	$ 4,350,000
Liabilities and Stockholders' Equity		
Intercompany accounts payable	$ 300,000	
Other current liabilities	1,450,000	$ 945,000
Bonds payable	1,500,000	950,000
Intercompany bonds payable		250,000
Common stock, $10 par	3,000,000	900,000
Additional paid-in capital	1,370,000	175,000
Retained earnings	4,830,000	1,130,000
Total liabilities and stockholders' equity	$12,450,000	$ 4,350,000

On December 31, 2002, one-half of the merchandise acquired by Patrick from Shannon prior to the business combination remained unsold.

Instructions

Prepare a working paper for a consolidated balance sheet and related working paper eliminations (in journal entry format) for Patrick Corporation and subsidiary on December 31, 2002. (Disregard income taxes.)

(Problem 8.11) Power Corporation acquired 80% of Snyder Company's 1,250 shares of outstanding $100 par common stock on July 1, 2002, for $158,600, including out-of-pocket costs of the business combination. The excess of the current fair value of Snyder's identifiable net assets over their carrying amounts on July 1, 2002, was attributable as follows:

To inventories	$3,000
To equipment (five-year remaining economic life on July 1, 2002)	4,000
To goodwill	3,400

In addition, on July 1, 2002, Power acquired in the open market at face amount $40,000 of Snyder Company's 6% bonds payable. Interest is payable by Snyder each July 1 and January 1.

Separate financial statements for Power Corporation and Snyder Company for the periods ended December 31, 2002, were as follows:

POWER CORPORATION AND SNYDER COMPANY
Separate Financial Statements
For Periods Ended December 31, 2002

	Power Corporation (Year Ended Dec. 31, 2002)	Snyder Company (Six Months Ended Dec. 31, 2002)
Income Statements		
Revenue:		
Net sales	$ 902,000	$400,000
Intercompany sales	60,000	105,000
Intercompany interest revenue (expense)	1,200	(1,200)
Intercompany investment income	13,280	
Intercompany loss on sale of equipment	(2,000)	
Total revenue	$ 974,480	$503,800
Costs and expenses:		
Cost of goods sold	$ 720,000	$300,000
Intercompany cost of goods sold	50,000	84,000
Operating expenses and income taxes expense	124,140	99,800
Total costs and expenses	$ 894,140	$483,800
Net income	$ 80,340	$ 20,000
Statements of Retained Earnings		
Retained earnings, beginning of period	$ 220,000	$ 50,000
Add: Net income	80,340	20,000
Subtotals	$ 300,340	$ 70,000
Less: Dividends declared	36,000	9,000
Retained earnings, end of period	$ 264,340	$ 61,000
Balance Sheets		
Assets		
Intercompany receivables (payables)	$ 100	$ (100)
Inventories, at first-in, first-out cost	300,000	75,000
Investment in Snyder Company common stock	164,680	
Investment in Snyder Company bonds	40,000	
Plant assets	794,000	280,600
Accumulated depreciation of plant assets	(260,000)	(30,000)
Other assets	610,900	73,400
Total assets	$1,649,680	$398,900
Liabilities and Stockholders' Equity		
Dividends payable		$ 1,600
Bonds payable	$ 600,000	45,000
Intercompany bonds payable		40,000
Other liabilities	376,340	114,300
Common stock, $100 par	360,000	125,000
Additional paid-in capital	49,000	12,000
Retained earnings	264,340	61,000
Total liabilities and stockholders' equity	$1,649,680	$398,900

Additional Information

1. Intercompany sales data for the six months ended December 31, 2002, are at the top of page 393.

	Power Corporation	Snyder Company
Intercompany accounts payable, Dec. 31, 2002	$13,000	$ 5,500
Intercompany purchases in inventories, Dec. 31, 2002	25,000	18,000

2. On October 1, 2002, Power had sold to Snyder for $ 12,000 equipment having a carrying amount of $ 14,000 on that date. Snyder established a five-year remaining economic life, no residual value, and the straight-line method of depreciation for the equipment. Snyder includes depreciation expense in operating expenses.

3. Dividends were declared by Snyder as follows:

Sept. 30, 2002	$1,000
Dec. 31, 2002	8,000
Total dividends declared	$9,000

4. Consolidated goodwill was unimpaired as of December 31, 2002.

Instructions

Prepare a working paper for consolidated financial statements and related working paper eliminations (in journal entry format) for Power Corporation and subsidiary for the year ended December 31, 2002. (Disregard income taxes.)

(Problem 8.12) On January 2, 2002, Pritchard Corporation issued 5,000 shares of its $10 par common stock having a current fair value equal to the current fair value (and carrying amount) of the combinee's net assets in exchange for all 3,000 shares of Spangler Company's $20 par common stock outstanding on that date. Out-of-pocket costs of the business combination may be disregarded. Separate financial statements of the two companies for the year ended December 31, 2002, follow:

PRITCHARD CORPORATION AND SPANGLER COMPANY
Separate Financial Statements
For Year Ended December 31, 2002

	Pritchard Corporation	Spangler Company
Income Statements		
Revenue:		
Net sales	$499,850	$298,240
Intercompany sales	40,000	6,000
Intercompany interest revenue (expense)	300	(480)
Intercompany investment income	10,200	
Intercompany gain on sale of equipment		2,000
Total revenue	$550,350	$305,760
Costs and expenses:		
Cost of goods sold	$400,000	$225,000
Intercompany cost of goods sold	30,000	4,800
Operating expenses and income taxes expense	88,450	65,760
Total costs and expenses	$518,450	$295,560
Net income	$ 31,900	$ 10,200

PRITCHARD CORPORATION AND SPANGLER COMPANY
Separate Financial Statements (concluded)
For Year Ended December 31, 2002

	Pritchard Corporation	Spangler Company
Statements of Retained Earnings		
Retained earnings, beginning of year	$ 89,100	$ 22,100
Add: Net income	31,900	10,200
Subtotals	$121,000	$ 32,300
Less: Dividends declared		4,500
Retained earnings, end of year	$121,000	$ 27,800
Balance Sheets		
Assets		
Intercompany receivables (payables)	$ 21,300	$ (22,980)
Inventories	81,050	49,840
Investment in Spangler Company common stock	112,300	
Plant assets	83,200	43,500
Accumulated depreciation of plant assets	(12,800)	(9,300)
Other assets	71,150	56,200
Total assets	$356,200	$117,260
Liabilities and Stockholders' Equity		
Liabilities	$ 56,700	$ 9,460
Common stock, $10 par	120,000	
Common stock, $20 par		60,000
Additional paid-in capital	58,500	20,000
Retained earnings	121,000	27,800
Total liabilities and stockholders' equity	$356,200	$117,260

Additional Information

1. On December 31, 2002, Spangler owed Pritchard $16,000 on open account and $8,000 on 12% demand notes dated July 1, 2002 (interest payable at maturity). Pritchard had discounted $3,000 of the notes received from Spangler with a bank on July 1, 2002, without notifying Spangler of this action.

2. During 2002, Pritchard sold to Spangler for $40,000 merchandise that cost $30,000. Spangler's December 31, 2002, inventories included $10,000 of this merchandise priced at Spangler's cost.

3. On July 1, 2002, Spangler had sold equipment with a carrying amount of $15,000 to Pritchard for $17,000. Pritchard recognized depreciation on the equipment in the amount of $850 for 2002. The remaining economic life of the equipment on the date of sale was 10 years. Pritchard includes depreciation expense in operating expenses.

4. Spangler had shipped merchandise to Pritchard on December 31, 2002, and recorded an intercompany account receivable of $6,000 for the sale. Spangler's cost for the merchandise was $4,800. Because the merchandise was in transit, Pritchard did not record the transaction. The terms of the sale were FOB shipping point.

5. Spangler declared a dividend of $1.50 a share on December 31, 2002, payable on January 10, 2003. Pritchard made no journal entry for the dividend declaration.

Instructions

a. Prepare adjusting entries for Pritchard Corporation and Spangler Company on December 31, 2002.

b. Prepare a working paper for consolidated financial statements and related working paper eliminations (in journal entry format) for Pritchard Corporation and subsidiary on December 31, 2002. Amounts in the working paper should reflect the adjusting entries in *a*. (Disregard income taxes.)

Chapter Nine

Consolidated Financial Statements: Income Taxes, Cash Flows, and Installment Acquisitions

Scope of Chapter

This chapter considers two topics that have relevance for every business combination and parent company–subsidiary relationship: (1) income taxes and (2) the consolidated statement of cash flows. In addition, this chapter deals with accounting for installment acquisitions of a subsidiary in a business combination.

INCOME TAXES IN BUSINESS COMBINATIONS AND CONSOLIDATIONS

Accounting for income taxes for business combinations and for a consolidated entity has received considerable attention from accountants in recent years, primarily because of the emphasis on interperiod income tax allocation and disclosure in financial statements. Accounting for income taxes in business combinations and consolidated financial statements may be subdivided into three sections: (1) income taxes attributable to current fair values of a combinee's identifiable net assets, (2) income taxes attributable to undistributed earnings of subsidiaries, and (3) income taxes attributable to unrealized and realized intercompany profits (gains).

Income Taxes Attributable to Current Fair Values of a Combinee's Identifiable Net Assets

Income tax accounting requirements for business combinations often differ from financial accounting requirements. A business combination, which in accordance with financial accounting requires a revaluation of the combinee's identifiable net assets, may meet the requirements for a "tax-free corporate reorganization" under the Internal Revenue Code, in which a new income tax basis may not be required for the combinee's net assets. In such situations, a *temporary difference* may result between provisions for depreciation and amortization in the combinee's financial statements and income tax returns.

In recognition of this problem, the Financial Accounting Standards Board made the following provision for income tax considerations in the valuation of a combinee's net assets:

> A deferred tax liability or asset shall be recognized in accordance with the requirements of this Statement for differences between the assigned values and the tax bases of the assets and liabilities (except the portion of goodwill for which amortization is not deductible for tax purposes, unallocated "negative goodwill," leveraged leases, . . .) recognized in a . . . business combination.[1]

To illustrate the application of the above, assume that the business combination of Regal Corporation and the combinee, Thorne Company, completed on June 1, 2002, met the requirements for a "tax-free corporate reorganization" for income tax purposes. Regal paid $800,000 (including direct out-of-pocket costs of the business combination) for all of Thorne's identifiable net assets except cash. The current fair values of Thorne's identifiable net assets were equal to their carrying amounts, except for the following assets:

Differing Current Fair Values and Carrying Amounts of Assets

Assets	Current Fair Values	Tax Bases/ Carrying Amounts	Current Fair Value Excess	Economic Life
Inventories (first-in, first-out cost)	$ 100,000	$ 80,000	$ 20,000	
Land	250,000	220,000	30,000	
Building	640,000	500,000	140,000	20 years
Machinery	120,000	100,000	20,000	5 years
Totals	$1,110,000	$900,000	$210,000	

If the carrying amounts (equal to current fair values) of Thorne's other identifiable assets and liabilities were $390,000 and $650,000, respectively, and the income tax rate is 40%, Regal's journal entries to record the business combination with Thorne Company on June 1, 2002, would be as follows:

Journal Entries for Business Combination Including Deferred Income Tax Liability

Investment in Net Assets of Thorne Company	800,000	
Cash		800,000

To record acquisition of net assets of Thorne Company except cash, and direct out-of-pocket costs of the business combination.

Inventories	100,000	
Land	250,000	
Building	640,000	
Machinery	120,000	
Other Identifiable Assets	390,000	
Goodwill {$800,000 − [($1,110,000 + $390,000) − ($84,000 + $650,000)]}	34,000	
Deferred Income Tax Liability ($210,000 × 0.40)		84,000
Other Liabilities		650,000
Investment in Net Assets of Thorne Company		800,000

To allocate cost of Thorne's net assets to identifiable net assets; to establish liability for deferred income tax attributable to differences between current fair values and tax bases of assets; and to allocate remainder of cost to goodwill.

[1] *FASB Statement No. 109*, "Accounting for Income Taxes" (Norwalk: FASB, 1992), par. 30.

The deferred income tax liability established in the foregoing journal entry will be extinguished when the temporary differences between current fair values and tax bases of the inventories and plant assets reverse through sale or depreciation. For example, assuming the inventories were sold during the fiscal year ended May 31, 2003, the deferred tax liability would be reduced by $12,400, computed as follows:

Income Tax Effect of Reversing Temporary Differences

Cost of goods sold (inventories current fair value excess)	$20,000
Building depreciation attributable to current fair value excess	
($140,000 ÷ 20)	7,000
Machinery depreciation attributable to current fair value excess	
($20,000 ÷ 5)	4,000
Total reversing temporary differences	$31,000
Income tax effect ($31,000 × 0.40)	$12,400

Assuming that business combination goodwill was not impaired as of May 31, 2003, and that Regal Corporation had pre-tax financial income of $420,000 (excluding tax-deductible goodwill amortization of $2,267) for the year ended May 31, 2003, and there were no temporary differences between pre-tax financial income and taxable income other than those resulting from the business combination with Thorne Company, Regal's journal entry for income taxes on May 31, 2003, is as follows:

Journal Entry for Income Taxes

Income Taxes Expense ($420,000 × 0.40)	168,000	
Deferred Income Tax Liability	12,400	
Income Taxes Payable [($420,000 + $31,000) × 0.40]		180,400
To record income taxes expense for 2003.		

In the foregoing journal entry, tax-deductible goodwill amortization expense of $2,267 is *not* included in the measurement of pretax financial income, because it is based on the 15-year amortization period required by Section 197 of the *Internal Revenue Code* ($34,000 ÷ 15 = $2,267).

Income Taxes Attributable to Undistributed Earnings of Subsidiaries

In 1992, the FASB revised prior accounting standards for income taxes attributable to undistributed earnings of subsidiaries in the following provisions:[2]

1. A deferred income tax liability is to be recognized for an excess of the financial reporting carrying amount of an investment in a domestic subsidiary over its tax basis if the excess arose in fiscal years beginning after December 15, 1992.

2. A deferred income tax liability need not be recognized for an excess of the financial reporting carrying amount over the tax basis of an investment in a foreign subsidiary if the excess essentially is permanent in duration.

The substance of the foregoing is that currently a deferred income tax liability must be provided by the parent company for the undistributed earnings of its domestic subsidiaries.

[2] Ibid., pars. 32(a) and 31(a).

Illustration of Income Tax Allocation for Undistributed Earnings of Subsidiaries

Pinkley Corporation owns 75% of the outstanding common stock of Seabright Company, which it acquired for cash on April 1, 2002. Goodwill acquired by Pinkley in the business combination was $30,000 and was to be amortized for income tax purposes over 15 years; Seabright's identifiable net assets were fairly valued at their carrying amounts. For the fiscal year ended March 31, 2003, Pinkley had pretax financial income, exclusive of tax-deductible goodwill amortization and intercompany investment income under the equity method of accounting, of $100,000. Seabright's pre-tax financial income was $50,000, and dividends declared and paid by Seabright during Fiscal Year 2003 totaled $10,000. The income tax rate for both companies is 40%. Income tax laws provide for a dividend-received deduction rate of 80% on dividends from less-than-80%-owned domestic corporations. Neither Pinkley nor Seabright had any temporary differences; neither had any income subject to preference income tax rates; and there were no intercompany profits resulting from transactions between Pinkley and Seabright. Consolidated goodwill was not impaired as of March 31, 2003.

Seabright's journal entry to accrue income taxes on March 31, 2003, is as follows:

Subsidiary's Journal Entry for Accrual of Income Taxes

Income Taxes Expense	20,000	
Income Taxes Payable		20,000
To record income taxes expense for Fiscal Year 2003 ($50,000 × 0.40 = $20,000).		

On March 31, 2003, Pinkley prepares the following journal entries for income taxes payable, the subsidiary's operating results, and deferred income tax liability:

PINKLEY CORPORATION
Journal Entries
March 31, 2003

Income Taxes Expense	39,200	
Income Taxes Payable		39,200
To record income taxes expense for Fiscal Year 2003 on income exclusive of intercompany investment income ($100,000 − $2,000 tax-deductible goodwill amortization) × 0.40 = $39,200.		
Cash	7,500	
Investment in Seabright Company Common Stock		7,500
To record dividend declared and paid by subsidiary ($10,000 × 0.75 = $7,500).		
Investment in Seabright Company Common Stock	22,500	
Intercompany Investment Income		22,500
To accrue share of subsidiary's net income for Fiscal Year 2003 ($30,000* × 0.75 = $22,500).		

(continued)

PINKLEY CORPORATION
Journal Entries (concluded)
March 31, 2003

Income Taxes Expense	1,800	
Income Taxes Payable		600
Deferred Income Tax Liability		1,200
To provide for income taxes on intercompany investment income from subsidiary as follows:		

Net income of subsidiary	$30,000
Less: Depreciation and amortization attributable to differences between current fair values and carrying amounts of subsidiary's net assets	-0-
Income of subsidiary subject to income taxes	$30,000
Parent company's share ($30,000 × 0.75)	$22,500
Less: Dividend-received deduction ($22,500 × 0.80)	18,000
Amount subject to income taxes	$ 4,500
Income taxes expense ($4,500 × 0.40)	$ 1,800
Taxes currently payable based on dividend received ($7,500 × 0.20 × 0.40)	$ 600
Taxes deferred until earnings remitted by subsidiary	1,200
Income taxes expense	$ 1,800

* $50,000 − $20,000 = $30,000.

Income Taxes Attributable to Intercompany Profits (Gains)

Federal income tax laws permit an affiliated group of corporations to file a consolidated income tax return rather than separate returns. Intercompany profits (gains) and losses are eliminated in a consolidated income tax return just as they are in consolidated financial statements. An "affiliated group" for federal income tax purposes is defined as follows:

The term "affiliated group" means one or more chains of includible corporations connected through stock ownership with a common parent corporation which is an includible corporation if—

(1) Stock possessing at least 80 percent of the voting power of all classes of stock and at least 80 percent of each class of the nonvoting stock of each of the includible corporations (except the common parent corporation) is owned directly by one or more of the other includible corporations; and

(2) The common parent corporation owns directly stock possessing at least 80 percent of the voting power of all classes of stock and at least 80 percent of each class of the nonvoting stock of at least one of the other includible corporations.

As used in this subsection, the term "stock" does not include nonvoting stock which is limited and preferred as to dividends.[3]

If a parent company and its subsidiaries do not qualify for the "affiliated group" status, or if they otherwise elect to file *separate income tax returns,* the provisions of *FASB Statement No. 109,* "Accounting for Income Taxes," for the recognition of deferred tax assets and liabilities apply.[4] (Accounting for income taxes is discussed in

[3] United States, *Internal Revenue Code of 1986,* sec. 1504(a).
[4] *FASB Statement No. 109,* pars. 9(e), 121 through 124.

depth in intermediate accounting textbooks.) The deferral of income taxes accrued or paid on unrealized intercompany profits is best illustrated by returning to the intercompany profits examples in Chapter 8.[5]

Income Taxes Attributable to Unrealized Intercompany Profits in Inventories

For unrealized intercompany profits in inventories at the end of the first year of an affiliated group's operations, return to the working paper elimination (in journal entry format) on page 341 for Post Corporation and Sage Company on December 31, 2004, which is as follows:

Elimination of Unrealized Intercompany Profit in Ending Inventories

Intercompany Sales—Sage	120,000	
Intercompany Cost of Goods Sold—Sage		96,000
Cost of Goods Sold—Post		16,000
Inventories—Post		8,000
To eliminate intercompany sales, cost of goods sold, and unrealized intercompany profit in inventories.		

If Post and Sage file **separate income tax returns** for Year 2004 and the income tax rate is 40%, the following additional elimination (in journal entry format) is required on December 31, 2004:

Elimination for Income Taxes Attributable to Unrealized Intercompany Profit in Ending Inventories

Deferred Income Tax Asset—Sage	3,200	
Income Taxes Expense—Sage		3,200
To defer income taxes provided on separate income tax returns of subsidiary applicable to unrealized intercompany profits in parent company's inventories on Dec. 31, 2004 ($8,000 × 0.40 = $3,200).		

The $3,200 reduction in the income taxes expense of Sage Company (the partially owned subsidiary) enters into the computation of the minority interest in net income of the subsidiary for the year ended December 31, 2004.

With regard to unrealized intercompany profits in beginning and ending inventories, I refer to the working paper elimination (in journal entry format, on page 343) for the year ended December 31, 2005, which follows:

Elimination of Intercompany Profits in Beginning and Ending Inventories

Retained Earnings—Sage ($8,000 × 0.95)	7,600	
Minority Interest in Net Assets of Subsidiary ($8,000 × 0.05)	400	
Intercompany Sales—Sage	150,000	
Intercompany Cost of Goods Sold—Sage		120,000
Cost of Goods Sold—Post		26,000
Inventories—Post		12,000
To eliminate intercompany sales, cost of goods sold, and unrealized intercompany profit in inventories.		

---

[5] In the examples that follow, it is assumed that the provisions of *FASB Statement No. 109,* "Accounting for Income Taxes" for recognizing deferred tax assets without a valuation allowance are met.

Assuming *separate income tax returns* for Post Corporation and Sage Company for Year 2005 and an income tax rate of 40%, the following additional eliminations (in journal entry format) are appropriate on December 31, 2005:

Eliminations for Income Taxes Attributable to Intercompany Profits in Ending and Beginning Inventories

Deferred Income Tax Asset—Sage	4,800	
Income Taxes Expense—Sage		4,800
To defer income taxes provided on separate income tax returns of subsidiary applicable to unrealized intercompany profits in parent company's inventories on Dec. 31, 2005 ($12,000 × 0.40 = $4,800).		
Income Taxes Expense—Sage	3,200	
Retained Earnings—Sage ($3,200 × 0.95; or $7,600 × 0.40)		3,040
Minority Interest in Net Assets of Subsidiary ($3,200 × 0.05; or $400 × 0.40)		160
To provide for income taxes attributable to realized intercompany profits in parent company's inventories on Dec. 31, 2004 ($8,000 × 0.40 = $3,200).		

The second of the foregoing eliminations reflects the income tax effects of the *realization* by the consolidated group, on a first-in, first-out basis, of the intercompany profits in the parent company's *beginning* inventories.

Income Taxes Attributable to Unrealized Intercompany Gain in Land

Under generally accepted accounting principles, gains and losses from sales of plant assets are not extraordinary items.[6] Thus, *intraperiod* income tax allocation is not appropriate for such gains and losses.

The intercompany gain on Post Corporation's sale of land to Sage Company during Year 2004 is eliminated by the following December 31, 2004, working paper elimination (in journal entry format, from page 345):

Elimination of Unrealized Intercompany Gain in Land

Intercompany Gain on Sale of Land—Post	50,000	
Land—Sage		50,000
To eliminate unrealized intercompany gain on sale of land.		

If Post and Sage filed *separate income tax returns* for Year 2004, the following elimination (in journal entry format) accompanies the one illustrated above, assuming an income tax rate of 40%:

Elimination for Income Taxes Attributable to Unrealized Intercompany Gain in Land— for Accounting Period of Sale

Deferred Income Tax Asset—Post	20,000	
Income Taxes Expense—Post		20,000
To defer income taxes provided on separate income tax returns of parent company applicable to unrealized intercompany gain in subsidiary's land on Dec. 31, 2004 ($50,000 × 0.40 = $20,000).		

[6] *APB Opinion No. 30*, "Reporting the Results of Operations" (New York: AICPA, 1973), pars. 10 and 23(d).

In years subsequent to Year 2004, as long as the subsidiary owns the land, the following elimination (in journal entry format) accompanies the elimination that debits Retained Earnings—Post and credits Land—Sage for $50,000:

Elimination for Income Taxes Attributable to Unrealized Intercompany Gain in Land— for Accounting Periods Subsequent to Sale

Deferred Income Tax Asset—Post	20,000	
Retained Earnings—Post		20,000
To defer income taxes attributable to unrealized intercompany gain in subsidiary's land.		

In a period in which the subsidiary resold the land to an outsider, the appropriate elimination would be a debit to Income Taxes Expense—Post and a credit to Retained Earnings—Post, in the amount of $20,000, because the $50,000 gain that previously was unrealized would be realized on behalf of Post by Sage, the seller of the land to an outsider.

Income Taxes Attributable to Unrealized Intercompany Gain in a Depreciable Plant Asset

As pointed out in Chapter 8, the intercompany gain on the sale of a depreciable plant asset is realized through the periodic depreciation of the asset. Therefore, the related deferred income taxes reverse as depreciation expense is taken on the asset.

To illustrate, refer to the illustration in Chapter 8, page 347, of the December 31, 2004, working paper elimination (in journal entry format) for the unrealized intercompany gain in Post Corporation's machinery, which is reproduced below:

Elimination of Unrealized Intercompany Gain in Machinery

Intercompany Gain on Sale of Machinery—Sage	23,800	
Machinery—Post		23,800
To eliminate unrealized intercompany gain on sale of machinery.		

Assuming ***separate income tax returns*** and an income tax rate of 40%, the tax- deferral elimination on December 31, 2004 (the date of the intercompany sale of machinery), is as follows:

Elimination for Income Taxes Attributable to Unrealized Intercompany Gain in Machinery—for Accounting Period of Sale

Deferred Income Tax Asset—Sage	9,520	
Income Taxes Expense—Sage		9,520
To defer income taxes provided on separate income tax returns of subsidiary applicable to unrealized intercompany gain in parent company's machinery on Dec. 31, 2004 ($23,800 × 0.40 = $9,520).		

The $9,520 increase in the subsidiary's net income is included in the computation of the minority interest in the subsidiary's net income for Year 2004. For the year ended December 31, 2005, the elimination (in journal entry format) of the intercompany gain (see page 348) is as follows:

Elimination of Intercompany Gain in Machinery and in Related Depreciation		
Retained Earnings—Sage ($23,800 × 0.95)	22,610	
Minority Interest in Net Assets of Subsidiary ($23,800 × 0.05)	1,190	
Accumulated Depreciation—Post	4,760	
Machinery—Post		23,800
Depreciation Expense—Post		4,760
To eliminate unrealized intercompany gain in machinery and in related depreciation. Gain element in depreciation computed as $23,800 × 0.20 = $4,760, based on five-year economic life.		

For the year ended December 31, 2005, the elimination (in journal entry format) for income taxes attributable to the intercompany gain is as follows:

Elimination for Income Taxes Attributable to Intercompany Gain in Machinery—for First Year Subsequent to Sale		
Income Taxes Expense—Sage	1,904	
Deferred Income Tax Asset—Sage ($9,520 − $1,904)	7,616	
Retained Earnings—Sage ($9,520 × 0.95; or $22,610 × 0.40)		9,044
Minority Interest in Net Assets of Subsidiary ($9,520 × 0.05; or $1,190 × 0.40)		476
To provide for income taxes expense on intercompany gain realized through parent company's depreciation ($4,760 × 0.40 = $1,904); and to defer income taxes attributable to remainder of unrealized gain.		

Comparable working paper eliminations would be necessary on December 31, Years 2006, 2007, 2008, and 2009.

Income Taxes Attributable to Intercompany Gain on Extinguishment of Bonds

As pointed out in Chapter 8, a gain or loss is recognized in consolidated financial statements for one affiliate's open-market acquisition of another affiliate's bonds. Thus, income taxes attributable to the gain or loss should be provided for in a working paper elimination.

Referring to Post Corporation's December 31, 2004, open-market acquisition of Sage Company's bonds (see page 358), there is the following working paper elimination (in journal entry format) on December 31, 2004:

Elimination for Realized Gain on Extinguishment of Affiliate's Bonds		
Intercompany Bonds Payable—Sage	300,000	
Discount on Intercompany Bonds Payable—Sage		18,224
Investment in Sage Company Bonds—Post		257,175
Gain on Extinguishment of Bonds—Sage		24,601
To eliminate subsidiary's bonds acquired by parent; and to recognize gain on the extinguishment of the bonds.		

The appropriate elimination (in journal entry format) to accompany the foregoing one is as follows, assuming that (1) the income tax rate is 40%, (2) *separate income tax returns are filed,* and (3) the gain on extinguishment of bonds is not material and thus is not reported as an extraordinary item in the consolidated income statement of Post Corporation and subsidiary for Year 2004:

Income Taxes Expense—Sage	9,840	
Deferred Income Tax Liability—Sage		9,840

Elimination for Income Taxes Attributable to Realized Gain on Extinguishment of Affiliate's Bonds—for Accounting Period of Extinguishment

To provide for income taxes attributable to subsidiary's realized gain on parent company's acquisition of the subsidiary's bonds ($24,601 × 0.40 = $9,840).

The additional expense of the subsidiary recognized in the foregoing elimination enters into the computation of the minority interest in net income of the subsidiary for Year 2004.

In periods subsequent to the date of the acquisition of the bonds, the *actual* income taxes expense of both the parent company and the subsidiary reflect the effects of the intercompany interest revenue and intercompany interest expense. The income tax effects of the difference between intercompany interest revenue and expense represent the reversal of the $9,840 deferred income tax liability recorded in the foregoing elimination. For example, the working paper elimination (in journal entry format) for intercompany bonds of Post Corporation and subsidiary on December 31, 2005 (see page 362), is repeated below:

Elimination for Intercompany Bonds One Year after Acquisition

Intercompany Interest Revenue—Post	38,576	
Intercompany Bonds Payable—Sage	300,000	
Discount on Intercompany Bonds Payable—Sage		14,411
Investment in Sage Company Bonds—Post		265,751
Intercompany Interest Expense—Sage		33,813
Retained Earnings—Sage ($24,601 × 0.95)		23,371
Minority Interest in Net Assets of Subsidiary ($24,601 × 0.05)		1,230

To eliminate subsidiary's bonds owned by parent company, and related interest revenue and expense; and to increase subsidiary's beginning related earnings by the amount of unamortized realized gain on the extinguishment of the bonds.

The foregoing elimination is accompanied by the following additional elimination (in journal entry format) on December 31, 2005:

Elimination for Income Taxes Attributable to Gain on Acquisition of Affiliate's Bonds—for First Year Subsequent to Acquisition

Retained Earnings—Sage ($9,840 × 0.95; or $23,371 × 0.40)	9,348	
Minority Interest in Net Assets of Subsidiary ($9,840 × 0.05; or $1,230 × 0.40)	492	
Income Taxes Expense—Sage [($38,576 − $33,813) × 0.40]		1,905
Deferred Income Tax Liability—Sage ($9,840 − $1,905)		7,935

To reduce the subsidiary's income taxes expense for amount attributable to **recorded** intercompany gain (for consolidation purposes) on subsidiary's bonds; and to provide for remaining deferred income taxes on unrecorded portion of gain.

Summary: Income Taxes Attributable to Intercompany Profits (Gains)

This section illustrates the interperiod allocation of income taxes attributable to intercompany profits (gains) of affiliated companies that *file separate income tax returns.* The elimination of unrealized intercompany profits (gains) causes a temporary difference in which taxable income exceeds pre-tax financial income in the accounting period of the intercompany gain; thus, assuming provisions of *FASB Statement No. 109,* "Accounting for Income Taxes," for recognizing deferred tax assets without a valuation allowance are met, deferred income tax assets must be accounted for in working paper eliminations that accompany the profit (gain) eliminations. In the case of intercompany bonds, pretax financial income exceeds taxable income of the accounting period of the realized gain; thus, a deferred income tax liability must be provided in a working paper elimination.

The illustrative working paper eliminations for Post Corporation and subsidiary for the year ended December 31, 2005, outlined in the preceding pages, are summarized as follows:

POST CORPORATION AND SUBSIDIARY **Partial Working Paper Eliminations** **December 31, 2005**		
(b) Retained Earnings—Sage ($8,000 × 0.95)	7,600	
Minority Interest in Net Assets of Subsidiary ($8,000 × 0.05)	400	
Intercompany Sales—Sage	150,000	
Intercompany Cost of Goods Sold—Sage		120,000
Cost of Goods Sold—Post		26,000
Inventories—Post		12,000
To eliminate intercompany sales, cost of goods sold, and unrealized intercompany profits in inventories.		
(c) Deferred Income Tax Asset—Sage	4,800	
Income Taxes Expense—Sage		4,800
To defer income taxes provided on separate income tax returns of subsidiary applicable to unrealized intercompany profits in parent company's inventories on Dec. 31, 2005 ($12,000 × 0.40 = $4,800).		
Income Taxes Expense—Sage	3,200	
Retained Earnings—Sage ($3,200 × 0.95; or $7,600 × 0.40)		3,040
Minority Interest in Net Assets of Subsidiary ($3,200 × 0.05; or $400 × 0.40)		160
To provide for income taxes attributable to realized intercompany profits in parent company's inventories on Dec. 31, 2004 ($8,000 × 0.40 = $3,200).		
(d) Retained Earnings—Post	50,000	
Land—Sage		50,000
To eliminate unrealized intercompany gain in land.		
(e) Deferred Income Tax Asset—Post	20,000	
Retained Earnings—Post		20,000
To defer income taxes attributable to unrealized intercompany gain in subsidiary's land ($50,000 × 0.40 = $20,000).		
(f) Retained Earnings—Sage ($23,800 × 0.95)	22,610	
Minority Interest in Net Assets of Subsidiary ($23,800 × 0.05)	1,190	
Accumulated Depreciation—Post	4,760	
Machinery—Post		23,800
Depreciation Expense—Post		4,760
To eliminate unrealized intercompany gain in machinery and in related depreciation. Gain element in depreciation computed as $23,800 × 0.20 = $4,760, based on five-year economic life.		

(continued)

POST CORPORATION AND SUBSIDIARY Partial Working Paper Eliminations (concluded) December 31, 2005		
(g) Income Taxes Expense—Sage	1,904	
Deferred Income Tax Asset—Sage ($9,520 − $1,904)	7,616	
Retained Earnings—Sage ($9,520 × 0.95; or $22,610 × 0.40)		9,044
Minority Interest in Net Assets of Subsidiary ($9,520 × 0.05; or $1,190 × 0.40)		476
To provide for income taxes expense on intercompany gain realized through parent company's depreciation ($4,760 × 0.40 = $1,904); and to defer income taxes attributable to remainder of unrealized gain.		
(h) Intercompany Interest Revenue—Post	38,576	
Intercompany Bonds Payable—Sage	300,000	
Discount on Intercompany Bonds Payable—Sage		14,411
Investment in Sage Company Bonds—Post		265,751
Intercompany Interest Expense—Sage		33,813
Retained Earnings—Sage ($24,601 × 0.95)		23,371
Minority Interest in Net Assets of Subsidiary ($24,601 × 0.05)		1,230
To eliminate subsidiary's bonds owned by parent company, and related interest revenue and expense; and to increase subsidiary's beginning retained earnings by amount of unamortized realized gain on the extinguishment of the bonds.		
(i) Retained Earnings—Sage ($9,840 × 0.95; or $23,371 × 0.40)	9,348	
Minority Interest in Net Assets of Subsidiary ($9,840 × 0.05; or $1,230 × 0.40)	492	
Income Taxes Expense—Sage [($38,576 − $33,813) × 0.40]		1,905
Deferred Income Tax Liability—Sage ($9,840 − $1,905)		7,935
To reduce the subsidiary's income taxes expense for amount attributable to **recorded** intercompany gain (for consolidation purposes) on subsidiary's bonds; and to provide for remaining deferred income taxes on unrecorded portion of gain.		

All the foregoing eliminations except (d) and (e) affect the net income of Sage Company, the partially owned subsidiary. The appropriate amounts in those eliminations are included in the computation of minority interest in net income of subsidiary for Year 2005.

CONSOLIDATED STATEMENT OF CASH FLOWS

The consolidated financial statements issued by publicly owned companies include a statement of cash flows. This statement may be prepared as described in intermediate accounting textbooks; however, when the statement is prepared on a consolidated basis, a number of problems arise. Some of these are described below and on page 408:

1. Depreciation and amortization expense, as reported in the consolidated income statement, is added to total consolidated income, *which includes minority interest*

in net income of subsidiary, in a consolidated statement of cash flows. The depreciation and amortization expense in a business combination is based on the current fair values of the assets, including any goodwill, of subsidiaries on the date of the business combination. Net income applicable to minority interest is included in the computation of net cash provided by operating activities because 100% of the cash of all subsidiaries is included in a consolidated balance sheet.

2. Only cash dividends paid by the parent company and cash dividends paid by partially owned subsidiary companies *to minority stockholders* are reported as cash flows from financing activities. Cash dividends paid by subsidiaries to the parent company have no effect on consolidated cash because cash is transferred entirely *within the affiliated group* of companies. Dividends paid to minority stockholders that are material in amount may be listed separately or disclosed parenthetically in a consolidated statement of cash flows.

3. A cash acquisition by the parent company of additional shares of common stock directly from a subsidiary does not change the amount of consolidated cash and thus is not reported in a consolidated statement of cash flows.

4. A cash acquisition by the parent company of additional shares of common stock from minority stockholders reduces consolidated cash. Consequently, such an acquisition is reported in a consolidated statement of cash flows in the cash flows from investing activities section.

5. A cash sale of part of the investment in a subsidiary company increases consolidated cash (and the amount of minority interest) and thus is reported with cash flows from investing activities in a consolidated statement of cash flows. A gain or loss from such a sale represents an adjustment to consolidated net income of the parent company and its subsidiaries in the measurement of net cash flow from operating activities.

Illustration of Consolidated Statement of Cash Flows

Parent Corporation has owned 100% of the common stock of Sub Company for several years. Sub has outstanding only one class of common stock, and its total stockholders' equity on December 31, 2002, was $500,000. On January 2, 2003, Parent sold 30% of its investment in Sub's common stock to outsiders for $205,000, which was $55,000 more than the carrying amount of the stock in Parent's accounting records. Sub had a net income of $100,000 for Year 2003 and paid cash dividends of $60,000 near the end of Year 2003. During Year 2003, Parent issued additional common stock and cash of $290,000 in exchange for plant assets with a current fair value of $490,000. The consolidated entity had additional long-term borrowings of $93,000 during Year 2003, and interest payments during the year totaled $62,000, none of which was capitalized. Income tax payments totaled $234,000.

The consolidated income statement for Year 2003, the consolidated statement of stockholders' equity for Year 2003, and the comparative consolidated balance sheets on December 31, 2003 and 2002, for Parent Corporation and subsidiary are on pages 409 to 410; the working paper for consolidated statement of cash flows for Year 2003 is on pages 410 to 411; and the consolidated statement of cash flows (indirect method) for Parent Corporation and subsidiary for Year 2003 is on page 411.

PARENT CORPORATION AND SUBSIDIARY
Consolidated Income Statement
For Year Ended December 31, 2003

Sales and other revenue (including gain of $55,000 on sale of investment in Sub Company common stock)		$2,450,000
Costs and expenses:		
Costs of goods sold	$1,500,000	
Depreciation and amortization expense	210,000	
Other operating expenses	190,000	1,900,000
Income before income taxes		$ 550,000
Income taxes expense		250,000
Total consolidated income		$ 300,000
Less: Minority interest in net income of subsidiary		30,000
Net income		$ 270,000
Basic earnings per share of common stock		$ 5.14

PARENT CORPORATION AND SUBSIDIARY
Consolidated Statement of Stockholders' Equity
For Year Ended December 31, 2003

	Common Stock, $10 Par	Additional Paid-in Capital	Retained Earnings	Total
Balances, beginning of year	$500,000	$300,000	$670,000	$1,470,000
Issuance of 5,000 shares of common stock for plant assets	50,000	150,000		200,000
Net income			270,000	270,000
Cash dividends declared and paid ($2.91 a share)			(160,000)	(160,000)
Balances, end of year	$550,000	$450,000	$780,000	$1,780,000

PARENT CORPORATION AND SUBSIDIARY
Consolidated Balance Sheets
December 31, 2003 and 2002

	December 31,	
	2003	**2002**
Assets		
Cash	$ 300,000	$ 240,000
Other current assets	900,000	660,000
Plant assets	3,000,000	2,510,000
Less: Accumulated depreciation of plant assets	(1,300,000)	(1,100,000)
Intangible assets (net)	240,000	250,000
Total assets	$3,140,000	$2,560,000

(continued)

PARENT CORPORATION AND SUBSIDIARY
Consolidated Balance Sheets (concluded)
December 31, 2003 and 2002

	December 31, 2003	December 31, 2002
Liabilities and Stockholders' Equity		
Current liabilities (no notes payable)	$ 505,000	$ 490,000
Long-term debt	693,000	600,000
Common stock, $10 par	550,000	500,000
Additional paid-in capital	450,000	300,000
Minority interest in net assets of subsidiary	162,000	
Retained earnings	780,000	670,000
Total liabilities and stockholders' equity	$3,140,000	$2,560,000

PARENT CORPORATION AND SUBSIDIARY
Working Paper for Consolidated Statement of Cash Flows (indirect method)
For Year Ended December 31, 2003

	Balances Dec. 31, 2002	Transactions for Year 2003 Debit	Transactions for Year 2003 Credit	Balances Dec. 31, 2003
Cash	240,000	(x) 60,000		300,000
Other current assets less current liabilities	170,000	(5) 225,000		395,000
Plant assets	2,510,000	(6) 290,000 (9) 200,000		3,000,000
Intangible assets (net)	250,000		(3) 10,000	240,000
Totals	3,170,000			3,935,000
Accumulated depreciation	1,100,000		(3) 200,000	1,300,000
Long-term debt	600,000		(7) 93,000	693,000
Common stock, $10 par	500,000		(9) 50,000	550,000
Additional paid-in capital	300,000		(9) 150,000	450,000
Minority interest in net assets of subsidiary		(8) 18,000	(2) 30,000 (4) 150,000	162,000
Retained earnings	670,000	(8) 160,000	(1) 270,000	780,000
Totals	3,170,000	953,000	953,000	3,935,000

Operating Activities				
Net income		(1) 270,000		From operating activities $230,000
Minority interest in net income of subsidiary		(2) 30,000		
Add: Depreciation and amortization expense		(3) 210,000		
Less: Gain on sale of investment in Sub Company common stock			(4) 55,000	
Net increase in net current assets			(5) 225,000	
Investing Activities				
Sale of investment in Sub Company common stock		(4) 205,000		From investing activities ($85,000)
Acquisition of plant assets			(6) 290,000	

(continued)

PARENT CORPORATION AND SUBSIDIARY
Working Paper for Consolidated Statement of Cash Flows (indirect method) (concluded)
For Year Ended December 31, 2003

	Balances Dec. 31, 2002	Transactions for Year 2003		Balances Dec. 31, 2003
		Debit	Credit	
Financing Activities				
Long-term borrowings		(7) 93,000		From financing
Payment of dividends, including $18,000 to				activities
minority stockholders of Sub Company			(8) 178,000	($85,000)
Subtotals		808,000	748,000	
Increase in cash			(x) 60,000	
Totals		808,000	808,000	

PARENT COMPANY AND SUBSIDIARY
Consolidated Statement of Cash Flows (indirect method)
For Year Ended December 31, 2003

Net cash provided by operating activities **(Exhibit 1)**		$230,000
Cash Flows from Investing Activities:		
Disposal of investment in Sub Company common stock	$205,000	
Acquisition of plant assets	(290,000)	
Net cash used in investing activities		(85,000)
Cash Flows from Financing Activities:		
Long-term borrowings	$ 93,000	
Dividends paid, including $18,000 to minority stock-holders of Sub Company	(178,000)	
Net cash used in financing activities		(85,000)
Net increase in cash		$ 60,000
Cash, beginning of year		240,000
Cash, end of year		$300,000
Exhibit 1 Cash flows from operating activities:		
Net income		$270,000
Adjustments to reconcile net income to net cash provided by operating activities:		
Minority interest in net income of subsidiary		30,000
Depreciation and amortization expense		210,000
Gain on disposal of investment in Sub Company common stock		(55,000)
Net increase in net current assets		(225,000)*
Net cash provided by operating activities		$230,000
Exhibit 2 Supplemental disclosure of cash flow information:		
Cash paid during the year for:		
Interest (none capitalized)		$ 62,000
Income taxes		234,000
Exhibit 3 Noncash investing and financing activities:		
Common stock issued for plant assets		$200,000

* This amount was aggregated to condense the illustration; **FASB Statement No. 95,** "Statement of Cash Flows" (Stamford: FASB, 1987), par. 29, requires disclosure, as a minimum, of changes in receivables and payables pertaining to operating activities and in inventories.

The following four items in the consolidated statement of cash flows warrant emphasis:

1. Net cash provided by operating activities *includes* the minority interest in net income of Sub Company.

2. Net cash provided by operating activities *excludes* the gain of $55,000 from sale of the investment in Sub Company common stock; thus, the proceeds of $205,000 are reported as a component of cash flows from investing activities in the consolidated statement of cash flows.

3. Only the dividends paid to stockholders of Parent Corporation ($160,000) and to minority stockholders of Sub Company ($18,000) are reported as cash flows from financing activities.

4. The issuance of common stock by Parent Corporation to acquire plant assets is a *noncash transaction* [coded (9) in the working paper on page 410] that is reported in Exhibit 3 at the bottom of the consolidated statement of cash flows on page 411.

INSTALLMENT ACQUISITION OF SUBSIDIARY

A parent company may obtain control of a subsidiary in a series of installment acquisitions of the subsidiary's common stock, rather than in a single transaction constituting a business combination. The installment acquisitions necessitate application of accounting standards applicable to both *influenced investees* and *controlled subsidiaries*.

In accounting for installment acquisitions of common stock of the eventual subsidiary, accountants are faced with a difficult question: At what point in the installment acquisition sequence should current fair values be determined for the subsidiary's identifiable net assets, in accordance with accounting for business combinations? A practical answer is: Current fair values for the subsidiary's net assets should be ascertained on the date when the parent company attains control of the subsidiary. On that date, the business combination is completed.

However, this answer is not completely satisfactory, because generally accepted accounting principles require use of the equity method of accounting for investments in common stock sufficient to enable the investor to influence significantly the operating and financial policies of the investee.[7] A 20% common stock investment is presumed, in the absence of contrary evidence, to be the minimum ownership interest for exercising significant operating and financial influence over the investee. *APB Opinion No. 18,* "The Equity Method of Accounting for Investments in Common Stock," requires retroactive application of the equity method of accounting when an investor's ownership interest reaches 20%. The following example illustrates these points.

---

[7] *APB Opinion No. 18,* "The Equity Method of Accounting for Investments in Common Stock" (New York: AICPA, 1971), par. 17.

Illustration of Installment Acquisition of Parent Company's Controlling Interest

Prinz Corporation, which has a February 28 or 29 fiscal year, acquired 9,500 shares of Scarp Company's closely held 10,000 shares of outstanding $5 par common stock in installments as follows (out-of-pocket costs are disregarded):

Parent Company's Installment Acquisition of Controlling Interest in Subsidiary

Date	Number of Shares of Scarp Company Common Stock Acquired	Method of Payment by Prinz Corporation	Carrying Amount of Scarp Company's Identifiable Net Assets
Mar. 1, 2002	1,000	$ 10,000 cash	$80,000
Mar. 1, 2003	2,000	22,000 cash	85,000
Mar. 1, 2004	6,500	28,000 cash 50,000, 15% 5-year promissory note	90,000
Totals	9,500	$110,000	

The foregoing analysis indicates that Prinz made investments at a cost of $10, $11, and $12 a share in Scarp's common stock on dates when the stockholders' equity (book value) per share of Scarp's common stock was $8, $8.50, and $9, respectively. The practicality of ascertaining current fair values for Scarp's identifiable net assets on March 1, 2004, the date Prinz attained control of Scarp, is apparent.

In addition to the Common Stock ledger account with a balance of $50,000 (10,000 × $5 = $50,000) and a Paid-in Capital in Excess of Par account with a balance of $10,000, Scarp had a Retained Earnings account that showed the following changes:

Retained Earnings Account of Investee

Retained Earnings

Date	Explanation	Debit	Credit	Balance
2002 Mar. 1	Balance			20,000 cr
2003 Feb. 10	Dividends declared ($1 a share)	10,000		10,000 cr
28	Net income		15,000	25,000 cr
2004 Feb. 17	Dividends declared ($1 a share)	10,000		15,000 cr
29	Net income		15,000	30,000 cr

Parent Company's Journal Entries for Installment Acquisition

Prinz prepares the following journal entries (in addition to the usual end-of-period adjusting and closing entries) to record its investments in Scarp's common stock. (All dividends declared by Scarp are assumed to have been paid in cash on the declaration date, and income tax effects are disregarded.)

PRINZ CORPORATION
Journal Entries

2002			
Mar. 1	Investment in Scarp Company Common Stock	10,000	
	Cash		10,000
	To record acquisition of 1,000 shares of Scarp Company's outstanding common stock.		
2003			
Feb. 10	Cash	1,000	
	Dividend Revenue		1,000
	To record receipt of $1 a share cash dividend declared this date on 1,000 shares of Scarp Company common stock.		
Mar. 1	Investment in Scarp Company Common Stock	22,000	
	Cash		22,000
	To record acquisition of 2,000 shares of Scarp Company's outstanding common stock.		
1	Investment in Scarp Company Common Stock	500	
	Retained Earnings of Investee		500
	To change retroactively accounting for investment in Scarp Company to equity method from cost method; and to record retroactively 10% share of Scarp Company's net income for year ended Feb. 28, 2003, as follows:		

Share of Scarp's net income, Fiscal Year 2003 ($15,000 × 0.10)	$1,500	
Less: Dividend revenue recognized in Year 2003	1,000	
Prior period adjustment to Retained Earnings of Investee ledger account	$ 500	

2004			
Feb. 17	Cash	3,000	
	Investment in Scarp Company Common Stock		3,000
	To record receipt of $1 a share cash dividend declared this date on 3,000 shares of Scarp Company's common stock.		
29	Investment in Scarp Company Common Stock	4,500	
	Investment Income		4,500
	To record share of Scarp Company's net income for year ended Feb. 29, 2004 ($15,000 × 0.30 = $4,500).		
Mar. 1	Investment in Scarp Company Common Stock	78,000	
	Cash		28,000
	Notes Payable		50,000
	To record acquisition of 6,500 shares of Scarp Company's outstanding common stock for cash and a 15%, five-year promissory note.		

Prinz's acquisition of 6,500 shares of Scarp's outstanding common stock on March 1, 2004, constitutes a business combination. Accordingly, on that date Prinz should apply the principles of purchase accounting described in Chapters 5 and 6, including the valuation of Scarp's identifiable net assets at their current fair values. Any excess of the $78,000 cost of Prinz's investment over Prinz's 65% share of the current fair value of Scarp's identifiable net assets is assigned to goodwill.

Criticism of Foregoing Approach

The foregoing illustration of accounting for the installment acquisition of an eventual subsidiary's common stock may be criticized for its handling of goodwill. On three separate dates spanning two years, goodwill was recognized in Prinz's three acquisitions of outstanding common stock of Scarp.

It might be argued that the current fair values of Scarp's identifiable net assets should be determined on each of the three dates Prinz acquired Scarp common stock. However, such a theoretically precise application of accounting principles for long-term investments in common stock appears unwarranted in terms of cost-benefit analysis. Until Prinz attained control of Scarp, the amortization elements of Prinz's investment income presumably would not be material. Thus, the goodwill approach illustrated in the preceding section of this chapter appears to be practical and consistent with the following passage from **APB Opinion No. 18:**

> The carrying amount of an investment in common stock of an investee that qualifies for the equity method of accounting . . . may differ from the underlying equity in net assets of the investee . . . if the investor is unable to relate the difference to specific accounts of the investee, the difference should be considered to be goodwill. . . .[8]

Working Paper for Consolidated Financial Statements

The working paper for consolidated financial statements and related working paper eliminations for Prinz Corporation and subsidiary on March 1, 2004, and for subsequent accounting periods are prepared in accordance with the procedures outlined in prior chapters. Prinz's retroactive application of the equity method of accounting for its investment in Scarp's common stock results in the Investment in Scarp Company Common Stock and Retained Earnings of Subsidiary (Investee) ledger accounts on March 1, 2004, that follow:

Selected Ledger Accounts of Parent Company

Investment in Scarp Company Common Stock

Date	Explanation	Debit	Credit	Balance
2002				
Mar. 1	Acquisition of 1,000 shares	10,000		10,000 dr
2003				
Mar. 1	Acquisition of 2,000 shares	22,000		32,000 dr
1	Retroactive application of equity method of accounting	500		32,500 dr
2004				
Feb. 17	Dividends received ($1 a share)		3,000	29,500 dr
29	Share of net income	4,500		34,000 dr
Mar. 1	Acquisition of 6,500 shares	78,000		112,000 dr

[8] Ibid., par. 19(n).

Retained Earnings of Subsidiary (Investee)

Date	Explanation	Debit	Credit	Balance
2003 Mar. 1	Retroactive application of equity method of accounting		500	500 cr
2004 Feb. 29	Closing entry—share of Scarp Company adjusted net income not declared as a dividend ($4,500 − $3,000)		1,500	2,000 cr

If the current fair value of Scarp's identifiable net assets on March 1, 2001, was $90,000, the same as the carrying amount of the net assets on that date, the working paper elimination (in journal entry format) for Prinz and subsidiary on March 1, 2004, is as illustrated below. Goodwill of $26,500 recognized in the working paper elimination comprises the three components shown following the elimination. (The goodwill was unimpaired as of February 29, 2004.)

Working Paper Elimination on Date of Business Combination for Partially Owned Subsidiary Acquired in Installments

---

PRINZ CORPORATION AND SUBSIDIARY
Working Paper Elimination
March 1, 2004

(a) Common Stock, $5 par—Scarp	50,000	
Additional Paid-in Capital—Scarp	10,000	
Retained Earnings—Scarp ($30,000 − $2,000)	28,000	
Retained Earnings of Subsidiary (Investee)—Prinz	2,000	
Goodwill—Prinz ($2,000 + $5,000 + $19,500)	26,500	
Investment in Scarp Company Common Stock—Prinz		112,000
Minority Interest in Net Assets of Subsidiary		4,500

To eliminate intercompany investment and equity accounts of subsidiary on date of business combination; to allocate excess of cost over current fair value (equal to carrying amounts) of identifiable net assets acquired to goodwill; and to establish minority interest in net assets of subsidiary on date of business combination ($90,000 × 0.05 = $4,500).

Components of Net Goodwill on Date of Business Combination Accomplished in Installments

Installment Acquisition of:	Mar. 1, 2002	Mar. 1, 2003	Mar. 1, 2004
Cost of Scarp Company common stock acquired	$10,000	$22,000	$78,000
Less: Share of carrying amount of Scarp's identifiable net assets acquired:			
Mar. 1, 2002 ($80,000 × 0.10)	8,000		
Mar. 1, 2003 ($85,000 × 0.20)		17,000	
Mar. 1, 2004 ($90,000 × 0.65)			58,000
Goodwill	$ 2,000	$ 5,000	$19,500

The $2,000 portion of Scarp's retained earnings attributable to Prinz's 30% ownership of Scarp common stock prior to the business combination *is not eliminated.* Thus, consolidated retained earnings on March 1, 2004, the date of the business combination, includes the $2,000 amount plus Prinz's own retained earnings of $210,000, for a total of $212,000.

For fiscal years subsequent to March 1, 2004, Prinz recognizes intercompany investment income equal to 95% of the operating results of Scarp. In addition, Prinz recognizes any impairment losses attributable to consolidated goodwill if they occur.

On March 1, 2004, the date the business combination of Prinz Corporation and Scarp Company was completed, only a consolidated balance sheet is appropriate, for reasons discussed in Chapter 6. Below is the working paper for consolidated balance sheet of Prinz and Scarp on March 1, 2004, that reflects the working paper elimination on page 416. Amounts for Prinz and Scarp other than those illustrated in the elimination are assumed. Also, there were no intercompany transactions between the two companies prior to March 1, 2004.

Partially Owned Subsidiary on Date of Business Combination Accomplished in Installments

PRINZ CORPORATION AND SUBSIDIARY
Working Paper for Consolidated Balance Sheet
March 1, 2004

	Prinz Corporation	Scarp Company	Elimination Increase (Decrease)	Consolidated
Assets				
Current assets	400,000	140,000		540,000
Investment in Scarp Company common stock	112,000		(a) (112,000)	
Plant assets (net)	1,200,000	160,000		1,360,000
Goodwill			(a) 26,500	26,500
Total assets	1,712,000	300,000	(85,500)	1,926,500
Liabilities and Stockholders' Equity				
Current liabilities	200,000	60,000		260,000
Long-term debt	800,000	150,000		950,000
Common stock, $1 par	150,000			150,000
Common stock, $5 par		50,000	(a) (50,000)	
Additional paid-in capital	350,000	10,000	(a) (10,000)	350,000
Minority interest in net assets of subsidiary			(a) 4,500	4,500
Retained earnings	210,000	30,000	(a) (28,000)	212,000
Retained earnings of subsidiary	2,000		(a) (2,000)	
Total liabilities and stockholders' equity	1,712,000	300,000	(85,500)	1,926,500

Review Questions

1. Under what circumstances do income taxes enter into the measurement of current fair values of a combinee's identifiable net assets in a business combination?

2. What standards were established in *FASB Statement No. 109,* "Accounting for Income Taxes," for income taxes attributable to undistributed earnings of subsidiaries?

3. Are interperiod income tax allocation procedures necessary in working paper eliminations for a parent company and subsidiaries that file consolidated income tax returns? Explain.

4. A parent company and its subsidiary file separate income tax returns. How does the consolidated deferred income tax asset associated with the intercompany gain on the parent company's sale of a depreciable plant asset to its subsidiary reverse? Explain.

5. Are cash dividends declared to minority stockholders displayed in a consolidated statement of cash flows? Explain.

6. How is the equity method of accounting applied when a parent company attains control of a subsidiary in a series of common stock acquisitions? Explain.

7. At what stage in the installment acquisition of an eventual subsidiary's outstanding common stock does the parent company ascertain the current fair values of the subsidiary's identifiable net assets? Explain.

8. What amounts comprise consolidated retained earnings on the date of a business combination that involved installment acquisitions of the subsidiary's outstanding common stock?

Exercises

Select the best answer for each of the following multiple-choice questions:

(Exercise 9.1)

1. If a business combination (for financial accounting) is a "tax-free corporate reorganization" for income tax purposes, in the journal entry to record the business combination, the current fair value excesses of the combinee's identifiable net assets are:
   a. Disregarded.
   b. The basis for a credit to Deferred Income Tax Liability.
   c. Credited to the affected asset accounts.
   d. Credited to retained earnings of the combinor.

2. In a business combination that is a "tax-free corporate reorganization" for income tax purpose, may the temporary differences between current fair values and tax bases of the combinee's inventories and plant assets be realized through the assets':

	Sale?	Depreciation?
a.	Yes	Yes
b.	Yes	No
c.	No	Yes
d.	No	No

3. Under the provisions of *FASB Statement No. 109,* "Accounting for Income Taxes," a debit to Deferred Income Tax Assets is required in a working paper elimination accompanying an elimination for all of the following except an:
   a. Intercompany profit on merchandise.
   b. Intercompany bondholding (open-market acquisition; bonds originally issued at face amount).

   c. Intercompany gain on a plant asset.

   d. Intercompany gain on an intangible asset.

4. Is a deferred income tax liability typically recognized by a combinor/parent company for:

	Differences between Current Fair Values and Carrying Amounts of the Identifiable Net Assets of a Subsidiary?	Undistributed Earnings of a 65%-Owned Domestic Subsidiary?
a.	Yes	Yes
b.	Yes	No
c.	No	Yes
d.	No	No

5. The appropriate format for a parent company's journal entry to provide for income taxes on intercompany investment income from a 65%-owned domestic subsidiary that declared and paid dividends less than the amount of that income is:

   a.

Deferred Income Tax Asset	XXX	
Income Taxes Expense	XXX	
Income Taxes Payable		XXX

   b.

Deferred Income Tax Liability	XXX	
Income Taxes Expense	XXX	
Income Taxes Payable		XXX

   c.

Deferred Income Tax Asset	XXX	
Income Taxes Expense		XXX
Income Taxes Payable		XXX

   d.

Income Taxes Expense	XXX	
Income Taxes Payable		XXX
Deferred Income Tax Liability		XXX

6. If a parent company and its subsidiary file separate income tax returns, a deferred income tax liability is recognized in working paper eliminations for a:

   a. Parent company's open-market acquisition of its subsidiary's outstanding bonds.

   b. Subsidiary's sale of merchandise to its parent company.

   c. Wholly owned subsidiary's sale of land to a partially owned subsidiary.

   d. Partially owned subsidiary's sale of an intangible asset to a wholly owned subsidiary.

7. In a consolidated statement of cash flows, cash flows from financing activities include, for a partially owned subsidiary:

   a. Cash dividends paid to the parent company only.

   b. Cash dividends paid to minority stockholders only.

   c. Both cash dividends paid to the parent company and cash dividends paid to minority stockholders.

   d. Neither cash dividends paid to the parent company nor cash dividends paid to minority stockholders.

8. How is the parent company's cash acquisition of additional shares of previously unissued common stock directly from a subsidiary displayed in a consolidated statement of cash flows?

   a. As an operating cash flow.

   b. As an investing cash flow.

   c. As a financing cash flow.

   d. It is not reported.

9. In a consolidated statement of cash flows (indirect method), a gain on the parent company's disposal of a portion of its investment in the subsidiary for cash is displayed with:

   a. Cash flows from investing activities.
   b. Cash flows from financing activities.
   c. Noncash investing and financing activities (exhibit).
   d. Cash flows from operating activities (exhibit).

10. In a consolidated statement of cash flows under the indirect method, the parent company's investment income from an influenced investee that paid no dividends is displayed in:

    a. Cash flows from investing activities.
    b. Cash flows from operating activities.
    c. The exhibit reconciling net income to net cash flows from operating activities.
    d. None of the foregoing sections.

11. In a consolidated statement of cash flows prepared under the indirect method, minority interest in net income of subsidiary is added to consolidated net income for the computation of net cash provided by operating activities because:

    a. Cash dividends paid to minority stockholders by a partially owned subsidiary are excluded from cash flows from financing activities.
    b. An increase in minority interest in net assets of subsidiary is displayed with cash flows from investing activities.
    c. A decrease in minority interest in net assets of subsidiary is displayed with cash flows from financing activities.
    d. 100% of the cash of all subsidiaries is included in a consolidated balance sheet.

12. In an installment acquisition of a controlling interest in a subsidiary, the investor uses a Retained Earnings of Investee/Subsidiary ledger account:

    a. Beginning with the date of the first investment, regardless of amount.
    b. Beginning when the investment aggregates at least 20%.
    c. Beginning when the controlling interest is acquired.
    d. In none of the foregoing circumstances.

13. If a parent company applies the equity method of accounting retroactively during the course of its installment acquisition of a controlling interest in its subsidiary, consolidated retained earnings on the date that the business combination is completed includes:

    a. The parent company's retained earnings only.
    b. Both the parent company's retained earnings and 100% of the subsidiary's retained earnings.
    c. The parent company's retained earnings plus a portion of the subsidiary's earnings equal to the balance of the parent's Retained Earnings of Subsidiary (Investee) ledger account.
    d. The parent company's retained earnings plus a percentage of the subsidiary's retained earnings equal to the percentage of the subsidiary's outstanding common stock acquired by the parent company to complete the business combination.

(Exercise 9.2) Salvo Corporation merged with Mango Company in a business combination. As a result, goodwill was recognized. For income tax purposes, the business combination was considered to be a tax-free corporate reorganization. One of Mango's assets was a building with an appraised value of $150,000 on the date of the business combination. The building had a carrying amount of $90,000, net of accumulated depreciation based on the double-declining-balance method of depreciation, for financial accounting. Current fair values of other assets were equal to carrying amounts.

Assuming a 40% income tax rate, prepare a working paper to compute the amount of the deferred income tax liability that Salvo Corporation recognizes with respect to the building as a result of the business combination.

(Exercise 9.3) On May 31, 2002, Combinor Corporation acquired for $560,000 cash all the net assets except cash of Combinee Company, and paid $60,000 cash to a law firm for legal services in connection with the business combination. The balance sheet of Combinee Company on May 31, 2002, was as follows:

COMBINEE COMPANY			
Balance Sheet (prior to business combination)			
May 31, 2002			
Assets		**Liabilities and Stockholders' Equity**	
Cash	$ 40,000	Liabilities	$ 620,000
Other current assets (net)	280,000	Common stock, $1 par	250,000
Plant assets (net)	760,000	Retained earnings	330,000
Intangible assets (net)	120,000	Total liabilities and	
Total assets	$1,200,000	stockholders' equity	$1,200,000

The present value of Combinee's liabilities on May 31, 2002, was $620,000. The current fair values of its noncash assets were as follows on that date:

Other current assets	$300,000
Plant assets	780,000
Intangible assets	130,000

The income tax rate is 40%, and the business combination was a "tax-free corporate reorganization" for income tax purposes.

Prepare journal entries (omit explanations) for Combinor Corporation on May 31, 2002, to record the acquisition of the net assets of Combinee Company except cash, but including a deferred income tax liability.

(Exercise 9.4) On November 1, 2002, the date of the business combination of Prudence Corporation and its 70%-owned subsidiary, Sagacity Company, the current fair values of Sagacity's identifiable net assets equaled their carrying amounts, and goodwill amortizable over 15 years for income tax purposes was recognized in the amount of $60,000 in the working paper elimination for the consolidated balance sheet of Prudence Corporation and subsidiary on that date. For the fiscal year ended October 31, 2003, Sagacity had a net income of $140,000 and declared and paid dividends of $50,000 on that date.

Assuming that the income tax rate is 40% and Prudence qualifies for the 80% dividend-received deduction, prepare journal entries (omit explanations) for Prudence Corporation, under the equity method of accounting, for the operations of Sagacity Company for the year ended October 31, 2003, including income tax allocation.

(Exercise 9.5) During the fiscal year ended October 31, 2003, Shipp Company, a wholly owned subsidiary of Ponte Corporation, sold merchandise to Stack Company, an 80%-owned subsidiary of Ponte, at billed prices totaling $630,000, representing Shipp's usual 40% markup on cost. Stack's beginning and ending inventories for the year included merchandise purchased from Shipp at the following total billed prices:

Nov. 1, 2002	$35,000
Oct. 31, 2003	77,000

Ponte, Shipp, and Stack file separate income tax returns, and each has an income tax rate of 40%.

Prepare October 31, 2003, working paper eliminations (in journal entry format, explanations omitted) for Ponte Corporation and subsidiaries, including income tax allocation, assuming that the provisions of *FASB Statement No. 109,* "Accounting for Income Taxes," for recognizing a deferred tax asset without a valuation allowance are met.

(Exercise 9.6) During the fiscal year ended November 30, 2003, Pederson Corporation sold merchandise costing $100,000 to its 80%-owned subsidiary, Solomon Company, at a gross profit rate of 20%. On November 30, 2003, Solomon's inventories included merchandise acquired from Pederson at a billed price of $30,000—a $10,000 increase over the comparable amount in Solomon's November 30, 2002, inventories. Both Pederson and Solomon file separate income tax returns, and both are subject to an income tax rate of 40%.

Prepare working paper eliminations (in journal entry format) for merchandise transactions and related income tax allocation for Pederson Corporation and subsidiary on November 30, 2003, assuming that the provisions of *FASB Statement No. 109,* "Accounting for Income Taxes," for recognizing a deferred tax asset without a valuation allowance are met.

(Exercise 9.7) The sales of merchandise by Sol Company, 80%-owned subsidiary of Pol Corporation, to Stu Company, 70%-owned subsidiary of Pol, during the fiscal year ended October 31, 2003, may be analyzed as follows:

	Selling Price	*Cost*	*Gross Profit*
Beginning inventories	$ 80,000	$ 60,000	$ 20,000
Sales	400,000	300,000	100,000
Subtotals	$480,000	$360,000	$120,000
Ending inventories	90,000	67,500	22,500
Cost of goods sold	$390,000	$292,500	$ 97,500

Pol, Sol, and Stu file separate income tax returns, and each has an income tax rate of 40%.

Prepare working paper eliminations, including income taxes allocation, in journal entry format (omit explanations) for Pol Corporation and subsidiaries on October 31, 2003, assuming that the provisions of *FASB Statement No. 109,* "Accounting for Income Taxes," for recognizing a deferred tax asset without a valuation allowance are met.

(Exercise 9.8) The following working paper eliminations (in journal entry format) were prepared by the accountant for Purdue Corporation on February 28, 2003, the end of a fiscal year:

PURDUE CORPORATION AND SUBSIDIARY **Working Paper Eliminations** **February 28, 2003**		
Intercompany Gain on Sale of Machinery—Purdue	12,000	
Machinery—Scarsdale		12,000
To eliminate unrealized intercompany gain on February 28, 2003, sale of machine with a six-year economic life, no residual value, and straight-line depreciation method.		
Deferred Income Tax Asset—Purdue ($12,000 × 0.40)	4,800	
Income Taxes Expense—Purdue		4,800
To defer income taxes provided in separate income tax returns of parent company applicable to unrealized intercompany gain in subsidiary's machinery on February 28, 2003.		

Prepare working paper eliminations (in journal entry format, explanations omitted) for Purdue Corporation and subsidiary on February 29, 2004, assuming that the provisions of *FASB Statement No. 109,* "Accounting for Income Taxes," for recognizing a deferred tax asset without a valuation allowance are met.

(Exercise 9.9) The working paper eliminations (in journal entry format) of Pegler Corporation and its wholly owned subsidiary, Stang Company, on October 31, 2003, included the following:

(b) Retained Earnings—Stang	10,000	
Intercompany Sales—Stang	240,000	
Intercompany Cost of Goods Sold—Stang		120,000
Cost of Goods Sold—Pegler		60,000
Inventories—Pegler		70,000
To eliminate intercompany sales, cost of goods sold, and unrealized intercompany profit in inventories.		
(c) Retained Earnings—Pegler	40,000	
Accumulated Depreciation—Stang	60,000	
Machinery—Stang		80,000
Depreciation Expense—Stang		20,000
To eliminate unrealized intercompany gain in machinery and in related depreciation. Gain element in depreciation computed as $80,000 ÷ 4 = $20,000, based on four-year economic life of machinery.		

Both Pegler and Stang file separate tax returns, and both have an income tax rate of 40%.

Prepare required additional working paper eliminations (in journal entry format; omit explanations) for Pegler Corporation and subsidiary on October 31, 2003, assuming that the provisions of *FASB Statement No. 109,* "Accounting for Income Taxes," for recognizing a deferred tax asset without a valuation allowance are met.

(Exercise 9.10) On October 31, 2003, Salvador Company, 80%-owned subsidiary of Panama Corporation, sold to its parent company for $20,000 a patent with a carrying amount of $15,000 on that date. Remaining legal life of the patent on October 31, 2003, was five years; the patent was expected to produce revenue for Panama during the entire five-year period. Panama and Salvador file separate income tax returns; their income tax rate is 40%. Panama uses an Accumulated Amortization of Patent ledger account.

Assuming that the provisions of *FASB Statement No. 109,* "Accounting for Income Taxes," for recognizing a deferred tax asset without a valuation allowance are met, prepare working paper eliminations (in journal entry format), including income tax allocation, for Panama Corporation and subsidiary with respect to the patent: (*a*) on October 31, 2003, and (*b*) on October 31, 2004.

(Exercise 9.11) The following working paper elimination (in journal entry format) was prepared for Plumm Corporation and subsidiary on March 31, 2003:

CHECK FIGURE

Credit deferred income tax liability—Sam, $7,384.

Intercompany Interest Revenue—Plumm ($456,477 × 0.10)	45,645	
Intercompany 8% Bonds Payable—Sam	500,000	
Discount on Intercompany 8% Bonds Payable—Sam ($22,429 − $2,981)		19,448
Investment in Sam Company Bonds—Plumm ($456,447 + $5,645)		462,092
Intercompany Interest Expense—Sam ($477,571 × 0.09)		42,981
Retained Earnings—Sam ($477,571 − $456,447)		21,124

To eliminate subsidiary's bonds owned by parent company, and related interest revenue and expense; and to increase subsidiary's beginning retained earnings by amount of unamortized realized gain on the extinguishment of the bonds.

Plumm and Sam file separate income tax returns, and both are subject to a 40% income tax rate.

Prepare a working paper elimination (in journal entry format) for Plumm Corporation and subsidiary on March 31, 2003, for the income tax effects of the foregoing elimination. Omit the explanation for the elimination.

(Exercise 9.12) On October 31, 2003, Pom Corporation acquired in the open market $500,000 face amount of the 10%, ten-year bonds due October 31, 2012, of its wholly owned subsidiary, Sepp Company. The bonds had been issued by Sepp on October 31, 2002, to yield 12%. Pom's investment was at a 15% yield rate. Both Pom and Sepp file separate income tax returns, both companies are subject to an income tax rate of 40%, and neither company has any items requiring interperiod or intraperiod income tax allocation other than the Sepp Company bonds, on which interest is payable each October 31. Working paper eliminations (in journal entry format) related to the bonds on October 31, 2003, and October 31, 2004, with certain amounts omitted, are as follows:

CHECK FIGURE

(4) $1,420.

POM CORPORATION AND SUBSIDIARY
Partial Working Paper Eliminations
October 31, 2003

Intercompany Bonds Payable—Sepp	500,000	
Discount on Intercompany Bonds Payable—Sepp		53,283
Investment in Sepp Company Bonds—Pom		380,710
Gain on Extinguishment of Bonds—Sepp		66,007*

To eliminate subsidiary's bonds acquired by parent, and to recognize gain on the extinguishment of the bonds.

Income Taxes Expense—Sepp	(1)	
Deferred Income Tax Liability—Sepp		(2)

To provide for income taxes attributable to subsidiary's realized gain on parent company's acquisition of the subsidiary's bonds.

* Not material.

POM CORPORATION AND SUBSIDIARY Partial Working Paper Eliminations October 31, 2004		
Intercompany Interest Revenue—Pom	57,107	
Intercompany Bonds Payable—Sepp	500,000	
Discount on Intercompany Bonds Payable—Sepp		49,725
Investment in Sepp Company Bonds—Pom		387,817
Intercompany Interest Expense—Sepp		53,558
Retained Earnings—Sepp		66,007
To eliminate subsidiary's bonds owned by parent company, and related interest revenue and expense; and to increase subsidiary's beginning retained earnings by amount of unamortized realized gain on the extinguishment of the bonds.		
Retained Earnings—Sepp	(3)	
Income Taxes Expense—Sepp		(4)
Deferred Income Tax Liability—Sepp		(5)
To reduce the subsidiary's income taxes expense for amount attributable to recorded intercompany gain (for consolidation purposes) on subsidiary's bonds; and to provide for remaining deferred income taxes on unrecorded portion of gain.		

Prepare a working paper to compute the five missing amounts in the foregoing working paper eliminations.

(Exercise 9.13) Prieto Corporation declared and paid cash dividends of $250,000 on its common stock and distributed a 5% common stock dividend in 2003. The current fair value of the shares distributed pursuant to the 5% stock dividend was $600,000. Prieto owns 100% of the common stock of Sora Company and 75% of the common stock of Sano Company. In 2003, Sora declared and paid cash dividends of $100,000 on its common stock and $25,000 on its $5 cumulative preferred stock. None of the preferred stock is owned by Prieto. In 2003, Sano declared and paid cash dividends of $44,000 on its common stock, the only class of capital stock issued.

Prepare a working paper to compute the amount to be displayed as cash flows for the payment of dividends in the Year 2003 consolidated statement of cash flows for Prieto Corporation and subsidiaries.

(Exercise 9.14) The consolidated statement of cash flows (indirect method) for Paradise Corporation and its partially owned subsidiaries is to be prepared for Year 2003. Using the following letters, indicate how each of the 13 items listed on page 426 should be displayed in the statement.

A–O = Add to combined net income in the computation of net cash provided by operating activities

D–O = Deduct from combined net income in the computation of net cash provided by operating activities

IA = A cash flow from investing activities

FA = A cash flow from financing activities

N = Not included or separately displayed in the consolidated statement of cash flows, but possibly disclosed in a separate exhibit

(1) The minority interest in net income of subsidiaries is $37,500.

(2) Paradise issued a note payable to a subsidiary company in exchange for plant assets with a current fair value of $180,000.

(3) Paradise distributed a 10% stock dividend; the additional shares of common stock issued had a current fair value of $675,000.

(4) Paradise declared and paid a cash dividend of $200,000.

(5) Long-term debt of Paradise in the amount of $2 million was converted to its common stock.

(6) A subsidiary sold plant assets to outsiders at the carrying amount of $80,000.

(7) Paradise's share of the net income of an influenced investee totaled $28,000. The investee did not declare or pay cash dividends in 2003.

(8) Consolidated depreciation and amortization expense totaled $285,000.

(9) A subsidiary amortized $3,000 of premium on bonds payable owned by outsiders.

(10) Paradise sold its entire holdings in an 80%-owned subsidiary for $3 million.

(11) Paradise merged with Sun Company in a business combination; 150,000 shares of common stock with a current fair value of $4.5 million were issued by Paradise for 98% of Sun's outstanding common stock.

(12) Paradise received cash dividends of $117,000 from its subsidiaries.

(13) The subsidiaries of Paradise declared and paid cash dividends of $21,500 to minority stockholders.

(Exercise 9.15) On August 1, 2002, Packard Corporation acquired 1,000 of the 10,000 outstanding shares of Stenn Company's $1 par common stock for $5,000. Stenn's identifiable net assets had a current fair value and carrying amount of $40,000 on that date. Stenn had a net income of $3,000 and declared and paid dividends of the same amount for the fiscal year ended July 31, 2003. On August 1, 2003, Packard acquired 4,500 more shares of Stenn's outstanding common stock for $22,500. The current fair values and carrying amounts of Stenn's identifiable net assets were still $40,000 on that date. Stenn had a net income of $7,500 and declared no dividends for the fiscal year ended July 31, 2004.

CHECK FIGURE

July 31, 2004, credit Intercompany Investment Income, $4,125.

Prepare journal entries for Packard Corporation for the foregoing business transactions and events for the two years ended July 31, 2004. (Omit explanations and disregard income tax effects.) Consolidated goodwill was unimpaired at July 31, 2004.

Cases

(Case 9.1) In a classroom discussion of accounting standards established in *FASB Statement No. 109,* "Accounting for Income Taxes," student Laura was critical of the requirement to establish a deferred tax asset or liability for differences between the assigned values and the tax bases of most assets and liabilities recognized in a business combination (see page 397). Laura pointed out that, in the usual situation of assigned values in excess of tax bases, the recognition of a deferred tax liability for the resultant differences has the effect of increasing goodwill (or decreasing "bargain-purchase excess") otherwise recognized in the business combination. Laura questions whether, on the date of the business combination, the so-called deferred income tax liability is really a *liability,* as defined in paragraph 35 of *FASB Concepts Statement No. 6,* "Elements of Financial Statements." Student Jason responds that in paragraphs 75 through 79 of

FASB Statement No. 109, the FASB dealt with the issue raised by Laura and concluded that deferred income tax liabilities resulting from purchase-type business combinations are indeed *liabilities.*

Instructions

Do you agree with student Jason that the FASB's conclusion should put to rest criticisms of *FASB Statement No. 109* such as that expressed by student Laura? Explain.

(Case 9.2) On April 1, 2002, the beginning of a fiscal year, Paddock Corporation acquired 70% of the outstanding common stock of domestic subsidiary Serge Company in a business combination. In your audit of the consolidated financial statements of Paddock Corporation and subsidiary for the year ended March 31, 2003, you discover that Serge had a net income of $50,000 for the year but did not declare or pay any cash dividends. Nonetheless, Paddock did not record a deferred income tax liability applicable to Serge's undistributed earnings, net of the 80% dividend-received deduction, despite Paddock's having adopted the equity method of accounting for Serge's operating results.

In response to your inquiries, the controller of Paddock pointed out that Serge's severe cash shortage made the declaration and payment of cash dividends by Serge doubtful for the next several years. Therefore, stated the controller, a provision for deferred income taxes on Serge's undistributed earnings for the year ended March 31, 2003, is inappropriate under generally accepted accounting principles.

Instructions

Do you agree with the controller's interpretation of generally accepted accounting principles for the undistributed earnings of Serge Company? Explain.

(Case 9.3) The recognition of goodwill on a *residual* basis in business combinations has been criticized by some accountants (see page 188). In the accounting for business combinations accomplished in installments, described on pages 412 through 417, more than one amount of goodwill may be recognized.

Instructions

Assume that you are asked to advise the Financial Accounting Standards Board on alternatives to recognizing multiple amounts of goodwill in business combinations accomplished in installments. What alternatives would you recommend? Explain.

(Case 9.4) As controller of Pantheon Corporation, a publicly owned enterprise that has a wholly owned subsidiary, Synthesis Company, you are considering whether a valuation allowance, as discussed in paragraph 17(e) of *FASB Statement No. 109,* "Accounting for Income Taxes," is required for the $400,000 deferred income tax asset related to the $1,000,000 unrealized intercompany gain from Pantheon's sale of part of its land to Synthesis as the site for a new factory building for Synthesis. For valid reasons, Pantheon and Synthesis file separate income tax returns; therefore, Pantheon has paid the $400,000 amount as part of its overall federal and state income tax obligations. You are aware that, unless Synthesis sells the land to an outsider in the future, the $1,000,000 gain will not be realized by the consolidated entity. Nonetheless, you know that land values are increasing in the area surrounding Synthesis's land, and that it is more likely than not that Synthesis would realize a gain if it did sell the land to an outsider. You also are aware that valuation allowances for deferred tax assets based on future taxable income were included in the AICPA's *Statement of Position 94-6,* "Disclosure of Certain Significant Risks and Uncertainties," especially in paragraphs A-43 through A-45 of Appendix A thereof.

Instructions

Do you consider a valuation allowance necessary for the $400,000 deferred tax asset of Pantheon Corporation and subsidiary? Explain.

Problems

(Problem 9.1) This problem consists of two unrelated parts.

a. The merchandise sales by Pro Corporation's wholly owned subsidiary, Spa Company, to Pro's 80%-owned subsidiary, Sol Company, may be analyzed as follows for the year ended October 31, 2003:

	Selling Price	Cost	Gross Profit (33⅓ of Cost; 25% of Selling Price)
Beginning inventories	$ 100,000	$ 75,000	$ 25,000
Sales	2,000,000	1,500,000	500,000
Subtotals	$2,100,000	$1,575,000	$525,000
Ending inventories	300,000	225,000	75,000
Cost of goods sold	$1,800,000	$1,350,000	$450,000

Pro, Spa, and Sol use the perpetual inventory system, file separate income tax returns, and have an income tax rate of 40%.

Instructions

Prepare working paper eliminations (in journal entry format), including income taxes allocation, for Pro Corporation and subsidiaries on October 31, 2003.

b. The following working paper eliminations (in journal entry format) were prepared by the accountant for Primrose Corporation, which had a single wholly owned subsidiary:

PRIMROSE CORPORATION AND SUBSIDIARY **Partial Working Paper Eliminations** **April 30, 2003**		
Intercompany 8% Bonds Payable—Safflower	1,000,000	
Discount on Intercompany 8% Bonds Payable—Safflower		124,622
Investment in Safflower Company 8% Bonds—Primrose		770,602
Gain on Extinguishment of Bonds—Safflower		104,776
To eliminate subsidiary's bonds (interest payable Apr. 30 and Oct. 31), which had been issued to yield 10% and were acquired by parent company at a 12% yield; and to recognize gain on the extinguishment of the bonds.		
Income Taxes Expense—Safflower ($104,776 × 0.40)	41,910	
Deferred Income Tax Liability—Safflower		41,910
To provide for income taxes attributable to subsidiary's realized gain on parent company's acquisition of the subsidiary's bonds.		

Instructions

Prepare comparable working paper eliminations for Primrose Corporation and subsidiary on October 31, 2003.

(Problem 9.2)   The working paper eliminations (in journal entry format) for intercompany bonds of Pullet Corporation and its wholly owned subsidiary on November 30, 2003, the end of a fiscal year, follow. The bonds, which had been issued by Sagehen Company for a five-year term on November 30, 2002, to yield 10%, were acquired in the open market by Pullet on November 30, 2003, to yield 12%. Interest on the bonds is payable at the rate of 8% each November 30, 2003 through 2007. Both companies use the interest method of amortization or accumulation of bond premium or discount.

CHECK FIGURE
b. Credit deferred income tax liability, $1,112.

PULLET CORPORATION AND SUBSIDIARY **Partial Working Paper Eliminations** **November 30, 2003**		
Intercompany Bonds Payable—Sagehen	60,000	
Discount on Intercompany Bonds Payable—Sagehen		3,804
Investment in Sagehen Company Bonds—Pullet		52,710
Gain on Extinguishment of Bonds—Sagehen		3,486*
To eliminate subsidiary's bonds acquired by parent; and to recognize gain on the extinguishment of the bonds.		
Income Taxes Expense—Sagehen ($3,486 × 0.40)	1,394	
Deferred Income Tax Liability—Sagehen		1,394
To provide for income taxes attributable to subsidiary's realized gain on parent company's acquisition of the subsidiary's bonds.		

* Not material.

Instructions

a. Prepare journal entries for both Pullet Corporation and Sagehen Company to recognize intercompany interest revenue and expense, respectively, on November 30, 2004. Disregard Sagehen's bonds owned by outsiders.

b. Prepare working paper eliminations (in journal entry format) for Pullet Corporation and subsidiary on November 30, 2004, including allocation of income taxes.

(Problem 9.3)   On January 2, 2002, Presto Corporation issued 10,000 shares of its $1 par (current fair value $40) common stock for all 50,000 shares of Shuey Company's outstanding common stock in a statutory merger that was a business combination. Out-of-pocket costs in connection with the combination, paid by Presto on January 2, 2002, were as follows:

Finder's fee, accounting fees, and legal fees relating to the business combination	$60,000
Costs associated with SEC registration statement for securities issued to complete the business combination	30,000
Total out-of-pocket costs of business combination	$90,000

For income tax purposes, the business combination qualified as a "Type A tax-free corporate reorganization." The balance sheet of Shuey Company on January 2, 2002, with associated current fair values of assets and liabilities, was as follows:

SHUEY COMPANY
Balance Sheet (prior to business combination)
January 2, 2002

	Carrying Amounts	Current Fair Values
Assets		
Cash	$ 20,000	$ 20,000
Trade accounts receivable (net)	80,000	80,000
Inventories	120,000	160,000
Short-term prepayments	10,000	10,000
Investments in held-to-maturity debt securities	30,000	45,000
Plant assets (net)	430,000	490,000
Intangible assets (net)	110,000	130,000
Total assets	$800,000	$935,000
Liabilities and Stockholders' Equity		
Liabilities:		
Notes payable	$ 60,000	$ 60,000
Trade accounts payable	90,000	90,000
Income taxes payable	30,000	30,000
Long-term debt	300,000	300,000
Total liabilities	$480,000	$480,000
Stockholders' equity:		
Common stock, $2 par	$100,000	
Additional paid-in capital	100,000	
Retained earnings	120,000	
Total stockholders' equity	$320,000	
Total liabilities and stockholders' equity	$800,000	

The income tax rate for both Presto and Shuey is 40%.

Instructions
Prepare journal entries for Presto Corporation to record the business combination with Shuey Company on January 2, 2002, including deferred income taxes.

(Problem 9.4) Separate balance sheets of Pellerin Corporation and its subsidiary, Sigmund Company, on the dates indicated, are as follows. Both companies have a December 31 fiscal year.

PELLERIN CORPORATION AND SIGMUND COMPANY				
Separate Balance Sheets				
Various Dates, Year 2002				
	Pellerin Corporation	Sigmund Company		
	Dec. 31, 2002	Jan. 2, 2002	Sept. 30, 2002	Dec. 31, 2002
Assets				
Cash	$ 400,000	$ 550,000	$ 650,000	$ 425,000
Fees and royalties receivable		250,000	450,000	500,000
Investment in Sigmund Company common stock	2,240,000			
Patents (net)		1,000,000	850,000	800,000
Other assets (net)	4,360,000			200,000
Total assets	$7,000,000	$1,800,000	$1,950,000	$1,925,000
Liabilities and Stockholders' Equity				
Liabilities	$ 400,000	$ 200,000	$ 150,000	$ 275,000
Common stock, $10 par	5,000,000	1,000,000	1,000,000	1,000,000
Retained earnings	1,600,000	600,000	800,000	650,000
Total liabilities and stockholders' equity	$7,000,000	$1,800,000	$1,950,000	$1,925,000

Additional Information

1. Pellerin had acquired 30,000 shares of Sigmund's outstanding common stock on January 2, 2002, at a cost of $480,000; and 60,000 shares on September 30, 2002, at a cost of $1,760,000. Pellerin obtained control over Sigmund because of the valuable patents owned by Sigmund.

2. Sigmund amortizes the cost of patents on a straight-line basis. Any amount allocated to patents as a result of the business combination is to be amortized over the five-year remaining economic life of the patents from January 2, 2002.

3. Sigmund declared and paid a cash dividend of $300,000 on December 31, 2002. Pellerin had not recorded either the declaration or the receipt of the dividend.

Instructions

Prepare journal entries for Pellerin Corporation on December 31, 2002, to account for its investments in Sigmund Company under the equity method of accounting. Disregard income taxes, and do not prepare journal entries for Pellerin's *acquisition* of the investments in Sigmund.

(Problem 9.5) Consolidated financial statements of Porcelain Corporation and its 80%-owned subsidiary, Skinner Company, for the year ended December 31, 2003, including comparative consolidated balance sheets on December 31, 2002, are as follows:

PORCELAIN CORPORATION AND SUBSIDIARY
Consolidated Income Statement
For Year Ended December 31, 2003

Revenue:		
Net sales		$1,200,000
Gain on disposal of plant assets		50,000
Total revenue		$1,250,000
Costs and expenses and minority interest:		
Cost of goods sold	$700,000	
Depreciation expense	40,000	
Amortization expense	20,000	
Other operating expenses	120,000	
Interest expense	50,000	
Income taxes expense	192,000	
Minority interest in net income of subsidiary	10,000	1,132,000
Net income		$ 118,000
Basic earnings per share of common stock		$ 1.97

PORCELAIN CORPORATION AND SUBSIDIARY
Consolidated Statement of Stockholders' Equity
For Year Ended December 31, 2003

	Common Stock, $1 par	Additional Paid-in Capital	Retained Earnings	Total
Balances, beginning of year	$ 60,000	$30,000	$180,000	$270,000
Issuance of 40,000 shares of common stock at $1.75 a share	40,000	30,000		70,000
Net income			118,000	118,000
Cash dividends declared and paid ($1 a share)			(60,000)	(60,000)
Balances, end of year	$100,000	$60,000	$238,000	$398,000

PORCELAIN CORPORATION AND SUBSIDIARY
Consolidated Balance Sheets
December 31, 2003 and 2002

	2003	2002
Assets		
Cash	$ 70,000	$ 50,000
Other current assets	230,000	150,000
Plant assets (net)	680,000	600,000
Goodwill	140,000	160,000
Total assets	$1,120,000	$960,000

(continued)

PORCELAIN CORPORATION AND SUBSIDIARY
Consolidated Balance Sheets (concluded)
December 31, 2003 and 2002

	2003	2002
Liabilities and Stockholders' Equity		
Liabilities:		
Current liabilities, including current portion of		
note payable	$ 187,000	$110,000
Note payable, due $50,000 annually, plus interest at 10%	450,000	500,000
Total liabilities	$ 637,000	$610,000
Stockholders' equity:		
Common stock, $1 par	$ 100,000	$ 60,000
Additional paid-in capital	60,000	30,000
Minority interest in net assets of subsidiary	85,000	80,000
Retained earnings	238,000	180,000
Total stockholders' equity	$ 483,000	$350,000
Total liabilities and stockholders' equity	$1,120,000	$960,000

Additional Information

1. The affiliated companies acquired plant assets for $220,000 cash during the year ended December 31, 2003. Also during the year, Skinner Company, the 80%-owned subsidiary of Porcelain, sold plant assets with a carrying amount of $100,000 to an outsider for $150,000 cash.

2. Skinner declared and paid dividends totaling $25,000 during the year ended December 31, 2003.

Instructions

Prepare a consolidated statement of cash flows (indirect method) for Porcelain Corporation and subsidiary for the year ended December 31, 2003, without using a working paper. Disregard disclosure of cash paid for interest and income taxes.

(Problem 9.6) The following transactions took place between Parkhurst Corporation and its wholly owned subsidiary, Sandland Company, which file separate income tax returns, during the fiscal year ended March 31, 2003:

1. Parkhurst sold to Sandland at a 30% gross profit rate merchandise with a total sale price of $200,000. Sandland's March 31, 2003, inventories included $40,000 (billed prices) of the merchandise obtained from Parkhurst—a $20,000 increase from the related April 1, 2002, inventories amount. Both Parkhurst and Sandland use the perpetual inventory system.

2. On April 1, 2002, Sandland sold to Parkhurst for $50,000 a machine with a carrying amount of $30,000 on that date. The economic life of the machine to Parkhurst was five years, with no residual value. Parkhurst uses the straight-line method of depreciation for all plant assets.

3. On February 28, 2003, Parkhurst sold land for a plant site to Sandland for $480,000. The land had a carrying amount to Parkhurst of $360,000.

4. On March 31, 2003, following Sandland's payment of interest to bondholders, Parkhurst acquired in the open market for $487,537, a 16% yield, 60% of Sandland's 12%, ten-year bonds dated March 31, 2002. The bonds had been issued to the public by Sandland on March 31, 2002, to yield 14%. On March 31, 2003,

after the payment of interest, Sandland's accounting records included the following ledger account balances relative to the bonds:

12% bonds payable	$1,000,000 cr
Discount on 12% bonds payable	100,590 dr

Both Parkhurst and Sandland use the interest method of amortization or accumulation of bond discount. The income tax rate for both affiliated companies, which file separate income tax returns, is 40%.

Instructions
Prepare working paper eliminations (in journal entry format), including income taxes allocation, for Parkhurst Corporation and subsidiary on March 31, 2003. Round all amounts to the nearest dollar.

(Problem 9.7)

Paine Corporation owns 99% of the outstanding common stock of Spilberg Company, acquired July 1, 2002, in a business combination that did not involve goodwill; and 90% of the outstanding common stock of Sykes Company, acquired July 1, 2002, in a business combination that reflected goodwill of $52,200. All identifiable net assets of both Spilberg and Sykes were fairly valued at their carrying amounts on July 1, 2002. Goodwill is amortized over 15 years for income tax purposes.

Separate financial statements of Paine, Spilberg, and Sykes for the fiscal year ended June 30, 2003, prior to income tax provisions and equity-method accruals in the accounting records of Paine, are below and on page 435.

PAINE CORPORATION AND SUBSIDIARIES			
Separate Financial Statements			
For Year Ended June 30, 2003			
	Paine Corporation	*Spilberg Company*	*Sykes Company*
Income Statements			
Revenue:			
Net sales	$1,000,000	$ 550,000	$ 220,000
Intercompany sales	100,000		
Total revenue	$1,100,000	$ 550,000	$ 220,000
Costs and expenses:			
Cost of goods sold	$ 700,000	$ 357,500	$ 143,000
Intercompany cost of goods sold	70,000		
Operating expenses	130,000	125,833	43,667
Interest expense	46,520		
Income taxes expense		26,667	13,333
Total costs and expenses	$ 946,520	$ 510,000	$ 200,000
Net income	$ 153,480	$ 40,000	$ 20,000
Statements of Retained Earnings			
Retained earnings, beginning of year	$ 396,520	$ 300,000	$ 150,000
Add: Net income	153,480	40,000	20,000
Subtotals	$ 550,000	$ 340,000	$ 170,000
Less: Dividends	50,000	20,000	10,000
Retained earnings, end of year	$ 500,000	$ 320,000	$ 160,000

(continued)

PAINE CORPORATION AND SUBSIDIARIES Separate Financial Statements (concluded) For Year Ended June 30, 2003			
	Paine Corporation	*Spilberg Company*	*Sykes Company*
Balance Sheets **Assets**			
Inventories	$1,000,000	$ 800,000	$ 700,000
Investment in Spilberg Company common stock	990,000		
Investment in Sykes Company common stock	574,200		
Other assets	1,501,300	1,260,000	790,000
Total assets	$4,065,500	$2,060,000	$1,490,000
Liabilities and Stockholders' Equity			
Intercompany dividends payable		$ 19,800	$ 9,000
Other liabilities	$1,965,500	1,020,200	891,000
Common stock, $1 par	1,000,000	500,000	300,000
Additional paid-in capital	600,000	200,000	130,000
Retained earnings	500,000	320,000	160,000
Total liabilities and stockholders' equity	$4,065,500	$2,060,000	$1,490,000

Additional Information

1. Intercompany profits in June 30, 2003, inventories resulting from Paine's sales to its subsidiaries during the year ended June 30, 2003, are as follows:

> In Spilberg Company's inventories—$6,000
> In Sykes Company's inventories—$7,500

2. Consolidated goodwill was unimpaired as of June 30, 2003.

Instructions

a. Prepare Paine Corporation's June 30, 2003, journal entries for income taxes and equity-method accruals. The income tax rate for all three companies is 40%. All three companies declared dividends on June 30, 2003. Disregard the dividend-received deduction.

b. Prepare a working paper for consolidated financial statements and related working paper eliminations (in journal entry format), including income taxes allocation, for Paine Corporation and subsidiaries for the year ended June 30, 2003. The three affiliated companies file separate income tax returns. Amounts for Paine Corporation should reflect the journal entries in *a*.

(Problem 9.8) The separate financial statements of Pickens Corporation and subsidiary for the year ended December 31, 2002, are as follows:

PICKENS CORPORATION AND SUBSIDIARY
Separate Financial Statements
For Year Ended December 31, 2002

	Pickens Corporation	Skiffen Company
Income Statements		
Revenue:		
Net sales	$ 840,000	$ 360,000
Intercompany sales	80,600	65,000
Intercompany gain on sale of equipment	9,500	
Intercompany interest revenue	2,702	
Intercompany investment income	44,800	
Total revenue	$ 977,602	$ 425,000
Costs and expenses:		
Cost of goods sold	$ 546,000	$ 252,000
Intercompany cost of goods sold	56,420	48,750
Interest expense	32,000	9,106
Intercompany interest expense		2,276
Other operating expenses and income taxes expense	270,752	56,868
Total costs and expenses	$ 905,172	$ 369,000
Net income	$ 72,430	$ 56,000
Statements of Retained Earnings		
Retained earnings, beginning of year	$ 595,000	$ 136,000
Add: Net income	72,430	56,000
Subtotals	$ 667,430	$ 192,000
Less: Dividends	20,000	11,000
Retained earnings, end of year	$ 647,430	$ 181,000
Balance Sheets		
Assets		
Intercompany receivables (payables)	$ 35,800	$ (35,800)
Inventories	180,000	96,000
Investment in Skiffen Company common stock	393,200	
Investment in Skiffen Company bonds	27,918	
Plant assets (net)	781,500	510,000
Accumulated depreciation of plant assets	(87,000)	(85,000)
Other assets	333,782	146,500
Total assets	$1,665,200	$ 631,700
Liabilities and Stockholders' Equity		
Dividends payable	$ 20,000	$ 2,200
Bonds payable	400,000	120,000
Intercompany bonds payable		30,000
Discount on bonds payable		(4,281)
Discount on intercompany bonds payable		(1,070)
Deferred income tax liability	15,800	
Other liabilities	164,470	24,851
Common stock, $2.50 par	400,000	250,000
Additional paid-in capital	14,000	29,000
Retained earnings	647,430	181,000
Retained earnings of subsidiary	3,500	
Total liabilities and stockholders' equity	$1,665,200	$ 631,700

Pickens had acquired 10% of the 100,000 outstanding shares of $2.50 par common stock of Skiffen Company on December 31, 2000, for $38,000. An additional 70,000 shares were acquired for $315,700 on January 2, 2002 (at which time there was no difference between the current fair values and carrying amounts of Skiffen's identifiable net assets). Out-of-pocket costs of the business combination may be disregarded.

Additional Information

1. Pickens Corporation's ledger accounts for Investment in Skiffen Company Common Stock, Deferred Income Tax Liability, Retained Earnings, and Retained Earnings of Subsidiary were as follows (before December 31, 2002, closing entries):

Investment in Skiffen Company Common Stock

Date	Explanation	Debit	Credit	Balance
2000				
Dec. 31	Acquisition of 10,000 shares	38,000		38,000 dr
2002				
Jan. 2	Acquisition of 70,000 shares	315,700		353,700 dr
2	Retroactive application of equity method of accounting [($40,000 − $5,000) × 0.10]	3,500		357,200 dr
Dec. 15	Dividend declared by Skiffen ($11,000 × 0.80)		8,800	348,400 dr
31	Net income of Skiffen ($56,000 × 0.80)	44,800		393,200 dr

Deferred Income Tax Liability

Date	Explanation	Debit	Credit	Balance
2002				
Jan. 2	Income taxes applicable to undistributed earnings of subsidiary ($3,500 × 0.40)*		1,400	1,400 cr
Dec. 31	Income taxes applicable to undistributed earnings of subsidiary [($44,800 − [$8,800) × 0.40]*		14,400	15,800 cr

* Dividend received deduction is disregarded.

Retained Earnings

Date	Explanation	Debit	Credit	Balance
2000				
Dec. 31	Balance			540,000 cr
2001				
Dec. 31	Close net income		55,000	595,000 cr

Retained Earnings of Subsidiary

Date	Explanation	Debit	Credit	Balance
2002 Jan. 2	Retroactive application of equity method of accounting		3,500	3,500 cr

2. Skiffen Company's Retained Earnings ledger account was as follows:

Retained Earnings

Date	Explanation	Debit	Credit	Balance
2000 Dec. 31	Balance			101,000 cr
2001 Dec. 31	Close net income		40,000	141,000 cr
31	Close Dividends Declared account	5,000		136,000 cr

3. Information relating to intercompany sales for 2002:

	Pickens Corporation	Skiffen Company
Dec. 31, 2002, inventory of intercompany merchandise purchases, on first-in, first-out basis	$26,000	$22,000
Intercompany payables, Dec. 31, 2002	12,000	7,000

4. Pickens acquired $30,000 face amount of Skiffen's 6% bonds in the open market on January 2, 2002, for $27,016—a 10% yield. Skiffen had issued the bonds on January 2, 2000, to yield 8% and had been paying the interest each December 31. Any gain or loss on extinguishment of the bonds is immaterial.

5. On September 1, 2002, Pickens sold equipment with a cost of $40,000 and accumulated depreciation of $9,300 to Skiffen for $40,200. On September 1, 2002, the equipment had an economic life of 10 years and no residual value. Skiffen includes depreciation expense (straight-line method) in other operating expenses.

6. Skiffen owed Pickens $32,000 on December 31, 2002, for noninterest-bearing cash advances.

7. Pickens and Skiffen file separate income tax returns. The income tax rate is 40%. The dividend-received deduction is disregarded, as is the $1,680 ($25,200 ÷ 15 = $1,680) unimpaired goodwill amortization for income tax purposes.

8. Consolidated goodwill was unimpaired as of December 31, 2002.

Instructions

Prepare a working paper for consolidated financial statements and related working paper eliminations (in journal entry format) for Pickens Corporation and subsidiary on December 31, 2002, including income taxes allocation other than for goodwill. Round all amounts to the nearest dollar.

(Problem 9.9) On January 2, 2002, Plummer Corporation acquired a controlling interest of 75% in the outstanding common stock of Sinclair Company for $96,000, including direct out-of-pocket costs of the business combination. Separate financial statements for the two companies for the fiscal year ended December 31, 2002, are as follows:

PLUMMER CORPORATION AND SINCLAIR COMPANY
Separate Financial Statements
For Year Ended December 31, 2002

	Plummer Corporation	Sinclair Company
Income Statements		
Revenue:		
Net sales	$772,000	$426,000
Intercompany sales	78,000	104,000
Dividend revenue		750
Intercompany gain on sale of machinery		800
Intercompany investment income	31,163	
Other revenue	9,000	2,900
Total revenue	$890,163	$534,450
Costs and expenses:		
Cost of goods sold	$445,000	$301,200
Intercompany cost of goods sold	65,000	72,800
Depreciation expense	65,600	11,200
Other operating expenses	195,338	84,667
Income taxes expense	35,225	25,833
Total costs and expenses	$806,163	$495,700
Net income	$ 84,000	$ 38,750
Statements of Retained Earnings		
Retained earnings, beginning of year	$378,000	$112,000
Add: Net income	84,000	38,750
Subtotals	$462,000	$150,750
Less: Dividends	7,500	4,000
Retained earnings, end of year	$454,500	$146,750
Balance Sheets		
Assets		
Short-term investments in trading securities		$ 18,000
Intercompany receivables (payables)	$ 16,000	(16,000)
Inventories	275,000	135,000
Other current assets	309,100	106,750
Investment in Sinclair Company common stock	124,163	
Plant assets	518,000	279,000
Accumulated depreciation	(298,200)	(196,700)
Total assets	$944,063	$326,050
Liabilities and Stockholders' Equity		
Dividends payable	$ 7,500	
Income taxes payable	35,225	$ 25,833
Other current liabilities	260,838	123,467
Common stock, $10 par	150,000	
Common stock, $5 par		20,000
Additional paid-in capital	36,000	10,000
Retained earnings	454,500	146,750
Total liabilities and stockholders' equity	$944,063	$326,050

Additional Information

1. Sinclair sold machinery with a carrying amount of $4,000, no residual value, and a remaining economic life of five years to Plummer for $4,800 on December 31, 2002.

2. Sinclair's depreciable plant assets had a composite estimated remaining economic life of five years on January 2, 2002; Sinclair uses the straight-line method of depreciation for all plant assets.

3. Data on intercompany sales of merchandise follow:

	In Purchaser's Inventory, Dec. 31, 2002	Amount Payable by Purchaser, Dec. 31, 2002
Plummer Corporation to Sinclair Company	$24,300	$24,000
Sinclair Company to Plummer Corporation	18,000	8,000

4. Both companies are subject to an income tax rate of 40%. Plummer is entitled to a dividend-received deduction of 80%. Each company will file separate income tax returns for Year 2002. Except for Plummer's Intercompany Investment Income ledger account, there are no temporary differences for either company.

5. Plummer's ledger accounts for Investment in Sinclair Company Common Stock and Intercompany Investment Income were as follows (before December 31, 2002, closing entries):

Investment in Sinclair Company Common Stock

Date	Explanation	Debit	Credit	Balance
2002				
Jan. 2	Acquisition of 3,000 shares	96,000		96,000 dr
Dec. 31	Net income of Sinclair ($38,750 × 0.75)	29,063		125,063 dr
31	Amortization of bargain-purchase excess {[($142,000 × 0.75) − $96,000] ÷ 5}	2,100		127,163 dr
31	Dividend declared by Sinclair ($4,000 × 0.75)		3,000	124,163 dr

Intercompany Investment Income

Date	Explanation	Debit	Credit	Balance
2002				
Dec. 31	Net income of Sinclair		29,063	29,063 cr
31	Amortization of bargain-purchase excess		2,100	31,163 cr

Instructions

a. Prepare a December 31, 2002, adjusting entry for Plummer Corporation to provide for income tax allocation resulting from Plummer's use of the equity method of accounting for the subsidiary's operating results. Round all amounts to the nearest dollar.

b. Prepare a working paper for consolidated financial statements and related working paper elimination (in journal entry format), including income tax allocation, for Plummer Corporation and subsidiary on December 31, 2002. Amounts for Plummer should reflect the journal entries in *a*.

Chapter Ten

Consolidated Financial Statements: Special Problems

Scope of Chapter

In this chapter, the following special problems that might arise in the preparation of consolidated financial statements are discussed:

Changes in parent company's ownership interest in a subsidiary

Subsidiary with preferred stock outstanding

Stock dividends distributed by a subsidiary

Treasury stock transactions of a subsidiary

Indirect shareholdings and parent company's common stock owned by a subsidiary

CHANGES IN PARENT COMPANY'S OWNERSHIP INTEREST IN A SUBSIDIARY

Subsequent to the date of a business combination, a parent company might acquire stockholdings of the subsidiary's minority stockholders; or the parent company might sell some of its shares of subsidiary common stock to outsiders. Also, the subsidiary itself might issue additional shares of common stock to the public, or to the parent company. The accounting treatment for each of these situations is discussed in the following sections.

Parent Company Acquisition of Minority Interest

Purchase accounting is applied to the parent company's or the subsidiary's acquisition of all or part of the minority interest in net assets of the subsidiary, even though the business combination had been accounted for as a pooling (prior to June 30, 2001, when pooling was denied for subsequent business combinations by the Financial

Accounting Standards Board).[1] Any other approach would be inconsistent with the basic premises of pooling accounting.

To illustrate the acquisition of a subsidiary's minority interest, return to the Prinz Corporation–Scarp Company illustration in Chapter 9 (pages 413 to 417) and assume that Scarp had a net income of $25,000 for the year ended February 28, 2005, and declared and paid dividends totaling $15,000 on February 14, 2005. Under the equity method of accounting, given that consolidated goodwill was not impaired as of February 28, 2005, Prinz Corporation's Investment in Scarp Company Common Stock and Retained Earnings of Subsidiary ledger accounts, and Scarp Company's Retained Earnings account, are as follows (before February 28, 2005, closing entries). The working paper eliminations (in journal entry format) for the year ended February 28, 2005, are on page 443 (disregarding income taxes).

Selected Ledger Accounts of Parent Company One Year after Business Combination

PRINZ CORPORATION LEDGER

Investment in Scarp Company Common Stock

Date	Explanation	Debit	Credit	Balance
2002				
Mar. 1	Acquisition of 1,000 shares	10,000		10,000 dr
2003				
Mar. 1	Acquisition of 2,000 shares	22,000		32,000 dr
1	Retroactive application of equity method of accounting	500		32,500 dr
2004				
Feb. 17	Dividends received: $1 a share (3,000 × $1)		3,000	29,500 dr
29	Share of net income ($15,000 × 0.30)	4,500		34,000 dr
Mar. 1	Acquisition of 6,500 shares	78,000		112,000 dr
2005				
Feb. 14	Dividends received: $1.50 a share (9,500 × $1.50)		14,250	97,750 dr
28	Share of net income ($25,000 × 0.95)	23,750		121,500 dr

Retained Earnings of Subsidiary

Date	Explanation	Debit	Credit	Balance
2003				
Mar. 1	Retroactive application of equity method of accounting		500	500 cr
2004				
Feb. 9	Closing entry—share of Scarp Company's adjusted net income not declared as a dividend ($4,500 − $3,000)		1,500	2,000 cr

---

[1] *FASB Statement No. 141,* "Business Combinations" (Norwalk, FASB, 2001), par. 14.

Retained Earnings Ledger
Account of Subsidiary
One Year after
Business Combination

SCARP COMPANY LEDGER

Retained Earnings

Date	Explanation	Debit	Credit	Balance
2002				
Mar. 1	Balance			20,000 cr
2003				
Feb. 10	Dividends declared: $1 a share	10,000		10,000 cr
2	Net income		15,000	25,000 cr
2004				
Feb. 17	Dividends declared: $1 a share	10,000		15,000 cr
28	Net income		15,000	30,000 cr

Working Paper Eliminations
for First Year Following
Business Combination

PRINZ CORPORATION AND SUBSIDIARY
Working Paper Eliminations
February 28, 2005

(a) Common Stock, $5 par—Scarp	50,000	
Additional Paid-in Capital—Scarp	10,000	
Retained Earnings—Scarp ($30,000 − $2,000)	28,000	
Retained Earnings of Subsidiary—Prinz	2,000	
Intercompany Investment Income—Prinz	23,750	
Goodwill—Prinz	26,500	
Investment in Scarp Company Common Stock—Prinz		121,500
Dividends Declared—Scarp		15,000
Minority Interest in Net Assets of Subsidiary ($4,500 − $750)		3,750

To eliminate intercompany investment and equity accounts of subsidiary at **beginning of year;** to allocate excess of cost over current fair values (equal to carrying amounts) of identifiable net assets acquired to goodwill; and to establish minority interest in net assets of subsidiary at beginning of year ($4,500—see page 417), less minority interest in dividends ($15,000 × 0.05 = $750).

(b) Minority Interest in Net Income of Subsidiary ($25,000 × 0.05)	1,250	
Minority Interest in Net Assets of Subsidiary		1,250

To establish minority interest in net income of subsidiary for year ended February 28, 2005.

Assume further that on March 1, 2005, Prinz acquired for $6,000 the 500 shares of Scarp's common stock owned by minority stockholders; the following journal entry is appropriate:

Parent Company's Journal
Entry for Acquisition of
Minority Interest

Investment in Scarp Company Common Stock	6,000	
Cash		6,000

To record acquisition of 500 shares of subsidiary's common stock from minority stockholders.

Because the minority interest in net assets of subsidiary in the consolidated balance sheet of Prinz and subsidiary on February 28, 2005, totaled $5,000 ($3,750 + $1,250 = $5,000), an additional $1,000 ($6,000 − $5,000 = $1,000) of goodwill must be recognized and subsequently tested for impairment. Under the equity method of accounting, Prinz accrues 100% of Scarp's net income subsequent to March 1, 2005, and there is no minority interest to be accounted for in consolidation.

If Prinz paid *less* than the carrying amount of the minority interest acquired, the appropriate accounting treatment of the difference is not clear. Presumably, the excess of minority interest carrying amount over Prinz's cost should be allocated pro rata to reduce the carrying amounts of selected assets of Scarp. This approach would be consistent with the theory of purchase accounting set forth in Chapter 5 (page 177). However, assuming that the difference between carrying amount and cost is immaterial, it may be treated as an offset to any goodwill arising from earlier acquisitions of Scarp's common stock that remains unimpaired.

Parent Company Sale of a Portion of Its Subsidiary Common Stockholdings

A parent company with a substantial ownership interest in a subsidiary may sell a portion of that interest for several reasons. Perhaps the parent company is short of cash, or the earnings of the subsidiary are unsatisfactory. The parent company may recognize that a subsidiary may be controlled effectively with less than a majority ownership of its outstanding common stock and that an 80% or 90% ownership of a subsidiary may tie up excessive amounts of capital. Some corporations in past years have sold a portion of a newly acquired subsidiary's common stock in order to generate cash for additional business combinations.

Sale of all or part of the *net assets* of a subsidiary often involves accounting for and income statement display of the disposal of a business segment. This topic is considered in Chapter 13.

Accounting for a parent company's sale of its investment in a subsidiary is similar to the accounting for disposal of any noncurrent asset. The carrying amount of the subsidiary common stock sold is removed from the parent company's Investment in Subsidiary Common Stock ledger account, and the difference between that carrying amount and the cash or current fair value of other consideration received is recognized as a gain or loss on disposal of the stock. Under generally accepted accounting principles, the gain or loss *is not an extraordinary item* for consolidated income statement display.[2]

Unless the business combination had resulted from an installment acquisition of the subsidiary's common stock, there is no significant change in the working paper eliminations after the parent's sale of part of its ownership interest in the subsidiary. However, the minority interest in the subsidiary's net income and net assets increases. The parent company's equity-method journal entries for the subsidiary's operations are changed only for the decrease in the percentage of the parent's ownership interest in the subsidiary.

When control was acquired by installment purchases of the subsidiary's common stock, *specific identification* should be used to account for the carrying amount of the subsidiary stock sold. There must be an accompanying adjustment in the parent company's application of the equity method of accounting for the subsidiary's operating results. For example, purchased goodwill should no longer be accounted for in the

---

[2] *APB Opinion No. 30*, "Reporting the Results of Operations" (New York: AICPA, 1973), par. 23(d).

working paper for consolidated financial statements if the block of subsidiary common stock to which it applies was sold by the parent company; the goodwill is impaired.

Illustration of Parent Company Sale of Subsidiary Stockholding

Returning to the Prinz Corporation–Scarp Company affiliation, assume that Scarp declared and paid a $15,000 dividend to Prinz on February 12, 2006, and had a net income of $35,000 for the year ended February 28, 2006. Under these circumstances, Prinz's Investment ledger account and Retained Earnings of Subsidiary account, and Scarp Company's Retained Earnings account (before February 28, 2006, closing entries), are as follows, given that consolidated goodwill was unimpaired as of February 28, 2006:

Selected Ledger Accounts of Parent Company Two Years after Business Combination

PRINZ CORPORATION LEDGER

Investment in Scarp Company Common Stock

Date	Explanation	Debit	Credit	Balance
2002				
Mar. 1	Acquisition of 1,000 shares	10,000		10,000 dr
2003				
Mar. 1	Acquisition of 2,000 shares	22,000		32,000 dr
1	Retroactive application of equity method of accounting	500		32,500 dr
2004				
Feb. 17	Dividends received: $1 a share (3,000 × $1)		3,000	29,500 dr
28	Share of net income ($15,000 × 0.30)	4,500		34,000 dr
Mar. 1	Acquisition of 6,500 shares	78,000		112,000 dr
2005				
Feb. 14	Dividends received: $1.50 a share (9,500 × $1.50)		14,250	97,750 dr
28	Share of net income ($25,000 × 0.95)	23,750		121,500 dr
Mar. 1	Acquisition of 500 shares	6,000		127,500 dr
2006				
Feb. 12	Dividends received: $1.50 a share (10,000 × $1.50)		15,000	112,500 dr
28	Share of net income ($35,000 × 1.00)	35,000		147,500 dr

Retained Earnings of Subsidiary

Date	Explanation	Debit	Credit	Balance
2003				
Mar. 1	Retroactive application of equity method of accounting		500	500 cr
2004				
Feb. 28	Closing entry—share of Scarp Company adjusted net income not paid as a dividend ($4,500 − $3,000)		1,500	2,000 cr
2005				
Feb. 28	Closing entry—share of subsidiary's net income not declared as a dividend ($23,750 − $14,250)		9,500	11,500 cr

SCARP COMPANY LEDGER

Retained Earnings

Date	Explanation	Debit	Credit	Balance
2002				
Mar. 1	Balance			20,000 cr
2003				
Feb. 10	Dividends declared: $1 a share	10,000		10,000 cr
28	Net income		15,000	25,000 cr
2004				
Feb. 17	Dividends declared: $1 a share	10,000		15,000 cr
29	Net income		15,000	30,000 cr
2005				
Feb. 14	Dividends declared: $1.50 a share	15,000		15,000 cr
28	Net income		25,000	40,000 cr

Under these circumstances, the working paper elimination (in journal entry format) for Prinz Corporation and subsidiary on February 28, 2005, is as shown below (disregarding income taxes):

PRINZ CORPORATION AND SUBSIDIARY
Working Paper Elimination
February 28, 2006

(a)	Common Stock, $5 par—Scarp	50,000	
	Additional Paid-in Capital—Scarp	10,000	
	Retained Earnings—Scarp ($40,000 − $11,500)	28,500	
	Retained Earnings of Subsidiary—Prinz	11,500	
	Intercompany Investment Income—Prinz	35,000	
	Goodwill—Prinz ($26,500 + $1,000)	27,500	
	Investment in Scarp Company Common Stock—Prinz		147,500
	Dividends Declared—Scarp		15,000

To eliminate intercompany investment and equity accounts of subsidiary at **beginning of year;** and to allocate excess of cost over current fair values (equal to carrying amounts) of identifiable net assets acquired to goodwill.

Continuing the illustration, assume that, in order to raise cash for additional business combinations, Prinz on March 1, 2006, sold in the open market the 1,000 and 2,000 shares of Scarp common stock acquired March 1, 2002, and March 1, 2003, respectively, for $55,000. The sale resulted in a gain of $12,000, computed as follows:

Computation of Gain on Parent Company's Sale of Portion of Subsidiary Stockholdings	Proceeds of sale		$ 55,000
	Less: Carrying amount of 1,000 shares of Scarp common stock acquired Mar. 1, 2002:		
	Cost	$10,000	
	Add: Share of Scarp's net income, Years 2003–2006 ($90,000 × 0.10)	9,000	
	Less: Share of Scarp's dividends, Years 2003–2006 ($50,000 × 0.10)	(5,000)	(14,000)
	Carrying amount of 2,000 shares of Scarp common stock acquired Mar. 1, 2003:		
	Cost	$22,000	
	Add: Share of Scarp's net income, Years 2004–2006 ($75,000 × 0.20)	15,000	
	Less: Share of Scarp's dividends, Years 2004–2006 ($40,000 × 0.20)	(8,000)	(29,000)
	Gain on sale of portion of subsidiary stockholdings		$ 12,000

The following journal entry is prepared by Prinz Corporation on March 1, 2006, to record the sale of part of its investment in Scarp Company common stock:

Parent Company's Journal Entry to Record Sale of Portion of investment in Subsidiary	Cash	55,000	
	Investment in Scarp Company Common Stock ($14,000 + $29,000)		43,000
	Realized Gain on Disposal of Investment in Subsidiary		12,000
	To record sale of 3,000 shares of Scarp Company common stock at a gain.		

The $12,000 realized gain in the foregoing journal entry is displayed in the consolidated income statement of Prinz Corporation and subsidiary for the year ending February 28, 2007, because it was *realized* in a transaction with *outsiders.*

For a consolidated balance sheet of Prinz Corporation and subsidiary on March 1, 2006, following Prinz's sale of Scarp common stock, the following working paper elimination (in journal entry format) is required:

Working Paper Elimination on Date of Parent Company's Disposal of a Portion of Its Subsidiary's Stockholdings

PRINZ CORPORATION AND SUBSIDIARY		
Working Paper Elimination		
March 1, 2006		
(a) Common Stock, $5 par—Scarp	50,000	
Additional Paid-in Capital—Scarp	10,000	
Retained Earnings—Scarp ($40,000 + $20,000 − $31,500)	28,500	
Retained Earnings of Subsidiary—Prinz ($11,500 + $35,000 − $15,000)	31,500	
Goodwill—Prinz ($27,500 − $2,000 − $5,000)	20,500	
Investment in Scarp Company Common Stock ($147,500 − $43,000)		104,500
Minority Interest in Net Assets of Subsidiary [($50,000 + $10,000 + $60,000) × 0.30]		36,000
To eliminate intercompany investment and equity accounts of subsidiary; to allocate excess of cost over current fair values (equal to carrying amounts) of identifiable net assets acquired to goodwill; and to establish minority interest in net assets of subsidiary.		

The foregoing elimination recognizes only the goodwill applicable to Prinz Corporation's March 1, 2004, and March 1, 2005, acquisitions of Scarp Company common stock. The total goodwill of $20,500 comprises the following:

<table>
<tr><td>**Computation of Goodwill, March 1, 2006**</td><td>Mar. 1, 2004, acquisition</td><td>$19,500</td></tr>
<tr><td></td><td>Mar. 1, 2005, acquisition</td><td>1,000</td></tr>
<tr><td></td><td>Total goodwill, Mar. 1, 2006</td><td>$20,500</td></tr>
</table>

Also reflected in the foregoing elimination is the minority interest in net assets of subsidiary that resulted from Prinz's disposal of 30% of its investment in Scarp's common stock. The amount of the minority interest is developed from the carrying amount of Scarp's identifiable net assets of $120,000 ($50,000 + $10,000 + $60,000 = $120,000) on March 1, 2006.

Subsidiary's Issuance of Additional Shares of Common Stock to the Public

Instead of obtaining funds by selling a portion of its ownership interest in a subsidiary, the parent company may instruct the subsidiary to issue additional shares of common stock to the public, with the parent company and minority stockholders of the subsidiary waiving their preemptive right to acquire part of the common stock. The cash obtained would be available to the consolidated group through intercompany transactions. Because the parent company does not acquire shares of common stock on a pro rata basis along with present minority stockholders in the subsidiary's stock issuance, as in a stock rights offering, the parent's percentage ownership interest in the subsidiary changes. In addition, unless the subsidiary issues additional common stock to the public at a price per share equal to the per-share carrying amount of the subsidiary's outstanding common stock, there generally is a realized nonoperating gain or loss to the parent company.[3] These two points are illustrated in the following section.

Illustration of Subsidiary's Issuance of Additional Common Stock to the Public

On January 2, 2002, Paulson Corporation acquired 80% of the outstanding common stock of Spaulding Company for $240,000. Out-of-pocket costs of the business combination are disregarded in this illustration. Spaulding's stockholders' equity on January 2, 2002, was as follows:

<table>
<tr><td>**Stockholders' Equity of Subsidiary on Date of Business Combination**</td><td>Common stock, $5 par</td><td>$ 50,000</td></tr>
<tr><td></td><td>Additional paid-in capital</td><td>75,000</td></tr>
<tr><td></td><td>Retained earnings</td><td>100,000</td></tr>
<tr><td></td><td>Total stockholders' equity</td><td>$225,000</td></tr>
</table>

The current fair values of Spaulding's identifiable net assets on January 2, 2002, were equal to their carrying amounts. Thus, the $60,000 excess of the cost of Paulson's investment ($240,000) over 80% of the $225,000 current fair value of Spaulding's identifiable net assets ($225,000 × 0.80 = $180,000) was attributable to goodwill, which was unimpaired on December 31, 2002.

For the year ended December 31, 2002, Spaulding had a net income of $20,000 and declared and paid cash dividends of $10,000 ($1 a share). On December 31, 2002, Spaulding issued 2,000 shares of common stock in a public offering at $33 a share,

---

[3] *Staff Accounting Bulletin 51,* Securities and Exchange Commission (Washington, 1983), as amended by *Staff Accounting Bulletin 84.*

net of costs of issuing the stock, for a total of $66,000. (Both Paulson and the existing minority stockholders of Spaulding waived their preemptive right to acquire additional shares of Spaulding's common stock.) Thus, after the closing process, Spaulding's stockholders' equity on December 31, 2002, amounted to $301,000 ($225,000 + $20,000 − $10,000 + $66,000 = $301,000) and consisted of the following amounts:

Stockholders' Equity of Purchased Subsidiary after Its Issuance of Common Stock to Public

Common stock, $5 par ($50,000 + $10,000)	$ 60,000
Additional paid-in capital ($75,000 + $56,000)	131,000
Retained earnings ($100,000 + $20,000 − $10,000)	110,000
Total stockholders' equity	$301,000

Paulson's Investment ledger account under the equity method of accounting is as follows after the subsidiary's issuance of common stock:

Parent Company's Investment Account after Subsidiary's Issuance of Common Stock to Public

Investment in Spaulding Company Common Stock

Date	Explanation	Debit	Credit	Balance
2002				
Jan. 2	Acquisition of 8,000 shares in business combination	240,000		240,000 dr
Dec. 31	Dividends received ($10,000 × 0.80)		8,000	232,000 dr
31	Share of net income ($20,000 × 0.80)	16,000		248,000 dr
31	Nonoperating gain on subsidiary's issuance of common stock to public	12,667		260,667 dr

The December 31, 2002, increase of $12,667 in Paulson's Investment ledger account is offset by a credit to a nonoperating gain account. The $12,667 is Paulson's share (for which Paulson paid nothing) of the increase in Spaulding's net assets resulting from Spaulding's issuance of common stock to the public at $33 a share. The $33 a share issuance price exceeds the $31 carrying amount ($248,000 ÷ 8,000 shares = $31) per share of Paulson's Investment account prior to Spaulding's common stock issuance. The $12,667 debit to Paulson's Investment ledger account is computed as follows:

Computation of Gain to Parent Company Resulting from Subsidiary's Issuance of Common Stock to Public

	Total	Paulson's Share		Minority's Share	
Carrying amount of Spaulding Company's identifiable net assets after common stock issuance to public	$301,000	(66⅔%)[†]	$200,667	(33⅓%)	$100,333
Carrying amount of Spaulding Company's identifiable net assets before common stock issuance to public	235,000*	(80%)	188,000[‡]	(20%)	47,000
Difference	$ 66,000		$ 12,667[§]		$ 53,333

* $225,000 + $20,000 − $10,000 = $235,000.
[†] 8,000 ÷ (10,000 + 2,000) = 66⅔%.
[‡] Paulson's share of Spaulding's identifiable net assets [($225,000 + $20,000 − $10,000) × 0.80] $188,000
  Add: Unimpaired goodwill 60,000
  Balance of Paulson's Investment in Spaulding Company Common Stock ledger account $248,000
[§] Nonoperating gain to parent company; Paulson's journal entry (explanation omitted) is as follows:
  Investment in Spaulding Company Common Stock 12,667
    Gain from Subsidiary's Issuance of Common Stock 12,667

The foregoing analysis reflects the effect of the decrease of Paulson's percentage interest in Spaulding's outstanding common stock from 80% before the public stock issuance to $66\frac{2}{3}\%$ after the issuance. Nevertheless, the issuance price of $33 a share exceeded the $31 carrying amount per share of Paulson's original investment in Spaulding, thus resulting in the $12,667 nonoperating gain to Paulson.

The following working paper eliminations (in journal entry format) are appropriate for Paulson Corporation and subsidiary following Spaulding's common stock issuance on December 31, 2002, assuming that consolidated goodwill was unimpaired as of that date and there were no other intercompany transactions or profits for Year 2002.

Working Paper Eliminations
on Date of Subsidiary's
Issuance of Common Stock
to Public

PAULSON CORPORATION AND SUBSIDIARY Working Paper Eliminations December 31, 2002		
(a) Common Stock—Spaulding	60,000	
Additional Paid-in Capital—Spaulding	131,000	
Retained Earnings—Spaulding	100,000	
Goodwill—Paulson	60,000	
Intercompany Investment Income—Paulson ($20,000 × 0.80)	16,000	
Investment in Spaulding Company Common Stock—Paulson		260,667
Dividends Declared—Spaulding		10,000
Minority Interest in Net Assets of Subsidiary ($45,000 − $2,000 + $53,333)		96,333
To eliminate intercompany investment and related equity accounts of subsidiary (retained earnings of subsidiary at the **beginning of year**); to eliminate subsidiary's dividends declared; to record unimpaired goodwill on Dec. 31, 2002; and to provide for minority interest in net assets of subsidiary at beginning of year ($225,000 × 0.20 = $45,000), less dividends to minority stockholders ($10,000 × 0.20 = $2,000), plus minority interest's share of proceeds of public stock issuance ($66,000 − $12,667 = $53,333).		
(b) Minority Interest in Net Income of Subsidiary	4,000	
Minority Interest in Net Assets of Subsidiary		4,000
To provide for minority interest in subsidiary's Year 2002 net income as follows: $20,000 × 0.20 interest throughout Year 2002 = $4,000.		

Note that Paulson's $12,667 nonoperating gain is not eliminated in the foregoing eliminations; it was *realized* through the subsidiary's transaction with *outsiders*.

Subsidiary's Issuance of Additional Shares of Common Stock to Parent Company

Instead of issuing additional common stock to the public, a subsidiary might issue the additional stock to the parent company. This eventuality might occur if the parent company desired to increase its total investment in the subsidiary, or if the parent wished to reduce the influence of minority stockholders of the subsidiary.

To illustrate, return to the Paulson Corporation–Spaulding Company illustration and assume that on December 31, 2002, Spaulding had issued 2,000 shares of common stock to Paulson, rather than to the public, at $33 a share, for a total of $66,000, and that the minority stockholders waived their preemptive rights to acquire additional common stock. Under these circumstances, Paulson's Investment account increases to a balance of $310,833 ($248,000 + $66,000 cost of common stock acquired − $3,167 nonoperating loss = $310,833). The nonoperating loss of $3,167 is computed as follows:

	Total	Paulson's Share	Minority's Share
Carrying amount of Spaulding Company's identifiable net assets after common stock issuance to parent	$301,000	(83⅓%)* $250,833	(16⅔%) $50,167
Carrying amount of Spaulding Company's identifiable net assets before common stock issuance to parent	235,000	(80%) 188,000†	(20%) 47,000
Difference	$ 66,000	$ 62,833	$ 3,167‡

* (8,000 + 2,000) ÷ (10,000 + 2,000) = 83⅓%.

† Paulson's share of Spaulding's identifiable net assets $188,000
Add: Unimpaired goodwill 60,000
  Balance of Paulson's Investment in Spaulding Company Common Stock ledger account $248,000

‡ Nonoperating loss to parent company; Paulson's journal entry (explanation omitted) is as follows:
Loss from Subsidiary's Issuance of Common Stock 3,167
  Investment in Spaulding Company Common Stock 3,167

Paulson's $3,167 loss is *realized* because, although it arose in a transaction with Spaulding, Paulson paid $66,000 for an investment valued at $62,833; the minority stockholders (*creditors* under the parent company concept) were the beneficiaries of the $3,167 difference. Thus, Paulson's $3,167 loss is displayed in the consolidated income statement of Paulson Corporation and subsidiary for the year ended December 31, 2002.

The working paper eliminations (in journal entry format) for Paulson Corporation and subsidiary following Spaulding's common stock issuance on December 31, 2002, are as follows:

PAULSON CORPORATION AND SUBSIDIARY
Working Paper Eliminations
December 31, 2002

(a) Common Stock—Spaulding	60,000	
Additional Paid-In Capital—Spaulding	131,000	
Retained Earnings—Spaulding	100,000	
Goodwill—Paulson	60,000	
Intercompany Investment Income—Paulson ($20,000 × 0.80)	16,000	
Investment in Spaulding Company Common Stock—Paulson ($250,833 + $60,000)		310,833
Dividends Declared—Spaulding		10,000
Minority Interest in Net Assets of Subsidiary ($45,000 − $2,000 + $3,167)		46,167

To eliminate intercompany investment and related equity accounts of subsidiary (retained earnings of subsidiary at the **beginning of year**); to eliminate subsidiary's dividends declared; to record unimpaired goodwill on Dec. 31, 2002; and to provide for minority interest in net assets of subsidiary at beginning of year ($225,000 × 0.20 = $45,000), less dividends to minority stockholders ($10,000 × 0.20 = $2,000), plus minority interest's share of proceeds of common stock issuance to parent company ($3,167).

(b) Minority Interest in Net Income of Subsidiary	4,000	
Minority Interest in Net Assets of Subsidiary		4,000

To provide for minority interest in subsidiary's Year 2002 net income as follows: $20,000 × 0.20 interest throughout Year 2002 = $4,000.

The recognition of nonoperating gains or losses on a subsidiary's issuance of additional shares of stock was tentatively opposed by the FASB, which supported instead reporting a change in a parent company's proportionate interest in a subsidiary as an increase or a decrease, as appropriate, in the parent's additional paid-in capital.[4]

SUBSIDIARY WITH PREFERRED STOCK OUTSTANDING

Some combinees in a business combination have outstanding preferred stock. If a parent company acquires all of a subsidiary's preferred stock, together with all or a majority of its common stock, the working paper for consolidated financial statements and working paper eliminations are similar to those illustrated in Chapters 6 through 9. If less than 100% of the subsidiary's preferred stock is acquired by the parent company, the preferences associated with the preferred stock must be considered in the computation of the minority interest in the net assets and net income of the subsidiary.

Illustration of Minority Interest in Subsidiary with Preferred Stock

Suppose, for example, that on July 1, 2002, Praeger Corporation paid $200,000 (including direct out-of-pocket costs of the business combination) for 60% of Simmon Company's 10,000 shares of outstanding $1 par, 6% cumulative preferred stock and 80% of Simmon's 50,000 shares of outstanding $2 par common stock, which were owned pro rata by the same stockholders. The preferred stock had a liquidation preference of $1.10 a share and was callable at $1.20 a share plus cumulative preferred dividends in arrears. The stockholders' equity of Simmon on July 1, 2002, was:

Stockholders' Equity of Subsidiary on Date of Business Combination	
6% cumulative preferred stock, $1 par; 10,000 shares outstanding	$ 10,000
Common stock, $2 par; 50,000 shares outstanding	100,000
Additional paid-in capital	30,000
Retained earnings	50,000
Total stockholders' equity	$190,000

There were no cumulative preferred dividends in arrears on July 1, 2002. The current fair values of Simmon's identifiable net assets on July 1, 2002, were equal to their carrying amounts on that date.

The presence of the preferred stock raises two questions:

1. What part, if any, does the preferred stock play in the measurement of the goodwill recognized in the business combination?

2. Which per-share amount—$1 par, $1.10 liquidation preference, or $1.20 call price—should be used to measure the minority interest in Simmon's net assets on July 1, 2002?

The following are logical answers to the two questions:

1. The preferred stock does not enter into the measurement of the goodwill recognized in the business combination. Typically, preferred stockholders have no voting rights;

---

[4] *Proposed Statement of Financial Accounting Standards,* "Consolidated Financial Statements: Policy and Procedures" (Norwalk: FASB, 1995), par. 29.

thus, in a business combination, preferred stock may in substance be considered ***debt*** rather than ***owners' equity.*** Accordingly, the amount paid by the combinor for the subsidiary's common stock should be the basis for computation of the goodwill.

2. The call price plus any cumulative preferred dividends in arrears should be used to measure the minority interest of the preferred stockholders in Simmon's net assets on July 1, 2002. The call price generally is the maximum claim on net assets imposed by the preferred stock contract. Furthermore, the call price is the amount that Simmon would pay, on a going-concern basis, to extinguish the preferred stock. Use of the preferred stock's liquidation value in the computation of the stockholders' interest in the subsidiary's net assets would stress a ***quitting-concern*** approach, rather than the going-concern principle. Finally, the par of the preferred stock has no significance as a measure of value for the preferred stock.

In accordance with the foregoing discussion, Praeger prepares the following journal entry to record the business combination with Simmon on July 1, 2002. (Out-of-pocket costs of the combination are not accounted for separately in this illustration.)

Parent Company's Journal Entry for Business Combination Involving Subsidiary's Preferred Stock

Investment in Simmon Company Preferred Stock (6,000 × $1.20)	7,200	
Investment in Simmon Company Common Stock ($200,000 − $7,200)	192,800	
Cash		200,000
To record business combination with Simmon Company.		

The working paper elimination (in journal entry format) for Praeger and subsidiary on July 1, 2002, is as follows:

Working Paper Elimination on Date of Business Combination Involving Partially Owned Subsidiary Having Preferred Stock Outstanding

PRAEGER CORPORATION AND SUBSIDIARY
Working Paper Elimination
July 1, 2002

Cumulative Preferred Stock—Simmon	10,000	
Common Stock—Simmon	100,000	
Additional Paid-in Capital—Simmon	30,000	
Retained Earnings—Simmon	50,000	
Goodwill—Praeger {$192,800 − [($190,000 − $12,000 call price of preferred stock) × 0.80]}	50,400	
Investment in Simmon Company Preferred Stock— Praeger		7,200
Investment in Simmon Company Common Stock— Praeger		192,800
Minority Interest in Net Assets of Subsidiary—Preferred (4,000 × $1.20)		4,800
Minority Interest in Net Assets of Subsidiary—Common ($178,000 × 0.20)		35,600
To eliminate intercompany investment and related equity accounts of subsidiary on date of business combination; to record excess of cost attributable to common stock over 80% share of current fair value of subsidiary's identifiable net assets as goodwill; and to provide for minority interest in subsidiary's preferred stock and in net assets applicable to common stock on date of business combination.		

The following aspects of the foregoing elimination should be emphasized:

1. Simmon's goodwill is measured as the difference between the cost assigned to Praeger's investment in Simmon's common stock and Praeger's share of the current fair value of Simmon's net assets applicable to common stock; Simmon's preferred stock does not enter the measurement of the goodwill.

2. The minority interest in the subsidiary's preferred stock is measured as the 4,000 shares of preferred stock owned by stockholders other than Praeger multiplied by the $1.20 call price per share.

3. The minority interest in the subsidiary's common stock is measured as 20% of the $178,000 ($190,000 − $12,000 = $178,000) net asset value of Simmon's common stock.

Preferred Stock Considerations Subsequent to Date of Business Combination

Regardless of whether Simmon's preferred dividend is paid or omitted in years subsequent to July 1, 2002, the preferred dividend affects the measurement of the minority interest of common stockholders in the net income of Simmon. For example, assume that Simmon had a net income of $50,000 for the fiscal year ended June 30, 2003, and declared and paid the preferred dividend of $0.06 a share and a common dividend of $0.50 a share on June 30, 2003; and that consolidated goodwill was unimpaired as of June 30, 2003. Praeger records these elements of Simmon's operating results on June 30, 2003, under the equity method of accounting, as follows:

PRAEGER CORPORATION Journal Entries		
Cash	20,360	
Investment in Simmon Company Common Stock		20,000
Intercompany Dividend Revenue		360
To record receipt of dividends declared and paid by Simmon Company as follows:		
Preferred stock (6,000 × $0.06)	$ 360	
Common stock (40,000 × $0.50)	20,000	
Total cash received	$20,360	
Investment in Simmon Company Common Stock	39,520	
Intercompany Investment Income		39,520
To record share of Simmon Company's net income applicable to common stock as follows:		
Simmon Company's net income	$50,000	
Less: Preferred dividend (10,000 × $0.06)	600	
Net income attributable to common stock	$49,400	
Parent company's share ($49,400 × 0.80)	$39,520	
(Income tax effects are disregarded.)		

After the foregoing journal entries are posted, Praeger's Investment in Simmon Company Common Stock ledger account is as follows:

Investment Account of
Parent Company One
Year Subsequent to
Business Combination

Investment in Simmon Company Common Stock

Date	Explanation	Debit	Credit	Balance
2002				
July 1	Acquisition of 40,000 shares	192,800		192,800 dr
2003				
June 30	Dividends received: $0.50 a share		20,000	172,800 dr
30	Share of net income	39,520		212,320 dr

If there are no other intercompany transactions or profits, the June 30, 2003, working paper eliminations (in journal entry format) for Praeger Corporation and subsidiary are as follows:

Working Paper Eliminations
One Year Subsequent to
Business Combination
Involving Partially Owned
Subsidiary Having Preferred
Stock Outstanding

PRAEGER CORPORATION AND SUBSIDIARY
Working Paper Eliminations
June 30, 2003

(a) Cumulative Preferred Stock—Simmon	10,000	
Common Stock—Simmon	100,000	
Additional Paid-in Capital—Simmon	30,000	
Retained Earnings—Simmon	50,000	
Intercompany Dividend Revenue—Praeger	360	
Intercompany Investment Income—Praeger	39,520	
Goodwill—Praeger	50,400	
Investment in Simmon Company Preferred Stock—Praeger		7,200
Investment in Simmon Company Common Stock—Praeger		212,320
Dividends Declared—Simmon [(10,000 × $0.06) + (50,000 × $0.50)]		25,600
Minority Interest in Net Assets of Subsidiary—Preferred ($4,800 − $240)		4,560
Minority Interest in Net Assets of Subsidiary—Common [$35,600 − ($25,000 × 0.20)]		30,600

To eliminate intercompany investment and related equity accounts of subsidiary at **beginning of year;** to eliminate subsidiary's dividends declared; to record unimpaired goodwill on June 30, 2003; and to provide for minority interest in subsidiary's preferred stock and common stock at beginning of year, less dividends to minority stockholders.

(b) Minority Interest in Net Income of Subsidiary	10,120	
Minority Interest in Net Assets of Subsidiary—Preferred		240
Minority Interest in Net Assets of Subsidiary—Common [($50,000 − $600) × 0.20]		9,880

To provide for minority interest in net income of subsidiary for Fiscal Year 2003.

In the review of the June 30, 2003, journal entries of Praeger and the working paper eliminations on that date, the following points should be noted:

1. Praeger Corporation's accounting for its investment in the subsidiary's preferred stock *essentially is the cost method.* This method is appropriate as long as the

subsidiary declares and pays the cumulative preferred dividend annually. If the subsidiary had *passed* the preferred dividend of $600 for the year ended June 30, 2003, Praeger would have recorded the passed preferred dividend *under the equity method of accounting* as follows:

<table>
<tr><td>**Parent Company's Journal Entry for *Passed* Cumulative Preferred Dividend of Subsidiary**</td><td>Investment in Simmon Company Preferred Stock
   Intercompany Investment Income
To accrue cumulative preferred dividend passed by subsidiary's board
of directors ($600 × 0.60 = $360).</td><td>360</td><td>
360</td></tr>
</table>

The working paper eliminations in the year of a passed cumulative preferred dividend would be the same as those illustrated on page 455, except that the minority interest in the subsidiary's preferred stock would be $240 ($600 × 0.40 = $240) larger because of the effect of the passed dividend. (Of course, no common dividend could be declared if the cumulative preferred dividend were passed.)

2. The net result of the foregoing journal entries and working paper eliminations is that the subsidiary's Fiscal Year 2003 net income of $50,000 is allocated as follows:

<table>
<tr><td>**Allocation of Subsidiary's Net Income to Preferred and Common Stockholders**</td><td></td><td>**Total**</td><td>**Consolidated Net Income**</td><td>**Minority Interest**</td></tr>
<tr><td></td><td>To preferred stockholders: 10,000
  shares × $0.06, in 60:40 ratio</td><td>$ 600</td><td>$ 360</td><td>$ 240</td></tr>
<tr><td></td><td>To common stockholders in
  80:20 ratio
Net income of subsidiary</td><td>49,400
$50,000</td><td>39,520
$39,880</td><td>9,880
$10,120</td></tr>
</table>

Other Types of Preferred Stock

Treatment similar to that illustrated in the foregoing section is appropriate for the minority interest in a subsidiary having other types of outstanding preferred stock. If the preferred stock were *noncumulative,* there would be no parent company accrual of passed dividends. If the preferred stock were *participating* (which seldom is the case), the subsidiary's retained earnings would be allocated to the minority interests in preferred stock and common stock according to the term of the *participation clause.*

STOCK DIVIDENDS DISTRIBUTED BY A SUBSIDIARY

If a parent company uses the equity method of accounting for the operating results of a subsidiary, the subsidiary's declaration and issuance of a common stock dividend has no effect on the parent's Investment in Subsidiary Common Stock ledger account. As emphasized in intermediate accounting textbooks, receipt of a stock dividend does not represent dividend revenue to the investor.

After the declaration of a common stock dividend not exceeding 20 to 25%, the subsidiary's retained earnings is reduced by an amount equal to the current fair value of the stock issued as a dividend. This reduction and the offsetting increase in the subsidiary's paid-in capital ledger accounts are incorporated in the working paper eliminations subsequent to the issuance of the stock dividend, and there is no specific elimination for the *stock dividend itself.* Thus, the amount of consolidated retained earnings is not affected by a subsidiary's stock dividend. As stated by the AICPA:

the retained earnings in the consolidated financial statements should reflect the accumulated earnings of the consolidated group not distributed to the shareholders of, or capitalized by, the parent company.[5]

Illustration of Subsidiary Stock Dividend

On June 30, 2002, the date of the business combination of Pasco Corporation and its wholly owned subsidiary, Salvo Company, the working paper elimination (in journal entry format) was as follows, because the current fair values of Salvo's identifiable net assets were equal to their carrying amounts and no goodwill was involved in the combination:

Working Paper Elimination on Date of Business Combination with Wholly Owned Subsidiary

PASCO CORPORATION AND SUBSIDIARY Working Paper Elimination June 30, 2002		
(a) Common Stock, $1 par—Salvo	150,000	
Additional Paid-in Capital—Salvo	200,000	
Retained Earnings—Salvo	250,000	
Investment in Salvo Company Common Stock—Pasco		600,000
To eliminate intercompany investment and related accounts for stockholders' equity of subsidiary on date of business combination.		

On June 18, 2003, Salvo distributed 15,000 shares of its $1 par common stock to Pasco as a 10% stock dividend. Salvo debited the Dividends Declared ledger account for $75,000, the current fair value of the common stock distributed as a dividend (15,000 × $5 = $75,000). Pasco prepared no journal entry for the stock dividend, but it did record the subsidiary's net income of $180,000 for the fiscal year ended June 30, 2003, under the equity method of accounting as follows:

Parent Company's Equity-Method Journal Entry to Record Net Income of Wholly Owned Subsidiary

Investment in Salvo Company Common Stock	180,000	
Intercompany Investment Income		180,000
To record 100% of Salvo Company's net income for the year ended June 30, 2003. (Income tax effects are disregarded.)		

On June 30, 2003, the working paper elimination (in journal entry format) for Pasco Corporation and subsidiary is as follows:

Working Paper Elimination Following Wholly Owned Subsidiary's Distribution of a Stock Dividend

PASCO CORPORATION AND SUBSIDIARY Working Paper Elimination June 30, 2003		
(a) Common Stock, $1 par—Salvo ($150,000 + $15,000)	165,000	
Additional Paid-in Capital—Salvo ($200,000 + $60,000)	260,000	
Retained Earnings—Salvo	250,000	
Intercompany Investment Income—Pasco	180,000	
Investment in Salvo Company Common Stock— Pasco ($600,000 + $180,000)		780,000
Dividends Declared—Salvo		75,000
To eliminate intercompany investment, related accounts for stockholders' equity of subsidiary, and investment income from subsidiary.		

[5] *ARB No. 51,* "Consolidated Financial Statements" (New York: AICPA, 1959), p. 46.

In its closing entries on June 30, 2003, Pasco credits its Retained Earnings of Subsidiary ledger account for $105,000, the amount of the undistributed earnings of the subsidiary ($180,000 − $75,000 = $105,000), which of course differs from the after-closing balance of Salvo's Retained Earnings ledger account ($250,000 + $180,000 − $75,000 = $355,000). However, because $75,000 of Pasco's intercompany investment income is closed with the remainder of Pasco's net income to its Retained Earnings ledger account, consolidated retained earnings of Pasco Corporation and subsidiary includes $430,000 of retained earnings attributable to the subsidiary ($355,000 + $75,000 = $430,000).

TREASURY STOCK TRANSACTIONS OF A SUBSIDIARY

Treasury stock owned by a subsidiary on the date of a business combination is treated as *retired stock* in the preparation of consolidated financial statements because the treasury stock is not outstanding and thus was not acquired by the parent company. A working paper elimination is prepared to account for the "retirement" of the treasury stock by the *par* or *stated value method,* which is described in intermediate accounting textbooks.

Illustration of Treasury Stock Owned by Subsidiary on Date of Business Combination

Palance Corporation acquired all 49,000 shares of the outstanding common stock of Sizemore Company on March 1, 2002, for $147,000, including direct out-of-pocket costs. Sizemore's stockholders' equity on that date was as follows:

Stockholders' Equity of Subsidiary with Treasury Stock on Date of Business Combination

Common stock, $1 par	$ 50,000
Additional paid-in capital	25,000
Retained earnings	50,000
Total paid-in capital and retained earnings	$125,000
Less: 1,000 shares of treasury stock, at cost	2,000
Total stockholders' equity	$123,000

On the date of the combination, the current fair values of Sizemore's identifiable net assets equaled their carrying amounts.

The working paper eliminations (in journal entry format) for Palance Corporation and subsidiary on March 1, 2002, are as follows:

Working Paper Eliminations on Date of Business Combination with Wholly Owned Subsidiary Having Treasury Stock

PALANCE CORPORATION AND SUBSIDIARY
Working Paper Eliminations
March 1, 2002

(a) Common Stock—Sizemore (1,000 × $1)	1,000	
Additional Paid-in Capital—Sizemore (1,000 × $0.50)	500	
Retained Earnings—Sizemore (1,000 × $0.50)	500	
Treasury Stock—Sizemore (1,000 × $2)		2,000
To account for subsidiary's treasury stock as though it had been retired.		

(continued)

PALANCE CORPORATION AND SUBSIDIARY Working Paper Eliminations (concluded) March 1, 2002		
(b) Common Stock—Sizemore ($50,000 − $1,000)	49,000	
Additional Paid-in Capital—Sizemore ($25,000 − $500)	24,500	
Retained Earnings—Sizemore ($50,000 − $500)	49,500	
Goodwill—Sizemore ($147,000 − $123,000)	24,000	
Investment in Sizemore Company Common Stock—Palance		147,000
To eliminate intercompany investment and equity accounts of subsidiary on date of business combination; and to allocate excess of cost over current fair values (and carrying amounts) of identifiable net assets acquired to goodwill.		

In the first elimination, additional paid-in capital of the subsidiary is reduced by the pro rata portion ($25,000 ÷ 50,000 shares = $0.50 a share) applicable to the treasury stock. The remainder of the cost of the treasury stock is allocated to the subsidiary's retained earnings.

As indicated on page 441, if, subsequent to the date of a business combination, a subsidiary acquires for its treasury some or all of the shares of its common stock owned by minority stockholders, purchase accounting is applied, even if the business combination had been accounted for as a pooling of interests. Thus, in the working paper elimination that accounts for the treasury stock as though it had been retired, current fair value differences and goodwill may be recognized. [It should be emphasized that, in a *greenmail* (defined on page 171) acquisition of treasury stock, the excess of the cost of the treasury stock over its current fair value typically is recognized as a loss.[6]]

Illustration of Treasury Stock Acquired by Subsidiary Subsequent to Business Combination

On December 31, 2002, Portola Corporation acquired 80% of the outstanding common stock of Stanley Company for $44,000, including direct out-of-pocket costs of the business combination. Stanley's stockholders' equity on December 31, 2002, was as follows, with current fair values of identifiable net assets equal to carrying amounts:

Stockholders' Equity of Subsidiary on Date of Business Combination

Common stock, $10 par	$10,000
Additional paid-in capital	15,000
Retained earnings	25,000
Total stockholders' equity	$50,000

For the fiscal year ended December 31, 2003, Stanley declared dividends of $4,000 and had a net income of $10,000. Portola's investment ledger account appeared as follows on December 31, 2003, assuming consolidated goodwill of $4,000 [$44,000 − ($50,000 × 0.80) = $4,000 goodwill] was unimpaired as of December 31, 2003:

---

[6] *FASB Technical Bulletin No. 85–6,* "Accounting for a Purchase of Treasury Shares at a Price Significantly in Excess of the Current Market Price of the Shares . . ." (Stamford: FASB, 1985), p. 2.

Investment in Stanley Company Common Stock

Date	Explanation	Debit	Credit	Balance
2002				
Dec. 31	Acquisition of 800 shares	44,000		44,000 dr
2003				
Dec. 28	Dividends received: $4 a share ($4,000 × 0.80)		3,200	40,800 dr
31	Share of net income ($10,000 × 0.80)	8,000		48,800 dr

The working paper eliminations (in journal entry format) for Portola Corporation and subsidiary on December 31, 2003, are as follows:

PORTOLA CORPORATION AND SUBSIDIARY
Working Paper Eliminations
December 31, 2003

(a) Common Stock, $10 par—Stanley	10,000	
Additional Paid-in Capital—Stanley	15,000	
Retained Earnings—Stanley	25,000	
Intercompany Investment Income—Portola	8,000	
Goodwill—Portola	4,000	
Investment in Stanley Company Common Stock—Portola		48,800
Dividends Declared—Stanley		4,000
Minority Interest in Net Assets of Subsidiary ($10,000 − $800)		9,200

To eliminate intercompany investment and equity accounts of subsidiary at **beginning of year;** to allocate excess of cost over current fair values (and carrying amounts) of identifiable net assets acquired to unimpaired goodwill; and to establish minority interest in net assets of subsidiary at beginning of year ($50,000 × 0.20 = $10,000), less minority interest in dividends declared by subsidiary during year ($4,000 × 0.20 = $800).

(b) Minority Interest in Net Income of Subsidiary ($10,000 × 0.20)	2,000	
Minority Interest in Net Assets of Subsidiary		2,000

To establish minority interest in subsidiary's net income for Year 2003.

On January 2, 2004, Stanley paid $7,400 (current fair value) to acquire 100 shares of its common stock from a minority stockholder. Stanley's journal entry to record the acquisition of treasury stock was as follows:

Treasury Stock (100 × $74)	7,400	
Cash		7,400

To record acquisition of common stock from a minority stockholder.

The $74 a share acquisition cost of the treasury stock exceeds the $56 a share ($11,200 ÷ 200 = $56) carrying amount of the minority interest in net assets of subsidiary by $18 ($74 − $56 = $18). Thus, assuming that the current fair values of

Stanley's identifiable net assets were equal to their carrying amounts on January 2, 2004, Stanley's acquisition of goodwill of $1,800 (100 × $18 = $1,800) is recognized in the first of the following working paper eliminations (in journal entry format) on that date:

Working Paper Eliminations
Following Partially Owned
Subsidiary's Acquisition of
Treasury Stock

PORTOLA CORPORATION AND SUBSIDIARY
Working Paper Eliminations
January 2, 2004

(a) Common Stock, $10 par—Stanley (100 × $10)	1,000	
Additional Paid-in Capital—Stanley (100 × $15)	1,500	
Retained Earnings—Stanley (100 × $31)	3,100	
Goodwill—Stanley (100 × $18)	1,800	
Treasury Stock—Stanley		7,400
To account for subsidiary's treasury stock as though it had been retired.		
(b) Common Stock, $10 par—Stanley ($10,000 − $1,000)	9,000	
Additional Paid-in Capital—Stanley ($15,000 − $1,500)	13,500	
Retained Earnings—Stanley ($25,000 + $10,000 − $4,000 − $3,100 − $4,800)	23,100	
Retained Earnings of Subsidiary—Portola ($8,000 − $3,200)	4,800	
Goodwill—Portola	4,000	
Investment in Stanley Company Common Stock—Portola		48,800
Minority Interest in Net Assets of Subsidiary ($11,200 − $5,600)		5,600
To eliminate intercompany investment and equity accounts of subsidiary; to allocate excess of cost over current values of identifiable net assets acquired to goodwill; and to establish minority interest in net assets of subsidiary (100 × $56 = $5,600).		

INDIRECT SHAREHOLDINGS AND PARENT COMPANY'S COMMON STOCK OWNED BY A SUBSIDIARY

In the early years of business combinations resulting in parent company–subsidiary relationships, complex indirect or reciprocal shareholdings frequently were involved. ***Indirect shareholdings*** are those involving such relationships as one subsidiary and the parent company jointly owning a controlling interest in another subsidiary, or a subsidiary company itself being the parent company of its own subsidiary. ***Reciprocal shareholdings*** involve subsidiary ownership of shares of the parent company's common stock.

Indirect Shareholdings

Business combinations in recent years generally have been far less complex than those described above. There usually has been a single parent company and one or more subsidiaries, and indirect shareholdings have been the exception rather than the rule. Accountants faced with the problems of preparing a working paper for consolidated financial statements for parent company–subsidiary relationships involving indirect shareholdings must follow carefully the common stock ownership percentages and apply the equity method of accounting for the operating results of the various subsidiaries.

Illustration of Indirect Shareholdings

On December 31, 2002, Placer Corporation acquired 160,000 shares (80%) of the outstanding common stock of Shabot Company for $476,240, and 36,000 shares (45%) of Sur Company's outstanding common stock for $182,000. Both amounts included direct out-of-pocket costs of the common stock acquisitions. On December 31, 2002, Shabot owned 20,000 shares (25%) of Sur's outstanding common stock; accordingly, Placer acquired indirect control of Sur as well as direct control of Shabot in the business combination, as illustrated in the following diagram:

Illustration of Indirect Shareholdings

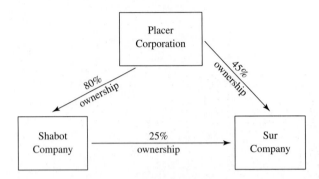

Because Shabot was able to exercise significant influence over the financing and operating policies of Sur, it applied the equity method of accounting for its investment in Sur.

Separate balance sheets of Shabot and Sur on December 31, 2002, prior to the business combination, follow:

SHABOT COMPANY AND SUR COMPANY Separate Balance Sheets (prior to business combination) December 31, 2002		
	Shabot Company	**Sur Company**
Assets		
Current assets	$ 360,400	$190,600
Investment in Sur Company common stock	91,950	
Plant assets (net)	640,650	639,400
Total assets	$1,093,000	$830,000
Liabilities and Stockholders' Equity		
Current liabilities	$ 210,200	$ 80,500
Long-term debt	300,000	389,500
Common stock, $1 par	200,000	80,000
Additional paid-in capital	150,000	120,000
Retained earnings	222,850	160,000
Retained earnings of investee	9,950	
Total liabilities and stockholders' equity	$1,093,000	$830,000

Shabot's Investment in Sur Company Common Stock and Retained Earnings of Investee ledger accounts were as follows on December 31, 2002:

Selected Ledger Accounts of Subsidiary-Investor on Date of Business Combination

Investment in Sur Company Common Stock

Date	Explanation	Debit	Credit	Balance
2001				
Dec. 31	Acquisition of 20,000 shares	82,000		82,000 dr
2002				
Dec. 6	Dividends received: $0.25 a share		5,000	77,000 dr
31	Share of net income ($60,000 × 0.25)	15,000		92,000 dr
31	Impairment of goodwill		50	91,950 dr

Retained Earnings of Investee

Date	Explanation	Debit	Credit	Balance
2002				
Dec. 31	Closing entry—share of Sur Company adjusted net income not paid as a dividend ($15,000 − $50 − $5,000)		9,950	9,950 cr

The foregoing ledger accounts of Shabot indicate that Shabot had applied the equity method of accounting for its investment in the influenced investee, Sur, and that the $2,000 excess of the cost of Shabot's investment over the underlying equity of Sur's identifiable net assets was allocated to goodwill that had been slightly impaired.

The current fair values of the identifiable net assets of both Shabot and Sur equaled their carrying amounts on December 31, 2002. Accordingly, goodwill acquired by Placer in the business combination with Shabot and Sur was measured as follows:

Computation of Goodwill Acquired by Parent Company

	Shabot Company	Sur Company
Cost of investment	$476,240	$182,000
Less: Current fair value of identifiable net assets acquired:		
Shabot ($582,800 × 0.80)	466,240	
Sur ($360,000 × 0.45)		162,000
Goodwill	$ 10,000	$ 20,000

Working Paper for Consolidated Balance Sheet on Date of Business Combination

The working paper for consolidated balance sheet of Placer Corporation and subsidiaries on December 31, 2002, the date of the business combination, and the related working paper eliminations (in journal entry format) are as follows:

Partially Owned Subsidiaries on Date of Business Combination

				Eliminations Increase (Decrease)	Consolidated
	Placer Corporation	**Shabot Company**	**Sur Company**		
Assets					
Current assets	1,400,000	360,400	190,600		1,951,000
Investment in Shabot Company common stock	476,240			(a) (476,240)	
Investment in Sur Company common stock	182,000	91,950		{(b) (91,950)} {(b) (182,000)}	
Plant assets (net)	3,800,000	640,650	639,400		5,080,050
Goodwill				{(a) 10,000} {(b) 21,950}	31,950
Total assets	5,858,240	1,093,000	830,000	(718,240)	7,063,000
Liabilities and Stockholders' Equity					
Current liabilities	600,000	210,200	80,500		890,700
Long-term debt	3,000,000	300,000	389,500		3,689,500
Common stock, $1 par	1,200,000	200,000	80,000	{(a) (200,000)} {(b) (80,000)}	1,200,000
Additional paid-in capital	500,000	150,000	120,000	{(a) (150,000)} {(b) (120,000)}	500,000
Minority interest in net assets of subsidiaries				{(a) 116,560} {(b) 108,000}	224,560
Retained earnings	558,240	222,850	160,000	{(a) (222,850)} {(b) (160,000)}	558,240
Retained earnings of investee		9,950		(a) (9,950)	
Total liabilities and stockholders' equity	5,858,240	1,093,000	830,000	(718,240)	7,063,000

PLACER CORPORATION AND SUBSIDIARIES
Working Paper for Consolidated Balance Sheet
December 31, 2002

Working Paper Eliminations on Date of Business Combination Involving Indirect Shareholdings

PLACER CORPORATION AND SUBSIDIARIES
Working Paper Eliminations
December 31, 2002

(a) Common Stock, $1 par—Shabot	200,000	
Additional Paid-in Capital—Shabot	150,000	
Retained Earnings—Shabot	222,850	
Retained Earnings of Investee—Shabot	9,950	
Goodwill—Placer	10,000	
Investment in Shabot Company Common Stock—Placer		476,240
Minority Interest in Net Assets of Subsidiaries ($582,800 × 0.20)		116,560

To eliminate intercompany investment and equity accounts of Shabot Company on date of business combination; to allocate excess of cost over current fair values (and carrying amounts) of identifiable net assets acquired to goodwill; and to establish minority interest in net assets of Shabot on date of business combination.

(continued)

PLACER CORPORATION AND SUBSIDIARIES
Working Paper Eliminations (concluded)
December 31, 2002

(b) Common Stock, $1 par—Sur	80,000	
Additional Paid-in Capital—Sur	120,000	
Retained Earnings—Sur	160,000	
Goodwill—Placer ($1,950 + $20,000)	21,950	
Investment in Sur Company Common Stock—Placer		182,000
Investment in Sur Company Common Stock—Shabot		91,950
Minority Interest in Net Assets of Subsidiaries ($360,000 × 0.30)		108,000

To eliminate intercompany investments and equity accounts of Sur Company on date of business combination; to allocate excess of cost over current fair values (and carrying amounts) of identifiable net assets acquired to goodwill; and to establish minority interest in net assets of Sur on date of business combination.

The following two aspects of the working paper eliminations warrant emphasis:

1. In elimination (a), Shabot Company's retained earnings of investee amount on the date of the business combination is reduced to zero. Because Placer Corporation is the parent company in the Placer–Shabot–Sur business combination, Shabot's ownership of 20,000 shares of Sur's outstanding common stock on the date of the combination is not construed as an installment acquisition by Placer; thus, consolidated retained earnings on the date of the combination does not include Shabot's share of Sur's retained earnings.

2. In elimination (b), both the $20,000 goodwill acquired by Placer (see page 463) and the unimpaired goodwill implicit in Shabot's investment in Sur ($2,000 − $50 = $1,950) are included in consolidated goodwill, because the current fair values of Sur's identifiable net assets equaled their carrying amounts on the date of combination. The entire goodwill is attributable to Placer because of the existence of minority interests in both Shabot and Sur.

Working Paper Eliminations Subsequent to Business Combination

For the fiscal year ended December 31, 2003, Shabot Company had an income of $150,000 (exclusive of investment income from Sur) and declared dividends of $60,000; Sur Company had a net income of $80,000 and declared dividends of $20,000. These operating results are recorded in the investment accounts of Placer and Shabot below and on page 466, under the equity method of accounting assuming that consolidated goodwill was unimpaired as of December 31, 2003; the working paper eliminations (in journal entry format) for Placer Corporation and subsidiaries on December 31, 2003, follow those accounts.

Investment Accounts of Parent Company and Subsidiary One Year Subsequent to Business Combination

PLACER CORPORATION LEDGER

Investment in Shabot Company Common Stock

Date	Explanation	Debit	Credit	Balance
2002				
Dec. 31	Acquisition of 160,000 shares	476,240		476,240 dr
2003				
Dec. 6	Dividends received: $0.30 a share		48,000	428,240 dr
31	Share of net income [($150,000 + $20,000) × 0.80]	136,000		564,240 dr

Investment in Sur Company Common Stock

Date	Explanation	Debit	Credit	Balance
2002 Dec. 31	Acquisition of 36,000 shares	182,000		182,000 dr
2003 Dec. 6	Dividends received: $0.25 a share		9,000	173,000 dr
31	Share of net income ($80,000 × 0.45)	36,000		209,000 dr

SHABOT COMPANY LEDGER

Investment in Sur Company Common Stock

Date	Explanation	Debit	Credit	Balance
2001 Dec. 31	Acquisition of 20,000 shares	82,000		82,000 dr
2002 Dec. 6	Dividends received: $0.25 a share		5,000	77,000 dr
31	Share of net income ($60,000 × 0.25)	15,000		92,000 dr
31	Impairment of goodwill		50	91,950 dr
2003 Dec. 6	Dividends received: $0.25 a share		5,000	86,950 dr
31	Share of net income ($80,000 × 0.25)	20,000		106,950 dr

Working Paper Eliminations for First Year Following Business Combination Involving Indirect Shareholdings

PLACER CORPORATION AND SUBSIDIARIES
Working Paper Eliminations
December 31, 2003

(a) Common Stock, $1 par—Shabot	200,000	
Additional Paid-in Capital—Shabot	150,000	
Retained Earnings—Shabot	222,850	
Retained Earnings of Investee—Shabot	9,950	
Intercompany Investment Income—Placer	136,000	
Goodwill—Placer	10,000	
Investment in Shabot Company Common Stock—Placer		564,240
Dividends Declared—Shabot		60,000
Minority Interest in Net Assets of Subsidiaries ($116,560 − $12,000)		104,560

To eliminate intercompany investment and equity accounts of Shabot Company at **beginning of year,** and subsidiary dividends; to allocate unamortized excess of cost over current fair values of identifiable net assets to unimpaired goodwill; and to establish minority interest in net assets of Shabot at beginning of year ($116,560), less minority interest in dividends ($60,000 × 0.20 = $12,000).

(continued)

PLACER CORPORATION AND SUBSIDIARIES		
Working Paper Eliminations (concluded)		
December 31, 2003		
(b) Common Stock, $1 par—Sur	80,000	
Additional Paid-in Capital—Sur	120,000	
Retained Earnings—Sur	160,000	
Intercompany Investment Income—Placer	36,000	
Intercompany Investment Income—Shabot	20,000	
Goodwill—Placer ($1,950 + $20,000)	21,950	
Investment in Sur Company Common Stock—Placer		209,000
Investment in Sur Company Common Stock—Shabot		106,950
Dividends Declared—Sur		20,000
Minority Interest in Net Assets of Subsidiaries ($108,000 − $6,000)		102,000
To eliminate intercompany investment and equity accounts of Sur Company at **beginning of year,** and subsidiary dividends; to allocate unamortized excess of cost over current fair values of identifiable net assets to unimpaired goodwill; and to establish minority interest in net assets of Sur at beginning of year ($108,000), less minority interest in dividends ($20,000 × 0.30 = $6,000).		
(c) Minority Interest in Net Income of Subsidiaries		
[($170,000 × 0.20) + ($80,000 × 0.30)]	58,000	
Minority Interest in Net Assets of Subsidiaries		58,000
To establish minority interest in subsidiaries' net income for Year 2003.		

Parent Company's Common Stock Owned by a Subsidiary

The traditional approach by accountants to problems of *reciprocal shareholdings* involved complex mathematical allocations of the individual affiliated companies' net income or loss to consolidated net income or loss and to minority interest. These allocations typically involved matrices or simultaneous equations.

Accountants have come to question the traditional approach to reciprocal shareholdings. The principal criticism is that strict application of mathematical allocations for reciprocal shareholdings violates the *going-concern* aspect of consolidated financial statements in favor of a *liquidation* approach. A related criticism is the emphasis of the traditional approach on *legal form* of the reciprocal shareholdings, rather than on *economic substance.* When a subsidiary acquires outstanding common stock of the parent company, it has been argued, the shares of parent company common stock owned by the subsidiary are in essence *treasury stock* to the consolidated entity. The treasury stock treatment for reciprocal shareholdings was sanctioned by the American Accounting Association and by the AICPA as follows:

> Shares of the controlling company's capital stock owned by a subsidiary before the date of acquisition of control should be treated in consolidation as treasury stock. Any subsequent acquisition or sale by a subsidiary should likewise by treated in the consolidated statements as though it had been the act of the controlling company.[7]

---

[7] *Accounting and Reporting Standards for Corporate Financial Statements,* "Consolidated Financial Statements" (Madison: AAA, 1957), p. 44.

... shares of the parent held by a subsidiary should not be treated as outstanding stock in the consolidated balance sheet.[8]

The material in this text is consistent with the view that a subsidiary's shareholdings of parent company common stock in essence are treasury stock to the consolidated entity. This position is analogous to that set forth in Chapter 8 for intercompany bondholdings. There the point is made that a subsidiary acquiring the parent company's bonds payable in the open market is acting on behalf of the parent in the acquisition of the bonds for the consolidated entity's treasury.

To illustrate the accounting and working paper eliminations for parent company's common stock owned by a subsidiary, assume that on May 1, 2002, the beginning of a fiscal year, Springer Company, the wholly owned subsidiary of Prospect Corporation, acquired for $50,000 in the open market 5,000 shares, or 5%, of the outstanding $1 par common stock of Prospect. On April 30, 2003, Prospect declared and paid a cash dividend of $1.20 a share.

Springer prepares the following journal entries for its investment in Prospect's common stock, under the appropriate cost method of accounting:

Subsidiary's Journal Entries for Investment in Parent Company's Common Stock

2002			
May 1	Investment in Prospect Corporation Common Stock	50,000	
	Cash		50,000
	To record acquisition of 5,000 shares of parent company's outstanding common stock at $10 a share.		
2003			
Apr. 30	Cash	6,000	
	Intercompany Dividend Revenue		6,000
	To record dividend of $1.20 a share on 5,000 shares of parent company's common stock.		

The working paper eliminations (in journal entry format) for Prospect Corporation and subsidiary on April 30, 2003, include the following:

Working Paper Eliminations for Parent Company Common Stock Owned by Subsidiary

PROSPECT CORPORATION AND SUBSIDIARY
Partial Working Paper Eliminations
April 30, 2003

(b)	Treasury Stock—Prospect	50,000	
	Investment in Prospect Corporation Common Stock—Springer		50,000
	To transfer subsidiary's investment in parent company's common stock to treasury stock category.		
(c)	Intercompany Dividend Revenue—Springer	6,000	
	Dividends Declared—Prospect		6,000
	To eliminate parent company dividends received by subsidiary.		

---

[8] *ARB No. 51*, par. 13.

The effect of the second elimination is to remove the parent company dividends applicable to the consolidated treasury stock. The result is that, in the consolidated statement of retained earnings, dividends are in the amount of $114,000 ($120,000 − $6,000 = $114,000), representing the $1.20 a share dividend on 95,000 shares of parent company common stock that are outstanding from the viewpoint of the consolidated entity.

Concluding Comments on Special Problems

This chapter presents a number of special problems that might arise in the preparation of consolidated financial statements. Not discussed are basic or diluted earnings per share computations for a consolidated entity, because in most circumstances the standards for earnings per share computations described in intermediate accounting textbooks apply to the computation of consolidated earnings per share. The problems that arise in earnings per share computations when a subsidiary owns shares of the parent company's common stock or the parent owns potentially ***dilutive*** financial instruments of the subsidiary are highly technical and too specialized to warrant inclusion in a discussion of basic concepts relating to consolidated financial statements. The FASB has dealt with such matters in ***FASB Statement No. 128,*** "Earnings per Share."[9]

Review Questions

1. ***FASB Statement No. 141,*** "Business Combinations," requires use of the purchase method of accounting for a parent company's or a subsidiary's acquisition of all or part of the minority interest in net assets of the subsidiary, even though the business combination had been a (now prohibited) pooling-type combination. Discuss the reasoning in support of this requirement.

2. If a parent company acquires the minority interest in net assets of a subsidiary at less than carrying amount, what accounting treatment is appropriate for the difference? Explain.

3. Why does a parent company recognize a nonoperating gain or loss when a subsidiary issues common stock to the public at a price per share that differs from the carrying amount per share of the parent company's investment in the subsidiary's common stock? Explain.

4. Is a gain or a loss that is recognized by a parent company on the disposal of part of its investment in common stock of a subsidiary eliminated in the preparation of consolidated financial statements? Explain.

5. Explain how the minority interest in net assets of a subsidiary is affected by the parent company's ownership of 70% of the subsidiary's outstanding common stock and 60% of the subsidiary's outstanding 7%, cumulative, fully participating preferred stock.

6. Does the declaration of a stock dividend by a subsidiary necessitate any special treatment in working paper eliminations? Explain.

7. Describe how a subsidiary's ledger accounts are affected when it acquires for its treasury all or part of its outstanding common stock owned by minority stockholders.

8. "The treasury stock treatment for shares of parent company common stock owned by a subsidiary overstates consolidated net income and understates the minority interest in net income of the subsidiary." Do you agree? Explain.

[9] *FASB Statement No. 128,* "Earnings per Share" (Norwalk: FASB, 1997), pars. 62, 156.

9. Shares of its common stock held by a corporation in its treasury are not entitled to dividends. However, a subsidiary receives dividends on shares of its parent company's common stock owned by the subsidiary. For consolidated financial statements, these parent company shares are considered equivalent to treasury stock of the consolidated entity. Is there an inconsistency in this treatment? Explain.

Exercises

(Exercise 10.1) Select the best answer for each of the following multiple-choice questions:

1. The minority interest of preferred stockholders in the net assets of a partially owned purchased subsidiary preferably is measured by the preferred stock's
   a. Cash dividend per share.
   b. Call price per share.
   c. Liquidation preference per share.
   d. Par or stated value per share.

2. Shares of a parent company's common stock owned by the parent's subsidiary are accounted for in consolidated financial statements of the parent company and its subsidiary as:
   a. Retired parent company stock.
   b. Reissued parent company stock.
   c. Consolidated short-term investments.
   d. Consolidated treasury stock.

3. Do the following business transactions or events of a subsidiary generally result in a nonoperating gain or loss to the parent company?

	Subsidiary's Issuance of Unissued Common Stock to Public?	Subsidiary's Issuance of Unissued Common Stock to Parent Company?	Subsidiary's Acquisition of Part of Minority Stockholdings for Treasury?
a.	No	No	No
b.	Yes	Yes	No
c.	Yes	No	Yes
d.	Yes	Yes	Yes

4. If a parent company acquires for cash all the common stock owned by minority stockholders of a partially owned subsidiary, the excess of the cash paid over the minority interest in net assets of the subsidiary generally is recognized as:
   a. An expense in a parent company journal entry.
   b. Goodwill in a working paper elimination.
   c. An increase in the current fair values of the subsidiary's identifiable net assets in a working paper elimination.
   d. A reduction of an additional paid-in capital ledger account balance in a parent company journal entry.

5. Parsell Corporation disposed of a 20% interest in the outstanding common stock of its previously wholly owned subsidiary, Sorbell Company, on May 31, 2003, to an outside entity at a substantial gain. A result of this event is:
   a. A decrease in consolidated goodwill of Parsell Corporation and subsidiary on May 31, 2003.

    b. The elimination of the gain in the working paper for consolidated financial statements of Parsell Corporation and subsidiary for the year ended May 31, 2003.

    c. An increase in minority interest in net income of subsidiary in the consolidated income statement of Parsell Corporation and subsidiary for the year ended May 31, 2003.

    d. All of the foregoing.

    e. None of the foregoing.

6. Is a parent company's gain on disposal of a portion of its investment in the subsidiary displayed as realized in the:

	Parent Company's Unconsolidated Income Statement?	*Consolidated Income Statement of Parent Company and Subsidiary?*
a.	Yes	Yes
b.	Yes	No
c.	No	Yes
d.	No	No

7. The appropriate recording (explanation omitted) for a parent company to reflect a loss on its subsidiary's issuance of additional shares of common stock to the public is:

    a. A working paper elimination debiting Nonoperating Loss from Subsidiary's Issuance of Common Stock and crediting Investment in Subsidiary Company Common Stock.

    b. A parent company journal entry debiting Nonoperating Loss from Subsidiary's Issuance of Common Stock and crediting Investment in Subsidiary Company Common Stock.

    c. A subsidiary journal entry debiting an additional paid-in capital ledger account and crediting Payable to Parent Company.

    d. A note to the consolidated financial statements only.

8. If a parent company acquires additional shares of previously unissued common stock from its subsidiary, with minority stockholders of the subsidiary waiving their preemptive rights, a resultant gain or loss is:

    a. Recognized by the parent company and eliminated in the preparation of consolidated financial statements.

    b. Recognized by the parent company and not eliminated in the preparation of consolidated financial statements.

    c. Recognized by the subsidiary and eliminated in the preparation of consolidated financial statements.

    d. Recognized in a working paper elimination for the preparation of consolidated financial statements.

9. A parent company realizes a gain or loss on its acquisition of additional common stock from a subsidiary, with the minority stockholders waiving their preemptive rights, because:

    a. The minority stockholders are *owners* under the economic unit concept.

    b. The minority stockholders are *creditors* under the parent company concept.

    c. The subsidiary will pay more dividends to the parent company subsequent to its acquisition of additional common stock of the subsidiary.

    d. The parent company will recognize more intercompany investment income or loss subsequent to its acquisition of additional common stock of the subsidiary.

10. Is a gain or loss *realized* by the parent company when a subsidiary issues additional shares of common stock to:

	The Public?	The Parent Company?
a.	No	No
b.	No	Yes
c.	Yes	No
d.	Yes	Yes

11. When a parent company acquires both preferred stock and common stock of the subsidiary in a business combination, goodwill recognized in the combination is computed based on:

a. Cost allocated to preferred stock only.
b. Cost allocated to common stock only.
c. Cost allocated to both preferred stock and common stock.
d. Some other measure.

12. Is goodwill attributable to a subsidiary recognized in a working paper elimination for treasury stock of the subsidiary:

	Owned on the Date of the Business Combination?	Acquired Subsequent to the Date of the Business Combination?
a.	Yes	Yes
b.	Yes	No
c.	No	Yes
d.	No	No

13. Treasury stock acquired by a subsidiary from minority stockholders of the subsidiary is accounted for in consolidated financial statements as:

a. Treasury stock of the subsidiary.
b. Treasury stock of the parent company.
c. Treasury stock of the consolidated entity.
d. Retired stock of the subsidiary.

14. Shares of the parent company's issued common stock that are owned by the subsidiary are treated in the consolidated balance sheet as being:

a. Outstanding.
b. In the treasury.
c. Retired.
d. Part of the minority interest.

(Exercise 10.2)

CHECK FIGURE

Minority interest,
$15,200.

On March 31, 2003, the consolidated balance sheet of Polberg Corporation and its 85%-owned subsidiary, Serrano Company, showed goodwill of $65,400 and minority interest in net assets of subsidiary of $22,800. On April 1, 2003, Polberg paid $10,000 to minority stockholders who owned 500 of Serrano's 10,000 shares of issued common stock.

Prepare a working paper to compute goodwill and minority interest in net assets of subsidiary for display in the consolidated balance sheet of Polberg Corporation and subsidiary on April 1, 2003.

(Exercise 10.3)

CHECK FIGURE

Nonoperating gain to
Prester, $2,500.

On January 2, 2002, Prester Corporation organized Shire Company, paying $40,000 for 10,000 shares of Shire's $1 par common stock. On January 3, 2002, before beginning operations, Shire issued 2,000 shares of its $1 par common stock to the public for net proceeds of $11,000; Prester did not exercise its preemptive right.

Prepare a working paper to compute the change in Prester's Investment ledger account balance that resulted from Shire's issuance of common stock to the public.

(Exercise 10.4)

On October 31, 2003, when the balance of Pinto Corporation's Investment in Sorrel Company Common Stock ledger account was $540,000 and the minority interest in net assets of subsidiary was $135,000, Sorrel Company, of whose 10,000 shares of outstanding common stock Pinto owned 8,000 shares, issued 2,000 shares of unissued common stock to Pinto at $72 a share. (Minority stockholders did not exercise their preemptive rights.) Prior to issuance of the 2,000 shares of common stock, the stockholders' equity of Sorrel, which had been organized by Pinto, totaled $675,000; after issuance of the 2,000 shares, Sorrel's stockholders' equity totaled $819,000.

a. Prepare a three-column working paper to compute the change in the Investment ledger account balance of Pinto Corporation resulting from Sorrel Company's issuance of 2,000 shares of common stock to Pinto on October 31, 2003. Use the following column headings: "Total," "Pinto's Share," and "Minority Interest Share."

b. Prepare a journal entry for Pinto Corporation on October 31, 2003, to record the change in Pinto's Investment ledger account balance resulting from Sorrel Company's issuance of 2,000 shares of common stock to Pinto.

(Exercise 10.5)

The stockholders' equity section of Stegg Company's August 31, 2002, balance sheet was as follows:

8% cumulative preferred stock, $1 par, dividends in arrears two years; authorized, issued, and outstanding 100,000 shares, callable at $1.10 a share plus dividends in arrears	$ 100,000
Common stock, $2 par; authorized, issued, and outstanding 100,000 shares	200,000
Additional paid-in capital—common stock	150,000
Retained earnings	750,000
Total stockholders' equity	$1,200,000

On August 31, 2002, Panay Corporation acquired 50,000 shares of Stegg's outstanding preferred stock and 75,000 shares of Stegg's outstanding common stock for a total cost—including out-of-pocket costs—of $1,030,500. The current fair values of Stegg's identifiable net assets were equal to their carrying amounts on August 31, 2002.

Answer the following questions (show supporting computations):

a. What amount of the $1,030,500 total cost is assignable to Stegg's preferred stock?

b. What is the minority interest of preferred stockholders in Stegg's net assets on August 31, 2002?

c. What is the amount of goodwill acquired by Panay August 31, 2002?

d. What is the minority interest of common stockholders in Stegg's net assets on August 31, 2002?

(Exercise 10.6)

Simplex Company, the partially owned subsidiary of Polyglot Corporation, had a net income of $342,800 for the fiscal year ended May 31, 2003, during which Simplex declared a dividend of $12 a share on its 10,000 shares of outstanding 12%, $100 par, cumulative preferred stock, and a dividend of $8 a share on its 80,000 shares of outstanding $1 par common stock. Polyglot owned 7,000 shares of preferred stock and 60,000 shares of common stock of Simplex. There were no dividends in arrears on the preferred stock.

Prepare a working paper (as on page 456) to show the allocation of Simplex Company's $342,800 net income for the year ended May 31, 2003, to consolidated net income and to the minority interest in net income of subsidiary.

(Exercise 10.7) On September 30, 2003, prior to the declaration of a 15% stock dividend by its subsidiary, Sabro Company, on that date, Placard Corporation's accountant prepared the following tentative working paper elimination (in journal entry format):

(a) Common Stock, $2 par—Sabro	80,000	
Additional Paid-in Capital—Sabro	40,000	
Retained Earnings—Sabro ($130,000 − $10,000)	120,000	
Retained Earnings of Subsidiary—Placard	10,000	
Intercompany Investment Income—Placard	70,000	
Goodwill—Sabro	20,000	
Investment in Sabro Company Common Stock—Placard		340,000
To eliminate intercompany investment and equity accounts of subsidiary at **beginning of year,** and investment income from subsidiary; and to allocate excess of cost over current fair values (and carrying amounts) of identifiable net assets acquired to goodwill.		

The current fair value of the dividend shares issued by Sabro was $5 a share. Placard had net sales of $840,200 and total costs and expenses of $668,500 for the fiscal year ended September 30, 2003.

a. Prepare a revised working paper elimination (in journal entry format) for Placard Corporation and subsidiary on September 30, 2003, to reflect the effects of Sabro's stock dividend. Omit explanation, but show supporting computations.

b. Prepare a single closing entry (forgoing use of the Income Summary ledger account) for Placard Corporation on September 30, 2003. Omit explanation, but show supporting computations.

(Exercise 10.8) On December 31, 2002, the date of the business combination of Portland Corporation and Salem Company, Salem had 50,000 shares of $5 par common stock authorized, 20,000 shares issued (total net issue proceeds were $160,000), and 500 shares in the treasury, with a total cost of $5,500. The balance of Salem's Retained Earnings ledger account was $240,000 on December 31, 2002.

Prepare a working paper elimination (in journal entry format) for Portland Corporation and subsidiary on December 31, 2002, to account for the subsidiary's treasury stock as though it had been retired.

(Exercise 10.9) On February 28, 2002, the stockholders' equity of Stocker Company was as follows:

Common stock, no par or stated value; 50,000 shares issued, 48,000 shares outstanding	$250,000
Retained earnings	600,000
Total paid-in capital and retained earnings	$850,000
Less: 2,000 shares of treasury stock, at cost	16,000
Total stockholders' equity	$834,000

On February 28, 2002, Priam Corporation paid $900,000 for all 48,000 shares of outstanding common stock of Stocker; on that date, current fair values of Stocker's identifiable net assets were equal to their carrying amounts. Out-of-pocket costs of the business combination may be disregarded.

Prepare working paper eliminations (in journal entry format; omit explanations) for Priam Corporation and subsidiary on February 28, 2002.

(Exercise 10.10) The stockholders' equity section of the balance sheet of Sergeant Company, the wholly owned subsidiary of Private Corporation, on May 31, 2002, the date of the business combination, which did not involve a current fair value excess or goodwill, was as follows:

Common stock, $10 par	$100,000
Additional paid-in capital	50,000
Retained earnings	150,000
Total paid-in capital and retained earnings	$300,000
Less: 500 shares of treasury stock, at cost	7,500
Total stockholders' equity.	$292,500

Prepare working paper eliminations, in journal entry format (omit explanations), for Private Corporation and subsidiary on May 31, 2002.

(Exercise 10.11) The stockholders' equity of Sibley Company on February 28, 2002, was as follows:

CHECK FIGURE

Total debits to
goodwill—Sibley,
$50,000.

Common stock, no par or stated value; 100,000 shares authorized, 80,000 shares issued	$160,000
Retained earnings	640,000
Total stockholders' equity	$800,000

On February 28, 2002, Parson Corporation acquired 75,000 shares of Sibley's outstanding common stock for $790,000, including direct out-of-pocket costs of the business combination. Simultaneously, Sibley acquired for the treasury the remaining 5,000 shares of its outstanding common stock for $60,000, a fair price. The current fair values of Sibley's identifiable net assets were equal to their carrying amounts on February 28, 2002.

Prepare working paper eliminations, in journal entry format (omit explanations), for Parson Corporation and subsidiary on February 28, 2002.

(Exercise 10.12) On January 2, 2002, Prince Corporation organized Sabine Company with authorized common stock of 10,000 shares, $5 par. Prince acquired 4,000 shares of Sabine's common stock at $8 a share, and Samnite Company, a wholly owned subsidiary of Prince, acquired the 6,000 remaining authorized shares of Sabine's common stock at $8 a share. For the fiscal year ended December 31, 2002, Sabine had a net income of $80,000 and declared dividends of $2 a share on December 28, 2002, payable on January 25, 2003.

Prepare journal entries under the equity method of accounting to record the operating results of Sabine Company for Year 2002 in the accounting records of (*a*) Prince Corporation, and (*b*) Samnite Company. (Omit explanations; disregard income taxes.)

(Exercise 10.13) During the fiscal year ended May 31, 2004, Sugar Company, the wholly owned subsidiary of Peaches Corporation, prepared the following journal entries:

2003				
June	1	Investment in Peaches Corporation Common Stock	100,000	
		Cash		100,000
		To record acquisition of 100 shares (1%) of parent company's outstanding common stock at $1,000 a share.		

2004			
May 31	Cash	5,000	
	Intercompany Dividends Revenue		5,000
	To record dividend of $50 a share on 100 shares of parent company's common stock.		

Prepare working paper eliminations (in journal entry format, omitting explanations) for Peaches Corporation and subsidiary on May 31, 2004.

(Exercise 10.14) On August 1, 2002, the beginning of a fiscal year, Pressman Corporation acquired 95% of the outstanding common stock of Sycamore Company in a business combination. Among the intercompany transactions and events between Pressman and Sycamore subsequent to August 1, 2002, were the following:

1. On May 31, 2003, Sycamore declared a 10% stock dividend on its 10,000 outstanding shares of $10 par common stock having a current fair value of $18 a share. The 1,000 shares of the stock dividend were issued June 18, 2003.
2. On July 28, 2003, Sycamore acquired in the open market for $15,000, 1,000 of the 100,000 outstanding shares of Pressman's $1 par common stock. Pressman declared no dividends during the fiscal year ended July 31, 2003.

Prepare working paper eliminations (in journal entry format) on July 31, 2003, for Pressman Corporation and subsidiary, required for the foregoing intercompany transactions.

Cases

(Case 10.1) Wilma Reynolds, CPA, a member of the American Institute of Certified Public Accountants (AICPA), is controller of Premium Corporation, a publicly owned enterprise with a now-60%-owned subsidiary, Service Company. Reynolds has informed Premium's chief financial officer, Wayne Cartwright, that the $150,000 increase in Premium's investment in Service, which resulted from Service's just-completed issuance of additional common stock to the public, should be recognized as an increase in Premium's additional paid-in capital, in accordance with a proposed standard of the FASB. Cartwright countered that Topic 5-H of the SEC *Staff Accounting Bulletins* (SAB), which is based on *SAB 51* and *SAB 84,* sanctions recognition of the $150,000 increase as nonoperating income of Premium. Cartwright expressed the belief that because the SEC has statutory authority to establish accounting standards, its pronouncements should prevail over those proposed or issued by the FASB.

Instructions
Do you agree with Wayne Cartwright? In formulating your answer, consider the following:

Sections 101 and 103 of the SEC's *Codification of Financial Reporting Policies.*

FASB Statement No. 111, "Recession of FASB Statement No. 32 and Technical Corrections," par. 25.

AICPA *Code of Professional Conduct,* Rule 203 "Accounting Principles" and Appendix A.

(Case 10.2) The board of directors of Banking Enterprises, Inc., a holding company with 25 subsidiary federally chartered banks, has offered $2,500,000 to Mary Phillips, the 40% minority stockholder of Bank of Provence, for the entire 40% interest, which has a carrying amount of $1,800,000 in the consolidated balance sheet of Banking Enterprises, Inc. and subsidiaries. In a discussion of the appropriate accounting for the $700,000 difference ($2,500,000 − $1,800,000 = $700,000) between the amount offered and the carrying amount, Banking's chief financial officer, Wendell Casey, supports recognition of goodwill. However, controller John Winston of Banking Enterprises, Inc., believes that some of the $700,000 represents a greenmail-type loss, and should be recognized as such. In an appearance before Banking's board, both Casey and Winston argue their positions forcefully. The board instructs the two men to consult with the engagement partner of Banking's independent auditing firm, Crandall & Lowe, CPAs, to resolve the matter.

Instructions
Assume you are the above-described partner of Crandall & Lowe, CPAs. How would you resolve the dispute between Wendell Casey and John Winston? Explain, including mention of the additional information you would need.

(Case 10.3) In a classroom discussion of the display, in a consolidated balance sheet, of the minority interest of preferred stockholders in the net assets of a subsidiary, student Ross suggested that such a minority interest differs from the minority interest of common stockholders, and thus possibly warrants display in the "mezzanine" section between liabilities and stockholders' equity. Student Kerry disagrees; she maintains that the term *minority* applies to preferred stockholders as well as common stockholders other than the parent company; both minority interests are part of consolidated stockholders' equity.

Instructions
Do you support the position of student Ross or of student Kerry? Explain.

Problems

(Problem 10.1) Scrip Company, the 80%-owned subsidiary of Pinch Corporation, had 10,000 shares of $5 par common stock outstanding on March 31, 2002, the date of the Pinch-Scrip business combination, with total stockholders' equity of $300,000 and total paid-in capital equal in amount to retained earnings on that date. Goodwill in the amount of $40,000 and minority interest in net assets of subsidiary of $60,000 were displayed in the consolidated balance sheet of Pinch Corporation and subsidiary on March 31, 2002. The current fair values of Scrip's identifiable net assets equaled their carrying amounts on March 31, 2002.

> **CHECK FIGURE**
> Debit goodwill—Pinch,
> $54,000.

    On April 1, 2002, Pinch paid $44,000 (the current fair value) to a minority stockholder for 1,000 shares of Scrip common stock. For the fiscal year ended March 31, 2003 Scrip had a net income of $90,000 and declared and paid dividends of $3 a share in March, Year 2003. Consolidated goodwill was unimpaired as of March 31, 2003.

Instructions
Prepare working paper eliminations (in journal entry format) for Pinch Corporation and subsidiary on March 31, 2003. (Disregard income taxes.)

(Problem 10.2)

On January 2, 2002, Prime Corporation issued 50,000 shares of $10 par (current fair value $25 a share) common stock and paid $140,000 out-of-pocket costs for all the outstanding common stock of Showboat Company in a business combination that did not involve goodwill or current fair value excess. On the date of the combination, Showboat's stockholders' equity consists of the following:

Common stock, $1 par	$400,000
Additional paid-in capital	300,000
Retained earnings	250,000
Total paid-in capital and retained earnings	$950,000
Less: 20,000 shares of treasury stock, at cost	50,000
Total stockholders' equity	$900,000

On December 29, 2002, Showboat declared a dividend of $0.10 a share, payable in Year 2003. For the fiscal year ended December 31, 2002, Showboat had a net income of $90,000.

Instructions

a. Prepare journal entries for Prime Corporation to record the operating results of Showboat Company for Year 2002, under the equity method of accounting. (Disregard income taxes.)

b. Prepare working paper eliminations (in journal entry format) for Prime Corporation and subsidiary on December 31, 2002. (Disregard income taxes.)

(Problem 10.3)

The working paper eliminations (in journal entry format) for Pumble Corporation and its subsidiary (established by Pumble on November 1, 2001, with a 2% minority interest) on October 31, 2003, are as follows:

PUMBLE CORPORATION AND SUBSIDIARY Working Paper Eliminations October 31, 2003		
(a) Common Stock—Salton	10,000	
Additional Paid-in Capital—Salton	60,000	
Retained Earnings—Salton ($80,000 × 0.02)	1,600	
Retained Earnings of Subsidiary—Pumble ($80,000 × 0.98)	78,400	
Intercompany Investment Income—Pumble ($40,000 × 0.98)	39,200	
Investment in Salton Company Common Stock— Pumble ($180,000 × 0.98)		176,400
Dividends Declared—Salton		10,000
Minority Interest in Net Assets of Subsidiary ($3,000 − $200)		2,800
To eliminate intercompany investment and related accounts for stockholders' equity of subsidiary at **beginning of year,** and investment income from subsidiary; and to establish minority interest in net assets of subsidiary at beginning of year ($150,000 × 0.02 = $3,000), less minority interest in dividends ($10,000 × 0.02 = $200).		
(b) Minority Interest in Net Income of Subsidiary ($40,000 × 0.02)	800	
Minority Interest in Net Assets of Subsidiary		800
To establish minority interest in net income of subsidiary for year ended October 31, 2003.		

On November 1, 2003, Salton issued 1,000 additional shares of $1 par common stock to Pumble for $20 a share (Salton's minority stockholders did not exercise their preemptive rights). (Out-of-pocket costs of the stock issuance may be disregarded.) On October 31, 2004, Salton declared a dividend of $2 a share, and for the fiscal year ended October 31, 2004, Salton had a net income of $35,000.

Instructions

a. Prepare journal entries for Pumble Corporation to record the operating results of Salton Company for the fiscal year ended October 31, 2004, under the equity method of accounting. Round Pumble's new percentage interest in Salton to two decimal places, and all dollar amounts to the nearest dollar. (Disregard income taxes.)

b. Prepare working paper eliminations (in journal entry format) for Pumble Corporation and subsidiary on October 31, 2004. Round all amounts to the nearest dollar. (Disregard income taxes.)

(Problem 10.4) On February 28, 2003, the end of a fiscal year, the balance of Pronto Corporation's Retained Earnings of Subsidiary ledger account (after closing) was $9,000, and the balance of Pronto's Investment in Speedy Company Common Stock ledger account was $75,000, which was analyzed as follows:

Share of identifiable net assets of Speedy (current fair values equaled carrying amounts on date of business combination) ($100,000 × 0.60)	$60,000
Goodwill (unimpaired)	15,000
Balance of Pronto's investment account, Feb. 28, 2003	$75,000

The minority interest in net assets of subsidiary in the consolidated balance sheet of Pronto Corporation and subsidiary on February 28, 2003, was $40,000 ($100,000 × 0.40 = $40,000). The stockholders' equity of Speedy Company on February 28, 2003, consisted of the following:

Common stock, $1 par	$ 10,000
Additional paid-in capital	30,000
Retained earnings	60,000
Total stockholders' equity	$100,000

On March 1, 2003, in order to reduce the minority interest in the net assets of Speedy Company, Pronto Corporation paid $32,000 to Speedy for 2,000 shares of Speedy's unissued common stock, thus increasing Pronto's ownership interest in Speedy to $66\frac{2}{3}\%\,[(6,000 + 2,000) \div (10,000 + 2,000) = 66\frac{2}{3}\%]$. (The minority stockholders of Speedy did not exercise their preemptive rights.)

Instructions

a. Prepare a journal entry for Speedy Company to record the issuance of 2,000 shares of common stock to Pronto Corporation on March 1, 2003.

b. Prepare a working paper to compute the balance of Pronto Corporation's Investment in Speedy Company Common Stock ledger account on March 1, 2003, following the acquisition of 2,000 shares of Speedy's unissued common stock. (Include the non-operating gain or loss resulting from Speedy's issuance of common stock to Pronto.)

c. Prepare a working paper elimination (in journal entry format) for the consolidated balance sheet of Pronto Corporation and subsidiary on March 1, 2003, following

Speedy's issuance of 2,000 shares of common stock to Pronto. Disregard Speedy's operations for March 1, 2003, and disregard income taxes.

(Problem 10.5) On October 31, 2002, Pun Corporation acquired 80% of the outstanding common stock of Sim Company for $960,000, including goodwill of $80,000. On that date, the carrying amount (equal to current fair value) of Sim's identifiable net assets was $1,100,000, represented by the following stockholders' equity:

Common stock, no par or stated value; 10,000 shares authorized, issued, and outstanding	$ 500,000
Retained earnings	600,000
Total stockholders' equity	$1,100,000

Additional Information

1. For the fiscal year ended October 31, 2003, Sim had a net income of $100,000 and declared and paid dividends of $40,000. Thus, because consolidated goodwill was unimpaired as of October 31, 2003, the balance of Pun's Investment in Sim Company Common Stock ledger account under the equity method of accounting on October 31, 2003, was $1,008,000, computed as follows:

Cost of 8,000 shares acquired Oct. 31, 2002	$ 960,000
Add: Share of net income ($100,000 × 0.80)	80,000
Subtotal	$1,040,000
Less: Share of dividends ($40,000 × 0.80)	32,000
Balance, Oct. 31, 2003	$1,008,000

2. The after-closing balance of Pun's Retained Earnings of Subsidiary ledger account on October 31, 2003, was $48,000 ($80,000 − $32,000 = $48,000).

3. On November 1, 2003, at Pun's direction, Sim paid $170,000 (the current fair value) to a dissident minority stockholder for 1,000 shares of Sim's outstanding common stock, preparing the following journal entry:

Treasury Stock (1,000 × $170)	170,000	
Cash		170,000
To record acquisition of 1,000 shares of outstanding common stock from a minority stockholder for the treasury.		

The current fair values of Sim's identifiable net assets were the same as their carrying amounts on November 1, 2003.

Instructions

Prepare working paper eliminations (in journal entry format) for Pun Corporation and subsidiary on November 1, 2003, to account for Sim Company's treasury stock as though it had been retired and to eliminate the intercompany investment and equity accounts of the subsidiary. Disregard Sim's operations for November 1, 2003, and disregard income taxes.

(Problem 10.6) Separate and consolidated financial statements of Peterson Corporation and its wholly owned subsidiary, Swanson Company, for the fiscal year ended May 31, 2004, are on page 481. The two companies used intercompany ledger accounts only for receivables and payables.

PETERSON CORPORATION AND SUBSIDIARY
Separate and Consolidated Financial Statements
For Year Ended May 31, 2004

	Peterson Corporation	Swanson Company	Consolidated
Income Statements			
Revenue:			
Net sales	$10,000,000	$4,600,000	$12,900,000
Other revenue	270,000	20,000	38,250
Total revenue	$10,270,000	$4,620,000	$12,938,250
Costs and expenses:			
Cost of goods sold	$ 6,700,000	$3,082,000	$ 8,085,300
Operating expenses and income taxes expense	2,918,750	1,288,000	4,208,000
Total costs and expenses	$ 9,618,750	$4,370,000	$12,293,300
Net income	$ 651,250	$ 250,000	$ 644,950
Statements of Retained Earnings			
Retained earnings, beginning of year	$ 2,421,250	$ 825,000	$ 2,530,550
Add: Net income	651,250	250,000	644,950
Subtotals	$ 3,072,500	$1,075,000	$ 3,175,500
Less: Dividends	300,000	175,000	297,000
Retained earnings, end of year	$ 2,772,500	$ 900,000	$ 2,878,500
Balance Sheets			
Assets			
Intercompany receivables (payable)	$ 520,000	$ (520,000)	
Short-term investments*	400,000	150,000	$ 530,000
Inventories	1,100,000	610,000	1,693,500
Investment in Swanson Company common stock	1,100,000		
Other assets	2,800,000	1,370,000	4,170,000
Goodwill			50,000
Total assets	$ 5,920,000	$1,610,000	$ 6,443,500
Liabilities and Stockholders' Equity			
Liabilities	$ 2,075,000	$ 560,000	$ 2,635,000
Common stock, $10 par	1,000,000	150,000	1,000,000
Retained earnings	2,772,500	900,000	2,878,500
Retained earnings of subsidiary	122,500		
Treasury stock	(50,000)		(70,000)
Total liabilities and stockholders' equity	$ 5,920,000	$1,610,000	$ 6,443,500

* Fair values same as carrying amounts

Additional Information

1. All of Swanson's identifiable net assets were fairly valued at their carrying amounts on May 31, 2002—the date of the Peterson–Swanson business combination. Thus, the $50,000 excess of Peterson's investment in Swanson over the carrying amounts of Swanson's identifiable net assets was attributable to goodwill, which was unimpaired as of May 31, 2004.

2. During the year ended May 31, 2004, Peterson sold merchandise to Swanson at Peterson's regular markup.

3. Swanson had acquired 1,000 shares of Peterson's common stock on June 10, 2003, and Peterson had acquired its treasury stock on May 26, 2004.

Instructions

Reconstruct the working paper eliminations (in journal entry format) for Peterson Corporation and subsidiary on May 31, 2004. (Disregard income taxes; omit explanations for eliminations.)

(Problem 10.7) Separate financial statements of Pomerania Corporation and its two subsidiaries for the year ended December 31, 2002, are as follows:

POMERANIA CORPORATION AND SUBSIDIARIES
Separate Financial Statements
For Year Ended December 31, 2002

	Pomerania Corporation	Slovakia Company	Sylvania Company
Income Statements			
Revenue			
Net sales	$1,120,000	$900,000	$700,000
Intercompany sales	140,000		
Intercompany investment income	44,000		
Total revenue	$1,304,000	$900,000	$700,000
Cost and expenses:			
Cost of goods sold	$ 800,000	$650,000	$550,000
Intercompany cost of goods sold	100,000		
Operating expenses and income taxes expense	300,000	150,000	130,000
Total costs and expenses	$1,200,000	$800,000	$680,000
Net income	$ 104,000	$100,000	$ 20,000
Statements of Retained Earnings			
Retained earnings, beginning of year	$ 126,200	$107,000	$100,000
Add: Net income	104,000	100,000	20,000
Subtotals	$ 230,200	$207,000	$120,000
Less: Dividends	22,000	75,000	
Retained earnings, end of year	$ 208,200	$132,000	$120,000
Balance Sheets			
Assets			
Intercompany receivables (payables)	$ 63,400	$ (41,000)	$ (22,400)
Inventories	290,000	90,000	115,000
Investment in Slovakia Company common stock	305,600		
Investment in Slovakia Company bonds	20,800		
Investment in Sylvania Company preferred stock	7,000		
Investment in Sylvania Company common stock	196,000		
Other assets	836,400	555,000	510,000
Total assets	$1,719,200	$604,000	$602,600

(continued)

POMERANIA CORPORATION AND SUBSIDIARIES
Separate Financial Statements (concluded)
For Year Ended December 31, 2002

	Pomerania Corporation	Slovakia Company	Sylvania Company
Liabilities and Stockholders' Equity			
Dividends payable	$ 22,000	$ 6,000	
Bonds payable	285,000	125,000	$125,000
Intercompany bonds payable		25,000	
Discount on bonds payable	(8,000)	(10,000)	
Discount on intercompany bonds payable		(2,000)	
Other liabilities	212,000	78,000	107,600
Preferred stock, $20 par	400,000		50,000
Common stock, $10 par	600,000	250,000	200,000
Retained earnings	208,200	132,000	120,000
Total liabilities and stockholders' equity	$1,719,200	$604,000	$602,600

Additional Information

1. Pomerania Corporation's Investment in Slovakia Company Common Stock ledger account is shown below:

Investments in Slovakia Company Common Stock

Date	Explanation	Debit	Credit	Balance
2002				
Jan. 2	Cost of 5,000 shares	71,400		71,400 dr
June 30	20% of dividend declared		9,000	62,400 dr
30	20% of net income for Jan. 2–June 30	12,000		74,400 dr
July 1	Cost of 15,000 shares	223,200		297,600 dr
Dec. 31	80% of dividend declared		24,000	273,600 dr
31	80% of net income for July 1–Dec. 31	32,000		305,600 dr

2. The accountant for Pomerania made no equity-method journal entries for Pomerania's investments in Sylvania's preferred stock and common stock. Pomerania had acquired 250 shares of Sylvania's fully participating noncumulative preferred stock for $7,000 and 14,000 shares of Sylvania's common stock for $196,000 on January 2, 2002. Out-of-pocket costs of the business combination may be disregarded.

3. Sylvania's December 31, 2002, inventories included $22,400 of merchandise purchased from Pomerania for which no payment had been made.

4. Pomerania had acquired in the open market twenty-five $1,000 face amount 6% bonds of Slovakia for $20,800 on December 31, 2002. The bonds had a December 31 interest payment date, and a maturity date of December 31, 2004.

5. Slovakia owed Pomerania $17,000 on December 31, 2002, for a noninterest-bearing cash advance.

Instructions

a. Prepare adjusting entries for Pomerania Corporation on December 31, 2002, to account for the investments in Sylvania Company preferred stock and common stock under the equity method. (Disregard income taxes.)

b. Prepare a working paper for consolidated financial statements and related working paper eliminations (in journal entry format) for Pomerania Corporation and subsidiaries on December 31, 2002. (Disregard income taxes.)

(Problem 10.8)

Plover Corporation acquired for $151,000, including direct out-of-pocket costs of the business combination, 100% of the common stock and 20% of the preferred stock of Starling Company on June 30, 2002. On that date, Starling's retained earnings balance was $41,000. The current fair values of Starling's identifiable assets and liabilities and preferred stock were the same as their carrying amounts on June 30, 2002.

The separate financial statements of Plover and Starling for the fiscal year ended December 31, 2003, are as follows:

PLOVER CORPORATION AND SUBSIDIARY Separate Financial Statements For Year Ended December 31, 2003		
	Plover Corporation	*Starling Company*
Income Statements		
Revenue:		
Net sales	$1,562,000	
Intercompany sales	238,000	
Contract revenue		$1,210,000
Intercompany contract revenue		79,000
Interest revenue	19,149	
Intercompany investment income	42,500	
Intercompany dividend revenue	500	
Intercompany gain on sale of land	4,000	
Intercompany interest revenue (expense)	851	(851)
Total revenue	$1,867,000	$1,288,149
Costs and expenses:		
Cost of goods sold	$ 942,500	
Intercompany cost of goods sold	212,500	
Cost of contract revenue		$ 789,500
Intercompany cost of contract revenue		62,500
Operating expenses and income taxes expense	497,000	360,000
Interest expense	49,000	31,149
Total costs and expenses	$1,701,000	$1,243,149
Net income	$ 166,000	$ 45,000
Statements of Retained Earnings		
Retained earnings, beginning of year	$ 139,311	$ 49,500
Add: Net income	166,000	45,000
Subtotals	$ 305,311	$ 94,500
Less: Dividends		2,500
Retained earnings, end of year	$ 305,311	$ 92,000

(continued)

PLOVER CORPORATION AND SUBSIDIARY
Separate Financial Statements (concluded)
For Year Ended December 31, 2003

	Plover Corporation	Starling Company
Balance Sheets		
Assets		
Intercompany receivables (payables)	$ 35,811	$ 21,189
Costs and estimated earnings in excess of billings on uncompleted contracts		30,100
Inventories	217,000	117,500
Investment in Starling Company preferred and common stock	202,000	
Land	34,000	42,000
Other plant assets (net)	717,000	408,000
Other assets	153,000	84,211
Total assets	$1,358,811	$ 703,000
Liabilities and Stockholders' Equity		
Dividends payable		$ 2,000
Mortgage notes payable	$ 592,000	389,000
Other liabilities	203,000	70,000
5% noncumulative, nonparticipating preferred stock, $1 par		50,000
Common stock, no par or stated value	250,000	100,000
Retained earnings	305,311	92,000
Retained earnings of subsidiary	8,500	
Total liabilities and stockholders' equity	$1,358,811	$ 703,000

Transactions between Plover and Starling during the fiscal year ended December 31, 2003, were as follows:

1. On January 2, 2003, Plover sold land with an $11,000 carrying amount to Starling for $15,000. Starling made a $3,000 down payment and signed an 8% mortgage note payable in 12 equal quarterly payments of $1,135, including interest, beginning March 31, 2003. 8% was a fair interest rate.

2. Starling produced equipment for Plover under two separate construction-type contracts. The first contract, which was for office equipment, was begun and completed during Year 2003 at a cost to Starling of $17,500. Plover paid $22,000 cash for the equipment on April 17, 2003. The second contract was begun on February 15, 2003, but will not be completed until May 2004. Starling had incurred $45,000 costs under the second contract as of December 31, 2003, and anticipated additional costs of $30,000 to complete the $95,000 contract. Starling accounts for all construction-type contracts under the percentage-of-completion method of accounting. Plover had made no journal entry in its accounting records for the uncompleted contract as of December 31, 2003. Plover depreciates all its equipment by the straight-line method over a 10-year estimated economic life with no residual value, takes a half year's depreciation in the year of acquisition of plant assets, and includes depreciation in operating expenses.

3. On December 1, 2003, Starling declared a 5% cash dividend on its preferred stock, payable January 15, 2004, to stockholders of record December 14, 2003.

4. Plover sold merchandise to Starling at an average markup of 12% of cost. During the year, Plover billed Starling $238,000 for merchandise shipped, for which Starling had paid $211,000 by December 31, 2003. Starling had $11,200 of this merchandise on hand on December 31, 2003.

Instructions

a. Prepare an analysis of the Intercompany Receivables (Payables) ledger accounts of the affiliates on December 31, 2003.

b. Prepare the adjusting entry or entries for December 31, 2003, based on your analysis in *a* above.

c. Prepare a working paper for consolidated financial statements and related working paper eliminations (in journal entry format) for Plover Corporation and subsidiary for the year ended December 31, 2003. Round all computations to the nearest dollar. The working paper should reflect the adjusting entries in *b*. (Disregard income taxes.)

(Problem 10.9)

On February 1, 2002, Pullard Corporation acquired all the outstanding common stock of Staley Company for $5,850,000, including direct out-of-pocket costs of the business combination, and 20% of Staley's preferred stock for $150,000. On the date of the combination, the carrying amounts and current fair values of Staley's identifiable assets and liabilities were as shown below:

CHECK FIGURES

Consolidated net income, $2,848,450; consolidated ending retained earnings, $15,531,950; minority interest in net assets, $600,000.

STALEY COMPANY Identifiable Assets and Liabilities February 1, 2002	Carrying Amounts	Current Fair Values
Cash	$ 200,000	$ 200,000
Notes receivable	85,000	85,000
Trade accounts receivable (net)	980,000	980,000
Inventories	828,000	700,000
Land	1,560,000	2,100,000
Other plant assets	7,850,000	10,600,000
Accumulated depreciation	(3,250,000)	(4,000,000)
Other assets	140,000	50,000
Total assets	$8,393,000	$10,715,000
Notes payable	$ 115,000	$ 115,000
Trade accounts payable	400,000	400,000
7% bonds payable	5,000,000	5,000,000
Total liabilities	$5,515,000	$ 5,515,000
Preferred stock, noncumulative, nonparticipating, $5 par and call price per share; authorized, issued, and outstanding 150,000 shares	$ 750,000	
Common stock, $10 par; authorized, issued, and outstanding 100,000 shares	1,000,000	
Additional paid-in capital—common stock	122,000	
Retained earnings	1,006,000	
Total stockholders' equity	$2,878,000	
Total liabilities and stockholders' equity	$8,393,000	

Separate financial statements of Pullard and Staley for the period ended October 31, 2002, are as follows:

PULLARD CORPORATION AND STALEY COMPANY
Separate Financial Statements
For Period Ended October 31, 2002

	Pullard Corporation (year ended 10/31/02)	Staley Company (9 months ended 10/31/02)
Income Statements		
Revenue:		
Net sales	$18,042,000	$5,530,000
Intercompany sales	158,000	230,000
Intercompany investment income	505,150	
Interest revenue	26,250	1,700
Intercompany interest revenue	78,750	
Total revenue	$18,810,150	$5,761,700
Costs and expenses:		
Cost of goods sold	$10,442,000	$3,010,500
Intercompany cost of goods sold	158,000	149,500
Depreciation expense	1,103,000	588,750
Operating expenses and income taxes expense	3,448,500	1,063,900
Interest expense	806,000	190,650
Intercompany interest expense		78,750
Total costs and expenses	$15,957,500	$5,082,050
Net income	$ 2,852,650	$ 679,650
Statements of Retained Earnings		
Retained earnings, beginning of period	$12,683,500	$1,006,000
Add: Net income	2,852,650	679,650
Retained earnings, end of period	$15,536,150	$1,685,650
Balance Sheets		
Assets		
Cash	$ 822,000	$ 530,000
Notes receivable		85,000
Trade accounts receivable (net)	2,723,700	1,346,400
Intercompany receivables	12,300	
Inventories	3,204,000	1,182,000
Investment in Staley Company common stock	6,355,150	
Investment in Staley Company preferred stock	150,000	
Investment in Staley Company bonds	1,500,000	
Land	4,000,000	1,560,000
Other plant assets	17,161,000	7,850,000
Accumulated depreciation	(6,673,000)	(3,838,750)
Other assets	263,000	140,000
Total assets	$29,518,150	$8,854,650

(continued)

PULLARD CORPORATION AND STALEY COMPANY
Separate Financial Statements (concluded)
For Period Ended October 31, 2002

	Pullard Corporation (year ended 10/31/02)	Staley Company (9 months ended 10/31/02)
Liabilities and Stockholders' Equity		
Notes payable		$ 115,000
Trade accounts payable	$ 1,342,000	169,700
Intercompany payables		12,300
7% bonds payable		3,500,000
Intercompany 7% bonds payable		1,500,000
Long-term debt	10,000,000	
Preferred stock, $5 par		750,000
Common stock, $10 par	2,400,000	1,000,000
Additional paid-in capital	240,000	122,000
Retained earnings	15,536,150	1,685,650
Total liabilities and stockholders' equity	$29,518,150	$8,854,650

By the fiscal year-end, October 31, 2002, the following transactions and events had taken place:

1. The balance of Staley's net trade accounts receivable on February 1, 2002, had been collected.

2. Staley's inventories on February 1, 2002, had been debited to cost of goods sold under the perpetual inventory system.

3. Prior to February 1, 2000, Pullard had acquired in the open market, at face amount, $1,500,000 of Staley's 7% bonds payable. The bonds mature on August 31, 2008, with interest payable annually each August 31.

4. As of February 1, 2002, Staley's other plant assets had a composite remaining economic life of six years. Staley used the straight-line method of depreciation, with no residual value. Staley's depreciation expense for the nine months ended October 31, 2002, was based on the former depreciation rates in effect prior to the business combination.

5. The other assets consist entirely of long-term investments in held-to-maturity debt securities made by Staley and do not include any investment in Pullard.

6. During the nine months ended October 31, 2002, the following intercompany sales of merchandise had occurred:

	Pullard to Staley	Staley to Pullard
Net sales	$158,000	$230,000
Included in purchaser's inventories, Oct. 31, 2002	36,000	12,000
Balance unpaid, Oct. 31, 2002	16,800	22,000

Pullard sold merchandise to Staley at cost. Staley sold merchandise to Pullard at selling prices that included a gross profit margin of 35%. There had been no intercompany sales prior to February 1, 2002.

7. Neither company had declared dividends during the period covered by the separate financial statements.

8. Staley's goodwill recognized in the business combination was $1,400,000. The goodwill was 3.75% impaired as of October 31, 2002.

9. The $505,150 balance of Pullard's Intercompany Investment Income ledger account is computed as follows:

Net income of Staley for nine months ended Oct. 31, 2002		$679,650
Less: Amortization and adjustment of differences between current fair values and carrying amounts of Staley's identifiable net assets on Feb. 1, 2002:		
Inventories—to cost of goods sold	$(128,000)	
Other plant assets—depreciation $\{[(\$6,600,000 - \$4,600,000) \div 6] \times \frac{3}{4}\}$	250,000	
Goodwill—impairment loss ($1,400,000 × 0.0375)	52,500	174,500
Balance, Oct. 31,		$505,150

Instructions

Prepare a working paper for consolidated financial statements and related working paper eliminations (in journal entry format) for Pullard Corporation and subsidiary on October 31, 2002. Round all amounts to the nearest dollar. (Disregard income taxes.)

Chapter Eleven

International Accounting Standards; Accounting for Foreign Currency Transactions

Scope of Chapter

Recent political events—such as the dissolution of the Union of Soviet Socialist Republics and the autonomy of its former satellite nations in Eastern Europe—and economic events—such as increased international trading in securities and the economic and currency (the **euro**) unification of the European Union[1]—have focused attention on the pressing need for more uniformity in international accounting standards. Two organizations in the forefront of attempts to achieve such uniformity are the International Accounting Standards Committee (IASC) and the International Organization of Securities Commissions (IOSCO). This chapter first discusses the work of the IASC, as abetted by the IOSCO; later, accounting for a multinational enterprise's business transactions denominated in a foreign currency is described and illustrated.

INTERNATIONAL ACCOUNTING STANDARDS

International Accounting Standards Committee

The IASC was formed in 1973 by professional accounting organizations of 10 countries. Currently its membership includes more than 140 accounting groups from more than 100 countries. Headquartered in London, the business of the IASC is conducted by an International Accounting Standards Board (IASB) of up to 17 members, of whom 13

---

[1] Member nations of the European Union (EU) are Austria, Belgium, Denmark, Finland, France, Germany, Greece, Ireland, Italy, Luxembourg, the Netherlands, Portugal, Spain, Sweden, and the United Kingdom. All except Denmark, Greece, Sweden, and the United Kingdom have adopted the euro as their official currency.

are representatives of member country organizations and up to 4 are representatives of other international organizations having an interest in accounting. To be issued, International Accounting Standards require the approval of three-fourths of the IASB members; these standards have no authoritative support unless they are adopted by standard-setting bodies in the member countries, such as the Financial Accounting Standards Board. The American Institute of Certified Public Accountants, as a member of the IASC, is committed to using its best efforts to persuade the FASB to adopt International Accounting Standards; however, to date there is no clear evidence of this commitment's being accomplished.

Through 2001 the IASB has issued or revised 40 ***International Accounting Standards,*** dealing with such accounting issues as consolidated financial statements, depreciation, segment reporting, leases, revenue recognition, business combinations, and related-party disclosures. To promote adoption of the ***Standards,*** the IASB had in the past accommodated alternative accounting treatments in several of its pronouncements. However, in 1993 the IASB revised 11 of its previously issued standards to eliminate some accounting alternatives completely and to establish ***benchmark,*** or preferred, accounting treatments with permissible alternatives. For example, ***International Accounting Standard (IAS) 2,*** "Inventories," designates first-in, first-out or weighted average as benchmark methods of applying inventory cost flows; in addition, last-in, first-out is an allowed alternative treatment for inventory cost flows, ***provided a reconciliation of last-in, first-out inventories to average or first-in, first-out cost is included.***

Among the ***International Accounting Standards*** issued by the IASB are four that deal with topics covered elsewhere in this book: joint ventures, business combinations, consolidated financial statements, and influenced investees. A fifth standard dealing with changes in foreign exchange rates is dealt with elsewhere in this chapter and in Chapter 12. The following section draws on ***AICPA Professional Standards,*** vol. 2. . . . "International Accounting Standards" as of June 1, 2000, to describe briefly the four standards listed above.

IAS 31, *"Financial Reporting of Interests in Joint Ventures"*

In this pronouncement, the IASB permitted either the ***proportionate consolidation method (proportionate share method*** in Chapter 3, pp. 105 to 106*)* or the ***equity method*** for a venturer's investment in a ***jointly controlled entity,*** which might be a corporation or a partnership. As pointed out in Chapter 3, U.S. accounting standards require the equity method of accounting for investments in corporate joint ventures but permit either the equity method or the proportionate share method of accounting for investments in unincorporated joint ventures.

IAS 22, *"Accounting for Business Combinations"*

The IASB required purchase-type accounting for all business combinations except those deemed a ***uniting of interests,*** defined as a combination in which the stockholders of the constituent companies combine into one entity the whole of the net assets and operations of those companies to achieve a continuing mutual sharing of the risks and benefits of the combined enterprise. For a uniting of interests-type combination, pooling-of-interests accounting ***must*** be used. Further, goodwill in a purchase-type business combination must be amortized over a period not exceeding 20 years, unless a longer period can be justified. The minority interest in net assets of a purchased subsidiary may be valued by either method **1** or method **2** (the benchmark method) on page 240 of Chapter 6.

IAS 27, "Consolidated Financial Statements and Accounting for Investments in Subsidiaries"

Among the provisions of *IAS 27* are the following:

1. Consolidation policy is based on *control* rather than solely on *ownership* (see Chapter 6, pages 220 to 222).

2. Intercompany transactions, profits or gains, and losses are eliminated in full, regardless of an existing minority interest.

3. The minority interest in net income of subsidiary is displayed separately in the consolidated income statement. The minority interest in net assets of subsidiary is displayed separately from liabilities and stockholders' equity in the consolidated balance sheet. Thus, the IASB rejected both the parent company concept and the economic unit concept (see Chapter 6, pages 239 to 240).

4. In the unconsolidated financial statements of a parent company, investments in subsidiaries that are included in the consolidated statements may be accounted for by either the equity method, as required by the SEC (see Chapter 7, page 303), or the cost method.

IAS 28, "Accounting for Investments in Associates"

Apart from using the term *associate* for an *influenced investee,* as that U.S. terminology is applied (see Chapter 9, page 412), the provisions of *IAS 28* resemble those of *APB Opinion No. 18,* "The Equity Method of Accounting for Investments in Common Stock."

FASB Study of International Accounting Standards

In 1999 the Financial Accounting Standards Board issued a second edition of *The IASC-U.S. Comparison Project: A Report on the Similarities and Differences between IAS Standards and U.S. GAAP.* The FASB's analysis of the 39 IASs then in effect produced the following summary:[2]

> There are differences between the accounting requirements of IASC standards and those of U.S. GAAP. The examples provided above illustrate several differences in five broad categories: recognition, measurement, alternatives, lack of requirements or guidance, and other differences. The resulting differences in reported financial information can be very significant from both a conceptual standpoint and a practical standpoint. Issues related to whether to recognize and how to measure items in the financial statements are among the most fiercely debated by standard setters. For financial statement users, compensating for the types of differences illustrated above is likely to be difficult because the information necessary to reconcile them may not be available. Some of those differences may be temporary—for example, differences in the timing of recognition may be short-term—while others may be permanent—for example, differences in accounting for a business combination can have indefinite effects on financial statement comparability.
>
> There are less-significant types of differences between IASC standards and U.S. GAAP that are not discussed above that can make financial statement analysis and comparison complicated. For example, differences in presentation and display of

---

[2] *The IASC-U.S. Comparison Project: A Report on the Similarities and Differences between IASC Standards and U.S. GAAP,* Second Edition (Norwalk: FASB, 1999), pp. 50–51.

similar items may require additional effort by financial statement users in making comparisons, and differences in definitions can lead to reported items that appear to be similar but may, in fact, be different. Those types of differences also are identified in the comparative analyses that follow.

Identifying all of the reasons why IASC standards and U.S. GAAP differ would be impossible. However, some of the reasons for the differences can be traced to the characteristics of the standard setters themselves. Although both the IASC and the FASB are concerned with improving the quality of financial reporting and increasing international comparability, they focus on different financial reporting environments. With FASB's primarily domestic focus, FASB standards overall tend to be fairly detailed, responding to the complexities of the U.S. economic environment and a demand from sophisticated financial-statement users for reliable, high-quality financial information. IASC standards, on the other hand, respond to a variety of national perspectives about what financial information is the most relevant and reliable for a particular topic. Consequently, the IASC develops standards without focusing on any particular economic environment, which may contribute to the tendency of IASC standards to be more general. That generality may be an inevitable characteristic of international standards, and additional guidance at the national level may continue to be necessary even in those nations that use IASC standards as national standards.

The existence of differences between accounting standards and resulting reported financial information is less important than the extent to which the reported financial information meets the demands of its consumers, that is, the financial statement users, in the market in which the information is provided. That should be the basis for assessing the acceptability of IASC standards for use in cross-border securities listings in the United States. . . .

INTERNATIONAL ORGANIZATION OF SECURITIES COMMISSIONS

Securities regulators from about 50 countries constitute the membership of the IOSCO, whose goal is to ease the impact of differences in securities trading regulations among its members. IOSCO and the IASC had agreed on a deadline of mid-1999 (obviously not met) for IOSCO's endorsement of IASC standards for cross-border offerings and trading of securities.

In addition to its participation in IOSCO, the SEC has eased its requirements for foreign issuers of securities in the United States by the following actions:

1. Adoption of a multijurisdictional disclosure system for eligible Canadian issuers of securities to permit them to register securities and report to the SEC using Canadian registration and reporting requirements. (Canada has a comparable system for U.S. issuers of securities there.)

2. Acceptance of a foreign issuer's statement of cash flows prepared in accordance with *IAS 7,* "Cash Flow Statements."

3. Elimination of requirements for reconciliations of differences between financial statements prepared under certain other *IAS*s and U.S. generally accepted accounting principles.

4. Elimination of eight previously required financial statement schedules, which are discussed in Chapter 13.

ACCOUNTING FOR FOREIGN CURRENCY TRANSACTIONS

In most countries, a foreign country's currency is treated as though it were a **commodity,** or a **money-market instrument.** In the United States, for example, foreign currencies are bought and sold by the international banking departments of commercial banks. These foreign currency transactions are entered into on behalf of the banks' multinational enterprise customers, and for the banks' own account.

The buying and selling of foreign currencies as though they were commodities result in variation in the **exchange rate** between the currencies of two countries. For example, a daily newspaper might quote exchange rates for the British pound (£) as follows, based on the prior day's transactions in the pound:

	Foreign Currency in Dollars	Dollars in Foreign Currency
Britain (pound)	1.6065	0.6225

The first column indicates that £1 could be exchanged for approximately $1.61; the second column indicates that $1 could be exchanged for approximately £0.62. Note that the two exchange rates are **reciprocals** (1 ÷ 1.6065 = 0.6225).

The exchange rate illustrated above is the **selling spot rate** charged by the bank for current sales of the foreign currency. The bank's **buying spot rate** for the currency typically is less than the selling spot rate; the **agio** (or **spread**) between the selling and buying spot rates represents gross profit to a trader in foreign currency. In addition to spot rates, there are **forward rates,** which apply to foreign currency transactions to be consummated on a future date. Forward rates apply to **forward contracts,** which are derivative instruments discussed in a subsequent section of this chapter.

To illustrate the application of exchange rates, assume that a U.S. business enterprise required £10,000 (10,000 British pounds) to pay for merchandise acquired from a British supplier. At the $1.6065 selling spot rate, the U.S. multinational enterprise would pay $16,065 (£10,000 × $1.6065 = $16,065) for the 10,000 British pounds.

Factors influencing fluctuations in exchange rates include a nation's balance of payments surplus or deficit, differing global rates of inflation, money-market variations (such as interest rates) in individual countries, capital investments levels, and monetary actions of central banks of various nations.

FASB Statements No. 52 and No. 133

In December 1981, the FASB issued *FASB Statement No. 52,* "Foreign Currency Translation," in which it established accounting standards for matters involving foreign currencies, and in 1998 it issued *FASB Statement No. 133,* "Accounting for Derivative Instruments and Hedging Activities." The accounting standards established by the FASB for foreign currency transactions such as purchases and sales of merchandise, loans, and related derivative instruments are discussed in the following sections.

Transactions Involving Foreign Currencies

A **multinational** (or **transnational**) **enterprise** is a business enterprise that carries on operations in more than one nation, through a network of branches, divisions, influenced investees, joint ventures, and subsidiaries. Multinational enterprises obtain material and capital in countries where such resources are plentiful. Multinational enterprises manufacture their products in nations where wages and other operating costs are low, and they sell their products in countries that provide profitable markets. Many of the largest multinational enterprises are headquartered in the United States.

A multinational enterprise headquartered in the United States engages in sales, purchases, and loans with independent foreign enterprises as well as with its branches, divisions, influenced investees, or subsidiaries in other countries. If the transactions with independent foreign enterprises are *denominated* (or expressed) in terms of the U.S. dollar, no accounting problems arise for the U.S. multinational enterprise. The sale, purchase, or loan transaction is recorded in dollars in the accounting records of the U.S. enterprise; the independent foreign enterprise must obtain or dispose of the dollars necessary to complete the transaction through the foreign exchange department of its bank.

Often, however, the transactions described above are negotiated and settled in terms of the foreign enterprise's *local currency unit* (LCU). In such circumstances, the U.S. enterprise must account for the transaction denominated in foreign currency in terms of U.S. dollars. This accounting, described as *foreign currency translation,* is accomplished by applying the appropriate exchange rate between the foreign currency and the U.S. dollar.

The Euro: The New Currency for Eleven Members of the European Union

In May 1998, the European Union formally adopted the *euro* (symbol €) as the common currency for Union members Austria, Belgium, Finland, France, Germany, Ireland, Italy, Luxembourg, the Netherlands, Portugal, and Spain, with January 1, 1999, the effective date of the adoption. Accordingly, the euro is illustrated in subsequent sections of this chapter.

Purchase of Merchandise from a Foreign Supplier

To illustrate a purchase of merchandise from a foreign supplier, assume that on April 18, 2002, Worldwide Corporation purchased merchandise from a German supplier at a cost of 100,000 euros. The April 18, 2002, selling spot rate was €1 = $1.05.[3] Because Worldwide was a customer of good credit standing, the German supplier made the sale on 30-day open account.

Assuming that Worldwide uses the perpetual inventory system, it records the April 18, 2002, purchase as follows:

Journal Entry for Purchase of Merchandise from German Supplier, Payment to Be Made in Euros

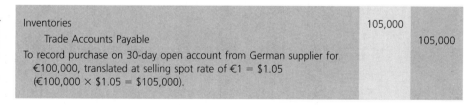

Inventories	105,000	
Trade Accounts Payable		105,000
To record purchase on 30-day open account from German supplier for €100,000, translated at selling spot rate of €1 = $1.05 (€100,000 × $1.05 = $105,000).		

The *selling* spot was used in the journal entry, because it was the rate at which the liability to the German supplier could have been settled on April 18, 2002.

[3] Exchange rates fluctuate significantly over time; thus, the exchange rates illustrated in this chapter may differ significantly from current exchange rates.

Foreign Currency Transaction Gains and Losses

During the period that the trade account payable to the German supplier remains unpaid, the *selling* spot rate for the euro may change. If the selling spot rate *decreases* (the euro *weakens* against the dollar), Worldwide will realize a *foreign currency transaction gain;* if the *selling* spot rate *increases* (the euro *strengthens* against the dollar), Worldwide will incur a *foreign currency transaction loss.* Foreign currency transaction gains and losses are included in the measurement of net income for the accounting period in which the spot rate changes.[4]

To illustrate, assume that on April 30, 2002, the selling spot rate for the euro was €1 = $1.04 and Worldwide prepares financial statements monthly. The accountant for Worldwide records the following journal entry with respect to the trade account payable to the German supplier:

<table>
<tr><td>**Journal Entry to Recognize Foreign Currency Transaction Gain on Date Financial Statements are Prepared**</td><td colspan="2">Trade Accounts Payable
    Foreign Currency Transaction Gains
To recognize foreign currency transaction gain applicable to April 18, 2002, purchase from German supplier, as follows:
    Liability recorded on Apr. 18, 2002 $105,000
      Less: Liability translated at Apr. 30, 2002, selling spot rate:
        €1 = $1.04 (€100,000 × $1.04 = $104,000)   104,000
    Foreign currency transaction gain $ 1,000</td><td>1,000

1,000</td></tr>
</table>

Assume further that the selling spot rate on May 18, 2002, was €1 = $1.02. The May 18, 2002, journal entry for Worldwide's payment of the liability to the German supplier is shown below:

<table>
<tr><td>**Journal Entry for Payment of Liability to German Supplier Denominated in the Euro**</td><td>Trade Accounts Payable
    Foreign Currency Transaction Gains
    Cash
To record payment for €100,000 draft to settle liability to German supplier, and recognition of transaction gain (€100,000 × $1.02 = $102,000).</td><td>104,000

2,000
102,000</td></tr>
</table>

Two-Transaction Perspective and One-Transaction Perspective

The journal entries on page 495 and above reflect the *two-transaction perspective* for interpreting a foreign trade transaction. Under this concept, which was sanctioned by the FASB in *FASB Statement No. 52,* Worldwide's dealings with the German supplier essentially were *two separate transactions.* One transaction was the purchase of the merchandise; the second transaction was the acquisition of the foreign currency required to pay the liability for the merchandise purchased. Supporters of the two-transaction perspective argue that an importer's or exporter's assumption of a risk of fluctuations in the exchange rate for a foreign currency is a *financing* decision, not a *merchandising* decision.

[4] *FASB Statement No. 52, "Foreign Currency Translation" (Stamford: FASB, 1981), par. 15.*

Advocates of an opposing viewpoint, the ***one-transaction perspective,*** maintain that Worldwide's total foreign currency transaction gain of $3,000 ($1,000 + $2,000 = $3,000) on its purchase from the German supplier should be applied to reduce the cost of the merchandise purchased. Under this approach, Worldwide would not prepare a journal entry on April 30, 2002, but would prepare the following journal entry on May 18, 2002 (assuming that all the merchandise purchased on April 18 had been sold by May 18):

Journal Entry under One-Transaction Perspective

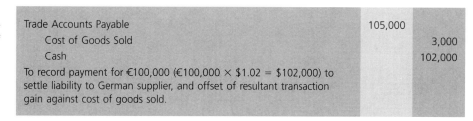

Trade Accounts Payable	105,000	
Cost of Goods Sold		3,000
Cash		102,000
To record payment for €100,000 (€100,000 × $1.02 = $102,000) to settle liability to German supplier, and offset of resultant transaction gain against cost of goods sold.		

In effect, supporters of the one-transaction perspective for foreign trade activities consider the original amount recorded for a foreign merchandise purchase as an ***estimate,*** subject to adjustment when the exact cash outlay required for the purchase is known. Thus, the one-transaction proponents emphasize the ***cash-payment*** aspect, rather than the ***bargained-price*** aspect, of the transaction.

The author concurs with the FASB's support for the two-transaction perspective for foreign trade transactions and for loans receivable and payable denominated in a foreign currency. The separability of the merchandising and financing aspects of a foreign trade transaction is an undeniable fact. In delaying payment of a foreign trade purchase transaction, an importer has made a decision to assume the risk of exchange rate fluctuations. This risk assumption is measured by the foreign currency transaction gain or loss recorded at the time of payment for the purchase of merchandise (or on the dates of intervening financial statements).

Sale of Merchandise to a Foreign Customer

Assume that on May 17, 2002, Worldwide Corporation, which uses the perpetual inventory system, sold merchandise acquired from a U.S. supplier for $12,000 to a French customer for €15,000, with payment due June 16, 2002. On May 17, 2002, the buying spot rate for the euro was €1 = $1.01. Worldwide prepares the following journal entries on May 17, 2002:

Journal Entries for Sale of Merchandise to French Customer, Payment to Be Received in Euros

Trade Accounts Receivable	15,150	
Sales		15,150
To record sale on 30-day open account to French customer for €15,000, translated at buying spot rate of €1 = $1.01 (€15,000 × $1.01 = $15,150).		
Cost of Goods Sold	12,000	
Inventories		12,000
To record cost of merchandise sold to French customer.		

Assuming that the buying spot rate for the euro was €1 = $0.99 (the euro ***weakened*** against the dollar) on May 31, 2002, when Worldwide prepared its customary monthly financial statements, the following journal entry is appropriate:

Journal Entry to Record Foreign Currency Transaction Loss on Date Financial Statements Are Prepared

Foreign Currency Transaction Losses	300	
Trade Accounts Receivable		300

To recognize transaction loss applicable to May 17, 2002, sale to French customer as follows:

Asset recorded on May 17, 2002	$15,150
Less: Asset translated at May 31, 2002, buying spot rate:	
€1 = $0.99 (€15,000 × $0.99 = $14,850)	14,850
Foreign currency transaction loss	$ 300

If on June 16, 2002, the date when Worldwide received a draft for €15,000 from the French customer, the euro had **strengthened** against the dollar to a buying spot rate of €1 = $0.995, Worldwide's journal entry would be as follows:

Journal Entry for Receipt from French Customer Denominated in the Euro

Cash	14,925	
Trade Accounts Receivable		14,850
Foreign Currency Transaction Gains		75

To record receipt and conversion to dollars of €15,000 draft in payment of receivable from French customer, and recognition of foreign currency transaction gain (€15,000 × $0.995 = $14,925).

Loan Payable Denominated in a Foreign Currency

If a U.S. multinational enterprise elects to borrow a foreign currency to pay for merchandise acquired from a foreign supplier, the following journal entries would be illustrative (Sfr is the symbol for the Swiss franc):

Journal Entries for Loan Payable in a Foreign Currency

2002				
Apr. 30	Inventories		69,000	
	Trade Accounts Payable			69,000

To record purchase from Swiss supplier for Sfr100,000, translated at selling spot rate of Sfr1 = $0.69 (Sfr100,000 × $0.69 = $69,000).

30	Trade Accounts Payable		69,000	
	Notes Payable			69,000

To record borrowing of Sfr100,000 from bank on 30-day, 6% loan to be repaid in Swiss francs, and payment of liability to Swiss supplier.

May 30	Notes Payable		69,000	
	Interest Expense ($69,000 × 0.06 × 30/360)		345	
	Foreign Currency Transaction Losses		201	
	Cash			69,546

To record payment for Sfr100,500 draft to settle Sfr100,000, 30-day, 6% note, together with Sfr500 interest (Sfr100,000 × 0.06 × 30/360 = Sfr500) at selling spot rate of Sfr1 = $0.692(Sfr100,500 × 0.692 = $69,546), and recognition of foreign currency transaction loss.

Loan Receivable Denominated in a Foreign Currency

A U.S. multinational enterprise's receipt of a promissory note denominated in a foreign currency might be illustrated by the following journal entries:

Journal Entries for Loan Receivable in a Foreign Currency

2002				
May 31	Notes Receivable		980,000	
	Sales			980,000
	To record sale to Belgian customer for 60-day, 9% promissory note for €1,000,000, translated at buying spot rate of €1 = $0.98 (€1,000,000 × $0.98 = $980,000).			
31	Cost of Goods Sold		820,000	
	Inventories			820,000
	To record cost of merchandise sold to Belgian customer.			
June 30	Notes Receivable		30,000	
	Interest Receivable ($1,010,000 × 0.09 × 30/360)		7,575	
	Interest Revenue			7,575
	Foreign Currency Transaction Gains			30,000
	To recognize foreign currency transaction gain applicable to May 31, 2002, sale to Belgian customer and to accrue interest on note receivable from the customer, valued at the buying spot rate of €1 = $1.01. Transaction gain is computed as follows:			
	Receivable translated at June 30, 2002, buying spot rate (€1,000,000 × $1.01) $1,010,000			
	Receivable recorded on May 31, 2002 980,000			
	Transaction gain $ 30,000			
July 30	Cash (€1,015,000 × $0.99)		1,004,850	
	Foreign Currency Transaction Losses		20,150	
	Notes Receivable			1,010,000
	Interest Receivable			7,575
	Interest Revenue [(€1,000,000 × $0.99) × 0.09 × 30/360]			7,425
	To record receipt and conversion to dollars of €1,015,000 draft to settle 60-day, 9% note, together with €15,000 interest (€1,000,000 × 0.09 × 60/360 = €15,000), and recognition of foreign currency transaction loss of $20,150 [(€1,000,000 + €7,500) × ($1.01 − $0.99) = $20,150].			

Conclusions Regarding Transactions Involving Foreign Currencies

From the foregoing examples, it is evident that *increases* in the selling spot rate for a foreign currency required by a U.S. multinational enterprise to settle a liability denominated in that currency generate *foreign currency transaction losses* to the enterprise because more U.S. dollars are required to obtain the foreign currency. Conversely, *decreases* in the selling spot rate produce *foreign currency transaction gains* to the enterprise because fewer U.S. dollars are required to obtain the foreign currency. In contrast, *increases* in the buying spot rate for a foreign currency to be received by a U.S. multinational enterprise in settlement of a receivable denominated in that currency generate *foreign currency transaction gains* to the enterprise; *decreases* in the buying spot rate produce *foreign currency transaction losses.* Mastery of these relationships assures a clearer understanding of the effects of changes in exchange rates for foreign currencies.

Forward Contracts

Forward contracts are another type of transaction involving foreign currencies. A *forward contract* is an agreement to exchange currencies of different countries on a specified future date at the forward rate in effect when the contract was made. Forward rates may be larger or smaller than spot rates for a foreign currency, depending on the foreign currency dealer's expectations regarding fluctuations in exchange rates for the currency. For example, a newspaper had the following data regarding the British pound (£) and the Swiss franc (Sfr):

	£1 =	Sfr 1 =
Spot rate	$1.6365	$0.6752
1 month forward rate	1.6338	0.6775
3 months forward rate	1.6284	0.6817
6 months forward rate	1.6207	0.6879

Forward contracts are *derivative instruments,* defined by the FASB as follows:

> A derivative instrument is a financial instrument or other contract with all three of the following characteristics:
>
> a. It has (1) one or more **underlyings** and (2) one or more **notional amounts** or payment provisions or both. Those terms determine the amount of the settlement or settlements, and, in some cases, whether or not a settlement is required.
> b. It requires no initial net investment or an initial net investment that is smaller than would be required for other types of contracts that would be expected to have a similar response to changes in market factors.
> c. Its terms require or permit net settlement, it can readily be settled net by a means outside the contract, or it provides for delivery of an asset that puts the recipient in a position not substantially different from net settlement.
>
> *Underlying, notional amount, and payment provision.* An underlying is a specified interest rate, security price, commodity price, *foreign exchange rate,* index of prices or rates, or other variable. An underlying may be a price or rate of an asset or liability but is not the asset or liability itself. A notional amount is a *number of currency units,* shares, bushels, pounds, or other units specified in the contract. The settlement of a derivative instrument with a notional amount is determined by interaction of that notional amount with the underlying. The interaction may be simple multiplication, or it may involve a formula with leverage factors or other constants. A payment provision specifies a fixed or determinable settlement to be made if the underlying behaves in a specified manner. (Emphasis added.)[5]

---

[5] *FASB Statement No. 133,* "Accounting for Derivative Instruments and Hedging Activities" (Norwalk: FASB, 1998), pars. 6 and 7.

In accordance with the foregoing, the underlying for a forward contract is the contracted forward rate, and the notional amount is the number of foreign currency units specified in the forward contract.

FASB Statement No. 133, "Accounting for Derivative Instruments and Hedging Activities," established accounting standards for the following types of forward contracts:[6]

1. Forward contract not designated as a hedge.

2. Forward contract designated as a hedge of a foreign-currency–denominated firm commitment.

3. Forward contract designated as a hedge of an investment in an available-for-sale security.

4. Forward contract designated as a hedge of a forecasted foreign-currency–denominated transaction.

5. Forward contract designated as a hedge of a net investment in a foreign operation.

The table on page 503 summarizes the accounting for gains and losses and the financial statement effects of the foregoing derivative instruments.

Forward contracts of the first two types listed above are discussed and illustrated in this chapter; the fifth type is dealt with in Chapter 12. (The complexity of the third and fourth types render them inappropriate for illustration in a textbook dealing with fundamental issues. An illustration of the fourth type of forward contract, termed a *cash flow hedge,* can be found in Example 10, paragraphs 165 through 172, of *FASB Statement No. 133,* "Accounting for Derivative Instruments and Hedging Activities.") The FASB required that *all* derivative instruments, including the forward contracts categorized above, be recognized as assets or liabilities, as appropriate, and measured at fair value.[7] Fair value was defined in part by the FASB as the amount at which the asset or liability could be bought or sold in a current transaction between willing parties, that is, other than in a forced liquidation or sale.[8]

Forward Contract Not Designated as a Hedge

To *hedge* is to take measures to reduce or eliminate a potential unfavorable outcome of a future event. For an illustration of a forward contract not designated as a hedge, assume that, in anticipation of a possible trip for its marketing executives to several countries of the European Union for potential customers of its products, on May 1, 2002, Carthay Company entered into a 60-day forward contract to acquire €100,000 on June 30, 2002, at a forward rate of €1 = $1.09. (The selling spot rate of the euro on May 1, 2002, was $1.04.) Because Carthay's purpose of entering into the forward contract did not involve designating the contract as one of the types of hedges described at the top of this page, any gain or loss on the forward contract during its 60-day term must be recognized currently in the measurement of Carthay's net income for a financial reporting period.[9]

Assuming forward rates for euro contracts maturing on June 30, 2002, were €1 = $1.07 on May 31 and €1 = $1.06 on June 30, and that Carthay prepared financial statements on May 31 and June 30, Carthay's journal entries for the forward contract not designated as a hedge are as follows:

---

[6] Ibid., par. 18.
[7] Ibid., par. 17.
[8] Ibid., par. 540.
[9] Ibid., par. 18a.

Journal Entries for Forward Contract Not Designated as a Hedge

2002				
May 1	Investment in Forward Contract		109,000[10]	
	Forward Contract Payable			109,000
	To record forward contract for €100,000, at forward rate of €1 = $1.09 (€100,000 × $1.09 = $109,000).			
31	Foreign Currency Transaction Losses		1,990	
	Investment in Forward Contract			1,990
	To recognize fair value of forward contract investment and resultant transaction loss, as follows:			
	Forward price of contract:			
	May 1	$109,000		
	May 31 (€100,000 × $1.07)	107,000		
	Difference	$ 2,000		
	Less: Discount to maturity			
	(30 days) at 6% rate			
	($2,000 × 0.06 × 30/360)	10[11]		
	Transaction loss	$ 1,990		
June 30	Investment in Euros (€100,000 × $1.06)		106,000	
	Forward Contract Payable		109,000	
	Foreign Currency Transaction Losses		1,010	
	Cash			109,000
	Investment in Forward Contract			107,010
	($109,000 − $1,990)			
	To recognize settlement of forward contract, fair value of investment in euros, and transaction loss as follows:			
	Carrying amount of contract May 31	$107,010		
	Fair value of contract			
	June 30 (€100,000 × $1.06)	106,000		
	Transaction loss	$ 1,010		

Presumably, the selling spot rate for the euro on June 30, 2002, is €1 = $1.06, the same as the forward rate for a forward contract maturing on that date. Thus, the investment in euros is valued at current fair value on that date. On subsequent financial statement preparation dates, foreign currency transaction gains or losses would be recognized for changes in the selling spot rate for the euro, as long as Carthay Company maintained its investment therein.

Forward Contract Designated as a Hedge of a Foreign-Currency–Denominated Firm Commitment

FASB Statement No. 133 defined a *firm commitment* as follows:[12]

> An agreement with an unrelated party, binding on both parties and usually legally enforceable, with the following characteristics:

---

[10] See ibid., par. 17a, re recognition of asset and liability.
[11] See ibid., par. 478, re effects of discounting in determination of fair value.
[12] Ibid., par. 540.

Statement of Financial Accounting Standards No. 133, **"Accounting for Derivative Instruments . . ."**

Type	Accounting for Gains (Losses)	Financial Statements Effects
Not Designated as a Hedge	Recognized immediately in earnings (paragraph 18a)	
Foreign Currency Hedge:		
Of exposure of unrecognized firm commitment or available-for-sale security	Same as for fair value hedge (see below) (paragraphs 37, 38, 18d1, 18d2)	Same as for fair value hedge
Of exposure of foreign currency denominated forecasted transaction	Same as for cash flow hedge (See below) (paragraphs 40, 41, 18d3)	Same as for cash flow hedge
Of net investment in foreign operation	Not applicable	Reported in accumulated other comprehensive income as accumulated foreign currency translation adjustments (paragraph 42 and FAS 52, paragraph 20a, 18d4)
Fair Value Hedge (of exposure to changes in fair value of recognized asset or liability or a firm commitment) (paragraph 20-21)	Recognized in earnings in the period of change in fair value, together with offsetting gain or loss on hedged item attributable to risk being hedged (paragraph 22) (paragraph 18b)	Net loss (if any) in income statement is measure of hedge ineffectiveness (paragraph 22)
Cash Flow Hedge (of exposure to variability in expected future cash flow attributable to a particular risk) (paragraphs 28–29)	Effective portion reported in other comprehensive income; ineffective portion reported in earnings (paragraph 30) Amounts in other comprehensive income reclassified into earnings in the period(s) that the hedged forecasted transaction affects earnings (paragraph 31) (paragraph 18c)	Overall *earnings* impact of hedge may be reported in more than one period (paragraph 31)

    a. The agreement specifies all significant terms, including the quantity to be exchanged, the fixed price, and the timing of the transaction. The fixed price may be expressed as a specified amount of an entity's functional currency or of a foreign currency. It may also be expressed as a specified interest rate or specified effective yield.

    b. The agreement includes a disincentive for nonperformance that is sufficiently large to make performance probable.

The FASB characterized a forward contract designated as a hedge of a foreign-currency–denominated firm commitment as a ***fair value hedge,***[13] for which it set forth a number of complex criteria not enumerated here.[14] Gains or losses on the hedging instrument (in this case, the forward contract) and on the hedged item to be acquired or disposed of under the firm commitment are to be recognized in the measurement of net income and of the carrying amount of the hedged item.[15]

To illustrate, assume that on August 1, 2002, Carthay Company entered into a firm commitment with a Japanese manufacturer to acquire a machine, delivery and passage of title on October 30, 2002, at a price of 10,000,000 yen (¥). To hedge against unfavorable changes in the exchange rate for the yen, the selling spot rate for which was ¥1 = $0.006958 on August 1, on that date Carthay entered into a ninety-day forward contract for ¥10,000,000 at a forward rate of ¥1 = $0.007051. Forward rates for yen-denominated forward contracts maturing on October 30, 2002, were ¥1 = $0.007030 on August 31, 2002, ¥1 = $0.007019 on September 30, 2002, and ¥1 = $0.007010 on October 30, 2002, on all of which dates Carthay prepared financial statements. Carthay's journal entries on August 1 and 31, September 30, and October 30, 2002, are as follows:

Journal Entries for Forward Contract Designated as a Hedge of a Foreign-Currency–Denominated Firm Commitment (Fair Value Hedge)

2002			
Aug. 1	Investment in Forward Contract	70,510	
	Forward Contract Payable		70,510
	To record forward contract for ¥10,000,000 at forward rate of ¥1 = $0.007051 (¥10,000,000 × $0.007051 = $70,510).		
31	Foreign Currency Transaction Losses	208	
	Firm Commitment for Machinery	208	
	Investment in Forward Contract		208
	Foreign Currency Transaction Gains		208
	To recognize fair value of forward contract investment, resultant transaction loss, increase in fair value of commitment to acquire machine, and resultant transaction gain, as follows:		

Forward price of contract:

Aug. 1		$70,510
Aug. 31 (¥10,000,000 × $0.007030)		70,300
Difference		$ 210
Less: Discount to maturity (60 days) at 6% rate ($210 × 0.06 × 60/360 = $2)		2
Transaction loss and gain		$ 208

(continued)

[13] Ibid., par. 4.
[14] Ibid., par. 20, 21.
[15] Ibid., par. 22.

Sept. 30	Foreign Currency Transaction Losses		110	
	Firm Commitment for Machinery		110	
	Investment in Forward Contract			110
	Foreign Currency Transaction Gains			110

To recognize fair value of forward contract investment, resultant transaction loss, increase in fair value of commitment to acquire machine, and resultant transaction gain, as follows:

Forward price of contract:		
Aug. 1	$70,510	
Sept. 30 (¥10,000,000 × $0.007019)	70,190	
Difference	$ 320	
Less: Discount to maturity (30 days) at 6% rate (320 × 0.06 × 30/360)	2	
Total change in fair value of forward contract (60 days)	$ 318	
Less: Change recognized Aug. 31, 2002	208	
Transaction loss and gain	$ 110	

Oct. 30	Foreign Currency Transaction Losses		92	
	Firm Commitment for Machinery		92	
	Investment in Forward Contract			92
	Foreign Currency Transaction Gains			92

To recognize fair value of forward contract investment, resultant transaction loss, increase in fair value of commitment to acquire machine, and resultant transaction gain, as follows:

Forward price of contract:		
Aug. 1	$70,510	
Oct. 30 (¥10,000,000 × $0.007010)	70,100	
Total change in fair value of forward contract (90 days)	$ 410	
Less: Changes in fair value recognized Aug. 31 and Sept. 30 ($208 + $110)	318	
Transaction loss and gain	$ 92	

Oct. 30	Investment in Yen (¥10,000,000 × $0.007010)		70,100	
	Forward Contract Payable		70,510	
	Investment in Forward Contract ($70,510 − $208 − $110 − $92)			70,100
	Cash			70,510

To recognize settlement of forward contract and fair value of investment in yen.

30	Machinery ($70,100 + $410)		70,510	
	Investment in Yen			70,100
	Firm Commitment for Machinery ($208 + $110 + $92)			410

To record acquisition of machinery from Japanese manufacturer.

Because Carthay Company had acquired a forward contract for the same amount of the same currency in which the firm commitment was denominated, the hedge was "perfect," in that it fully covered the risk of unfavorable changes in the exchange rate for the yen. Accordingly, the cost of the machine acquired from the Japanese manufacturer was the U.S. dollar amount of the forward contract.

International Accounting Standards 21 and 39

The provisions of *IAS 21,* "The Effects of Changes in Foreign Exchange Rates," dealing with foreign-currency–denominated transactions are essentially the same as those of *FASB Statement No. 52,* "Foreign Currency Translation." However, *IAS 21* has no coverage of forward contracts, which are dealt with in *IAS 39,* "Financial Instruments: Recognition and Measurement," with standards similar to those of *FASB Statement No. 133.*

Disclosures Regarding Foreign Currency Transactions

For transactions denominated in a foreign currency, *FASB Statement No. 52* requires disclosure, in the financial statements or notes thereto, of the aggregate foreign currency transaction gains and losses included in the measurement of net income.[16] For example, under the caption "Other Expense (Income)" in its income statements for the three fiscal years ended September 27, 1997, Tyson Foods, Inc., a publicly owned company, displayed "Foreign currency exchange" [losses] of $15.6 million for 1995 and $9.0 million for 1996, but none for 1997.

  FASB Statement No. 133, effective for fiscal years beginning after June 15, 2000, requires numerous quantitative and qualitative disclosures regarding *all* derivative instruments, including those designated as hedges of foreign currency exchange risks. (Presumably, such disclosures are to be in the financial statements and the notes thereto.)[17] Further, the SEC requires disclosure, outside the financial statements and the notes thereto, of both qualitative and quantitative information about market risk inherent in derivative instruments.[18] (*Market risk* is the risk of a decline in value or an increase in onerousness of a derivative instrument resulting from future changes in market prices.)

Review
Questions

1. What are the 15 member countries of the European Union?
2. Differentiate between the International Accounting Standards Board (IASB) and the International Organization of Securities Commissions (IOSCO).
3. What is the U.S. term for the IASB's *jointly controlled entity*?
4. How does *IAS 22,* "Accounting for Business Combinations," compare with current U.S. accounting standards for business combinations? Explain.
5. In *IAS 27,* "Consolidated Financial Statements . . . ," did the IAS adopt the parent company concept or the economic unit concept for display of the minority interest in net income and net assets of subsidiaries in consolidated financial statements? Explain.

---

[16] *FASB Statement No. 52,* par. 30.
[17] *FASB Statement No. 133,* par. 45.
[18] *Codification of Financial Reporting Policies* (Washington: SEC, 1997), sec. 507

6. Define the following terms associated with foreign currencies:
    a. *Exchange rate.*
    b. *Forward rate.*
    c. *Selling spot rate.*
    d. *Spot rate.*

7. A newspaper listed spot exchange rates for the Japanese yen (¥) as follows:

    Buying rate: ¥1 = $0.0039
    Selling rate: ¥1 = $0.0043

    How many U.S. dollars does a U.S. enterprise have to exchange for ¥50,000 at the above rates to settle a trade account payable denominated in that amount to a Japanese supplier? Explain.

8. What is a *multinational* enterprise?

9. On March 27, 2002, a U.S. multinational enterprise purchased merchandise on 30-day credit terms from a Philippines exporter at an invoice cost of ₱80,000. (₱ is the symbol of the Philippine peso). What U.S. dollar amount does the U.S. enterprise credit to Trade Accounts Payable if the March 27, 2002, spot rates for the Philippine peso are as follows?

    Buying rate: ₱1 = $0.11
    Selling rate: ₱1 = $0.12

10. Are foreign currency transaction gains or losses entered in the accounting records prior to collection of a trade account receivable or payment of a trade account payable denominated in a foreign currency? Explain.

11. Explain the *one-transaction perspective* regarding the nature of a foreign currency transaction gain or loss.

12. What arguments are advanced in support of the *two-transaction perspective* for foreign currency transaction gains and losses? Explain.

13. What is a *forward contract*?

14. How may a U.S. multinational enterprise *hedge* against the risk of fluctuations in exchange rates for foreign currencies? Explain.

15. What is *market risk* with respect to derivative instruments?

Exercises

(Exercise 11.1) Select the best answer for each of the following multiple-choice questions:

1. Export Company had a trade account receivable from a foreign customer stated in the local currency of the foreign customer. The trade account receivable for 900,000 local currency units (LCU) had been restated to $315,000 in Export's June 30, 2002, balance sheet. On July 26, 2002, the account receivable was collected in full when the exchange rate was LCU1 = $0.33⅓. The journal entry (explanation omitted) that Export prepares to record the collection of this trade account receivable is:

    a. Cash 300,000
            Trade Accounts Receivable 300,000
    b. Cash 300,000
            Foreign Currency Transaction Gains and Losses 15,000
                    Trade Accounts Receivable 315,000

c. Cash		300,000	
Foreign Currency Translation Adjustments		15,000	
Trade Accounts Receivable			315,000
d. Cash		315,000	
Trade Accounts Receivable			315,000

2. If the exchange rate for one British pound is $1.55, $1.00 may be exchanged for:

   a. 0.45 pound.

   b. 0.65 pound.

   c. 0.78 pound.

   d. An indeterminate fraction of a pound.

3. If $1.9672 is required to acquire one British pound, the amount of pound(s) required to acquire $1 is:

   a. £0.5083   *b.* £5.0834   *c.* £3.8702   *d.* £0.2584

4. Vermont Corporation, a U.S. enterprise, purchased merchandise from a New Zealand supplier on November 5, 2002, for $NZ50,000, when the selling spot rate was $NZ1 = $0.4295. On Vermont's December 31, 2002, year-end the selling spot rate was $0.4245. On January 15, 2003, Vermont acquired $NZ50,000 at the selling spot of $0.4345 and paid the invoice. What amounts does Vermont report in its income statements for years 2002 and 2003 as foreign currency transaction gains or (losses)?

   a. $250 $(500)

   b. (250)   -0-

   c. -0-   (250)

   d. -0-   -0-

   e. Some other amounts

5. On April 30, 2002, the buying spot rate for the local currency unit (LCU) was $0.15, the selling spot rate was $0.17, and the 30-day forward rate was $0.19. If a U.S. multinational enterprise received a LCU100,000 draft from a foreign customer in settlement of a purchase made by the customer on March 31, 2002, the U.S. enterprise may convert the LCU100,000 draft to:

   a. $15,000.   *b.* $17,000.   *c.* $19,000.   *d.* Some other amount.

6. A U.S. multinational enterprise has an account receivable from a German customer and an account payable to an unrelated German supplier, both of which are denominated in the euro. If the exchange rate for the euro *decreases,* the result to the enterprise will be realization of foreign currency transaction gains or losses as follows:

	On Account Receivable	*On Account Payable*
a.	Transaction gain	Transaction gain
b.	Transaction loss	Transaction loss
c.	Transaction loss	Transaction gain
d.	Transaction gain	Transaction loss

7. In *FASB Statement No. 52,* "Foreign Currency Translation," did the FASB sanction, for interpreting a foreign trade transaction, the:

	Two-Transaction Perspective?	*One-Transaction Perspective?*
a.	No	Yes
b.	No	No
c.	Yes	Yes
d.	Yes	No

8. The International Accounting Standards Board has designated as preferable the inventory cost flow valuation method(s):
   a. First-in, first-out or weighted average.
   b. First-in, first-out or last-in, first-out.
   c. Last-in, first-out or weighted average.
   d. First-in, first-out only.
   e. Weighted average only.

9. The U.S. member of the International Accounting Standards Committee is the:
   a. Securities and Exchange Commission.
   b. Financial Accounting Standards Board.
   c. American Institute of Certified Public Accountants.
   d. General Accounting Office.

10. The Scandinavian country that is not a member of the European Union is:
    a. Denmark   b. Finland   c. Norway   d. Sweden

11. A forward contract is a derivative instrument because:
    a. It has an underlying: the contracted foreign exchange rate.
    b. It has a notional amount: the number of foreign currency units.
    c. It requires no initial net investment.
    d. Of all the foregoing reasons.

12. The FASB required that forward contracts:
    a. Be recognized as assets or liabilities, as appropriate.
    b. Be valued at fair value.
    c. Be valued at their notional amount.
    d. Be treated in the manner described in both *a* and *b*.
    e. Be treated in the manner described in both *a* and *c*.

(Exercise 11.2) On June 26, 2002, L.A. Company purchased merchandise from Brit Company for £10,000, terms net 30 days. On June 30, 2002, L.A. Company prepared financial statements. On July 26, 2002, L.A. Company electronically transferred £10,000 to Brit Company. Relevant spot exchange rates for the pound sterling (£) were as follows:

	£1 =	
	Buying Rate	*Selling Rate*
June 16, 2002	$1.63	$1.67
June 30, 2002	1.64	1.68
July 26, 2002	1.62	1.66

Prepare journal entries (omit explanations) for L.A. Company on June 26 and 30 and July 26, 2002. L.A. Company uses the perpetual inventory system.

(Exercise 11.3) Walker, Inc., a U.S. corporation that prepares annual financial statements, ordered a machine (plant asset) from Pfau Company of Germany on July 15, 2002, for €100,000 when the selling spot rate for the euro was $1.065. Pfau shipped the machine on September 1, 2002, and billed Walker for €100,000. The selling spot rate for the euro was $1.070 on that date. Walker acquired a draft for €100,000 and paid the invoice on October 25, 2002, when the selling spot rate for the euro was $1.065.

Prepare journal entries for Walker, Inc., to record the foregoing business transactions and events.

(Exercise 11.4)

On November 18, 2002, U.S. Company, which uses the perpetual inventory system and
prepares financial statements monthly, shipped merchandise costing $1,000 to France
Company for €1,500, terms n/30. On December 18, 2002, U.S. Company received
from France Company a draft for €1,500, which U.S. converted to U.S. dollars immediately. Spot rates for the euro were as follows:

	€1 =	
	Buying Rate	*Selling Rate*
Nov. 18, 2002	$1.055	$1.060
Nov. 30, 2002	1.060	1.050
Dec. 18, 2002	1.050	1.055

Prepare journal entries for U.S. Company on November 18 and 30 and December
18, 2002. Omit explanations for the journal entries.

(Exercise 11.5)

On March 25, 2002, Lincoln Company, a U.S. multinational enterprise, sold merchandise
costing $260,000 to Svenska Company, a Swedish enterprise, for 2,000,000 krona (Kr) on
30-day open account. On April 24, 2002, Lincoln received a Kr2,000,000 draft from Sven-
ska and converted it to U.S. dollars. Lincoln prepares monthly financial statements and
uses the perpetual inventory system. Exchange rates for the krona were as follows:

	Kr1 =		
	Buying	*Selling*	*Forward*
Mar. 25, 2002	$0.19	$0.20	$0.22
Mar. 31, 2002	0.20	0.22	0.24
Apr. 24, 2002	0.18	0.19	0.20

Prepare journal entries (omit explanations) for Lincoln Company on March 25,
March 31, and April 24, 2002.

(Exercise 11.6)

On March 1, 2002, Yankee Company sold merchandise with a cost of $100,000 to a for-
eign customer in its local currency unit (LCU) for a LCU600,000, 60-day promissory note
bearing interest of 18% a year. On April 30, 2002, Yankee received a draft for LCU618,000,
in settlement of the note receivable from the foreign customer, and converted it to U.S.
dollars immediately. Relevant exchange rates for the LCU were as follows:

	LCU1 =	
	Mar. 1, 2002	*Apr. 30, 2002*
Spot rates:		
Buying	$0.30	$0.33
Selling	0.32	0.34
30-day forward rate	0.40	0.44

Prepare journal entries for Yankee Company on March 1, 2002, and April 30, 2002,
for the foregoing information. Yankee uses the periodic inventory system and prepares
end-of-period adjustments only on June 30, the end of its fiscal year.

(Exercise 11.7)

The accountant for Transglobal Company is a proponent of the one-transaction perspective of accounting for foreign trade transactions. On November 19, 2002, Transglobal's accountant prepared the following journal entry:

Trade Accounts Payable	60,000	
Cost of Goods Sold ($3,000 × 33⅓%)	1,000	
Inventories ($3,000 × 66⅔%)	2,000	
Cash		63,000

To record payment for €60,000 draft (€60,000 × $1.05 = $63,000) to settle liability to French supplier, and allocation of resultant foreign currency transaction loss to cost of goods sold and to inventories.

Prepare a journal entry for Transglobal Company on November 19, 2002, to correct the foregoing journal entry. Do not reverse the foregoing entry.

(Exercise 11.8) On March 31, 2002, Kingston Company acquired a 30-day forward contract for 100,000 local currency units (LCU) of a foreign country. The contract was not designated to hedge. On April 30, 2002, Kingston paid cash to settle the contract and obtain the LCU100,000 draft, Kingston prepares adjusting entries and financial statements only at the end of its fiscal year, April 30. Relevant exchange rates for one unit of the local currency were as follows:

CHECK FIGURE

Apr. 30, debit foreign currency transaction losses, $3,000.

	LCU1 =	
	Mar. 31, 2002	*Apr. 30, 2002*
Spot rates:		
Buying	$0.18	$0.19
Selling	0.20	0.22
Forward rates:		
Contracts maturing April 30, 2002	0.25	0.22

The discount rate is 6%.

Prepare journal entries for Kingston Company on March 31, 2002, and April 30, 2002.

(Exercise 11.9) On August 6, 2002, Concordia Company, a U.S. multinational enterprise that uses the perpetual inventory system, purchased from a Belgium supplier on 30-day open account goods costing €80,000. On that date, various exchange rates for the euro were as follows:

CHECK FIGURE

Sept. 5, credit investment in forward contract, $87,200.

Spot rates:
  Buying: €1 = $1.07
  Selling: €1 = $1.08
30-day forward rate: €1 = $1.10

Also on August 6, 2002, Concordia acquired a 30-day forward contract for €80,000, designated to hedge the euro commitment.

Prepare journal entries to record the August 6, 2002, transactions of Concordia Company, as well as the related transactions on September 5, 2002, on which date the forward rate for forward contracts maturing that date was €1 = $1.09. Concordia does not close its accounting records monthly or prepare monthly financial statements. None of the merchandise had been sold.

Cases

(Case 11.1) Both the International Accounting Standards Board (IASB) and the U.S. Financial Accounting Standards Board were established in 1973. Since that time, the IASB has issued 40 *International Accounting Standards,* but the FASB has issued more than 140 *Statements of Financial Accounting Standards.*

Instructions

Do you favor the FASB's continued outpouring of **Statements,** most of which differ at least in some respects from IASB **Standards**? Alternatively, should the FASB act as a recommender to the IASB for provisions of **Standards** that it issues? Base your answer on your perception of which course of action would best enhance the adoption of uniform accounting standards throughout the world.

(Case 11.2) Many accountants believe that generally accepted accounting principles in the United States, especially those developed by the Financial Accounting Standards Board, are superior to **International Accounting Standards** or to the accounting standards of other countries. In their view, foreign enterprises wanting to have their securities traded on U.S. stock exchanges should prepare financial reports that comply with U.S. accounting standards. However, the U.S. Securities and Exchange Commission is a member of the International Organization of Securities Commissions, which is studying the possibility of allowing foreign enterprises to prepare financial reports that incorporate **International Accounting Standards** in requesting permission to have their securities traded in any country.

Instructions

Do you support or oppose the SEC's participation in the work of the IOSCO? Should or should not foreign enterprises meet financial reporting standards applicable to U.S. enterprises if the foreign enterprises want their securities to be traded on U.S. stock exchanges? Explain.

(Case 11.3) **FASB Statement No. 133,** "Accounting for Derivative Instruments and Hedging Activities," which is effective for fiscal years beginning after June 15, 2000, requires (in paragraphs 44 and 45) numerous disclosures regarding derivative instruments.

Instructions

Obtain the annual report of a publicly owned enterprise that has forward contract derivative instruments, make a copy of the note to financial statements that deals with such instruments, and analyze the note for compliance with paragraphs 44 and 45 of **FASB Statement No. 133.** Attach the copy of the note to your solution to the case.

Problems

(Problem 11.1) On August 1, 2002, Caribbean Company, a U.S. multinational enterprise that prepares financial statements monthly, acquired a 60-day forward contract for £50,000. Exchange rates for the British pound (£) on various dates in 2002 were as follows:

CHECK FIGURE

a. Aug. 31, debit foreign currency transaction losses, $995; *b.* Sept. 30, credit foreign currency transaction gains, $505.

	£1 =		
	Aug. 1	*Aug. 31*	*Sept. 30*
Spot rates:			
Buying	$1.80	$1.82	$1.83
Selling	1.90	1.91	1.92
Forward rates:			
Contracts maturing Sept. 30, 2002	1.95	1.93	1.92

Instructions

Prepare journal entries (omit explanations) for Caribbean Company's forward contract during its 60-day term under the following assumptions:

a. The contract was not designated as a hedge.

b. The contract was designated as a hedge of a £50,000 purchase order issued by Caribbean on August 1, 2002, to a British supplier for merchandise to be delivered and paid for on September 30, 2002.

Use a 6% discount rate.

(Problem 11.2)   The following problem consists of two unrelated parts.

CHECK FIGURE

b. Apr. 30, debit foreign currency transaction losses, $2,010.

a. On June 27, 2002, U.S. Company, which uses the perpetual inventory system, purchased from French Company, for 100,000 euros (€), merchandise to be shipped by air that date directly to Canadian Company at a selling price of 180,000 Canadian dollars ($C). On July 27, 2002, U.S. Company obtained for U.S. dollars and sent to French Company a draft for €100,000 and received from Canadian Company a draft for $C180,000, which U.S. immediately converted to U.S. dollars. U.S. Company does not prepare monthly financial statements. Relevant spot exchange rates were as follows:

	€1 =		$C1 =	
	Buying	*Selling*	*Buying*	*Selling*
June 27, 2002	$1.03	$1.05	$0.84	$0.86
July 27, 2002	1.04	1.06	0.85	0.87

Instructions

Prepare journal entries (omit explanations) for U.S. Company on June 27, 2002, to record the purchase and sale of merchandise and on July 27, 2002, to record the payment to French Company and the receipt from Canadian Company.

b. On March 1, 2002, Spheric Company prepared the following journal entry:

Investment in Forward Contract (Singapore dollars)	35,000	
Forward Contract Payable (S$100,000 × $0.35)		35,000
To record acquisition of forward contract, not designated as a hedge, for 60 days at forward rate of S$1 = $0.35.		

The forward rates for the Singapore dollar for forward contracts maturing April 30, 2002, were as follows:

Date	S$1 =
Mar. 31, 2002	$0.33
Apr. 30, 2002	0.31

Instructions

Prepare journal entries (omit explanations) for Spheric Company on March 31 and April 30, 2002. Spheric prepares monthly financial statements. The discount rate is 6%.

(Problem 11.3)   The following problem consists of two unrelated parts.

CHECK FIGURE

b. Aug. 29, credit foreign currency transaction gains, $15,300.

a. Zonal Corporation is a multinational company that sells merchandise to Stacey, Ltd., a customer in the United Kingdom. On November 19, 2002, Zonal sold to Stacey merchandise costing $40,000 for £38,000. On December 19, 2002, Zonal received from Stacey a draft for £38,000, which Zonal immediately converted to U.S. dollars. Zonal uses the perpetual inventory system and prepares monthly financial statements. Selected exchange rates for the British pound were as follows:

	£1 =		
	Nov. 19, 2002	*Nov. 30, 2002*	*Dec. 19, 2002*
Spot rates:			
Buying	$1.45	$1.44	$1.43
Selling	1.48	1.47	1.46
Forward rate:			
30-day contract	1.50	1.49	1.48

Instructions

Prepare journal entries (omit explanations) for Zonal Corporation on November 19, November 30, and December 19, 2002.

b. On June 30, 2002, Iberia Company, a U.S. multinational enterprise that does not prepare monthly financial statements, sold merchandise costing $75,000 to a foreign customer, and received in exchange a 60-day, 12% note for 7,500,000 local currency units (LCU). The buying spot rate for the LCU on June 30, 2002, was LCU1 = $0.014. On August 29, 2002, Iberia received from the foreign customer a draft for LCU7,650,000, which Iberia converted on that date to U.S. dollars at the buying spot rate of LCU1 = $0.016.

Instructions

Prepare journal entries (omit explanations) for Iberia Company to record the June 30, 2002, sale, under the perpetual inventory system, and the August 29, 2002, conversion of the foreign customer's LCU7,650,000 draft to U.S. dollars.

(Problem 11.4) Imex Company, a U.S. multinational enterprise with an April 30 fiscal year, had the following transactions and events, among others, during March and April, 2002:

CHECK FIGURE

a. Apr. 5, debit inventories, $100.

Date	Explanation of Transactions and Events	Buying	Selling	Forward
			Spot	
		Buying	Selling	Forward
2002				
Mar. 6	Received merchandise purchased from Venezuelan supplier on 30-day open account, cost 100,000 bolivars (B). Acquired 30-day forward contract for B100,000 as hedge.	$0.006	$0.007	$0.008
18	Received merchandise purchased from Danish supplier on 30-day open account, cost 75,000 euros (€).	1.04	1.06	1.10
25	Sold merchandise to Swiss customer on 30-day open account for 50,000 francs (Sfr).Cost of goods sold $15,000.	0.52	0.53	0.54
Apr. 4	Received merchandise purchased from Spanish supplier on 30-day open account for 150,000 euros (€).	1.05	1.07	1.11
5	Settled B100,000 forward contract, and paid Venezuelan supplier for Mar. 6 purchase, none of which had been sold.	0.006	0.007	0.007
17	Acquired draft for €75,000 for payment to Danish supplier for Mar. 18 purchase.	1.03	1.05	1.08

(continued)

		Buying	Selling	Forward
Date	*Explanation of Transactions and Events*			
Apr. 24	Received draft for Sfr50,000 from Swiss customer for sale of Mar. 25. Exchanged draft for U.S. dollar credit to bank checking account.	0.53	0.54	0.55
30	Obtained exchange rates quotation for euro.	1.03	1.05	1.07

Exchange Rates — Spot

Instructions

a. Prepare journal entries (omit explanations) for Imex Company to record the foregoing transactions and events in U.S. dollars, under the perpetual inventory system.

b. Prepare an adjusting entry (omit explanation) for Imex Company on April 30, 2002. Imex does not prepare monthly financial statements.

(Problem 11.5)

CHECK FIGURE

Aug. 29, debit foreign currency transaction losses, $153.

On June 30, 2002 Impo Company, which prepares monthly financial statements, acquired from Japanese Company for 500,000 yen (¥) a machine with an economic life of five years and no residual value. To pay Japanese Company, Impo borrowed ¥500,000 from Japanese Bank on a 12%, 60-day promissory note. Impo acquired a ¥510,000 draft from U.S. Bank on August 29, 2002, to pay the maturity value of the note to Japanese Bank. Relevant spot rates for the yen were as follows:

	Buying Rate	Selling Rate
June 30, 2002	$0.0081	$0.0084
July 31, 2002	0.0080	0.0082
Aug. 29, 2002	0.0082	0.0085

¥1 =

Instructions

Prepare journal entries (omit explanations) for Impo Company on June 30, July 31, and August 29, 2002, including interest accrual and depreciation of the machine. Use 30-day months for July and August interest.

(Problem 11.6)

CHECK FIGURE

Debit foreign currency transaction losses, $15.

During your first-time audit of the financial statements of Allison Company, a closely held corporation, you review the following ledger account:

Forward Contracts

Date	Explanation	Debit	Credit	Balance
2002				
Apr. 30	Payment for 60-day contract for ¥100,000 at ¥1 = $0.00801	801		801 dr
Sept. 30	Payment of 60-day contract for €50,000 at €1 = $1.04	52,000		52,801 dr

Your study of underlying records discloses the following:

1. Allison, as a nonpublic company, prepares financial statements at the end of its September 30 fiscal year only.

2. The offsetting credits for the debits to Forward Contracts were to Cash.

3. No other journal entries had been prepared by Allison for the forward contracts.

4. The contract for Japanese yen (¥) was not designated as a hedge. The yen were used for travel expenses in Japan prior to September 30, 2002.

5. The contract for euros (€) hedged a €50,000 purchase commitment to a French supplier for merchandise received and paid for September 30, 2002, all of which was on hand on that date.

6. Forward rates for forward contracts payable on the indicated dates were as follows:

   ¥1: Mar. 1, 2002, $0.00801; Apr. 30, 2002, $0.00786

   €1: Aug. 1, 2002, $1.04; Sept. 30, 2002, $1.01

Instructions

Prepare two journal entries, one for each forward contract, for Allison Company on September 30, 2002, to correct the accounting for the two contracts. Show supporting computations in the explanations for the entries.

Chapter Twelve

Translation of Foreign Currency Financial Statements

Scope of Chapter

When a U.S. multinational enterprise prepares consolidated or combined financial statements that include the operating results, financial position, and cash flows of foreign subsidiaries or branches, the U.S. enterprise must **translate** the amounts in the financial statements of the foreign entities from the entities' **functional currency** to the U.S. dollar, the **reporting currency.** Similar treatment must be given to investments in other foreign investees for which the U.S. enterprise uses the equity method of accounting. In addition, if the foreign entity's accounting records are maintained in a **local currency** (of the foreign country) that is not the entity's functional currency, the foreign entity's account balances must be **remeasured** to the functional currency from the local currency. Both **remeasurement** and **translation** are described and illustrated in this chapter, together with other issues involving foreign currency restatements.

FUNCTIONAL CURRENCY

The FASB defined the **functional currency** of a foreign entity as follows:

> An entity's functional currency is the currency of the primary economic environment in which the entity operates; normally, that is the currency of the environment in which an entity primarily generates and expends cash. . . .
>
> For an entity with operations that are relatively self-contained and integrated within a particular country, the functional currency generally would be the currency of that country. However, a foreign entity's functional currency might not be the currency of the country in which the entity is located. For example, the parent's currency generally would be the functional currency for operations that are a direct and integral component or extension of the parent company's operations.[1]

To assist in the determination of the functional currency of a foreign entity, the FASB provided the following guidelines:[2]

---

[1] *FASB Statement No. 52,* "Foreign Currency Translation" (Stamford: FASB, 1981), pars. 5–6.
[2] Ibid., par. 42.

The salient economic factors set forth below, and possibly others, should be considered both individually and collectively when determining the functional currency.

a. Cash flow indicators
  (1) *Foreign Currency*—Cash flows related to the foreign entity's individual assets and liabilities are primarily in the foreign currency and do not directly impact the parent company's cash flows.
  (2) *Parent's Currency*—Cash flows related to the foreign entity's individual assets and liabilities directly impact the parent's cash flows on a current basis and are readily available for remittance to the parent company.

b. Sales price indicators
  (1) *Foreign Currency*—Sales prices for the foreign entity's products are not primarily responsive on a short-term basis to changes in exchange rates but are determined more by local competition or local government regulation.
  (2) *Parent's Currency*—Sales prices for the foreign entity's products are primarily responsive on a short-term basis to changes in exchange rates; for example, sales prices are determined more by worldwide competition or by international prices.

c. Sales market indicators
  (1) *Foreign Currency*—There is an active local sales market for the foreign entity's products, although there also might be significant amounts of exports.
  (2) *Parent's Currency*—The sales market is mostly in the parent's country or sales contracts are denominated in the parent's currency.

d. Expense indicators
  (1) *Foreign Currency*—Labor, materials, and other costs for the foreign entity's products or services are primarily local costs, even though there also might be imports from other countries.
  (2) *Parent's Currency*—Labor, materials, and other costs for the foreign entity's products or services, on a continuing basis, are primarily costs for components obtained from the country in which the parent company is located.

e. Financing indicators
  (1) *Foreign Currency*—Financing is primarily denominated in foreign currency, and funds generated by the foreign entity's operations are sufficient to service existing and normally expected debt obligations.
  (2) *Parent's Currency*—Financing is primarily from the parent or other dollar-denominated obligations, or funds generated by the foreign entity's operations are not sufficient to service existing and normally expected debt obligations without the infusion of additional funds from the parent company. Infusion of additional funds from the parent company for expansion is not a factor, provided funds generated by the foreign entity's expanded operations are expected to be sufficient to service that additional financing.

f. Intercompany transactions and arrangements indicators
  (1) *Foreign Currency*—There is a low volume of intercompany transactions and there is not an extensive interrelationship between the operations of the foreign entity and the parent company. However, the foreign entity's operations may rely on the parent's or affiliates' competitive advantages, such as patents and trademarks.
  (2) *Parent's Currency*—There is a high volume of intercompany transactions and there is an extensive interrelationship between the operations of the foreign entity and the parent company. Additionally, the parent's currency generally would be the functional currency if the foreign entity is a device or shell corporation for holding investments, obligations, intangible assets, etc., that could readily be carried on the parent's or an affiliate's books.

The foregoing guidelines indicate the importance of determining the appropriate functional currency for a foreign entity. The functional currency of the foreign entity underlies the application of the ***monetary principle*** (discussed in intermediate accounting textbooks) for the entity.

Alternative Methods for Translating Foreign Entities' Financial Statements

If the exchange rate for the functional currency of a foreign subsidiary or branch remained constant instead of fluctuating, translation of the foreign entity's financial statements to U.S. dollars would be simple. All financial statement amounts would be translated to U.S. dollars at the constant exchange rate. However, exchange rates fluctuate frequently. Thus, accountants charged with translating amounts in a foreign entity's financial statements to U.S. dollars face a problem similar to that involving inventory valuation during a period of purchase price fluctuations: Which exchange rate or rates should be used to translate the foreign entity's financial statements? A number of answers were proposed for this question prior to the issuance of ***FASB Statement No. 52,*** "Foreign Currency Translation." The several methods for foreign currency translation may be grouped into three basic classes: ***current/noncurrent, monetary/nonmonetary,*** and ***current rate.*** (A fourth method, the ***temporal method,*** essentially is the same as the monetary/nonmonetary method.) The three classes differ principally in translation techniques for balance sheet amounts.

Current/Noncurrent Method

In the ***current/noncurrent method*** of translation, current assets and current liabilities are translated at the exchange rate in effect on the balance sheet date of the foreign entity (the ***current rate***). All other assets and liabilities, and the elements of owners' equity, are translated at the ***historical rates*** in effect at the time the assets, liabilities, and equities first were recognized in the foreign entity's accounting records. In the income statement, depreciation expense and amortization expense are translated at historical rates applicable to the related assets, while all other revenue and expenses are translated at an ***average*** exchange rate for the accounting period.

The current/noncurrent method of translating foreign investees' financial statements was sanctioned by the AICPA for many years. This method supposedly best reflected the ***liquidity*** aspects of the foreign entity's financial position by showing the current U.S. dollar equivalents of its working capital components. Today, the current/noncurrent method has few supporters. The principal theoretical objection to the current/noncurrent method is that, with respect to inventories, it represents a departure from historical cost. Inventories are translated at the ***current rate,*** rather than at ***historical rates*** in effect when the inventories were acquired, if the current/noncurrent method of translating foreign currency accounts is applied.

Monetary/Nonmonetary Method

The ***monetary/nonmonetary method*** of translating foreign currencies focuses on the characteristics of assets and liabilities of the foreign entity, rather than on their balance sheet classifications. This method is founded on the same monetary/nonmonetary aspects of assets and liabilities that are employed in historical-cost/constant-purchasing-power accounting, described in intermediate accounting textbooks. ***Monetary assets and liabilities***—those representing claims or obligations expressed in a fixed monetary amount—are translated at the current exchange rate. All other assets, liabilities, and owners' equity amounts are translated at appropriate historical rates. In the income statement, average exchange rates are applied to all revenue and expenses except depreciation expense, amortization expense, and cost of goods sold, which are translated at appropriate historical rates.

Supporters of the monetary/nonmonetary method emphasized its retention of the historical-cost principle in the foreign entity's financial statements. Because the foreign entity's financial statements are consolidated or combined with those of the U.S. multinational enterprise, consistent accounting principles are applied in the consolidated or combined financial statements. The monetary/nonmonetary method essentially was sanctioned by the FASB prior to the issuance of *FASB Statement No. 52.*

Critics of the monetary/nonmonetary method point out that this method emphasizes the *parent company* aspects of a foreign entity's financial position and operating results. By reflecting the foreign entity's changes in assets and liabilities, and operating results, as though they were made in the parent company's *reporting currency,* the monetary/nonmonetary method misstates the actual financial position and operating results of the foreign entity.

Current Rate Method

Critics of the monetary/nonmonetary method of foreign currency translation generally have supported the *current rate method.* Under the current rate method, all balance sheet amounts other than owners' equity are translated at the current exchange rate. Owners' equity amounts are translated at historical rates.

To emphasize the *functional currency* aspects of the foreign entity's operations, all revenue and expenses may be translated at the current rate on the respective transaction dates, if practical. Otherwise, an average exchange rate is used for all revenue and expenses.

Standards for Translation Established by the Financial Accounting Standards Board

FASB Statement No. 52 adopted the current rate method, as described in the preceding section of this chapter, for *translating* a foreign entity's financial statements from the entity's *functional currency* to the *reporting currency* of the parent company, which for a U.S. enterprise is the U.S. dollar.[3] If a foreign entity's accounting records are maintained in a currency other than its functional currency, account balances must be *remeasured* to the functional currency before the foreign entity's financial statements may be translated.[4] *Remeasurement* essentially is accomplished by the monetary/nonmonetary method of translation described above. If a foreign entity's functional currency is the U.S. dollar, *remeasurement* eliminates the need for *translation* of the entity's financial statements. Because remeasurement, if required, *must precede translation,* remeasurement techniques are illustrated in the next section.

REMEASUREMENT OF A FOREIGN ENTITY'S ACCOUNTS

The FASB provided the following guidelines for remeasurement:

> The remeasurement process should produce the same result as if the entity's books of record had been initially recorded in the functional currency. To accomplish that result, it is necessary to use historical exchange rates between the functional currency and

[3] Ibid., par. 12.
[4] Ibid., par. 10.

another currency in the remeasurement process for certain accounts (the current rate will be used for all others), . . . it is also necessary to recognize currently in income all . . . gains and losses from remeasurement of monetary assets and liabilities that are not denominated in the functional currency (for example, assets and liabilities that are not denominated in dollars if the dollar is the functional currency).[5]

The following list includes the nonmonetary balance sheet items and related revenue and expense amounts that should be ***remeasured using historical rates*** to produce the same result in terms of the functional currency that would have occurred if those items had been recorded initially in the functional currency. (All other items are remeasured using the current rate.)

Marketable securities carried at cost:

Equity securities

Debt securities not intended to be held until maturity

Inventories carried at cost

Short-term prepayments such as insurance, advertising, and rent

Plant assets and accumulated depreciation of plant assets

Patents, trademarks, licenses, formulas, goodwill, other tangible assets, and accumulated amortization of intangible assets

Deferred charges and credits

Deferred revenue

Common stock

Preferred stock carried at issuance price

Examples of revenue and expenses related to nonmonetary items:

Cost of goods sold

Depreciation of plant assets

Amortization of intangible assets such as goodwill, patents, and licenses

Amortization of deferred charges or credits

The appropriate historical or current exchange rate generally is the rate applicable to conversion of the foreign currency for dividend remittances.[6] Accordingly, a U.S. multinational enterprise having foreign branches, investees, or subsidiaries typically uses the buying spot rate on the balance sheet date or applicable historical date to remeasure the foreign currency financial statements.

Illustration of Remeasurement of a Foreign Entity's Account Balances

To illustrate the remeasurement of a foreign entity's account balances to the entity's functional currency from another currency, return to the Smaldino Company

---

[5] Ibid., par. 47.
[6] Ibid., par. 27(b).

illustration in Chapter 4, with merchandise shipments by the home office to Mason Branch in excess of home office cost. Assume that both the home office and Mason Branch use the perpetual inventory system, that Mason Branch is located in France, and that the functional currency of Mason Branch is the U.S. dollar, although the branch maintains its accounting records in the euro (€), the *local currency.*

Year 2002 transactions and events of Smaldino's home office and branch illustrated in Chapter 4 are repeated below. Following each transaction is the exchange rate for the euro on the date of the transaction or event.

Transactions or Events for Year 2002

1. Cash of $1,000 was sent by the home office to Mason Branch (€1 = $1.065).

2. Merchandise with a cost of $60,000 was shipped by the home office to Mason Branch at a billed price of $90,000 (€1 = $1.065).

3. Equipment was acquired by Mason Branch for €527, to be carried in the home office accounting records (€1 = $1.054).

4. Sales by Mason Branch on credit amounted to €92,500 (€1 = $1.058). Cost of goods sold was €64,818.

5. Collections of trade accounts receivable by Mason Branch amounted to €68,400 (€1 = $1.055).

6. Payments for operating expenses by Mason Branch totaled €6,414 (€1 = $1.060).

7. Cash of €39,750 was remitted by Mason Branch to home office (€1 = $1.060).

8. Operating expenses incurred by the home office charged to Mason Branch totaled $3,000 (€1 = $1.063).

The exchange rate on December 31, 2002, was €1 = $1.058.

The foregoing transactions or events are recorded by the home office and by Mason Branch with the following journal entries (explanations omitted):

SMALDINO COMPANY
Home Office and Mason Branch Journal Entries
For Year 2002

Home Office Accounting Records (U.S. Dollar)			Mason Branch Accounting Records (Euro)		
(1) Investment in Mason Branch	1,000		Cash ($1,000 ÷ $1.065)	939	
Cash		1,000	Home Office		939
(2) Investment in Mason Branch	90,000		Inventories ($90,000 ÷ $1.065)	84,507	
Inventories		60,000	Home Office		84,507
Allowance for Overvaluation of					
Inventories: Mason Branch		30,000			
(3) Equipment: Mason Branch					
(€527 ÷ $1.054)	500		Home Office	527	
Investment in Mason Branch		500	Cash		527

(continued)

SMALDINO COMPANY Home Office and Mason Branch Journal Entries (concluded) For Year 2002				
Home Office Accounting Records (U.S. Dollar)			**Mason Branch Accounting Records (Euro)**	
(4) None			Trade Accounts Receivable	92,500	
			Cost of Goods Sold	64,818	
			Sales		92,500
			Inventories		64,818
(5) None			Cash	68,400	
			Trade Accounts Receivable		68,400
(6) None			Operating Expenses	6,414	
			Cash		6,414
(7) Cash (€39,750 ÷ $1.060)	37,500		Home Office	39,750	
Investment in Mason Branch		37,500	Cash		39,750
(8) Investment in Mason Branch	3,000		Operating Expenses ($3,000 × $1.063)	3,189	
Operating Expenses		3,000	Home Office		3,189

In the home office accounting records, the Investment in Mason Branch ledger account (in dollars, before the accounts are closed) is as shown below:

Home Office Reciprocal Ledger Account with Branch (in Dollars)

Investment in Mason Branch

Date	Explanation	Debit	Credit	Balance
2002	Cash sent to branch	$ 1,000		$ 1,000 dr
	Merchandise shipped to branch	90,000		91,000 dr
	Equipment acquired by branch, carried in home office accounting records		$ 500	90,500 dr
	Cash received from branch		37,500	53,000 dr
	Operating expenses billed to branch	3,000		56,000 dr

In the Mason Branch accounting records, the Home Office ledger account (in euros, before the accounts are closed) is as follows:

Branch Reciprocal Ledger Account with Home Office (in Euros)

Home Office

Date	Explanation	Debit	Credit	Balance
2002	Cash received from home office		€ 939	€ 939 cr
	Merchandise received from home office		84,507	85,446 cr
	Equipment acquired by branch	€ 527		84,919 cr
	Cash sent to home office	39,750		45,169 cr
	Operating expenses billed by home office		3,189	48,358 cr

Following is the Mason Branch trial balance (in euros) on December 31, 2002:

SMALDINO COMPANY
Mason Branch Trial Balance
December 31, 2002

	Debit	Credit
Cash	€ 22,648	
Trade accounts receivable	24,100	
Inventories	19,689	
Home office		€ 48,358
Sales		92,500
Cost of goods sold	64,818	
Operating expenses	9,603	
Totals	€140,858	€140,858

Remeasurement of Branch Trial Balance

Remeasurement of the Mason Branch trial balance on December 31, 2002, is illustrated below.

Working Paper for *Remeasurement* **of Branch Trial Balance to U.S. Dollar Functional Currency from Euros**

SMALDINO COMPANY
Remeasurement of Mason Branch Trial Balance to U.S. Dollars
December 31, 2002

	Balance (Euros) dr (cr)	Exchange Rates	Balance (U.S. Dollars) dr (cr)
Cash	€ 22,648	$1.058 (1)	$ 23,962
Trade accounts receivable	24,100	1.058 (1)	25,498
Inventories	19,689	1.065 (2)	20,969
Home office	(48,358)	(3)	(56,000)
Sales	(92,500)	1.0615 (4)	(98,189)
Cost of goods sold	64,818	1.065 (2)	69,031
Operating expenses	9,603	1.0615 (4)	10,194
Subtotals	€ -0-		$ (4,535)
Foreign currency transaction loss			4,535
Totals	€ -0-		$ -0-

(1) Current rate (on Dec. 31, 2002)
(2) Historical rate (when goods were shipped to branch by home office)
(3) Balance of Investment in Branch ledger account in home office accounting records
(4) Average of beginning (€1 = $1.065) and ending (€1 = $1.058) exchange rates for euro

In a review of the remeasurement of the Mason Branch trial balance, the following four features should be noted:

1. Monetary assets are remeasured at the current rate; the single nonmonetary asset—inventories—is remeasured at the appropriate historical rate.

2. To achieve the same result as remeasurement of the Home Office ledger account transactions at appropriate historical rates, the balance of the home office's

Investment in Mason Branch account (in dollars) is substituted for the branch's Home Office account (in euros). All equity ledger accounts—regardless of legal form of the investee—are remeasured at historical rates.

3. A simple average of beginning-of-year and end-of-year exchange rates is used to remeasure revenue and expense accounts other than cost of goods sold, which is remeasured at the appropriate historical rates. In practice, a quarterly, monthly, or even daily weighted average might be computed.

4. A balancing amount labeled *foreign currency transaction loss,* which is *not a ledger account,* is used to reconcile the total debits and total credits of the branch's remeasured trial balance. This transaction loss is included in the measurement of the branch's net income for 2002, because it results from the branch's transactions' having been recorded in *euros,* the branch's local currency, rather than in *dollars,* the branch's functional currency.[7]

After the trial balance of the Mason Branch has been remeasured from euros to U.S. dollars, combined financial statements for home office and branch may be prepared as illustrated in Chapter 4, because the branch's functional currency is the U.S. dollar.

TRANSLATION OF A FOREIGN ENTITY'S FINANCIAL STATEMENTS

As indicated on page 520, if a foreign entity's financial statement amounts are expressed in a functional currency other than the U.S. dollar, those amounts must be translated to dollars (the U.S. reporting currency) by the current rate method. The following sections illustrate translation of the financial statements of a foreign influenced investee and a foreign subsidiary.

Translation of Financial Statements of Foreign Influenced Investee

To illustrate the translation of the financial statements of a foreign investee whose functional currency is its local currency, assume that on May 31, 2002, the end of a fiscal year, Colossus Company, a U.S. multinational company, acquired 30% of the outstanding common stock of a corporation in Venezuela, which is termed Venezuela Investee. Although the investment of Colossus enabled it to exercise influence (but not control) over the operations and financial policies of Venezuela Investee, that entity's functional currency was the bolivar (B). Colossus acquired its investment in Venezuela Investee for B600,000, which Colossus acquired at the selling spot rate of B1 = $0.25, for a total cost of $150,000. Out-of-pocket costs of the investment may be disregarded. Stockholders' equity of Venezuela Investee on May 31, 2002, was as follows:

Stockholders' Equity of Foreign Investee on Date of Investment		
Common stock	B	500,000
Additional paid-in capital		600,000
Retained earnings		900,000
Total stockholders' equity	B	2,000,000

[7] Ibid., par. 47.

There was no difference between the cost of Colossus Company's investment and its equity in the net assets of Venezuela Investee (B2,000,000 × 0.30 = B600,000, the cost of the investment).

The exchange rates for the bolivar were as follows:

Exchange Rates for Venezuelan Bolivar

May 31, 2002	$0.25
May 31, 2003	0.27
Average for year ended May 31, 2003	0.26

Translation of Venezuela Investee's financial statements from the functional currency to the U.S. dollar *reporting currency* for the fiscal year ended May 31, 2003, is illustrated below:

Working Paper for *Translation of Investee Financial Statements to U.S. Dollar Reporting Currency from Bolivar Functional Currency*

VENEZUELA INVESTEE
Translation of Financial Statements to U.S. Dollars
For Year Ended May 31, 2003

	Venezuelan Bolivars	Exchange Rates	U.S. Dollars
Income Statement			
Net sales	B6,000,000	$0.26 (1)	$1,560,000
Costs and expenses	4,000,000	0.26 (1)	1,040,000
Net income	B2,000,000		$ 520,000
Statement of Retained Earnings			
Retained earnings, beginning of year	B 900,000	0.25 (2)	$ 225,000
Add: Net income	2,000,000		520,000
Subtotals	B2,900,000		$ 745,000
Less: Dividends*	600,000	0.27 (3)	162,000
Retained earnings, end of year	B2,300,000		$ 583,000
Balance Sheet			
Assets			
Current assets	B 200,000	0.27 (3)	$ 54,000
Plant assets (net)	4,500,000	0.27 (3)	1,215,000
Other assets	300,000	0.27 (3)	81,000
Total assets	B5,000,000		$1,350,000
Liabilities and Stockholders' Equity			
Current liabilities	B 100,000	0.27 (3)	$ 27,000
Long-term debt	1,500,000	0.27 (3)	405,000
Common stock	500,000	0.25 (2)	125,000
Additional paid-in capital	600,000	0.25 (2)	150,000
Retained earnings	2,300,000		583,000
Foreign currency translation adjustments			60,000†
Total liabilities and stockholders' equity	B5,000,000		$1,350,000

* Dividends were declared on May 31, 2003
† Income tax effects are disregarded.
(1) Average rate for year ended May 31, 2003
(2) Historical rate (on May 31, 2002, date of Colossus Company's investment)
(3) Current rate (on May 31, 2003)

In a review of the translation of the foreign investee's financial statements illustrated on page 526, the following features may be emphasized:

1. All assets and liabilities are translated at the current rate.

2. The paid-in capital amounts and the beginning retained earnings are translated at the historical rate on the date of Colossus Company's acquisition of its investment in Venezuela Investee.

3. The average rate for the year ended May 31, 2003, is used to translate all revenue and expenses in the income statement.

4. A balancing amount labeled *foreign currency translation adjustments,* which is *not a ledger account,* is used to reconcile total liabilities and stockholders' equity with total assets in the translated balance sheet of Venezuela Investee. Foreign currency translation adjustments are displayed in the accumulated other comprehensive income section of the translated balance sheet.[8]

Following the translation of Venezuela Investee's financial statements from bolivars (the *functional currency* of Venezuela Investee) to U.S. dollars (the *reporting currency* of Colossus Company), on May 31, 2003, Colossus prepares the following journal entries in U.S. dollars under the equity method of accounting for an investment in common stock:

Investor Company's Journal Entries under Equity Method of Accounting

Investment in Venezuela Investee Common Stock ($520,000 × 0.30)	156,000	
Investment income		156,000
To record 30% of net income of Venezuela Investee. (Income tax effects are disregarded.)		
Investment in Venezuela Investee Common Stock ($60,000 × 0.30)	18,000	
Foreign Currency Translation Adjustments		18,000
To record 30% of other comprehensive income component of Venezuela Investee's stockholders' equity. (Income tax effects are disregarded.)		
Dividends Receivable ($162,000 × 0.30)	48,600	
Investment in Venezuela Investee Common Stock		48,600
To record dividends receivable from Venezuela Investee.		

After the foregoing journal entries are posted, the Investment ledger account of Colossus Company (in U.S. dollars) is as follows:

Investment Ledger Account of Investor

Investment in Venezuela Investee Common Stock

Date	Explanation	Debit	Credit	Balance
2002				
May 31	Acquisition of 30% of common stock	150,000		150,000 dr
2003				
May 31	Share of net income	156,000		306,000 dr
31	Share of other comprehensive income	18,000		324,000 dr
31	Share of dividends		48,600	275,400 dr

[8] Ibid., par. 13, as amended by *FASB Statement No. 130,* "Reporting Comprehensive Income" (Norwalk: FASB, 1997), par. 29.

The $275,400 balance of the Investment account is equal to Colossus Company's share of the total stockholders' equity, ***including foreign currency translation adjustments,*** in the translated balance sheet of Venezuela Investee [($125,000 + $150,000 + $583,000 + $60,000) × 0.30 = $275,400]. Foreign currency translation adjustments, which are not operating revenues, gains, expenses, or losses, do not enter into the measurement of the translated ***net income*** or dividends of Venezuela Investee; however, the investor's share of the translation adjustments is reflected in the investor's Investment ledger account as ***other comprehensive income.***[9] Foreign currency translation adjustments are displayed in accumulated other comprehensive income in the stockholders' equity section of Venezuela Investee's translated balance sheet until sale or liquidation of all or part of Colossus Company's investment in Venezuela Investee. At that time, the appropriate amount of the foreign currency translation adjustments is included in the measurement of the gain or loss on sale or liquidation of the investment in Venezuela Investee.[10]

Translation and Consolidation of Financial Statements of Foreign Subsidiary

To illustrate the translation and consolidation of financial statements of a foreign subsidiary whose functional currency is its local currency, assume that on August 31, 2002, the end of a fiscal year, SoPac Corporation, a U.S. enterprise with no other subsidiaries, acquired at the selling spot rate of $NZ1 = $0.52 a draft for 500,000 New Zealand dollars ($NZ), which it used to acquire all 10,000 authorized shares of $NZ50 par common stock of newly organized Anzac, Ltd., a New Zealand enterprise. The out-of-pocket costs of the acquisition were immaterial and thus recognized as expense by SoPac, which prepared the following journal entry for the investment:

Journal Entry for Investment in Foreign Subsidiary

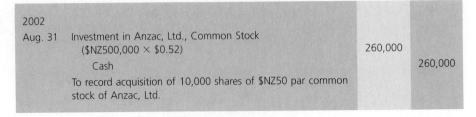

2002			
Aug. 31	Investment in Anzac, Ltd., Common Stock		
	($NZ500,000 × $0.52)	260,000	
	Cash		260,000
	To record acquisition of 10,000 shares of $NZ50 par common stock of Anzac, Ltd.		

Anzac, Ltd., was self-contained in New Zealand, where it conducted all its operations. Thus, the functional currency of Anzac was the New Zealand dollar. Further, to enhance Anzac's growth, the board of directors of SoPac decided that Anzac should pay no dividends to SoPac in the foreseeable future.

For the fiscal year ended August 31, 2003, Anzac prepared the following income statement and balance sheet (a statement of cash flows is disregarded):

[9] *FASB Statement No. 130,* par. 121.
[10] *FASB Statement No. 52,* par. 14; *FASB Interpretation No. 37,* "Accounting for Translation Adjustments upon Sale of Part of an Investment in a Foreign Entity" (Stamford: FASB, 1983), par. 2.

ANZAC, LTD.
Income Statement
For Year Ended August 31, 2003

Revenue:		
Net sales		$NZ240,000
Other		60,000
Total revenue		$NZ300,000
Costs and expenses:		
Cost of goods sold	$NZ180,000	
Operating expenses and income taxes expense	96,000	
Total costs and expenses		276,000
Net income (retained earnings, end of year)		$NZ 24,000

ANZAC, LTD.
Balance Sheet
August 31, 2003

Assets

Cash	$NZ 10,000
Trade accounts receivable (net)	40,000
Inventories	180,000
Short-term prepayments	4,000
Plant assets (net)	320,000
Intangible assets (net)	20,000
Total assets	$NZ574,000

Liabilities and Stockholder's Equity

Notes payable	$NZ 20,000
Trade accounts payable	30,000
Total liabilities	$NZ 50,000
Common stock, $NZ50 par	$NZ500,000
Retained earnings	24,000
Total stockholder's equity	$NZ524,000
Total liabilities and stockholder's equity	$NZ574,000

The exchange rates for the New Zealand dollar were as follows:

Aug. 31, 2002	$0.52
Aug. 31, 2003	0.50
Average for year ended Aug. 31, 2003	0.51

Translation of the financial statements of Anzac, Ltd., from the functional currency to the U.S. dollar *reporting currency* for the fiscal year ended August 31, 2003, is illustrated on page 530.

Working Paper for *Translation* of Subsidiary Financial Statements to U.S. Dollar Reporting Currency from New Zealand Dollar Functional Currency

ANZAC, LTD. Translation of Financial Statements to U.S. Dollars For Year Ended August 31, 2003			
	New Zealand Dollars	**Exchange Rate**	**U.S. Dollars**
Income Statement			
Net sales	$NZ240,000	$0.51 (1)	$122,400
Other revenue	60,000	0.51 (1)	30,600
Total revenue	$NZ300,000		$153,000
Cost of goods sold	$NZ180,000	0.51 (1)	$ 91,800
Operating expenses and income taxes expense	96,000	0.51 (1)	48,960
Total costs and expenses	$NZ276,000		$140,760
Net income (retained earnings, end of year)	$NZ 24,000		$ 12,240
Balance Sheet			
Cash	$NZ 10,000	0.50 (2)	$ 5,000
Trade accounts receivable (net)	40,000	0.50 (2)	20,000
Inventories	180,000	0.50 (2)	90,000
Short-term prepayments	4,000	0.50 (2)	2,000
Plant assets (net)	320,000	0.50 (2)	160,000
Intangible assets (net)	20,000	0.50 (2)	10,000
Total assets	$NZ574,000		$287,000
Notes payable	$NZ 20,000	0.50 (2)	$ 10,000
Trade accounts payable	30,000	0.50 (2)	15,000
Common stock	500,000	0.52 (3)	260,000
Retained earnings	24,000		12,240
Foreign currency translation adjustments			(10,240)*
Total liabilities and stockholder's equity	$NZ574,000		$287,000

* Income tax effects are disregarded.
(1) Average for year ended Aug. 31, 2003
(2) Current rate (on Aug. 31, 2003)
(3) Historical rate (on Aug. 31, 2002, date of SoPac Corporation's investment)

Following the translation of the financial statements of Anzac, Ltd., from New Zealand dollars (the functional currency of Anzac) to U.S. dollars (the reporting currency of SoPac Corporation), SoPac prepares the following journal entries in U.S. dollars under the equity method of accounting for an investment in common stock:

Parent Company's Journal Entry under Equity Method of Accounting

2003			
Aug. 31	Investment in Anzac, Ltd., Common Stock	12,240	
	Intercompany Investment Income		12,240
	To record 100% of net income of Anzac, Ltd. (Income tax effects are disregarded.)		
31	Foreign Currency Translation Adjustments	10,240	
	Investment in Anzac, Ltd. Common Stock		10,240
	To record 100% of other comprehensive income component of Anzac Ltd.'s stockholder's equity. (Income tax effects are disregarded.)		

After the foregoing journal entries are posted, the balance of SoPac's Investment in Anzac, Ltd., Common Stock ledger account is $262,000 ($260,000 + $12,240 − $10,240 = $262,000), which is equal to the total stockholder's equity of Anzac, Ltd., ***including foreign currency translation adjustments,*** in the translated balance sheet of Anzac ($260,000 + $12,240 − $10,240 = $262,000). SoPac is now enabled to prepare the following working paper elimination (in journal entry format) and working paper for consolidated financial statements, as well as the consolidated financial statements on pages 532 and 533 (other amounts for SoPac are assumed).

SOPAC CORPORATION AND SUBSIDIARY
Working Paper Elimination
August 31, 2003

(a) Common Stock—Anzac	260,000	
Intercompany Investment Income—SoPac	12,240	
Investment in Anzac, Ltd., Common Stock—SoPac		262,000
Foreign Currency Translation Adjustments—SoPac		10,240
To eliminate intercompany investment and equity accounts of subsidiary.		
(Income tax effects are disregarded.)		

Equity Method: Wholly Owned Subsidiary Subsequent to Date of Business Combination

SOPAC CORPORATION AND SUBSIDIARY
Working Paper for Consolidated Financial Statements
For Year Ended August 31, 2003

	SoPac Corporation	Anzac, Ltd.	Eliminations Increase (Decrease)	Consolidated
Income Statement				
Revenue:				
Net sales	840,000	122,400		962,400
Intercompany investment income	12,240		(a) (12,240)	
Other	120,000	30,600		150,600
Total revenue	972,240	153,000	(12,240)	1,113,000
Costs and expenses:				
Cost of goods sold	720,000	91,800		811,800
Operating expenses and income taxes expense	160,000	48,960		208,960
Total costs and expenses	880,000	140,760		1,020,760
Net income	92,240	12,240	(12,240)	92,240
Statement of Retained Earnings				
Retained earnings, beginning of year	480,000			480,000
Net income	92,240	12,240	(12,240)	92,240
Subtotal	572,240	12,240	(12,240)	572,240
Dividends declared	30,000			30,000
Retained earnings, end of year	542,240	12,240	(12,240)	542,240
Balance Sheet				
Assets				
Cash	80,000	5,000		85,000
Trade accounts receivable (net)	270,000	20,000		290,000
Inventories	340,000	90,000		430,000

(continued)

Equity Method: Wholly Owned Subsidiary Subsequent to Date of Business Combination

	SoPac Corporation	Anzac, Ltd.	Eliminations Increase (Decrease)	Consolidated
SOPAC CORPORATION AND SUBSIDIARY Working Paper for Consolidated Financial Statements (concluded) For Year Ended August 31, 2003				
Short-term prepayments	12,000	2,000		14,000
Investment in Anzac, Ltd., common stock	262,000		(a) (262,000)	
Plant assets (net)	618,000	160,000		778,000
Intangible assets (net)	80,000	10,000		90,000
Total assets	1,662,000	287,000	(262,000)	1,687,000
Liabilities and Stockholders' Equity				
Notes payable	50,000	10,000		60,000
Trade accounts payable	80,000	15,000		95,000
Long-term debt	400,000			400,000
Common stock	600,000	260,000	(a) (260,000)	600,000
Retained earnings	542,240	12,240	(12,240)	542,240
Foreign currency translation adjustments	(10,240)	(10,240)	(a) (10,240)*	(10,240)†
Total liabilities and stockholders' equity	1,662,000	287,000	(262,000)	1,687,000

* A **decrease** in foreign currency translation adjustments and an **increase** in equity.
† Income tax effects are disregarded.

SOPAC CORPORATION AND SUBSIDIARY
Consolidated Income Statement
For Year Ended August 31, 2003

Revenue:		
Net sales		$ 962,400
Other		150,600
Total revenue		$1,113,000
Costs and expenses:		
Cost of goods sold	$811,800	
Operating expenses and income taxes expense	208,960	
Total costs and expenses		1,020,760
Net income		$ 92,240
Basic earnings per share of common stock (60,000 shares outstanding)		$ 1.54

SOPAC CORPORATION AND SUBSIDIARY
Consolidated Statement of Comprehensive Income
For Year Ended August 31, 2003

Net income	$ 92,240
Other comprehensive income: Foreign currency translation adjustments (disregarding income tax effects)	(10,240)
Comprehensive income	$ 82,000

	SOPAC CORPORATION AND SUBSIDIARY			
	Consolidated Statement of Changes in Equity			
	For Year Ended August 31, 2003			

	Common Stock	Retained Earnings	Accumulated Other Comprehensive Income	Total
Balances, beginning of year	$600,000	$480,000		$1,080,000
Add: Net income		92,240		92,240
Other comprehensive income:				
Foreign currency translation adjustments			$(10,240)	(10,240)
Comprehensive income				$ 82,000
Dividends declared		(30,000)		(30,000)
Balances, end of year	$600,000	$542,240	$(10,240)	$1,132,000

SOPAC CORPORATION AND SUBSIDIARY
Consolidated Balance Sheet
August 31, 2003

Assets

Current assets:	
Cash	$ 85,000
Trade accounts receivable (net)	290,000
Inventories	430,000
Short-term prepayments	14,000
Total current assets	$ 819,000
Plant assets (net)	778,000
Intangible assets (net)	90,000
Total assets	$1,687,000

Liabilities and Stockholders' Equity

Current liabilities:		
Notes payable		$ 60,000
Trade accounts payable		95,000
Total current liabilities		$ 155,000
Long-term debt		400,000
Total liabilities		$ 555,000
Stockholders' equity:		
Common stock, $10 par	$600,000	
Retained earnings	542,240	
Accumulated other comprehensive income	(10,240)	
Total stockholders' equity		1,132,000
Total liabilities and stockholders' equity		$1,687,000

The foregoing consolidated financial statements are in the formats required by the FASB.[11]

[11] *FASB Statement No. 130,* pars. 14, 22, 23, 26.

Summary: Remeasurement and Translation

Principal features of the foregoing discussion of remeasurement of a foreign entity's accounts and translation of a foreign entity's financial statements are summarized in the following table:

Comparison of *Remeasurement* and *Translation*

Feature	Remeasurement	Translation
Underlying concept	Foreign entity's accounts should reflect transactions and events as though recorded in the **functional currency** rather than the **local currency.**	Foreign entity's financial statements should reflect financial results and relationships created in the economic environment of the foreign operations.
When required	(1) Foreign entity's accounts are maintained in the **local currency** instead of the **functional currency.** (2) Foreign entity is operating in a **highly inflationary economy** (see page 535).	Foreign entity's **functional currency** is not the **reporting currency.**
Method used	Monetary/nonmonetary method	Current rate method
Display of balancing amount	In income statement as transaction gain or loss	In balance sheet, stockholders' equity section, as part of accumulated other comprehensive income

Other Aspects of Foreign Currency Translation

In addition to the topics discussed thus far, the four topics described in the following sections are included in *FASB Statement No. 52.*

Transaction Gains and Losses Excluded from Net Income

The FASB required that gains and losses from the following foreign currency transactions be accounted for in the same manner as *foreign currency translation adjustments.*[12]

1. Foreign currency transactions that are designated as, and are effective as, economic hedges of a net investment in a foreign entity, commencing as of the designation date

2. Intercompany foreign currency transactions that are of a long-term investment nature (that is, settlement is not planned or anticipated in the foreseeable future), when the entities to the transaction are consolidated, combined, or accounted for by the equity method. . . .

---

[12] *FASB Statement No. 52*, par. 20, as reaffirmed by *FASB Statement No. 133,* "Accounting for Derivative Instruments and Hedging Activities" (Norwalk: FASB, 1998), pars. 42, 474–478, which deals also with forward contracts designated as a hedge of the net investment in a foreign operation.

To illustrate an economic hedge of a net investment in a foreign entity, return to the Venezuela Investee illustration on pages 526 to 527 and assume that, to hedge its investment, Colossus Company borrowed B1,020,000 from a Venezuela bank on May 31, 2003. B1,020,000 is equal to the carrying amount, in bolivars, of Colossus Company's investment on May 31, 2003 [(B500,000 + B600,000 + B2,300,000) × 0.30 = B1,020,000]. If the exchange rate for the bolivar was B1 = $0.28 on May 31, 2004, Colossus had a foreign currency transaction loss of $10,200 [B1,020,000 × ($0.28 − $0.27) = $10,200] during the fiscal year ended May 31, 2004, on the loan payable to the Venezuela bank. Disregarding income taxes, no part of the $10,200 transaction loss is recognized by Colossus if foreign currency translation adjustments in the May 31, 2004, translated balance sheet of Venezuela Investee are at least $70,200, which is a $10,200 increase ($70,200 − $60,000 = $10,200) over the May 31, 2003, balance. If however, foreign currency translation adjustments are less than $70,200 on May 31, 2004, Colossus Company recognizes an appropriate part of the transaction loss. For example, if foreign currency translation adjustments in the May 31, 2004, translated balance sheet are $64,500, Colossus prepares the following journal entry on May 31, 2004:

Investor Company's Journal Entry for Foreign Currency Transaction Loss on Hedging Loan

Foreign Currency Transaction Losses	5,700	
Loan Payable to Venezuela Bank		5,700
To recognize foreign currency transaction loss on loan obtained to hedge investment in Venezuela Investee as follows:		
Liability recorded on May 31, 2003 (B1,020,000 × $0.27) $275,400		
Less: Liability translated at May 31, 2004, spot rate		
B1 = $0.28 (B1,020,000 × $0.28) 285,600		
Difference $ (10,200)		
Less: Increase in foreign currency translation		
adjustments of investee ($64,500 − $60,000) 4,500		
Foreign currency transaction loss recognized $ (5,700)		

Functional Currency in Highly Inflationary Economies

The FASB required that the functional currency of a foreign entity in a highly inflationary economy be identified as the reporting currency (the U.S. dollar for a U.S. multinational enterprise). The FASB defined a ***highly inflationary economy*** as one having cumulative inflation of 100% or more over a three-year period.[13] Thus, financial statements of a foreign entity in a country experiencing severe inflation are remeasured in U.S. dollars, regardless of the criteria for determination of the functional currency described on pages 517 to 518.

Income Taxes Related to Foreign Currency Translation

Conventional interperiod and intraperiod income tax allocation procedures were prescribed by the FASB for the income tax effects of foreign currency translation, as follows:[14]

---

[13] Ibid., par. 11.
[14] Ibid., pars. 22–24.

1. Interperiod tax allocation for temporary differences associated with foreign currency transaction gains and losses that are reported in different accounting periods for financial accounting and income taxes. [Interperiod tax allocation is discussed in intermediate accounting textbooks.]

2. Interperiod tax allocation for temporary differences associated with foreign currency translation adjustments that do not meet the criteria for nonrecognition of deferred tax liabilities for undistributed earnings of foreign subsidiaries. (See Chapter 9, page 398.)

3. Intraperiod tax allocation for foreign currency translation adjustments included in the stockholders' equity section of the balance sheet. (Intraperiod tax allocation is discussed in intermediate accounting textbooks.)

Disclosure of Foreign Currency Translation

The FASB required disclosure, in the income statement or in a note to the financial statements, of the aggregate foreign currency transaction gains or losses of an accounting period. Further, as illustrated on page 533, the FASB required disclosure of changes in foreign currency translation adjustments (as well as other components of accumulated other comprehensive income) during an accounting period. The FASB also has specified additional disclosures for forward contracts or other financial instruments designated as hedges of the foreign currency exposure of a net investment in a foreign operation.[15]

International Accounting Standard 21

The provisions of *IAS 21,* "The Effects of Changes in Foreign Exchange Rates," dealing with translation of foreign currency financial statements are comparable with those of *FASB No. 52,* "Foreign Currency Translation." A difference is that *IAS 21* states a preference for applying price-level adjustments (a topic discussed in intermediate accounting textbooks and covered in *IAS 29,* "Financial Reporting in Hyperinflationary Economies") prior to the translation of financial statements of foreign entities operating in highly inflationary economies.

Appraisal of Accounting Standards for Foreign Currency Translation

FASB Statement No. 52 was approved by the FASB by a bare four-to-three majority, which indicates the degree of dissatisfaction with the standards it established for foreign currency translation. Among the criticisms of *FASB Statement No. 52* are the following:

1. It established an identifiable distinction between *transaction gains and losses* arising from *remeasurement* and *translation adjustments* resulting from *translation.* Both *remeasurement* and *translation* involve comparable activities—the restatement of amounts in a foreign currency to another currency—thus, they should be accounted for in the same manner.

2. It abandoned the historical-cost principle by sanctioning use of the current rate method for translation of foreign currency financial statements.

It appears that *FASB Statement No. 52* has been accepted by the business community. *FASB Statement No. 8,* "Accounting for the Translation of Foreign Currency

---

[15] Ibid., pars. 30–31; *FASB Statement No. 130,* par. 26; *FASB Statement No. 133,* par. 45c.

Transactions and Foreign Currency Financial Statements," which was superseded by *FASB Statement No. 52,* was in effect for little more than six years, during which time it was the subject of continuous controversy. *FASB Statement No. 8* was criticized for its requirements that translation adjustments be included in the measurement of net income and that the monetary/nonmonetary method be used to translate a foreign entity's financial statements.

Review Questions

1. What is the *functional currency* of a foreign entity?
2. Differentiate between the *current/noncurrent method* and the *current rate method* of translating foreign currency financial statements.
3. What exchange rate is used to remeasure to U.S. dollars (the functional currency) the balance of the Intercompany Accounts Payable ledger account of a foreign subsidiary of a U.S. parent company? Explain.
4. Differentiate *remeasurement to functional currency* from *foreign currency translation.*
5. Differentiate between *foreign currency transaction gains and losses* and *foreign currency translation adjustments.*
6. What *foreign currency transaction gains and losses* are excluded from the measurement of net income?
7. What is the functional currency of a foreign investee in a highly inflationary economy?
8. What disclosures relating to foreign currency matters are required in the financial statements or in a note to the financial statements of U.S. multinational enterprises?
9. What criticisms of *FASB Statement No. 52,* "Foreign Currency Translation," have been made?

Exercises

(Exercise 12.1) Select the best answer for each of the following multiple-choice questions:

1. The functional currency of a foreign subsidiary might be any of the following except the:
   a. Local currency.
   b. Reporting currency.
   c. Supplemental Drawing Rights of the International Monetary Fund.
   d. Currency in which the subsidiary maintains its accounting records.
2. If a foreign subsidiary of a U.S. multinational enterprise has a functional currency other than its local currency and the U.S. dollar, the subsidiary's financial statements must be:
   a. Remeasured to the U.S. dollar only.
   b. Translated to the U.S. dollar only.
   c. Remeasured to the functional currency and translated to the U.S. dollar.
   d. Translated to the functional currency and remeasured to the U.S. dollar.
3. Gains and losses resulting from remeasurement of foreign currency financial statements to the functional currency are displayed as a(n):

    a. Part of equity in the balance sheet.

    b. Extraordinary item in the income statement for the accounting period in which remeasurement takes place.

    c. Ordinary item in the income statement for losses but deferred for gains.

    d. Ordinary item in the income statement for the accounting period in which re-measurement takes place.

4. According to **FASB Statement No. 52,** "Foreign Currency Translation," remeasurement of a foreign subsidiary's accounting records to the subsidiary's functional currency should be accomplished by the:

    a. Monetary/nonmonetary method.

    b. Current rate method.

    c. Current/noncurrent method.

    d. Functional currency method.

5. The monetary/nonmonetary method of foreign currency translation currently is used for:

    a. Remeasurement but not for translation.

    b. Translation but not for remeasurement.

    c. Both remeasurement and translation.

    d. Neither remeasurement nor translation.

6. According to **FASB Statement No. 52,** "Foreign Currency Translation," the appropriate method of restatement from a foreign currency to the U.S. dollar for each of the following is:

	Remeasurement	*Translation*
a.	Current rate	Monetary/nonmonetary
b.	Monetary/nonmonetary	Current rate
c.	Monetary/nonmonetary	Monetary/nonmonetary
d.	Current rate	Current rate

7. Currently displayed in the **income** statement of a U.S. multinational enterprise are:

    a. Foreign currency transaction gains and losses only.

    b. Foreign currency translation adjustments only.

    c. Both foreign currency gains and losses and foreign currency translation adjustments.

    d. Neither foreign currency transaction gains and losses nor foreign currency translation adjustments.

8. With respect to a foreign subsidiary's financial statements, are foreign currency transaction gains and losses recognized in:

	Remeasurement from Local Currency to Functional Currency?	*Translation from Functional Currency to Reporting Currency?*
a.	Yes	Yes
b.	Yes	No
c.	No	Yes
d.	No	No

9. Do **foreign currency translation adjustments** result from:

	Remeasurement of a Branch's Trial Balance?	Translation of a Foreign Investee's Financial Statements?
a.	Yes	No
b.	No	Yes
c.	No	No
d.	Yes	Yes

10. Foreign currency translation adjustments arising from translation of the financial statements of a foreign subsidiary are currently reported in:

   a. Stockholders' equity of the foreign subsidiary.
   b. Revenue or expenses of the foreign subsidiary.
   c. Consolidated net income of the parent company and the foreign subsidiary.
   d. Paid-in capital of the parent company.

11. ***Foreign currency translation adjustments*** is a:

   a. Parent company ledger account.
   b. Foreign subsidiary ledger account.
   c. Balancing amount for translation.
   d. Balancing amount for remeasurement.

(Exercise 12.2)   Among the journal entries of the foreign branch of Logan Company for the month of April 2003 were the following, denominated in the local currency unit (LCU):

Apr. 4	Cash	LCU10,000	
	Home Office		LCU10,000
	To record receipt and conversion to LCU of $2,400 draft sent by the home office on Apr. 1, 2002.		
16	Home Office	LCU50,000	
	Cash		LCU50,000
	To record payment for equipment to be carried in the home office accounting records.		
28	Home Office	LCU4,000	
	Cash		LCU4,000
	To record dispatch of LCU4,000 draft to home office.		

Spot exchange rates for the LCU during April 2003 were as follows:

	LCU1 =	
	Buying	*Selling*
Apr. 1	$0.22	$0.24
4	0.23	0.25
16	0.21	0.22
28	0.23	0.24
30	0.22	0.23

The home office of Logan Company received and converted the LCU4,000 draft to U.S. dollars on April 30, 2003.

Prepare journal entries, denominated in U.S. dollars, for the home office of Logan Company to reflect appropriately the foregoing transactions and events of the foreign branch.

(Exercise 12.3) A wholly owned foreign subsidiary of Multiverse Company had selected expense accounts stated in local currency units (LCU) for the fiscal year ended November 30, 2003, as follows:

Doubtful accounts expense	LCU 60,000
Patent amortization expense (patent acquired Dec. 1, 2000)	40,000
Rent expense	100,000

The functional currency of the foreign subsidiary is the U.S. dollar. The exchange rates for the LCU for various dates or periods were as follows:

Dec. 1, 2002	$0.25
Nov. 30, 2003	0.20
Average for year ended Nov. 30, 2003	0.22

Prepare a working paper to compute the total dollar amount to be included in the remeasured income statement of Multiverse Company's foreign subsidiary for the year ended November 30, 2003, for the foregoing expense accounts.

(Exercise 12.4)

CHECK FIGURE

Depreciation expense for 2003, $216,720.

The foreign subsidiary of Paloma Company, a U.S. multinational enterprise, had plant assets on December 31, 2003, with a cost of 3,600,000 local currency units (LCU). Of this amount, plant assets with a cost of LCU2,400,000 were acquired in 2001, when the exchange rate was LCU1 = $0.625; and plant assets with a cost of LCU1,200,000 were acquired in 2002, when the exchange rate was LCU1 = $0.556. The exchange rate on December 31, 2003, was LCU1 = $0.500, and the weighted-average exchange rate for 2003 was LCU1 = $0.521. The foreign subsidiary depreciated plant assets by the straight-line method over a 10-year economic life with no residual value. The U.S. dollar was the functional currency of the foreign subsidiary.

Prepare a working paper to compute for 2003 the depreciation expense for Paloma Company's foreign subsidiary, in U.S. dollars, for the remeasured income statement.

(Exercise 12.5) Following is the euro-denominated trial balance of the French Branch of USA Corporation on June 30, 2002, the end of the first month of the branch's operations:

CHECK FIGURE

Foreign currency transaction gain, $12,150.

USA CORPORATION French Branch Trial Balance June 30, 2002		
Cash	€ 15,000	
Trade accounts receivable	250,000	
Inventories	115,000	
Home office		€360,000
Sales		450,000
Cost of goods sold	340,000	
Operating expenses	90,000	
Totals	€810,000	€810,000

Additional Information

1. All the merchandise in the branch's inventories on June 30, 2002, had been shipped by the home office on June 1, 2002, when the exchange rate was €1 = $1.05.
2. The balance of the home office's Investment in French Branch ledger account on June 30, 2002, was $365,000.
3. The exchange rate on June 30, 2002, was €1 = $1.04.

Prepare a working paper to remeasure the June 30, 2002, trial balance of French Branch of USA Corporation to U.S. dollars, the branch's functional currency. Round all remeasured amounts to the nearest dollar.

(Exercise 12.6) The trial balance of the German Branch of Global Company, a U.S. multinational enterprise, on April 30, 2002, the end of the first month of the branch's operations, was as follows [denominated in the euro (€)]:

GLOBAL COMPANY
German Branch Trial Balance
April 30, 2002

	Debit	Credit
Cash	€ 15,000	
Trade accounts receivable	260,000	
Inventories	120,000	
Home office		€280,000
Sales		550,000
Cost of goods sold	340,000	
Operating expenses	95,000	
Totals	€830,000	€830,000

The balance of Global Company's home office's Investment in German Branch ledger account on April 30, 2002, was $298,000. Relevant exchange rates for the euro were as follows:

	€1 =
April 1, 2002 (date of Global's home office's only shipment of merchandise to the branch)	$1.04
Apr. 30, 2002	1.06
Average for April 2002	1.05

Prepare a working paper to remeasure the April 30, 2002, trial balance of the German Branch of Global Company to U.S. dollars, its functional currency, from euros. Round all amounts to the nearest dollar. Use the following columns in your working paper:

Balance (€) dr (cr)	Exchange Rates	Balance ($) dr (cr)

(Exercise 12.7) The translated balance sheet items of Spanish Company, wholly owned foreign subsidiary of U.S. corporation, which owned all of Spanish's authorized common stock, were as follows on November 30, 2003:

Additional paid-in capital	$100,000
Common stock	50,000
Foreign currency translation adjustments (credit balance)	30,000
Current assets	180,000
Current liabilities	80,000
Long-term debt	120,000
Other assets	60,000
Plant assets (net)	260,000
Retained earnings	120,000

Prepare a balance sheet for Spanish Company on November 30, 2003.

(Exercise 12.8)   For the year ended December 31, 2002, its first year of operations after its establishment by its parent company, Stateside Corporation, wholly owned Overseas Company had the following financial statement amounts, denominated in its functional currency, the local currency unit (LCU):

Total revenue	LCU800,000
Total expenses	600,000
Total assets	900,000
Total liabilities	500,000
Stockholder's equity:	
Common stock, LCU1 par	200,000
Retained earnings (no dividends declared)	200,000

Exchange rates for the LCU were as follows:

Jan. 2, 2002 (date Overseas was established)	LCU1 = $0.44
Dec. 31, 2002	LCU1 = $0.48
Average for 2002	LCU1 = $0.46

Prepare a working paper to compute the foreign currency translation adjustments to be displayed in the translated balance sheet, stockholder's equity section, of Overseas Company on December 31, 2002.

(Exercise 12.9)   On December 31, 2003, Investor Corporation, a U.S. multinational enterprise, had a 20% influencing investment in the common stock of Foreign Investee Company, whose stockholders' equity totaled 1,500,000 local currency units (LCU), its functional currency, on that date. The translated balance sheet of Foreign Investee on December 31, 2003, included in stockholders' equity foreign currency translation adjustments of $47,600 (credit balance). On January 2, 2004, to hedge its net investment in Foreign Investee, Investor borrowed LCU300,000 when the exchange rate was LCU1 = $0.20, which was the same exchange rate in effect on December 31, 2003. On December 31, 2004, the exchange rate for the local currency unit was LCU1 = $0.24, and foreign currency translation adjustments in Foreign Investee's translated balance sheet amounted to $50,300 (credit balance).

Prepare a journal entry for Investor Corporation on December 31, 2004, to recognize the change in the exchange rate for the LCU from LCU1 = $0.20 on December 31, 2003, to LCU1 = $0.24 on December 31, 2004.

Cases

(Case 12.1)   Ostmark Company, a U.S. multinational enterprise, has a subsidiary in Austria. On April 1, 2003, Ostmark acquired for $550,000 a draft for 500,000 euros (€) and remitted it to the Austrian subsidiary as a long-term, noninterest-bearing advance. The advance was to be repaid ultimately in U.S. dollars. The euro is the functional currency of the subsidiary.

You were engaged as independent auditor for the audit of the March 31, 2004, consolidated financial statements of Ostmark Company and subsidiaries (including the Austrian subsidiary). On March 31, 2004, the selling spot rate for the euro was €1 = $1.05. Ostmark's controller translated the Payable to Ostmark Company liability in the Austrian subsidiary's balance sheet from €500,000 to $525,000 (€500,000 × $1.05 = $525,000). Because the $525,000 translated balance of the subsidiary's Payable to Ostmark Company liability did not offset the $550,000 balance of Ostmark's Receivable from Austrian Subsidiary ledger account on March 31, 2000, Ostmark's controller prepared the following working paper elimination (in journal entry format) on March 31, 2004:

Foreign Currency Translation Adjustments—Austrian Subsidiary	25,000	
Receivable from Austrian Subsidiary—Ostmark		25,000
To record translation adjustment resulting from decline in exchange rate for the euro to €1 = $1.05 on March 31, 2004, from €1 = $1.10 on April 1, 2003.		

Instructions
Evaluate the accounting treatment described above.

(Case 12.2)   Suppose that the following resolution were to be debated in your accounting class:

> RESOLVED, that *FASB No. 52,* "Foreign Currency Translation," established an indefensible distinction between transaction gains and losses arising from remeasurement and translation adjustments arising from translation.

Instructions
Which side—affirmative or negative—would you support in the debate? Explain.

(Case 12.3)   *FASB No. 52,* "Foreign Currency Translation," essentially gives to management of a U.S. multinational enterprise the responsibility for determining the functional currency of the enterprise's foreign branches, divisions, influenced investees, joint ventures, and subsidiaries, except for foreign entities that operate in highly inflationary economies, which must use the reporting currency as the functional currency.

Instructions
Given that remeasurement from a local currency to the functional currency produces foreign currency transaction gains and losses displayed in the enterprise's income statement, while translation from the functional currency to the reporting currency generates foreign currency translation adjustments currently displayed in the stockholders' equity section of the balance sheet, is there any incentive for management to determine that the local currency of a foreign entity is *not* its functional currency? Explain.

Problems

(Problem 12.1)

On March 1, 2002, Transcontinent Company, a U.S. multinational enterprise, established a branch in Mideastia, a foreign country. Transcontinent's home office sent cash and merchandise (billed at cost) to the Mideastia Branch only on March 1, 2002, and the branch made sales and incurred rent and other operating expenses in Mideastia during the month of March 2002. Transcontinent's home office maintained accounts in its ledger for the branch's plant assets. Because the Mideastia Branch's operations were an integral component of Transcontinent's home office's operations, the U.S. dollar was the functional currency of the Mideastia Branch; however, the branch maintained its accounting records in the local currency unit (LCU).

The trial balance of the Mideastia Branch on March 31, 2002, was as follows:

TRANSCONTINENT COMPANY Mideastia Branch Trial Balance March 31, 2002		
	Debit	*Credit*
Cash	LCU 2,000	
Trade accounts receivable	58,000	
Allowance for doubtful accounts		LCU 1,000
Inventories	126,000	
Home office		220,000
Sales		184,000
Cost of goods sold	160,000	
Operating expenses	59,000	
Totals	LCU405,000	LCU405,000

Relevant exchange rates for the Mideastia Branch's local currency unit were as follows:

Mar. 1, 2002	$0.60
Mar. 31, 2002	0.64
Average for March 2002	0.62

Instructions

Prepare a working paper to remeasure the March 31, 2002, trial balance of Mideastia Branch of Transcontinent Company to U.S. dollars, the branch's functional currency, from local currency units. The March 31, 2002, balance (before closing entries) of the Investment in Mideastia Branch ledger account in Transcontinent's home office's ledger was $132,000. Use the following headings for your working paper:

Account Title	*Balance (LCUs) dr (cr)*	*Exchange Rates*	*Balance (U.S. Dollars) dr (cr)*

(Problem 12.2)

The trial balance in local currency units (LCU) of Foreign Branch of Sarasota Company on April 30, 2002, the end of the branch's first month of operations, is as follows. The functional currency of Foreign Branch is the U.S. dollar.

SARASOTA COMPANY
Foreign Branch Trial Balance
April 30, 2002

	Balance dr (cr)
Cash	LCU 10,000
Trade accounts receivable	50,000
Inventories (1,600 units at first-in, first-out cost)	124,375
Home office	(104,565)
Sales (2,100 units at LCU133)	(279,300)
Cost of goods sold	152,289
Operating expenses	47,201
Total	LCU -0-

Additional Information

1. Foreign Branch sells a single product, which it acquires from the home office of Sarasota Company.
2. The Investment in Foreign Branch ledger account in the accounting records of the home office of Sarasota Company (prior to end-of-period adjusting and closing entries) is shown below:

Investment in Foreign Branch ($)

Date	Explanation	Debit	Credit	Balance
2002				
Apr. 1	Cash sent to branch	10,000		10,000 dr
1	1,000 units of merchandise shipped to branch × $80 a unit	80,000		90,000 dr
3	Equipment acquired by branch (recorded in Home Office accounting records)		5,500	84,500 dr
10	1,200 units of merchandise shipped to branch × $81 a unit	97,200		181,700 dr
20	1,500 units of merchandise shipped to branch × $82 a unit	123,000		304,700 dr
29	Cash received from branch		210,000	94,700 dr
30	Operating expenses billed to branch	25,000		119,700 dr

3. The Home Office ledger account in the accounting records of the Foreign Branch of Sarasota Company (prior to end-of-period closing entries) is shown on page 546:

Home Office (LCU)

Date	Explanation	Debit	Credit	Balance
2002				
Apr. 2	Cash received from home office		9,091	9,091 cr
2	1,000 units of merchandise received from home office × LCU72.73		72,730	81,821 cr
2	Equipment acquired by branch	5,000		76,821 cr
11	1,200 units of merchandise received from home office × LCU72.32		86,784	163,605 cr
21	1,500 units of merchandise received from home office × LCU78.10		117,150	280,755 cr
28	Cash sent to home office	200,000		80,755 cr
30	Operating expenses billed by home office		23,810	104,565 cr

4. Exchange rates for the local currency unit (LCU) of the country in which Foreign Branch operates were as follows during April 2002:

Apr. 1–Apr. 6	$1.10
Apr. 7–Apr. 18	1.12
Apr. 19–Apr. 30	1.05

Instructions

Prepare a working paper to remeasure the April 30, 2002, trial balance of Foreign Branch of Sarasota Company to U.S. dollars, its functional currency, from local currency units. Compute all exchange rates to the nearest cent.

(Problem 12.3)

CHECK FIGURE

Accumulated depreciation, Nov. 30, 2004, $16,010.

On December 1, 2002, the beginning of a fiscal year, Pan-Europe Corporation, a U.S. multinational enterprise, formed a foreign subsidiary, which issued all of its currently outstanding common stock to Pan-Europe on that date. Selected items from the subsidiary's trial balances, all of which are shown in local currency units (LCU), are as follows:

	Nov. 30, 2004	Nov. 30, 2003
Trade accounts receivable (net of allowance for doubtful accounts of LCU2,200 on Nov. 30, 2004, and LCU2,000 on Nov. 30, 2003)	LCU 40,000	LCU 35,000
Inventories, at first-in, first-out cost	80,000	75,000
Plant assets (net of accumulated depreciation of LCU31,000 on Nov. 30, 2004, and LCU14,000 on Nov. 30, 2003)	163,000	150,000
Long-term debt	100,000	120,000
Common stock, authorized 10,000 shares, LCU10 par; issued and outstanding 5,000 shares on Nov. 30, 2004, and Nov. 30, 2003	50,000	50,000

Additional Information

1. Relevant exchange rates were as follows:

Dec. 1, 2002–June 30, 2003	2LCU to $1
July 1, 2003–Sept. 30, 2003	1.8LCU to $1
Oct. 1, 2003–May 31, 2004	1.7LCU to $1
June 1, 2004–Nov. 30, 2004	1.5LCU to $1
Average monthly rate for year ended Nov. 30, 2003	1.9LCU to $1
Average monthly rate for year ended Nov. 30, 2004	1.6LCU to $1

2. Analysis of the trade accounts receivable (net) balances follows:

	Year Ended November 30,	
	2004	*2003*
Trade Accounts Receivable:		
Balances, beginning of year	LCU 37,000	
Sales (LCU36,000 a month in 2004 and		
LCU31,000 a month in 2003)	432,000	LCU 372,000
Collections	(423,600)	(334,000)
Write-offs (April 2004 and November 2003)	(3,200)	(1,000)
Balances, end of year	LCU 42,200	LCU 37,000
Allowance for Doubtful Accounts:		
Balances, beginning of year	LCU 2,000	
Doubtful accounts expense	3,400	LCU 3,000
Write-offs (April 2004 and November 2003)	(3,200)	(1,000)
Balances, end of year	LCU 2,200	LCU 2,000

3. An analysis of inventories, for which the first-in, first-out inventory method is used, follows:

	Year Ended November 30,	
	2004	*2003*
Inventories, beginning of year	LCU 75,000	
Purchases (May 2004 and May 2003)	335,000	LCU375,000
Goods available for sale	LCU410,000	LCU375,000
Inventories, end of year	80,000	75,000
Cost of goods sold	LCU330,000	LCU300,000

4. On December 1, 2002, Pan-Europe's foreign subsidiary acquired land for LCU24,000 and depreciable plant assets for LCU140,000. On June 4, 2004, additional depreciable plant assets were acquired for LCU30,000. Plant assets are being depreciated by the straight-line method over a 10-year economic life with no residual value. A full year's depreciation is taken in the year of acquisition of plant assets.

5. On December 15, 2002, 14% serial bonds with a face amount of LCU120,000 were issued. The bonds were to mature serially each year through December 15, 2008, and interest was payable semiannually on June 15 and December 15. The first principal payment was made on December 15, 2003.

Instructions

Prepare a working paper to remeasure the foregoing items to U.S. dollars, the functional currency of Pan-Europe Corporation's foreign subsidiary, on November 30, 2004, and November 30, 2003, respectively. Show supporting computations. Round all exchange rates to the nearest cent.

(Problem 12.4) On August 1, 2002, Westpac Corporation, a U.S. multinational enterprise, established a sales branch in Singapore. The transactions and events of Westpac's home office with the Singapore branch, and the branch's own transactions and events, during August 2002, are described below. Following each transaction or event is the appropriate spot exchange rate for the Singapore dollar (S$).

(1) Cash of $50,000 sent to branch (S$1 = $0.45).

(2) Merchandise with a cost of $75,000 shipped to branch at a billed price of $100,000 (S$1 = $0.45).

(3) Rent of leased premises for August paid by branch, S$1,000 (S$1 = $0.45).

(4) Store and office equipment acquired by branch for S$5,000, to be carried in home office accounting records (S$1 = $0.45).

(5) Sales by branch on credit, S$25,000 (S$1 = $0.46). Cost of goods sold, S$15,000.

(6) Collections of trade accounts receivable by branch, S$20,000 (S$1 = $0.455).

(7) Payment of operating expenses by branch, S$5,000 (S$1 = $0.47).

(8) Cash remitted to home office by branch, S$10,000 (S$1 = $0.44).

(9) Operating expenses incurred by home office charged to branch, $2,000 (S$1 = $0.445).

(10) Uncollectible account receivable written off by branch, S$1,000 (S$1 = $0.44).

Instructions

Prepare journal entries for the home office of Westpac Corporation in U.S. dollars, and for the Singapore branch in Singapore dollars, to record the foregoing transactions or events. Both home office and branch use the perpetual inventory system and the direct write-off method of accounting for uncollectible accounts. Round all amounts to the nearest dollar. Omit journal entry explanations.

(Problem 12.5) Portero Corporation, a U.S. multinational enterprise, combined with Sudamerica Company on January 2, 2002, by the acquisition at carrying amount of all of Sudamerica's outstanding common stock. Sudamerica is located in Nicaduras, whose monetary unit, the local currency of Sudamerica, is the peso ($N). Sudamerica's functional currency is the U.S. dollar. Sudamerica's accounting records were continued without change. A trial balance, in Nicaduran pesos, on January 2, 2002, follows:

CHECK FIGURE
Foreign currency
transaction loss, $13,720.

SUDAMERICA COMPANY
Trial Balance (Nicaduran Pesos)
January 2, 2002

	Debit	Credit
Cash	$N 3,000	
Trade accounts receivable	5,000	
Inventories (first-in, first-out cost)	32,000	
Plant assets	204,000	
Accumulated depreciation of plant assets		$N 42,000
Trade accounts payable		81,400
Common stock		50,000
Retained earnings		70,600
Totals	$N244,000	$N244,000

Sudamerica's trial balance, in Nicaduran pesos, on December 31, 2003, follows:

SUDAMERICA COMPANY
Trial Balance (Nicaduran Pesos)
December 31, 2003

	Debit	Credit
Cash	$N 25,000	
Trade accounts receivable	20,000	
Allowance for doubtful accounts		$N 500
Receivable from Portero Corporation	33,000	
Inventories (first-in, first-out cost)	110,000	
Plant assets	210,000	
Accumulated depreciation of plant assets		79,900
Notes payable		60,000
Trade accounts payable		22,000
Income taxes payable		40,000
Common stock		50,000
Retained earnings		100,600
Sales—local		170,000
Sales—foreign		200,000
Cost of goods sold	207,600	
Depreciation expense	22,400	
Other operating expenses	60,000	
Income taxes expense	40,000	
Gain on disposal of plant assets		5,000
Totals	$N728,000	$N728,000

Additional Information

1. All of Sudamerica's foreign sales are made to Portero and are accumulated in the Sales—Foreign ledger account. The balance of the Receivable from Portero Corporation account (a current asset) is the total of unpaid invoices. All foreign sales are billed in U.S. dollars. The reciprocal accounts in Portero's accounting records show total Year 2003 purchases as $471,000 and the total of unpaid invoices as

$70,500 (before end-of-period adjusting entries). Portero remits pesos to pay for the purchases.

2. Depreciation is computed by the straight-line method over a 10-year economic life with no residual value for all depreciable assets. Machinery costing $N20,000 was acquired by Sudamerica on December 31, 2002, and no depreciation was recorded for this machinery in 2002. There have been no other depreciable plant assets acquired since January 2, 2002, and no assets are fully depreciated.

3. No journal entries have been made in the Retained Earnings ledger account of Sudamerica since its acquisition other than the net income for 2002.

4. The exchange rates for the Nicaduran peso follow:

Jan. 2, 2002	$2.00
Year 2002 average	2.10
Dec. 31, 2002	2.20
Year 2003 average	2.30
Dec. 31, 2003	2.40

Instructions

Prepare a working paper to remeasure the trial balance of Sudamerica Company for the year ended December 31, 2003, from Nicaduran pesos to U.S. dollars, Sudamerica's functional currency. The working paper should show the trial balance amounts in pesos, the exchange rates, and the amounts in dollars.

(Problem 12.6)

CHECK FIGURE

b. Foreign currency transaction gain, $20,113.

Hightower Company, a U.S. multinational enterprise, established a branch in Brazentina in 1995. The branch carried its accounting records in the Brazentina peso (BP), although its functional currency was the U.S. dollar.

You were engaged to audit Hightower's combined financial statements for the year ended December 31, 2002. You retained a licensed professional accounting firm in Brazentina to audit the branch accounts. The firm reported that the branch accounts were fairly stated in pesos, except that a Brazentina franchise fee and any possible adjustments required by home office accounting procedures were not recorded. Trial balances for the home office and branch office of Hightower Company on December 31, 2002, are on page 551.

Additional Information

1. The Brazentina peso was devalued July 1, 2002, from BP1 = $0.25 to BP1 = $0.20. The former exchange rate had been in effect since 1994.

2. Included in the balance of the home office's Investment in Brazentina Branch ledger account was a $4,000 billing for merchandise shipped during 2002. The branch did not receive the shipment during 2002. Home office sales to the branch are marked up $33\frac{1}{3}$% on home office cost and shipped FOB home office. Branch sales to home office are made at branch cost. There were no seasonal fluctuations in branch sales to outsiders during the year.

3. The branch had beginning and ending inventories valued at first-in, first-out cost of BP80,000 [exclusive of the amount in (2), above], of which one-half on each date had been acquired from the home office. The home office had December 31, 2002, inventories valued at first-in, first-out cost of $520,000.

HIGHTOWER COMPANY
Home Office and Branch
Trial Balances
December 31, 2002

	Home Office (U.S. Dollars) dr (cr)	Branch (Brazentina Pesos) dr (cr)
Cash	$ 90,000	BP 110,000
Trade accounts receivable (net)	160,000	150,000
Inventories, beginning of year	510,000	80,000
Short-term prepayments	18,000	
Investment in Brazentina Branch	10,000	
Branch market research	12,000	
Plant assets	750,000	1,000,000
Accumulated depreciation of plant assets	(350,000)	(650,000)
Current liabilities	(240,000)	(220,000)
Long-term debt	(200,000)	(230,000)
Home office		(30,000)
Common stock	(300,000)	
Retained earnings	(145,000)	
Sales	(4,035,000)	(1,680,000)
Intracompany sales	(160,000)	
Purchases	3,010,000	1,180,000
Intracompany purchases	140,000	
Depreciation expense	50,000	100,000
Other operating expenses and income		
taxes expense	680,000	190,000
Totals	$ -0-	BP -0-

4. The Branch Market Research ledger account balance is the unamortized portion of a $15,000 fee paid by the home office in January 2000 to a U.S. firm for market research for the branch. Currency restrictions prevented the branch from paying the fee. The home office agreed to accept merchandise from the branch over a five-year period, during which the market research fee was to be amortized.

5. There were no changes in the branch's plant assets during 2002.

6. The government of Brazentina imposes a franchise fee of 10 pesos per 100 pesos of income before franchise fee of the branch, in exchange for certain exclusive trading rights granted to the branch. The fee is payable each May 1 for the preceding calendar year's trading rights; it had not been recorded by the branch on December 31, 2002.

Instructions

a. Prepare journal entries on December 31, 2002, to correct the accounting records of:

(1) The home office of Hightower Company

(2) The Brazentina branch of Hightower Company

b. Prepare a working paper to combine the financial statements of Hightower Company's home office and Brazentina branch for year 2002, with all amounts stated in U.S. dollars. Formal combined financial statements are not required. Do not prepare formal combination eliminations; instead, explain the eliminations, including supporting computations, at the bottom of the working paper. Disregard income taxes. Assume that the branch purchases occurred evenly throughout 2002.

The following column headings are suggested for the working paper:

> Home Office Adjusted Trial Balance—dr (cr)
> Branch Adjusted Trial Balance:
>   In Brazentina Pesos—dr (cr)
>   Exchange Rates (remeasurement)
>   In Dollars—dr (cr)
> Eliminations—dr (cr)
> Home Office and Branch Combined—dr (cr)

(Problem 12.7)

CHECK FIGURE

a. Foreign currency translation adjustments, $5,000 debit.

The financial statements of Eagle Corporation, a U.S. multinational enterprise, and its wholly owned Canadian subsidiary, Mapleleaf Company, at the end of the first year following Eagle's establishment of Mapleleaf, were as follows ($C is the symbol for the Canadian dollar, the functional currency of Mapleleaf):

EAGLE CORPORATION AND MAPLELEAF COMPANY
Separate Financial Statements
For Year Ended December 31, 2002

	Eagle Corporation	Mapleleaf Company
Income Statements		
Total revenue	$1,200,000	$C800,000
Total costs and expenses	900,000	700,000
Net income	$ 300,000	$C100,000
Statements of Retained Earnings		
Retained earnings, beginning of year	$ 500,000	
Net income	300,000	$C100,000
Subtotal	$ 800,000	$C100,000
Dividends declared	200,000	
Retained earnings, end of year	$ 600,000	$C100,000
Balance Sheets		
Assets		
Current assets	$ 700,000	$C400,000
Investment in Mapleleaf Company common stock	160,000	
Plant assets (net)	1,600,000	500,000
Intangible assets (net)	240,000	
Total assets	$2,700,000	$C900,000
Liabilities and Stockholders' Equity		
Current liabilities	$ 400,000	$C200,000
Long-term debt	500,000	400,000
Common stock	1,200,000	200,000
Retained earnings	600,000	100,000
Total liabilities and stockholders' equity	$2,700,000	$C900,000

Exchange rates for the Canadian dollar were as follows during 2002:

	$C1 =
Jan. 2, 2002 (date Mapleleaf Company was established)	$0.80
Dec. 31, 2002	0.78
Average for 2002	0.79

Instructions

a. Prepare a working paper to translate the financial statements of Mapleleaf Company for the year ended December 31, 2002, from Canadian dollars, its functional currency, to U.S. dollars, the reporting currency.

b. Prepare journal entries for Eagle Corporation on December 31, 2002, to account for its investment in Mapleleaf Company under the equity method of accounting. (Disregard income taxes.)

c. Prepare a working paper for consolidated financial statements of Eagle Corporation and subsidiary on December 31, 2002, and a related working paper elimination (in journal entry format). (Disregard income taxes.)

(Problem 12.8)

Separate financial statements of Panamer Corporation, a U.S. multinational enterprise, and its two subsidiaries for the year ended December 31, 2003, are as follows (IN is the symbol for the Itican peso):

PANAMER CORPORATION AND SUBSIDIARIES
Separate Financial Statements
For Year Ended December 31, 2003

	Panamer Corporation (Dollars)	U.S. Subsidiary (Dollars)	Itican Subsidiary (Pesos)
Income Statements			
Revenue:			
Sales	$400,000	$21,000	IN381,000
Intercompany sales to U.S. Subsidiary	10,000		
Total revenue	$410,000	$21,000	IN381,000
Costs and expenses:			
Cost of goods sold	$300,000	$15,000	IN300,000
Intercompany cost of goods sold	7,500		
Depreciation expense	3,000	550	17,500
Selling expenses	34,500	2,400	16,500
Other operating expenses	40,000	1,383	23,667
Income taxes expense	10,000	667	9,333
Total costs and expenses	$395,000	$20,000	IN367,000
Net income	$ 15,000	$ 1,000	IN 14,000
Statements of Retained Earnings			
Retained earnings, beginning of year	$ 25,000	$ 2,000	IN 7,000
Net income	15,000	1,000	14,000
Subtotals	$ 40,000	$ 3,000	IN 21,000
Dividends declared		1,000	
Retained earnings, end of year	$ 40,000	$ 2,000	IN 21,000

(continued)

PANAMER CORPORATION AND SUBSIDIARIES **Separate Financial Statements (concluded)** **For Year Ended December 31, 2003**			
	Panamer Corporation (Dollars)	*U.S. Subsidiary (Dollars)*	*Itican Subsidiary (Pesos)*
Balance Sheets			
Assets			
Cash	$ 10,000	$ 1,500	IN 10,000
Trade accounts receivable (net)	30,000	8,000	35,000
Intercompany receivables (payables)	4,000	(900)	
Inventories	20,000		83,000
Investment in U.S. Subsidiary common stock	9,000		
Investment in Itican Subsidiary common stock	12,000		
Plant assets	45,000	5,500	175,000
Accumulated depreciation of plant assets	(15,000)	(2,000)	(75,000)
Total assets	$115,000	$12,100	IN228,000
Liabilities and Stockholders' Equity			
Trade accounts payable	$ 25,000		IN 7,000
Dividends payable		$ 100	
Long-term debt			100,000
Common stock, 1,000 shares	50,000	10,000	100,000
Retained earnings	40,000	2,000	21,000
Total liabilities and stockholders' equity	$115,000	$12,100	IN228,000

Additional Information

1. On December 31, 2002, Panamer had acquired 900 of the 1,000 outstanding shares of common stock of U.S. Subsidiary for $9,000, and all 1,000 shares of the outstanding common stock of Itican Subsidiary for $12,000. The identifiable net assets of both combinees were fairly valued at their carrying amounts on December 31, 2002. Panamer adopted the equity method of accounting for its investments in both subsidiaries.

2. Both of Panamer's subsidiaries depreciate plant assets by the straight-line method over 10-year economic lives, with no residual values. None of the subsidiaries' plant assets was fully depreciated on December 31, 2002, or on December 31, 2003. There were no additions to or retirements of Itican Subsidiary's plant assets during 2003.

3. On December 31, 2003, Panamer shipped merchandise billed at $4,000 to U.S. Subsidiary. There were no intercompany sales to Itican Subsidiary.

4. On December 18, 2003, U.S. Subsidiary declared a dividend of $1 a share, payable January 16, 2004, to stockholders of record January 10, 2004.

5. Relevant exchange rates for the Itican peso, which is the functional currency of Itican Subsidiary, were as follows:

Dec. 31, 2002, through Mar. 31, 2003	$0.12
Apr. 1, 2003, through Dec. 31, 2003	0.08

Instructions

a. Prepare a working paper to translate Itican Subsidiary's financial statements for the year ended December 31, 2003, from Itican pesos, its functional currency, to U.S. dollars. Use weighted-average exchange rates where appropriate.

b. Prepare correcting entries for Panamer Corporation and for U.S. Subsidiary on December 31, 2003.

c. Prepare a working paper for consolidated financial statements and working paper eliminations (in journal entry format) for Panamer Corporation and subsidiaries on December 31, 2003. The working papers should reflect the translated balances in *a* and the adjustments in *b*. (Disregard income taxes.)

Chapter Thirteen

Segments; Interim Reports; Reporting for the SEC

Scope of Chapter

This chapter deals with three topics that have received considerable attention from accountants. Reporting for segments of a business enterprise and interim reports have been the subjects of pronouncements of the Financial Accounting Standards Board, the American Institute of Certified Public Accountants, and the Securities and Exchange Commission (SEC). In addition, the specialized requirements of accounting and reporting for the SEC by enterprises subject to its jurisdiction have undergone substantial modifications in recent years. All three topics are of considerable significance for accountants who deal with publicly owned corporations.

SEGMENT REPORTING

The Accounting Principles Board defined a **business segment** as "a component of an entity whose activities represent a separate major line of business or class of customer."[1] The wave of **conglomerate** business combinations in past years, involving companies in different industries or markets, led to consideration of appropriate methods for reporting **disaggregated** financial data for business segments. Financial analysts and others interested in comparing one diversified business enterprise with another found that consolidated financial statements did not supply enough information for meaningful comparative statistics regarding operations of the diversified enterprises in specific industries.

Background of Segment Reporting

The FASB has traced the history of segment reporting from the start of hearings in 1964 before the U.S. Senate Judiciary Committee's Subcommittee on Antitrust and Monopoly. The Subcommittee was considering economic concentration in

[1] *APB Opinion No. 30,* "Reporting the Results of Operations . . ." (New York: AICPA, 1973), par. 13.

American industry, especially in the so-called conglomerate (diversified) business enterprises.

Out of these hearings came discussions and debate among academicians, members of Congress, SEC officials, financial analysts, business executives, and AICPA representatives regarding the propriety of disaggregated financial reporting for segments of a business enterprise. The concept of segment reporting was controversial because it was opposed to the philosophy that consolidated financial statements, rather than separate financial statements, fairly present the financial position and operating results of an economic entity, regardless of the legal or business-segment structure of the entity.

In 1976, the FASB issued *FASB Statement No. 14,* "Financial Reporting for Segments of a Business Enterprise." Defining an *industry segment* as "a component of an enterprise engaged in providing a product or service or a group of related products and services primarily to unaffiliated customers (i.e., customers outside the enterprise) for a profit,"[2] the FASB required business enterprises having industry segments to disclose certain information regarding their operations in different industries, their foreign operations and export sales, and their major customers. Comparable information was required to be disclosed for an enterprise's operations in individual foreign countries or groups of countries, its export sales, and its major customers. Both maximum and minimum limitations were placed on the number of segments or foreign areas for which the information was to be provided, and enterprise management was given considerable latitude in identifying enterprise industry segments and allocating nontraceable expenses to segments, and in the method of disclosure of the required information; that is, within the enterprise's financial statements, in the notes to the financial statements, or in a separate exhibit.

Proposal to Improve Segment Reporting

In 1994, the AICPA's Special Committee on Financial Reporting issued a report that addressed concerns about the relevance and usefulness of business enterprise reporting. Among the committee's recommendations for improvements in disclosures of business segment information were the following:

> Segment reporting should be improved by better aligning the information in business reporting with the segment information that companies report internally to senior management or the board [of directors].
>
> *****
>
> [W]hen reporting about each segment, companies should avoid arbitrary allocations made solely for purposes of business reporting. Instead, companies should report information in the same way they determine it for internal reporting and disclose the methods used. Companies also should disclose more detailed financial information about each investment in, or affiliation with, an unconsolidated entity that is individually significant.[3]

Reacting to the foregoing, in 1997 the FASB issued *Statement No. 131,* "Disclosures about Segments of an Enterprise and Related Information." Adopting the

---

[2] *FASB Statement No. 14,* "Financial Reporting for Segments of a Business Enterprise" (Stamford: FASB, 1976), par. 10a.
[3] The AICPA Special Committee on Financial Reporting, *Improving Business Reporting—A Customer Focus,* AICPA (New York: 1994), pp. 11–12.

management approach to segment reporting, which requires segmentation of business activities based on the way a business enterprise is managed, the FASB replaced the term *industry segment* as used in *FASB Statement No. 14* with the term *operating segment,* determined as follows:

An *operating segment* is a component of an enterprise:

(a) That engages in business activities from which it may earn revenues and incur expenses (including revenues and expenses relating to transactions with other components of the same enterprise),

(b) Whose operating results are regularly reviewed by the enterprise's chief operating decision maker to make decisions about resources to be allocated to the segment and assess its performance, and

(c) For which discrete financial information is available.[4]

For *reportable* operating segments of a business enterprise as specified by the FASB, it mandated several disclosures, including the following:

(1) Factors used to identify reportable segments

(2) Types of products and services from which each reportable segment derives its revenue

(3) Segment profit or loss and segment total assets, as measured by the internal financial reporting system

(4) Selected components of revenues and expenses included in the measurement of reportable segment profit or loss, such as interest revenue and interest expense

(5) Reconciliation of total reportable segments' profit or loss to the enterprise's pre-tax income from continuing operations

(6) Explanation of how segment profit or loss is measured

(7) Reconciliation of total of reportable segments' assets to total assets

(8) Investments in influenced investees included in segment assets

(9) Total expenditures for additions to long-lived segment assets

(10) In certain cases, selected information about reportable segments that operate in more than one country

(11) Information about the enterprise's reliance on major customers: those who provide 10 percent or more of the enterprise's total revenues.[5]

In addition to the foregoing information required to be provided in annual financial reports, the FASB required selected comparable information to be disclosed in interim reports to an enterprise's shareholders.[6] Interim reports are discussed in another section of this chapter (pages 565 to 574).

It is clear from a comparison of the foregoing with the disclosures required under *FASB Statement No. 14* (see page 557) that, under *FASB Statement No. 131,* enterprise managements will have a great deal of flexibility in complying with the requirements thereof, which will provide far more information to users of financial reports than was required by *FASB Statement No. 14.*

Following are examples of disclosures required by the FASB for reportable segment profit or loss and components thereof; segment assets and liabilities; and reconciliations of segment totals to pre-tax income from continuing operations and to consolidated total assets and total liabilities.

---

[4] *FASB Statement No. 131*, "Disclosures about Segments of an Enterprise and Related Information" (Norwalk: FASB, 1997), par. 10.

[5] Ibid., pars. 26–39.

[6] Ibid., par. 33.

VARIEGATED COMPANY
Information about Segment Profit or Loss and Segment Assets and Liabilities
For Year Ended March 31, 2003
(amounts in thousands)

	Operating Segment		
	No. 1	**No. 2**	**Total**
Revenues from external customers	$8,100	$7,400	$15,500
Intersegment revenues	100	200	300
Segment profit	200	1,300	1,500
Interest expense	400	300	700
Depreciation and amortization expense	1,800	900	2,700
Income taxes expense	300	800	1,100
Segment assets	9,600	8,400	18,000
Additions to plant and intangible assets	700	400	1,100

VARIEGATED COMPANY
Reconciliation of Operating Segment Totals to Consolidated Totals
For Year Ended March 31, 2003
(amounts in thousands)

	Revenues	**Profit**	**Assets**
Segment totals	$15,800	$1,500	$18,000
Elimination of intersegment items	(400)	(200)	(2,000)
Unallocated expenses		(300)	
Consolidated amounts	$15,400	$1,000*	$16,000

* Pretax income from continuing operations.

The financial statements of The McGraw-Hill Companies, Inc., in Appendix 1 to this chapter, illustrate the first of the foregoing methods of disclosure of segment information under *FASB Statement No. 131.* The segment information is included in Note 4 on pages 587 through 588.

Allocation of Nontraceable Expenses to Operating Segments

The FASB required a ***reasonable basis*** for allocations such as nontraceable expenses— those enterprise expenses not identifiable with operations of a specific operating segment—to those segments in the measurement of reportable segment profit or loss.[7] Accordingly, enterprise management must devise an appropriate method for apportioning nontraceable expenses to the operating segments. Methods that have been used for such allocations include ratios based on operating segment revenues, payroll totals, average plant assets and inventories, or a combination thereof. For example, assume the following data for Multiproduct Corporation:

[7] Ibid., par. 29.

Data for Company and Its Two Operating Segments

| | | Operating Segments | | |
	Company	Chemical Products	Food Products	Total
(1) Net sales (operating segment revenues)		$550,000	$ 450,000	$1,000,000
Traceable expenses		$300,000	$ 350,000	$ 650,000
Nontraceable expenses	$200,000			200,000
Total expenses	$200,000	$300,000	$ 350,000	$ 850,000
Income before income taxes				$ 150,000
Income taxes expense				60,000
Net income				$ 90,000
(2) Payroll totals	$ 60,000	$160,000	$ 240,000	$ 460,000
(3) Average plant assets and inventories	$ 80,000	$620,000	$1,380,000	$2,080,000

Computation of a ratio for allocating nontraceable expenses to operating segments based on the three factors described on page 559 is as follows:

Computations of Three-Factor Ratio

	Chemical Products	Food Products
(1) Ratio of operating segment revenue	$\dfrac{\$\ 550,000}{\$1,000,000} = 55\%$	$\dfrac{\$\ 450,000}{\$1,000,000} = 45\%$
(2) Ratio of segment payroll totals	$\dfrac{\$\ 160,000}{\$\ 400,000} = 40\%$	$\dfrac{\$\ 240,000}{\$\ 400,000} = 60\%$
(3) Ratio of average plant assets and inventories	$\dfrac{\$\ 620,000}{\$2,000,000} = 31\%$	$\dfrac{\$1,380,000}{\$2,000,000} = 69\%$
Totals	126%	174%
Arithmetic averages (divide by 3)	42%	58%

The $200,000 amount of nontraceable expenses of the home office of Multiproduct Corporation is allocated to the two operating segments as follows:

Allocation of Nontraceable Expenses

To Chemical Products segment ($200,000 × 0.42)	$ 84,000
To Food Products segment ($200,000 × 0.58)	116,000
Total nontraceable expenses	$200,000

Segment profit (loss) for the two operating segments of Multiproduct Corporation is computed as follows:

Segment Profit (Loss) of Two Operating Segments

	Chemical Products	Food Products	Total
Net sales	$550,000	$450,000	$1,000,000
Traceable expenses	$300,000	$350,000	$ 650,000
Nontraceable expenses	84,000	116,000	200,000
Total expenses	$384,000	$466,000	$ 850,000
Segment profit (loss)	$166,000	$ (16,000)	$ 150,000

SEC Requirements for Segment Information

The requirements of the Securities and Exchange Commission for reporting of segment information are in ***Regulation S-K,*** which outlines nonfinancial statement information that must be included in reports to the SEC. The SEC disclosure requirements for operating segments, in addition to the requirements of the FASB, are as follows:[8]

1. Amount or percentage of total revenue contributed by any ***class of product or services*** that accounted for 10% or more of total revenue during the past three years.

2. The ***name*** of a major customer (see page 558), together with its relationship to the reporting enterprise, ***if loss of the customer would have a material adverse effect on the enterprise.***

3. Information about foreign operations or export sales that are ***expected to be material in the future.***

Regulation S-K is discussed in a subsequent section of this chapter.

Reporting the Disposal of a Business Segment

To this point, accounting standards developed by the FASB for financial reporting for ***existing*** operating segments have been discussed. The consideration of segment reporting is concluded with the reporting for effects of the ***disposal*** of a business segment.

In 1973, the Accounting Principles Board issued ***APB Opinion No. 30,*** "Reporting the Results of Operations. . . ." The APB's conclusions included the following with respect to disposal of a business segment.

> For purposes of this Opinion, the term ***discontinued operations*** refers to the operations of a segment of a business . . . that has been sold, abandoned, spun off, or otherwise disposed of or, although still operating, is the subject of a formal plan for disposal. . . . The Board concludes that the results of continuing operations should be reported separately from discontinued operations and that any gain or loss from disposal of a segment of a business . . . should be reported in conjunction with the related results of discontinued operations and not as an extraordinary item. Accordingly, operations of a segment that has been or will be discontinued should be reported separately as a component of income before extraordinary items and the cumulative effect of accounting changes (if applicable) in the following manner:

Income from continuing operations before income taxes	$XXXX	
Provision for income taxes	XXX	
Income from continuing operations		$XXXX
Discontinued operations (Note _____)		
Income (loss) from operations of discontinued Division X		
(less applicable income taxes of $_____)	$XXXX	
Loss on disposal of Division X, including provision of		
$_____ for operating losses during phase-out period		
(less applicable income taxes of $_____)	XXXX	XXXX*
Net income		$XXXX

[8] *Codification of Financial Reporting Policies,* Securities and Exchange Commission (Washington: 1982), Sec. 503.02.

* In August, 2001, the Financial Accounting Standards Board Issued ***FASB Statement 144,*** "Accounting for the Impairment or Disposal of Long-Lived Assets," in which it required only this total (or net) amount to be disclosed for discontinued operations, effective for fiscal years beginning after December 15, 2001.

Amounts of income taxes applicable to the results of discontinued operations and the gain or loss from disposal of the segment should be disclosed on the face of the income statement or in related notes. Revenues applicable to the discontinued operations should be separately disclosed in the related notes.[9]

The provisions of *ABP Opinion No. 30* are discussed in the following sections.

Income from Continuing Operations

The purpose of the income from continuing operations amount is to provide a basis of comparison in the comparative income statements of a business enterprise that has discontinued a business segment. In order for the income from continuing operations amounts to be comparable, the operating results of the discontinued segment of the enterprise *must be excluded from income from continuing operations for all accounting periods presented in comparative income statements.* For example, in comparative income statements for the three years ended December 31, 2004, for Wexler Company, a diversified enterprise with five operating segments, which disposed of one of the segments during 2004, the income from continuing operations amounts for 2002 and 2003, as well as for 2004, exclude the operating results of the discontinued segment.

Income (Loss) from Discontinued Operations

The income or loss, net of applicable income taxes, of Wexler Company's discontinued operations (business segment) is included in its entirety in this section of Wexler's income statement for 2002 and 2003. For 2004, the net-of-tax income or loss of the discontinued operations is for the period from January 1, 2001, until the *measurement date,* defined as the date on which management of Wexler committed itself to a formal plan for disposal of the segment. Assuming a measurement date of September 30, 2004, Wexler's 2004 income statement would include the income or loss of the discontinued operations, net of income taxes, for the nine months ended September 30, 2004, under the caption "Income (loss) from operations of discontinued business segment (described)."

Gain (Loss) on Disposal of Discontinued Operations

Included in the gain or loss recognized on discontinued operations are the following:

1. Income or loss from discontinued operations during phase-out period. The *phase-out period* is the period between the *measurement date* and the *disposal date*—the date of closing the sale of the discontinued operations or ceasing the operations of an abandoned segment.

2. The gain or loss on the sale or abandonment of the industry segment.

3. The income taxes allocated to 1 and 2 above.

If the measurement date and the disposal date are in the same accounting period, the income statement for that period displays *actual* amounts for income from continuing operations, income (loss) from discontinued operations, and gain (loss) on disposal of discontinued operations. However, if the disposal date is in an accounting period subsequent to the period of the measurement date, management of the enterprise must *estimate* on the measurement date whether disposal of the discontinued operations, including operating results of the phase-out period, will result in a gain or a loss,

---

[9] *APB Opinion No. 30, par. 8.*

net of income taxes. If a ***gain*** is anticipated, it is not recognized until the ***disposal date;*** if a ***loss*** is expected, it must be recognized on the ***measurement date.***

Computation of the gain or loss on disposal of a segment may be a difficult process, especially if the disposal date is a considerable period of time after the measurement date. To assist in such a computation, the Accounting Principles Board provided substantial guidance.[10]

Disclosure of Disposal of a Business Segment

Because of the significance of discontinued operations in the financial history of a business enterprise, the Accounting Principles Board required the following disclosures:

> In addition to the amounts that should be disclosed in the financial statements . . . , the notes to financial statements for the period encompassing the measurement date should disclose:
>
> 1. The identity of the segment of business that has been or will be discontinued
> 2. The expected disposal date, if known
> 3. The expected manner of disposal
> 4. A description of the remaining assets and liabilities of the segment at the balance sheet date
> 5. The income or loss from operations and any proceeds from the disposal of the segment during the period from the measurement date to the date of the balance sheet[11]

An example of disclosure of discontinued operations, from the annual report of Georgia Gulf Corporation, a publicly owned company, follows:[12]

(In thousands)	1999	1998	1997
Income from continuing operations before income taxes	$67,969	$90,172	$99,836
Provision for income taxes	24,808	33,587	37,813
Income from continuing operations	43,161	56,585	62,023
Discontinued operation			
(Loss)/earnings from discontinued operation, net	(2,525)	(306)	19,178
Loss on disposal of discontinued operation, net	(7,631)	—	—
Net income	$33,005	$56,279	$81,201

NOTES TO CONSOLIDATED FINANCIAL STATEMENTS
Note 4. Discontinued Operation
On September 2, 1999, we announced our decision to exit the methanol business at the end of 1999. In connection with the discontinuance of the methanol business, we incurred a one-time charge of $7,631,000, net of income tax benefits, related to the write-off of the methanol plant assets, net of expected proceeds, and an accrual for estimated losses during the phase-out period. The methanol plant remains idle and we intend to dismantle the facility at some time in the future. A number of methanol sales contracts have been assigned, and our methanol customer list has been sold. Proceeds from actual and future sales of the methanol railcars, customer list and other discontinued plant

---

[10] Ibid., pars. 15–17.
[11] Ibid., par. 18.
[12] AICPA, *Accounting Trends & Techniques,* Fifty-fourth ed. (Jersey City: 2000), p. 418.

assets are estimated to be $2,900,000. The disposition of the methanol operations represents the disposal of a business segment under Accounting Principles Board ("APB") Opinion No. 30. Accordingly, results of this operation have been classified as discontinued, and prior periods have been restated, including the reallocation of fixed overhead charges to other business segments. For business segment reporting purposes, the methanol business results were previously classified as the segment "Gas Chemicals."

Net sales and income from the discontinued operation are as follows:

(In thousands)	1999	1998	1997
Net sales	$ 26,181	$49,726	$94,266
Pretax (loss) income from discontinued operation	$ (3,976)	$ (487)	$30,932
Pretax loss on disposal of business segment	(12,017)	—	—
Income tax benefit (expense)	5,837	181	(11,754)
Net (loss) income from discontinued operation	$(10,156)	$ (306)	$19,178

Assets and liabilities of the discontinued operation were as follows:

(In thousands)	1999	1998
Current assets	$3,553	$ 4,536
Property, plant and equipment, net	—	12,956
Current liabilities	(3,110)	(1,189)
Long-term liabilities	—	(2,984)
Net assets of discontinued operation	$ 443	$13,319

International Accounting Standard 14

In 1997, the International Accounting Standards Board issued a revised *IAS 14,* "Segment Reporting," which, although similar in many respects to *FASB Statement No. 131,* differed significantly in the method of identifying reportable segments.

SEC Enforcement Action Dealing with Wrongful Application of Accounting Standards for Operating Segments

AAER 1061

In *AAER 1061,* "In the Matter of Sony Corporation and Sumio Sano, . . ." (August 5, 1998), the SEC reported that Sony Corporation, a Japanese enterprise that operated through subsidiaries in the United States, inappropriately reported two distinct operating segments—music and motion pictures—as a single "entertainment" segment. Through this device, Sony was able to conceal the substantial operating losses of the motion picture segment through offsets against the profitable music segment. Further, according to the SEC, Sony did not disclose those losses in the Management Discussion and Analysis section of its annual report to shareholders. Further compounding the inadequate reporting was the lack of a vice president of finance to oversee such reporting; the individual responsible was a director and the general manager of Sony's Capital Market and Investor Relations Division. In addition to complying with *FASB Statement No. 131,* "Disclosures about Segments of an Enterprise and Related Information," Sony was ordered by the SEC to have an independent auditor examine and express an opinion on the Management Discussion and Analysis section of Sony's fiscal year 1999 annual report to stockholders and to take measures to ensure that its chief financial officer would be responsible for Sony's financial reporting.

INTERIM FINANCIAL REPORTS

Generally, financial statements are issued for the full fiscal year of a business enterprise. In addition, many enterprises issue complete financial statements for interim accounting periods during the course of a fiscal year. For example, a closely held company with outstanding bank loans may be required to provide monthly or quarterly financial statements to the lending bank. However, interim financial statements usually are associated with the *quarterly reports* issued by publicly owned companies to their stockholders, the Securities and Exchange Commission, and the stock exchanges that list their capital stock. The New York Stock Exchange's listing agreement requires listed companies to publish quarterly financial reports. Companies subject to the periodic reporting requirements of the SEC must file *Form 10-Q* with the SEC no later than 45 days after the end of each of the first three quarters of their fiscal years. In addition, the SEC requires disclosure of operating results for each quarter of the two most recent fiscal years in a "supplementary financial information" section of the annual report of a business enterprise.[13]

Problems in Interim Financial Reports

Except for 10-Q quarterly reports filed with the SEC, the form, content, and accounting practices for interim financial reports were left to the discretion of business enterprises until 1973. In that year, the Accounting Principles Board issued *Opinion No. 28,* "Interim Financial Reporting." Prior to the issuance of *Opinion No. 28,* there were unresolved problems regarding interim financial reports, including the following:

1. Enterprises employed a wider variety of accounting practices and estimating techniques for interim financial reports than they used in the annual financial statements audited by independent CPAs. The enterprises' implicit view was that any misstatements in interim financial reports would be corrected by auditors' proposed adjustments for the annual financial statements.

2. Seasonal fluctuations in revenue and irregular incurrence of costs and expenses during the course of a business enterprise's fiscal year limited the comparability of operating results for interim periods of the fiscal year. Further, time constraints in the issuance of interim statements limited the available time to accumulate end-of-period data for inventories, payables, and related expenses.

3. Accountants held two divergent views on the theoretical issues underlying interim financial statements. These differing views are described below:

    a. Under the *discrete theory,* each interim period is considered a *basic accounting period;* thus, the results of operations for each interim period are measured in essentially the same manner as for an annual accounting period. Under this theory, deferrals, accruals, and estimations at the end of each interim period are determined by following essentially the same principles and estimates or judgments that apply to annual periods.

---

[13] *Regulation S-K,* Item 302(a), Securities and Exchange Commission (Washington).

b. Under the ***integral theory,*** each interim period is considered an ***integral part of the annual period.*** Under this theory, deferrals, accruals, and estimates at the end of each interim period are affected by judgments made at the interim date as to results of operations for the remainder of the annual period. Thus, an expense item that might be considered as falling entirely within an annual period (no fiscal year-end accrual or deferral) might be allocated among interim periods based on estimated time, sales volume, production volume, or some other basis.[14]

The problems discussed in the preceding section led to a number of published interim income statements with substantial quarterly earnings, and income statements for the year with a substantial net loss.

APB Opinion No. 28

The stated objectives for ***APB Opinion No. 28*** were to provide guidance on accounting issues peculiar to interim reporting and to set forth minimum disclosure requirements for interim financial reports of publicly owned enterprises.[15] One part of the ***Opinion*** dealt with standards for measuring interim financial information and another covered disclosure of summarized interim financial data by publicly owned enterprises. In ***APB Opinion No. 28,*** the APB adopted the ***integral theory*** that interim periods should be considered as integral parts of the annual accounting period.

The APB established guidelines for the following components of interim financial reports: revenue, costs associated with revenue, all other costs and expenses, and income taxes expense. These guidelines are discussed in the following sections.

Revenue

Revenue from products sold or services rendered ***should be recognized for an interim period on the same basis as followed for the full year.*** Further, business enterprises having significant seasonal variations in revenue should disclose the seasonal nature of their activities.[16]

Costs Associated with Revenue

Costs and expenses associated directly with or allocated to products sold or services rendered include costs of material, direct labor, and factory overhead. ***APB Opinion No. 28*** required the same accounting for these costs and expenses in interim financial reports as in fiscal-year financial statements. However, the ***Opinion*** provided the following exceptions with respect to the measurement of cost of goods sold for interim financial reports:[17]

1. Enterprises that use the ***gross margin*** method at interim dates to estimate cost of goods sold should disclose this fact in interim financial reports. In addition, any material adjustments reconciling estimated interim inventories with annual physical inventories should be disclosed.

2. Enterprises that use the ***last-in, first-out inventory method*** and ***temporarily*** deplete a base layer of inventories during an interim reporting period should include in cost of goods sold for the interim period the estimated ***cost of replacing the depleted lifo base layer.***

---

[14] *APB Opinion No. 28,* "Interim Financial Reporting" (New York: AICPA, 1973), par. 5.
[15] Ibid., par. 6.
[16] Ibid., pars. 11 and 18.
[17] Ibid., pars. 13–14.

To illustrate, assume that Megan Company, which uses the last-in, first-out inventory valuation method, temporarily depleted a base layer of inventories with a cost of $80,000 during the second quarter of the fiscal year ending December 31, 2003. Replacement cost of the depleted base layer was $100,000 on June 30, 2003. In addition to the usual debit to Cost of Goods Sold and credit to Inventories for the quarter ended June 30, 2003, which would include the $80,000 amount from the base layer, Megan prepares the following journal entry on June 30, 2003:

Journal Entry for Temporary Depletion of Base Layer of Lifo Inventories

Cost of Goods Sold ($100,000 − $80,000)	20,000	
Liability Arising from Depletion of Base Layer of Lifo Inventories		20,000
To record obligation to replenish temporarily depleted base layer of last-in, first-out inventories.		

Assuming merchandise with a total cost of $172,000 was purchased by Megan on July 6, 2003, the following journal entry is required:

Journal Entry for Restoration of Base Layer

Inventories ($172,000 − $20,000)	152,000	
Liability Arising from Depletion of Base Layer of Lifo Inventories	20,000	
Trade Accounts Payable		172,000
To record purchase of merchandise and restoration of depleted base layer of last-in, first-out inventories.		

3. Lower-of-cost-or-market write-downs of inventories should be provided for interim periods as for complete fiscal years, unless the interim date market declines in inventory are considered *temporary,* and not applicable at the end of the fiscal year. If an inventory market write-down in one interim period is offset by an inventory market price *increase* in a subsequent interim period, *a gain is recognized in the subsequent period to the extent of the loss recognized in preceding interim periods of the fiscal year.*

   For example, assume that Reynolds Company, which uses lower-of-cost-or-market, first-in, first-out cost, for valuing its single merchandise item, had 10,000 units of merchandise with first-in, first-out cost of $50,000, or $5 a unit, in inventory on January 1, 2003. Assume further for simplicity that Reynolds made no purchases during 2003. Quarterly sales and end-of-quarter replacement costs for inventory during 2003 were as follows:

Quarterly Sales and End-of-Quarter Replacement Costs for Inventory

Quarter Ended	Quarterly Sales (Units)	End-of-Quarter Inventory Replacement Costs (Per Unit)
Mar. 31	2,000	$6
June 30	1,500	4
Sept. 30	2,000	7
Dec. 31	1,200	3

If the replacement cost (market) decline in the second quarter was not considered to be *temporary,* Reynolds Company's cost of goods sold for the four quarters of 2003 would be computed as follows:

**Computation of Quarterly Cost
of Goods Sold**

		Cost of Goods Sold	
Quarter Ended	**Computation for Quarter**	**For Quarter**	**Cumulative**
Mar. 31	2,000 × $5	$10,000	$10,000
June 30	(1,500 × $5) + (6,500 × $1)*	14,000	24,000
Sept. 30	(2,000 × $4) − (4,500 × $1)†	3,500	27,500
Dec. 31	(1,200 × $5) + (3,300 × $2)‡	12,600	40,100

* 6,500 units remaining in inventory multiplied by $1 write-down to lower replacement cost.
† 4,500 units in inventory multiplied by $1 write-up to original first-in, first-out cost.
‡ 3,300 units remaining in inventory multiplied by $2 write-down to lower replacement cost.

The $40,100 cumulative cost of goods sold for Reynolds Company for 2003 may be verified as follows:

**Verification of Cumulative Cost
of Goods Sold**

6,700 units sold during 2003, at $5 first-in, first-out cost per unit	$33,500
Write-down of 2003 ending inventory to replacement cost (3,000 units × $2)	6,600
Cost of goods sold for 2003	$40,100

Alternative Verification:

Cost of goods available for sale (10,000 × $5)	$50,000
Less: Ending inventory, at lower of first-in, first-out cost or market (3,300 × $3)	9,900
Cost of goods sold for 2003	$40,100

4. Enterprises using standard costs for inventories and cost of goods sold generally should report standard cost variances for interim periods as they do for fiscal years. Planned variances in materials prices, volume, or capacity should be deferred at the end of interim periods if the variances are expected to be absorbed by the end of the fiscal year.

All Other Costs and Expenses

The following guidelines for all costs and expenses other than those associated with revenue are set forth in *APB Opinion No. 28:*

> Costs and expenses other than product costs should be charged to income in interim periods as incurred, or be allocated among interim periods based on an estimate of time expired, benefit received or activity associated with the periods. Procedures adopted for assigning specific cost and expense items to an interim period should be consistent with the bases followed by the company in reporting results of operations at annual reporting dates. However, when a specific cost or expense item charged to expense for annual reporting purposes benefits more than one interim period, the cost or expense item may be allocated to those interim periods. . . .
>
> The amounts of certain costs and expenses are frequently subjected to year-end adjustments even though they can be reasonably approximated at interim dates. To the extent possible such adjustments should be estimated and the estimated costs and expenses assigned to interim periods so that the interim periods bear a reasonable portion of the anticipated annual amount. Examples of such items include inventory shrinkage, allowance for uncollectible accounts, allowance for quantity discounts, and discretionary year-end bonuses.[18]

[18] Ibid., pars. 15a and 17.

APB Opinion No. 28 includes a number of specific applications of the foregoing guidelines.

Income Taxes Expense

The techniques for recognizing income taxes expense in interim financial reports were described as follows:

> At the end of each interim period the company should make its best estimate of the effective tax rate expected to be applicable for the full fiscal year. The rate so determined should be used in providing for income taxes on a current year-to-date basis. The effective tax rate should reflect anticipated . . . foreign tax rates, percentage depletion, . . . and other available tax planning alternatives. However, in arriving at this effective tax rate no effect should be included for the tax related to significant unusual or extraordinary items that will be separately reported or reported net of their related tax effect in reports for the interim period or for the fiscal year.[19]

To illustrate, assume that on March 31, 2003, the end of the first quarter of fiscal year 2003, Carter Company's actual first quarter and forecasted fiscal year operating results were as follows:

	First Quarter (Actual)	Fiscal Year (Estimated)
Revenue	$400,000	$1,800,000
Less: Costs and expenses other than income taxes	300,000	1,500,000
Income before income taxes	$100,000	$ 300,000

Actual First Quarter and Forecasted Fiscal Year Pre-Tax Financial Income

Assume further that there were no *temporary differences* between Carter's pretax financial income and taxable income, but that Carter had the following estimated *permanent differences* between pre-tax financial income and federal and state taxable income for the 2003 fiscal year:

Estimated Permanent Differences

Dividend received deduction	$17,000
Premiums on officers' life insurance	5,000

If Carter's *nominal* federal and state income tax rates total 40%, Carter estimates its *effective* combined income tax rate for 2003 as follows:

Computation of Estimated Effective Income Tax Rate

Estimated income before income taxes	$300,000
Add: Nondeductible premiums on officers' life insurance	5,000
Less: Dividend received deduction	(17,000)
Estimated taxable income	$288,000
Estimated combined federal and state income taxes ($288,000 × 0.40)	$115,200
Estimated effective combined federal and state income tax rate for 2003 ($115,200 ÷ $300,000)	38.4%

Carter's journal entry for income taxes on March 31, 2003, is as follows:

---

[19] Ibid., par. 19.

<table>
<tr><td></td><td>Income Taxes Expense
    Income Taxes Payable
To provide for estimated federal and state income taxes for the first
quarter of 2003 ($100,000 × 0.384 = $38,400).</td><td>38,400

 </td><td>
38,400</td></tr>
</table>

For the second quarter of 2003, Carter again estimates an effective combined federal and state income tax rate based on more current projections for permanent differences between pretax financial income and taxable income for the entire year. However, the new effective rate *is not applied retroactively* to restate the first quarter's income taxes expense. For example, assume that Carter's second-quarter estimate of the effective combined federal and state income tax rate was 39.2% and that Carter's pretax financial income for the second quarter was $120,000 (or $220,000 for first two quarters). Carter prepares the following journal entry on June 30, 2003, for income taxes expense for the second quarter of 2003:

<table>
<tr><td></td><td>Income Taxes Expense
    Income Taxes Payable
To provide for estimated federal and state income taxes for the second
quarter of 2003 as follows:
    Cumulative income taxes expense ($220,000 × 0.392) $86,240
    Less: Income taxes expense for first quarter   <u>38,400</u>
    Income taxes expense for second quarter   <u>$47,840</u></td><td>47,840

 </td><td>
47,840</td></tr>
</table>

The foregoing computation of income taxes expense for interim periods is a highly simplified example. Many complex aspects of income taxes, such as net operating loss carrybacks and carryforwards, complicate the computations of income taxes for interim periods. *FASB Interpretation No. 18,* "Accounting for Income Taxes in Interim Periods," provides guidance for complex interim period income tax computations.

Reporting Accounting Changes in Interim Periods

In 1974, the FASB issued *FASB Statement No. 3,* "Reporting Accounting Changes in Interim Financial Statements," as an amendment to *APB Opinion No. 28.* Following are the two principal provisions of *FASB Statement No. 3:*

> If a cumulative effect type accounting change is made during the *first* interim period of an enterprise's fiscal year, the cumulative effect of the change on retained earnings at the *beginning of that fiscal year* shall be included in net income of the first interim period (and in last-twelve-months-to-date financial reports that include that first interim period).
>
> If a cumulative effect type accounting change is made in *other than the first* interim period of an enterprise's fiscal year, *no* cumulative effect of the change shall be included in net income of the period of the change. Instead, financial information for the pre-change interim periods of the fiscal year in which the change is made shall be restated by applying the newly adopted accounting principle to those pre-change interim

periods. The cumulative effect of the change on retained earnings at the ***beginning of that fiscal year*** shall be included in restated net income of the first interim period of the fiscal year in which the change is made (and in any year-to-date or last-twelve-months-to-date financial reports that include the first interim period). Whenever financial information that includes those pre-change interim periods is presented, it shall be presented on the restated basis.[20]

Disclosure of Interim Financial Data

As minimum disclosure, ***APB Opinion No. 28*** provided that the following data should be included in publicly owned enterprises' interim financial reports to stockholders. The data are to be reported for the most recent quarter and the year to date, or 12 months to date of the quarter's end.[21]

1. Sales or gross revenue, income taxes expense, extraordinary items (including related income tax effects), cumulative effect of a change in accounting principle or practice, and net income.

2. Basic and diluted earnings per share data for each period presented (as amended by ***FASB Statement No. 128,*** "Earnings per Share").

3. Seasonal revenue, costs, or expenses.

4. Significant changes in estimates or provisions for income taxes.

5. Disposal of a business segment and extraordinary, unusual, or infrequently occurring items.

6. Contingent items.

7. Changes in accounting principle or estimate.

8. Significant changes in financial position.

For enterprises that complete a material business combination in an interim period, the FASB requires disclosure of the following through the most recent interim period of the relevant fiscal year:[22]

1. The name and a brief description of the acquired entity and the percentage of voting equity interests acquired.

2. The primary reasons for the acquisition, including a description of the factors that contributed to a purchase price that results in recognition of goodwill.

3. The period for which the results of operations of the acquired entity are included in the income statement of the combined entity.

4. The cost of the acquired entity and, if applicable, the number of shares of equity interests (such as common shares, preferred shares, or partnership interests) issued or issuable, the value assigned to those interests, and the basis for determining that value.

---

[20] *FASB Statement No. 3,* "Reporting Accounting Changes in Interim Financial Statements" (Stamford: FASB, 1974), pars. 9–10.
[21] *APB Opinion No. 28,* par. 30.
[22] *FASB Statement No. 141,* "Business Combinations" (Norwalk: FASB, 2001, pars, 51, 58.

5. Supplemental pro forma information that discloses the results of operations for the current interim period and the current year up to the date of the most recent interim statement of financial position presented (and for the corresponding periods in the preceding year) as though the business combination had been completed as of the beginning of the period being reported on. That pro forma information shall display, at a minimum, revenue, income before extraordinary items and the cumulative effect of accounting changes (including those on an interim basis), net income, and earnings per share.

6. The nature and amount of any material, nonrecurring items included in the reported pro forma results of operations.

The FASB also has required the following additional disclosures for reportable operating segments in interim reports: revenues from external customers; intersegment revenues; segment profit or loss; segment assets if material changes have occurred since the most recent year-end financial statements; description of differences from last annual report in the basis for segmentation or for the measurement of segment profit or loss; and reconciliation of total reportable segments' profit or loss to the enterprise's pretax income from continuing operations.[23]

Examples of the disclosure of interim financial data are illustrated in the excerpts from the annual report of The McGraw-Hill Companies, Inc., page 587, of Appendix 1, and in the quarterly report (in the form of a news release) of the same enterprise in Appendix 2.

Conclusions on Interim Financial Reports

APB Opinion No. 28, FASB Statement No. 3, and *FASB Interpretation No. 18* represented a substantial effort to upgrade the quality of interim financial reports. However, controversy continues on the subject of interim financial reporting—especially concerning the APB's premise that an interim period should be accounted for as an integral part of the applicable annual period. In recognition of this controversy and other problems of interim financial reporting, the FASB undertook a comprehensive study of the topic, and issued a *Discussion Memorandum* entitled "Interim Financial Accounting and Reporting." However, because of more pressing matters on its agenda, the FASB abandoned the project a few years later.

IAS 34, "Interim Financial Reporting"

In *IAS 34,* the International Accounting Standards Board specified the condensed financial statements and other data to be included in quarterly or semiannual reports: comparative balance sheets, income statements, cash flows statements, and equity changes statements, together with basic and diluted earnings per share and selected notes to financial statements. Presumably the IASB provided more specificity than is present in *APB Opinion No. 28* because of the detailed requirements for financial statements included in the SEC's *Form 10-Q* and the instructions thereto.

SEC Enforcement Actions Dealing with Wrongful Application of Accounting Standards for Interim Financial Reports

Numerous SEC enforcement actions have addressed overstatements of quarterly earnings reported in *Form 10-Q.* Among techniques used in such overstatements are

---

[23] *FASB Statement No. 131,* par. 33.

premature recognition ("front-ending") of revenues; creation of fictitious inventories; use of improper gross margin percentages; improper deferral of costs that should be recognized as expenses; and overstatement of percentage of completion on construction-type contracts. Examples of SEC enforcement actions involving interim financial reports follow:

AAER 170

AAER 170, "Securities and Exchange Commission v. Kaypro Corporation and Andrew F. Kay" (November 6, 1987), deals with a federal court's entry of a permanent injunction against a corporation that developed, manufactured, and marketed microcomputers, and against its CEO/CFO. According to the SEC, the latter was responsible for the corporation's issuance of misleading interim reports to the SEC in ***Form 10-Q*** because he sanctioned misuse of the gross margin method for estimating quarterly ending inventories. The SEC found that quarterly cost of goods sold amounts had been estimated at 57% of sales instead of the actual 74% of sales determined by the corporation's independent auditors at the end of the fiscal year that included the subject quarters.

AAER 207 *and* 208

AAER 207, ". . . In the Matter of Matrix Science Corp., et al.," and ***AAER 208,*** "Securities and Exchange Commission v. Ronald A. Hammond, John H. MacQueen and Thomas Fleming, Jr." (November 1, 1988), report SEC enforcement actions against a corporation engaged in the design, manufacture, and sale of electrical connectors, and against 10 of its senior and middle-management executives, including its CFO. The SEC found that, among other misstatements, the corporation's quarterly sales, reported to the SEC in ***Form 10-Q,*** were overstated because sales journals had been held open for up to two days after the end of each quarter, to enable the corporation to report net sales amounts that approximated preestablished sales quotas for the quarter.

AAER 389

AAER 389, "Securities and Exchange Commission v. Albert Barette and Michael Strauss," (June 17, 1992) reported a permanent injunction and fines of $50,000 and $10,000, respectively, against the former CEO and former CFO of a wholly owned subsidiary of a publicly owned company. The SEC alleged that the two officials misstated the subsidiary's quarterly operating results reported to the parent company, in order to conceal the subsidiary's failure to meet internal budgetary targets. The SEC charged that because of the overstatements of some quarterly results and the understatements of others, the following pattern emerged with respect to the parent company's earnings reported to the SEC on ***Form 10-Q:***

	Quarter Ended (000 Omitted)				
	9/30/89	**12/31/89**	**3/31/90**	**9/30/90**	**12/31/90**
Pre-tax income:					
As reported	$2,611	$2,723	$4,100	$3,677	$3,231
Actual	2,262	2,974	4,529	3,165	2,569
Overstatement (understatement)	$ 349	$(251)	$(429)	$ 512	$ 662

AAER 1275

AAER 1275, "In the Matter of Mary Sattler Polverari, CPA," describes the fraud perpetrated by the supervisor of financial reporting for a controller of franchise brand names in the hotel, real estate brokerage, and car rental businesses. According to the SEC, the supervisor, after preparing conventional interim consolidating financial statements for the enterprise's business units, using electronic spreadsheets, made unsupported changes in the consolidated amounts as directed by her supervisors. The purpose of the changes was to inflate the enterprise's interim earnings reports to meet expectations of Wall Street financial analysts. The SEC denied the supervisor's privilege of practicing before it as an accountant, with the provision that, after meeting certain requirements, she might apply for reinstatement after a period of three years.

REPORTING FOR THE SEC

The Securities and Exchange Commission (SEC) is an agency of the U.S. government created in 1934 to oversee the interstate issuances and trading of securities. Since its creation, the SEC's functions have expanded to include administration of the following statutes, among others:

- *Securities Act of 1933,* governing interstate issuances of securities to the public.

- *Securities Exchange Act of 1934,* governing trading of securities on national securities exchanges and over the counter.

- *Public Utility Holding Company Act of 1935,* governing interstate public utility holding company systems for electricity and gas.

- *Trust Indenture Act of 1939,* governing the issuance of bonds, debentures, and similar debt securities under an indenture meeting the requirements of the Act.

- *Investment Company Act of 1940* and *Investment Advisers Act of 1940,* governing operations of investment companies and investment advisers.

This section focuses on SEC administration of the Securities Act of 1933 (the 1933 Act) and the Securities Exchange Act of 1934 (the 1934 Act).

Nature of Reporting to the SEC

Most publicly owned companies are subject to either or both the 1933 Act and the 1934 Act. Companies planning to issue securities interstate to the public generally must file a *registration statement* with the SEC. Companies whose securities are traded on national stock exchanges also must file a registration statement; in addition, periodic reports must be made to the SEC by such companies. Most large companies whose securities are traded over the counter also must report periodically to the SEC.

Registration of Securities

The SEC has developed a series of *forms* for the registration of securities. *Forms S-1, S-2, S-3, S-4, F-1, F-2, F-3,* and *F-4* are used by large companies to register securities to be issued to the public; *Form SB-1* and *Form SB-2* are used by small business issuers, as defined in the 1933 Act. The principal form for registering securities for trading on a national exchange or over the counter is ***Form 10.*** The various forms are not a series of blanks to be filled in; they are guides for the ***format of information to be included in the registration statements.***

Periodic Reporting

The principal forms established by the SEC for reporting by companies whose stock is traded on national exchanges or over the counter are ***Form 10-K, Form 10-Q,*** and ***Form 8-K. Form 10-K*** is an annual report to the SEC, which must be filed within 90 days following the close of the company's fiscal year. Much of the information required by ***Form 10-K*** may be ***incorporated by reference*** to the annual report to stockholders, which also must be filed with the SEC.

 Form 10-Q is a quarterly report to the SEC that is due within 45 days after the end of each of the first three quarters of the company's fiscal year; a quarterly report for the fourth quarter of the fiscal year is not required. The condensed financial statements that must be included in ***Form 10-Q*** are more extensive than the minimum disclosure requirements of ***APB Opinion No. 28,*** "Interim Financial Reporting" (see page 571), but the ***10-Q*** financial statements need not be audited.

 Form 8-K is a current report that must be filed with the SEC within a specified number of days after the occurrence of events such as the following:

1. Change in control of the reporting company.

2. Acquisition or disposal of assets by the reporting company, including business combinations.

3. Bankruptcy or receivership of the reporting company.

4. Change of independent auditors for the reporting company.

5. Resignation of directors of the reporting company.

In addition, a company may choose to report to the SEC in ***Form 8-K*** any other event that it considers important to stockholders.

 Another important periodic report to the SEC is a ***proxy statement,*** which must be filed by companies that solicit proxies for annual meetings of their stockholders. If matters other than election of directors, selection of independent auditors, and consideration of stockholder proposals are to take place at an annual meeting, a ***preliminary proxy statement*** must be filed with the SEC for review and comment prior to distribution of the ***definitive proxy statement*** to stockholders. Essentially, the proxy statement includes disclosure of all matters to be voted on at the forthcoming meeting of stockholders whose proxies are solicited. If the stockholders are to vote on authorization or issuances of securities, modification or exchanges of securities, or business combinations, the proxy statement must include financial statements of the company and of any proposed combinee.

Organization and Functions of the SEC

The SEC is administered by five commissioners appointed for five-year terms by the President and confirmed by the Senate of the United States. No more than three commissioners may be members of the same political party. Headquartered in Washington, D.C., the SEC has nine regional offices and six branch offices. In the following sections, three segments of the SEC are discussed: chief accountant, Division of Corporation Finance, and Division of Enforcement.

Chief Accountant

The chief accountant of the SEC, as an expert in accounting, is responsible for issuing pronouncements that establish the SEC's position on matters affecting accounting and auditing. The chief accountant also supervises disciplinary proceedings against accountants charged with violating the SEC's Rules of Practice. The chief accountant cooperates with the FASB and other private organizations interested in research and standards setting in accounting and auditing.

Division of Corporation Finance

The staff of the SEC's Division of Corporation Finance reviews the **Forms** and proxy statements filed with the SEC under the 1933 Act and the 1934 Act. The extent of the reviews varies, depending on whether the filing company has a history of acceptable reporting to the SEC or is "unseasoned." Division of Corporation Finance personnel consult with the chief accountant on the propriety of accounting presentations in filings with the SEC. Changes in the various **Forms** and in **Regulation S-X** and **Regulation S-K** are the responsibility of the Division of Corporation Finance.

Division of Enforcement

The duties of the SEC's Division of Enforcement involve monitoring the compliance of companies subject to the SEC's jurisdiction with the 1933 Act and the 1934 Act. When noncompliance is ascertained, the Division of Enforcement often will request and obtain federal court injunctions prohibiting the company and its management from further violations of the two Acts. Many of the criminal indictments involving management fraud in recent years have been obtained through the efforts of the SEC's Division of Enforcement.

Interaction between SEC and FASB

Both the 1933 Act and the 1934 Act empower the SEC to establish rules for the accounting principles underlying financial statements and schedules included in reports filed with the SEC. The SEC rarely has used this authority directly. Instead, it generally has endorsed actions on accounting principles by organizations in the private sector (currently the FASB), while reserving the right to issue its own pronouncements when necessary. This posture of the SEC has been described as follows:

> In ASR [Accounting Series Release] 4, the Commission stated its policy that financial statements prepared in accordance with accounting practices for which there was no substantial authoritative support were presumed to be misleading and that footnote or other disclosure would not avoid this presumption. It also stated that, where there was a difference of opinion between the Commission and a registrant as to the proper accounting to be followed in a particular case, disclosure would be accepted in lieu of correction of the financial statements themselves only if substantial authoritative support existed for the accounting practices followed by the registrant and the position of the Commission had not been expressed in rules, regulations or other official releases. For purposes of this policy, principles, standards and practices promulgated by the FASB in its Statements and Interpretations will be considered by the Commission as having substantial authoritative support, and those contrary to such FASB promulgations will be considered to have no such support.
>
> . . . Information in addition to that included in financial statements conforming to generally accepted accounting principles is also necessary. Such additional disclosures are required to be made in various fashions, such as in financial statements and sched-

ules reported on by independent public accountants or as textual statements required by items in the applicable forms and reports filed with the Commission. The Commission will continue to identify areas where investor information needs exist and will determine the appropriate methods of disclosure to meet these needs.[24]

Thus, the SEC differentiated between ***generally accepted accounting principles*** and ***disclosures*** in financial statements and schedules, and expressed an intention to concentrate on pronouncements on disclosures. The principal devices used by the SEC to communicate its requirements for accounting principles and disclosures have been ***Regulation S-X, Regulation S-K, Accounting Series Releases, Financial Reporting Releases,*** and ***Staff Accounting Bulletins.***

Regulation S-X

The SEC issued ***Regulation S-X*** to provide guidance for the form and content of financial statements and schedules required to be filed with the SEC under the laws that it administers. Since the adoption of ***Regulation S-X*** in 1940, the SEC has amended the document extensively, including a thorough overhaul in 1980 (***Accounting Series Release No. 280***).

Regulation S-X consists of numerous rules subdivided into several articles. Among the significant provisions of ***Regulation S-X*** are Rule 3-02, which requires audited income statements and statements of cash flows for three fiscal years, and Article 12, which illustrates the form and content of schedules to be filed in support of various financial statement items. Excerpts from the annual report of The McGraw-Hill Companies, Inc., in Appendix 1 illustrate the required comparative financial statements.

At one time, numerous ***schedules*** were required to be included in some of the ***Forms*** filed with the SEC. However, in 1994, the SEC terminated several of the required schedules, in ***Financial Reporting Release No. 44.*** One of the few remaining schedules is "Schedule II—Valuation and Qualifying Accounts," the format and instructions for which are as follows:[25]

		Column C — Additions			
Column A—Description[1]	Column B—Balance at Beginning of Period	(1)—Charged to Costs and Expenses	(2)—Charged to Other Accounts—Describe	Column D—Deductions—Describe	Column E—Balance at End of Period

[1] List, by major classes, all valuation and qualifying accounts and reserves not included in specific schedules. Identify each class of valuation and qualifying accounts and reserves by descriptive title. Group (A) those valuation and qualifying accounts which are deducted in the balance sheet from the assets to which they apply and (B) those reserves which support the balance sheet caption, Reserves. Valuation and qualifying accounts and reserves as to which the additions, deductions, and balances were not individually significant may be grouped in one total and in such case the information called for under columns C and D need not be given.

Typically reported in Schedule II are asset valuation accounts such as Allowance for Doubtful Accounts and Accumulated Depreciation.

[24] *Codification of Financial Reporting Policies,* Securities and Exchange Commission (Washington: 1982), Sec. 101.
[25] *Regulation S-X,* Rule 12-09.

Regulation S-K

The SEC issued **Regulation S-K** in 1977 to provide guidance for the completion of nonfinancial statement disclosure requirements in the various **Forms** filed under the 1933 Act and the 1934 Act. As amended since its adoption, **Regulation S-K** contains several items of disclosure.

Accounting Series Releases (ASRs)

In 1937 the SEC initiated a program of pronouncements by the chief accountant designed to contribute to the development of uniform standards and practice in major accounting questions. Through early 1982, 307 **ASRs** were issued, with more than half of them published after January 1974. However, fewer than half of the **ASRs** dealt solely with accounting principles and disclosures; the remainder covered auditing standards, independence of auditors, and enforcement actions of the SEC involving accountants.

Two examples of **ASR**s dealing with accounting principles and disclosures are **ASR No. 142** and **ASR No. 149.** In **ASR No. 142,** "Reporting Cash Flow and Other Related Data," the SEC concluded that financial reports **should not** present **cash flow** (net income adjusted for noncash expenses and revenue) **per share** and other comparable per-share computations, other than those based on net income, dividends, or net assets. In **ASR No. 149,** "... Improved Disclosure of Income Tax Expense" (as amended by **ASR No. 280**), the SEC mandated several disclosures concerning income taxes. Note 5 of the annual report of The McGraw-Hill Companies, Inc., in Appendix 1 (page 588) illustrates the requirements of **ASR No. 149,** which later were incorporated in paragraph 47 of **FASB Statement No. 109,** "Accounting for Income Taxes."

Financial Reporting Releases (FRRs)

In 1982, the SEC terminated the issuance of **Accounting Series Releases** and instituted **Financial Reporting Releases** for stating its views on financial reporting matters. (Enforcement actions of the SEC were to be publicized in **Accounting and Auditing Enforcement Releases.**)

Staff Accounting Bulletins (SABs)

The following excerpt from **ASR No. 180** describes the **SAB**s issued by the SEC:

> The Securities and Exchange Commission today announced the institution of a series of Staff Accounting Bulletins intended to achieve a wider dissemination of the administrative interpretations and practices utilized by the Commission's staff in reviewing financial statements. The Division of Corporation Finance and the Office of the Chief Accountant began the series today with the publication of Bulletin No. 1. . . . The statements in the Bulletin are not rules or interpretations of the Commission nor are they published as bearing the Commission's official approval; they represent interpretations and practices followed by the Division and the Chief Accountant in administering the disclosure requirements of the federal securities laws.

The following example from **SAB No. 1** (subsequently superseded by **SAB No. 40**) illustrates the contents of a typical Bulletin:

> *Facts:* Company E proposes to include in its registration statement a balance sheet showing its subordinated debt as a portion of stockholders' equity.
>
> *Question:* Is this presentation appropriate?

Interpretive Response: Subordinated debt may not be included in the stockholders' equity section of the balance sheet. Any presentation describing such debt as a component of stockholders' equity must be eliminated. Furthermore, any caption representing the combination of stockholders' equity and any subordinated debt must be deleted.

Integration Project and Other Activities of the SEC

The foregoing discussion indicates the complexity of the reporting requirements of the SEC. Compliance with these requirements often is a major undertaking for companies that report to the SEC.

In the early 1980s, the SEC substantially completed an integration project designed to provide, wherever possible, uniform reporting requirements in the various *Forms* filed with the SEC. The integration was focused on providing comparable requirements for the *transaction-oriented* Securities Act of 1933 and the *status-oriented* Securities Exchange Act of 1934.[26] In a number of *ASR*s, the SEC accomplished the following:

1. Through the *incorporation by reference* technique, enabled many companies to satisfy the reporting requirements of the 1933 Act by already-filed *Forms* provided to the SEC under the 1934 Act.

2. Permitted many of the requirements of *Form 10-K* to be met by reference to the annual report to stockholders.

3. Conformed many of the accounting requirements of *Regulation S-X* to generally accepted accounting principles, thus generally permitting the form and content of financial statements included in annual reports to stockholders to suffice for reports to the SEC.

In addition to the integration project, the SEC has encouraged the voluntary filing of *projections of future economic performance* (also termed *financial forecasts*) in reports to it. In Section 229.10(b) of *Regulation S-K* the SEC provided guidelines for the preparation and disclosure of such projections. The SEC has long believed that users of financial reports would benefit from management's projections as a supplement to the historical data in the financial statements. However, the SEC has been reluctant to require projections in the various *Forms,* because there is widespread opposition to submission of financial forecasts to stockholders by accountants and business executives who fear the litigation consequences if forecasted results are not achieved.

In 1983, the SEC initiated *EDGAR,* its Electronic Data Gathering, Analysis, and Retrieval project designed to permit "paperless" filings with the SEC by means of direct communication over telephone lines, on diskettes, or on magnetic tapes. After substantial testing of EDGAR through a pilot project, the SEC mandated electronic filings of all *Forms* and reports.

In 1998, the SEC proposed new rules to simplify the complex reporting requirements for enterprises registering securities under the *Securities Act of 1933.* A reported goal of the simplification would be to free the staff of the SEC's Division of Corporate Finance to review more periodic reports under the *Securities Exchange Act of 1934.*[27]

---

[26] *Accounting Series Release No. 306,* Securities and Exchange Commission (Washington: 1982).
[27] "SEC Proposes New Rules to Streamline Stock Offerings by Public Companies," *The Wall Street Journal,* October 16, 1998.

Appendix 1

Excerpts from 2000 Annual Report of The McGraw-Hill Companies, Inc.

The McGraw-Hill Companies

Consolidated Statement of Income (Restated)

Years ended December 31 (in thousands, except per-share data)	2000	1999	1998
OPERATING REVENUE (Note 1, 4 and 12)	**$4,280,968**	$3,991,685	$3,724,971
EXPENSES			
Operating	**1,762,721**	1,738,125	1,661,615
Selling and general	**1,390,262**	1,269,479	1,216,686
Depreciation and amortization (Note 1)	**362,325**	308,355	299,240
TOTAL EXPENSES	**3,515,308**	3,315,959	3,177,541
Other income – net (Note 2)	**54,523**	63,949	56,779
INCOME FROM OPERATIONS	**820,183**	739,675	604,209
Interest expense – net	**52,841**	42,013	47,961
INCOME BEFORE TAXES ON INCOME	**767,342**	697,662	556,248
Provision for taxes on income (Note 5)	**295,426**	272,088	216,937
INCOME BEFORE EXTRAORDINARY ITEM AND CUMULATIVE ADJUSTMENT	**471,916**	425,574	339,311
EXTRAORDINARY ITEM—LOSS ON EARLY EXTINGUISHMENT OF DEBT, NET OF TAX (Note 3)	**—**	—	(8,716)
CUMULATIVE CHANGE IN ACCOUNTING, NET OF TAX (Note 12)	**(68,122)**	—	—
NET INCOME	**$ 403,794**	$ 425,574	$ 330,595
BASIC EARNINGS PER COMMON SHARE (Note 11)			
INCOME BEFORE EXTRAORDINARY ITEM AND CUMULATIVE ADJUSTMENT	$ **2.43**	$ 2.17	$ 1.72
NET INCOME	$ **2.08**	$ 2.17	$ 1.68
DILUTED EARNINGS PER COMMON SHARE (Note 11)			
INCOME BEFORE EXTRAORDINARY ITEM AND CUMULATIVE ADJUSTMENT	$ **2.41**	$ 2.14	$ 1.70
NET INCOME	$ **2.06**	$ 2.14	$ 1.66

See accompanying notes.

Consolidated Balance Sheet (Restated)

December 31 (in thousands, except share data)	2000	1999
ASSETS		
CURRENT ASSETS		
Cash and equivalents (Note 1)	$ 3,171	$ 6,489
Accounts receivable (net of allowances for doubtful accounts and sales returns:		
2000 – $256,263; 1999 – $232,526)	**1,095,118**	1,048,991
Inventories:		
Finished goods	**324,852**	239,139
Work-in-process	**24,231**	25,205
Paper and other materials	**39,864**	30,911
Total inventories (Note 1)	**388,947**	295,255
Deferred income taxes (Note 5)	**192,789**	142,520
Prepaid and other current assets (Note 1)	**121,665**	89,784
Total current assets	**1,801,690**	1,583,039
PREPUBLICATION COSTS (net of accumulated amortization:		
2000 – $757,034; 1999 – $661,207) (Note 1)	**518,031**	439,351
INVESTMENTS AND OTHER ASSETS		
Investment in Rock-McGraw, Inc. – at equity (Note 1)	**95,862**	85,997
Prepaid pension expense (Note 9)	**159,598**	119,495
Other	**226,910**	206,770
Total investments and other assets	**482,370**	412,262
PROPERTY AND EQUIPMENT—AT COST		
Land	**13,685**	12,654
Buildings and leasehold improvements	**299,639**	300,898
Equipment and furniture	**733,045**	680,152
Total property and equipment	**1,046,369**	993,704
Less – accumulated depreciation	**614,464**	563,296
Net property and equipment	**431,905**	430,408
GOODWILL AND OTHER INTANGIBLE ASSETS—AT COST		
(net of accumulated amortization:		
2000 – $586,127; 1999 – $555,346) (Notes 1 and 2)	**1,697,448**	1,253,051
TOTAL ASSETS	**$4,931,444**	$4,118,111

582 Part 3 *International Accounting: Reporting of Segments, for Interim Periods, and to the SEC*

	2000	1999
LIABILITIES AND SHAREHOLDERS' EQUITY		
CURRENT LIABILITIES		
Notes payable (Note 3)	$ 227,848	$ 86,631
Current portion of long-term debt (Note 3)	—	95,043
Accounts payable	313,286	340,220
Accrued royalties	115,022	99,468
Accrued compensation and contributions to retirement plans	243,252	245,871
Income taxes currently payable	55,388	105,066
Unearned revenue (Note 12)	475,559	314,811
Other current liabilities (Note 1)	350,430	310,660
Total current liabilities	1,780,785	1,597,770
OTHER LIABILITIES		
Long-term debt (Note 3)	817,529	354,775
Deferred income taxes	163,231	135,426
Accrued postretirement healthcare and other benefits (Note 10)	178,525	187,485
Other non-current liabilities	230,330	194,165
Total other liabilities	1,389,615	871,851
Total liabilities	3,170,400	2,469,621
COMMITMENTS AND CONTINGENCIES (Note 6)		
SHAREHOLDERS' EQUITY (Notes 7 and 8)		
$1.20 preference stock, $10 par value: authorized – 891,256 shares; outstanding – 1,328 and 1,352 shares in 2000 and 1999	13	14
Common stock, $1 par value: authorized – 300,000,000 shares; issued – 205,838,910 and 205,838,594 shares in 2000 and 1999	205,839	205,838
Additional paid-in capital	44,176	24,305
Retained income (Note 12)	2,105,145	1,883,813
Accumulated other comprehensive income	(110,358)	(87,731)
Less – common stock in treasury – at cost (11,553,707 shares in 2000 and 10,129,840 shares in 1999)	470,903	363,728
Unearned compensation on restricted stock	12,868	14,021
Total shareholders' equity	1,761,044	1,648,490
TOTAL LIABILITIES AND SHAREHOLDERS' EQUITY	**$4,931,444**	**$4,118,111**

Consolidated Statement of Cash Flows (Restated)

Years ended December 31 (in thousands)	2000	1999	1998
CASH FLOW FROM OPERATING ACTIVITIES			
Net income	**$ 403,794**	$ 425,574	$ 330,595
Cumulative change in accounting principle	**68,122**	—	—
Adjustments to reconcile net income to cash provided by operating activities:			
Depreciation	**86,993**	82,110	77,168
Amortization of goodwill and intangibles	**66,715**	55,586	52,530
Amortization of prepublication costs	**208,617**	170,653	169,542
Provision for losses on accounts receivable	**47,589**	68,657	104,597
Gain on sale of building	**—**	—	(26,656)
Gain on sale of Petrochemical publications	**—**	(39,668)	—
Gain on sale of Tower Group International	**(16,587)**	—	—
Extraordinary loss on early extinguishment of debt	**—**	—	14,289
Other	**(9,173)**	1,372	(4,595)
Change in assets and liabilities net of effect of acquisitions and dispositions:			
Increase in accounts receivable and inventory	**(117,031)**	(166,872)	(73,990)
Increase in prepaid and other current assets	**(19,707)**	(948)	(161)
(Decrease)/increase in accounts payable and accrued expenses	**(19,717)**	54,906	66,500
Increase in unearned revenue and other current liabilities	**31,346**	22,197	47,339
(Decrease)/increase in interest and income taxes currently payable	**(29,848)**	67,254	(20,050)
Net change in deferred income taxes	**34,680**	(8,428)	33,339
Net change in other assets and liabilities	**(30,233)**	(24,340)	(15,377)
Cash provided by operating activities	**705,560**	708,053	755,070
INVESTING ACTIVITIES			
Investment in prepublication costs	**(250,005)**	(246,341)	(194,978)
Purchase of property and equipment	**(97,721)**	(154,324)	(178,889)
Acquisition of businesses and equity interests	**(703,719)**	(67,085)	(24,720)
Proceeds from disposition of property, equipment and businesses	**142,418**	67,244	66,479
Cash used for investing activities	**(909,027)**	(400,506)	(332,108)
FINANCING ACTIVITIES			
Dividends paid to shareholders	**(182,462)**	(169,049)	(154,386)
Additions to/(repayment of) commercial paper and other short-term debt – net	**606,276**	11,899	(1,660)
Repayment of long-term debt	**(95,043)**	—	(154,988)
Repurchase of treasury shares	**(167,611)**	(173,784)	(105,637)
Exercise of stock options	**45,317**	22,813	16,080
Other	**(3,239)**	(1,709)	(14,973)
Cash provided by/(used for) financing activities	**203,238**	(309,830)	(415,564)
EFFECT OF EXCHANGE RATE CHANGES ON CASH	**(3,089)**	(1,679)	(1,715)
Net change in cash and equivalents	**(3,318)**	(3,962)	5,683
Cash and equivalents at beginning of year	**6,489**	10,451	4,768
CASH AND EQUIVALENTS AT END OF YEAR	**$ 3,171**	$ 6,489	$ 10,451

See accompanying notes.

Consolidated Statement of Shareholders' Equity (Restated)

Years ended December 31, 2000, 1999 and 1998 (in thousands, except per-share data)	$1.20 preference $10 par	Common $1 par	Additional paid-in capital	Retained income	Accumulated other comprehensive income	Less – common stock in treasury at cost	Less – unearned compensation on restricted stock	Total
BALANCE AT DECEMBER 31, 1997	$14	$102,919	$35,469	$1,502,587	$(74,247)	$159,447	$12,911	$1,394,384
Net income	—	—	—	330,595	—	—	—	330,595
Other comprehensive income, net of tax – foreign currency translation adjustments	—	—	—	—	(1,715)	—	—	(1,715)
COMPREHENSIVE INCOME								328,880
Dividends ($.78 per share)	—	—	—	(154,386)	—	—	—	(154,386)
Share repurchase	—	—	—	—	—	105,637	—	(105,637)
Employee stock plans	—	—	15,840	—	—	(30,275)	599	45,516
Other	—	—	102	—	—	(136)	—	238
Two-for-one stock split at par value	—	102,919	(51,411)	(51,508)	—	—	—	—
BALANCE AT DECEMBER 31, 1998	14	205,838	—	1,627,288	(75,962)	234,673	13,510	1,508,995
Net income	—	—	—	425,574	—	—	—	425,574
Other comprehensive income, net of tax – foreign currency translation adjustments	—	—	—	—	(11,769)	—	—	(11,769)
COMPREHENSIVE INCOME								413,805
Dividends ($.86 per share)	—	—	—	(169,049)	—	—	—	(169,049)
Share repurchase	—	—	—	—	—	173,784	—	(173,784)
Employee stock plans	—	—	24,121	—	—	(44,646)	511	68,256
Other	—	—	184	—	—	(83)	—	267
BALANCE AT DECEMBER 31, 1999	14	205,838	24,305	1,883,813	(87,731)	363,728	14,021	1,648,490
Net income	—	—	—	403,794	—	—	—	403,794
Other comprehensive income, net of tax – foreign currency translation adjustments	—	—	—	—	(22,627)	—	—	(22,627)
COMPREHENSIVE INCOME								381,167
Dividends ($.94 per share)	—	—	—	(182,462)	—	—	—	(182,462)
Share repurchase	—	—	—	—	—	167,611	—	(167,611)
Employee stock plans	—	—	19,828	—	—	(60,348)	(1,153)	81,329
Other	(1)	1	43	—	—	(88)	—	131
BALANCE AT DECEMBER 31, 2000	$13	$205,839	$44,176	$2,105,145	$(110,358)	$470,903	$12,868	$1,761,044

See accompanying notes.

NOTES TO CONSOLIDATED FINANCIAL STATEMENTS

1. ACCOUNTING POLICIES

PRINCIPLES OF CONSOLIDATION. The consolidated financial statements include the accounts of all subsidiaries and the company's share of earnings or losses of joint ventures and affiliated companies under the equity method of accounting. All significant intercompany accounts and transactions have been eliminated.

USE OF ESTIMATES. The preparation of financial statements in conformity with generally accepted accounting principles requires management to make estimates and assumptions that affect the amounts reported in the financial statements and accompanying notes. Actual results could differ from those estimates.

CASH EQUIVALENTS. Cash equivalents consist of highly liquid investments with maturities of three months or less at the time of purchase.

INVENTORIES. Inventories are stated at the lower of cost (principally first-in, first-out) or market.

PREPUBLICATION COSTS. Prepublication costs, principally outside preparation costs, are amortized from the year of publication over their estimated useful lives, primarily three to five years, using either an accelerated or the straight-line method. It is the company's policy to evaluate the remaining lives and recoverability of such costs, which is often dependent upon program acceptance by state adoption authorities.

INVESTMENT IN ROCK-McGRAW, INC. Rock-McGraw owns the company's headquarters building in New York City. Rock-McGraw is owned 45% by the company and 55% by Rockefeller Group, Inc. The company accounts for this investment under the equity method of accounting.

GOODWILL AND OTHER INTANGIBLE ASSETS. Goodwill and other intangible assets that arose from acquisitions either consummated or initiated prior to November 1, 1970 are not amortized unless there has been a reduction in the value of the related assets. Goodwill and other intangible assets arising subsequent to November 1, 1970 of $1.7 billion at December 31, 2000 and 1999 are being amortized over periods of up to 40 years. The company periodically reviews its goodwill to determine if any impairment exists based upon projected, undiscounted net cash flows of the related business unit.

RECEIVABLE FROM/PAYABLE TO BROKER-DEALERS AND DEALER BANKS. A subsidiary of J.J. Kenny Co. acts as an undisclosed agent in the purchase and sale of municipal securities for broker-dealers and dealer banks, and the company had matched purchase and sale commitments of $98.2 million and $66.0 million at December 31, 2000 and 1999, respectively. Only those transactions not closed at the settlement date are reflected in the balance sheet as a component of other current assets and liabilities.

FOREIGN CURRENCY TRANSLATION. Assets and liabilities are translated using current exchange rates, except certain accounts of units whose functional currency is the U.S. dollar, and translation adjustments are accumulated in a separate component of shareholders' equity. Revenue and expenses are translated at average monthly exchange rates. Inventory, prepublication costs and property and equipment accounts of units whose functional currency is the U.S. dollar are translated using historical exchange rates and translation adjustments are charged and credited to income.

REVENUE. Revenue is generally recognized when goods are shipped to customers or services are rendered. Units whose revenue is principally from subscription income and service contracts record revenue as earned. Subscription income is recognized over the related subscription period. For further details on the company's change of revenue recognition policy, see Note 12.

DEPRECIATION. The costs of property and equipment are depreciated using the straight-line method based upon the following estimated useful lives:

Buildings and leasehold improvements – 15 to 40 years
Equipment and furniture – three to 10 years

ADVERTISING EXPENSE. The cost of advertising is expensed as incurred. The company incurred $104 million, $101 million and $107 million in advertising costs in 2000, 1999 and 1998, respectively.

STOCK-BASED COMPENSATION. As permitted by Statement of Financial Accounting Standards No. 123 (SFAS No. 123), Accounting for Stock-Based Compensation, the company measures compensation expense for its stock-based employee compensation plans using the intrinsic method prescribed by Accounting Principles Board Opinion No. 25 (APBO No. 25), Accounting for Stock Issued to Employees, and has provided in Note 8 pro forma disclosures of the effect on net income and earnings per share as if the fair value-based method prescribed by SFAS No. 123 had been applied in measuring compensation expense.

RECENT ACCOUNTING PRONOUNCEMENTS. In June 1998, the Financial Accounting Standards Board issued SFAS No. 133, Accounting for Derivative Instruments and Hedging Activities. The new standard is effective January 1, 2001. SFAS No. 133 establishes accounting and reporting standards for derivative instruments and for hedging activities, requiring companies to recognize all derivatives as either assets or liabilities on their balance sheet and measuring them at fair value. The adoption of SFAS No. 133 did not have a material impact on the company's financial statements.

The Securities and Exchange Commission (SEC) issued Staff Accounting Bulletin No. 101, Revenue Recognition in Financial Statements, in December 1999 and updated the Bulletin in 2000 (SAB 101). The new standard was effective January 1, 2000, with implementation required by the fourth quarter of 2000. This pronouncement summarizes the SEC's views of revenue recognition practices in financial statements and how they apply to generally accepted accounting principles. For further discussion on the impact of SAB 101 on the company's financial statements refer to Note 12.

RECLASSIFICATION. Certain prior-year amounts have been reclassified for comparability purposes.

2. ACQUISITIONS AND DISPOSITIONS

Acquisitions. In 2000, the company acquired three companies, principally Tribune Education and CBRS, for $703.7 million, net of cash acquired. In 1999, the company acquired six companies, principally Appleton & Lange, Rational Investor and Emerging Markets Database, for $67.1 million, net of cash acquired. In 1998, the company acquired Xebec Multi Media Solutions, Ltd. and Optical Data Corporation for $24.7 million, net of cash acquired. All of these acquisitions were accounted for under the purchase method. Goodwill recorded for all current transactions is amortized using the straight-line method for periods not exceeding 25 years.

NONCASH INVESTING ACTIVITIES. Liabilities assumed in conjunction with the acquisition of businesses:

(in millions)	2000	1999	1998
Fair value of assets acquired	$840.5	$70.7	$28.0
Cash paid (net of cash acquired)	703.7	67.1	24.7
Liabilities assumed	$136.8	$ 3.6	$ 3.3

DISPOSITIONS. In 2000, the company sold Tower Group International for $138.2 million. As a result of this transaction a pre-tax gain of $16.6 million ($10.2 million after-tax, or 5 cents per diluted share) was recognized. In 1999, the company sold its Petrochemical publications for $62.8 million. As a result of this transaction a pre-tax gain of $39.7 million, ($24.2 million after-tax, or 12 cents per diluted share) was recognized. In 1998, the company sold the remainder of its Information Technology and Communications Group for $28.6 million. There was no gain or loss on the divestiture as the net proceeds minus disposition costs approximated the net book value of the Group's assets.

3. DEBT

At December 31, 2000, the company had short-term borrowings of $1.043 billion, primarily representing domestic commercial paper borrowings of $1.019 billion maturing at various dates during 2001, and acquisition related debt of $24 million at an average interest rate of 6.4%. The commercial paper borrowings in 2000 are supported by the revolving credit agreement described below, and approximately $816 million and $350 million have been classified as long-term in 2000 and 1999, respectively.

On August 15, 2000, the company retired its existing revolving credit facility that was due to expire on February 13, 2002, and replaced it with two new revolving credit facilities. The two revolving credit facility agreements, each with the same 11 domestic and international banks, consisting of a $625 million, five-year revolving credit facility ("New Five-year Facility") and a $625 million, 364-day revolving credit facility ("New 364-day Facility"). The New Five-year Facility provides that the company may borrow at any time until August 15, 2005, when the commitment terminates and any outstanding loans mature. The New 364-day Facility agreement provides that the company may borrow until August 14, 2001, on which date the facility commitment terminates and the maturity of such borrowings may not be later than August 14, 2002. The company pays a facility fee of five and seven basis points on the New 364-day Facility and New Five-year Facility, respectively (whether or not amounts have been borrowed), and borrowings may be made at a range of 13 to 20 basis points above LIBOR at the company's current credit rating. The fees and spreads on the New Five-year Facility fluctuate based upon a schedule related to the company's long-term credit rating by Moody's and Fitch. The facility agreements each contain certain covenants, and the only financial covenant requires that the company not exceed an indebtedness to cash flow ratio, as defined, of four to one at any time. This restriction, which was also in place under the retired facility, has never been exceeded. At December 31, 2000, there were no borrowings under either facility. The commercial paper borrowings outstanding is supported by the new revolving credit facilities, and 80% of these borrowings have been classified as long-term.

A summary of long-term debt at December 31 follows:

(in millions)	2000	1999
9.43% Notes due 2000	$ —	$ 95.0
Commercial paper supported by bank revolving credit agreement	815.6	350.0
Other (primarily acquisition related notes)	1.9	4.8
	817.5	449.8
Less: current portion of long-term debt	—	(95.0)
Total long-term debt	$817.5	$354.8

The company paid interest on its debt totaling $56.3 million in 2000, $42.8 million in 1999 and $48.9 million in 1998.

The carrying amount of the company's commercial paper borrowings approximates fair value. The fair value of the company's 9.43%. Notes and other long-term debt at December 31, 1999, based on current borrowing rates for debt with similar terms and maturities, was estimated to be $99.7 million.

4. SEGMENT REPORTING AND GEOGRAPHIC INFORMATION

The company has three reportable segments: McGraw-Hill Education, Financial Services and Information and Media Services. The McGraw-Hill Education segment provides education, training and lifetime learning textbooks and instructional materials for students and professionals. The Financial Services segment consists of Standard & Poor's operations, which provide financial information, ratings and analyses, enabling access to capital markets. The Information and Media Services segment includes business and professional media offering information, insight and analysis.

Information as to the operations of the three segments of the company is set forth below based on the nature of the products and services offered. The CEO Council, comprising the company's principal corporate and operations executives, is the company's chief operating decision maker and evaluates performance based primarily on operating profit. The accounting policies of the operating segments are the same as those described in the summary of significant accounting policies – refer to Note 1 of the financial statements for the company's significant accounting policies.

(in millions)	McGraw-Hill Education	Financial Services	Information and Media Services	Segment Totals	Adjustments	Consolidated Total
2000						
Operating revenue	$1,993.2	$1,280.3	$1,007.5	$4,281.0	$ —	$4,281.0
Operating profit	307.7	395.5	208.3	911.5	(144.2)	767.3*
Depreciation and amortization[†]	281.0	51.3	27.5	359.8	2.5	362.3
Assets	3,004.1	827.9	452.4	4,284.4	647.0	4,931.4
Capital expenditures[‡]	286.7	32.4	28.6	347.7	—	347.7
1999						
Operating revenue	$1,734.9	$1,224.6	$1,032.2	$3,991.7	$ —	$3,991.7
Operating profit	273.7	369.7	179.6	823.0	(125.3)	697.7*
Depreciation and amortization[†]	232.8	40.8	32.6	306.2	2.2	308.4
Assets	2,172.0	827.1	592.1	3,591.2	526.9	4,118.1
Capital expenditures[‡]	298.2	57.8	44.7	400.7	—	400.7
1998						
Operating revenue	$1,620.3	$1,087.8	$1,016.9	$3,725.0	$ —	$3,725.0
Operating profit	202.1	355.9	126.9	684.9	(128.7)	556.2*

(continued)

(concluded)

(in millions)	McGraw-Hill Education	Financial Services	Information and Media Services	Segment Totals	Adjustments	Consolidated Total
Depreciation and amortization[†]	226.9	35.5	34.6	297.0	2.2	299.2
Assets	2,049.4	729.7	606.0	3,385.1	432.2	3,817.3
Capital expenditures[‡]	257.4	50.1	66.4	373.9	—	373.9

* Income before taxes on income.
[†] Includes amortization of goodwill and intangible assets and prepublication costs.
[‡] Includes purchase of property and equipment and investments in prepublication costs.

The operating profit adjustments listed above relate to the operating results of the corporate entity, which is not considered an operating segment, and includes all corporate expenses of $91.4 million, $83.3 million and $80.7 million, respectively, for 2000, 1999 and 1998, and net interest expense of $52.8 million, $42.0 million, and $48.0 million, respectively, of the company.

Corporate assets consist principally of cash and equivalents, investment in Rock-McGraw, Inc., prepaid pension expense, deferred income taxes and leasehold improvements related to subleased areas.

The following is a schedule of revenue and long-lived assets by geographic location:

(in millions)	2000		1999		1998	
	Revenue	Long-lived assets	Revenue	Long-lived assets	Revenue	Long-lived assets
United States	$3,492.9	$2,685.7	$3,243.5	$2,171.2	$3,041.2	$2,018.8
European region	406.9	69.9	372.7	67.8	330.3	67.3
Rest of world	381.2	57.7	375.5	67.7	353.5	60.3
Total	$4,281.0	$2,813.3	$3,991.7	$2,306.7	$3,725.0	$2,146.4

Foreign operating profit from our continuing businesses were $143.5 million, $138.8 million, and $119.4 million in 2000, 1999 and 1998, respectively. Foreign revenue, operating profit and long-lived assets include operations in 33 countries. The company does not have operations in any foreign country that represents more than 5% of its consolidated revenue. Transfers between geographic areas are recorded at agreed upon prices and intercompany revenue and profit are eliminated.

5. TAXES ON INCOME

Income before taxes on income resulted from domestic operations (including foreign branches) and foreign subsidiaries' operations as follows:

(in millions)	2000	1999	1998
Domestic operations	$724.8	$642.0	$509.3
Foreign operations	42.5	55.7	46.9
Total income before taxes	$767.3	$697.7	$556.2

A reconciliation of the U.S statutory tax rate to the company's effective tax rate for financial reporting purposes follows:

	2000	1999	1998
U.S. statutory rate	35.0%	35.0%	35.0%
Goodwill amortization	0.9	0.9	1.2
Effect of state and local income taxes	3.9	4.1	4.1
Other – net	(1.3)	(1.0)	(1.3)
Effective tax rate	38.5%	39.0%	39.0%

The provision for taxes on income consists of the following:

(in millions)	2000	1999	1998
Federal:			
Current	**$235.5**	$216.3	$135.6
Deferred	**(3.9)**	(6.5)	27.7
Total federal	**231.6**	209.8	163.3
Foreign:			
Current	**17.9**	18.6	21.8
Deferred	**0.1**	(0.6)	(3.0)
Total foreign	**18.0**	18.0	18.8
State and local:			
Current	**46.9**	45.7	25.9
Deferred	**(1.1)**	(1.4)	8.9
Total state and local	**45.8**	44.3	34.8
Total provision for taxes	**$295.4**	$272.1	$216.9

The principal temporary differences between the accounting for income and expenses for financial reporting and income tax purposes as of December 31 follow:

(in millions)	2000	1999
Fixed assets and intangible assets	**$(177.7)**	$(135.9)
Prepaid pension and other expenses	**(101.4)**	(93.5)
Unearned revenue	**(23.5)**	(16.4)
Reserves and accruals	**219.5**	165.1
Postretirement and postemployment benefits	**90.2**	90.5
Other – net	**22.5**	(2.7)
Deferred tax asset – net	**$ 29.6**	$ 7.1

The company made net income tax payments totaling $290.3 million in 2000, $215.0 million in 1999, and $193.0 million in 1998.

The company has not recorded deferred income taxes applicable to undistributed earnings of foreign subsidiaries that are indefinitely reinvested in foreign operations. Undistributed earnings amounted to approximately $77 million at December 31, 2000, excluding amounts that, if remitted, generally would not result in any additional U.S. income taxes because of available foreign tax credits. If the earnings of such foreign subsidiaries were not indefinitely reinvested, a deferred tax liability of approximately $20 million would have been required.

6. RENTAL EXPENSE AND LEASE OBLIGATIONS

Rental expense for property and equipment under all operating lease agreements was as follows:

(in millions)	2000	1999	1998
Gross rental expense	**$134.4**	$130.2	$113.3
Less: sublease revenue	**28.5**	30.4	30.0
Net rental expense	**$105.9**	$ 99.8	$ 83.3

The company is committed under lease arrangements covering property, computer systems and office equipment. Certain lease arrangements contain escalation clauses covering increased costs for various defined real estate taxes and operating services.

The company entered into a lease agreement in 1998 for its headquarters building, referred to in Note 1, covering approximately 0.4 million square feet starting in 2002.

Minimum rental commitments under existing noncancelable leases with a remaining term of more than one year, including the company's headquarters building, are shown in the following table. The annual rental commitments for real estate through the year 2003 have been reduced by approximately $11 million of rental income from existing noncancelable subleases.

(in millions)	
2001	$ 95.4
2002	100.4
2003	99.6
2004	83.8
2005	76.8
2006 and beyond	920.5
Total	$1,376.5

7. CAPITAL STOCK

On January 27, 1999, the Board of Directors declared a two-for-one stock split of the company's common stock, payable on March 8, 1999, to stockholders of record on February 24, 1999. The Board of Directors also approved a share repurchase program authorizing the repurchase of up to 15 million shares, approximately 7.5% of the company's outstanding common stock. The company implemented the program through open market purchases and private transactions. Through December 31, 2000, the company had repurchased approximately 6.3 million shares of common stock from the 1999 program at a total cost of $341.5 million. The repurchased shares will be used for general corporate purposes, including the issuance of shares for stock compensation plans. In the event of a significant investment opportunity, the company may slow the pace of repurchase activity.

The number of common shares reserved for issuance for employee stock plan awards was 23,162,119 at December 31, 2000 and 15,628,036 at December 31, 1999. Under the Director Deferred Stock Ownership Plan, 312,023 and 313,095 common shares were reserved for issuance at December 31, 2000 and 1999.

The $1.20 convertible preference stock may be converted into common stock at the option of the shareholder at the rate of one share of preference stock for 13.2 shares of common stock.

Two million shares of preferred stock, par value $1 per share, are authorized; none have been issued. 600,000 shares have been reserved for issuance under a Preferred Share Purchase Rights Plan adopted by the company's Board of Directors on July 29, 1998. Under the 1998 Rights Plan, one Right for each share of common stock outstanding was issued to shareholders of record on August 14, 1998. These Rights will become exercisable only if a person or group acquires 20% or more of the company's common stock or announces a tender offer that would result in the ownership of 20% or more of the common stock. Each Right will then entitle the holder to buy a 1/400th interest in a share of Series A preferred stock at an exercise price of $150. The Rights are redeemable by the company's Board of Directors for one-quarter cent each prior to a 20% acquisition by a third party. The 1998 Plan also gives the Board of Directors the option to exchange one share of common stock of the company for each Right (not owned by the acquirer) after an acquirer holds 20% but less than 50% of the outstanding shares of common stock. In the event, after a person or group acquires 20% or more of the company's stock, that the company is acquired in a merger or other business combination transaction of 50% or more of its consolidated assets or earning power are sold, each Right becomes exercisable for common stock equivalent to two times the exercise price of the Right.

Dividends were paid at the quarterly rate of $0.235 per common share and $0.30 per preference share. All dividends on preference stock are cumulative. Total dividends paid in 2000, 1999, and 1998 were $182.5 million, $169.0 million and $154.4 million, respectively.

8. STOCK PLAN AWARDS

The company applies the provisions of APBO No. 25, Accounting for Stock Issued to Employees, in accounting for its stock-based awards. Accordingly, no compensation cost has been recognized for its stock option plans other than for its restricted stock performance awards.

The company has two stock option plans: the 1993 and 1987 Employee Stock Incentive Plans.

The plans provide for the granting of incentive stock options, nonqualified stock options, stock appreciation rights, restricted stock awards, deferred stock (applicable to the 1987 Plan only) or other stock-based awards to purchase a total of 37.8 million shares of the company's common stock − 9.2 million shares under the 1987 Plan and 28.6 million shares under the 1993 Plan, as amended.

Stock options, which may not be granted at a price less than the fair market value of the company's common stock at date of grant, vest in two years in equal annual installments and have a maximum term of ten years.

Beginning in 1997, participants who exercise an option by tendering previously owned shares of common stock of the company may elect to receive a one-time restoration option covering the number of shares tendered. Restoration options are granted at fair market value of the company's common stock on the date of the grant, have a maximum term equal to the remainder of the original option term, and are subject to a six-month vesting period.

Under the fair value based method of accounting in SFAS No. 123, Accounting for Stock-Based Compensation, net income would have been reduced by $23.1 million, or $0.12 per diluted share for 2000, $16.2 million, or $0.08 per diluted share for 1999 and $1.9 million, or $0.01 per diluted share for 1998, after accounting for stock-based compensation effective for awards made January 1, 1995 and thereafter.

The fair value of each option grant was estimated on the date of grant using the Black-Scholes option-pricing model with the following assumptions for 2000, 1999, and 1998, respectively: risk-free average interest rate of 6.6%, 5.1% and 5.6%; dividend yield of 1.7%, 1.7%, and 2.1%; volatility of 28%, 24%, and 22%; and expected life of five years for all years.

A summary of the status of the company's stock option plans as of December 31 and activity during the year follows:

(in thousands of shares)	Shares	Weighted average exercise price
Outstanding at December 31, 1997	7,130	$ 20.46
Options granted	3,825	37.74
Options exercised	(1,871)	19.93
Options cancelled and expired	(216)	28.41
Outstanding at December 31, 1998	8,868	$ 27.79
Options granted	4,100	53.71
Options exercised	(2,260)	23.05
Options cancelled and expired	(358)	46.58
Outstanding at December 31, 1999	10,350	$ 38.41
Options granted	4,154	49.96
Options exercised	(1,847)	31.20
Options cancelled and expired	(451)	50.32
Outstanding at December 31, 2000	**12,206**	**$42.97**

At December 31, 2000, 1999 and 1998, options for 6,841,000, 5,328,000 and 4,644,000 shares of common stock were exercisable. The weighted average fair value of options granted during 2000, 1999 and 1998 was $15.70, $13.69 and $8.95, respectively.

A summary of information about stock options outstanding and options exercisable at December 31, 2000 follows:

(in thousands of shares) Range of exercise prices	Options Outstanding			Options Exercisable	
	Shares	Weighted average remaining term	Weighted average exercise price	Shares	Weighted average exercise price
$14.25 to $17.44	853	2.99 years	$16.27	853	$16.27
$21.19 to $31.16	1,365	5.58 years	$22.97	1,365	$22.97
$33.55 to $49.66	4,963	8.15 years	$40.98	2,628	$37.53
$50.41 to $66.84	5,025	8.54 years	$54.89	1,995	$54.29
$14.25 to $66.84	**12,206**	**7.67 years**	**$42.97**	**6,841**	**$36.86**

Under the Director Deferred Stock Ownership Plan, a total of 312,023 shares of common stock was reserved as of December 31, 2000, and may be credited to deferred stock accounts for eligible Directors. In general, the Plan requires that 50% of eligible Directors' annual compensation plus dividend equivalents be credited to deferred stock accounts. Each Director may also elect to defer all or a portion of the remaining compensation and have an equivalent number of shares credited to the deferred stock account. Recipients under this Plan are not required to provide consideration to the company other than rendering service. Shares will be delivered as of the date a recipient ceases to be a member of the Board of Directors or within five years thereafter, if so elected. The Plan will remain in effect until terminated by the Board of Directors or until no shares of stock remain available under the Plan.

Restricted stock performance awards have been granted under the 1993 and 1987 Plans. These restricted stock awards will vest only if the company achieves certain financial goals over various vesting periods. Recipients are not required to provide consideration to the company other than rendering service and have the right to vote the shares and to receive dividends.

A total of 270,176 restricted shares were issued at an average market value of $51.77 in 2000, 280,405 shares at an average market value of $52.70 in 1999 and 373,596 shares at an average market value of $37.54 in 1998. The awards are recorded at the market value on the date of grant. Initially, the total market value of the shares is treated as unearned compensation and is charged to expense over the respective vesting periods. Under APBO No. 25, for performance incentive shares, adjustments are also made to expense for changes in market value and achievement of financial goals. Restricted stock compensation charged to expense was $31.5 million for 2000, $33.0 million for 1999 and $37.0 million for 1998. Restricted shares outstanding at the end of the year were 690,307 in 2000, 868,039 in 1999, and 1,121,750 in 1998.

9. RETIREMENT PLANS

The company and its subsidiaries have a number of defined benefit pension plans and defined contribution plans covering substantially all employees. The company's primary pension plan is a noncontributory plan under which benefits are based on employee career employment compensation. The company also has a voluntary deferred compensation plan under which the company matches employee contributions up to certain levels of compensation and an Employee Retirement Account Plan under which the company contributes a percentage of eligible employees' compensation to the employees' accounts.

For purposes of determining annual pension cost, prior service costs and the net asset at January 1, 1986 are being amortized straight-line over the average remaining service period of employees expected to receive benefits. The assumed return on plan assets of 9.5% is based on a calculated market-related value of assets, which recognizes changes in market value over five years.

A summary of pension income for the company's domestic defined benefit plans follows:

(in millions)	2000	1999	1998
Service cost	$ 18.2	$ 20.2	$ 17.6
Interest cost	41.2	38.2	36.1
Expected return on assets	(84.1)	(69.4)	(60.8)
Curtailment credit	(2.0)	—	—
Settlement charge	0.5	—	—
Amortization of:			
Transitional net asset	—	(0.1)	(0.7)
Prior service cost	1.1	1.1	1.0
Actuarial (gain)/loss	(15.0)	(1.5)	(0.7)
Net pension income	$(40.1)	$ (11.5)	$ (7.5)
Assumed rates – January 1:			
Discount rate	7½%	6¾%	7¼%
Compensation increase factor	5½	5½	5½
Return on assets	9½	9½	9½

The company also has unfunded supplemental benefit plans to provide senior management with supplemental retirement, disability and death benefits. Supplemental retirement benefits are based on final monthly earnings. Pension cost was approximately $6 million for 2000 and 1999 and $4 million for 1998. The accrued benefit obligation as of December 31, 2000 was $32.1 million.

Total retirement plans cost was $26.3 million for 2000, $48.6 million for 1999 and $45.3 million for 1998.

The funded status of the domestic defined benefit plans as of December 31 follows:

(in millions)	2000	1999
Change in benefit obligation		
Net benefit obligation at beginning of year	$ 540.8	$ 557.5
Service cost	18.2	20.2
Plan amendments	0.9	—
Interest cost	41.2	38.2
Actuarial loss/(gain)	24.0	(39.5)
Curtailments	(2.4)	—
Settlements	0.5	—
Gross benefits paid	(37.4)	(35.6)
Net benefit obligation at end of year	$ 585.8	$ 540.8
Change in plan assets		
Fair value of plan assets at beginning of year	1,190.4	905.5
Actual return on plan assets	(57.5)	320.5
Employer contributions	—	—
Gross benefits paid	(37.4)	(35.6)
Fair value of plan assets at end of year	$1,095.5	$1,190.4
Funded status at end of year	509.7	649.7
Unrecognized net actuarial (gain)/loss	(353.2)	(533.9)
Unrecognized prior service costs	3.1	3.7
Unrecognized net transition obligation/(asset)	—	—
Prepaid pension cost	$ 159.6	$ 119.5
Assumed rates – December 31:		
Discount rate	7½ %	7½ %
Compensation increase factor	5½	5½

The company has several foreign pension plans that do not determine the accumulated benefits or net assets available for benefits as disclosed above. The amounts involved are not material and are therefore not included.

10. POSTRETIREMENT HEALTHCARE AND OTHER BENEFITS

The company and some of its domestic subsidiaries provide certain medical, dental and life insurance benefits for retired employees and eligible dependents. The medical and dental plans are contributory while the life insurance plan is noncontributory. The company currently does not fund any of these plans.

Postretirement benefits cost was $3.4 million in 2000, $5.5 million in 1999, and $6.9 million in 1998. A summary of the components of the cost in 2000, 1999 and 1998 follows:

(in millions)	2000	1999	1998
Service cost	$ 2.3	$ 2.4	$ 2.5
Interest cost	9.0	8.7	9.4
Curtailment credit	(0.8)	—	—
Settlement gain	(1.4)	—	—
Amortization of:			
Prior service cost	(2.6)	(3.4)	(2.6)
Actuarial (gain)/loss	(3.1)	(2.2)	(2.4)
Postretirement benefits cost	$ 3.4	$ 5.5	$ 6.9

A summary of the components of the unfunded postretirement benefit obligation as of December 31 follows:

(in millions)	2000	1999
Change in benefit obligation		
Net benefit obligation at beginning of year	$ 128.2	$ 142.7
Service cost	2.3	2.4
Interest cost	9.0	8.7
Plan participants contributions	1.5	2.0
Plan amendments	—	2.1
Settlements	(1.0)	—
Actuarial (gain)/loss	9.1	(16.9)
Gross benefits paid	(13.9)	(12.8)
Net benefit obligation at end of year	$ 135.2	$ 128.2
Change in plan assets		
Fair value of plan assets at beginning of year	—	—
Employer contributions	12.4	10.8
Plan participants contributions	1.5	2.0
Gross benefits paid	(13.9)	(12.8)
Fair value of plan assets at end of year	—	—
Funded status at end of year	$(135.2)	$(128.2)
Unrecognized net actuarial (gain)/loss	(37.7)	(50.3)
Unrecognized prior service costs	(5.6)	(9.0)
Accrued benefit cost	$(178.5)	$(187.5)

The assumed weighted average healthcare cost trend rate ranges from 6.0% in 2000 decreasing ratably to 5.5% in 2002 and remaining at that level thereafter. The weighted average discount rate used to measure expense was 7.5% in 2000 and 6.75% in 1999; the rate used to measure the accumulated postretirement benefit obligation was 7.50% in 2000 and 1999. Assumed healthcare cost trends have a significant effect on the amounts reported for the healthcare plans. A one-percentage point change in assumed healthcare cost trend creates the following effects:

(in millions)	One-Percentage Point Increase	One-Percentage Point Decrease
Effect on total of service and interest cost	$ 0.9	$ (0.8)
Effect on postretirement benefit obligation	$10.8	$(10.0)

11. EARNINGS PER SHARE

A reconciliation of the number of shares used for calculating basic earnings per common share and diluted earnings per common share follows:

(in thousands)	2000	1999	1998
Net income	$403,794	$425,574	$330,595
Average number of common shares outstanding	194,099	196,311	197,206
Effect of stock options and other dilutive securities	1,973	2,246	1,898
Average number of common shares outstanding including effect of dilutive securities	196,072	198,557	199,104

Restricted performance shares outstanding at December 31, 2000 of 633,000 were not included in the computation of diluted earnings per common share because the necessary vesting conditions have not yet been met.

As stated in Note 1, the company restated the prior-year financial statements to reflect a change in recording certain subscription revenue from the cash basis to the accrual basis of accounting. The impact of the restatement on 1999 and 1998 net income was a decrease of $0.2 million and $2.5 million, respectively. The restatement resulted in a $0.01 dilution of basic and diluted earnings per share in 1998. Refer to Note 12 for further information.

12. ACCOUNTING CHANGE AND RESTATEMENT

In December 1999, the Securities and Exchange Commission issued Staff Accounting Bulletin ("SAB") No. 101, Revenue Recognition in Financial Statements, which summarized the Staff's views regarding the recognition and reporting of revenue and related expenses in certain transactions. SAB 101, which was further clarified in 2000, was required to be implemented by the fourth quarter retroactive to January 1, 2000.

In consideration of the views expressed in SAB 101 and related interpretations, the company modifed its revenue recognition policies related to various service contracts. Under SAB 101, the company will recognize revenue relating to agreements where it provides more than one service based upon the fair value to the customer of each service, rather than recognizing revenue based on the level of service effort to fulfill such contracts. If the fair value to the customer for each service is not objectively determinable, revenue will be recognized ratably over the service period.

The cumulative effect of the accounting change as of January 1, 2000 results in a charge to income of $68.1 million (net of income taxes of $46.7 million). The effect of the change on the year ended December 31, 2000 was to decrease net income before the cumulative effect of the accounting change by $(9.2) million, or $(0.04) per diluted share. On a pro forma basis, the impact for the years ended December 31, 1999 and December 31, 1998 is $(12.2) million, ($0.06 per diluted share) and $(10.5) million ($0.05 per diluted share), respectively. For the quarters ended March 31, June 30, September 30 and December 31, 2000, the impact of the accounting change was to (decrease)/ increase revenue by $(15.5) million, $(7.5) million, $2.1 million and $(5.5) million, respectively and to (decrease)/ increase net income by $(12.5) million, $(3.6) million, $(2.5) million and $9.4 million, respectively.

For the quarters ended March 31, June 30, September 30, and December 31, 2000 the company recognized $43.4 million, $31.8 million, $18.6 million and $5.9 million, in revenue, respectively, that was included in the cumulative effect adjustment as of January 1, 2000. The effect on the first, second, third and fourth quarters was to increase net income by $26.5 million, $19.4 million, $11.3 million and $3.6 million, respectively (after

reduction for income taxes of $16.9 million, $12.4 million, $7.3 million and $2.3 million, respectively), during those periods.

In addition, the company also restated its consolidated financial statements. Previously, subscription income for units whose revenue was principally from advertising was recognized as received. As part of the restatement, such income is being deferred over the related subscription periods.

As a result, the consolidated financial statements were restated to defer revenue of $0.3 million and $4.2 million for the years ended December 31, 1999 and 1998, respectively. The impact of the restatement was to reduce net income by $0.2 million ($0.00 per diluted share) and $2.5 million (or $0.01 per diluted share) for 1999 and 1998, respectively. The effect of that revenue for the first, second, third and fourth quarters of the year ended December 31, 2000 was to (decrease) increase net income by $(1.7) million, $2.6 million, $0.4 million and $(1.5) million, respectively, (after an (expense) benefit for income taxes of $(1.0) million, $1.6 million, $0.2 million and $(0.9) million, respectively) during those periods. The cumulative effect of the restatement to opening retained income at January 1, 1998 was $40.2 million.

REPORT OF MANAGEMENT

TO THE SHAREHOLDERS OF THE McGRAW-HILL COMPANIES, INC.

The financial statements in this report were prepared by the management of The McGraw-Hill Companies, Inc., which is responsible for their integrity and objectivity.

These statements, prepared in conformity with generally accepted accounting principles and including amounts based on management's best estimates and judgments, present fairly The McGraw-Hill Companies' financial condition and the results of the company's operations. Other financial information given in this report is consistent with these statements.

The McGraw-Hill Companies' management maintains a system of internal accounting controls designed to provide reasonable assurance that the financial records accurately reflect the company's operations and that the company's assets are protected against loss. Consistent with the concept of reasonable assurance, the company recognizes that the relative costs of these controls should not exceed the expected benefits in maintaining these controls. It further assures the quality of the financial records in several ways: a program of internal audits, the careful selection and training of management personnel, maintaining an organizational structure that provides an appropriate division of financial responsibilities, and communicating financial and other relevant policies throughout the corporation. The financial statements in this report have been audited by Ernst & Young LLP, independent auditors, in accordance with auditing standards generally accepted in the United States. The independent auditors were retained to express an opinion on the financial statements, which appears in the next column.

The McGraw-Hill Companies' Board of Directors, through its Audit Committee, composed entirely of outside directors, is responsible for reviewing and monitoring the company's financial reporting and accounting practices. The Audit Committee meets periodically with management, the company's internal auditors and the independent auditors to ensure that each group is carrying out its respective responsibilities. In addition, the independent auditors have full and free access to the Audit Committee and meet with it with no representatives from management present.

Harold McGraw III
Chairman of the Board, President and Chief Executive Officer

Robert J. Bahash
Executive Vice President and Chief Financial Officer

REPORT OF INDEPENDENT AUDITORS

THE BOARD OF DIRECTORS AND SHAREHOLDERS OF THE McGRAW-HILL COMPANIES, INC.

We have audited the accompanying consolidated balance sheets of The McGraw-Hill Companies, Inc. as of December 31, 2000 and 1999, and the related consolidated statements of income, shareholders' equity and cash flows for each of the three years in the period ended December 31, 2000. These financial statements are the responsibility of the company's management. Our responsibility is to express an opinion on these financial statements based on our audits.

We conducted our audits in accordance with auditing standards generally accepted in the United States. Those standards require that we plan and perform the audit to obtain reasonable assurance about whether the financial statements are free of material misstatement. An audit includes examining, on a test basis, evidence supporting the amounts and disclosures in the financial statements. An audit also includes assessing the accounting principles used and significant estimates made by management, as well as evaluating the overall financial statement presentation. We believe that our audits provide a reasonable basis for our opinion.

In our opinion, the consolidated financial statements referred to above present fairly, in all material respects, the consolidated financial position of The McGraw-Hill Companies, Inc. at December 31, 2000 and 1999, and the consolidated results of its operations and its cash flows for each of the three years in the period ended December 31, 2000, in conformity with accounting principles generally accepted in the United States.

As discussed in Note 12 to the consolidated financial statements, effective January 1, 2000, the company changed its method of accounting for revenue recognition on certain service contracts. In addition, the consolidated financial statements have been restated.

Ernst & Young LLP
New York, New York
February 14, 2001

Supplemental Financial Information Quarterly Financial Information (unaudited) (Restated)

(in thousands, except per-share data)	First quarter	Second quarter	Third quarter	Fourth quarter	Total year
2000					
Operating revenue (Note 12)	$784,214	$1,015,924	$1,394,470	$1,086,360	$4,280,968
Income before taxes and cumulative adjustment	70,561	173,710	350,588	172,483	767,342
Income before cumulative adjustment (Note 12)	43,395	106,832	215,611	106,078	471,916
Net income	(24,727)	106,832	215,611	106,078	403,794
Earnings per share:					
Basic:					
Income before cumulative adjustment	0.22	0.55	1.11	0.55	2.43
Net income	(0.13)	0.55	1.11	0.55	2.08
Diluted:					
Income before cumulative adjustment	0.22	0.55	1.10	0.54	2.41
Net income	(0.13)	0.55	1.10	0.54	2.06
1999					
Operating revenue (Note 12)	$716,830	$915,951	$1,324,332	$1,034,572	$3,991,685
Income before taxes	40,437	140,803	318,218	198,204	697,662
Net income	24,667	85,889	194,113	120,905	425,574
Earnings per share:					
Basic	0.12	0.44	0.99	0.62	2.17
Diluted	0.12	0.43	0.98	0.61	2.14
1998					
Operating revenue (Note 12)	$703,230	$884,868	$1,207,626	$929,247	$3,724,971
Income before taxes and extraordinary item (Note 3)	32,824	131,355	278,914	113,155	556,248
Net income	20,023	80,126	161,422	69,024	330,595
Earnings per share:					
Basic:					
Income before extraordinary item	0.10	0.41	0.86	0.35	1.72
Net income	0.10	0.41	0.82	0.35	1.68
Diluted:					
Income before extraordinary item	0.10	0.40	0.85	0.35	1.70
Net income	0.10	0.40	0.81	0.35	1.66

HIGH AND LOW SALES PRICES OF THE McGRAW-HILL COMPANIES COMMON STOCK ON THE NEW YORK STOCK EXCHANGE*

	2000**	1999**	1998**
First quarter	$61.69–43.50	$59.13–48.88	$39.00–34.25
Second quarter	59.88–41.88	60.75–50.44	41.50–36.38
Third quarter	67.69–54.25	54.13–47.13	43.50–37.06
Fourth quarter	66.00–52.00	63.13–49.00	51.69–36.13
Year**	67.69–41.88	63.13–47.13	51.69–34.25

* The New York Stock Exchange is the principal market on which the Corporation's shares are traded.
** All high and low prices reflect the two-for-one stock split approved by the Corporation's Board of Directors on January 27, 1999.

Appendix **2**

Excerpts from June 30, 2001, Quarterly News Release of The McGraw-Hill Companies, Inc.

1221 Avenue of the Americas
New York, NY 10020-1095
Tel 212 512 2000
Fax 212 512 3840
investor_relations@mcgraw-hill.com
www.mcgraw-hill.com/investor_relations

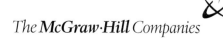 The *McGraw·Hill* Companies

NEWS RELEASE

THE McGRAW-HILL COMPANIES REPORTS 7.3% INCREASE IN 2nd QUARTER EPS BEFORE ONE-TIME ITEMS

New York, NY, July 24, 2001—The McGraw-Hill Companies (NYSE: MHP) today reported diluted earnings per share before a one-time gain on the sale of DRI and restructuring initiatives increased by 7.3% to 59 cents in the second quarter compared to 55 cents last year. Including the one-time items, diluted earnings per share for the second quarter were 61 cents. Revenue for the second quarter increased 13.1% to $1.1 billion.

"Strong performances in education and financial services were key to our second quarter," said Harold McGraw III, chairman, president and chief executive officer of The McGraw-Hill Companies. "The results offset a decline in our advertising-based businesses, demonstrating again the resilience of our portfolio.

"In keeping with our strategic focus on equities and mutual funds at Standard & Poor's Information Services, we pruned the portfolio in the second quarter. In addition to divesting DRI, an economic research and consulting company, we announced the August shutdown of the *Blue List*, a municipal bond service for the secondary market, contributed Rational Investor to mPower.com, Inc. in exchange for an equity position in the online investment advisory service for the retirement planning market and wrote down selected assets.

"Net income for the second quarter before the one-time items grew to $115.6 million. Including one-time events, net income for the second quarter was $120.0 million.

"For the first half of 2001, earnings per share before one-time events were 67 cents versus 72 cents last year. Including a one-time gain on the sale of real estate, the divestiture of DRI and other one-time events in 2001, earnings per share for the first half were 71 cents versus 42 cents last year after a cumulative adjustment and a gain on the sale of Tower Group International in 2000. The cumulative adjustment of $68.1 million, or 35 cents per diluted share, in compliance with SEC-mandated accounting charges for SAB 101 and a $16.6 million pre-tax gain, or 5 cents per diluted share, on the gain on the sale of Tower Group International, were taken in the first quarter of 2000."

Education: Revenue for this segment in the second quarter increased 26.4% to $566.2 million and operating profits grew by 33.0% to $68.0 million.

"The School Education Group gained share in the elementary-high school market with strong performances in reading, language arts, literature, math and testing," said Mr. McGraw. "We are finishing first or second in every major reading or literature adoption this year.

"In the key Texas adoption, we took first place, winning more than 30% of the K-12 market dollars. Macmillan/McGraw-Hill and SRA/McGraw-Hill combined to lead the elementary reading market while Glencoe again took share in literature, winning more than 27% of the market with a program that was first introduced last year. Recently acquired NTC/Tribune high school titles also contributed to Glencoe's success in Texas.

"In Florida, we are the market leader in art and language arts at both the elementary and secondary levels.

"A good year is also taking shape in California. Our research-based *Open Court* reading program from SRA/McGraw-Hill continues to win new customers, who are purchasing it with state supplementary funds. We're also enjoying success in the second year of the science adoption, the third year of the social studies adoption, and with secondary math in the first year of this adoption. Only the elementary school math program is not matching expectations in California, although it is producing good results in other adoption states and the open territories.

"The Tribune Education acquisition also augmented sales in some important markets, including research-based math for SRA/McGraw-Hill, literacy and math supplements for Wright/McGraw-Hill and secondary remedial reading and elective course materials for Glencoe.

"CTB/McGraw-Hill, our full service testing company, produced another solid gain in the second quarter, benefiting from sales of custom contracts and *TerraNova,* its ground-breaking standardized achievement test.

"Our Higher Education business is showing strength across the board, gaining market share with solid results from both the front and back lists, which we expect to carry through in the key summer selling season. In building our market position, we continue to benefit from the delivery of digital solutions for both course management and classroom materials. There are now more than 60,000 college and university instructors registered to use our *PageOut* service to develop their own course-specific Web sites in the United States.

"Strong gains in Canada, and the Asia-Pacific markets helped produce a revenue gain for International Publishing, but shortfalls in Latin America and the Lbero Group resulted in a decline in operating profits.

"The Professional Book operations improved despite difficult economic conditions. *Brand Warfare*, a new title from Professional Book, hit the *BusinessWeek* and *Wall Street Journal's* best-seller lists."

Financial Services: "Revenue for this segment in the second quarter increased 15.8% to $365.8 million and operating profits, excluding one-time items, grew by 29.0% to $124.1 million. Including one-time items, operating profits grew by 14.4%.

"Surging bond market activity in the U.S. and Europe and solid growth in nontraditional services such as bank loan ratings resulted in double-digit top and bottom line gains for Standard & Poor's Credit Market Services in the second quarter. New issue dollar volume in the U.S. market grew by 62.6% in this period, according to Securities Data Corporation. In Europe, the dollar volume of bond issuance increased 31.5%, according to Bondware.

"Spurred by recent Interest rate cuts by the Federal Reserve Board, refinancing in the municipal bond market continues to grow. High yield issuance soared by 209% in the second quarter. Standard & Poor's also benefited from a robust global securitization market.

"Standard & Poor's Information Services produced a single-digit revenue gain, but operating profits declined due to investments in new products and softness in foreign exchange markets. Revenue for index and portfolio services, Compustat, ComStock and Fund Services all showed gains."

Information and Media Services: "Revenue for this segment decreased 13.8% to $217.5 million and operating profits fell 43.7% to $33.1 million, reflecting a sharp decline in the advertising market.

"At *BusinessWeek,* which had a record second quarter in 2000, ad pages declined 38.3%, according to Publishers Information Bureau. The Broadcasting Group also faced tough comparisons. Absent political advertising, which helped produce double-digit revenue and operating profit gains last year, both local and national time sales were down at Broadcasting. The Healthcare Group was also off as pharmaceutical companies cut back advertising.

"But there were some bright spots in the quarter. With a lift from the biennial Paris Air Show in May, the Aviation Week Group turned in outstanding results. And Platts, benefiting from volatility in energy markets, continues to produce gains.

"The Construction Information Group benefited from growth at Sweet's and cost reductions."

The Outlook: "With an excellent start in the education market and strength in Financial Services, we continue to look forward to our ninth consecutive year of double-digit top and bottom line growth."

The forward-looking statements in this news release involve risks and uncertainties and are subject to change based on various important factors, including worldwide economic and political conditions, the health of capital and equity markets, including future interest rate cuts, strength in advertising in the second half of 2001, continued strength in the education market, the successful marketing of new products and the effect of competitive products and pricing.

Founded in 1888, The McGraw-Hill Companies is a global information services provider meeting worldwide needs in the financial services, education and business information markets through leading brands such as Standard & Poor's, *BusinessWeek* and McGraw-Hill Education. The Corporation has more than 300 offices in 33 countries. Sales in 2000 were $4.3 billion. Additional information is available at http://www.mcgraw-hill.com.

The McGraw·Hill Companies

STATEMENTS OF INCOME
PERIODS ENDED JUNE 30 2001 AND 2000
(in thousands, except earnings per share)

(unaudited)	Three Months			Six Months		
	2001	2000	% Change	2001	2000	% Change
Operating revenue	$1,149,470	$1,015,924	13.1	$1,995,867	$1,800,138	10.9
Expenses—net	959,420	830,976	15.5	1,755,781	1,535,284	14.4
Income from operations	190,050	184,948	2.8	240,086	264,854	(9.4)
Interest expense—net	16,021	11,238	42.6	32,901	20,583	59.8
Income before taxes on income	174,029	173,710	0.2	207,185	244,271	(15.2)
Provision for taxes on income	54,032	66,878	(19.2)	66,797	94,044	(29.0)
Income before cumulative change in accounting	119,997	106,832	12.3	140,388	150,227	(6.5)
Cumulative change in accounting, net of tax	—	—	N/A	—	68,122	(100.0)
Net income	$ 119,997	$ 106,832	12.3	$ 140,388	$ 82,105	71.0
Earnings per common share:						
Basic						
Income before cumulative change in accounting	0.62	0.55	12.7	0.72	0.77	(6.5)
Net Income	$ 0.62	$ 0.55	12.7	$ 0.72	$ 0.42	71.4
Diluted						
Income before cumulative change in accounting	0.61	0.55	10.9	0.71	0.77	(7.8)
Net Income	$ 0.61	$ 0.55	10.9	$ 0.71	$ 0.42	69.0
Dividend per common share	$ 0.245	$ 0.235	4.3	$ 0.490	$ 0.470	4.3
Average number of common shares outstanding:						
Basic	194,571	193,705		194,433	194,227	
Diluted	196,962	195,440		196,632	195,952	

OPERATING RESULTS BY SEGMENT
PERIODS ENDED JUNE 30, 2001 AND 2000
(dollars in thousands)

(unaudited)	Revenue			Operating Profit		
	2001	**2000**	**% Change**	**2001**	**2000**	**% Change**
Three Months						
McGraw-Hill Education	$ 566,150	$ 447,734	26.4	$ 67,990	$ 51,126	33.0
Financial Services[1]	365,781	315,924	15.8	110,051	96,200	14.4
Information and Media Services	217,539	252,266	(13.8)	33,073	58,779	(43.7)
Total operating segments	1,149,470	1,015,924	13.1	211,114	206,105	2.4
General corporate expense	—	—	—	(21,064)	(21,157)	(0.4)
Interest expense–net	—	—	—	(16,021)	(11,238)	42.6
Total company	$1,149,470	$1,015,924	13.1	$174,029*	$173,710*	0.2
(unaudited)						
Six Months						
McGraw-Hill Education	$ 873,908	$ 684,096	27.7	$ 10,160	$ 12,730	(20.2)
Financial Services[1]	710,962	620,612	14.6	216,659	184,180	17.6
Information and Media Services[2]	410,997	495,430	(17.0)	46,744	107,886	(56.7)
Total operating segments	1,995,867	1,800,138	10.9	273,563	304,796	(10.2)
General corporate expense[3]	—	—	—	(33,477)	(39,942)	(16.2)
Interest expense–net	—	—	—	(32,901)	(20,583)	59.8
Total company	$1,995,867	$1,800,138	10.9	$207,185*	$244,271*	(15.2)

* Income before taxes on income.

[1] Three month and year-to-date results for Financial Services include an $8.8 million pre-tax gain (13 cents per diluted share) on the sale of DRI and $22.8 million pre-tax charge (11 cents per diluted share) for restructuring initiatives.

[2] Results for Information and Media Services include a $16.6 million pre-tax gain (5 cents per diluted share) on the disposition of Tower Group International in February 2000.

[3] Year-to-date corporate expense in 2001 includes a $6.9 million pre-tax gain (2 cents per diluted share) on the sale of real estate.

THE McGRAW-HILL COMPANIES DECLARES QUARTERLY DIVIDENDS

New York, NY, July 25, 2001—At a regular meeting of the Board of Directors of The McGraw-Hill Companies (NYSE: MHP) held today, the following dividends were declared:

- On the $1.20 convertible preference stock, a quarterly dividend of thirty cents ($0.30) per share payable October 1, 2001 to shareholders of record on August 28, 2001.

- On the Corporation's common stock, a quarterly dividend of twenty-four and one-half cents ($0.24 1/2) per share payable September 12, 2001 to shareholders of record on August 28, 2001.

The year 2001 marks the 28th consecutive year of increased dividends for The McGraw-Hill Companies. In January the Corporation announced a 4.3% increase in the regular quarterly cash dividends on its common stock. The annual rate of $.98 per share in 2001 represents a compound growth rate in The McGraw-Hill Companies' common share dividend of 10.7% since 1974.

To our shareholders:
For more information on The McGraw-Hill Companies, visit http://www.mcgraw-hill.com/investor_relations. The Web site provides information on the corporation's dividend payments, stock quotes and charts, SEC filings, including the 10-Q and 10-K, as well as earnings announcements.

Review Questions

1. What is an *operating segment* of a business enterprise?

2. Is the concept of segment reporting consistent with the theory of consolidated financial statements? Explain.

3. Differentiate between the *measurement date* and the *disposal date* for the discontinuance of a business segment. Define *phase-out period.*

4. Discuss the provisions of *APB Opinion No. 28,* "Interim Financial Reporting," dealing with the accounting for costs associated with revenue in interim financial reports.

5. How is lower-of-cost-or-market accounting for inventories applied in interim financial reports?

6. Explain the technique included in *APB Opinion No. 28,* "Interim Financial Reporting," for the measurement of income taxes expense in interim financial reports.

7. Identify four U.S. statutes administered by the SEC.

8. Differentiate between *Form 10-K* and *Form 8-K* filed with the SEC under the Securities Exchange Act of 1934.

9. Under what circumstances must financial statements of a business enterprise be included in a *proxy statement* issued to the enterprise's stockholders under the provisions of the Securities Exchange Act of 1934?

10. What position did the SEC take regarding its role in the establishment of accounting principles?

11. How do accountants use *Regulation S-X* in filings with the SEC?

12. What is *Regulation S-K* of the SEC?

13. What are *Financial Reporting Releases*?

14. Does the SEC *require* the inclusion of *financial forecasts* in filings with the SEC?

Exercises

(Exercise 13.1) Select the best answer for each of the following multiple-choice questions:

1. In financial reporting for segments of a business enterprise, *must* the segment profit or loss of an operating segment include:

	Interest Expense?	Income Taxes Expense?
a.	Yes	Yes
b.	Yes	No
c.	No	Yes
d.	No	No

2. Rawson Company is a diversified enterprise that discloses segment financial information for its operating segments. The following information is available for 2003:

Operating Segment	Sales	Traceable Expenses	Nontraceable Expenses
Segment A	$400,000	$225,000	
Segment B	300,000	240,000	
Segment C	200,000	135,000	
Totals	$900,000	$600,000	$150,000

Nontraceable expenses are allocated based on the ratio of a segment's income before nontraceable expenses to total income before nontraceable expenses. The segment profit for Operating Segment B for 2003 is:

a. $0.

b. $10,000.

c. $30,000.

d. $50,000.

e. Some other amount.

3. Irving Company discloses operating segment information in its annual report. The following data were available for the year ended December 31, 2003:

Operating Segment	Sales	Traceable Expenses
Chemicals	$ 500,000	$300,000
Tools	400,000	250,000
Services	300,000	175,000
Totals	$1,200,000	$725,000

Additional expenses for the year ended December 31, 2003, not included above, were as follows:

Nontraceable operating expenses	$180,000
Unallocated expenses	120,000

Appropriate common expenses are allocated to operating segments based on the ratio of a segment's sales to total sales. The segment profit for the Services operating segment for the year ended December 31, 2003, is:

a. $125,000

b. $80,000

c. $65,000

d. $50,000

e. Some other amount.

4. Revenue of an operating segment of a business enterprise includes:

a. Intersegment sales or transfers.

b. An appropriate portion of revenue earned solely at the corporate level.

c. Equity in net income of influenced investees.

d. All of the foregoing.

5. For the reporting of segment revenues for operating segments in interim reports, the FASB requires that:

a. Sales to unaffiliated customers and intersegment sales or transfers be disclosed separately.

b. Sales to unaffiliated customers and intersegment sales or transfers be reported as a single amount.

c. Intersegment sales or transfers be excluded.

d. None of the foregoing take place.

6. On September 15, 2003, the board of directors of Harte Company approved a plan to dispose of an operating segment. It was expected that the disposal would be accomplished on June 1, 2004, for $1 million proceeds. Disposal costs of $150,000

were paid by Harte during the fiscal year ended April 30, 2004, and it was estimated that the carrying amount of the operating segment's net assets on June 1,
2004, would be $1,750,000. The operating segment had actual or estimated oper-
ating losses as follows:

May 1 through Sept. 14, 2003	$130,000
Sept. 15, 2003, through Apr. 30, 2004	50,000
May 1 through May 31, 2004	15,000

Disregarding income taxes, Harte Company displays in its income statement for
the fiscal year ended April 30, 2004 a loss on disposal of business segment of:

a. $0
b. $900,000
c. $915,000
d. $965,000

7. May a net-of-tax provision for operating losses of a discontinued operating segment during the phase-out period be included with:

	Income (Loss) of the Discontinued Business Segment?	Gain (Loss) on Disposal of the Discontinued Business Segment?
a.	Yes	Yes
b.	Yes	No
c.	No	Yes
d.	No	No

8. Trent Company had a net income of $700,000 for the fiscal year ended June 30,
2004, after the following events or transactions that occurred during the year:

(1) The decision was made July 1, 2003, to discontinue the plastics operating
segment.
(2) The plastics operating segment was sold December 31, 2003.
(3) Operating loss from July 1 to December 31, 2003, for the plastics operating
segment amounted to $60,000 before income tax benefit.
(4) Plastics operating segment net assets with a carrying amount of $350,000 were
sold for $200,000.

Trent's income tax rate was 40%. For the fiscal year ended June 30, 2004, Trent
Company's income from continuing operations was:

a. $574,000
b. $700,000
c. $784,000
d. $826,000
e. Some other amount

9. When an operating segment has been discontinued during the year, the segment's
losses of the current period up to the measurement date are displayed in the:

a. Income statement as part of the income (loss) from operations of the discontinued business segment.
b. Income statement as part of the loss on disposal of the discontinued business
segment.
c. Income statement as part of the income (loss) from continuing operations.
d. Retained earnings statement as a direct decrease in beginning retained earnings.

10. *APB Opinion No. 28,* "Interim Financial Reporting," provided special treatment for interim periods' cost of goods sold for:

   a. Gross margin method.
   b. Temporary depletions of base layers of last-in, first-out inventories.
   c. Temporary market declines of inventories.
   d. All of the foregoing.

11. In accordance with *APB Opinion No. 28,* "Interim Financial Reporting," may costs and expenses other than product costs be allocated among interim periods based on an estimate of:

	Time Expired?	*Benefit Received?*	*Activity Associated with the Periods?*
a.	Yes	Yes	Yes
b.	Yes	No	Yes
c.	No	Yes	No
d.	No	Yes	Yes

12. In *APB Opinion No. 28,* "Interim Financial Reporting," the APB adopted the:

   a. Integral theory
   b. Interim theory
   c. Discrete theory
   d. Unified theory

13. According to *APB Opinion No. 28,* "Interim Financial Reporting," must lower-of-cost-or-market writedowns of inventories be provided for interim periods if the interim date market declines are considered:

	Permanent?	*Temporary?*
a.	Yes	Yes
b.	Yes	No
c.	No	Yes
d.	No	No

14. In interim financial reporting, year-end adjustments to which of the following item or items must be estimated and assigned to interim periods?

   a. Inventory shrinkage.
   b. Doubtful accounts expense.
   c. Discretionary year-end bonuses.
   d. All of the foregoing.

15. According to *APB Opinion No. 28,* "Interim Financial Reporting," income taxes expense in an income statement for the first interim period of an enterprise's fiscal year should be computed by applying the:

   a. Estimated income tax rate for the full fiscal year to the pretax financial income for the interim period.
   b. Estimated income tax rate for the full fiscal year to the taxable income for the interim period.
   c. Statutory income tax rate to the pretax financial income for the interim period.
   d. Statutory income tax rate to the taxable income for the interim period.

16. Wade Company, which has a fiscal year ending February 28 or 29, had the following pretax financial income and estimated effective annual income tax rates for the first three quarters of the year ended February 28, 2003:

Quarter	Pre-Tax Financial Income	Estimated Effective Annual Income Tax Rate at End of Quarter
First	$60,000	40%
Second	70,000	40%
Third	40,000	45%

Wade's income taxes expense in its interim income statement for the third quarter of fiscal year 2003 is:

a. $18,000.   *b.* $24,500.   *c.* $25,500.   *d.* $76,500.   *e.* Some other amount

17. Which of the following SEC publications provides guidelines for the financial statements required in reports to the SEC?

   a. **Regulation S-X**
   b. **Regulation S-K**
   c. **Staff Accounting Bulletins**
   d. **Regulation C**

18. Guidance for the completion of nonfinancial statement disclosure requirements in the various *Forms* filed with the SEC is provided in:

   a. **Regulation S-X**
   b. **Regulation S-K**
   c. **ASR 142**
   d. **SAB 1**

19. Which of the following is not a registration statement filed with the SEC?

   a. **Form S-1**   *b.* **Form S-2**   *c.* **Form S-3**   *d.* **Form 10**   *e.* **Form 10-K**

20. The current report form of the SEC is:

   a. **Form 10-K**
   b. **Form 10-Q**
   c. **Form 8-K**
   d. Proxy statement

21. The SEC's present position with respect to the inclusion of financial forecasts in filings with the SEC is that financial forecasts are:

   a. Permissible
   b. Mandatory
   c. Forbidden
   d. Unimportant

(Exercise 13.2)   Data for the three operating segments of Polyglot Company for the fiscal year ended June 30, 2003, were as follows (amounts in thousands):

CHECK FIGURE

Alpha segment profit, $150,000.

	Operating Segment			
	Alpha	*Beta*	*Gamma*	*Total*
Sales to unaffiliated customers	$400	$500	$600	$1,500
Intersegment sales	50	40	30	120
Traceable expenses:				
Intersegment purchases	60	20	40	120
Other	200	300	500	1,000
Nontraceable expenses				150

Prepare a working paper to compute the revenue and segment profit or loss of each of the operating segments of Polyglot Company for the year ended June 30, 2003, assuming that Polyglot allocates nontraceable expenses to operating segments in the ratio of segment sales to unaffiliated customers.

(Exercise 13.3) Rinker Company operates in three different industries, each of which is appropriately regarded as an operating segment. Segment No. 1 contributed 60% of Rinker's total sales in 2003. Sales for Segment No. 1 were $900,000 and traceable expenses were $400,000 in 2003. Rinker's total nontraceable expenses for 2003 were $600,000. Rinker allocates nontraceable expenses based on the ratio of a segment's sales to total sales, an appropriate method of allocation.

Prepare a working paper to compute the segment profit or loss for Rinker Company's Segment No. 1 for 2003.

(Exercise 13.4) The nontraceable expenses of Coopers Company for the fiscal year ended June 30, 2003, totaled $310,000. The net sales, payroll totals, and average plant assets and inventories for the two operating segments of Coopers were as follows:

	Chemicals Segment	Sporting Goods Segment
Net sales	$1,400,000	$600,000
Payroll totals	150,000	100,000
Average plant assets and inventories	710,000	290,000

Prepare a working paper to compute the amount of Coopers Company's nontraceable expenses to be allocated to the Chemicals segment and the Sporting Goods segment of Coopers Company for the year ended June 30, 2003, assuming that such expenses are allocated to the two segments on the basis of the arithmetic average of the percentage of net sales, payroll taxes, and average plant assets and inventories applicable to each segment.

(Exercise 13.5) Canton Company allocates nontraceable expenses to its three operating segments in the ratio of net sales to unaffiliated customers. For the fiscal year ended April 30, 2003, relevant segment data were as follows:

	Operating Segment A	Operating Segment B	Operating Segment C
Revenue:			
Net sales to unaffiliated customers	$500,000	$300,000	$200,000
Intersegment transfers out	80,000	40,000	20,000
Costs and expenses:			
Traceable expenses	400,000	100,000	200,000
Intersegment transfers in	30,000	60,000	50,000

Nontraceable expenses of Canton Company for the year ended April 30, 2003, totaled $100,000.

Prepare a working paper to compute for each operating segment of Canton Company the following amounts for the year ended April 30, 2003: revenue, expenses, segment profit or loss. Use a column for each operating segment, as shown above.

(Exercise 13.6) Crossley Company had a net income of $600,000 for the year ended December 31, 2003, after inclusion of the following events or transactions that occurred during the year:

(1) The decision was made on January 2 to dispose of the cinder block operating segment.

(2) The cinder block operating segment was disposed of on July 1.

(3) Operating income from January 2 to June 30 for the cinder block operating segment amounted to $90,000 before income taxes.

(4) Cinder block operating segment net assets with a carrying amount of $250,000 were disposed of for $100,000.

Crossley was subject to income taxes at the rate of 40%.

a. Prepare a working paper to compute Crossley Company's income from continuing operations for the year ended December 31, 2003.

b. Prepare a working paper to compute Crossley Company's total income taxes (expense and allocated) for the year ended December 31, 2003.

(Exercise 13.7) Tovar Company's accounting records for the fiscal year ended August 31, 2003, include the following data with respect to its Wallis division, an operating segment. Sale of the net assets of that division to Expansive Enterprises, Inc., for $300,000 was authorized by Tovar's board of directors on August 31, 2003. Closing date of the disposal was expected to be February 29, 2004.

Wallis Division:	
Net sales, year ended Aug. 31, 2003	$200,000
Costs and expenses, year ended Aug. 31, 2003	150,000
Estimated operating losses, six months ending Feb. 29, 2004	40,000
Estimated carrying amount of net assets, Feb. 29, 2004	330,000

Tovar's income tax rate is 40%. For the year ended August 31, 2003, Tovar had a $640,000 income from continuing operations before income taxes.

Prepare a partial income statement for Tovar Company for the year ended August 31, 2003, to present the foregoing information. Disregard earnings per share data.

(Exercise 13.8) For the fiscal year ended June 30, 2003, Dispo Company, which has an income tax rate of 40%, had the following **pretax** amounts:

Income from continuing operations	$1,000,000
Loss from disposal of net assets of discontinued Division 105 (an operating segment)	60,000
Loss from operations of Division 105 from July 1, 2002, through the measurement date, Mar. 31, 2003	150,000
Loss from operations of Division 105 from Apr. 1, 2003, through the disposal date, May 31, 2003	20,000

Prepare a partial income statement for Dispo Company for the year ended June 30, 2003, beginning with income from continuing operations. Disregard basic earnings per share.

(Exercise 13.9) The income tax rate for Downsize Company was 40%, and it had no differences between pre-tax financial income and taxable income. For the fiscal year ended November 30, 2003, **pretax** amounts in the bottom portion of Downsize's income statement for the year then ended were as follows:

Income from continuing operations (before income taxes)	$500,000
Income from operations of discontinued Webb Division	
(an operating segment) (prior to measurement date)	60,000
(Loss) on disposal of Webb Division	(40,000)
(Operating losses) of Webb Division during phase-out period	(50,000)

Prepare a partial income statement, including intraperiod tax allocation, for Downsize Company for the year ended November 30, 2003. Disregard earnings per share data.

(Exercise 13.10)   Reducto Company had the following data for the fiscal year ended April 30, 2003, a year in which its directors had resolved on February 28, 2003, to dispose of Woeful Division, an operating segment, and completed the disposal on April 15, 2003:

Income tax rate	40%
Pretax:	
Income from continuing operations	$600,000
Loss from disposal of net assets of Woeful Division, Apr. 15, 2003	70,000
Operating losses of Woeful Division:	
May 1, 2002–Feb. 28, 2003	160,000
Mar. 1–Apr. 15, 2003	40,000

Prepare the bottom portion of Reducto Company's income statement for the year ended April 30, 2003, beginning with income from continuing operations before income taxes. Disregard basic earnings per share disclosures.

(Exercise 13.11)   On January 2, 2003, Luigi Company paid property taxes of $40,000 on its plant assets for 2003. In March, 2003, Luigi made customary annual major repairs to plant assets in the amount of $120,000. The repairs will benefit the entire year ended December 31, 2003. In April 2003, Luigi incurred a $420,000 loss from a replacement cost decline of inventories that was considered to be permanent.

Prepare a working paper to show how the foregoing items are reported in Luigi Company's quarterly income statements for the fiscal year ended December 31, 2003.

(Exercise 13.12)   Lundy Company sells a single product, which it purchases from three different vendors. On May 1, 2003, Lundy's inventory of the product consisted of 1,000 units at first-in, first-out cost of $7,500. Lundy's merchandise transactions for the fiscal year ended April 30, 2004, were as follows:

Quarter Ended	Units Purchased	Cost per Unit Purchased	Units Sold	End-of-Quarter Replacement Cost per Unit
July 31, 2003	5,000	$8.00	4,500	$8.50
Oct. 31, 2003	6,000	8.50	7,000	9.00
Jan. 31, 2004	8,000	9.00	6,500	8.50*
Apr. 30, 2004	6,000	8.50	5,500	9.50

* Decline not considered to be temporary.

Prepare a working paper to compute Lundy Company's cost of goods sold for each of the four quarters of the year ended April 30, 2004. Show computations.

(Exercise 13.13)

Marmon Corporation's statutory income tax rate is 40%. Marmon forecasts pre-tax financial income of $100,000 for the fiscal year ending April 30, 2003, and no temporary differences between pretax financial income and taxable income. Marmon forecasts the following permanent differences between pretax financial income and taxable income for the year ending April 30, 2003: dividend received deduction, $20,000; premiums expense for officers' life insurance, $10,000.

Prepare a working paper to compute Marmon Corporation's estimated effective income tax rate for the year ending April 30, 2003.

(Exercise 13.14)

Basey Company has a fiscal year ending April 30. On July 31, 2002, the end of the first quarter of fiscal year 2003, Basey estimated an effective income tax rate of 55% for that year. On October 31, 2002, the end of the second quarter of fiscal year 2003, Basey estimated an effective income tax rate of 52% for that year. Pretax financial income for Basey was as follows:

For three months ended July 31, 2002	$200,000
For three months ended October 31, 2002	250,000

Prepare journal entries for income taxes expense of Basey Company on July 31 and October 31, 2002.

(Exercise 13.15)

Public Company, which uses the perpetual inventory system and the last-in, first-out method of valuing inventory, temporarily depleted a base layer of its inventories with a cost of $170,000 during the third quarter of its fiscal year ending February 28, 2003. Replacement cost of the depleted inventory was $210,000 on November 30, 2003. On December 18, 2003, Public made its first purchase of merchandise during the fourth quarter, at a total cost of $360,000, on open account.

Prepare journal entries for Public Company on November 30 and December 18, 2003.

(Exercise 13.16)

For its first two quarters of calendar year 2003, its fiscal year, Intero Company had the following data:

Three Months Ended	Pre-Tax Financial Income for Quarter	Estimated Effective Income Tax Rate for 2003
Mar. 31, 2003	$500,000	38.6%
June 30, 2003	600,000	41.2%

Prepare journal entries (omit explanations) for Intero Company to accrue income taxes expense for the first two quarters of 2003.

(Exercise 13.17)

On January 31, 2003, the end of the first quarter of its fiscal year ending October 31, 2003, Cassidy Company had the following ledger account balances:

Income taxes expense	$160,000 dr
Liability arising from depletion of base layer of lifo inventories	30,000 cr

On February 1, 2003, Cassidy purchased merchandise costing $110,000 on account, and on April 30, 2003, Cassidy estimated total income taxes expense of $340,000 for the six months ended on that date. Cassidy uses the perpetual inventory system.

Prepare journal entries for Cassidy Company on February 1 and April 30, 2003, for the foregoing facts.

(Exercise 13.18) Farber Company's journal entry for income taxes on September 30, 2003, the end of its fiscal year, was as follows:

| Income Taxes Expense ($31,960 + $14,100) | | 46,060 | |
| Income Taxes Payable | | | 46,060 |

To provide for income taxes for the year as follows:

	Federal	*State*
Pre-tax financial income	$100,000	$100,000
Less: Nontaxable municipal bond interest	(10,000)	(10,000)
Add: Nondeductible expenses	4,000	4,000
Taxable income, state		$ 94,000
State income tax at 15%		$ 14,100
Less: State income tax	(14,100)	
Taxable income, federal	$ 79,900	
Federal income tax at 40%	$ 31,960	

Prepare a reconciliation, in percentages rounded to the nearest hundredth, between the statutory federal income tax rate, 40%, and Farber Company's effective income tax rate, 46.06% ($46,060 ÷ $100,000 = 0.4606), required by *Regulation S-X,* Rule 4-08(h)(2), for a note to Farber's September 30, 2003, financial statements filed with the SEC in *Form 10-K.* Combine any reconciling items that individually are less than 5% of the statutory federal income tax rate. Use the format on page 588.

Cases

(Case 13.1) Ellen Laughlin, CPA, controller of Electronics, Inc., a publicly owned enterprise, is preparing the company's *Form 10-Q Quarterly Report* for the quarter ended May 31, 2003, the first quarter of the fiscal year ending February 29, 2004. In the course of her work, Laughlin is instructed by Wilbur Jackson, Electronics, Inc.'s chief financial officer, to include in first quarter sales a $500,000 shipment delivered to the truck driver of long-time customer Wilmont Company on June 1, 2003. Prior to the inclusion, first quarter sales of Electronics, Inc., totaled $6,400,000. Jackson pointed out to Laughlin that (1) the goods had been manufactured by Electronics to Wilmont's specifications; (2) the goods were packaged and invoiced to Wilmont in Electronics, Inc.'s shipping department on May 31, awaiting scheduled pickup by Wilmont's truck driver on that date in accordance with the contract with Wilmont; and (3) because Wilmont's truck had been disabled in a traffic accident while en route to Electronics on the afternoon of May 31, a substitute truck could not be obtained by Wilmont until June 1.

Instructions
Can Ellen Laughlin ethically comply with Wilbur Jackson's instructions? Explain, considering the provisions of paragraphs 83 and 84 of *FASB Concepts Statement No. 5,* "Recognition and Measurement in Financial Statements of Business Enterprises," and Chapters 4 and 5 of Division 2, "Sales," of the *Uniform Commercial Code.*

(Case 13.2) In a classroom discussion of the provisions for reporting of operating segments of a business enterprise, as set forth in *FASB Statement No. 131,* "Disclosures about Segment of an Enterprise . . . ," student Jeff asserts that the proposed changes are flawed in that they give far too much latitude to managements of business enterprises in determining operating segments, deciding what information is needed for management decisions regarding operating segments, and segment profit or loss of operating segments. The result of such latitude, in Jeff's opinion, is noncompliance with the qualitative characteristic *reliability,* established as a requirement for useful financial information in paragraph 33 of *FASB Concepts Statement No. 2,* "Qualitative Characteristics of Accounting Information." Jeff points out that such management-determined information is neither *verifiable* nor *neutral*—two ingredients of reliable financial information. Jeff admitted that, in taking this position, he was influenced by the dissent of FASB member James J. Leisenring to the issuance of *FASB Statement No. 131.*

Instructions

Do you agree with student Jeff? Explain.

(Case 13.3) In *APB Opinion No. 28,* "Interim Financial Reporting," the APB adopted the *integral theory,* rather than the *discrete theory,* for interim financial statements.

Instructions

a. Present arguments in favor of the integral theory of interim financial reporting.

b. Present arguments in favor of the discrete theory of interim financial reporting.

c. Which theory do you prefer? Explain, disregarding the APB's adoption of the integral theory.

(Case 13.4) Critics have charged that the SEC, contrary to its position as stated on pages 576 through 577, essentially establishes generally accepted accounting principles in its *Financial Reporting Releases* and *Staff Accounting Bulletins.*

Instructions

Do you agree with the critics? Explain.

(Case 13.5) Nanson Company, a publicly owned corporation listed on a major stock exchange, forecasted operations for the fiscal year ending December 31, 2003, as shown below.

NANSON COMPANY
Forecasted Income Statement
For Year Ending December 31, 2003

Net sales (1,000,000 units)	$6,000,000
Cost of goods sold	3,600,000
Gross margin on sales	$2,400,000
Operating expenses	1,400,000
Operating income	$1,000,000
Nonoperating revenue and expenses	-0-
Income before income taxes	$1,000,000
Income taxes expense (current and deferred)	550,000
Net income	$ 450,000
Basic earnings per share of common stock	4.50

Nanson has operated profitably for many years and has experienced a seasonal pattern of sales volume and production similar to the following ones forecasted for 2003: Sales volume is expected to follow a quarterly pattern of 10%, 20%, 35%, 35%, respectively, because of the seasonality of the industry. Also, because of production and storage capacity limitations, it is expected that production will follow a pattern of 20%, 25%, 30%, 25%, per quarter, respectively.

At the conclusion of the first quarter of 2003, the controller of Nanson prepared and issued the following interim income statement:

NANSON COMPANY Income Statement For Quarter Ended March 31, 2003	
Net sales (100,000 units)	$ 600,000
Cost of goods sold	360,000
Gross margin on sales	$ 240,000
Operating expenses	275,000
Operating loss	$ (35,000)
Loss from warehouse explosion	(175,000)
Loss before income taxes	$(210,000)
Income taxes expense	-0-
Net loss	$(210,000)
Basic loss per share of common stock	$ (2.10)

Additional Information

The following additional information was available for the first quarter just completed, but was not included in the information released by Nanson:

1. Nanson uses a standard cost system in which standards are set at currently attainable levels on an annual basis. At the end of the first quarter, underapplied fixed factory overhead (volume variance) of $50,000 was recognized as an asset. Production during the first quarter was 200,000 units, of which 100,000 units were sold.

2. The operating expenses were forecasted on a basis of $900,000 fixed expenses for the year plus $0.50 variable expenses per unit sold.

3. The warehouse explosion loss met the conditions of an extraordinary loss. The warehouse had a carrying amount of $320,000; $145,000 was recovered from insurance on the warehouse. No other gains or losses were anticipated during the year from similar events or transactions, nor has Nanson had any similar losses in preceding years; thus, the full loss will be deductible as an ordinary loss for income tax purposes.

4. The effective rate for federal and state income taxes combined was expected to average 55% of pretax financial income for. There were no permanent differences between pretax financial income and taxable income.

5. Basic earnings per share of common stock was computed on the basis of 100,000 shares of common stock outstanding. Nanson has only one class of common stock issued, no long-term debt outstanding, no stock option plans, and no warrants to acquire common stock outstanding.

Instructions

a. Identify the weaknesses in form and content of Nanson Company's interim income statement, without reference to the additional information.

b. For each of the five items of additional information, indicate the preferable treatment for interim reports and explain why that treatment is preferable.

Problems

(Problem 13.1) Data with respect to the four operating segments of Wabash Company for the fiscal year ended November 30, 2004, follow:

	Operating Segment				
	Alpha	*Beta*	*Gamma*	*Delta*	*Total*
Net sales to outsiders	$40,000	$20,000	$25,000	$5,000	$90,000
Intersegment transfers out	2,000	4,000	1,000	3,000	10,000
Intersegment transfers in	4,000	3,000	2,000	1,000	10,000
Other traceable expenses	9,000	6,000	5,000	10,000	30,000
Nontraceable expenses					20,000

Wabash allocated nontraceable expenses to operating segments by the following reasonable method: Alpha—40%; Beta—30%; Gamma—20%; Delta—10%.

Instructions

Prepare a working paper to compute the segment profit or loss for Wabash Company's four operating segments for the year ended November 30, 2004.

(Problem 13.2) Cregar Company is "going public" early in Year 2004, and is preparing to file a *Form S-1* registration statement with the SEC to register the common stock it plans to issue to the public. The accountant for Cregar prepared the following comparative income statements for inclusion in the *Form S-1*:

CREGAR COMPANY
Income Statements
For Three Years Ended December 31, 2003

	2003	*2002*	*2001*
Net sales	$10,000,000	$9,600,000	$8,800,000
Cost of goods sold	6,200,000	6,000,000	5,400,000
Gross margin on sales	$ 3,800,000	$3,600,000	$3,400,000
Operating expenses	2,200,000	2,400,000	2,100,000
Income from operations	$ 1,600,000	$1,200,000	$1,300,000
Gain on disposal of operating segment	900,000		
Income before income taxes	$ 2,500,000	$1,200,000	$1,300,000
Income taxes expense	1,000,000	480,000	520,000
Net income	$ 1,500,000	$ 720,000	$ 780,000

During your audit of the foregoing income statements, you discover that Cregar contracted on January 2, 2003, to sell for $3,200,000 the assets and product line of one of its operating segments. The sale was completed on December 31, 2003, for a gain of $900,000 before income taxes. The discontinued operations' contribution to Cregar's income before income taxes for each year was as follows: 2003, $640,000 loss: 2002, $500,000 loss; 2001, $200,000 income. Cregar's income tax rate is 40%.

Instructions

Prepare corrected partial comparative income statements for Cregar Company for the three years ended December 31, 2003. Disregard notes to financial statements and basic earnings per share of common stock. Begin the income statements with income from continuing operations before income taxes. Show supporting computations.

(Problem 13.3) For the fiscal year ending July 31, 2003, Lang Corporation forecasted pretax financial income of $800,000. Lang did not anticipate any temporary differences between pretax financial income and taxable income. However, the following permanent differences between financial and taxable income for fiscal year 2003 were forecasted:

Dividend received deduction	$150,000
Lobbying expenses	20,000
Officers' life insurance premium expense	15,000

Additional Information

1. Lang's combined federal and state income tax rate is 40%, and federal and state laws coincide with respect to the computation of taxable income.

2. Lang's quarterly pretax financial income for the year ended July 31, 2003, is summarized below:

Quarter Ended	
Oct. 31, 2002	$180,000
Jan. 31, 2003	230,000
Apr. 30, 2003	195,000
July 31, 2003	225,000

3. During fiscal year 2003, Lang did not alter its forecast of pretax financial income for the year. However, effective January 31, 2003, Lang revised its permanent difference estimate for the 2003 dividend received deduction to $180,000 from $150,000. The actual amounts for the permanent differences computed by Lang on July 31, 2003, were as follows:

Dividend received deduction	$175,000
Lobbying expenses	20,000
Officers' life insurance premium expense	16,000

Instructions

a. Prepare a working paper to compute the effective combined federal and state income tax rate that Lang Corporation should use for its quarterly interim financial reports for the year ended July 31, 2003. Round all percentage computations to the nearest tenth.

b. Prepare Lang Corporation's journal entries for income taxes on October 31, 2002, and January 31, April 30, and July 31, 2003.

(Problem 13.4) Bixler Company, a diversified manufacturing enterprise that does not report to the SEC, had four operating segments engaged in the manufacture of products in each of the following industries: food products, health aids, textiles, and office equipment.

Additional Information

1. Financial data for the two years ended December 31, 2004, are shown below:

Operating Segment	Net Sales		Cost of Goods Sold		Operating Expenses	
	2004	2003	2004	2003	2004	2003
Food products	$3,500,000	$3,000,000	$2,400,000	$1,800,000	$ 550,000	$ 275,000
Health aids	2,000,000	1,270,000	1,100,000	700,000	300,000	125,000
Textiles	1,580,000	1,400,000	500,000	900,000	200,000	150,000
Office equipment	920,000	1,330,000	800,000	1,000,000	650,000	750,000
Totals	$8,000,000	$7,000,000	$4,800,000	$4,400,000	$1,700,000	$1,300,000

2. On January 1, 2004, Bixler adopted a plan to dispose of the assets and product line of the office equipment segment at an anticipated gain. On September 1, 2004, the segment's assets and product line were disposed of for $2,100,000 cash, at a gain of $640,000 (exclusive of operations during the phase-out period).

3. Bixler's textiles segment had six manufacturing plants that produced a variety of textile products. In April 2004, Bixler sold one of these plants and realized a gain of $130,000. After the sale, the operations at the plant that was sold were transferred to the remaining five textile plants that Bixler continued to operate.

4. In August 2004, the main warehouse of the food products segment, located on the banks of the Colton River, was flooded when the river overflowed. The resulting uninsured damage of $420,000 is not included in the financial data in (1) above. Historical records indicate that the Colton River normally overflows every four to five years, causing flood damage to adjacent property.

5. For the two years ended December 31, 2004 and 2003, Bixler realized interest revenue on investments of $70,000 and $40,000, respectively. For the two years ended December 31, 2004 and 2003, Bixler's net income was $960,000 and $670,000, respectively. Income taxes expense for each of the two years should be computed at a rate of 40%.

Instructions

Prepare comparative income statements for Bixler Company for the years ended December 31, 2004 and 2003. Notes to the financial statements and basic earnings per share of common stock disclosures are not required.

(Problem 13.5) The accounting records of Draco Company included the following amounts for the year ended December 31, 2003:

Cost of goods sold—continuing operations	$ 8,000,000
Estimated loss on disposal of Southern Division (an operating segment), to be completed in first quarter of Year 2004	50,000
Income taxes payable ($540,000 × 0.40)	216,000
Interest expense	100,000
Judgment paid in lawsuit of **Justin Company v. Draco Company,** initiated in 2001	80,000

(continued)

Loss from bankruptcy liquidation of major customer	150,000
Loss from operations of Southern Division, discontinued effective Dec. 31, 2003 (measurement date)	120,000
Net sales—continuing operations	10,000,000
Operating expenses—continuing operations	800,000
Uninsured loss from earthquake at Northern Division	160,000

Draco's income tax rate is 40%. Draco had no temporary differences or permanent differences between pretax financial income and taxable income for 2003. Prior to 2003, there had not been an earthquake in the Northern Division's locality for more than 50 years.

Instructions

a. Prepare an income statement for Draco Company for the year ended December 31, 2003, in accordance with the provisions of **APB Opinion No. 30,** "Reporting the Results of Operations." Disregard earnings per share data and notes to financial statements.

b. Prepare a journal entry for Draco Company's income taxes on December 31, 2003, with appropriate intraperiod tax allocation.

(Problem 13.6)

Principia Corporation was incorporated January 2, 2003, with a public issuance of 3 million shares of $1 par common stock on that date for net proceeds of $5,750,000, net of out-of-pocket costs of the stock issuance. Immediately thereafter, Principia organized three wholly owned subsidiaries: Seattle Company and Boston Company in the United States, and London Company in the United Kingdom. Principia paid $1,500,000 cash for each subsidiary's 1,500,000 authorized shares of $1 par common stock.

The working paper for consolidated financial statements for Principia Corporation and subsidiaries for the year ended December 31, 2003, is on page 618.

Additional Information

1. Each of the affiliated companies constitutes an operating segment.

2. None of the companies declared or paid dividends in 2003.

3. Each of the companies files separate income tax returns at an effective income tax rate of 40%.

4. Intercompany receivables and payables represent loans or advances. (Receivables and payables arising from intercompany sales of merchandise had been paid in full on December 31, 2003.)

5. Of Principia's operating expenses, $50,000 represents nontraceable expenses allocable to each operating segment in the ratio of the **average** of each segment's 2003 sales to outsiders and December 31, 2003, plant asset amounts. The remainder of Principia's operating expenses represents general corporate expenses.

6. Cash not required for each operating segment's current operations is forwarded to Principia for the acquisition of short-term investments classified as trading securities. Interest on the investments is not allocated to operating segments.

Instructions

Prepare for Principia Corporation and subsidiaries, in the format illustrated on page 559, (*a*) information about segment profit or loss and segment assets, and (*b*) a reconciliation of operating segment totals to consolidated totals. Disregard segment depreciation and amortization expense, interest expense, and additions to plant assets.

PRINCIPIA CORPORATION AND SUBSIDIARIES
Working Paper for Consolidated Financial Statements
For Year Ended December 31, 2003
(000 omitted)

	Principia Corporation	Seattle Company	Boston Company	London Company*	Eliminations Increase (Decrease)		Consolidated
Income Statement							
Revenue:							
Net sales	500	400	300	200			1,400
Intercompany sales	40	30	20	10	(b)	(100)	
Intercompany investment income	32				(a)	(32)	
Interest revenue	20						20
Total revenue	592	430	320	210		(132)	1,420
Costs and expenses:							
Cost of goods sold	375	320	210	130	(b)	(10)	1,025
Intercompany cost of goods sold	32	24	16	8	(b)	(80)	
Operating expenses	133	60	40	50			283
Interest expense		6	9	7			22
Income taxes expense	15	12	27	9	(b)	(6)	57
Total costs and expenses	555	422	302	204		(96)	1,387
Net income (and retained earnings)	37	8	18	6		(36)	33
Balance Sheet							
Assets							
Short-term investments (trading)	80						80
Inventories	500	600	700	800	(b)	(10)	2,590
Other current assets	700	800	600	500			2,600
Deferred income tax asset					(b)	6	6
Intercompany receivables (payables)	80	(60)	50	(70)			
Investments in subsidiaries' common stock	4,532				(a) (4,532)		
Plant assets (net)	800	900	700	600			3,000
Intangible assets (net)	40	60	50	70			220
Total assets	6,732	2,300	2,100	1,900		(4,536)	8,496
Liabilities and Stockholders' Equity							
Current liabilities	945	692	432	227			2,296
6% bonds payable		100	150	167			417
Common stock, $1 par	3,000	1,500	1,500	1,500	(a) (4,500)		3,000
Additional paid-in capital	2,750						2,750
Retained earnings	37	8	18	6		(36)	33
Total liabilities and stockholders' equity	6,732	2,300	2,100	1,900		(4,536)	8,496

Explanation of eliminations:
(a) To eliminate intercompany investments and related equity accounts of subsidiaries.
(b) To eliminate intercompany sales, cost of goods sold, and unrealized profits in inventories, and to defer income taxes applicable to unrealized profits.
* Amounts remeasured to U.S. dollars, London's functional currency, from British pounds.

(Problem 13.7)   This problem consists of three unrelated parts.

a. For the fiscal year ended April 30, 2003, Lobeck Company had a net income of $600,000. Lobeck's income tax rate is 40%, and there were no permanent differences or temporary differences between pretax financial income and taxable income.

On February 28, 2003, in accordance with a decision of Lobeck's board of directors on December 31, 2002, Lobeck disposed of its Texas Division, an operating segment, for a pretax loss of $50,000. The $120,000 pretax operating loss of Texas Division for the 10 months ended February 28, 2003, was incurred as follows:

Eight months ended Dec. 31, 2002	$ 80,000
Two months ended Feb. 28, 2003	40,000
Total pre-tax operating loss	$120,000

Instructions
Prepare the bottom portion of Lobeck Company's income statement for the year ended April 30, 2003, beginning with "Income from continuing operations before income taxes." Disregard basic earnings per share of common stock.

b. For the fiscal year ended December 31, 2003, Spratt Company had the following:

Quarter Ended	Pre-Tax Financial Income (and Taxable Income)	Estimated Effective Income Tax Rate for 2003
Mar. 31, 2003	$100,000	45%
June 30, 2003	120,000	46%
Sept. 30, 2003	140,000	44%
Dec. 31, 2003	150,000	43%

Instructions
Prepare journal entries for Spratt Company's income taxes expense on March 31, June 30, September 30, and December 31, 2003. Omit explanations for the journal entries.

c. During the three months ended March 31, 2003, the third quarter of its fiscal year ended June 30, 2003, Jackson Company temporarily depleted its base layer of last-in, first-out inventories having a lifo cost of $120,000 and a replacement cost on March 31, 2003, of $210,000. On April 30, 2003, Jackson purchased replacement merchandise with a cost of $370,000, on open account.

Instructions
Prepare journal entries for Jackson Company on March 31 and April 30, 2003, for the foregoing business transactions and events. Omit explanations for the journal entries.

Chapter Fourteen

Bankruptcy: Liquidation and Reorganization

Scope of Chapter

Business failures are a common occurrence in the U.S. economy. Poor management, excessive debt, and inadequate accounting are the most commonly cited causes of business failures. The situation that precedes the typical business failure is inability of a business enterprise to pay liabilities as they become due. Unsecured creditors often resort to lawsuits to satisfy their unpaid claims against a business enterprise. Secured creditors may force foreclosure proceedings for real property or may repossess personal property that collateralizes a *security agreement.* The Internal Revenue Service may seize the assets of a business enterprise that has failed to pay FICA and income taxes withheld from its employees.

A business enterprise may be unable to pay its liabilities as they become due even though the current fair values of its assets exceed its liabilities. For example, an enterprise may experience a severe cash shortage in times of price inflation because of the lag between the purchase or production of goods at inflated costs and the recovery of the inflated costs through increased selling prices.

More typical of the failing business enterprise than the conditions described in the foregoing paragraph is the state of insolvency. *Insolvent* is defined in the Bankruptcy Code as follows:

"insolvent" means—
(A) with reference to an entity other than a partnership and a municipality, financial condition such that the sum of such entity's debts is greater than all of such entity's property, at a fair valuation, exclusive of—
(i) property transferred, concealed, or removed with intent to hinder, delay, or defraud such entity's creditors; and
(ii) property that may be exempted from property of the estate under . . . this title; and
(B) with reference to a partnership, financial condition such that the sum of such partnership's debts is greater than the aggregate of, at a fair valuation—
(i) all of such partnership's property, exclusive of property of the kind specified in subparagraph (A) (i) of this paragraph; and

(ii) the sum of the excess of the value of each general partner's nonpartnership property, exclusive of property of the kind specified in subparagraph (A) (ii) of this paragraph, over such partner's nonpartnership debts;[1]

The terms *insolvent* and *bankrupt* often are used as interchangeable adjectives. Such usage is technically incorrect; *insolvent* refers to the financial condition of a person or business enterprise, and *bankrupt* refers to a legal state. In this chapter, various legal and accounting issues associated with bankruptcy reorganizations and liquidations are discussed and illustrated.

THE BANKRUPTCY CODE

The U.S. Constitution (Article 1, Section 8) authorizes Congress to establish uniform laws on the subject of bankruptcies throughout the United States. For the first 89 years under the Constitution, the United States had a national bankruptcy law for a total of only 16 years. During the periods in which national bankruptcy laws were not in effect, state laws on insolvency prevailed. In 1898 a Bankruptcy Act was enacted that, as amended, remained in effect for 80 years. Enactment of the Bankruptcy Act caused state laws on insolvency to be relatively dormant. In 1978 the Bankruptcy Reform Act established the present Bankruptcy Code; in 1980 the Bankruptcy Tax Act established a uniform group of income tax rules for bankruptcy and insolvency; and in 1994 the Bankruptcy Code was amended by the Bankruptcy Reform Act of 1994.

The U.S. Supreme Court may prescribe by general rules the various legal practices and procedures under the Bankruptcy Code. Thus, the Federal Rules of Bankruptcy Procedure established by the Supreme Court constitute important interpretations of provisions of the Bankruptcy Code.

BANKRUPTCY LIQUIDATION

The process of *bankruptcy liquidation* under Chapter 7 of the Bankruptcy Code involves the realization (sale) of the assets of an individual or a business enterprise and the distribution of the cash proceeds to the creditors of the individual or enterprise. Creditors having *security interests* collateralized by specific assets of the debtor generally are entitled to obtain satisfaction of all or part of their claims from the assets pledged as collateral. The Bankruptcy Code provides for priority treatment for certain unsecured creditors; their claims are satisfied in full, if possible, from proceeds of realization of the debtor's noncollateralized assets. Unsecured creditors without priority receive cash, in proportion to the amounts of their claims, from proceeds available from the realization of the debtor's assets. Thus, there are four classes of creditors in a bankruptcy liquidation: *fully secured creditors, partially secured creditors, unsecured creditors with priority,* and *unsecured creditors without priority.*

Debtor's (Voluntary) Petition

The Bankruptcy Code provides that any "person," except certain entities such as a railroad, an insurance company, a bank, a credit union, or a savings and loan association, may file a petition in a federal bankruptcy court for *voluntary liquidation* under

---

[1] Bankruptcy Code, sec. 101 (32).

Chapter 7 of the Code. The official form for a ***debtor's bankruptcy petition,*** also known as a ***voluntary petition,*** must be accompanied by supporting exhibits of the petitioner's debts and property. The debts are classified as follows: (1) creditors having priority; (2) creditors holding security; and (3) creditors having unsecured claims without priority. The debtor's property is reported as follows: real property, personal property, and property claimed as exempt. Valuations of property are at ***market*** or ***current fair values.*** Also accompanying the debtor's bankruptcy petition is a ***statement of financial affairs*** (not to be confused with the ***accounting*** statement of affairs illustrated on page 627 of this chapter), which contains a series of questions concerning all aspects of the debtor's financial condition and operations.

Creditors' (Involuntary) Petition

If a debtor other than a farmer, a nonprofit organization, or one of the types precluded from filing voluntary petitions owes unpaid amounts to 12 or more unsecured creditors who are not employees, relatives, stockholders, or other "insiders," three or more of the creditors having unsecured claims totaling $10,000 or more may file in a federal bankruptcy court a ***creditors' petition for bankruptcy,*** also known as an ***involuntary petition.*** If fewer than 12 creditors are involved, one or more creditors having unsecured claims of $10,000 or more may file the petition. The creditors' petition for bankruptcy must claim either (1) the debtor is not paying debts as they come due or (2) within 120 days prior to the date of the petition, a custodian was appointed for or had taken possession of the debtor's property.

Unsecured Creditors with Priority

The Bankruptcy Code provides that the following unsecured debts are to be paid in full, in the order specified if adequate cash is not available for all, out of a debtor's estate before any cash is paid to other unsecured creditors:

1. Administrative costs.

2. Claims arising in the course of the debtor's business or financial affairs after the commencement of a creditors' bankruptcy proceeding but before appointment of a trustee or order for relief.

3. Claims for wages, salaries, and commissions, including vacation, severance, and sick leave pay not in excess of $4,000 per claimant, earned within 90 days before the date of filing the petition for bankruptcy or cessation of the debtor's business.

4. Claims for contributions to employee benefit plans arising within 180 days before the date of filing the petition for bankruptcy or cessation of the debtor's business. The limit of such claims is $4,000 times the number of employees covered by the plans, less the aggregate amount paid to the covered employees under priority **3** above.

5. Claims by producers of grain against a grain storage facility or by fishermen against a fish storage or processing facility, not in excess of $4,000 per claimant.

6. Claims for cash deposited for goods or services for the personal, family, or household use of the depositor, not in excess of $1,800 per claimant.

7. Claims for alimony, maintenance, or support of a spouse, former spouse, or child of the debtor, under a separation agreement, divorce decree, or court order.

8. Claims of governmental entities for various taxes or duties, subject to varying time limitations.

Property Claimed as Exempt

Certain property of a bankruptcy petitioner is not includable in the debtor's estate. The Bankruptcy Code excludes from coverage of the Code the various allowances provided in the laws of either the United States or the state of the debtor's residence, whichever is more beneficial to the debtor. Typical of these allowances are residential property exemptions provided by homestead laws and exemptions for life insurance policies payable on death to the spouse or a relative of the debtor. (Bills introduced in Congress in 2001 would modify these allowances.)

Role of Court in Liquidation

The ***federal bankruptcy court*** in which a debtor's or creditors' petition for bankruptcy liquidation is filed oversees all aspects of the bankruptcy proceedings.

One of the first acts of the court is either to dismiss the debtor's or creditors' bankruptcy petition or to grant an **order for relief** under the Bankruptcy Code. The filing of a debtor's petition in bankruptcy is in effect an order for relief; in a creditors' petition, order for relief is made by the court after a hearing at which the debtor may attempt to refute the creditors' allegations that the debtor was not paying debts as they came due. Any suits that are pending against a debtor for whom a debtor's or creditors' bankruptcy petition is filed generally are **stayed** until order for relief or dismissal of the petition; after order for relief such suits are further stayed until the question of the debtor's **discharge** is determined by the court. Further, the court appoints an interim trustee after the order for relief, to serve permanently or until a trustee is elected by the creditors.

Role of Creditors

Within a period of 10 to 30 days after an order for relief, the bankruptcy court must call a meeting of the creditors. At the meeting, the "outsider" creditors appoint a trustee to manage the debtor's estate. A majority vote in number and amount of claims of all unsecured and nonpriority creditors present is required for actions by creditors.

Role of Trustee

The trustee elected by the creditors or appointed by the court assumes custody of the debtor's nonexempt property. The principal duties of the trustee are to continue operating the debtor's business if directed by the court, realize the free assets of the debtor's estate, and pay cash to unsecured creditors. The trustee is responsible for keeping accounting records to enable the filing of a final report with the bankruptcy court.

The Bankruptcy Code empowers the trustee to invalidate a **preference,** defined as the transfer of cash or property to an "outsider" creditor for an existing debt, made while the debtor was insolvent and within 90 days of filing of the bankruptcy petition, provided the transfer caused the creditor to receive more cash or property than would be received in the bankruptcy liquidation. The trustee may recover from the creditor the cash or property constituting the preference and include it in the debtor's estate.

Discharge of Debtor

Once the debtor's property has been liquidated, all secured and priority creditor claims have been paid, and all remaining cash has been paid to unsecured, nonpriority creditors, the debtor may receive a *discharge,* defined as the release of the debtor from all unliquidated debts except debts such as the following:

1. Taxes payable by the debtor to the United States or to any state or subdivision, including taxes attributable to improper preparation of tax returns by the debtor.

2. Debts resulting from the debtor's obtaining money or property under false pretenses or representations, or willful conversion of the property of others.

3. Debts not scheduled by the debtor in support of the bankruptcy petition, such creditors not being informed of the bankruptcy proceedings.

4. Debts arising from embezzlement or other fraudulent acts by the debtor acting in a fiduciary capacity.

5. Amounts payable for alimony, maintenance, or child support.

6. Debts for willful and malicious injuries to the persons or property of others.

7. Debts for fines, penalties, or forfeitures payable to governmental entities, other than for tax penalties.

8. With certain exceptions, debts for educational loans made, insured, or guaranteed by governmental entities or by nonprofit universities or colleges. (In 1997, a National Bankruptcy Review Commission recommended discharge of educational loans other than for medical schools.)

A debtor will not be discharged if any crimes, misstatements, or other malicious acts were committed by the debtor in connection with the court proceedings. In addition, a debtor will not be discharged if the current bankruptcy petition was filed *within six years* of a previous bankruptcy discharge to the same debtor.

Role of Accountant in Bankruptcy Liquidation

The accountant's role in liquidation proceedings is concerned with proper reporting of the financial condition of the debtor and adequate accounting and reporting for the trustee for the debtor's estate, as described in the following sections.

Financial Condition of Debtor Enterprise: The Statement of Affairs

A business enterprise that enters bankruptcy liquidation proceedings is a *quitting concern,* not a *going concern.* Consequently, a balance sheet, which reports the financial position of a going concern, is inappropriate for an enterprise in liquidation.

The financial statement designed for a business enterprise entering liquidation is the *statement of affairs* (not to be confused with the legal bankruptcy form with a similar title described on page 622). The purpose of the statement of affairs is to display the assets and liabilities of the debtor enterprise from a *liquidation* viewpoint, because liquidation is the outcome of the Chapter 7 bankruptcy proceedings. Thus, assets displayed in the statement of affairs are valued at *current fair values;* carrying amounts of the assets are presented on a memorandum basis. In addition, assets and liabilities in the statement of affairs are classified according to the rankings and priorities set forth in the Bankruptcy Code; the current/noncurrent classification used in a balance sheet for a going concern is not appropriate for the statement of affairs.

Illustration of Statement of Affairs

The balance sheet of Sanders Company on June 30, 2003, the date that Sanders filed a debtor's (voluntary) bankruptcy petition, is as follows:

SANDERS COMPANY
Balance Sheet
(prior to filing of debtor's bankruptcy petition)
June 30, 2003

Assets

Current assets:		
Cash		$ 2,700
Notes receivable and accrued interest, less allowance		
for doubtful notes, $6,000		13,300
Trade accounts receivable, less allowance for		
doubtful accounts, $23,240		16,110
Inventories, at first-in, first-out cost:		
Finished goods		12,000
Goods in process		35,100
Material		19,600
Factory supplies		6,450
Short-term prepayments		950
Total current assets		$106,210
Plant assets, at cost:		
Land	$ 20,000	
Buildings (net)	41,250	
Machinery (net)	48,800	
Tools (net)	14,700	
Net plant assets		124,750
Total assets		$230,960

Liabilities and Stockholders' Equity

Current liabilities:		
Notes payable:		
Pacific National Bank, including accrued interest		
(due June 30, 2004)		$ 15,300
Suppliers, including accrued interest		
(due May 31, 2004)		51,250
Trade accounts payable		52,000
Salaries and wages payable		8,850
Property taxes payable		2,900
Interest payable on first mortgage bonds		1,800
FICA and income taxes withheld and accrued		1,750
Total current liabilities		$133,850
First mortgage bonds payable		90,000
Total liabilities		$223,850
Stockholders' equity:		
Common stock, $100 par; 750 shares		
authorized, issued, and outstanding	$ 75,000	
Deficit	(67,890)	7,110
Total liabilities and stockholders' equity		$230,960

Other information available from notes to financial statements and from estimates of current fair values of assets follows:

1. Notes receivable with a face amount plus accrued interest totaling $15,300, and a current fair value of $13,300, collateralize the notes payable to Pacific National Bank.

2. Finished goods are expected to be sold at a markup of 33¹/₃% over cost, with disposal costs estimated at 20% of selling prices. Estimated cost to complete goods in process is $15,400, of which $3,700 would be cost of material and factory supplies used. The estimated selling price of goods in process when completed is $40,000, with disposal costs estimated at 20% of selling prices. Estimated current fair values for material and factory supplies not required to complete goods in process are $8,000 and $1,000, respectively. All short-term prepayments are expected to be consumed in the course of liquidation.

3. Land and buildings, which collateralize the first mortgage bonds payable, have a current fair value of $95,000. Machinery with a carrying amount of $18,200 and current fair value of $10,000 collateralizes notes payable to suppliers in the amount of $12,000, including accrued interest. The current fair value of the remaining machinery is $9,000, net of disposal costs of $1,000, and the current fair value of tools after the amounts used to complete the goods in process inventory is $3,255.

4. Salaries and wages payable are debts having priority under the Bankruptcy Code.

5. Costs of administering the bankruptcy liquidation are estimated at $1,905.

The statement of affairs for Sanders Company on June 30, 2003, is as shown on page 627.

The following points should be stressed in the review of the June 30, 2003, statement of affairs for Sanders Company:

1. The "Carrying Amount" columns in the statement of affairs serve as a tie-in to the balance sheet of Sanders on June 30, 2003, as well as a basis for estimating expected losses or gains on realization of assets.

2. Assets are assigned to one of three groups: pledged for fully secured liabilities, pledged for partially secured liabilities, and free. This grouping of assets facilitates the computation of estimated amounts available for unsecured creditors—those with priority and those without priority.

3. Liabilities are grouped in the categories reported by a debtor in the exhibits supporting a debtor's bankruptcy petition (see pages 621 to 622): unsecured with priority, fully secured, partially secured, and unsecured without priority.

4. An *offset* technique used where the *legal right of setoff* exists. For example, amounts due to fully secured creditors are deducted from the estimated current fair value of the assets serving as collateral; and unsecured liabilities with priority are deducted from estimated amounts available to unsecured creditors from the proceeds of free asset realization.

5. An estimated settlement per dollar of unsecured liabilities without priority is computed by dividing the estimated amount available for unsecured, nonpriority creditors by the total unsecured liabilities, thus:

$$\frac{\$60,960}{\$95,250} = 64 \text{ cents on the dollar}$$

This computation enables the bankruptcy trustee to estimate the amount of cash that will be available to unsecured, nonpriority creditors in a liquidation proceeding.

SANDERS COMPANY
Statement of Affairs
June 30, 2003

Carrying Amounts	Assets	Current Fair Values	Estimated Amount Available	Loss or (Gain) on Realization
	Assets Pledged for Fully Secured Liabilities:			
$ 20,000	Land	} $95,000		
41,250	Buildings			
	Less: Fully secured liabilities (contra)	91,800	$ 3,200	$(33,750)
	Assets Pledged for Partially Secured Liabilities:			
13,300	Notes and interest receivable (deducted contra)	$13,300		
18,200	Machinery (deducted contra)	$10,000		8,200
	Free Assets:			
2,700	Cash	$ 2,700	2,700	
16,110	Trade accounts receivable	16,110	16,110	
	Inventories:			
12,000	Finished goods	12,800	12,800	(800)
35,100	Goods in process	20,300*	20,300	14,800
19,600	Material	8,000	8,000	11,600
6,450	Factory supplies	1,000	1,000	5,450
950	Short-term prepayments	-0-	-0-	950
30,600	Machinery	9,000	9,000	21,600
14,700	Tools	3,255	3,255	11,445
				$ 39,495
	Total estimated amount available		$76,365	
	Less: Unsecured liabilities with priority (contra)		15,405	
	Estimated amount available for unsecured, nonpriority creditors (64¢ on the dollar)		$60,960	
	Estimated deficiency to unsecured, nonpriority creditors (36¢ on the dollar)		34,290	
$230,960			$95,250	

Carrying Amounts	Liabilities and Stockholders' Equity	Amount Unsecured
	Unsecured Liabilities with Priority:	
	Estimated administrative costs	$ 1,905
$ 8,850	Salaries and wages payable	8,850
2,900	Property taxes payable	2,900
1,750	FICA and income taxes withheld and accrued	1,750
	Total (deducted contra)	$15,405
	Fully Secured Liabilities:	
90,000	First mortgage bonds payable	$90,000
1,800	Accrued interest on first mortgage bonds payable	1,800
	Total (deducted contra)	$91,800
	Partially Secured Liabilities:	
15,300	Notes and accrued interest payable to Pacific National Bank	$15,300
	Less: Net realizable value of notes receivable pledged as collateral (contra)	13,300	$ 2,000
12,000	Notes and accrued interest payable to suppliers	$12,000
	Less: Estimated realizable value of machinery pledged as collateral (contra)	10,000	2,000
	Unsecured Liabilities without Priority:	
39,250	Notes payable to suppliers	39,250
52,000	Trade accounts payable	52,000
7,110	Stockholders' equity	
$230,960		$95,250

* Estimated selling price .... $ 40,000
Less: Estimated "out-of-pocket" completion costs ($15,400 − $3,700) .... (11,700)
Estimated disposal costs ($40,000 × 0.20) .... (8,000)
Net realizable value .... $ 20,300

Estimated Amounts to Be Recovered by Each Class of Creditors

By reference to the statement of affairs on page 627, the accountant for the trustee in bankruptcy for Sanders Company may prepare the summary of estimated amounts to be recovered by each class of Sanders's creditors shown below:

		SANDERS COMPANY	
		Estimated Amounts to Be Recovered by Creditors	
		June 30, 2003	

Class of Creditors	Total Claims	Computation	Estimated Recovery
Unsecured with priority	$ 15,405	100%	$ 15,405
Fully secured	91,800	100%	91,800
Partially secured	27,300	$23,300 + ($4,000 × 0.64)	25,860
Unsecured without priority	91,250	64%	58,400
Totals	$225,755*		$191,465[†]

* $15,405 + $91,800 + $15,300 + $12,000 + $39,250 + $52,000 = $225,755.
[†] $95,000 + $13,300 + $10,000 + ($76,365 − $3,200) = $191,465.

Accounting and Reporting for Trustee

Traditionally, the accounting records and reports for trustees have been extremely detailed and elaborate. However, the provisions of the applicable Federal Rule of Bankruptcy Procedure are general. Therefore, simple accounting records and reports such as the following should be adequate.

1. The accounting records of the debtor should be used during the period that a trustee carries on the operations of the debtor's business.

2. An *accountability* technique should be used once the trustee begins realization of the debtor's assets. In the accountability method of accounting, the assets and liabilities for which the trustee is responsible are entered in the accounting records of the trustee at their statement of affairs valuations, with a balancing debit to a memorandum-type ledger account with a title such as Estate Deficit. The amount of the debit to Estate Deficit is equal to the estimated deficiency to unsecured creditors reported in the statement of affairs. Appropriate cash receipts and cash payments journal entries are made for the trustee's realization of assets and payment of liabilities. No "gain" or "loss" ledger account is necessary because a business enterprise in liquidation does not require an income statement. Differences between cash amounts realized or paid and carrying amounts of the related assets or liabilities are debited or credited to the Estate Deficit ledger account.

3. The *interim* and *final reports* of the trustee to the bankruptcy court are a statement of cash receipts and cash payments, a statement of realization and liquidation, and, for interim reports, supporting exhibits of assets not yet realized and liabilities not yet liquidated.

Illustration of Accountability Technique

Assume that Arline Wells, the trustee in the voluntary bankruptcy liquidation proceedings for Sanders Company (see page 625), took custody of the assets of Sanders on June 30, 2003. The accountant for the trustee prepared the following journal entry on June 30, 2003.

SANDERS COMPANY, IN BANKRUPTCY
Arline Wells, Trustee
Journal Entry
June 30, 2003

Cash	2,700	
Notes and Interest Receivable	13,300	
Trade Accounts Receivable	16,110	
Finished Goods Inventory	12,800	
Goods in Process Inventory	20,300	
Material Inventory	8,000	
Factory Supplies	1,000	
Land and Buildings	95,000	
Machinery ($10,000 + $9,000)	19,000	
Tools	3,255	
Estate Deficit	34,290 (1)	
Estimated Administrative Costs		1,905
Notes and Interest Payable ($15,300 + $12,000 + $39,250)		66,550
Trade Accounts Payable		52,000
Salaries and Wages Payable		8,850
Property Taxes Payable		2,900
FICA and Income Taxes Withheld and Accrued		1,750
Interest Payable on First Mortgage Bonds		1,800
First Mortgage Bonds Payable		90,000
To record current fair values of assets and liabilities of Sanders Company, in bankruptcy liquidation proceedings.		

(1) Equal to estimated deficiency to unsecured, nonpriority creditors in the statement of affairs on page 627.

When the trustee realizes assets of Sanders, the appropriate journal entry is a debit to Cash, credits to the asset ledger accounts, and a debit or credit to the Estate Deficit account for a loss or gain on realization, respectively. Costs of administering the estate that exceed the $1,905 liability also are debited to the Estate Deficit ledger account.

Statement of Realization and Liquidation

The traditional statement of realization and liquidation was a complex and not too readable accounting presentation. A form of realization and liquidation statement that should be more useful to the bankruptcy court than the traditional statement is as follows. This financial statement is based on the assumed activities of the trustee for the estate of Sanders Company during the month of July 2003, including operating the business long enough to complete and sell the goods in process inventory.

Interim Statement of
Realization and Liquidation
for Trustee in
Bankruptcy Liquidation

SANDERS COMPANY, IN BANKRUPTCY
Arline Wells, Trustee
Statement of Realization and Liquidation
For Month Ended July 31, 2003

	Current Fair Values, June 30, 2003	Realization Proceeds	Loss or (Gain)	
Estate deficit, June 30, 2003				$34,290
Assets realized:				
Trade accounts receivable	$14,620	$12,807	$ 1,813	
Finished goods inventory	12,800	11,772	1,028	
Goods in process inventory	14,820	15,075	(255)	
Totals	$42,240	$39,654		2,586
Liabilities with priority liquidated at carrying amounts:				
Salaries and wages payable			$ 8,850	
Property taxes payable			2,900	
FICA and income taxes withheld and accrued			1,750	
Total liabilities with priority liquidated			$13,500	
Administrative costs paid, $1,867 ($1,905 had been estimated)				(38)
Estate deficit, July 31, 2003				$36,838

An accompanying statement of cash receipts and cash payments for the month ended July 31, 2003, would show the sources of the $39,654 total realization proceeds, and the dates, check numbers, payees, and amounts of the $13,500 paid for liabilities with priority and the $1,867 paid for administrative costs. Supporting exhibits would summarize assets not yet realized and liabilities not yet paid.

Liquidation involves realization of the assets of the debtor's estate. In many cases, an insolvent debtor may be restored to a sound financial footing if it can defer payment of its debts. Chapter 11 of the Bankruptcy Code, dealing with reorganization, enables a debtor to continue operations under court protection from creditor lawsuits while it formulates a plan to pay its debts. Reorganization is discussed in the next section.

BANKRUPTCY REORGANIZATION

Chapter 11 of the Bankruptcy Code provides for the court-supervised reorganization of a debtor business enterprise. Typically, a reorganization involves the reduction of amounts payable to some creditors, other creditors' acceptance of equity securities of the debtor for their claims, and a revision of the par or stated value of the common stock of the debtor.

A debtor's (voluntary) petition for reorganization may be filed by a railroad or by any "person" eligible to petition for liquidation (see page 621) except a stockbroker or a commodity broker. Requirements for a creditors' (involuntary) petition for reorganization are the same as the requirements for a liquidation petition (see page 622).

Appointment of Trustee or Examiner

During the process of reorganization, management or owners of the business enterprise may continue to operate the enterprise as ***debtor in possession.*** Alternatively, the bankruptcy court may appoint a trustee to manage the enterprise. A trustee is appointed because of fraud, dishonesty, incompetence, or gross mismanagement by current owners or managers, or to protect the interests of creditors or stockholders of the enterprise. In some reorganization cases not involving a trustee, the court may appoint an examiner to investigate possible fraud or mismanagement by the current managers or owners of the enterprise; the appointment of an examiner is limited to enterprises having unsecured liabilities, other than payables for goods, services, or taxes, exceeding $5 million.

Among the powers and duties of the trustee are the following:

1. Prepare and file in court a list of creditors of each class and their claims and a list of stockholders of each class.

2. Investigate the acts, conduct, property, liabilities, and business operations of the enterprise, consider the desirability of continuing operations, and formulate a plan for such continuance for submission to the bankruptcy judge if management of the debtor has not done so.

3. Report to the bankruptcy judge any facts ascertained as to fraud against or mismanagement of the debtor enterprise.

Plan of Reorganization

The plan of reorganization submitted by the management or the trustee to the bankruptcy court is given to the debtor enterprise's creditors and stockholders, to the U.S. Secretary of the Treasury, and possibly to the SEC. The plan must include provisions altering or modifying the interests and rights of the creditors and stockholders of the debtor enterprise, as well as a number of additional provisions. The SEC may review the plan and may be heard in the bankruptcy court's consideration of the plan. Before a plan of reorganization is confirmed by the bankruptcy court, the plan must be accepted by a majority of the creditors, whose claims must account for two-thirds of the total liabilities, and by stockholders owning at least two-thirds of the outstanding capital stock of each class. If one or more classes of stockholders or creditors has not accepted a plan, the bankruptcy court may confirm the plan if the plan is ***fair and equitable*** to the nonacceptors. Confirmation of the plan of reorganization by the bankruptcy court makes the plan binding on the debtor enterprise, on all creditors and owners of the enterprise, and on any other enterprise issuing securities or acquiring property under the plan.

Accounting for a Reorganization

The accounting for a reorganization typically requires journal entries for adjustments of carrying amounts of assets; reductions of par or stated value of capital stock (with recognition of resultant paid-in capital in excess of par or stated value); extensions of due dates and revisions of interest rates of notes payable; exchanges of equity securities for debt securities; and the elimination of a retained earnings deficit. The latter entry is associated with ***fresh start reporting*** for a reorganized enterprise whose liabilities exceed the ***reorganization value*** (essentially current fair value) of its assets.[2]

---

[2] *Statement of Position 90-7,* "Financial Reporting by Entities in Reorganization under the Bankruptcy Code" (New York: AICPA, 1990), par. 36.

Because of changes in the ownership of common stock of such an enterprise as a result of the reorganization, it is no longer controlled by its former stockholder group, and it essentially is a new reporting enterprise whose assets and liabilities should be valued at current fair values and whose stockholders' equity consists only of paid-in capital.[3]

It is important for accountants to be thoroughly familiar with the plan of reorganization, in order to account properly for its implementation. Accountants must be careful to avoid charging post-reorganization operations with losses that arose before the reorganization.

To illustrate the accounting for a reorganization, assume that Sanders Company (see pages 625 to 628) filed a petition for reorganization, rather than for liquidation, on June 30, 2003, with Sanders management as debtor in possession. The plan of reorganization, which was approved by stockholders and all unsecured creditors and confirmed by the bankruptcy court, included the following:

1. Deposit $25,000 with escrow agent, as soon as cash becomes available, to cover liabilities with priority and costs of reorganization proceedings.

2. Amend articles of incorporation to provide for 10,000 shares of authorized common stock of $1 par. The new common stock is to be exchanged on a share-for-share basis for the 750 shares of outstanding $100 par common stock.

3. Extend due date of unsecured notes payable to suppliers totaling $15,250 for four years, until May 31, 2008. Increase the interest rate on the notes from the stated rate of 14% to 18%, the current fair rate of interest.

4. Exchange 1,600 shares of new $1 par common stock (at current fair value of $15 a share) for unsecured notes payable to suppliers totaling $24,000.

5. Pay suppliers 70 cents per dollar of trade accounts payable owed.

The journal entries below and on page 633, numbered to correspond with the provisions of the reorganization plan outlined above, were recorded by Sanders Company as cash became available from operations. Assuming that fresh start reporting is appropriate for Sanders Company after the plan of reorganization has been carried out, the last journal entry on page 633 is appropriate for eliminating the $67,890 retained earnings deficit of Sanders on June 30, 2003.

Journal Entries for Bankruptcy Reorganization

SANDERS COMPANY
Journal Entries

(1)	Cash with Escrow Agent	25,000	
	Cash		25,000
	To record deposit of cash with escrow agent under terms of bankruptcy reorganization.		
	Salaries and Wages Payable	8,850	
	Property Taxes Payable	2,900	
	FICA and Income Taxes Withheld and Accrued	1,750	
	Cash with Escrow Agent		13,500
	To record escrow agent's payment of liabilities with priority.		

(continued)

[3] Ibid., par. 39.

SANDERS COMPANY
Journal Entries (concluded)

	Costs of Bankruptcy Proceedings	11,000	
	Cash with Escrow Agent		11,000
	To record escrow agent's payment of costs of bankruptcy proceedings.		
(2)	Common Stock, $100 par	75,000	
	Common Stock, $1 par		750
	Paid-in Capital in Excess of Par		74,250
	To record issuance of 750 shares of $1 par common stock in exchange for 750 shares of $100 par common stock.		
(3)	14% Notes Payable to Suppliers, due May 31, 2004	15,250	
	18% Notes Payable to Suppliers, due May 31, 2008		15,250
	To record extension of due dates of notes payable to suppliers and increase of interest rate to 18% from 14%.		
(4)	Notes Payable to Suppliers	24,000	
	Common Stock, $1 par		1,600
	Paid-in Capital in Excess of Par		22,400
	To record exchange of 1,600 shares of $1 par common stock for $24,000 face amount of notes payable, at current fair value of $15 a share.		
(5)	Trade Accounts Payable	52,000	
	Cash		36,400
	Gain from Discharge of Indebtedness in Bankruptcy		15,600
	To record payment of $0.70 per dollar of accounts payable to suppliers.		

Journal Entry to Eliminate Deficit Paid-in Capital in Excess of Par	63,290	
Gain from Discharge of Indebtedness in Bankruptcy	15,600	
Costs of Bankruptcy Proceedings		11,000
Retained Earnings		67,890
To eliminate deficit on June 30, 2003, and close bankruptcy gain and costs to Paid-in Capital in Excess of Par ledger account.		

The effect of the foregoing journal entries is to show a "clean slate" for Sanders Company as a result of the approved bankruptcy reorganization and the write-off of the retained earnings deficit existing on the date of the petition for reorganization. The extension of due dates of some liabilities, conversion of other liabilities to common stock, and liquidation of trade accounts payable at less than their face amount should enable Sanders to resume operations as a going concern. For a reasonable number of years following the reorganization, Sanders might "date" the retained earnings in its balance sheets to disclose that the earnings were accumulated after the reorganization.

Disclosure of Reorganization

The elaborate and often complex issues involved in a bankruptcy reorganization are disclosed in a note to the financial statements for the period in which the plan of reorganization was carried out. Examples of recent such disclosures are included in the AICPA's 1994 publication ***Illustrations of Financial Reporting by Entities in Reorganization Under the Bankruptcy Code.*** In addition, the Summary of Significant

Accounting Policies note to financial statements of a reorganized enterprise might include disclosures such as the following for Wang Laboratories, Inc., a publicly owned enterprise:

> Bankruptcy-Related Accounting
>
> The Company has accounted for all transactions related to the Chapter 11 case in accordance with Statement of Position 90-7 ("SOP 90-7"), "Financial Reporting by Entities in Reorganization Under the Bankruptcy Code," which was issued by the American Institute of Certified Public Accountants in November 1990. Accordingly, liabilities subject to compromise under the Chapter 11 case have been segregated on the Consolidated Balance Sheet and are recorded for the amounts that have been or are expected to be allowed on known claims rather than estimates of the amounts those claims are to receive under the Reorganization Plan. In addition, the Consolidated Statements of Operations and Consolidated Statements of Cash Flows for the year ended June 30, 1993 separately disclose expenses and cash transactions, respectively, related to the Chapter 11 case (see Note C, Reorganization and Restructuring). In accordance with SOP 90-7, no interest has been accrued on pre-petition, unsecured debt. Additionally, interest income earned by WLI subsequent to the filing of Chapter 11 is reported as a reduction of reorganization items. The reorganized Company will account for the Reorganization Plan utilizing the "Fresh-Start" reporting principles contained in SOP 90-7.[4]

Review Questions

1. Define *insolvency* as that term is used in the Bankruptcy Code for an entity other than a partnership.
2. What are *Federal Rules of Bankruptcy Procedure*?
3. Identify the various classes of creditors whose claims are dealt with in bankruptcy liquidations.
4. Describe the process of *liquidation* under Chapter 7 of the Bankruptcy Code.
5. Differentiate between a *debtor's petition* and a *creditors' petition.*
6. May *any* business enterprise file a debtor's bankruptcy petition for liquidation? Explain.
7. Who may file a *creditors' petition* for bankruptcy liquidation?
8. What is a *statement of financial affairs* under the Bankruptcy Code?
9. List the unsecured debts having priority over other unsecured debts under the provisions of the Bankruptcy Code.
10. Describe the priority of claims for wages and salaries under the Bankruptcy Code.
11. Describe the authority of a bankruptcy trustee with respect to a *preference.*
12. What are the effects of a *discharge* in bankruptcy liquidation proceedings? Explain.
13. What use is made of the accounting financial statement known as a *statement of affairs*? Explain.
14. Describe the *accountability* method of accounting used by a trustee in a bankruptcy liquidation.
15. For what types of bankruptcy reorganizations might an *examiner* be appointed by the bankruptcy court?
16. What is the role of the Securities and Exchange Commission in a bankruptcy reorganization?

---

[4] AICPA, *Accounting Trends & Techniques,* 48th ed. (New York: 1994), p. 35.

17. Must all classes of creditors accept a reorganization plan before the plan may be confirmed by the bankruptcy court? Explain.

18. What is *fresh-start reporting* for a business enterprise reorganized under Chapter 11 of the Bankruptcy Code, and under what circumstances is it appropriate?

Exercises

(Exercise 14.1)   Select the best answer for each of the following multiple-choice questions:

1. A category of assets that typically has zero in the Estimated Amount Available column of a statement of affairs is:
   a. Factory supplies inventory
   b. Tools
   c. Short-term prepayments
   d. None of the foregoing

2. In a bankruptcy proceeding, the term *statement of affairs* refers to:
   a. A document containing a series of questions concerning all aspects of the debtor's financial condition and operations.
   b. A financial statement prepared in lieu of a balance sheet.
   c. Both *a* and *b.*
   d. Neither *a* nor *b.*

3. The number of classes of creditors in a bankruptcy liquidation is:
   a. Two
   b. Three
   c. Four
   d. Five

4. The Paid-in Capital in Excess of Par ledger account of a debtor corporation undergoing bankruptcy reorganization typically is debited or credited for:
   a. Costs of bankruptcy proceedings.
   b. Gain from discharge of indebtedness in bankruptcy.
   c. Retained earnings deficit.
   d. All the foregoing items.
   e. None of the foregoing items.

5. The bankruptcy trustee for Insolvent Company sold assets having a carrying amount of $10,000 for $8,500 cash. The journal entry (explanation omitted) to record the sale is:

a. Cash	8,500	
Loss on Realization of Assets	1,500	
Assets		10,000
b. Cash	8,500	
Estate Administration Expenses	1,500	
Assets		10,000
c. Cash	8,500	
Cost of Goods Sold	10,000	
Sales		8,500
Assets		10,000

d. Cash	8,500	
Estate Deficit	1,500	
Assets		10,000

6. In a statement of affairs (financial statement), assets pledged for partially secured liabilities are:

   a. Included with assets pledged for fully secured liabilities.
   b. Offset against partially secured liabilities.
   c. Included with free assets.
   d. Disregarded.

7. Regis Company is being liquidated in bankruptcy. Unsecured creditors without priority are expected to be paid 50 cents on the dollar. Sardo Company is the payee of a note receivable from Regis in the amount of $50,000 (including accrued interest), which is collateralized by machinery with a current fair value of $10,000. The total amount expected to be realized by Sardo on its note receivable from Regis is:

   a. $35,000
   b. $30,000
   c. $25,000
   d. $10,000
   e. Some other amount

8. In journal entries for a bankruptcy reorganization, the difference between the carrying amount of a liability of the debtor and the amount accepted by the creditor in full settlement of the liability is credited to:

   a. Retained Earnings (Deficit).
   b. Paid-in Capital in Excess of Par or Stated Value.
   c. Paid-in Capital from Reorganization.
   d. Cash with Escrow Agent.
   e. Some other ledger account.

9. With respect to the terms ***bankrupt*** and ***insolvent*** as adjectives:

   a. ***Bankrupt*** refers to a legal state; ***insolvent*** refers to the financial condition of a person or a business enterprise.
   b. ***Bankrupt*** refers to the financial condition of a person or a business enterprise; ***insolvent*** refers to a legal state.
   c. Both ***bankrupt*** and ***insolvent*** refer to the financial condition of a person or a business enterprise.
   d. ***Bankrupt*** and ***insolvent*** properly may be used as interchangeable adjectives.

10. The accounting records of a trustee in a bankruptcy liquidation are maintained:

    a. Under the accrual basis of accounting.
    b. Under the cost basis of accounting.
    c. Under an accountability technique.
    d. In accordance with the bankruptcy court's instructions.

11. Under the Bankruptcy Code, are creditors having priority:

	Secured Creditors?	*Unsecured Creditors?*
a.	Yes	Yes
b.	Yes	No
c.	No	Yes
d.	No	No

12. The period of time that must elapse before a debtor that has had a previous bankruptcy discharge may again be discharged is:

    a. Four years
    b. Five years
    c. Six years
    d. Seven years

13. The sequence of listing (1) fully secured liabilities, (2) partially secured liabilities, (3) unsecured liabilities with priority, and (4) unsecured liabilities without priority in the liabilities and stockholders' equity section of a statement of affairs is:

    a. (1), (2), (3), (4)
    b. (3), (1), (2), (4)
    c. (1), (3), (2), (4)
    d. (1), (3), (4), (2)

14. The following journal entry (explanation omitted) was prepared by an enterprise that had filed a debtor's petition in bankruptcy:

Cash with Escrow Agent	100,000	
Cash		100,000

    Such a journal entry generally is related to:

    a. A liquidation only.
    b. A reorganization only.
    c. Either a liquidation or a reorganization.
    d. Neither a liquidation nor a reorganization.

15. The *estimated amount available* for free assets in a statement of affairs for a business enterprise undergoing bankruptcy liquidation is equal to the assets':

    a. Carrying amounts less current fair values.
    b. Carrying amounts plus gain or less loss on realization.
    c. Carrying amounts plus loss or less gain on realization.
    d. Current fair values less carrying amounts.

16. A *retained earnings deficit* of a business enterprise undergoing bankruptcy reorganization typically is eliminated by its:

    a. Offset against gain from discharge of indebtedness in bankruptcy.
    b. Inclusion with costs of bankruptcy proceedings.
    c. Offset against legal capital.
    d. Offset against additional paid-in capital.

17. On April 30, 2003, Carson Welles, trustee in bankruptcy liquidation for Lyle Company, paid $12,140 in full settlement of Lyle's liability under product warranty, which had been carried in Welles's accounting records at $10,000. The appropriate journal entry for Welles (explanation omitted) is:

a. Liability under Product Warranty	12,140	
Cash		12,140
b. Liability under Product Warranty	10,000	
Estate Deficit	2,140	
Cash		12,140
c. Liability under Product Warranty	10,000	
Product Warranty Expense	2,140	
Cash		12,140

d. Liability under Product Warranty   10,000
     Retained Earnings (Prior Period Adjustment)   2,140
         Cash   12,140

(Exercise 14.2)   The December 18, 2003, statement of affairs of Downside Company, which is in bankruptcy liquidation, included the following:

CHECK FIGURE

To partially secured
liabilities, $48,000.

Assets pledged for fully secured liabilities	$100,000
Assets pledged for partially secured liabilities	40,000
Free assets	120,000
Fully secured liabilities	80,000
Partially secured liabilities	50,000
Unsecured liabilities with priority	60,000
Unsecured liabilities without priority	90,000

Prepare a working paper to show the estimated amount of assets expected to be received by each of the four classes of creditors of Downside Company in its bankruptcy liquidation.

(Exercise 14.3)   Amounts related to the statement of affairs of Foldup Company, in bankruptcy liquidation on April 30, 2003, were as follows:

CHECK FIGURE

Estimated deficiency,
$100,000.

Assets pledged for fully secured liabilities	$ 80,000
Assets pledged for partially secured liabilities	50,000
Free assets	280,000
Fully secured liabilities	60,000
Partially secured liabilities	80,000
Unsecured liabilities with priority	40,000
Unsecured liabilities without priority	330,000

Prepare a working paper to compute the ***total estimated deficiency*** to unsecured, nonpriority creditors, and the ***cents per dollar*** that such creditors may expect to receive from Foldup Company.

(Exercise 14.4)   Data from the April 30, 2003, statement of affairs of Windup Company, which was undergoing bankruptcy liquidation, included the following:

CHECK FIGURE

To partially secured
liabilities, $35,000.

Assets pledged for fully secured liabilities	$70,000
Assets pledged for partially secured liabilities	30,000
Free assets	50,000
Fully secured liabilities	60,000
Partially secured liabilities	40,000
Unsecured liabilities with priority	30,000
Unsecured liabilities without priority	50,000

Prepare a working paper to show how Windup Company's assets on April 30, 2003, are expected to be apportioned to Windup's creditors' claims on that date.

(Exercise 14.5) Components of the December 17, 2003, statement of affairs of Liquo Company, which was undergoing liquidation under Chapter 7 of the Bankruptcy Code, included the following:

Assets pledged for fully secured liabilities, at current fair value	$150,000
Assets pledged for partially secured liabilities, at current fair value	104,000
Free assets, at current fair value	80,000
Fully secured liabilities	60,000
Partially secured liabilities	120,000
Unsecured liabilities with priority	14,000
Unsecured liabilities without priority	224,000

Prepare a working paper dated December 17, 2003, to compute the amount expected to be paid to each class of creditors of Liquo Company. The following column headings are suggested: Class of Creditor, Total Claims, Computation, Estimated Amount. The total of the Estimated Amount column should equal total assets, $334,000.

(Exercise 14.6) Scott Company filed a debtor's bankruptcy petition on June 25, 2003, and its statement of affairs included the following amounts:

	Carrying Amounts	Current Fair Values
Assets		
Assets pledged for fully secured liabilities	$160,000	$190,000
Assets pledged for partially secured liabilities	90,000	60,000
Free assets	200,000	140,000
Totals	$450,000	$390,000
Liabilities		
Unsecured liabilities with priority	$ 20,000	
Fully secured liabilities	130,000	
Partially secured liabilities	100,000	
Unsecured liabilities without priority	260,000	
Total	$510,000	

Assuming that Scott Company's assets realized cash at the current fair values and the business was liquidated by the bankruptcy trustee, prepare a working paper to compute the amount of cash that the partially secured creditors should receive.

(Exercise 14.7) The statement of affairs for Wick Corporation shows that approximately 78 cents on the dollar probably will be paid to unsecured creditors without priority. Wick owes Stark Company $23,000 on a promissory note, plus accrued interest of $940. Inventories with a current fair value of $19,200 collateralize the note payable.

Prepare a working paper to compute the amount that Stark Company should receive from the trustee of Wick Corporation, assuming that actual payments to unsecured creditors without priority amount to 78 cents on the dollar. Round all amounts to the nearest dollar.

(Exercise 14.8) Decker Company filed a debtor's bankruptcy petition on August 15, 2003, and its statement of affairs included the following amounts:

	Carrying Amounts	Current Fair Values
Assets		
Assets pledged for fully secured liabilities	$150,000	$185,000
Assets pledged for partially secured liabilities	90,000	60,000
Free assets	210,000	160,000
Totals	$450,000	$405,000
Liabilities		
Unsecured liabilities with priority	$ 35,000	
Fully secured liabilities	130,000	
Partially secured liabilities	100,000	
Unsecured liabilities without priority	270,000	
Total	$535,000	

Assuming that Decker Company's assets realized cash at the current fair values and the business was liquidated by the bankruptcy trustee, prepare a working paper to compute the amount of cash available to pay unsecured liabilities without priority.

(Exercise 14.9) Prepare a working paper to compute the estimated amount expected to be paid to each class of creditors, using the following data taken from the statement of affairs for Kent Corporation:

Assets pledged for fully secured liabilities (current fair value, $75,000)	$ 90,000
Assets pledged for partially secured liabilities (current fair value, $52,000)	74,000
Free assets (current fair value, $40,000)	70,000
Unsecured liabilities with priority	7,000
Fully secured liabilities	30,000
Partially secured liabilities	60,000
Unsecured liabilities without priority	112,000

(Exercise 14.10) The following information for Progress Book Company on May 31, 2003, was obtained by an accountant retained by Progress Book's creditors:

1. Furniture and fixtures: Carrying amount, $70,000; current fair value, $60,500; pledged on a note payable of $42,000 on which unpaid interest of $800 has accrued.

2. Book manuscripts owned: Carrying amount, $15,000; current fair value, $7,200; pledged on a note payable of $9,000; interest on the note is paid to date.

3. Books in process of production: Accumulated cost (direct material, direct labor, and factory overhead), $37,500; estimated sales value on completion, $60,000; additional out-of-pocket costs of $14,200 will be required to complete the books in process.

Prepare the headings for the asset side of a statement of affairs for Progress Book Company on May 31, 2003, and illustrate how each of the three items described is displayed in the statement.

(Exercise 14.11) Edward Ross, the trustee in bankruptcy for Winslow Company, set up accounting records based on the April 30, 2003, statement of affairs for Winslow. The trustee completed the following transactions and events early in May 2003:

> May 2 Sold for $10,000 cash the finished goods inventory with a statement of affairs valuation of $10,500.
>
> 3 Paid wages with a statement of affairs valuation of $8,000.
>
> 4 Collected $6,000 on trade accounts receivable with a statement of affairs valuation of $6,200. The remainder was considered to be uncollectible.
>
> 7 Paid trustee fee for one week, $500. (Debit Estimated Administrative Costs.)

Prepare journal entries (omit explanations) for Edward Ross, trustee in bankruptcy for Winslow Company, for the transactions and events described above.

(Exercise 14.12) From the following traditional form of statement of realization and liquidation, prepare a more concise statement of realization and liquidation similar to the one illustrated on page 630:

similar to the one illustrated on page 630:

CHECK FIGURE

Estate deficit, Jan. 31, $7,150.

REED COMPANY, IN BANKRUPTCY			
Selma Ross, Trustee			
Statement of Realization and Liquidation			
For Month of January 2003			
Assets to be realized:		Liabilities to be liquidated:	
Trade accounts receivable	$ 7,500	Notes payable	$ 5,000
Inventories	12,500	Trade accounts payable	30,000
Equipment	10,000	Interest payable	150
Subtotal	$30,000	Subtotal	$35,150
Supplementary charges:		Liabilities assumed:	
Administrative costs	2,950	Interest payable	50
Interest expense	50	Assets realized:	
Liabilities liquidated:		Trade accounts receivable	6,500
Trade accounts payable	6,000	Inventories	14,500
Liabilities not liquidated:		Assets not realized:	
Notes payable	5,000	Equipment	10,000
Trade accounts payable	24,000	Net loss	2,000
Interest payable	200		
Total	$68,200	Total	$68,200

(Exercise 14.13) Following are selected provisions of the plan of reorganization for Kolb Company, which is emerging from Bankruptcy Code Chapter 11 reorganization on July 27, 2003:

(1) Amended articles of incorporation to provide for 100,000 shares of authorized common stock, $5 par, to be exchanged on a share-for-share basis for 50,000 shares of outstanding no-par, no-stated-value common stock with a carrying amount of $600,000.

(2) Exchanged 10,000 shares of the new $5 par common stock for trade accounts payable totaling $70,000.

(3) Paid 80 cents per dollar for full settlement of other trade accounts payable totaling $60,000.

Prepare journal entries (omit explanations) for Kolb Company on July 27, 2003, to reflect the foregoing elements of its plan of reorganization.

(Exercise 14.14) Among the provisions of the reorganization of Hayward Company under Chapter 11 of the Bankruptcy Code were the following:

(1) Issued 1,000 shares of $5 par common stock in exchange for 1,000 shares of $100 par common stock outstanding.
(2) Issued 200 shares of $5 par common stock (current fair value $10 a share) for notes payable to suppliers with unpaid principal of $2,500 and accrued interest of $500.
(3) Paid $8,000 to suppliers in full settlement of trade accounts payable of $10,000.

Prepare journal entries (omit explanations) for Hayward Company for the foregoing provisions, all of which were completed on January 20, 2003.

Cases

(Case 14.1) The January 29, 1994, balance sheet of Hills Stores Company, a publicly owned enterprise, included the following asset:

Reorganization value in excess of amounts
allocable to identifiable assets, net $176,718,000

The Intangible Assets section of Hills's Summary of Significant Accounting Policies note to financial statements read in part as follows:

Reorganization value in excess of amounts allocable to identifiable assets is being amortized over 20 years on a straight-line basis. Accumulated amortization was $29,395,000 at January 29, 1994.

The reorganization value accounted for more than 19% of Hills's total assets of $907,621,000 on January 29, 1994.

Instructions
What is your opinion of the foregoing balance sheet display and related note disclosures? Explain, after researching the following:

AICPA *Statement of Position 90-7*, "Financial Reporting by Entities in Reorganization Under the Bankruptcy Code," paragraphs 9, 38, 61, and 62.

FASB *Statement of Financial Accounting Concepts No. 6*, "Elements of Financial Statements," paragraphs 25 through 31 and 171 through 177.

FASB *Statement of Financial Accounting Standards No. 142*, "Goodwill and Other Intangible Assets," paragraphs 1, 5, and 10.

FASB *Statement of Financial Accounting Standards No. 87*, "Employers' Accounting for Pensions," paragraphs 36, 37, and 38, and dissent of Robert T. Sprouse.

(Case 14.2) In auditing the financial statements of Delbert Company for the six months ended December 31, 2003, you find items *a* through *e* below had been debited or credited to the Retained Earnings ledger account during the six months immediately following a bankruptcy reorganization, which was effective July 1, 2003:

a. Debit of $25,000 arising from an additional income tax assessment applicable to 2002.

b. Credit of $48,000 resulting from gain on disposal of equipment that was no longer used in the business. This impaired equipment had been written down by a $50,000 increase in the Accumulated Depreciation ledger account on July 1, 2003.

c. Debit of $15,000 resulting from the loss on plant assets destroyed in a fire on November 2, 2003.

d. Debit of $32,000 representing cash dividends declared on preferred stock.

e. Credit of $60,400, the net income for the six-month period ended December 31, 2003.

Instructions
For each of the foregoing items, state whether it is correctly debited or credited to the Retained Earnings ledger account. Give a brief reason for your conclusion.

(Case 14.3) You have been asked to conduct a training program explaining the preparation of a statement of affairs (financial statement) for the staff of Bixby & Canfield, CPAs.

Instructions
Explain how each of the following is presented in a statement of affairs (financial statement) for a corporation in bankruptcy liquidation proceedings:

a. Assets pledged for partially secured liabilities.

b. Unsecured liabilities with priority.

c. Stockholders' equity.

Problems

(Problem 14.1) On July 24, 2003, the date the plan of reorganization of Re-Org Company was approved by the bankruptcy court, Re-Org's stockholders' equity was as follows:

Common stock, no par or stated value; authorized 100,000	
shares, issued and outstanding 60,000 shares	$ 580,000
Deficit	(260,000)
Total stockholders' equity	$ 320,000

Included in Re-Org's plan of reorganization were the following:

1. Authorize payment of $50,000 unrecorded bankruptcy administrative costs by escrow agent holding special Re-Org cash account.

2. Amend articles of incorporation to change common stock to $1 par from no-par, no-stated-value stock.

3. Exchange 10% unsecured $120,000 promissory note payable to supplier (interest unpaid for three months) for a 12%, two-year promissory note in the total amount of unpaid principal and accrued interest on the 10% note.

4. Pay suppliers 80 cents on the dollar (from Re-Org cash account) for their claims totaling $100,000.

5. Eliminate deficit against paid-in capital resulting from (2) and gain resulting from (4).

Instructions

Assuming the foregoing were completed on July 24, 2003, prepare journal entries (omit explanations) for Re-Org Company on that date. Use the following ledger account titles:

Cash	Interest Payable
Cash with Escrow Agent	10% Note Payable
Common Stock, no par	12% Note Payable
Common Stock, $1 par	Paid-in Capital in Excess of Par
Costs of Bankruptcy Proceedings	Retained Earnings (Deficit)
Gain from Discharge of Indebtedness in Bankruptcy	Trade Accounts Payable

(Problem 14.2)   The following information was available on October 31, 2003, for Dodge Company, which cannot pay its liabilities when they are due:

	Carrying Amounts
Cash	$ 4,000
Trade accounts receivable (net): Current fair value equal to carrying amount	46,000
Inventories: Net realizable value, $18,000; pledged on $21,000 of notes payable	39,000
Plant assets: Current fair value, $67,400; pledged on mortgage note payable	134,000
Accumulated depreciation of plant assets	27,000
Supplies: Current fair value, $1,500	2,000
Wages payable, all earned during October 2003	5,800
Property taxes payable	1,200
Trade accounts payable	60,000
Notes payable, $21,000 secured by inventories	40,000
Mortgage note payable, including accrued interest of $400	50,400
Common stock, $5 par	100,000
Deficit	59,400

Instructions

a. Prepare a statement of affairs for Dodge Company on October 31, 2003, in the form illustrated on page 627.

b. Prepare a working paper to compute the estimated percentage of claims each group of creditors should expect to receive if Dodge Company petitions for liquidation in bankruptcy.

(Problem 14.3)   Robaire Corporation was in financial difficulty because of declining sales and poor cost controls. Its stockholders and principal creditors had asked for an estimate of the financial results of the realization of the assets, the payment of liabilities, and the liquidation of Robaire. Thus, the accountant for Robaire prepared the statement of affairs shown on page 646.

On January 2, 2004, Robaire filed a debtor's petition for liquidation under the Bankruptcy Code. Charles Stern was appointed as trustee by the bankruptcy court to take custody of the assets, make payments to creditors, and implement an orderly liquidation. The trustee completed the following transactions and events during January, 2004:

Jan. 2 Recorded the assets and liabilities of Robaire Corporation in a separate set of accounting records. The assets were recorded at current fair value, and all liabilities were recorded at the estimated amounts payable to the various groups of creditors.

7 Disposed of the land and buildings at an auction for $52,000 cash and paid $42,550 to the mortgagee. The payment included interest of $50 that accrued in January.

10 Made cash payments as follows:

Wages payable	$1,500
FICA and income taxes withheld and accrued	800
Completion of inventories	400
Administrative costs of liquidation	600

31 Received cash from Jan. 8 to Jan. 31, 2004, as follows:

Collection of trade accounts receivable at carrying amount, including $10,000 of assigned accounts	$17,500
Sale of inventories	18,000
Disposal of Public Service Company bonds	920

31 Made additional cash payments as follows:

Administrative costs of liquidation	$ 1,250
Note payable to bank (from proceeds of collection of assigned accounts receivable)	10,000
Fifty cents on the dollar to unsecured creditors	30,500

Instructions

a. Prepare journal entries for the foregoing events and transactions of the trustee for Robaire Corporation.

b. Prepare a statement of realization and liquidation for the trustee of Robaire Corporation for the month of January 2004. Use the format illustrated on page 630.

c. Prepare a trial balance for the trustee of Robaire Corporation on January 31, 2004.

ROBAIRE COMPANY
Statement of Affairs
December 31, 2003

Carrying Amounts	Assets	Current Fair Values	Estimated Amount Available	Loss or (Gain) on Realization
	Assets Pledged for Fully Secured Liabilities:			
$ 4,000	Land	$20,000		$(16,000)
25,000	Buildings	30,000		(5,000)
	Total	$50,000		
	Less: Fully secured liabilities (contra)	42,500	$ 7,500	
	Assets Pledged for Partially Secured Liabilities:			
10,000	Trade accounts receivable (deducted contra)	$10,000		
	Free Assets:			
700	Cash	$ 700	700	
10,450	Trade accounts receivable	10,450	10,450	
40,000	Inventories	$19,350		
	Less: Cost to complete	400	18,950	21,050
9,100	Factory supplies	-0-	-0-	9,100
5,750	Public Service Company bonds	900	900	4,850
38,000	Machinery and equipment	18,000	18,000	20,000
			$56,500	$ 34,000
	Total estimated amount available			
	Less: Unsecured liabilities with priority (contra)		5,500	
	Estimated amount available for unsecured, nonpriority creditors		$51,000	
	Estimated deficiency to unsecured, nonpriority creditors		10,000	
$143,000			$61,000	

Carrying Amounts	Liabilities and Stockholders' Equity	Amount Unsecured
	Unsecured Liabilities with Priority:	
	Estimated administrative costs	$ 3,200
$ 1,500	Wages payable	1,500
800	FICA and income taxes withheld and accrued	800
$ 7,500	Total (deducted contra)	$ 5,500
	Fully Secured Liabilities:	
42,000	Mortgage note payable	$42,000
500	Interest payable	500
	Total (deducted contra)	$42,500
	Partially Secured Liabilities:	
25,000	Notes payable to bank	$25,000
	Less: Assigned trade accounts receivable	10,000 $ 15,000
	Unsecured Liabilities without Priority:	
20,000	Notes payable to suppliers	20,000
26,000	Trade accounts payable	26,000
27,200	Stockholders' equity	
$143,000		$61,000

(Problem 14.4) Javits Corporation advised you that it is facing bankruptcy proceedings. As the independent auditor for Javits, you knew of its financial condition.

The unaudited balance sheet of Javits on July 10, 2003, was as follows:

JAVITS CORPORATION
Balance Sheet
July 10, 2003

Assets

Cash	$ 12,000
Short-term investments, at cost	20,000
Trade accounts receivable, less allowance for doubtful accounts	90,000
Finished goods inventory	60,000
Material inventory	40,000
Short-term prepayments	5,000
Land	13,000
Buildings (net)	90,000
Machinery (net)	120,000
Goodwill (net)	20,000
Total assets	$470,000

Liabilities and Stockholders' Equity

Notes payable to banks	$135,000
Trade accounts payable	94,200
Wages payable	15,000
Mortgage notes payable	130,000
Common stock	100,000
Retained earnings (deficit)	(4,200)
Total liabilities and stockholders' equity	$470,000

Additional Information

1. Cash included a $500 travel advance that had been spent.
2. Trade accounts receivable of $40,000 had been pledged as collateral for notes payable to banks in the amount of $30,000. Credit balances of $5,000 were netted in the accounts receivable total. All accounts were expected to be collected except those for which an allowance had been established.
3. Short-term investments (all acquired in May 2003), classified as *trading,* consisted of U.S. government bonds costing $10,000 and 500 shares of Owens Company common stock. The current fair value of the bonds was $10,000; the current fair value of the stock was $18 a share. The bonds had accrued interest receivable of $200. The short-term investments had been pledged as collateral for a $20,000 note payable to bank.
4. Estimated realizable value of finished goods was $50,000 and of material was $30,000. For additional out-of-pocket costs of $10,000 the material would realize $59,900 as finished goods.
5. Short-term prepayments were expected to be consumed during the liquidation period.
6. The current fair values of plant assets were as follows: land, $25,000; buildings, $110,000; impaired machinery, $65,000.
7. Trade accounts payable included $15,000 withheld FICA and income taxes and $6,000 payable to creditors who had been reassured by the president of Javits that

they would be paid. There were unrecorded employer's FICA taxes in the amount of $500.

8. Wages payable were not subject to any limitations under the Bankruptcy Code.

9. Mortgage notes payable consisted of $100,000 secured by land and buildings, and a $30,000 installment contract secured by machinery. Total unrecorded accrued interest for these liabilities amounted to $2,400.

10. Probable judgment on a pending suit against Javits was estimated at $50,000.

11. Costs other than accounting fees to be incurred in connection with the liquidation were estimated at $10,000.

12. You had not submitted an invoice for $5,000 for the April 30, 2003, annual audit of Javits, and you estimate a $1,000 fee for liquidation work.

Instructions

a. Prepare correcting journal entries for Javits Corporation on July 10, 2003.

b. Prepare a statement of affairs for Javits Corporation on July 10, 2003. Amounts in the statement should reflect the journal entries in *a*.

(Problem 14.5) The adjusted trial balance of Laurel Company on June 30, 2003, is as follows:

CHECK FIGURE

Estimated deficiency, $32,400.

LAUREL COMPANY Adjusted Trial Balance June 30, 2003		
	Debit	*Credit*
Cash	$ 14,135	
Notes receivable	29,000	
Interest receivable	615	
Trade accounts receivable	24,500	
Allowance for doubtful accounts		$ 800
Inventories	48,000	
Land	10,000	
Building	50,000	
Accumulated depreciation of building		15,000
Machinery and equipment	33,000	
Accumulated depreciation of machinery and equipment		19,000
Furniture and fixtures	21,000	
Accumulated depreciation of furniture and fixtures		9,500
Goodwill	9,600	
Note payable to City Bank		18,000
Notes payable to Municipal Trust Company		6,000
Notes payable to suppliers		24,000
Interest payable on notes		1,280
Trade accounts payable		80,520
Wages payable		1,400
FICA and income taxes withheld and accrued		430
Mortgage bonds payable		32,000
Interest payable on mortgage bonds		1,820
Common stock		70,000
Retained earnings—deficit	39,900	
Totals	$279,750	$279,750

Additional Information

1. Notes receivable of $25,000 were pledged to collateralize the $18,000 note payable to City Bank. Interest of $500 was accrued on the pledged notes receivable, and interest of $600 was accrued on the $18,000 note payable to the bank. All the pledged notes receivable were considered collectible. Of the remaining notes receivable, a $1,000 noninterest-bearing note was uncollectible. The note had been received for an unconditional cash loan.

2. Trade accounts receivable included $7,000 from Boren Company, which currently was being liquidated. Creditors were expected to realize 40 cents on the dollar. The allowance for doubtful accounts was adequate to cover any other uncollectible accounts. A total of $3,200 of the remaining collectible trade accounts receivable was pledged as collateral for the notes payable to Municipal Trust Company of $6,000 with accrued interest of $180 on June 30, 2003.

3. Inventories, valued at first-in, first-out cost, were expected to realize 25% of cost on a forced liquidation sale after the write-off of $10,000 of obsolete stock.

4. Land and buildings, which had been appraised at 110% of their carrying amount, were mortgaged as collateral for the bonds. Interest of $1,820 was accrued on the bonds on June 30, 2003. Laurel expected to realize 20% of the cost of its impaired machinery and equipment, and 50% of the cost of its impaired furniture and fixtures after incurring refinishing costs of $800.

5. Estimated costs of liquidation were $4,500. Depreciation and accruals had been adjusted to June 30, 2003.

6. Laurel had net operating loss carryovers for income tax purposes of $22,000 for the year ended June 30, 2002, and $28,000 for the year ended June 30, 2003. The income tax rate expected to be in effect when the operating loss carryovers were used was 40%.

Instructions

Prepare a statement of affairs for Laurel Company on June 30, 2003.

(Problem 14.6)

CHECK FIGURE

b. Total assets, $1,137,530.

Bilbo Corporation, which is in bankruptcy reorganization, had $105,000 of dividends in arrears on its 7% cumulative preferred stock on March 31, 2003. While retained earnings was adequate to permit the payment of accumulated dividends, Bilbo's management did not want to weaken its working capital position. It also realized that a portion of the plant assets was no longer used by Bilbo. Therefore, management proposed the following plan of reorganization, which was accepted by stockholders and confirmed by the bankruptcy court, to be effective on April 1, 2003:

1. The preferred stock was to be exchanged for $300,000 face amount and current fair value of 15%, ten-year bonds. Dividends in arrears were to be settled by the issuance of 12,000 shares of $10 par, 15%, noncumulative preferred stock having a current fair value equal to par.

2. Common stock was to be assigned a par of $50 a share.

3. Impaired goodwill was to be written off; impaired plant assets were to be written down, based on appraisal and estimates of current fair value, by a total of $103,200, consisting of a $85,400 increase in the Accumulated Depreciation ledger account balance and a $17,800 decrease in plant assets; other current assets were to be written down by $10,460 to reduce trade accounts receivable and inventories to net realizable values.

The balance sheet of Bilbo Corporation on March 31, 2003, follows:

BILBO CORPORATION
Balance Sheet
March 31, 2003

Assets

Cash		$ 30,000
Other current assets		252,890
Plant assets	$1,458,250	
Less: Accumulated depreciation	512,000	946,250
Goodwill		50,000
Total assets		$1,279,140

Liabilities and Stockholders' Equity

Current liabilities	$ 132,170
7% cumulative preferred stock, $100 par ($105,000 dividends in arrears); 3,000 shares authorized, issued, and outstanding	300,000
Common stock, no par or stated value; 9,000 shares authorized, issued, and outstanding	648,430
Additional paid-in capital: preferred stock	22,470
Retained earnings	176,070
Total liabilities & stockholders' equity	$1,279,140

Instructions

a. Prepare journal entries for Bilbo Corporation to give effect to the plan of reorganization on April 1, 2003.

b. Prepare a balance sheet for Bilbo Corporation on April 30, 2003, assuming that net income for April was $15,000. The operations resulted in $11,970 increase in cash, $18,700 increase in other current assets, $7,050 increase in current liabilities, and $8,620 increase in the Accumulated Depreciation ledger account.

Chapter **Fifteen**

Estates and Trusts

Scope of Chapter

Estates and trusts are accounting entities as well as taxable entities. The individuals or business enterprises that manage the property in estates and trusts are *fiduciaries;* they exercise stewardship for the property in accordance with the provisions of a will, a trust document, or state laws.

This chapter deals first with the legal aspects of estates, including wills, and then discusses and illustrates the accounting for estates; the last section covers the legal and accounting aspects of trusts.

LEGAL AND ACCOUNTING ASPECTS OF ESTATES

State laws (generally termed *probate codes*) regulate the administration and distribution of property in estates of decedents, missing persons, and other individuals subject to protection of courts. The many variations among the probate codes of the 50 states led to the drafting of a *Uniform Probate Code,* developed by the National Conference of Commissioners on Uniform State Laws and approved by the American Bar Association. Although the Code has not yet been adopted in total by all states, it is used in this chapter to illustrate the important legal issues underlying the accounting for estates.

Provisions of Uniform Probate Code Governing Estates

The Uniform Probate Code identifies an *estate* as all the property of a decedent, trust, or other person whose affairs are subject to the Code.[1] *Person* is defined as an individual or an organization. The Code also provides that the real and personal property of a decedent is to be awarded to the persons specified in the decedent's *will.* In the absence of a will—a condition known as *intestacy*—the decedent's property goes to *heirs,* as described in the Code. Thus, the intentions of a *testator* (a person creating a will) control the disposition of a decedent's property.[2]

Wills

The Code provides that a will shall be in writing, signed by the testator, or in the testator's name by some other person in the testator's presence and by the testator's direction, and also signed by at least two witnesses. The chief exception of these requirements is a *holographic will*—a will having its essential provisions and signature in the handwriting of the testator.

[1] Uniform Probate Code, Sec. 1-201(14).
[2] Ibid., Sec. 2-101

Probate of Wills

The ***probate*** of a will is action by the probate court (also known as ***surrogate*** or ***orphan's*** court) to validate the will. The Code provides for two types of probate—***informal*** and ***formal.*** Informal probate is initiated by the application of an interested party filed with a court official known as a ***registrar.*** After thorough review of the completeness and propriety of an application for informal probate, the registrar issues a written statement of informal probate, thus making the will effective.

Formal probate (formal testacy proceedings) is litigation to determine whether a decedent left a valid will; it is initiated by a petition filed by an interested party requesting the probate court to order probate of the will. The petition also may request a finding that the decedent died ***intestate*** (without a valid will). During the court hearings, any party to the formal probate proceedings may oppose the will; however, the burden of proof that the will is invalid is on the contestant of the will. After completion of the hearings, the court enters an order for formal probate of a will found to be valid, or an order that the decedent died intestate. Generally, no formal or informal probate proceedings may be undertaken more than three years after the decedent's death.

Appointment of Personal Representative

In both informal and formal probate proceedings, the probate court appoints a ***personal representative*** of the decedent to administer the decedent's estate. A personal representative named in the decedent's will is called an ***executor.*** If the decedent died intestate, the court-appointed personal representative is known as an ***administrator.*** The Code requires the probate court to issue ***letters testamentary*** to the personal representative before administration of the estate may begin. Because personal representatives are fiduciaries, they must observe standards of care in administering estates that prudent persons would observe in dealing with the property of others. The personal representative is entitled to reasonable compensation for services.

Powers and Duties of Personal Representative

The personal representative of a decedent is empowered to take possession and control of the decedent's property, and to have title to the property in trust for the benefit of creditors and beneficiaries of the estate. The personal representative also has many additional powers, such as the right to continue any single proprietorship of the decedent for not more than four months following the date of the personal representative's appointment and the authority to allocate items of revenue and expenses of the estate to either ***estate principal*** (corpus) or ***estate income,*** as provided by the will or by law. Such allocations constitute the chief accounting problem for an estate and are discussed in a subsequent section of this chapter (pages 654 to 655).

Not later than 30 days after appointment, the personal representative must inform the decedent's ***devisees*** or heirs of the appointment. A ***devisee*** is any person or trust named in a will to receive real or personal property of the decedent in a transfer known as a ***devise.*** Within three months after appointment, the personal representative must prepare an inventory of property owned by the decedent on the date of death, together with a list of any liens against the property. The property in the inventory must be stated at current fair value on the date of death. The personal representative may retain the services of an appraiser to obtain the current fair values of property. The inventory of decedent's property is filed with the probate court. If other property of the decedent is discovered after the filing of the original inventory, the personal representative must file a supplementary inventory with the probate court.

Exempt Property and Allowances

In a manner similar to the bankruptcy law discussed in Chapter 14, the Uniform Probate Code provides for certain exemptions from claims against the estate property, even by devisees. These exceptions are as follows:

1. *Homestead allowance.* The decedent's surviving spouse, or surviving minor and dependent children, are entitled to a *homestead allowance* of a specified amount. This allowance is in addition to any share of the estate property passing to the spouse or children pursuant to the provisions of the will.

2. *Exempt property.* The decedent's surviving spouse or children are entitled to an aggregate specified value of automobiles, household furniture and furnishings, appliances, and personal effects.

3. *Family allowance.* The surviving spouse and minor children who were being supported by the decedent are entitled to a reasonable cash allowance, payable in a lump sum not exceeding a specified amount, or in installments not exceeding one-twelfth of the specified lump sum each month for one year, during the administration of the estate. The family allowance has priority over all claims against the estate other than the homestead allowance.

Claims of Creditors against the Estate

The personal representative for an estate is required to publish a notice once a week for three successive weeks, in a newspaper of general circulation, requesting creditors of the estate to present their claims within four months after the date of the first publication, or be forever barred. If the estate property not exempt under the Code is insufficient to pay all creditors' claims in full, the personal representative pays the claims in the following order:

1. Costs of administering the estate.

2. Decedent's reasonable funeral costs.

3. Debts and taxes with preference under federal law.

4. Reasonable and necessary medical and hospital costs of decedent's last illness.

5. Debts and taxes with preference under state laws.

6. All other claims.

Four months after publication of the first notice to estate creditors, the personal representative initiates payment of claims in the order outlined above, after first providing for homestead, family, and exempt property allowances.

Distributions to Devisees

The personal representative also has the duty of distributing estate property to the devisees named in the will. The property is to be distributed in kind to the extent possible, rather than first being realized in cash and then distributed.

If estate property that is not exempt is insufficient to cover creditors' claims as well as all devises, the devises *abate* (are reduced) in the sequence provided for in the decedent's will. If the will is silent as to order of abatement, the Uniform Probate Code provides the following *abatement sequence:*

1. Property not disposed of by the will.

2. *Residuary devises,* which are devises of all estate property remaining after general and specific devises are satisfied.

3. *General devises,* which are gifts of an amount of money or a number of countable monetary items, such as 500 shares of Mercury Company common stock.

4. *Specific devises,* which are gifts of identified objects, such as named paintings, automobiles, stock certificates, or real property.

Devises may be granted to the devisees *in trust,* which requires the establishment of a *testamentary trust,* that is, one provided for by a will. Trusts are discussed in a subsequent section of this chapter.

Estate and Inheritance Taxes

The federal estate tax assessed against the net assets of an estate, and inheritance taxes assessed by various states against devisees and heirs of a decedent, often called *death taxes,* must be charged to the devisees as outlined in the will. If the will is silent on this point, the Code provides that death taxes are to be apportioned to the devisees in the ratio of their interests (equity) in the estate.

Closing the Estate

No earlier than six months after the date of appointment, a personal representative may close an estate by filing a statement with the probate court. The written content of this statement is described in the Uniform Probate Code; this legal statement usually is accompanied by a financial statement known as a *charge and discharge statement.*

Provisions of Revised Uniform Principal and Income Act Governing Estates

As noted on page 652, the primary accounting problem for an estate is the allocation of revenue and expenses to principal and income. This allocation is important because many wills provide that income of a testamentary trust is paid to an *income beneficiary,* and that trust principal is paid to a different *principal beneficiary* (or *remainderman*). A proper accounting for principal and income is essential before the estate is closed.

The Revised Uniform Principal and Income Act provides guidelines for allocation in the absence of instructions in the will or trust instrument. Many states have adopted all or part of the Act, often with modifications. The provisions of the Act include the following:

1. *Income* is defined as the return in money or property derived from the use of principal, including rent, interest, cash dividends, or any other revenue received during administration of an estate.

2. *Principal* is defined as property set aside by its owner to be held in trust for eventual delivery to a remainderman. Principal includes proceeds of insurance on principal property, stock dividends, and liquidating dividends. Any accrued revenue on the date of death of the testator is included in the principal of the estate.

3. Premium or discount on investments in bonds included in principal is not amortized. All proceeds from sale or redemption of bonds are principal.

4. Income is charged with a reasonable provision for depreciation, computed in accordance with generally accepted accounting principles, on all depreciable property except property used by a beneficiary, such as a residence or a personal automobile. Income also is charged with costs of administering and preserving income-producing property. Such costs include property taxes, ordinary repairs, and property insurance.

5. Principal is charged with expenditures incurred in preparing principal property for sale or rent, cost of investing and reinvesting principal property, major repairs to principal property, and income taxes on receipts or gains allocable to principal.

6. Court costs, attorneys' fees, trustees' fees, and accountants' fees for periodic reporting to the probate court are allocated as appropriate to principal and to income.

Illustration of Accounting for an Estate

Now that certain legal issues involved in estates have been discussed, it is appropriate to illustrate the accounting for estates, including the charge and discharge statement rendered by the personal representative at the closing of the estate. Estate accounting is carried out in accordance with the ***accountability*** technique illustrated in Chapter 14. The accounting records of the personal representative include only those items for which the representative is accountable, under the equation Assets = Accountability.

The illustration on pages 657 to 659 of journal entries in accounting for an estate is based on the following information for the estate of Jessica Davis:

1. Jessica Davis, a single woman, died March 18, 2002, after a brief illness that required her to be hospitalized. Her will, approved for informal probate on March 25, 2002, contained the following devises:
   a. General devises of $10,000 cash to each of three household employees: Alice Martin, Angelo Bari, and Nolan Ames. Devisees must waive claims for unpaid wages on date of death.
   b. Specific devise of ***all*** 200 shares of Preston Company common stock to Nancy Grimes, a niece.
   c. Specific devise of paintings, other art objects, clothing, jewelry, and personal effects to Frances Davis Grimes, sister of Jessica Davis.
   d. Specific devise of residence, furniture, and furnishings to Wallace Davis, brother of Jessica Davis.
   e. General devise of $5,000 cash to Universal Charities, a nonprofit organization.
   f. Residue of estate in trust (First National Bank, Trustee) to Nancy Grimes; income to be paid to her at the end of each calendar quarter until her twenty-first birthday on October 1, 2007, at which time the principal also is to be paid to Nancy Grimes.

2. Paul Hasting, attorney for Jessica Davis and executor of her estate, published the required newspaper notice to creditors on March 26, April 2, and April 9, 2002. The following claims were received from creditors within the four-month statutory period:

List of Claims against Estate of Jessica Davis

Funeral costs (Wade Mortuary)	$ 810
Hospital costs (Suburban Hospital)	1,928
Physician's fees (Charles Carson, M.D.)	426
Morningside Department Store charge account	214
Various residence bills	87
Total claims against estate of Jessica Davis	$3,465

3. Hasting prepared final individual federal and state income tax returns for Jessica Davis for the period January 1 to March 18, 2002. The federal return showed income tax due in the amount of $457; the state return showed no tax due.
4. Hasting prepared the following inventory of property owned by Jessica Davis on March 18, 2002:

List of Property Included in Estate of Jessica Davis	Description of Estate Property	Current Fair Values, Mar. 18, 2002
	Bank checking account	$ 2,157
	Bank savings account (including accrued interest)	30,477
	Savings and loan association 2-year certificate of deposit maturing June 30, 2002 (including accrued interest)	26,475
	Salary earned for period Mar. 1 to Mar. 8, 2002	214
	Claim against medical insurance carrier	1,526
	Social security benefits receivable	14,820
	Proceeds of life insurance policy (payable to estate)	25,000
	Marketable securities:	
	Common stock of Preston Company, 200 shares	8,000
	Common stock of Arthur Corporation, 100 shares	6,500
	Residence	40,800*
	Furniture and furnishings	2,517
	Paintings and other art objects	16,522
	Clothing, jewelry, personal effects	625
	Automobile	2,187
	Total current fair value of estate property	$177,820

* Subject to unpaid mortgage note of $15,500, due $500 monthly on the last day of the month, plus interest at 10% a year on the unpaid balance.

5. Subsequent to preparing the foregoing inventory, Hasting discovered a certificate for 600 shares of Campbell Company common stock with a fair value of $18,000.
6. Hasting prepared the federal estate tax return for the Estate of Jessica Davis, Deceased. The return showed a tax due of $18,556. Hasting also prepared state inheritance tax returns for the devisees showing taxes due of $5,020.
7. Hasting administered the estate, charging a fee of $2,500, and closed the estate by filing the required legal documents and a charge and discharge statement prepared by a CPA who was a member of Hasting's law firm.

PAUL HASTING, EXECUTOR
Of the Will of Jessica Davis, Deceased
Journal Entries

2002				
Mar. 18	Principal Cash (bank checking account)		2,157	
	Savings Account		30,477	
	Certificate of Deposit (including accrued interest)		26,475	
	Salary Receivable		214	
	Medical Insurance Claim Receivable		1,526	
	Social Security Benefits Receivable		14,820	
	Life Insurance Claim Receivable		25,000	
	Marketable Securities		14,500	
	Residence		40,800	
	Furniture and Furnishings		2,517	
	Paintings and Other Art Objects		16,522	
	Clothing, Jewelry, Personal Effects		625	
	Automobile		2,187	
	Mortgage Note Payable			15,500
	Interest Payable ($15,500 \times 0.10 \times {}^{18}/_{360}$)			78
	Estate Principal Balance ($177,820 - $15,578)			162,242
	To record inventory of property owned by decedent Jessica Davis on date of death, net of lien against residence.			
25	Marketable Securities		18,000	
	Property Discovered			18,000
	To record property discovered subsequent to filing of original inventory of property.			
31	Principal Cash		70,511	
	Income Cash		55	
	Savings Account			30,477
	Salary Receivable			214
	Social Security Benefits Receivable			14,820
	Life Insurance Claim Receivable			25,000
	Interest Revenue			55
	To record realization of various property, including $55 interest received on savings account for period Mar. 18 through 31, 2002.			
31	Distributions to Income Beneficiaries		55	
	Income Cash			55
	To distribute income cash to residuary devisee Nancy Grimes, as required by the will.			
Apr. 2	Principal Cash		2,050	
	Loss on Disposal of Principal Property		137	
	Automobile			2,187
	To record disposal of automobile.			

(continued)

PAUL HASTING, EXECUTOR
Of the Will of Jessica Davis, Deceased (continued)
Journal Entries

2002				
Apr. 4	Devises Distributed		5,000	
	Principal Cash			5,000
	To record distribution of general devise to Universal Charities.			
16	Liabilities Paid		3,922	
	Principal Cash			3,922
	To record following liabilities paid:			
	Funeral costs (Wade Mortuary)	$ 810		
	Hospital costs (Suburban Hospital)	1,928		
	Physician's fees (Charles Carson, M.D.)	426		
	Final federal income tax	457		
	Morningside Department Store charge account	214		
	Various residence bills	87		
	Total	$ 3,922		
19	Principal Cash		1,526	
	Medical Insurance Claim Receivable			1,526
	To record collection of medical insurance claim.			
24	Principal Cash		1,000	
	Income Cash		1,500	
	Payable to Devisees			1,000
	Dividend Revenue			1,500
	To record receipt of quarterly cash dividends on common stock, as follows:			
	Preston Company (payable to Nancy Grimes)	$ 1,000		
	Arthur Corporation	300		
	Campbell Company	1,200		
	Total	$ 2,500		
25	Receivable from Devisees		23,576	
	Principal Cash			23,576
	To record payment of federal estate tax and state inheritance taxes on behalf of devisees, as follows:			
	Federal estate tax	$18,556		
	State inheritance taxes	5,020		
	Total	$23,576		
Apr. 26	Principal Cash		6,295	
	Receivable from Devisees			6,295
	To record receipt of cash from specific devisees for their shares of federal estate tax and state inheritance taxes as follows:			
	Frances Davis Grimes ($23,576 × 0.102)*	$ 2,405		
	Wallace Davis ($23,576 × 0.165)*	3,890		
	Total	$ 6,295		

* See explanation on pages 660 to 661.

(continued)

PAUL HASTING, EXECUTOR
Of the Will of Jessica Davis, Deceased (concluded)
Journal Entries

2002				
Apr. 27	Devisees Distributed		30,000	
	Receivable from Devisees			4,173
	Principal Cash			25,827
	To record payment of cash to general devisees, less amounts receivable for their shares of federal estate tax and state inheritance taxes, as follows:			
	$10,000 devises payable to Alice Martin, Angelo Bari, Nolan Ames ($10,000 × 3)	$30,000		
	Less: Share of death taxes ($23,576 × 0.059* × 3)	4,173		
	Net cash paid	$25,827		
30	Mortgage Note Payable		15,500	
	Interest Payable		78	
	Devises Distributed		52,886	
	Payable to Devisees		1,000	
	Marketable Securities			8,000
	Residence			40,800
	Furniture and Furnishings			2,517
	Paintings and Other Art Objects			16,522
	Clothing, Jewelry, Personal Effects			625
	Principal Cash			1,000
	To transfer to devisee Nancy Grimes cash for dividend received on Preston Company common stock; and to record distribution of specific devises as follows:			
	Specific devise to Nancy Grimes:			
	200 shares of Preston Company common stock	$ 8,000		
	Specific devise to Frances Davis Grimes:			
	Paintings, other art objects, clothing, jewelry, personal effects	17,147		
	Specific devise to Wallace Davis:			
	Residence, net of mortgage note payable, with furniture and furnishings	27,739		
	Total	$52,886		
May 1	Administrative Costs		2,500	
	Principal Cash			2,500
	To record payment of executor's fee.			
3	Devises Distributed		85,797	
	Distributions to Income Beneficiaries		1,500	
	Principal Cash (balance of account)			21,714
	Income Cash			1,500
	Certificate of Deposit			26,475
	Marketable Securities			24,500
	Receivable from Devisees (balance of account)			13,108
	To record distribution of residuary devise (principal and income) to First National Bank, trustee for Nancy Grimes, devisee.			

* See explanation on pages 660 to 661.

The foregoing journal entries are entered in the accounting records for the Estate of Jessica Davis, Deceased. (Dates for journal entries are assumed.) Comments relating to specific journal entries that require particular emphasis follow:

March 18 Journal Entry

This entry records the executor's inventory of estate property, including accrued interest and unpaid salary on the date of death. Because the decedent was a single woman, there was no homestead allowance, family allowance, or exempt property. The mortgage note payable (and any accrued interest) applicable to the residence is recognized as a liability for accountability purposes. Claims of unsecured creditors *are not* recorded as liabilities because the accounting records for an estate are not designed to record all aspects of the estate's financial position; accounting records for an estate reflect only the executor's accountability for property and any direct claims against the property.

March 31 Journal Entries

A separate ledger account, Income Cash, is used to record cash receipts attributable to income. In accordance with provisions of the will of Jessica Davis, the income of $55 attributable to the residuary devise to Nancy Grimes is distributed to her at the end of the calendar quarter.

April 2 Journal Entry

No depreciation was recognized on the automobile prior to its disposal, because it was not a revenue-producing asset for the estate.

April 16 Journal Entry

The Liabilities Paid ledger account represents a reduction of the executor's accountability for estate property; it is neither an asset account nor an expense account, but rather an account in which distributions to estate creditors are recorded.

April 24 Journal Entry

Dividends received on marketable securities required segregation in the accounting records, because the securities are allocable to separate devises, as follows:

1. Preston Company common stock, $1,000: Allocable to specific devise to Nancy Grimes.

2. Arthur Corporation and Campbell Company common stocks, $1,500: Allocable to residuary devise to Nancy Grimes.

Although Nancy Grimes is the recipient of both devises, the residuary devise ultimately will be placed in a testamentary trust for the devisee.

April 25 Journal Entry

The will of Jessica Davis was silent regarding allocation of estate and inheritance taxes. Consequently, in accordance with the provisions of the Uniform Probate Code, the federal estate tax and state inheritance taxes are allocated in the ratio of interests of devisees, other than the nontaxable nonprofit organization, in the estate. The following summary shows this ratio:

	PAUL HASTING, EXECUTOR **Of the Will of Jessica Davis, Deceased** **Ratio of Devisee Interests** **April 25, 2002**	
Devisee	**Current Fair Value of Estate Interest**	**Ratio to Total of All Estate Interests**
Alice Martin	$ 10,000	5.9%
Angelo Bari	10,000	5.9
Nolan Ames	10,000	5.9
Nancy Grimes (specific devise)	8,000	4.7
Frances Davis Grimes	17,147 (1)	10.2
Wallace Davis	27,739 (2)	16.5
Nancy Grimes (residuary devise)	85,797	50.9
Totals	$168,683 (3)	100.0%

(1) $16,522 + $625 = $17,147.
(2) ($40,800 + $2,517) − ($15,500 + $78) = $27,739.
(3) $162,242 + $18,000 − $137 − $5,000 − $3,922 − $2,500 = $168,683.

April 26 and April 27 Journal Entries

The executor requested the specific devisees to pay in cash their shares of the federal estate tax and state inheritance taxes. The executor withheld the general devisees' death taxes from the cash payable to them.

May 1 Journal Entry

The entire fee of the executor was charged to estate principal because the time spent by Paul Hasting on income property was insignificant. The allocation of fees is more appropriate for a trust than for an estate of relatively short duration.

May 3 Journal Entry

No adjusting entries are required for interest on the certificate of deposit or any declared but unpaid dividends on the marketable securities. An accrual-basis cutoff for an estate is appropriate only at the time the executor prepares the inventory of estate property in order to facilitate the distinction between estate principal and estate income. If the will provides that the accrual basis of accounting must be used, the executor must comply.

In the preceding illustration, federal and state income taxes on the estate were disregarded. In addition, it was assumed that devisee Wallace Davis immediately occupied the decedent's residence, so that depreciation on the residence was not required as it would be if rent revenue were realized from a lease. A further assumption was that devisee Wallace Davis paid the March 31 and April 30, 2002, installments on the mortgage note secured by the residence.

Trial Balance

A trial balance of the ledger accounts of the Estate of Jessica Davis on May 3, 2002, is as follows:

PAUL HASTING, EXECUTOR Of the Will of Jessica Davis, Deceased Trial Balance May 3, 2002	
	Dr (Cr)
Principal:	
Estate principal balance	$(162,242)
Property discovered	(18,000)
Loss on disposal of principal property	137
Liabilities paid	3,922
Devises distributed	173,683
Administrative costs	2,500
Total	$ -0-
Income:	
Interest revenue	$ (55)
Dividend revenue	(1,500)
Distributions to income beneficiaries	1,555
Total	$ -0-

Charge and Discharge Statement for Executor

The executor's charge and discharge statement and supporting exhibits for the Estate of Jessica Davis are below and on pages 663 to 664. The items in the statement were taken from the trial balance above. Although the executor's activities essentially ended May 3, the Uniform Probate Code precludes closing an estate earlier than six months after the issuance of letters testamentary.

PAUL HASTING, EXECUTOR Of the Will of Jessica Davis, Deceased Charge and Discharge Statement For Period March 18 through September 18, 2002		
First, as to Principal		
I charge myself as follows:		
Inventory of estate property, Mar. 18, 2002 **(Exhibit 1)**	$162,242	
Property discovered **(Exhibit 2)**	18,000	$180,242
I credit myself as follows:		
Loss on disposal of principal property **(Exhibit 3)**	$ 137	
Liabilities paid **(Exhibit 4)**	3,922	
Devises distributed **(Exhibit 5)**	173,683	
Administrative costs **(Exhibit 6)**	2,500	180,242
Balance, Sept. 18, 2002		$ -0-
Second, as to Income		
I charge myself as follows:		
Interest revenue (bank savings account)	$ 55	
Dividend revenue **(Exhibit 7)**	1,500	$ 1,555
I credit myself as follows:		
Distributions of income **(Exhibit 8)**		1,555
Balance, Sept. 18, 2002		$ -0-

PAUL HASTING, EXECUTOR
Of the Will of Jessica Davis, Deceased
Exhibits Supporting Charge and Discharge Statement
For Period March 18 through September 18, 2002

Exhibit 1—Inventory of Estate Property, Mar. 18, 2002:

Bank checking account		$ 2,157
Bank savings account (including accrued interest)		30,477
Savings and loan association 2-year certificate of deposit maturing June 30, 2002 (including accrued interest)		26,475
Salary earned for period Mar. 1 to 8, 2002		214
Claim against medical insurance carrier		1,526
Social security benefits receivable		14,820
Proceeds of life insurance policy (payable to estate)		25,000
Marketable securities:		
Common stock of Preston Company, 200 shares		8,000
Common stock of Arthur Corporation, 100 shares		6,500
Residence	$ 40,800	
Less: Balance of mortgage note payable, including accrued interest of $78	15,578	25,222
Furniture and furnishings		2,517
Paintings and other art objects		16,522
Clothing, jewelry, personal effects		625
Automobile		2,187
Total inventory of estate property		$162,242

Exhibit 2—Property Discovered:

On Mar. 25, 2002, a certificate for 600 shares of Campbell Company common stock was discovered among the decedent's personal effects. All other securities were located in the decedent's safe deposit box at First National Bank. (Valued at fair value on date of Jessica Davis's death.)	$ 18,000

Exhibit 3—Loss on Disposal of Principal Property:

Disposal of automobile, Apr. 3, 2002:	
Carrying amount	$ 2,187
Less: Cash proceeds	2,050
Loss on disposal of principal property	$ 137

Exhibit 4—Liabilities Paid:

Wade Mortuary	$ 810
Suburban Hospital	1,928
Charles Carson, M.D.	426
Final federal income tax	457
Morningdale Department Store	214
Various residence bills	87
Total liabilities paid	$ 3,922

(continued)

PAUL HASTING, EXECUTOR
Of the Will of Jessica Davis, Deceased
Exhibits Supporting Charge and Discharge Statement (concluded)
For Period March 18 through September 18, 2002

Exhibit 5—Devises Distributed:

General devise to Universal Charities: Cash	$ 5,000
General devise to Alice Martin: Cash	10,000
General devise to Angelo Bari: Cash	10,000
General devise to Nolan Ames: Cash	10,000
Specific devise to Nancy Grimes: 200 shares of Preston Company common stock	8,000
Specific devise to Frances Davis Grimes: Paintings, other art objects, clothing, jewelry, personal effects	17,147
Specific devise to Wallace Davis: Residence, net of mortgage note payable, with furniture and furnishings	27,739
Residuary devise to Nancy Grimes: Cash, certificate of deposit, 100 shares of Arthur Corporation common stock, and 600 shares of Campbell Company common stock (in trust)	85,797
Total devises distributed	$173,683

Exhibit 6—Administrative Costs:

Fee of executor (charged entirely to principal because income administration activities were nominal)	$ 2,500

Exhibit 7—Dividend Revenue:

Arthur Corporation common stock	$ 300
Campbell Company common stock	1,200
Total dividend revenue	$ 1,500

Exhibit 8—Distributions of Income:

Mar. 31, 2002: To residuary devisee Nancy Grimes	$ 55
May 3, 2002: To First National Bank, trustee for Nancy Grimes	1,500
Total distributions of income	$ 1,555

The foregoing charge and discharge statement shows the executor's ***accountability,*** not the financial position or cash transactions of the estate. The statement discloses the charges to the executor for estate principal and estate income property for which the executor is accountable, and the credits to the executor for the dispositions made of estate property.

Closing Entry for Estate

Once the executor's closing statement and charge and discharge statement have been accepted by the probate court, the accountant for the estate may prepare an appropriate closing entry. The closing entry for the estate of Jessica Davis on September 18, 2002, follows:

Journal Entry to Close Estate of Jessica Davis

Estate Principal Balance	162,242	
Property Discovered	18,000	
Interest Revenue	55	
Dividend Revenue	1,500	
Loss on Disposal of Principal Property		137
Liabilities Paid		3,922
Devises Distributed		173,683
Administrative Costs		2,500
Distributions to Income Beneficiaries		1,555
To close estate of Jessica Davis in accordance with probate court authorization.		

The example of estate accounting in this chapter was simplified in terms of details and time required for the liquidation of the estate. In practice, many estates—especially those involved in formal probate proceedings—take several months and sometimes years to settle. For many estates, preparation of the federal estate tax return is a complex task. Furthermore, the estate of an intestate decedent involves complicated legal issues. An accountant involved in accounting for an estate must be familiar with provisions of the decedent's will and with appropriate state probate laws and principal and income laws, and should work closely with the attorney and executor (or administrator) for the estate.

LEGAL AND ACCOUNTING ASPECTS OF TRUSTS

A trust created by a will, as illustrated in the preceding section of this chapter, is a *testamentary trust.* A trust created by the act of a living person or persons is an *inter vivos,* or *living, trust.* The parties to a trust are (1) the *settlor* (also known as the *donor* or *trustor*)—the individual creating the trust, (2) the *trustee*—the fiduciary individual or corporation holding legal title to the trust property and carrying out the provisions of the *trust document* for a fee, and (3) the *beneficiary*—the party for whose benefit the trust was established. As noted on page 654, the income from trust property may be distributed to an *income beneficiary,* but the principal of a trust ultimately goes to a *principal beneficiary* (also known as the *remainderman*).

Provisions of Uniform Probate Code Governing Trusts

The Uniform Probate Code contains detailed sections dealing with trust registration, jurisdiction of courts concerning trusts, duties and liabilities of trustees, and powers of trustees. The Code requires that a trustee of a trust must register the trust with the appropriate state probate court. Registration subjects the trust to the jurisdiction of the court. The court's jurisdiction may include appointing or removing a trustee, reviewing the trustee's fees, and reviewing or settling interim or final accountings of the trustee. The trustee is required by the Code to administer the trust expeditiously for the benefit of the beneficiaries, and to use standards of care appropriate for a prudent person in dealing with the property of others. The trustee must keep the trust beneficiaries reasonably informed as to the administration of the trust, and furnish the beneficiaries a statement of the trust accounts annually (or more frequently if necessary) and at the termination of the trust.

Provisions of Revised Uniform Principal and Income Act Governing Trusts

The provisions for allocations between principal and income that are set forth in the Revised Uniform Principal and Income Act (pages 654 and 655) are applicable to trusts as well as to estates.

Illustration of Accounting for a Trust

The journal entries in the accounting records of a trust usually differ from those of an estate because of the longer life of a trust. Whereas the personal representative for an estate attempts to complete the administration of the estate as expeditiously as possible, the trustee for a trust must comply with the provisions of the trust document during the stated term of the trust. Accordingly, the trustee's activities include investment of trust property and maintenance of accounting records for both trust principal and trust income.

To illustrate the accounting issues for a trust, return to the testamentary trust provided by the will of Jessica Davis (page 655). The trust was created by the residuary devise to Nancy Grimes, which required the trustee to pay income from the trust to Grimes at the end of each calendar quarter until her twenty-first birthday (October 1, 2007), at which time the trust principal would be paid to Grimes. Thus, Grimes is both the income beneficiary and the principal beneficiary.

The following journal entries illustrate the activities of First National Bank, trustee for Nancy Grimes, during the quarter ended June 30, 2002. The journal entries for the Nancy Grimes Trust are essentially *cash-basis* entries; there is no need to accrue interest or dividends on trust investments at the end of a quarter because conventional financial statements generally are not prepared for a trust.

NANCY GRIMES TRUST
First National Bank, Trustee
Journal Entries

2002				
May 3	Principal Cash		21,714	
	Income Cash		1,500	
	Certificate of Deposit (including accrued interest)		26,475	
	Marketable Securities		24,500	
	Trust Principal Balance			72,689
	Trust Income Balance			1,500
	To record receipt of principal and income property in trust from Paul Hasting, executor of estate of Jessica Davis.			
May 6	Marketable Securities		19,900	
	Interest Receivable		180	
	Principal Cash			20,080
	To record acquisition of the following securities:			
	$15,000 face amount of 12% bonds of Warren Company, due Mar. 31, 2022	$15,000		
	Accrued interest	180		
	$5,000 face amount of commercial paper of Modern Finance Company, due July 5, 2002 acquired at 12% discount	4,900		
	Total cash paid	$20,080		
June 30	Principal Cash		26,475	
	Income Cash		612	
	Certificate of Deposit			26,475
	Interest Revenue			612
	To record proceeds of matured certificate of deposit and interest since Mar. 18, 2002.			
30	Administrative Costs		250	
	Expenses Chargeable to Income		250	
	Principal Cash			250
	Income Cash			250
	To record payment of trustee fee for period May 3–June 30, 2002, chargeable equally to principal and to income.			
30	Marketable Securities		25,000	
	Principal Cash			25,000
	To record acquisition of 14% U.S. Treasury notes due June 30, 2007, at face amount.			
30	Distributions to Income Beneficiary		1,862	
	Income Cash			1,862
	To record regular quarterly distribution to income beneficiary Nancy Grimes.			

The May 3, 2002, opening journal entry for the trust is the counterpart of the journal entry for the Estate of Jessica Davis on the same date (page 659), except that the amount receivable from the trust beneficiary for federal estate tax and state inheritance tax was offset against the gross amount of the devise, and the $72,689 difference ($85,797 − $13,108 = $72,689) was recorded as the trust principal balance.

Trial Balance

The trial balance of the Nancy Grimes Trust on June 30, 2002, is as follows:

	NANCY GRIMES TRUST First National Bank, Trustee Trial Balance June 30, 2002

	Dr (Cr)
Principal:	
Principal cash	$ 2,859
Marketable securities	69,400
Interest receivable	180
Trust principal balance	(72,689)
Administrative costs	250
Totals	$ -0-
Income:	
Trust income balance	$ (1,500)
Interest revenue	(612)
Expenses chargeable to income	250
Distributions to income beneficiary	1,862
Totals	$ -0-

Charge and Discharge Statement for Trustee

A charge and discharge statement for the trustee of the Nancy Grimes Trust would resemble the charge and discharge statement for an estate illustrated on pages 662 to 664. The major difference would be an exhibit for the details of the $72,439 ($72,689 − $250 = $72,439) trust principal balance on June 30, 2002.

Periodic Closing Entry for Trust

A closing entry should be made for a trust at the end of each period for which a charge and discharge statement is prepared to clear the nominal accounts for the next reporting period. The closing entry for the Nancy Grimes Trust on June 30, 2002, is as illustrated below:

Periodic Closing Entry for a Trust

	Dr	Cr
Trust Principal Balance	250	
Trust Income Balance	1,500	
Interest Revenue	612	
Administrative Costs		250
Expenses Chargeable to Income		250
Distributions to Income Beneficiary		1,862
To close nominal accounts of trust.		

At the time specified in the trust document for transfer of the trust principal to the principal beneficiary, a journal entry is made to debit the Distributions to Principal Beneficiary ledger account and credit the various trust principal asset accounts. A closing entry for the termination of the trust would then be required, in the form of the comparable estate journal entry illustrated on page 665.

Review Questions

1. Is the Uniform Probate Code in effect throughout the United States?
2. Define the following terms:

   a. *Estate*   f. *Letters testamentary*
   b. *Intestacy*   g. *Devise*
   c. *Testator*   h. *Remainderman*
   d. *Executor*   i. *Inter vivos trust*
   e. *Administrator*   j. *Settlor*

3. Compare *informal probate* with *formal probate* of a will.
4. Compare the standards of care required of a *personal representative* of a decedent with the standards of care required of a *trustee* of a trust.
5. Why must there be a distinction between *principal* and *income* in the administration of an estate?
6. Describe the *exempt property and allowances* provisions of the Uniform Probate Code.
7. What type of *devise* is each of the following?

   a. The beach house at 1411 Ocean Avenue, Long Beach, California.
   b. $25,000 cash.
   c. $60,000 face amount of U.S. Treasury bonds.
   d. 1,000 shares of Rogers Corporation common stock represented by certificate No. G-1472.
   e. All my remaining property.

8. Is the accrual basis of accounting ever used for an estate or a trust? Explain.
9. Explain the requirements for depreciation accounting contained in the Revised Uniform Principal and Income Act.
10. Describe the use of the Property Discovered ledger account in accounting for an estate.
11. Compare a personal representative's *charge and discharge statement* for an estate with the financial statements issued by a business enterprise.
12. Discuss the similarities and differences in the journal entries for estates and for trusts.

Exercises

(Exercise 15.1)   Select the best answer for each of the following multiple-choice questions:

1. In the accounting records of the executor of an estate, the Property Discovered ledger account is:

   a. An asset account.   c. An equity account.
   b. A liability account.   d. An accountability account.

2. If estate property that is not exempt is insufficient to cover creditors' claims as well as all devises, and the will is silent as to abatement, the Uniform Probate Code provides the following abatement sequence:

    a. Property not specifically mentioned in the will, residuary devises, general devises, specific devises.

    b. Residuary devises, specific devises, property not specifically mentioned in the will, general devises.

    c. General devises, residuary devises, property not specifically mentioned in the will, specific devises.

    d. None of the above.

3. Which of the following ledger accounts of an executor of a decedent's will typically has a debit balance?

    a. Assets Discovered.

    b. Liabilities Paid.

    c. Estate Principal Balance.

    d. None of the above.

4. In the abatement sequence for devises established by the Uniform Probate Code, the last devises to be abated are:

    a. Specific devises.

    b. General devises.

    c. Residuary devises.

    d. *Inter vivos* devises.

5. The Devises Distributed ledger account of a decedent's estate is a(n):

    a. Asset account

    b. Liability account

    c. Accountability account

    d. Expense account

6. Devises distributed are displayed in the charge and discharge statement for the executor of a decedent's will in the section:

    a. First, as to principal, I charge myself as follows.

    b. First, as to principal, I credit myself as follows.

    c. Second, as to income, I charge myself as follows.

    d. Second, as to income, I credit myself as follows.

7. The ranking, in order of priority of payment by the personal representative of a decedent's estate, of debts and taxes with preference under federal law is:

    a. First   b. Second   c. Third   d. Fourth

8. The financial statement prepared periodically for the trustee of a trust is:

    a. A charge and discharge statement.

    b. A statement of realization and liquidation.

    c. An income statement.

    d. A statement of affairs.

9. The Liabilities Paid ledger account in the accounting records of the personal representative of an estate is a(n):

    a. Asset account

    b. Liability account

    c. Accountability account

    d. Expense account

10. In the charge and discharge statement for the executor of a will, ***property discovered*** is displayed with:

    a. Principal—I charge myself as follows.
    b. Income—I charge myself as follows.
    c. Principal—I credit myself as follows.
    d. Income—I credit myself as follows.

11. Court costs, attorneys' fees, trustees' fees, and accountants' fees for periodic reporting to the probate court by a trustee are:

    a. Charged entirely to principal.
    b. Charged entirely to income.
    c. Allocated to principal and income.
    d. Charged as ordered by the court.

12. A devise of 1,000 shares of The Walt Disney Company common stock is a(n):

    a. Residuary devise
    b. General devise
    c. Specific devise
    d. Abated devise

13. Which of the following journal entries (amounts and explanations omitted) is inappropriate for an estate?

    a. Savings Account
           Property Discovered
    b. Receivable from Devisees
           Principal Cash
    c. Liabilities Paid
           Principal Cash
    d. Devises Distributed
           Income Cash
    e. None of the above.

14. A personal representative of an estate who is appointed by the probate court is a(n):

    a. Executor
    b. Administrator
    c. Trustee
    d. Devisee

(Exercise 15.2) Indicate whether each of the following items would be charged to trust principal or to trust income of a testamentary trust, assuming that the Revised Uniform Principal and Income Act is to be followed:

a. Depreciation of building.

b. Legal fees for managing trust property.

c. Special assessment tax levied on real property for street improvements.

d. Interest on mortgage note payable.

e. Loss on disposal of trust investments.

f. Major repairs to real property prior to disposal of the property.

(Exercise 15.3) After the payment of all estate liabilities, excepting the executor's fee of $40,000, the following property remained in the Estate of Allen Baker, deceased, on April 30, 2002:

	Amount	% of Total
Cash in checking account	$13,860	21%
Bank certificate of deposit maturing April 30, 2003, including accrued interest	21,120	32
100 shares of BBM Company common stock, at current fair value on date of death	9,900	15
$20,000 face amount Southeastern Airlines 7% bonds due 2004, at current fair value on date of death	21,120	32
Total estate property	$66,000	100%

The following devises remained to be distributed by the executor:

1. Barbara Baker (wife)—certificate no. X4738 for $20,000 face amount of Southeastern Airlines 7% bonds due 2004.
2. Carl Baker (son)—50 shares of BBM Company common stock.
3. Danielle Baker (daughter)—50 shares of BBM Company common stock.
4. Edie Baker (niece)—residue of estate.

Prepare a working paper to show how total estate property should be distributed by the executor on April 30, 2002.

(Exercise 15.4)

After payment of all liabilities of the Estate of Rhoda Ross, deceased, and the completion of distributions to income beneficiaries, the trial balance of the estate was as follows on December 17, 2002:

	Dr (Cr)
Principal:	
Principal cash	$ 100,000
200 shares of Excel Corporation common stock, at current fair value	60,000
$50,000 face amount of 10% Engle Corporation bonds, plus accrued interest at date of death, at current fair value	55,000
Estate principal balance	(200,000)
Gain on disposal of principal property	(15,000)
Total	$ -0-

Remaining devises to be distributed were as follows:

1. All 200 shares of Excel Corporation common stock to Leah Ross, daughter.
2. $25,000 face amount of 10% Engle Corporation bonds to Ward Ross, son.
3. $60,000 checking account balance (included in principal cash) in acct. no. 6158 at Bank of America to University of Carlin, a nonprofit organization.
4. $50,000 cash to Music Center Fund, a nonprofit organization.
5. Residue of estate to Roberta Jones, sister.

Prepare a working paper to show how the foregoing devices are to be distributed on December 17, 2002. The following column headings are suggested: Devisee, Type of Devise, Gross Devise Amount, Abated Amount, Net Devise Amount. The Net Devise Amount column should total $215,000, the carrying amount (and current fair value) of the estate principal property.

(Exercise 15.5) Prepare journal entries (omit explanations) for the following selected transactions of the executor of the will of Lincoln Johnson, deceased:

2002

Dec. 6 Executor Grant Hayes discovered a certificate for 1,000 shares of Coburn Company common stock with a current fair value of $6 a share. Hayes had filed the inventory of estate property with the probate court on November 14, 2002.

     14 Hayes distributed a general devise of $2,500 cash to Garfield Arthur, Johnson's nephew.

     26 Hayes was authorized by the probate court to receive a fee of $1,000 (all allocable to principal) for services to date. Hayes prepared the check.

     31 Hayes paid liabilities of the Estate of Lincoln Johnson in the amount of $9,200.

(Exercise 15.6) Selected transactions and events completed by the executor of the will of D. C. Kane, who died on October 15, 2002, are as follows:

Oct. 20 Inventory of estate property (at current fair value) was filed with the court as follows:

Cash	$ 88,800
Real property	148,000
Arriba Company common stock	60,000
Carter Corporation bonds ($40,000 face amount)	40,000
Accrued interest on Carter Corporation bonds	600
Personal and household effects	23,500

     29 A certificate for 150 shares of Basin Corporation common stock valued at $9,000 was found in the coat pocket of an old suit belonging to the decedent.

Nov. 10 A cash dividend of $520 was received on the Arriba Company common stock. The stock had been willed as a specific devise to Edward Kane, son of D.C. Kane.

     15 Liabilities of D. C. Kane in the amount of $30,000 were paid.

     22 Administrative costs of $3,240 were paid. All costs are chargeable to principal.

     29 Bonds of Carter Corporation were sold at 94, plus accrued interest of $1,050.

     30 Arriba Company common stock and the cash dividend of $520 received on November 10 were transferred to Edward Kane.

Prepare journal entries to record the foregoing transactions and events in the accounting records of the executor of the will of D. C. Kane, deceased. Omit explanations for the journal entries.

(Exercise 15.7) The inexperienced accountant for Lillian Crane, executor of the will of Marion Wilson, deceased, prepared the following journal entries, among others:

2002			
Apr. 25	Marketable Securities	10,400	
	Estate Principal Balance		10,400
	To record supplemental inventory for property discovered subsequent to filing of original inventory.		
30	Distribution Expense	800	
	Income Cash		800
	To record distribution of income cash to residuary devise, as required by the will.		
May 27	Accounts Payable	7,400	
	Principal Cash		7,400
	To record following liabilities paid:		

Funeral costs	$2,500	
Hospital bills	3,800	
Doctor's fees	1,100	
Total	$7,400	

Prepare journal entries for Lillian Crane, executor of the will of Marion Wilson, deceased, on May 31, 2002, to correct the foregoing journal entries. Do not reverse the foregoing entries.

(Exercise 15.8) The accountant for the executor of the will of Howard Jones, deceased, prepared the following trial balance on December 18, 2002, the date the estate was closed:

MARIAN SMITH, EXECUTOR
Of the Will of Howard Jones, Deceased
Trial Balance
December 18, 2002

	Dr (Cr)
Principal:	
Estate principal balance (June 18, 2002)	$(150,000)
Property discovered	(20,000)
Gain on disposal of principal property	(1,000)
Liabilities paid	40,000
Devises distributed	125,000
Administrative costs	6,000
Total	$ -0-
Income:	
Interest revenue	$ (10,000)
Dividend revenue	(15,000)
Distributions to income beneficiaries	25,000
Total	$ -0-

Prepare a charge and discharge statement for Marian Smith, executor of the will of Howard Jones, deceased, on December 18, 2002. (Disregard supporting exhibits.)

(Exercise 15.9) Barbara Coleman, executor of the will of Robert Kaplan, who died on August 10, 2001, prepared the following trial balance on February 10, 2002:

BARBARA COLEMAN, EXECUTOR
Of the Will of Robert Kaplan, Deceased
Trial Balance
February 10, 2002

	Dr (Cr)
Principal cash	$ 26,000
Income cash	490
Estate principal balance	(117,000)
Property discovered	(1,800)
Gain on disposal of principal property	(1,200)
Administrative costs	3,000
Liabilities paid	24,500
Devises distributed	66,500
Interest revenue	(3,590)
Distributions to income beneficiaries	2,000
Expenses chargeable to income	1,100
Total	$ -0-

Prepare an *interim* charge and discharge statement for the period August 10, 2001, through February 10, 2002. (Do not prepare supporting exhibits.)

(Exercise 15.10) The trial balance of Wanda Wardlow, executor of the will of William Wardlow, deceased, on June 30, 2002, the filing date for the final charge and discharge statement, included the following:

Administrative costs	$ 5,000
Property discovered	36,000
Devises distributed	347,366
Distributions to income beneficiaries	3,110
Dividend revenue	3,000
Estate principal balance	324,484
Interest revenue	110
Liabilities paid	7,844
Loss on disposal of principal property	274

Prepare a closing entry for Wanda Wardlow, executor of the will of William Wardlow, deceased, on June 30, 2002.

(Exercise 15.11) Pursuant to the will of Gina Adams, the residue of her estate after probate of the will is to be transferred to a testamentary trust. The following trial balance was prepared from the ledger of the estate on June 30, 2002:

	Dr (Cr)
Principal cash	$115,000
Income cash	6,750
Marketable securities	105,000
Estate principal balance	(265,000)
Property discovered	(13,000)
Gain on disposal of principal property	(12,000)
Administrative costs	5,400
Liabilities paid	16,000
Devises distributed	48,600
Interest revenue	(4,000)
Dividend revenue	(4,500)
Expenses chargeable to income	1,750
Total	$ -0-

a. Prepare journal entries to transfer the residuary devise to the trustee and to close the accounting records of the estate.

b. Prepare a journal entry to open the accounting records of the trust.

(Exercise 15.12) The trial balance of the Wilson Woodrow Trust on April 30, 2002, a date on which the trustee rendered a charge and discharge statement to the probate court, included the following items:

	Debit	Credit
Administrative costs (chargeable to principal)	$ 1,700	
Distributions to income beneficiary	2,000	
Expenses chargeable to income	800	
Interest revenue		$ 1,600
Marketable securities	80,000	
Principal cash	30,000	
Trust income balance		1,200
Trust principal balance		111,700
Totals	$114,500	$114,500

Prepare a closing entry for the Wilson Woodrow Trust on April 30, 2002.

Cases

(Case 15.1) At a meeting in his office, Carl Roberts, managing partner of Roberts & Webb, LLP, CPAs, is asked by Albert Hopp, a wealthy tax client, to approve Hopp's naming Roberts as executor of his and his terminally ill wife's wills and as trustee of their testamentary trusts. Hopp tells Roberts that a bank trust department would not be as effective in the roles as Roberts because of the complexities of Hopp's investments, liabilities, and tax matters. Roberts informs Hopp that, as a partner in his firm, Roberts would have to use firm personnel in administering the estate and trust, and that such an arrangement might create a conflict of interest between Roberts as trustee and Roberts as partner. Roberts explained to Hopp that, under the quality control procedures established by Roberts & Webb, LLP, for the acceptance of new clients, he would have to consult with his three partners before accepting the engagement as executor of the Hopp wills and testamentary trusts.

Instructions

If you were a partner in the Roberts & Webb, LLP, firm, would you approve Carl Roberts' acceptance of the proffered executor and trustee appointments by the Hopps? Explain.

(Case 15.2) The estate of Mary Carr included the following securities on the date of death, April 16, 2002 (all of which are a part of the residuary devise):

1. Sand Company 12% bonds due June 16, 2012, face amount $100,000; current fair value on April 16, 2002 (excluding accrued interest), $103,500; interest payable June 16 and December 16 of each year.

2. Palko Corporation common stock, 5,000 shares; current fair value on April 16, 2002, $68,000; dividend of $1 a share declared April 1, 2002, payable May 1, 2002, to stockholders of record April 14, 2002.

3. Palko Corporation 8%, $100 par, cumulative preferred stock, 1,000 shares; current fair value on April 16, 2002, $97,500. Dividends are paid semiannually January 1 and July 1, and there are no dividends in arrears.

Instructions

a. Inform the executor of the will of Mary Carr, deceased, which of the foregoing items constitute income and which constitute principal of the estate.

b. If the dividends were in arrears on the Palko Corporation 8%, $100 par, cumulative preferred stock, would your answer to *a* be any different? Explain.

(Case 15.3) James Saliba transferred a manufacturing enterprise and 10,000 shares of MP Company common stock to Fidelity Trust Company to be held in trust for the benefit of his son, Robert, for life, with the remainder to go to Robert's son, Edward. Fidelity Trust Company insured the enterprise with Boston Insurance Company under two policies. One policy was a standard fire insurance policy covering the buildings and equipment. The other policy covered any loss of income during periods when the enterprise was inoperable as a result of fire or other catastrophe. The buildings and equipment subsequently were destroyed by fire, and Boston Insurance Company paid claims under both policies to Fidelity Trust Company.

Shortly after the 10,000 shares of MP Company common stock had been transferred to Fidelity Trust Company, MP Company declared a dividend of 10 shares of Monte Oil Corporation common stock for each 100 shares of MP Company common stock held. The Monte Oil common stock had been acquired as an investment by MP Company.

During the same year, MP Company directors split the common stock 2 for 1. After the distribution of the new shares, Fidelity Trust Company disposed of 10,000 shares of MP Company common stock.

Instructions

How should Fidelity Trust Company handle the events described above as to distribution between the income beneficiary and the remainderman? State reasons for making the distribution in the manner that you recommend.

(Case 15.4) In reviewing the accounting records of Stanley Koyanagi, executor of the will of Edward Dunn, who died January 16, 2002, you study the will and other documents, which reveal that (1) Dunn's son received a specific devise of the decedent's only rental property and 12% bonds of Padre Corporation, $50,000 face amount, due March 1, 2016; (2) Dunn's daughter was the beneficiary of a life insurance policy (face amount $100,000) on which the decedent had paid the premiums; and (3) Dunn's widow had been left the remainder of the estate in trust.

Your review also reveals the following transactions and events occurring from the time of Dunn's death to March 1, 2002:

(1) Jan. 17 $3,195 was received from the redemption of $3,000 face amount of Camm Corporation 13% bonds that matured on January 15, 2002.

(2) Jan. 20 $500 was received from Pittson Corporation as a cash dividend of $1 a share on common stock, declared December 1, 2001, payable January 15, 2002, to stockholders of record January 2, 2002.

(3) Jan. 20 $5,040 was paid to Witter & Company, stockbrokers, for the acquisition of five Seaboard, Inc., 14%, $1,000 bonds due June 30, 2013.

(4) Jan. 21   30 shares of common stock were received from Ragusa Company, constituting a 2% stock dividend declared December 14, 2001, distributable January 20, 2002, to stockholders of record January 15, 2002.

(5) Feb. 1 $200 quarterly interest was paid by the executor on a promissory note payable due January 31, 2003.

(6) Feb. 1   Dunn's physician was paid $2,500 for services rendered during Dunn's last illness.

(7) Feb. 2 $600 was received from East Corporation as a cash dividend of $0.25 a share on common stock, declared January 18, 2002, payable January 30, 2002, to stockholders of record January 27, 2002.

(8) Feb. 3 $575 rent revenue for February was received and deposited in the bank.

(9) Feb. 10 $890 was paid for property taxes covering the period from February 1 to July 31, 2002.

(10) Mar. 1 $1,802 was paid to the Internal Revenue Service as the remaining income taxes owed by the decedent for 2001 taxable income.

Instructions

Indicate whether each transaction or event should be:

Allocated between principal and income.

Allocated between principal and beneficiaries (devisees).

Attributed solely to income.

Attributed solely to principal.

Attributed solely to beneficiaries (devisees).

State reasons supporting your conclusions as to how each transaction or event should be handled.

Problems

(Problem 15.1)

Mildred Young died on June 5, 2002. Michael Synn was named executor in the will that had been prepared by Young's attorney. On December 31, 2002, the accountant for the executor prepared the following trial balance:

MICHAEL SYNN, EXECUTOR Of the Will of Mildred Young, Deceased Trial Balance December 31, 2002	
	Dr (Cr)
Principal cash	$ 25,700
Income cash	13,000
Investments in bonds	268,300
Investments in common stocks	224,300
Household effects	39,500
Gains on disposal of principal property	(2,200)
Property discovered	(16,800)
Liabilities paid	36,200
Administrative costs	10,000
Devises distributed	15,000
Estate principal balance	(600,000)
Dividend revenue	(14,200)
Interest revenue	(18,500)
Expenses chargeable to income	720
Distributions to income beneficiaries	18,980
Total	$ -0-

Instructions

The amount in the Estate Principal Balance ledger account represents the inventory of estate property on June 5, 2002. Prepare an interim charge and discharge statement for the executor of the will of Mildred Young for the period June 5 through December 31, 2002. Supporting exhibits are not required for any items except the listing of property comprising the estate principal balance on December 31, 2002.

(Problem 15.2)

Pablo Garcia died on March 1, 2002, leaving a will in which he named Mark Castro as executor and trustee pending final distribution of estate property to Manuel Montejano, a nephew. The will instructed the executor to transfer Garcia's personal effects and automobile to the nephew, to pay estate taxes, outstanding liabilities, and administrative costs of the estate, and to transfer the remaining estate property to a trust for the benefit of the nephew. Income from the estate and the trust was to be paid to the nephew, who was to receive the principal (corpus) upon graduation from State University.

The inventory of estate property on March 1, 2002, consisted of the following:

Cash	$44,440
Certificate of deposit at Standard Savings Bank (includes accrued interest of $1,100)	101,100
Personal effects	13,200*
Automobile	2,800*
Investments in common stocks	77,000*

* At current fair value.

The following transactions or events were completed by the executor through December 10, 2002:

(1) Discovered a savings account of $6,290 in the name of Pablo Garcia. (Debit Principal Cash.)

(2) Paid administrative costs for the estate, $5,200. All costs are chargeable to principal.

(3) Disposed of common stock with a carrying amount of $20,000 for $26,020, net of commissions.

(4) Transferred personal effects and automobile to Manuel Montejano.

(5) Received income as follows (there were no expenses chargeable to income): Interest, $5,200 (includes accrued interest on certificate of deposit on March 1, 2002); dividends, $1,400.

(6) Distributed the income of the estate to Manuel Montejano.

(7) Paid liabilities of decedent, $8,050.

(8) Paid estate taxes, $32,000. (Debit Estate Taxes Paid.)

(9) Closed the accounting records of the estate and transferred property to the Manuel Montejano Trust.

Instructions

a. Prepare journal entries to record the foregoing transactions or events and to close the accounting records of the estate. Disregard homestead allowance, exempt property, and family allowance.

b. Prepare a charge and discharge statement immediately after the transfer of estate property to the Manuel Montejano Trust. Do not prepare any supporting exhibits.

c. Prepare a journal entry on December 10, 2002, to open the accounting records for the testamentary trust: the Manuel Montejano Trust.

(Problem 15.3) Janet Mann died on May 31, 2002. Her will provided that all liabilities and costs were to be paid and that the property was to be distributed as follows:

CHECK FIGURE

Estate principal balance, July 1, $291,700.

1. Personal residence to George Mann, widower of Janet Mann.
2. U.S. Treasury 12% bonds and Permian Company common stock—to be placed in trust. All income to go to George Mann during his lifetime.
3. Sonar Corporation 9% bonds—devised to Eleanor Mann, daughter of Janet Mann.
4. Cash—a devise of $15,000 to Dudley Mann, son of Janet Mann.
5. Residue of estate—to be divided equally between the two children of Janet Mann: Eleanor and Dudley.

Additional Information

1. The will further provided that during the administration period George Mann was to be paid $1,500 a month from estate income. Estate and inheritance taxes were to be paid from the principal of the estate. Dudley Mann was named as executor and trustee.
2. The following inventory of the decedent's property was prepared (amounts are current fair values):

Personal residence	$245,000
Jewelry—diamond ring	14,600
City National Bank—checking account; balance May 31, 2002	43,000
$200,000 U.S. Treasury 12% bonds, due 2018, interest payable Mar. 1 and Sept. 1 (includes accrued interest of $6,000)	206,000
$10,000 Sonar Corporation 9% bonds, due 2011, interest payable May 31 and Nov. 30	9,900
Permian Company common stock, 800 shares	64,000
Dividends receivable on Permian Company common stock	800
Roe Company common stock, 700 shares	70,000

3. The executor opened an estate checking account and transferred the decedent's checking account balance to it. Other deposits in the estate checking account through July 1, 2003, were as follows:

Interest received on $200,000 U.S. Treasury 12% bonds:	
Sept. 1, 2002	$12,000
Mar. 1, 2003	12,000
Dividends received on Permian Company common stock:	
June 15, 2002, declared May 7, 2002, payable to holders of record May 27, 2002	800
Sept. 15, 2002	800
Dec. 15, 2002	1,200
Mar. 15, 2003	1,500
June 15, 2003	1,500
Net proceeds of June 19, 2002, disposal of 700 shares of Roe Company common stock	68,810

4. Payments were made from the estate checking account through July 1, 2003, for the following:

Liabilities of decedent paid (including funeral costs)	$12,000
Additional prior years' federal and state income taxes, plus interest to May 31, 2002	1,810
Income taxes of Janet Mann for the period Jan. 1, 2002, through May 31, 2002, in excess of amounts paid by the decedent on declarations of estimated tax	9,100
Federal and state fiduciary income taxes, fiscal years ending June 30, 2002, and June 30, 2003	2,400
Estate and inheritance taxes	43,000
Monthly payments to George Mann, 13 payments of $1,500	19,500
Attorney's and accountant's fees (allocated entirely to principal)	25,000

5. The executor, Dudley Mann, waived a fee. However, he desired to receive his mother's diamond ring in lieu of the $15,000 cash devise. All parties agreed to this in writing, and the probate court's approval was secured. All devises other than the assets to be held in trust and the residue of the estate were delivered on July 1, 2002.

Instructions

Prepare a charge and discharge statement as to principal and income, with supporting exhibits, to accompany the formal court accounting on behalf of the executor of the will of Janet Mann, deceased, for the period from May 31, 2002, through July 1, 2003.

In accordance with the will, the executor accrued the interest and dividends on the estate investments to July 1, 2003. Disregard homestead allowance, exempt property, and family allowance.

(Problem 15.4)

The will of Frederick Doheny directed that the executor, Richard Cordes, liquidate the entire estate within two years of the date of death and pay the net proceeds and income to United Charities. Frederick Doheny, a bachelor, died on February 1, 2002, after a brief illness.

An inventory of the decedent's property was prepared, and the current fair value of all items was determined. The preliminary inventory, before the computation of any appropriate income accruals on the property in inventory, follows:

	Current Fair Values
Union Bank checking account	$ 33,500
$60,000 face amount Sun City bonds, interest rate 12%, payable Jan. 1 and July 1, maturity date July 1, 2006	59,000
2,000 shares Ron Corp. common stock	220,000
Term life insurance: beneficiary, Estate of Frederick Doheny	20,000
Residence ($86,500) and furniture ($23,500)	110,000

During the remainder of 2002, the following transactions or events occurred:

(1) The interest on the Sun City bonds was received. The bonds were disposed of on July 1, for $59,000, and the proceeds and interest accrued on February 1 ($600), were paid to United Charities.

(2) Ron Corp. paid cash dividends of $1 a share on March 1 and December 1, and distributed a 10% stock dividend on July 1. All dividends had been declared 45 days before each payment date and were payable to holders of record as of 40 days before each payment date. In September, 1,000 shares of Ron Corp. common stock were disposed of for $105 a share, and the proceeds were paid to United Charities.

(3) The residence was rented furnished at $900 a month commencing April 1. The rent was paid monthly, in advance. Property taxes of $1,200 for the calendar year 2002 were paid. The house and furnishings had estimated economic lives of 40 years and 8 years, respectively. The part-time gardener was paid four months' wages totaling $500 on April 30 for services performed, and then was released.

(4) The Union Bank checking account was closed, and the balance of $8,500 was transferred to a bank checking account for the estate.

(5) The proceeds of the term life insurance were received on March 1 and deposited in the bank checking account for the estate.

(6) The following cash payments were made:
(a) Funeral costs and costs of last illness, $3,500.
(b) Amount due on 2001 income taxes of decedent, $700.
(c) Attorney's and accountant's fees, $20,000, of which $3,025 was allocated to income.

(7) On December 31, the balance of the undistributed income, except for $500, was paid to United Charities. The balance of the cash on hand derived from the principal of the estate was paid to United Charities on December 31. On December 31, the executor resigned and waived all fees.

Instructions

Prepare a charge and discharge statement, together with supporting exhibits, for the executor of the will of Frederick Doheny, deceased, for the period February 1 through December 31, 2002. Disregard depreciation.

Chapter **Sixteen**

Nonprofit Organizations

Scope of Chapter

This chapter discusses and illustrates some of the accounting and financial statement display issues for nonprofit organizations. A ***nonprofit*** (or ***not-for-profit***) ***organization*** is a legal and accounting entity that is operated for the benefit of society as a whole, rather than for the benefit of an individual proprietor or a group of partners or stockholders. Thus, the concept of net income is not meaningful for a nonprofit organization. Instead, as does the internal service fund of a governmental entity described in Chapter 19, a nonprofit organization generally strives only to obtain revenues sufficient to cover its expenses.

Nonprofit organizations constitute a significant segment of the U.S. economy. As pointed out by the Financial Accounting Standards Board:

> Not-for-profit organizations include cemetery organizations, civic organizations, colleges and universities, cultural institutions, fraternal organizations, hospitals, labor unions, libraries, museums, performing arts organizations, political parties, private and community foundations, private elementary and secondary schools, professional associations, public broadcasting stations, religious organizations, research and scientific organizations, social and country clubs, trade associations, voluntary health and welfare organizations, and zoological and botanical societies. They do not include governmental units.[1]

ACCOUNTING STANDARDS FOR NONPROFIT ORGANIZATIONS

For many years, the accounting standards and practices that constitute generally accepted accounting principles were not considered to be entirely applicable to nonprofit organizations. The following quotation, which formerly appeared in various auditing publications of the AICPA, outlines this situation:

> The statements . . . of a not-for-profit organization . . . may reflect accounting practices differing in some respects from those followed by enterprises organized for profit. In some cases generally accepted accounting principles applicable to not-for-profit organizations have not been clearly defined. In those areas where the independent auditor believes generally accepted accounting principles have been clearly defined, he may state his opinion as to the conformity of the financial statements either with generally ac-

---

[1] *Invitation to Comment,* "Financial Reporting by Not-for-Profit Organizations: Form and Content of Financial Statements" (Norwalk: FASB, 1989), p. 17.

cepted accounting principles or (less desirably) with accounting practices for not-for-profit organizations in the particular field, and in such circumstances he may refer to financial position and results of operations. In those areas where he believes generally accepted accounting principles have not been clearly defined, the provisions covering special reports as discussed under cash basis and modified accrual basis statements are applicable.[2]

In the period 1972 to 1974, the unsettled state of accounting for nonprofit organizations was improved by the AICPA's issuance of three *Audit and Accounting Guides* or *Industry Audit Guides:* "Hospital Audit Guide," "Audits of Colleges and Universities," and "Audits of Voluntary Health and Welfare Organizations." All three were subsequently amended, and the "Hospital Audit Guide" was superseded by "Health Care Organizations." The status of an *Audit and Accounting Guide* or an *Industry Audit Guide* is set forth in each guide; the following language in "Health Care Organizations" is typical:

> The AICPA Auditing Standards Board has found the descriptions of auditing standards, procedures, and practices in this Audit and Accounting Guide to be consistent with existing standards covered by rule 202 of the AICPA Code of Professional Conduct. Descriptions of auditing standards, procedures, and practices in Audit and Accounting Guides are not as authoritative as pronouncements of the Auditing Standards Board, but AICPA members should be aware that they may have to justify a departure from such descriptions if the quality of their work is questioned.[3]

The three *Guides* listed above dealt with only three types of nonprofit organizations. Thus, in 1978, the AICPA issued *Statement of Position 78-10,* later incorporated in "Audits of Certain Nonprofit Organizations," which applied to at least 18 types of nonprofit organizations, ranging from cemetery societies to zoological and botanical societies.

The existence of four separate sources of authoritative support for generally accepted accounting principles for nonprofit organizations led to many inconsistencies among the accounting standards for such organizations. The FASB resolved several of these inconsistencies in four *Statements of Financial Accounting Standards* discussed in subsequent sections of this chapter: No. 93, "Recognition of Depreciation by Not-for-Profit Organizations"; No. 116, "Accounting for Contributions Received and Contributions Made"; No. 117, "Financial Statements of Not-for-Profit Organizations"; and No. 124, "Accounting for Certain Investments Held by Not-for-Profit Organizations." Subsequently, the AICPA issued an *Audit and Accounting Guide,* "Not-for-Profit Organizations," that superseded "Audits of Colleges and Universities," "Audits of Voluntary Health and Welfare Organizations," and "Audits of Certain Nonprofit Organizations." Taken together, the actions of the FASB and the AICPA brought order out of chaos with respect to accounting standards for nonprofit organizations.

CHARACTERISTICS OF NONPROFIT ORGANIZATIONS

Nonprofit organizations are in certain respects hybrid because they have some characteristics similar to those of governmental entities (which are discussed in Chapter 17) and other characteristics similar to those of business enterprises.

---

[2] *Statement on Auditing Standards No. 1,* "Codification of Auditing Standards and Procedures" (New York: AICPA, 1973), par. 620.08.
[3] *Audit and Accounting Guide,* "Health Care Organizations" (New York: AICPA, 1996), p. iii.

Among the features of nonprofit organizations that resemble characteristics of governmental entities are the following:

1. ***Service to society*** Nonprofit organizations often render services to society as a whole. The members of this society may range from a limited number of citizens in a community to almost the entire population of a city, state, or nation. Similar to the services rendered by governmental entities, the services of nonprofit organizations are of benefit to the many rather than the few.

2. ***No profit motivation*** Nonprofit organizations do not operate with the objective of earning a profit. Consequently, nonprofit organizations generally are exempt from federal and state income taxes. Governmental entities, except for enterprise funds, have the same characteristics. (As pointed out in Chapter 19, enterprise funds sometimes are assessed an amount in lieu of property taxes by the legislative branch of the government.)

3. ***Financing by the citizenry*** As with governmental entities, most nonprofit organizations depend on the general population for a substantial portion of their support, because revenues from charges for their services are not intended to cover all their operating costs. Exceptions are professional societies and the philanthropic foundations established by wealthy individuals or families. Whereas the citizenry's contributions to government revenues are mostly ***involuntary taxes,*** their contributions to nonprofit organizations are ***voluntary contributions.***

4. ***Stewardship for resources*** Because a substantial portion of the resources of a nonprofit organization is donated, the organization must account for the resources on a stewardship basis similar to that of governmental entities. The stewardship requirement makes ***fund accounting*** appropriate for many nonprofit organizations, as it is for governmental entities.

5. ***Importance of budget*** The four preceding characteristics of nonprofit organizations cause their ***annual budget*** to be as important as for governmental entities.

Among the characteristics of nonprofit organizations that resemble those of business enterprises are the following:

1. ***Governance by board of directors*** As with a business corporation, a nonprofit corporation is governed by elected or appointed directors, trustees, or governors. In contrast, the legislative and executive branches of a governmental entity share the responsibilities for its governance.

2. ***Measurement of cost expirations*** Governance by a board of directors means that a nonprofit organization does not answer to a lawmaking body as does a governmental entity. One consequence is that ***cost expirations,*** or ***expenses,*** rather than ***expenditures,*** are reported in the ***statement of activities*** (see pages 698 to 699) of most nonprofit organizations. Allocation of expenses (including depreciation) and revenues to the appropriate accounting period thus is a common characteristic of nonprofit organizations and business enterprises.

3. ***Use of accrual basis of accounting*** Nonprofit organizations employ the same accrual basis of accounting used by business enterprises.

FUND ACCOUNTING BY NONPROFIT ORGANIZATIONS

The internal accounting unit for many nonprofit organizations is the *fund,* which is an accounting entity with a self-balancing set of accounts recording cash and other financial resources, together with all related liabilities and residual balances, and changes therein, which are segregated for the purpose of carrying on specific activities or attaining certain objectives in accordance with special regulations, restrictions, or limitations.[4]

Separate funds may be necessary to distinguish between assets that may be used as authorized by the board of directors and assets whose use is restricted by donors. Funds commonly used by some of the nonprofit organizations covered in this chapter include the following:

- Unrestricted fund (sometimes called *unrestricted current fund, general fund,* or *current unrestricted fund*).

- Restricted fund (sometimes called *restricted current fund* or *current restricted fund*).

- Endowment fund.

- Agency fund (sometimes called *custodian fund*).

- Annuity fund and life income fund (sometimes called *living trust fund*).

- Loan fund.

- Plant fund (sometimes called *land, building, and equipment fund*).

Unrestricted Fund

In many respects, an *unrestricted fund* is similar to the *general fund* of a governmental entity, which is discussed in Chapter 17. The unrestricted fund includes all the assets of a nonprofit organization that are available for use as authorized by the board of directors and are not restricted for specific purposes. Thus, similar to the general fund of a governmental entity, an unrestricted fund is *residual* in nature.

Revenues and Gains of Unrestricted Fund

The revenues and gains of an unrestricted fund are derived from a number of sources. For example, a hospital derives general (unrestricted) fund revenues from patient services, educational programs, research and other grants, unrestricted gifts, unrestricted income from endowment funds, and miscellaneous sources such as contributed material and services. A university's sources of unrestricted fund revenues and gains include student tuition and fees; governmental grants and contracts; gifts and private grants; unrestricted income from endowment funds; and revenue from auxiliary activities such as student residences, food services, and intercollegiate athletics. The principal revenue source of voluntary health and welfare organizations' unrestricted funds (and all other funds) is contributions. Revenues may also include membership dues, interest, dividends, and realized and unrealized gains on investments in debt and equity securities. A nonprofit professional society receives revenues from membership dues, fees for educational programs, advertising, and sales of publications.

[4] *Codification of Governmental Accounting and Financial Reporting Standards* (Norwalk: Governmental Accounting Standards Board, 2000), Sec. 1100.102.

Revenues for Services

A nonprofit organization's revenues for services are accrued at full rates, ***even though part or all of the revenue is to be waived or reduced.***[5] Suppose, for example, that nonprofit Community Hospital's patient service records for June 2002 include the following amounts:

Patient Service Revenues Components of a Nonprofit Hospital

Gross patient service revenues (before charity care or contractual adjustments)	$100,000
Charity care for indigent patients	8,000
Amount to be received from Civic Welfare, Inc., as a partial reimbursement for charity care	3,000
Contractual adjustment allowed to Blue Cross	16,000
Provision for doubtful accounts	12,000

The following journal entries are appropriate for the Community Hospital General Fund on June 30, 2002:

Journal Entries for Patient Service Revenues of General Fund of a Nonprofit Hospital

Accounts Receivable	92,000	
Patient Service Revenues ($100,000 − $8,000)		92,000
To record gross patient service revenues for month of June at full rates, exclusive of charity care.		
Accounts Receivable	3,000	
Patient Service Revenues		3,000
To record amount receivable from Civic Welfare, Inc. ($3,000), as a partial reimbursement for charity care.		
Contractual Adjustments	16,000	
Accounts receivable		16,000
To record contractual adjustments allowed to Blue Cross for June.		
Doubtful Accounts Expense	12,000	
Allowance for Doubtful Accounts		12,000
To provide for doubtful accounts receivable for June.		

In the first journal entry for Community Hospital, the value of the ***charity care*** provided to indigent patients is not accrued as accounts receivable or revenues because the underlying health care services provided by the hospital were never expected to result in cash flows to the hospital.[6] The account receivable in the second journal entry resulted from a commitment by another nonprofit organization to contribute toward the cost of charity care provided by Community Hospital. The contractual adjustments recorded in the third journal entry above illustrate a unique feature of a hospital's operations. Many accounts receivable of a hospital are collectible from a ***third-party payor,*** rather than from the patient receiving services. Among third-party payors are the U.S. government (Medicare and Medicaid programs), state programs such as MediCal in California, Blue Cross, and private medical insurance carriers. The hospital's contrac-

---

[5] *FASB Statement No. 117,* "Financial Statements of Not-for-Profit Organizations" (Norwalk: FASB, 1993), par. 24.
[6] "Health Care Organizations," par. 10.03.

tual agreements with third-party payors generally provide for payments by the third parties at less than full billing rates.

In the statement of activities of Community Hospital for June 2002, the balances of the Contractual Adjustments ledger account on June 30, 2002, is deducted from the balance of the Patient Service Revenues account to compute net patient service revenue for the month. The balance of the Allowance for Doubtful Accounts ledger account is offset against the balance of the Accounts Receivable account in the balance sheet, and write-offs of accounts receivable are recorded in the customary fashion. For example, the uncollectible accounts receivable of nonpaying patients who had been billed for services would be written off by Community Hospital by the following journal entry in the Unrestricted Fund on June 30, 2002:

Journal Entry to Write Off Uncollectible Accounts Receivable of a Nonprofit Hospital

Allowance for Doubtful Accounts	5,100	
Accounts Receivable		5,100
To write off uncollectible accounts receivable of nonpaying patients, as follows:		
J.R. English	$1,500	
R.L. Knight	1,100	
S.O. Newman	2,500	
Total	$5,100	

In contrast to the offset presentation of contractual adjustments in the statement of activities of a nonprofit hospital, the comparable tuition remissions or exemptions of a nonprofit university or college often are included with *expenses for student aid* in that entity's statement of activities.[7]

Contributed Material, Services, and Facilities

In addition to cash contributions, nonprofit organizations often receive contributions of material, services, and facilities. For example, a hospital may receive free drugs, or a university may receive free operating supplies. The contributed material is recorded in the Inventories ledger account at its current fair value, with a credit to a revenues account in an unrestricted fund, as illustrated in the following journal entry for the General Fund of Community Hospital:

Journal Entry for Material Contributed to a Nonprofit Hospital

Inventories	5,000	
Contributions Revenue		5,000
To record contributed drugs at current fair value.		

Contributed services are recorded in an unrestricted fund as salaries expense, with an offset to a revenues account, if the services are rendered to the nonprofit organization by skilled individuals. The value assigned to the services is the going rate for comparable employees or contractors of the entity, less any meals or other living costs absorbed for the donor of the services by the nonprofit organization. The FASB established the following requirements for recognizing contributed services in the accounting records of a nonprofit organization:

[7] *Audit and Accounting Guide,* "Not-for-Profit Organizations" (New York: AICPA, 1996), par. 13.07.

Contributions of services shall be recognized if the services received (a) create or enhance nonfinancial assets or (b) require specialized skills, are provided by individuals possessing those skills, and would typically need to be purchased if not provided by donation. Services requiring specialized skills are provided by architects, carpenters, doctors, electricians, lawyers, nurses, plumbers, teachers, and other professionals and craftsmen. Contributed services . . . that do not meet the above criteria shall not be recognized.[8]

To illustrate the accounting for contributed services that meet the foregoing criteria, assume that the services of volunteer nurses' aides were valued at $26,400 for the month of June 2002 by Community Hospital, and that the value of meals provided at no cost to the volunteer during the month was $2,100. The following journal entry is appropriate for the General Fund of Community Hospital on June 30, 2002:

Journal Entry for Services Contributed to a Nonprofit Hospital

Salaries Expense	24,300	
Contributions Revenue		24,300
To record contributed services at current fair value of $26,400 less $2,100 value of meals provided to donors.		

Significant contributed facilities are recognized as revenue at their current fair value, offset by a debit to an asset or an expense account, as appropriate. For example, if the fair rental value of the building used by Archer School, a nonprofit private elementary school, is $8,000 a month, but the building's owner waives rental payments, Archer School prepares the following journal entry each month in its Unrestricted Fund:

Journal Entry for Contributed Facilities

Rent Expense	8,000	
Contributions Revenue		8,000
To record current fair value of rental of school building whose use was contributed.		

Pledges

A *pledge* (or *promise to give*) is a commitment by a prospective donor to contribute a specific amount of cash or property to a nonprofit organization on a future date or in installments. Because a pledge is in writing and signed by the *pledgor,* it resembles in form the *promissory note* used in business. However, pledges often are not enforceable contracts.

Under the accrual basis of accounting, *unconditional* pledges are recognized as receivables and revenues in the unrestricted fund, with appropriate provision for doubtful pledges.[9] Pledges due in future accounting periods or having restrictions as to their use generally are accounted for in a restricted fund (see pages 694 to 695).[10]

To illustrate the accounting for pledges, assume that Civic Welfare, Inc., a voluntary health and welfare organization, received unconditional pledges totaling $200,000 in a fund-raising drive. Based on past experience and current economic conditions, 15% of the pledges are considered to be doubtful of collection. The journal entries on page 691 are appropriate:

---

[8] *FASB Statement No. 116,* "Accounting for Contributions Received and Contributions Made" (Norwalk: FASB, 1993), par. 9.

[9] Ibid., par. 8.

[10] Ibid., par. 15.

Pledges Receivable	200,000	
Contributions Revenue		200,000
To record receivable for pledges.		
Doubtful Pledges Expense	30,000	
Allowance for Doubtful Pledges		30,000
To record provision for doubtful pledges ($200,000 × 0.15 = $30,000).		

Contributions revenue is displayed in the statement of activities, as is doubtful pledges expense. Pledges receivable are displayed in the balance sheet net of the allowance for doubtful pledges. The write-off of uncollectible pledges is recorded by a debt to the Allowance for Doubtful Pledges ledger account and a credit to the Pledges Receivable account.

Revenues and Gains from Pooled Investments

Many of the funds of nonprofit organizations have cash available for investments in securities and other money-market instruments. To provide greater efficiency and flexibility in investment programs, the investment resources of all funds of a nonprofit organization may be pooled for investment by a single portfolio manager. The pooling technique requires a careful allocation of investment revenues and realized and unrealized gains and losses to each participating fund.

To illustrate the pooling of investments, assume that on January 2, 2002, four funds of Civic Welfare, Inc., a nonprofit voluntary health and welfare organization, pooled their securities investments (to be managed by the Unrestricted Fund), as follows:

Pooling of Investments by Nonprofit Voluntary Health and Welfare Organization on Jan. 2, 2002

	Cost	Current Fair Values	Original Equity, %
Unrestricted Fund	$ 20,000	$ 18,000	15
Restricted fund	15,000	21,600	18
Plant Fund	10,000	20,400	17
Wilson Endowment Fund	55,000	60,000	50
Totals	$100,000	$120,000	100

The original equity percentages in the above tabulation are based on *current fair values,* not on *cost.* The current fair values of the pooled investments on January 2, 2002, represent a common "measuring rod" not available in the cost amounts, which represent current fair values on various dates the investments were acquired by the respective funds. Realized and unrealized gains (or losses) and interest and dividend revenue of the pooled investments during 2002 are allocated to the four funds in the ratio of the original equity percentages. For example, if $11,000 net realized gains of the investment pool during 2002 were *reinvested,* net unrealized gains amounted to $7,000, and interest and dividend revenue of $9,000 was *distributed* by the pool during 2002, these amounts are allocated as shown on page 692:

Allocation of Year Revenue from Pooled Investments to Respective Funds	Original Equity, %*	Net Realized and Unrealized Gains	Interest and Dividends Revenue
Unrestricted Fund	15	$ 2,700	$1,350
Restricted Fund	18	3,230	1,620
Plant Fund	17	3,060	1,530
Wilson Endowment Fund	50	9,000	4,500
Totals	100	$18,000	$9,000

* The original equity percentages may be converted to *units,* with a per-unit value of $180 ($18,000 ÷ 100 = $180) allocated for net gains, and a per-unit value of $90 ($9,000 ÷ 100 = $90) allocated for interest and dividends revenue.

Each of the funds participating in the investment pool debits Investments and credits Gains on Investments or Investment Income for its share of the $18,000 net gains of the pooled investments. However, assuming that *all* the interest and dividends revenue, regardless of the fund to which it is attributable, is available for unrestricted use by Civic Welfare, Inc., the entire $9,000 interest and dividends revenue is recognized as revenue by the Unrestricted Fund.

If another fund of Civic Welfare, Inc., entered the investment pool on December 31, 2002, the original equity percentages would be revised, based on the December 31, 2002, current fair values of the investment portfolio. For example, if the Harris Endowment Fund entered the Civic Welfare, Inc., investment pool (which had total investments with a current fair value of $144,000) on December 31, 2002, with investments having a cost of $32,000 and a current fair value of $36,000 on that date, the equity percentages would be revised as illustrated below:

Revision of Fund Equities in Pooled Investments on Dec. 31, 2002	Cost*	Current Fair Values[†]	Revised Equity, %
Unrestricted Fund	$ 22,700	$ 21,600	12.0
Restricted Fund	18,240	25,920	14.4
Plant Fund	13,060	24,480	13.6
Wilson Endowment Fund	64,000	72,000	40.0
Subtotals	$118,000	$144,000	
Harris Endowment Fund	32,000	36,000	20.0
Totals	$150,000	$180,000	100.0

* Cost for four original pool member funds includes $18,000 gains of 2002.

[†] Current fair value of original pooled investments totaling $144,000 on December 31, 2002, allocated to original pool member funds based on original equity percentages computed on page 691.

Gains (or losses) and interest and dividends revenue for accounting periods subsequent to December 31, 2002, are *allocated in the revised equity percentages.* The revised equity percentages are maintained until the membership of the investment pool changes again.

Expenses and Losses of Unrestricted Fund

A nonprofit organization typically recognizes all expenses in its unrestricted fund. As indicated on page 691, losses may be recognized in other funds as well as in the unrestricted fund.

Expenses of a nonprofit organization may be classified in two groups: program services and supporting services. *Program services* are the organization's activities that result in the distribution of goods and services to beneficiaries, customers, or members that fulfill the purposes or mission of the organization. ***Supporting services*** are all activities of the organization other than program services, such as management and general, fund-raising, and membership development activities.[11]

Depreciation Expense of Nonprofit Organizations

In ***FASB Statement No. 93,*** "Recognition of Depreciation by Not-for-Profit Organizations," the FASB required recognition of depreciation on ***all*** long-lived tangible assets of nonprofit organizations, except for individual works of art or historical treasures having extraordinarily long economic lives, with disclosure of the following in a note to the financial statements:[12]

1. Depreciation expense for the period.

2. Balances of major classes of depreciable assets, by nature or function, at the balance sheet date.

3. Accumulated depreciation, either by major classes of depreciable assets or in total, at the balance sheet date.

4. A general description of the method or methods used in computing depreciation for major classes of depreciable assets.

Expenses that are unique to nonprofit organizations include fund-raising expense, ***conditional*** pledges, and income taxes on certain unrelated business income.

Fund-Raising Expense

Although fund-raising costs may benefit future accounting periods of a nonprofit organization, just as advertising costs of a business enterprise may benefit future periods, fund-raising costs are recognized as an expense when incurred.[13]

Conditional Pledges

Some nonprofit organizations promise to make grants to individuals or to other organizations. For example, a nonprofit performing arts organization may promise to make grants to theaters to help defray operating costs. Generally, grants are recognized as expense when the governing board of the nonprofit organization unconditionally approves them. However, unpaid amounts of pledges for grants that may be revoked by the nonprofit organization are not recognized as expense until they become unconditional.[14]

Income Taxes

Some otherwise tax-exempt nonprofit organizations may be subject to federal and state income taxes on their ***unrelated business income,*** which is derived from activities not substantially related to the educational, charitable, or other basis of the organization's tax-exempt status. For example, the income that a country club derives from staging professional tennis tournaments on its tennis courts otherwise used by members might be subject to income taxes. Income taxes expense for such nonprofit organizations is subject to the interperiod tax allocation requirements for business enterprises.[15]

---

[11] *FASB Statement No. 117,* pars. 26–28.
[12] *FASB Statement No. 93,* "Recognition of Depreciation by Not-for-Profit Organizations" (Stamford: FASB, 1987), pars. 5–6.
[13] "Not-for-Profit Organizations," par. 13.07.
[14] *FASB Statement No. 116,* par. 22.
[15] *FASB Statement No. 109,* "Accounting for Income Taxes" (Norwalk: FASB, 1992), par. 3.

Assets and Liabilities of Unrestricted Fund

Most assets and liabilities of a nonprofit organization's unrestricted fund are similar to the current assets and liabilities of a business enterprise. Cash, investments, accounts receivable, receivables from other funds, inventories, and short-term prepayments are typical assets of an unrestricted fund. Nonprofit organizations that use fund accounting generally account for plant assets in a plant fund, although health care entities may account for such assets in the general fund.[16]

With respect to nonexhaustible *collections* of museums, art galleries, botanical gardens, libraries, and similar nonprofit organizations, the FASB waived recognition of such assets in the organizations' accounting records under specified conditions. However, the organization's statement of activities and a note to the financial statements must include specified disclosures regarding the collections.[17]

The liabilities of an unrestricted fund include payables, accruals, and deferred revenue similar to those of a business enterprise, as well as amounts payable to other funds.

Fund Balance of Unrestricted Fund

Because most nonprofit organizations do not have owners, the net assets of the organizations' unrestricted funds are represented by a *fund balance* similar to that of most funds of a governmental entity, as discussed in Chapters 17 through 19.

The board of directors of a nonprofit organization may *designate* a portion of an unrestricted fund's net assets for a specific purpose. The earmarked position is accounted for as a segregation of the unrestricted fund balance, rather than as a separate restricted fund. For example, if the board of directors of Civic Welfare, Inc., a voluntary health and welfare organization, earmarks $25,000 of the unrestricted fund's assets for the acquisition of office equipment, the following journal entry is prepared for Civic Welfare, Inc., Unrestricted Fund:

Journal Entry for Designation of Portion of Fund Balance of Unrestricted Fund

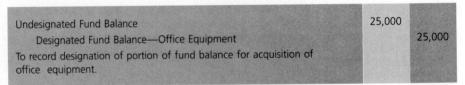

Undesignated Fund Balance	25,000	
Designated Fund Balance—Office Equipment		25,000
To record designation of portion of fund balance for acquisition of office equipment.		

The Designated Fund Balance—Office Equipment ledger account is similar to a retained earnings appropriation account of a corporation and is reported in the accounting records of Civic Welfare, Inc., as a portion of the fund balance of the Unrestricted Fund.

Restricted Fund

Nonprofit organizations establish *restricted funds* to account for assets available for current use but expendable only as authorized by the donor of the assets. Thus, a restricted fund of a nonprofit organization resembles the special revenue fund of a governmental entity (as described in Chapter 18), because the assets of both types of funds may be expended only for specified purposes.

The assets of restricted funds are not derived from the operations of the nonprofit organization. Instead, the assets are obtained from (1) restricted gifts or grants from

[16] "Health Care Organizations," par. 1.12.
[17] *FASB Statement No. 116*, pars. 11, 26–27.

individuals or governmental entities, (2) revenues from restricted fund investments, (3) realized and unrealized gains or investments of the restricted funds, and (4) restricted income from endowment funds. These assets are transferred to the unrestricted fund at the time the designated expenditure is made, with a credit to an account with a title such as Net Assets Released from Restrictions.

To illustrate, assume that on July 1, 2002, Robert King donated $50,000 to Community Hospital, a nonprofit organization, for the acquisition of beds for a new wing of the hospital. On August 1, 2002, Community Hospital paid $51,250 for the beds. These transactions and events are recorded by Community Hospital as shown below:

Journal Entries for Restricted Donation to Nonprofit Hospital

In Robert King Restricted Fund:

2002			
July 1	Cash	50,000	
	Contributions Revenue		50,000
	To record receipt of gift from Robert King for acquisition of beds for new wing.		
Aug 1	Net Assets Released from Restrictions	50,000	
	Payable to Unrestricted Fund		50,000
	To record obligation to Unrestricted Fund for cost of beds for new wing in accordance with Robert King's gift.		

In Unrestricted Fund:

2002			
Aug. 1	Plant Assets	51,250	
	Cash		51,250
	To record acquisition of beds for new wing.		
1	Receivable from Robert King Restricted Fund	50,000	
	Net Assets Released from Restrictions		50,000
	To record receivable from Robert King Restricted Fund for reimbursement of expenditures for beds.		

Endowment Fund

An *endowment fund* of a nonprofit organization is similar to a *nonexpendable trust fund* of a governmental entity, which is described in Chapter 19. A *permanent endowment fund* is one for which the principal must be maintained indefinitely in revenue-producing investments. Only the revenues from a permanent endowment fund's investments may be expended by the nonprofit organization. In contrast, the principal of a *term endowment fund* may be expended after the passage of a period of time or the occurrence of an event specified by the donor of the endowment principal. A *quasi-endowment fund* is established by the board of directors of a nonprofit organization, rather than by an outside donor. At the option of the board, the principal of a quasi-endowment fund later may be expended by the entity that established the fund.

The revenues of endowment funds are accounted for in accordance with the instructions of the donor or the board of directors. If there are no restrictions on the use of endowment fund income, it is transferred to the nonprofit organization's unrestricted fund. Otherwise, the endowment fund revenues are transferred to an appropriate restricted fund.

Agency Fund

An *agency fund* of a nonprofit organization is used to account for assets held by a nonprofit organization as a custodian. The assets are disbursed only as instructed by their owner. For example, a nonprofit university may act as custodian of cash of a student organization. The university disburses the cash as directed by the appropriate officers of the student organization. The undistributed cash of the student organization is reported as a *liability* of the university's agency fund, rather than as a *fund balance,* because the university has no equity in the fund.

Annuity and Life Income Funds

Annuity Fund

Assets may be contributed to a nonprofit organization with the stipulation that the organization pay specified fixed amounts periodically to designated recipients, for a specified time period. An *annuity fund* is established by the nonprofit organization to account for this arrangement. At the end of the specified time period for the periodic payments, the unexpended assets of the annuity fund are transferred to the unrestricted fund or to a restricted fund or endowment fund specified by the donor.

The following journal entries illustrate the accounting for the Ruth Collins Annuity Fund of Ridgedale College, a nonprofit college, for the fund's first fiscal year, ending June 30, 2003:

Journal Entries for Annuity Fund of a Nonprofit College

2002			
July 1	Cash	50,000	
	Annuity Payable		35,000
	Contributions Revenue		15,000
	To record receipt of cash from Andrea Collins for an annuity of $6,000 a year each June 30 to Ruth Collins for her lifetime. Liability is recorded at the actuarially computed present value of the annuity, based on life expectancy of Ruth Collins.		
1	Investments	45,000	
	Cash		45,000
	To record acquisition of interest in Ridgedale College's investment pool.		
2003			
June 30	Cash	1,500	
	Investments	2,000	
	Annuity Payable		3,500
	To record share of realized and unrealized revenues and gains of Ridgedale College investment pool.		

(continued)

2003			
June 30	Annuity Payable	6,000	
	Cash		6,000
	To record payment of current year's annuity to Ruth Collins.		
30	Contributions Revenue	15,000	
	Annuity Payable		1,000
	Fund Balance		14,000
	To close revenue account and adjust annuity liability based on revised actuarial valuation of Ruth Collins annuity.		

Note that, in the first journal entry on June 30, 2003, the revenues and gains on the annuity fund's share of the investment pool are credited to the Annuity Payable ledger account. This is necessary because the actuarial computation of the annuity on the date of establishment of the annuity fund valued the annuity liability at its ***then present value.***

Life Income Fund

A ***life income fund*** is used to account for stipulated payments to a named beneficiary (or beneficiaries) during the beneficiary's lifetime. In a life income fund, only the ***income*** is paid to the beneficiary. Thus, payments to a life income fund's beneficiary vary from one accounting period to the next, but payments from an annuity fund are fixed in amount.

Loan Fund

A ***loan fund*** may be established by any nonprofit organization, but loan funds most frequently are included in the accounting records of colleges and universities. Student loan funds generally are ***revolving;*** that is, as old loans are repaid, new loans are made from the receipts. Loans receivable are carried in the loan fund at estimated realizable value; provisions for doubtful loans are debited directly to the Fund Balance ledger account, not to an expense account. Interest on loans is credited to the Fund Balance account, ordinarily on the cash basis of accounting.

Plant Fund

The components of plant funds vary among nonprofit organizations. In addition to plant assets, plant funds may include cash and investments earmarked for additions to plant assets and mortgage notes payable and other liabilities collateralized by the plant assets. Sinking-fund assets set aside for retirement of debt incurred to acquire plant assets also may be in plant funds.

FINANCIAL STATEMENTS OF NONPROFIT ORGANIZATIONS

The wide variety of nonprofit organizations described on page 684, together with the various inconsistent pronouncements of the AICPA on accounting for nonprofit organizations, contributed in the past to an assortment of form, content, display, and terminology techniques for financial statements of such organizations. To lend more uniformity to financial reporting by nonprofit organizations without imposing inflexible standards, the FASB issued ***FASB Statement No. 117,*** "Financial Statements of Not-for-Profit Organizations." Among its provisions were the following:[18]

[18] *FASB Statement No. 117,* passim.

1. Financial statements of nonprofit organizations shall be a statement of financial position, a statement of activities, a statement of cash flows, and notes to the financial statements.

2. The statement of financial position shall report the amounts of the organization's total assets, total liabilities, and total net assets.

3. The statement of financial position shall report the amounts for each of the three classes of the organization's net assets: permanently restricted, temporarily restricted, and unrestricted.

4. The statement of activities shall report the amount of the change in the organization's net assets for the period with a caption such as *changes in net assets* or *change in equity.*

5. The statement of activities shall report the amount of the changes in each of the three classes of the organization's net assets: permanently restricted, temporarily restricted, and unrestricted.

6. The statement of activities shall report gross amounts of revenues and expenses of the organization, except that investment revenues may be reported net of expenses and gains or losses on disposal of plant assets may be reported net.

7. The statement of activities or a note thereto shall report expenses by functional classifications such as program services and supporting services.

8. The statement of cash flows shall be similar in format—direct method or indirect method—to one that is issued for a business enterprise.

The following financial statements illustrate a format that complies with the foregoing standards:

NONPROFIT ORGANIZATION Statement of Activities For Year Ended June 30, 2002 (amounts in thousands)	
Changes in unrestricted net assets:	
Revenues and gains:	
Contributions	$ 9,000
Fees	6,000
Investment revenue	7,000
Net realized and unrealized gains on investments	8,000
Other	1,000
Total unrestricted revenue and gains	$ 31,000
Net assets released from restrictions	16,000
Total unrestricted revenues, gains, and other support	$ 47,000
Expenses:	
Programs	$ 28,000
Management and general	3,000
Fund raising	2,000
Total expenses	$ 33,000
Increase in unrestricted net assets	$ 14,000

(continued)

NONPROFIT ORGANIZATION
Statement of Activities (concluded)
For Year Ended June 30, 2002
(amounts in thousands)

Changes in temporarily restricted net assets:	
Contributions	$ 9,000
Investment revenue	3,000
Net realized and unrealized gains on investments	3,000
Net assets released from restrictions	(16,000)
Decrease in temporarily restricted net assets	$ (1,000)
Changes in permanently restricted net assets:	
Contributions	$ 2,000
Investment revenue	10,000
Net realized and unrealized gains on investments	6,000
Increase in permanently restricted net assets	$ 18,000
Increase in net assets	$ 31,000
Net assets, beginning of year	252,200
Net assets, end of year	$283,200

NONPROFIT ORGANIZATION
Statement of Financial Position
June 30, 2002
(amounts in thousands)

Assets

Cash and cash equivalents	$ 100
Short-term investments in securities, at fair value	1,500
Accounts and interest receivable (net)	2,300
Pledges receivable (net)	3,000
Inventories and short-term prepayments	700
Long-term investments in securities, at fair value	220,000
Cash and investments in securities, restricted to acquisition of plant assets	5,300
Plant assets (net)	62,000
Total assets	$294,900

Liabilities and Net Assets

Liabilities:	
Accounts payable	$ 3,000
Grants payable	1,000
Annuities payable	1,700
Long-term debt	6,000
Total liabilities	$ 11,700
Net assets:	
Unrestricted	$ 92,000
Temporarily restricted	50,000
Permanently restricted	141,200
Total net assets	$283,200
Total liabilities and net assets	$294,900

NONPROFIT ORGANIZATION Statement of Cash Flows (indirect method) For Year Ended June 30, 2002 (amounts in thousands)		
Net cash provided by operating activities **(Exhibit 1)**		$ 19,000
Cash flows from investing activities:		
Acquisition of investments in securities	$(29,000)	
Acquisition of plant assets	(2,000)	
Disposal of plant assets	12,600	
Net cash used in investing activities		(18,400)
Cash flows from financing activities:		
Contributions received	$ 3,000	
Interest and dividends received and reinvested	1,000	
Payment of annuities payable	(2,000)	
Payment of long-term debt	(3,000)	
Net cash used in financing activities		(1,000)
Net decrease in cash and cash equivalents		$ (400)
Cash and cash equivalents, beginning of year		500
Cash and cash equivalents, end of year		$ 100
Exhibit 1 Cash flows from operating activities:		
Increase in net assets		$ 31,000
Adjustments to reconcile increase in net assets to net cash provided by operating activities:		
Depreciation expense		7,000
Increase in accounts and interest receivable		(1,000)
Increase in pledges receivable		(1,000)
Decrease in inventories and short-term prepayments		2,000
Increase in accounts payable		2,000
Decrease in grants payable		(4,000)
Net realized and unrealized gains on investments in securities		(17,000)
Net cash provided by operating activities		$ 19,000
Exhibit 2 Cash paid during the year for interest (none capitalized)		$ 400
Exhibit 3 Noncash investing and financing activities:		
Plant assets acquired through contribution		$ 2,200

The following features of the foregoing financial statements may be noted:

1. In the statement of activities, contributions, investment income, and gains or losses are common to changes in all three categories of net assets: unrestricted, temporarily restricted, and permanently restricted. Fees and other operating revenues and expenses are associated with changes in unrestricted net assets only.

2. In the statement of financial position, *restricted* cash and investments are displayed separately.

3. As mandated by the FASB, ***current fair value*** is the basis of valuation for all securities investments: short term, long term, and restricted.[19]

4. In the statement of cash flows (indirect method), the $17,000 of net realized and unrealized gains on investments is the total of the following in the statement of activities:

Net realized and unrealized gains on investments from:	
Unrestricted net assets	$ 8,000
Temporarily restricted net assets	3,000
Permanently restricted net assets	6,000
Total	$17,000

5. For a nonprofit organization that uses fund accounting, unrestricted net assets typically are those in the unrestricted (or general) fund. Temporarily restricted net assets generally are those in restricted funds, loan funds, term and quasi-endowment funds, annuity and life income funds, and plant funds. The most significant source of permanently restricted net assets is permanent endowment funds.

An example of financial statements of a nonprofit organization is in Appendix 1.

Concluding Observations on Accounting for Nonprofit Organizations

The FASB's issuance of ***Statements No. 93, 116, 117,*** and ***124*** has supplanted many of the previously accepted—but inconsistent—accounting standards for the numerous types of nonprofit organizations listed on page 684. More reforms may be necessary, however, in the form and content of financial statements issued by those organizations. For example, should there be a caption, "Excess of revenues over expenses," somewhere in a nonprofit organization's statement of activities? Should budgeted amounts be compared with actual operating results in the statement of activities? May some measure of performance—for example, effectiveness of use of contributions—be reported? Perhaps more research into the needs of users of financial statements of nonprofit organizations may yield answers to these and other questions.

---

[19] *FASB Statement No. 124,* "Accounting for Certain Investments Held by Not-for-Profit Organizations" (Norwalk: FASB, 1995), par. 7.

Excerpts from the 2000 Annual Report of the Kenneth T. and Eileen L. Norris Foundation

INDEPENDENT AUDITORS' REPORT

To the Trustees of the Kenneth T. and Eileen L. Norris Foundation:

We have audited the accompanying statement of financial position of the Kenneth T. and Eileen L. Norris Foundation (the "Foundation") as of November 30, 2000, and the related statements of activities and cash flows for the year then ended. These financial statements are the responsibility of the Foundation's management. Our responsibility is to express an opinion on these financial statements based on our audit.

We conducted our audit in accordance with auditing standards generally accepted in the United States of America. Those standards require that we plan and perform the audit to obtain reasonable assurance about whether the financial statements are free of material misstatement. An audit includes examining, on a test basis, evidence supporting the amounts and disclosures in the financial statements. An audit also includes assessing the accounting principles used and significant estimates made by management, as well as evaluating the overall financial statement presentation. We believe that our audit provides a reasonable basis for our opinion.

In our opinion, such financial statements present fairly, in all material respects, the financial position of the Foundation as of November 30, 2000, and the changes in its net assets and its cash flows for the year then ended in conformity with accounting principles generally accepted in the United States of America.

As discussed in Note 7 to the financial statements, in 2000, the Foundation changed its basis of accounting from the income tax basis of accounting, which is a comprehensive basis of accounting other than generally accepted accounting principles, to accounting principles generally accepted in the United States of America. Accordingly, the Foundation has restated its beginning net assets.

Deloitte & Touche LLP
March 4, 2002
Los Angeles, California

THE KENNETH T. AND EILEEN L. NORRIS FOUNDATION
Statement of Financial Position
November 30, 2000

Assets

Cash and cash equivalents	$ 474,457
Investments at fair value (Note 3)	
Corporate stocks	$115,292,813
Domestic corporate bonds	63,546,618
U.S. and state government obligations	2,670,110
Limited partnerships	11,223,253
Mutual funds	2,242,865
Trust deed notes receivable	2,562,783
Total investments	197,538,442
Interest receivable and other	1,814,191
Property and equipment	5,449
Total	$199,832,539

Liabilities and unrestricted net assets

Liabilities:	
Grants payable (Note 4)	$ 14,009,866
Federal excise taxes payable (Note 6)	186,940
Total liabilities	14,196,806
Unrestricted net assets (Note 7)	185,635,733
Total	$199,832,539

See notes to financial statements.

THE KENNETH T. AND EILEEN L. NORRIS FOUNDATION
Statement of Activities
Year Ended November 30, 2000

Revenue and gains:	
Interest, net of amortization of bond premiums of $97,173	$ 4,255,696
Dividends	1,069,967
Realized gain on sale of investments, net	4,716,938
Other income	446,167
Total revenue and gains	10,488,768
Expenses:	
Grants	18,091,890
Unrealized loss on investments, net	14,687,494
Administrative fees (Note 5)	902,179
Custodian fees	214,421
Federal excise tax	186,940
Foreign and property taxes	46,958
Rent	42,419
Insurance	15,500
Depreciation	17,839
Other expenses	239,651
Total expenses	34,445,291
Change in unrestricted net assets	(23,956,523)
Unrestricted net assets, beginning of year, as restated (Note 7)	209,592,256
Unrestricted net assets, end of year	$185,635,733

See notes to financial statements.

THE KENNETH T. AND EILEEN L. NORRIS FOUNDATION
Statement of Cash Flows
Year Ended November 30, 2000

Cash flows from operating activities:	
Change in unrestricted net assets	$(23,956,523)
Adjustments to reconcile change in unrestricted net assets to net cash used in operating activities:	
Net realized gains from investments	(4,393,274)
Net unrealized loss on investments	14,687,494
Gain on sale of property and equipment	(323,664)
Amortization of premiums paid on investments	97,173
Depreciation	17,839
Changes in operating assets and liabilities:	
Increase in interest receivable and other	(572,743)
Increase in grants payable	9,409,205
Increase in federal excise taxes payable	58,519
Net cash used in operating activities	(4,975,974)
Cash flows from investing activities:	
Proceeds from sales of investments	27,801,019
Purchase of investments	(26,767,972)
Proceeds from the sale of property and equipment	3,225,255
Net cash provided by investing activities	4,258,302
Net decrease in cash and cash equivalents	(717,672)
Cash and cash equivalents, beginning of year	1,192,129
Cash and cash equivalents, end of year	$ 474,457

See notes to financial statements.

THE KENNETH T. AND EILEEN L. NORRIS FOUNDATION
Notes to Financial Statements
Year Ended November 30, 2000

---

1. **Trust Agreement**

   The Kenneth T. and Eileen L. Norris Foundation (the "Foundation"), a charitable trust, was created in September 1963 by gift of property from Kenneth T. and Eileen L. Norris. The Foundation is a private foundation as defined in Section 509(a) of the Internal Revenue Code, and, accordingly, the Foundation and its trustees are subject to the provisions of the Internal Revenue Code of 1986 and the laws of the State of California. The terms of the trust indenture provide that, either directly or indirectly, the assets and income are to be applied exclusively for charitable purposes.

2. **Significant Accounting Policies**

   Grants – Unconditional grants made by the Foundation are recognized as an expense in the period in which they are approved. If these grants are to be paid over a period exceeding one year they are recorded at the net present value of the future cash payments, using an applicable U.S. Treasury Bill rate. Grants which are conditioned upon future events are expensed when those conditions are substantially met.

   Cash and Cash Equivalents – For purposes of reporting cash flows, cash and cash equivalents include cash and investments in U.S. Treasury bills and commercial paper that mature within 90 days.

Investments – The Foundation records its investments in equity securities with readily determinable fair values and all investments in debt securities at fair value. The fair value of U.S. and state government obligations, and mutual funds is determined on the basis of quoted market values. Trust deed notes receivable bear interest at or near market rates and approximate fair value. Limited partnerships which do not have readily determinable market values as of November 30, 2000 are valued based on the available partner capital account balances as reported by the partnerships to the Foundation, adjusted for capital contributions and distributions from the partnerships through November 30, 2000.

Purchases and sales of securities are recorded on the trade date. Dividend income is recorded based on the payment date. Interest income is recorded as earned on an accrual basis. Realized gains and losses are recorded upon disposition of securities. The allocation of cost to a sale, where part of a holding is disposed of, is determined on the highest cost, first-out basis. Investment income and realized and unrealized gains and losses are recognized as unrestricted net assets, unless their use is temporarily or permanently restricted by donors to a specified purpose or future period.

Property and Equipment – Property and equipment are recorded at cost at date of purchase, or fair market value at date of donation, and are depreciated or amortized using the straight-line method over 3 to 10 years depending on the type of asset.

Use of Estimates – The preparation of financial statements in conformity with accounting principles generally accepted in the United States of America requires management to make estimates and assumptions that affect the reported amounts of assets and liabilities and disclosure of contingent assets and liabilities at the date of the financial statements and the reported amounts of revenues and expenses during the reporting period. Actual results could differ from those estimates.

3. **Investments**
   Investments comprised the following at November 30, 2000:

	Cost	Fair Value
Corporate stocks	$ 43,825,197	$115,292,813
Domestic corporate bonds	63,704,160	63,546,618
U.S. and state government obligations	2,701,875	2,670,110
Limited partnerships	6,181,603	11,223,253
Mutual funds	1,000,000	2,242,865
Trust deed notes receivable	2,562,783	2,562,783
Total investments	$119,975,618	$197,538,442

   Included in investments are notes receivable secured by deeds of trust. Such notes bear interest at rates between 9 percent and 15 percent and mature between 2001 and 2020.

4. **Grants Payable**
   Grants payable include unconditional donations approved by the Foundation during the current or previous years that will be paid in future years. As of November 30, 2000, such grants are expected to be paid as follows:

Less than one year	$ 3,861,500
One to five years	10,685,000
More than five years	2,130,000
	16,676,500
Less unamortized discount	(2,666,634)
Total grants payable at net present value	$14,009,866

Cash payments made during 2000 on unconditional grants were $8,682,688.

5. **Related Parties**

Certain trustees of the Foundation are also officers of KTN Enterprises, Inc., which provides all administrative and accounting services to the Foundation. The Foundation is charged an administrative fee for these services.

6. **Federal Excise Taxes**

The Foundation qualifies as a tax-exempt organization under Section 501(c)(3) of the Internal Revenue Code (the "Code") but is subject to a federal excise tax at the rate of two percent on its "net investment income" as defined by the Code. The excise tax may be reduced to one percent should the amount of qualified distributions during the years exceed a threshold amount, which is determined based on a formula provided by the Code.

Federal income tax regulations require the Foundation to distribute, before the close of the following year, five percent of the market value of its aggregate noncharitable assets, reduced by federal excise taxes. The Foundation has undertaken to make timely qualifying distributions in order to satisfy the minimum distribution requirements of the Trust.

7. **Change in Accounting Method**

During the year ended November 30, 2000, the Foundation changed its basis of accounting from the income tax basis of accounting, which is a comprehensive basis of accounting other than generally accepted accounting principles, to accounting principles generally accepted in the United States of America. This change resulted in an increase in beginning unrestricted net assets of $97,650,708 as reflected in the accompanying financial statements.

Review Questions

1. What is a *nonprofit organization*?
2. List four types of nonprofit organizations in the United States.
3. What role did the AICPA's *Accounting and Auditing Guides* or *Industry Audit Guides* play in the establishment of accounting standards for nonprofit organizations? Explain.
4. What are three characteristics of nonprofit organizations that resemble those of governmental entities?
5. What characteristics of nonprofit organizations resemble those of business enterprises?
6. Nonprofit hospitals and universities often reduce their basic revenue charges to patients and students, respectively. How are these reductions reflected in the revenue accounting for the two types of nonprofit organizations? Explain.

= Exam Question on test

7. *a.* Does a nonprofit organization recognize contributed material in its accounting records? Explain.

   b. Does a nonprofit organization recognize contributed services in its accounting records? Explain.

8. How are expenses classified in the statement of activities of a nonprofit organization that receives significant support from the public? Explain.

9. Explain the accounting for pledges of grants that may be revoked by the board of trustees of a nonprofit performing arts organization.

10. How are collections reported in the financial statements of a nonprofit museum? Explain.

11. Differentiate between an **annuity fund** and a **life income fund** of a nonprofit organization.

12. Define the following terms applicable to nonprofit organizations:

    a. **Designated Fund Balance.**

    b. **Third-party payor.**

    c. **Pledge.**

    d. **Charity care.**

    e. **Term endowment fund.**

13. Identify the financial statements that are issued by a nonprofit organization.

Exercises

(Exercise 16.1)   Select the best answer for each of the following multiple-choice questions:

1. Are fund-raising expenses of a nonprofit organization displayed in the statement of activity as:

	Program Services Expenses?	*Supporting Services Expenses?*
a.	Yes	Yes
b.	Yes	No
c.	No	Yes
d.	No	No

*: Exact question is on test

2. Caddy School, a nonprofit private elementary school, occupies its school building rent-free, as permitted by the building owner. The existence of rent-free facilities is recognized in Caddy School's Unrestricted Fund as:

   a. Financial aid expense and other operating support.

   b. Rent expense and an increase in fund balance.

   c. Rent expense and contributions revenue.

   d. An item requiring disclosure in a note to the financial statements.

3. Costs of fund-raising dinners by a nonprofit organization are:

   a. Recognized as expense when incurred.

   b. Deferred and recognized as expense over the accounting periods expected to benefit from the fund-raising proceeds.

   c. Offset against the revenue received from the dinners.

   d. Offset against the undesignated fund balance of the organization's unrestricted fund.

4. The type of endowment fund that may be established only by the board of trustees of a nonprofit university is a:

u 95

    a. Permanent endowment fund.
    b. Term endowment fund.
    c. Quasi-endowment fund.
    d. Trustee endowment fund.

5. The Contractual Adjustments ledger account of a nonprofit hospital is:

    a. An expense account.
    b. A revenue offset account.
    c. A loss account.
    d. An asset account.

6. With respect to a nonprofit organization's payments to beneficiaries of annuity funds and life income funds:

    a. Annuity fund payments are fixed in amount; life income fund payments vary in amount.
    b. Annuity fund payments vary in amount; life income fund payments are fixed in amount.
    c. Payments from both annuity funds and life income funds are fixed in amount.
    d. Payments from both annuity funds and life income funds vary in amount.

7. One characteristic of nonprofit organizations that is comparable with characteristics of governmental entities is:

    a. Stewardship of resources.
    b. Governance by board of directors.
    c. Measurement of cost expirations.
    d. None of the foregoing.

8. The plant assets of a nonprofit hospital are accounted for as part of:

414

    a. The general fund.
    b. A restricted fund.
    c. A plant fund.
    d. Other nonoperating funds.

9. Does the current funds group of a nonprofit university include:

	Annuity Funds?	Loan Funds?
a.	Yes	Yes
b.	Yes	No
c.	No	No
d.	No	Yes

10. The records of Rehab Hospital, a nonprofit organization, had the following amounts on June 30, 2002:

Charity care	$ 40,000
Contractual adjustments	80,000
Patient service revenues (gross)	620,000
Provision for doubtful accounts	70,000

Net patient service revenues for Rehab Hospital for the year ended June 30, 2002, amount to:

    a. $620,000.   *d.* $430,000.
    b. $550,000.   *e.* Some other amount.
    c. $500,000.

620,000
− 40,000
580,000

11. An annuity fund of a nonprofit organization resembles the organization's:

   a. Endowment funds.
   b. Restricted funds.
   c. Life income funds.
   d. Loan funds.

12. The fund of a nonprofit university that is ***revolving*** is a(n):

   a. Annuity fund.
   b. Life income fund.
   c. Loan fund.
   d. Endowment fund.

13. The statement of financial position of a nonprofit organization displays the organization's assets, liabilities, and:

   a. Fund balance.
   b. Equity.
   c. Excess of assets over liabilities.
   d. Net assets.

(Exercise 16.2) Gross patient service revenues of Neighborhood Hospital, a nonprofit organization, for the month of May 2002, totaled $860,000. Charity care to indigent patients totaled $80,000, of which $50,000 was to be received by Neighborhood Hospital from City Charities. Contractual adjustments allowed to Blue Cross amounted to $140,000. Doubtful accounts expense was estimated at $20,000.

Prepare journal entries (omit explanations) for Neighborhood Hospital on May 31, 2002.

(Exercise 16.3) For the month of September 2002, its first month of operations, Redwood Hospital's patient service records included the following:

Amount to be received from United Way for indigent patients	$ 16,500
Charity care for indigent patients	32,000
Contractual adjustments allowed for Medicare patients	18,500
Gross patient service revenues (excluding charity care and contractual adjustments)	225,000
Doubtful accounts expense (no accounts were written off)	14,600

Prepare a working paper to show how the foregoing information is displayed in the financial statements of nonprofit Redwood Hospital for the month of September, 2002.

(Exercise 16.4) Selected ledger account balances for Recuperative Hospital, a nonprofit organization, on October 31, 2002, the end of its first month of operations, were as follows:

Accounts receivable	$174,000 dr
Allowance for doubtful accounts	24,000 cr
Contractual adjustments	32,000 dr
Doubtful accounts expense	24,000 dr
Patient service revenues	206,000 cr

In addition, Recuperative had charity care totaling $10,000, of which $6,000 was to be reimbursed by Local Services, a nonprofit organization. Because Recuperative billed patients on October 31, 2002, it had not collected any accounts receivable as of that date.

Reconstruct the journal entries (omit explanations) prepared by Recuperative Hospital on October 31, 2002.

(Exercise 16.5) The library of the nonprofit University of South Park (USP) received books with a current fair value of $16,000 from various publishers at no cost on June 15, 2002. The library's operations are accounted for in USP's Unrestricted Fund.

Prepare a journal entry for the Unrestricted Fund of University of South Park on June 15, 2002.

(Exercise 16.6) In your audit of the financial statements of Cordova Hospital, a nonprofit organization, for the fiscal year ended March 31, 2002, you note the following journal entry in the General Fund:

Inventories	200	
Cash		200
To record purchase of medicine and drugs from manufacturer at nominal cost. Current fair value of the items totaled $6,400.		

Prepare a journal entry to correct the accounting records of the General Fund of Cordova Hospital on March 31, 2002.

(Exercise 16.7) During the month of October 2002, volunteer instructors' aides rendered services at no cost to Warner College, a nonprofit organization. Salary rates for comparable employees of Warner College, applied to the services, yielded a total value of $3,400. Complimentary meals given to the volunteers at the Warner College cafeteria during October 2002 cost $180. The volunteer's services met the specifications for donated services in *FASB Statement No. 116,* "Accounting for Contributions Received and Contributions Made."

Prepare a journal entry for the Warner College Unrestricted Fund on October 31, 2002, for the services donated to Warner College during the month of October 2002. (Disregard income taxes and other withholdings.)

(Exercise 16.8) The value of services contributed by docents of Modern Museum, a nonprofit organization, totaled $68,000 for the fiscal year ended June 30, 2002. Also during that year, Modern Museum used rent-free facilities for storage that would have been leased to a business enterprise by the owner for the rent of $96,000 a year.

Prepare journal entries dated June 30, 2002, for the foregoing support of Modern Museum.

(Exercise 16.9) Community Welfare, Inc., accounts for pledges in accordance with *FASB Statement No. 116,* "Accounting for Contributions Received and Contributions Made." During the month of November 2002, Community Welfare received unrestricted pledges totaling $500,000, of which 20% was estimated to be uncollectible, and wrote off uncollectible pledges totaling $30,000. During that month, $240,000 was collected on pledges.

Prepare journal entries (dated November 30, 2002) for Community Welfare, Inc., with respect to pledges. (Omit explanations for the journal entries.)

(Exercise 16.10) The "Summary of Significant Accounting Policies" note to the financial statements prepared by the controller of Wabash Hospital (a nonprofit organization) for the fiscal year ended June 30, 2002, included the following sentence: "Pledges for contributions are recorded when the cash is received." Another note read as follows:

CHECK FIGURE

Credit contributions revenue, $25,000.

Pledges   Unrestricted pledges receivable, received, and collected during the year ended June 30, 2002, were as follows:

Pledges receivable, July 1, 2001 (10% doubtful)	$ 50,000
New pledges received during year ended June 30, 2002	300,000
Pledges receivable, July 1, 2001, determined to be uncollectible during year	(15,000)
Pledges collected in cash during year ended June 30, 2002	(275,000)
Pledges receivable, June 30, 2002 (12% doubtful)	$ 60,000

All pledges are due six months from the date of the pledge. Pledge revenue is recorded in the General Fund.

Assume that you are engaged in the first annual audit of the financial statements of Wabash Hospital for the fiscal year ended June 30, 2002, and are satisfied with the propriety of the amounts recorded in the hospital's "Pledges" note. Prepare an adjusting entry for the General Fund of Wabash Hospital on June 30, 2002.

(Exercise 16.11)   On July 1, 2001, three funds of Wilmington College pooled their individual securities investments, as follows:

	Cost	Current Fair Values
Restricted Fund	$ 80,000	$ 90,000
Quasi-Endowment Fund	120,000	126,000
Annuity Fund	150,000	144,000
Totals	$350,000	$360,000

During the fiscal year ended June 30, 2002, the Wilmington College investment pool, managed by the Unrestricted Fund, reinvested realized gains of $3,000, had net unrealized gains of $7,000, and received dividends and interest totaling $18,000.

Prepare journal entries on June 30, 2002, for each of the three Wilmington College funds to record the results of the investment pool's operations during Fiscal Year 2002. Do not use Receivable from Unrestricted Fund ledger accounts.

(Exercise 16.12)   Artistry Unlimited, a nonprofit performing arts organization, received a contribution of $50,000 on July 1, 2002, the beginning of a fiscal year, to be awarded as grants to students of ballet for the school year beginning in September 2002. On September 1, 2002, unconditional grants totaling $45,000 were awarded to nine students of ballet. Artistry Unlimited does not use fund accounting.

Prepare journal entries for Artistry Unlimited on July 1 and September 1, 2002.

(Exercise 16.13)   On July 1, 2002, the beginning of a fiscal year, Technology Specialists, a nonprofit research and scientific organization, awarded a $30,000, three-year research grant to Martin Grey. The grant was payable in three annual installments of $10,000, beginning July 1, 2002; however, the governing board of Technology Specialists reserved the right to revoke the remaining unpaid amount of the grant on appropriate notice to Grey on June 30, 2003, or June 30, 2004, if Grey's research efforts were unproductive.

Prepare a journal entry for Technology Specialists on July 1, 2002.

(Exercise 16.14)   From the following ledger account balances (amounts in thousands) of the General Fund of No-Prof Hospital, a nonprofit organization, prepare a statement of financial position as of June 30, 2002. No-Prof has only a general fund.

Accounts with Debit Balances		Accounts with Credit Balances	
Accounts receivable (net)	$ 900	Accounts payable and accrued	
Cash and cash equivalents	100	liabilities	$ 550
Cash restricted to acquisition of		Advances from third-party	
plant assets	200	payors	200
Investments restricted to		Deferred revenues	100
acquisition of plant assets	400	Fund balance designated for	
Inventory of supplies	200	plant assets	600
Plant assets (net)	3,100	Housing bonds payable	400
Short-term prepayments	50	Mortgage bonds payable	500
		Notes payable (current)	300
		Undesignated fund balance	2,300
Total	$4,950	Total	$4,950

Cases

(Case 16.1) During the June 20, 2002, meeting of the board of directors of Roakdale Association, a nonprofit voluntary health and welfare organization, the following discussion occurred:

> *Chair:* We shall now hear the report from the controller.
>
> *Controller:* Our unrestricted contributions are at an all-time high. I project an increase in unrestricted net assets of $100,000 for the year ending June 30, 2002.
>
> *Chair:* That's too large an amount for us to have a successful fund-raising drive next year. I'll entertain a motion that $80,000 of unrestricted contributions be transferred to a Restricted Fund.
>
> *Director Walker:* So moved.
>
> *Director Hastings:* Second.
>
> *Chair:* All those in favor say aye.
>
> *All Directors:* Aye.
>
> *Chair:* The chair directs the controller to prepare the necessary journal entries for the Unrestricted Fund and a Restricted Fund.

Instructions
Do you concur with the action taken by the board of directors of Roakdale Association? Explain.

(Case 16.2) The board of trustees of Toledo Day Care Center, a nonprofit organization, has asked you, as independent auditor for the center, to attend a meeting of the board of trustees and participate in the discussion of a proposal to create one or more endowment funds. At the meeting, the board members ask you numerous questions regarding the operations and the accounting treatment of endowment funds. Among the questions posed by trustees were the following:

1. Are only the revenues of an endowment fund expendable for current operations?

2. Under what circumstances, if any, may endowment fund principal be expended at the discretion of the board?

3. Must a separate set of accounting records be established for each endowment fund, or may all endowment fund operations be accounted for in a single restricted fund?

Instructions

Prepare a reply for each of the trustee's questions. Number your replies to correspond with the question numbers.

(Case 16.3) In your audit of the financial statements of Science Unlimited, a nonprofit research and scientific organization, for the fiscal year ended June 30, 2002, you find that products created by Science Unlimited are sold at prices less than production costs. Unsold products are carried at an arbitrary amount in two sections of Science Unlimited's statement of financial position—$10,000 "base stock" as a plant asset and the remainder as a current asset. No provision is made for distribution, handling, or storage costs.

Instructions

Do you concur with the way Science Unlimited presents unsold products in its statement of financial position? Explain. (Adapted from *AICPA Technical Practice Aids.*)

(Case 16.4) Station KKLL, a nonprofit public broadcasting station, is authorized to acquire surplus broadcasting equipment from the U.S. government at nominal prices. In your audit of the financial statements of Station KKLL for the fiscal year ended June 30, 2002, you discover that a radio station tower antenna with a current fair value of $8,000 had been acquired from the U.S. government for $500, which was the amount debited to the Broadcasting Equipment ledger account. Under terms of the acquisition, Station KKLL is not permitted to resell the antenna for a period of four years.

Instructions

Do you concur with Station KKLL's accounting for the acquisition of the antenna? Explain. (Adapted from *AICPA Technical Practice Aids.*)

(Case 16.5) The accountant for Nonprofit Religious Organization proposes to estimate the fair value of services contributed by deacons, elders, ushers, and other volunteer laypersons and recognize the amount as both expense and revenue in the organization's statement of activities.

Instructions

Do you concur with the accountant's proposal? Explain.

(Case 16.6) As a CPA, a member of the AICPA, and chief accountant of Vol-Wel, a nonprofit voluntary health and welfare organization, you are engaged in preparing financial statements for Vol-Wel for its first fiscal year, ended June 30, 2002. You have shown the following draft condensed statement of activities to Wells Conner, president of Vol-Wel and chairman of its board of trustees:

VOL-WEL
Draft Condensed Statement of Activities
For Year Ended June 30, 2002

Changes in unrestricted net assets:	
Total unrestricted revenues and gains	$380,000
Net assets released from restrictions	25,000
Total unrestricted revenues, gains, and other support	$405,000
Expenses:	
Programs	$ 80,000
Management and general	210,000
Fund raising	40,000
Total expenses	$330,000
Increase in unrestricted net assets	$ 75,000

Conner expresses concern about the amount of the management and general expenses, which constitute nearly 64% ($210,000 ÷ $330,000 = 0.636) of total expenses and over half ($210,000 ÷ $405,000 = 0.519) of total unrestricted revenues, gains, and other support. He fears that prospective donor users of the statement of activities will not be inclined to make unrestricted contributions to Vol-Wel, given its substantial overhead expenses. He therefore instructs you to do the following:

1. Recognize the $60,000 estimated value of services contributed by fund-raising volunteers, who do not have specialized skills.
2. Move a substantial part of Conner's $100,000 annual salary from management and general expenses to program expenses and fund raising expenses, given his participation in both programs and fund raising.

Instructions

Can you ethically comply with Wells Conner's instructions? In forming your solution, consider the following:

FASB Statement No. 116, "Accounting for Contributions Received and Contributions Made," pars. 9–10 and 118–124.

FASB Statement No. 117, "Financial Statements of Not-for-Profit Organizations," pars. 26–28.

AICPA Professional Standards, vol. 2, ET Section 203.05, "Responsibility of Employees for the Preparation of Financial Statements in Conformity with GAAP."

Problems

(Problem 16.1) Ledger account balances (in alphabetical sequence) to be included in the statement of activities for Seaside Hospital (a nonprofit organization that has only a general fund) for the fiscal year ended June 30, 2002, are as follows:

CHECK FIGURE

Increase in unrestricted net assets, $200,000.

	Debit	Credit
	(in thousands)	
Administrative services expenses	$280	
Contractual adjustments	140	
Depreciation expense	340	
Doubtful accounts expense	80	
Fiscal service expense	180	
General services expense	360	
Nursing services expense	560	
Other operating revenue		$ 180
Other professional services expense	260	
Patient service revenue		1,560
Unrestricted contributions revenue		380
Unrestricted revenue from investments		280

Instructions

Prepare a statement of activities for Seaside Hospital (amounts in thousands) for the year ended June 30, 2002, ending with increase (decrease) in unrestricted net assets.

(Problem 16.2) Among the transactions and events of Holley School, a nonprofit, private secondary school, for the fiscal year ended June 30, 2002, were the following:

(1) Paid $50,000 from the Unrestricted Fund for classroom computers, to be carried in the Plant Fund.

(2) Received an unrestricted cash gift of $200,000.

(3) Disposed of for $110,000 common stocks investments that had been carried in the Quasi-Endowment Fund at $100,000. There were no restrictions on use of the proceeds attributable to the gain.

(4) Constructed a new school building at a total cost of $2 million. Payment was by $250,000 cash from the Plant Fund and $1,750,000 obtained on a 5% mortgage note payable.

Instructions
Prepare journal entries for the foregoing transactions and events of Holley School for the year ended June 30, 2002. Use the following ledger account titles in the journal entries:

Plant Fund
 Buildings
 Cash
 Equipment
 Fund Balance
 Mortgage Note Payable
Quasi-Endowment Fund
 Cash
 Investments
 Payable to Unrestricted Fund
Unrestricted Fund
 Cash
 Contributions revenue
 Investment Income
 Receivable from Quasi-Endowment Fund
 Undesignated Fund Balance

(Problem 16.3) The adjusted trial balance of Nonprofit Trade Association, which does not use fund accounting, for June 30, 2002, was as follows:

NONPROFIT TRADE ASSOCIATION
Adjusted Trial Balance
June 30, 2002

	Debit	Credit
Cash	$ 7,000	
Short-term investments in securities	217,000	
Accounts receivable	28,000	
Allowance for doubtful accounts		$ 3,000
Publications inventory	61,000	
Long-term investments in securities	120,000	
Plant assets	55,000	

(continued)

NONPROFIT TRADE ASSOCIATION
Adjusted Trial Balance (concluded)
June 30, 2002

	Debit	*Credit*
Accumulated depreciation of plant assets		22,000
Other assets	28,000	
Accounts payable		36,000
Accrued liabilities		12,000
Deferred membership dues		131,000
Fund balance, July 1, 2001		285,000
Membership dues		184,000
Conferences and meetings revenue		321,000
Publications and advertising sales		143,000
Special assessments revenue		50,000
Investment revenue and net gains		11,000
Member services expense	56,000	
Conferences and meetings expense	166,000	
Technical services expense	218,000	
Communications expense	61,000	
General administration expenses	154,000	
Membership development expense	27,000	
Totals	$1,198,000	$1,198,000

Instructions

Prepare a statement of activities and a statement of financial position for Nonprofit Trade Association for the fiscal year ended June 30, 2002.

(Problem 16.4) On July 1, 2001, the beginning of a fiscal year, the four funds of Suburban Welfare Services, a nonprofit organization, formed an investment pool of securities managed by the Unrestricted Fund. On that date, cost and current fair values of the investment pool securities were as follows:

	Cost	*Current Fair Values*
Unrestricted Fund	$ 50,000	$ 59,400
Restricted Fund	20,000	16,200
Plant Fund	80,000	89,100
Arnold Life Income Fund	100,000	105,300
Totals	$250,000	$270,000

Additional Information

1. During the six months ended December 31, 2001, the investment pool, managed by the Unrestricted Fund, reinvested gains totaling $5,000, had net unrealized gains of $10,000, and received dividends and interest totaling $25,000, which was distributed to the participating funds.

2. On December 31, 2001, the Restricted Fund withdrew from the pool and was awarded securities in the amount of its share of the pool's aggregate December 31, 2001, current fair value of $300,000.

3. On January 2, 2002, the Edwards Endowment Fund entered the Suburban Welfare Services investment pool with investments having a cost of $70,000 and a current fair value of $78,000.

4. During the six months ended June 30, 2002, the investment pool reinvested gains totaling $40,000 and received dividends and interest totaling $60,000, which was distributed to the participating funds.

Instructions

a. Prepare a working paper for the Suburban Welfare Services investment pool to compute the following (round all percentages to two decimal places):

(1) Original equity percentages, July 1, 2001.

(2) Revised equity percentages, January 2, 2002.

b. Prepare journal entries to record the operations of the Suburban Welfare Services investment pool in the accounting records of the Unrestricted Fund. Use Payable to Restricted Fund, Payable to Plant Fund, and Payable to Arnold Life Income Fund ledger accounts for amounts payable to other funds.

(Problem 16.5) Among the transactions and events of the General Fund of Harbor Hospital, a nonprofit organization, for the month of October 2002, were the following:

(1) Gross patient revenues of $80,000 were billed to patients. Indigent patient charity care amounted to $4,000, of which amount $2,500 was receivable from Bovard Welfare Organization. Provision was made for contractual adjustments allowed to Medicaid of $6,000, and doubtful accounts of $8,000.

(2) Contributed services approximating $10,000 at going salary rates were received from volunteer nurses. Meals costing $200 were served to the volunteer nurses at no charge by the Harbor Hospital cafeteria.

(3) New unrestricted pledges, due in three months, totaling $5,000 were received from various donors. Collections on pledges amounted to $3,500, and the provision for doubtful pledges for October 2002 was $800.

(4) The $500 monthly annuity established for Arline E. Walters by Walters's contribution to Harbor Hospital three years ago was paid on behalf of the Arline E. Walters Annuity Fund.

(5) The amount of $3,000, received from the Charles Watson Restricted Fund, was expended for new surgical equipment, as authorized by the donor.

Instructions

a. Prepare journal entries for the October 2002 transactions and events of the Harbor Hospital General Fund. Number each group of entries to correspond to the number of each transactions or events group.

b. Prepare journal entries required for the Harbor Hospital Arline E. Walters Annuity Fund and Charles Watson Restricted Fund as indicated by the transactions and events of the General Fund.

(Problem 16.6) The statements of financial position of Wigstaff Foundation, a nonprofit research and scientific organization that does not use fund accounting, on June 30, 2002 and 2001, were as follows:

WIGSTAFF FOUNDATION
Statements of Financial Position
June 30, 2002 and 2001

Assets

	2002	2001
Current assets:		
Cash	$ 650,000	$ 630,000
Accounts receivable (net)	744,000	712,000
Unbilled contract revenue and reimbursable grant costs	976,000	780,000
Short-term payments	80,000	76,000
Total current assets	$2,450,000	$2,198,000
Long-term investments in securities	$ 840,000	$ 780,000
Plant assets:		
Land	$ 440,000	$ 440,000
Building	958,000	958,000
Furniture and equipment	334,000	312,000
Subtotals	$1,732,000	$1,710,000
Less: Accumulated depreciation	518,000	370,000
Net plant assets	$1,214,000	$1,340,000
Total assets	$4,504,000	$4,318,000

Liabilities and Net Assets

	2002	2001
Current liabilities:		
Accounts payable and accrued liabilities	$ 836,000	$ 776,000
Restricted grant advances	522,000	420,000
Current portion of long-term debt	176,000	164,000
Total current liabilities	$1,534,000	$1,360,000
Long-term debt (collateralized by plant assets)	618,000	794,000
Total liabilities	$2,152,000	$2,154,000
Net assets:		
Net equity in plant assets	$ 596,000	$ 546,000
Undesignated	1,756,000	1,618,000
Total unrestricted net assets	$2,352,000	$2,164,000
Total liabilities and net assets	$4,504,000	$4,318,000

Additional Information for Fiscal Year Ended June 30, 2002:

1. The increase in unrestricted net assets was $188,000.

2. There were no disposals of plant assets or long-term securities investments. Furniture and equipment was acquired for cash, as were long-term investments.

3. The "net equity in plant assets" designation of the fund balance represents the difference between total plant assets and long-term debt collateralized by plant assets.

Instructions

Prepare a statement of cash flows (indirect method) for Wigstaff Foundation for the year ended June 30, 2002. A working paper is not required. Disregard changes in current fair values of securities investments.

(Problem 16.7) The post-closing trial balance of Mid-City Sports Club, a nonprofit social club, on June 30, 2001, was as follows:

MID-CITY SPORTS CLUB
Post-Closing Trial Balance
June 30, 2001

	Debit	Credit
Cash	$ 9,000	
Investments in securities	58,000	
Inventories	5,000	
Land	10,000	
Building	164,000	
Accumulated depreciation of building		$130,000
Furniture and equipment	54,000	
Accumulated depreciation of furniture and equipment		46,000
Accounts payable		12,000
Membership certificates (100 × $1,000)		100,000
Cumulative increase in net assets		12,000
Totals	$300,000	$300,000

Additional Information for Fiscal Year Ended June 30, 2002

1. Dues revenue was $20,000.

2. Snack bar and soda fountain sales totaled $28,000.

3. Interest received on securities investments amounted to $6,000.

4. Amounts vouchered for payment were as follows:

Clubhouse expenses	$17,000
Snack bar and soda fountain supplies (perpetual inventory system)	26,000
General and administrative expenses	11,000

5. Vouchers paid totaled $55,000.

6. The members were assessed $10,000 on June 30, 2002, payable within one year, for capital improvements to the clubhouse. All the assessments were considered collectible, although none was collected on June 30, 2002. (Credit Contributions Revenue.)

7. An unrestricted gift of $5,000 was received.

8. Depreciation expense of $4,000 for the building and $8,000 for the furniture and equipment was allocable as follows: $9,000 to clubhouse expense, $2,000 to snack bar and soda fountain expense, and $1,000 to general and administrative expense.

9. The June 30, 2002, physical inventory of snack bar and soda fountain supplies totaled $1,000.

Instructions

a. Prepare journal entries (omit explanations) for the events and transactions of Mid-City Sports Club for the year ended June 30, 2002.

b. Prepare a statement of activities and a statement of financial position for Mid-City Sports Club for the year ended June 30, 2002.

Disregard changes in current fair values of securities investments.

(Problem 16.8)   Following is the post-closing trial balance of the unrestricted fund and the restricted fund of State University, a nonprofit organization, on June 30, 2001:

STATE UNIVERSITY
Post-Closing Trial Balance
June 30, 2001
(amounts in thousands)

	Unrestricted Fund	Restricted Fund
Cash and cash equivalents	$210	$ 7
Accounts receivable (student tuition and fees)	350	
Allowance for doubtful accounts	(9)	
State appropriation receivable	75	
Investments in securities		60
Totals	$626	$67
Accounts payable	$ 45	
Deferred revenues	66	
Fund balance	515	$67
Totals	$626	$67

The following transactions and events occurred during the fiscal year ended June 30, 2002, at actual amounts:

(1) On July 7, 2001, a gift of $100,000 was received from an alumnus. The alumnus requested that one-half of the gift be used for the acquisition of books for the university library and that the remainder be used for the establishment of a scholarship. The alumnus further requested that the revenue generated by the scholarship fund be used annually to award a scholarship to a qualified student, with the principal remaining intact. On July 20, 2001, the board of trustees resolved that the cash of the newly established scholarship (endowment) fund would be invested in bank certificates of deposit. On July 21, 2001, the certificates of deposit were acquired.

(2) Revenues from student tuition and fees applicable to the year ended June 30, 2002, amounted to $1,900,000. Of this amount, $66,000 had been collected in the prior year and $1,686,000 had been collected during the year ended June 30, 2002. In addition, on June 30, 2002, the university had received cash of $158,000, representing tuition and fees for the session beginning July 1, 2002.

(3) During the year ended June 30, 2002, State University had collected $349,000 of the outstanding accounts receivable at the beginning of the year. The balance was determined to be uncollectible and was written off against the allowance ledger account. On June 30, 2002, the allowance account was increased by $3,000.

(4) During the year, interest of $6,000 was earned and collected on late student fee payments.

(5) During the year, the state appropriation was received. An additional unrestricted appropriation of $50,000 was made by the state, but had not been paid to State University as of June 30, 2002.

(6) Unrestricted cash gifts totaling $25,000 were received from alumni of the university.

(7) During the year, restricted fund securities investments carried at $21,000 were sold for $26,000. Investment earnings amounting to $1,900 were received. (Credit Fund Balance.)

(8) During the year, unrestricted operating expenses of $1,777,000 were recognized. On June 30, 2002, $59,000 of these expenses remained unpaid.

(9) Restricted cash of $13,000 was spent for authorized purposes during the year. An equal amount was transferred from fund balance to revenues of the restricted fund.

(10) The accounts payable on June 30, 2001, were paid during the year.

(11) During the year, $7,000 interest was earned and received on the certificates of deposit acquired in accordance with the board of trustees resolution discussed in item (1). (Credit Fund Balance.)

Instructions

Prepare journal entries for State University to record the transactions or events for the year ended June 30, 2002. Each journal entry should be numbered to correspond with the transaction or event described on page 720 and above. (Omit explanations for the journal entries.)

The working paper should be organized as follows:

Transaction Number	Ledger Accounts	Unrestricted Fund dr(cr)	Restricted Fund dr(cr)	Endowment Fund dr(cr)
(1)				

Use the following ledger account titles in the journal entries:

Unrestricted Fund
  Accounts Payable
  Accounts Receivable
  Allowance for Doubtful Accounts
  Cash
  Deferred Revenues
  Expenses
  Revenues
  State Appropriation Receivable
Restricted Fund
  Cash
  Expenditures
  Fund Balance
  Investments
  Revenues
Endowment Fund
  Cash
  Fund Balance
  Investments

Disregard changes in current fair values of securities investments.

(Problem 16.9) Following is the post-closing trial balance of the three funds of Resthaven Hospital, a nonprofit organization, on December 31, 2001, the end of a fiscal year:

RESTHAVEN HOSPITAL
Post-Closing Trial Balance
December 31, 2001
(amounts in thousands)

	General Fund	Plant Replacement and Expansion Fund	Endowment Fund
Cash	$ 20	$ 54	$ 6
Accounts receivable	37		
Allowance for doubtful accounts	(7)		
Inventory of supplies	14		
Investments in securities		71	260
Land	370		
Buildings	1,750		
Accumulated depreciation of buildings	(430)		
Equipment	680		
Accumulated depreciation of equipment	(134)		
Totals	$2,300	$125	$266
Accounts payable	$ 16		
Accrued liabilities	6		
Mortgage bonds payable	150		
Fund balance designated for plant assets	2,116		
Undesignated fund balance	12	$125	$266
Totals	$2,300	$125	$266

Additional Information for 2002:

1. Gross debits to Accounts Receivable for hospital services were as follows:

Room and board	$ 780,000
Other professional services	321,000
Gross debits to Accounts Receivable	$1,101,000

2. Deductions from gross revenues were contractual adjustments of $15,000. Doubtful accounts expense was $30,000.

3. The General Fund paid $18,000 to retire mortgage bonds payable with that face amount.

4. The General Fund received unrestricted gifts of $50,000 and revenues from Endowment Fund securities investments of $6,500. The General Fund had been designated to receive the revenues on Endowment Fund investments.

5. Equipment costing $26,000 was acquired. An x-ray machine that had cost $24,000 and had a carrying amount of $2,400 was disposed of for $500.

6. Vouchers totaling $1,191,000 were issued for the following:

Administrative services expense	$ 120,000
Interest expense	95,000
General services expense	225,000
Nursing services expense	520,000
Other professional services expense	165,000
Inventory of supplies	60,000
Accrued liabilities, Dec. 31, 2001	6,000
Total vouchers issued	$1,191,000

7. Collections on accounts receivable totaled $985,000. Accounts receivable written off as uncollectible amounted to $11,000.

8. Cash payments on accounts payable were $825,000.

9. Supplies of $37,000 were issued for nursing services.

10. On December 31, 2002, accrued interest on Plant Replacement and Expansion Fund securities investments was $800.

11. Depreciation of buildings and equipment was as follows:

Buildings	$ 44,000
Equipment	73,000
Total depreciation	$117,000

12. On December 31, 2002, an accrual of $6,100 was made for interest on the mortgage bonds payable.

Instructions

For the period January 1 through December 31, 2002, prepare journal entries (omit explanations) to record the transactions and events described above for the following funds of Resthaven Hospital:

General Fund
Plant Replacement and Expansion Fund
Endowment Fund

Each journal entry should be numbered to correspond with the transactions or events described on page 722 and above.

The working paper should be organized as follows:

Transaction Number	Ledger Accounts	General Fund dr(cr)	Plant Replacement and Expansion Fund dr(cr)	Endowment Fund dr(cr)
(1)				

In addition to the ledger accounts included in the December 31, 2001, post-closing trial balance of Resthaven Hospital, the following accounts are pertinent:

Unrestricted Fund
   Administrative Services Expense
   Contractual Adjustments
   Depreciation Expense
   Doubtful Accounts Expense
   General Services Expense
   Interest Expense
   Loss on Disposal of Plant Assets
   Nursing Services Expense
   Other Professional Services Expense
   Patient Service Revenues
   Unrestricted Gift Revenues
   Unrestricted Revenues from Endowment Fund

Plant Replacement and Expansion Fund
  Interest Receivable

Disregard changes in current fair values of securities investments.

(Problem 16.10) A partial statement of financial position for Libra College, a nonprofit organization, on June 30, 2001, follows:

LIBRA COLLEGE		
Partial Statement of Financial Position		
June 30, 2001		

	Current Funds	
	Unrestricted	*Restricted*
Assets		
Cash	$200,000	$ 10,000
Investments in securities		210,000
Accounts receivable, tuition and fees (net of $15,000 allowance for doubtful accounts)	360,000	
Short-term prepayments	40,000	
Total assets	$600,000	$220,000
Liabilities and Net Assets		
Accounts payable	$100,000	$ 5,000
Payable to other funds	40,000	
Deferred revenues	25,000	
Net assets (fund balances)	435,000	215,000
Total liabilities and net assets	$600,000	$220,000

Additional Information for Fiscal Year Ended June 30, 2002:

1. Cash collected from tuition and fees totaled $3 million, of which $362,000 was for accounts receivable on June 30, 2001, $2,500,000 was for Fiscal Year 2002 tuition, and $138,000 was for Fiscal Year 2003 tuition.

2. Deferred revenues (for tuition and fees) on June 30, 2001, were earned.

3. The balance of accounts receivable on June 30, 2001, was written off, and the required June 30, 2002, balance of the Allowance for Doubtful Accounts ledger account was estimated at $10,000.

4. On June 30, 2002, an unrestricted appropriation of $60,000 was received from the state government.

5. Unrestricted cash gifts of $80,000 were received, of which $30,000 was transferred to the Student Loan Fund by the board of trustees of Libra College.

6. Investment income of $18,000 was realized and collected; investments carried at $25,000 were disposed of for $31,000; and the Restricted Fund acquired securities investments for $40,000.

7. Unrestricted general expenses of $2,500,000 were incurred; on June 30, 2002, unrestricted accounts payable totaled $75,000.

8. The restricted accounts payable balance on June 30, 2001, was paid.

9. The $40,000 payable to other funds was paid to the Plant Fund.

10. One-fourth of the June 30, 2001, short-term prepayments expired and pertained to general expenses; there were no additional short-term prepayments made.

Instructions

For the year ended June 30, 2002, prepare journal entries (omit explanations) for the transactions and events described on page 724 for the Unrestricted Fund and the Restricted Fund of Libra College. Each journal entry should be numbered to correspond with the transactions of events described above. Disregard changes in current fair values of investment securities.

The working paper should be organized as follows:

Transaction Number	Ledger Accounts	Unrestricted Fund dr(cr)	Restricted Fund dr(cr)
(1)			

In addition to the ledger accounts included in the June 30, 2001, partial statement of financial position of Libra College, the following accounts are pertinent:

Unrestricted Fund
Education and General Expenses
Government Grants Revenues
Private Gifts Revenues
Provision for Doubtful Tuition and Fees
State Appropriation Receivable
Tuition and Fees Revenues

(Problem 16.11) The adjusted trial balances of the two funds of Disadvantaged Children Association, a nonprofit voluntary health and welfare organization, on June 30, 2002, the end of a fiscal year, were as follows:

DISADVANTAGED CHILDREN ASSOCIATION CURRENT FUNDS
Adjusted Trial Balances
June 30, 2002

	Unrestricted Fund Debit	Unrestricted Fund Credit	Restricted Fund Debit	Restricted Fund Credit
Cash	$ 40,000		$ 9,000	
Pledges receivable	12,000			
Bequest receivable			5,000	
Allowance for doubtful pledges		$ 3,000		
Interest receivable	1,000			
Investments in securities, at fair value	100,000			
Accounts payable and accrued liabilities		50,000		$ 1,000
Deferred revenues		2,000		
Restricted fund balance				3,000
Designated fund balance		12,000		
Undesignated fund balance		26,000		
Contributions revenue		320,000		15,000
Membership dues revenue		25,000		
Program service fees revenue		30,000		

(continued)

DISADVANTAGED CHILDREN ASSOCIATION CURRENT FUNDS Adjusted Trial Balances (concluded) June 30, 2002				
	Unrestricted Fund		**Restricted Fund**	
	Debit	*Credit*	*Debit*	*Credit*
Investment revenue and gains		10,000		
Hearing-impaired children's program expenses	120,000			
Vision-impaired children's program expenses	150,000			
Management and general expenses	45,000		4,000	
Fund-raising expenses	8,000		1,000	
Provision for doubtful pledges	2,000			
Totals	$478,000	$478,000	$19,000	$19,000

Instructions

Prepare financial statements, excluding a statement of cash flows, for Disadvantaged Children Association for the fiscal year ended June 30, 2002.

Chapter **Seventeen**

Governmental Entities: General Fund

Scope of Chapter

In 1999, the Governmental Accounting Standards Board (GASB), whose establishment in 1984 is described on page 730, issued **GASB Statement No. 34,** "Basic Financial Statements—and Management's Discussion and Analysis—for State and Local Governments." That pronouncement was a major milestone in the upgrading of the financial accounting and reporting by governmental entities other than the United States government and sparked renewed interest in a somewhat arcane area of accounting: state and local governmental entities.

This chapter deals with the following aspects of **state and local** governmental entities: their nature; their financial reporting objectives; their accounting and reporting standards; and accounting for a governmental entity's general fund. Accounting and reporting for other funds and account groups of governmental entities are covered in Chapters 18 and 19. However, it must be emphasized that Chapters 17 through 19 do not discuss accounting standards for the United States **federal government.**

NATURE OF GOVERNMENTAL ENTITIES

Students beginning the study of accounting for governmental entities temporarily must set aside many of the familiar accounting principles for business enterprises. Such fundamental concepts of accounting theory for business enterprises as the nature of the accounting entity and the primacy of the income statement have limited relevance in accounting for governmental entities. Consequently, the following discussion identifies the features of governmental entities that give rise to unique accounting concepts.

When thinking of governmental entities of the United States, one tends to focus on the federal government or on the governments of the 50 states. However, in addition to those major governmental entities and the governments of the several U.S. territories, there are the following governmental entities in the United States:[1]

- More than 3,000 counties.

- Nearly 17,000 townships.

---

[1] *Local Governmental Accounting Trends & Techniques—1990 Third Edition* (New York: AICPA, 1990), p. 1-1.

- Over 19,000 municipalities.

- Nearly 15,000 school districts.

- Over 28,000 special districts (port authorities, airports, public buildings, libraries, and others).

Despite the wide range in size and scope of governance, the governmental entities listed above have a number of characteristics in common. Among these characteristics are the following:

1. ***Organization to serve the citizenry.*** A basic tenet of governmental philosophy in the United States is that governmental entities exist to serve the citizens subject to their jurisdiction. Thus, the citizens as a whole establish governmental entities through the constitutional and charter process. In contrast, business enterprises are created by only a limited number of individuals.

2. ***General absence of the profit motive.*** With few exceptions, governmental entities render services to the citizenry without the objective of profiting from those services. Business enterprises are motivated to earn profits.

3. ***Taxation as the principal source of revenue.*** The citizens subject to a governmental entity's jurisdiction provide resources to the governmental entity principally through taxation. Many of these taxes are paid on a self-assessment basis. There is no comparable revenue for business enterprises.

4. ***Impact of the legislative process.*** Operations of governmental entities are for the most part initiated by various legislative enactments, such as operating budgets, borrowing authorizations, and tax levies. Business enterprises also are affected by federal, state, and local laws and regulations, but not to such a direct extent.

5. ***Stewardship for resources.*** A primary responsibility of governmental entities in financial reporting is to demonstrate adequate stewardship for resources provided by their citizenry ("other people's money"). Business enterprises have a comparable responsibility to their owners, but not to the same extent as governmental entities.

The five foregoing characteristics of governmental entities are major determinants of accounting standards for such entities.

OBJECTIVES OF FINANCIAL REPORTING FOR GOVERNMENTAL ENTITIES

Shortly after its establishment (as described on page 730) the Governmental Accounting Standards Board (GASB) issued ***Concepts Statement No. 1,*** "Objectives of Financial Reporting," in which it established the following reporting objectives for ***state and local*** governmental entities:

1. *Financial reporting should assist in fulfilling government's duty to be publicly accountable and should enable users to assess that accountability.*

   a. *Financial reporting should provide information to determine whether current-year revenues were sufficient to pay for current-year services.* This also implies that financial reporting should show whether current-year citizens received services but shifted part of the payment burden to future-year citizens; whether previously accumulated resources were used up in providing services to current-year citizens; or, conversely, whether current-year revenues were not only sufficient to pay for current-year services, but also increased accumulated resources.

b. *Financial reporting should demonstrate whether resources were obtained and used in accordance with the entity's legally adopted budget; it should also demonstrate compliance with other finance-related legal or contractual requirements.*

c. *Financial reporting should provide information to assist users in assessing the service efforts, costs, and accomplishments of the governmental entity.* This information, when combined with information from other sources, helps users assess the economy, efficiency, and effectiveness of government and may help form a basis for voting or funding decisions. The information should be based on objective criteria to aid interperiod analysis within an entity and comparisons among similar entities. Information about physical resources (as discussed in paragraph 3b) should also assist in determining cost of services.

 2. *Financial reporting should assist users in evaluating the operating results of the governmental entity for the year.*

a. *Financial reporting should provide information about sources and uses of financial resources.* Financial reporting should account for all outflows by function and purpose, all inflows by source and type, and the extent to which inflows met outflows. Financial reporting should identify material nonrecurring financial transactions.

b. *Financial reporting should provide information about how the governmental entity financed its activities and met its cash requirements.*

c. *Financial reporting should provide information necessary to determine whether the entity's financial position improved or deteriorated as a result of the year's operations.*

 3. *Financial reporting should assist users in assessing the level of services that can be provided by the governmental entity and its ability to meet its obligations as they become due.*

a. *Financial reporting should provide information about the financial position and condition of a governmental entity.* Financial reporting should provide information about resources and obligations, both actual and contingent, current and noncurrent. The major financial resources of most governmental entities are derived from the ability to tax and issue debt. As a result, financial reporting should provide information about tax sources, tax limitations, tax burdens, and debt limitations.

b. *Financial reporting should provide information about a governmental entity's physical and other nonfinancial resources having useful lives that extend beyond the current year, including information that can be used to assess the service potential of those resources.* This information should be presented to help users assess long- and short-term capital needs.

c. *Financial reporting should disclose legal or contractual restrictions on resources and risks of potential loss of resources.*[2]

The foregoing objectives provide the framework within which the GASB develops standards of financial reporting for governmental entities[3] (as described in the following section).

ACCOUNTING AND REPORTING STANDARDS FOR GOVERNMENTAL ENTITIES

For many years, accounting and reporting standards for governmental entities were established by the National Council on Governmental Accounting, a 21-member organization composed primarily of local, state, and national finance officers, including two

---

[2] *Codification of Governmental Accounting and Financial Reporting Standards* (Norwalk: GASB, 2000), pp. B-27 and B-28 (footnote omitted).
[3] Ibid., p. B-5.

Canadian finance officers. In 1984, the Governmental Accounting Standards Board was established as an arm of the Financial Accounting Foundation, which also oversees the Financial Accounting Standards Board. The GASB issues *Statements of Governmental Accounting Standards* for financial accounting and reporting of state and local governmental entities.

One of the first acts of the GASB was to codify governmental accounting and financial reporting standards in effect in 1984. Subsequently, the GASB has issued a number of *Statements* that superseded, modified, or supplemented the standards set forth in the *Codification;* and the *Codification* was frequently revised. This chapter and Chapters 1 and 13 discuss and illustrate many of the governmental accounting and financial reporting standards currently in effect.

The Governmental Financial Reporting Entity

A significant question to be resolved in accounting for governmental entities is what agencies, institutions, commissions, public authorities, or other governmental organizations are to constitute the *financial reporting entity* for a governmental entity. The *Codification* provided that the governmental financial reporting entity is to consist of the following:[4]

1. The *primary government*—a state government, a municipality or county, or a special-purpose government such as a school district or a park district meeting specified criteria.

2. Organizations for which the primary government is *financially accountable* by reason of appointing a voting majority of the governing bodies and thus either imposing its will on the organizations or being responsible to provide financial benefits to, or financial burdens on, the organizations.

3. Other organizations whose relationship with the primary government necessitates their inclusion in the financial reporting entity.

The organizations described in **2** and **3** above are termed *component units.* The *Codification* provided several nonauthoritative illustrative examples of governmental financial reporting entities.[5]

Funds: The Principal Accounting Unit for Governmental Entities

Accounting for business enterprises emphasizes the economic entity as an accounting unit. Thus, a partnership is considered to be an accounting entity separate from the partners; and consolidated financial statements are issued for a group of affiliated—but legally separate—corporations that constitute a single economic entity under common control.

There is generally no single accounting entity for a specific governmental entity, such as a city or a county. Instead, *the principal accounting unit for governmental entities is the fund.* The *Codification* defined *fund* as follows:

> Governmental accounting systems should be organized and operated on a fund basis. A *fund* is defined as a fiscal and accounting entity with a self-balancing set of accounts recording cash and other financial resources, together with all related liabilities and

[4] Ibid., Sec. 2100.111 ff.
[5] Ibid., Sec. 2100.902 ff.

residual equities or balances, and changes therein, which are segregated for the purpose of carrying on specific activities or attaining certain objectives in accordance with special regulations, restrictions, or limitations. [Emphasis added.][6]

GASB Statement No. 34 identified the following 11 types of funds:[7]

Governmental Funds

1. *The General Fund*—to account for all financial resources except those required to be accounted for in another fund.

2. *Special Revenue Funds*—to account for the proceeds of specific revenue sources (other than trusts for individuals, private organizations, or other governments or for major capital projects) that are legally restricted to expenditure for specified purposes.

3. *Capital Projects Funds*—to account for financial resources to be used for the acquisition or construction of major capital facilities (other than those financed by proprietary funds or in trust funds for individuals, private organizations, or other governments).

4. *Debt Service Funds*—to account for the accumulation of resources for, and the payment of, general long-term debt principal and interest.

5. *Permanent Funds*—to report resources that are legally restricted to the extent that only earnings, and not principal, may be used for purposes that support the governmental entity's programs, that is, for the benefit of the government or its citizenry.

Proprietary Funds

1. *Enterprise Funds*—to report any activity for which a fee is charged to external users for goods or services.

2. *Internal Service Funds*—to report any activity that provides goods or services to other funds, departments, or agencies of the governmental entity, or to other governments on a cost-reimbursement basis.

Fiduciary Funds

1. *Pension* (and other *Employee Benefit*) Trust Funds—to report resources required to be held in trust for the members and beneficiaries of pension, other postemployment benefit, and other employee benefit plans.

2. *Investment Trust Funds*—to report the external portion of investment pools reported by the sponsoring government.

3. *Private-Purpose Trust Funds*—to report all other trust arrangements under which principal and income benefit individuals, private organizations, or other governments.

4. *Agency Funds*—to report resources held by the governmental entity in a purely custodial capacity (assets equal liabilities).

The ***governmental funds*** account for financial resources of a governmental entity that are used in day-to-day operations. The ***proprietary funds*** carry out governmental

---

[6] Ibid., Sec. 1100.102.
[7] *GASB Statement No.34,* pars. 65, 67–68, 70–73 and pp. 309–310.

entity activities that closely resemble the operations of a business enterprise. ***Fiduciary funds*** account for resources that are not ***owned*** by a governmental entity, but are administered by the entity as a ***custodian*** or ***fiduciary.***

 Every governmental entity has a general fund. According to the ***Codification,*** any additional funds should be established as required by law and sound financial administration.[8] Accounting and reporting for the general fund are discussed in a subsequent section of this chapter; accounting and reporting for other funds and the account groups are explained in Chapters 18 and 19. At this point, it is appropriate to emphasize that a governmental entity ***does not have a single accounting unit*** to account for its financial resources, obligations, revenues, and expenditures.

The Modified Accrual Basis of Accounting

The governmental funds of a governmental entity have used a ***modified accrual basis of accounting,*** in which revenues are recognized only when they became both ***measurable*** and ***available*** to finance expenditures of a fiscal period. Expenditures are recognized when the related liabilities are incurred, and short-term prepayments are not recognized as assets. The conventional accrual basis of accounting is used for other funds.[9]

Recording the Budget

GASB Statement No.34 provided the following statement regarding budgets of governmental entities:[10]

1. An annual budget(s) should be adopted by every governmental entity.

2. The accounting system should provide the basis for appropriate budgetary control.

3. Budgetary comparison schedules should be presented as required supplementary information for the general fund and for each major special revenue fund that has a legally adopted annual budget.

Budgets are key elements of legislative control over governmental entities. The executive branch of a governmental entity proposes the budgets; the legislative branch reviews, modifies, and enacts the budgets; and finally the executive branch approves the budgets and carries out their provisions.

 The two basic classifications of budgets for governmental entities are the same as those for business enterprises—annual budgets and long-term or capital budgets. ***Annual budgets*** include the ***estimated revenues*** and ***appropriations*** for expenditures for a specific fiscal year of the governmental entity. Annual budgets are appropriate for the general fund and special revenue funds; they sometimes are used for other governmental funds. ***Capital budgets,*** which are used to control the expenditures for construction projects or other plant asset acquisitions, may be appropriate for capital projects funds. The annual or capital budgets often are recorded in the accounts of all these funds, to aid in accounting for compliance with legislative authorizations.

 The operations of the two proprietary funds (enterprise funds and internal service funds) are similar to those of business enterprises. Consequently, annual budgets are used by these funds as a managerial planning and control device ***rather than as a leg-***

---

[8] Codification, Sec. 1100.104.
[9] *GASB Statement No. 34,* pp. 321–322.
[10] Ibid., p. 303.

islative control tool. Thus, annual budgets of enterprise funds and internal service funds generally *are not recorded in ledger accounts by those funds.*

Types of Annual Budgets

Several types of annual budgets may be used by a governmental entity.[11] An *object budget* emphasizes, by department, the *object* of each authorized expenditure. For example, under the legislative activity of the general government function, the object budget may include authorized expenditures for salaries, services, supplies, and equipment.

A *program budget* stresses measurement of total cost of a specific governmental entity *program,* regardless of how many departments of the governmental entity are involved in the program. Object of expenditure information is of secondary importance in a program budget.

In a *performance budget,* there is an attempt to relate the input of governmental resources to the output of governmental services. For example, the total estimated expenditures of the enforcement section of the taxation department might be compared with the aggregate collections of additional tax assessments budgeted for the fiscal year.

Regardless of which types of annual budgets are used by a governmental entity, the final annual budget adopted by the governmental entity's legislative body will include *estimated revenues* for the fiscal year and the *appropriations* for expenditures authorized for that year. If the estimated revenues of the budget exceed appropriations (as required by law for many governmental entities), there will be a *budgetary surplus;* if appropriations exceed estimated revenues, there will be a *budgetary deficit* in the *deficit budget.*

Journal Entry for a General Fund Budget

To illustrate the recording of an annual budget in the accounts of a general fund, assume that the Town of Verdant Glen in June 2002 adopted the following condensed annual budget for its General Fund for the fiscal year ending June 30, 2003:

Budget of General Fund of a Governmental Entity

Estimated revenues:		
General property taxes		$700,000
Other		140,000
Total estimated revenues		$840,000
Add: Estimated other financing sources (transfer from		
Enterprise Fund)		10,000
Subtotal		$850,000
Less: Appropriations:		
General government	$470,000	
Other	340,000	
Total appropriations	$810,000	
Estimated other financing uses (transfer to Debt		
Service Fund)	10,000	820,000
Excess of estimated revenues and other financing sources over appropriations and other financing uses (budgetary surplus)		$ 30,000

---

[11] *Audit and Accounting Guide,* "Audits of State and Local Governmental Units" (New York: AICPA, 1994), pars. 6.05, 6.09, 6.17, 6.20.

The journal entry to record the annual budget on July 1, 2002, follows:

Journal Entry for Budget of General Fund of a Governmental Entity

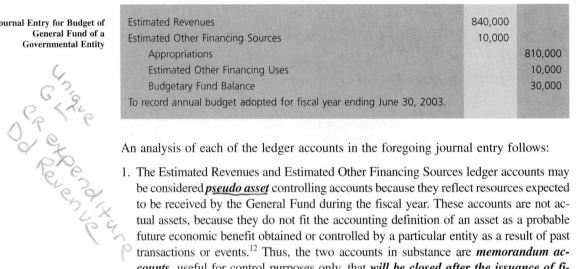

Estimated Revenues	840,000	
Estimated Other Financing Sources	10,000	
Appropriations		810,000
Estimated Other Financing Uses		10,000
Budgetary Fund Balance		30,000
To record annual budget adopted for fiscal year ending June 30, 2003.		

An analysis of each of the ledger accounts in the foregoing journal entry follows:

1. The Estimated Revenues and Estimated Other Financing Sources ledger accounts may be considered *pseudo asset* controlling accounts because they reflect resources expected to be received by the General Fund during the fiscal year. These accounts are not actual assets, because they do not fit the accounting definition of an asset as a probable future economic benefit obtained or controlled by a particular entity as a result of past transactions or events.[12] Thus, the two accounts in substance are *memorandum accounts,* useful for control purposes only, that *will be closed after the issuance of financial statements* for the General Fund for the fiscal year ending June 30, 2003.

2. The Estimated Other Financing Sources ledger account includes the budgeted amounts of such items as proceeds from the disposal of plant assets (which also may be recognized as revenue) and *operating transfers in* from other funds.

3. The Appropriations and Estimated Other Financing Uses ledger accounts may be considered *pseudo liability* controlling accounts because they reflect the legislative body's *commitments* to expend General Fund resources as authorized in the annual budget. These accounts are not genuine liabilities because they do not fit the definition of a liability as a probable future sacrifice of economic benefits arising from present obligations of a particular entity to transfer assets or provide services to other entities in the future as a result of past transactions or events.[13] The Appropriations and Estimated Other Financing Uses accounts are *memorandum accounts,* useful for control purposes only, that *will be closed after issuance of year-end financial statements* for the General Fund.

4. The Estimated Other Financing Uses account includes budgeted amounts of *operating transfers out* to other funds, which are not expenditures.

5. The Budgetary Fund Balance ledger account, as its title implies, is an account that balances the debit and credit entries to accounts of a *budget journal entry.* Although similar to the owners' equity accounts of a business enterprise in this balancing feature, the Budgetary Fund Balance account does not purport to show an ownership interest in a general fund's assets. At the end of the fiscal year, the Budgetary Fund Balance account is closed by a *journal entry that reverses the original entry for the budget.*

The journal entry to record the Town of Verdant Glen General Fund's annual budget for the year ending June 30, 2003, is accompanied by detailed entries to subsidiary ledgers for estimated revenues, estimated other financing sources, appropriations, and

---

[12] *Statement of Financial Accounting Concepts No. 6,* "Elements of Financial Statements" (Stamford: FASB, 1985), par. 25.
[13] Ibid., par. 35.

estimated other financing uses. The budget of the Town of Verdant Glen General Fund purposely was condensed; in practice, the general fund's estimated revenues and appropriations would be detailed by source and function, respectively, into one or more of the following widely used subsidiary ledger categories:

Estimated revenues:	Appropriations:
Taxes	General government
Licenses and permits	Public safety
Intergovernmental revenues	Public works
Charges for services	Health and welfare
Fines and forfeits	Culture—recreation
Miscellaneous	Conservation of natural resources
	Debt service
	Intergovernmental expenditures
	Miscellaneous

In summary, budgets of a governmental entity generally are recorded in the accounts of the general fund and special revenue funds; they may also be recorded in the accounts of capital projects funds. ***The recording of the budget initiates the accounting cycle for each of the funds.*** Recording the budget also facilitates the preparation of financial statements that compare actual amounts of revenues and expenditures with budgeted amounts.

Encumbrances and Budgetary Control

Because of the need for the expenditures of governmental entities to be in accord with appropriations of governing legislative bodies, an ***encumbrance*** accounting technique often is used for the general fund and special revenue funds and sometimes for capital projects funds. When a purchase order for goods or services is issued to a supplier by one of those funds, a journal entry similar to the following is prepared for the fund:

Journal Entry for Encumbrances

Encumbrances	18,413	
Fund Balance Reserved for Encumbrances		18,413
To record encumbrance for purchase order No. 1685 issued to Wilson Company.		

When the supplier's invoice for the ordered merchandise or services is received by the governmental entity, it is recorded ***and the related encumbrance is reversed*** as illustrated below:

Journal Entries for Receipt of Invoice and Reversal of Encumbrance

Expenditures	18,507	
Vouchers payable		18,507
To record invoice No. 348J received from Wilson Company under purchase order No. 1685.		
Fund Balance Reserved for Encumbrances	18,413	
Encumbrances		18,413
To reverse encumbrance for purchase order No. 1685 issued to Wilson Company.		

As indicated by the example on page 735, the invoice amount may differ from the amount of the governmental entity's purchase order because of such items as shipping charges, sales taxes, and price changes.

The controls inherent in the encumbrance technique may be illustrated by assuming, with respect to the foregoing journal entries, that they applied to a purchase order for supplies (not available from the governmental entity's internal service fund) for the general government, the general fund fiscal year appropriation for which totaled $85,000. The subsidiary ledger record for general government supplies would include the following information (dates are assumed):

Subsidiary Ledger Account for Supplies	General Government—Supplies			
Date	Appropriation, Credit	Encumbrance, Debit	Expenditure, Debit	Unexpended, Unencumbered Balance, Credit
2003				
July 1 Budgeted appropriation	85,000			85,000
2 P.O. 1685 to Wilson Company		18,413		66,587
6 Inv. 348J from Wilson Company		(18,413)	18,507	66,493

The posting of the $18,413 encumbrance on July 2 reduces the balance of the appropriation by that amount and protects against the issuance of one or more purchase orders in excess of the unexpended, unencumbered balance of $66,587. Receipt of the invoice for $18,507 and reversal of the related encumbrance of $18,413 reduces the unexpended, unencumbered balance by $94 ($18,507 − $18,413 = $94).

Thus, the encumbrance technique is a memorandum method for ensuring that total expenditures for a fiscal year do not exceed appropriations. Encumbrance journal entries *are not necessary for normal recurring expenditures such as salaries and wages, utilities, and rent.* The encumbrance technique used in accounting for governmental entities has no counterpart in accounting for business enterprises.

ACCOUNTING AND REPORTING FOR A GOVERNMENTAL ENTITY'S GENERAL FUND

As indicated on page 731, a general fund is used to account for all transactions and events of a governmental entity not accounted for in one of the other 10 types of funds. Thus, the general fund as an accounting unit serves the same *residual* purpose that the general journal provides as an accounting record. Although the general fund is residual, it generally accounts for the largest aggregate dollar amounts of the governmental entity's revenues and expenditures.

In illustrating the accounting for a general fund, the example of the Town of Verdant Glen used in the preceding section is continued.

Illustration of Accounting for a General Fund

Assume that the balance sheet of the Town of Verdant Glen General Fund on June 30, 2002 (*prior to the journal entry for the Fiscal Year 2003 budget* illustrated on page 734), was as shown on page 737.

Balance Sheet of a
Governmental Entity's General
Fund at End of Preceding
Fiscal Year

TOWN OF VERDANT GLEN GENERAL FUND
Balance Sheet
June 30, 2002

Assets

Cash		$160,000
Inventory of supplies		40,000
Total assets		$200,000

Liabilities and Fund Balance

Vouchers payable		$ 80,000
Fund balance:		
Reserved for inventory of supplies	$40,000	
Unreserved and undesignated	80,000	120,000
Total liabilities and fund balance		$200,000

The fund balance reserved for inventory of supplies is analogous to a ***mandatory*** restriction of retained earnings in a business enterprise. It represents a reservation of the General Fund's fund balance, so that the $40,000 nonexpendable portion of the General Fund's total assets will not be appropriated for expenditures in the legislative body's adoption of the annual budget for the General Fund for the year ending June 30, 2003.

Assume that, in addition to the budget illustrated on page 733 and recorded on page 734, the Town of Verdant Glen General Fund had the summarized transactions and events for the fiscal year ended June 30, 2003, that follow. For simplicity, income taxes, sales taxes, short-term prepayments, and short-term loans are disregarded in this illustration.

1. Property taxes were billed in the amount of $720,000, of which $14,000 was of doubtful collectibility.

2. Property taxes collected in cash totaled $650,000; revenues from licenses and permits fees collected totaled $102,000.

3. Property taxes in the amount of $13,000 were determined to be uncollectible.

4. Purchase orders for nonrecurring expenditures were issued to outside suppliers in the total amount of $360,000.

5. Expenditures for the year totaled $760,000, of which $90,000 applied to additions to inventory of supplies, and $350,000 applied to $355,000 of the purchase orders in the total amount of $360,000 issued during the year.

6. Billings for services and supplies received from the Enterprise Fund and the Internal Service Fund totaled $30,000 and $20,000, respectively.

7. Cash payments on vouchers payable totaled $770,000. Cash payments to the Enterprise Fund and the Internal Service Fund were $25,000 and $14,000, respectively.

8. Transfers of cash to the Debt Service Fund for maturing principal and interest on general obligation serial bonds totaled $11,000.

9. A payment of $40,000 in lieu of property taxes and a subsidy of $10,000 were received from the Enterprise Fund.

10. Supplies with a cost of $80,000 were used during the year.

11. All uncollected property taxes on June 30, 2003, were delinquent.

12. The Town Council **designated** $25,000 of the unreserved and undesignated fund balance for the replacement of equipment during the year ending June 30, 2004.

After the journal entry for the budget is recorded, as illustrated on page 737, the following journal entries, numbered to correspond to the foregoing transactions or events, are prepared for the Town of Verdant Glen General Fund during the year ended June 30, 2003:

Journal Entries for General Fund of a Governmental Entity

1	Taxes Receivable—Current	720,000	
	Allowance for Uncollectible Current Taxes		14,000
	Revenues		706,000
	To accrue property taxes billed and to provide for estimated uncollectible portion.		

As indicated on page 732, *the modified accrual basis of accounting for a general fund requires the accrual of property taxes because they are billed* to the property owners by the Town of Verdant Glen and are thus **measurable** and **available** as collected. The estimated uncollectible property taxes are **offset** against the total taxes billed in order to measure **actual revenues** from property taxes for the year.

2	Cash	752,000	
	Taxes Receivable—Current		650,000
	Revenues		102,000
	To record collections of property taxes and licenses and permits fees revenues for the year.		

Under the modified accrual basis of accounting, revenues from licenses and permits fees are recognized on the cash basis. However, any taxes or other revenues collected in advance of the fiscal year to which they apply are credited to a liability ledger account.

If a governmental entity's general fund has a cash shortage prior to collection of property taxes, it may issue short-term **tax anticipation notes** to borrow cash. Typically, tax anticipation notes payable are repaid from proceeds of the subsequent tax collections.

3	Allowance for Uncollectible Current Taxes	13,000	
	Taxes Receivable—Current		13,000
	To write off receivables for property taxes that are uncollectible.		

The foregoing journal entry represents a shortcut approach. In an actual situation, uncollectible property taxes first would be transferred, together with estimated uncollectible amounts, to the Taxes Receivable—Delinquent ledger account from the Taxes

Receivable—Current account. Any amounts collected on these delinquent taxes would include revenues for interest and penalties required by law. Uncollected delinquent taxes would be transferred, together with estimated uncollectible amounts, to the Tax Liens Receivable ledger account. After the passage of an appropriate statutory period, the governmental entity might satisfy its tax lien by selling the property on which the delinquent taxes were levied.

4	Encumbrances	360,000	
	Fund Balance Reserved for Encumbrances		360,000
	To record purchase orders for nonrecurring expenditures issued during the year.		

As explained on page 735, encumbrance journal entries often are used to prevent the overexpending of an appropriated amount in the budget. The journal entry to the Encumbrances ledger account is posted in detail to reduce the unexpended balances of each applicable appropriation in the subsidiary ledger for appropriations. The unexpended balance of each appropriation thus is reduced for the amount committed by the issuance of purchase orders.

5a	Expenditures	670,000	
	Inventory of Supplies	90,000	
	Vouchers Payable		760,000
	To record expenditures for the year.		

The Expenditures ledger account is debited with all expenditures, regardless of purpose, ***except for additions to the inventory of supplies.*** Principal and interest payments on long-term debt, additions to the governmental entity's plant assets not accounted for in other funds, payments for goods or services to be received in the future—all are debited to Expenditures or to Other Financing Uses rather than to asset or liability ledger accounts. (Expenditures for long-term debt principal and plant asset additions often are recorded ***on a memorandum basis*** in the general long-term debt and general capital (plant) assets account groups, respectively, as explained and illustrated in Chapter 18.)

The accounting for general fund expenditures described above emphasizes once again the importance of the annual budget in the accounting for a general fund. Expenditures are chargeable to amounts appropriated by the legislative body of the governmental entity. Detailed items making up the $670,000 total debit to the Expenditures ledger account in the foregoing journal entry are posted to the appropriations subsidiary ledger as reductions of unexpended balances of each appropriation.

5b	Fund Balance Reserved for Encumbrances	355,000	
	Encumbrances		355,000
	To reverse encumbrances applicable to vouchered expenditures totaling $350,000.		

Recording actual expenditures of $350,000 (included in the $670,000 total in entry **5a** on page 739) applicable to purchase orders totaling $355,000 makes this amount of the previously recorded encumbrances no longer necessary. Accordingly, $355,000 of encumbrances is reversed; the reversal is posted to the detailed appropriations subsidiary ledger as well as to the general ledger. Encumbrances of $5,000 ($360,000 − $355,000 = $5,000) remain outstanding on June 30, 2003, the fiscal year-end.

6	Expenditures	50,000	
	Payable to Enterprise Fund		30,000
	Payable to Internal Service Fund		20,000
	To record billings for services and supplies received from other funds.		

Billings from other funds of the governmental entity are not subject to encumbrance or vouchered for payment, as are billings from outside suppliers. Instead, billings from other funds are recorded in separate liability ledger accounts. The related debit is to the Expenditures account if the billings are for *quasi-external transactions,* such as providing services and supplies.

7	Vouchers Payable	770,000	
	Payable to Enterprise Fund	25,000	
	Payable to Internal Service Fund	14,000	
	Cash		809,000
	To record payment of liabilities during the year.		
8	Other Financing Uses	11,000	
	Cash		11,000
	To record transfer to Debt Service Fund for maturing principal and interest on long-term general-obligation serial bonds.		

The Other Financing Uses ledger account is debited because the payment to the Debt Service Fund is an *operating transfer out* rather than a *quasi-external transaction.* (The corresponding journal entry in the Debit Service Fund is shown in Chapter 18.)

9	Cash	50,000	
	Revenues		40,000
	Other Financing Sources		10,000
	To record payment in lieu of property taxes ($40,000) and subsidy ($10,000) received from Enterprise Fund.		

Amounts transferred in to the General Fund from other funds are recognized as revenues if they are *quasi-external transactions,* such as payments in lieu of property taxes; otherwise, they are recognized as other financing sources if they are *operating transfers in,* such as subsidies. (The financial statement display of the foregoing transfers out of the Enterprise Fund is illustrated in Chapter 19.)

10a	Expenditures	80,000	
	Inventory of Supplies		80,000
	To record cost of supplies used during the year.		

10b	Unreserved and Undesignated Fund Balance	10,000	
	Fund Balance Reserved for Inventory of Supplies		10,000
	To increase inventory of supplies reserve to $50,000 to agree with balance of inventory of Supplies ledger account at end of year ($50,000 − $40,000 = $10,000).		

The immediately preceding journal entry represents a restriction of a portion of the Fund Balance account to prevent its being appropriated improperly to finance a deficit annual budget for the General Fund for the year ending June 30, 2004. Only cash and other monetary assets of a general fund are available for appropriation to finance authorized expenditures of the succeeding fiscal year.

11	Taxes Receivable—Delinquent	57,000	
	Allowance for Uncollectible Current Taxes	1,000	
	Taxes Receivable—Current		57,000
	Allowance for Uncollectible Delinquent Taxes		1,000
	To transfer delinquent taxes and related estimated uncollectible amounts from the current classification.		

The foregoing journal entry clears the Taxes Receivable—Current ledger account and the related valuation account for uncollectible amounts so that they will be available for accrual of property taxes for the fiscal year ending June 30, 2004.

12	Unreserved and Undesignated Fund Balance	25,000	
	Fund Balance Designated for Replacement of Equipment		25,000
	To designate a portion of the fund balance for the replacement of equipment during the year ending June 30, 2004.		

The Fund Balance Designated for Replacement of Equipment ledger account is similar to a *voluntary* retained earnings appropriation of a business enterprise. It indicates that the annual budget for the Town of Verdant Glen General Fund for the year ending June 30, 2004, must include an appropriation of $25,000 for new equipment and estimated revenues for the proceeds from disposal of the replaced equipment. The designated fund balance of $25,000 will be closed to the Unreserved and Undesignated Fund Balance ledger account on July 1, 2003, when the annual budget for the year ending June 30, 2004, is recorded.

Trial Balance at End of Fiscal Year for a General Fund

After all the foregoing journal entries (including the budget entry on page 734) have been posted to the general ledger of the Town of Verdant Glen General Fund, the trial balance on June 30, 2003, is as follows:

Trial Balance of a
Governmental Entity's General
Fund at End of Current
Fiscal Year

TOWN OF VERDANT GLEN GENERAL FUND
Trial Balance
June 30, 2003

	Debit	Credit
Cash	$ 142,000	
Taxes receivable—delinquent	57,000	
Allowance for uncollectible delinquent taxes		$ 1,000
Inventory of supplies	50,000	
Vouchers payable		70,000
Payable to Enterprise Fund		5,000
Payable to Internal Service Fund		6,000
Fund balance reserved for encumbrances		5,000
Fund balance reserved for inventory of supplies		50,000
Fund balance designated for replacement of equipment		25,000
Unreserved and undesignated fund balance		45,000
Budgetary fund balance		30,000
Estimated revenues	840,000	
Estimated other financing sources	10,000	
Appropriations		810,000
Estimated other financing uses		10,000
Revenues		848,000
Other financing sources		10,000
Expenditures	800,000	
Other financing uses	11,000	
Encumbrances	5,000	
Totals	$1,915,000	$1,915,000

Financial Statements for a General Fund

The results of operations (that is, net income or net loss) is not relevant for a general fund. Instead, two financial statements—a statement of revenues, expenditures, and changes in fund balance, and a balance sheet—are appropriate.[14] These two financial statements are shown below and on page 743 for the Town of Verdant Glen's General Fund for the year ended June 30, 2003.

Financial Statements of a
Governmental Entity's General
Fund at End of Current
Fiscal Year

TOWN OF VERDANT GLEN GENERAL FUND
Statement of Revenues, Expenditures, and Changes in Fund Balance
For Year Ended June 30, 2003

	Budget	Actual	Variance Favorable (Unfavorable)
Revenues:			
Taxes	$700,000	$706,000	$ 6,000
Other	140,000	142,000	2,000
Total revenues	$840,000	$848,000	$ 8,000

(continued)

[14] *GASB Statement No.34,* pars. 83 and 86.

Financial Statements of a
Governmental Entity's General
Fund at End of Current Fiscal
Year (concluded)

TOWN OF VERDANT GLEN GENERAL FUND
Statement of Revenues, Expenditures, and Changes in Fund Balance (concluded)
For Year Ended June 30, 2003

	Budget	Actual	Variance Favorable (Unfavorable)
Expenditures:*			
General government	$470,000	$459,000	$11,000
Other	340,000	341,000	(1,000)
Total expenditures	$810,000	$800,000	$10,000
Excess of revenues over expenditures	$ 30,000	$ 48,000	$18,000
Other financing sources (uses):			
Operating transfers in	10,000	10,000	
Operating transfers out	(10,000)	(11,000)	(1,000)
Net change in fund balance	$ 30,000	$ 47,000	$17,000
Fund balance, beginning of year	120,000	120,000	
Fund balance, end of year	$150,000	$167,000	$17,000

* Breakdown of actual amounts between general government and other categories is assumed.

TOWN OF VERDANT GLEN GENERAL FUND
Balance Sheet
June 30, 2003

Assets

Cash	$142,000
Taxes receivable, net of allowance for estimated uncollectible amounts, $1,000	56,000
Inventory of supplies	50,000
Total assets	$248,000

Liabilities and Fund Balance

Liabilities:		
Vouchers payable		$ 70,000
Payable to other funds		11,000
Total liabilities		$ 81,000
Fund balance:		
Reserved for encumbrances	$ 5,000	
Reserved for inventory of supplies	50,000	
Designated for replacement of equipment	25,000	
Unreserved and undesignated	87,000	167,000
Total liabilities and fund balance		$248,000

The following aspects of the Town of Verdant Glen General Fund financial statements are significant:

1. The statement of revenues, expenditures, and changes in fund balance compares budgeted with actual amounts. This comparison aids in the appraisal of the stewardship for the General Fund's resources and the compliance with legislative

appropriations. (Expenditures in excess of appropriated amounts generally are not permitted unless a supplementary appropriation is made by the legislative body and approved by the executive of the governmental entity.)

2. The amounts received from and paid to other funds of the Town of Verdant Glen are termed *operating transfers in* and *operating transfers out,* respectively, to distinguish them from other types of financing sources and uses that might have been received or paid by the General Fund.

3. The assets of the General Fund include only *financial resources assets*—cash, some short-term investments, receivables, and inventories. Expenditures for plant assets are not recognized as assets in the General Fund; they are recorded in the General Capital Assets Account Group.

4. The unreserved and undesignated fund balance in the balance sheet, $87,000, is a balancing amount to make the total of the reserved, designated, and unreserved and undesignated fund balance amounts equal to $167,000, the final amount in the statement of revenues, expenditures, and changes in fund balance. After the posting of the closing entries illustrated in the next section, the ending balance of the Unreserved and Undesignated Fund Balance ledger account is $87,000 (see page 745).

Closing Entries for a General Fund

After financial statements have been prepared for the Town of Verdant Glen General Fund, the budgetary and actual revenues, expenditures, and encumbrances ledger accounts must be closed, to clear them for the next fiscal year's activities. The closing entries below are appropriate for the Town of Verdant Glen General Fund on June 30, 2003:

Closing Entries for a Governmental Entity's General Fund at End of Current Fiscal Year

Unreserved and Undesignated Fund Balance	5,000	
Encumbrances		5,000
To close Encumbrances ledger account.		
Appropriations	810,000	
Estimated Other Financing Uses	10,000	
Budgetary Fund Balance	30,000	
Estimated Revenues		840,000
Estimated Other Financing Sources		10,000
To close budgetary ledger accounts. (See page 734.)		
Revenues	848,000	
Other Financing Sources	10,000	
Expenditures		800,000
Other Financing Uses		11,000
Unreserved and Undesignated Fund Balance		47,000
To close revenues, expenditures, and other financing sources and uses ledger accounts.		

The foregoing journal entries do not close the Fund Balance Reserved for Encumbrances ledger account. Thus, the reserve represents a *mandatory* restriction of the fund balance on June 30, 2003, because the Town of Verdant Glen General Fund is committed in Fiscal Year 2004 to make estimated expenditures of $5,000 attributable to budgetary appropriations carried over from Fiscal Year 2003. If the Fund

Balance Reserved for Encumbrances account had been closed, the Unreserved and Undesignated Fund Balance account would have been overstated by $5,000. The Unreserved and Undesignated Fund Balance ledger account balance must represent the amount of the General Fund's net assets that is available for appropriation for a ***deficit budget*** in Fiscal Year 2004. When expenditures applicable to the $5,000 outstanding encumbrances on June 30, 2003, are vouchered for payment in the succeeding fiscal year, the Fund Balance Reserved for Encumbrances ledger account is debited for $5,000, the Vouchers Payable account is credited for the amount to be paid, and the balancing debit or credit is entered in the Unreserved and Undesignated Fund Balance account. In this way, the Expenditures ledger account is not improperly debited in Fiscal Year 2004 for an amount attributable to Fiscal Year 2003.

The budgetary accounts are closed at the end of the fiscal year because they are no longer required for control over revenues, expenditures, and other financing sources and uses. The amounts in the journal entry that closed the budgetary accounts were taken from the journal entry to record the budget (page 734).

After the June 30, 2003, closing entries for the Town of Verdant Glen General Fund are posted, the Unreserved and Undesignated Fund Balance ledger account is as follows:

Unreserved and Undesignated Fund Balance Ledger Account of a Government Entity's General Fund at End of Current fiscal year

Unreserved and Undesignated Fund Balance

Date	Explanation	Debit	Credit	Balance
2002				
June 30	Balance			80,000 cr
2003				
June 30	Increase in amount reserved for inventory of supplies (page 741)	10,000		70,000 cr
30	Designation for replacement of equipment (page 741)	25,000		45,000 cr
30	Close Encumbrances account (page 744)	5,000		40,000 cr
30	Close excess of revenues and other financing sources over expenditures and other financing uses (page 744)		47,000	87,000 cr

Review Questions

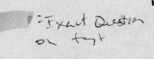

1. Does the Financial Accounting Standards Board establish accounting standards for governmental entities? Explain.
2. What characteristics of governmental entities have a significant influence on the accounting for governmental entities? Explain.
3. What is a ***fund*** in accounting for governmental entities?
4. What is the support for each of the following accounting standards for general funds of governmental entities?
   a. The modified accrual basis of accounting.
   b. The encumbrance accounting technique.
   c. Recording the budget in the accounting records.
5. *a.* Differentiate between a ***program budget*** and a ***performance budget***.
   b. Differentiate between a ***budgetary deficit*** and a ***deficit budget***.
6. The Estimated Revenues ledger account of a governmental entity's general fund may be considered a ***pseudo asset***, and the Appropriations account may be considered a ***pseudo liability***. Why is this true?

7. What is the function of the Budgetary Fund Balance ledger account for a governmental entity's general fund?

8. What does the reference to a governmental entity's general fund as *residual* mean? Explain.

9. What revenues of a governmental entity's general fund generally are accrued? Explain.

10. Distinguish between the Expenditures ledger account of a governmental entity's general fund and the expense accounts of a business enterprise.

11. Explain the purpose of the Other Financing Sources and Other Financing Uses ledger accounts of a governmental entity's general fund.

12. The accounting records for the City of Worthington General Fund include a ledger account titled Fund Balance Reserved for Inventory of Supplies. Explain the purpose of this account.

13. Differentiate between a *reservation* and a *designation* of the fund balance of a governmental entity's general fund.

14. a. What are the financial statements issued for a governmental entity's general fund?
    b. What are the principal differences between the financial statements of a governmental entity's general fund and the financial statements of a business enterprise?

Exercises

(Exercise 17.1)

Select the best answer for each of the following multiple-choice questions:

1. The Estimated Revenues ledger account of a governmental entity's general fund is debited when:
   a. The budgetary accounts are closed at the end of the fiscal year.
   b. The budget is recorded.
   c. Actual revenues are recognized under the modified accrual basis of accounting.
   d. Actual revenues are received in cash.

2. Which of the following ledger accounts is debited by a governmental entity's general fund that uses the encumbrances accounting technique when a purchase order is issued?
   a. Appropriations.
   b. Vouchers Payable.
   c. Fund Balance Reserved for Encumbrances.
   d. Encumbrances.
   e. None of the foregoing.

3. *GASB Statement No. 34,* "Basic Financial Statements . . . for State and Local Governments," identified:
   a. Eleven types of funds.
   b. Seven types of funds and two account groups.
   c. Two types of funds and seven account groups.
   d. Eight types of funds and two account groups.

4. Is a *fund* of a governmental entity:

	A Fiscal Unit?	An Accounting Unit?
a.	Yes	Yes
b.	Yes	No
c.	No	Yes
d.	No	No

5. In the journal entry to record the annual budget of a governmental entity's general fund, appropriate entries to the following general fund ledger accounts are:

	Estimated Revenues	*Appropriations*	*Estimated Other Financing Uses*
a.	Debit	Debit	Credit
b.	Debit	Credit	Credit
c.	Credit	Debit	Debit
d.	Credit	Debit	Credit

6. Which of the following is a budgetary ledger account of a governmental entity's general fund?

   a. Encumbrances.
   b. Other Financing Sources.
   c. Unreserved and Undesignated Fund Balance.
   d. Appropriations.

7. Which of the following ledger accounts of a governmental entity's general fund is credited when previously ordered supplies are received?

   a. Fund Balance Reserved for Encumbrances.
   b. Encumbrances.
   c. Expenditures.
   d. Appropriations.
   e. None of the foregoing.

8. In a governmental entity's general fund journal entry on the date an invoice is received for a nonrecurring procurement under a purchase order for which encumbrance accounting was used, the appropriate entries to the following ledger accounts are:

	Encumbrances	*Expenditures*
a.	Debit	Debit
b.	Debit	Credit
c.	Credit	Debit
d.	Credit	Credit

9. The ledger account debited in the journal entry of a governmental entity's general fund crediting the Allowance for Uncollectible Current Taxes ledger account is:

   a. Doubtful Current Taxes Expense.
   b. Unreserved and Undesignated Fund Balance.
   c. Revenues.
   d. Taxes Receivable—Current.
   e. Some other account.

10. Repairs that have been made for a governmental entity's general fund, and for which an invoice has been received, are recorded in the general fund with a debit to:

    a. Expenditures.
    b. Encumbrances.
    c. Repairs Expense.
    d. Appropriations.
    e. Some other ledger account.

11. The appropriate ledger accounts to be credited by a governmental entity's general fund for cash received from the entity's enterprise fund are:

	Payments in Lieu of Property Taxes	*Subsidies*
a.	Revenues	Other Financing Sources
b.	Revenues	Revenues
c.	Other Financing Sources	Revenues
d.	Other Financing Sources	Other Financing Sources

12. The appropriate format of the end-of-fiscal-year journal entry (explanation omitted) to close the Encumbrances ledger account of a governmental entity's general fund is:

   a. Unreserved and Undesignated Fund Balance
       Encumbrances
   b. Fund Balance Reserved for Encumbrances
       Encumbrances
   c. Expenditures
       Encumbrances
   d. Encumbrances
       Appropriations

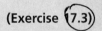

(Exercise 17.2) The activity with respect to the General Government—Supplies subsidiary ledger account of the Ridge City General Fund included the following for the first part of the July 1, 2002–June 30, 2003, fiscal year:

CHECK FIGURE

July 8 unexpended, unencumbered balance, $62,520 credit.

2002

July 1   The appropriation in the fiscal year budget was $100,000.

    2   Purchase order 4-1 for $20,000 was issued to Crosby Company; encumbrance accounting is used.

    3   Supplies were received from Crosby Company under purchase order 4-1, invoice 6392 for $20,120.

    5   Defective supplies with an invoice 6392 cost of $640 were returned to Crosby Company, accompanied by debit memorandum 4-6.

    8   Purchase order 4-14 for $18,000 was issued to Lassen Company.

Prepare a subsidiary ledger account for General Government—Supplies for Ridge City General Fund and post entries for the foregoing events or transactions. Your ledger account should have the following columns: Date; Explanation; Appropriation, credit; Encumbrance, debit; Expenditure, debit; Unexpended, unencumbered balance, credit.

(Exercise 17.3) The post-closing trial balance of the Winston County General Fund included the following ledger account balances on June 30, 2002:

Taxes receivable—delinquent	$30,200 dr
Allowance for uncollectible delinquent taxes	1,300 cr

The property taxes assessment for the fiscal year ending June 30, 2003, totaled $640,000; 4% of Winston County's property taxes assessments has been uncollectible in past fiscal years.

Prepare a journal entry for the property taxes of Winston County's General Fund on July 1, 2002, the date on which the property taxes for the fiscal year ending June 30, 2003, were billed to taxpayers.

(Exercise 17.4) On July 25, 2002, office supplies estimated to cost $2,390 were ordered from a vendor for delivery to the office of the city manager of Gaskill. The City of Gaskill maintains a perpetual inventory system and encumbrance accounting for such supplies. The supplies ordered July 25 were received on August 9, 2002, accompanied by an invoice for $2,500.

Prepare journal entries to record the foregoing transactions in the City of Gaskill General Fund.

(Exercise 17.5) The Glengarry School District General Fund had an inventory of supplies (and related reserve) of $60,200 on July 1, 2002. For the fiscal year ended June 30, 2003, supplies costing $170,900 were acquired; related purchase orders totaled $168,400. The physical inventory of unused supplies on June 30, 2003, totaled $78,300. The perpetual inventory system and encumbrance accounting is used to account for the inventory of supplies.

Prepare journal entries for the foregoing facts for the year ended June 30, 2003. Omit explanations for the journal entries.

(Exercise 17.6) Among the journal entries prepared by the inexperienced accountant of Rainbow County General Fund for the fiscal year ended June 30, 2003, were the following:

2002			
July 1	Accounts Receivable	800,000	
	Cash		800,000
	To record nonreturnable operating transfer of cash to Internal Service Fund to provide working capital for that fund.		
Sept. 1	Equipment	120,000	
	Vouchers Payable		120,000
	To record acquisition of equipment having a 10-year economic life and no residual value.		

Prepare correcting journal entries on June 30, 2003, for Rainbow County General Fund.

(Exercise 17.7) From the following ledger account balances for the Town of Irving General Fund on June 30, 2003, the end of the town's fiscal year, prepare closing entries:

Appropriations	$1,520,000
Encumbrances	10,000
Estimated revenues	1,600,000
Expenditures	1,500,000
Fund balance reserved for encumbrances	10,000
Revenues	1,616,000

(Exercise 17.8) *Selected* ledger account balances of Bixby Village General Fund on June 30, 2003, were as follows:

	Debit	Credit
Appropriations		$400,000
Budgetary fund balance		30,000
Encumbrances	$ 1,000	
Estimated other financing sources	10,000	
Estimated other financing uses		6,000
Estimated revenues	426,000	
Expenditures	395,000	
Fund balance reserved for encumbrances		1,000
Other financing sources		14,000
Other financing uses	5,000	
Revenues		440,000
Unreserved and undesignated fund balance		80,000

Prepare closing entries (omit explanations) for Bixby Village General Fund on June 30, 2003.

(Exercise 17.9) Following is the statement of revenues, expenditures, and changes in fund balance for the Village of Mortimer General Fund for the year ended June 30, 2003. The village did not have any other financing sources or uses for the year. Unfilled purchase orders on June 30, 2003, for which the village used encumbrance accounting, totaled $11,400.

VILLAGE OF MORTIMER GENERAL FUND
Statement of Revenues, Expenditures, and Changes in Fund Balance
For Year Ended June 30, 2003

	Budget	Actual	Variance Favorable (Unfavorable)
Revenues:			
Taxes	$820,000	$814,200	$(5,800)
Other	160,000	162,500	2,500
Total revenues	$980,000	$976,700	$(3,300)
Expenditures:			
General government	$615,000	$618,800	$(3,800)
Other	275,000	277,400	(2,400)
Total expenditures	$890,000	$896,200	$(6,200)
Net change in fund balance	$ 90,000	$ 80,500	$(9,500)
Fund balance, beginning of year	280,400	280,400	
Fund balance, end of year	$370,400	$360,900	$(9,500)

Prepare closing entries for the Village of Mortimer General Fund on June 30, 2003.

(Exercise 17.10) The *post-closing* trial balance of the Town of Parkside General Fund on June 30, 2003, was as follows:

TOWN OF PARKSIDE GENERAL FUND
Post-Closing Trial Balance
June 30, 2003

	Debit	Credit
Cash	$150,000	
Taxes receivable—delinquent	50,000	
Allowance for uncollectible delinquent taxes		$ 5,000
Inventory of supplies	60,000	
Vouchers payable		80,000
Payable to Town of Parkside Enterprise Fund		20,000
Fund balance reserved for encumbrances		4,000
Fund balance reserved for inventory of supplies		60,000
Unreserved and undesignated fund balance		91,000
Totals	$260,000	$260,000

Prepare a balance sheet for the Town of Parkside General Fund on June 30, 2003.

(Exercise 17.11) On July 1, 2002, the general ledger of the City of Winkle General Fund had the following fund balance ledger accounts:

	Balance July 1, 2002
Reserved for inventory of supplies	$ 80,600
Reserved for encumbrances	18,100
Unreserved and undesignated	214,700

The budget for the fiscal year ending June 30, 2003, showed a budgetary surplus of $20,400. Revenues for the year ended June 30, 2003, exceeded expenditures by $37,600. There were no other financing sources or uses for the year. The physical inventory of supplies on June 30, 2003, was $88,200, and outstanding encumbrances on June 30, 2003, totaled $14,800.

Prepare a working paper to compute the balance of the Unreserved and Undesignated Fund Balance ledger account (after posting of closing entries) for the City of Winkle General Fund on June 30, 2003.

(Exercise 17.12) The Unreserved and Undesignated Fund Balance ledger account of the Town of Oldberry General Fund was as follows on June 30, 2003. The Town of Oldberry did not have any other financing sources or uses during the year ended June 30, 2003.

Unreserved and Undesignated Fund Balance

Date	Explanation	Debit	Credit	Balance
2002				
June 30	Balance			62,400 cr
2003				
June 30	Decrease in amount reserved for inventory of supplies		3,700	66,100 cr
30	Close Encumbrances ledger account	6,200		59,900 cr
30	Close excess of revenues ($840,200) over expenditures ($764,800)		75,400	135,300 cr
30	Designation for replacement of equipment	60,000		75,300 cr

Reconstruct the journal entries of the Town of Oldberry General Fund indicated by the foregoing information.

Cases

(Case 17.1) The inexperienced accountant of Corbin City prepared the following financial statements for the city's general fund:

CORBIN CITY GENERAL FUND
Income Statement
For Year Ended June 30, 2003

Revenues:		
Taxes		$640,000
Other		180,000
Total revenues		$820,000
Expenses:		
General government	$600,000	
Depreciation	60,000	
Other	120,000	780,000
Net income		$ 40,000

CORBIN CITY GENERAL FUND
Statement of Changes in Fund Balance
For Year Ended June 30, 2003

Fund balance, beginning of year	$4,850,000
Add: Net income	40,000
Fund balance, end of year	$4,890,000

CORBIN CITY GENERAL FUND
Balance Sheet
June 30, 2003

Assets

Cash	$ 260,000
Property taxes receivable—delinquent	80,000
Inventory of supplies	110,000
Plant assets (net)	4,620,000
Total assets	$5,070,000

Liabilities, Reserves, and Fund Balance

Vouchers payable	$ 160,000
Reserve for delinquent property taxes	20,000
Fund balance	4,890,000
Total liabilities, reserves, and fund balance	$5,070,000

Instructions

Identify the deficiencies in each of the foregoing financial statements of Corbin City General Fund. There are no arithmetic errors in the statements. Disregard notes to the financial statements.

(Case 17.2) In a classroom discussion of the modified accrual basis of accounting for general funds of governmental entities, student Ella questioned the propriety of accruing self-assessed taxes such as income taxes and sales taxes. She pointed out that until the taxes are paid, the governmental entity has no liability-paying ability and no knowledge of the amount of taxes ultimately to be collected. Student Janice disagreed with Ella, stating that the budget-preparation process entails estimation of total fiscal year revenues, including revenues from sales taxes and income taxes. Janice concluded by asserting that the currently required modified accrual basis of accounting for governmental entities' general fund revenues is overly conservative and fails to provide meaningful budget-to-actual comparisons in general funds' statements of revenues, expenditures, and changes in fund balance.

Instructions

Do you support the views of student Ella or student Janice? Explain.

(Case 17.3) You have been assigned by your CPA firm, in which you are an audit manager, to conduct a staff training program in accounting for governmental entities. In preparing for the program, you have decided to anticipate questions about the reasons governmental entities must use a maximum of 11 separate funds, rather than a single accounting unit, to account for the governmental entity's transactions and events.

Instructions

Prepare a brief essay on the reasons for the use of fund accounting by governmental entities.

Problems

(Problem 17.1) The trial balance of Weedpatch County General Fund on June 30, 2003, was as follows (amounts in thousands):

	Debit	Credit
Cash	$ 100	
Taxes receivable—delinquent	60	
Allowance for uncollectible delinquent taxes		$ 10
Inventory of supplies	50	
Vouchers payable		40
Payable to other funds		12
Fund balance reserved for encumbrances		4
Fund balance reserved for inventory of supplies		50
Unreserved and undesignated fund balance		18
Budgetary fund balance		20
Estimated revenues	800	
Appropriations		780
Revenues		830
Expenditures	750	
Encumbrances	4	
Totals	$1,764	$1,764

The balance of the Unreserved and Undesignated Fund Balance ledger account on July 1, 2002, was $22,000; there were balances of $6,000 and $40,000, respectively, in the Fund Balance Reserved for Encumbrances and the Fund Balance Reserved for Inventory of Supplies accounts on that date.

Instructions

Prepare a statement of revenues, expenditures, and changes in fund balance and a balance sheet (amounts in thousands) for Weedpatch County General Fund for the year ended June 30, 2003.

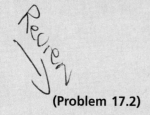

(Problem 17.2) The following information was taken from the accounting records of the General Fund of the City of Lory after the ledger accounts had been closed for the fiscal year ended June 30, 2003. The budget for the fiscal year ended June 30, 2003, included estimated revenues of $2,000,000 and appropriations of $1,940,000. There were no estimated or actual other financing sources or other financing uses.

City of Lory General Fund

	Post-Closing Trial Balance, June 30, 2002	Transactions, Events, and Closing Entries, July 1, 2002, through June 30, 2003		Post-Closing Trial Balance, June 30, 2003
		Debit	Credit	
Debits				
Cash	$700,000	$1,820,000	$1,852,000	$668,000
Taxes receivable	40,000	1,870,000	1,828,000	82,000
Total debits	$740,000			$750,000

(continued)

City of Lory General Fund (concluded)

	Post-Closing Trial Balance, June 30, 2002	Transactions, Events, and Closing Entries, July 1, 2002, through June 30, 2003		Post-Closing Trial Balance, June 30, 2003
		Debit	Credit	
Credits				
Allowance for uncollectible taxes	$ 8,000	8,000	10,000	$ 10,000
Vouchers payable	132,000	1,852,000	1,840,000	120,000
Fund balance:				
Reserved for encumbrances		1,000,000	1,070,000	70,000
Unreserved and undesignated	600,000	70,000	20,000	550,000
Total credits	$740,000	$6,620,000	$6,620,000	$750,000

Instructions

Prepare journal entries to record the budgeted and actual transactions and events of the City of Lory General Fund for the fiscal year ended June 30, 2003. Also, prepare closing entries. Do not differentiate between current and delinquent taxes receivable.

(Problem 17.3) At the start of your audit of the financial statements of the City of Riverdale, you discovered that the city's accountant failed to maintain separate funds. The trial balance of the City of Riverdale General Fund for the fiscal year ended December 31, 2003, is as follows:

CITY OF RIVERDALE GENERAL FUND
Trial Balance
December 31, 2003

	Debit	Credit
Cash	$ 207,500	
Taxes receivable—current	148,500	
Allowance for uncollectible current taxes		$ 6,000
Revenues		992,500
Expenditures	760,000	
Donated land	190,000	
Construction in progress—River Bridge	130,000	
River Bridge bonds payable		100,000
Contracts payable—River Bridge		30,000
Vouchers payable		7,500
Unreserved and undesignated fund balance		300,000
Totals	$1,436,000	$1,436,000

Additional Information

1. The budget for Year 2003, not recorded in the accounting records, was as follows: estimated revenues, $815,000; appropriations, $775,000. There were no estimated or actual other financing sources or other financing uses.

2. Outstanding purchase orders on December 31, 2003, for expenditures not recognized in the accounting records, totaled $2,500. Riverdale uses encumbrance accounting.

3. Included in the Revenues ledger account balance was a credit of $190,000 representing the current fair value of land donated by the state as a site for construction of the River Bridge.

4. The taxes receivable became delinquent on December 31, 2003.

Instructions
Prepare correcting journal entries on December 31, 2003, for the City of Riverdale General Fund. Correcting entries for other funds or account groups and closing entries are not required.

(Problem 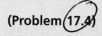 The following transactions and events affecting Canning County General Fund took place during the fiscal year ended June 30, 2003:

(1) The following annual budget was adopted:

Estimated revenues:	
Property taxes	$4,500,000
Licenses and permits	300,000
Fines	200,000
Total estimated revenues	$5,000,000
Appropriations:	
General government	$1,500,000
Police services	1,200,000
Fire department services	900,000
Public works services	800,000
Acquisition of fire engines	400,000
Total appropriations	$4,800,000

There were no other financing sources or other financing uses budgeted.

(2) Property tax bills totaling $4,650,000 were issued; it was estimated that $150,000 of this amount would be uncollectible. Fines of $200,000 were assessed.

(3) Property taxes totaling $3,900,000 were collected. The $150,000 previously estimated to be uncollectible remained unchanged, but $630,000 of uncollected property taxes was reclassified as delinquent. It was known that delinquent taxes would be collected soon enough after June 30, 2003, to make these taxes available to finance obligations incurred during the year ended June 30, 2003. (There was no balance of uncollected taxes on July 1, 2002.)

(4) Other cash collections were as follows:

Licenses and permits	$270,000
Fines	200,000
Disposal of public works equipment (carrying amount in the General Capital Assets Account Group was $5,000)	15,000
Total other cash collections	$485,000

(5) No encumbrances were outstanding on June 30, 2002. The following purchase orders were executed:

	Total Amount	Outstanding June 30, 2003
General government	$1,050,000	$ 60,000
Police services	300,000	30,000
Fire department services	150,000	15,000
Public works services	250,000	10,000
Fire engines	400,000	
Totals	$2,150,000	$115,000

(handwritten note: Revenues Expenditures are not encumbered)

(6) The following vouchers were approved for payment:

General government	$1,440,000
Police services	1,155,000
Fire department services	870,000
Public works services	700,000
Fire engines	400,000
Total vouchers approved	$4,565,000

(7) Vouchers totaling $4,600,000 were paid.

Instructions

Prepare journal entries to record the foregoing transactions and events of Canning Company General Fund for the year ended June 30, 2003. Do not prepare closing entries.

(Problem 17.5) The trial balance of Arden School District General Fund is as follows:

ARDEN SCHOOL DISTRICT GENERAL FUND
Trial Balance
December 31, 2003

	Debit	Credit
Cash	$ 47,250	
Short-term investments	11,300	
Taxes receivable—delinquent	30,000	
Inventory of supplies	11,450	
Vouchers payable		$ 20,200
Payable to Internal Service Fund		950
Fund balance reserved for encumbrances		2,800
Fund balance reserved for inventory of supplies		11,450
Unreserved and undesignated fund balance		59,400
Budgetary fund balance		7,000
Estimated revenues	1,007,000	
Appropriations		985,000
Estimated other financing uses		15,000
Revenues		1,008,200
Expenditures	990,200	
Other financing uses	10,000	
Encumbrances	2,800	
Totals	$2,110,000	$2,110,000

The balance of the Fund Balance Reserved for Inventory of Supplies ledger account on December 31, 2002, was $9,500.

Instructions

a. Prepare the following financial statements for Arden School District General Fund for the year ended December 31, 2003:

(1) Statement of revenues, expenditures, and changes in fund balance.
(2) Balance sheet.

b. Prepare closing entries for Arden School District General Fund on December 31, 2003.

(Problem 17.6) The following summary of transactions and events was taken from the accounting records of Melton School District General Fund before the accounting records had been closed for the fiscal year ended June 30, 2003:

MELTON SCHOOL DISTRICT GENERAL FUND
Summary of Transactions and Events
For Year Ended June 30, 2003

	Post-Closing Balances, June 30, 2002	Pre-Closing Balances, June 30, 2003
Ledger accounts with debit balances:		
Cash	$400,000	$ 700,000
Taxes receivable	150,000	170,000
Estimated revenues		3,000,000
Expenditures		2,700,000
Other financing uses		142,000
Encumbrances		91,000
Totals	$550,000	$6,803,000
Ledger accounts with credit balances:		
Allowance for uncollectible taxes	$ 40,000	$ 70,000
Vouchers payable	80,000	408,000
Payable to other funds	210,000	142,000
Fund balance reserved for encumbrances	60,000	91,000
Unreserved and undesignated fund balance	160,000	162,000
Revenues from taxes		2,800,000
Other revenues		130,000
Budgetary fund balance		20,000
Appropriations		2,810,000
Estimated other financing uses		170,000
Totals	$550,000	$6,803,000

Additional Information

1. The estimated taxes receivable for the year ended June 30, 2003, were $2,870,000, and taxes collected during the year totaled $2,810,000.

2. An analysis of the transactions in the Vouchers Payable ledger account for the year ended June 30, 2003, follows:

	Debit (Credit)
Current year expenditures (all subject to encumbrances)	$(2,700,000)
Expenditures applicable to June 30, 2002, outstanding encumbrances	(58,000)
Vouchers for payments to other funds	(210,000)
Cash payments	2,640,000
Net change	$ (328,000)

3. During Fiscal Year 2003, the General Fund was billed $142,000 for services furnished by other funds of Melton School District.

4. On May 2, 2003, purchase orders were issued for new textbooks at an estimated cost of $91,000. The books were to be delivered in August, 2003.

Instructions

a. Based on the foregoing data, reconstruct the journal entries to record all transactions and events of Melton School District General Fund for the year ended June 30, 2003, including the recording of the budget for the year. Disregard current and delinquent taxes receivable. (Hint: The $2,000 difference between the $60,000 fund balance reserved for encumbrances on June 30, 2002, and the $58,000 amount vouchered for the related expenditures is credited to the Unreserved and Undesignated Fund Balance ledger account.)

b. Prepare closing entries for Melton School District General Fund on June 30, 2003.

c. Prepare a post-closing trial balance for Melton School District General Fund on June 30, 2003.

(Problem 17.7) Because the controller of the City of Romaine had resigned, the assistant controller attempted to compute the cash required to be derived from property taxes for the General Fund for the fiscal year ending June 30, 2003. The computation was made as of January 1, 2002, to serve as a basis for establishing the property tax rate for the fiscal year ending June 30, 2003. The mayor of Romaine has requested you to review the assistant controller's computations and obtain other necessary information to prepare for the City of Romaine General Fund a formal estimate of the cash required to be derived from property taxes for the fiscal year ending June 30, 2003. Following are the computations prepared by the assistant controller:

City resources other than proposed property tax levy:	
Estimated General Fund cash balance, Jan. 1, 2002	$ 352,000
Estimated cash receipts from property taxes, Jan. 1 to June 30, 2002	2,222,000
Estimated cash revenues from investments, Jan. 1, 2002, to June 30, 2003	442,000
Estimated proceeds from issuance of general obligation bonds in August, 2002	3,000,000
Total City resources	$6,016,000
General Fund requirements:	
Estimated expenditures, Jan. 1 to June 30, 2002	$1,900,000
Proposed appropriations, July 1, 2002, to June 30, 2003	4,300,000
Total General Fund requirements	$6,200,000

Additional Information

1. The General Fund cash balance required for July 1, 2003, is $175,000.

2. Property tax collections are due in March and September of each year. You note that during February 2002 estimated expenditures will exceed available cash by $200,000. Pending collection of property taxes in March 2002, this deficiency will have to be met by the issuance of 30-day tax-anticipation notes of $200,000 at an estimated interest rate of 12% a year.

3. The proposed general-obligation bonds will be issued by the City of Romaine Enterprise Fund to finance the construction of a new water pumping station.

Instructions

Prepare a working paper as of January 1, 2002, to compute the property tax levy required for the City of Romaine General Fund for the fiscal year ending June 30, 2003.

(Problem 17.8) The following data were taken from the accounting records of the Town of Tosca General Fund after the ledger accounts had been closed for the fiscal year ended June 30, 2003:

TOWN OF TOSCA GENERAL FUND Data from Accounting Records For Year Ended June 30, 2003				
	Balances July 1, 2002	Fiscal Year 2003 Changes		Balances June 30, 2003
		Debit	Credit	
Assets				
Cash	$180,000	$ 955,000	$ 880,000	$255,000
Taxes receivable	20,000	809,000	781,000	48,000
Allowance for uncollectible taxes	(4,000)	6,000	9,000	(7,000)
Total assets	$196,000			$296,000
Liabilities and Fund Balance				
Vouchers payable	$ 44,000	880,000	889,000	$ 53,000
Payable to Internal Service Fund	2,000	7,000	10,000	5,000
Payable to Enterprise Fund	10,000	60,000	100,000	50,000
Fund balance reserved for encumbrances	40,000	40,000	47,000	47,000
Unreserved and undesignated fund balance	100,000	47,000	88,000	141,000
Total liabilities and fund balance	$196,000	$2,804,000	$2,804,000	$296,000

Additional Information

1. The budget for Fiscal Year 2003 provided for estimated revenues of $1,000,000 and appropriations of $965,000. There were no other financing sources or other financing uses budgeted.
2. Expenditures totaling $895,000, in addition to those chargeable against the Fund Balance Reserved for Encumbrances ledger account, were made.
3. The actual expenditure chargeable against the July 1, 2002, Fund Balance Reserved for Encumbrances ledger account was $37,000.

Instructions

Reconstruct the journal entries, including closing entries, for the Town of Tosca General Fund indicated by the foregoing data for the year ended June 30, 2003. Do not attempt to differentiate between current and delinquent taxes receivable.

(Problem 17.9) The post-closing trial balance of the City of Douglas General Fund on June 30, 2002, was as follows:

CITY OF DOUGLAS GENERAL FUND Post-Closing Trial Balance June 30, 2002		
	Debit	Credit
Cash	$ 62,000	
Taxes receivable—delinquent	46,000*	
Allowance for uncollectible delinquent taxes		$ 8,000
Inventory of supplies	18,000	
Vouchers payable		28,000
Fund balance reserved for inventory of supplies		18,000
Fund balance reserved for encumbrances		12,000
Unreserved and undesignated fund balance		60,000
Totals	$126,000	$126,000

* Collectible delinquent taxes were expected to be collected by Aug. 31, 2002.

Additional Information

1. The annual budget for the fiscal year ending June 30, 2003, was as follows:

Estimated revenues		$400,000
Estimated other financing sources		200,000
Subtotal		$600,000
Less: Appropriations	$560,000	
Estimated other financing uses	20,000	580,000
Budgetary surplus		$ 20,000

2. Property taxes were levied for the year ended June 30, 2003, in an amount to provide revenues of $220,800, after estimated uncollectible taxes of 4% of total taxes receivable.

3. Purchase orders issued for the year ended June 30, 2003, totaled $518,000. Encumbrance accounting is used.

4. Cash receipts for the year ended June 30, 2003, were as follows:

Delinquent property taxes	$ 38,000
Current property taxes	226,000
Refund from vendor for overpayment of Fiscal Year 2003 invoice for acquisition of equipment	4,000
Other revenues (licenses and permits fees)	196,000
Other financing sources	200,000
Total cash receipts	$664,000

5. Vouchers were prepared as follows for the year ended June 30, 2003:

Encumbrance outstanding, June 30, 2002	$ 10,000
Expenditures for year ended June 30, 2003 (including supplies, $80,000; related encumbrances totaled $292,000)	298,000
Other expenditures (no encumbrances)	244,000
Other financing uses (payable to Capital Projects Fund)	20,000
Total vouchers	$572,000

6. Cash payments for vouchers payable during the year ended June 30, 2003, totaled $580,000.

7. The physical inventory of supplies on June 30, 2003, amounted to $12,000. Supplies are accounted for under the perpetual inventory system.

8. On June 30, 2003, $20,000 of the unreserved and undesignated fund balance was designated for the acquisition of equipment during the fiscal year ending June 30, 2004.

Instructions

Prepare journal entries for the foregoing transactions and events of the City of Douglas General Fund for the year ended June 30, 2003, and closing entries on June 30, 2003.

Chapter Eighteen

Governmental Entities: Other Governmental Funds and Account Groups

Scope of Chapter

This chapter presents a discussion and illustration of accounting and reporting for a governmental entity's governmental funds other than the general fund, and for the general capital assets and general long-term debt account groups.

OTHER GOVERNMENTAL FUNDS

Accounting and reporting for the four governmental funds (special revenue funds, capital projects funds, debt service funds, and permanent funds) other than the general fund incorporates many of the accounting standards discussed in Chapter 17. For example, the modified accrual basis of accounting is appropriate for all governmental funds, and recording the budget (together with encumbrance accounting) is appropriate for special revenue funds and may be useful for debt service funds and capital projects funds.

Accounting and Reporting for Special Revenue Funds

As indicated on page 732, *separate* special revenue funds are established by governmental entities, as required by law and sound financial administrations, to account for the receipts and expenditures associated with specialized revenue sources that are earmarked by law or regulation to finance specified governmental operations. Fees for rubbish collection, state gasoline taxes, "sin taxes" on tobacco products and alcoholic beverages, and traffic violation fines are examples of governmental entity revenues that may be accounted for in separate special revenue funds. Ledger account titles, budgetary processes, and financial statements for special revenue funds are similar to those for the general fund.

To illustrate the accounting for a special revenue fund, assume that on July 1, 2003, the Town Council of the Town of Verdant Glen authorized the establishment of a special revenue fund—its first such fund—to account for *special assessments* levied on certain residents of the neighboring Village of Arbor. Those residents had requested the Town Council to provide street cleaning and streetlight maintenance services, which could not be furnished by the Village of Arbor. Because the property tax revenues of the Town of Verdant Glen, which among other services financed street cleaning and streetlight maintenance for *residents of the town only,* could not be used for such services elsewhere, the Town Council authorized the special assessment to finance comparable services for the requesting residents of the Village of Arbor. The Town Council adopted a budget for the Special Revenue Fund for the fiscal year ending June 30, 2004, providing for estimated revenues of $80,000 (from the special assessments) and appropriations of $75,000 (for reimbursements to the General Fund for expenditures made by that fund for the services provided to the Village of Arbor residents). Following are additional transactions or events of the Town of Verdant Glen Special Revenue Fund for the fiscal year ended June 30, 2004:

1. Special assessments totaling $82,000 were levied on the appropriate residents of the Village of Arbor, to be paid in full in 60 days. All the special assessments were expected to be collected.

2. Cash receipts from the special assessments were collected in full, $82,000.

3. Of the cash receipts, $63,000 was invested in U.S. Treasury bills with a face amount of $65,000. The U.S. Treasury bills matured on June 30, 2004, and were redeemed in full on that date.

4. Billings from the Town of Verdant Glen General Fund, requesting reimbursement of expenditures of that fund, totaled $76,000; $62,000 of that amount was paid to the General Fund by June 30, 2004.

5. On June 30, 2004, the Town Council of the Town of Verdant Glen designated the fund balance ($8,000) of the Special Revenue Fund for reimbursement of the General Fund during the fiscal year ending June 30, 2005.

Journal Entries for Special Revenue Fund

Journal entries of the Town of Verdant Glen Special Revenue Fund to record the foregoing events and transactions and to close the accounts for the fiscal year ended June 30, 2004, are as follows. Note that the encumbrances technique is not used by this special revenue fund *because it does not issue purchase orders for goods or services from outsiders.*

Because the $76,000 billings of the Town of Verdant Glen General Fund to the Special Revenue Fund were for reimbursement of General Fund expenditures, the General Fund credits its Expenditures ledger account in the journal entry in which it debits Receivable from Special Revenue Fund.

TOWN OF VERDANT GLEN SPECIAL REVENUE FUND
Journal Entries

Estimated Revenues:	80,000	
Appropriations		75,000
Budgetary Fund Balance		5,000
To record annual budget adopted for fiscal year ending June 30, 2004.		
Special Assessments Receivable—Current	82,000	
Revenues		82,000
To record special assessments billed, all of which are estimated to be collectible.		
Cash	82,000	
Special Assessments Receivable—Current		82,000
To record collection of special assessments in full during the year.		
Investments	63,000	
Cash		63,000
To record acquisition of $65,000 face amount of U.S. Treasury bills, maturity June 30, 2004.		
Cash	65,000	
Investments		63,000
Revenues		2,000
To record receipt of cash for matured U.S. Treasury bills.		
Expenditures	76,000	
Payable to General Fund		76,000
To record billings from General Fund for reimbursement of expenditures for street cleaning and streetlight maintenance for residents of the Village of Arbor.		
Payable to General Fund	62,000	
Cash		62,000
To record payments to General Fund during the year.		
Appropriations	75,000	
Budgetary Fund Balance	5,000	
Estimated Revenues		80,000
To close budgetary ledger accounts.		
Revenues ($82,000 + $2,000)	84,000	
Expenditures		76,000
Unreserved and Undesignated Fund Balance		8,000
To close Revenues and Expenditures ledger accounts.		
Unreserved and Undesignated Fund Balance	8,000	
Fund Balance Designated for Reimbursement of General Fund		8,000
To designate entire fund balance for reimbursement of the General Fund during the fiscal year ending June 30, 2005.		

Financial Statements for Special Revenue Fund

The financial statements for a special revenue fund are the same as those for the general fund: a statement of revenues, expenditures, and changes in fund balance, and a balance sheet. Financial statements for the Town of Verdant Glen Special Revenue Fund for the fiscal year ended June 30, **2004,** are as follows:

Financial Statements of a Governmental Entity's Special Revenue Fund

TOWN OF VERDANT GLEN SPECIAL REVENUE FUND
Statement of Revenues, Expenditures, and Changes in Fund Balance
For Year Ended June 30, 2004

	Budget	Actual	Variance Favorable (Unfavorable)
Revenues:			
Special assessments	$80,000	$82,000	$ 2,000
Other		2,000	2,000
Total revenues	$80,000	$84,000	$ 4,000
Expenditures:			
Reimbursement of General Fund expenditures	$75,000	$76,000	$(1,000)
Excess of revenues over expenditures (fund balance, end of year)	$ 5,000	$ 8,000	$ 3,000

TOWN OF VERDANT GLEN SPECIAL REVENUE FUND
Balance Sheet
June 30, 2004

Assets	
Cash	$22,000
Liabilities and Fund Balance	
Payable to General Fund	$14,000
Fund balance designated for reimbursement of General Fund	8,000
Total liabilities and fund balance	$22,000

Accounting and Reporting for Capital Projects Funds

Capital projects funds of a governmental entity record the receipt and payment of cash for the construction or acquisition of the governmental entity's plant assets other than those financed by proprietary funds (enterprise funds and internal service funds) or trust funds. The resources for a capital projects fund generally are derived from proceeds of general obligation bonds, but the resources also may come from current tax revenues of the general fund or from **grants** or **shared revenues** of other governmental entities.

A capital budget, rather than an annual budget, is the ***control device*** appropriate for a capital projects fund. The capital budget deals with both the authorized expenditures for the project and the bond proceeds or other financing sources for the project.

Journal Entries for Capital Projects Fund

On July 1, 2002, the Town of Verdant Glen authorized a $500,000, 20-year, 7% general obligation bond issue to finance an addition to the town's high school. A capital budget was approved for the amount of the bonds, but was not to be integrated in the accounting records of the capital projects fund authorized for the project. The following journal entries illustrate receipt of proceeds of the bonds and other activities of the Town of Verdant Glen Capital Projects Fund for the fiscal year ended June 30, 2003:

Journal Entries for Capital Project Fund of a Governmental Entity

TOWN OF VERDANT GLEN CAPITAL PROJECTS FUND
Journal Entries

Cash	450,518	
Other Financing Uses: Discount on Bonds Issued	49,482	
Other Financing Sources: Bonds Issued		500,000
To record proceeds of 20-year, 7% general obligation term bonds due July 1, 2022, interest payable Jan. 1 and July 1, to yield 8%, face amount $500,000. (Bond issue costs are disregarded.)		
Investments	335,000	
Cash		335,000
To record acquisition of $350,000 face amount of U.S. Treasury bills, maturity 26 weeks.		
Encumbrances	482,000	
Fund Balance Reserved for Encumbrances		482,000
To record contracts with architect and construction contractor and issuance of purchase orders.		
Cash	350,000	
Investments		335,000
Revenues		15,000
To record receipt of cash for matured U.S. Treasury bills.		
Expenditures	378,000	
Vouchers Payable		378,000
To record expenditures for the year.		
Fund Balance Reserved for Encumbrances	368,200	
Encumbrances		368,200
To reverse encumbrances applicable to vouchered expenditures.		
Vouchers Payable	327,500	
Cash		327,500
To record payment of vouchers during the year.		

(continued)

TOWN OF VERDANT GLEN CAPITAL PROJECTS FUND
Journal Entries (concluded)

R.E. ~ Surplus (handwritten)

Unreserved and Undesignated Fund Balance ($482,000 − $368,200)	113,800	
Encumbrances		113,800
To close Encumbrances ledger account.		
Revenues	15,000	
Other Financing Sources: Bonds Issued	500,000	
Expenditures		378,000
Other Financing Uses: Discount on Bonds Issued		49,482
Unreserved and Undesignated Fund Balance		87,518
To close Revenues, Expenditures, and Other Financing Sources and Uses ledger accounts.		

(handwritten: Close out; DIFF unres FB)

The following features of the foregoing journal entries should be noted:

1. The capital budget for the high school addition was not entered in the accounting records of the Capital Projects Fund. The indenture for the 20-year, 7% general obligation bonds (*general long-term capital debt*) provided adequate control.

2. The liability applicable to the 20-year general obligation bonds was not recorded in the Capital Projects Fund. The liability for the bonds is recorded at face amount in the general long-term debt account group (see page 774).

3. The face amount of the general obligation bonds is another financing source of the Capital Projects Fund; the discount on the bonds is another financing use.[1] The interest earned on the short-term investment in U.S. Treasury bills represents revenues to the Capital Projects Fund.

4. The encumbrances and expenditures accounting for the Capital Projects Fund is similar to that for the General Fund illustrated in Chapter 17. Also, the closing entries for the two types of governmental funds are similar.

Expenditures for construction recorded in the Town of Verdant Glen Capital Proj-ects Fund are accompanied in the general fixed assets account group by a journal entry at the end of the fiscal year with a debit to Construction in Progress and a credit to Investment in Capital Assets from Capital Projects Funds (see page 771).

At the end of each fiscal year prior to completion of a capital project, the Revenues, Other Financing Sources, Expenditures, and Encumbrances ledger accounts of the Capital Projects Fund are closed to the Unreserved and Undesignated Fund Balance account. On completion of the project, the Capital Projects Fund is terminated by a transfer of any unused cash to the Debt Service Fund or the General Fund, as appropriate; the Unreserved and Undesignated Fund Balance ledger account of the receiving fund would be credited for this *residual equity transfer.* Any cash deficiency in the Capital Projects Fund (a possibility suggested by the deficit fund balance in the balance sheet on page 767) probably would be made up by the General Fund; this *operating*

---

[1] *Codification of Governmental Accounting and Financial Reporting Standards* (Norwalk: GASB, 2000), p. A-37.

transfer would be credited to the Other Financing Sources ledger account of the Capital Projects Fund and debited to the Other Financing Uses account of the General Fund.

Financial Statements for Capital Projects Fund

A capital projects fund issues the same financial statements as a general fund: a statement of revenues, expenditures, and changes in fund balance, and a balance sheet. For the Town of Verdant Glen Capital Projects Fund, these financial statements are as follows for the year ended June 30, *2003:*

Financial Statements of a Governmental Entity's Capital Projects Fund

TOWN OF VERDANT GLEN CAPITAL PROJECTS FUND Statement of Revenues, Expenditures, and Changes in Fund Balance For Year Ended June 30, 2003	
Revenues:	
Miscellaneous	$ 15,000
Expenditures:*	
Construction contracts	$ 287,600
Engineering and other	90,400
Total expenditures	$ 378,000
Excess (deficiency) of revenues over expenditures	$(363,000)
Other financing sources (uses):	
Face amount of general obligation bonds	$ 500,000
Discount on general obligation bonds	(49,482)
Excess of revenues and other sources over expenditures and other uses (fund balance, end of year)	$ 87,518

* Breakdown of expenditures is assumed.

TOWN OF VERDANT GLEN CAPITAL PROJECTS FUND Balance Sheet June 30, 2003		
Assets		
Cash		$138,018
Liabilities and Fund Balance		
Liabilities:		
Vouchers payable		$ 50,500
Fund balance:		
Reserved for encumbrances	$113,800	
Unreserved and undesignated	(26,282)	87,518
Total liabilities and fund balance		$138,018

To reiterate, the plant assets constructed with resources of the Capital Projects Fund are not displayed in that fund's balance sheet. The constructed plant assets are recorded in the governmental entity's general capital assets account group. Furthermore, the general obligation bonds issued to finance the Capital Projects Fund are not a liability of that fund. Prior to the maturity date or dates of the bonds, the liability is carried in the general long-term debt account group (see page 774). On the date the bonds mature, the related liability is transferred to a debt service fund or to the general fund, as appropriate, from the general long-term debt account group.

Accounting and Reporting for Debt Service Funds

Payments of principal and interest on long-term bonds and other long-term debt of a governmental entity, other than special assessment bonds, revenue bonds, and general obligation bonds serviced by an enterprise fund, are accounted for either in the general fund or in debt service funds. *Special assessment bonds* are repaid from the proceeds of special assessment levies against specific properties receiving benefits from the special assessment improvements; if these bonds finance construction projects for an enterprise fund, they are accounted for in that enterprise fund. *Revenue bonds* are payable from the earnings of a governmental entity's enterprise and are accounted for in the appropriate enterprise fund. In some cases, *general obligation bonds,* which are backed by the full faith and credit of the issuing governmental entity, will be repaid from the resources of a governmental entity enterprise. These general obligation bonds are displayed as liabilities of the appropriate enterprise fund.

The liability for bonds payable from resources of the general fund or a debt service fund is not recorded in that fund until the debt matures. Prior to maturity date, the bond liability is carried in the general long-term debt account group.

The two customary types of general obligation bonds whose servicing is recorded in debt service funds are the following:

- *Serial bonds,* with principal payable in annual installments over the term of the bond issue.

- *Term bonds,* with principal payable in total on a fixed maturity date, generally from proceeds of an accumulated sinking fund.

Generally, legal requirements govern the establishment of debt service funds. In the absence of legal requirements or of a formal plan for accumulation of a sinking fund for repayment of a general obligation term bond, there may be no need to establish a debt service fund.

Journal Entries for Debt Service Fund

To illustrate the journal entries that are typical for a debt service fund, assume that the Town of Verdant Glen had only two general obligation bond issues outstanding during the fiscal year ended June 30, **2003:** A $100,000, 10% serial bond issue whose final annual installment of $10,000 was payable on January 1, 2003, and a $500,000, 7% term bond issue due July 1, 2022 (see page 765). The Town Council had authorized establishment of a debt service fund for the serial bonds. However, sinking fund accumulations on the term bonds were not required to begin until July 1, 2005; therefore, a debt service fund for those bonds was unnecessary during the fiscal year ended June 30, 2003.

Interest on both general obligation bond issues was payable each January 1 and July 1. Interest payments on the term bonds were recorded in the General Fund during the fiscal year ended June 30, 2003, and were included in expenditures of that fund, as illustrated on page 740. Interest payments on the serial bonds were made from the Debt Service Fund to a fiscal agent, for transfer to the bondholders.

The June 30, 2002, balance sheet of the Town of Verdant Glen Debt Service Fund for the serial bonds was as follows:

TOWN OF VERDANT GLEN DEBT SERVICE FUND	
Balance Sheet	
June 30, 2002	
Assets	
Cash	$342
Liabilities and Fund Balance	
Fund balance reserved for debt service	$342

Aggregate journal entries for the Town of Verdant Glen Debt Service Fund for the year ended June 30, *2003,* are as follows:

(Sink Fund)

Aggregate Journal Entries for Debt Service Fund of a Governmental Entity

TOWN OF VERDANT GLEN DEBT SERVICE FUND
Journal Entries

Cash	11,000	
Other Financing Sources *(GF)*		11,000
To record receipt of cash from General Fund for payment of serial bond principal ($10,000) and interest ($1,000) maturing on July 1, 2002, and Jan. 1, 2003.		
Cash with Fiscal Agent *(BANK)*	11,000	
Cash		11,000
To record payment of cash to bank trust department acting as fiscal agent for payment of serial bond principal and interest.		
Expenditures	11,000	
Matured Bonds Payable		10,000
Matured Interest Payable		1,000
To record expenditures for interest due July 1, 2002, and principal and interest due Jan. 1, 2003.		
Matured Bonds Payable	10,000	
Matured Interest Payable	1,000	
Cash with Fiscal Agent		11,000
To record fiscal agent's payments of bond principal and interest.		
Expenditures	342	
Cash		342
To record payment of fiscal agent for services during year ended June 30, 2003.		
Other Financing Sources	11,000	
Fund Balance Reserved for Debt Service	342	
Expenditures		11,342
To close fund on extinguishment of related serial bonds.		

Following are significant aspects of these journal entries.

1. There was no journal entry to record an annual budget. Generally, indentures for general obligation bonds provide sufficient safeguards (such as restricting the fund balance of the debt service fund solely for the payment of debt and related servicing costs), so that recording the budget in the Debt Service Fund is unnecessary. (Note, however, on page 733 of Chapter 17 that the General Fund's estimated other financing use for payment of $10,000 to the Debt Service Fund had been included in the General Fund's annual budget.)

2. The first journal entry is the counterpart of the General Fund journal entry no. 8 on page 740 in Chapter 17.

3. Expenditures for principal and interest payments of the Debt Service Fund are recorded only on the maturity dates of the obligations. Prior to the maturity dates, the liability for the bonds' ***principal*** is carried in the general long-term debt account group (see page 774). Because a debt service fund generally does not issue purchase orders, encumbrance accounting is not required.

4. The closing entry extinguishes all remaining ledger account balances of the Debt Service Fund, because the final serial principal payment had been made.

The modified accrual basis of accounting is appropriate for revenues of a debt service fund. Thus, any property taxes specifically earmarked for servicing of a governmental entity's general obligation bonds may be accrued as revenues in the debt service fund. The accounting for such a tax accrual is the same as that for the general fund.

For a term bond issue that requires the accumulation of a sinking fund, the journal entries for a debt service fund include the investment of cash in interest-bearing securities and the collection of interest. Under the modified accrual basis of accounting, interest revenue accrued on sinking fund investments at the end of the governmental entity's fiscal year is recognized in the accounting records of the debt service fund.

Financial Statements for Debt Service Fund

A balance sheet for a debt service fund is illustrated on page 768. There is no balance sheet for the Town of Verdant Glen Debt Service Fund on June 30, *2003*, because the fund had been extinguished. The statement of revenues, expenditures, and changes in fund balance for the Town of Verdant Glen Debt Service Fund for the year ended June 30, *2003*, is shown below:

Statement of Revenues, Expenditures, and Changes in Fund Balance of a Governmental Entity's Debt Service Fund

TOWN OF VERDANT GLEN DEBT SERVICE FUND Statement of Revenues, Expenditures, and Changes in Fund Balance For Year Ended June 30, 2003	
Expenditures:	
Principal retirement	$ 10,000
Interest and charges by fiscal agent	1,342
Total expenditures	$ 11,342
Excess (deficiency) of revenues over expenditures	$(11,342)

(continued)

TOWN OF VERDANT GLEN DEBT SERVICE FUND	
Statement of Revenues, Expenditures, and Changes in Fund Balance (concluded)	
For Year Ended June 30, 2003	
Other financing sources:	
Operating transfers in	11,000
Net change in fund balance	$ (342)
Fund balance, beginning of year	342
Fund balance, end of year	-0-

Permanent Funds

As indicated on page 731 of Chapter 17, **permanent funds** of a governmental entity report resources that are legally restricted so that **principal** cannot be used for programs such as ongoing maintenance of a public cemetery.[2] Because of their limited application, accounting and reporting for permanent funds are not illustrated in this chapter.

GENERAL CAPITAL ASSETS AND GENERAL LONG-TERM DEBT ACCOUNT GROUPS

The accounting standards for state and local governmental entities described in Chapter 17 (page 732) make it advisable for governmental entities to use **account groups** to record capital (plant) assets (including **infrastructure:** streets, sidewalks, bridges, and the like) and long-term debt of a governmental entity not recorded in a fund. A governmental entity's general capital assets and general long-term debt account groups are not **funds;** they are **memorandum accounts.** Their purpose is to provide in one record the governmental entity's plant assets and long-term liabilities that are not recorded in one of the governmental entity's funds. Plant assets are recorded in enterprise, trust, and internal service funds; bonds payable and other long-term liabilities are recorded in debt service and enterprise funds.

Accounting and Reporting for General Capital Assets Account Group

Plant assets in the general capital assets account group are recorded at their cost to the governmental entity or at their current fair value if donated to the governmental entity. The offsetting credit is to a memorandum ledger account such as Investment in General Capital Assets from (the source of the asset).

According to the Governmental Accounting Standards Board, except for certain infrastructure and inexhaustible (land and certain works of art) assets, depreciation **must** be recorded in the general capital assets account group, with a debit to the appropriate Investment in General Capital Assets ledger account and a credit to an

---

[2] *GASB Statement No. 34,* "Basic Financial Statements . . . for State and Local Governments (Norwalk: GASB, 1999), p. 25.

Accumulated Depreciation account.[3] When a plant asset carried in the general capital assets account group is disposed of by the governmental entity, the carrying amount of the asset is removed from the appropriate memorandum ledger accounts in the general capital assets account group; any proceeds are recognized as miscellaneous revenue or as other financing sources in the general fund, and no gain or loss is recognized.

Journal Entries for General Capital Assets Account Group

The following journal entries for the Town of Verdant Glen are typical of those for a governmental entity's general capital assets account group:

Journal Entries for General
Capital Assets Account Group
of a Governmental Entity

Memorandum

Example Sold Gain

Depreciation

TOWN OF VERDANT GLEN GENERAL CAPITAL ASSETS ACCOUNT GROUP
Journal Entries

Machinery and Equipment	126,400	
Investment in General Capital Assets from General Fund Revenues		126,400
To record acquisition of equipment by General Fund.		
Construction in Progress	378,000	
Investment in General Capital Assets from Capital Projects Funds		378,000
To record construction work in progress on high school addition.		
Land	500,000	
Buildings	800,000	
Investment in General Capital Assets from Gifts		1,300,000
To record, at current fair value, private citizen's gift of land and a building to be used as a public library.		
Investment in General Capital Assets from General Fund Revenues	20,000	
Accumulated Depreciation of Machinery and Equipment	70,000	
Machinery and Equipment		90,000
To record disposal of machinery and equipment.		
Investment in General Capital Assets from General Fund Revenues	40,000	
Investment in General Capital Assets from Capital Projects Funds	1,280,000	
Investment in General Capital Assets from Gifts	60,000	
Accumulated Depreciation of Infrastructure		1,000,000
Accumulated Depreciation of Buildings		240,000
Accumulated Depreciation of Machinery and Equipment		140,000
To recognize depreciation of infrastructure, buildings, and machinery and equipment for the year ended June 30, 2003.		

The first of the foregoing journal entries incorporates the assumption that equipment acquisitions were included in the expenditures of the Town of Verdant Glen General Fund for the year ended June 30, 2003 (see page 739); the second journal entry was made on June 30, 2003, to record accumulated cost of the construction project of the Town of Verdant Glen Capital Projects Fund (page 765); and the fourth journal

---

[3] Ibid., pars, 21 and 478.103.

entry incorporates the assumption that proceeds of disposal of machinery and equipment were included in revenues of the Town of Verdant Glen General Fund for the year ended June 30, 2003.

Required Disclosures for General Capital Assets

The Governmental Accounting Standards Board requires presentation of an analysis of changes in general capital assets of a governmental entity in a note to the financial statements discussed in Chapter 19.[4] The analysis of changes in general capital assets for the Town of Verdant Glen for the fiscal year ended June 30, 2003, is as follows (beginning-of-year and end-of-year balances are assumed):

	Balances, July 1, 2002	Additions	Retirements*	Balances, June 30, 2003
CHANGES IN TOWN OF VERDANT GLEN GENERAL CAPITAL ASSETS *For Year Ended June 30, 2003*				
General Capital Assets				
Infrastructure	$50,000,000			$50,000,000
Land	6,200,000	$ 500,000		6,700,000
Buildings	18,700,000	800,000		19,500,000
Machinery and equipment	720,000	126,400	90,000	756,400
Construction in progress		378,000		378,000
Totals	$75,620,000	$1,804,400	$ 90,000	$77,334,400
Accumulated Depreciation				
Infrastructure	$ 7,000,000	$1,000,000		$ 8,000,000
Buildings	1,460,000	240,000		1,700,000
Machinery and equipment	216,000	140,000	$ 70,000	286,000
Totals	$ 8,676,000	$1,380,000†	$ 70,000	$ 9,986,000
Investment in General Capital Assets				
From General Fund revenues	$10,424,000	$ 126,400	$ 60,000	$10,490,400
From Capital Projects Funds	52,618,000	378,000	1,280,000	51,716,000
From gifts	3,902,000	1,300,000	60,000	5,142,000
Totals	$66,944,000	$1,804,400	$1,400,000	$67,348,400

* For investment in general capital assets section, includes depreciation.
† Broken down by function in the statement of activities described in Chapter 19.

Accounting and Reporting for General Long-Term Debt Account Group

General obligation bonds of a governmental entity, both serial and term, and other long-term liabilities that are not recorded in an enterprise fund are recorded as memorandum credits in the general long-term debt account group. The offsetting memorandum debit entry is to the Amount to Be Provided ledger account. When cash and other assets for the ultimate payment of a bond issue or other long-term liabilities have been accumulated in a debt service fund, the Amount Available in Debt Service Fund ledger

[4] Ibid., par. 117.

account is debited and the Amount to Be Provided account is credited. When the bonds or other liabilities are paid by the debt service fund, the memorandum accounts are reversed in the general long-term debt account group in a closing entry at the end of the fiscal year.

Journal Entries for Long-Term Debt Account Group

The following journal entries for the Town of Verdant Glen General Long-Term Debt Account Group parallel the corresponding journal entries in the Debt Service Fund (page 769) and the Capital Projects Fund (page 765), respectively:

Journal Entries for General Long-Term Debt Account Group of a Governmental Entity

TOWN OF VERDANT GLEN GENERAL LONG-TERM DEBT ACCOUNT GROUP
Journal Entries

Amount Available in Debt Service Fund	10,000	
Amount to Be Provided		10,000
To record amount received by Debt Service Fund from General Fund for retirement of principal of general obligation serial bonds.		
Serial Bonds Payable	10,000	
Amount Available in Debt Service Fund		10,000
To record Debt Service Fund payment of 10% serial bonds on January 1, 2003.		
Amount to Be Provided	500,000	
Term Bonds Payable		500,000
To record issuance of 7% general obligation term bonds for construction of addition to high school.		

Required Disclosures for General Long-Term Debt

The Governmental Accounting Standards Board requires presentation of an analysis of changes in general long-term debt of a governmental entity in a note to the financial statements discussed in Chapter 19.[5] Following is an analysis of changes in general long-term debt of the Town of Verdant Glen for the year ended June 30, 2003:

CHANGES IN TOWN OF VERDANT GLEN GENERAL LONG-TERM DEBT
For Year Ended June 30, 2003

	Balances, July 1, 2002	Additions	Payments	Balances, June 30, 2003
Term Bonds				
7%, 20-year general obligation bonds due July 1, 2022		$500,000		$500,000
Serial Bonds				
10%, 10-year general obligation bonds, final installment due January 1, 2003	$10,000		$10,000	
Totals	$10,000	$500,000	$10,000	$500,000

---

[5] Ibid., par. 119.

Capital Leases of Governmental Entities

If a capital lease is executed by a governmental entity for property not recorded in a proprietary fund (internal service fund or enterprise fund), the property is recorded in the general capital assets account group and the lease liability is recorded in the general long-term debt account group, valued in accordance with the provisions of **FASB Statement No. 13**, "Accounting for Leases" (as amended and interpreted).[6] The periodic lease payments typically are included in expenditures of the general fund.

To illustrate accounting for a capital lease by a governmental entity, assume that on July 1, **2003**, the Town of Verdant Glen entered into a three-year capital lease for furniture and equipment for the library building donated to the town (see page 772). The minimum lease payments were $10,000, payable each July 1, 2003 through 2005. Title to the furniture and equipment was to be vested in the town on July 1, 2006. The town adopted the straight-line method of depreciation, a 10-year economic life, and no residual value for the furniture and equipment. The interest rate implicit in the lease, known to the town and less than the town's incremental borrowing rate, was 8%.

The following journal entries would be required for the capital lease for the three-year lease term:

Journal Entries for Governmental Entity's Capital Lease

TOWN OF VERDANT GLEN
Journal Entries for Capital Lease

In General Fund

2003
July 1 Expenditures 10,000
      Cash 10,000
    To record first lease payment on three-year capital lease for library furniture and equipment.

2004
July 1 Expenditures ($1,427 interest + $8,573 principal) 10,000
      Cash 10,000
    To record second lease payment on three-year capital lease for library furniture and equipment.

2005
July 1 Expenditures ($740 interest + $9,260 principal) 10,000
      Cash 10,000
    To record third lease payment on three-year capital lease for library furniture and equipment.

In General Long-Term Debt Account Group

2003
July 1 Amount to Be Provided ($10,000 × 2.783265*) 27,833
      Liability under Capital Lease (net) 27,833
    To record liability under three-year capital lease for library furniture and equipment.

* Present value of **annuity due** of 1 for three periods at 8%.

(continued)

[6] *Codification*, par. L20.115.

TOWN OF VERDANT GLEN
Journal Entries for Capital Lease (concluded)

1 Liability under Capital Lease (net)	10,000	
Amount to Be Provided		10,000
To record General Fund payment of first lease payment on three-year capital lease for library furniture and equipment.		
2004		
July 1 Liability under Capital Lease (net)	8,573	
Amount to Be Provided		8,573
To record General Fund payment of second lease payment on three-year capital lease for library furniture and equipment.		
2005		
July 1 Liability under Capital Lease (net)	9,260	
Amount to Be Provided		9,260
To record General Fund payment of third lease payment on three-year capital lease for library furniture and equipment.		
In General Capital Assets Account Group		
2003		
July 1 Leased Furniture and Equipment—Capital Lease	27,833	
Investment in General Capital Assets from General Fund Revenues		27,833
To record acquisition of library furniture and equipment under three-year capital lease.		
2004		
June 30 Investment in General Capital Assets from General Fund Revenues ($27,833 ÷ 10)	2,783	
Leased Furniture and Equipment—Capital Lease		2,783
To recognize depreciation of leased library furniture and equipment for the year ended June 30, 2004.		

(The same depreciation journal entries would be prepared on June 30, 2005, through June 30, 2013.)

Accounting for Special Assessment Bonds

In *GASB Statement No. 6,* "Accounting and Financial Reporting for Special Assessments," the Governmental Accounting Standards Board terminated the use of *special assessment funds* to account for the construction of public improvements financed by special assessments against selected property owners and by related special assessment bonds.[7] Instead, special revenue funds, capital projects funds, and debt service funds are to be used, as appropriate, for the transactions and events related to such construction projects.

With respect to special assessment bonds, which sometimes are issued by a governmental entity to finance construction projects pending the receipt of special assessments payable in annual installments, the GASB provided the following standards:

[7] Ibid., Sec. S40.113.

    b. Special assessment debt for which the government is obligated in some manner . . .
should be reported as general long-term liabilities in the government-wide statement
of net assets, except for the portion, if any, that is directly related to and expected to
be paid from proprietary funds.

       (1) The portion of the special assessment debt that will be repaid from property
owner assessments should be reported as "special assessment debt with governmental commitment."

       (2) The portion of special assessment debt that will be repaid from general re-
sources of the government (the public benefit portion, or the amount assessed
against government-owned property) should be reported like other general long-
term liabilities.

       (3) The portion of special assessment debt that is directly related to and expected to
be paid from proprietary funds should be reported as liabilities of those funds in
the proprietary fund statement of net assets. Liabilities directly related to and
expected to be repaid from proprietary funds should also be reported in the government-wide statement of net assets.

    c. Special assessment debt for which the government is not obligated in any manner
should not be displayed in the government's financial statements.[8]

To illustrate application of the foregoing standards, assume that on July 1, *2003,* the
Town Council of Verdant Glen enacted a special assessment for paving streets and installing sidewalks in a section of the town. The total assessment was $250,000, payable
by the assessed property owners in five annual installments, beginning July 1, 2003.
Interest on unpaid balances at 10% a year was payable annually by the assessed property owners, beginning July 1, 2004. To help finance the cost of the construction project, the Town Council authorized the issuance on July 1, 2003, of $200,000 face amount,
four-year, 8% special assessment bonds, payable $50,000 a year plus interest payable
annually, beginning July 1, 2004. The Town Council authorized the establishment of a
special revenue fund and a capital projects fund to account for the construction project. Under the terms of the bond indenture for the special assessment bonds, the Town
of Verdant Glen was obligated to pay the special assessment bonds at maturity if the
property owners defaulted on their special assessments and proceeds of lien foreclo-
sures on the property were insufficient.

The following journal entries are required on July 1, *2003,* the date of the special
assessment:

**Journal Entries for
Governmental Entity
Construction Project Financed
by Special Assessment**

**TOWN OF VERDANT GLEN
Journal Entries for Construction Project Financed by Special Assessment**

In Special Revenue Fund (different from that illustrated on pages 761 to 764):		
Special Assessments Receivable—Current	50,000	
Special Assessments Receivable—Deferred	200,000	
Revenues		50,000
Deferred Revenues		200,000
To record special assessment levied on property owners benefited by paving and sidewalk project; special assessments receivable and related revenues applicable to year ended June 30, 2003, are current, and the balance is deferred.		

(continued)

[8] *GASB Statement No. 34,* pp. 391–392, pars., 116b, c.

TOWN OF VERDANT GLEN
Journal Entries for Construction Project Financed by Special Assessment (concluded)

Cash	50,000	
Special Assessments Receivable—Current		50,000
To record receipt of current special assessment payments.		
Other Financing Uses	50,000	
Cash		50,000
To record transfer of cash for financing of paving and sidewalk project to Capital Projects Fund established for that purpose.		
In Capital Projects Fund (different from that illustrated on pages 764 to 767):		
Cash	50,000	
Other Financing Sources		50,000
To record receipt of cash from Special Revenue Fund for proceeds of current installment of special assessments.		
Cash	195,776	
Other Financing Uses: Discount on Bonds Issued	4,224	
Other Financing Sources: Bonds Issued		200,000
To record proceeds of $200,000 face amount of four-year, 8% special assessment bonds to yield 9%.		
In General Long-Term Debt Account Group (same as that illustrated on pages 773 to 774):		
Amount to Be Provided	200,000	
Special Assessment Bonds Payable		200,000
To record issuance of 8% special assessment bonds for paving and sidewalk project; the town is obligated to honor deficiencies on payment of the bonds.		

Some significant features of the foregoing journal entries are as follows:

1. The capital budget for the paving and sidewalks project is not entered in the accounting records of either the Special Revenue Fund or the Capital Projects Fund. The Town Council's approval of the special assessment and the related bonds provides adequate control.

2. Because the Special Revenue Fund will collect the special assessments as they become current, that fund also will service the special assessment bonds as they become payable. Further, the Special Revenue Fund will accrue interest receivable (at 10%) on the unpaid special assessments receivable, and interest payable (at 8%) on the special assessment bonds.

3. On June 30, 2004, 2005, 2006, and 2007, the Special Revenue Fund will prepare the following journal entry:

Special Assessments Receivable—Current	50,000	
Deferred Revenues	50,000	
Special Assessments Receivable—Deferred		50,000
Revenues		50,000
To transfer special assessment installment receivable in next fiscal year and related revenues to the current category from the deferred category.		

4. The special assessment bonds and related interest are payable serially over a four-year period by the Special Revenue Fund, from proceeds of the annual collections of special assessments and related interest. Accordingly, the present value of the 8% special assessment bonds ($195,776) at the 9% yield rate is computed as follows:

Computation of Present Value of Special Assessment Bonds Principal and interest due July 1, 2004 [($50,000 + $16,000) × 0.917431*]	$ 60,550
Principal and interest due July 1, 2005 [($50,000 + $12,000) × 0.841680*]	52,184
Principal and interest due July 1, 2006 [($50,000 + $8,000) × 0.772183*]	44,787
Principal and interest due July 1, 2007 [($50,000 + $4,000) × 0.708425*]	38,255
Present value (proceeds) of 8% special assessment bonds at 9% yield rate	$195,776

* From present value tables.

Review Questions

1. Describe the taxes, fees, or other revenues of a governmental entity that often are accounted for in special revenue funds.

2. The following journal entry was prepared for the Town of Groman Special Revenue Fund, established to account for special assessments on selected property owners of the nearby Village of Angelus:

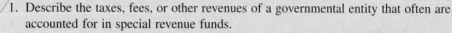

Expenditures	42,000	
Payable to General Fund		42,000
To record billings from General Fund for reimbursement of expenditures for street cleaning and streetlight maintenance for residents of the Village of Angelus.		

EXPEND

LT DEBT

What ledger account does the Town of Groman General Fund credit to offset the $42,000 debit to Receivable from Special Revenue Fund? Explain.

3. How are proceeds of general obligation bonds issued at face amount by a governmental entity to finance a construction project accounted for in a capital projects fund? Explain.

4. Is a separate debt service fund established for every issue of general obligation bonds issued by a governmental entity? Explain.

5. The following journal entry (explanation omitted) appeared in the Charter County Debt Service Fund:

Cash with Fiscal Agent	83,000	
Cash		83,000

What is the probable explanation for this journal entry? Explain.

6. Is the recognition of depreciation of plant assets appropriate for a governmental entity's general capital assets account group? Explain.

7. Explain the use of the Investment in General Capital Assets from Gifts ledger account of a governmental entity's general capital assets account group.

8. Is a balance sheet issued for a governmental entity's general capital assets account group? Explain.

9. The following journal entry appeared in the accounting records of the Village of Marvell General Long-Term Debt Account Group:

Amount to Be Provided	25,000	
Amount Available in Debt Service Fund		25,000

To record amount received by Debt Service Fund from General Fund
for retirement of principal of general obligation serial bonds.

Is the foregoing journal entry prepared correctly? Explain.

10. Explain how each of the following accounting units of a governmental entity is affected by a capital lease for fire engines of the fire department: general fund, general long-term debt account group, general capital assets account group.

11. Under what circumstances, if any, is a liability for special assessment bonds recorded in a governmental entity's general long-term debt account group? Explain.

Exercises

(Exercise 18.1)   Select the best answer for each of the following multiple-choice questions:

1. May funds other than the general fund be established by a governmental entity in response to:

	Legislative Action?	Executive Action?
a.	Yes	Yes
b.	Yes	No
c.	No	Yes
d.	No	No

2. The governmental funds of a governmental entity include all the following except:

   a. Special revenue funds.
   b. Agency funds.
   c. Debt service funds.
   d. Capital projects funds.

3. An example of a governmental fund of a governmental entity is:

   a. An enterprise fund.
   b. A special revenue fund.
   c. An agency fund.
   d. None of the foregoing.

4. The type of governmental fund of a governmental entity whose accounting most resembles that of the entity's general fund is a:

   a. Capital projects fund.
   b. Debt service fund.
   c. Special revenue fund.
   d. Special expenditures fund.

5. The governmental funds of a governmental entity for which the statement of revenues, expenditures, and changes in fund balance typically displays both budgeted and actual amounts are:

   a. Special revenue funds.
   b. Capital projects funds.
   c. Debt service funds.
   d. None of the foregoing.

6. A capital projects fund of a governmental entity is:
   a. A governmental fund.
   b. A proprietary fund.
   c. A fiduciary fund.
   d. An account group.

7. A Fund Balance Record for Encumbrances ledger account most likely is appropriate for a governmental entity's:
   a. Special revenue fund.
   b. Capital projects fund.
   c. Debt service fund.
   d. Three foregoing governmental funds.

8. To record the issuance of general obligation bonds at face amount to finance a governmental entity's capital project fund, the accountant for that fund credits:
   a. Revenues.
   b. Other Financing Sources.
   c. Unreserved and Undesignated Fund Balance.
   d. General Obligation Bonds Payable.

9. Is an annual budget always recorded by a governmental entity's:

	Special Revenue Funds?	Capital Projects Funds?	Debt Service Funds?
a.	Yes	Yes	Yes
b.	Yes	No	Yes
c.	Yes	Yes	No
d.	Yes	No	No

10. A governmental entity's general capital assets account group may be used for all plant assets of the governmental entity not recorded in:
    a. Capital projects funds.
    b. Trust funds.
    c. The general fund.
    d. Plant asset funds.

11. Are plant assets of a governmental entity accounted for in the entity's:

	General Fund?	Capital Projects Funds?
a.	Yes	Yes
b.	Yes	No
c.	No	Yes
d.	No	No

12. Excluded from the general capital assets account group of a governmental entity are:
    a. Donated plant assets.
    b. Plant assets constructed with resources of capital projects funds.
    c. Infrastructure.
    d. None of the foregoing.

13. A governmental entity's Amount to Be Provided ledger account is included in the accounting records of the entity's:
    a. Debt service funds.
    b. Capital projects funds.

    c. General long-term debt account group.

    d. General capital assets account group.

14. The typical balances of the following ledger accounts of a governmental entity's general long-term debt account group are:

	Amount Available in Debt Service Fund	*Amount to Be Provided*
a.	Debit	Credit
b.	Credit	Debit
c.	Debit	Debit
d.	Credit	Credit

15. Are journal entries for a capital lease (for property not recorded in a proprietary fund) entered into by a governmental entity typically required in the entity's:

	General Fund?	*General Long-Term Debt Account Group?*	*General Capital Assets Account Group?*
a.	No	Yes	Yes
b.	Yes	No	Yes
c.	Yes	Yes	No
d.	Yes	Yes	Yes

16. For the transactions and events related to construction of public improvements financed by special assessments, does a governmental entity use a:

	Special Revenue Fund?	*Capital Projects Fund?*	*Debt Service Fund?*
a.	Yes	Yes	Yes
b.	Yes	Yes	No
c.	No	Yes	No
d.	No	Yes	Yes

(Exercise 18.2) On July 1, 2002, property taxes totaling $480,000, of which $1\frac{1}{2}\%$ was estimated to be uncollectible, were levied by the County of Larchmont Special Revenue Fund. Property taxes collected by the Special Revenue Fund during July 2002 totaled $142,700.

    Prepare journal entries for the County of Larchmont Special Revenue Fund for the foregoing transactions and events.

(Exercise 18.3) On July 1, 2002, the City of Garbo Capital Projects Fund received the proceeds of a $1 million face amount, 6% five-year serial bond issue, $200,000 principal plus interest payable annually, to finance the construction of a new elementary school. The bonds were issued to yield 8%.

CHECK FIGURE

Present value of bonds, $949,636.

    Prepare a working paper to compute the proceeds (present value) of the City of Garbo 6% serial bonds on July 1, 2002.

(Exercise 18.4) On July 1, 2002, the County of Pinecrest issued at face amount $1,200,000 of 30-year, 5% general obligation term bonds, interest payable each January 1 and July 1, to finance the construction of a public health center.

    Prepare journal entries on July 1, 2002, to record the foregoing transaction for all County of Pinecrest funds or account groups affected. Identify the funds or account groups.

(Exercise 18.5) On April 30, 2002, the fiscal agent for the Town of Wallen Debt Service Fund paid the final serial payment of $50,000 on the town's 8% general obligation bonds, together with semiannual interest. The Debt Service Fund had provided sufficient cash to the fiscal agent a few days earlier.

Prepare a journal entry for the Town of Wallen Debt Service Fund to record the fiscal agent's payment of bond principal and interest on April 30, 2002.

(Exercise 18.6) On March 18, 2002, the Bucolic Township General Fund transferred $140,000 to the Debt Service Fund for the semiannual $100,000 serial maturity (payable March 31, 2002) on $800,000 face amount of outstanding 10% general obligation bonds, plus interest of $40,000.

Prepare journal entries (omit explanations) *on March 18, 2002 only,* for the appropriate funds and account group of Bucolic Township.

(Exercise 18.7) Among the activities of Nemo County for the fiscal year beginning July 1, 2002, and ending June 30, 2003, was the following:

Sept. 1, 2002 Acquired for cash, from proceeds of general tax revenues, equipment costing $80,000 (the related purchase order was for $79,600). The equipment was to be used by the general government of Nemo County. The county uses encumbrance accounting.

Prepare journal entries (omit explanations) for the foregoing activity of Nemo County. Identify by initials the funds or account groups (for example, GF, SRF, CPF, GCAAG) in which the journal entries are recorded.

(Exercise 18.8) On March 24, 2002, Wildwood Village sold to a scrap dealer for $40,000 an old fire engine with a cost of $200,000 and carrying amount of $20,000 in Wildwood's general capital assets account group. The $40,000 cash was received by Wildwood's general fund, which simultaneously acquired another fire engine for $450,000 cash, compared with the $446,000 amount of the purchase order that had been issued on February 10, 2002. The village uses encumbrance accounting.

Prepare journal entries (omit explanations) for Wildwood Village's general fund and general capital assets account group *on March 24, 2002 only.*

(Exercise 18.9) On June 30, 2002, the end of the fiscal year, the following journal entry was prepared by the accountant for the Town of Backwoods Town Hall Capital Projects Fund:

Expenditures	950,000	
Vouchers Payable		950,000
To record first progress billings of architect and contractor for town hall under construction.		

Prepare a journal entry on June 30, 2002, for the Town of Backwoods General Capital Assets Account Group.

(Exercise 18.10) A citizen of Hays City donated 10 acres of undeveloped land to the city for a future school site. The donor's cost of the land was $555,000. The current fair value of the land was $850,000 on the date of the gift.

Prepare a journal entry for the appropriate fund or account group of Hays City to record the gift. Identify the fund or account group.

(Exercise 18.11) On April 30, 2002, the Town of Noblisse General Fund received the $30,000 proceeds from disposal of a computer that had a carrying amount of $40,000. The General Fund had acquired the computer three years earlier at a cost of $100,000.

Prepare journal entries on April 30, 2002, to record the foregoing transaction for all Town of Noblisse funds or account groups affected. Identify the funds or account groups.

(Exercise 18.12)

On July 1, 2002, the City of Rogell entered into a five-year capital lease for fire-fighting equipment, with lease payments of $20,000 due each July 1, 2002 through 2006. Title to the equipment was to pass to the City of Rogell on June 30, 2007. The interest rate implicit in the lease, known to Rogell and less than Rogell's incremental borrowing rate, was 8%.

Prepare journal entries on July 1, 2002, to record the foregoing transaction for all City of Rogell funds or account groups affected. Identify the funds or account groups.

(Exercise 18.13)

On July 1, 2002, the Town of Warren issued $600,000 face amount of three-year, 9% special assessment bonds, payable $200,000 a year plus interest, at a 10% yield rate, to finance a street improvement project. The town was "obligated in some manner" for the bonds.

Prepare journal entries on July 1, 2002, to record the foregoing transaction for all Town of Warren funds or account groups affected. Identify the funds or account groups.

(Exercise 18.14)

The ledger accounts listed below are included frequently in the accounting records of governmental entities.

Ledger Account	*Fund or Account Group*
F, D 1 Bonds Payable	a General fund
A, C, B 2 Fund Balance Reserved for Encumbrances	b Special revenue fund
F 3 Amount to Be Provided	c Capital projects fund
E 4 Equipment	d Debt service fund
B, A 5 Appropriations	e General capital assets account group
A, B 6 Estimated Revenues	f General long-term debt account group
A, B 7 Taxes Receivable—Current	

Select the appropriate identifying letter to indicate the governmental entity fund or account group in which these ledger accounts might properly appear. An account might appear in more than one fund or account group.

Cases

(Case 18.1)

The controller of the city of Darby has asked your advice on the accounting for an installment contract payable by the city. The contract covers the cost of installing automatic gates, currency receptacles, and ticket dispensers for the 20 city-owned parking lots in the downtown district. Installation of the self-parking equipment resulted in a decrease in the required number of parking attendants for the city-owned parking lots and a reduction in the salaries and related expenditures of the City of Darby General Fund.

The contract is payable monthly in amounts equal to 40% of the month's total parking revenue for the 20 lots. Because no legal or contractual provisions require the City of Darby to establish an enterprise fund for the parking lots, both parking revenue and parking-lot maintenance and repairs expenditures are to be recorded in the City of Darby General Fund. The parking-lot sites are to be carried at cost in the City of Darby General Capital Assets Account Group.

The city controller describes the plans for accounting for payments on the contract as follows: Monthly payments under the contract are to be debited to the Expenditures ledger account of the General Fund and to the debt service section of the expenditures subsidiary ledger. The payments also will be recorded in the General Capital Assets Account Group as additions to the Improvements Other than Buildings ledger account. A note to the General Fund balance sheet will disclose the unpaid balance of the installment contract at the end of each fiscal year. The unpaid balance of the contract will not be included in the General Long-Term Debt Account Group because the contract does not represent a liability for borrowing of cash, as do the bond and other long-term debt liabilities of the City of Darby.

Instructions

What is your advice to the controller of the City of Darby? Explain.

(Case 18.2) The chief accountant of the City of DelVille requests your advice on how to account for two special assessments, which the city has never before enacted. One special assessment was to finance street lighting and maintenance services to selected residents of the nearby Town of Minimus; the other was to finance construction of a new city hall for the City of DelVille. Special assessment bonds were not to be issued.

Instructions

What is your advice to the chief accountant of the City of DelVille? Explain.

(Case 18.3) James Milton, the newly elected controller of Wilburtown, a municipality with a population of approximately 120,000, is astonished that Wilburtown's accounting records include 25 special revenue funds. He requests you, a member of the newly appointed independent auditors of Wilburtown, which had never before been audited, for assistance in determining which—if any—of the special revenue funds might be closed, with their revenues and related expenditures to be accounted for in the Wilburtown General Fund. Before responding to Milton, you decide to consult Sections 1300.105 through 1300.108 of *Codification of Governmental Accounting and Financial Reporting Standards* (Norwalk: GASB, 2000).

Instructions

After undertaking the consulting described above, prepare a memorandum to James Milton in answer to his question.

(Case 18.4) In a classroom discussion of accounting procedures for the general long-term debt account group of a governmental entity, Professor Lisa Newton posed the following question to her students:

> In the journal entry to provide for the liability under a general obligation term bond payable in the general long-term debt account group, should there also be a debit to Amount to Be Provided and a credit to Interest to Be Paid for the total interest obligation under the bonds? Explain your views.

Instructions

If you were a student in Professor Newton's class, how would you answer her question?

(Case 18.5) The City Council of Martinburg has asked you, the engagement manager of the CPA firm that has just concluded the audit of the city's financial statements for the fiscal year ended June 30, 2003, to explain the negative balance of the unreserved and undesignated fund balance in the following balance sheet:

CITY OF MARTINBURG CLINIC CAPITAL PROJECTS FUND
Balance Sheet
June 30, 2003

Assets

Cash	$ 24,000
Investments, at fair value	382,000
Total assets	$406,000

Liabilities and Fund Balance

Liabilities:		
Vouchers payable		$ 10,000
Contracts payable		60,000
Total liabilities		$ 70,000
Fund balance:		
Reserved for encumbrances	$480,000	
Unreserved and undesignated	(144,000)	336,000
Total liabilities and fund balance		$406,000

Your firm's audit working papers show that the clinic was 80% complete on June 30, 2003.

Instructions

How would you respond to the City Council's request? Explain.

Problems

(Problem 18.1) During the fiscal year ended June 30, 2003, Ridge City had the following plant asset transactions and events, among others:

2002

Oct. 31 General Fund acquired for cash equipment costing $20,000.

Dec. 10 A citizen donated land and a building with current fair values of $100,000 and $500,000, respectively.

2003

June 30 Construction in progress expenditures in the Capital Projects Fund totaled $970,000 at fiscal year-end.

30 Depreciation of buildings—$250,000—and of equipment—$40,000— was attributable to plant assets acquired as follows: From General Fund revenues—$60,000; from Capital Projects Funds—$140,000; from gifts—$90,000.

30 Depreciation of infrastructure—$850,000—was attributable to assets acquired from capital projects funds.

Instructions

Prepare journal entries for the Ridge City General Capital Assets Account Group for the foregoing transactions and events.

(Problem 18.2) Shown on page 787 is the trial balance of the Town of Dilbey Capital Projects Fund at the end of its first year of operations.

TOWN OF DILBEY CAPITAL PROJECTS FUND
Trial Balance
June 30, 2003

	Debit	Credit
Cash	$ 276,036	
Vouchers payable		$ 101,000
Fund balance reserved for encumbrances		227,600
Revenues (interest on investments)		30,000
Other financing sources: Bonds issued		1,000,000
Expenditures: Construction contracts	575,200	
Expenditures: Engineering and other	180,800	
Other financing uses: Discount on bonds issued	98,964	
Encumbrances	227,600	
Totals	$1,358,600	$1,358,600

Instructions

Prepare financial statements for the Town of Dilbey Capital Projects Fund for the fiscal year ended June 30, 2003.

(Problem 18.3) On July 1, 2002, the Town of Logan began two construction projects: (1) an addition to the town hall and (2) a curbing construction project financed with a special assessment. The special assessment totaled $400,000, payable by the assessed citizens in five annual installments beginning July 1, 2002, together with interest at 8% a year on the unpaid assessments. Other details for the fiscal year ended June 30, 2003, were as follows:

	Addition to Town Hall	Curbing Construction Project
Bonds issued July 1, 2002, at face amount	$600,000 face amount, 7%, 20-year general obligation term bonds, interest payable Jan. 1 and July 1	$320,000 face amount 7½%, 4-year special assessment bonds, $80,000 principal and interest payable each July 1
Total encumbrances	$530,200	$384,600
Total expenditures	$380,600	$360,300
Encumbrances applicable to expenditures	$382,100	$354,700
Total cash paid on vouchers payable	$322,700	$347,600

Instructions

Prepare journal entries for the fiscal year ended June 30, 2003, including year-end accruals but excluding closing entries, for (a) the Town of Logan Town Hall Capital Projects Fund and (b) the Town of Logan Special Revenue Fund (established to account for the proceeds of the special assessment). Do not prepare journal entries for the Town of Logan Curbing Construction Capital Projects Fund.

(Problem 18.4) Among the journal entries of the General Fund of Webster Village for the fiscal year ended June 30, 2003, were the following:

2002

July 3 Other Financing Uses 15,000

    Payable to Capital Projects Fund 15,000

To record liability to Capital Projects Fund for operating transfer to make up that fund's cash deficiency.

Aug. 31 Other Financing Uses 210,000

    Cash 210,000

To record transfer to Debt Service Fund for maturing principal and final six-months' interest payment on $200,000 face amount, 20-year, 10% general obligation term bonds issued Aug. 31, 1982.

Nov. 30 Expenditures 60,000

    Vouchers Payable 60,000

To record expenditure for new computer for village. Straight-line depreciation to be used; economic life is five years, with no residual value.

30 Fund Balance Reserved for Encumbrances 58,800

    Encumbrances 58,800

To reverse encumbrance applicable to computer.

2003

Jan. 2 Other Financing Uses 20,000

    Cash 20,000

To record operating transfer to Special Revenue Fund for village's share of street-paving project cost in Westside section; remaining $180,000 estimated cost is to be financed by a special assessment.

Instructions

Prepare journal entries for the fiscal year ended June 30, 2003, in the other funds or account groups affected by the foregoing transactions or events of the General Fund of Webster Village. Identify the affected funds or account groups. Include a journal entry for depreciation of the computer.

(Problem 18.5) Among the activities of Calabash County for the fiscal year beginning July 1, 2002, and ending June 30, 2003, were the following:

2002

July 1 Approved the annual budget for the Gasoline Tax Special Revenue Fund as follows: Appropriations, $600,000; estimated revenues, $640,000.

5 Executed a contract for the construction of a new public library at a total cost of $5 million.

Aug. 1 Authorized a special assessment of $400,000 on residents of the North Subdivision for construction of sidewalks. The special assessment, which was payable in five annual installments beginning October 1, 2002, with interest at 9% a year on the unpaid installments, was to be accounted for in the Special Assessment Special Revenue Fund.

Sept. 1   Acquired from proceeds of general tax revenues equipment costing $20,000 (the related purchase order was for $19,600). The equipment was to be used by the general government of Calabash County, which does not depreciate plant assets in the General Capital Assets Account Group. The county uses encumbrance accounting.

Instructions

Prepare journal entries for the fiscal year ended June 30, 2003, for the foregoing transactions or events of Calabash County. Identify the funds or account groups in which the journal entries are recorded.

(Problem 18.6)

On July 1, 2002, the City of Arlette, which records depreciation on plant assets in the General Capital Assets Account Group, leased under a three-year term capital lease a computer with a four-year economic life and no residual value. Lease payments of $3,000 were payable by the General Fund on July 1, 2002, 2003, and 2004; a bargain purchase option of $500 was payable on June 30, 2005. The interest rate implicit in the lease, 9%, was less than the city's incremental borrowing rate and was known to the City Council.

Instructions

Prepare journal entries with respect to the capital lease for the City of Arlette for the three fiscal years ended June 30, 2005, in all affected funds and account groups. Identify the affected funds or account groups. The City of Arlette depreciates plant assets by the straight-line method.

(Problem 18.7)

The City of Ordway's fiscal year ends on June 30. During the year ended June 30, 2003, the city authorized the construction of a new library and the issuance of general obligation term bonds to finance the construction of the library. The authorization imposed the following restrictions:

1. Construction cost was not to exceed $5 million.
2. Annual interest rate was not to exceed 10%.

The city does not record capital budgets, but other appropriate ledger accounts, included for encumbrance accounting, are maintained. The following transactions or events relating to the financing and constructing of the library occurred during the fiscal year ended June 30, 2004:

(1) On July 1, 2003, the city issued $5 million of 30-year, 9% general obligation term bonds for $5,100,000. The semiannual interest dates were June 30 and December 31.

(2) On July 3, 2003, the Library Capital Projects Fund invested $4,900,000 in short-term notes. This investment was at face amount, with no accrued interest. Interest on cash invested by the Library Capital Projects Fund must be transferred to the Library Debt Service Fund. During the year ending June 30, 2004, estimated interest to be earned was $140,000.

(3) On July 5, 2003, the City signed a construction-type contract with Premier Construction Company to build the library for $4,980,000.

(4) On January 15, 2004, the Library Capital Projects Fund received $3,040,000, from the maturity of short-term notes acquired on July 3, 2003. The cost of these notes was $3 million. The interest of $40,000 was transferred to the Library Debt Service Fund.

(5) On January 20, 2004, Premier Construction Company billed the City $3 million for work performed on the new library. The contract calls for 10% retention until

final inspection and acceptance of the building. The Library Capital Projects Fund paid $2,700,000 to Premier.

(6) On June 30, 2004, the accountant for the Library Capital Projects Fund prepared adjusting and closing entries.

Instructions

a. Prepare journal entries for the fiscal year ended June 30, 2004, for the foregoing transactions or events of the City of Ordway Library Capital Projects Fund. Use the following ledger account titles:

Cash

Encumbrances

Expenditures

Fund Balance Reserved for Encumbrances

Interest Receivable

Investments

Other Financing Sources

Payable to Library Debt Service Fund

Unreserved and Undesignated Fund Balance

Vouchers Payable

Do not record journal entries in any other fund or account group.

b. Prepare a balance sheet for the City of Ordway Library Capital Projects Fund on June 30, 2004.

(Problem 18.8) In a special election held on May 1, 2002, the citizens of the City of Wilmont approved a $10 million issue of 20-year, 8% general obligation term bonds maturing in 2022. The proceeds of the bonds will be used to help finance the construction of a new civic center. The total cost of the project was estimated at $15 million. The remaining $5 million was to be financed by an irrevocable state grant, which has been awarded. A capital projects fund was established to account for this project and was designated the Civic Center Capital Projects Fund.

The following transactions and events occurred during the fiscal year beginning July 1, 2002, and ending June 30, 2003:

(1) On July 1, the General Fund loaned $500,000 (noninterest-bearing) to the Civic Center Capital Projects Fund for defraying engineering and other costs.

(2) Preliminary engineering and planning costs of $320,000 were paid to Akron Company. There had been no encumbrance for this cost.

(3) On December 1, the bonds were issued to yield 9%. Interest was payable each June 1 and December 1, through 2022.

(4) On March 15, a contract for $12 million was entered into with Carlson Construction Company for the major part of the project.

(5) Purchase orders were placed for material estimated to cost $55,000. Encumbrance accounting was used.

(6) On April 1, a partial payment of $2,500,000 was received from the state government.

(7) The material that was ordered previously was received at a cost of $51,000 and paid for.

(8) On June 15, a progress billing of $2 million was received from Carlson Construction Company for work done on the project. In accordance with the contract, the city withheld 6% of any billing until the project was completed.

(9) The General Fund was repaid the $500,000 previously loaned.

Instructions

Prepare general journal entries to record the foregoing transactions and events of the Civic Center Capital Projects Fund for the period July 1, 2002, through June 30, 2003, and the closing entries on June 30, 2003. Omit explanations for the journal entries. Use the following ledger account titles in the journal entries:

Cash	Other Financing Uses
Encumbrances	Payable to General Fund
Expenditures	Receivable from State Government
Fund Balance Reserved for	Revenues
Encumbrances	Unreserved and Undesignated Fund Balance
Other Financing Sources	Vouchers Payable

(Problem 18.9) The following deficit budget was proposed for 2002 for the Angelus School District General Fund:

ANGELUS SCHOOL DISTRICT GENERAL FUND Annual Budget For Year Ending December 31, 2002	
Fund balance, Jan. 1, 2002	$128,000
Revenues:	
Property taxes	112,000
Investment interest	4,000
Total	$244,000
Expenditures:	
Operating	$120,000
County treasurer's fees	1,120
Bond interest	50,000
Projected fund balance, Dec. 31, 2002	72,880
Total	$244,000

A general obligation bond issue of the School District had been proposed in 2001. The proceeds were to be used for a new school. There are no other outstanding bond issues. Information about the bond issue follows:

Principal amount	$1,000,000
Interest rate	$7\frac{1}{2}\%$
Bonds dated	Jan. 1, 2002
Interest payable	Jan. 1 and July 1, beginning July 1, 2002
Maturity	Serially at the rate of $1000,000 a year, starting Jan. 1, 2004.

The School District uses a separate bank account for each fund. The General Fund trial balance on December 31, 2001, follows:

ANGELUS SCHOOL DISTRICT GENERAL FUND
Trial Balance
December 31, 2001

	Debit	Credit
Cash	$ 28,000	
Short-term investments—U.S. Treasury 6% bonds, interest payable on May 1 and Nov. 1	100,000	
Unreserved and undesignated fund balance		$128,000
Totals	$128,000	$128,000

The county treasurer collects the property taxes and withholds a fee of 1% on all collections. The transactions and events for 2002 were as follows:

Jan. 1 The proposed budget was adopted, the general obligation bond issue was authorized, and the property taxes were levied.

Feb. 28 Net property tax receipts from county treasurer, $49,500, were deposited.

Apr. 1 General obligation bonds were issued at 101 plus accrued interest. It was directed that the premium be used for payment of interest by the General Fund.

2 The School District paid $147,000 for the new school site.

3 A contract for $850,000 for the new school was approved. Encumbrance accounting was used.

May 1 Interest was received on short-term investments.

July 1 Interest was paid on bonds.

Aug. 31 Net property tax receipts from county treasurer, $59,400, were deposited.

Nov. 1 Payment on new school construction contract, $200,000, was made.

1 Interest was received on short-term investments.

Dec. 31 Operating expenditures during the year were $115,000. (Disregard vouchering and encumbrances.)

Instructions
Prepare journal entries for Angelus School District to record the foregoing Year 2002 transactions and events in the following funds or account groups. (Closing entries are not required.)

a. General Fund.

b. Capital Projects Fund.

c. General Capital Assets Account Group.

d. General Long-Term Debt Account Group.

Angelus School District does not use a Debt Service Fund.

Chapter Nineteen

Governmental Entities: Proprietary Funds, Fiduciary Funds, and Comprehensive Annual Financial Report

Scope of Chapter

In this chapter, the coverage of accounting and reporting for governmental entities is completed with the discussion and illustration of (1) accounting and reporting for proprietary funds and fiduciary funds, and (2) the comprehensive annual financial report (CAFR) currently published by governmental entities other than the federal government.

PROPRIETARY FUNDS

Enterprise funds and internal service funds constitute the proprietary funds of governmental entities. These funds are more similar to business enterprises than are governmental funds or fiduciary funds (trust funds and agency funds). Enterprise funds sell services to the citizens, and sometimes to other funds, of the governmental entity, for amounts designed to produce a net income. Internal service funds, as their title indicates, sell goods or services to other funds of the governmental entity, but not to the public. Accordingly, earning significant amounts of net income is not an objective of an internal service fund.

Both enterprise funds and internal service funds use the accrual basis of accounting and issue financial statements similar to those for a nonprofit organization—a statement of revenues, expenses, and changes in net assets [which includes an amount labeled increase (decrease) in net assets], a balance sheet, and a statement of cash flows.

The balance sheets of both types of proprietary funds are classified into current and noncurrent sections. The plant assets of the two types of proprietary funds are recorded in their accounting records, and depreciation and amortization expenses are recognized by each proprietary fund.

Because of the many similarities in the accounting cycle and the financial statements of business enterprises and proprietary funds, journal entries for proprietary funds are not illustrated in this section. Instead, the unique features of proprietary funds, including differences from features of business enterprises, are emphasized, and financial statements for proprietary funds are illustrated.

Accounting and Reporting for Enterprise Funds

Enterprise funds account for the operations of commercial-type activities of a governmental entity, such as utilities, airports, seaports, and recreational facilities. These commercial-type enterprises sell services to the public (and sometimes to other activities of the governmental entity) at a profit. Consequently, the accounting for enterprise funds is more akin to business enterprise accounting than the accounting for any other governmental entity fund. For example, the accrual basis of accounting is used for an enterprise fund, with short-term prepayments, depreciation expense, and doubtful accounts expense recognized in the fund's accounting records. The enterprise fund's accounting records also include the plant assets owned by the fund, as well as the liabilities for revenue bonds and any general obligation bonds payable by the fund. (General obligation bonds are a liability of an enterprise fund if their proceeds were used by the enterprise fund for construction of plant assets or other purposes.) Encumbrance accounting is not used for enterprise funds, and their annual budgets generally are not entered in the accounting records. The fund balance of an enterprise fund may be debited with cash remittances for operating transfers to the general fund, similar to dividends declared and paid by a corporate enterprise.

However, there are several differences between accounting for an enterprise fund and accounting for a business enterprise. Among these differences are the following:

1. Enterprise funds are not subject to federal and state income taxes. However, an enterprise fund may make payments in lieu of property or franchise taxes to the general fund and display the payments as expenses in the statement of revenues, expenses, and changes in net assets. (See page 740 of Chapter 17.)
2. There is no capital stock in an enterprise fund's balance sheet. Instead, Contributions ledger accounts set forth, in the net assets section of the balance sheet, the assets contributed to the enterprise fund by the governmental entity, by customers of the enterprise fund, or by other public agencies.
3. An enterprise fund has restricted assets, which are segregated from current assets in the balance sheet. Cash deposits made by customers of a utility enterprise fund, which are to help assure the customers' payment for utility services, are restricted for cash or interest-bearing investments to offset the enterprise fund's liability for the customers' deposits. Cash received from proceeds of revenue bonds issued by the enterprise fund is restricted to payments for construction of plant assets financed by issuance of the bonds. Part of the cash generated by the enterprise fund's operations must be segregated and invested for payment of interest and principal of the revenue bonds issued by the enterprise fund.
4. Current liabilities payable from restricted assets are segregated from other current liabilities of an enterprise fund in a section of the balance sheet that precedes long-term liabilities.

5. A *restricted net assets* amount generally is displayed in the balance sheet of an enterprise fund. The amount is equal to the total of cash and investments restricted to payment of revenue bond interest and principal.
6. Subsidy-type operating transfers from an enterprise fund to the general fund are displayed in the operating transfers section of the enterprise fund's statement of revenues, expenses, and changes in net assets.
7. The form of the statement of cash flows for proprietary funds of governmental entities was set forth in *GASB Statement No. 9,* "Reporting Cash Flows of Proprietary and Nonexpendable Trust Funds and Governmental Entities That Use Proprietary Fund Accounting," issued in 1989 by the Governmental Accounting Standards Board.[1] Among the features of an enterprise fund's statement of cash flows are the following:
   (1) There are *four categories* of cash flows: from operating activities, from noncapital financing activities, from capital and related financing activities, and from investing activities. (The statement of cash flows for a business enterprise has *three categories* of cash flows.)
   (2) In the direct method, *operating income,* rather than *increase (decrease) in net assets* is reconciled to net cash provided by operating activities.
   (3) Noncapital financing activities cash flows include operating grants from other governmental entities and operating transfers to or from other funds of the governmental entity.
   (4) Temporary investments of cash received from borrowings for plant assets construction are reported with cash flows from capital and related financing activities, rather than with cash flows from investing activities.

Financial Statements for Enterprise Fund

Some of the foregoing discussion is illustrated in the following financial statements of the Town of Verdant Glen Enterprise Fund (for the town's water utility):

Financial Statements of a Governmental Entity's Enterprise Fund

TOWN OF VERDANT GLEN ENTERPRISE FUND Statement of Revenues, Expenses, and Changes in Net Assets For Year Ended June 30, 2003		
Operating revenues:		
Charges for services		$520,000
Operating expenses:		
Personal services	$ 82,000	
Contractual services	94,000	
Supplies	21,000	
Material	75,000	
Heat, light, and power	14,000	
Depreciation	45,000	
Payment in lieu of property taxes	40,000	
Total operating expenses		371,000
Operating income		$149,000

(continued)

[1] *Codification of Governmental Accounting and Financial Reporting Standards* (Norwalk: GASB, 2000), Sec. 2450.

**Financial Statements of a
Governmental Entity's
Enterprise Fund** (continued)

TOWN OF VERDANT GLEN ENTERPRISE FUND
Statement of Revenues, Expenses, and Changes in Net Assets (concluded)
For Year Ended June 30, 2003

Nonoperating revenues (expenses):		
Operating grants	$ 43,000	
Investment revenue and net gains	12,000	
Interest expense	(46,000)	
Fiscal agent fees	(14,000)	
Total nonoperating revenues (expenses)		(5,000)
Income before operating transfers		$144,000
Operating transfer (out) to General Fund		(10,000)
Increase in net assets		$134,000
Net assets, beginning of year		532,000
Net assets, end of year		$666,000

TOWN OF VERDANT GLEN ENTERPRISE FUND
Balance Sheet
June 30, 2003

Assets

Current assets:		
Cash		$ 62,000
Short-term investments, at fair value		120,000
Accounts receivable (net)		56,000
Receivable from General Fund		5,000
Inventory of supplies, at first-in, first-out cost		18,000
Short-term prepayments		2,000
Total current assets		$ 263,000
Restricted assets:		
Cash	$ 22,000	
Short-term investments, at fair value	145,000	
Total restricted assets		167,000
Capital assets:		
Land	$ 192,000	
Buildings	1,285,000	
Machinery and equipment	347,000	
Subtotal	$1,824,000	
Less: Accumulated depreciation	748,000	
Net capital assets		1,076,000
Total assets		$1,506,000

RA

(continued)

Financial Statements of a Governmental Entity's Enterprise Fund (concluded)

TOWN OF VERDANT GLEN ENTERPRISE FUND
Balance Sheet (concluded)
June 30, 2003

Liabilities and Net Assets

Current liabilities:		
Vouchers payable		$ 144,000
Accrued liabilities		82,000
Total current liabilities		$ 226,000
Liabilities payable from restricted assets:		
Interest payable	$ 20,000	
Current portion of revenue bonds	50,000	
Customers' deposits	44,000	
Total liabilities payable from restricted assets		114,000
Long-term debt:		
Revenue bonds, less current portion		500,000
Total liabilities		$ 840,000
Net assets:		
Restricted for revenue bonds retirement	$ 53,000	
Unrestricted	613,000	
Total net assets		666,000
Total liabilities and net assets		$1,506,000

TOWN OF VERDANT GLEN ENTERPRISE FUND
Statement of Cash Flows
For Year Ended June 30, 2003

Net cash provided by operating activities **(Exhibit 1):**		
Cash receipts from customers		$782,000
Cash receipts from interfund services provided		87,000
Total cash receipts		$869,000
Cash payments to employees for services	$314,000	
Cash payments to other suppliers of goods or services	203,000	
Cash payment in lieu of property taxes to General Fund	40,000	
Other operating cash payments	108,000	
Total cash payments		665,000
Net cash provided by operating activities		$204,000
Cash flows from noncapital financing activities:		
Payment of principal ($50,000) and interest ($2,000) of note payable to bank	$ (52,000)	
Operating grants from state government	43,000	
Operating transfer (out) to General Fund	(10,000)	
Net cash used in noncapital financing activities		(19,000)

(continued)

TOWN OF VERDANT GLEN ENTERPRISE FUND
Statement of Cash Flows (concluded)
For Year Ended June 30, 2003

Cash flows from capital and related financing activities:		
Acquisition of machinery and equipment	$ (41,000)	
Payment of serial maturity of revenue bonds ($50,000) and annual interest on the bonds ($44,000)	(94,000)	
Payment of fiscal agent fees	(14,000)	
Deposits received from customers	10,000	
Net cash used in capital and related financing activities		(139,000)
Cash flows from investing activities:		
Revenue and net gains from short-term investments		12,000
Increase in cash and cash equivalents		$ 58,000
Cash and cash equivalents, beginning of year		291,000
Cash and cash equivalents, end of year		$349,000
Exhibit 1 Cash flows from operating activities:		
Operating income	$149,000	
Adjustments to reconcile operating income to net cash provided by operating activities:		
Depreciation expense	45,000	
Decrease in accounts receivable (net)	3,000	
Increase in receivable from General Fund	(5,000)	
Increase in inventory of supplies	(4,000)	
Decrease in short-term prepayments	1,000	
Increase in vouchers payable	21,000	
Decrease in accrued liabilities	(6,000)	
Net cash provided by operating activities	$204,000	

The following four aspects of the financial statements for the Town of Verdant Glen Enterprise Fund should be noted:

1. The payment in lieu of property taxes, $40,000, and the operating transfer out, $10,000, in the statement of revenues, expenses, and changes in net assets are counterparts of the amounts recorded by the Town of Verdant Glen General Fund in journal entry no. 9 on page 740 of Chapter 17.

2. The receivable from General Fund, $5,000, in the balance sheet is the counterpart of the related payable to Enterprise Fund in the General Fund trial balance on page 742 of Chapter 17.

3. The $53,000 net assets restricted for revenue bonds retirement in the balance sheet may be verified as follows:

Total restricted assets	$167,000
Less: Total liabilities payable from restricted assets	114,000
Net assets restricted for revenue bonds retirement	$ 53,000

4. Short-term investments, both current and restricted, in the balance sheet are *cash equivalents.* Thus, the end-of-year amount of cash and cash equivalents in the statement of cash flows is computed as follows: $62,000 + $120,000 + $22,000 + $145,000 = $349,000.

Accounting and Reporting for Internal Service Funds

An internal service fund is established to sell supplies and services to other funds of the governmental entity, but not to the public. This type of fund is created to ensure uniformity and economies in the procurement of supplies and services for the governmental entity as a whole, such as computer and stationery supplies and the maintenance and repairs of motor vehicles.

The operations of internal service funds resemble those of a business enterprise, except that internal service funds are not profit-motivated. The revenues of internal service funds should be sufficient to cover all their operating costs and expenses, with perhaps a modest profit margin. In this way, the resources of internal service funds are "revolving"; the original contribution from the general fund of the governmental entity to establish an internal service fund is expended for supplies, operating equipment, employees' salaries or wages, and other operating expenses, and the amounts expended then are recouped through billings to other funds of the governmental entity.

Although an internal service fund should use an annual budget for managerial planning and control purposes, the budget need not be entered in the accounting records of the fund. The accrual basis of accounting, including the perpetual inventory system and depreciation of plant assets, is appropriate for an internal service fund. Encumbrance accounting may be useful in controlling nonrecurring purchase orders of an internal service fund.

Because internal service funds do not issue revenue bonds and do not receive contributions or deposits from customers, the financial statements of internal service funds are nearly identical in form and content to those of business enterprises. However, similar to enterprise funds, internal service funds do not have owners' equity in their balance sheets. A net assets ledger account balance typically supports that amount in the liabilities and net assets section of the balance sheet for an internal service fund.

Financial Statements for Internal Service Fund

The following financial statements for the Town of Verdant Glen Internal Service Fund are illustrative of the statements for such a fund. The receivable from General Fund, $6,000, in the balance sheet on page 800 is the counterpart of the related payable to Internal Service Fund in the General Fund trial balance on page 742 of Chapter 17.

Financial Statements of a Governmental Entity's Internal Service Fund

TOWN OF VERDANT GLEN INTERNAL SERVICE FUND Statement of Revenues, Expenses, and Changes in Net Assets For Year Ended June 30, 2003		
Operating revenues:		
Charges for services		$162,400
Operating expenses:		
Personal services	$21,200	
Supplies	84,300	
Heat, light, and power	20,500	
Depreciation	34,000	
Total operating expenses		160,000
Increase in net assets		$ 2,400
Net assets, beginning of year		636,800
Net assets, end of year		$639,200

TOWN OF VERDANT GLEN INTERNAL SERVICE FUND
Balance Sheet
June 30, 2000

Assets

Current assets:

Cash		$ 8,600
Receivable from General Fund		6,000
Inventory of supplies, at first-in, first-out cost		64,300
Total current assets		$ 78,900
Capital assets:		
Land	$142,100	
Building	627,500	
Machinery and equipment	132,800	
Subtotal	$902,400	
Less: Accumulated depreciation	327,800	
Net capital assets		574,600
Total assets		$653,500

Liabilities and Net Assets

Current liabilities:

Vouchers payable		$ 14,300
Net assets		639,200
Total liabilities and net assets		$653,500

TOWN OF VERDANT GLEN INTERNAL SERVICE FUND
Statement of Cash Flows
For Year Ended June 30, 2003

Net cash provided by operating activities **(Exhibit 1):**		
Cash receipts from interfund services provided		$370,300
Cash payments to employees for services	$ 76,000	
Cash payments to other suppliers of goods or services	212,000	
Other operating cash payments	53,600	
Total cash payments		341,600
Net cash provided by operating activities		$ 28,700
Cash flows from capital and related financing activities:		
Acquisition of machinery and equipment		(23,400)
Increase in cash		$ 5,300
Cash, beginning of year		3,300
Cash, end of year		$ 8,600

Exhibit 1 Cash flows from operating activities:

Increase in net assets	$ 2,400
Adjustments to reconcile increase in net assets to net cash provided by operating activities:	
Depreciation expense	34,000
Decrease in receivable from General Fund	1,000
Increase in inventory of supplies	(11,300)
Increase in vouchers payable	2,600
Net cash provided by operating activities	$ 28,700

Applicability of FASB Pronouncements to Proprietary Funds

In *GASB Statement No. 20,* "Accounting and Financial Reporting for Proprietary Funds
. . . ," the GASB addressed the troublesome issue of which—if any—pronouncements
of the FASB should apply to proprietary funds of governmental entities.[2] As an interim
measure, the GASB provided that proprietary funds *should* apply all *Accounting Research Bulletins, Accounting Principles Board Opinions,* and *Financial Accounting
Standards Board Statements* and *Interpretations* issued as of November 30, 1989, unless those pronouncements conflicted with or contradicted GASB pronouncements. In
addition, proprietary funds *might elect* to apply *all* (not *some*) FASB *Statements* and
Interpretations issued after November 30, 1989, as long as they do not conflict with
or contradict with GASB pronouncements. Thus, *GASB Statement No. 20* provided
temporary guidance to governmental entities for applying business enterprise-type accounting standards, as appropriate, to their proprietary funds. In *GASB Statement No.
34,* "Basic Financial Statements . . .," paragraphs 93 through 95, the GASB reaffirmed
the foregoing provisions of *GASB Statement No. 20.*

FIDUCIARY FUNDS

Private-purpose trust funds, pension trust funds, agency funds, and investment trust
funds constitute the fiduciary funds of a governmental entity. The position of the governmental entity with respect to such funds is one of a *custodian* or a *trustee,* rather
than an *owner.*

For fiduciary funds, the Governmental Accounting Standards Board has mandated
use of the accrual basis of accounting and preparation of a *statement of fiduciary net
assets* and a *statement of changes in fiduciary net assets.*[3] The following sections of
this chapter describe and illustrate accounting and reporting for fiduciary funds.

Accounting and Reporting for Agency Funds

Agency funds are of short duration. Typically, agency funds are used to account for
sales taxes collected by a state government on behalf of the municipalities and townships of the state, and for payroll taxes and other deductions withheld from salaries
and wages payable to employees of a governmental entity. The amounts withheld subsequently are paid to a federal or state collection unit.

Agency funds do not have operations during a fiscal year; thus, the only financial
statements for an agency fund are a statement of fiduciary assets showing the cash or
receivables of the fund and the amounts payable to other funds or governmental entities or to outsiders, and a statement of changes in fiduciary assets, illustrated as follows for the Town of Verdant Glen:

**Financial Statements of a
Governmental Entity's
Agency Fund**

TOWN OF VERDANT GLEN AGENCY FUND
Statement of Fiduciary Assets
June 30, 2003

Assets

Cash	$12,600

Liabilities

Vouchers payable	$12,600

---

[2] Ibid., Sec. P80.104 and P80.105.
[3] *GASB Statement No. 34,* "Basic Financial Statements . . .," (Norwalk: GASB, 1999), pars. 107
through 109.

TOWN OF VERDANT GLEN AGENCY FUND Statement of Changes in Fiduciary Assets For Year Ended June 30, 2003				
	Balances, July 1, 2002	Additions	Deductions	Balances, June 30, 2003
Assets				
Cash	$14,200	$49,000	$50,600	$12,600
Liabilities				
Vouchers payable	$14,200	$49,000	$50,600	$12,600

Accounting and Reporting for Private-Purpose Trust Funds

Private-purpose trust funds of a governmental entity are longer-lived than agency funds. An *expendable trust fund* is one whose principal and income both may be expended to achieve the objectives of the trust. A *nonexpendable trust fund* is one whose revenues are expended to carry out the objectives of the trust; the principal remains intact. For example, an *endowment* established by the grantor of a trust may specify that the revenues from the endowment are to be expended by the governmental entity for student scholarships, but the endowment principal is not to be expended. A nonexpendable trust fund requires two separate trust fund accounting entities—one for principal and one for revenues. Accounting for the two separate trust funds requires a careful distinction between transactions affecting the principal—such as changes in the investment portfolio—and transactions affecting revenues—such as cash dividends and interest on the investment portfolio. The *trust indenture,* which is the legal document establishing the trust, should specify distinctions between principal and revenues. If the trust indenture is silent with respect to such distinctions, the trust law of the governmental entity governs separation of principal trust fund and revenues trust fund transactions.

Because the governmental entity serves as a custodian for a trust fund, accounting for a trust fund should comply with the trust indenture under which the fund was established. Among the provisions that might affect the accounting for a trust fund are requirements that the annual budget for the trust fund be entered in its accounting records and that depreciation be recognized for an endowment principal trust fund that includes depreciable plant assets.

To illustrate accounting for expendable and nonexpendable trust funds, assume that Karl and Mabel Root, residents of the Town of Verdant Glen, contributed marketable securities with a current fair value of $100,000 on July 1, 2002, to a trust to be administered by the Town of Verdant Glen as trustee. Principal of the gift was to be maintained in an Endowment Principal Nonexpendable Trust Fund. Revenues from the marketable securities were to be used for scholarships for qualified students to attend Verdant Glen College; the revenues and expenditures for scholarships were to be accounted for in an Endowment Revenues Expendable Trust Fund. The Bank of Verdant Glen trust department was to receive an annual trustee's fee of $500 for administering the two trust funds on behalf of the Town of Verdant Glen.

Journal entries for the two trust funds for the year ended June 30, 2003, are summarized on page 804 (changes in current fair value of the marketable securities are disregarded).

FINANCIAL STATEMENTS OF NONEXPENDABLE TRUST FUND

Financial statements of the Town of Verdant Glen Endowment Principal Nonexpendable Trust Fund are shown below for the year ended June 30, 2003:

Financial Statements of a Governmental Entity's Nonexpendable Trust Fund

TOWN OF VERDANT GLEN ENDOWMENT PRINCIPAL NONEXPENDABLE TRUST FUND Statement of Changes in Fiduciary Net Assets For Year Ended June 30, 2003	
Operating revenues:	
Interest	$ 5,000
Dividends	8,000
Gifts	100,000
Total operating revenues	$113,000
Operating transfers out	13,000
Increase in net assets	$100,000
Net assets, beginning of year	-0-
Net assets, end of year	$100,000

TOWN OF VERDANT GLEN ENDOWMENT PRINCIPAL NONEXPENDABLE TRUST FUND Statement of Fiduciary Net Assets June 30, 2003	
Assets	
Investments, at fair value	$100,000
Net Assets	
Net assets reserved for endowment	$100,000

Financial Statements of Expendable Trust Fund

For the Town of Verdant Glen Endowment Revenues Expendable Trust Fund, financial statements for the year ended June 30, 2003, are as follows:

Financial Statements of a Governmental Entity's Expendable Trust Fund

TOWN OF VERDANT GLEN ENDOWMENT REVENUES EXPENDABLE TRUST FUND Statement of Changes in Fiduciary Net Assets For Year Ended June 30, 2003	
Revenues	$ -0-
Expenditures:	
Education	$ 12,000
Administration	500
Total expenditures	$ 12,500
Excess (deficiency) of revenues over expenditures	$(12,500)
Operating transfers in	13,000
Increase in net assets	$ 500
Net assets, beginning of year	-0-
Net assets, end of year	$ 500

Journal Entries for Nonexpendable Trust Fund and Expendable Trust Fund of a Governmental Entity

Explanation of Transactions and Events	Account Titles	Endowment Principal Nonexpendable Trust Fund		Endowment Revenues Expendable Trust Fund	
Receipt of marketable securities in trust	Investments	100,000			
	Revenues		100,000		
Accrual of revenues on marketable securities	Interest Receivable	5,000			
	Dividends Receivable	8,000			
	Revenues		13,000		
Receipt of interest and dividends	Cash	13,000			
	Interest Receivable		5,000		
	Dividends Receivable		8,000		
Recording of liability to Revenues Trust Fund for interest and dividends	Other Financing Uses	13,000			
	Payable to Revenues Trust Fund		13,000		
	Receivable from Principal Trust Fund			13,000	
	Other Financing Sources				13,000
Transfer of cash from Principal Trust Fund to Revenues Trust Fund	Payable to Revenues Trust Fund	13,000			
	Cash		13,000		
	Cash			13,000	
	Receivable from Principal Trust Fund				13,000
Payment of scholarships to students James Rich and Janet Wells	Expenditures			12,000	
	Cash				12,000
Payment of trustee's fee	Expenditures			500	
	Cash				500
Closing entries	Revenues	113,000			
	Other Financing Uses		13,000		
	Net assets Reserved for Endowment		100,000		
	Other Financing Sources			13,000	
	Expenditures				12,500
	Net assets Reserved for Scholarships				500

**TOWN OF VERDANT GLEN ENDOWMENT REVENUES
EXPENDABLE TRUST FUND**
Statement of Fiduciary Net Assets
June 30, 2003

Assets

Cash	$500

Net Assets

Net assets reserved for scholarships	$500

There is no unreserved and undesignated net assets balance for either of the Town of Verdant Glen trust funds, because the trust indenture required the reservation of the entire net assets of each fund to achieve the purpose of the trust.

Accounting and Reporting for Pension Trust Funds

The GASB has defined a *pension trust fund* as follows:

> A fund held by a governmental entity in a trustee capacity for pension plan members; used to account for the accumulation of assets for the purpose of paying benefits when they become due in accordance with the terms of the plan; a pension plan included in the financial reporting entity of the plan sponsor or a participating employer.[4]

Pension trust funds are accounted for in essentially the same manner as proprietary funds. Thus, the accounting records of pension trust funds are maintained under the accrual basis of accounting and include all assets, liabilities, revenues, and expenses of the fund.

Because of the complexities of pension trust funds, illustrative journal entries for a pension trust fund are beyond the scope of this discussion. The following financial statements for the Town of Verdant Glen Employees' Retirement System Pension Trust Fund for the year ended June 30, 2003, which exclude a statement of cash flows, which is optional, illustrate some of the accounting concepts involved.[5]

TOWN OF VERDANT GLEN PENSION TRUST FUND
Statement of Changes in Fiduciary Net Assets
For Year Ended June 30, 2003

Additions:		
Employee contributions		$131,600
Employer contributions		247,300
Investment net gains and revenues, net of investment expenses		146,200
Total additions		$525,100
Deductions:		
Annuity and disability benefits	$222,000	
Refunds of contributions	38,300	
Administrative expenses	187,200	
Total deductions		447,500
Increase in net assets		$ 77,600
Net assets held in trust for pension benefits, beginning of year		842,300
Net assets held in trust for pension benefits, end of year		$919,900

---

[4] *Codification,* Sec. P20.551.
[5] Ibid., Sec. Pe5.901.

TOWN OF VERDANT GLEN PENSION TRUST FUND
Statement of Fiduciary Net Assets
June 30, 2003

Assets	
Cash and short-term investments, at fair value	$ 21,200
Receivables	34,800
Long-term investments, at fair value	884,600
Capital assets, less accumulated depreciation	82,100
Total assets	$1,022,700
Liabilities	
Refunds payable and other	102,800
Net assets held in trust for pension benefits	$ 919,900

In addition to the foregoing financial statements, the pension trust fund of a governmental entity must provide two schedules as required supplementary information following the notes to the pension fund's financial statements:

A *schedule of funding progress* that includes historical trend information about the actuarially determined funded status of the pension plan and the progress made in accumulating sufficient assets to pay benefits when due

A *schedule of employer contributions* that includes historical trend information about the annual required contributions compared with the actual contributions[6]

Following is a discussion of important features of the financial statements for the Town of Verdant Glen Pension Trust Fund:

1. The defined benefit pension plan of the Town of Verdant Glen is a *contributory pension plan,* to which both covered employees and the town make contributions. (In a *noncontributory pension plan,* only the town would make contributions.)

2. Investment revenues of the Pension Trust Fund include realized and unrealized gains and losses on investments as well as interest and dividends.

3. Annuity benefits are pension payments to retired former employees of the Town of Verdant Glen. Disability benefits are payments to former employees whose disabilities precluded their working until scheduled retirement dates.

4. All pension payments to retired employees had been made through June 30, 2003; otherwise, the liabilities in the Pension Trust Fund statement of fiduciary net assets would include an amount for annuities payable.

5. Not illustrated for the Town of Verdant Glen Pension Trust Fund are the extensive disclosures required in notes to the financial statements of the Pension Trust Fund. These required disclosures are set forth in *GASB Statement No. 25,* "Financial Reporting for Defined Benefit Pension Plans and Note Disclosures for Defined Contribution Plans," paragraph 32.

Accounting and Reporting for Investment Trust Funds

Governmental entities such as counties and states often maintain *external investment pools,* similar to the pooled investments of the various funds of nonprofit organizations discussed in Chapter 16. Smaller governmental entities, such as towns and villages

---

[6] Ibid.

located in the same county or state, may achieve higher returns by pooling their investments with those of other small entities. The investments are managed by the treasurer or chief financial officer of the state or county **sponsoring government.** In *GASB Statement No. 31,* "Accounting and Financial Reporting for Certain Investments and for External Investment Pools," the GASB required sponsoring governments to establish *investment trust funds* for external investment pools. Financial statements for the investment pools would be the same as for pension trust funds: a statement of fiduciary net assets and a statement of changes in fiduciary net assets.[7]

To illustrate, assume that Riparian County maintains an external investment pool for the Town of Verdant Glen and other towns and villages within its borders. Following are hypothetical financial statements for the Riparian County Investment Trust Fund:

RIPARIAN COUNTY INVESTMENT TRUST FUND
Statement of Changes in Fiduciary Net Assets
For Year Ended June 30, 2003

Additions:	
Participants' contributions	$ 1,800,000
Investment net realized and unrealized gains and revenues, net of investment expenses	1,140,000
Total additions	$ 2,940,000
Deductions:	
Administrative expenses	460,000
Net increase	$ 2,480,000
Net assets held in trust for pool participants, beginning of year	65,820,000
Net assets held in trust for pool participants, end of year	$68,300,000

RIPARIAN COUNTY INVESTMENT TRUST FUND
Statement of Fiduciary Net Assets
June 30, 2003

Assets	
Cash and short-term investments, at fair value	$26,200,000
Long-term investments at fair value	42,180,000
Total assets	$68,380,000
Liabilities	
Payable to Treasurer of Riparian County	80,000
Net assets held in trust for pool participants	$68,300,000

COMPREHENSIVE ANNUAL FINANCIAL REPORT OF GOVERNMENTAL ENTITIES

As pointed out in Chapter 17 (page 727), the Governmental Accounting Standards Board's issuance in 1999 of *GASB Statement No. 34,* created renewed interest in financial reporting by state and local governmental entities. The GASB reported its objective in issuing *GASB Statement No. 34,* as follows:

---

[7] Ibid., Sec. 150.116.

The Board's objective with this Statement is to establish a basic financial reporting model that will result in greater accountability by state and local governments by provding more useful information to a wider range of users than did the previous model. The new model also improves on earlier standards and proposals for modifying the previous model, ...[8]

GASB Statement No. 33—A Preliminary Step

Before issuing *GASB Statement No. 34,* the GASB resolved the pressing issue of accounting for a governmental entity's **nonexchange** transactions, such as most taxes, grants, and private donations. The four classes of nonexchange transactions and their recognitions established by the GASB are summarized in the following chart:[9]

Classes and Timing of Recognition of Nonexchange Transactions

Class	Recognition
Derived tax revenues Examples: sales taxes, personal and corporate income taxes, motor fuel taxes, and similar taxes on earnings or consumption	**Assets*** Period when *underlying exchange has occurred* or when resources are received, whichever is first. **Revenues** Period when *underlying exchange has occurred.* (Report advance receipts as deferred revenues.) When modified accrual accounting is used, resources *also* should be "available."
Imposed nonexchange revenues Examples: property taxes, most fines and forfeitures	**Assets*** Period when an *enforceable legal claim has arisen* or when resources are received, whichever is first. **Revenues** Period when *resources are required* to *be used* or first period that use is permitted (for example, for property taxes, the *period for which levied*). When modified accrual accounting is used, resources *also* should be "available." (For property taxes, apply NCGA Interpretation 3, as amended.)
Government-mandated nonexchange transactions Examples: federal government mandates on state and local governments **Voluntary nonexchange transactions** Examples: certain grants and entitlements, most donations	**Assets* and liabilities** Period when *all eligibility requirements have been met* or (for asset recognition) when resources are received, whichever is first. **Revenues and expenses or expenditures** Period when *all eligibility required have been met.* (Report advance receipts or payments for use in the following period as deferred revenues or advances, respectively. However, when a provider precludes the sale, disbursement, or consumption or resources for a specified number of years, until a specified event has occurred, or permanently [for example, permanent and term endowments], report revenues and expenses or expenditures when the resources are, respectively, received or paid and report resulting net assets, equity, of fund balance as restricted.) When modified accrual accounting is used for revenue recognition, resources *also* should be "available."

* If there are purpose restrictions, report restricted net assets (or equity or fund balance) or, for governmental funds, a reservation of fund balance.

[8] *GASB Statement No. 34,* par. 183.
[9] *GASB Statement No. 33,* "Accounting and Financial Reporting for Nonexchange Transactions" (Norwalk: GASB, 1998), p. 48.

Subsequent to its issuance, *GASB Statement No. 33* was modified with respect to accounting for a governmental entity's derived tax revenues or imposed nonexchange revenues shared with other governmental entities.[10]

Subsequent Steps—*GASB Statements No. 35, 37, and 38*

Subsequent to the issuance of *GASB Statement No. 34,* the GASB issued three additional statements that either modified or supplemented *Statement No. 34,* as follows:

1. *GASB Statement No. 35,* "Basic Financial Statements—and Management's Discussion and Analysis—for Public Colleges and Universities." This statement merely amended *Statement No. 34* to include public colleges and universities within its scope.[11]

2. *GASB Statement No. 37,* "Basic Financial Statements—and Management's Discussion and Analysis—for State and Local Governments: Omnibus." This statement's purpose was to encourage financial managers of governmental entities to report management discussion and analysis items that have the most relevance and to avoid boilerplate language.[12]

3. *GASB Statement No. 38,* "Certain Financial Statement Note Disclosures." Following a general disclosure principle that disclosure in the notes to the financial statements of a governmental entity is needed only when the information required to be disclosed is not displayed on the face of the financial statements, *GASB Statement No. 38* established and modified disclosure requirements related to the following:

> Summary of significant accounting policies
>
> Violations of finance-related legal or contractual provisions
>
> Debt and lease obligations
>
> Short-term debt
>
> Disaggregation of receivable and payable balances
>
> Interfund balances and transfers[13]

Composition of a Governmental Entity's Comprehensive Annual Financial Report

The Governmental Accounting Standards Board provided the following general guidelines for a governmental entity's comprehensive annual financial report:

a. A comprehensive annual financial report should be prepared and published, covering all activities of the primary government (including its blended component units*) and providing an overview of all discretely presented component units* of the reporting entity—including introductory section, management's discussion and analysis (MD&A), basic financial statements, required supplementary information

---

* The term **component units** is defined on page 750 of Chapter 17.

[10] *Codification,* Sec. N50.125

[11] *GASB Statement No. 35,* "Basic Financial Statements—and Management's Discussion and Analysis—for Public Colleges and Universities" (Norwalk:GASB, 1999), par. 2.

[12] *GASB Statement No. 37,* "Basic Financial Statements—and Management's Discussion and Analysis—for State and Local Governments: Omnibus" (Norwalk: GASB, 2001), par. 4.

[13] *GASB Statement No. 38,* "Certain Financial Statement Note Disclosures" (Norwalk: GASB, 2001), pars. 5–15.

other than MD&A, combining and individual fund statements, schedules, narrative explanations, and statistical section. The reporting entity is the primary government (including its blended component units) and all discretely presented component units . . . .

b. The minimum requirements for MD&A, basic financial statements, and required supplementary information other than MD&A are:

(1) Management's discussion and analysis.

(2) Basic financial statements. The basic financial statements should include:

    (a) Government-wide financial statements.

    (b) Fund financial statements.

    (c) Notes to the financial statements.

(3) Required supplementary information other than MD&A.[14]

The GASB diagrammed the foregoing features of a comprehensive annual financial report as follows:[15]

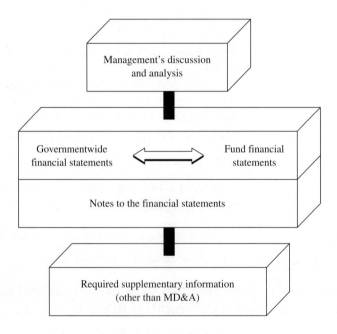

The GASB provided general guidance for the sections of a comprehensive annual financial report as follows:

1. Management's Discussion and Analysis should discuss the current-year results in comparison with the prior year, with emphasis on the current year. This fact-based analysis should discuss the positive and negative aspects of the comparison with the prior year.[16]

2. The governmentwide financial statements consist of a statement of net assets and a statement of activities. Those statements should:

---

[14] *GASB Statement No. 34,* p. 333.

[15] Ibid., p. 5.

[16] Ibid., p. 6.

   a. Report information about the overall government without displaying individual funds or fund types

   b. Exclude information about fiduciary activities, including component units that are fiduciary in nature (such as certain public employee retirement systems)

   c. Distinguish between the primary government and its discretely presented component units

   d. Distinguish between governmental activities and business-type activities of the primary government

   e. Measure and report all assets (both financial and capital), liabilities, revenues, expenses, gains, and losses using the . . . accrual basis of accounting.[17]

3. Fund financial statements should be used to report additional and detailed information about the primary government. Governments should report governmental, proprietary, and fiduciary funds to the extent that they have activities that meet the criteria for using those funds.[18]

4. The notes to the financial statements should communicate information essential for fair presentation of the financial statements that is not displayed on the face of the financial statements. As such, the notes are an integral part of the basic financial statements. The notes should focus on the primary government—specifically, its governmental activities, business-type activities, major funds, and nonmajor funds in the aggregate.[19]

5. Required supplementary information includes budgetary comparison schedules for governmental funds, showing original and final appropriated budgets compared with actual amounts realized. Also, under certain conditions, governmental entities must report supplementary information about infrastructure assets.[20]

The foregoing discussion regarding the comprehensive annual financial report of a governmental entity suggests that such a report may be a complex, voluminous disclosure instrument. The statement of net assets and the statement of activities of the City of Alexandria, Virginia, for the fiscal year ended June 30, 2000, are clear evidence of such complexity.[21]

SEC ENFORCEMENT ACTION DEALING WITH WRONGFUL APPLICATION OF ACCOUNTING AND REPORTING STANDARDS FOR GOVERNMENTAL ENTITY

AAER 970

In *AAER 970,* "In the Matter of The City of Syracuse, New York, Warren D. Simpson, and Edward D. Polgreen" (September 30, 1997), the SEC reported that official statements produced by the City of Syracuse in connection with the issuance of $23,000,000 face amount of one-year bond anticipation notes were materially false and misleading. According to the SEC, the combined statements of revenue, expenditures,

---

[17] Ibid., pp. 8–9.
[18] Ibid., p. 25.
[19] Ibid., p. 39.
[20] Ibid., pp. 45–46.
[21] Bruce W. Chase and Laura B. Triggs, "How to Implement GASB Statement No. 34," *Journal of Accountancy,* November 2001 (Jersey City: American Institute of Certified Public Accountants, Inc.), pp. 77–79

and changes in fund balances for the City's general and debt service funds reported a $400,000 *excess of revenues over expenditures* instead of the *actual* $9,400,000 *excess of expenditures over revenues.* In addition, the combined ending fund balances of the general and debt service funds were *overstated* by $24,200,000. According to the SEC, the primary cause of the misstatements were the preparation of the combined financial statements *before* the City's accounting records had been closed for the relevant fiscal year and the premature recognition of property tax revenues. The City, its most senior accountant in its Finance Department, and its First Deputy Commissioner of Finance agreed to cease and desist from violating the Securities Act of 1933 and the Securities and Exchange Act of 1934.

Review Questions

1. Under what circumstances are general obligation bonds payable of a governmental entity recorded in the governmental entity's enterprise fund? Explain.

2. The accounting for a governmental entity's enterprise fund in many respects is similar to the accounting for a business enterprise; yet there are a number of differences between the two types of accounting. Identify at least three of the differences.

3. Why does a governmental entity's enterprise fund have restricted assets in its balance sheet? Explain.

4. What are the four categories of cash flows in the statement of cash flows for a governmental entity's enterprise fund?

5. How is the excess of total assets over total liabilities displayed in the financial statements of a governmental entity's internal service fund? Explain.

6. How does the balance sheet of a governmental entity's internal service fund differ from the balance sheet of the governmental entity's enterprise fund? Explain.

7. Is a statement of revenues, expenses, and changes in fiduciary net assets issued for an agency fund of a governmental entity? Explain.

8. Accounting for a nonexpendable trust for which a governmental entity acts as custodian requires the establishment of two separate private-purpose trust funds. Why is this true?

9. Explain the nature of the *contributions* in the statement of changes in fiduciary net assets of a governmental entity's pension trust fund.

10. Are fund financial statements the only financial statements included in the comprehensive annual financial report of a governmental entity? Explain.

11. Does the management's discussion and analysis section of a governmental entity's comprehensive annual financial report include required supplementary financial information? Explain.

Exercises

(Exercise 19.1) Select the best answer for each of the following multiple-choice questions:

1. An agency fund of a governmental entity is an example of which of the following types of fund?
   a. Fiduciary *b.* Governmental *c.* Proprietary *d.* Internal service

✗2. Is a Contributed Capital from General Fund amount displayed in the balance sheet of a governmental entity's:

	Enterprise Fund?	Internal Service Fund?
a.	Yes	No
b.	No	Yes
c.	No	No
d.	Yes	Yes

3. The following transactions were among those reported by the Scobey County Water and Power Enterprise Fund for the fiscal year ended June 30, 2003:

Proceeds from issuance of revenue bonds	$5,000,000
Cash deposits received from customer households	3,000,000
Cash contributed by subdividers	1,000,000

In the water and power enterprise fund's statement of cash flows for the year ended June 30, 2003, the amount to be reported as cash flows from capital and related financing activities is:

a. $9,000,000
b. $8,000,000
c. $6,000,000
d. $5,000,000

4. Does a governmental entity's agency fund issue a:

	Balance Sheet?	Statement of Revenues, Expenses, and Changes in Net Assets?
a.	Yes	Yes
b.	Yes	No
c.	No	Yes
d.	No	No

✗5. Slade City Internal Service Fund received a residual equity transfer of $50,000 cash from the General Fund. This $50,000 transfer is accounted for in the Internal Service Fund with a credit to:

a. Revenues.
b. Other Financing Sources.
c. Accounts Payable.
d. Contributed Capital.

✗6. Is the entire fund balance reserved in:

	A Nonexpendable Private-Purpose Trust Fund?	An Expendable Private-Purpose Trust Fund?
a.	Yes	Yes
b.	Yes	No
c.	No	Yes
d.	No	No

7. Which of the following funds of a governmental entity uses the same basis of accounting as an enterprise fund?

a. Special revenue funds.
b. Internal service funds.

c. Expendable private-purpose trust funds.

d. Capital projects funds.

7. *Restricted assets* are displayed in a governmental entity balance sheet for:

a. Both an enterprise fund and an internal service fund.

b. Neither an enterprise fund nor an internal service fund.

c. An enterprise fund only.

d. An internal service fund only.

8. Which of the following funds of a governmental entity may be either expendable or nonexpendable?

a. Debt service funds.

b. Enterprise funds.

c. Private-purpose trust funds.

d. Special revenue funds.

e. None of the foregoing funds.

10. Customers' deposits that may not be spent for operating purposes are displayed in the balance sheet of the enterprise fund of a governmental entity as:

a. Restricted cash or investments.

b. Nonrestricted cash or investments.

c. Payable to general fund.

d. Payable to special revenue fund.

11. Does an agency fund for a governmental entity issue:

	A Balance Sheet?	A Statement of Revenues, Expenditures, and Changes in Net Assets?	A Statement of Cash Flows?
a.	Yes	Yes	Yes
b.	Yes	No	Yes
c.	Yes	Yes	No
d.	Yes	No	No

12. A Net Assets Reserved for Endowment ledger account is appropriate for:

a. An endowment principal nonexpendable trust fund only.

b. An endowment revenues expendable trust fund only.

c. Either an endowment principal nonexpendable trust fund or an endowment revenues expendable trust fund.

d. Neither an endowment principal nonexpendable trust fund nor an endowment revenues expendable trust fund.

13. Which of the following taxes is *not* a tax revenue of a governmental entity that is classified as *derived* under *GASB Statement No. 33,* "Accounting and Financial Reporting for Nonexchange Transactions"?

a. Sales tax   b. Personal income tax   c. Motor fuel tax   d. Property tax

(Exercise 19.2) The Enterprise Fund of Orchard City billed the Orchard City General Fund $16,400 for utility services on May 31, 2003.

Prepare journal entries for the May 31, 2003, billing for both the Orchard City General Fund and the Orchard City Enterprise Fund.

(Exercise 19.3) Selected ledger accounts of the Town of Goland Enterprise Fund had the following balances on June 30, 2003:

Liabilities payable from restricted assets:

Interest payable	$ 24,400
Current portion of revenue bonds	80,000
Customers' deposits	62,600
Restricted assets:	
Cash	42,300
Short-term investments, at fair value	168,100

Prepare a working paper to compute the required balance of the Net Assets Restricted for Revenue Bonds Retirement ledger account of the Town of Goland Enterprise Fund on June 30, 2003.

(Exercise 19.4) On June 18, 2003, the Wilbert Township Enterprise Fund made a $120,000 payment in lieu of property taxes to the Wilbert Township General Fund.

Prepare journal entries on June 18, 2003, for Wilbert Township's General Fund and Enterprise Fund.

(Exercise 19.5) Selected items taken from comparative financial statements of the Town of Liddell Enterprise Fund were as follows for the fiscal year ended June 30, 2003:

Decrease in inventory of supplies	$ 42,600
Decrease in receivable from General Fund	21,700
Decrease in vouchers payable	12,200
Depreciation expense	81,700
Increase in accounts receivable	36,800
Increase in accrued liabilities	8,100
Increase in short-term prepayments	11,600
Net income	94,200
Operating income	125,400
Operating transfer out to General Fund	18,600
Payment in lieu of property taxes to General Fund	46,800

Prepare the cash flows from operating activities exhibit for the statement of cash flows (direct method) for the Town of Liddell Enterprise Fund for the year ended June 30, 2003.

(Exercise 19.6) From the following trial balance, prepare appropriate financial statements (excluding a statement of cash flows):

TOWN OF DILBEY INTERNAL SERVICE FUND
Trial Balance
June 30, 2003

	Debit	Credit
Cash	$ 17,200	
Receivable from General Fund	12,000	
Inventory of supplies	128,600	
Capital assets	1,804,800	
Accumulated depreciation of capital assets		$ 655,600
Vouchers payable		28,600
Net assets, July 1, 2002		1,273,600
Charges for services		324,800
Operating expenses	320,000	
Totals	$2,282,600	$2,282,600

(Exercise 19.7) Agatha Morris, a citizen of Roark City, donated common stock with a current fair value of $620,000 to the city under a trust indenture dated July 1, 2002. Under the terms of the indenture, the principal amount is to be kept intact; use of dividends revenues from the common stock is restricted to financing academic scholarships for college students. On December 14, 2002, dividends of $42,000 were received on the common stock donated by Morris.

Prepare journal entries for Roark City to record the foregoing transactions and events in the appropriate funds. Identify the funds. Disregard entries for *accrual* of dividends and for unrealized gains or losses on investments. Omit explanations for the journal entries.

(Exercise 19.8) Ledger account balances on June 30, 2003, applicable to the City of Carvell Pension Trust Fund statement of changes in pension plan net assets for the fiscal year ended on that date, were as follows:

CHECK FIGURE

Ending net assets, $841,700.

Administrative expenses	$294,600
Annuity benefits	284,300
Disability benefits	52,800
Employer contributions	318,500
Net assets held in trust for pension benefits, July 1, 2002	841,000
Investment revenues (net)	163,900
Employee contributions	211,600
Refunds of contributions	61,600

Prepare a statement of changes in fiduciary net assets for the City of Carvell Pension Trust Fund for the year ended June 30, 2003.

(Exercise 19.9) Among the transactions or events of Local Town for the month of November, 2002 were the following:

Nov. 3 Issued at face amount $1 million of general obligation bonds, the proceeds of which were to finance construction of a new water treatment plant for water sold to residents of the town.

5 Received an invoice of $25,000 in the General Fund for equipment for which a purchase order in the amount of $24,700 had been issued earlier. The town uses encumbrance accounting.

7 Acquired for $50,000 cash supplies for the central warehouse, to be issued to various departments of the town. The perpetual inventory system is used for supplies.

30 Issued bills totaling $80,000 to consumers of the water utility, for water consumption for the 30 days ended November 30, 2002.

Prepare journal entries (omit explanations) for the foregoing transactions or events of Local Town for the month of November 2002. Identify the fund or account group in which each journal entry is recorded.

Cases

(Case 19.1) You have been requested to audit the financial statements of the funds and account groups of Ashburn City for the fiscal year ended June 30, 2003. During the course of your audit, you learned that on July 1, 2002, the city had issued at face amount $1 million, 20-year, 8% general obligation serial bonds to finance additional power-generating facilities for the Ashburn City electric utility. Principal and interest on the bonds were payable by the Ashburn City Electric Utility Enterprise Fund. However, for the first five years of the serial maturities of the bonds—July 1, 2003, through July 1, 2007—a special tax levy accounted for in the Ashburn City Special Revenue Fund was to contribute to the payment of 80% of the interest and principal of the general obligation bonds. At the end of the five-year period, revenues from the electric utility's new power-generating facilities are expected to produce cash flows for the Ashburn City Electric Utility Enterprise Fund sufficient to pay all the serial maturities and interest of the general obligation bonds during the period July 1, 2008, through July 1, 2022.

You found that the accounting records of the Ashburn City Electric Utility Enterprise Fund included the following ledger account balances relative to the general obligation bonds on June 30, 2003:

8% general obligation serial bonds payable ($50,000 due July 1, 2003)	$1,000,000 cr
Interest payable (interest on the bonds is payable annually each July 1)	80,000 cr
Interest expense	80,000 dr

The statement of revenues, expenses, and changes in net assets for the year ended June 30, 2003, prepared by the accountant for the Ashburn City Electric Utility Enterprise Fund showed a decrease in net assets of $40,000 . You also learned that on July 1, 2000, the Ashburn City Special Revenue Fund paid $104,000 ($130,000 × 0.80 = $104,000) and the Ashburn City Electric Utility Enterprise Fund paid the remaining $26,000 ($130,000 × 0.20 = $26,000) to the fiscal agent for the 8% general obligation serial bonds. The $130,000 was the total of the $50,000 principal and $80,000 interest due on the bonds July 1, 2003. In the Enterprise Fund's journal entry to record payment of the bond principal and interest, the amount of $104,000 was credited to the Contribution from Special Revenue Fund ledger account.

Instructions
Do you concur with the Ashburn City Electric Utility Enterprise Fund's accounting and reporting treatment for the 8% general obligation serial bonds? Discuss.

(Case 19.2) Wallace and Brenda Stuart, residents of Colby City, have donated their historic mansion, "Greystone," in trust to Colby City to serve as a tourist attraction. For a nominal charge, tourists will be guided through Greystone to observe the paintings, sculptures, antiques, and other art objects collected by the Stuarts, as well as the mansion's unique architecture.

The trust indenture executed by the Stuarts provided that the admissions charges to Greystone (which was appraised at $5 million on the date of the trust indenture) are to cover the operating expenditures associated with the tours, as well as maintenance and repairs costs for Greystone. Any excess of admissions revenues over the foregoing expenditures and costs was to be donated to Colby University for scholarships to art and architecture students. The trust indenture requires depreciation of Greystone.

Instructions
Discuss the fund accounting issues, and related accounting matters such as depreciation, that should be considered by officials of Colby City with respect to the Stuart Trust.

Problems

(Problem 19.1) Among the transactions and events of Kaspar City for the first four months of the fiscal year ending June 30, 2003, were the following:

2002

July 1   Billed general property taxes, $1,600,000, of which 5% was estimated to be uncollectible.

Aug. 1   Issued $1 million, 20-year, 7% general obligation bonds to yield 6%, interest payable February 1 and August 1, to finance construction of a power-generating facility for the electricity utility.

Sept. 1   Received invoice in General Fund for a new computer for governmental accounting. Cost of the computer and related software was $10,000; the related purchase order had been issued for $10,200.

Oct. 1   Received invoice in General Fund for supplies received from Internal Service Fund, $1,200. The amount had not been subject to encumbrance.

Instructions

Prepare journal entries for the foregoing transactions or events of Kaspar City for the first four months of the fiscal year ended June 30, 2003, in all affected funds or account groups. Identify the funds or account groups. The Internal Service Fund uses the periodic inventory system.

(Problem 19.2) The adjusted trial balance of the Town of Tolliver Enterprise Fund on June 30, 2003, was as follows:

TOWN OF TOLLIVER ENTERPRISE FUND Adjusted Trial Balance June 30, 2003		
	Debit	*Credit*
Cash—unrestricted	$ 22,000	
Cash—restricted	38,000	
Short-term investments, at fair value—unrestricted	64,000	
Short-term investments, at fair value—restricted	97,000	
Accounts receivable	64,000	
Allowance for doubtful accounts		$ 12,000
Receivable from General Fund	26,000	
Receivable from Internal Service Fund	18,000	
Inventory of supplies, at average cost	47,000	
Short-term prepayments	8,000	
Land	160,000	
Buildings	830,000	
Accumulated depreciation of buildings		186,000
Machinery and equipment	247,000	
Accumulated depreciation of machinery and equipment		62,000
Vouchers payable		38,000
Contracts payable		27,000

(continued)

TOWN OF TOLLIVER ENTERPRISE FUND
Adjusted Trial Balance (concluded)
June 30, 2003

	Debit	Credit
Accrued liabilities		18,000
Interest payable		24,000
Customers' deposits		38,000
6% revenue bonds, payable $40,000 a year		400,000
Net assets restricted for revenue bonds retirement		33,000
Unrestricted net assets, beginning of year		726,000
Charges for services		643,000
Operating grants		50,000
Investment revenue and net gains		12,000
Personal services	281,000	
Contractual services	143,000	
Material and supplies	46,000	
Heat, light, and power	38,000	
Depreciation expense	57,000	
Interest expense and fiscal agent's fees	83,000	
Totals	$2,269,000	$2,269,000

Instructions

Prepare a statement of revenues, expenses, and changes in net assets and a balance sheet for the Town of Tolliver Enterprise Fund for the fiscal year ended June 30, 2003.

(Problem 19.3) In compliance with a newly enacted state law, Diggs County assumed the responsibility of collecting all property taxes levied within its boundaries as of July 1, 2002. A composite property tax rate per $100 of net assessed valuation was developed for the fiscal year ending June 30, 2003, and is presented below:

Diggs County General Fund	$ 6.00
Evans City General Fund	3.00
Hickman Township General Fund	1.00
Total	$10.00

All property taxes were due in quarterly installments. After collection, taxes were to be distributed to the governmental entities represented in the composite rate. In order to administer collection and distribution of such taxes, Diggs County established a Tax Agency Fund.

Additional Information

1. In order to reimburse Diggs County for estimated costs of administering the Tax Agency Fund, the Tax Agency Fund was to deduct 2% from the tax collections each quarter for Evans City and Hickman Township. The total amount deducted was to be remitted to the Diggs County General Fund.
2. Current year tax levies to be collected by the Tax Agency Fund were as follows:

	Gross Levy	Estimated Amount to Be Collected
Diggs County	$3,600,000	$3,500,000
Evans City	1,800,000	1,740,000
Hickman Township	600,000	560,000
Totals	$6,000,000	$5,800,000

3. As of September 30, 2002, the Diggs County Tax Agency Fund had received $1,440,000 in first-quarter payments. On October 1, 2002, the Diggs County Tax Agency Fund made a distribution to the three governmental entities.

Instructions

For the period July 1, 2002, through October 1, 2002, prepare journal entries (explanations omitted) to record the foregoing transactions and events for the following funds:

Diggs County Tax Agency Fund　　Evans City General Fund

Diggs County General Fund　　Hickman Township General Fund

Your working paper should be organized as follows:

	Diggs County Tax Agency Fund	Diggs County General Fund	Evans City General Fund	Hickman Township General Fund
Account Titles	dr(cr)	dr(cr)	dr(cr)	dr(cr)

(Problem 19.4) The Town of Northville was incorporated and began operations on July 1, 2002. The following transactions and events occurred during the first fiscal year, July 1, 2002, to June 30, 2003:

(1) The town council adopted a budget for general operations during the year ending June 30, 2003. Revenues were estimated at $400,000. Legal authorizations for budgeted expenditures were $394,000. There were no other financing sources or uses.

(2) Property taxes were levied in the amount of $390,000; it was estimated that 2% of this amount would be uncollectible. These taxes were available on the date of levy to finance current expenditures.

(3) During the year a resident of the town donated marketable securities with a current fair value of $50,000 to the town under a trust. The terms of the trust indenture specified that the principal amount was to be kept intact; use of revenues generated by the securities was restricted to financing college scholarships for students. Revenues earned and received on these marketable securities amounted to $5,500 through June 30, 2003.

(4) A General Fund transfer of $55,000 was made to establish an Internal Service Fund to provide for an inventory of supplies.

(5) The town council decided to install lighting in the Town Park, and a special assessment project was authorized to install the lighting at a cost of $75,000. The assessments were levied for $72,000, with the town contributing $3,000 from the General Fund. All assessments were collected during the year, as was the General Fund contribution.

(6) A contract for $75,000 was approved for the installation of the lighting. On June 30, 2003, the lighting was completed but not approved. The contractor was paid all but 5%, which was retained to ensure compliance with the terms of the contract. Encumbrances accounts are maintained.

(7) During the year, the Internal Service Fund purchased supplies at a cost of $41,900.

(8) Cash collections recorded by the General Fund during the year were as follows:

Property taxes	$386,000
Licenses and permits fees	7,000

(9) The town council decided to build a town hall at an estimated cost of $500,000 to replace space occupied in rented facilities. The town does not record project authorizations. General obligation term bonds bearing interest at 6% were to be issued. On June 30, 2003, the bonds were issued at their face amount of $500,000, payable June 30, 2023. No contracts had been signed for this project and no expenditures had been made.

(10) A fire truck was acquired for $16,000, and the voucher was approved and paid by the General Fund. This expenditure previously had been encumbered for $15,000.

Instructions

Prepare journal entries for the Town of Northville to record each of the foregoing transactions and events in the appropriate fund or account group. Omit explanations for the journal entries. Do not prepare closing entries for any fund. Organize your working paper as follows:

Transaction or Event No.	Fund or Account Group	Account Titles	Debit	Credit

Number each journal entry to correspond with the transactions or events described on page 821 and above. Use the following funds (show fund symbol in working paper) and account titles:

Endowment Principal Trust Fund (EPF)
  Cash
  Investments
  Other Financing Uses
  Payable to Endowment Revenues Trust Fund
  Revenues
Endowment Revenues Trust Fund (ERF)
  Cash
  Other Financing Sources
  Receivable from Endowment Principal Trust Fund
General Capital Assets Account Group (GCA)
  Improvements (Other than Buildings)
  Investment in General Capital Assets from Capital Projects Funds
  Investment in General Capital Assets from General Fund Revenues
  Machinery and Equipment
General Fund (GF)
  Allowance for Uncollectible Current Taxes
  Appropriations
  Budgetary Fund Balance
  Cash

Encumbrances
Estimated Revenues
Expenditures
Fund Balance Reserved for Encumbrances
Other Financing Uses
Payable to Special Revenue Fund
Revenues
Taxes Receivable—Current
Vouchers Payable
General Long-Term Debt Account Group (GLTD)
   Amount to Be Provided
   Term Bonds Payable
Internal Service Fund (ISF)
   Cash
   Contribution from General Fund
   Inventory of Supplies
Special Revenue Fund (SRF)
   Cash
   Other Financing Sources
   Receivable from General Fund
   Revenues
   Special Assessments Receivable—Current
Town Hall Capital Projects Fund (TH)
   Cash
   Other Financing Sources
Town Park Lighting Capital Projects Fund (TPL)
   Cash
   Encumbrances
   Expenditures
   Fund Balance Reserved for Encumbrances
   Vouchers Payable

(Problem 19.5) The City of Cavendish operates a central garage in an Internal Service Fund to provide garage space and repairs for all city-owned and -operated vehicles. The Internal Service Fund was established by a contribution of $200,000 from the General Fund on July 1, 2000, at which time the building was acquired. The post-closing trial balance of the Internal Service Fund on June 30, 2002, was as follows:

CITY OF CAVENDISH INTERNAL SERVICE FUND
Post-Closing Trial Balance
June 30, 2002

	Debit	Credit
Cash	$150,000	
Receivable from General Fund	20,000	
Inventory of material and supplies	80,000	
Land	60,000	
Building	200,000	
Accumulated depreciation of building		$ 10,000
Machinery and equipment	56,000	
Accumulated depreciation of machinery and equipment		12,000
Vouchers payable		38,000
Net assets, beginning of year		506,000
Totals	$566,000	$566,000

Additional Information for the Fiscal Year Ended June 30, 2003:

(1) Material and supplies were purchased on account for $74,000.

(2) The perpetual inventory balance of material and supplies on June 30, 2003, was $58,000, which agreed with the physical count on that date.

(3) Salaries and wages paid to employees totaled $230,000, including related fringe benefits.

(4) A billing was received from the Enterprise Fund for utility charges totaling $30,000, and was paid.

(5) Depreciation of the building was recognized in the amount of $5,000. Depreciation of the machinery and equipment amounted to $8,000.

(6) Billings to other funds for services rendered to them were as follows:

General Fund	$262,000
Enterprise Fund	84,000
Special Revenue Fund	32,000

(7) Unpaid interfund receivable balances on June 30, 2003, were as follows:

General Fund	$ 6,000
Special Revenue Fund	16,000

(8) Vouchers payable on June 30, 2003, were $14,000.

Instructions

For the fiscal year July 1, 2002, through June 30, 2003, prepare journal entries to record all the transactions and events for the City of Cavendish Internal Service Fund. Omit explanations for the entries. Use the following account titles, in addition to those included in the June 30, 2002, post-closing trial balance:

Charges for Services	Payable to Enterprise Fund
Operating Expenses	Receivable from Enterprise Fund
(controlling account)	Receivable from Special Revenue Fund

(Problem 19.6) Your audit of the financial statements of the Town of Novis for the fiscal year ended June 30, 2003, disclosed that the town's inexperienced accountant was uninformed regarding governmental accounting standards and recorded all transactions and events in the General Fund. The following Town of Novis General Fund trial balance was prepared by the accountant:

CHECK FIGURE

b. Trial balance totals, $34,200.

TOWN OF NOVIS GENERAL FUND
Trial Balance
June 30, 2003

	Debit	Credit
Cash	$ 12,900	
Accounts receivable	1,200	
Taxes receivable—current	8,000	
Town property	16,100	
Vouchers payable		$ 15,000
Bonds payable	48,000	

(continued)

TOWN OF NOVIS GENERAL FUND
Trial Balance (concluded)
June 30, 2003

	Debit	Credit
Unreserved and undesignated fund balance		23,200
Appropriations		350,000
Expenditures	332,000	
Estimated revenues	290,000	
Revenues		$320,000
Totals	$708,200	$708,200

Your audit disclosed the following:

1. The accounts receivable balance was due from the town's water utility for the sale of obsolete equipment on behalf of the General Fund. Accounts for the water utility operated by the town are maintained in the Water Utility Enterprise Fund.

2. The total property tax levy for the year was $270,000. The town's tax collection experience in recent years indicates an average loss of 3% of the total property tax levy for uncollectible taxes.

3. On June 30, 2003, the town retired at face amount 12% general obligation serial bonds totaling $30,000. The bonds had been issued on July 1, 1998, in the total amount of $150,000. Interest paid during the year also was recorded in the Bonds Payable ledger account. There was no debt service fund for the serial bonds.

4. On July 1, 2002, to service various departments the town council authorized a supply room with an inventory not to exceed $10,000. During the year supplies totaling $12,300 were purchased and debited to Expenditures. The physical inventory taken on June 30, 2003, disclosed that supplies totaling $8,400 had been used. No internal service fund was authorized by the town council.

5. Expenditures for Fiscal Year 2003 included $2,600 applicable to purchase orders issued in the prior year. Outstanding purchase orders on June 30, 2003, not entered as encumbrances in the accounting records, amounted to $4,100.

6. The amount of $8,200, receivable from the state during Fiscal Year 2003 for the town's share of state gasoline taxes, had not been entered in the accounting records, because the state was late in remitting the $8,200.

7. Equipment costing $7,500, which had been acquired by the General Fund, was removed from service and sold for $900 during the year, and new equipment costing $17,000 was acquired. These transactions were recorded in the Town Property ledger account. The town does not recognize depreciation in the General Capital Assets Account Group.

Instructions
a. Prepare adjusting and closing entries for the Town of Novis General Fund on June 30, 2003.
b. Prepare a post-closing trial balance for the Town of Novis General Fund for the year ended June 30, 2003.
c. Prepare adjusting entries for any other funds or account groups of the Town of Novis. (The town's accountant had recorded all the foregoing transactions or events in the General Fund, and had prepared no journal entries for other funds or account groups.)

(Problem 19.7) Selected financial statements of the Village of Rosner Enterprise Fund are as follows:

VILLAGE OF ROSNER ENTERPRISE FUND
Statement of Revenues, Expenses, and Changes in Net Assets
For Year Ended June 30, 2003

Operating revenues:		
Charges for services		$282,000
Operating expenses:		
Personal services	$ 41,000	
Contractual services	26,000	
Material and supplies	37,000	
Heat, light, and power	11,000	
Depreciation	36,000	
Payment in lieu of property taxes	15,000	
Total operating expenses		166,000
Operating income		$116,000
Nonoperating revenues (expenses):		
Operating grant	$ 20,000	
Investment revenue and net gains	8,000	
Interest expense	(40,000)	
Total nonoperating revenues (expenses)		(12,000)
Income before operating transfers		$104,000
Operating transfer (out) to General Fund		(5,000)
Increase in net assets		$ 99,000
Transfer of net assets to General Fund		(50,000)
Net assets, beginning of year		282,000
Net assets, end of year		$331,000

VILLAGE OF ROSNER ENTERPRISE FUND
Balance Sheets
June 30, 2003 and 2002

	June 30,	
	2003	*2002*
Assets		
Current assets:		
Cash and short-term investments	$ 41,000	$ 32,000
Accounts receivable (net)	82,000	76,000
Receivable from General Fund	12,000	8,000
Inventory of supplies	21,000	23,000
Short-term prepayments	4,000	5,000
Total current assets	$160,000	$144,000
Restricted assets:		
Cash and short-term investments	118,000	106,000
Capital assets (net)	641,000	614,000
Total assets	$919,000	$864,000

(continued)

VILLAGE OF ROSNER ENTERPRISE FUND
Balance Sheets (concluded)
June 30, 2003 and 2002

	June 30,	
	2003	*2002*
Liabilities and Net Assets		
Current liabilities:		
Vouchers payable	$ 67,000	$ 73,000
Accrued liabilities	46,000	39,000
Total current liabilities	$113,000	$112,000
Liabilities payable from restricted assets:		
Interest payable	$ 20,000	$ 20,000
Customers' deposits	55,000	50,000
Total liabilities payable from restricted assets	$ 75,000	$ 70,000
Long-term debt:		
10% revenue bonds payable	$400,000	$400,000
Total liabilities	$588,000	$582,000
Net assets:		
Restricted for revenue bonds retirement	43,000	36,000
Unrestricted	288,000	246,000
Total net assets	$331,000	$282,000
Total liabilities and net assets	$919,000	$864,000

Additional Information for the Fiscal Year Ended June 30, 2003

(1) The 10% revenue bonds, which pay interest January 1 and July 1, are due serially $50,000 a year beginning July 1, 2004.

(2) New customers' deposits totaled $7,000; refunds of customers' deposits amounted to $2,000.

(3) Capital assets with a carrying amount of $22,000 were disposed of for that amount; new capital assets were acquired for cash.

(4) A $50,000 transfer of net assets was made to the General Fund.

(5) The short-term investments are cash equivalents.

Instructions

Prepare a statement of cash flows (indirect method) for the Village of Rosner Enterprise Fund for the fiscal year ended June 30, 2003.

Glossary

A

abatement sequence   The order of reduction of devises in the will of a decedent whose estate property is insufficient to pay all the decedent's liabilities and cover all devises; the order is as follows: property not specifically mentioned in the will, residuary devises, general devises, specific devises

account group   A set of memorandum ledger accounts established by a governmental entity to account for plant assets (general capital assets account group) and long-term debt (general long-term debt account group) not recorded in a fund of the governmental entity

accountability method   The method of accounting used by a trustee in bankruptcy or by the personal representative of a decedent's estate, evidenced by the equation Assets = Accountability

Accounting and Auditing Enforcement Releases (AAERs)   A series of pronouncements initiated by the Securities and Exchange Commission (SEC) in 1982 to report its enforcement actions involving accountants and accounting issues

Accounting Series Releases (ASRs)   Pronouncements of the chief accountants of the SEC from 1937 to 1982 designed to contribute to the development of uniform standards and practice in major accounting questions

acquisition of assets   A business combination in which one business enterprise acquires the gross or net assets of another enterprise by paying cash or issuing equity or debt securities

acquisition of common stock   A business combination in which an investor enterprise issues cash or equity or debt securities to acquire a controlling interest in the outstanding common stock of an investee enterprise, which is not liquidated but becomes a subsidiary of the investor parent company

administrator   An intestate decedent's personal representative, who is appointed by the probate court

affiliate   A business enterprise that is controlled or significantly influenced by another enterprise

agency funds   Fiduciary funds of a governmental entity, of short duration, that account for sales taxes, payroll taxes, and other such amounts collected by the governmental entity for later payment to other governmental entities entitled to the taxes and other amounts; also, funds of nonprofit organizations used for assets held by the organizations as custodian

agio (spread)   The difference between the selling spot rate and the buying spot rate of a foreign currency

American Institute of Certified Public Accountants (AICPA)   The national professional organization of certified public accountants licensed by the states and territories of the United States

annual budget   A budget prepared for the general fund and special revenue funds of a governmental entity; includes estimated revenues, estimated other financing sources, appropriations, and estimated other financing uses for a fiscal year

annuity fund   A fund established by a nonprofit organization to account for assets contributed to the organization, the income from which is the source of fixed periodic payments to designated recipients for a specified time period

appropriations   Authorized expenditures of a governmental entity's general fund and special revenue funds, as approved by the legislative and executive authorities of the entity and set forth in the annual budget

associate   The International Accounting Standards Board's term for *influenced investee*

B

bankrupt   A legal state in which an insolvent debtor is given protection from creditors' claims by the Bankruptcy Court

Bankruptcy Code   The federal law governing bankruptcies in the United States

bankruptcy liquidation   The procedure under Chapter 7 of the Bankruptcy Code in which a trustee realizes the debtor's nonexempt assets and pays creditors as specified in the Bankruptcy Code

bankruptcy reorganization   The procedure under Chapter 11 of the Bankruptcy Code in which a business enterprise is protected from creditor's claims while it develops a plan for restructuring its liabilities and stockholders' equity

bargain-purchase excess   The excess of the current fair value of the combinee's identifiable net assets in a business combination over the cost to the combinor

beneficiary   The party for whose benefit a trust is established

branch A unit of a business enterprise, located at some distance from the home office, that carries merchandise obtained from the home office, makes sales, approves customers' credit, and makes collections from its customers

budgetary deficit An excess of appropriations and estimated other financing uses over estimated revenues and estimated other financing sources in the annual budget of a governmental entity's general fund

budgetary surplus An excess of estimated revenues and estimated other financing sources over appropriations and estimated other financing uses in the annual budget of a governmental entity's general fund and special revenue funds

business combination An entity's acquisition of net assets that constitute a business or of equity interests in one or more entities and obtains control over that entity or entities

buying spot rate The exchange rate paid by a foreign currency dealer "on the spot"

C

capital budget A budget prepared for a capital projects fund of a governmental entity; includes the estimated resources available for a capital project and the estimated costs of completion of the project

capital expenditures Expenditures for capital (plant) assets of a governmental entity

capital lease A lease that, from the viewpoint of the lessee, is equivalent to the *acquisition,* rather than the *rental,* of property from the lessor

capital projects funds Governmental funds that record the receipt and payment of cash for the construction or acquisition of the governmental entity's capital (plant) assets other than those accounted for in proprietary funds or trust funds

cash distribution program A plan prepared for a liquidating partnership to show the appropriate sequence for paying cash as it becomes available to partnership creditors and to partners

cash equivalents Short-term investments that are readily marketable and have maturity dates no longer than three months

certificate A document evidencing formation of a limited partnership, filed with the county recorder of the principal place of business of the limited partnership

change in the reporting entity A type of accounting change, dealt with in *APB Opinion No. 20,* "Accounting Changes," that requires an adjustment to beginning-of-period retained earnings

charge and discharge statement The financial statement prepared on behalf of the personal representative of a decedent's estate, submitted to the probate court; a comparable financial statement prepared on behalf of the trustee of a trust

charity care Health services provided by nonprofit hospitals to indigent patients, there being no expectation of resultant cash flows to the hospital

collections Nonexhaustible resources of nonprofit museums, art galleries, botanical gardens, libraries, and similar nonprofit organizations, for which a determination of value is impracticable and depreciation is inappropriate

combined enterprise The accounting entity that results from a business combination

combinee A constituent company other than the combinor in a business combination

combinor A constituent company entering into a business combination whose owners as a group end up with control of the ownership interests in the combined enterprise

component unit An organization included in a governmental financial reporting entity because the primary government is financially accountable for the organization or because of the relationship of the organization to the primary government

comprehensive annual financial report (CAFR) The annual report required by the Governmental Accounting Standards Board to be prepared by every governmental entity as a matter of public record

comprehensive income The change in equity of a business enterprise during a period from transactions and other events and circumstances from nonowner sources

conflict of interest A situation in which an individual reaps an inappropriate personal benefit from his or her acts in an official capacity

conglomerate A group of affiliated business enterprises in unrelated industries or markets

conglomerate combination A business combination between enterprises in unrelated industries or markets

consolidated financial statements Financial statements of a single economic entity composed of several legal entities (parent company and subsidiaries)

constituent companies The business enterprises that enter into a business combination

contingent consideration Additional cash, other assets, or securities that may be issuable in the future, contingent on future events such as a specified level of earnings or a designated market price for a security that had been issued to complete a business combination

contractual adjustments Discounts from full billing rates of nonprofit hospitals provided in contracts with third-party payors such as Medicare and Medicaid

contributory pension plan A pension plan that requires contributions from employees as well as employers

"cookie jar reserves" A "cooking the books" technique that involves establishing fictitious liabilities for bogus expenses or revenue in a highly profitable period, and reversing the liabilities in subsequent low earnings periods

"cooking the books" Fraudulent financial reporting

cost method The method of accounting for an investment in a subsidiary that recognizes revenue only to the extent the subsidiary declares dividends from retained earnings accumulated after the date of the business combination

credit risk The risk of nonperformance by a party to a financial instrument or derivative instrument contract

creditors' (involuntary) petition A bankruptcy petition initiated by creditors of an insolvent debtor in accordance with provisions of the Bankruptcy Code

cumulative preferred stock Preferred stock that requires dividends "passed" in one year to be declared and paid in a subsequent year, together with that year's regular dividends, to preferred stockholders before dividends may be declared and paid to common stockholders

current/noncurrent method A method of translating foreign currency financial statements in which current assets and liabilities are translated at the current exchange rate on the balance sheet date, while other assets, other liabilities, and owners' equity elements are translated at historical rates. Depreciation and amortization expenses are translated at historical rates; all other revenue and expenses are translated at an average rate for the accounting period

current rate method A method of translating foreign currency financial statements in which all balance sheet amounts other than owners' equity are translated at the current exchange rate, while owners' equity elements are translated at historical rates. All revenue and expense items are translated at the appropriate current rate or at an average of current rates

"cute accounting" Stretching the form of accounting standards to the limit, regardless of the substance of the underlying business transaction or events

D

death taxes Federal estate taxes on the principal of a decedent's estate and state inheritance taxes on devisees receiving devises

debt service expenditures Expenditures for interest on operating debt of a governmental entity, such as short-term loans

debt service funds Governmental funds that account for payments of principal and interest on long-term bonds and other long-term debt of a governmental entity other than special assessment bonds, revenue bonds, and general obligation bonds serviced by an enterprise fund

debtor in possession Management of a business enterprise undergoing reorganization under Chapter 11 of the Bankruptcy Code that continues to operate the enterprise during the reorganization

debtor's (voluntary) petition A bankruptcy petition initiated by an insolvent debtor

defined benefit pension plan A pension plan under which the basis of computation of pension benefits for retired employees usually involves employee compensation, years of service, and age on date of retirement

derivative instrument A financial instrument or other contract that has (1) one or more underlyings and (2) one or more notional amounts or payment provisions or both; requires no initial net investment or a smaller-than-expected initial net investment; and has terms requiring or permitting net settlement or related settlement options

designated fund balance A segregated amount of the fund balance of a nonprofit organization's unrestricted fund or of the general fund of a governmental entity that evidences the earmarking of the fund's net assets for a purpose specified by the organization's governing board or legislative body

devise A transfer of real or personal property in a will

devisee The recipient of a devise

direct out-of-pocket costs Some legal fees, some accounting fees, and finder's fee incurred specifically to accomplish a business combination

discharge Forgiveness of all except specified unpaid liabilities of a debtor that underwent liquidation under Chapter 7 of the Bankruptcy Code

discontinued operations Operations of a business (operating) segment that has been sold, abandoned, spun off, or otherwise disposed of, or, although still operating, is the subject of a formal plan for disposal

discrete theory A theory of interim financial reporting that considers each interim period a basic accounting period whose operating results are measured in essentially the same manner as for an annual accounting period

disposal date The date of closing the sale of discontinued operations or ceasing the operations of an abandoned business segment

dissolution   A change in the relationship among partners of a partnership, caused by any partner's ceasing to be associated in the carrying on of the partnership business

division   A segment of a business enterprise that generally has more autonomy than a branch; a segment that often was formerly an independent enterprise, but subsequently was a constituent company—typically the combinee—in a business combination

downstream intercompany sales   Sales of merchandise by a parent company to a subsidiary of the parent

drawing   A partner's withdrawal of cash or other assets from a partnership in accordance with terms of the partnership contract

E

economic unit concept   A concept of consolidated financial statements of a parent company and one or more partially owned subsidiaries that views the consolidated enterprise as a single entity with ownership by parent company stockholders and subsidiary minority stockholders

EDGAR   The Electronic Data Gathering, Analysis, and Retrieval project of the SEC, designed to permit "paperless" filings with the SEC over telephone lines, on diskettes, or on magnetic tapes

encumbrance accounting   An accounting method for governmental funds of a governmental entity that entails a debit to Encumbrances and a credit to Fund Balance Reserved for Encumbrances when purchase orders or contracts for nonrecurring expenditures are issued by the funds

endowment   A gift placed in trust that generally requires the principal of the gift to be maintained intact, with revenues from the investment of the gift used for the purposes specified by the donor of the gift

endowment fund   A nonprofit organization's fund whose principal must be maintained intact permanently or temporarily and whose income is expendable by the organization for a specified or elective purpose

enterprise funds   Proprietary funds of a governmental entity that account for any activity for which a fee is charged to external users for goods or services

equity method   The method of accounting for an investment in a corporate or an unincorporated joint venture that increases the venturer's Investment account balance for the venturer's share of venture net income and decreases the account balance for the venturer's share of venture net losses, dividends, or other cash remittances; also, the method of accounting for an investment in a subsidiary that increases the parent company's Investment account balance for the parent's share of subsidiary net income and decreases the account balance for the parent's share of subsidiary net losses and dividends

estate   All the property of a decedent, trust, or other person whose affairs are subject to the Uniform Probate Code

exchange rate   The ratio between one unit of each of two foreign currencies

executor   The personal representative of a decedent, named in the decedent's will

exempt property   Property of a decedent excluded from claims of the decedent's creditors and devisees, including aggregate specified value of automobiles, household furniture and furnishings, and personal effects

expendable private-purpose trust funds   Fiduciary funds of a governmental entity, of long duration, that account for the receipt and expenditure of revenues produced by the principal of the trust, which is nonexpendable

external investment pools   Pooled investments of small governmental units such as towns and villages, maintained by larger governmental entities such as counties and states, the object being the realization of a larger return on the investments than would be possible apart from the pool

F

family allowance   A reasonable cash allowance, payable in a lump sum not exceeding a specified amount, to the decedent's spouse or children during the administration of the estate

fiduciaries   The individuals or business enterprises that manage the property in estates and trusts

fiduciary funds   Private-purpose and other trust funds, and agency funds, of a governmental entity that account for resources that are not owned by the entity but are administered by the entity as a custodian or fiduciary

financial accountability   A situation in which a primary government appoints a majority of the governing body of another organization and thus imposes its will on the organization or is responsible for providing financial benefits to, or financial burdens on, the other organization

Financial Executives Institute (FEI)   The national professional organization of financial vice presidents, controllers, and treasurers of business enterprises

financial forecast   Prospective financial statements that present an entity's expected financial position, results of operations, and cash flows

financial instrument   Cash, evidence of an ownership interest in an entity, or a contract that imposes both a right on one entity and an obligation on another entity to exchange cash or other financial instruments

financial reporting entity   The primary government and other component units that comprise the governmental entity that issues financial reports

Financial Reporting Releases (FRRs)   A series of pronouncements initiated by the SEC in 1982 to state its views on financial reporting matters

financial resources   Cash, claims to cash such as receivables and investments, inventories, and short-term prepayments of governmental funds of a governmental entity

finder's fee   A fee paid to an investment banker or other organization or individuals that investigated the combinee, assisted in determining the price, and otherwise rendered services to bring about a business combination

foreign currency transaction   A transaction of a business enterprise that is denominated in a currency other than the local currency of the enterprise

foreign currency transaction gains (losses)   Gains and losses recognized on transactions denominated in a foreign currency or in the remeasurement to the functional currency of foreign entities' financial statements maintained in the local currency

foreign currency translation   Restating a transaction denominated in a foreign currency to the local currency of the transacting enterprise

foreign currency translation adjustments   A balancing amount resulting from the translation of a foreign entity's financial statements from the entity's functional currency to the reporting currency of the parent company or investor enterprise

Form 8-K   A current report filed by a publicly owned company with the SEC within a specified number of days following the occurrence of specified events or events elected to be reported by the company

Form 10   A registration statement filed by a publicly owned company with the SEC in connection with trading of the company's securities on a national exchange or over the counter

Form 10-K   The annual report filed by a publicly owned company with the SEC within 90 days following the close of the company's fiscal year

Form 10-Q   A quarterly report filed by a publicly owned company with the SEC within 45 days following the close of each of the company's first three fiscal-year quarters

formal probate   Litigation to determine whether a decedent left a valid will

Forms S-1 through S-4 and F-1 through F-4   Registration statements filed with the SEC by companies that issue securities to the public interstate

forward contract   An agreement to exchange currencies of different countries on a specified future date at the forward rate in effect when the contract was made

forward rate   The rate of exchange between foreign currencies to be exchanged on a future date

fresh start reporting   A method of financial reporting applied to certain business enterprises emerging from reorganization under Chapter 11 of the Bankruptcy Code in which assets and liabilities are stated at current fair values and retained earnings deficits are written off against additional paid-in capital

friendly takeover   A business combination in which the boards of directors of the constituent companies generally work out the terms of the combination amicably and submit the proposal to stockholders of all constituent companies for approval

fully secured creditors   Creditors of a debtor in bankruptcy whose claims are collateralized by debtor's assets having current fair values in excess of the amount of the claims

functional currency   The currency of the primary economic environment in which the entity operates; normally, that is the currency of the environment in which the entity primarily generates and expends cash

fund   In governmental and nonprofit organization accounting, a fiscal and accounting entity with a self-balancing set of accounts recording cash and other financial resources, together with all related liabilities and residual equities or balances, and changes therein, which are segregated for the purpose of carrying on specific activities or attaining certain objectives in accordance with special regulations, restrictions, or limitations

G

general capital assets account group   The memorandum set of accounts of a governmental entity in which are recorded plant assets that are not in a fund

general devise   A decedent's gift of an amount of money or a number of countable monetary items

general long-term capital debt   Liabilities expected to be paid from the financial resources of governmental funds and that provide long-term financing to acquire a governmental entity's capital assets, including infrastructure, or for nonrecurring projects or activities that have long-term economic benefit

general long-term debt account group The memorandum set of accounts of a governmental entity in which are recorded long-term liabilities that are not recorded in a fund

general obligation bonds Bonds issued by a governmental entity that are backed by the full faith and credit of the entity and supported by its taxation power

general partnership A partnership in which all the partners are responsible for liabilities of the firm and all have authority to act for the firm

goodwill In general, an unidentifiable intangible asset whose cost measures the value of excess earnings of an acquired business enterprise; in a business combination, the excess of the combinor's cost in a business combination over the current fair values of the combinee's identifiable net assets

governmental funds The general fund, special revenue funds, capital projects funds, debt service funds, and permanent funds of a governmental entity that account for financial resources of the entity used in day-to-day operations

grant A contribution of cash or other assets received by a governmental entity from another government to be used or expended for a specific purpose, activity, or facility

greenmail A tactic used to resist a hostile takeover business combination in which the target combinee acquires its common stock presently owned by the prospective combinor at a price substantially in excess of the prospective combinor's cost, with the stock thus acquired placed in the treasury or retired

H

hedge Measures taken to reduce or eliminate a potential unfavorable outcome of a future event

heirs Recipients of property of an intestate decedent, as specified by state probate codes

highly inflationary economy An economy having cumulative inflation of 100% or more over a three-year period

holographic will A will having its essential provisions and signature in the handwriting of the testator

home office The principal business unit of an enterprise that has branches or divisions

homestead allowance A specified amount of a decedent's property allocated to a decedent's spouse or surviving minor or dependent children, in addition to property passing to those persons by devises

horizontal combination A business combination between enterprises in the same industry

hostile takeover A prospective business combination in which the target company resists the proposed takeover

I

income beneficiary The recipient of income of a testamentary trust

informal probate A proceeding by the registrar of a probate court that results in the registrar's making a decedent's will effective by means of a written statement

infrastructure Streets, sidewalks, bridges, and the like of a governmental entity

insider trading Purchasing or selling a security while in possession of material, nonpublic information or communicating such information in connection with a securities transaction

insolvent Unable to pay liabilities when due because of insufficient assets and poor borrowing potential

Institute of Management Accountants (IMA) The national professional organization of accountants in industry

integral theory A theory of interim financial reporting that considers each interim period an integral part of the annual period

inter vivos (living) trust A trust created by a living person

interest method A technique for computing interest revenue or expense that applies the yield rate of bonds to their present value at the beginning of the period for which interest is to be measured

internal service funds Proprietary funds of a governmental entity that provide supplies and services to other funds, departments, or agencies of the governmental entity on a cost-reimbursement basis

International Accounting Standards Board (IASB) An organization of up to 17 members that conducts the business of the International Accounting Standards Committee

International Accounting Standards Committee (IASC) An organization of accounting groups from more than 100 countries, headquartered in London, whose mission is to develop accounting standards for potential adoption in the countries of the member accounting groups

International Organization of Securities Commissions (IOSCO) An organization of securities regulators from about 50 countries whose goal is to ease the impact of differences in securities trading regulations among its members

intestacy The absence of a will for a decedent

intestate Without a valid will

investment trust funds Fiduciary funds of a governmental agency that account for external investment pools for which the entity is the sponsoring government

J

joint venture A partnership of limited duration and with limited projects or other activities

jointly controlled entity The International Accounting Standards Board term for *joint venture*

L

lateral intercompany sales Sales of merchandise by one subsidiary of a parent company to another subsidiary of that parent

letters testamentary Authorization document for the personal representative of an estate to begin administration of the estate

life income fund A fund established by a nonprofit organization to account for assets contributed to the organization, the income from which, in whatever amount, is distributed in periodic payments to designated recipients for a specified time period

limited liability company (LLC) An entity that combines features of both partnerships (for federal income tax proposes) and corporations (for protection of owners from personal liability for entity debts)[1]

limited liability partnership (LLP) A partnership whose partners are liable for their own actions and the actions of partnership employees under their supervision, but not for the actions of other partners; further, an LLP is responsible for the actions of all partners and employees

limited partnership A partnership having, in addition to one or more general partners, one or more partners with no responsibility for unpaid liabilities of the partnership and with restrictions on activities related to the partnership

liquidation (of partnership) The winding up of partnership activities, usually by selling assets, paying liabilities, and distributing any remaining cash to partners

loan fund A fund typically established by a nonprofit school, college, or university for loans to students

local currency unit The unit of currency of the country in which a business enterprise is located

[1] Coopers & Lybrand, *Choosing a Business Entity in the 1990's* (Washington: Coopers & Lybrand LLP, 1994), p. 27.

London Interbank Offered Rate (LIBOR) The international interest rate banks charge each other for loans

M

management approach The method of operating segment designation that is based on the way a segmented business enterprise is managed

market risk The risk of a decline in value or an increase in onerousness of a financial instrument or derivative instrument resulting from future changes in market prices

marshaling of assets A provision of the Uniform Partnership Act that specifies the respective rights of partnership creditors and partners' personal creditors to partnership assets and to partners' personal assets

master limited partnership A large limited partnership engaged in ventures such as oil and gas exploration and real estate development that issues units registered with the Securities and Exchange Commission

measurement date The date on which management of a business enterprise commits itself to a formal plan for disposal of a segment of the enterprise

minority (noncontrolling) interest The claim of stockholders other than the parent company to the net assets and net income or losses of a partially owned subsidiary

modified accrual basis of accounting An accounting method applied to the governmental funds of a governmental entity in which revenues are recognized only when they are measurable and available

monetary assets Cash and other assets representing claims expressed in a fixed monetary amount

monetary liabilities Liabilities representing obligations expressed in a fixed monetary amount

monetary/nonmonetary method A method of translating foreign currency financial statements in which monetary assets and monetary liabilities are translated at the current exchange rate on the balance sheet date; nonmonetary assets and liabilities and owners' equity elements are translated at historical rates. Depreciation and amortization expenses and cost of goods sold are translated at historical rates; all other revenue and expenses are translated at an average rate for the accounting period

monetary principle The principle that money is assumed to be a useful standard measuring unit for reporting the effects of business transactions and events

multinational (transnational) enterprise A business enterprise that carries on operations in more than one nation, through a network of branches, divisions, influenced investees, joint ventures, and subsidiaries

N

negative goodwill The remainder of a bargain-purchase excess that cannot be apportioned to reduce the amounts assigned to the combinee's qualifying assets

net assets Total assets less total liabilities; equal to stockholders' equity of a corporation

nonbusiness organizations Governmental entities and nonprofit organizations

noncontributory pension plan A pension plan that requires contributions from the employer but not from employees

noncumulative preferred stock Preferred stock whose owners have no future claim for dividends "passed" in any year

nonexpendable private-purpose trust funds Fiduciary funds of a governmental entity, of long duration, that account for the principal of a trust, which must be maintained intact

nonprofit organization A legal and accounting entity that generally is operated for the benefit of society as a whole, rather than for the benefit of an individual proprietor or a group of partners or stockholders

notional amount A number of currency units, shares, or other units specified in a contract underlying a derivative instrument

O

operating debt Short-term loans obtained by the general fund of a governmental entity

operating expenditures Expenditures for day-to-day operations of the governmental funds of a governmental entity, such as for salaries and wages, utilities, and consumption of short-term prepayments and inventories of supplies

operating segment A component of a business enterprise that engages in business activities for which it earns revenues and incurs expenses, whose operations are regularly reviewed by the enterprise's chief operating decision maker for purposes of evaluating past performance and making decisions about future allocation of resources, and for which discrete financial information, generated by or based on the internal financial reporting system, is available

operating transfers Transfers of financial resources among governmental funds of a governmental entity for other than quasi-external transactions

order for relief Action by the Bankruptcy Court to protect the debtor from creditors' claims during the bankruptcy procedure

other financial sources Sources of financial resources of a governmental fund other than revenues, such as operating transfers in and gains on disposals of plant assets

other financing uses Uses of financial resources of a governmental fund other than expenditures, such as operating transfers out and losses on disposals of plant assets

P

pac-man defense A tactic used to resist a hostile takeover business combination in which the target company itself threatens a takeover of the prospective combinor

par value method A method of accounting for the retirement of treasury stock in which the cost of the treasury stock is allocated pro rata to reduce (1) the Common Stock ledger account balance by the par or stated value, if any, of the treasury shares; (2) an appropriate additional paid-in capital account for the excess over par or stated value attributable to the original issuance of the treasury shares; and (3) Retained Earnings for any unallocated cost remaining

parent company An investor enterprise that obtains control of an investee (subsidiary)

parent company concept A concept of consolidated financial statements of a parent company and one or more partially owned subsidiaries that views the consolidated entity as an extension of the parent company, with the minority interest in the net assets of subsidiary considered to be a liability, and the minority interest in net income of subsidiary an expense, of the consolidated entity

partially secured creditors Creditors of a debtor in bankruptcy whose claims are collateralized by debtor's assets having current fair values less than the amount of the claims

participating preferred stock Preferred stock whose owners, after receiving the specified dividend on the preferred stock, may receive an additional dividend if the common stockholders are paid dividends in excess of the specified preferred dividend

partnership An association of two or more persons to carry on, as co-owners, a business for profit

pension trust funds Fiduciary funds of a governmental entity that account for the receipt and expenditure of amounts contributed by employer and employees to provide resources for post-retirement pensions and other such benefits to former employees

performance budget   An annual budget of a governmental entity's general fund that attempts to relate the input of governmental resources to the output of governmental services

periodic inventory system   The method of accounting for inventory in which the Inventories ledger account is used only at the end of an accounting period to reflect the value of the ending inventory of merchandise or manufactured products

permanent difference   A difference between pre-tax financial income and taxable income that does not reverse in one or more subsequent accounting periods

permanent endowment fund   An endowment fund whose principal never may be disbursed by the nonprofit organization

permanent funds   Governmental funds that account for resources that are legally restricted to the extent that only earnings, and not principal, may be used for purposes that support the governmental entity's programs

perpetual inventory system   The method of accounting for inventory in which the Inventories ledger account is debited for purchases of merchandise or the cost of goods manufactured and credited for the cost of goods sold

personal representative   The executor or administrator of a decedent's estate

phase-out period   The period between the measurement date and the disposal date for a business segment

plant fund   A fund of a nonprofit organization that accounts for plant assets, and often for cash and investments earmarked for additions to plant assets as well as mortgage notes and other liabilities collateralized by the organization's plant assets

pledge   A commitment by a prospective donor to contribute a specific amount of cash or property to a nonprofit organization on a future date or in installments

pledgor   The maker of a pledge

poison pill   A tactic used to resist a hostile takeover business combination in which the target company amends its articles of incorporation or bylaws to make it more difficult to obtain stockholder approval for a takeover

preacquisition contingencies   Contingent assets (other than potential income tax benefits of a loss carryforward), contingent liabilities, or contingent impairments of assets that existed prior to completion of a business combination

preference   The transfer of cash or property to a creditor by an insolvent debtor within 90 days of the filing of a bankruptcy petition by or on behalf of the debtor, provided that the transfer caused the creditor to receive more cash or property than would be received in the bankruptcy liquidation

primary government   A state government, a municipality or county, or a special-purpose government such as a school district or a park district meeting specified criteria

principal beneficiary (remainderman)   The recipient of the principal of a trust

prior period adjustment   In a statement of partners' capital, an adjustment to partners' beginning capital balances to correct an error in the financial statements of a prior period

private-purpose trust funds   Fiduciary funds of a governmental entity that account for trust arrangements under which principal and income benefit individuals, private organizations, or other governments

probate   Action by the probate court to validate a decedent's will

probate (orphan's, surrogate) court   The state court established to probate decedents' wills

professional corporation   A form of corporation authorized by some states, having various requirements as to professional licensing of stockholders, transfers of stock ownership, and malpractice insurance coverage

program services   Activities of a nonprofit organization that result in the distribution of goods and services to beneficiaries, customers, or members that fulfill the purposes or mission of the organization

projected benefits   The amount of all benefits under a defined benefit pension plant attributable to employee services to the date of computation of the actuarial present value

promissory note   An unconditional promise in writing, signed by the maker, to pay a certain sum of money on demand or at a fixed or determinable future time to order of a payee or to bearer

proportionate consolidation method   The International Accounting Standards Board term for the ***proportionate share method*** of accounting for an investment in a joint venture

proportionate share method   The method of accounting for an investment in an unincorporated joint venture that allocates to the venturer's assets, liabilities, revenue, gains, expenses, and losses the venturer's pro rata share of the venture's comparable items

proprietary funds   Enterprise funds and internal services funds of a governmental entity that carry out governmental activities closely resembling the operations of a business enterprise

proxy statement   A statement filed by a publicly owned company with the SEC prior to the company's solicitation of proxies from stockholders prior to a meeting of stockholders

push-down accounting   Accounting for net assets of a subsidiary at their current fair values as established in the business combination, rather than at carrying amounts, in separate financial statements of the subsidiary

Q

quasi-endowment fund   An endowment fund established by the governing board of a nonprofit organization, the principal of which may be expended at the direction of the board

quasi-external transactions   Transactions of the general fund of a governmental entity with proprietary funds of the entity, such as for goods and services provided by the proprietary funds

R

realization   Conversion of noncash assets of a liquidating partnership or debtor in bankruptcy to cash

reciprocal accounts   The Investment in Branch ledger account in the home office accounting records and the Home Office account in the branch accounting records; also, the Investment in Subsidiary Common Stock ledger account in the parent company's accounting records and the stockholders' equity accounts in the subsidiary's accounting records

registrar   The officer of a probate court authorized to carry out informal probate of decedents' wills

registration statement   A document filed with the SEC by a company that issues securities to the public interstate

Regulation S-K   A pronouncement of the SEC that provides guidance for the completion of nonfinancial statement disclosure requirements in the various *Forms* filed with the SEC

Regulation S-X   A pronouncement of the SEC that provides guidance on the form and content of financial statements included in the various *Forms* filed with the SEC

remeasurement   Restatement of account balances of a foreign entity to its functional currency from its local currency

reorganization value   The current fair value of the total assets of a business enterprise undergoing reorganization under Chapter 11 of the Bankruptcy Code

reporting currency   The currency of the parent company, home office, or investor enterprise of a foreign entity

residual equity transfer   An amount received by the general fund of a governmental entity from a capital projects fund of the entity to clear a final fund balance of the latter fund

residuary devise   A devise of all property of a decedent remaining after specific and general devises are distributed

restricted fund   A fund established by a nonprofit organization to account for contributed assets available for current use but expendable only as authorized by the donor of the assets

revenue bonds   Bonds issued by an enterprise fund of a governmental entity to finance a construction project of the entity; the bonds' principal and interest are paid from revenues generated by the construction project

Revised Uniform Principal and Income Act   A law in effect in part or in full in many states, which provides for allocation of transactions of the personal representative of an estate or trust between principal and income, in the absence of appropriate instructions in the will or trust document

right of offset   A legal doctrine that permits offsetting of a loan receivable from or payable to a partner of a liquidating partnership against that partner's capital account balance

S

sales-type lease   A lease that, from the viewpoint of the lessor, is equivalent to the *sale,* rather than the *rental,* of property to the lessee

scorched earth   A tactic used to resist a hostile takeover business combination in which the target company sells or spins off to stockholders one or more profitable business segments

Securities and Exchange Commission (SEC)   The federal agency charged with overseeing issuance and trading of securities interstate by publicly owned companies

security interest   A legal claim of a secured creditor of a debtor to designated personal property of the debtor

selling spot rate   The exchange rate charged by a foreign currency dealer "on the spot"

settlor (donor, trustor)   The creator of a trust

shared revenues   Revenues received by a governmental entity from another government that had levied the taxes or fees to be shared

shark repellent   A tactic used to resist a hostile takeover business combination in which the target company acquires substantial amounts of its outstanding common stock for the treasury or for retirement or incurs substantial long-term debt in exchange for its outstanding common stock

special assessment bonds   Bonds issued by a governmental entity, principal and interest of which are paid from special assessments on specific taxpayers benefited by the construction project financed in part by the bonds

special assessments   Taxes levied by a governmental entity on specific taxpayers to be benefited by the construction project financed in part by the assessments

special revenue funds   Governmental funds that account for receipts and expenditures associated with specialized revenue sources that are earmarked by law or regulation to finance specified government operations

specific devise   A decedent's gift of identified objects, such as named paintings, automobiles, stock certificates, or real property

sponsoring government   A governmental entity that manages external investment pools

spot rate   The rate of exchange between two foreign currencies to be exchanged "on the spot"

Staff Accounting Bulletins (SABs)   Pronouncements of the SEC staff regarding administrative interpretations and practices used by the staff in reviewing *Forms* and financial statements filed with the SEC

statement of activities   A financial statement that displays the changes in net assets—unrestricted, temporarily restricted, and permanently restricted—of a nonprofit organization

statement of affairs (financial statement)   A "quitting concern" financial statement prepared on behalf of a debtor undergoing bankruptcy liquidation that classifies nonexempt assets and liabilities of the debtor according to provisions of the Bankruptcy Code

statement of cash flows   A financial statement that displays the cash flows from operating activities, investing activities, and financing activities of a business enterprise, governmental entity, or nonprofit organization

statement of financial affairs (legal document)   A document accompanying a debtor's petition that contains a series of questions concerning all aspects of the debtor's financial position and operations

statement of financial position   A financial statement that displays the assets, liabilities, and net assets—permanently restricted, temporarily restricted, and unrestricted—of a nonprofit organization

statement of partners' capital   The financial statement issued by a partnership to display changes in partners' capital from investments, net income or loss, and drawings during an accounting period

statement of realization and liquidation   A financial statement prepared for a liquidating partnership that displays realization of noncash assets, allocation of resultant gains or losses to partners, payment of partnership liabilities, and distribution of any remaining cash to partners; also, a financial statement prepared on behalf of a trustee in a bankruptcy liquidation that sets forth assets realized and liabilities paid, with "gains" and "losses" thereon applied to the estate deficit

statutory consolidation   A business combination in which a new corporation issues common stock for all outstanding common stock of two or more other corporations that are then dissolved and liquidated, with their net assets owned by the new corporation

statutory merger   A business combination in which one corporation (the survivor) acquires all the outstanding common stock of one or more other corporations that are then dissolved and liquidated, with their net assets owned by the survivor

subsidiary   An investee enterprise controlled by an investor enterprise (parent company)

support   Resources obtained by nonprofit organizations through contributions from individuals, governmental entities, and other organizations

supporting services   All activities of a nonprofit organization other than program services, such as management and general, fund-raising, and membership development activities

survivor   The constituent company in a statutory merger that is not dissolved and liquidated

T

temporary difference   A difference between the tax basis of an asset or a liability and its reported amount in the financial statements that will result in taxable or deductible amounts in future years when the reported amount of the asset or liability is recovered or settled, respectively; a difference between pretax financial income and taxable income that reverses in one or more subsequent accounting periods

term endowment fund   An endowment fund whose principal may be expended after a specified time period or the occurrence of a specified event

testamentary trust   A trust created by a will

testator   The maker of a will

third-party payor   An organization such as Medicare or Medicaid that pays for services rendered by a nonprofit hospital to patients

translation   Restatement of financial statement amounts of a foreign entity from its functional currency to the reporting currency of the parent company or investor enterprise

trust document   The document establishing a trust

trust indenture   The legal document that creates a trust

trustee The fiduciary individual or corporation holding title to trust property and carrying out provisions of the trust document

U

underlying A specified interest rate, security price, foreign exchange rate, index of prices or rates, or other variable; it may be a price or rate of an asset or liability but not the asset or liability itself

undistributed earnings of subsidiary The parent company's share, under the equity method of accounting, of the adjusted net income less dividends of the subsidiary

Uniform Probate Code A law in effect in part or in full in many states, which provides for procedures used in probating wills

uniting of interests The International Accounting Standards Board term for a business combination not construed as a purchase of the combinee by the combiner

units Securities evidencing ownership interests in a limited partnership

unrelated business income Income derived by a nonprofit organization from activities not substantially related to the educational, charitable, or other basis of the organization's tax-exempt status

unrestricted fund A nonprofit organization's fund that includes all assets of the organization available for use as authorized by the governing board and not restricted for specific purposes

unsecured creditors with priority Creditors of a debtor in a bankruptcy proceeding whose unsecured claims are paid in accordance with provisions of the Bankruptcy Code prior to the payment of claims of other unsecured creditors

unsecured creditors without priority Creditors of a debtor in a bankruptcy proceeding whose unsecured claims do not have priority under the Bankruptcy Code

upstream intercompany sales Sales of merchandise by a subsidiary to its parent company

V

vertical combination A business combination between an enterprise and its customers or suppliers

W

white knight A tactic used to resist a hostile takeover business combination in which the target company seeks out a candidate to be the combinor in a friendly takeover

will A document that awards a testator's property to devisees following the testator's death

Index

B

D

T

U

V

W

Ch. 8 Online MC

1 D	6 C
2 B	7 A
3 B	8 A
4 A	9 A
5 B	10 B

http://highered.mcgraw-hill.com/sites/0072502908/student-view0/
chapter8/multiple_choice_quiz.html